Conservation
of Endangered Species
in Captivity

SUNY Series in Endangered Species
Edward F. Gibbons, Jr.
and Jack Demarest,
Editors

Conservation
of Endangered Species
in Captivity

An Interdisciplinary Approach

EDITED BY

Edward F. Gibbons, Jr.,
Barbara S. Durrant,
and Jack Demarest

STATE UNIVERSITY OF NEW YORK PRESS

Published by
State University of New York Press, Albany

For information, address State University of New York
Press, State University Plaza, Albany, N.Y., 12246

Production by Diane Ganeles
Marketing by Dana Yanulavich

Library of Congress Cataloging-in-Publication Data

Conservation of endangered species in captivity : an interdisciplinary
    approach / edited by Edward F. Gibbons, Jr., Barbara S. Durrant,
    Jack Demarest.
        p.   cm. — (SUNY series in endangered species)
    Includes bibliographical references (p.   ) and index.
    ISBN 0-7914-1911-8 (CH : acid-free). — ISBN 0-7914-1912-6 (PB :
    acid-free)
    1. Endangered species.   2. Captive wild animals.   3. Wildlife
conservation.   I. Gibbons, Edward F., 1949–   II. Durrant, Barbara Susan,
1949–   .   III. Demarest, Jack, 1945–   .   IV. Series.
QL82.C665   1995
639.9'7—dc20   93-40073
                                                               CIP

10   9   8   7   6   5   4   3   2   1

Contents

VII. Primates

Acknowledgments

The idea for a book focusing on endangered species in captivity grew out of a conference held at the American Museum of Natural History in New York in 1985. The conference organizers and editors of this volume wish to thank Dr. Ethel Tobach and the Museum for providing a forum for our initial venture. Much time and effort has been invested since that gathering, and this book owes a debt of appreciation to many individuals. In particular, the editors extend their sincere gratitude to Dr. Katherine Wilson for her dedicated attention to detail and unfailing sense of humor in compiling, confirming, and editing the volume's references and citations. A note of appreciation is also extended to the library staffs at the State University of New York at Stony Brook, the Zoological Society of San Diego (in particular Linda Coates and Courtney Martin), Monmouth College, and the University of Michigan for their help in locating, obtaining and/or verifying obscure references and esoteric journals.

The editors gratefully acknowledge clerical and technical assistance of the following individuals: Carol Carlson, Ruth Shepard, and Stephen Nash at the State University of New York at Stony Brook; Susan Butler and Vivian Graham at the Center for Reproduction of Endangered Species, Zoological Society of San Diego; and Rose McCormack at Monmouth College. Appreciation for administrative support during the book's lengthy gestation is also extended to: D.M. Germano, R.B. Turan, B.W. Deutschman, M.A. Achtziger, and T. Donohue at Briarcliffe College; to the Zoological Society of San Diego, especially W. Heuschele and the Reproductive Physiology staff at the Center for Reproduction of Endangered Species; and to G. Nemerowicz, E. Rosi and the Grants and Sabbaticals Committee at Monmouth College. We thank each of you for your patience and encouragement.

This book would not have been possible without the support and dedication of the editorial staff at the State University of New York Press, in particular to Priscilla Ross for her effort and encouragement throughout the preparation of this volume. Lastly, to the many colleagues who took time to review one or more chapters in this volume, we say thank you: Drs. R. Arnold, M.R. Bakst, E.M. Barrows, M. Bekoff, R. Brill, G. Burghardt, D. Chizar, T. Christenson, D.P. DeMaster, B.L. Dresser, T.C. Emmel, A.A. Eudey, D.M. Germano, J.E. Hafernik, Jr., J. Hearn, J.D. Hewitt, IV, F.W. Koontz, V. Lance, A. Lieberman, E.W. Menzel, Jr., P. Opler, M.A. Ottinger, H. Quinn, C. Schreck, J.M. Scriber, P. Shannon, N. Stacey, M.K. Stoskopf, R. Wells, and T.H. Welsh.

The logo for the State University of New York Press Series on Endangered Species was designed by Stephen Nash of Conservation International.

Introduction

Volume Editors

Advances in ecological theory and in the techniques employed in studying ecosystems, habitat rehabilitation, population dynamics, species diversity, reproductive physiology, genetics, and behavior have begun to change the course of conservation. Until recently, conservation efforts concentrated either on a particular species without regard for its ecosystem, or on the protection of a defined geographical area with little or no consideration for the interactions between animals and plants. Similarly, the conservation literature was devoted either to specific endangered species or to general conservation issues. Volumes such as *The Giant Panda of Wolong* (Schaller et al., 1985) and *Endangered Parrots* (Low, 1984) focused primarily on individual taxonomic groups, while works like *Conservation Biology* (Soulé and Wilcox, 1980) and *Genetics and Conservation* (Schoenwald-Cox, 1983) emphasized a specific methodological or research orientation. On a more global scale, recent emphasis has been on monitoring ecosystems and biodiversity (Verner et al., 1986; Jones, 1987; Wilson, 1988; McNeely et al., 1990; Goldsmith, 1991), and on habitat rehabilitation and restoration (Cairns, 1988; Berger, 1990).

A review of the *ex situ* conservation literature reveals a parallel evolution of philosophy from single species propagation to attempts to simulate and reconstruct ecosystems for the purpose of preparing captive populations for reintroduction into the wild (e.g. Conway, 1980, 1989; Stanley-Price, 1989). Again, the focus of this literature has progressed from primarily one-dimensional (i.e., lacking an integrated approach that addresses conservation issues from a variety of perspectives) to multidimensional. In only the past few years *ex situ* conservation efforts have begun to integrate methods from diverse disciplines while keeping in perspective each species' unique evolutionary history and function within its ecosystem. The present volume was designed to advance this trend in *ex situ* conservation, and argues for a more integrated scientific approach to conservation research.

This book's dual organization includes taxonomic groups and scientific disciplines. Seven taxonomic groups comprise the volume's main divisions and include: (1) invertebrates, (2) fishes, (3) reptiles and amphibians, (4) birds, (5) mammals (excluding marine mammals and primates), (6) marine mammals, and (7) primates. The scientific disciplines represented in each taxonomic division are (a) conservation, (b) reproductive physiology, (c) behavior, and (d) habitat design in captivity.

Each of the twenty-eight chapters in this volume is intended to represent a review of the literature in one of the scientific disciplines within a taxonomic group. Although the number of species in some taxonomic groups is greater than in others, space in the volume was allocated based on the amount of literature to be reviewed, resulting in a greater emphasis on those taxa for which more scientific information is known. This organization of the volume illustrates the taxonomic imbalance in the current literature, and may serve to encourage increased investigation in less well-studied groups.

The disciplines chosen for inclusion in the book represent those areas for which there are no major works covering multiple taxa. Scientific fields such as genetics (e.g. Hartl, 1980; Schoenwald-Cox et al., 1983; Ryman and Utter, 1987; Soulé, M.E., 1987; Val Giddings et al., 1989), nutrition (e.g. Crawford, 1968; Lint and Lint, 1981; Robbins, 1983), and veterinary medicine (e.g. Fox, 1923; Page, 1976; Kinne, 1980; Montali and Migaki, 1980; Edwards and McDonnell, 1982; Wallach and Boever, 1983; May, 1988; Smith and Hearn, 1988) are well represented in the literature and therefore were not topics of focus in the present volume. Many of the authors, however, have referred to these aforementioned scientific disciplines in order to achieve a more interdisciplinary discussion of their respective topics. In spite of the multidisciplinary nature of this volume, it is not intended to stand alone, but to become part of the growing literature in the new field of integrative conservation research (e.g., Wilson, 1988; Western and Pearl, 1991).

The conservation chapters review the status of the taxonomic group, and the need for and problems of conservation programs in captivity. Authors have focused on issues concerning the decline of species and provide current assessments of species status, threats to survival in the wild, and a personal view of the value of conservation efforts in captivity for that taxonomic group. A portion of each chapter is devoted to a discussion of endangered and threatened species currently bred in captivity and includes suggestions for research priorities designed to meet the conservation needs of the twenty-first century.

The purpose of the reproductive physiology chapters is to provide a review of the genetic, physiological, and environmental influences on captive propagation programs. Authors describe the normal reproductive processes of endangered animals or closely related nonendangered species by summarizing the literature on anatomy, endocrinology, and physiology. Discussion of current and developing technologies designed to diagnose and remedy reproductive failure include monitoring of endocrine cycles, hormonal manipulation of the ovary and the estrous cycle, artificial insemination, embryo transfer, and cryopreservation of germplasm. Authors were encouraged to make suggestions for future research in reproductive physiology and to evaluate the impact of advanced technology on this scientific discipline.

Authors of the behavior chapters review the status of field research and discuss the rationale for behavioral research on endangered and threatened species in captivity. For each taxonomic group there is a summary of methods employed and problems encountered in research on captive species. Abiotic, biotic, and social factors that influence the behavior of individuals or social groups in the targeted taxon are examined in the context of maintaining species in captivity while preparing them for reintroduction to the wild. Opinions are expressed concerning the desired direction of behavioral studies including which areas of investigation hold the greatest promise for integrating behavioral research into future conservation programs.

The final chapter in each taxonomic section is devoted to habitat design. These chapters review the practical and aesthetic issues concerning the design of captive exhibits for endangered and threatened species. Topics that are discussed include: economic limitations, security, health concerns, and particular species' biological and psychological needs. Requirements for space, light, climate

control, and social considerations such as group dynamics and preda-
tor/prey relationships are analyzed. Authors have drawn from their
own experiences in habitat design as well as from the literature on
captive environments.

Each taxonomic division in the book is preceded by a brief
preview introducing the authors in that section. A glimpse of the
author's background serves to acquaint the reader with the individual style and research orientation to be encountered in the chapter. Although authors were provided with an outline of topics to be
covered, they were encouraged to bring their own ideas and opinions to their chapters. Generally speaking, authors associated with
zoological parks and aquariums or with government wildlife agencies (e.g., curators and field biologists) approach their disciplines
with a more applied orientation, while basic science predominates
in those chapters written by university personnel and zoo laboratory scientists. This intentional mix of professionals provides a cross
section of the philosophies and perspectives that will shape conservation research in captivity.

I

Invertebrates

Introduction of Authors
and Chapter Previews

The conservation of invertebrates within their native habitats is a priority of Michael Robinson, director of the Smithsonian Institution's National Zoological Park. Phasmids and mantids have been of great interest to him as an ethologist, and he has published extensively on the behavior and ecology of tropical spiders as well as insects. The dearth of taxonomists and scientists studying invertebrates is of great concern, and he is an outspoken proponent of increased education and research efforts on behalf of this enormous taxonomic group. Toward that end, he has opened a highly-praised invertebrate exhibit at the National Zoo.

Dr. Robinson's chapter alerts readers to the crucial need for research focusing on the conservation of invertebrates. Priority areas are identified as faunal surveys, ecological studies, and public education.

The reproductive physiology of invertebrates is authored by Boyce Drummond, scientific director of Pike's Peak Research Station and scientific consultant at Natural Perspectives, Colorado. His research emphasis on butterflies encompasses laboratory culture techniques, the description of reproductive structure and function, and studies of multiple mating and sperm competition. Environmentally induced changes in reproductive function and coevolution of specific plants and butterflies are other fields of interest.

In his chapter, Dr. Drummond highlights the integration of environmental factors and invertebrate reproduction. He discusses the implications of these "endangered interactions" for captive breeding and reintroduction attempts.

Jack Demarest, chair and professor of Psychology at Monmouth College and Marcia Bradley, assistant professor of Biology at Ocean County College, discuss the behavior of invertebrates. In addition to Dr. Demarest's research focus on behavioral ecology, he edited the *Comparative Psychology Newsletter*. Dr. Bradley is a laboratory entomologist specializing in enzymatic and hormonal stress reactions in insects.

While these authors acknowledge that behavior research on endangered invertebrates in captivity is virtually nonexistent, they present a compelling argument for its pursuit. They illustrate how such research can be an integral part of the conservation of this taxon.

The captive design chapter is coauthored by Leslie Saul-Gershenz, Richard A. Arnold, and J. Mark Scriber. As the director of the San Francisco Insect Zoo, Ms. Saul-Gershenz has over thirteen years experience in habitat design for and breeding of invertebrates in captive environments. She has developed breeding programs for over seventy species of invertebrates from diverse taxa. She is a founding member and serves on the Invertebrate Taxon Advisory Group for the American Zoo and Aquariums Association. Dr. Arnold is an environmental consultant who, since 1977, has specialized in rare and endangered insects and invertebrates. He is the author of U.S. Fish and Wildlife Service recovery plans for eight of the thirteen federally recognized endangered insects that occur in California, and has reared numerous insect species in captivity. Dr. Scriber heads the Entomology Department at Michigan State University. His research interests focus on the genetics, physiology, and ecology of swallowtail butterflies. An important component of his research has been the design of captive breeding programs for numerous swallowtail species under laboratory conditions. Dr. Scriber also heads a multistate regional research project dealing with gypsy moth management and the effects of Bt sprays (and, alternatively, forest defoliation) on nontarget Lepidoptera and associated communities of parasites and predators in the Great Lakes region.

These authors enumerate the salient factors to consider when designing captive habitats for invertebrates and stress the widely variant environmental needs of some species during different developmental stages. The chapter includes a list of selected butterfly and anthropod exhibits throughout the world.

1

The Conservation of Invertebrates: Problems and Prospects

Michael H. Robinson

Writing a review of the problems facing invertebrate conservation is a very different task from that confronting the reviewer of any discrete vertebrate group. For a start the group is not, of course, a natural one. Invertebrates are best defined by exclusion from vertebrates. It is preferable to state that they are "animals without backbones." Simple! For an example of the complexities of the modern view of major biological categories, compared with a Victorian system, the reader is referred to Margulis and Schwartz (1988). The syncretic nature of the invertebrate group is not the major problem. What is a problem is the enormous diversity of this rag-bag assemblage. Until relatively recently, estimates of invertebrate species numbered around 1.5 million. Since the work of Terry Erwin (1982, 1983a, b) on the insects of the canopy of tropical forests, we clearly need to revise that estimate. Now insects alone account for between 15 and 30 million species. These estimates are believed by Erwin himself (pers. comm.) to be conservative. May (1986) has calculated an estimate of insect species based on a regression of physical size against species number. Since the larger species are comparatively well-known, May simply extrapolates from the known to the unknown. He states (p. 514) " . . . there is no reason to expect such a simple extrapolation to estimate accurately the number of unclassified smaller species, but it is interesting that the number is not inconsistent with Erwin's more biologically based estimate." Allowing for the marvelous cautiousness of "no reason to expect" and "not inconsistent with," this is a remarkably positive statement. Certainly May concludes that the earlier estimates of insect diversity were "pure hand-waving." Some idea of the immensity of the remaining unknowns can be gathered from the fact that these new estimates only deal with insect diversity, and there are other invertebrate groups in the rain forest canopy which could also be more complex than we have previously realized. Consider only the multitudinous mites and other arachnids not susceptible to this sampling technique. Indeed, a recent estimate of the total number of animal species by Ehrlich and Wilson (1991) suggests that there may be as many as 100 million.

This enormous diversity creates problems that are magnified and compounded by the current state of taxonomic science. Wilson (1985) has drawn attention to the fact that for many major invertebrate groups we have no extant expert capable of identifying the raw materials of ecological and field studies. In his excellent review of the threats to biodiversity, Wilson cites the study of tropical spiders as an example of an area suffering a dearth of taxonomists. But, of course, the problem is not simply confined to spiders. Orthopteroid insects are in the same regrettable position. Phasmids and mantids have fascinated the author for much of his working life as a biologist (Robinson, 1969, 1985) and there is no known entomologist anywhere capable of determining any but the most common species in these groups. The situation may be (must be?) as bad for many other groups.

There is some general agreement about the broad factors that cause endangerment. These are summarized, for instance, by IUCN/UNEP/WWF (1980). However, in general the causes of present extinctions are usually analyzed in terms of vertebrates, where the issues are much simpler. To some extent the past can illuminate the present. The geological history of extinctions has received a great deal of recent attention and a proliferation of interesting and innovative theorization has resulted from this (see Raup, 1986 for a provocative summary). Once again most authors have concentrated on vertebrates for obvious reasons. Analyses of past extinction events concentrate on so-called natural events, whether catastrophic or uniformitarian in the geological sense. On the other hand, present environmental problems are largely due to the activities of one species, *Homo sapiens*. Man-induced environmental changes threaten extinctions on a much shorter time scale than that of the great geological processes of the past. Humans are responsible for two major processes that cause extinctions: habitat alterations and human pollution. In addition, a number of lesser species-threatening processes result from human activities. These include exploitation of living resources, plant and animal, and the introduction and propagation of non-indigenous species. The division of manmade biological perturbations into categories is partly a classificatory convenience, because exploitation, pollution and introductions are all, in essence, environmental changes. Such divisions are, however, useful, because they allow comparisons between regions in terms of the relative importance of these factors, and that can be of major importance in proposing *in situ* remedies. It is important to note that the relative effect of habitat alteration and pollution differs between the developed (largely, but not exclusively temperate) world and the undeveloped or less developed world. Figure 1.1, modified from Robinson (1982), illustrates this. In the developed world most of the physical conversion of one habitat to another is now historic, with the exception of spreading urbanization and wetland-drainage, and problems mainly result from pollution. In the less-developed (largely, but not exclusively tropical) world, problems result from massive conversion of habitats: forest to grassland, complex forest to simplified forest, desertification and so on. Pollution can certainly be a factor but it is relatively less important; however, pollution can be exported from the developed to the less-developed world in the form of oceanic and atmospheric effects that are global in scope. Since the tropics are undoubtedly the area where most species occur, most threatened extinctions resulting from profound habitat changes can be predicted for that region. The paradox is that the world population of biologists is distributed in a manner that is inversely proportional to the distribution of animal and plant species. For instance, Myers (1987a) has pointed out that Colombia, with 30,000 plant species, has about a dozen botanists capable of determining a new plant species, whereas Britain, with 1300 plant species, has 1400 botanists. Biological ignorance is greatest where species are most diverse.

We cannot dismiss man-induced environmental perturbations even in such advanced, prosperous, and developed countries as the United States. In that country, environmental awareness, and its complement protectionism, must be as high as anywhere on earth. Despite this, there seems never to have been a study of the effects on invertebrate populations of the massive winter-feeding of songbirds in which millions of people indulge. This feeding must have affected bird mortality due to winter starvation. If we suppose, merely as a model, that summer populations of birds are

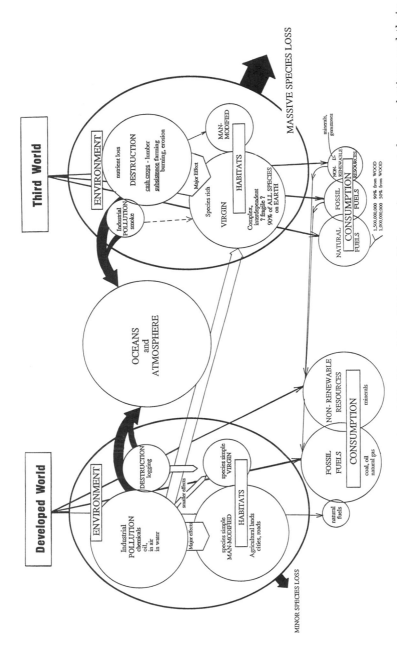

Figure 1.1. Comparisons between the Developed World and the Third World in environmental perturbations and their effect on biological diversity. The thickness of major connecting lines is roughly proportional to the intensity of the presumed effects.

consequently higher, and in a sense unnatural, could this be affecting insect populations? If we think that the removal of plankton-eating whales could affect invertebrate populations in antarctic oceans, we must postulate an effect on insects in America resulting from our unintended manipulation of bird populations.

While we can categorize the threats to species, it is much more difficult to evaluate their effect on invertebrates compared to their effect on vertebrates. For example, it is comparatively easy to reckon the effects of habitat fragmentation on giant pandas, because we know quite a lot about their food requirements, home ranges and the ecology of bamboos (Schaller et al., 1985). When it comes to terrestrial arthropods, or marine plankton for that matter, we are in a far darker area. In essence, we need a major concentration on the biology of tropical invertebrates to even make informed guesses about invertebrate conservation.

It is interesting to consider that many phytophagous insects, and possibly their arthropod predators, may be restricted to particular tree species, which could become isolated by deforestation. They could mimic island effects. A key paper in this field is that of Beaver (1979). There are strong inferences from Erwin's (1982, 1983a, b) results that suggest individual trees may contain endemic aggregates of insect species. He assumes that 20% of tropical canopy species are restricted to genus-groups of plants (1982). Erwin argues that effects based on phytotaxonomy should be greatest in phytophagous species and least in carnivorous ones. His studies in Brazil (Erwin 1983a, b) show that when trees in four types of forest at Manaus are compared, 83% of all beetle species are restricted to only one type of forest and only 17% are shared between two or more. Further studies of beetles in the Amazonian forest canopy support the hypothesis that phytophagous species may be much more host-species restricted than others (Farrell and Erwin, 1988). On the other hand, in fogging studies of the canopy of Bornean forest, Stork (1987) found that taxonomic similarity between trees had a major effect in only eight out of eighteen groups of insects that were analyzed. Wilson (1987a) reported a massive diversity and biomass of ants in Peruvian Amazon trees independent of tree taxonomy. In this sampling, carried out by insecticidal fogging, one tree yielded 26 genera and 43 species of ants. This is approximately equal to the entire ant fauna, from all habitats, of the British Isles. Wilson concludes (p. 251) that close study of ant colonies in the arboreal zone of Neotropical forests "will yield a great deal of valuable new information on the evolution of species diversity."

Also important is the ecological effect of barriers. Janzen (1966) has argued effectively that the tolerance range of tropical organisms to climatic variables may be much less than that of temperate organisms. His paper was titled, significantly, "Why mountain passes are higher in the tropics." A recent paper by Peters and Darling (1985) looks at what might be called the other end of this problem: what will happen to faunal preserves if there is a latitudinal shift in temperature ranges following global warming? The effects of longterm variations in climatic factors (rainfall, sea temperatures) on animals and plants is very poorly understood. Again this is particularly the case for invertebrates. An effect of irregular perturbations of the El Niño current on sea urchin populations thousands of miles from the origin of this phenomenon has been suggested (Glynn, 1985a, b). All in all, we are in a sea of ignorance in terms of many aspects of the elements of invertebrate ecology that could affect species survival in a changing world.

All we can really answer to the question "What can we do to save invertebrate species?" is to say "stop the destruction and start the research."

Species Status in the Wild

How can we estimate what invertebrate species are at risk if we have only recently discovered that there are probably ten or twenty times more species in an important Class than we once thought? How can we estimate extinction risks if there are no specialists available to identify already described species? These are tremendous problems, but there are other equally daunting ones. Quite simply, the present status of most invertebrates, for most areas of high species diversity, is not being monitored. In contrast, it is relatively easy to decide whether or not a mammal or bird species is endangered, at least for the conspicuous ones. Small, retiring mammals, reptiles, and amphibians are not so easy, but they are simple compared to cryptic, cryptozoic, and small invertebrates or those living in inaccessible habitats. Some invertebrates are easier to monitor than others. A glance through endangered species lists for invertebrates shows a basic bias in the sampling (see Table 1.1, a list of endangered insects, as an example). Large and conspicuous flying insects are much more likely to be noticed than are flightless, less brightly colored, and otherwise less obtrusive forms. Forest dwelling species are less likely to be monitored than those of open habitats. Endemic forms restricted to well-explored and populous places are more likely to be carefully monitored than are species living in less developed and economically disadvantaged regions. (A survey of 518 articles in the journal *Biological Conservation* dating from 1975–1986 shows that only 4.6% were about invertebrates. These few were preponderantly about insects and more than half were about butterflies.) In confirmation of the above-stated conclusion that developed and highly populated areas are more likely to attend to invertebrate endangerments, it is noteworthy that two-thirds of the articles concerned the fauna of Great Britain or the United States.

Conservation Programs in Captivity

Saul-Gershenz, Arnold and Scriber (chap. 4, this volume) deals with methods of *ex situ* conservation for some species of invertebrates. The only group of invertebrates which seems to have aroused widespread support for so-called "captive breeding" is the butterflies. Morton (1983) has called, eloquently, for the creation of a "Captive Breeding Institute." Many species of invertebrates have been cultured for laboratory studies, and commercial culture methods have been developed for the mass production of organisms ranging from earthworms to silkworms, domestic crickets to Tenebrio larvae. It is clear that given sufficient investment of research time, methods can usually be worked out for even the most difficult species. In recent years even some species of the reputably tricky cephalopod mollusks have been successfully raised in aquaria. There is no doubt that we could save endangered invertebrate species, as is done with vertebrates, by so-called captive breeding if the resources of time, space, and money were made available. In the author's view this effort would be unjustified in all except the most exceptional cases. Such cases might result from short-term rescue operations. Otherwise the number of species at risk is too large to contemplate saving in this way. Neither should we divert our energies from the task of ecosystem preservation and the massive research effort that progress on that issue entails. Trying to preserve most tropical species by *ex situ* breeding programs is like being given the choice of saving one work of art from a vast gallery, rather than putting out the fire that was threatening to destroy the entire irreplaceable collection.

Table 1.1
Rare and endangered Insects. Excerpted from the IUCN Red Data Book. Analysis shows predominance of Lepidoptera and island/populous area forms (see text)

EPHEMEROPTERA

R	*Tasmanophlebia lacus-coerluli*	Large Blue Lake Mayfly
E	*Hemiphlebia mirabilis*	Hemiphlebia Damselfly
E	*Coenagrion Freyl*	Freya's Damselfly
E	*Ischnura gemina*	San Francisco Forktail DamselFly
R	*Macromia spledens*	Shining Macromania Dragonfly
E	*Somatochlora hineana*	Ohio Emerald Dragonfly

PHASMATODEA

E	*Dryococelus australis*	Lord Howe Island Stick-insect

PLECOPTERA

E	*Eusthenia nothofagi*	Otway Stonefly
R	*Leptoperia cacuminis*	Mount Kosciusko Wingless Stonefly
R	*Riekoperia darlingtoni*	Mount Donna Buang Wingless Stonefly

ANOPLURA

E	*Haematopinus oliveri*	Pygmy Hog Sucking Louse

COLEOPTERA

E	*Cicindela columbica*	Columbia Tiger Beetle
E	*Nicrophorus americanus*	Giant Carrion Beetle
R	*Polposipus herculeanus*	Frigate Island Giant Terebrionid Beetle

DIPTERA

E	*Edwardsina gigantea*	Giant Torrent Midge
E	*E. tasmaniensis*	Tasmanian Torrent Midge
E	*Brennania belkini*	Belkin's Dune Tabanid Fly

LEPIDOPTERA

R	*Dalla octomaculata*	Eight-spotted Skipper
E	*Graphium lysithous harrisianus*	Harris' Mimic Swallowtail Butterfly
E	*Ornithoptera alexandrae*	Queen Alexandra's Birdwing Butterfly
E	*Papilio aristodemus ponceanus*	Schaus' Swallowtail Butterfly
R	*P. hahneli*	Hahnel's Amazonian Swallowtail Butterfly
E	*Maculinea nausithous*	Dusky Large Blue Butterfly

Table 1.1 *continued*

E	*Euphydryas editha bayensis*	Bay Checkerspot Butterfly
E	*Heliconius natterei*	Natterer's Longwing Butterfly
E	*Euproserpinus wiesti*	Wiest's Spinx Moth

HYMENOPTERA

| R | *Epimyrma ravouxi* | Ravoux's Slavemaker Ant |

SUMMARY

| Lepidoptera: | 9 | 33% |
| All others | 18 | 66% |

| Restricted range or populous area or Lepidoptera | 21 | 77.7% |
| Not restricted or populous area or Leidoptera | 6 | 22.3% |

Problems with Invertebrate Conservation: *In Situ* and *Ex Situ*

The establishment of faunal reserves is clearly the only way to preserve the vast majority of the invertebrates that are at risk, just as it is, ultimately, the only way to preserve most other species. Given the immense figures of insect species at risk because of the reduction of rain forests, there is no way that any form of captive conservation could save them. The resources necessary to do this simply do not exist. Similarly, marine invertebrates in the coral reef ecosystem are of sufficient diversity that only the creation of marine national parks, as in Kenya, can effectively protect the substantial majority. Of course, such reserves in themselves do not guarantee survival; they need protection and management and are susceptible to exported pollution. In many countries, large terrestrial reserves have been established by legislative fiat, and no supporting budgets exist. This system produces impressive statistics and is probably better than nothing at all. If the question of reserve size is the subject of controversy even in the case of vertebrates, it is surely an even more complex issue as far as invertebrates are concerned. Scale of organism has its effects, but it is clearly not the only factor. To illustrate this, we can compare protists, insects, and pelagic cephalopods. It is a constant delight to discover how diverse an assemblage of protists and other microscopic invertebrates are resident in the National Zoo's 480-gallon marine tank, which ostensibly houses a collection of cnidarians in an artificial reef. The "micros" are a by-product of the productivity of this tank and 'accidental' introductions. It abounds with diatoms, rhizopoda, ciliates, and flagellates. Tardigrades are regularly discovered as we explore drops of water in our microtheater. Clearly the 480 gallons is an invertebrate reserve. When we think of the coleopterans living in the canopy of tropical rain forests, the picture is much, much more complex. There may be species that use the canopy/crown of one tree species as a reserve or macrocosm, but we certainly do not know that they can do so if the tree were standing isolated in the middle of a vast cattle ranch. One would be fairly confident in asserting that such isolation would substantially reduce the biodiversity of the tree. But we do not know what the 'minimum critical size' of a patch of trees needs to be for even one species of tropical carabid beetle. We do know that some tropical species that are folivores cannot feed on a single individual of the right tree species 'forever' because, with time, the host plant becomes somehow inimical. It appears to fight back, possibly by producing chemical defenses (Smith, 1983). Thus, the resources needed by the species includes a multitude of host individuals.

Apart from the establishment of reserves of proper size, properly protected and managed, *in situ* conservation can be facilitated by protective legislation and by various single-species propagation programs. Legal protection measures that include invertebrates exist in many countries where collection and/or export permits are needed for the export of dead or living invertebrates. At airports, bags are invariably checked in at airlines prior to customs and immigration control, and customs inspections on exit are rare. Furthermore, the logistics of airline baggage-handling militate against inspection by agents of wildlife control. Nor are the personnel available to carry out inspections, were they logistically possible. Even worse, wildlife control agents are totally incapable of recognizing the very minor differences between one, for example, insect species and the next (most scientists cannot do this either!). Export regulations may control commercial collectors and have some deterrent effect on scientific and amateur collecting. In general, this possibility seems to be, on the whole, highly dubious. In one of the countries where I worked, I was consulted by the wildlife protection agency about measures to strengthen the wildlife protection laws. When I made suggestions about controlling exit procedures, I was told that no staff were available, nor could they be funded. I suspect that this is the general case. For most countries, it is difficult to protect the fauna from deleterious imports, never mind control exports of small fauna. Rhinos are conspicuous but spiders are not.

In-country propagation efforts are best exemplified by the Butterfly Farming project that was started in Papua New Guinea by Angus Hutton (BOSTID/NAS, 1983). The so-called Birdwing butterflies are objects of international trade, along with certain other mainly tropical butterfly species. One estimate puts the volume of international trade in butterflies at between $10 to $20 million annually (BOSTID/NAS, 1983). In principle, the aim of butterfly farming in Papua New Guinea is to satisfy the international demand for endangered species by attracting adult butterflies to plantations of the larval food plants where 'wild' females will oviposit. The butterfly 'farmer' then cares for the resulting caterpillars until they pupate. The farmer obtains perfect adult specimens from 'farmed' pupae; these adults are much more valuable than specimens caught on the wing. The latter are invariably in less than perfect condition. The typical butterfly farm in Papua New Guinea is an area hedged by quick-growing, showy nectar-producing plants such as *Hibiscus*, *Ixora* and so on, and it contains a mass of plants that serve as larval food for the species to be attracted. It can house fruit trees for shade and intercropped vegetables for sale. A central agency purchases and markets the farm produce—insects. The panel of scientists who reviewed butterfly farming in Papua New Guinea concluded (BOSTID/NAS, 1983, p. 3): "Through butterfly farming many rural Papua New Guineans are for the first time participating in a cash economy. . . . Compared with farming coffee, another possible industry in Papua New Guinea's rural regions, it requires far less effort and land, and it involves minimal costs to the producer. And where a few expatriate opportunists once made small fortunes exploiting Papua New Guinea's butterflies, the profits now go to the villagers." This is very optimistic and, of course, is not an estimate of the conservation success of the program.

Planting larval food plants certainly helps in conserving rare and endangered species, but farming the larvae that result from this does not help unless a number of adults is added back into the breeding population. Even more serious is the possibility that once a cash market is established, villagers will feel it worthwhile to collect caterpillars from the wild to raise in the farms, thereby increasing the pressure on wild populations. The authors of the survey hint at the encouragement of general collecting that the program has stimulated: "Colorful beetles, strange-looking stick and leaf insects, and some moths and cicadas are caught in the wild and sent to Bulolo" (BOSTID/NAS, 1983, p. 3). Bulolo is the town where the *Insect Farming and Trading* (author's italics) agency is located. Collecting wild caterpillars would be particularly deleterious, because most villagers collect large later-stage caterpillars that have passed their maximum vulnerability to bird predation. In a sense, therefore, there is a real danger that operation of a butterfly farm can legitimize collecting of an otherwise protected insect. All in all, one can conclude that the program of butterfly farming is potentially advantageous to invertebrate conservation, but its efficacy in practice depends on very strict administrative control.

None of this is to argue that there are no other prospects for the *in situ* breeding of invertebrates. Confining consideration to those arthropods which have been raised, by the author, in large numbers, one can say that tropical species are usually much more easily propagated in the tropics than in temperate regions. One does not need complex equipment to simulate the correct (and often essential) environmental conditions. Food plants for phytophagous insects are usually available, and a range of substitutes can be tried out with relative ease. Animals can actually be netted out onto living trees and bushes if care is taken to exclude predators. All these techniques are used with temperate insects in temperate regions and are adaptable to tropical conditions. Predatory insects and spiders can be raised with great facility because it is not difficult to capture insect prey for them. Prey organisms can be attracted to bait and light or captured by sweep-netting. For instance, large quantities of *Drosophila* spp. can be raised out of doors by simply placing large tubs of fruit in shady locations and then netting off the swarms of flies as they emerge. Some arthropod-raising techniques that have been tested in the tropics are detailed in Robinson (1978).

Genetics

Studies of inbreeding in small populations of mammals, particularly those in zoos, has established beyond doubt that inbreeding can produce very rapid deleterious effects (Ralls, 1979). For this reason *ex situ* breeding programs have been designed that maximize outbreeding. These programs, which require careful recordkeeping and pair selection, are the subject of national and international cooperation between zoos. The effects of inbreeding on most groups (or species, for that matter) of invertebrates is largely unknown; what data there are often derive from using insects as the subject of genetic investigations because of their short lifespans. There is, of course, a huge literature on the genetics of *Drosophila*, several species of butterflies, and *Cepea nemoralis* (snails), but this may have little bearing on the phenomenon of inbreeding in insects in general or invertebrates at large. In this respect it is important to realize that many species are probably obligate inbreeders and in several groups parthenogenesis is the rule rather than the exception. The author's particular interest, apart from spiders, is in phasmids, where some marvellous species like *Phyllium bioculatum* and *Carausius morosus* have been maintained in culture for decades. It should be possible to compare these *ex situ* populations with those in the wild. But, in general, the data and even the signposts to inferences are few indeed. If money were available for conservation-oriented research into the genetics of invertebrate species, where would we start? This question contains a worthy challenge to the community of conservation biologists.

Conclusion

What is to be done?

Faunal surveys. To assess the degree of loss of biological diversity and consequently the degree of faunal loss and endangerment among the invertebrates, faunal surveys are urgently needed. This need was highlighted, for the tropics, more than ten years ago when the National Research Council set up a Committee on Research Priorities in Tropical Biology. The first report of this committee, published by the National Academy of Sciences (1980), contained a number of strong recommendations on biological inventorying in the tropics (pp. 2-3):

> "Greatly accelerate the pace of biological inventory in the tropics, combining regional studies of relatively well-known groups or those of economic importance with detailed local studies of others."

> "Take steps to increase the pool of taxonomists studying tropical organisms from its present level of about 1500 people worldwide to four or five times as many. . . . "

> "Give priority to areas containing the richest and most endemic biota, the least-known biota, and biota in immediate danger of extinction."

Since this report, the state of biodiversity worldwide has received continuing attention from agencies as varied as the International Union for the Conservation of Nature and Natural Resources (1983) and the United States Congress, Office of Technology Assessment (1987). In 1987, the Smithsonian Institution and the National Academy of Sciences jointly organized a substantial symposium on the subject (Wilson, 1988a). This again focused attention on the problems of assessing losses in species and the need for inventories.

Clearly, it is not only the tropics that require this kind of attention; there have been frequent calls, for instance, for a national biological survey of the United States (Kosztareb, 1984). The state of marine and freshwater habitats also requires surveying. The entire balance of planktonic invertebrates in the southern oceans has almost certainly been affected by the unprecedented reduction in the whale population that has resulted from the overexploitation of this resource. This leads us into the absolute linkage between the state of ecological studies and the state of particular ecosystems. If our knowledge of the composition of non-temperate faunas is inadequate, so is our knowledge of their functioning.

Ecological studies. If the taxonomy of tropical species lags behind that of temperate ones, this is also true of basic biology. Because ecological factors affect endangerment, our relative ignorance in that field must be corrected. The processes that put species at risk are numerous and generally identifiable (see above). Having said this, it is important to reiterate that for some systems the effects are imperfectly understood. Thus, although there is a clear relationship between habitat destruction and species loss, there are considerable problems in deciding when such losses are local or absolute. It is now common to speak of extinction and then qualify the word with adjectives such as local or general. This seems to be a misuse of language: in the opinion of the author, the term extinction should be reserved for the loss of a species in the absolute sense. Local disappearances of a species are just that, and the word extinction is inappropriate to such losses. These issues are commonly raised in connection with vertebrate populations and most frequently in connection with the minimum size of faunal reserves. (Minimal critical size is a pointed phrase that Lovejoy and Oren (1981) coined to apply to the species-sustaining character of a habitat patch.) There is by now an enormous literature on reserves and reserve size, redolent with in-language, acronyms, and bureaucratese (a sampling of the output can be skimmed from the 70 plus references in Soulé and Simberloff, 1986). Such problems are seldom even modeled in connection with invertebrates. Quite simply, if we do not know how widely a species is distributed, how can we possibly assess the dangers inherent in local or regional deforestation? A concept that has been useful in this respect has been derived from recent theories of island biogeography, which owed their origins to MacArthur and Wilson (1967).

Whatever else can be concluded about the conservation of invertebrates, we are confronted with a major public education task. What use are bugs (or slugs, or worms, or squids or starfish, and so on) are the commonest questions directed by nonscientists to invertebrate biologists. Answering these questions is not a simple matter and requires both skill and immense patience. Unless we convince people of the fact that invertebrates are fundamentally important constituents of ecosystems on which other more obviously significant life forms depend, we will never succeed in developing a movement for their conservation. It helps if people can also be convinced of the direct utility to mankind of many invertebrate species. There is no doubt that invertebrates need to be presented as fascinating, exciting, and frequently wonderful organisms. One way that this can be done is by the creation of exhibits of living invertebrates at museums, botanical gardens, and zoos. This can be done in many ways: these include creating specific invertebrate exhibits at zoos (Robinson, 1988a) and transforming zoological and botanical parks into biological parks (Robinson, 1987).

Just as the author views the future of tropical rain forests with extreme pessimism (Robinson, 1987), so does he view the issues that confront those of us who are concerned with invertebrate conservation. The problems are immense, the research needs are stupendous in their extent, and the attitude of the public, though improving, is not sufficiently supportive. Even when we coattail invertebrate conservation onto broader and more charismatic issues (rain forest conservation, saving coral reefs), the prospects, as Robert Burns would have put it, are drear: "forward tho' I canna see, I guess, an' fear" (Ode to a mouse, 1885). There is now increasing concern about these spectacular ecosystems, biomes, or whatever they should be called, but little sign of the political actions that are necessary to save them. This is a relatively dismal conclusion. That the will and the talents that could solve the general problems facing life on earth exist within the scientific community is the ultimate, and only, ray of hope.

2

Complex Life Histories and Diverse Reproductive Physiologies of Endangered Invertebrates: Implications for Captive Conservation

Boyce A. Drummond

The ranges in size, form, and life histories among invertebrates are astonishing, and any attempt to summarize the reproductive variability of this heterogeneous group is beyond the scope of this short chapter. Robinson (chapter 1, this volume) describes invertebrates as "animals without backbones," which means they include organisms that range in size from microscopic roundworms (nematodes) to the giant squid (*Architeuthis harveyi*), the largest living invertebrate, which grows to a total length of over 13 m and to a body weight exceeding 2000 kg (Wood, 1976). Of the roughly 1.4 million described species of organisms (Parker, 1982), nearly one million are encompassed by Robinson's definition of invertebrates. Millions more undescribed species of invertebrates are believed to exist, mostly arthropods in tropical forests (Erwin, 1983b; Wilson, 1988b), but the majority of these are likely to become extinct through habitat destruction within the next human generation or two. Despite the accelerating deterioration and disappearance of critical habitats worldwide, less than 0.005% of the named invertebrate species have been listed as threatened or endangered. Yet, the number of invertebrate taxa, great though it is, underestimates their ecological importance. The complex life histories of invertebrates, especially insects, mean that different life stages often occupy different habitats and have very different functional roles in the ecosystem (e.g., different food sources, predators, competitors). In that sense, preservation of a single invertebrate species is tantamount to conserving several functionally different organisms at once. The flip side, of course, is that captive breeding programs must accommodate the often disparate ecological and nutritive requirements of each life stage, thus making *ex situ* propagation of invertebrates much more complex than breeding and raising most vertebrates.

Physiological Considerations for Invertebrate Conservation Strategies

There are at least three reasons why the study of reproductive physiology of endangered invertebrates is important: (1) to understand the underlying physiological bases for the behaviors and ecological interactions of the organisms, (2) to determine the environmental conditions appropriate for captive breeding, (3) to infer the ecological characteristics required of sites to be used for introductions of captively bred organisms. An often overlooked facet of the first reason is that widespread species may have evolved a diversity of reproductive physiologies that are distributed among several locally adapted populations. In such cases, captive breeding based on individuals from only one population may be of no help in insuring the survival of populations in the remainder of the species' range. Although reintroduction of such captively bred individuals into their original habitat may be successful, introductions into other parts of the species' range or into new habitats may fail because the reproductive physiologies of the released individuals do not match the environmental conditions present in the new habitats.

Acknowledging the diversity of reproductive physiologies encompassed by a species leads to the realization that preventing extinction of a species is only the most basic goal of captive conservation. A colony of individuals maintained *ex situ* conserves only part of what is important about a species. The ways in which a species interacts with other species and with its environment constitute a set of attributes that should be preserved if species conservation is to be of any real value. Can we hope to preserve endangered ecological interactions as well the endangered species themselves? Consider the monarch butterfly (*Danaus plexippus,* Lepidoptera: Nymphalidae). The monarch is widespread and in no danger of becoming extinct, as a species. But serious threats to the overwintering sites in Mexico (Brower, 1986) endanger the migratory phenomenon that makes the monarch so famous (Urquhart and Urquhart, 1976). If the overwintering sites go, with their unique constellation of nurturing environmental characteristics (Calvert and Brower, 1986), so does the unique multigenerational migration (Brower and Malcolm, 1989) and the dynamic reproductive physiology that evolved to accommodate this extraordinary migratory habit (Herman et al., 1989). The implications of this possible loss are so serious that the monarch migration was designated a threatened phenomenon in The IUCN Invertebrate Red Data Book in 1983. [For historical perspective, recall that the mass migrations of passenger pigeons disappeared well before the actual extinction of the species (Halliday, 1980)].

The monarchs that fly south in the fall to the overwintering sites in California and Mexico are in a state of reproductive diapause and most are virgins (Herman, 1981). The cool, moist conditions of the montane forests at the Mexican overwintering sites help maintain reproductive diapause and sexual inactivity (Herman, 1985) and promote lipid conservation (Masters et al., 1988). Reproductive diapause ends in late January and early February as photoperiod lengthens and temperature increases. Mating takes place at the overwintering sites between mid-February and mid-March, after which juvenile hormone levels increase in the females (Herman and Barker, 1977), stimulating development of the reproductive organs (Herman, 1985) and synthesis of yolk protein (vitellogenin) by the fat body cells (Pan and Wyatt, 1971). Only later, when temperatures approach 20°C and day lengths reach 11 to 12 hours, does egg formation begin (Barker and Herman, 1976). In contrast, non-migratory populations of monarchs in South America are reproductively active throughout the year and do not enter reproductive diapause (L. Brower, pers. comm.). Thus, the dynamic nature of the monarch's reproductive physiology, which is closely adapted to the seasonal and geographical changes in climate associated with the migratory habit, is genetically encoded only in North American populations and could easily be lost without the species becoming extinct. Conserving the behavioral and physiological diversity within a species may be as important a goal as preserving the species itself.

Indeed, conserving the species may be focussing on the wrong level of organization; populations, not species, are the units of evolution and are locally adapted to habitats. Some populations may be more stable than others, possessing a level of genetic and physiologic resilience that allows them to persist through essentially all natural environmental perturbations. Ehrlich and Murphy (1987) call these "reservoir populations" and argue persuasively that, if conservation options are limited, top priority should be given to identifying and preserving them. The value of drawing individuals from reservoir populations as breeding stock for *ex situ* conservation lies in their ability to reproduce successfully under a broader range of conditions, facilitating both captive breeding and subsequent introductions to a broad array of natural areas. If conservation options are more inclusive, representatives from as many locally adapted populations of a species as possible should be included in a captive breeding program, although this raises the knotty question of whether these populations should be maintained separately in captivity. Combining them may break up advantageous genetic combinations that made each of them reproductively successful in their respective habitats, hampering later attempts at reintroduction; maintaining them separately may be considerably more expensive.

It is important to recognize that even the best captive breeding programs inadvertently substitute some degree of artificial selection for natural selection, leading inevitably to unpredictable genetic change in the captive population (Ashton, 1988). The reproductive physiology of most invertebrates is genetically programmed to respond to daily, seasonal, or annual environmental cues. Isolating captive populations from these proximal cues eventually may alter their reproductive physiology to the extent that captively bred individuals lose some or all of their ability to reproduce successfully in the original environment. Unfortunately, the long-term genetic and physiologic consequences of captive breeding of invertebrates are largely unknown, although electrophoretic sampling of robust captive populations should allow a periodic assessment of their genetic health.

Reproductive Physiology

Reproduction in most invertebrates is bisexual; before an egg will develop into an embryo it requires fusion with a sperm cell. This simple statement, however, belies the astonishing variation in modes of germ cell production, storage, delivery, and fusion that occur among invertebrates. Although knowledge of the details of gametogenesis may not be required for successful culture of most invertebrates, it may be important in understanding the genetic structure of populations of some species.

There are, of course, exceptions to the bisexual rule. Parthenogenesis, the development of unfertilized eggs, occurs in several groups of invertebrates and is often associated with freshwater (rather than marine) habitats among aquatic groups such as Gastrotricha, Gastropoda, and Crustacea (Ghiselin, 1974). Among insects, parthenogenesis occurs in some grasshoppers (Acrididae) and cockroaches (Blattidae) and all phasmids (Phasmidae) (Orthoptera), a few moths (e.g., Psychidae, Saturniidae: Lepidoptera), mosquitoes (Diptera), aphids (Homoptera), and many parasitic groups (including Thysanoptera, Hymenoptera, and Homoptera) to name but a few (Chapman, 1971). Parthenogenesis may be obligate, as in some phasmids, sporadic, as in cockroaches, or cyclical (alternating with sexual generations), as in aphids (Moran, 1992). Other variations occur, such as the haploid parthenogenesis in honeybees (Hymenoptera), in which fertilized eggs develop into diploid females and unfertilized eggs into haploid males.

As in vertebrates, sex is usually determined by the distribution of sex chromosomes. Among insects, not all groups have two sex chromosomes. There may be an unpaired X-chromosome (monosome) that occurs singly in the diploid state in one sex (the male in most groups, such as Orthoptera and Homoptera, but sometimes the female, as in some Lepidoptera); the opposite sex then has two X-chromosomes. In many invertebrates, one sex (usually the male) has a pair of dissimilar chromosomes, called X and Y (the heterogametic sex), whereas the other sex has two X-chromosomes (the homogametic sex). Among insects, males are the heterogametic sex in most Hemiptera, Diptera, and Coleoptera, but in many Lepidoptera, females are the heterogametic sex (Wigglesworth, 1972).

Insects account for three-quarters of all named invertebrates, which justifies their selection for detailed description in this section. The reproductive system of most insects consists of paired sexual glands, the testes of the male and the ovaries of the female, paired gonoducts into which the sexual products (sperm and eggs, respectively) are discharged, and a median duct lined with cuticle, derived by invagination from the ventral body wall, forming the vagina in the female and the ejaculatory duct in the male. Considerable variation occurs in the external genitalia of both sexes. The structure of insect reproductive organs has been reviewed by Snodgrass (1935) and a general overview of insect reproductive biology is given in Davey (1965). The following account of insect reproductive anatomy and physiology is greatly condensed from Engelmann (1970) and Wigglesworth (1972). Details of reproductive anatomy and physiology of other invertebrate groups can be found in the four volume series *Reproductive Biology of Invertebrates* (Adiyodi and Adiyodi, 1983, 1984, 1988, 1989).

Female Reproductive System

Anatomy (Figure 2.1). Each ovary is made up of a series of ovarioles (egg tubes) that contain a chain of developing ova. The num-

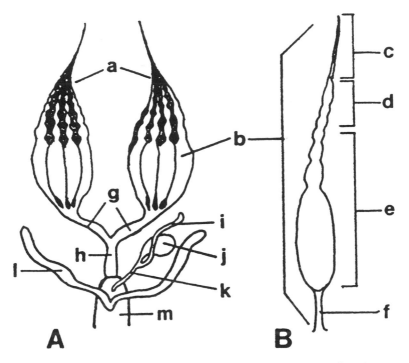

Figure 2.1. A. Generalized female reproductive system of an insect. B. Detail of ovariole (after Snodgrass, 1935); (a) ovaries, (b) ovariole, (c) terminal filament, (d) germarium, (e) vitellarium, (f) ovariole stalk, (g) paired oviducts, (h) common oviduct, (i) spermathecal gland, (j) spermatheca, (k) spermathecal duct, (l) accessory (colleterial) gland, (m) vagina.

ber of ovarioles per ovary varies from one in some aphids to more than 2000 in certain termites. Eggs are released from the two ovaries into paired oviducts, which unite to form the common oviduct, sometimes called the vagina. Associated with the vagina are a number of accessory glands and organs. The spermathecal duct connects the dorsum of the vagina with the spermatheca, a pouch lined with cuticle in which the sperm received at copulation are stored. Often there is a spermathecal gland whose products may activate or nourish the sperm. A bursa copulatrix, formed as a diverticulum from the vagina, receives the sperm (or the sac-like spermatophore containing the sperm) during copulation before the sperm migrate to the spermatheca. The bursa copulatrix is present only in some groups; in the higher Lepidoptera it has an external opening used for copulation that is separate from the vaginal opening through which eggs are laid (see Drummond, 1984 for a review of reproductive structure and function in the Lepidoptera).

The accessory glands, usually one or two pairs, open into the distal portion of the vagina. Often termed "colleterial glands" because of the adhesive cement they produce, these glands also have other functions related to oviposition.

Oogenesis and Oviposition. The ovarioles comprise four zones. A thread-like terminal filament collectively attaches the ovarioles of one ovary to the body wall. At the upper (distal) end of the ovariole is the germarium, a region of densely packed cells from which the primordial germ cells (oogonia) become differentiated into oocytes and nutritive (nurse) cells. The vitellarium occupies the greatest part of the ovariole and contains a series of oocytes, each enclosed in a follicle, that become progressively larger towards the lower (proximal) end. Connecting the vitellarium with the oviduct is the ovariole stalk, a thin-wall tube. While the leading oocyte is ripening it is separated from the lumen of this tube by an epithelial plug, which breaks down during ovulation to release the ripe eggs into the oviduct.

Eggs are carried down the oviducts by waves of peristalsis and are deposited singly or in masses depending on the habits of the species. The accessory glands produce a secretion that coats the eggs and may cause them to adhere to the oviposition surface, as in Lepidoptera. In some groups the secretion forms a gelatinous sheath in which the eggs are embedded, as in the aquatic Trichoptera and Chironomidae (Diptera), or a hard, shell-like egg capsule (ootheca), as in cockroaches (Orthoptera).

Male Reproductive System

Anatomy (Figure 2.2). The testis consists of a series of tubular follicles, which vary greatly in number and arrangement in different

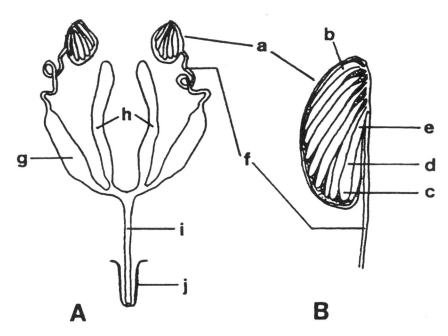

Figure 2.2. A. Generalized male reproductive system of an insect. B. Detail of testis (after Snodgrass, 1935); (a) testis, (b) follicle, (c) germarium, (d) zone of maturation, (e) zone of transformation, (f) vas deferens, (g) vesicula seminalis, (h) accessory glands, (i) ejaculatory duct, (j) aedeagus.

insects. A sheath of connective tissue, often pigmented, encloses the group of follicles, determining the shape of the organ. In Lepidoptera the two testes are often bound together in a single capsule.

The vasa deferentia are a pair of fine ducts that carry sperm from the testes to storage reservoirs (vesicula seminalis) formed by dilation or coiling of the vasa. The vasa deferentia unite and connect with the ejaculatory duct, which is lined with cuticle and surrounded by a powerful muscular coat. The terminus is often enclosed in an evagination of the body wall to form the intromittent penis (aedeagus). Glandular secretions may be produced by the walls of the vasa deferentia and by accessory glands of varied number and form. These secretions may include seminal fluids, sperm activating factors, factors that stimulate oviposition and inhibit courtship receptivity in females, or the material for spermatophores and mating plugs (Chen, 1984).

Spermatogenesis. The follicles of the testes contain a succession of zones with sex cells in different stages of development. The germarium consists of densely packed but growing spermatogonia. These undergo meiosis in the zone of maturation and reduction. In the zone of transformation, the rounded spermatids are converted into flagellated spermatozoa. The numbers produced vary from a few hundred to many millions depending on the species. Spermatogenesis may take place in late larval or nymphal stages in many temperate zone insects, so that mating can occur immediately after adult eclosion (T. C. Emmel, pers. comm.).

Hormonal Control of Reproduction

Postembryonic development and sexual maturation of insects are regulated by hormones that are secreted by several endocrine glands (Wigglesworth 1970; Novak, 1975; Happ, 1992). The most important of these for regulating sexual function are the paired corpora allata, located behind the brain, which secrete terpenoid hormones called juvenile hormones (Menn and Beroza, 1972). In sexually immature stages, juvenile hormones interact with other neurosecretory products (e.g., ecdysones) to regulate metamorphosis. In adult insects, juvenile hormones become gonadotropic and stimulate vitellogenesis in females and spermatogenesis in males. In females, after yolk formation, a multilayered proteinaceous chorion, or egg shell, is manufactured around each oocyte. Unlike vitellogenesis, this process of choriogenesis takes place in the absence of hormonal modulators. But juvenile hormone is required for development and maintenance of many female accessory glands (Willis, 1974), the secretions of which coat eggs and protect them from desiccation and mechanical damage. Likewise, juvenile hormones are required to stimulate male genital accessory glands to produce fluids that nourish and protect the sperm (Leopold, 1976).

Mating and Fertilization

Reproductive behavior of endangered invertebrates is discussed by Demarest and Bradley (chap. 3, this volume). More detailed reviews of insect mating systems, including sexual selection and sperm competition, can be found in Blum and Blum (1979), Thornhill and Alcock (1983), and Smith (1984a). Courtship and mating of invertebrates involve the use of diverse stimuli, including vision (color, pattern, luminescence, and movement), scents (male and female, long distance and close range), sounds (including stridulation), vibrations (as on spider webs), and may depend on endogenous rhythms set by lunar or solar cycles (as in the mass shedding of gametes by many marine invertebrates). The complexity of stimuli required for successful courtship in higher insects may be difficult to duplicate in captive settings, even if they can be fully identified. For Lepidoptera, the technique of hand-pairing butterflies and larger moths (Clarke and Sheppard, 1956) has proved useful in bypassing specific courtship requirements in many species. Even so, problems remain; for example, although hand-pairing has been particularly successful in the Papilionidae, many tropical members of this family refuse to oviposit in captivity (K.S. Brown, Jr., pers. comm.).

External fertilization is common among aquatic invertebrates; gametes are usually shed directly into the water but may be enclosed in a membranous sac or spermatophore. Spermatophores are common among terrestrial invertebrates and make possible external fertilization in such insect orders as Thysanura and Collembola, in which males deposit spermatophores on the courtship surface to be picked up later by females, who insert the spermatophores into their vaginas. Odonata also use external fertilization but the male and female fly in tandem while the male deposits a spermatophore externally on his body; the female, held by the neck by the male's claspers, bends her abdomen underneath his to pick up the spermatophore. But most terrestrial insects rely on internal fertilization. Sperm may be passed in fluid form, usually into the vagina, as in *Drosophila* (Diptera) or, more rarely, directly into the spermatheca, as in the bug *Lygaeus* (Hemiptera). Transfer of sperm in a spermatophore, formed by the secretion of the male accessory glands, occurs in the largest insect orders, including Lepidoptera, many Orthoptera, Neuroptera, Trichoptera, Hymenoptera, and Coleoptera. The spermatophore is usually transferred to the bursa copulatrix, after which the sperm migrate from the spermatophore across the vagina and into the spermatheca, sometimes under their own movement and sometimes aided by contractions of the female genital tract, or both.

Unusual methods of sperm transfer occur in some groups. For example, males of the bedbug, *Cimex* (Hemiptera), bypass the female genital opening by using their sharp aedeagus to pierce the female's integument and discharge sperm into a pouch of special tissue on her lower abdominal surface; the sperm must reach the female's genital tract by wandering through the body cavity. Lost sperm and seminal fluids are thus added to the female's hemolymph, a nutritional enrichment resulting in increased oogenesis (Carayon,

1964). Researchers are increasingly recognizing the nutrient contribution to female reproduction (egg production, longevity, etc.) made by males during copulation in the form of external feeding or by transfer of nutrients in seminal fluids (e.g., see Gwynne, 1984).

Fertilization occurs when sperm migrating down the spermathecal duct from the spermatheca to the vagina encounter a ripe egg released from the ovaries. Sperm enter the egg through one or more micropyles, points on the egg where the chorion is either very thin or perforated. Fertilization may occur in a modified portion of the vagina called the vestibulum, in which the egg is held just prior to oviposition with the micropylar end facing the opening of the spermathecal duct. Polyspermy is almost universal among insects, yet only one of the many sperm that enter the egg is actually involved in fertilization.

The spermathecae of many arthropods are capable of storing sperm for long periods and females of many groups mate only once, drawing on this sperm supply to fertilize their eggs as they are laid (Parker, 1970). Multiple mating is common in some groups, however, such as Lepidoptera, offering the possibility of sperm competition (Smith, 1984b). In such cases, the last male to mate usually fertilizes the female's remaining eggs (Drummond, 1984; Gwynne, 1984), an important consideration in attempts to manipulate genetic diversity in captive colonies.

Invertebrates display a variety of special modes of reproduction (Engelmann, 1970), including polyembryony (e.g., in some parasitic Hymenoptera), ovoviviparity and viviparity (e.g., some Diptera), neoteny and paedogenesis (e.g., some Coleoptera), and hermaphroditism (e.g., some Plecoptera and Homoptera among the insects, and Gastropoda among the mollusks).

Environmental and Social Influences On Reproductive Physiology

Invertebrate fecundity is strongly influenced by environmental conditions. Hence, it is best studied and understood at the population level, with careful consideration given to the range of ecological conditions that shape population dynamics and species distributions (Labeyrie, 1978). By definition, *ex situ* captive breeding isolates populations from many relevant ecological influences, including interspecific interactions, and may also alter social structure. It is important to remember that the ecological separation of immature and adult stages in holometabolous insects (those with complete metamorphosis) means that conditions experienced in the larval stage may influence profoundly the reproductive physiology of the adult in ways not readily apparent from studying adult populations only. Conversely, maternal effects (genetic or environmental differences among adult females that are expressed as phenotypic differences in their offspring) complicate our understanding of reproductive strategies by adding a cross-generational component to regulation of diapause, sexual differentiation and maturation, dispersal behavior, development time, growth rate, and survival (Mousseau and Dingle, 1991).

Temporal Organization of Reproductive Activity

In the face of regular variation in environmental parameters in all but the most uniform tropical habitats, it is the task of the invertebrate reproductive system to produce offspring at the most appropriate time and place (Davey, 1965; Bailey and Ridsdill-Smith, 1991). Species with external fertilization, such as many marine invertebrates, synchronously release gametes using lunar or other external cues. Among terrestrial species, proper timing of reproduction becomes ever more important as environments become more temporally heterogeneous. In strongly seasonal environments, such as those at high latitudes and elevations, reproduction is limited to seasons that offer appropriate temperatures. In tropical areas that experience a severe dry season, it is the availability of moisture that determines reproductive activity (Opler, 1989). Invertebrates may respond to an unfavorable season by entering a state of developmental or reproductive diapause. Such an arrest of activity may be a direct effect of an adverse environment, easily reversed when favorable conditions return, or it may be a true diapause, under hormonal control and triggered by a regular environmental cue like day length, that persists even during intermittent favorable conditions (Wigglesworth, 1972). In climates without unfavorable seasons, timing of reproduction may be set by interactions with other species, either by the necessity of a mutualistic association or by the need to avoid predators or parasites (Gilbert, 1977).

Superimposed on seasonal patterns of reproductive activity are local environmental and social influences. Both vitellogenesis and oviposition may be stimulated by presence of larval host plants (in phytophagous species) or by an appropriate meal by carnivorous or blood sucking invertebrates (Labeyrie, 1978). Ovarian activity is often controlled by copulation, either by hormonal factors in the seminal fluid, by sperm, or by copulation itself (Engelmann, 1970; Leopold, 1976; Monsma et al., 1990). Other intraspecific stimuli of ovarian activity include population density and crowding effects (as in Acrididae) and social feeding (as in social Hymenoptera) (Labeyrie, 1978). In sum, the quality, quantity, and distribution of ovarian reserves depend not only on the nutritional status of the female (which, in turn, may depend heavily on conditions experienced in the larval stage) and her genotype, but also on the stimuli (environmental and social) to which she is subjected during ovarian activity (Labeyrie, 1978).

Temperature

Invertebrates are poikilothermous animals, and their rates of egg production and sperm formation are temperature dependent, increasing with increasing temperature but falling off after an inhibitory high temperature is reached. The temperature limits of reproduction, however, are often much narrower than the range of temperatures over which other activities can flourish. Sometimes there are sexual differences in the tolerance of temperature extremes, with the male usually more sensitive than the female (Wigglesworth, 1972). Tropical species generally have narrower temperature tolerance ranges than temperate species, resulting from the broader range of temperatures that the latter have experienced during their evolution. Humidity is an important, temperature-related environmental component, especially for tropical forest species. Many tropical insects in seasonal environments enter reproductive diapause at the beginning of the dry season to avoid desiccation. The butterfly *Eurema daira* (Pieridae) in Costa Rica, for example, migrates to moist shady areas (stream margins, pasture edges) at the beginning of the dry season and enters reproductive diapause. Associated with these changes in behavior across the wet season/dry season boundary are phenotypic changes of color pattern and morphology (Opler, 1989) and physiological changes in reproductive function (Drummond, Emmel, Szelistowski, unpublished), which together form an adaptive complex that allows the species to successfully track the sharply changing environmental conditions.

Nutrition

Insect digestive systems are morphologically and physiologically complex (Terra, 1990), reflecting an extraordinary range of adaptations to their diverse food sources, especially plants (Jaenike, 1990; Price et al., 1991). A broad array of insect species requires the presence of internally living microbial symbionts to digest otherwise nutritionally inaccessible food sources, e.g., wood-feeding beetles, termites, and roaches (Slansky and Rodriguez, 1987a).

Because much of the expense of reproduction in insects is financed by energy collected and stored in the larval stage, egg production in the adult may be greatly influenced by larval nutrition (Wigglesworth, 1972). Larval feeding that is quantitatively or qualitatively inadequate can result in adults of smaller size and of reduced fecundity (Slansky and Rodriguez, 1987a). But not all insects depend entirely on larval feeding for adult reproduction. Lepidoptera can be classified into three overlapping groups according to the state of the ovaries at the time of eclosion (Wigglesworth, 1972): (1) those with few fully developed eggs, the rest being matured after emergence; (2) those with all eggs fully mature, with no more to be developed; and (3) an intermediate condition. Clearly, Lepidoptera belonging to the first group (many butterflies and some long-lived moths) must rely on adult feeding to obtain nutritional resources for egg maturation. Obligate pollen-feeding by adult female passion-flower butterflies (*Heliconius*: Nymphalidae) is perhaps an extreme example; pollen is collected on the proboscis and digested extracellularly to release amino acids that are absorbed and used in egg development (Gilbert, 1972). Similarly, egg production of most blood-sucking species (e.g., bed bugs and mosquitoes) is determined by the quantity of blood consumed by the adult (Wigglesworth, 1972). An additional effect of adult feeding is to prolong adult lifespan, lengthening the time available for oviposition and thereby increasing total fecundity (Miller, 1989).

Nutrition can alter the rate of egg maturation by affecting the activity of the corpus allatum, which secretes a hormone that regulates yolk deposition in developing oocytes (Wigglesworth, 1972; Raikhel and Dhadialla, 1992). The endocrine-like functions of the corpora allata also control a suite of other reproductive processes in a variety of insects, including male maturation, female scent production, and initiation of sexual feeding behavior.

Larval and adult nutrition can also affect courtship and mating success. In some Lepidoptera, mating success of males depends on the production of courtship pheromones, which requires alkaloid precursors obtained from either the larval food plant, as in the case of the moth, *Utethesia* (Arctiidae) (Conner et al., 1981), or from specific adult nectar sources, as in the case of ithomiine butterflies (Pliske, 1975). Slansky and Rodriguez (1987a) review the effect of nutrition on quality of courtship signals and mating success, resource allocation to reproduction, and other aspects of arthropod reproductive physiology.

Conclusions

Detailed knowledge of reproductive physiology (including timing of gametogenesis, social effects on reproductive behavior, and environmental strategies such as diapause) is clearly important to successful conservation of invertebrates, especially for managing small nature reserves and for captive breeding programs. A key question is: "How representative of invertebrate reproductive physiology are those species that have received intense study?" The answer is, "Not very." Reproductive processes vary tremendously in detail from species to species; there is no "invertebrate type" of reproduction, any more than there is a "vertebrate type" of reproduction (Davey, 1967). The result is that captive breeding of major groups of invertebrates requires different approaches, and that even within a seemingly homogeneous group such as the Lepidoptera, enormous variety exists between and within families and subfamilies, requiring intimate knowledge of the physiological ecology and behavior of the species to be reared.

Most invertebrates can survive and reproduce only within a relatively limited suite of ecological conditions. These conditions must be identified and replicated if *ex situ* conservation is to be successful. The range of tolerance that an insect displays toward these ecological requirements is mediated by its physiology, which, in turn, is dictated by its genetic makeup. The more specialized an insect is in its reproductive requirements (i.e., the more narrow its tolerances), the more difficult it will be to duplicate and sustain its ecological needs in an artificial environment, and the more susceptible the *ex situ* colony will be to failure. Although their small size makes it possible to contain many more species of invertebrates than vertebrates in the same space, this advantage is more than offset by the fact that most invertebrates have much more exacting environmental and nutritional requirements than most vertebrates.

3

Behavioral Research with Endangered Invertebrate Species

Jack Demarest and Marcia Bradley

Regardless of the list used to identify endangered species, the vast majority of the invertebrates listed are commercially valuable molluscs and relatively large, conspicuous insects, particularly the butterflies. Only a few of the estimated 30 million or more species (Erwin, 1982; Wilson, 1987b) have been surveyed and fewer still have been observed in sufficient detail to reveal how they interact with their environments and other organisms. Captive behavioral research on endangered invertebrates fundamentally does not exist.

Scope of Current Research

Much of the research on an endangered or threatened invertebrate species is concerned with its known distribution, historical range, and general ecological requirements (e.g., food plants, temperature range, humidity). Behavioral information, where it exists, has largely been gathered in the field with occasional laboratory supplementation. Population size and distribution studies have found that geographic ranges are generally small. For example, before 1983 the El Segundo blue butterfly (*Euphilotes battoides*), occupied only two small dune remnants, 302 acres (122 ha) and 1.6 acres (0.6 ha) in area along the California coastline (Arnold and Goins, 1987). One population has since been lost to development (Anonymous, 1987b). In Britain, a colony of several hundred heath fritillary butterflies (*Mellicta athalia*), have existed for over 10 years in only 0.25 ha of breeding habitat (Warren, 1991). The autecological studies of Arnold

37

(1981a, 1983a) on six lycaenid butterflies, Arnold and Goins (1987) on the El Segundo blue, and the research by Ehrlich and his colleagues (e.g., Brussard and Ehrlich, 1970; Ehrlich, et al., 1975; Brown and Ehrlich, 1980; Ehrlich, 1984; Murphy and Weiss, 1988) on the population biology of the Bay checkerspot butterfly (*Euphydryas editha*) are the most comprehensive. These authors demonstrated that the most important factor contributing to declining populations is degradation of their habitats, particularly the loss of larval food plants. These species are univoltine, reproducing only once a year, and their entire life history is associated with their larval food plants. The El Segundo blue butterfly uses buckwheat (*Eriogonum parvifolium*) not only for larval food, but also as oviposition and pupation sites, nectar for adults, basking sites for larval and adult thermoregulation, perching sites for males searching for females, and visual or chemical landmarks for females locating males.

The autecological approach includes study of weather conditions, an accounting of food plants in their various mature and immature stages, as well as population characteristics such as population size, aggregation density, sex and age ratios, movement and dispersal statistics, mortality statistics, and survival or longevity rates. Most of this research involves short-term sampling of a population, omitting labor intensive ethological descriptions or longitudinal evaluation typical of vertebrate studies. The more intensive studies by Arnold (1983a, 1988a) and Ehrlich (1965, 1984) also provide data on site preferences, mate selection, foraging strategies, and sex and age differences in behavior. Much of their data result from capture-recapture studies which identify individuals and determine their approximate ages and vagilities (rates of movement). Although detailed descriptions of behavior are uncommon, the similarity within families is evident in the research that does exist (Arnold, 1983a; Arnold and Goins, 1987). But little is known about behavioral variation within most invertebrate species, much less between taxonomically or ecologically similar species, and it may be that individual differences are much greater and more profound than is typically assumed (Scott, 1975; Barrows, 1976; Colgan, 1983; Frohlich and Tepedino, 1986; Huettel, 1986).

Functions of Behavioral Research in Captivity

If most of the research on invertebrate population biology has ignored behavior, then why is it important to include behavioral studies in captive conservation programs? We believe there are at least five reasons.

First, knowledge of behavior can be used to enhance existing populations and facilitate the reintroduction efforts of captive breeding programs. The United States and Great Britain have set aside several reserves for maintaining and enhancing endangered invertebrate species. These reserves were established decades ago without much thought about how they were used by these animals (Pyle, 1976; Thomas, 1980, 1984, 1991). The U.S. Fish and Wildlife Service now requires the development of recovery plans to help ensure that these animals' ecological requirements are met. Arnold and Goins (1987) described one such recovery plan for the El Segundo blue butterfly that has resulted in its population increase in the wild, and similar recovery plans have been suggested for a number of other endangered insects in California (Arnold, 1983b, c, 1984, 1985a, b). Each of the plans calls for the identification of the stringent microhabitat requirements of the animal, and this is reliably determined mainly by observation of its reproductive behavior, thermoregulatory behavior, foraging behavior, and dispersal patterns.

One of the major problems faced by invertebrate conservation programs is the lack of public appreciation for this, the largest group of organisms. The public typically makes a distinction between animals (vertebrates) and bugs or insects (most invertebrates), often characterizing the latter taxa as pests (Barrows et al., 1983). The media frequently reinforce this attitude (Mertins, 1986). Therefore, a second function for behavioral studies, especially of rare and threatened species, is that accurate behavioral films and exhibits are effective ways to promote public education about these animals and the complex and elegant roles they play in global ecology (Schneirla, 1958, 1959; Saul-Gershenz et al., chap. 4, this volume).

Behavioral research can also be valuable as an "early warning signal" of habitat destruction, and as a means for assessing the ecological flexibility of the species. Typically, habitat assessment is done by employing broad criteria like the relative rarity or diversity or "naturalness" of the existing fauna (Usher, 1986). The Mission blue butterfly (*Plebejus icarioides missionensis*) is one example. It was an indicator of the threat to at least a dozen other populations of animals and plants on San Bruno Mountain in California (Arnold, 1987b). While mapping the decline in its numbers did not necessitate behavioral research, by the time a decline was recognized it was already too late to do much to revitalize the community. Behavioral

assays of feeding, mate selection, and oviposition could have anticipated the problem. For some species, a better understanding of their
sensory physiology and search strategies (Bell, 1990, 1991), and their
chemical ecology and host-plant adaptations and preferences (Via,
1990) may permit their translocation to geographically different but
ecologically acceptable alternative habitats (e.g., Warren et al., 1984).
In fact, it is not difficult to imagine that experimental manipulation
of microhabitat characteristics *in situ* or in captivity would be especially useful in identifying the critical physiological mechanisms and
ecological stimuli used by the animals.

Finally, longitudinal ecological and behavioral research carried out *in situ* and in captivity not only aid in understanding the
factors that limit population size for a given endangered animal,
but can also help us to understand the mechanisms that affect
population sizes of economically important species.

Behavioral research, then, may benefit conservation efforts
by: (1) increasing sizes of existing populations of endangered species, (2) assessing critical habitat and the ecological flexibility of
the animals, (3) providing knowledge essential to captive breeding
and/or population control programs, and (4) raising public awareness. To this list we add the basic scientific benefit of assessing
ecological theory (e.g., Ehrlich and Birch, 1967). Studies of invertebrates are particularly useful in this regard because most species
are relatively small and have short generation times in comparison
to vertebrates. Much of our knowledge of genetics has been obtained
from invertebrate species. Furthermore, ecobehavioral studies in
the field (Brussard and Ehrlich, 1970) and in experimental settings
(Tuskes, 1981) have revealed limitations in current ecological
thought. Thus, behavioral research, especially experimental studies,
can be an important means for examining the ecological principles
used to identify and describe species at risk.

Methods of Research in Captivity

Captivity typically brings to mind images of artificial control. One
thinks of captivity in terms of laboratory animals or zoo exhibits or,
less frequently, tracts of land (reserves) set aside for one or more
species (Sullivan and Shaffer, 1975). But it may be more useful to
think of captivity as confinement of any sort. An island is a captive
environment for many species (MacArthur and Wilson, 1967), and
the existence of habitat islands (Arnold, 1981a, 1983a; Ehrlich,

1984; Ehrlich et al., 1988) and isolated community ecosystems (Whittaker, 1970) that support endangered species are in some sense as much like captive settings as a biological pest control center (Boller, 1972) or an animal behavior laboratory (Boice, 1980, 1981). In this view, an isolated habitat can be thought of as a large cage or enclosure within which observations and manipulations can take place. Captive animal research, then, includes field methods as well as laboratory methods, and lends itself to revealing ecological and evolutionary principles as well as providing detailed ethological descriptions of specific animals in specific, sometimes artificial, settings.

Field studies of invertebrates are almost always concerned with a particular behavioral phenomenon (e.g., chemosensory perception, foraging, mating behavior) or, more often, with population parameters and ecology. Behavioral investigation, in the latter type of study, is often incidental to the main focus of the research. Field studies of endangered species typically fall into this category. Two of the better examples of field research with endangered species that shed light on behavior are those by Arnold (1983a) and Ehrlich (Ehrlich et al., 1975). Using mark-recapture techniques (Ehrlich and Davidson, 1960; Southwood, 1978a; Gall, 1984a), they studied populations of several endangered species of butterflies in California over several decades. On each butterfly, a unique number or identification pattern was written in indelible ink on the distal portion of its fore- and hindwing undersurface. Butterflies were marked and released as soon as possible after capture. Physical condition and age were estimated by a wing-wear rating system (Watt et al., 1977). Given that assumptions of equal catchability and survivability of marked individuals have been met (see section on "problems of research in captivity," this chapter), statistical analysis of mark-recapture data can yield information on spatial distribution and home range, vagility, and crowding/dispersal relationships. Similar information can also be collected with postdiapausal larvae (Weiss et al., 1987, 1988; White and Singer, 1987). Combined with information on adult wing wear and sex, age-specific and gender-specific patterns for these behaviors can be determined (e.g., Gall, 1984b) and compared to closely related but nonendangered species (Murphy et al., 1986), other populations in different habitats (Brussard and Ehrlich, 1970), and sympatric species that are unrelated (Scott, 1973). Labor-intensive field studies, lasting up to two years and involving a number of study habitats, have enabled Arnold (1988a) to provide a more complete description of the behavioral repertoire of the threatened Oregon silverspot butterfly (*Speyeria zerene hippolyta*). He has identified eight primary and twenty secondary behaviors and their associations with particular habitats, topographic features, plant species, and weather conditions. Less labor-intensive, indirect measures of behavior, such as dispersal estimates based on wing-wear condition at first capture, turn out to have limited value if a species' entire flight period is not monitored (Murphy et al., 1986). Much of this research is now performed with the aid of portable calculators and computers with data management software (e.g., Arnold, 1988b; Ball, 1990), some of which require the use of digitizers for entering location data (Arnold, 1986). Many sampling techniques have been used for collecting nonthreatened species including ultraviolet lights, baits, and pitfall, windowpane, and Malaise traps, some of which permit night sampling for nocturnal species (Southwood, 1978a). However, some of these methods are of questionable value when sampling endangered populations because they can contribute to the problem.

A major problem in this comparative fieldwork, despite the use of similar techniques, is that butterfly species are heterogeneous in nearly all ecological characteristics (e.g., vagility, host density, reproductive capacity). This heterogeneity makes it difficult to make meaningful comparisons, particularly of characteristics that might contribute to extinction. Most research has yielded only rather obvious results: species at risk are short-lived, comparatively sedentary, typically endemic to small plots of land isolated by urban and industrial sprawl, and almost always host-plant specialists.

Occasionally, fortuitous or planned field experiments have been carried out. Shuster (1981b), for example, documented intraspecific cannibalism by healthy members of the endangered Socorro isopod (*Thermosphaeroma thermophilum*) after sweep netting accidently injured some animals in the sampled population. In addition, Fletcher and Underwood (1987) isolated some of the variables influencing interspecific competition between two sympatric species of limpet (*Patelloida* spp.) by experimentally manipulating the numbers and types of substrates available in a subtidal zone. Less often, controlled laboratory studies are performed. Shuster's (1981a) detailed analysis of mate selection strategies in the Socorro isopod, and the studies of host fish specificity in the endangered fresh water pearly mussel (*Lampsilis higginsi*) (Sylvester et al., 1984) are unusual in this regard. Laboratory studies that focus on more specific genetic, biochemical, and physiological factors are common for invertebrates, but rare for species listed as endangered.

Problems of Research in Captivity

Most of the methods used to study the behavior of endangered invertebrates may be criticized to some degree for being inaccurate, invalid or even for placing the animals at risk. Sampling and marking techniques, for example, are commonly used to estimate the size of populations, dispersal patterns and intraspecific behavior (Southwood, 1978a, 1978b), but the requirement that the animal's behavior and survival is not affected by the technique does not always receive appropriate attention. Adverse effects of marking include direct effects on activity levels and social behavior (e.g., producing an immobile or sexually unreceptive organism), and conditioned reactions that affect recapture (e.g., "trap happiness" or, conversely, emigration). Conspicuous marks may also increase risk of predation, and can affect the reactions of unmarked members of the population (e.g., mate selection, resource competition). Gall (1984a) found that newly-marked butterflies behaved differently than unmarked ones for up to 1–2 hours after release. Similarly, Greenslade (1964) found that marked carabid beetles showed abnormal movement soon after their release. In many cases, this effect may be due to handling rather than marking per se, since Gall (1984a) did not observe this decrement in activity when previously marked butterflies were netted but not handled before release. Furthermore, the application of anesthesia for marking, commonly used with insects, has been shown to prematurely age honey bees and may have the same effect on some other insects (Southwood, 1978b). Chilling, covering an animal with a net (Murdoch, 1963), or using a suction tube (Muir, 1958) to hold an animal for marking are alternative handling procedures.

Sampling provides another set of problems. For relatively immobile organisms like molluscs, direct-search surveys are probably adequate given that a habitat is systematically explored. More mobile creatures that are relatively conspicuous like butterflies and some kinds of beetles can be sampled by visual searches, aerial or sweep netting, using a variety of traps, or baiting individuals of one sex to caged, pheromone-producing individuals of the opposite sex. In all cases, however, the particular collecting method is very selective (Usher, 1986). For example, a pitfall trap may be very successful at catching large numbers of individuals in a population but unsuccessful in reflecting the size, sex ratio or age-range of the population being sampled (Disney, 1968, 1976; Disney et al., 1982). Furse et al. (1981) showed that representative sampling using pond netting varied with both site and operator, and Disney et al. (1982) noted that small differences in design or even the state of cleanliness of a Malaise trap can produce significant differences in a catch. Furthermore, visual searches of the same habitat can give different impressions of species richness and abundances than Malaise traps (e.g., Barrows, 1986). Muirhead-Thomson (1991) has provided a recent summary and assessment of various trap designs for flying insects, including those that have been used for the study of endangered species.

Capture-recapture methods have been used with many butterfly species to determine their population dynamics, especially spatial distribution and life history characteristics. However, this procedure has been shown to bias sex-ratio estimates in some endangered species because of differences in the flight behavior of males and females (Brussard and Ehrlich, 1970; Arnold, 1983a; Gall, 1984b). Murphy et al. (1986) argued that capture-recapture is not a particularly useful methodology by itself for revealing differences between populations of endangered and nonendangered species. The implication is that most population studies of invertebrates have not provided much information on the operative characteristics of the species at risk (Ehrlich et al., 1975). They have, at best, pointed to fairly obvious ecological conditions that are typically beyond reclamation, and they may have vastly misrepresented the actual population dynamics of the species in question (Brussard and Ehrlich, 1970).

Pest-control laboratories are already aware that behavior is one of the more important components of a rearing program. The requirement that mass-produced organisms interact normally with their natural counterparts necessitates an understanding of species-typical behavior. Do ethograms of field and captive animals differ? Do mass produced animals distribute themselves normally in their habitat? Do they respond appropriately in a social situation? Will they become sexually integrated within their wild population? Will they reproduce and perform parental obligations in appropriate ways? Boller (1972) discusses the concept of inbreeding bottlenecks in mass-rearing programs and points out that selection in the laboratory typically favors individuals that are adapted to laboratory conditions, and not necessarily to the natural conditions. Reared on artificial substrates (e.g., larval diet, oviposition devices), successfully reared individuals may be ones that are physiologically compatible with an artificial diet, but maladapted to naturally existing ecosystems. Individual organisms selected in this way may not exhibit normal courtship or mating behavior (Fletcher et al., 1968). Oviposition behavior may be altered so that smooth surfaces may be selected instead of textured ones, or eggs may be dropped instead of attached to the leaf undersurfaces (Richardson, 1925), or host preferences conditioned in the lab may isolate captive-reared from wild-type animals (Bush, 1969). The absence or reduction of home range and reduced flight distance in captivity could also produce two spatially segregated populations in nature as the captive-reared organisms concentrate more and more at release sites while wild-type organisms emigrate to less dense areas (Monroe, 1966). Boller (1972) provided numerous examples of changed behaviors of mass-reared insects, and it is not unreasonable to conclude that similar captive-rearing "errors" will exist in breeding programs for endangered species.

Factors to Consider in Behavioral Studies

Invertebrate behavior is affected by a variety of environmental and social influences, and conservation efforts will require attention to these factors. Here, consideration of some of these is simplified by discussing nonsocial ecological influences like climate and habitat separately from intra- and inter-species relationships.

Nonsocial Factors

The lifespan of most endangered invertebrates is short, and the biology and behaviors of these species are typically governed by environmental factors like light, temperature, wind, and in many cases the location of host plants. In butterflies, host plants serve as nutrition, breeding "leks" (Arnold, 1983a), oviposition sites for females, perching sites for "roosting" and for thermoregulatory "basking" and "wing pumping" (Porter, 1982; Arnold, 1988a), and in some cases for antipredator defense (Eisner, 1970, 1980; Bowers, 1990). Many other herbivorous invertebrates including most of the endangered insects are larval food-plant specialists. In Britain, the decline of populations of the brown argus butterfly (*Aricia agestis*) is due neither to weather nor to larval host plant density, but to the organic nitrogen content and mesophyll thickness of these plants which are often found on chalk and limestone downs (Bourn and Thomas, 1993).

Habitat preferences also characterize the distribution of other endangered invertebrates. Tree snails, for instance, prefer certain trees over others presumably because the surface of smooth-barked trees facilitates algae growth and ease of movement (Voss, 1976; Tuskes, 1981). Erwin's (1982, 1983a, b) studies of insects inhabiting the canopy of tropical rain forests suggest that 20% or more of these species are restricted to specific plant genera, and over 80% of all beetle species are found in only one type of forest. In the United States, the Delta green ground beetle (*Elaphrus viridis*) is a carabid species located exclusively around intermittent bodies of water in or near the Jepson Prairie Preserve of California (Arnold, 1983c, 1985b).

Given the ubiquity of habitat preferences, migration may not be an issue for the majority of invertebrates in a captive conservation program. Homing has been documented in experiments with butterflies (Keller et al., 1966), many kinds of Hymenoptera (Wilson, 1971), and freshwater limpets (Hulings, 1985), and often results in a highly circumscribed population structure (Ehrlich et al., 1975) in which individuals "choose" not to move even though there are no physical barriers to movement. Moreover, Scott's (1975) comparative research on lepidopteran flight patterns shows that taxonomically similar species have similar flight distances, and the flights of captive reared individuals are similar to those of wild individuals. Rearing characteristics, however, can significantly alter dispersal patterns of individual butterflies. For example, thermal environments affect the rates of larval and pupal development as well as the phenology of their host plants which, in turn, determine the phase relationships between flight behavior in adults and host plant senescence (Weiss et al., 1988).

Finally, site preferences may also affect reproductive behavior. For example, in many insects the oviposition response is highly site specific and selection of a place to deposit eggs is precisely governed by discriminatory activity (Richardson, 1925; Bell, 1990). The narrowly endemic alpine butterfly (*Boloria acrocnema*) has been observed to exhibit a variety of pre-ovipositional behaviors (e.g., tarsal drumming, abdominal curling) that presumably aid in selection of its preferred ovipositional substrate (Gall, 1984b). The Oregon silverspot butterfly rapidly taps and scrapes withered violet foliage or stems with its forelegs, presumably releasing a chemical cue that identifies the plant as a violet (Arnold, 1988a). In captivity, some species oviposit on almost any convenient surface while others adhere rigidly to specific substrates. Most of the variables that influence oviposition and site specificity may be controlled under captive conditions, typically resulting in an abnormal rearing environment. Thus, it will be important to identify the stimuli that affect these behaviors, the sensory mechanisms used to detect these stimuli, the degree of influence of these and other stimuli in captivity, and the extent to which captive rearing experiences transfer to natural conditions as part of reintroduction efforts.

Social Factors

Government-sponsored conservation recovery plans and captive propagation programs often ignore intra- and inter-specific influences, focusing instead on space and food resources (Sullivan and Shaffer, 1975) or efficient mass rearing techniques (Boller, 1972). Field studies, however, have identified many intra- and inter-species factors that need to be considered in conservation efforts.

Intraspecies Influences. Perching, investigative flights, chasing, swarming, and pre-nuptial flights (Scott, 1973; Arnold, 1988a) are behaviors exhibited by some endangered butterfly species that represent qualitatively different stages of mating behavior. Hilltopping is another mate-locating behavior (Shields, 1967; Scott, 1968; Arnold, 1983a; Alcock, 1987; Alcock and Smith, 1987). Mate guarding in the male Socorro isopod (Shuster, 1981a) and selective resistance by females to insemination attempts are two reproductive strategies that influence reproductive success. A number of other behavioral strategies exhibited by one or more endangered invertebrates have evolutionary significance: sperm precedence (Ehrlich, 1965), "spread-the-risk" egg laying and dispersal by females (Gall, 1984b), and post-reproductive mortality among semelparous species (Voss, 1976). Whether or not these activities are essential to effective captive conservation programs remains to be seen, however, the crowded conditions of most mass-rearing programs can defeat their adaptive purposes. Activity like hilltopping is unlikely to be incorporated in these programs, and the cannibalistic nature of the larva of some species (Arnold, 1987a) also makes mass-rearing programs more costly and labor intensive.

Interspecies Influences. The parasitic relationship between *Lampsilis* mussels and their fish hosts seems vitally important to the mussel's survival. Glochidia (larvae) move with difficulty in streams and rivers and must be transported upstream to avoid displacement seaward. Fish serve as hosts for this purpose. The pearly mussel has a minnow-like appendage which it flashes, attracting large, hungry fish. Glochidia are taken into the fish's mouth where they attach to the gill filaments of the host, absorbing nutrients over the next few weeks. They finally break out and settle to the river bottom in a new location, ideally upstream (Welsh, 1969). Pearly mussels have become endangered due to pollution and pearl fishing, and *in vitro* culture with artificial growth medium (Isom and Hudson, 1982) has been used to maintain the species, but restocking has yet to succeed in producing a self-sustaining population (Young and Williams, 1983; Woodward, 1990). Identifying the mechanisms of this process, as well as the details of substrate preference and fish host specificity, has yet to be worked out (Sylvester et al., 1984). An additional problem for conservation efforts is the viability of host fish populations which have also become threatened by pollution (e.g., Altaba, 1990).

A number of butterfly species have larvae that are symbiotic with specific ant species and sometimes with several species (Wilson, 1971; Arnold, 1981a; Picrcc and Mcad, 1981; Ravenscroft, 1990; Jordano and Thomas, 1992; Jordano et al., 1992). By stroking them while they feed on their plant hosts, the ants stimulate larvae to discharge sugars and amino acids from dorsal glands which the ants ingest. In return, the larvae are protected from predators and parasites by their attendants (Pierce and Mead, 1981). In fact, the larvae attract the ants with calls. DeVries (1990) recorded substrate-borne calls in many lycaenid caterpillar species, and concluded that calling may be ubiquitous among ant-associated species. Nitrogen intake also seems to encourage myrmecophily because larvae can produce more or better quality amino acids. Baylis and Pierce (1991) reported that *Jalmenus evagoras* larvae reared on plants treated with nitrogen fertilizer attracted more ant attendants and had higher survival than larvae reared on untreated plants. According to Hinton (1951), this mutualistic relationship has become obligatory for many, if not all, of the lycaenids attended by ants. He argued that if the secretion is not removed regularly by the ants, the larvae will die. However, several of the endangered ant-tended lycaenid butterflies have been reared in the lab without ants, therefore this is probably a facultive rather than obligatory relationship (Arnold, pers. comm.).

Finally, defense against predation is an important factor in the ecology of most insect species (Evans and Schmidt, 1990) and attention to predator-prey relationships ought to be a consideration of captive conservation programs. Behavioral adaptations and strategies may be physiologically costly and are likely to impact upon reproductive potential (Schmidt, 1990). In captive breeding programs, these are the phenotypes that would be negatively affected by selection for increased reproductive capacity. Moreover, strategies for avoiding high parasitoid mortality in the wild; e.g., by migration or off-host oviposition (Lederhouse, 1990), may not be possible in captivity or may be incorrectly viewed as artifacts of captivity, and threats due to parasite infestation may require special attention.

Future Directions

Behavior is a product of natural selection, and invertebrates usually exhibit behavior adapted to particular ecological conditions. Consequently, a major limiting factor in studies of invertebrate behavior has been our inability to detect the environmental conditions to which the animals respond. In fact, much of the pioneering research in biology focused on the sensory physiology and endocrinology of invertebrates (e.g., Loeb, 1918; Kopec, 1922; Jennings, 1923; Wigglesworth, 1933, 1936; Fraenkel and Gunn, 1940; Dethier, 1957; Carthy, 1958). Invertebrate behavioral research continues this tradition, especially as it pertains to the chemical ecology and regulation of development in insects (e.g., Eisner, 1970, 1980; Bowers, 1980, 1990). In contrast, research with endangered invertebrates has concentrated almost exclusively on descriptions of their vanishing habitat and the ecological parameters that directly influence their population sizes. The mechanisms controlling their behavior have been virtually ignored.

It would be foolish to argue that a thorough knowledge of a given species' physiology and behavior would enable us to save the animal from extinction. It seems equally naive, however, to believe that conservation efforts will be successful simply by acquiring and maintaining new and larger habitat reserves (Soulé and Simberloff, 1986). Robinson (chap. 1, this volume) has pointed out that there are simply not enough resources available, especially when one considers the dramatic numbers of insect species that have or will soon become endangered due to destruction of the tropical rain forests. The answer to conservation efforts, particularly for endangered invertebrates, will have to be a compromise between the ideal and reality. Human intervention will continue to be the most important limiting factor in species survival. Animals at risk will have to coexist with humans, and this requires knowledge of their physiological and behavioral flexibility. Consequently, we must not focus only on identifying the special needs of endangered species; we must also determine why these needs are special, what mechanisms the animals use to detect and regulate these needs, and how they might be mitigated (Arnold, 1983a, 1985c). Given this approach, behavioral investigation is central to successful conservation efforts.

4

Design of Captive Environments for Endangered Invertebrates

Leslie S. Saul-Gershenz, Richard A. Arnold, and J. Mark Scriber

Invertebrates have been captively bred for centuries, primarily to obtain products they produce (e.g., silk honey, lac, and dyes) and for agricultural purposes. Radio-carbon dating of Neolithic Chinese silk suggests that silkmoths (*Bombyx mori*) have been reared for at least 7,000 years (Tsai, 1982). Similarly, the lac insect (*Laccifer lacca*) has been reared in China and India for several thousand years for the production of shellac (Singh and Moore, 1985). During the past 2,000 years, dozens of insects and invertebrates have been bred and used for medicinal, commercial, and agricultural purposes. A notable example is the honey bee (*Apis mellifera*), which has been bred both for crop pollination and the honey it produces. Other taxa and their uses have been reviewed (Smith et al., 1973; Southwood, 1977a; Free, 1982; and Tsai, 1982).

Today, captive propagation of invertebrates is performed by a variety of institutions for both basic and applied purposes. Many government laboratories and universities maintain captive cultures to conduct research in agriculture, genetics, evolutionary biology, physiology, endocrinology, nutrition, population biology, and medicine. For example, laboratory-reared fruit flies (*Drosophila*), and to a lesser extent, snails and Lepidoptera, have contributed immeasurably to our understanding of genetics and evolutionary biology. Many of these research efforts are adjunct to field studies, to elucidate details of the animal's natural history.

However, as summarized in Table 4.1 (from Edwards et al., 1987; and IUCN, 1990), much of the government-sponsored research that relies on cultures of invertebrates emphasizes pest species, which threaten our crops, domesticated animals, forests, and human health. Although these efforts have focused on just a small fraction of the total invertebrate fauna, an important by-product has been the development of rearing techniques and procedures that can be applied to related, nonpest taxa.

Singh and Moore (1985) summarize specific rearing methods, cage design, dietetics, and environmental needs for hundreds of Coleoptera, Collembola, Dictyoptera, Hemiptera, Homoptera, Hymenoptera, Neuroptera, Orthoptera, Diptera and Lepidoptera. But they also note that of the millions of insect species, only 1,400 have been reared in the laboratory and only several dozen on a large scale. The vast majority of the 2,250 invertebrates, presently recognized as threatened in the IUCN's Red Data Book (1990), have never been reared or bred in captivity.

Although most countries spend more money and effort controlling or eradicating "pest" invertebrates than protecting "beneficial" species, numerous invertebrates are still bred for commercial and agricultural purposes as more uses for them and their products or services are discovered. For example, the medicinal leech (*Hirodu medicinalis*), although endangered in the United Kingdom (Wells et al., 1983), is bred in captivity to supply research labs in universities and hospitals, thereby reducing the demand on wild populations (Hughes and Bennett, 1991). In the U.S. alone, the honey bee (*Apis mellifera*) annually pollinates over $4.5 billion worth of food crops (Borror and DeLong, 1971). Snails are an important but inexpensive source of protein for humans in poorer areas of the world (FAO, 1986). Other terrestrial, marine, and freshwater invertebrates (i.e., crabs, shrimp, mussels, oysters, crickets, caterpillars, mealworms, etc.) are either harvested or cultivated for food. Increasing reliance on biological control practices has spurred the breeding of numerous invertebrate predators and parasites of various insect and worm pests.

Captive propagation of invertebrates for conservation purposes has been used primarily for crisis intervention. For example, captive-reared specimens have been released to enhance wild populations under stress, such as the endangered Lange's metalmark butterfly (*Apodemia mormo langei*) in California (Arnold, 1981b), and the giant wetas of New Zealand (*Deinacrida fallai* and *D. rugosa*) (Balance, 1990; Barrett, 1991). In addition, reintroductions of captive-bred invertebrates into portions of their historical ranges, include such species as the large blue (*Maculinea arion*; Clarke, 1977), and large copper (*Lycaena dispar*) in England (Duffey, 1971), the Ameri-

Table 4.1
Numbers of families and species of threatened invertebrates, based on the IUCN's Red Data Book (1990), with mention of threatened taxa that have been maintained in captivity, plus numbers of other nonthreatened arthropods (in parentheses) presently in culture at government, university, and corporate laboratories in the United States and Canada (source: Edwards et al., 1987).

Class	Order	Numbers of Threatened Taxa	
		Families	Species
Phylum Ciliophora			
Polyhymenophora	Heterotrichida	1	1
Phylum Cnidaria:			
Anthozoa	Gorgonacea	1	1
	Heliporacea	1	20
	Actinaria	1	2
	Anthipatharia	1	ca. 150
Phylum Platyhelminthes			
Turbellaria	Tricladida	1	4
Phylum Nemertea			
Enopla	Hoplonemertea	1	10
Phylum Mollusca			
Bivalvia	Pterioida	3	101
	Veneroida	3	9
Gastropoda	Archaeogastropoda	2	2
	Mesogastropoda	8	120
	Basommatophora	4	15
	Stylommatophora	28	253
	Partula (9 species)	Moorean Tree Snails	
	Gymnosomata	1	1

Table 4.1 *continued*

Class	Order	Numbers of Threatened Taxa	
		Families	**Species**
Phylum Annelida			
Polychaeta	Eunicida	1	1
Hirundinea	Arhynchobdellae	1	1
Oligochaeta	Haplotaxida	5	140
Phylum Arthropoda			
Merostomata	Xiphosura	1	4
	Limulus polyphemus Horseshoe Crab		
Arachnida	Araneae	10	ca. 16
	Euathlus smithii Mexican Red-legged Tarantula		
	Acarina	— (9)	— (41)
	Pseudoscorpionida	1	1
	Opiliones	1	1
Crustacea	Anaspidacea	3	8
	Thoracica	1	2
	Anostraca	1	2
	Isopoda	9 (4)	27 (9)
	Amphipoda	3	51
	Decopoda	10	37
	Birgus latro Coconut crab		
Insecta	Thysanura	1 (1)	2 (2)
	Collembola	1 (3)	6 (4)
	Ephemeroptera	8	16
	Odonata	18	141
	Ischnura gemina	San Francisco Fork-tailed Damsefly	
	Blattaria	1 (1)	1 (55)
	Mantodea	1	1
	Grylloblattaria	1	1
	Orthoptera	8 (4)	42 (9)
	Deinacrida fallai Poor Knight's Weta		
	Deinacrida rugosa Stephens Island Weta		
	Phasmatoptera	1	1
	Dermaptera	1	1
	Plecoptera	10	16
	Zoraptera	1	1
	Anoplura	1 (1)	1 (1)
	Hemiptera	8 (8)	26 (26)

Table 4.1 *continued*

Class	Order	Numbers of Threatened Taxa	
		Families	Species
	Homoptera	7 (9)	22 (64)
	Neuroptera	5 (1)	14 (2)
	Coleoptera	28 (16)	ca. 357 (88)
	Nicrophorus americanus American Burying Beetle		
	Dynastes hercules Hercules Beetle		
	Mecoptera	1	1
	Diptera	13 (18)	21 (167)
	Tricoptera	14	52
	Lepidoptera	27 (17)	408 (100)
	Danaus plexippus Monarch Butterfly		
	Hymenoptera	9 (19)	97 (120)
	Mallophaga	— (1)	— (3)
	Siphonaptera	— (1)	— (2)
	Thysanura	— (1)	— (2)
	Thysanoptera	— (1)	— (2)
Phylum Onychophora			
Onychophora	Onychophora	2	ca. 4
	Peripatus Peripatus		
Phylum Echinodermata			
Echinoida	Echinoida	1	2

can burying beetle (*Nicrophorus americanus*) in the northeastern United States (Kozol et al., 1988), and the atala hairstreak (*Eumaeus atala*), in portions of mainland Florida (Emmel and Boender, 1991). Although captive breeding of endangered invertebrates has rarely been used to reestablish wild populations, this is likely to become a more important conservation strategy as habitat requirements of more invertebrate species are determined. For example, *Partula* snails indigenous to various pacific islands (Wells et al., 1983) are endangered due to habitat destruction plus the introduction of non-native mammals and a predatory snail, *Euglandina rosea* (Murray et al., 1988). Researchers at the University of Virginia, University of Western Australia, University of Nottingham, the Shedd Aquarium (Chicago, IL), and other institutions are propagating

Partula snails with the intent of reintroducing them after the alien predatory snail is controlled or eradicated (Kinney, 1980; Murray et al., 1988).

In recent years, the exhibition of living invertebrates at zoos, museums, aquaria, insectaria, and butterfly houses has rapidly increased in popularity with visitors, thus these institutions have become increasingly active in the research and captive propagation of rare and endangered invertebrates (Collins, 1990). At the San Francisco Insect Zoo 70 species of arthropods, representing 11 Orders and 24 families, are maintained, and 35 of these are captively propagated. Twenty-five zoos in England and Ireland maintain 230 invertebrate species (Hughes and Bennett, 1991), including five listed as threatened on the 1990 IUCN Red List of Threatened Animals (IUCN, 1990).

Butterfly houses, which have been popular since the 1960s in Britain and more recently in the U.S.A., typically display large, colorful, tropical species in greenhouse, walk-through exhibits. Collins (1987) queried butterfly houses in England and found that only one-third of the approximately 300 lepidopteran species on display were actually reared at the butterfly houses. Rather, most of the species are imported as pupae and the adults emerge at the butterfly house for display purposes. Only a few facilities focus solely on native species, such as Sonoran Arthropod Studies, Inc. in Arizona and the Penang Butterfly House in Malaysia. Even so, many butterfly houses are promoting captive propagation on site and in the country of origin, where they aid habitat conservation by providing commerce for the native people. This new industry is known as butterfly farming, and an excellent example is in Papua New Guinea where the national constitution includes insect conservation as a goal (Pyle, 1988). There the rare and spectacular birdwing (*Ornithoptera*) and swallowtail (*Papilio*) butterflies are bred to supply scientific and exhibition needs, which has fostered protection and enhancement of the butterfly's native habitats and reduced collection pressure on wild populations.

Many insects can be maintained continuously in captive cultures for long periods. For example, the southern armyworm moth (*Spodoptera eridania*) has been in culture at one laboratory since 1937 (Wright, 1985). Although numerous insects can be successfully reared for one or a few generations, other species are subject to various difficulties during long-term propagation, such as disease, inbreeding, dietary deficiencies, parasites, synchronization problems, and other issues discussed later in this chapter. Only one invertebrate, a species of *Partula* snail, is known to have been protected from extinction by captive propagation (T. Mason, pers. comm.).

For these reasons, the best way to protect endangered inverte-brates from extinction is still by habitat preservation (see Robinson chap. 1, this volume; Pyle et al., 1981, Arnold, 1983a; Collins and Thomas, 1991). Collins and Morris (1985) describe how tropical and temperate deforestation, agricultural conversion and intensification, industrialization, urbanization, pollution, and commercial exploita-tion have drastically affected endangered and threatened swallow-tail butterflies. These and other factors are affecting all taxonomic groups of invertebrates throughout the world. While butterfly houses and butterfly farming (Parsons, 1992) may help prevent extinction of a few rare species, habitat protection and management are far more important actions for endangered invertebrates and will undoubt-edly continue to be for the foreseeable future.

Much of our collective experience with captive propagation of invertebrates has been with terrestrial arthropods, especially Lepi-doptera, which are probably the best known order of invertebrates and have received considerable conservation attention (Pyle, 1976, 1988; Arnold, 1983a; Wells et al., 1983; Collins and Morris, 1985). Thus, the remaining sections of this chapter will primarily focus on captive environmental design issues important for captive propaga-tion efforts for terrestrial invertebrates. Special attention will be devoted to insects, especially Lepidoptera. Other publications (see Spotte, 1979; Hinegardner, 1981; Merritt and Cummins, 1984; Adey and Loveland, 1991) review culture and aquaria techniques for freshwater and marine invertebrates. However, because of the di-versity of species and lifestyles of invertebrates, much remains to be learned about the vast majority of these taxa before they can be adequately protected and propagated in captivity.

Economics of Captive Design

The cost of constructing and maintaining a captive breeding facility for insects and other invertebrates varies greatly depending upon the organism, its lifestyle and ecological requirements, the purpose of the facility, and its scale. For example, branches of the United States Department of Agriculture (Agricultural Research Service, Animal and Plant Health Inspection Service, and the U. S. Forest Service) main-tain major insect rearing facilities across the country (Edwards et al., 1987). In addition, numerous corporations (e.g., Johnson and Johnson, Ecogen, Mycogen, Neogen, Crop Genetics International, AgriGenetics, Pioneer, FMC, Dupont, Chevron, Dow, and Stauffer) maintain cul-tures for research purposes, such as testing pesticide effectiveness or host plant resistance studies. Because rearing and research labs are often located outside a particular species' geographic range, it is important to prevent these insects from escaping from the facilities. Thus, security measures account for a significant proportion of the cost in constructing insect rearing and containment facilities, particularly in states such as California, where there is a mild climate and significant agriculture.

The techniques required for successful rearing of a particular species also influence the economics of captive breeding. Numerous techniques for rearing insects and invertebrates have been developed since the early 1900s (Peterson, 1953; Smith, 1966; Hinegardner, 1981; King and Leppla, 1984; Fisher and Leppla, 1985; Singh and Moore, 1985; Frye, 1992). However, each species or "guild" has its own specific ecological and favored gustatory conditions. Specific thermal, textural, nutritional, and allelochemical combinations are needed to initiate and sustain feeding for different guilds of insects, spiders, mites, and other arthropods (Brooks, 1985; Slansky and Scriber, 1985; Slansky and Rodriguez, 1987b). Some examples are: special soil substrates for *Collembola*; parafilm sachets for piercing-sucking aphids and bugs; lyophilized powders of prey insects for feeding by predatory insects; fast flowing, cool-water arenas for blackflies; and carefully balanced chemical mixtures in meridic diets customized for particular species. Similarly, captive rearing of arachnids requires specialized techniques that accommodate their feeding ecology (Slansky and Rodriguez, 1987b), mating behavior, physiological ecology (Merritt, 1978), and other environmental needs (Frye, 1992). Similar concerns must be dealt with when rearing nematodes (Thorne, 1961; Gaugler and Kaya, 1991), mites (Rodriguez, 1979; Schuster and Murphy, 1991), and other arthropod taxa (Eisenbeis and Wichard, 1987; Frye, 1992). Thus, successful captive propagation of invertebrates, especially taxa that have not previously been reared, depends upon discovering and providing the right combination of environmental, dietary, physical, and biotic parameters. Because this process often proceeds on a trial and error basis, considerable research and development costs can be incurred until these specific factors are determined.

Animal Acquisition and Replacement Costs

Export and import permits must be obtained from local, federal, and sometimes international regulatory agencies. For insects, such agencies might include the United States Department of Agriculture, a state or county agricultural department, U.S. Fish and Wildlife Service, and the Forestry Department or National Park Service in the country of the animal's origin. Generally there is a nominal fee for permits, but the process can be time consuming and is therefore more costly in terms of personnel expenses.

Animal acquisition or the procurement of specimens for founder colonies can range from the cost of a tank of gas to thousands of dollars, particularly if extensive field work and travel to distant regions are necessary. Unlike many endangered vertebrates, endangered invertebrates are rarely available from commercial sources or from institutions, unless a captive breeding program has already been established, as for *Partula* snails or the American burying beetle. Thus, procurement costs frequently include travel to the species' habitat, field time for staff to collect specimens, equipment rental or purchase, temporary holding and shipping expenses. These costs vary depending upon the distance of the species' geographic range to the breeding facility and the amount of time spent in the field to procure specimens.

Spatial and Equipment Costs

Building a facility that is capable of containing small, prolific, agile invertebrates, especially those capable of flight, presents challenges and requires creative solutions. In California, a typical insect rearing facility requires double doors at all entrances and exits, a closed air system with filters and tight screening on all vents, refrigerator-like doors, nonopening windows, special screens and traps on all drains, sealed conduit systems, a variety of trap systems, and a quarantine room. These precautions are necessary in a state or region which has a large agricultural industry and a mild climate, to prevent exotic insects from escaping. These precautions also help to exclude parasites from accidental entry, but only if wild caught colonies are quarantined properly. If only native insects are being reared, all of the above precautions may not be necessary.

The cost of rearing equipment is usually minimal compared to construction costs. Terraria and other simple containers, and locally available or commercial diets are required to successfully rear many terrestrial arthropods. However, specialized equipment, such as environmental chambers or salt water systems, are considerably more expensive to obtain and operate. At butterfly houses, many butterflies are reared most efficiently in greenhouse settings, which can be costly to build. Also, the foodplant requirements can necessitate the need for additional greenhouses to maintain high population numbers of hungry caterpillars.

The acquisition of required foodplants for exotic species can be inexpensive or costly depending upon the source. Sometimes local vegetation of related plants will suffice. The San Francisco Insect Zoo has imported plant material from out of state or out of the country, thus requiring permits and substantial expenditures of staff time and shipping costs. In general, we have found that the smaller amount of human manipulation required usually correlates with the lower economic costs. Artificial diets are practical when mass rearing a species, but typically result in higher mortality rates (Singh and Moore, 1985).

Captive colonies in the animal's natural environment, such as in country butterfly farms, often provide not only ideal environmental conditions but also minimize construction and equipment costs. Clearly, such facilities can vary greatly depending upon the habitat and biological requirements of a particular species.

Personnel Costs

A well-trained and reliable staff is an essential component for successful captive propagation of invertebrates, but is frequently the most costly economic consideration. Indeed, a day of neglect can lead to disastrous results for not only research projects, but also for long-term maintenance of healthy colonies. For instance, a single incident of low oxygen stress in a salt water system or heat stress for a colony of burying beetles can result in immediate death or promote the outbreak of a pathogen. Unfortunately, there are few places where one can learn the science and art of breeding invertebrates. Because information on the biology of most taxa is scarce, often the only recourse is trial and error coupled with educated guesses. The development of propagation techniques and the culmination of release programs require long-term staff commitments ranging from several months to several years. Staff must often master specialized rearing techniques, such as hand-pairing of certain butterfly species to successfully reproduce them in captivity. While no special equipment is needed to accomplish hand-pairing, this or other specialized skills are labor intensive and require considerable practice to master.

Species Considerations in Captive Design for Invertebrates

The design of outdoor and indoor insectaries (Peterson, 1953; Langhans, 1978; Goodenough and Parnell, 1985) must address essential environmental conditions and their control, as well as disease control (Sikorowski and Goodwin, 1985) and protection from predators and parasites (Hinegardner, 1981; Poinar and Thomas, 1984). When rearing or exhibiting involves group enclosures or tanks, species composition must also be considered to insure compatibility (Hinegardner, 1981). Thus, appropriate species choice is important because tolerance of confinement varies among species. The remainder of this section focuses primarily on Lepidoptera and other leaf-eating insects to illustrate various abiotic and biotic considerations in the design of captive breeding facilities for invertebrates.

Abiotic Factors

Temperature. Because most insects and other invertebrates are ectothermic, temperature is the most obvious factor influencing their activity levels and population dynamics. Thermal extremes, thermal periods, and total seasonal degree day (thermal unit) accumulations are of critical importance to all insects (Clark, 1967; Wieser, 1973; May, 1979; Taylor, 1981, 1982). Rate of development is often temperature dependent. Pest management computer programs and population dynamics models are driven almost exclusively by thermal units. The importance of host plant quality interacting with thermal units to influence growth rates and ecological success has recently been described (Scriber and Slansky, 1981; Scriber and Lederhouse, 1991).

Photoperiod. Although not as important as temperature for growth rates, photoperiod has profound effects on biochemistry, physiology, and the ecology of most insects (Beck, 1980). As an important cue to changing seasonal conditions, photoperiod is a predominant factor in the activity level and diapause responses of many insects (Tauber et al., 1986). Insect rearing operations must carefully control photoperiod and thermoperiod to maintain continuous cultures.

Humidity. Relative humidity that is too low results in desiccation of invertebrates, yet if too high can lead to other problems such as increased vulnerability to disease. The correct amount of humidity varies with different developmental stages of insects since susceptibility to desiccation is variable in different life stages. Many lepidopteran larvae will remain in diapause until a certain combination of photoperiod and moisture is achieved. Many phasmid (walkingstick) eggs require a minimum of 90% humidity in order for the egg to hatch (Brock, 1985). Humidity is also critical for ecdysis (molting) (Floyd, 1987).

Living Space: Quality and Quantity. The need for physical space is variable for the successful rearing of different insects and other invertebrates; however, with many insects it is frequently possible to rear individuals from egg to adult in very small plastic containers (e.g., 20 cm^3) on artificial diets. Adult sex pheromones can attract males from long distances; however, confined quarters interfere with matings. Adequate (depends on the species) space for successful molting is imperative. Habitat heterogeneity for oviposition or other activities can be critical for some species and for different life stages of the same species. At the San Francisco Insect Zoo, we found the leaf-footed bug (*Thasus acutangulus*) preferred vertical woody branches for oviposition. Interestingly, its eggs are laid in a straight row and are perfectly camouflaged in this situation. The degree to which this lack of spatial heterogeneity limits successful captive rearing is not known, but could be significant. As with many animals, adequate ventilation to inhibit fungal, bacterial, and viral growth is important for overall health.

Biotic Factors

Collection. Shipping and transport of live animals to insure that they arrive alive and healthy can be a challenge. Heat or cold stress can be fatal, so appropriate precautions must be taken to protect living invertebrates while in transit. Some species of temperate arthropods, such as the black widow spider (*Lactrodectus mactans*), can withstand freezing temperatures, while others, such as burying beetles (*Nicrophorus* spp.), are extremely sensitive to heat stress. Insulated shipping containers or dry ice can be used to minimize temperature fluctuations during shipment. The shorter the travel time the better.

Adult arthropods, when collected in the spring in southern latitudes and transported to northern laboratories, often require fresh greenhouse-grown trees or weekly shipments of leaves from southern cooperators to elicit oviposition and for successful rearing. Further, while adult butterflies travel and store well in glassine or paper envelopes in an ice chest or refrigerator, they must be fed to maximize their subsequent lifespan and reproductive output. A 10% honey water solution is used for female butterflies and a combination of honey water supplemented with electrolytes (a modified butterfly Ringer's solution) and amino acids for the male butterflies, to enhance their mating success and reproductive output (Lederhouse *et al.*, 1990).

Oviposition. Individuals can be marked easily for subsequent identification (Southwood, 1978). Various techniques can be used for different Lepidoptera including: screen cages over potted plants

(Peterson, 1953), plastic boxes with small sprigs of host plants in water-filled, rubber-capped plastic vials (Scriber, 1977; Scriber et al., 1991), hand-held adults (Singer, 1986), or paper bags for saturniid moths.

Sex Ratio. Careful attention must be paid to sex ratio in breeding enclosures. Some species appear to be indifferent while other species must go through courtship behaviors that require comparison opportunities. In predatory species of insects, such as mantids, often a single male and a single female is the best nuptial arrangement.

Rearing Immature Stages. Excised host plants with adequate leaf water content (in water vials), or else whole potted plants can be used. Excised leaves in closed containers with plaster-of-paris base platforms help to maintain humidity. In some situations, the leaf material must be changed daily. Artificial diets are frequently much more convenient than real plant tissues, but often do not work because they lack the proper texture or chemical feeding stimulants.

Disease organisms can be expected eventually; however, the regular cleaning of fecal material and sodium hypochlorite solution treatments help to minimize the outbreak of disease (Sikorowski and Goodwin, 1985). Maintaining adequate fresh food at all times seems to be one of the most important factors in preventing disease. Overcrowding, low oxygen, adverse light, and heat are other important variables (Steinhaus, 1958, 1963; Burges, 1973) that must be monitored. Most leaf-feeding Lepidoptera may contain microsporidians, various viruses (e.g., granular, nuclear polyhedrosis, cytoplasmic polyhedrosis) and bacterial septicemia (Bucher, 1960). Other disease causes and their symptoms are described by Goodwin (1984); Poinar and Thomas (1984); Sikorowski and Goodwin (1985). Another problem is cannibalism, which is common in certain groups.

Greenhouse grown plants must be properly fertilized and watered. These foodplants often must be cultured because they are not available from commercial sources and should avoid contamination with pesticides. Unhealthy foodplants result in unhealthy herbivores. Plants must be protected from spider mites, white flies, scales, aphids, powdery mildew, rust, nematodes, algae, and pesticide contamination (Horst, 1978). Residues, even from nonsystemic insecticide treatments, can quickly exterminate a captive culture. As an alternative to chemical control, we have often removed all plants and insects from a rearing facility, closed down our vents, and turned on all 1000-watt Metalarc illuminators to let direct sunlight bake out (140° F) our pests.

The dietary requirements of nonherbivorous insects and invertebrates range from a simple scavenger diet of apple and dog kibble to animal carcasses. Usually colonies of several prey species must be cultured to provide a continuous supply of food for various ages and sizes of predatory invertebrates.

The immature stages of many insects and invertebrates live in environments that are in sharp contrast to those of their mature stages. For example, many aquatic insects live in the water as immatures, but outside of their aquatic environments as adults. Thus, captive propagation requires maintenance of these different environmental conditions for both life stages.

Pupal Storage and Diapause. For *Papilio* pupae and saturniid cocoons we carefully remove the pupae with girdle and silk pads at the attachment site and place them in a screened petri dish (a cylindrical screen cage between the lid and base) to allow wing expansion and eclosion. Photoperiods and thermoperiods can be adjusted to affect direct development or diapause. However, some with obligate diapause, such as *Papilio canadensis* (Rockey et al., 1987) must be cold treated or otherwise manipulated to break the diapause.

Protection from Parasites and Predators. Fine mesh ("no-see-um" or silkscreen material 50 mm screen) netting or screening can protect pupae from dipteran and hymenopteran parasitoids. Larvae left free to forage on greenhouse plants have been attacked by pentatomids, ants, and spiders that gain entry via open vents, doors, or cracks.

Inbreeding Depression in Continuous Culture. Heterozygosity of insects in laboratory cultures can be lost with continuous breeding, especially when only a few individuals are used (Benz, 1963; Bartlett, 1985). Thus, it may be necessary to periodically introduce new genetic material. In some cases, laboratory-reared larvae fed on meridic diets for more than one year lose some of their ability to survive and grow on real foodplants (Guthrie et al., 1982, 1984), although little difference was observed between 10-generation versus 62-generation laboratory cultures (Manuwoto and Scriber, 1985).

Although it is a common problem in captive propagation, inbreeding depression may be incorrectly assumed to explain the general decline of vigor in some laboratory invertebrate cultures. Deficiencies such as mating problems and reduced fertility, can be corrected with proper electrolytes and/or amino acid supplements (Lederhouse et al., 1990). Cultures of the southern armyworm moth which have been maintained for decades, are often the result of a single mated female or two. These lab-reared larvae appear to be able to eat and thrive on dozens of hosts in more than 33 families of plants (Scriber, 1986).

Artificial Selection. In addition to problems related to genetic inbreeding depression (Bush et al., 1976; Ralls et al., 1986a), types of hybrid dysgenesis, such as outbreeding depression (Sved, 1979; Templeton, 1986), may develop in laboratory or otherwise confined organisms. The decline in "quality" of mass-reared insects may be due to many traits that were inadvertently selected for (or against) in the rearing process (e.g., fecundity, fertility, viability, size, mating competitiveness or capability, flight, feeding behavior, overall competitiveness, resistance to disease, or vulnerability to predators and parasites). These are described and discussed in general and specifically for fruit flies (Diptera) and gypsy moths (Lepidoptera) by Moore et al. (1985).

Captive Design and Animal Health

Providing a healthy, captive environment can be complicated depending upon the invertebrate species and its life history and biological requirements. In general, proper maintenance of several factors, for example, daily and seasonal temperature, photoperiod, and humidity regimes, shelter and dietary needs, suitable oviposition sites, and mate selection opportunities are essential for the continuous culture of invertebrates. For example, the appropriate sex ratio must be maintained for certain coreid bugs to mate (Schaeffer, pers. comm.). Crowding and improper ventilation are prevalent problems in captive propagation situations. Some species require high humidity, which is difficult to maintain while simultaneously providing adequate ventilation without sophisticated equipment (Saul, 1992). Also, molting deformities and death are common problems due to faulty design or overcrowding. Because confined insects can no longer disperse, the probability of disease increases. Confinement and crowding are also concerns for predatory species that are inclined to cannibalism if housed communally. Most diseases of insects are still unknown (Lipa, 1975; Goodwin, 1984; Poinar and Thomas, 1984), however, new information is becoming available due to the use of insect pathogens and parasites in biological control programs. For discussions of the health problems of terrestrial and marine invertebrates in captive propagation, see Frye (1992) and Hinegardner (1981).

Captive Design and Conservation

Only a very small proportion of the listed endangered and vulnerable invertebrate species have been successfully propagated (Arnold, 1981b, 1983a; Wells et al., 1983; Edwards et al., 1987; Balance, 1990; Barrett, 1991; Collins and Thomas, 1991; Hughes and Bennett, 1991), and most of these for only a generation or two to study their life history rather than in continuous culture. An exception is the rare (and recently nominated for endangered status) San Francisco fork-tailed damselfy (*Ischnura gemina*), which has been cultured at San Francisco State University (Hafernik, Jr., pers. comm.). However, some nonendangered relatives of endangered species are in captive culture, which provide an opportunity to refine captive rearing techniques that can be applied to the endangered species if needed. For example, the hercules beetle (*Dynastes hercules*) from Central and South America is listed as endangered in the IUCN Invertebrate Red Data Book (Wells et al., 1983). At the San Francisco Insect Zoo, the nonendangered, southwestern hercules beetle (*Dynastes granti*) has been cultured for several years. Similarly, the Vancouver Aquarium has developed propagation techniques for the moon jellyfish (*Aurelia aurita*) and the crimson anemone (*Cribrinopsis frenaldi*) (Butschler, pers. comm.). The insectarium of the Metropolitan Toronto Zoo has cultured several species of the large theraphosid spiders. The Cincinnati Zoo's World of the Insect has propagated the goliath beetle (*Goliathus goliathus*).

The popularity of butterfly houses, insectaria, and nature centers has increased in the last couple of decades with over 100 million people visiting these facilities each year. Further, there is a vast potential to reach still more people through various media including print, radio, television, and film. Table 4.2 is a worldwide list of selected facilities known to us that exhibit and propagate living insects and invertebrates. Simultaneously, activities to protect and enhance habitats of invertebrates, such as butterfly gardening, have also been increasing in popularity. Popular books on butterfly gardening (Rothschild and Farrell, 1983; Tekulsky, 1985; Schneck, 1990; Xerces Society/Smithsonian Institution, 1990) have recently been published as a result of this trend. These activities have helped to increase public awareness about the importance of certain insects and invertebrates and the need for their conservation. One of the most important by-products of captive propagation efforts may be the public exhibition of invertebrates for educational purposes.

Table 4.2
Selected major institutional exhibits of living insects or invertebrates.

Butterfly Exhibits

Australian Bufferfly Sanctuary
Kennedy Highway, P.O. Box 345
Far North, Kuranda
Queensland 4872, Australia

Museum of Victoria
71 Victoria Crescent
Abbotsford, Victoria 3067
Australia

Butterfly Garden
Grevenmacher sur Moselle
Route du Vin
Luxemburg

New Forest Butterfly Farm
Longdown, Ashurst
Southampton S04 4UH
England

Butterfly World
Tradewinds Park
3600 W. Sample Road
Coconut Creek, Florida 33073 USA

Papiliorama
Marin Centra
Neufchatel
Switzerland

Day Butterfly Center
Callaway Gardens
Pine Mountain, Georgia 31822 USA

Penang Butterfly House
Mk. 2, Jalan Teluk Bahang
11050 Penang, Malaysia

Jersey Butterfly Farm
Haute Tombette, St. Mary
Jersey Channel Islands, England

Royal Melbourne Zoological Gardens
Butterfly House, P.O. Box 74
Parkville, 3052 Victoria, Australia

London Butterfly House
Syon Park Brentford
Middlesex, TW8 8JF England

The Butterfly Farm, Ltd.
Bilsington, Asford
Kent TN25 7JW, England

Mackinac Island Butterfly House
Sawyers Greenhouse
1306 McGaulpin
Mackinac Island, Michigan 49757
   USA

The Butterfly Farm S.A.
La Guacima de Alejuela
Apdo 323, 6150 Santa Ana
Costa Rica

Marine World Africa, USA
Marine World Parkway
Vallejo, California USA

The Butterfly House
Williamson Park
Lancaster LA1 1UX, England

Anthropod Exhibits

Argus Entomological Centre
Commercial Unit Globus a/R 1890
Vladivostok 690012, USSR

Metropolitan Toronto Zoo
P.O. Box 280 West Hill
Toronto, Ontario M1E 4R5 Canada

Table 4.2 *continued*

Anthropod Exhibits (continued)

Arizona-Sonora Desert Museum
Rt. 9, Box 900
Tucson, AZ 85743 USA

Artis Zoo Insectarium
Amsterdam, The Netherlands

Zoologischer Garten
Budapester Str. 32
D 1000, Berlin 30, Germany

Budapest Zoological Garden
1371 Budapest 5 pf 469
Budapest, Hungary

Cheng-Ching Lake Butterfly Farm
Formosa Insect Farm
P.O. Box 2-046, Peitou 11216
Taipei, Republic of Taiwan

Chessington Zoo
United Kingdom

Cincinnati Zoo
World of the Insect
3400 Vine Street
Cincinnati, Ohio 45220 USA

Columbus Zoo
9990 Riverside Drive
Powell, Ohio 43065 USA

Copenhagen Zoo Zoologisk Have
Sdr. Fasnvej 79, DK-2000 kbh.
Copenhagen F, Denmark

Edinburgh Butterfly Farm
Doobies Garden Centre
Lasswade nr. Midlothian
EH18 1AZ Scotland

Fort Worth Zoological Park
  & Insectarium
2727 Zoological Park Drive
Fort Worth, Texas 76110 USA

Musee des Papillons-Insectarium
Foret de Chize
79360 Beavoir Sur Niort, France

Museum of Arthropoda, Ecology Hall
471 Shaniwar Peth, Pune 411 030
Maharashtra, India

National Zoological Park
Invertebrate House
3000 Connecticut Ave., N.W.
Washington, D.C. 20008 USA

Noorder Zoo
P.O. Box 1010
7801 BA Emmen
The Netherlands

Northern Arizona University
Flagstaff, Arizona 86011 USA

Respublikinis Zoologijos Sodas
Kaunas 233028, 16 tos Divizijos pl 21
Lithuania

San Fransico Zoological Garden
Insect Zoo, 1 Zoo Road
San Francisco, CA 94132 USA

Santa Barbara Natural History
  Museum
2559 Puesta del Sol Road
Santa Barbara, CA 93105 USA

Smithsonian Institution
Insect Zoo
NHB Stop 101
Washington, D.C. 20560 USA

Sonoran Arthropod Studies, Inc.
P.O. Box 5624
Tucson, Arizona 85703 USA

Table 4.2 *continued*

Anthropod Exhibits (continued)

Glasgow Zoo
Calder Park, Uddington
Glasgow, Scotland G71 7RZ

Stratford-upon-Avon Butterfly Farm
Tramway Walk, Stratford-upon-Avon
Warwickshire CV37 7LS England

Insectarium de Montreal
Ville de Montreal
4101 rue Sherbrooke East
Montreal, Quebec H1X 2B2 Canada

Tama Zoological Park
300 Hodokubo, Hino City
Tokyo, Japan

Insectarium Hortus Haren
P.O. Box 174, 9750 AD Haren

The Living World
Seven Sisters Country Park
Exceat, Seaford, E. Sussex England

The Netherlands
Los Angeles County Museum of
   Natural History, Insect Zoo
900 Exhibition Blvd.
Los Angeles, CA 90007 USA

Toshimaen Amusement Park
   Insectarium
3-25-1 Koyama, Nerima-ku
Tokyo, Japan

Living Desert Museum
47-900 Portola
Palm Desert, CA 92260 USA

Worldwide Butterflies &
   Lullingstone Silk
Compton House, Sherborne Dorset
DT9 4CN England

London Zoological Gardens
Insect House, Regent's Park
London NW1 4RY England

Zoological-Botanic Garden Wilhelma
Insektarium D-7000, Stuttgart 50
Postfach 50 12 27, Germany

Zoologicka Zahrada Praha
17100 Praha, 7 Troja
Czechoslovakia

Zoologischer Garten Koln
D-5000 Koln, Riehler Strasse 173
Germany

Marine Invertebrate Exhibits

Aquarium of the Berlin Zoo
Budapester Str 32 D-1000
Berlin 30, Germany

National Aquarium in Baltimore
Pier 3, 501 E. Pratt Street
Baltimore, Maryland 21202 USA

Bergen Aquarium
   (Akvariet i Bergen)
Nordnesparken 2, Bergen Norway

Aquarium for Wildlife Conservation
West 8th St. & Surf Ave.
Brooklyn, New York 11224 USA

Indianapolis Zoo
1200 West Washington Street
Indianapolis, Indiana 46222 USA

Seattle Aquarium
Pier 59
Seattle, Washington 98101 USA

Table 4.2 *continued*

Marine Invertebrate Exhibits (continued)

John G. Shedd Aquarium
1200 South Lakeshore Drive
Chicago, Illinois 60605 USA

Steinhart Aquarium
Golden Gate Park
San Francisco, California 94118 USA

Monterey Bay Aquarium
886 Cannery Row
Monterey, California 93940 USA

Vancouver Public Aquarium
P.O. Box 3232, Vancouver
British Columbia V6B 3X8, Canada

For some species, however, exhibits and captive propagation may also foster habitat protection efforts. Butterfly farming and captive propagation at the site of release are examples of captive techniques that aid the preservation of intact ecosystems. Also, the concept of "extractive reserves" has been developed in Brazil by the Instituto de Estudos Amazonicos. Because of the popularity of living butterfly exhibits, insectaria and butterfly houses can provide a market for such operations. If livestock for exhibit purposes is obtained from such cooperative projects that benefit the local, economically deprived human populations, it would promote the conservation of rain forests and other native plant communities.

Conclusions

We agree with Robinson (chap. 1, this volume) that habitat protection and management are the most significant conservation needs for threatened and endangered invertebrates. Captive propagation of invertebrates can help by publicizing the importance of invertebrate diversity, simulating natural communities, mass-rearing for commercial purposes (e.g., biocontrol agents, medical research, to satisfy collectors, butterfly houses); however, in our opinion it will not adequately restore more than a handful of endangered species. Nonetheless, it can enhance and possibly even save a few flagship species, and in the process, it should improve the public's awareness about invertebrates and the need for their conservation.

Acknowledgments

Preparation of this chapter was supported in part by Michigan State University (Projects 1644 and 8072). We would like to thank the many individuals we contacted for sharing their unpublished information and helpful comments on this topic.

II

Fishes

Introduction of Authors
and Chapter Previews

Conservation issues for endangered species of fish are reviewed by Christopher Kohler, associate director of Fisheries Research Laboratory and associate professor of Zoology at Southern Illinois University. His research focus is fisheries ecology and management, and he feels that propagating endangered fishes in captivity is futile in the absence of reintroduction programs. He is primarily interested in American fishes and authored the American Fisheries Society position on introduction of aquatic species.

Dr. Kohler expresses optimism for the preservation of specific endangered species of fish through captive conservation. However, he warns that propagation without reintroduction is only a partial solution and that degradation of critical habitat may be justified by decision-makers citing captive breeding successes.

The reproductive physiology of endangered fishes is discussed by Leo Demski, Leonard S. Florsheim Sr. Chair and professor of Biology at New College of the University of South Florida. His research focus is primarily on neurohormonal mechanisms controlling reproductive physiology and behavior in skates, stingrays and hermaphroditic sea bass. Dr. Demski is also an adjunct scientist at the Mote Marine Laboratory in Sarasota Florida and has served for a number of years on the scientific advisory board of the Cincinnati Zoo.

Dr. Demski details the reproductive functions of a number of fish species with special emphasis on endocrinology. He urges continued research in the fields of ova and embryo cryopreservation and the establishment of germplasm banks for the maintenance of maximum genetic diversity.

A review of behavioral research in captivity, in this case limited to North American endangered fish, is provided by Ruth Francis-Floyd and James Williams. Francis-Floyd is a veterinarian specializing in aquatic animal medicine at the College of Veterinary Medicine and the Department of Fisheries and Aquatic Sciences at the University of Florida. Her expertise is in the clinical medicine of fish. Dr. Williams taps into his long association and research experience with the Office of Endangered Species, U.S. Fish and Wildlife Service, and his current work as Chief of the Endangered Species Branch at the National Fisheries Research Center in Gainesville, Florida.

In their chapter, Drs. Francis-Floyd and Williams emphasize the need for behavioral research in fishes, a group representing half of all vertebrate species. The authors highlight the importance of behavioral stress studies in the management of fish species citing the recognition of early behavioral warning signs of impending disease as crucial to timely treatment.

The captive design chapter is authored by Michael Stoskopf, previously chief of medicine at the National Aquarium in Baltimore. He is currently professor of wildlife and aquatic medicine and coordinator of the environmental medicine consortium at the College of Veterinary medicine at North Carolina State University. Dr. Stoskopf is a pioneer in the study of environmental and physiological factors related to the health of aquatic animals. He has used his research examining the impact of environmental parameters on the well-being of captive marine and freshwater fishes to improve closed system designs used in display, research, and production facilities. Stoskopf believes that understanding the impact of environmental factors on host physiology is the most important issue in the quest to optimize longevity and quality of existence for captive fishes.

Dr. Stoskopf has detailed many of the design features that must be considered for proper management of fishes in captivity. He recognizes two problems facing managers of captive fish: the lack of information regarding specific requirements of each species; and the economic constraints associated with the construction of large, complex captive environments.

5

Captive Conservation of Endangered Fishes

Christopher C. Kohler

Fishes can generally be defined as aquatic, cold-blooded, gill-breathing vertebrates. With over 20,000 extant species, they represent the largest and most diverse group of their phylum. Fish have, through the course of evolution, made adaptations to nearly every aquatic environ from the ocean abyss to desert pools. Unique habitats provide settings for unique adaptations. Small disjunct water bodies are to the aquatic sphere what small islands are to the terrestrial. Much like Darwin's finches of the Galapagos Islands, these "water islands" sometimes support remarkable fishes that illustrate a number of evolutionary and ecological principles. Similar to their terrestrial island counterparts, many fish species may progress through a series of evolutionary changes [taxon cycling] that eventually can greatly increase their probability of extinction (Wilson, 1961; MacArthur and Wilson, 1967; Ricklefs and Cox, 1972). Extinction, like speciation, is a natural phenomenon. What is important is that man has the capacity to affect the relationship between these processes. Since the Industrial Revolution, mankind has been responsible for the extirpation or endangerment of hundreds of species of fishes through habitat degradation and overexploitation.

Deacon et al. (1979) identified major threats facing fish species including destruction, modification or curtailment of habitat or range, naturally restricted range, overutilization, disease, and other natural or manmade factors including hybridization, introduction of exotic species, predation, and competition. Of the 251 fish taxa that they listed as endangered, threatened, or of special concern, habitat modification was involved in 98% of the cases; other natural or manmade factors were threats for 37%, a restricted range was involved in 16%, overexploitation in 3%, and disease was involved in 2% of the cases. The above generalization illustrates that destruction or modification of habitat is the primary threat to the continued existence of most fish species. Williams et al. (1989) have updated the previous list, and their findings support Deacon et al.'s (1979) conclusion that habitat destruction is the most frequent factor endangering the integrity of fish species. Nevertheless, an array of factors are often involved in each case, and mitigation of a potential extinction is a complex issue.

Many fishes are beautiful, but many are diminutive and plain while others have an appearance that only a mother could love. Although man's zeal to exploit fish species has led to the downfall of many, the commercial and recreational value of exploitable species has provided impetus for safeguarding the entire group. The general public may not relate to a specific fish, but they can relate to fish as a class. This provides a much needed window for education on the broader issues of fish conservation. Small "inconsequential" fish can delay but not halt human development of habitat. Consider the case of the snail darter (*Percina tanasi*). After much debate, court injunctions, and amendments to and violations of the Endangered Species Act, the Tellico Dam was completed in 1980 impounding a portion of the Little Tennessee River and destroying the snail darter's habitat. Nevertheless, public opinion inspired an effort that resulted in the species being downlisted from endangered to threatened due to a successful transplantation and identification of other sites where it occurs naturally (Ono et al., 1983). This case illustrates that all avenues must be sought in the preservation of endangered species. One important avenue, the theme of this volume, is captive conservation. Aquaculture, the controlled rearing of aquatic organisms, provides an opportunity to save some species from certain extinction. As with other taxonomic groups, captive conservation does not represent a panacea for preserving endangered fishes. It may only buy time for species unless coupled with habitat protection, but time or more appropriately the lack of it, is what extinction is all about.

Species Status in the Wild

The U.S. Fish and Wildlife Service (1989) lists 88 fish species as being either endangered or threatened. Of these only eight are native outside of North America. The American Fisheries Society Endangered Species Committee provides a list (Williams et al., 1989) for North American fishes that are threatened or endangered which is an updated version of one produced by the same committee, albeit different membership, in the late 1970s (Deacon et al., 1979). The original list contained 251 fish taxa. The 1989 list adds 139 new taxa and removes 26 for a total of 364 fishes. This represents an increase of 45% in the number of threatened and endangered fishes during the past decade in North America alone. The International Union for the Conservation of Nature Red Data Book (IUCN, 1986) lists 286 fish species in their compilation, about one-third of which are endemic to areas outside North America. The relatively short list of endangered fishes outside North America is in all likelihood due to a lack of information rather than a paucity of threatened species. Any list of endangered and threatened species must be considered provisional.

On behalf of the American Fisheries Society's Endangered Species Committee, Johnson (1987) conveyed a list of protected fishes of the United States and Canada. The list included 517 taxa having legal protection and 709 of special concern. The number of fishes that are threatened with extinction either locally or throughout their range is expanding at an unprecedented rate. Fifty-six percent of the described fish species of the United States and Canada are receiving some degree of protection; nearly one-third are fully protected by one or more governments in all or a portion of their ranges (Johnson, 1987). Not knowing with the same degree of confidence what the status of fish species is in the rest of the globe is even more disturbing.

Species threatened with extirpation do not stay on lists forever. Their populations eventually recover or they become extinct. Forty fishes from North America have become extinct in the past century, all as a result of expanding human pressures on aquatic resources (Miller et al., 1989). Table 5.1 lists four species from the Laurentian Great Lakes, three salmonids of the genus *Coregonus* and one percid, the blue pike (*Stizostedion vitreum glaucum*). The loss of these species to the world's ichthyofauna and how it happened exemplifies the role of mankind in the acceleration of species extinctions.

Human interventions in the Great Lakes that have taken their toll on species populations include overexploitation, pollution, and unintentional species introductions. The entrance of the sea lamprey (*Petromyzon marinus*) apparently through the Welland Canal resulted in devastating effects. Soon after the lamprey became established, the alewife (*Alosa pseudoharengus*) entered and expanded exponentially becoming a chief competitor with many of the smaller coregonids.

Table 5.1
Fishes native to the United States and Canada known, suspected, or on verge of being extinct.[1]

Taxa and Common Name	Former Range	Last known collection
Petromyzontidae		
Lampetra minima (Miller Lake lamprey)	Miller Lake, Oregon (USA)	1952
Salmonidae		
Coregonus alpenae (longjaw cisco)	Great Lakes	1975
Coregonus johannae (deepwater cisco)	Great Lakes	1952
Coregonus nigripinnis (blackfin cisco)	Great Lakes	1969
Cyprinidae		
Gila crassicauda (thicktail chub)	Central Valley, California (USA)	1957
Lepidomeda altivelis (Pahranagat spinedace)	Pahranagat Valley, Nevada (USA)	1938
Pogonichthys ciscoides (Clear Lake splittail)	Clear Lake, California (USA)	1970
Castostomidae		
Lagochila lacera (harelip sucker)	Midcentral and Southern USA	1895
Cyprinodontidae		
Empetrichthys latos (Pahrump killifish)[2]	Pahrump Valley, Nevada (USA)	1975
Empetrichthys merriami (Ash Meadows killifish)	Ash Meadows, Nevada (USA)	1948
Fundulus albolineatus (whiteline topminnow)	Spring Creek, Alabama (USA)	?
Poeciliidae		
Gambusia amistadensis (Amistad gambussia)[2]	Amistad Reservoir, Texas (USA)	1970s

Table 5.1 *continued*

Taxa and Common Name	Former Range	Last known collection
Percidae		
Stizostedion vitreum glaucum (blue pike)	Great Lakes	1970s
Cottidae		
Cottus echinatus (Utah Lake sculpin)	Utah Lake, Utah (USA)	1930s

1. Source: Robins et al. (1980).

2. Maintained under cultivation.

However, the largest and most highly valued of the corgonids, the blackfin cisco (*Coregonus nigripinnis*), had already been decimated through fisheries exploitation long before the arrival of the lamprey and alewife. The same was true of the blue pike. Pollution must likewise be considered as a contributing cause toward the decline of Great Lakes' fishes. The extent and pervasiveness of these changes can be seen in Lake Michigan where the fishery is now largely based on introduced salmonids that must be continually maintained by hatchery stockings. The fishery is extremely popular and has been an economic boon to the area, making a comparison of the relative merits of the historical and present fishery of philosophical interest only. For detailed accounts of human-induced changes of ichthyofauna of the Great Lakes, the reader is referred to Smith (1968), Wells and Maclean (1972), and Crowder (1980).

Conservation Programs in Captivity

The role artificial propagation can play in enabling the recovery of rare and endangered species of fish has only recently been appreciated (Johnson and Jensen, 1991). Initial attempts to propagate rare fishes have often failed (Ono et al., 1983). Such failures, however, should be construed as inevitable setbacks that befall any new initiative. Progress can and has been made. The Dexter National Fish Hatchery in New Mexico (U.S.A.) is a pioneering example of implementation of a change in philosophy of hatchery operation (Stuart and Johnson, 1981). This hatchery has as its major objectives to serve as a refugium, to provide opportunity to conduct much needed research, and to propagate endangered fishes for reintroduction into the wild (Rinne et al., 1986). As of 1982, 17 species that are threatened with extinction to some degree were being held in captivity.

Propagating endangered fishes merely for the sake of propagating or holding is an exercise in futility if reintroductions are not made. This is where the vagaries of the political process oftentimes impede progress. The U.S. Endangered Species Act was finally amended in 1982 to allow "experimental" populations, a provision designed to expedite reintroduction actions. The provision has had the desired effect. Between 1981 and 1984, Dexter National Fish Hatchery personnel distributed 6,108,965 fry and 296,376 fingerling razorback suckers (*Zyrauchen texanus*), and 116,638 Colorado squawfish fingerlings into historic habitats (Rinne et al., 1986). Other transplants have also been made with the Gila topminnow (*Poeciliopsis occidentalis*). The effort to reintroduce the Gila topminnow may represent the most intensive effort ever attempted for the recovery of an endangered species. Over 100 separate reintroductions have taken place (Rinne et al., 1986).

A Paiute (Native American) tribal hatchery has been in operation in Nevada (U.S.A.) since 1973 for the sole purpose of culturing endangered cui-ui (*Chasmistes cujus*) which is endemic to Pyramid Lake. Cui-ui culture techniques were developed by Koch and Contreras (1973). Impressive progress in the hatchery program has occurred with the number of cui-ui larvae stocked or distributed increasing from 1.6 million in 1973 to nearly 11 million by 1982 (Rinne et al., 1986). Considering that dam construction has made much of their natural spawning area inaccessible, it can be argued that hatchery propagation is the reason that cui-ui are still in existence. A success story has yet to emerge from two decades of intensive culture of endangered Apache trout (*Oncorhynchus apache*) in Arizona (Rinne et al., 1986). Efforts still continue and recent breakthroughs are cause for optimism.

The presentation of the foregoing examples of captive conservation efforts is not meant to be an all inclusive discourse. Artificial propagation of various endangered or threatened species is being undertaken by several agencies, universities, and interested biologists. Endangered species may also be in some level of cultivation in commercial ornamental fish farms. Nonetheless, the number of biologists involved in captive conservation of fishes pales in comparison to the number of species that may eventually need such protection.

Problems Facing Conservation Programs in Captivity

The long list of protected fishes of the United States and Canada (Johnson, 1987) signifies the presence of concern among the various regulatory bodies. Concern does not always translate into desired actions but the collective voices of conservationists are occasionally heard and the political climate is such that captive conservation programs for fishes potentially can become an inherent component of species recovery plans. Such is not the case in developing countries, many of which are located in tropical or subtropical regions where the highest species diversity of fishes exists. Habitat degradation in third-world countries is an enormous threat to all endemic species, plant and animal alike. Evoking concern for threatened fishes for any other than those having food or other commercial value is, and will continue to be, an arduous task. Arguments for conservation measures should initially be directed at preservation of fish as a group rather than placing too much urgency on a given species that might not be an effective standard-bearer.

For political as well as biological reasons it is important that captive conservation programs be successful in a relatively short period of time. All fish hatcheries are under pressure to meet quotas for stocking. This has a pervasive influence on hatchery operations and administration, and it will likely carry over in captive conservation programs. Unfortunately, not all endangered species are readily amenable to artificial propagation. Development of aquaculture technology has been profit-driven in terms of organisms for food or recreational value. The technology is often not applicable to the species of noncommercial value which are often the ones most threatened with extinction. There is also concern that attempting to rear endangered species outside their native habitats is not biologically sound (Conant, 1988; Williams et al., 1988). Such attempts should be restricted to circumstances where all native habitats have been destroyed or are in jeopardy of such destruction (Williams et al., 1989). Specific gaps of information and technology with respect to culture of endangered fishes are addressed in subsequent chapters of this volume.

As the science of endangered fish conservation matures it is imperative that a genetic foundation underpins recovery efforts (Meffe, 1986). Long-term conservation of any endangered species will likely fail if genetic aspects are ignored at the outset (Frankel and Soulé, 1981). Captive conservation of endangered fishes should be compatible with three dominant conservation goals: (1) maintenance of variable populations in the short-term (=avoidance of extinction), (2) maintenance of the capacity of the fishes to adapt to changing environments, and (3) maintenance of the capacity for continued speciation (Soulé, 1980). Meffe (1986) provides a succinct synoptic description of conservation genetics and the management of endangered fishes. His recommended actions to maximize long-term genetic health of endangered fishes bears repeating here: (1) monitor genetics of field and captive populations, (2) maintain the largest feasible genetically effective population size of captive stocks, (3) avoid inbreeding through selective mating, (4) keep stocks in hatchery environments for as short a time as possible, and (5) maintain separate stocks of distinct populations to preserve among-population variance. Following such a course of action will minimize the chances of bottlenecks, drift, inbreeding, and catastrophic loss of the stock.

A number of problems exist that are beyond those already mentioned with respect to rearing endangered fishes. Rinne et al. (1986) summarize these as avoidance of accidental intertransfer (hatchery to outside) and intratransfer (within culture units) coupled with the usual concerns in hatchery operations dealing with diseases, genetics, and domestication. These are untested factors as they may apply to rare wild strain species of fish. It is quite obvious that captive conservation of fishes presents a new challenge to the emerging science of aquaculture. Nonetheless, it is imperative that the "solution" does not become part of the "problem." Decision-makers might be tempted to justify actions that could lead to degrading critical habitat under the guise that fishes can be fully protected through captive conservation.

Ultimately, successful captive conservation efforts will lead to reintroductions. The American Fisheries Society has provided guidelines for introductions of threatened and endangered fishes (Williams et al., 1988). The guidelines are divided into three components: (1) selecting the introduction site, (2) conducting the introduction, and (3) postintroduction monitoring, reporting, and analysis. Following these or similar guidelines should increase success rates in recovering endangered fishes.

Lastly, it must be recognized that aquaculture has also played a major role in the demise of fish species. The development of aquaculture technology has made it possible to transfer fishes throughout the globe. Many of these introductions have had drastic negative effects on native ichthyofauna (see Courtenay and Stauffer, 1984; Courtenay and Kohler, 1986; Welcomme, 1986). Of the 40 species that have recently gone extinct in North America (Williams et al., 1989), introduced species were a contributory factor in 27 cases. Adherence to the American Fisheries Society position on introduced species (Kohler and Courtenay, 1986) would serve to slow the rate of fish endangerment and extinctions.

Conclusion

With the approach of the twenty-first century, conservationists have much reason for concern and some glimmerings for optimism with respect to the preservation of our natural heritage. Captive conservation can certainly play a role in recovery of endangered fishes but alone cannot prevent endangerment of a species. The role that hatcheries can play in recovery of rare fishes is only as good as the availability of suitable habitats in the wild for reintroductions (Rinne et al., 1986). Recognition of the need for captive conservation of a fish demands among other things, acceptance of the need to protect critical habitat. Natural resource agencies need to manage for conservation of entire ecosystems rather than the recovery of individual species (Williams et al., 1989). In the final analysis, education of the public and decision-makers with respect to turning the tide of species extinctions is the dominant challenge facing the conservationist. In that context, captive conservation not only buys time for endangered fishes but also for conservationists whose message has yet to be fully appreciated.

6

Reproductive Physiology of Teleost Fishes

Leo S. Demski

Information on reproductive physiology of individual species of endangered or threatened (E–T) fishes is sparse[1] (for available details on certain groups, see Breder and Rosen, 1966; Naiman and Soltz, 1981; Kuehne and Barbour, 1983; Ono et al., 1983; and Page, 1983). Indeed, of the 20–30,000 modern bony fishes (teleosts), most of the data concern a few species which have been studied extensively because of their importance as food (salmon, carp, trout, *Tilapia*, catfish, red drum), gamefish (trout, bass, sunfish), laboratory animals (goldfish, carp, guppies, swordtails, many cichlids) or special features such as sex-reversal (sea bass and wrasses). Thus, of necessity, most comments in this chapter refer to commonly used species; where possible, examples are chosen from fishes which are reasonably closely related to the largest groups of E–T species (see Kohler, chap. 5, this volume). Cartilaginous fishes (sharks and rays), none of which are considered E–T, have recently been reviewed elsewhere (Callard et al., 1988; Demski, 1989a–d).

Strategies and tactics for conservation of E–T native fishes have been discussed in detail (Meffe, 1986, 1987). One of the prime considerations is avoidance of inbreeding depression which within several generations can result in deleterious effects such as body deformities, reduction in growth, abnormal behavior, failure in reproductive systems (see Burns and Kallman, 1985; Meffe, 1986). Estimates of population sizes needed to reduce the effects of inbreeding to tolerable levels in captive populations are given based on generally accepted models.

Experimental procedures may also be used to create special genetic stocks. Genome manipulation and sex reversal are readily accomplished in oviparous fishes in which gametes can be hand-stripped and fertilized *in vitro*. Simple techniques are available for inducing gynogenesis (total maternal inheritance, see Komen et al., 1992), androgenesis (total paternal inheritance), and polyploidy (Thorgaard, 1983). Sex reversal is usually carried out by treatment of embryos with sex-steroids (Schreck, 1974; Hunter and Donaldson, 1983). Naturally occurring hybriogenic and gynogenetic all-female populations can also be studied (Moore, 1984; Vrijenhoek, 1984; Quattro et al., 1992). Thus, fish biologists have a battery of techniques for determination of basic genetic mechanisms. These procedures should be especially important for species in which only a few individuals may be available for study.

Neuroendocrinology of Fish Reproduction (Male and Female)

The essential control elements in the brain-pituitary-gonadal axis of fishes are described below. Sex-steroid secretion and gametogenesis are immediately controlled by gonadotropins (GtH) secreted by adenohypophyseal gonadotrops (Dubourg et al., 1985; Yan and Thomas, 1991). Two fish GtHs have been proposed based on biochemical and immunological studies mostly in salmon, carp flounder, and killifish (Idler and Ng, 1983; Suzuki et al., 1988a, b; Lin et al., 1992; Van Der Kraak et al., 1992; Yan et al., 1992). Maturational GtH is richer in carbohydrate and, in hypophysectomized (HYPX) fish, can maintain oocyte maturation and ovulation, spermatogenesis, spermiation, and steroidogenesis. The other GtH has been termed vitellogenic GtH because its major function appears to be yolk uptake.

Brain control of GtH secretion involves both facilatory and inhibitory systems (Peter, 1983; Peter et al., 1986, 1990, 1991; Lin et al., 1989; Sloley et al., 1992; Yu and Peter, 1992). In most teleosts two forms of gonadotropin releasing hormone (GnRH) are differentially located in the nervous system. Salmon GnRH is present in forebrain cells while a chicken II-like form is found in a group of midbrain neurons. Like the similar mammalian leutinizing hormone releasing hormone (LHRH) both fish types can evoke GtH release in a variety of species (Yu et al., 1988; Okuzawa et al., 1990; Amano et al., 1991, 1992; Chang et al., 1991; Suzuki et al., 1992). Asian catfish of the genus *Clarias* appear to have a novel form of GnRH in place of the salmon GnRH (Sherwood et al., 1989;

Ngamvongchon et al., 1992; Bogerd et al., 1992) while common eels (*Anguilla anguilla*) substitute mammalian GnRH for the salmon form (King et al., 1990). Various analogues of LHRH are also effective in releasing or inhibiting the release of GtH in fishes. Dopamine is a potent inhibitor of GtH release; other amines (serotonin and norepinepherine), several amino acid neurotransmitters, neuropeptide Y and sex steroids, and pineal hormones are also involved in the regulation of GtH secretion (Gern et al., 1987; Peter et al., 1991).

Female Reproductive Systems

Anatomy and development

The anatomy of female reproduction systems has been fairly well-studied (de Vlaming, 1974; Harder, 1975; Nagahama, 1983; van Tienhoven, 1983). Ovaries originate as folds of the developing peritoneum. Eggs are ovulated into the hollow interior of the ovary and delivered by its duct to the exterior. Live bearers (Poeciliidae) have specialized ovarian systems.

Growth and development of the oocytes are characterized by four general stages: primary growth, secondary growth including vitellogenesis, final maturation, and ovulation. All stages are susceptible to various hormonal and environmental manipulations. Eggs of fishes can atrophy (atresia) at any stage of development or survive to be ovulated. Following either fate, follicles develop "corpus luteum-like" structures (see below).

Three types of rhythmic development have been described for teleost ovaries (Harder, 1975; de Vlaming, 1983; Nagahama, 1983). (1) Total synchronism is found in species that spawn only once and die (e.g., some salmon). All oocytes develop synchronously. (2) Group synchronism is common in fishes that spawn once a year and several times during their life (e.g., herrings; trout, probably including the E–T Gila trout [*Salmo gilae*] [Rinne, 1980]; and some catfish). One set of oocytes matures to become the brood for the current season while a second undeveloped group will mature the following year. (3) Asynchronism characterizes fish that spawn over a relatively long period and have several matings per season; egg cells at various stages are present at the same time. Examples include: goldfish; probably the E–T peppered shiner (*Notropis perpallidus*) (Snelson and Jenkins, 1973); and two species of E–T desert pupfish,

Cyprinodon diabolis (Minckley and Deacon, 1973) and *Cyprinodon bovinus* (Kennedy, 1977). At least some E–T darters (small members of the Percidae) may also fit into this category because eggs of three size classes are found in the ovaries of spawning trispot darters (*Etheostoma trisella*) (Ryon, 1986) and fountain darters (*Etheostoma fonticola*) (Schenck and Whiteside, 1977a).

Several ovarian cell types are involved in steroid production. In salmon, both thecal and granulosa tissues are necessary for GtH-induced synthesis of both estradiol-17β (E_2) and an egg maturation-inducing hormone 17α,20β-dihydroxy-4-pregnen-3-one (17α,20β-P) (Nagahama, 1983). *In vitro* synthesis of progesterone and related steroids has been demonstrated in young, but not old, postovulatory follicles in trout (Nagahama, 1983; Nagahama and Adachi, 1985). The physiological significance of the latter is not known.

Endocrinology

Cycles-Seasons. Seasonal reproductive activities in female as well as male fishes vary greatly depending on the environment of the animals (see reviews by Breder and Rosen, 1966; de Vlaming, 1974, 1983; Lam, 1983; Peter, 1983; Scott and Sumpter, 1983; van Tienhoven, 1983; Bye, 1984; Stacey, 1984, 1987; Thresher, 1984; Whittier and Crews, 1987; chapters in Munro et al., 1990). Early studies on seasonality correlated gonadal development with time of year while more recently plasma and pituitary GtH as well as sex-steroid levels have been measured throughout the reproductive cycle in a few teleosts. Endogenous factors that affect gonadal maturation in two of the better studied fishes are considered as examples. Exogenous factors that determine the timing of reproductive events are discussed in a later section of this chapter.

Goldfish (*Carassius auratus*): Both long-term (seasonal) and short-term (daily) changes in reproductive hormones have been measured under various environmental conditions. Ovarian growth begins during the winter with vitellogenesis being completed late in spring (Stacey, 1987). Ovulation and spawning normally occur when water temperatures reach 20°C. Laboratory-housed goldfish with regressed gonads tend to have reduced GtH levels and lack daily fluctuations of GtH characteristic of females undergoing ovarian recrudescence (Hontela and Peter, 1983; Kobayashi et al., 1986; Hontela and Stacey, 1990).

The endocrine events related to ovulation have been especially well-studied (Stacey, 1984, 1987; Kobayashi et al., 1987, 1988;

Hontela and Stacey, 1990). The fish spawn in the early morning following ovulation in the later part of the night. Ovulation is immediately preceded by a surge in circulating GtH. Prostaglandins (PGs) are probably involved in both ovulation and triggering of the female sex behavior. Plasma $17\alpha,20\beta$-P and testosterone (T) peak before and decrease by the time of ovulation. E_2 levels are elevated several days before ovulation while moderate levels of E_2 occur during the GtH increase but no change immediately precedes or follows the GtH surge. Kobayashi and coworkers (1988, p. 304) have also outlined the endocrine events associated with the repeated ovulations of goldfish that occur during their extended spawning period. "First an increase in E_2 stimulates vitellogenesis. A gradual rise in testosterone lags behind and follows the increase in E_2. Then an ovulatory GtH surge occurs. The GtH surge causes an acute increase in testosterone followed by a shift of steroid hormone production from testosterone to $17\alpha,20\beta$-P, an inducer of final oocyte maturation. Ovulation occurs around the peak of the GtH surge, which probably is associated with the production of prostaglandins (Stacey and Goetz, 1982)." They feel that the increase in T before ovulation may cause the accumulation of pituitary GtH via a positive feedback system. Similar suggestions have been made for carp (*Cypinus carpio*) (Santos et al., 1986).

Rainbow Trout (*Salmo gairdneri*): There is considerable information on this and related species (see Scott, 1990 and references below). Spawning times vary significantly among populations that are widely distributed geographically. Previtellogenic winter-spawning females have low plasma levels of sex steroids (March–August). In the early fall, plasma E_2 and T begin to increase. Levels of the two steroids decline by the time of ovulation (December–February), whereas $17\alpha,20\beta$-P levels peak dramatically just before ovulation and remain high until about March. As mentioned, this steroid is involved in egg maturation. GtH generally remains low until about December and reaches a rapid peak during the ovulatory period. Episodic increases in GtH may occur early in the fall (Scott and Sumpter, 1983; Scott, 1987). Scott (1987) suggests that the GtH increase results from decreases in negative feedback regulation via T and E_2 and that the elevated GtH in turn triggers the increase in $17\alpha,20\beta$-P.

In studies in a feral trout population, GtH and $17\alpha,20\beta$-P both increase in females allowed to build nests and interact with males, whereas the hormonal changes are not observed in females prevented from such activity (Liley et al., 1986b).

Hormonal manipulation of the ovary and reproductive cycle. Oogonial proliferation appears to be facilitated by pituitary hormones because hypophysectomy (HYPX) may either severely reduce or eliminate mitotic activity in the stem cells. Conversely, transformation of oogonia into oocytes and the early stages of oocyte growth are not prevented by HYPX. However, the later stages of vitellogenesis, final maturation, ovulation, and oviposition are clearly controlled by a variety of hormones including GtHs, gonadal steroids, PGs, and neurohypophyseal peptides (Wallace and Selman, 1981; Donaldson and Hunter, 1983; Goetz, 1983; Idler and Ng, 1983; Nagahama, 1983, 1987; Ng and Idler, 1983; Ho, 1987; Jones, 1987; Scott, 1987; Xavier, 1987; Hontela and Stacey, 1990).

With regard to teleost GtH, there has been some controversy concerning the number of molecular forms as well as their potential roles in sexual development and physiology. For many years, only a single LH-like GtH was generally recognized. As mentioned above, it now appears that this is incorrect, at least for some species, which appear to have two GtHs. According to Ng and Idler (1983), in several diverse species, a maturational GtH controls vitellogenesis or at least its endogenous phase by stimulation of estrogen secretion. The latter (mostly E_2) in turn activates and maintains hepatic vitellogen production. A second or vitellogenic GtH is primarily responsible for the incorporation of the vitellogen into the oocytes. Suzuki and coworkers (Suzuki et al., 1988a, b, 1992; Swanson et al., 1991) have recently purified two GtHs from female salmon pituitaries. The types have different molecular weights, amino acid N-terminal residues, and subsets of receptors in the ovary (Yan et al., 1992). Both GtHs stimulate gonadal growth and enhance E_2 production, although they seem to be maximally effective at different times in the sexual cycle. The authors consider the GtHs dissimilar to those proposed by Idler and colleagues (Idler et al., 1987) but rather feel that they may be respectively homologous to LH and follicle stimulating hormone of tetrapods. Continued research is needed before broad generalizations concerning teleost GtH(s) can be made (see also Copeland and Thomas, 1989).

Final maturation, in at least some teleosts, is controlled by GtH mediation of follicular secretion of steroid hormones which, in turn, act directly on the oocyte (see review by Scott and Canario, 1987). As mentioned, $17\alpha,20\beta$-P is most likely the maturational steroid in a variety of species (e.g., trout, perch, goldfish, pike) while a similar molecular form, $17\alpha,20\beta,21$-trihydroxy-4-prenen-3-one ($17\alpha,20\beta,21$-P) appears to control ovarian development in the

Sciaenidae; i.e., the croakers and drums (Trant et al., 1986; Trant and Thomas, 1988; Thomas and Trant, 1989). T may also be a factor regulating final maturation because in goldfish it increases oocyte meiosis *in vitro* (Habibi et al., 1989). Maturational steroid control involves activation of a maturation-promoting factor located in the oocyte cytoplasm. In goldfish and carp, the later is a complex of cdckinase and cyclin B (Yamashita et al., 1992).

Ovulation usually directly follows oocyte maturation. Steroid stimulation *in vitro* results in ovulation in only a few species, including the perch and trout. *In vitro* and *in vivo* studies in the medaka (*Oryzias latipes*) indicate that interactions between GtH and steroids may be necessary to promote ovulation in certain species (Iwamatsu, 1978a, b). Oocyte expulsion from follicles probably occurs through PG activated contraction of "smooth muscle-like" cells in the theca (Goetz, 1983; Jones, 1987; Scott, 1987).

Steroid production and release by the fish ovary are generally under similar hormonal control as oocyte development (see above). Crude fish pituitary extracts, mammalian GtH, and fish maturational GtH preparations are all capable of stimulating ovarian steroid production (Fostier et al., 1983). Hormonal control of female sex behavior including either oviposition or copulation has been reviewed (Demski, 1983, 1987; Liley and Stacey, 1983; and Stacey, 1987). Suffice it to say that sex steroids, PGs, and certain neuropeptides (GnRH, arginine vasotocin and oxytocin) have powerful effects on these processes. The hormones appear to act via brain pathways which include hormone-sensitive neurons in the preoptic area and ventral telencephalon.

Fish culturists have long exploited the use of exogenous hormone treatment to artificially induce oocyte development, final maturation, and ovulation (Pickford and Atz, 1957). The hormones are usually administered in conjunction with a regimen of environmental stimulation (e.g., a photoperiod and temperature conducive to egg development or ovulation). Practical application of increased knowledge of hormonal control mechanisms has led to a number of highly effective procedures (de Vlaming, 1974; Fontaine, 1976; Hunter and Donaldson, 1983; Peter et al., 1987; Gissis et al., 1991; Lin et al., 1991a, b; Trudeau et al., 1991; Harmin and Crim, 1992). The treatments, which include antiestrogens, GtHs, GnRH and analogues coupled with dopamine antagonists[2], PGs, epinephrine, and sex steroids, affect different levels of the brain-pituitary-gonadal axis.

Such procedures have been used successfully on a few E–T species. For example, ovulation has been induced in razorback suckers (*Xyrauchen texanus*) by injection of 220 units of chorionic gonadotropin/kg at 24 hr intervals. Fish ovulated after three injections (Hamman, 1985a). Similarly, spawning has been induced in the South African border barb (*Barbus trevelyani*) using a single injection of either crude extracts of pituitaries from sexually mature *Labeo umbratus* (0.1–0.3 glands/fish), human chorionic gonadotropin (doses up to 750 IU) or combinations of the two (Bok and Heard, 1982).

Physiology

Puberty: (female and male). Little is known concerning the detailed timing and control of sexual development in most fishes. Many fish mature within a year (see Breder and Rosen, 1966) while others may take several years to reach puberty (e.g., 2 or 7 years in bluegill sunfish (*Lepomis macrochirus*) (Gross, 1984). Still other fish normally change sex at critical stages of their life history (Demski, 1987). With regard to E–T species there are limited data on a few species. The Australian grayling (*Prototrotes maraena*) matures and spawns at 2 years and then dies; a few individuals survive to mate at 3 years (Bishop and Bell, 1978). Modoc suckers (*Catostomus microps*) mature in their second or third years and seldom live longer than 5 years (Moyle and Mariochi, 1975). The peppered shiner probably spawns at ages 1, 2, and 3 with few fish surviving to 4 years (Snelson and Jenkins, 1973). Kennedy (1977) reports that Leon Springs pupfish live for only 20–23 months and that most individuals participate in only one spawning period. Trispot darters live 2+ years with some animals probably spawning in two seasons (Ryon, 1986). Mechanisms controlling puberty have been most extensively studied in the platyfish (*Xiphophorus maculatus*) (Schreibman et al., 1987).

Viviparity. Gestation lengths in live-bearing teleosts are best known for common members of the family Poeciliidae (Breder and Rosen, 1966; Wourms, 1981; Wourms et al., 1988). The family includes five E–T species of *Gambusia*. Following a single mating, guppies (*Poecilia reticulata*) produce several broods at intervals of about 28 days while platyfish deliver as many as seven broods at monthly intervals. Hormonal control of parturition has been studied in live-bearers (Heller, 1972; Kujala, 1978; Guillette, 1987). In guppies, injections of either deoxycortisol, oxytocin or vasotocin can result in premature parturition.

Artificial insemination and embryo transfer. Most, if not all, commercially important teleosts are oviparous and for this reason, there has been little interest in artificial insemination and embryo transfer. Attempts to cryopreserve teleost ova or embryos have proven rather unsuccessful; however, freezing and short-term storage (1–60 days) of eggs from certain species has been accomplished (Stoss, 1983).

Male Reproductive Systems

Anatomy

The basic morphology of the male reproductive system in teleosts has been extensively reviewed (de Vlaming, 1974; Harder, 1975; Grier et al., 1980; Grier, 1981, 1992; Billard et al., 1982; Nagahama, 1983; van Tienhoven, 1983). Thus, only a brief summary of essential features is given here.

Microscopic structure of testis follows two basic patterns. In the "unrestricted type," the spermatogonia are distributed along the entire length of the tubule. The pattern is characteristic of most teleosts. The "restricted type" has spermatogonia located only at the blind distal tip of lobule-like branches of the tubules. This type is characteristic of the Atheriniformes which include two families with E–T species; i.e., the livebearers (Poeciliidae) and the killifish (Cyprinodontidae). In species with internal fertilization, sperm are packaged into either spermatozeugmata (unencapsulated sperm bundles) or spermatophores (encapsulated sperm bundles). Spermiation is a thinning or hydration of the milt in most teleosts (see below). Testis cells have been implicated in steroidogenesis. Interstitial cells are considered equivalent to Leydig cells of tetrapods and are thus assumed to be the major source of testicular androgen. Less evidence is available for steroidogenesis in Sertoli cells. The sperm ducts receive sperm from the testis lobules and, in some species, secretions from accessory glands; contractions of smooth muscles in the sperm duct deliver milt to the exterior via a urogenital papilla near the anus. Specialized copulatory organs are present in species with internal fertilization.

Endocrinology (Seasonal Aspects) Including Puberty

In general, male teleosts follow seasonal reproductive patterns in concert with the females. This includes time of first sexual development (i.e., puberty) and seasonal cycles of gonadal recrudescence, spermiation, spawning, and regression (see reviews by Demski, 1987; Moore, 1987b; Stacey, 1987; Whittier and Crews, 1987; and chapters in Munro et al., 1990). Species differences in seasonal production of sperm can be great (e.g., in carp, spermatozoa are present throughout the year whereas in trout, there is regular succession of germ cell-types).

In terms of endocrine control, male reproduction can be separated into spermatogenesis, steroidogenesis, spermiation, and sexual behavior. These stages have some common as well as unique hormonal control mechanisms (de Vlaming, 1974; Billard et al., 1982; Demski and Hornby, 1982; Peter, 1983; Scott and Sumpter, 1983; Demski, 1987; Lofts, 1987; Scott, 1987; Stacey, 1987; Hontela and Stacey, 1990; Miura et al., 1991; Cochran, 1992; Schulz et al., 1992).

The pituitary appears to be necessary for testicular steroid production and development of sperm. In general, HYPX leads to a decline in plasma androgen levels, regression of secondary sexual characteristics, loss of sexual behavior, and cessation of spermatogenesis. Earlier stages of sperm development (spermatogonial mitosis to spermatocytc formation) appear to be more dependent on pituitary hormones than later ones (spermatocyte to spermatozoa). The effects of pituitary loss, which can be reversed by administration of exogenous GtHs, are probably secondary to decreases in androgen production. In *Fundulus*, different pituitary GTHs appear to control testis steroid production and growth respectively (Cochran, 1992).

There is considerable evidence that androgens are responsible for sex cell development (Miura et al., 1991; Cochran, 1992; Lee et al., 1992). For example, in salmonids injection of the hormones in juveniles causes premature development and androgen levels are high during normal and precocious spermatogenesis. In addition, significant interactions between gonadal steroids and pituitary GtH occur at different phases of male sexual development. In immature fish, androgens appear to increase GtH secretion via a positive feedback system which leads to puberty (Magri et al., 1985); whereas in adults, the steroids produce negative feedback (e.g., their loss due to castration results in a significant rise in GtH). The steroid effects may be mediated by steroid-concentrating cells in both the pars distalis of the pituitary and preoptic and hypothalamic areas of the brain (Demski and Hornby, 1982).

Spermiation, a term originally defined for release of sperm from Sertoli cells in amphibians, has been applied to teleosts. In fishes it more generally refers to the condition of thinning of milt. Spermiation in goldfish is blocked by HYPX and can be reinstated by exogenous GtH (Yamazaki and Donaldson, 1969). The GtH effect is most likely mediated by testicular steroid secretion. For example, Ueda and coworkers (1985) found that T, 11-ketotestosterone (11-KT), and 17α,20β-P were very effective in initiating spermiation in male goldfish and Cochran (1992) indicates that 11-KT is associated with the response in *Fundulus*. GtHs and/or sex steroids have also been used to activate the response in other species (de Vlaming, 1974; Billard et al., 1982; Ueda et al., 1985).

In at least several teleosts, sperm release during spawning appears to be controlled by a central nervous system pathway (preoptic area-spinal cord-sympathetic nerves) to smooth muscle of the sperm duct. The system is sensitive to GnRH and receives input from the nose (Demski, 1983; Demski and Sloan, 1985; Demski and Dulka, 1986; Dulka and Demski, 1986; Sloan and Demski, 1987).

Sex-hormone profiles over seasonal cycles and especially in perispawning periods are available for a few male teleosts. In carp, although spermatozoa are present throughout the year, peak production with highest fertilizing capacity occurs during the spawning period in the spring (Weil, 1981; Billard et al., 1982). This period is characterized by an increase in pituitary GtH which, however, peaks after spawning and remains high for several months; plasma GtH, although higher than in months immediately before spawning, does not show a peak corresponding to the spawning period. Daily fluctuations of GtH are known in goldfish and such changes, which can be affected by photoperiod, temperature and social stimuli, may be physiologically more important than average sustained levels of hormone (Hontela and Peter, 1983; Kyle et al., 1985). Plasma androgen levels in carp are rather constant across the annual reproductive cycle (Weil, 1981) whereas, in the closely related goldfish, they peak during the spawning season (Schreck and Hopwood, 1974; Kobayashi et al., 1986). It should also be noted that, at least in goldfish, GtH and E and T levels, although elevated during the spawning period, do not closely correlate with specific events in the sexual cycle (see details in Kobayashi et al., 1986).

In rainbow trout, T and 11-KT increase in the plasma during the time of testicular development and most active spermatogenesis and start to fall at about the time of spermiation; however, basal levels are reached only after testicular regression (see reviews by Scott et al., 1980; Billard et al., 1982; Scott and Sumpter,

1983; Liley et al., 1986a; Scott, 1987; Scott and Sumpter, 1989). In some cases, 11-KT may peak as much as a month or two after T. The hormone levels cannot be directly correlated with peak sperm volume, sperm number or milt density and presumably are thus related to other aspects of testicular development (e.g., 11-KT may control development of secondary sexual characteristics). However, 17α,20β-P does increase in plasma in correspondence with the sperm production peak. The hormone appears to regulate the ionic content of the milt rather than its amount or number of sperm. *In vitro* studies suggest that seasonal variation in steroids may result from changes in testicular sensitivity to GtH (Schulz et al., 1992).

Liley and coworkers (1986a) have measured GtH and several steroids at various stages in a natural spawning population of rainbow trout. Plasma GtH, T, and especially 11-KT were elevated in spawning fish and the steroids were undetectable in postspawning animals. Striking changes were found in fish placed with females. GtH levels rose in fish exposed to sexually active, as well as inactive and unovulated females, while 17α,20β-P levels increased only in males allowed to interact with sexually active females. The results indicate dynamic hormonal changes related to behavior and social stimuli. A similar response has been observed in male white suckers (*Catostomus commersi*) (Stacey et al., 1984). The findings could potentially be useful in breeding certain E–T species; e.g., Gila trout, (Rinne, 1980); cui-ui lakesuckers (*Chasmistes cujus*) (Koch and Contreras, 1973); razorback suckers (Hamman, 1985a); and Modoc suckers (Moyle and Marciochi, 1975).

Semen Collection, Evaluation, and Cryopreservation

Artificial *in vitro* insemination of teleost eggs has been practiced for many years in a number of countries (Lam, 1982a, b; Donaldson and Hunter, 1983; de Vlaming, 1983). In addition to hand stripping, testis fragments can also be used to obtain sperm.

Techniques for both short-term and long-term preservation of fish sperm have been reviewed in considerable depth (Scott and Baynes, 1980; Stoss, 1983; Chao et al., 1987). The following are general considerations that should be taken into account in sperm handling. Differences in metabolism between fish sperm types have been demonstrated. Thus, optimal conditions for storage media vary with sperm type. Sperm viability is usually assessed in terms of motility. The cells remain immobile while inside the testes and in some cases in the milt as well. They are normally activated by particular chemical-ionic stimuli in the media into which they are released. In designing artificial storage vehicles, it is important to maintain immobility as it greatly reduces metabolic demands. It is equally imperative that sperm motility can be triggered just before mixing with ova.

Short-term storage of sperm is useful when there is a delay in obtaining eggs or where the gametes must be transported to rearing facilities. It may also be an important preliminary step for long-term preservation. Cryopreservation for indefinite long-term storage has been successfully carried out in a number of species of both freshwater and marine teleosts (Stoss, 1983).

Environmental and Social Influences

Sexual cycles in teleosts vary considerably from species to species but animals living under common conditions frequently have similar reproductive seasons. Timing of cycles results from interactions of endogenous rhythms and exogenous factors which include environmental and social stimuli. The interactions can be varied and complex and our knowledge of such is restricted to laboratory experiments in only a few species (Lowe-McConnell, 1979; Peter, 1981, 1983; de Vlaming, 1983; Lam, 1983; Bye, 1984; Stacey, 1984, 1987; chapters in Munro et al., 1990).

Reproductive cycles are most prominent in temperate or cold-water species in which there is usually a well-defined breeding season, lasting from 1 or 2 days to several weeks or months (Bye, 1990; Sumpter, 1990). Exogenous factors can modify endogenous rhythms at different times in the cycles. In spring spawners such as carp and goldfish, decreasing day lengths and temperatures in the fall trigger gametogenesis while increasing day lengths and temperatures in early spring initiate final maturation, ovulation, spermiation, and sexual behavior. Similar patterns probably occur in a number of temperate E–T species including: Gila trout (Rinne, 1980); cui-ui lakesucker (Koch and Contreras, 1973); razorback sucker (Tyus, 1987); Modoc sucker (Moyle and Marciochi, 1975); humpback chub (*Gila cypha*) (Hamman, 1982a); and trispot darter (Ryon, 1986). Such cycles may be reversed in typical autumn spawners (e.g., some trout and the E–T Australian grayling Bishop and Bell, 1978). Site specific stimuli may also be involved in the later stages; for example, floating aquatic vegetation facilitates ovulation in goldfish (Stacey et al., 1979; Stacey, 1984). With respect to E–T species, the following environmental features are likely to be involved in the control of reproduction: depth of water (*S. gilae*, Rinne, 1980); presence of aquatic vegetation (*E. trisella*, Ryon, 1986);

type of bottom substrate (*E. trisella*, Ryon, 1986; *S. gilae*, Rinne, 1980; *X. texanus*, Tyus, 1987; *C. microps*, Moyle and Marciochi, 1975); current velocity (*S. gilae*, Rinne, 1980); pH (*C. cujus*, Koch and Contreras, 1973) and presence of shaded areas (*C. microps*, Moyle and Marciochi, 1975).

Tropical, subtropical, and desert species generally have less well-defined periods of reproduction (e.g., coral reef fishes typically spawn throughout the year). In warmer climates in which day length and/or temperature changes are not pronounced, tide cycles, food availability, rainy versus dry periods, and changes in social environments (see below) may be the primary environmental cues for reproduction. Several North American E–T species fit into this category and some aspects of their spawning habitats are discussed briefly. The peppered shiner populations of the Red and Ouachita river drainages of Arkansas and Oklahoma have protracted spawning periods which extend from May through August (Snelson and Jenkins, 1973). The summer spawning is possible because the moderate fall climate in the area permits growth of the fry. Most darters have a single spring spawning period; however, the fountain darter, which lives under relatively constant temperatures in southwest Texas, has at least two spawning peaks (late August and late winter-early spring) and probably exercises some mating on a year-round basis. Slight increases in water temperature and/or decreases in water flow rate are the most probable environmental signals regulating the reproductive activity (Schenck and Whiteside, 1977a). Desert cyprinodonts (killifish), including pupfish of the genus *Cyprinodon* and the Pahrump poolfish (*Empetichthys latos latos*), have extended "specialized" spawning periods as adaptations to environments with rather constant high year-round temperatures (see papers in Naiman and Stoltz, 1981). For example, the devil's hole pupfish probably mates throughout the year but has a peak of activity in the spring. The cycle is most likely controlled by photoperiod expressed as variations in algal growth; i.e., food availability (Minckley and Deacon, 1973). The Leon Springs pupfish has a similar pattern with a somewhat later peak (mid-July). It also exhibits two daily peaks in spawning activity (1000–1030 and 1800–1900 hr) which probably correspond to temperature windows set to avoid the extreme heat of midday (Kennedy, 1977). Pahrump poolfish also have a long spawning period (February–July) with a peak in April (Baugh et al., 1987).

Additional environmental factors that may influence reproduction include: dissolved oxygen levels, salinity, barometric pressure, limitation of food, water pollution, and other stresses (Lam,
1983; Munro, 1990; Taylor, 1990). Certain "representative" environmental and social effects on reproductive cycles are discussed
below and elsewhere throughout this chapter (see also Breder and
Rosen, 1966).

The role of social stimuli in controlling reproduction has only
been studied in a few species. In some cases, the specific stimuli
involved have been identified while in others only general conditions that affect the response are known. For example, crowding
inhibits sex maturation in a number of species (Lam, 1983), and
GtH and sex-steroids can increase in certain male salmonids and
cyprinids allowed access to females (see discussion in endocrinology section).

Visual contact with conspecifics can influence sexual development (Lam, 1983; Demski, 1987). In certain wrasses (genus
Thalassoma) female sex-change in response to removal of a dominant male is in part determined by visual cues related to fish size.
Several studies in cichlids (Perciformes) indicate that seeing other
fish can facilitate ovulation and sex behavior (review by Munro,
1990) or in certain males delay sexual development related to growth
of brain GnRH-containing neurons (Davis and Fernald, 1990). Similarly, isolated male sticklebacks (Gasterosteiformes) attain breeding conditions more readily if allowed to view conspecific males or
females (review by Baggerman, 1990). Seasonal and nonseasonal
sexual dimorphisms occur in many fishes. Frequently encountered
are male-typical color patterns, breeding tubercles and, in viviparous forms, intromittent organs. Presumably, these characters are
used in sexual displays and other aspects of mating. Color dimorphisms are prominent in the North American darters including the
E–T fountain darter (Schenck and Whiteside, 1977a) and the trispot
darter (Ryon, 1986).

There are few studies on the effects of acoustic stimuli on
stimulation of reproduction. Courtship sounds are made by many
species (Fine et al., 1977), and it would be surprising if they did not
have profound effects on reproductive physiology. Indeed, Marshall
(1972) observed that female *Tilapia mossambica* exposed to recordings of male sounds reached spawning condition up to ten days
sooner than control fish.

Pheromonal or chemical stimulation of sexual development,
ovulation, spermiation, and reproductive behavior is known or sus-

pected in a variety of teleosts (Liley and Stacey, 1983; Stacey, 1987; Resink et al., 1989; Cole and Smith, 1992; Van den Hurk and Resink, 1992). The goldfish system, which has received the most extensive study, is outlined as an example (Demski and Hornby, 1982; Dulka et al., 1987; Kyle et al., 1987; Sloan and Demski, 1987; Sorensen et al., 1988, 1989, 1990, 1991; Stacey et al., 1989 and Van Der Kraak et al., 1989; Hontela and Stacey, 1990). Females release at least two pheromones associated with ovulation and spawning. $17\alpha,20\beta$-P is produced in response to increased GtH levels and controls final oocyte maturation. When released into the water, it triggers a GtH rise in mature males. Olfactory pathways, which include the medial olfactory tract, mediate the response which increases the milt available for spawning. Continued development of the eggs results in an increase in PG synthesis which in turn triggers ovulation, female sexual behavior, and release of PGs into the water where they act as pheromones triggering courtship and possibly sperm release in the males; thus, sexual activity occurs at a time when sperm and ova are most available.

In a few cases, complex behavioral activities rather than isolated stimuli are the effective triggers for alteration of reproductive systems. Examples in sex-changing fish are the most notable (Demski, 1987).

Conclusions

Advances in fish reproductive physiology have frequently led to rapid development of new techniques of fish culture (e.g., the now widespread use of GnRH for initiation of maturation and spawning). Chromosome manipulation and artificial sex-change, molecular biology of sex hormones and their receptors and brain-endocrine interactions involved in reproductive development and behavior are likely areas from which exciting new information should be forthcoming. Translation of the experimental data into practical fisheries techniques will be especially important.

Successful cryopreservation of fish gametes, while currently feasible for sperm, must be extended to eggs and embryos. The information available on the latter suggests that this can be achieved. Gene banks could then be established and gametes of E–T as well as other species stockpiled for future breeding and research. In the meantime, large aquatic facilities need to be utilized for artificial breeding of E–T species. Attempts should be made to maintain as much genetic diversity as possible. In addition, for the effective design of captive breeding programs for most E–T species, coordinated field and laboratory studies are needed to determine the critical environmental and social influences that facilitate or inhibit reproduction.

Notes

1. A Biosis search (file #5, 1969–July 1989) with the descriptors endangered or threatened, osteichthyes, and reproductive system-physiology and biochemistry resulted in only 38 citations. Of these, 14 articles were relevant to this paper and only 5 concerned culture methods (e.g., procedures for inducing spawning or rearing of young). The other references dealt primarily with reproductive biology as part of field-oriented life-history studies. Only five teleost families (Catostomidae, Cyprinidae, Cyprinodontidae, Percidae, and Salmonidae) are represented in the 14 papers.

2. Kits with these components are available as Ovaprim from Syndel Laboratories Ltd., 9211 Shaughnessy Street, Vancouver, British Columbia, Canada V6P 6R5.

7

Behavioral Research on Captive Endangered Fishes of North America

Ruth Francis-Floyd and James D. Williams

Habitats of endangered freshwater fishes are diverse and vary greatly in their physical and chemical characteristics. Environmental conditions of the habitat and the small size of most endangered and threatened fishes make direct behavioral observations *in situ* difficult under even the best conditions. For many species, studies of captive populations offer the best opportunity to gain insight into the behavior of these fishes.

Of the 84 endangered and threatened fishes listed by the U.S. Fish and Wildlife Service, 49 have been held in captivity (Table 7.1). Most captive situations involved adult fishes held for propagation, and few included behavioral observations. Although information about how a given species solves the problems of feeding, body maintenance, defense against predators, and reproduction is essential to conservation efforts, historically, the behavior of endangered fishes has not been emphasized. However, as the endangered and threatened fishes program evolves beyond the initial phase of identifying and defining the problem, it appears that some attention is beginning to be focused on behavioral questions.

Representativeness of Field Studies

Much of the available information specific to endangered or threatened fishes is summarized in the species recovery plans of the U.S. Fish and Wildlife Service. Recovery plans for 41 species were available for our review. Behavioral information incorporated into these plans covers a wide range: (1) incidental observations made in the

Table 7.1

Endangered and threatened fishes (on Federal list) which have been or are presently held in captivity. The number of individuals, life stage, and lengths of time in captivity varies for each species. An asterisk preceeding the scientific name indicates the species is currently (1990) in captivity. In the agency/individual contact or reference column the abbreviation NFH = National Fish Hatchery and USFWS = United States Fish and Wildlife Service.

Family *Scientific Name*	Historic Range	Purpose	Agency/Individual Contact or Reference
Acipenseridae			
Acipenser brevirostrum	Atlantic coast, USA, Canada	Captive propagation	Smith et al., 1985 Smith et al., 1986 USFWS, Orangeburg NFH, Orangeburg, SC.
Salmonidae			
Oncorhynchus aguabonita whitei	CA	Captive propagation Refuge population	California Game & Fish Kernville, CA
O. apache	AZ	Captive propagation Refuge population	Arizona Game & Fish Phoenix, AZ. USFWS, Williams Creek NFH, White River, AZ.
O. clarki henshawi	CA, NV	Captive propagation Refuge population	California Fish & Game Sacramento, CA. Gerstung, 1988. USFWS, Lahontan NFH, Gardnerville, NV.

Species	Distribution	Activity	References
*O. clarki stomias	CO	Captive propagation Refuge population	Dwyer & Rosenlund, 1988 USFWS, Fish Technology Center Bozeman, MT.
*O. gilae	AZ, NM	Captive propagation Refuge population	New Mexico Game & Fish Santa Fe, NM. USFWS, Mescalero NFH, Mescalero, NM.
Cyprinidae			
Gila bicolor mohavensis	CA	Physiological studies Refuge population	Castleberry & Cech, 1986 Feldmeth et al, 1985 Havelka et al, 1982 McClanahan et al., 1986
G. boraxobius	OR	Biological studies	Williams, 1980
G. cypha	AZ, CO, UT, WY	Hybridization studies Physiological studies Spawning in captivity	Pimentel & Bulkley, 1983 Hamman, 1981a Hamman, 1982a USFWS, Dexter NFH, Dexter, NM.
G. ditaenia	AZ, Mexico	Refuge population	USFWS, Dexter NFH, Dexter, NM.
*G. elegans	AZ, CA, CO, NY, UT, WY	Captive propagation Hybridization studies Induced spawning Physiological studies Refuge population	Hamman, 1981a Hamman, 1982b Hamman, 1985 Pimentel & Bulkley, 1983 USFWS, Dexter NFH, Dexter, NM. USFWS, Willow Beach NFH, Boulder, NV.

Table 7.1 continued

Family Scientific Name	Historic Range	Purpose	Agency/Individual Contact or Reference
*G. nigrescens	NM, Mexico	Captive propagation Refuge population	USFWS, Dexter NFH, Dexter NM.
*G. robusta jordani	NV	Captive propagation Refuge population	USFWS, Dexter NFH, Dexter, NM.
G. purpurea	AZ, Mexico	Captive propagation Refuge population	USFWS, Dexter NFH, Dexter, NM.
Hybopsis cahni	TN, VA	Reproductive behavior	Dr. Richard Neves, VPI & SU, Blacksburg, VA.
Lepidomeda mollispinis pratensis	NV	Captive propagation	Dr. James Deacon, Biology Dept., UNLV, Las Vegas, NV.
Moapa coriacea	NV	Captive propagation Reproductive biology	Dr. James Deacon, Biology Dept., UNLV, Las Vegas, NV. USFWS, Reno, NV.
*Notropis formosus	AZ, NM, Mexico	Captive propagation Refuge population	USFWS, Dexter NFH, Dexter, NM.
N. simus pecosensis	NM	Captive propagation	USFWS, Dexter NFH, Dexter, NM.

Species	Distribution	Activity	References
Plagopterus argentissimus	AZ, NV, UT	Captive propagation Habitat requirements Refuge population Reproductive biology Thermal tolerances	Deacon et al, 1987 Greger & Deacon, 1982 USFWS, Dexter NFH, Dexter, NM.
Ptychocheilus lucius	AZ, CA, CO, NM, NV, UT, WY, Mexico	Captive propagation Physiological studies Refuge population	Arizona Game & Fish, Page Springs Hatchery, Prescott, AZ. Berry, 1988 Black & Bulkley, 1985a Black & Bulkley, 1985b Hamman, 1981b Hamman, 1986 Marsh, 1985 Osmundson, 1987 Pimentel & Bulkley, 1983 Toney, 1974 USFWS, Dexter NFH, Dexter, NM. USFWS, Willow Beach NFH, Boulder, NV.

Catostomidae

Species	Distribution	Activity	References
Chasmistes brevirostris	OR, CA	Captive propagation	Klamath Tribe, Braymill Hatchery, Chiloquin, OR. USFWS, Dexter NFH, Dexter, NM.
C. cujus	NV	Captive propagation	Chatto, 1979 Koch & Contreras, 1973 Nevada Department of Wildlife,

Table 7.1 *continued*

Family Scientific Name	Historic Range	Purpose	Agency/Individual Contact or Reference
C. cujus (continued)			Carson City, NV. Pyramid Lake Tribal Hatchery, Sutcliff, NV. USFWS, Reno, NV.
Deltistis luxatus	OR, CA	Captive propagation	Klamath Tribe, Braymill Hatchery, Chiloquin, OR. USFWS, Dexter NFH, Dexter, NM.
Ictaluridae			
Ictalurus pricei	AZ, Mexico	Captive propagation Refuge population	USFWS, Dexter NFH, Dexter, NM.
Noturus baileyi	TN	Captive propagation	USFWS, Ashville, NC.
N. flavipinnis	GA, TN, VA	Captive propagation	USFWS, Ashville, NC.
Amblyopsidae			
Amblyopsis rosae	AR, MO, OK	Behavioral studies	Bechler, 1983
Cyprinodontidae			
Crenichthys baileyi grandis	NV	Artificial hybridization Captive propagation	Baugh et al., 1985 Hubbs & Drewry, 1962

Species	Location		
Cyprinodon bovinus	TX	Captive propagation Refuge population Thermal tolerances	Dr. Clark Hubbs, UT, Austin, TX. Kennedy, 1977 USFWS, Dexter NFH, Dexter, NM.
C. diabolis	NV	Captive propagation Maintenance in captivity Refuge population Thermal tolerances	Baugh & Deacon, 1983 Baugh & Deacon, 1988 Baugh & Feldmeth, 1971 Castro, 1983 Williams, 1977
C. elegans	TX	Captive propagation Thermal tolerance	Gehlbach et. al., 1978 Dr. Clark Hubbs, UT, Austin, TX. USFWS, Dexter NFH, Dexter, NM.
*C. macularius	AZ, CA, Mexico	Behavioral studies Captive propagation Refuge population	Arizona Sonora Desert Museum, Tucson, AZ. Butte County Mosquito Abatement District, Butte County, CA. Miller et al., 1985 (and references therein) Dr. W. L. Minckley, ASU, Tempe, AZ. University of California, Riverside, CA. USFWS, Dexter NFH, Dexter, NM.
C. nevadensis mionectes	NV	Behavioral studies Thermal tolerances	Brown & Feldmeth, 1971 Kodric-Brown, 1981 Soltz, 1974

Table 7.1 continued

Family *Scientific Name*	Historic Range	Purpose	Agency/Individual Contact or Reference
C. nevadensis pectoralis	NV	Thermal tolerances	Brown & Feldmeth, 1971
C. radious	CA	Behavioral studies	Dr. George Barlow and June Mirge, UC, Berkeley, CA.
Empetrichthys latos	NV	Biological observations Captive propagation Growth studies	Baugh et al., 1987 Sokol, 1954
Poeciliidae			
*Gambusia gaigei	TX	Captive propagation Morphological studies Refuge population	Hubbs & Brodrick, 1963 Hubbs & Springer, 1957 USFWS, Dexter NFH, Dexter, NM.
G. heterochir	TX	Reproductive behavior	Warburton et al., 1957
G. nobilis	NM, TX	Captive propagation Refuge population Thermal tolerances	Gehlbach et al., 1978 USFWS, Dexter NFH, Dexter, NM.
*Poeciliopsis occidentalis	AZ, NM, Mexico	Behavioral ecology Captive propagation Refuge population Reproduction and population biology	Arizona Game & Fish, Phoenix, AZ. Constantz, 1975 Meffe, et al., 1983 Schoenherr, 1977 USFWS, Dexter NFH, Dexter, NM.

Gasterosteridae			
Gasterosteus aculeatus williamsoni	CA	Physiological studies	Feldmeth & Baskin, 1976.
Percidae			
Etheostoma boschungi	AL, TN	Reproductive behavior	Boschung, 1976
E. fonticola	TX	Captive propagation Feeding behavior Refuge population Reproductive behavior	Hubbs, 1967 Schenck & Whiteside, 1977 USFWS, Dexter NFH, Dexter, NM. USFWS, San Marcos NFH & Technology Center, San Marcos, TX.
*E. okaloosae	FL	Interspecific interactions Reproductive behavior	USFWS, National Fisheries Research Center, Gainesville, FL.
E. rubrum	MS	Reproductive behavior Substrate preference.	Dr. Steve Ross, USM, Hattisburg, MS.
*E. wapiti	AL, TN	Captive propagation Reproductive behavior	USFWS, National Fisheries Research Center, Gainesville, FL
Percina pantherina	AR, OK	Captive propagation	USFWS, NFH & Technology Center, San Marcos, TX.
P. tanasi	AL, GA, TN	Captive propagation Reproductive behavior	Hickman & Fitz, 1978 Starnes, 1977

field (U.S. Fish and Wildlife Service, 1983a); (2) seasonal studies (Boccone and Mills, 1979); (3) long-term field observations of certain behavior patterns (Williams and Williams, 1980); and (4) experimental studies of target species held in the laboratory in aquaria (Williams, 1980) or artificial streams (U.S. Fish and Wildlife Service, 1984).

Most conclusions about behavioral traits of individual species are somewhat tentative, and based largely on inferences. For example, a common means of determining feeding and foraging habits of target species has been the analysis of stomach contents (La Rivers, 1962; Minckley and Deacon, 1975; National Marine Fisheries Service, 1982). The Moapa dace (*Moapa coriacea*), an endangered cyprinid of the Southwest (and the only known representative of the genus *Moapa*), was determined to be carnivorous by La Rivers (1962) on the basis of large quantities of insects found in its stomach and the short length of its intestinal tract. The endangered Cape Fear shiner (*Notropis mekistocholas*), a cyprinid endemic to the Cape Fear River system of North Carolina, is believed to be herbivorous because it has a long coiled intestine (Snelson, 1971). The measurement of physical and morphologic traits, such as length of intestine or stage of gonad development, have been used to infer conclusions regarding feeding or reproductive habits in other fishes. The conclusions drawn from morphological observations have sometimes been questioned after behavioral observations were made in the field. For example, the humpback chub (*Gila cypha*) has a subterminal mouth that suggests it is a bottom-feeder; however, biologists have seen the fish feeding at the surface, and have caught it near the surface, which suggests that it may be a surface feeder or feed throughout the water column (U.S. Fish and Wildlife Service, 1979).

Need for Controlled Studies

In aquatic habitats, identifying the factors that place endangered fishes at risk is sometimes problematic, and controlled studies that examine the influence of isolated variables are badly needed.

As a group, desert fishes of the southwestern states are the most severely threatened, and behavioral studies of the pupfishes (genus *Cyprinodon*) are far more detailed than those of any other group of endangered or threatened fishes. All five species and two subspecies of endangered pupfishes have been held in captivity, where they were the subjects of a variety of behavioral studies (Kodric-Brown, 1981). Some of these studies have included laboratory (aquarium) and field observations (Barlow, 1961; Soltz, 1974).

Darters of the genus *Etheostoma* have also been the subject of behavioral studies, especially in recent years. Most have been focused on reproductive behavior, which has been used in the development of phylogenetic relationships within the genus *Etheostoma* (Page, 1985). Field studies of the reproductive biology of the threatened slackwater darter (*E. boschungi*) (Boschung, 1976), and the threatened Niangua darter (*E. nianguae*) (Pflieger, 1978), were undertaken to gain information critical to managing habitat and the development of plans for captive propagation. Yet, field studies are often unsuccessful. The reproductive behavior of the snail darter (*Percina tanasi*) has never been observed despite extensive observation in captive environments and in the field (Starnes, 1977; Hickman and Fitz, 1978).

Sublethal concentrations of certain pollutants are known to adversely affect behavior patterns of fish (Rand, 1985; Murty, 1986), and the changes have been linked to decreased fitness. After five weeks of exposure to water contaminated with sublethal concentrations of pentachlorophenol (PCP), largemouth bass (*Micropterus salmoides*) became hyperactive, and feeding attempts and the incidence of prey capture decreased (Brown et al., 1987). It was hypothesized that the increased energy expenditure coupled with decreased food intake could compromise the long-term survival of the fish. Woodward et al. (1991) demonstrated that alteration in feeding behavior was a sensitive indicator of sublethal aluminum toxicity in greenback cutthroat trout (*Onchorynchus clarki stomias*) reared under acid conditions.

The influence of temperature on the behavior of the Borax Lake chub (*Gila boraxobius*) has been examined under controlled conditions. This cyprinid is found only in Borax Lake, a small thermal spring-fed lake in southern Oregon (Williams, 1983a). Since the 1980s, outlets from the lake have been altered, diverting water for irrigation and lowering the water level in the lake. As the lake level has decreased, the fish have been forced closer to the hot thermal springs (40–50°C) that supply the lake (U.S. Fish and Wildlife Service, 1987a). Although the Borax Lake chub is eurythermic, Williams and Bond (1983) observed that it avoided water temperatures higher than 34°C, and noted that fish held in laboratory aquaria seemed to lose equilibrium at temperatures higher than 34.5°C (Williams, 1980). Williams and Williams (1980) observed seasonal fluctuations in food habits of the chub and noted that they were primarily bottom feeders, although at times they were observed feeding throughout the water column and at the surface. As the fish are crowded toward the hot springs by the decrease in lake volume, information about the effects of chronic exposure to increased water temperatures on their ability to forage and reproduce becomes very important to their conservation.

Functions of Behavioral Research in Captivity

Public Education

The display of captive animals in zoos and aquaria helps to educate the public about the diversity of species and their ecological requirements. Behavioral exhibits can facilitate appreciation for unfamiliar species. For example, cavefishes of the family Amblyopsidae are interesting because of unusual habitats and morphological adaptations to cave environments. Bechler (1983) examined the agonistic behavior of cavefishes, including the threatened Ozark cavefish (*Amblyopsis rosae*), and found species differences in six aggressive acts and two submissive acts. *Amblyopsis rosae*, a highly adapted cave species, exhibited only one of the aggressive behaviors which were observed in other species of cavefish. A comparative display of cavefish morphology and behavior can help educate people about the process of degenerative evolution.

The need exists to educate the public about less unusual but ecologically important animals. For instance, the survival of the Colorado squawfish (*Ptychocheilus lucius*), the largest minnow in North America which historically achieved an adult size of six feet and weights of eighty pounds (Miller, 1961), might never have been an issue if the public had an accurate understanding of this fish and its behavior. Despite its historical importance as a native food resource (Jordan, 1891; U.S. Fish and Wildlife Service, 1978), the squawfish was considered in the late 1950s and early 1960s to be a serious threat to game fish because of its piscivorous nature. In 1962 there was a joint federal and state effort to eradicate this fish with rotenone in the upper Colorado River system. Minckley and Deacon (1968) pointed out that the fish was difficult to observe and to exhibit; consequently, there was little interest in its preservation by sportsmen and the fishing industry. Today it is endangered and its future is in doubt; however, there is some interest in restoration of the species as a potential sport fishery in Colorado.

Audet et al. (1985) demonstrated that the Colorado squawfish migrates long distances (400 km) to spawn in some of the few remaining pristine areas. They further suggested that this homing behavior may be the result of very early imprinting. If this is true, introduced hatchery-reared fish may fail to migrate to spawning areas. Given this combination of historical, commercial, and behavioral information, the Colorado squawfish could be a model example for educating the public about the dramatic environmental changes that resulted from damming the Colorado River and introducing nonnative fish. Karp and Tyus (1990) examined the behavioral influence of six species of nonnative fish on juvenile Colorado squawfish and reported that feeding behavior, and consequently survival, of the young squawfish was negatively impacted by aggressive competition from introduced fish. They further suggested that high mortality of Colorado squawfish during the first year may be partially responsible for the apparent poor annual recruitment of the species.

Husbandry and Captive Propagation

Controlled propagation of endangered fish is a very important reason for maintaining captive populations. In general, this important function is widely overlooked by commercial oceanaria and zoos despite their active conservation efforts with endangered mammals, birds, and some reptiles (Maitland and Evans, 1986). The efforts undertaken at Dexter (New Mexico) National Fish Hatchery of the U.S. Fish and Wildlife Service in the conservation of endangered fishes make it the most noteworthy facility of this kind (Rinne et al., 1986).

Behavioral studies could greatly enhance captive propagation programs. The removal of endangered fishes from their native habitat for captive propagation must be preceded by knowledge of the tolerance of the species for stress. For example, one small captive population (20 adults) of Moapa dace transported to a federal facility for endangered fishes died of unknown causes within one month (U.S. Fish and Wildlife Service, 1983a), and captive-born fingerling Gila trout (*Oncorhynchus gilae*) died before they could be stocked (U.S. Fish and Wildlife Service, 1983b). Preliminary behavioral stress studies might have anticipated these consequences and suggested alternative procedures for transportation and maintenance in captivity. Ironically, the effect of environmental and nutritional factors on the behavior and general well-being of rare fish can be determined only by controlled studies of captive animals. Most field studies cannot define the limits of tolerance and the effect of suboptimal conditions on the animal's survival and reproduction. However, observations and experiments carried out in the field may provide the behavioral clues needed to identify the relevant variables.

Fish that are stressed may also display abnormal behavioral traits that compromise their ability to survive (Henderson, 1980). This is a critical concern when one is planning release of captive-bred fish or fry. Henderson (1980) reported that the failure of fry of silver carp (*Hypophthalmichthys molitrix*) to form schools after transport resulted in 100% mortality because of the lack of defense against predators.

Health and Well-being

Although species-specific behavior varies, behavior is probably the best indicator of the health and well-being of captive fishes (Francis-Floyd, 1988). Fish kept in ponds, tanks, or raceways are not readily available for observation. Under these conditions, one of the few reliable indicators of fish health is feeding activity. Consequently, daily observation of surface feeding behavior of channel catfish (*Ictalurus punctatus*) is important to managers of commercial fish farms because it is the only time when healthy fish are seen (Busch, 1985).

Behavioral indicators of health of captive aquarium fish were reviewed by Francis-Floyd (1988), who showed that behavioral observation is critically important for early detection of disease. Recognition of early warning signs of impending disease, such as decreased feeding or activity, may allow time for the diagnostic evaluation and implementation of appropriate treatment before significant mortality occurs.

For territorial species, such as the keyhole cichlid (*Cichlasoma nigrofasciatum*) proximity to conspecifics sometimes causes sufficient stress to submissive individuals to increase susceptibility to disease. Ardelt (1986), who experimentally infected keyhole cichlids with a sublethal concentration of *Aeromonas hydrophila* to examine the influence of behavioral stress on mortality, concluded that aggressive tendencies must be defused in territorial species to maintain their well-being. If insufficient space is available, one means of accomplishing this is to add enough conspecifics so that none are able to establish a territory (Francis-Floyd, 1988). Peters et al. (1988) also correlated social stress in rainbow trout (*Onchorhynchus mykiss*) with increased susceptibility to *A. hydrophila* infection.

Methods of Research in Captivity

A common method of determining the feeding habits of fish is the examination of stomach contents. In endangered fishes with a restricted distribution, this procedure may adversely affect the size of the remaining population. For example, the total population of the Devils Hole pupfish (*Cyprinodon diabolis*) in the 1980s fluctuated from a low of about 300 to a high of about 500. Minckley and Deacon (1975) examined stomach contents from 66 Devils Hole pupfish that had been collected over a period of three years prior to the species being listed as endangered. Although the removal of 66 fish over a three-year period when population levels were higher was not detrimental to the survival of the population, it would be difficult indeed to justify this activity under conditions of population depletion. Data collection involving noninvasive procedures, such as the extensive field observations that Williams and Williams (1980) made to better understand the forage habits of the Borax Lake chub, are sometimes preferable to techniques that require sacrifice of the animal. Light et al. (1983) described a gastric lavage procedure that enables the analysis of stomach contents without sacrificing the fish. The technique can be used repeatedly on the same fish without causing obvious harm.

The major constraint in the use of noninvasive techniques involves the difficulty of gaining access to fish in their natural environment. Although scuba gear has been used for observational studies of the Devils Hole pupfish (U.S. Fish and Wildlife Service, 1980a), the presence of divers may disrupt normal behavior and activity. One alternative is the use of underwater television cameras with remote monitors. Poor visibility, however, might be a constraint to this approach with small fishes in freshwater systems.

Laboratory observation may make it easier to find and identify individuals, but observations made in the laboratory may have little relation to fish behavior in the wild. The laboratory aquarium is an unnatural environment and considerable effort is required to try to re-create a "normal" habitat in such a setting. Successful attempts have been made to reproduce suitable habitats (see Table 7.1), including the adaptation of the desert pupfish to the home aquarium (Axelrod, 1976).

Comparative studies of nonendangered fishes may provide further insight into traits of closely related endangered species. An example is the Red River pupfish (*Cyprinodon rubrofluviatilis*) a nonendangered cyprinodont native to several river systems in

northern Texas and southwestern Oklahoma. It has been extensively studied in the field (Echelle, 1973) and under laboratory
conditions (Hill and Holland, 1971; Echelle et al., 1972, 1973). The
Cyprinodontidae are noted for hardiness and tolerance of a wide
range of temperatures and salinities that are needed for survival
under harsh desert conditions. Observations on reproductive and
feeding behavior of free-ranging Red River pupfish and experimental evaluation of the effects of temperature and salinity variation
on laboratory-reared fish of this species have provided information
that has enhanced understanding of the reproductive processes of
closely related endangered fishes. For example, diel spawning was
observed in the Leon Springs pupfish (*C. bovinus*); spawning peaked
at 29°C and decreased to nil at 37°C (Kennedy, 1977). This is
similar to the diel spawning observed by Echelle (1973) in free-
ranging Red River pupfish. At high temperatures, the fish spawned
in the morning, whereas at lower temperatures they spawned in
the afternoon. Echelle (1973) reported that at high temperatures
(>32°C) spawning activity decreased and the fish moved to deeper
water.

Crear and Haydock (1971) suggested the use of the endangered desert pupfish (*C. maculatus*) as a laboratory model. Among
the advantages enumerated were that this euryhaline species was
suitable for comparative studies involving marine and freshwater
systems. Hill and Holland (1971) discuss the survival value of this
trait.

Problems with Studies of Behavior in Captivity

A frequently encountered problem in the field is the identification
of subjects. The small size (length < 10 cm) of many of these fishes
and the presence of closely related species can make the selection
of subjects for captive studies extremely difficult. The habitats of
endangered and threatened fishes are also difficult to simulate.
These range from small springs with a relatively constant environment to large rivers with widely variable chemical and physical
characteristics. Because environmental factors such as temperature, light, flow, and dissolved oxygen may function as behavioral
cues, every effort should be made to duplicate or compensate for
the obvious habitat requirements of the species involved.

The quality and quantity of available habitat in captive settings sometimes significantly influences behavior. Pupfishes of the

genus *Cyprinodon* have four types of breeding systems, each of which is associated with a certain kind of environment. Kodric-Brown (1981), in experiments with the endangered Ash Meadows pupfish (*Cyprinodon nevadensis mionectes*), found that a few fish from a population, which normally exhibits a territorial breeding system, established a dominance hierarchy breeding system when held in a confined environment, such as an aquarium. Shifts in breeding behavior observed in the field and in captive populations of other pupfishes indicated that these breeding systems are not genetically fixed but represent a facultative response to changing environmental conditions (Kodric-Brown, 1981).

Behavioral, morphological, and physiological characteristics, however, are influenced by heredity, and the prolonged inbreeding of small captive populations (e.g., hatchery stocks) usually results in the loss of genetic diversity or reduced heterozygosity (National Council on Gene Resources, 1982). In comparing wild and domesticated hatchery stocks of brook trout (*Salvelinus fontinalis*), Vincent (1960) noted behavioral variation that could affect fitness. Wild fish, when placed in a tall aquarium, remained near the bottom, whereas hatchery fish were spread through the water column. In an aquarium with rocks, wild brook trout sought concealment in the rocks whereas the hatchery fish remained in the open water, fully exposed (Vincent, 1960).

Behavior of captive populations of closely related species may also change if they hybridize. The endangered Clear Creek gambusia (*Gambusia heterochir*) has been successfully maintained in captivity only in the absence of mosquitofish (*G. affinis*) (U.S. Fish and Wildlife Service, 1980b). When the two species occur together, they hybridize and produce fertile offspring (Yardley and Hubbs, 1976). In this example, hybridization results in further decreases in the annual recruitment of *G. heterochir* and the resulting hybrids provide additional competition for the remaining wild-type fish. Hubbs (1971) reported that female *G. heterochir* were more selective in choosing their mates than males of the same species; thus the females used their reproductive resources to ensure the production of pure *G. heterochir* offspring.

Maitland and Evans (1986) summarized problems associated with captive maintenance of endangered fishes. The first constraint involves difficulties in maintaining isolated, phylogenetically similar stocks in a relatively small area. An example is reflected in the extinction of the Amistad gambusia (*G. amistadensis*) after contamination of the captive population with the morphologically similar mosquitofish (Hubbs and Jensen, 1984). Secondly, Maitland and Evans (1986) emphasize the importance of preventing the inadvertent escape of captive exotic fish from holding facilities because this sometimes results in the introduction of new diseases that may decimate populations of native fish. The introduced species may have a negative effect on the natural ecosystem, thereby placing the local fauna at a disadvantage.

Conclusions

Almost half of all vertebrate species are fishes, but proportionally less is known about their behavior than that of other classes of vertebrate animals. An explanation for the dearth of behavioral research on fishes is the difficulty of dealing with the aquatic environment, under natural or captive conditions, when compared to the terrestrial environment. We believe it unlikely that the lack of attention devoted to this group of vertebrates is in any way related to their behavior. Fishes that have been the subjects of behavioral studies have revealed an array of behaviors that vary widely in complexity. Behavioral studies of captive endangered and threatened fishes are becoming more important as fish conservation biologists begin to initiate recovery actions. Most work with captive endangered fishes has centered on captive propagation for reintroduction. Behavioral studies of habitat preference, migrating, schooling, feeding, and interspecific interactions of larval and juvenile stages could provide valuable information and guidance for reintroduction. Behavioral research involving the larval and juvenile stages of endangered fishes resulting from captive propagation efforts is easily justified because it does not adversely affect the wild population of these species.

Although 49 species have been held in captivity for various purposes, only 12 have been used in behavioral studies. Most of these studies have involved darters of the family Percidae and pupfishes of the family Cyprinodontidae. The cyprinodontids—both endangered and nonendangered species—have been involved in more captive studies (behavioral, physiological, etc.) than any other family of North American freshwater fishes. This is most likely due to the combination of their interesting behaviors, their ability to inhabit harsh environments, and their adaptability to captive situations. Although pupfishes tolerate extreme environmental conditions in their native habitats, several species remain threatened with extinction, due partly to the presence of alien species that have been introduced into their habitat. Captive studies of interspecific behavioral interactions between endangered pupfishes and alien fishes could provide valuable data for designing refugia and restoring existing habitat. As more alien fishes become established in open waters of the United States, this threat to native fishes will undoubtedly increase.

8

Design of Captive Environments for Endangered Fishes

Michael K. Stoskopf

Early efforts in the management of fish in captivity were closely linked to natural water, using dams, pens, and cages submerged in rivers, ponds, and estuaries. This type of management was suitable for the exploitation of aquatic species as food sources and remains the basis for the majority of techniques employed today (Colt, 1986). Curiosity about the diverse creatures that occupy the underwater world was a driving force in the development of early aquariums. The removal of fish from their natural habitat allowed the intimate observation required for scientific study and the appreciation of their aesthetic beauty.

The requirements of any fish in captivity are sufficiently rigorous to necessitate investigation into the nature of the fish's interaction with its environment. The precarious relationship of the fish to a visible medium with many "invisible" components must take credit for the relatively advanced state of captive environmental design found in aquaria today (Chang, 1986). Nevertheless, there remains considerably more to learn. The advent of new materials and technologies has provided solutions to many perplexing problems in aquarium design. This chapter concentrates on general principles which are relatively universally applicable to the wide range of fish species considered endangered.

The Economics of Captive Design

The most commonly used systems in aquaculture involve diversion or encapsulation of a part of the natural environment (Colt, 1986).

The major advantages of these systems are their relatively low construction and maintenance costs, while their dependence upon natural conditions and the difficulty of observing the fish are disadvantages. These systems are at the mercy of the same environmental conditions which may be contributing to the decline of the species in the wild. On the other hand, when abiotic environmental factors are not the limiting factors in a species' recovery, this technique can succeed even when relatively little is known about the requirements of the species.

A step removed from the environmental vulnerability of the completely open system is the modified open system design, where water is processed through filters before circulation through manmade enclosures protected from the external environment. These systems have many advantages over pure open systems but are considerably more expensive to construct and still require specific geographic location.

As the filtration and disinfection systems in these facilities become more complex and complete, they begin to approach the expense of closed systems, which constantly recirculate conditioned water (Hawkins and Anthony, 1981). System selection will depend upon the geographic availability and suitability of water sources and the amount of capital dedicated to the project. Further, the services of an engineer with a background in hydrodynamics and a biologist with experience in system construction will help prevent costly mistakes in materials selection and configuration choice.

Perhaps the most significant factor in the economics of design for holding fish in captivity is gravity. Water is heavy. It requires expensive containment barriers and considerable expenditure of energy to be moved uphill. A small 100 gallon tank of freshwater will weigh about 800 pounds exclusive of the weight of the tank. As tanks grow larger, the weight of the system expands as a cubic function, while the strength of materials increases as a square function. Consequently, tanks must have the tensile strength to withstand forces applied to the underlying support structure as well as forces exerted laterally. In larger systems, more massive materials become necessary to support the weight of the system, and these in turn add more weight and expense.

Materials Selection

Materials should be able to contain the water and remain impervious to it. They should provide sufficient strength to retain the water, and they should furnish the aesthetic and/or observational requirements of the system. Finally, the materials should be inert and not contribute toxic substances to the system.

Glass and Plastics. Glass and plastics are commonly used to achieve lateral viewing in tanks. Smaller tanks are often constructed entirely of clear materials, while larger tanks usually combine clear materials with structurally more suitable or inexpensive materials. Glass thickness and the selection of special plate or strengthened glass is based on the weight of water to be supported. Tanks up to 100 liters can be constructed from 4 mm thick glass, but 6 mm glass is preferable, particularly on the long span. For rectangular tanks over 100 liters, 6 mm glass is a necessity. Tanks over 250 liter capacity require 10 mm glass. Large aquaria in the 1000 liter class generally require glass at least 20 mm thick (Ford, 1981).

Glass has advantages over plastic as a viewing window for smaller systems. It is generally harder and less easily scratched during maintenance than acrylic plastics (although plastic coated safety plate is also readily scratched). Plastics generally require solvent sealing and are not readily sealed with silicone sealants, making construction more difficult. On the negative side, glass is more breakable than most plastics.

Plastics cover a wide range of materials with quite diverse properties (Stoskopf, 1992). Clear plastics used in viewing ports are usually highly specialized acrylics. They are expensive, relatively soft, and susceptible to scratching. Most can be polished to optical clarity by grinding, so it is advisable to select materials nearly 50% over the thickness required for strength. Acrylics have the advantage over glass in that they can be molded in panes to fill much larger spans (Hawkins and Lloyd, 1981). They are not subject to shattering with the same forces that affect glass, but can be broken. Acrylics are subject to melting from the heat of photographic lights and can catch fire (Stoskopf, 1992). Little is known about their interaction with chemicals and drugs used in the treatment of fish (Stoskopf, 1992).

Plastics are also used as structural components of tanks that are not intended for viewing. New or unknown materials should be tested for toxicity with a bioassay, and low-cost recycled plastics should be avoided because of their contribution to toxicity (Stoskopf, 1992). Additives mixed with polymers include antioxidants, colorants, catalysts, plasticizers for flexibility, flame-retardants, fillers, and stabilizers in the form of lead salts, phenols, aromatic amines, aromatic hydrocarbons, and isocyanates (Hawkins and

Lloyd, 1981). Do not rely on the theory that these compounds are supported by the polymer and cannot leach out. Materials graded as acceptable for foodstuffs are generally acceptable for aquarium systems.

Fiberglass has the highest tension loading capacity of the plastics, a factor important in the construction of circular tanks (Wheaton, 1977a). It is relatively inexpensive and probably the most commonly used structural plastic in aquarium construction (Hawkins and Lloyd, 1981). New tanks incorporating fiberglass should be treated to eliminate plasticizer and trapped metals in the resin (Carmignani and Bennett, 1976). Alternately run the system with and discard freshwater of pH 3.0 or lower, pH 11 or higher, and pH 3.0. Leech marine tanks with saltwater for an additional day (Stoskopf, 1992). A bioassay is still advisable before using such a system for endangered fish.

Vinyl is a flexible plastic which often finds its way into inexpensive makeshift holding facilities. It is easily damaged, and residuals of toxic plasticizer, diocytlphthalate, and heavy metals trapped in the polymerization process make vinyl a poor choice in any system to house endangered fish. In contrast, high density linear polyethylene and polypropylene tanks are relatively inert and can be stripped free of heavy metal and plasticizer contaminants with the same protocol described for fiberglass. They are expensive and opaque, but quite suited to use in fish systems.

Polyvinylchloride (PVC) is generally not used in tank construction, but in the plumbing systems that operate tanks. PVC is basically inert to saltwater, but comes in a variety of schedules with different properties. High impact or unplasticized (uPVC) is most commonly used for plumbing applications, but can contain trace amounts of metals, particularly lead that can be leached in acid water (Hawkins and Lloyd, 1981). Acrylonitrile butadiene styrene (ABS) pipes are less likely to cause subtle toxicity problems and are recommended in construction of systems for rare species. Finally, when choosing a sealant, it is important not to use low grade silicone caulks that contain heavy metals, cyanide, and organic toxins.

Concrete. Concrete is widely used for larger systems because of its durability, low cost, and formability. Concrete has a strong resistance to compression, but lacks tensile strength. Reinforcing steel increases shear resistance and tensile strength of concrete.

Concrete is highly alkaline and contains small amounts of foreign materials, including chromates that can leach out slowly over a long period. In sea water, the alkalinization effect of concrete is buffered by the carbonate system. Nevertheless, concrete structures should be thoroughly leached with dilute muriatic acid and coated with several coats of sodium silicate or other sealant before being used for fish (Stoskopf, 1992).

Concrete can be made more durable in sea water by the exclusion of tricalcium aluminate, substituting tetracalcium alumino-ferrite to inhibit sulfate attack (Wheaton, 1977a). When concrete does fail in an aquarium, it is usually due to the failure of the reinforcing steel being oxidized by sea water. A layer of 50–75 mm of compacted concrete must separate reinforcing metal from the exposure surface to ensure protection of this structural material (Hawkins and Lloyd, 1981).

Wood. Wood has historically been used in the construction of many medium-sized systems. Select well-dried, seasoned heart wood, preferably of teak or aformosia, which are most resistant to decay (Hawkins and Lloyd, 1981). Mahogany, oak, and western red cedar are also useful (Hawkins and Lloyd, 1981). Plywoods must be marine ply. Many wood preservatives are toxic (Radeleff, 1970; Murphy, 1980).

Metal. Metals exposed to water corrode, and corroded metals lose structural integrity and strength and generally are toxic to fish. Stainless steel is considered the most resistant metal to seawater corrosion, but it will corrode. The most available stainless steel is AISI type 316, which is a high molybdenum alloy resistant to pitting and crevice corrosion. Type 316 steel is not a high strength steel, nor is it completely immune to corrosion (Hawkins and Lloyd, 1981). Where strength and maximal corrosion resistance are needed, titanium is generally preferred.

Other common metals include galvanized fittings and brass or copper. Unfortunately, the galvanized coat placed on iron contains considerable zinc. Zinc is quite toxic to fish (Lewis, 1978). Lethal concentrations of zinc can dissolve from galvanized fittings within short periods, even when calcium protection is in effect in seawater (Stoskopf, 1992). Bronze and copper fittings can also be a source of zinc. In marine aquaria, however, death due to metal toxicity is rarely the major problem in fish. Sublethal concentrations of metals can affect the behavior and physiology of the fish. Copper suppresses the immune system of fish, making them more susceptible to infection (Benoit and Holcombe, 1978; Hodson et al., 1979). Zinc can have a severe impact on reproduction (Hodson et al., 1979). As a general rule, metals should be avoided in systems designed for endangered species.

Protective coating of metals should be applied with caution. Very severe corrosion can occur underneath cracked, chipped, or peeled coatings when only a very small area of metal is exposed. Most protective coatings incorporate oxidation inhibitors, but most of these (lead chromate, zinc chromate) are toxic to fish. Breakdown in coatings can have more consequences than just structural damage to the tank.

Filtration and Water Handling

Once water is contained, it must be circulated for filtration and aeration, as well as for development of currents needed by some species. Here, without careful design, gravity can become a drain on operating capital. Use gravity as much as possible. Limit the number of pumps needed to complete the cycle. In designing the plumbing system, make sure it is possible to completely drain the enclosure. The enclosure should not drain if a pump fails or power is interrupted and water circulation stops.

Power is commonly a major limiting factor in completed facilities. Heaters, chillers, additional lights, and additional pumps rapidly overload conservative reserve power provisions. A rule of thumb is to provide twice the power which would ordinarily be designed for a facility, including reserve power.

Once the basics of flow are established, it is necessary to filter the water in any closed or partially closed system. Mechanical filtration, sometimes referred to as primary filtration, removes suspended particles from water by passing it through a fine mesh medium that obstructs the particles (Stoskopf, 1992). The mesh of the medium used depends on the size of the particulates to be removed and the amount of resistance which can be placed on the pump (Stoskopf, 1992). When the physical limits of flow are reached in a pumping system, reduced through-put results in longer turnover times and reduced impact of the filter. Designing a proper mechanical filter involves compromises between the size of particles cleared (degree of polishing) and the need to achieve reasonable turnover and keep backwash labor at reasonable limits. This is usually achieved by creating a more complex mechanical filtration system, using different mesh sized media in series (Stoskopf, 1992).

Biological filtration in aquarium systems generally refers to the biological fixation of nitrogenous wastes into less toxic compounds by bacteria. Other forms of biological filtration include the concentration of metals and certain toxic organics in algal scrubbers (Stoskopf, 1992). In bacterial filters, heterotrophic bacterial colonies process the nitrogenous wastes of the fish into soluble wastes, which are in turn converted by autotrophic bacteria to less toxic compounds. The usual limiting factors are the provision of surface area on which the bacteria grow, and the circulation of the waste-laden water into contact with the bacteria. Augmenting systems include plastic-fluted spheres and cylinders that maximize surface area while minimizing flow impedance. The potential and limitations of algal scrubbers remain to be completely defined because factors such as harvesting rate and cellular disturbance affect their efficacy. They concentrate heavy metals, but the effects on metal levels in the water can be frequently surprising, because improperly harvested algal scrubbers can become a point source for metals through "leaking."

Chemical filtration covers a wide range of methodology for removing molecular contaminants of water. These include ion exchange, both specific (resins) and nonspecific (activated carbon), and oxidative systems (ozone) (Stoskopf, 1992). Foam fractionation and ultraviolet filtration can also be considered chemical, because they rely on basic modifications of chemical structure.

The most commonly applied form of chemical filtration is ion exchange filtration with activated carbon. A finite number of binding sites are available on the carbon, based primarily on the surface area of the carbon particles. These bind cations and anions with differing binding strengths, and these ions undergo constant exchange with ions in the water. Ions with strong binding are effectively removed from the system until all binding sites are saturated. Then competitive binding reaches a point where all toxic ions cannot be bound simultaneously, and some must be released by mass action (Spotte, 1979, 1992). The system also fails when very strongly binding ions are introduced into the system, which displaces more weakly bound toxic compounds (Beleau, 1988). In either of these cases, the filter designed to remove toxic compounds becomes a source of the toxin (Stoskopf, 1992). This can be corrected by removing the saturated carbon and replacing it with unsaturated medium.

Although water handling is usually given extensive consideration in design of fish facilities, it is equally important to consider air handling. This includes the air that will be the source of surface exchange and the air that will be pumped in airlifts and through aeration devices. This latter air is particularly important because enforced exchange under relatively optimal circumstances will be involved. This will dramatically increase the exchange of any toxic contaminant in the air. In facilities designed for endangered species, the pumped air should be filtered through carbon filters. Careful attention should also be paid to the location and protection of the intake source. Also, it is important to prevent aerosolized contamination of adjacent enclosures with bacteria, viruses, and fungi when active aeration is used.

Ergonomics

There can be no doubt that animals are better cared for with lower costs if their handlers can easily accomplish their tasks. In fish facilities, accessibility is the key. Adequate head space over all tanks is important to allow the unimpeded use of nets and traps. Head room should ideally exceed the depth of the tank. In deep installations where this is unrealistic, the geometry of reaching the bottom with a handheld net should be considered in the design. Valves and adjustment fittings should be easily reached without having to stand on ladders or stools. Lighting and overhead ornaments should be designed so that they can routinely be slid out of the way to permit complete access to the tank. This will facilitate changing of bulbs and avoid risk of electrocution, a hazard that should be given top priority in design.

Visibility is not just for display. If caretakers are unable to observe the fish easily, they will not be able to detect important signs of impending disease, subtle indicators of system degeneration, or monitor the effectiveness of their feeding and cleaning procedures. Superb visibility should be provided.

A facility housing endangered fish should be secured, and may require night guards and surveillance alarms. Loss of fish to thieves can rapidly destroy a fish breeding program. Perhaps even more dangerous is the potential for malicious mischief. Security measures aimed at preventing loss of equipment or fish should also be effective against unwanted additions to the system (coins, poisons, other animals etc.).

An important aspect of security is the ability to identify fish. For most species, this requires the placement of a microscopic tag that can only be read by handling the fish (Parker et al., 1990). In endangered fish, only tags that can be read noninvasively should be used. These include tags read by radiographing the fish and the newer passive computer chips, which can be implanted under the skin and transmit an identification code when activated with a radio frequency (Williams, 1988). These chips have no battery and are about the size of a thick pencil lead.

Species Considerations In Captive Design

The construction of a suitably sized, accessible container on a solid foundation with a safe and energy efficient water circulation and filtration system is only the beginning of providing endangered fish with their captive requirements. Three physical factors are critical: temperature, photorequirements, and substrate. Two major biological considerations also merit discussion: nutrients and social interaction.

Abiotic Factors

Temperature. Many fish have remarkable ranges of thermal tolerance but these appear to narrow in captivity, probably due to demands placed on their physiology by suboptimal habitat (Stickney and Kohler, 1990). In captive systems, fish usually do not have the option to move into pockets of different temperature, a situation available in the thermoclines of most natural waters. The use of thermal gradients, an accepted principle in reptile and amphibian management (Regal, 1980), has not received much attention with fish primarily due to the difficulties imposed by the need to keep water thoroughly mixing, even at minimal flow. The use of in-tank heaters does generate a gradient of sorts, but little attention has been paid to the fishes' utilization of this gradient. The common cost-saving design feature of regulating water temperature by ambient air temperature effectively eliminates gradients.

The possibility of shifting thermal requirements during annual or diurnal cycles has also received very little attention. The dogma that water temperatures in the wild, particularly in large bodies of water (oceans), remain seasonally static has no basis in fact for shore and reef fishes. Even pelagic fish may be migrating between thermoclines in a systematic manner due to needs of their metabolism. The systematic management of an endangered fish in captivity should examine the impact annual or diurnal thermal cycles might have on reproduction.

Redundancy is an important consideration in temperature management for endangered species. It is preferable to use several smaller heating units to achieve the required thermal capacity for a system than to use a single large heater (Thiel, 1989). If one of several small heaters fails, the results are much less catastrophic than if the only heater fails.

It is much more expensive to cool a tank from ambient temperature than it is to heat it. This is true both in equipment cost and in power consumption. Also, many fish tolerate extremes in their low thermal range better than extremes in their high range, making heating a steady-state cool system preferable to refrigerating a warm system. First, it is safer. The failure of the thermal engine in a heated system will allow considerably more reaction time before fish are irretrievably damaged than if a chilling system fails. In either case, emergency detection of thermal problems through sensors and alarms is a basic requirement of any system housing endangered fish.

Photorequirements. Two components of light must be considered in the design of animal facilities, intensity and photoperiodicity. The effect of photoperiodicity on reproduction has been a major concern in fish husbandry (Crim, 1982; Peter, 1982). This effect is not merely an alteration in general activity levels or spatial utilization, but actually an effect at the level of hormone production in several organs. Light cycles are at least partially responsible for hormonal electrolyte regulation (Zaugg, 1981). Photointensity requirements in fish are less well studied. Certain deepwater fish appear to perform much better in extremely low photointensity and avoid bright lights. This is also true of many nocturnal species. Other species thrive under bright lights, particularly if proper spectral patterns are provided.

A third category of photorequirement is phototransitional quality, a combination of photoperiodicity and photointensity gradients. This effect is well documented in the behavior of many freshwater and marine coral reef fish species (Helfman, 1979, 1981). It is particularly important to crepuscular feeders where certain behaviors (e.g., feeding, social spacing, parasite cleaning, and comfort) are linked to specific intensities of light that occur in the natural transition from light at dawn or dusk (Hobson, 1965; Stevenson, 1972). Instantaneous change from nocturnal to diurnal lighting has more impact on the biological and physiological well-being of captive fish than the simple startle response observed at transition. It can eliminate or adversely modify important behaviors.

Substrate. The substrate requirements of fish exist in three dimensions. Adequate surface area must be provided for gaseous exchange, or this must be handled through aeration towers. Beyond this basic requirement, the configuration of the space must provide for the behavioral requirements of the intended occupants.

Biotic Factors

Nutrition. With all physical factors considered, it remains important to consider certain biological factors. Food must be nutritious, palatable, and accessible. Powerful skimmers can compete with surface feeders if operated during feeding. Similarly, bottom feeding fish may have difficulty receiving food if housed with aggressive surface feeders. In any animal husbandry situation, overfeeding can be deleterious. This is accentuated in fish systems because of the impact of uneaten food and waste products from excessive ingested food on environmental quality. Excessive feeding or failure to remove uneaten food can trigger biochemical changes in water which can result in the death of fish within 24 hours.

Social. Intraspecific and interspecific social requirements in fish are highly varied and should be considered in the design and management of captive facilities. Schooling fish housed individually may suffer the same behavioral and physiological disadvantages that are documented for social mammals. In such situations, their energetic demands may increase due to inability to draft behind other fish in rotation (Smith, 1982). In addition, predator/prey relationships are not always completely deleterious and on occasion may be beneficial. In one case, a variety of compatible species introduced into a large oval system failed to settle into artificial reefs. The fish swam doggedly in circles, generally refusing to feed and sleep over a period of weeks. Losses to disease and general exhaustion made dramatic measures appropriate. A larger predatory fish was placed in one end of the oval. Exhausted prey fish immediately took cover and began to settle into their system, avoiding the predator's territory. They also began to eat and sleep normally. Multistationed feeding has made this arrangement a long-term success for more than 7 years.

Captive Design and Health

Every aspect of captive design has an impact on health. Most facilities require some form of tank cover to prevent fish from jumping out and becoming stranded on dry land. Even species that do not commonly jump benefit from covers. In outdoor situations, predation may be significantly thwarted by proper tops. Indoors or out, covers can minimize cross-contamination of enclosures through aerosol transmission of bacteria, viruses, and fungi.

Filtration design must be carefully designed to avoid inflicting trauma on the proposed inhabitants. Skimmers and intake pipes should be covered and screened so fish are not accidentally pulled into them. This would spell the end of the individual fish, and the resultant blockage of the water-handling system may endanger every fish in the enclosure. There must be proper flow and water exchange with all portions of the tank, minimizing the possibility of formation of dead pockets where anaerobic bacteria flourish. Anaerobic production of toxins, or even simple sulfates and CO_2, can cause devastating losses. Excess aeration, particularly in cold water, can result in fish losses due to embolism and oxygen toxicity.

An often overlooked aspect of design and fish health is the effect of noise. Anecdotal accounts of failure to thrive in noisy environments abound, and major improvements in fish behavior have been observed when noisy tank situations are corrected. More study in this area is needed.

Hospitalization of fish is fraught with many of the same problems that plague veterinarians dealing with terrestrial animals. Social isolation can be a boon or hazard, depending on the natural history and condition of the patient. Some fish do much better in schools and find themselves very vulnerable when isolated. The social interactions of a crowded enclosure can be the underlying cause of immunosuppression and observable disease (Schreck, 1981). It is critical to provide appropriate furniture to fish held in hospital tanks. Hospital facilities should be designed to comfortably accommodate any species being held in the main facility. The hospital tanks should be adjustable for all environmental factors including temperature, salinity, photoperiod, and photointensity. They should be capable of providing complete isolation from the main enclosures and should be easily disassembled and subjected to disinfection.

Captive Design and Conservation

Although relatively untapped for all but a few sport fish, the potential for captive propagation and wild release of fish into recovered habitats probably exceeds that of any other vertebrate group. Tremendous numbers of animals can be grown from egg or small live-born young to a size suitable for wild release in relatively little space when compared with the requirements of mammals and most birds. The requirements for preparing the animals for survival in the wild are generally not complex, and mating rituals are frequently easily manipulated for genetic management. On the downside is the relative expense of constructing and operating water systems.

The utilization of waste energy is a significant design goal in locating and constructing rearing facilities. Water temperature stabilization has been accomplished both directly and indirectly by using warm waters heated by waste energy from public utilities (Liewes, 1984). On a smaller scale, waste heat from air-conditioning systems and heat pumps can be used to accomplish the same goal. Counter-current heat exchangers with thermoregulated gating can be placed in line in system circulation to provide regulated water temperatures for fish requiring warmer or colder water. Growth rates for fish tolerant of cooler water are frequently accelerated with minimal increases in water temperature, reducing holding time and increasing feed utilization efficiency (Wheaton, 1977b; Fast, 1986; Torrans, 1986).

The successful rearing of a single fish species may require the sequential provision of a dozen different food sources in high volume over a short but critical time period (Girin, 1979; Moe, 1992). In many cases, these foods are the natural foods of the fish (Laxter, 1981). The advantage of this situation is the ease of acclimation of the fish to wild food sources. The major design problem is the provision of culture facilities for the food items. This aspect of production can become one of the most labor intensive aspects of rearing endangered fish in captivity.

Multiple primary enclosures are required in any active rearing facility. Generally, round tanks are more suitable for pelagic and free-swimming reef species (Wheaton, 1977a). Square tanks are appropriate for species that are more sessile and tend to hide among substrates. Multiple enclosures may be designed within larger enclosures to minimize plumbing and environmental control costs. This approach can be extremely efficient if carefully managed. It allows for the effective regulation of a single large system rather than multiple small systems, which are by their nature more volatile. The disadvantage is that any failure in the system, including an outbreak of infectious disease, will affect all fish.

The compromise between the expense of redundancy and the labor of evaluating multiple independent systems must by weighted against the risk of catastrophic losses due to disease or system failure.

It is important that the flow design of the primary enclosures be appropriate to both the species of fish being reared and to the stage of the fish being held. Egg masses of some reef and surf species may require extensive flow to keep them properly oxygenated and blown free of debris (Frakes and Hoff, 1983). Newly hatched young, on the other hand, generally do not have the mobility or strength to fight strong currents for prolonged periods. Flow design has been a significant factor in the successful efforts to rear marine clownfish (Frakes and Hoff, 1983). Further, as fish grow, the biomass capacity of an enclosure generally remains stable, while the number of fish that biomass represents decreases dramatically. Unless culling is required for genetic reasons, a geometrically expanding space requirement imposes itself on a successful breeding program long before fish reach an appropriate size for release.

The introduction of fish back into secured habitat has been considered a relatively uncomplicated process. Unfortunately, survival yield is not anywhere near 100% for any species. Timing of release and the characteristics of the water where the fish are released are important factors. Food transition apparently presents little problem in game fish, and efforts to release other species into the wild have not examined the impact of this aspect. More attention has been paid to water acclimation. A design that allows acclimation to the water of destination prior to release reduces loss due to maladaptation to temperature, pH, or trace mineral differences between rearing and destination waters. Such a system also offers the advantage of implementing active immunization of the fish, allowing them to encounter new pathogens without the stress of transport and delivery into a new environment. Once exposed, if fish break with disease, it is possible to observe the problem and implement medical treatment. Fish recovering from such an outbreak would be expected to have markedly greater survival upon release.

The Future of Captive Design for Fish

Coastal land with accessible water suitable for fish husbandry is both costly and rare, whether freshwater or marine. This factor alone will provide adequate pressure to ensure the continued development of closed systems capable of maintaining and propagating fish away from their native waters. With this trend, managers of captive fish will face two major problems: (1) the lack of knowledge of the specific requirements of individual species, and (2) the inability to economically achieve appropriate facility scale and complexity for captive reproductive efforts and multigeneration programs.

There are more than 17,000 species of teleost fishes alive today (Keeton, 1967). The diversity of this large group of animals is orders of magnitude beyond that which regularly perplexes the managers of mammals, birds, or reptiles. Very few species have been studied in significant detail. New species are regularly discovered, and more frequently, species are brought into captivity for the first time.

The successes we currently enjoy are often based on intuitive extrapolation, rather than knowledge. Managers of captive fish are nearly always limited to providing a "suitable" habitat, rather than an optimal one because of technical limitations. For this reason, more is known about the tolerable range of limits for important environmental factors than is known about optimal values. This lack of knowledge will be very much felt when new design projects meet their fiscal referees. Costly implementation of individual systems with fine control of even basic parameters such as temperature cannot be justified without hard data. Cost accounting will dictate minimal flexibility and force averaging of the requirements of multiple species in a single facility. In order for captive endangered fish management to improve, there must be more research into the optimum environmental requirements of fish.

Increased knowledge of basic requirements of specific fish will see the construction of larger facilities dedicated to select species with significant allocation of resources to secondary holding. The tremendous expense of achieving the primary objective in a coastal aquatic facility usually exhausts available capital before proper facilities for quarantine, isolation, or holding and rearing of fry can be implemented. The very factors that give the captive breeding of endangered fish the best chance for making a significant impact on wild populations contribute to this problem (e.g., large number of young per mating and normally high losses to predations, including cannibalism). Reproduction programs require multiple systems of varying dimension to provide the requirements of developing fry, and space and suitable systems for the culture of live foods.

Similarly, hospital design in fisheries facilities must be integrated into the initial stages of facility planning. The impact of disease on longevity and productivity will become more apparent as access to wild fish stocks becomes more limited. Holding endangered species in captivity carries the moral obligation to provide optimal programs of preventive and clinical medicine. Quarantine and hospital facilities capable of long-term holding of target species will become standard design components of successful aquatic programs in the twenty-first century.

III

Reptiles and Amphibians

Introduction of Authors
and Chapter Previews

The conservation chapter for reptiles and amphibians is authored by Peter Pritchard, Vice President for Florida and International Conservation of the Florida Audubon Society. As an officer of an environmental organization, his mandate is not only to document the natural world but also to undertake activities calculated to conserve and improve it. This has resulted in his current mix of activities including field research on sea turtles, preparation of turtle management plans for various entities, including foreign governments, and, in recent years, making films and videotapes that illustrate the diversity of turtle life, interactions between turtles and man, and the steps that are necessary for proper conservation of turtle populations.

Dr. Pritchard proposes to exhaust all other means of species conservation before relying on captive reproduction. However, he recognizes that the withdrawal of even minimal breeding stock from the wild may place a severely endangered species at risk. He concludes that methodologies of captive propagation should be perfected before a species becomes excessively rare, thus captive breeding should be the norm, or at least the goal, for all species maintained in captivity.

Paul Licht, professor of Integrative Biology and Group in Endocrinology, has written the reproductive physiology chapter with a distinctively endocrinological bent. His current research takes an evolutionary approach to understanding the role of the pituitary gland in the regulation of reproduction and growth. Although much of his effort has been focused on reptiles and amphibians as pivotal groups in tetrapod evolution, he uses a comparative approach which leads to studies in all major vertebrate groups from fish to mammals, including birds. Dr. Licht studies animals in natural environments when possible as he is especially interested in understanding how the environment affects hormonal systems and how such systems help animals cope with environmental stresses and change. He feels that studies involving the role of stress on endocrine responses may explain problems in captive populations.

In his chapter, Dr. Licht describes the endocrinological basis of reproductive processes in reptiles and amphibians with comparisons to birds and mammals. He includes results of studies using heterologous hormone therapy to stimulate these processes in captive herptiles, cautioning that the use of mammalian hormones may stimulate antibody production in long-lived specimens.

The behavior of reptiles and amphibians is discussed by Gordon Burghardt and Mark Milostan. Dr. Burghardt, professor in the Department of Psychology at the University of Tennessee, is also a professor of Zoology and former director of the Graduate Program in Ethology. His research interests include chemical food cue preferences and foraging in snakes, social behavior in hatchling green iguanas, defensive behavior in snakes, conservation and ethical aspects of animal use, and the function and evolution of playfulness. Milostan, assistant professor in the Department of Health Education and Health Science at Central Michigan University, is interested in the behavioral and evolutionary ecology of amphibians and reptiles and neuroendocrine influences on behavior. His current areas of research include the comparative ontogeny of prey capture and immobilization in snakes and the proximate factors affecting defensive behavior in reptiles.

These authors remind the reader that the very little behavioral and psychological information is available for reptiles and amphibians. They point out the need for empirical studies (in zoos and in natural habitats) to replace traditional, anthropomorphic interpretations of herptile needs that may hinder conservation efforts of captive species.

Exhibit design for reptiles and amphibians is coauthored by Janice Perry-Richardson and Craig Ivanyi. Former assistant curator at Audubon Zoo, Ms. Perry-Richardson is now affiliated with the Arizona-Sonora Desert Museum (ASDM). She received a M.S. in Interdisciplinary studies from the University of Texas at Tyler.

Perry-Richardon's current research projects concern the reproductive behavior of beaded lizards and the dietary requirements and reproductive behavior of chuckwallas. She is participating in a mark/ recapture study involving free-ranging rattlesnakes on the museum grounds. Mr. Ivanyi is assistant curator of Herpetology and Ichthyology at the ASDM and received his M.S. in Wildlife and Fisheries from the University of Arisona. His research interests include conservation of threatened amphibians of Arizona and population/movement studies of rattlesnakes native to Arizona.

In their chapter, these authors emphasize flexibility in exhibit design to accommodate multiple species over time. Regional specialization in the breeding and maintenance of herps is suggested as a method to increase zoos' carrying capacity for these species.

9

Conservation of Reptiles and Amphibians

Peter C. H. Pritchard

It is often believed that the Age of Reptiles came to an end with the demise of the dinosaurs, and that the heyday of the Amphibia occurred even earlier. Yet, the surviving species of reptiles and amphibians hardly represent a depauperate or limited group. An exact species count for these two Classes is not feasible in view of the constant discoveries of new forms and the ongoing juggling of trinomials and binomials for known taxa. Nevertheless, while the Rhynchocephalia include only a single living species (the tuatara, [*Sphenodon punctatus*] of New Zealand) confined to a few tiny rocky islands, there are over 20 crocodilian species, over 200 species of turtles and tortoises, and over 2000 species each for lizards and snakes. The Amphibia too are remarkably diverse, with a rapidly increasing total of over 4000 recognized species, of which almost one-third were described within the last twenty-five years.

The determination of which species of reptile and amphibian are in need of conservation attention and investment is no easy task. Some species appear rare because they are adept at hiding. Many semiterrestrial turtles remain in complete concealment most of the time, venturing forth for just a few days or weeks in the year, often in response to the onset of the rainy season. Other species may actually seem more abundant than they really are. In the Galapagos Islands, the marine iguanas (*Amblyrhynchus*) bask in great numbers along the shorelines, and one could easily conclude that they were in no need of conservation attention. Yet their vulnerability to attack by feral predators (especially dogs; Kruuk and Snell, 1981), their very low reproductive potential (usually 3–4 eggs per clutch) compared to dozens for the common mainland species *Iguana iguana* (Rand, 1968; Rauch, 1981), and the fact that circumambulation of a small island may literally expose to view every member of the population, combine to make it important that even such conspicuous species be carefully protected.

Thus, it is not yet possible to produce a list of endangered reptiles and amphibians that follows objective criteria. Knowledge of the nearly 10,000 extant species is much too uneven. Species such as the American alligator (*Alligator mississippiensis*) are the subject of many state and federal conservation and monitoring programs and an enormous degree of scientific attention. By contrast, small frogs or burrowing caecilians in isolated ecosystems may have almost no primary literature, no management attention, no specimens in captivity, and perhaps only a small type series in a single museum collection.

Members of the Classes Reptilia and Amphibia that are considered to be threatened or endangered fall into one of the following categories:

1. Large, often conspicuous species, often but not always with wide natural distribution, that have been heavily hunted for food or for commercially valuable products such as tortoiseshell or leather. Sea turtles, many crocodilians, some pythons and boas, and some tortoises fall into this category. Sometimes vulnerability may be enhanced by colonial nesting habits, as is the case with some of the large river turtles, whose populations may be decimated by a few people exploiting the nesting females or their eggs.

2. Oceanic island species, whose natural ranges may be very small, and that have evolved under protected and isolated conditions and are vulnerable to ecological disturbance. Giant tortoises (*Geochelone spp.*), *Phelsuma* day geckoes, land iguanas of the Galapagos (*Conolophus spp.*) or rock iguanas of the Bahamas or Greater Antilles (*Cyclura spp.*), and the boas, *Bolyeria* and *Casarea*, of Round Island, Mauritius, are examples of this category. In many cases, the threat to these species comes less from direct human take than from introduced fauna, especially feral mammals.

3. Continental species with naturally small and often relictual ranges. Such species, in many cases, were already on the

retreat before the advent of man, and in some cases may be difficult to save even with protective efforts. The Western Australian swamp tortoise (*Pseudemydura umbrina*), the Houston toad (*Bufo houstonensis*), the Texas blind salamander (*Typhlomolge rathbuni*), and the Bolson tortoise (*Gopherus flavomarginatus*) are examples of this category.

Species Status in the Wild

The IUCN listings for chelonians, crocodilians, and rhynchocephalians were published by Groombridge (1982); taxa were categorized as "Endangered," "Vulnerable," "Indeterminate," and "Insufficiently Known." IUCN categories for the remaining reptile groups and for the amphibians are found in IUCN (1985), and these forms are included in the USDI (U.S. Fish and Wildlife Service, 1987b) and CITES (1984) listings (see Table 9.1). In all of these lists it is easy to spot inconsistencies. For example, the extremely rare Brazilian sideneck turtle (*Phrynops hogei*) is listed as "Indeterminate" by IUCN, whereas the still numerous and circumglobal Olive ridley (*Lepidochelys olivacea*), Green (*Chelonia mydas*), and Leatherback (*Dermochelys coriacea*) sea turtles are listed as "Endangered." The authority of the CITES list is weakened in the inclusion of some of the most common turtles in the Indian Subcontinent, and the omission of some of the rarest ones (IUCN, 1989). These inclusions, with the exception of the Flap-shelled softshell turtle (*Lissemys punctata*) which was removed from the U.S. list of 1984, are for the most part repeated in the current U. S. Fish and Wildlife Service list. None of the lists includes the Puerto Rican toad (*Peltaphryne lemur*), even though this species has become so rare in the wild that no specimens were found for four years. This species is in fact the first amphibian species for which the American Zoo and Aquariums Association (AZA) has drawn up a survival plan.

Of the crocodilian species of the world, many are depleted in the wild and in need of management attention, but only five forms have reached the point at which captive reproduction may be essential to save them from extinction. These taxa are: the Chinese alligator (*Alligator sinensis*), the Orinoco crocodile (*Crocodylus intermedius*), the Philippine crocodile (*C. mindorensis*), the black caiman (*Melanosuchus niger*), and the false gharial (*Tomistoma schlegeli*).

Table 9.1
Inventory of species of reptiles and amphibians currently listed as "endangered" (E) or "vulnerable" (V) by IUCN, Appendix I and II of CITIES, and "endangered" or "threatened" (T) by USDI.

Reptiles	IUCN	CITES	USDI
TESTUDINES			
Pseudemydura umbrina	E	I	E
Podocnemis (all species)		II	
Podocnemis expansa	E		E
Podocnemis unifilis	V		E
Caretta caretta	V	I	T
Chelonia mydas	E	I	E (Florida, Pacific Mexico)
			T (elsewhere)
Eretmochelys imbricata	E	I	E
Lepidochelys kempi	E	I	E
Lepidochelys olivacea	E	I	E (Pacific Mexico)
			T (elsewhere)
Natator depressa		I	
Dermatemys mawii	V	II	E
Dermochelys coriacea	E	I	E
Batagur baska	E	I	E
Callagur borneoensis	V		
Chrysemys scripta	V		
Clemmys muhlenbergi		II	
Geoclemys hamiltoni		I	E
Graptemys oculifera			T
Kachuga tecta tecta		I	E
Melanochelys tricarinata		I	E
Morenia ocellata		I	E
Pseudemys rubriventris bangsi			E
Terrapene coahuila	V	I	E
Kinosternon flavescens spooneri	E		
Testudinidae (all species)		II (except those in Appendix I)	
Geochelone elephantopus (= G. nigra)	E	I	E
Geochelone (= Astrochelys) *radiata*	V	I	E

Table 9.1 *continued*

Reptiles	IUCN	CITES	USDI
Geochelone (= Astrochelys) yniphora	E	I	E
Gopherus agassizii	V		T (Beaver Dam Slope population)
Gopherus flavomarginatus	E	I	E
Gopherus polyphemus	V		
Psammobates geometricus	V	I	E
Testudo hermanni	V		
Trionyx ater		I	E
Trionyx gangeticus		I	E
Trionyx hurum		I	E
Trionyx nigricans		I	E .
CROCODYLIA (all species)		II (unless I)	
Alligator mississippiensis		II	T (Fla, parts of E Ga, SC, elsewhere)
Alligator sinensis	E	I	E
Caiman crocodilus apaporiensis		I	E
Caiman crocodilus crocodylus	V	II	
Caiman crocodilus fuscus	V	II	
Caiman crocodilus yacare		II	E
Caiman latirostris	E	I	E
Melanosuchus niger	E	I	E
Paleosuchus trigonatus		II	
Crocodylus acutus	E	I	E
Crocodylus cataphractus		I	E
Crocodylus intermedius	E	I	E
Crocodylus johnsoni	V	II	
Crocodylus moreletii	E	I	E
Crocodylus niloticus	V	I (II for Zimbabwe ranched population)	E
Crocodylus n. novaeguineae	V	II	
Crocodylus n. mindorensis	E	I	E
Crocodylus palustris	V	I	E
Crocodylus porosus	V	I (II in Papua New Guinea)	E (Except Papua New Guinea)

Table 9.1 *continued*

Reptiles	IUCN	CITES	USDI
Crocodylus rhombifer	E	I	E
Crocodylus siamensis	E	I	E
Osteolaemus tetraspis		I	E
Tomistoma schlegelii	E	I	E
Gavialis gangeticus	E	I	E

RHYNCHOCEPHALIA

Sphenodon punctatus		I	E

SAURIA

Hydrosaurus pustulosus	V		
Uromastyx spp.		II	
Paradelma orientalis		II	
Anniella pulchra nigra	E	II	
Chameleo spp.		II	
Cordylus spp.		II	
Pseudocordylus spp.		II	
Crocodilurus lacertinus		II	
Cyrtodactylus serpensinsula		II	
Oedura reticulata	V		T
Phelsuma spp.		II	
Phelsuma edwardnewtoni	E		E
Phelsuma guentheri			E
Sphaerodactylus micropithecus			E
Heloderma spp.		II	
Heloderma suspectum	V		
Amblyrhynchus cristatus		II	
Anolis roosevelti	E		E
Brachylophus fasciatus	E	I	E
Brachylophus vitiensis			E
Conolophus pallidus		II	E
Conolophus subcristatus	V	II	
Cyclura spp.		I	
Cyclura cornuta	V	I	
Cyclura bacolopha		I	
Cyclura carinata	V	I	
Cyclura carinata bartschi		I	T
Cyclura carinata carinata		I	T
Cyclura collei		I	E

Table 9.1 *continued*

Reptiles	IUCN	CITES	USDI
Cyclura cychlura cychlura		I	T
Cyclura cychlura figginsi		I	T
Cyclura cychlura inornata		I	T
Cyclura nubila nubila	V	I	T (except intro-duced pop'n on Puerto Rico)
Cyclura nubila caymanensis	V	I	T
Cyclura nubila lewisi	V	I	E
Cyclura pinguis	E	I	E
Cyclura rileyi rileyi	E	I	E
Cyclura rileyi cristata		I	T
Cyclura rileyi nuchalis		I	T
Cyclura stejnegeri	E	I	T
Gambelia silus	E	I	E
Iguana spp.		II	
Iguana iguana	V		
Phrynosoma coronatum blainvillei		II	
Sauromalus varius	E/V	I	E
Gallotia simonyi	E		E
Podarcis pityusensis			T
Leiolopisma telfairii			T
Ameiva polops	E		E
Cnemidophorus hyperythrus	V	II	E
Dracaena guianensis		II	
Tupinambis spp.		II	
Varanidae		II	
Varanus bengalensis		I	E
Varanus flavescens		I	E
Varanus griseus	V	I	E
Varanus griseus caspius	V		
Varanus komodoensis		I	E
Xantusia riversiana			T

SERPENTES

Boidae		II	
Acrantophis spp.		I	
Bolyeria multocarinata	E	I	E

Table 9.1 *continued*

Reptiles	IUCN	CITES	USDI
Casarea dussumieri	E	I	E
Constrictor constrictor		II	
Epicrates cenchris cenchris		II	
Epicrates inornatus	E	I	E
Epicrates monensis	E	I	
Epicrates monensis monensis			T
Epicrates monensis granti			E
Epicrates subflavus	V	I	E
Eunectes notaeus		II	
Python molurus	V		
Python molurus molurus	V	I	E
Python molurus bivittatus	V		
Sanzinia madagascariensis		I	
Drymarchon corais couperi	V		T
Nerodia fasciata taeniata			T
Nerodia harteri paucimaculata			T
Thamnophis couchi hammondi		II	·
Thamnophis sirtalis tetrataenia	E		E
Naja oxiana	E		
Ogmodon vitianus	V		
Pseudoboa cloelia		II	
Crotalus unicolor			T
Crotalus willardi	V		
Crotalus willardi obscurus			T
Viper latifii	E		E
Viper lebertina schweizeri	V		
Viper ursinii	V		

AMPHIBIANS

CAUDATA

	IUCN	CITES	USDI
Ambystoma californiense	V		
Ambystoma dumerilii dumerilii		II	
Ambystoma lermaensis		II	
Ambystoma macrodactylum croceum	E		E
Ambystoma mexicanum		II	

Table 9.1 *continued*

Amphibians	IUCN	CITES	USDI
Andrias davidianus			E
Andrias japonicus		I	
Batrachoseps aridus	E		E
Eurycea nana			T
Phaeognathus hubrichti			T
Plethodon neomexicanus	V		
Typhlomolge rathbuni			E
Proteus anguinus	V		
Chioglossa lusitanica	V		
Atelopus varius zeteki		I	E
Bufo exsul	V		
Bufo hemiophrys baxteri			E
Bufo houstonensis	E		E
Bufo periglenes	E	I	E
Bufo retiformis	V	II	
Bufo superciliaris		I	E
Nectophrynoides occidentalis	V	I	E
Discoglossus nigriventer	E		E
Argenteohyla siemersi	V		
Leiopelma hamiltoni			E
Elutherodactylus jasperi			T
Rheobatrachus silus	V		
Pelobates fuscus insubricus	E		
Xenopus gilli	V		
Conrana goliath	V		
Rana latastei	V		
Rana onca	E		
Rana pipiens fisheri	E		

Two other taxa, the Apaporis River caiman (*Caiman crocodilus apaporiensis*), and the Siamese crocodile (*Crocodylus siamensis*) may already be extinct in the wild, the former by genetic swamping by the common caiman, and the latter by actual extirpation (although about 5,000 individuals survive in captivity at the Samutprakan Crocodile Farm in Thailand, where hybridization with *C. porosus* occurs, and where there are no published plans for their future).

The black caiman, once very widespread and abundant in Amazonia, now is reduced to four small areas of relative abundance near Kaw, French Guiana; Lago Limoncocha, Ecuador; Manu

National Park, Peru; and near Karanambo, Guyana, being very rare to absent in the huge expanses of intervening territory (Plotkin et al., 1983; Pritchard, pers. obs.).

Reasons for decline or endangerment of reptiles and amphibians are numerous. For large, commercially valuable species, including many crocodilians, commercial hunting has often reduced populations to low levels even when habitats are substantially intact. Nevertheless, market hunting alone rarely exterminates continental species, because at a given point the rarity of the animal makes further hunting unprofitable, unless conducted incidentally to operations based upon species that are still abundant. On the other hand, island species may be threatened or even exterminated either by over-collection or by a variety of other causes. Moreover, real-world examples usually involve multiple stresses. Thus, the giant tortoises of several of the Galapagos Islands were reduced to near-extinction by over-collection, after which collection of the last few individuals was too arduous to be worth pursuing. But by that point, goats had been introduced to such islands as Hood and Abingdon, which rapidly degraded the vegetation, thus destroying the tortoises' food supply. Domestic rats brought to Duncan Island proliferated and predated the hatchling tortoises with virtual 100% efficiency, thus dooming the population even though the larger animals were unaffected (Pritchard, 1985). Feral dogs menaced young and even larger subadult tortoises on Chatham and southern Albemarle Islands. In all these cases, legal protection of the species was not enough; a hands-on recovery plan was essential.

Feral mammals also menace certain island saurian species. The Antillean iguanas of the genus *Cyclura* are an important example. These large ground lizards of the Bahamas and Greater Antilles disappear rapidly from their natural habitats, especially from small islands and cays, when even small numbers of feral dogs are introduced to the ecosystem. Similarly, the Galapagos land iguanas on Indefatigable and Albemarle Islands have been severely stressed by feral dogs in recent decades, to the extent that the surviving individuals had to be taken into protective captivity. On other islands, such as Baltra, the iguanas were exterminated by direct human action (including vandalistic slaughter by occupying forces during WW II).

Removal of feral mammals is difficult, but not impossible, and vigorous efforts have been made in the Galapagos, where several islands are now goat-free, and feral dogs have been removed from several critical areas by judicious use of poisoned bait (Reynolds, 1982).

There has now been good success in head-starting tortoises of several populations in captivity at the Charles Darwin Research Station, and already good numbers of captive-reared tortoises from Chatham, James, Duncan, and elsewhere have been returned to their respective islands.

Conservation Programs in Captivity

Relatively few species of reptiles and amphibians have reached the point at which they can be expected to be saved *only* by captive reproduction. Others, however, may well benefit from "ranching"—that is, taking advantage of the large clutch size (offset in nature by heavy neonatal mortality) of many species by collecting eggs from nests in the wild, hatching them, and raising the young in captivity. This technique offers several advantages over closed-cycle reproduction in that much money is saved if one does not have to house adults of species that are sometimes very large. The operation is necessarily combined with monitoring of the breeding effort of the wild population. Further, in the case of commercial operations, there is a permanent vested interest in the maintenance of natural habitat for the wild breeding population.

Crocodilians

All 22 or 23 crocodilian species are represented amongst U.S. zoos, although numbers are very unequal. There are fewer than ten adults of each of five species (*Melanosuchus niger*, *Crocodylus intermedius*, *C. mindorensis*, *C. johnsoni*, and *C. novaeguineae*); (Behler, 1991).

Two crocodilian species, the mugger (*Crocodylus palustris*) and the gharial (*Gavialis gangeticus*) may have been saved, by captive breeding in the former case and head-starting in the latter, in facilities throughout India (Anonymous, 1980; Choudhury, 1981; Larson and Vijaya, 1981; Sharma, 1987; Andrews, 1988). In addition, Morelet's crocodile (*Crocodylus moreleti*) is now being bred in quantity in Zoo Atlanta (Hunt, 1975). Behler (1989) reported that over 300 hatchlings had been produced, and a current priority was to identify a potential site in Belize to receive them. Some thousands of Cuban crocodiles (*Crocodylus rhombifer*) are being maintained, with some captive reproduction but also some hybridization with *Crocodylus acutus*, at a facility near Playa Giron on the south coast of Cuba (Varona, 1980).

Efforts to save the Chinese alligator have started. Very few wild specimens of this species survive, and the habitat has been severely degraded, but currently guards are posted when breeding individuals are located (J. Behler, pers. comm.). Meanwhile, in the U.S.A., successful captive reproduction has occurred since the late 1970s at the Rockefeller Wildlife Refuge in Louisiana, at the St. Augustine Alligator Farm, Florida, and at the Bronx Zoo. The young from the seven wild-caught founders have been widely distributed and currently 13 U.S. institutions are holding a total of 125 animals (Behler, 1991). In China, the Anhui Breeding Center had its first hatching of alligators in 1981, and in 1986, 684 were hatched. By 1987, Anhui had 975 captive-bred alligators (Behler, 1991), although the prospect of finding suitable receiving habitat for these animals seems remote.

In Venezuela, an effort is being made to census and captive-breed the very rare *Crocodylys intermedius*, one of the world's largest crocodilians. The natural recovery of this species, following legal protection, may have been prevented by competition between the young and the very abundant common caiman (*Caiman crocodilus*). Currently, 104 specimens are housed in captivity in a variety of zoos and other facilities, under the overall aegis of Tomas Blohm of Caracas, and 16 adults and 140 juveniles are maintained at Blohm's field facility at Hato Masaguaral. Some breeding also occurs at the UNELLE University in Guanare.

Initial conservation efforts are underway for the Philippine crocodile (*Crocodylus mindorensis*) in the wild. Breeding has occurred since 1981 in the captive group held at Silliman University Marine Laboratory on Negros Island, and the Gladys Porter Zoo in Brownsville, Texas now has two adult pairs that are displaying breeding behavior (Behler, 1989).

For the other two severely threatened species, the false gharial and the black caiman, captive breeding to date has been insignificant, apart from some reproduction of the latter in a seminatural setting at Hato El Dorado in Bolivia (Behler, 1989). Breeding efforts should be initiated with some urgency; perhaps the French Government can be persuaded to undertake a captive breeding effort in its *Department d'outre mer* of French Guiana, possibly starting with subadult animals to avoid the trauma of handling the very large adults.

Tortoises

Several of the races of Galapagos tortoises (*Geochelone nigra*) have been saved either through captive breeding or by "ranching." Certain zoological institutions, especially those of San Diego and Honolulu, have achieved sporadic but significant success in the captive breeding of Galapagos tortoises. In addition, since 1988 there has been excellent success at the Life Fellowship facility in Florida with over 85 hatchlings from the first season, and with some individual females depositing as many as five clutches in a season (Pritchard, 1989a). These programs have been criticized by some because the island origins of the breeding animals have not always been clear, but in reality it is likely that most of the breeding stock was derived from southwestern Isabela Island (subspecies *vicina*). Zoos, however, have not been able to accumulate more than isolated specimens of the rare forms, and it is fortunate that the efforts of the Charles Darwin Research Station and the Galapagos National Park have made great headway in breeding some of the endangered races in captivity. The remaining total stock of 14 wild-caught Hood Island tortoises (supplemented by an old male from the San Diego Zoo) proved very productive in captivity at the Darwin Research Station. Several hundred eggs have now hatched, and the oldest of the released young tortoises (from 1971) have reached mature size and have started to show reproductive activity.

Fewer options remain for the Abingdon Island subspecies, of which the only survivor is a male (called "Lonesome George") found on Abingdon in 1972, and housed since then at the Darwin Research Station. This animal is not especially old, but efforts to cross-breed him with morphologically appropriate females from other islands have been unsuccessful. Apparently no mating has occurred, and in one case "George" overturned and drowned a potential mate in the small pond provided for drinking and wallowing. The circumstances of the discovery of this animal are described by Pritchard (1977).

Of the other endangered tortoises, captive breeding seems definitely indicated for the very rare Malagasy form *Astrochelys yniphora*, of which no more than a few hundred individuals survive, confined to the vicinity of Baly Bay. Captive groups have been held at the Honolulu Zoo and at the New York Zoological Society's facility at St. Catherine's Island, Georgia, and some oviposition has occurred and at least one hatchling produced. Another group of eight animals is housed at a government facility at Ampijoroa,

Madagascar. The first clutch of three eggs was deposited April 20, 1987 (Mast, pers. comm.), and by late 1989 there were nearly a dozen healthy young tortoises produced by the program. Fast-growing husbandry insights give promise that the numbers will increase rapidly.

The other large Malagasy tortoise (*Astrochelys radiata*) is now being bred successfully at the Gladys Porter Zoo, at St. Catherine's Island, and at the Jersey Wildlife Trust, and is the subject of an SSP program and a Studbook. Even more urgent is the captive breeding effort for the small species *Pyxis planicauda*, apparently limited to a very small area in western coastal Madagascar, although a small second population has now been identified (Kuchling and Bloxam, 1988). The Knoxville and San Diego zoos have had this species in recent years, without successful reproduction, but the Jersey Wildlife Trust now reports the first successful captive hatching in Madagascar (Swingland, pers. comm.).

Captive breeding is also an essential component of the survival plan for the giant Mexican gopher tortoise (*Gopherus flavomarginatus*), the largest tortoise in North America and one that is confined to an arid, internally-drained basin in southern Chihuahua (Groombridge, 1982). Specimens have bred in captivity at the Research Ranch in Arizona and at the Laboratorio del Desierto in Mapimi (Durango), and plans are currently under way to "repatriate" individuals to the Big Bend National Park (Texas), precolombian habitat for the species.

Some other tortoises, including the South African *Psammobates geometricus*, are very rare, and captive breeding may contribute to their ultimate survival. But tortoises of this genus often do poorly in captivity, and the real solution lies more in careful monitoring and protection and active management of fire in the renosterveld areas in which this tortoise is still found in extreme southwestern Cape Province (Boycott and Bourquin, 1989).

Marine and Freshwater Turtles

Of the sea turtles, the green turtle has been farmed or ranched commercially on both Grand Cayman and Reunion Islands, although CITES prohibitions on international trade have thwarted real commercial success, and there have been sporadic efforts to farm and ranch the hawksbill (*Eretmochelys imbricata*) (e.g., in the Palau Islands). However, the one species that is so depleted that it may ultimately only be saved by captive breeding is Kemp's ridley (*Lepidochelys kempi*). Over the past decade, this species has been head-started in large numbers by the U.S. National Marine Fisheries Service in Galveston, Texas, and recently closed-cycle captive breeding has been achieved at the Cayman Turtle Farm, Grand Cayman, West Indies (Wood and Wood, 1984).

Of the freshwater turtles, *Aspideretes nigricans*, a very large softshell species, is apparently restricted to a single, captive population housed in a rectangular artificial pond or "tank" beside a Moslem shrine in Chittagong, Bangladesh (Whitaker, 1982). Although the most conspicuous (i.e., tamest) turtles are very old and large, some reproduction occurs; Pritchard saw juveniles and a fresh nest in 1989. The sacred status of the animals may inhibit the establishment of independent colonies, but Ahsan (1984) reported some juveniles hatched in his laboratory in Chittagong.

Captive breeding may be the only hope for the extremely rare Western Swamp Tortoise (*Pseudemydura umbrina*) in Western Australia, but this will not be easy. Animals have been held at the Perth Zoo for a long time, but breeding was sporadic at best in the early years of the program, and then ceased. The turtles may take as much as 15 years to mature, and the clutch size is only 3–5. They feed upon live prey, such a tadpoles, but show no great skill in catching them. Presently, the species is also being held at a facility operated by the Conservation and Land Management Agency of Western Australia. No young were produced from 1981 to 1988 (Burbidge, pers. comm.). However, exciting recent news (Kuchling, 1989) indicated that eleven hatchlings were produced in 1989, and although survival was disappointing, the 1990 hatchlings have done well (and grown much more rapidly) under a modified husbandry technique (Kuchling, pers. comm.; Pritchard, pers. obs.), and an integrated recovery plan for the species was launched by Prince Philip in Perth in December 1990.

The Gladys Porter Zoo, the New York Zoological Society, and the Jersey Wildlife Trust have produced relatively large numbers of the Coahuila Box Turtle (*Terrapene coahuila*) in recent years. A softshell species, *Apalone ater*, like *Terrapene coahuila* endemic to the Cuatro Cienegas Basin, may be threatened by genetic swamping by an ecologically aggressive form, *Apalone spinifer emoryi*, invading from the north (Smith and Smith, 1980). It would be important to collect and breed the best morphotypes of *A. ater* that could still be found.

Another species for which captive breeding is recommended is the very rare Brazilian sideneck (*Phrynops hogei*). The species is nearly restricted to the small, heavily polluted Rio Paraiba in Rio de

Janeiro, and only 17 individuals were known when Rhodin and Mittermeier (1983) summarized information on the species, although some others have subsequently come to light (Mittermeier, pers. comm.).

The small and perhaps very rare terrestrial batagurine *Geoemyda silvatica* has recently been "rediscovered" in southern India (Vijaya, 1984), and oviposition started soon after a captive colony was set up at the Madras Crocodile Bank (Anonymous, 1983), although this group has subsequently died out (Whitaker, pers. comm.).

For the giant river turtles, closed-cycle captive breeding will only rarely be feasible, and probably not necessary because good protection of the colonial nesting grounds may be more easily achieved. However, H. Boos and J. Seyjagat of the Emperor Valley Zoo in Port-of-Spain, Trinidad, recently succeeded in breeding the very large *Podocnemis expansa* in quite a small pond, and using breeding stock that had been in captivity over 60 years (Pritchard, 1988). This species is also being bred in a much larger, also very long-term captive colony in the gardens of the Museu Goeldi, Belem, Brazil (Ellis, pers. comm.). By contrast, the relatively diminutive congener *Podocnemis erythrocephala* is now breeding successfully under indoor conditions at the Bronx Zoo (Behler, pers. comm.).

The largest of the batagurine turtles, *Orlitia borneensis*, has also reproduced successfully at the Bronx Zoo in 1991 and 1992. But more typically, head-starting or ranching will be more feasible for these very large turtles, as is being undertaken in Malaysia for both *Batagur baska* and *Callagur borneensis* (Moll, 1983).

Snakes

Although there are well over 2,000 species of snakes in the world, only a few are at the point at which captive breeding for survival is indicated. These few include two rare species of boa from Round Island, Mauritius: *Bolyeria multocarinata* (possibly already extinct) and *Casarea dussumieri*. The Jersey Wildlife Trust has already had some success with captive reproduction of *Casarea* as well as with other endangered Round Island reptiles, including the day gecko (*Phelsuma guentheri*) and Telfair's skink (*Leiolopisma telfairi*).

Several other snake species or subspecies have such limited distribution or have suffered such severe habitat degradation that captive breeding may be an essential factor in their survival. These include the San Francisco garter snake (*Thamnophis sirtalis tetrataenia*), the Jamaican boa (*Epicrates subflavus*), and the Aruba rattlesnake (*Crotalus durissus unicolor*). Another very localized rattlesnake, *Crotalus durissus vegrandis*, naturally limited to the state of Monagas, Venezuela, has already been captive bred.

Lizards

The Antillean iguanas are susceptible to rapid extermination by feral dogs (and cats) (Iverson, 1978), and in many cases these animals will have to be saved by captive breeding. The extremely endangered population of Grand Cayman Island is an obvious candidate for this, and these and other forms are currently being bred in captivity in at least two facilities in Florida.

In addition to the endangered Round Island snakes and lizards mentioned above, some endangered Mascarene lizards are currently the focus of captive breeding efforts at the Fresno Zoo, California. These include the Reunion day gecko (*Phelsuma ornata inexpectata*), the Reunion chamaeleon (*Chamaeleo pardalis*), and the Mauritius lowland forest day gecko (*Phelsuma g. guimbeaui*) (McKeown, as cited in Gowen, 1988).

Amphibians

Amphibians are obvious candidates for conservation by captive reproduction or at least "ranching" and head-starting, in that few species are large, and many lay very large numbers of eggs. If one could successfully raise to adulthood the majority of eggs or young of even a few individuals of the more prolific frog species, enough captive-bred stock could be generated to repopulate substantial areas of habitat. Indeed, this has already been done for the fire-bellied toad (*Bombina orientalis*) of the Balearic islands (Bloxham, pers. comm.). But in most cases, amphibians can be preserved best by maintaining their habitat, thereby avoiding the somewhat difficult task of finding large quantities of small live food for thousands of developing young. Of special concern is the amphibian fauna of the Antilles where some of the species have been depleted (in most cases by habitat destruction) to the point at which they must be considered endangered.

Space does not permit a full discussion of the potentially devastating and still mysterious topic of worldwide amphibian depletion, of which the isolated, protected, and spectacular golden toad

(*Bufo periglenes*) of Monte Verde, Costa Rica, may already be a victim (Crump et al., 1992).

One of the most exciting recent successes in the conservation of endangered amphibians by captive breeding has been the case of the Puerto Rican toad (*Peltaphryne lemur*). Judging by fossil evidence this species was once abundant, but it has been very rare since its discovery in 1868, possibly as a result of competition with the aggressive introduced species *Bufo marinus*, as well as extensive habitat alteration. After several years with no sightings, two pairs were located in 1980 and 1981, and thirty young toads derived from these adults were sent to the Buffalo Zoo (New York). In 1983 the Buffalo Zoo was able to return 175 juvenile toads to natural habitats in Puerto Rico, and in 1984, 500 more were sent (Olsen, 1984; Vogel, 1984).

Clearly, care will have to be taken to ensure that the released animals are not destroyed or out-competed by the introduced marine toads, but the program does show every indication of being a clear case of a species saved by captive reproduction. A comparable program is under way at the Houston Zoo (Texas) to save the endangered Houston toad by captive breeding and reintroduction to its natural habitat in the Atwater Prairie Chicken Reserve.

Another amphibian that ultimately may benefit from captive breeding is the extremely restricted Stephens Island frog (*Leiopelma hamiltoni*) of New Zealand. Although now known to occupy a small site on Maud Island in addition to the half-acre rock-scree habitat on Stephens Island, it remains extremely rare, far more so than the tuataras that sometimes prey upon this species. Efforts are being made to create new habitat on other areas of these two islands (Newman, 1977), but ultimately it would seem to be desirable to establish an "insurance colony" in captivity, which would not only provide valuable insights into the virtually unknown breeding habits of the species, but would also provide a source of specimens for reintroduction experiments.

Problems Facing Conservation Programs in Captivity

Most conservationists agree that captive reproduction is usually only economically justified for severely endangered species, and there are many problems associated with the successful introduction of captive-raised specimens to the wild even though most reptile and amphibian behavior is instinctive.

Efforts should be made to preserve endangered species in their natural habitat, because without this habitat or a good facsimile thereof, a captive-bred population will have to be maintained in captivity forever, an exercise of enormous cost and increasingly questionable long-term prospects. Ideally, very rare species may be taken for captive reproduction as a sort of protective custody as well as to develop husbandry techniques before the species is reduced to the last few individuals. Once vigorous efforts to reduce or eliminate habitat perturbations and direct or indirect take of specimens from the wild have been successful, regular releases of captive-bred stock can be made from the large numbers of individuals generated from healthy captive parental stock.

In a sense, captive reproduction should be attempted when all other means of saving a species have been exhausted; yet paradoxically when that point is reached, the withdrawal of even minimal breeding stock from the wild may be more than the species can stand. Thus, captive breeding should be the norm, or at least the goal, for all species maintained in captivity, and the methodologies should be perfected before the species become excessively rare.

In most cases, it will be easiest to have a captive breeding operation in a country in which the species occurs naturally. This will minimize problems with permits and will allow the animals to be maintained out-of-doors, with such factors as humidity, temperature cycles, and day-length similar to those in the wild. While such factors can be reproduced reasonably well using modern equipment, this approach presupposes that all the natural constraints and parameters are known. Even then, some species, including the leatherback sea turtle and several South African tortoises of the genera *Homopus* and *Psammobates*, are so sensitive that they cannot usually be kept for protracted periods even in countries to which they are native (Boycott and Bourquin, 1988). In cases such as these, there is no alternative to conservation of the wild populations and their habitats. There is a distinct concentration of available resources, facilities, and technology for captive reproduction of rare species in North America and a few countries of western Europe, whereas most of the species in question live in the Third World. But the record shows that the efforts that saved Galapagos tortoises, gharials, and other large endangered reptiles from extinction were captive breeding or head-starting efforts in the countries to which these species are native (Pritchard, 1985; Sharma, 1987).

Conclusions

There is substantial and largely healthy diversity of opinion as to the importance of captive reproduction as a means of saving endangered species of reptiles and amphibians. This diversity stems in part from the tendency of individual workers to emphasize the importance of activities in which they themselves are engaged. Those struggling to maintain native habitats sometimes distrust captive breeding programs as defeatist, or as giving a dangerous "don't worry — we can save the species without its habitat" message to the public. Conversely, those involved in the captive reproduction of reptiles and amphibians often feel that habitat destruction, already severe, will become overwhelming in the decades to come. They believe that, without efforts such as theirs, whole species will be lost. They may sometimes lack detailed plans as to how their efforts will be utilized to augment wild populations, but they can point to an increasing inventory of cases in which pressure on a wild species has been reduced sharply by the efforts of captive breeders. They can also note a small but growing list of species for which captive-bred individuals have been returned to the wild. There is much merit to both sides, and the arguments may ultimately simplify to a classical optimist/pessimist scenario.

The saving of species in their habitats is fraught with political, economic, and sociological implications and difficulties, and only rarely can one rest assured that a given problem has been solved, as opposed to merely "receiving attention." On the other hand, reptile breeders, once having obtained their initial stock, are able to operate in a less political milieu and one over which they have more individual control. In some cases their successes have been spectacular, and the growing body of reptile husbandry and captive breeding technology now has its own glossy journal, *The Vivarium* (first issue published winter 1988), to supplement the extensive information published over the years in *Salamandra*, *Das Aquarium und Terrarium Zeitschrift*, *Herpetological Review*, *International Zoo Yearbook*, and newer journals including *Sauria* and *Die Schildkrote*.

As a final word, one is impressed by the variety of institutions undertaking the captive breeding of endangered reptiles and amphibians — not just zoos, but nature reserves; tourist attractions; commercial sea turtle farms; religious facilities, old and new, in the East and in the West; commercial animal dealers; and a host of dedicated private individuals. In years to come there will be many species to save, and the contributions of all of these diverse organizations and individuals will be needed.

10

Reproductive Physiology of Reptiles and Amphibians

Paul Licht

The successful propagation of endangered and threatened species under captive conditions will likely depend on an array of factors concerning the general health of the animals. However, even reptiles and amphibians in excellent somatic condition (i.e., feeding well, good appearance, and exceptional longevity) may fail to exhibit normal reproductive behavior because of the special relationship between reproductive physiology and the environment (both biotic and abiotic). For example, nutritional requirements for the nonreproductive and reproductive individual may differ considerably depending on sex, clutch size, rate of gonadal development, and reproductive mode. Environmental conditions (e.g., light, temperature, humidity, group social structure) that may be excellent for maintaining animals may fail to elicit reproductive behavior. Even when breeding appears successful, the quality of eggs (e.g., number and hatchability) may be inferior to wild animals (e.g., Wood and Wood, 1980; Lance et al., 1983).

Unfortunately, while a sizable literature exists for captive breeding of reptiles and amphibians, the number of carefully controlled experiments is meager; hence, it is often difficult to define exact requirements. A compilation of tips for individual species may be found in the many issues of the Reptile Symposium on Captive Propagation and Husbandry (Zoological Consortium, Inc., Thurmont, Md. 21788; also see Murphy and Collins, 1980). It is apparent from these practical experiences and limited experimental studies that no single methodology will suffice for all reptiles or amphibians because of their wide variations in habitat adaptation. However, some general patterns emerge that provide guidelines for working with new species.

Reproductive Anatomy

The condition and appearance of the reptilian and amphibian urogenital systems are often highly variable through both development and seasonal cycles, but the gonads are usually sufficiently differentiated to allow recognition of sexes at the time of hatching or birth. Fox (1977) presents a very thorough review and description of the reptilian urogenital system and only brief observations will be made here. Photographic illustrations of representative reptilian ovaries and oviducts are shown in Licht, 1984 (snakes); Owens, 1980 (turtles); Lance, 1989 (alligator).

Females

Reptiles and amphibians have paired ovaries with associated oviducts. The appearance of the ovary and especially the size and number of oocytes is highly variable in both reptiles and amphibians and in both is correlated with reproductive mode (e.g., viviparous species differ from oviparous). Generally, the ovary is a membranous sac-like structure in which individual follicles are easily recognized as vitellogenesis proceeds. In alligators, the two ovaries contain different numbers of follicles but this is not necessarily the condition in other crocodilians (Lance, 1989). In reptiles that produce multiple clutches in one season, a hierarchy of follicular sizes permits estimation of the number and size of clutches to be produced that year; this condition is especially accentuated in turtles (Moll, 1979; Owens, 1980).

Follicular size changes enormously throughout the ovarian cycle; the time to complete vitellogenesis can be weeks to years depending on species and conditions (Fox, 1977). Major interspecific differences also occur in the maximal size of preovulatory follicles. In reptiles, these range from a few millimeters to almost half a centimeter and direct experience is required to recognize the fully mature, preovulatory condition in a particular species; variation is less in amphibians.

In addition to normal vitellogenic follicles, the ovary may contain large numbers of atretic follicles (these will vary in appearance depending on stage of degeneration) and if ovulation has occurred recently, distinct corpora lutea (CL) form in the reptilian ovary. While CL are commonly used as evidence of previous ovulation, caution must be exercised in identifying these structures. In reptiles, the newly formed luteal body, corpus hemorrhagicum, is characteristically a compact donut shaped structure (Owen, 1980;

Xavier, 1987). The alligator CL differs in lacking the appearance of a steroid secreting tissue (Lance, 1989). In advanced stages of degeneration, the CL may be superficially confused with advanced atretic follicles. The "life-span" of the reptilian and amphibian CL are highly variable, and correlate with the mode of reproduction. In egg-laying species, the structure may only persist for a day or so in amphibians and for several days or weeks in reptiles, while in viviparous species, they remain active and apparently secretory for much longer (e.g., weeks), depending on gestation times (Yaron, 1985; Guillette, 1987; Xavier, 1987).

Clutch sizes in reptiles vary from one in some lizards to over a hundred in large turtles and from a few to many thousands in amphibians; these variations will obviously affect the appearance of the ovary. In reptiles with more than one egg/clutch, both ovaries are likely to participate to about the same extent in each cycle and ovulation is essentially synchronous (autochronic), but there are species (notably anoline lizards) in which the two ovaries alternate throughout the cycle (allochronic) or where only a single ovary contributes (monochronic); see Smith et al. (1972) for further descriptions of ovarian participation. Amphibians also differ in the proportion of ova ovulated for each spawning (Duellman and Trueb, 1986).

The paired oviducts of reptiles and amphibians typically undergo pronounced changes in gross appearance and size with the ovarian cycle. They become highly distended and often convoluted under the influence of ovarian steroids in the preovulatory condition. The oviduct is divided into distinct regions relating to function (Palmer and Guillette, 1988). In many reptiles, notably turtles, the oviducts have specialized regions for sperm storage (see Gist and Jones, 1987 for review and illustrations). Albumin is secreted by glands in the anterior region and egg shell more posteriorly. The ovum appears almost fully shelled within 1–2 days after ovulation, but the egg (in oviparous species) is retained for days to weeks. Reptiles exhibit a wide range of reproductive modes.

While all turtles and crocodilians are oviparous, squamates (lizards and snakes) fall on a continuum ranging from oviparity to viviparity with attendant variations in the duration of gestation (Shine, 1983; St. Girons, 1985) which is associated with the complexity of placentation (Yaron, 1985). In a few extreme cases, notably skinks, placental formation is associated with an enormous reduction in yolk deposition so that preovulatory follicles remain minute (Blackburn et al., 1984). The structure of the oviduct is also related to the degree of placentation (Guillette, 1987). It is also important to mention here that parthenogenesis is well documented and occurs in several distinct families of lizards (reviewed by Darevsky et al., 1985).

Males

The reptilian testes are paired structures that are typically asymmetrically positioned in the peritoneal cavity. They tend to be egg shaped in lizards, crocodilians, and turtles but are more elongate and cylindrical in snakes; pigmentation is also variable. Testicular morphology is more complex in amphibians, usually involving several discrete lobes (Lofts, 1987). The reptilian accessory ducts are equally variable (Fox, 1977). In the regressed condition, they tend to be colorless and thread-like, but it is usually easy to recognize the sperm filled epididymides and vas deferens as they become distended and white in appearance. The maximal development of testes and their associated gonaducts do not necessarily coincide (see below). Not surprisingly, the external fertilization in many amphibians leads to differences in morphology, and in urodeles (salamanders), the formation of spermatophores is associated with additional morphological specializations (Duellman and Trueb, 1986).

Reproductive Hormones

General Organization of the Reproductive Endocrine System

Future attempts to use hormonal intervention will require knowledge of the nature of the endogenous reproductive hormones in the animals to be studied. In this regard, at least three hormonal foci must be considered: the brain factors regulating the pituitary, especially gonadotropin-releasing hormone (GnRH); the pituitary gonadotropins (and possibly other hormones) that control the gonads; and the gonadal sex steroids that control peripheral sexual features and feedback on the hypothalamus and pituitary (other possible gonadal hormones like inhibins and activins have not yet been studied in any ectotherm).

The hormonal components of the hypothalamo-pituitary-gonadal axis in reptiles and amphibians are basically similar to those described for mammals; but important variations in the details of these interactions must be taken into account in attempts to understand or manipulate the system. From a practical standpoint, at least two fundamental issues relating to the choice of hormones must be addressed in designing hormonal therapy in an endangered species. First, which type of hormone is required (i.e., what is the action of each hormone)? Second, what is the source of the hormone (i.e., can hormones derived from one species be used in another)? The latter question is of obvious import because it is unlikely that large quantities of any homologous hormone will be available from endangered species.

Brain Peptides

Studies in a variety of reptiles and amphibians indicate that these groups have a neuropeptide homologous to GnRH that acts to stimulate pituitary release of both gonadotropins (follicle-stimulating hormone, FSH, and luteinizing hormone, LH; Licht and Porter, 1987). While the structure of this neuropeptide varies among species (in fact, several forms may exist in a single species), unlike mammals, reptilian and amphibian pituitaries exhibit relatively little discrimination between different forms (Licht et al., 1987; Pavgi and Licht, unpublished). Because of this lower specificity and because of their commercial availability, use of these peptides is likely to represent the most practical method for hormonal manipulation of reproduction in non-mammalian species.

In addition to the lesser specificity of the GnRH receptors, the physiology of these peptides in reptiles and amphibians may differ in important respects from those in mammals. The pulsatile nature of GnRH release and the requirement for noncontinuous stimulation to avoid pituitary desensitization (which may lead to sterility) appears to be an essential feature of GnRH action in mammals and birds. In contrast, limited data on reptiles and amphibians indicate that they do not show the same temporal requirements and indeed prolonged or continuous exposure to the peptide may yield the best results in both amphibians (McCreery and Licht, 1983a, b) and reptiles (Phillips et al., 1987).

In amphibians, treatment with GnRH analogs promises to be a highly effective method to induce ovulation (Odum et al., 1983) and sperm release (Licht and Porter, 1987). Most data deal with the use of the peptide for acute release of eggs or sperm (spawning behavior can also be elicited) in animals with mature gonads, and there is little information on whether such treatment would be effective for inducing earlier stages of gonadal development.

There is less information on the practical use of the peptide in reptiles, and results are variable. Alderet et al. (1980) induced sex behavior with GnRH in female anole lizards, but the effect may have been due to direct actions in the brain; there was no evidence of a gonadal response. While GnRH is generally effective when tested on pituitary gonadotropin release *in vitro*, results with *in vivo* injections have been inconsistent. No change in circulating gonadotropins could be demonstrated in the cobra (*Naja naja*) and musk turtle (*Sternotherus oderatus*) (Licht et al., 1984), but Lance et al. (1985) reported a rise in plasma testosterone (T) in alligators on the day after injection of GnRH, and Ciarci et al. (1989) found similar changes in a lizard. Results in green sea turtles (*Chelonia mydas*) were unpredictable (Licht, 1980), even when GnRH was given shortly before the normal preovulatory surge (Licht, unpublished). Perhaps the most encouraging results for use in artificial propagation are those for the green iguana (Phillips and Lasley, 1987; Phillips et al., 1985, 1987). Chronic GnRH treatment of females via implanted minipumps elicited a complete premature ovarian cycle which elicited out of season mating and led to production of viable eggs. In contrast, daily treatment with various GnRH analogs for 15–30 days caused testicular regression and suppressed plasma testosterone in a lacertid lizard, suggesting "down-regulation" of the system (Ciarci et al., 1989).

Pituitary Gonadotropins

The presence of two distinct gonadotropins that chemically resemble mammalian FSH and LH have been identified in several anuran (e.g., frogs, toads) and urodele amphibians (reviewed in Licht, 1979); thus a dual gonadotropin system is likely a common feature of Amphibia. Moreover, the actions of the hormones parallel those classically associated with the corresponding molecules in mammals. However, species-specificity in hormone action may severely limit the use of heterologous hormones in amphibians. For example, while some well studied frogs like those in the genus *Xenopus* respond to LH of mammalian origin (or the related human chorionic gonadotropin), not all species of gonadotropin are equally effective, and other frogs, like ranids, respond poorly if at all (Licht, 1979; Licht and Papkoff, 1976). It is not even clear whether amphibian hormones would be fully effective in other amphibians. Moreover, not all mammalian hormones are equally effective within a single amphibian like *Xenopus* (Licht and Papkoff, 1976). These difficulties tend to limit the practicality of using commercially available gonadotropins for use in hormone therapy.

The situation vis-à-vis gonadotropins in reptiles may be even more complex than in amphibians. Reptiles may differ from all other tetrapods in terms of both the nature of their gonadotropins and the specific actions of the hormones on the gonads. Fractionation studies on pituitaries of several turtles, including the endangered green sea turtle (Licht and Papkoff, 1985), and the alligator (*Alligator mississippiensis*) (Licht et al., 1976), demonstrated the presence of chemically distinct FSH- and LH-type gonadotropins. However, in similar studies on representatives of five snake families only a single gonadotropin (with both FSH and LH-like properties) could be isolated (Licht et al., 1979a). Moreover, the presence of two distinct gonadotropins in chelonians (turtles and tortoises) and crocodilians does not necessarily imply similarity in physiological action to the mammalian counterparts. In particular, FSH is typically the most potent for eliciting ovulation and gonadal steroid secretion, events normally controlled by LH in mammals (and other tetrapods). As in amphibians, species specificity in hormone action may limit the use of the most available hormones. For example, mammalian LH, the most readily available form, is conspicuously inactive in reptiles compared with LH molecules derived from other species (Licht, 1979).

Use of Gonadotropins in Reproductive Therapy. Suggestions for the potential application of gonadotropins for induction of reproductive activity come from a wealth of physiological studies on their basic actions in amphibians and reptiles. While LH is required for inducing steroid secretion in males and ovulation in female amphibians, the FSH molecule appears to act as a "complete" gonadotropin in both sexes of reptiles and little additional benefit is derived from LH (Licht, 1979). Lizards respond rapidly to gonadotropin with production of sperm and eggs, but other reptiles, especially turtles, respond relatively slowly and complete gonadal cycles have not been induced (Licht, 1972).

Prolonged treatment of young green sea turtles with the long-lasting mammalian pregnant mare serum gonadotropin has only marginal effects on spermatogenesis (Owens, 1976). In addition to problems with the type and species of hormone, special problems may exist in terms of dosage. In particular, studies in female lizards (*Anolis carolinensis*) indicate that excessive amounts of FSH block ovulation and lead to production of multiple clutches within the ovary (e.g., Licht, 1970). Gonadotropin responses in reptiles are highly temperature dependent, and if the animals are not sufficiently warm, even prolonged treatment may have no measurable effect (e.g., Licht, 1975). Before undertaking gonadotropin therapy using mammalian hormones in long-lived species, the possibility of detrimental long-term effects should be considered because of the antigenicity of heterologous hormones. Owens *et al.* (1979) showed that sea turtles developed antibody titers to mammalian growth hormone.

Gonadal Sex Steroids

The major gonadal sex steroids in amphibians and reptiles are similar to those in mammals: testosterone, estradiol-17B (E_2) and progesterone (PRO) predominate in reptiles, and 5α-dihydrotestosterone (DHT) is often more important than T in amphibians. Commercially available steroids can be conveniently used in reptiles and amphibians, and data taken from mammals offer a useful guide to their potential action in reptiles. However, reptiles and amphibians may differ conspicuously from one another and from mammals in the circulating levels of sex steroids, and such variation must be taken into account in designing hormone therapy regimes. Plasma estrogen and androgen are commonly much higher (often by more than an order of magnitude) than those normally encountered in mammals. Males and females of a species typically differ in maximal levels of each steroid, and the difference in plasma T between males and females has been used to help identify the sex of immature sea turtles which are otherwise difficult to sex externally (Owens et al., 1979; Wibbels et al., 1987a). Given the efficacy of gonadotropins, especially FSH, in inducing steroid secretion, an injection of hormone would likely facilitate the sexing process (Owens, 1976). However, many female reptiles and amphibians may have higher levels of androgen than males of other or even the same species. Most notably, female bullfrogs (*Rana catesbeiana*) exhibit levels of plasma T that are many times higher than the maximum in males. In this and several other amphibian species, a high plasma DHT/T ratio, rather than high T characterizes the male (Muller, 1977).

Extensive work has been done on the effects of steroids on reptilian and amphibian morphology and physiology. In particular, steroid treatments have been used to induce precocial development of gonaducts, sexual characteristics (Norris, 1987) and sexual behaviors, including attractiveness and receptivity in squamates and chelonians (see reviews by Fox, 1977; Crews and Silver, 1985; Cooper et al.,1986; Moore, 1987). The role of steroids in sex behavior in amphibians is less clear (Crews and Silver, 1985; Moore, 1987). While androgens generally stimulate male-like properties and estrogen the female-like condition, each steroid may have anomalous actions (Norris, 1987). Concerning endangered species, Owens (1976) showed that both T and E_2 elicit precocial sexual changes in immature green sea turtles. Unfortunately, while such therapy may produce dramatic effects, it is not clear that it can be used safely to accomplish fertile breeding. In particular, the long-term effects have not been fully assessed and caution must be exercised because of the feedback actions on the hypothalamo-pituitary axis.

Reproductive Cycles

General Patterns of Reproductive Seasonality

Whether reproduction is seasonal and how many clutches can be produced in a season, and, if seasonal, whether the cycling is obligatory or facultative are all obviously important for attempts at captive breeding. A review of the literature on reptiles and amphibians reveals that some seasonality in reproductive activity is probably the rule in nature, even in many tropical areas (Licht, 1984). However, there are many degrees of seasonality. Some species, for example, only exhibit changes in the intensity of breeding, while others undergo periods of complete quiescence. In other cases, individuals may breed only once per year, but the population breeds year-round.

Surprisingly, few generalizations can be made, even for closely sympatric species (e.g., Gorman et al., 1981). Some reptiles, particularly the large turtles and crocodilians or more northern species (e.g., vipers), may not breed annually but rather at intervals of 2–3 years (e.g., Fitch, 1970; Moll, 1979; Licht, 1984; Lance, 1989). This phenomenon may also occur in amphibians (e.g., Houck, 1977). There is scant evidence to support the view that such long-term cycles are obligatory, rather their basis may reside in temperature-limited rates of development in the case of northern species and in nutritional constraints in those producing clutches representing large energy investments. Well nourished captive-reared animals may show more frequent breeding, or even larger clutches, than the same species in nature (Wood and Wood, 1980; Lance, 1989).

Differences in the timing of natural seasonal cycles appear related to both the phylogeny and distribution of the species. For example, cycles in temperate lizards are different from those of snakes and turtles. In lizards, spermatogenesis and ovarian maturation are relatively synchronized (see St. Girons, 1982; Angelini and Ghiara, 1984; and Licht, 1984, for examples). The ovarian and testicular cycles are considered to be associated (Crews and Moore, 1986) when gonadal activity increases immediately prior to mating. Reproductive activation typically occurs in the spring and early summer, although some viviparous lizards show fall breeding.

The implication for captive breeding is that both sexes must be brought into breeding condition simultaneously, and it is likely that both will be stimulated by similar environmental conditions (e.g., increasing temperatures and photoperiod). Crocodilians tend to exhibit similar synchrony between the two sexes (Lance, 1989).

Anuran amphibians usually have associated cycles but many urodeles with internal fertilization rely on sperm storage in females. In many amphibians, the testes may contain sperm for much of the year while the ovary undergoes pronounced cycles (Dwellman and Trueb, 1986; Whittier and Crews, 1987); consequently, the main effort for captive breeding will be on inducing ovarian recrudescence.

In contrast to this rather simple synchronization between the testicular and ovarian cycles in lizards, temperate-zone snakes and turtles exhibit a striking asynchrony between the sexes—the spermatogenic and ovarian cycles are seasonally dissociated (Moll, 1979; St. Girons, 1982; Licht, 1984; Whittier and Crews, 1987). The ovary is maximally active and ovulation occurs in spring as in lizards, but testes do not attain peak activity until many months later, in late summer or fall. Testes are fully regressed when females are ovulating. The sperm must either be stored in the male (in epididymides and vas deferens) until mating in the spring, or mating may occur in fall (when the ovary may be inactive) with sperm storage in the female tract until the following ovulatory season (see especially Gist and Jones, 1987). An intermediate condition may occur in north-temperate species when the normal fall spermatogenic cycle is interrupted by winter hibernation, causing completion of spermiogenesis to be delayed until spring (e.g., Nilson, 1980; Licht, 1984).

A dissociation between the two sexual cycles has several implications for establishing a breeding program. First, it implies that the two sexes may have different environmental requirements for gamete production and indeed limited experimental evidence for turtles supports this prediction (see below). Secondly, it complicates decisions as to when attempts to elicit mating should be undertaken. This may be phrased in terms of whether mating is dependent on when the male is producing fresh sperm or when the female is about to ovulate. This question is relevant whether natural breeding or artificial insemination is to be practiced. A brief review of normal mating periods suggests that mating should be attempted at several times during the year.

Preservation of sperm and artificial insemination might be especially important in species with dissociated cycles. Limited data are available for reptiles, but some success in obtaining sperm for insemination has been reported for snakes (Murphy and Collins, 1980) and alligators (Larsen et al., 1984); the alligator study also describes semen extenders.

There is still uncertainty about when mating normally occurs in species with dissociated cycles. It has long been presumed that snakes and turtles mated in spring (i.e., based on sperm stored in epididymides when testes are otherwise regressed). However, there is now strong evidence that many turtles and snakes thought to have dissociated cycles may mate over extended periods, and that a fall as well as spring peak in mating may occur. Further, behavioral studies in captive musk turtles (*Sternotherus odoratus*), combined with cloacal lavages of wild animals, reveal that the major period of mating is undoubtedly in the fall (Mendonca and Licht, 1986a; Mendonca, 1987b).

Similarly, even in snakes known for dramatic spring mating activity following emergence from hibernation (e.g., the garter snake, *Thamnophis sirtalis*), evidence from cloacal inspections indicate that the vast majority of females are probably inseminated before entering the hibernacula in fall (Whittier and Crews, 1986), and in European vipers (*Vipera berus*) with conspicuous spring mating, extended or secondary fall mating is common in many parts of the range (St. Girons, 1982).

The basic dichotomy between temperate-zone lizards and crocodilians vs. snakes and turtles probably breaks down to a large extent in tropical fauna. Limited information on testicular activity suggests that both free-living and farm-reared green turtles undergo recrudescence in spring and mating activity is concentrated in this season (Licht et al., 1979b; Wood and Wood, 1980). Likewise, in nature, subtropical/tropical snakes may show a more associated pattern than do temperate species (reviewed in Licht, 1984), but no simple generalization about the extent of seasonality in tropical species is possible because species from the same area may exhibit distinctive patterns (Gorman et al., 1981).

Hormonal Cycles

Until recently, the majority of reproductive studies have relied largely on gross assessment of breeding condition (e.g., general appearance [histology, morphometrics] of the gonads or reproductive behavior per se). The disadvantage of these methods is that it is often unclear where problems exist when the breeding effort is unsuccessful, and how to correct the problems. Lately, there has been an increasing effort to study the endocrine correlates of reproduction in reptiles and amphibians. Changes in endocrine status have the advantage of allowing more refined predictions to be made about the progress of reproductive development, and may suggest mechanisms for explaining failures or for intervention to improve reproductive performance. The use of such hormonal indices requires a thorough understanding of the normal pattern of endocrine events associated with successful reproduction. It may be necessary to obtain such normative data from free-living populations in order to assess the effects of captivity. Seasonal endocrine cycles have recently been described in a variety of reptiles and amphibians, but most data deal with sex steroids and little information is available on GnRH or gonadotropins. Nevertheless, some important principles emerge. Much of this literature is reviewed in Duvall et al. (1984), Lance (1984, 1989), and Licht (1984).

Sex Steroids in Males. Male reptiles and amphibians exhibit pronounced annual cycles in circulating androgen, but the seasonal timing of these cycles and their relation to other gonadal activities and to sexual behavior is inconsistent. In lizards, there is invariably a good correlation between peak androgen levels and maximal testicular development (based on size and spermatogenic condition) (Duvall et al., 1984; Lance, 1984; Licht, 1984). Data for alligators suggest that a similar condition exists for the crocodilians (Lance, 1989), but the situation may be more complex for some snakes and turtles due to the "dissociated" nature of the spermatogenic and steroid activities.

Direct measurements of plasma T indicates that temperate-zone turtles show a peak coincident with autumnal testicular recrudescence (McPherson and Marion, 1981; Kuchling, 1982; Licht et al., 1985; Mendonca and Licht, 1986a) and in some cases, a second brief and more transient rise in spring upon emergence from hibernation (Licht et al., 1985). On the other hand, the more tropical sea turtles exhibit only a single spring peak in circulating androgen (Licht et al., 1979b; Wibbels et al., 1987b). In the green turtle, this peak appears to be associated with spring testicular recrudescence (Licht et al., 1979b, 1984). A similar pattern is evident in snakes. Temperate species tend to show two peaks—in spring and fall (e.g., Aldridge, 1979; Nalleau et al., 1987) while more tropical species show a single spring peak (e.g., Bona-Gallo et al. 1980). Male reptiles and amphibians typically show low or nondetectable levels of estrogens, but Ciarcia et al. (1986) have recently reported a rise in E_2 during testicular regression in a lizard. They suggest that this conspicuously elevated E_2 may be responsible for the regression.

In studies on captive sea turtles in which mating activity has been quantified (Wood and Wood, 1980), the single spring peak in plasma T clearly precedes the onset of mating. Plasma T reaches its nadir during the mating season (Licht et al., 1979b). The intensity of individual male mating behavior for wild-caught males correlated with levels of plasma T in the preceding two months. A similar correlation between androgen levels and subsequent mating behavior was also noted for freshly captured musk turtles (Mendonca, 1987b).

Captivity may induce important changes in steroids. In the captive-bred sea turtles on the Cayman Islands, seasonal plasma T profiles appear to closely follow those in wild animals (Licht et al., 1980), but this may not always be the case in reptiles or amphibians. Androgen profiles in captive stinkpot turtles (*Sternotherus oderatus*) paralleled those in nature but at much lower absolute levels (e.g., Mendonca and Licht, 1986a). Moreover, plasma T in reptiles (e.g., turtles, Licht et al., 1985; Mendonca and Licht, 1986a; alligators, Lance and Elsey, 1986) and amphibians (Licht et al., 1983) may respond rapidly to handling, especially during the capture of wild animals. After capture, plasma T levels begin to decline within hours and may remain suppressed for many days in captivity. There is other evidence for a suppression of reproduction related to stress in reptiles (Greenberg and Wingfield, 1987). Consequently, normative data for steroid levels are required for the species in question before levels in captivity can be interpreted.

Male amphibians (urodeles and anurans) also tend to show pronounced seasonal cycles in androgen (e.g., Licht et al., 1983; Mendonca et al., 1984; Polzonetti-Magni et al., 1984; Garnier, 1985a;

Norris et al., 1985; Rastogi et al., 1986; Varriale et al., 1986; Pierantoni et al., 1987). However, the relation between these cycles and sexual behavior is not always clear in keeping with the controversy regarding the role of androgens in amphibian sexual behavior (see Moore, 1987).

Sex Steroids in Females. In female reptiles several sex hormones change in association with the ovarian cycle with parallel increases in E_2 and T mirroring ovarian growth (see reviews in Duvall et al., 1984; Licht, 1984; Whittier and Crews, 1987). In the garter snake rapid changes in E_2 are induced by mating in association with the induction of vitellogenesis (Whittier and Crews, 1987). Anuran and urodele amphibians show similar marked seasonality in these hormones. Pronounced concomitant increases in E_2 and androgen are typically associated with vitellogenesis (see Garnier and Joly, 1980; Specker and Moore, 1980; Licht et al., 1983; Polzonetti-Magni et al., 1984; Cayrol et al., 1985; Garnier, 1985b; Lecouteux et al., 1985; Iela et al., 1986; Pierantioni et al., 1987; Xavier, 1987). The importance of estrogen for induction of hepatic vitellogenesis and for priming the oviducts is well known, but the role of the androgen is less well understood (see Ho, 1987 for a recent review of the endocrinology of vitellogenesis in reptiles and amphibians).

Plasma PRO shows a pronounced surge in association with ovulation, but the change is transient, perhaps lasting only a few hours or days. The most complete temporal data for reptiles are for sea turtles (e.g., Licht et al., 1979b, 1980, 1982) and for amphibians are for bullfrogs *Rana catesbeiana* (Licht et al., 1983; McCreery and Licht, 1983b), but similar transient surges have been inferred from limited data on snakes (e.g., Bona-Gallo et al., 1980) and alligators (Lance, 1989). Thus, while PRO may represent a good indicator of ovulation, it is impractical to use it for this purpose.

Gonadotropins. Gonadotropin levels have been measured in only a few reptiles. In cobras, gonadotropins increased during the vitellogenic period and there was some evidence of a surge around the time of ovulation; similarly, levels rose during testicular growth (Bona-Gallo et al., 1980). In turtles in which a separate FSH and LH have been identified, only the former has been shown to change during the male reproductive cycle. FSH levels peak coincident with peaks of both spring and fall plasma T, but are otherwise usually below measurable levels (Licht et al., 1985). In female turtles, gonadotropins have only been measurable during the ovulatory phase of the cycle; i.e., the periovulatory LH surge (e.g.,

Licht et al., 1979b, 1980, 1982). Because there is a concomitant surge in FSH (Wibbels and Licht, unpublished), it is difficult to attribute ovulation to either hormone.

Direct measurements of amphibian seasonal gonadotropin cycles are known only for the bullfrog. These data confirm the importance of gonadotropins, especially LH for the induction of ovulation. Gonadotropins, like steroids, are sensitive to stress effects and tend to fall precipitously within hours of capture (Licht et al., 1983).

Gonadotropin Releasing Hormone. There are no data on the seasonality of GnRH in reptiles, but several studies indicate that brain levels of this peptide vary seasonally and with stress effects in amphibians (reviewed in Licht and Porter, 1987). From a practical standpoint, it is important to note that seasonal changes in the responsiveness of the pituitary to GnRH may occur. In amphibians, this may be related to feedback effects of steroid hormones, but the basis of this seasonality is less well understood in reptiles.

Environmental Control of Gonadal Cycles

Studies of reproductive activity involving manipulation of environmental conditions provide information on how to induce breeding and address the issue of whether species undergo facultative or obligatory cycling. If normal seasonality is primarily environmentally induced, it may be possible to induce breeding year-round in captivity, at least in some individuals. Year-round breeding, however, may be impossible if cycling results from inherent refractoriness. In fact, even hormone therapy may be ineffective in the latter case, depending on the sites of refractoriness. There is evidence for the entire range of conditions in reptiles and amphibians, including the few endangered species that have been examined (e.g., Ross and Marzec, 1991). Environmental (proximate) factors implicated in controlling the onset and termination of reproduction include temperature, photoperiod, moisture, and social effects. These many aspects of reptilian and amphibian reproductive cycles have been extensively reviewed in recent years (e.g., see Angelini and Ghiara, 1984; Duvall et al., 1984; Licht, 1984; Lofts, 1984; Duellman and Trueb, 1986; Whittier and Crews, 1987), and only the major issues most likely to influence captive propagation are mentioned here.

Temperature has been shown to be a pervasive proximate factor influencing all aspects of reproduction in reptiles and amphibians. It may represent the dominate regulator of both the onset and termination of breeding cycles, or it may interact with other factors such as photoperiod and rainfall to regulate these events. Little or no response to circulating hormones is observed if animals are cooled much below their normally preferred temperature range, while excessive temperatures may cause sterility (e.g., Licht, 1965).

Rising temperatures in spring have been shown experimentally to act as stimuli for the onset or completion of gonadal maturation and breeding in a variety of squamates and chelonians (see reviews mentioned above). Temperatures probably play a similar role in alligators based on environmental correlations and limited manipulations in captivity (Lance, 1989). The delay in spermatogenic development until fall in temperate-zone turtles appears to reflect a requirement for an even more prolonged exposure to high temperatures. Spring spermatogenic recrudescence can be stimulated by exposure to warm temperatures in captivity (Ganzhorn and Licht, 1983; Mendonca and Licht, 1986b). In the turtles, the two sexes may have different thermal requirements, and the same conditions that stimulate the males may be responsible for ovarian regression and cessation of egg production in the females (Ganzhorn and Licht, 1983; Mendonca, 1987a).

While some degree of warming may be required for the onset of breeding, several studies have shown that reptiles may become refractory to further stimulation by either environmental or hormonal manipulations. Temperature frequently plays a major role in controlling and eventually terminating this refractoriness. A prolonged exposure to very low temperatures may be required before renewed gonadal activity commences (see Gavaud and Xavier, 1986). While experimental data remain meager, it has become common practice among snake breeders to expose animals to some winter cooling in order to stimulate renewed mating activity (refer to Reptile Symposium on Captive Propagation and Husbandry—see the introduction to this chapter). This method has even been effective for breeding tropical pythons and boids (Ross and Marzec, 1991). A notable example, for which experimental data are available, is seen in the courtship and mating behavior of the male northern garter snake *T. sirtalis parietalis* (see Whittier and Crews, 1987; Whittier et al., 1987). Species showing such refractoriness presumably have obligatory reproductive cycling and could not be made to breed continuously under any circumstances in the laboratory.

Based on experimental evidence, one is led to the conclusion that photoperiod plays a surprisingly small role in the regulation of reptilian breeding cycles (see review by Licht, 1984 for squamates and Mendonca and Licht, 1986b; Mendonca, 1987a for turtles). Some breeders have reported that the use of regimented photoperiods have enabled them to obtain regular breeding cycles in diverse snakes (e.g., Kardon, 1981), but photoperiodism has not been confirmed by controlled experimentation (see Aldridge, 1975; Whittier et al., 1987). Photoperiodic responses have been demonstrated in only a few species of lizards (reviewed by Licht, 1984), and in these cases it seems more likely that short daylengths control gonadal regression rather than long daylengths being required for stimulation; as is more typical in birds. Even this photoperiodism is temperature dependent (Licht, 1973).

Egg production and egg laying may be influenced by moisture or humidity in some lizards (Licht, 1984), but this aspect of the environment has not been thoroughly explored for other reptiles. It is likely to be most important in tropical species because reproductive cycles frequently correlate with wet-dry seasons. In contrast, breeding in many amphibians is clearly linked to rainfall, and breeding behavior of terrestrial species in captivity is often elicited by sprinkling the animals.

Evidence for a social influence on ovarian activity comes largely from the work of Crews and colleagues (see Crews and Silver, 1985). Studies done mostly on lizards have demonstrated that the behavior of males may modulate ovarian development and female condition can influence male behavior. In each case, social conditions may either facilitate or depress gonadal development in the opposite sex. Even in parthenogenetic lizards, females may alternate between typically male and female behavior in a manner that can influence ovarian development in other individuals (Crews and Moore, 1993). Of special interest is the observation that male iguanas kept in the presence of females treated with GnRH showed unseasonal sexual behavior, presumably due to the altered physiological state of the females; overt changes in the behavior of females were not noted (Phillips et al., 1987).

Conclusions

Reptiles and amphibians are not a homogeneous group and few generalizations can be made about their reproductive anatomy and physiology. This review has only touched upon a few of the problems that must be anticipated in future attempts at captive husbandry.

A common theme throughout this chapter is the need for good normative data on the levels of hormones and the seasonal changes in reproductive activity for the species of interest. Without such data interpretation of existing hormone levels and establishment of hormonal therapy or environmental manipulation will be difficult. With a thorough understanding of the relation of endocrine events to reproductive performance, it may be possible to use endocrine manipulation to intervene in the treatment of breeding problems. However, in the case of endangered species, it is particularly important to consider the long-range effects of such intervention, because some treatments that enhance immediate breeding efforts would not be warranted if they ultimately result in sterility.

Acknowledgment

The preparation of this chapter was supported in part by a grant from the National Science Foundation (DCB–8848022).A.

11

Ethological Studies on Reptiles and Amphibians: Lessons for Species Survival Plans

Gordon M. Burghardt and Mark A. Milostan

The reptile house has traditionally been one of the most popular buildings in zoos. Typically it is dark, hot, and humid with illuminated tableaux containing motionless snakes, lizards, turtles, and crocodilians along with a few barely visible or hidden salamanders and frogs. Such a building may also house a few invertebrates and fishes, but the main attraction is typically the large or the highly venomous reptiles ("giants and killers," see also Marcellini and Jenssen, 1988). Recent trends toward more ecological, educational, and multi-species exhibits are beginning to take hold (Olney et al., 1989), but as with other taxa, decisions about what species to exhibit are based on a mix of what the public expects and what interests or challenges curators and zoo directors.

Zoo and university researchers have made great strides in breeding many crocodilians, turtles, lizards, the tuatara, and rare and endangered larger snakes (Gowan, 1989; Olney et al., 1989; Beaman et al., 1990; Boardman and Sibley, 1991). Researchers are also uncovering many aspects of amphibian courtship and mating behavior that facilitate reproduction. Still, given the roughly 10,000 species of amphibians and reptiles, far fewer than 10% have been bred in captivity. The chance or occasional reproduction prevents us from understanding the behavioral and physiological factors underlying such successes.

Other chapters in this volume consider issues of exhibiting, conserving, and breeding reptiles and amphibians in more detail. Behavior research in the zoo environment is treated from several perspectives in Burghardt (1975), Schaff (1984), Kleiman (1985), and Finlay and Maple (1986). Books by Hediger (e.g., 1950) and the National Academy of Sciences (1975) are useful, although with little specifically on amphibians and reptiles (herptiles). Here we will focus on issues that are important in and specific to behavioral herpetology in captivity.

Reptiles will be emphasized both because of where our own knowledge and experience lie, and because better than 90% of all herps exhibited at zoos are reptiles. This is not to say that amphibians are not deserving of much more attention; they may even be more sensitive to human altered environments than reptiles (Harte and Hoffman, 1989; Welsh, 1990; Wyman, 1990a). But their relatively smaller size, often nocturnal and secretive habits, and more complex metamorphic life histories have received less attention. Even with reptiles, however, our coverage will necessarily be selective and brief. The bibliography should help those wanting further information (see also Tryon, 1979; Smith, 1992).

Rationale for Behavioral Studies on Endangered Species in Captivity

Scope of Existing Field Studies

Existing field studies on herptiles are variable in extent, rigor, and conservation import. In the last 30 years herpetologists have regained their historical interest in natural history and are incorporating their fieldwork into current trends in ecology, ethology, and conservation biology. Studies of taxonomy, dietary habits, and reproductive cycles based on collected and preserved specimens were predominant until about 1970. The former are still needed given the chaos of much herptile systematics, but the penchant for collecting hundreds of animals to examine scales, stomachs, and gonads is, we hope, in permanent decline.

Behavioral/ecological field studies are of two major types: intensive, long-term studies on single populations or surveys of many species. The latter may concern the relations among species in a community (e.g., Duellman, 1987) or survey limited aspects of related species such as vocalizations in frogs, dewlap displays in lizards, or feeding habits in snakes (e.g., Carpenter, 1982). Both have an important role to play, although intensive field studies are particularly valuable for both conservation of wild populations and captive breeding programs because of their in-depth coverage of several factors and their longitudinal aspects. For example, only long-term monitoring of green iguana (*Iguana iguana*) hatching success at a communal nest site in Panama revealed that no eggs hatched after an unusually humid "dry" season (Bock, 1984).

A number of up-to-date reviews are available on the biology, ecology, and physiology of amphibians and especially reptiles. These include the entire *Biology of the Reptilia* series (Senior Series editor Carl Gans) consisting (in 1992) of 18 volumes (Gans, 1992). There are also various other volumes such as Dunson (1975), Seigel et al. (1987), Gloyd and Conant (1990), and Campbell and Brodie (1992) on snakes; Greenberg and McLean (1978), Burghardt and Rand (1982), Huey et al. (1983), and Pianka (1988) on lizards; and Duellman and Trueb (1986) on amphibians. Bradshaw (1986) has summarized information on the physiology of desert reptiles. Many chapters in these books are seminal reviews that could not be mentioned individually.

Intensive monographs on single species include the series of autecology reports by Fitch (e.g., 1954, 1956) and colleagues on reptiles such as collared lizards (*Crotaphytus collaris*), eastern garter snakes (*Thamnophis sirtalis*), copperheads (*Agkistrodon contortrix*), five-lined skinks (*Eumeces fasciatus*), and the racer (*Coluber constrictor*). (See Seigel et al., 1984 for a complete Fitch bibliography up to that year). Other species include the lizards *Anolis lineatus* (Rand, 1967), *Sceloporus undulatus* (Blair, 1960), and *Uta stansburiana* (Tinkle, 1967). For turtles there are recent volumes on *Trachemys scripta* (Gibbons, 1990) and *Macroclemys temminckii* (Pritchard, 1989b). The Central American frog (*Physalaemus pustulosus*) is covered by Ryan (1985). Auffenberg (1981, 1988) has written major monographs on the endangered Komodo Island Monitor (*Varanus komodoensis*) and Grey's monitor (*V. olivaceous*), and several iguanines have received similar treatment such as *Sauromalus obesus* (Berry, 1974), *Cyclura carinata* (Iverson, 1979), and on *Iguana iguana* (Rodda, 1992).

Need for Controlled Studies

While adequate field data are critical, captive work is important for establishing and implementing research agendas on breeding, social organization, space requirements, development, diets, and other factors important to captive maintenance and propagation. The herpetological community has made great strides in this area of late.

Sajdak (1983) surveyed three major herpetological journals between 1977 and 1981 for articles involving research in zoos. Of

1,084 papers published on herpetological subjects, only 53 (4.9%) involved animals in zoos. And of these papers, only 30 involved research actually performed at the zoo. Most zoo research papers (70%) dealt with behavior, and exotic species were emphasized (71.4%); the majority involved collaborations, usually between zoo and university personnel.

The pace of research has certainly increased since 1981 (see Olney et al., 1989; Murphy et al., 1994). Zoos are still not the main setting for research on captive herptiles, especially the smaller species that can be maintained in university and research institute settings. Behavioral researchers often prefer to carry out their work in settings less disruptive of systematic study than the crowded, exhibit oriented environment of most zoos. Zoos generally have smaller sample sizes than are needed for more than exploratory studies. Most useful are the breeding colonies many zoos maintain for propagation or release where the majority of individuals are behind the scenes and more readily manipulated. Even feeding studies are often difficult because zoo keepers have set schedules and often understandable, but strict, protocols for feeding and maintenance. For example, many zoos never feed live vertebrate prey and have a policy against doing so for health and other reasons. While this can lead to some interesting research (see O'Connell et al., 1982 discussed below), such restrictions are too often constraining to the basic researcher attempting to understand the typical behavioral repertoire of a species. Research with perceived immediate applied payoffs on breeding, diseases, parasites, and nutrition are understandably more enthusiastically supported by zoos and their staffs.

Academic researchers are also becoming more interested in exotic species (often for conservation reasons) and feel more confident in moving from local common species to rare, unique, delicate, or expensive to maintain animals. Thus, more collaboration among zoo personnel and field and laboratory workers is not only desirable but essential (Murphy and Chiszar, 1989). Guidelines for proper research techniques with herps have been developed recently and, while general, they make some specific recommendations as well as incorporate an empathic and conservation-minded ethos (Joint Herpetological Societies, 1987; Pough, 1991).

Much captive research is done in the field with freshly captured animals, or at field stations where animals can be maintained in enclosures exposed to natural climatic conditions and where appropriate prey or plants are readily available. Studies combining zoo and natural habitat observations are particularly useful, as shown by the study of Schafer et al. (1983) on the correlations among agonistic behavior, shell shape, and ecology in the Galapagos tortoise (*Geochelone elephantopus*). Captive studies have complemented field studies in many ways and often are the only way behavioral data can be accurately collected. This is especially true when comparative information and controlled physiological data are required.

Comparative studies of specific behavior patterns in reptiles are on the rise; e.g., the displays of lizards (e.g., Clarke, 1965; Carpenter, 1967, 1982), snakes (Carpenter, 1977), and turtles (Auffenberg, 1977), vocalization in young crocodilians (Herzog and Burghardt, 1977), interspecific recognition in lizards (e.g., Cooper and Vitt, 1987), foraging and prey immobilization in snakes (e.g., Greene, 1977; O'Connell et al., 1982; Drummond 1983; Chiszar et al., 1985; Milostan, 1989), and chemical prey preferences in specific genera (e.g., *Thamnophis*; Burghardt, 1969) or across families of squamate reptiles (e.g., von Achen and Rakestraw, 1984).

Of the many studies on reproductive physiology and behavior, the extensive ongoing research program on garter snakes (*Thamnophis sirtalis*) by Crews and coworkers is perhaps the most well-known and integrates laboratory and field observation and experimentation (e.g., Crews and Gartska, 1982). Several long-term studies of green iguanas are underway combining both field and laboratory research involving zoos. In Panama, Rand has carried out and collaborated in an extensive program of naturalistic field research that has run for over 25 years (e.g., Rand, 1968). Werner has spearheaded a captive breeding, propagation, and restocking effort in Panama and now in Costa Rica— motivated in part by the fact that green iguanas are a potentially important food resource for human beings (Werner, 1991). This has led to some practical information on inducing nesting in captive females (Werner and Miller, 1984) and on increasing hatching success (Miller, 1987). In Belize and at the San Diego Zoo, Phillips et al. (1987) found that social factors can entrain male hormonal states that induce territorial, fighting, and mating behavior in *Iguana iguana*. Variation in hormone cycles associated with the ontogeny of dominance and social communication have also been investigated (Alberts et al., 1992; Phillips et al., 1993).

Information from both *Thamnophis* and *Iguana* will be important for modeling effective collaboration between zoos and other institutions and integrating field and captive research. But it cannot be emphasized enough that diversity among reptiles (and amphibians) is immense and specific procedures might not be readily transferred even across subspecies. Thus, comparative work remains essential (cf., Crews and Moore, 1986).

With the large economically valuable bullfrog (*Rana catesbeiana*) there has been considerable applied behavioral/ecological research (Culley, 1981; Bury and Whelan, 1984). However, this too has built on basic ethological studies (e.g., Willis et al., 1956; Wiewandt, 1969; Emlen, 1976; Howard, 1978a, b). The National Academy of Sciences (1974) has published a compendium on amphibian breeding that is still useful. Larval social behavior is a topic that also needs to be considered in captive systems (e.g., Wasserzug, 1973; Blaustein and Waldman, 1992). Such knowledge needs to be applied to endangered amphibians.

Functions of Behavioral Research in Captivity

Public Education

Public displays of reptiles and amphibians will only effectively educate if they accommodate the behavioral and psychological needs of herptiles. Meeting the animal's physical needs (e.g., nutrition, temperature, light) will partially satisfy it psychologically (Bowler, 1980). Providing the appropriate environment to allow species-typical behavior patterns to be expressed is perhaps essential for the animals' welfare as well as for edifying the public. Very often, what is lacking are exhibits that stimulate animal activity, and signs that aid visitors in interpreting such behavior.

Most people see little behavior from herps in the zoo except position shifts and occasional feeding in omnivores or herbivores. When herps are properly displayed with accurate natural history and behavioral information, the public can gain much more from their visit than the superficial awe and fear at seeing exotic, often wildly colored, statuesque animals. The green iguana is a case in point. When properly maintained, even in indoor enclosures, a rich and quite active behavioral repertoire is seen (e.g., Burghardt et al., 1986).

Many herps are secretive, nocturnal, or fossorial. Natural habitats are thus not conducive to visitors observing normal behavior or even seeing the animal. Imaginative techniques are needed to overcome these limitations. The use of red light and reversed daynight cycles has become standard in many small mammal houses and could be applied more widely to herps as well. Chiszar et al.

(1987) discovered that red spitting cobras (*Naja mossambica pallida*) would use clear Plexiglas hiding boxes in lieu of dark hiding boxes, although the latter were preferred if the snakes were given a choice. Therefore, it seems apparent that thigmotaxic cues can satisfy the cover-seeking requirements of these snakes; transparent retreats may have a potential use for the public display of cobras and possibly other herps. It is, however, realistic to assume that efforts to better display some species (no matter how well-intended) may be deterred or superseded by husbandry practices that have been proven most effective in maintaining healthy animals and breeding endangered species.

Husbandry

Being familiar with a species is essential for optimizing health and reproduction in captivity. Whenever possible, dietary requirements, home range or territory sizes, and mating systems should be determined through field studies prior to the initiation of captive programs. Huff (1980) points out that certain behavioral patterns may change and indicate readiness to breed (e.g., fasting, irritability). Behavior can also be used as an indication of health, stress, or impending parturition. Some species, for example, may stop feeding prior to parturition (Honegger, 1975). Indeed, green iguana males stop eating during much of the mating season (Dugan, 1982) and then females cease to feed as their body cavities fill up with eggs. Snakes may become more irritable, secretive, or reluctant to eat before ecdysis (skin-shedding), even when the eyes are not cloudy.

But in general, it is not possible to make global statements about behavior as a stress or health indicator. Here, the compilation of ethograms that extensively list and define the natural behaviors of healthy animals can be extremely useful. Captives that fail to perform the most common behavioral repertoire observed in nature or behave in a seemingly aberrant manner, may flag a warning to the critically observant caretaker cognizant of such ethograms. Social stress may develop due to crowding, hierarchy formation, and dominant individuals restricting access of others to resources such as food and perch sites (e.g., Tubbs, 1976, Phillips et al., 1993). Just plain dislike or preferences for specific conspecifics of either sex may also occur (e.g., among green iguanas, Dugan, 1982; Burghardt, pers. obs.). In our captive colony of iguanas raised from wild caught hatchlings for 5 years, one male, when adult, viciously attacked a female, even after a long separation. This appeared inexplicable but could be based on inbreeding avoidance, because the hatchlings had been caught very close to one another in Panama.

Restoration into the Wild

It is becoming a more common conservation practice to relocate animals from less favorable sites to more suitable habitats, or from captive bred populations to the wild (Gipps, 1991). A lively debate on the issue of amphibian and reptile "relocations, repatriations, and translocations" has recently appeared and should be consulted for a fuller treatment (Burke, 1991; Dodd and Seigel, 1991; Reinert, 1991).

Recent work by Berry (1986) has stressed the behavioral implications of such restorations dealing with desert tortoises (*Gopherus agassizii*) (see also Turner, 1986). In addition to identifying appropriate abiotic and ecological factors, site selection for these restorations should take into account the movements and social behavior of this species. Introducing tortoises into areas with a very small resident population may transmit respiratory ailments, disrupt the resident social system through dispersal, passive avoidance, or dominant displacement; juveniles seem most likely to become integrated into social systems (Berry, 1986). Animals intentionally or unintentionally released in areas where they were not historically found may also impact on resident species, as in the brown anole (*Anolis sagrei)* from the Caribbean, which is displacing the native green anole (*Anolis carolinensis*) in many areas of Florida. The same is happening with the introduction of the African clawed frog (*Xenopus laevis*), and bullfrogs in the American southwest (e.g., Moyle, 1973). Other examples are discussed in Case et al., 1992. The effect of the colubrid snake (*Boiga irregularis*) on the birds, lizards, and mammals of Guam will go down as a major conservation nightmare (e.g., Rodda and Fritts, 1992). Long-term tracking of animals is an important part of assessing the success of all reintroductions, and again must be based on a thorough knowledge of behavior, such as homing. Genetic considerations also need to be addressed before introductions.

Mitigation of stress on native populations in human-altered habitats is another concern. After determining seasonal fluctuations in the daily activity of *Thamnophis radix* (an endangered species in Ohio), Dalrymple and Reichenbach (1984) suggested that grass mowing operations (a major source of mortality) near wet areas such as ponds, marshes, and drainage ditches (areas where

T. radix are especially common) could be performed during those daytime periods when these snakes (and other species with similar daily and seasonal activity patterns) are relatively uncommon at the surface. They also suggest management alternatives to limit "road kills" (another major source of mortality that they documented). Siegel (1986) reached comparable conclusions on mitigating mortality on an endangered pigmy rattlesnake (*Sistrurus catenatus*) in Missouri.

There is also some question concerning the effects of long-term captivity on reptiles. Studies that directly test or survey for any detrimental effects caused by captivity are few, but more are needed to examine the scope of this problem. For instance, do rattlesnakes (*Crotalus*) show any diminished capacity to search for food after being fed a diet of dead prey all their life? The practice of feeding dead prey allows for the ingestion of food without strikes, thus precluding the use of strike-induced chemosensory searching (SICS), an innate predatory mechanism well documented within rattlesnakes by David Chiszar and associates. Using Old World or New World Pit vipers (Crotalinae), which had been offered dead rodents for relatively long periods of time (in some cases at least four years), both O'Connell et al. (1982) and Chiszar et al. (1985) reported results that suggest no such degradation in the SICS mechanism. Thus, it appears that, as far as feeding is concerned, long-term captive viperids could be expected to forage normally in the wild because they exhibited no diminished capacity to search for envenomated prey. The effects of captive rearing on non-native diets for the ability of released animals to locate, ingest, and process food is an area that needs urgent work for all captive release programs (Burghardt 1978; Murphy and Chiszar, 1989; Box, 1991).

Methods of Research in Captivity

Identification and Marking Techniques

Standard reviews of marking methods are found in Ferner (1979). Rodda et al. (1988) have compared various marking methods for iguanas in the field and have also documented how capture can lead to unexpected changes in behavior. Marking methods, therefore, are not necessarily benign, even when they do not physically harm or overtly stress the animal, or affect survival in the wild or captivity. The herpetological guidelines for field research present an updated view that takes into account ethical and welfare issues (Joint Herpetological Societies, 1987). Marking methods that disfigure the animal even if temporarily, such as large painted numbers, are not acceptable in zoo exhibits, nor are methods that maim the animal, such as cutting off toes. Use of implanted transponders, small machine readable microchips, is a newer and broadly applicable method for both field and captive studies.

Data Collection Techniques

Lehner (1979), Bakeman and Gottman (1986), and Martin and Bateson (1986) provide useful discussions of general issues including observation, experimental design, sampling, reliability, and sequential analysis. The study of herp behavior necessitates the full range of data recording, sampling, and analytic techniques, including check lists, film, video and audio recording, and monitoring of physiological and hormonal status, often enhanced with computers. Day length, temperature, moisture, rainfall, humidity, and other physical parameters can be critical to herp behavior, and must be measured in the wild and controlled in captivity. Seasonal variation in these factors are also important, for many subtle and minor modifications in captivity have led to feeding, reproduction, and survival of young that previously were impossible. Excellent examples of iguanid lizard descriptive studies are those by Greenberg (1977) and Jenssen (1970). Tryon (1980) gives a fine example of the detailed qualitative observations possible under zoo conditions with an endangered dwarf crocodile (*Osteolaemus tetraspis*).

Problems of Research in Captivity

Research on captive animals is under scrutiny in many quarters, and zoo research is no exception (Hutchins and Fascione, 1991). Working with animals that are little understood can often lead to illness and death due merely to inadequate maintenance procedures irrespective of any treatment conditions. This situation is thus different from research on well-known laboratory and domesticated species. Captive reptiles are often fed food not typical for them in the wild, and this can lead to malnutrition or, conversely, obesity, as well as affecting behavior and its development. Herbivorous green iguanas, for example, are often fed dog food in captivity, thus receiving far more protein and far less fiber than in the wild. It is interesting to note that this feeding regimen occurs in an environment that encourages less activity and energy expenditure than the wild. Problems associated with excess protein are summarized in Allen et al. (1990). Courtship and other displays generally appear normal in topography when captive and field observations are available for comparison. Carpenter (1980), however, cautions that mixing species may often lead to aberrant or misdirected communicatory behavior. A major problem in captive behavior research is just inducing and appreciating the richness of behavior that herps possess.

Environmental Factors

The behavior of herps in captivity may vary in several ways from that seen in the field. When population density is increased, social systems may be more hierarchical than territorial. Subordinate individuals may not be able to escape thereby causing more fights, injuries, and deaths than might occur in the field. Solutions may include providing refuges, structural complexity, and even biasing sex ratios toward females.

Honegger (1975) has documented the importance of various environmental factors that affect reproductive behavior in reptiles, and his categories and some of his examples will be used in this chapter (see Honegger, 1975, for more details). All these factors can also affect other categories of behavior.

Space. In order to successfully maintain and breed large lizard species (e.g., monitors, *Varanus*; rhinoceros iguanas (*Cyclura cornuta*) or other members of the genus *Cyclura*), it is vital that ample space, refuges, and display perches be provided when appropriate. This allows individuals of the group to retreat during encounters, and may encourage their full range of natural behaviors. Some monitors need much larger than normal space when performing pre-mating and mating activities.

Temperature. Improper temperatures cause specimens to feed irregularly or insufficiently. Such nutritional deficits can indirectly affect reproduction because the physiology of the animals may be altered. Enclosures should be heated properly to conform with daily and seasonal variation. For instance, the successful captive breeding of Mediterranean tortoises (*Testudo graeca libera*, *Testudo hermanni hermanni*, *Testudo hermanni robertmertensi*, and *Testudo marginata*) is enhanced when open-air enclosures are used during warm weather and temperature-controlled rooms are utilized during unfavorable weather conditions. Crews and Gartska (1982) maintain that the increase in temperature in the springtime triggers mating behavior in Canadian red-sided garter snakes (*Thamnophis sirtalis parietalis*). Males must be maintained at a temperature of less than 10°C for at least seven weeks if they are to show mating behavior when subsequently exposed to higher temperatures. Ideally, some sort of thermal gradient should be provided to allow animals to select their thermal preferences. Too great of a temperature variation has been implicated in the failure of many radiated tortoises (*Testudo radiata*) to reproduce in zoos, but free choice of even extreme temperatures may be beneficial (e.g., behaviorally induced fever in lizards, Kluger et al., 1975).

Light. Many reptile species are nocturnal, whereas others are diurnal. Nocturnal species may not reproduce unless darkness is provided. The type of lighting provided is also important. Ultraviolet (UV) light is critical for the proper growth and development of many reptiles (e.g., Kauffeld, 1969), especially diurnal heliotropic lizards. In fact, outdoor enclosures with retreat areas may be preferred for such species when practical. In our experience with rearing green iguanas in artificial light, we found that several hours of intense UV light was essential daily. Without it animals usually developed irreversible symptoms of the shakes, loss of body tone, and other debilitating effects associated with calcium deficiency. Commercial fluorescent lights such as Vitalites were not sufficient, and should be supplemented with direct UV. Gehrmann (1987) provides a useful comparison of UV sources. UV light also seems to stimulate aggressive and investigatory behavior in many species (Moehn, 1974; Alberts, 1989). On the other hand, forest dwelling, fossorial, and nocturnal reptiles may not need UV radiation and may even be harmed by it. Pawley (1969) noted that sensitive-skinned snakes such as *Drymarchon, Spilotes,* and *Dendroaspis* do not do well if exposed to even moderate to small amounts of UV.

Relative Humidity. Many crocodiles, amphibians, and turtles both in captivity and in the wild display increased activities when it rains. For many snakes in captivity, however, chronic high humidity or overly wet substrates lead to skin lesions and fungal problems. This is often a problem for snakes kept on paper, wood, or other substrates on which spilled water bowls can create soggy environments. Thus, water bowls that are heavy and stable are necessary. They should only be partially filled so that when the snake enters the bowl completely it does not displace most of the water.

Food. The prevailing view that young reptiles are but miniature adults (see discussion in Burghardt, 1978, 1988) leads to the general assumption that the same food types are appropriate throughout life if adjusted for size. This is probably not always the case. In the wild, young red-eared turtles (*Trachemys scripta*) have been shown to be initially carnivorous, but later to become primarily herbivorous (Moll and Legler, 1971), and this is true of other freshwater turtles and perhaps some herbivorous lizards (e.g., some ctenosaurs). Seasonal shifts in diet are probably common in many temperate snakes, especially those living on amphibians. Invertebrate prey populations fluctuate dramatically and offer predators shifting nutrients and caloric densities. Such shifts may be themselves important, both nutritionally and psychologically. To go through life on the exact same diet, even if properly "balanced" nutritionally, may lead to a kind of "boredom," even in reptiles, especially for dietary generalists. At the very least, the animal is deprived of the opportunity to engage in the diverse repertoire of feeding behavior it has the mechanisms to perform, as well as the opportunity to perfect skills (Burghardt, 1978).

Furthermore, even in neonatal animals, experience as well as growth in size can lead to dietary preference shifts (review in Burghardt, 1978; see also Mushinsky and Lotz, 1980). Conversely, even neonates from the same litter may have different chemical food cue (Burghardt, 1975) and feeding (Arnold, 1977; Burghardt, 1990) preferences. The importance of chemical cues in inducing many reptiles, especially snakes, to eat, has led to the development of simple but effective methods that should be considered whenever a little known species is kept in captivity (Weldon et al., 1994).

Observation

It is important to emphasize that the process of observation itself may interfere with ongoing behavior as shown in collared lizards (*Crotaphytus collaris*) observed with or without a one-way mirror (Sugarman and Hacker, 1980). More subtle effects can also be expected as repeated observation can lead to the enhancement of some behavior patterns and the inhibition of others (Jordan and Burghardt, 1986). Most reptiles become accustomed to human presence to some extent, and will carry on feeding, breeding, and other activities. But many reptiles remain wary and nervous in captivity even after many months or years. Some may be unwilling to feed or reproduce under captive conditions. Most "difficult" species fall under this category. Often, as noted below, animals reared from neonates in captivity adjust much better than wild-caught adults. After taking into account the role of physical and social needs temperament is probably the major, and often most difficult, problem faced in keeping "difficult" species in captivity.

Other Factors

Proper nesting facilities (substratum) should be provided so that eggs are laid in substrate of the proper moisture and are not consumed or crushed by others. Tegus (*Tupinambis spp.*) and some monitors typically lay eggs inside termite mounds. How critical are such interspecific relationships? Additionally, separation and reintroduction of individuals may be necessary to induce breeding in some species. Antipredator responses should also be considered (see recent comprehensive review by Greene, 1987).

Huff (1980) points out that long-term captive reptiles are susceptible to a condition he calls "captive stagnancy," characterized by the animals becoming so accustomed to routine that they become lazy, lethargic, and generally inactive and breed poorly. Although variations in routine are usually prescribed for "higher animals," it may well be that Huff's observations also point to more sensitive consideration of variation, novelty, and stimulation in captive reptiles. Stress is an area where close observation of individual animals and knowledge of normal behavior is essential. But assessments of stress must be done on the basis of careful study, not just anthropomorphic intuition. The ability of reptiles to learn has been generally unappreciated and many experimental studies with particular relevance to spatial and perceptual cues are reviewed by Burghardt (1977).

Hand Rearing, Taming, and Natural Behavior

It might be thought that herps, unlike many birds and mammals, should be relatively impervious to effects of early experience on later behavior, such as sexual imprinting. Although this may be true for sexual behavior, the critical experiments have yet to be done. However, with diet there is anecdotal and experimental

(Arnold, 1978; Burghardt, 1978, Mushinsky and Lotz, 1980) data for experiential effects. Many species become less aggressive to humans in captivity, but this is hard to generalize across or within species. Recent work has shown that in the highly defensive Mexican garter snake (*Thamnophis melanogaster*), individual and litter differences in striking were stable over the first year of life, but that the amount of keeper attention was related to the nature and amount of the behavior (Herzog and Burghardt, 1988; Herzog et al., 1989).

Wild caught green iguanas rarely make good captives in confined surroundings or when frequently exposed to people. Iguanas captured shortly after birth, however, and properly fed and housed, adapt well to captive conditions and, in our lab, carried out normal feeding, display, courtship, and fighting behaviors just a meter or two from people, and allowed people to approach, groom, feed, and spray them with water. Although being picked up and held was usually not very acceptable, some individuals would approach and climb onto caregivers. Our iguanas were weighed and measured once a month for the first 5 years of life. They lived in a succession of cages and rooms, all artificially heated and lit, and then were sent to the San Diego Zoo where they were released into a 264 m² outdoor exhibit area with trees and other amenities. They set up territories and adjusted remarkably well (Phillips, personal comm., 1988; Pratt et al., 1992). This shows that their basic behavioral repertoire was relatively unaffected. Whether other species will react in this way needs study.

Social Factors that Influence Conservation in Captivity

Green iguanas are a highly social and gregarious species, even as neonates (Burghardt, 1988). Many other herps are relatively solitary most of the time except for breeding (e.g., monitor lizards, many snakes, some salamanders). It would seem that these animals may be even less affected by early experience and the lack of being with conspecifics during nonreproductive seasons. However, the social systems of supposed solitary species may also be underestimated. Tortoises, crocodilians, many lizards, and the tuatara (*Sphenodon punctatus*) (Gans et al., 1984) have dominance or territorial systems in the wild. Carpenter (1984) has reviewed the evidence for dominance in the apparently "nonsocial" snakes and found that groups in captivity do establish hierarchies (see also Barker et al., 1979). Still in question, however, is whether or not such observations are artifacts of captivity. Field observations of marked individuals or studies of snakes in large naturalistic enclosures are needed. Snakes do, however, often aggregate outside of the breeding and hibernation periods, especially juveniles.

Carpenter (1980) has surveyed the various channels relevant to communication and reproductive success in the different reptile groups (Testudinata, Crocodilia, Lacertilia, Serpentes). He also reviewed the use of these channels by various reptiles as they go through the progressive sequence of courtship and mating. He pointed out the differing importance of several modalities, such as light, sound, chemical cues, and physical contact. More than one channel is usually used. Duvall et al. (1987) have documented composite visual and chemical communication via fecal piles in lizards. Various signals are used for recognition of species, sex, social status, and sexual readiness (Carpenter, 1980). Dominance rank or holding a territory may determine if a male will court as well as to whom a female may submit or with whom she will mate. Further, the amount of space available and the individual animal's familiarity with it may play a role, as well the presence of other individuals. The careful analysis of communication may be the key to fine-tuning the breeding of many species in the field as well in captivity as we go beyond the pioneering work on the role of light, temperature, nutrition, and space.

With the toad *Bufo calmita* in Britain, Banks and Beebee (1986) have shown that careful study of calling and spawning behavior in relation to weather patterns is useful in predicting reproductive activity in this amphibian that breeds over many months. Such information can be used in management even if direct observation is not practical.

Little experimental work has been done on mixed species groups in captivity, although many herps kept together originated in different populations. Mixed species groups are common in zoo exhibits including freshwater turtles, sea turtles with fish and invertebrates in large aquariums, and similar sized desert lizards. The popular trend towards regional habitat groupings accentuates the need for careful study; the old "let's just see what happens" approach is no longer appropriate with rare, valuable, and endangered species. However, disease transmission, food perch or retreat site competition, and interspecific predation all deter this approach.

Misdirected sign stimuli involved in courtship may lead to homo-sexual pairings (Carpenter, 1980), which may, however, not be com-pletely abnormal (e.g., sexual mimicry, Weldon and Burghardt, 1984).

Conclusions

Knowledge gained from common species can often be judiciously extended to threatened ones, be it procedures for inducing breed-ing, incubating eggs, feeding neonates, structuring habitat and so-cial groups, or providing proper temperature and lighting. Thus, work on nonendangered species should precede possible stress and other risks to rare forms whenever possible.

It is likely that the use of reptiles and amphibians in basic biomedical research will increase as ethical issues are raised over certain kinds of work with birds and mammals (Greenberg et al., 1989). This situation will create opportunities as well as conun-drums for zoos. We need much more behavioral and psychological information about the potential of herps to be bored, to suffer, to need various kinds of stimulation for optimal captive performance, and so on. Our anthropomorphic tendency to decide these issues by mammalian standards may not suffice; failure to do so may com-promise support for needed conservation efforts of captive reptiles and amphibians. Consider that the communicatory repertoire of reptiles has been shaped by a social system in which communica-tion with parents is rare (except for crocodilians), and bonding and empathy between human and reptile (let alone amphibian) is also rare compared to endotherms (Bowers and Burghardt, 1992). Zoos must themselves become more ardent in their support of herp ex-hibits, education, conservation, and research. There are thus nu-merous important challenges for the future success of behavioral research on exotic reptiles and amphibians.

Acknowledgments

Preparation of this paper was supported in part by NSF research grant BNS–8709629 and BNS–91–11387. We thank A. Alberts, P. Andreadis, D. Chiszar, J. Demarest, B. Durrant, A. C. Echternacht, E. Gibbons, J. Gittleman, D. Layne, J. Phillips, and P. Weldon for helpful comments on earlier drafts.

12

Captive Design for Reptiles and Amphibians

Janice J. Perry-Richardson and Craig S. Ivanyi

Reptiles, primarily snakes and crocodiles, have been kept in captivity since the days of ancient Egypt. Even venomous species, such as the cobra (*Naja haje*), were considered sacred and welcomed into the home. During the middle ages in Europe, when travels to distant countries became commonplace, royalty began assembling menageries of exotic animals. These collections eventually led to comparative studies of animal anatomy (Bodson, 1984).

The first American reptile facility opened at the Philadelphia Zoological Garden in 1874 (Conant, 1980). At this time, no attempt was made to simulate the animal's natural habitat. Exhibit enclosures were sparsely decorated with a gravel substrate, a water bowl and perhaps a branch. Tropical species were housed the same as desert forms, regardless of their behavioral or physiological needs (Bowler, 1980). Most institutions devoted little space, time, or money to amphibians. Temperature and humidity control was virtually impossible due to the primitiveness of the animal facilities (Conant, 1971). The majority of animals survived a year or two and were readily replaced from the wild. When breedings did occur, it was by chance, not by plan. Veterinary care of reptiles and amphibians was in its infancy, and most zoo veterinarians had minimal experience with herpetofauna. Exhibit graphics presented little information beyond an animal's name, where it was from, and perhaps its feeding habits. A few zoos even allowed public participation in the force feeding of large pythons, in viewing the removal of stuck eye caps from king cobras, and even venomous snake milking (Conant, 1980).

Exhibitry, husbandry, and educational interpretation of reptiles and amphibians have improved considerably since the early
days. Today zoos exhibit a variety of reptiles and amphibians in
naturalistic enclosures. Emphasis is placed on the physiological
and behavioral needs of each species. Public institutions now provide educational, participatory experiences such as HERPlab at the
National Zoo (White and Marcellini, 1986) and "the other side" at
the Dallas Zoo (Murphy and Mitchell, 1989). Additionally, zoos are
becoming more involved in research and conservation of threatened
wildlife. For example, ongoing amphibian studies may help determine the degree of impact man is having on the natural world
(Barinaga, 1990; Tyler, 1991).

Economics of Captive Design

Although this book specifically addresses endangered species in
captivity, design aspects for endangered species do not differ greatly
from nonendangered forms. Therefore, this chapter discusses design as it pertains to all reptiles and amphibians.

The cost of designing, building, and maintaining an herpetological facility depends upon many factors; however, a gross estimate of total cost can vary from a few to several million dollars.
For example, a 10,000 square foot reptile facility built in New
Orleans in 1987, cost $2 million, the same facility constructed else-
where may easily have been double that price (Bowler, pers. comm.).

Some of the factors affecting facility costs are: the number of
specimens, which species are selected, and the mission of the organization (i.e., education, conservation, research, reproduction, entertainment). If it is a public facility, species selection depends
upon the educational focus of the institution. Many endangered or
threatened forms are difficult and costly to obtain legally from the
wild. Therefore, captive-bred specimens should be obtained whenever possible. However, this may prove unsatisfactory if the genetic
constitution of the animals is unknown. If obtained from commercial sources, it may be difficult to verify background information or
legal status of animals. Also, recent imports may arrive in poor
condition and/or have been exposed to diseases or parasites.

Ideally, management and propagation protocols should be established by working with similar, nonendangered animals from
healthy, stable populations or local species. Experience gained
through working with nonthreatened species will help determine

the parameters necessary for effective management and propagation of threatened or endangered forms. If animals are to be housed outdoors year round, select species which are adapted to the prevailing climatic conditions.

In designing a building, provide for animal needs, keeper and animal safety, and keeper work efficiency. Ideally, design several separate rooms, with means of regulating temperature, humidity, as well as photoperiod. Insulate facilities for the control of heat, humidity, and ambient sound levels. Allow no cross-contamination of air between rooms and utilize separate air systems for public areas, although these systems can be very expensive. A heating, ventilation, and air conditioning system for a 10,000 square foot facility can easily cost $130,000 (Bowler, pers. comm). Provide tepid (27°C) water via hose bibs, sinks, and for enclosures with large permanent pools or built-in water bowls, such as those needed for aquatic turtles, giant snakes, and crocodilians. Construct floors, walls, and ceilings with materials which are waterproof to facilitate cleaning and disinfection. Utilize durable materials such as: sealed wood, metal, fiberglass, and heavy reinforced plastic in the fabrication of shelving and counters. Numerous electrical outlets fitted with Ground Fault Interrupters (GFI) are necessary. Additionally, fire and security alarms may be desirable. Rooms that house amphibians may be unsuitable for other vertebrates due to humidity requirements. Aquatic amphibian facilities outlined by Nace (1968) and Cullum and Justus (1973) are suitable for smaller operations if scaled down in size.

Service areas which are spacious enough to allow keepers ample room to move around, carry tools on a cart, or move out of the way of an escaped animal are a necessity. "Snake-proof" all areas so escapees are easily located, contained, and retrieved. This includes putting wire mesh over air vents and floor drains, as well as caulking pipes, cracks, and crevices. Design at least two lockable doors between animals and the outside or public areas. Weatherstrip all doors to prevent animals going from one portion of the building to another. A backup generator is recommended for powering air systems, emergency lighting, food storage coolers, and the snake bite alarm, in case of power outage. In addition, install battery operated emergency lights in all areas housing potentially dangerous animals (venomous snakes, large snakes, crocodilians).

Designate a room for raising and holding food animals (mice, rats, insects, fish, etc). If the animal collection will be over 500 animals, consider contracting food needs out to a supplier. While this may seem more expensive, in reality, raising food items may cost more due to personnel salaries, time commitment, and source reliability. Additionally, provide space for vegetarian diet preparation, along with a refrigerator to store vegetables, fruits, and other food products. Install high quality stainless steel countertops and sinks.

Two additional rooms, separate from each other and apart from the main collection, with separate entrances, will serve as quarantine and isolation/hospital. Provide a small medication refrigerator in each room. Consider separate quarantine and isolation facilities for amphibians due to their specialized needs.

Venomous reptile facilities must have a snakebite alarm system which may cost upwards of $50,000 (Bowler, pers. comm.), a snakebite emergency protocol, and if available, recommended amounts of current antivenin for all venomous species held. A coding system for antivenin is highly recommended. Antivenin suppliers, recommended antivenins and dosages, as well as procedures for legally obtaining antivenin are available in the Antivenom Index (1989). Antivenin has a short shelf life, is expensive, and the cost will continue to rise in the future. Prior to venomous animal arrival, discuss first-aid and treatment with emergency room doctors, along with species to be held by the facility.

Individual animal enclosures should be easy to maintain with good ventilation. Plumb aquatic enclosures with inflow and outflow pipes as well as drains to facilitate cleaning, reduce stress for nervous individuals, and provide for thorough disinfection. Reserve enclosures should be available to separate cagemates, sexes, or for holding offspring. Plan on housing surplus animals indefinitely.

Materials Selection

Stoskopf (chap. 8, this volume) discusses costs associated with the use of materials in fish environments. Many of these considerations apply to reptiles and amphibians. Several issues particular to reptiles and amphibians are discussed here.

Many institutions house amphibians and reptiles in standard glass aquaria. There are several drawbacks to using glass units, a few of which are: (1) difficulty in removing feces without disturbing cage inhabitants, (2) difficulty in plumbing flow-through systems and drains, (3) ease of breakage, (4) unsightly water splashes and droplets, (5) specimens can view adjacent animals and service personnel, therefore possibly increasing stress levels. Plexiglass offers advantages over glass, chiefly in reduced breakage and ease of plumbing. However, plexiglass is not without disadvantages. It scratches, may be damaged by disinfectants, and tends to warp in humid environments. Another suitable material for reserve enclosures is stainless steel (Cullum and Justus, 1973). Unfortunately stainless steel is heavy and the cost may be prohibitive. Whatever material is chosen, it is more economical to buy numerous modular units than to have individual enclosures custom made.

Finally, framed nylon, plastic, or aluminum mesh may be utilized in the construction of small cage lids. Consider the size and behavior of the inhabitant when selecting materials. Installing multiple panels in larger tops will allow access without disturbing or offering escape routes to animals. If high humidity is a requirement, plexiglass or fiberglass tops may be utilized. For safety, venomous animals should have double screened tops.

Material costs fluctuate daily. If budgetary problems occur, start small and build with future expansion in mind. Consider decreasing the number of species held rather than taking shortcuts in facility design. Design flexibility into enclosures and facilities so over time many species can be accommodated. However, there will be compromises between cost and function in the design process (Graves, 1990).

Species Considerations in Captive Design

Abiotic Factors

Thermoregulation. Amphibian and reptile body temperatures are influenced by many factors: the physical environment (Brattstrom, 1968), time of day (Arad et al., 1989), body size (Diefenbach, 1975), digestive state (Bradshaw et al., 1980; Naulleau, 1983), reproductive state (Murphy and Campbell, 1987), bacterial infections (Vaughn et al., 1974; Kluger et al., 1975), and countless other parameters (Regal, 1980). Body temperature regulation occurs through various behavioral activities such as basking, burrowing, movement patterns, postural orientation, and periods of activity (Cowles and Bogert, 1944; Diefenbach, 1975; Johnson et al., 1975; Muth, 1977). Past studies may actually indicate an acceptable range for activity rather than a preferred body temperature (Light et al., 1966).

Captivity itself may alter temperature selection (DeWitt, 1967; Regal, 1980); even so, consult temperature data from the animals' native habitat when setting up thermal gradients. It is best to provide a range of day and night temperatures along with seasonal fluctuations. Laszlo (1979) presents an excellent review of temperature ranges for numerous reptiles and amphibians. The importance of basking is poorly understood in amphibians, but serves many functions in reptiles. Crocodiles, snakes, lizards, turtles, and even the tuatara have all been reported to bask (Porter, 1972). Basking behavior is closely associated with feeding in many reptiles (Gatten, 1974), and may be important in gonadal activity (Jacob and Painter, 1980) and gestation (Van Mierop and Bessette, 1981). Gravid female snakes, provided with hot spots, show a decrease in anomalous neonates (Murphy and Campbell, 1987). Additionally, while incubating eggs, some pythons increase their body temperatures by muscular contractions (Vinegar et al., 1970; Harlow and Grigg, 1984).

In some turtles and crocodilians, egg incubation temperatures determine the sex of offspring. In the American alligator (*Alligator mississippiensis*), temperatures of 32–34°C result in males, while temperatures of 28–30°C result in females, with the intermediate range producing varying proportions of both sexes (Lang, 1989a). Crocodilian embryos incubated at the limits of the viable incubation range resulted in high numbers of malformed embryos (Ferguson, 1989). Conversely, green sea turtle (*Chelonia mydas*) eggs incubated in nests below 28°C result in 90% males, while nests above 29.5°C yield 95–100% females (Morreale et al., 1982).

The effects of low temperatures in reptiles and amphibians have not been studied extensively. Many species avoid extreme temperatures by brumation or hibernation. As with basking, hibernation may also stimulate gonadal activity (Bowler, 1980; Jacob and Painter, 1980). Some species have the ability to withstand ice formation in extracellular fluid. The wood frog *(Rana sylvatica)*, common grey tree frog (*Hyla versicolor*), spring peeper (*H. crucifer*), and the chorus frog (*Pseudacris triseriata*) can survive many days with 65% of total body water as ice. The red-sided garter snake (*Thamnophis sirtalis*) tolerates short-term freezing with an ice content of below 60%. Organ preservation depends on high levels of accumulated cryoprotectants (glucose, glycerol) (Storey, 1989; Storey and Storey, 1990).

Photoperiod. Photoperiod requirements of amphibians and reptiles needs further study. Regal (1980) suggested photoperiod may affect physiological processes such as: reproduction, thermal resistance, and metabolism. Turney and Hutchison (1974) demonstrated endogenous metabolic rhythms in temperate amphibians, while Weathers and Snyder (1977) showed rhythmic metabolism in three species of tropical *Rana*.

Desert reptiles are diurnal during periods when daytime temperatures are moderate (Perry-Richardson, pers. obs.), suggesting that nocturnal behavior might be a means of avoiding extreme temperatures. Gehrmann (1971) theorized that photoperiod influences seasonal processes by regulating the time an animal spends at various temperatures. Gibbons and Semlitsch (1987) discovered snakes moved to winter den sites in response to photoperiod, regardless of the environmental temperatures. Crews and Garrick (1980) noted light may influence reproductive processes through a direct action on the pineal gland. When snakes and lizards at the San Antonio Zoo were given seasonal photoperiods, staff noticed definite seasonal breeding cycles in eight species (Kardon, 1981).

Light Quality. The quality of light reptiles receive is important. This is particularly true in the case of lizards, crocodilians, and chelonians. Jarchow et al. (1991) suggested it also may be important in boas and pythons. Laszlo (1969) reported a reinitiation of feeding in fasting snakes and increased basking in snakes and lizards when exposed to light bulbs emitting ultraviolet (UV) radiation (Optima and Vita-Lite). Proper exposure to UV light reduced deformed bone growth in Round Island skink (*Leiolopisma telfairi*) (Bloxam and Tonge, 1986) and alleviated symptoms of metabolic bone disease in Chihuahuan spotted whiptail (*Cnemidophorus exsanguis*) (Townsend and Cole, 1985). Behler (1982) stated hatchling chinese alligators (*Alligator sinensis*) appeared to benefit from exposure to UV light.

Few studies have examined the light quality required by amphibians. De Vosjoli (1978) noted a reduction of bacterial and fungal infections in frogs exposed to full-spectrum lighting (FSL), and suggested FSL is necessary for long-term survival in captivity. In western toad (*Bufo boreas*) tadpoles exposed to UV-B (290–315 nm) radiation, Worrest and Kimeldorf (1976) documented abnormal development of the presumptive cornea, areas of integumental hyperplasia, a concave curvature of the spine, and increased mortality. However, daily exposure to radiation above 315 nm following UV-B insult mitigated its potentially lethal effects. Spinal curvature occurred in lowland leopard frog (*Rana yavapiensis*) tadpoles raised under FSL combined with UV-B producing blacklights (Perry-Richardson, pers. obs.). Excessive UV radiation is theorized as a causative agent for wild amphibian population declines (Wyman, 1990b).

Ultraviolet radiation, in the 280–315 nm range, plays an important role in the synthesis of Vitamin D_3 in the skin, which is necessary for calcium metabolism (Moyle, 1989). In captivity, it can be provided artificially or through UV penetrating skylights. Gehrmann (1987) tested many UV producing bulbs and found that scattered UV radiation can be concentrated by using a reflector around the back of bulbs. However, UV radiation is reduced to nearly zero as the distance from bulb to specimen exceeds 50 cm. Additionally, the amount of UV radiance drops to 85% after 2000 hours of use for both Vita-Lites and blacklights (Behler, 1987). Therefore, bulbs must be replaced every six months to a year depending on use. Behler (1987) reported blacklights produce tenfold more UV in the 290–320 nm range than Vita-Lites and gave credit to blacklights for the successful breeding of ameiva (*Ameiva ameiva*) at the Bronx Zoo (McCrystal and Behler, 1982). However, for exhibit purposes, blacklights alone may not be the bulb of choice as the purplish light produced may be undesirable. In off-exhibit lizard enclosures, Jarchow et al. (1991) suggested placing the fixture on the floor of the cage, allowing lizards to thermoregulate on the warm ballast while deriving benefits from the UV radiation.

There is still much to be learned concerning reptiles and UV radiation. What is the minimum amount of UV light required by reptiles? Is there a lethal level of UV-B exposure in reptiles? Do fossorial, or secretive species, and heliothermic species differ in their UV requirements? Kauffeld (1969) strongly stated that snakes do not need UV light and questioned whether snake skin was capable of absorbing it. Will future research support this statement?

Water Quality. Water quality is a very important aspect of amphibian husbandry. Amphibian's highly permeable skin is extremely sensitive to toxins in water and desiccates easily (Duellman and Trueb, 1986). Water quality varies both geographically and temporally, depending on source, surface vs. subterranean, as well as method of transport (Nace et al., 1974). Heavy metals are often found in water, while others may leach into it from pipes and plumbing fixtures. Many of these substances are toxic to amphibians, especially gill-breathing larvae (Jarchow, pers. comm.). Acceptable levels of these metals have not been evaluated in any detail (Nace et al., 1974); therefore, avoid using galvanized, copper or brass pipes and fixtures. Instead use black iron pipe, high-density polyethylene, polypropylene or nylon pipe and fixtures. For general water quality guidelines see Nace et al. (1974).

Aquatic systems should be filtered. Smaller terraria can be effectively serviced by under-gravel units. Larger units may use canister filters, with removable cartridges, powered by small pumps. Gravity-feed sand filters using small pumps are suitable for very large aquaria (1000's liters), although they require considerable space. High pressure (35–40 lbs.) sand filters alleviate many of the spatial concerns mentioned above, but require high capacity pumps and are expensive to operate. One benefit of both sand filter types is that they allow for biological filtration. Diatomaceous earth filters, though good for water clarity, will not facilitate bio-filtration unless used with sand or gravel substrates (Drieschman, 1982). Additionally, they are labor-intensive and utilize a potentially harmful dust in dry form. Ultraviolet light filters can be used alone or in tandem with one of the above to reduce bacterial counts. Additionally, cold water amphibians require chiller units.

Humidity. Many amphibians thrive in high humidity environments, while 35–60% humidity is adequate for most reptiles (Frye, 1973). Even desert dwellers may live in humid micro-habitats such as under rotting vegetation, subterranean burrows, or in densely clumped vegetation. Tropical reptiles have higher skin permeability than desert species and therefore may desiccate easily in low humidity. If the humidity is too low, normal ecdysis may not occur, animals may dehydrate quickly, or other potentially serious medical problems may develop. Conversely, excessive humidity may cause "blister disease" in captive reptiles (Frye, 1973).

Humidity levels may be increased by incorporating automatic misting systems, waterfalls, large pools, and live plants into enclosure designs. To reduce humidity levels for xeric animals, Bowler (1980) suggested putting calcium chloride desiccators in enclosures. Heating, air conditioning, and refrigeration systems also lower humidity.

Cage Furniture. All areas within the enclosure should be accessible to the keeper from the cage door so feces, uneaten food, and animals can be retrieved easily. Cage furniture should make good use of three-dimensional space, reflecting species' needs. Most amphibians and reptiles seek shelter which provides a tactile sense of security.

Rocks, branches, artificial or live plants, as well as plastic containers, tubes or rods may accommodate climbing. Plastic or styrofoam containers, or rocks can be used for hiding areas. Large or heavy furnishings should be firmly anchored to prevent accidents.

Biotic Factors

Food and Water. Although the natural diets of amphibians and reptiles vary greatly, a few generalizations can be made. For the most part, adult amphibians feed primarily on invertebrate and small vertebrate prey, while larvae are usually herbivorous. As with any group of organisms there are exceptions, such as the treefrog (*Hyla truncata*), which has been recently observed feeding on fruits and seeds (da Silva et al., 1989). Similarly, reptile diets are varied. Snakes and crocodilians are essentially carnivorous, relying on a wide range of organisms for subsistence. Saurians and chelonians may be categorized as omnivores, although numerous species of lizards are exclusively insectivorous, although some, such as day geckos (*Phelsuma*), also utilize nectar (McKeown, 1984).

In captivity it is difficult to provide the variety of foods amphibians and reptiles consume in the wild. Therefore, whenever possible, utilize commercially available foods for captives. As a rule-of-thumb it is best to offer as much variety in foods as possible. This helps insure that if one item lacks certain nutrients others will contain it. Nutritional supplementation may be required if there is too much variance from the natural diet. However, consult a veterinarian before supplementing food with vitamin and/or mineral additives due to the ease of overdosing (Gershoff, 1981; Hall et al., 1985). Minute amounts of trace minerals are required by many reptiles, especially those with salt-secreting glands, and can be added to their diets. For example, the Arizona-Sonora Desert Museum (ASDM) uses grated mineral block sprinkled over chuckwalla (*Sauromalus varius, S. hispidus*) and desert tortoise (*Xerobates agassizi*) diets to provide these minerals.

Carnivores feeding on whole food animals should not require supplementation, provided food animals are properly nourished.

However, improperly fed food animals may lead to nutritional deficiencies in captives. For instance, Frye (1984) reported severe vitamin E deficiency in red-tailed boa (*Boa constrictor*) fed exclusively obese rats which had eaten only sunflower seeds. Freezing food animals in water helps prevent dehydration of food items, though frozen food loses some nutritional value over time. Food fishes such as tuna, mackerel, mullet, and smelt may lack certain vitamins, especially vitamin E (Frye, 1984; Dierenfeld et al., 1991). Others, such as goldfish, may contain high levels of thiaminase, which can break down thiamine in piscivorous species (Frye, 1984). Some reptiles, especially turtles, develop vitamin A deficiencies when fed exclusively meat (Frye, 1984).

Insectivorous species may require vitamin and mineral supplementation for optimal health (Beltz-Decker, 1989). Insects housed at a facility must be fed appropriate diets to ensure optimal nourishment for those consuming them. At the ASDM, crickets are maintained on rodent block and calcium carbonate (85%:15% by volume), along with carrot as a source of moisture and vitamin A. Morris (1983), Zimmermann (1986) and Beltz-Decker (1989) provide an evaluation of several insects and food recipes.

Captive diets of herbivorus reptiles should simulate natural diets as closely as possible. Unfortunately, many herbivorous diets are formulated arbitrarily based on incomplete information. Lawler (pers. comm.) analyzed data from six major plants consumed by *Sauromalus varius* in the wild during a reproductive year and found an extremely high calcium/phosphorus ratio of 31.79:1 and minimal protein intake of 10.27%. Highfield (1988) reports wild tortoises from arid habitats experience a calcium to phosphorus ratio of 5:1 to 8:1.

Activated vitamin D_3 along with the hormones calcitonin and parathyroid increase blood calcium levels. Acceptable levels of plasma calcium and phosphorus permit bone formation and the proper functioning of the neuromuscular system (DeLuca, 1982). Additionally, egg-laying females need good calcium stores for egg shell development, especially in *Phelsuma* where females will actually eat calcium out of bowls (McKeown, 1984; Miller, 1984). Dietary sources of vitamin D include ingestion of whole animals, primarily the liver (where vitamin D is stored) and the skin. Plants generally do not contain vitamin D. An overzealous approach to vitamin D supplementation can lead to toxic levels (Jarchow, pers. comm.).

Obesity is a common problem in long-term captives. Feeding frequency must be matched to metabolic needs, growth, and activity level of the individual. Active species, like small lizards and frogs, need food daily, while large, sedentary species such as adult ana-condas (*Eunectes spp.*) may be fed once every 1–2 months. Larval amphibians should not be offered much more than they will accept. Specimens suffering from starvation may be recognized by shrunken skin stretched over bony prominences, feel underweight, and ex-hibit sunken eyes. Some amphibians and reptiles exhibit tempo-rary anorexia. Gravid females, hibernating animals, and pre-shed-ding are all conditions where food may be refused (Malaret and Fitch, 1984).

Provide fresh water for drinking. Some tropical snakes and lizards will drink water droplets off foliage, so daily misting is required. Wild desert reptiles often do not have water readily avail-able, but may drink when water is offered in captivity. Some small ant and termite eating reptiles drink water applied to their lips, and day geckos will commonly lick water off their faces and eyes. Tortoises drink when offered water in dishes and usually defecate at this time. Signs of dehydration in reptiles and amphibians in-clude loss of skin and subcutaneous turgor and integumental wrin-kling (Frye, 1984; Jarchow, 1988).

Social Considerations. Competition may occur anytime there is a limiting resource like food or space, and has been shown to be density dependent for many species (Wilbur, 1972; Stenhouse et al., 1983). Males often establish territories which are aggressively defended (Verrell and Donovan, 1991), sometimes to the death. Female crocodilians aggressively defend nesting sites and hatchlings (Lang, 1989b; Magnusson et al., 1989). Galapagos tortoise (*Geochelone elephantopus*) will engage in gape threatening and face biting to establish positions within herd hierarchies (Burchfield et al., 1987). In addition, glass may cause an individual to be aggres-sive towards its own reflection. Cannibalism may occur in species of dissimilar size, although it is usually an opportunistic event (Polis and Myers, 1985). To eliminate such behaviors, place visual barriers and retreats within enclosures.

Mixed species enclosures provide a holistic representation of nature by grouping sympatric species together. Also, a larger num-ber of animals can be maintained in a given amount of space. Multiple species enclosures can be successful if careful consider-ation is devoted to species selection. Obviously, avoid placing po-tential prey and predators together. Additionally, it is unwise to have predator and prey species within visual contact with one another. If possible, house species from the same geographic area together. Choose species that have the same environmental needs, but utilize different niches and have different dietary needs. For example, a good combination might be a tortoise with an arboreal lizard or snake. However, *Pseudomonas* may be carried by turtles nonpathogenically, although it is pathogenic in snakes. Interspecific anuran skin toxins are potentially incompatible (e.g., toxins of some *Scaphiopus* species can be fatal to others; Lawler, pers. comm.). All introductions in mixed species exhibits should be carefully observed. At the ASDM, when beaded lizards (*Heloderma horridum*) were introduced into an exhibit housing a Central American boa (*Boa constrictor imperator*), the lizards would rapidly exit the exhibit (pers. obs.). Eventually they acclimated to the boa's presence. At feeding time, each individual is carefully watched, because their dietary requirements are similar.

Captive Design and Animal Health

With foresight, most captivity-induced injuries can be avoided. Skin burns may result from close contact with heat sources such as light bulbs, heating pads, and hot rocks. Rough surfaces may abrade or cut the feet and venters of amphibians and reptiles. Moreover, enclosure components that slide past one another (e.g., doors, movable dioramas) must be designed to keep specimens from entering between the two where they could be injured or killed. Animals may be injured by jumping out of elevated cages during servicing or falling from elevated places within the enclosure.

Amphibians and reptiles are subject to a host of pathogens. Many of these are ubiquitous in nature, causing disease states in immunosuppressed animals. Among these are viruses such as herpes-type viruses, paramyxovirus in snakes, a papova-type isolated from Lucke tumors in frogs, and an adeno-type found in frog kidneys (Clark et al, 1968; Granoff, 1969). Bacterial invaders include: *Pseudomonas*, *Proteus*, *Aeromonas*, and *Salmonella* (Hoff and Hoff, 1984; Jacobson, 1984; Shotts, 1984; White, 1984a; Duellman and Trueb, 1986). Abrasions, nasal openings, and mucous membranes are apparently routes that fungi use to gain access to bodies. Additionally, amphibians and reptiles are subject to a myriad of internal and external parasites. Among these are protozoans, helminths, annelids, and arthropods (Migaki et al., 1984; Duellman and Trueb, 1986). Organic cage materials can contribute to health problems in immunocompromised animals (Hoff and Hoff, 1984). Many of the aforementioned pathogens are present in "wild" foods (Miller, 1980), thus they should be avoided. If it is necessary to utilize these foods, freezing will kill numerous parasites (Stoskopf and Hudson, 1982). Due to potential for injury, prekill food animals. Some bacteria are beneficial, especially in the case of herbivores species; therefore, allow young herbivores to eat healthy adult feces to inoculate their guts with these fauna.

Place all newly acquired animals in quarantine. The quarantine management protocol listed in Table 12.1 was developed in a paramyxovirus meeting held at Audubon Zoo (Anonymous, 1989a) and is recommended as standard procedure. Place ill or injured collection animals in an isolation room and consult a veterinarian. The same procedures outlined in Table 12.1 apply, with the following changes: (1) animals do not leave isolation until cleared by a veterinarian, (2) the isolation room is the last animal area worked in the day, (3) post-surgery enclosures should be sterile and simple, (4) animals should only be reintroduced to others after complete recovery, and if reintroduction will not cause undo stress or potential reinjury.

Captive Design and Conservation

In many people's minds, conservation through captive design equals captive breeding, with the ultimate destiny of progeny being that of release into the wild. Captive populations may serve as genetic reservoirs for species extinct in the wild, and is a valuable tool in the recovery of a species if combined with habitat and ecosystem preservation. Captive breeding may also reduce the number of animals collected from the wild.

Captive reproduction is not without problems. Captive bred animals may harbor deleterious pathogens which could seriously injure wild populations. Introducing captive born animals to established populations could exceed the carrying-capacity of the habitat, increasing resource competition and possible displacement of established residents. Maintaining a large enough population size to maximize genetic diversity takes considerable space. Conway (1987) estimates the world zoo carrying capacity at 96 reptile and 32 amphibian species. This may be, in part, due to the fact that many institutions work with the same species. One way

Table 12.1
Quarantine Management Protocol for Paramyxovirus

1) All animals entering quarantine remain there for a minimum of sixty days.
2) All animals receive two consecutive negative stool samples.
3) All animals are housed individually.
4) All animals are weighed prior to entering and exiting quarantine.
5) All animals must be feeding regularly before leaving quarantine.
6) The quarantine room has its own set of tools and cages. These never leave the room. Cross-contamination between enclosures is avoided at all costs. Disinfect utensils. Wash hands between enclosures, if hand contact with anything in the enclosure was made.
7) A footbath (water and bleach) is at the door for use upon entering and exiting the room. Change the footbath daily.
8) All animals are closely observed for abnormal behavior and/or posturing. A general physical exam must prove satisfactory. There should be no clinical signs of disease.
9) Only introduce clean, healthy animals to the main collection.
10) Necropsy all animals that die. Save tissues (lung, liver, kidney, and spleen) for analysis.
11) In the case of a die-off, thoroughly disinfect ALL cages with a strong bleach solution, dry out. Keep these cages empty for at least a week. AVOID WOODEN CAGES.
12) The quarantine room is serviced after the main collection and prior to servicing the isolation/hospital room. Additionally, blood work is done and accurate animal records maintained. These include feedings, treatments, weights. Consider the possibility of euthanizing "poor doers." If animals die during quarantine, consider putting a "hold" on all animals exiting quarantine until the necropsy reports confirm the cause of death.

to increase these numbers may be to move towards regional specialization. Finally, reintroduction programs may encounter lack of cooperation from governmental agencies. Zoo Atlanta, after finding suitable habitat in Belize (without sport hunters and crocodiles) for potential release of the endangered Morelet's Crocodile (*Crocodylus moreletii*), ran into obstacles with the Belize Forestry Department whose officials felt Belize had enough crocodiles, and that they were taking good care of their resident population (Hunt, 1987).

There have been twenty-five [sic] amphibians and reptiles released into the wild through reintroduction, translocation, and repatriation projects (Dodd and Seigel, 1991). Follow-up data on these
projects are scanty (Wemmer and Derrickson, 1987). Of these
projects, Dodd and Seigel (1991) state that five were successful, six
unsuccessful, and fifteen not classified. Effective evaluation will
only occur when long-term projects yield necessary data. While
large scale reintroduction of captive bred reptile and amphibian
species into the wild may not be practical at this time, there are
several areas for spearheading conservation efforts; among them
headstarting and commercial "ranching." For more information on
these techniques, see Pritchard, chap. 9, this volume. Conservation
efforts can also be directed towards education.

Zoological institutions fit into this scheme primarily through
research and conservation education. Zoos may be the best vehicle
for educating the public about the plight of the natural world.
There is much information available regarding the dangers nature
faces today. The problem is involving the general public in the
conservation mission. Only through changes in public perception
will any of our true goals be met. Knowledge is our only weapon
against ignorance which is accelerating the destruction of the natural world. If we share our knowledge, we inform others of the
tragedy that looms over our heads and hopefully effect greater
involvement in the solution. Zoos are visited by millions of people
each year. Biota "hook" people into visiting zoos. Once there, they
are a captive audience which can be educated by naturalistic exhibits and interpretive biologists. This requires that exhibits focus on
major themes supported by smaller stories. In effect, by giving
people small pieces of the puzzle, we help them to create the "ge-
stalt" image or overall picture. Currently, naturalistic exhibitry is
extremely popular. However, it is debatable whether the value of
this approach can be positively correlated with information gained
by the public. In other words, do people incorporate more information through viewing "habitats," or do they merely view these
exhibits as pretty pictures?

Conclusions

Speculation on the future of captive design is difficult. There is no
way to predict the future focus of animal exhibitry. Will it still be
conservation, research, and education? Will there be anything left

to study or interpret? No one knows. Undoubtedly, increased attention will be paid to justification for animals in captivity. More important, without knowledge of future needs, how do we avoid "locking" into one train of thought that is currently popular? Zoos originated as collections of oddities, then moved to "postage stamp" exhibitry, and now experiment with naturalistic "habitats" featuring biodiversity as the central theme. None of the former philosophies prevailed, and there isn't a guarantee that the latter will either. Each institutional renovation requires new master plans, and construction currently costs approximately one million dollars/acre for large-scale naturalistic habitats (Hancocks, pers. comm.). How many times can an institution afford to start over? Perhaps the message is design with foresight and hindsight! Today's vogue exhibit might be tomorrow's dinosaur. Avoid nebulous general exhibits, but create maximum flexibility preventing costly future remodeling. Finally, a most important and often ignored question is posed: what criteria do we use to evaluate whether zoological institutions have met the challenges and goals they purport to take on?

IV

Birds

Introduction of Authors
and Chapter Previews

Christine Sheppard, Curator of Ornithology at the Wildlife Conservation Society, formerly the New York Zoological Society, contributes the avian conservation chapter. She has been instrumental in developing captive husbandry techniques for a variety of endangered species including the first hand-rearing of the African pigmy grouse, the Mauritius pink pigeon, and the Pesquet's parrot. She is secretary of the Hornbill Specialist Group and helped coordinate an international meeting to develop conservation action priorities for the hornbill. Dr. Sheppard also coordinated an analysis of space available for captive management of birds in zoos.

In her chapter, Dr. Sheppard highlights three successful captive conservation programs. For the peregrine falcon, cranes, and birds of paradise, she details causes of population decline, requirements for captive propagation, and the factors contributing to the success of each program.

George Gee of Patuxent Wildlife Research Center in Maryland provides an overview of the research on avian reproductive physiology. As leader of the Captive Propagation Research Group at Patuxent, he directs research on the breeding and release of endangered whooping cranes, Mississippi sandhill cranes, and masked bobwhites. His research interests include photoperiod, artificial insemination, and cryopreservation of avian semen and embryos. In addition to this research, he continues work with artificial incubation, genetic diversity, and genetic management of endangered avian species. His recent cooperative studies with others using allozymes, minisatellite DNA, and the major histocompatibility complex help to describe genetic diversity in the whooping crane.

Dr. Gee recognizes at least three goals for the reproduction of avian species in captivity: to create a self-sustaining captive population, to maintain a genetically healthy gene pool, and to produce birds for reintroduction into native habitats. He discusses the methodologies of semen collection and storage for artificial insemination but advises aviculturists to consider less labor-intensive techniques for overcoming infertility problems in captive birds.

The application of animal behavior to wildlife management and conservation is the primary research interest of behavior chapter author Michael Hutchins who is director of Conservation and Science for the American Zoo and Aquariums Association. Dr. Hutchins' coauthors, Christine Sheppard, Anna Marie Lyles, and Gerry Casadei are all members of the Ornithology Department at the Wildlife Conservation Society as curator, assistant curator, and intern, respectively. Dr. Sheppard is introduced above. Dr. Lyles, educated at Princeton, is primarily interested in the conservation and management of small populations of birds. She is active in a number of AAZPA Species Survival Plans and Studbooks and serves on the Small Population Management Advisory Group. Mr. Casadei participated in the effort to bring to the United States the only successful breeding group of hoatzins from Venezuela. His other field experience included a study of bee-eaters in Zimbabwe.

In addition to reviewing the difficulties associated with studying the behavior of captive birds, the authors of this chapter offer suggestions for resolving some of these problems. They also discuss the influence of space and diet on the activity patterns, social interactions, and physical and psychological well-being of captive birds.

The chapter on design of avian habitats reflects the long-term interest of Bruce Bohmke, general curator at the Phoenix Zoo, in captive husbandry, management of birds, and zoo exhibition. His emphasis on functional (versus structural) issues for design implementation are evident in his chapter. Analysis of avian mortality in captivity is another research interest. Mr. Bohmke feels avian habitats in zoos primarily reflect the needs of public exhibition. Creative exhibit design remains underutilized with regard to enhancing conservation, education, and reproduction.

In his chapter, Mr. Bohmke discusses captive design as it relates to reintroduction schemes as well as to captive propagation. He emphasizes that enclosures for animals destined to be released into the wild must be designed to optimize the birds' physical conditions, thus enhancing their fitness in the wild.

13

Captive Propagation and Avian Conservation

Christine Sheppard

The world boasts about 9,000 species of birds, each unique and irreplaceable. As of 1988, the IUCN estimated that nearly 10% of all bird species were considered endangered (Mountfort, 1988). Hundreds of these species may be lost within decades (Meyers, 1988), even if strong action is taken now. Extinction rates for birds have increased from approximately one species every 83 years, before the rise of *Homo sapiens*, to one every four years during the last four centuries (King, 1985). By the end of this century, the rate is expected to be two species per year. While virtually all extinctions in recorded history can be traced back to human activity, patterns and scale have changed over time. In a review of avian extinction, Temple (1986) noted that behavioral or ecological characteristics made certain categories of bird taxa especially vulnerable, even before technology enabled large-scale environmental modifications by humans and increased the efficiency of hunting.

Species Status in the Wild

Island Endemics

Island endemics are particularly at risk. Both their ranges and their total populations are small and therefore very vulnerable to density independent forces. Evolution in environments lacking predators, competitors, and disease frequently results in the loss of defensive mechanisms found in related mainland species (Diamond, 1985b).

The history of bird species in the Hawaiian archipelago illustrates many of the factors which, singly or in combination, can
threaten survival of island endemics. While distance restricted colonization, it is believed that representatives of 20 different bird
families eventually reached the islands. These arrivals, faced with
a rich complexity of habitat, eventually evolved into 84 forms unique
to Hawaii. Polynesian colonists, believed to have arrived about 400
A.D., caused the extinction of 44 of these through hunting, burning,
and clearing lowland forests and introduction of rats, dogs, jungle
fowl, and other species (Scott et al., 1986; Scott et al., 1988). These
effects were largely restricted to areas near the coasts. However,
the arrival of Europeans in 1778 presaged the beginning of forest
clearing on a large scale for pasture, agriculture, and timber. By
the end of the nineteenth century, most accessible forest areas had
been cleared. Feral goats and pigs caused degradation of all but the
most remote habitats on the large islands (Berger, 1981). Within
two hundred years, twenty more bird taxa were lost. Some of these
modern extinctions are very precisely documented. For instance,
rabbits introduced to Laysan island destroyed virtually all vegetation, causing the loss of the Laysan rail, millerbird, and honey-
creeper (Scott et al., 1988).

Continued clearing of land for agriculture and housing has reduced the populations of all Hawaii's endemics. Introduced avian
diseases, especially malaria, spread by introduced mosquitoes, have
made lowland habitats virtually barren of endemics, which have no
resistance to these diseases. Today, most of Hawaii's indigenous
birds exist only in a few refugia, too high for mosquitoes and too far,
as yet, for habitat degradation by humans or feral animals. Equally
damaging, over 50 exotic bird species, 18 mammals, and hundreds of
plants have become established, displacing native forms and preventing their return (Gagne, 1988). Gagne has calculated that Hawaii, representing less than 0.2% of the land mass of the United
States, accounts for over 25% of listed endangered species and 72%
of recorded historical extinctions for that country.

Resource Restricted Species

Species that specialize in scarce resources face risks similar to
those affecting island species. Habitat is the most obvious restriction, but prey items or nest sites can be equally critical. This is
especially true because birds tend to be conservative in their patterns of dispersal, migration, feeding, and nesting. Patches of suit-

able habitat might be available to a species but never encountered. The whooping crane (*Grus americana*) is a typical case, threatened by drainage of wetlands needed for breeding and particularly by overuse of the river flats used for resting and feeding along its migration route (U.S. Fish and Wildlife Service, 1986). The snail kite (*Rostrhamus sociabilis*) is endangered in the United States, where drainage of its Everglades habitat has reduced the population of apple snails (*Pomacea paludosa*), its preferred food (Snyder, 1974). In Asia, hornbills are threatened, not by hunting but because forest cutting removes the old, large diameter trees required by these species for nesting. Replanting can produce a lush looking habitat which, because it lacks proper nesting trees, is incapable of supporting native bird species (Wells, 1985).

Hunting and Collecting

Tasty birds and others especially sought after by human hunters are another threatened category. Many of these birds are relatively prolific breeders, usually thought to be more resistant to disturbance and tolerant of harvesting than slow breeding taxa. The pressure of hunting, however, with modern weapons is such that even species with huge populations are unable to keep up. The passenger pigeon (*Ectopistes migratorius*) is the best known example, hunted from flocks of billions in the 1800s to zero in 1914 (Teres, 1980). The dodo from Mauritius and New Zealand's moa, both flightless island birds, were hunted to extinction by primitive cultures.

Psittacines are often hunted for food, but greater damage to populations results from large-scale collection for the pet trade. For instance, over the last ten years, nearly 500,000 parrots were imported annually into the United States alone (Clubb, 1987). Such collection has virtually eliminated parrot populations in many regions of South America (Bolze, 1992). Unfortunately, the rarer a species, the more desirable it becomes to collectors. The wild population of rare spix macaws (*Cyanopsitta spixii*) had been reduced to a single individual by 1990, through trapping for private collectors (Thomsen and Munn, 1987; Anonymous, 1991a). Parrots are multiply threatened, as collectors frequently destroy scarce nesting sites and mortality during transport is high (Nilsson, 1981). Recent studies have indicated that parrots have very slow reproductive rates, and that wild populations could not easily sustain even limited harvesting (Munn, 1987).

Future Trends: Deforestation in the Tropics

Island endemics were affected early in man's history. King (1985) estimates that of the 92 species extinguished between 1600 and 1980, 93% were island endemics. Ironically, only 54% of the 240 species in the most recent *Red Data Book* are island endemics; a good example of misleading statistics.

Tropical forests contrast greatly with oceanic islands. Here, species diversity and species density is great—a third of the world's bird species inhabit only tropical forest (Diamond, 1985a). These forests are being felled at a chilling rate of 24–48 million acres each year. Some countries have already lost over 90% of their forest resources and the trend is not slowing (Collins et al., 1991). Loss of tropical forests has more than local effects. Fifty-one percent of bird species found in the contiguous United States winter in the neotropics, living in or passing through forest habitats (Lovejoy, 1983). Conservationists in many countries are attempting to protect at least some tropical forest birds by establishing refuges, parks, and reserves. Protection of such areas from hunting and clearing is difficult, however, as funding and manpower is often unavailable. Because of the direct relationship between the size of an area and the number of species it can support, reserves will inevitably be unable to support populations of all bird species native to an area (Diamond, 1985a; Lovejoy, 1985). Even the most optimistic outlook predicts the loss of hundreds of bird species in the coming decades.

Conservation Programs in Captivity

History of Captive Management of Bird Species

Zoos have always been interested in rare species. Initially, the lure was the prestige of displaying the unique or unusual, and this is still a factor today in attracting public interest. In the last three decades, however, zoos have developed a new ethic and a new purpose. The change is partly ascribable to self-interest but largely to the sense that zoos could be more than just living museums— they could become active and significant forces for conservation (Conway, 1969).

Fifteen years ago, conservationists were more optimistic about saving threatened species through habitat preservation and *in situ* management (King, 1977; Temple, 1977a). The notion that zoos might contribute to conservation programs met with great skepticism. Even within the zoo community, captive breeding was regarded as a last resort (Conway, 1978). Since that time, it has become increasingly clear that there is no foreseeable end to present trends of extinction, and that many species will be lost as their habitats disappear. The need for ways to preserve such species has become obvious, even to those who would prefer to focus resources on habitat preservation.

Simultaneously, technology for captive management has developed exponentially, although much remains to be accomplished and programs for birds in particular need to be forwarded. The application of captive management to endangered bird species is very different from that for mammals (Sheppard, 1985a). Endangered birds seldom have the popular appeal of tigers or gorillas. Zoos lose no attendance because they fail to exhibit the Chatham Island Robin and a display of Rodrigues Foties would not draw a crowd. Many endangered birds represent groups that have never bred predictably in captivity (Conway, 1978). For these reasons, more work has been done with management of endangered birds in the wild than in captivity. However, as destruction of habitat continues and zoos are increasingly perceived as conservation tools, zoos are being asked to try to preserve bird species through captive breeding.

Management of Captive Avian Populations

Conway (1986) estimated that the world's zoos could realistically expect to preserve at most 300 bird species as self-sustaining captive populations. This is considerably less than 5% of all bird species but considerably more than we now have the ability to breed reliably. Because avoidance of inbreeding inevitably requires working with a substantial number of animals, endangered species breeding programs usually involve multiple institutions. Most zoos cannot devote the amount of space demanded by a complete breeding program. Subdividing a population also minimizes the risk that all animals could be lost to an epidemic or natural disaster. Participating institutions must cooperate in management or program goals will not be possible. In 1981, the American Association of Zoological Parks and Aquariums (AAZPA) formalized a program for planned cooperative management of captive populations, the Species Survival Plan (SSP), for U.S. zoo programs (Willis et al., 1992). The SSP program includes a structure for cooperative participation and management, with elected representatives from each zoo forming a committee or propagation group, which jointly manages the population. By 1992, SSP programs had been approved for 14 bird species. Some SSPs now manage groups of related taxa. To better organize the SSP process, in 1990 the Taxon Advisory Group (TAG) program was instituted to assign and evaluate conservation possibilities and priorities within families or orders.

To function effectively, a program for managing any species in captivity for an extended period must combine several elements. In particular, cooperation among organizations working with a species and a management scheme to produce a population stable for multiple generations are essential. Captive populations must be sufficiently large, and sufficiently representative of the wild gene pool to withstand the loss of genetic diversity inherent in management of small breeding groups over time (Franklin, 1980; Senner, 1980). Models for maximizing genetic diversity and minimizing inbreeding have been developed by conservation biologists (Foose et al., 1986; MacCluer et al., 1986; Soulé et al., 1986), and applications of these models are an important part of the SSP program. Captive populations must be analyzed demographically and a plan developed that incorporates the amount of space available, the number of founder individuals, rates of reproduction and mortality, the need for stability of population size once available space is filled, and the need to minimize genetic loss. Once a model is developed, the population must be monitored continually and management recommendations made, because real animals virtually never perform in complete accordance with an ideal model. As yet, no avian endangered species program now operating combines all of these elements.

In almost no case is knowledge of a species sufficient to allow precise population planning. Ways to identify sexes, to select and introduce prospective breeders, to incubate eggs, handrear young, to feed birds of all ages, and to release captive reared individuals to the wild must all be discovered. For species like pheasants and waterfowl, which have long captive histories, some or all of these techniques may be readily available. For manakins and oilbirds, we lack even the knowledge to maintain living adults. In most cases, we have some information but must seek out the rest.

The ultimate goal of captive management programs is to produce animals which can be released to re-establish extinct populations or to bolster threatened ones. To date, this has been possible in only a few instances, because, in general, the factors which have caused species to become endangered still exist. Much needs to be learned about release technology, including how to teach captive born animals to function independently in the wild (Cade, 1986b).

Problems Facing Conservation Programs in Captivity

Every species is unique and while there are common causes for endangerment, the impact of these causes will be different for each species. The history of each species in aviculture is also different, as are the abilities of captive managers to care for particular species. A look at several functioning programs will illustrate the problems involved and the strategies adopted in their respective solutions.

Peregrine Falcon (*Falco peregrinus*)

The peregrine falcon, like other top chain carnivores, has never had a dense population, but its distribution is cosmopolitan. The East Coast of the United States historically had a population of about 350 breeding pairs (Barclay and Cade, 1983). Until the late 1940s, peregrine populations had been extremely stable, with some individual nest sites in continual use for centuries (Cade, 1982). During the 1950s and 1960s, however, populations began to dwindle throughout the world, as accumulations of DDT caused eggshell thinning and reproductive failure (Ratcliffe, 1967, 1980). By 1964, the peregrine falcon was extinct in the United States, east of the Mississippi (Cade, 1982). While restrictions on the use of organochlorine pesticides have slowed the decline of the peregrine population as a whole, only a restocking program could restore the non-existent population.

In 1970, faced with the loss of the peregrine, falconers, headed by Dr. Tom Cade, organized an international effort to develop breeding and release techniques (Barclay and Cade, 1983). Cade's proposal to breed peregrines in captivity and release them into the wild was met with skepticism and even ridicule (Cade, 1982). However, in 1973, the first 20 chicks were hatched and by 1981, over 1000 falcons had been produced by captive propagation. Releases began in 1975 and continued each year until 1986. By 1980, released birds had paired and hatched young of their own. Enough peregrines are now established in the wild to allow the population to grow to the carrying capacity of the habitat (Barclay and Cade, 1983).

Perhaps the single most important factor in the success of the peregrine project was its focus on a single species. Where zoos must concentrate on education and recreation, as well as breeding, and must manage many species at one time, peregrine breeders could give all their attention to the requirements of peregrines. How to produce eggs and chicks were obviously among the first questions to be addressed. It was discovered that birds taken as nestlings and handreared were the best candidates for captive breeding (Cade and Fyfe, 1977). This finding had proved to be true for many other species, including cranes and parrots. Wild caught adults may be too stressed by captivity or too dependent on cues unavailable in a captive environment for normal reproduction. Handrearing accustoms birds to humans and artificial environments. Close association with humans may result in imprinted birds, desirable under some conditions for use in programs using artificial insemination. Reducing human contact and rearing young with conspecifics, however, can produce a bird which is comfortable in captivity, yet responds normally to other birds for reproduction (Cade and Fyfe, 1977; Sheppard, 1988a).

In the wild, peregrines will re-lay if a clutch is lost to predation or natural disturbance. In captivity, this behavior can be exploited by removing eggs for artificial incubation. Determining the optimal pattern of temperature and humidity to ensure maximum hatchability is difficult, however, and artificial incubation programs frequently suffer from low hatching success (Weaver and Cade, 1983). Research on peregrines identified subspecific differences in shell structure, related to environmental humidity and measured temperature under incubating falcons (Schwartz et al., 1977). Eventually, differences in eggs among individual females could be identified (Cade, pers. comm.).

In wild populations, mortality among fledged young may be as high as 80% during the first year (Barclay and Cade, 1983) as birds learn to find food, seek shelter, and avoid predators. Captive reared birds must learn these same lessons and may be more naive than their wild counterparts. Release techniques must be developed to minimize mortality while permitting birds to learn essential skills. Several strategies were suggested for peregrine release. The method ultimately used relied on modified training techniques from falconry (Temple, 1977b; Cade, 1986a). Young birds were allowed to develop hunting skills while still in a protected environment, monitored extensively by volunteers. Thus, birds could be recaptured if problems arose, or allowed to become independent.

The peregrine release program was successful, in part, because the environmental poisoning by pesticides (which had caused the extinction of the population) had been identified and corrected. The project, therefore, was designed for short-term, not long-term management. Genetic management of multiple generations was not necessary. Unfortunately, most endangered species breeding projects face continuing habitat destruction and must spend considerable energy on demographic management.

Two other things should be particularly noted. The Eastern peregrine subspecies became extinct. Released birds represented many other North American subspecies, and the expectation is that eventually a new Eastern subspecies may develop. The original subspecies is gone, however, and cannot be recreated. Wild peregrines nest on cliffs. During early releases, high mortality was experienced by birds released into traditional areas, particularly to predation by great horned owls (*Bubo virginianus*). Better results came when tall buildings and specially constructed release towers were used. The "new" peregrine is thus slightly modified in behavior; safer but different in its choice of nesting area.

In most aspects, however, the peregrine program is a model of how to approach and solve the challenge of captive breeding. Techniques developed for the peregrine are now being used for other endangered raptor species. The program is also typical in requiring time and extensive funding. Restoring the peregrine falcon ultimately cost millions of dollars.

Cranes (Gruidae)

All of the 14 species in the family Gruidae are tied to wetlands, especially for breeding. These habitats are disappearing around the world, filled in for agriculture or construction, and cranes are disappearing with them. Cranes are also prized as game birds and continued hunting threatens several species. At least nine species are currently considered to be endangered or threatened and none can be assumed to have a secure future (Archibald et al., 1980).

Because cranes are large and handsome, they are popular exhibit birds and have been displayed in zoos throughout history. As interest in endangered species breeding grew during the 1960s, several zoos developed crane breeding programs. At Patuxent, the U.S. endangered species breeding facility, a program for the whooping crane (*Grus americana*) was started, and the International Crane Foundation was founded in Wisconsin. Techniques for basic management of adult cranes were well established (Wiley, 1978)—some zoo specimens had lived to well over 40 years of age. Breeding, however, raised many questions. The development of laparoscopy in the 1970s made it possible to reliably sex cranes, which are monomorphic. Pair formation, therefore, became easier; although cranes will not always accept a preselected mate. Not all pairs are successful. Mirande (1990) suggests that pairs in which the female is dominant are less likely to produce fertile eggs. To prevent aggressive interactions, all crane species must be kept as pairs when breeding age is reached, and pairs require fairly large spaces. While cranes will breed if they can hear other pairs, sight of an adjacent pair can inhibit breeding, as birds may spend their time pacing the mutual fence line (Archibald and Viess, 1979). Sight barriers give pairs the illusion of private territories. The illusion can also be created psychologically, with pairs occupying every other pen in a row. Neighboring crane pairs each act as if the empty pen between them is a part of their territory from which the others have been excluded.

While crane species share many characteristics, in some cases recognition of differences proved to be the key to breeding. Hooded cranes (*Grus monacha*) normally breed at nearly 60° north latitude (Johnsgard, 1983a), where day length eventually reaches close to 24 hours. First breeding of hooded cranes came after light was used to extend photoperiod to approximate that of their breeding habitat. Artificial rain showers are credited with producing the first captive breeding of the brolga (*Grus rubicundus*).

By the 1980s, cranes had become one of the most reliably bred groups in aviculture (Sheppard and Bruning, 1983). Extensive work had refined diets, improving fertility and decreasing the incidence of chick malformation. Artificial and surrogate incubation techniques were developed. Studbooks were published for the white-naped (*Grus vipio*), hooded, red crowned (*Grus japonensis*), Siberian (*Grus leucogeranus*), and wattled cranes (*Bugeranus carunculatus*) and were proposed for other species.

As studbooks and management plans were begun, questions arose which had not yet been addressed in the context of other endangered bird programs. Zoos had begun to breed large numbers of cranes, but common species like sarus (*Grus antigone*) were reproducing faster than rarer, endangered forms. Because most species have essentially identical requirements for space and management, and zoos have space limitations, it became clear that eventually crane species would be in competition for space for captive breeding. In 1987, zoos addressed this problem by developing strategies for cranes as a group, instead of species by species.

The captive and wild status of each species was evaluated. Five species—the white-naped, wattled, red-crowned, paradise (*Anthropoides paradisea*), and hooded cranes—were found to be both threatened in the wild and sufficiently well represented in captivity for long-term management to be meaningful. However, zoos have approximately 500 "spots" for breeding cranes, and perhaps the same number of exhibition spaces. Preliminary calculations show that a minimum of 150 birds per species will be needed for long-term management (Sheppard, 1988). These numbers limit breeding programs to only three species, unless more space can be created. Many spaces are presently occupied by the "wrong" species, and not all zoos will want to follow the recommendations of the advisory group. This experiment in planning at the family level set important precedents for decision-making and helped lead to the AAZPA TAG program.

Birds of Paradise (Paradiseadae)

Birds of paradise represent a program in progress. Large bodied colorful birds, with dramatic breeding plumage, they have been prized but have done poorly in captivity for at least a century (Worth et al., 1991). Restricted to the island of New Guinea, these birds play an important role in native cultures but have been declining locally, as shotguns replace bows and arrows. The extensive forests of Papua New Guinea (PNG) are relatively intact (Beehler, 1985) but significant logging is beginning, so birds of paradise may well become endangered in the near future. The Wildlife Conservation Society (WCS) coordinates two related programs, working in PNG to set up reserves and developing management and breeding techniques for birds of paradise in the United States. Founder stock was collected in areas slated for large-scale mining or logging.

WCS has had significant success with the red bird of paradise (*Paradisaea rubra*) and the lesser bird of paradise (*Paradisaea minor*). Success can be traced to concentration of effort, a factor common to other successful programs. Both space and manpower have been specifically dedicated to the problems posed by this group. These problems, experienced by zoos and individuals working with birds of paradise before 1980 (Muller, 1984) include iron storage disease, aspergillosis, and the birds' lek social system.

Birds of paradise are one of several groups susceptible to iron overload when maintained on normal avicultural diets (Taylor, 1984; Lowenstein, 1986). Such diets tend to be rich in iron, often from animal sources. Fruit eating birds, like birds of paradise, are adapted to food sources not only lower in iron, but also where iron is bound to other compounds and not readily available. Starting in 1985, a low iron diet was formulated and used, and losses to iron storage disease almost immediately stopped.

While birds of paradise live in tropical forests, they can seek cooler microclimates during the heat of the day. Mortality from aspergillosis in birds of paradise was correlated with high summer heat and humidity, especially for molting birds already under physiological stress. Air conditioning, providing a maximum temperature of 85°F was an effective solution.

Birds of paradise are lek breeders—males concentrate in traditional display areas which females visit only for copulation. Females nest solitarily and rear their young alone (LeCroy, 1981; Beehler, 1983a, b; Avery, 1984; Beehler and Foster, 1988), being reluctant to build nests near males. Males kept together may fight with fatal results. Based on this information, only single males are exhibited and breeding groups are set up off-exhibit in areas which can be subdivided. Early efforts were frustrated, as males tore up nests when allowed in a female's enclosure. Workable solutions were found, but involved intensive management and knowledge of individual behavior patterns (Hundgen et al., 1990). Now females are kept in flights with visual access to one or more males. Males stimulate one another to display. When females exhibit nest building behavior, they are allowed to shift into a male's flight, but never vice versa. Through 1992, 24 red bird of paradise have been hatched, and in 1992 a captive reared bird laid her first egg. Ten lesser bird of paradise have been hatched.

The difficulties inherent in breeding birds of paradise can be solved. However, before plans for establishing captive populations can be taken further, we must make sure that techniques used are repeatable, and are communicated to other zoos. We must devise exhibits suitable for breeding lekking birds. If large-scale exhibition is not possible, are we still willing to devote substantial off-exhibit space to the program?

The bird of paradise project illustrates the hardest problem faced by zoos trying to establish long-term propagation as a conservation reality. Achieving measurable success required more than ten years of effort, the collaboration of at least a dozen individuals with special knowledge and dedication, and off-exhibit management space for at least twenty birds. Such resources and focus of effort are not easily obtained in today's zoos, where curators and keepers manage collections which can include over two hundred species.

Conclusions: The Future of
Avian Captive Breeding Programs

Certainly, zoos cannot hope to preserve all endangered species through captive breeding (Sheppard, 1985a; Conway, 1986). The first order of business must be to establish criteria for deciding what species warrant the intensive effort and expense required by management programs. Until now, zoos have been almost passive, establishing breeding programs for those few endangered birds already in collections, initiating breeding programs when asked, and asked only when it is almost too late.

Endangered species breeding programs are expensive, requiring manpower, facilities, and space. For institutions often supported by public funds, it may be difficult to convince budget makers that funds should be committed to captive propagation, particularly when these programs occur off-exhibit. Ways to allocate priorities for space among breeding programs, education programs, and recreation must be developed.

One major resource conflict lies in exhibit design. The lush, natural habitat exhibits which the public has come to demand and which dramatically convey the value of habitat conservation, are among the most difficult to manage for captive breeding. Certainly, we must develop ways to make effective use of such exhibits but even with creative use, most exhibits will be restricted to one pair of any species. If we are to seriously discuss maintaining more than a token number of long-term breeding programs, we must find ways to obtain off-exhibit space, where both intensive management and development of new management techniques can take place.

For zoos, one answer may be the establishment of long-range conservation programs that include a close relationship with a species' country of origin. It is unlikely that zoos will ever be able to breed as many species as they would like to exhibit. The cost of such an endeavor, even if technology were available, would be more than prohibitive. For short lived species, such as many passerines, long-term management would require thousands of individuals. On the other hand, the number of birds that zoos need for exhibit is relatively small and these birds serve to promote conservation to the public. Conway has proposed that zoos might sponsor a reserve or buy land near reserves, in habitat that is essential for threatened wildlife; thus providing support for wardens and local education programs. In return, zoos would receive permission to trap small numbers of common species for exhibition. Associated programs should include development of field studies on the target species, education of local inhabitants, and encouragement of reserves, parks, and other forms of protection.

Management requirements should also be considered when priorities are evaluated. Conway (1987) makes the point that colonial species make the most efficient use of many scarce zoo resources, especially space and manpower. Aggressive, solitary species like hummingbirds, which also require precise regulation of climatic variables, can be extremely expensive to keep, requiring construction of indoor aviaries and extensive monitoring. Economics must always be considered. While off-exhibit breeding space may not apparently contribute directly to revenue production, by producing popular exhibit species and enhancing a zoo's conservation image, it may actually contribute considerably. Also, off-exhibit costs are often substantially less per bird, as public-related expenses are not required.

One lesson to be learned from already successful species management programs is the need for more information about the biology of any species we hope to breed. Zoos must develop serious research programs, aimed not at the acquisition of abstract knowledge, but at knowledge that will improve our chances of preserving particular species. As interest in conservation biology grows, collaborations between zoos and universities should become common. We need field studies to provide data with which to compare similar information on captive birds, and quantitative information about captive birds so that management decisions are based on more than hunches. The special nutritional requirements of each species must be elucidated. Physiological studies are needed to help correct fertility problems and to permit application of cryopreservation technology. We must learn how to test and evaluate a captive situation so that breeding is predictable, not lucky. Then captive breeding will truly become a tool of conservation.

14

Avian Reproductive Physiology

George F. Gee

Aviculturists use the special avian features noted throughout this chapter to design successful captive propagation programs. Successful propagation has at least three goals: (1) security of the captive population, (2) maintenance of the gene pool, and (3) production of quality stock for release (Erickson, 1968; Mettler and Gregg, 1969; Carpenter and Derrickson, 1981; Gee, 1986; Lande, 1988). Release of individuals from captive stock should be an adjunct to, and not a replacement for, habitat preservation and reclamation, or other types of conservation. Maintenance of captive stock has advantages; most importantly, control over reproduction, security, and genetic distribution.

Managers of captive stock have to use modern biochemical and systematic techniques to enhance the likelihood of genetically pure lines of captive stock, especially of birds destined for release. Aside from pedigree information, managers need estimates of genetic diversity and relatedness. They can make these estimates with protein electrophoresis, DNA restriction fragment length polymorphisms, and immunogenetics (Bertsch, 1987; Burke and Burford, 1987; Hill, 1987; Wetton et al., 1987; Longmire, 1988; Longmire, 1992).

Proper management and successful propagation of captive birds require comprehensive knowledge of avian reproductive anatomy and physiology. Physiological and behavioral control of reproduction varies from species to species. Also, our knowledge of physiological control in most endangered species is limited. The U.S. Fish and Wildlife service (1991) lists 238 endangered birds. Because of scarce species-specific information about endangered birds, this review includes information from nondomestic and, when needed, domestic birds. Aviculturists should use caution when extrapolating the results of these studies from one bird to another, especially from chickens (*Gallus domesticus*) to other birds. Data from closely-related species, such as surrogates for an endangered bird, provides some information, but eventually, the aviculturist must determine its usefulness for the endangered bird.

Reproductive Physiology of Female Birds

Most birds lay multi-egg clutches with one to three day intervals between eggs in the clutch. Some species lay more than one clutch per season, and have evolved special mechanisms to maintain high fertility in multi-egg clutches.

Functional Anatomy

The female's reproductive tract begins with the ovary, ventral to the cephalic lobe of the left kidney. The oviduct begins under the ovary and ends in the urodeum of the cloaca. The mesovarium ligament attaches the ovary to the dorsal body wall. The ovary has an inner medullary region containing major blood vessels and nerves, and the outer cortical region containing oocytes in various stages of development. Although the ovary contains millions of oocytes, birds ovulate few of them during their reproductive lifespan (Lofts and Murton, 1973; Johnson, 1986a).

The oviduct in a producing female is a large, convoluted tube composed of five distinct areas: infundibulum, magnum, isthmus, uterus, and vagina. The magnum is the longest section, about 40% of the total length, and the rest is divided equally between the other four areas. The wall of the infundibulum is thinner than the rest of the oviduct, and the wall of the uterus or shell gland is thick and muscular. Although bilateral in the female embryo, few mature birds have both right and left ovaries. In those that do, usually only the left side is functional (Marshall, 1961b; Lofts and Murton, 1973; Johnson, 1986a).

Birds lay eggs within a day or two of ovulation, although passage through the oviduct may take 50 to 60 hours in cranes (Gruidae) (Putnam, pers. comm.). The infundibulum captures the ovum, and if present, spermatozoa fertilize the female gamete. A thick, uniform layer of albumen coats the ovum as it passes through the magnum. The magnum forces the egg into the isthmus where the inner and outer shell membranes form. At this stage, the egg is small and contains only yolk and albumen. From the isthmus the egg enters the shell gland (uterus) where it spends about 80% of its time in its passage through the oviduct. A watery uterine fluid, added through the shell membranes, acts to increase the albumen volume. During the last hours, the uterus adds shell and shell pigment to complete the egg. The egg, when laid, contains several layers of egg white. These include the chalaziferous layer attached to the yolk, an inner liquid albumen layer, a thick albumen layer, and a thin outer albumen layer (Roca et al., 1984; Li-Chan and Naki, 1989).

The vagina (a short muscular part of the oviduct with a highly folded, compact lumen) provides a passageway for the egg and for the sperm. The sperm host glands (tubular invaginations of the vaginal mucosal epithelium at the uterovaginal [UV] juncture) enable birds to lay several fertile eggs after a single insemination (Zavaleta and Ogasawara, 1987). Sperm host glands may play a role in sperm choice and accretion of viable sperm (Bakst and Bird, 1987; Birkhead et al., 1988). The UV sperm host glands may begin storing sperm before follicular growth begins on the ovary and before the oviduct begins active stages of growth (Bakst,1988; Birkhead, pers. comm.). Although birds entering the early reproductive phase can store sperm, UV sperm host glands increase in size and number during the reproductive season (Hatch, 1983; Birkhead, 1987). Nalbandov (1958), Lofts and Murton (1973), and Johnson (1986a) provide detailed descriptions of the avian female anatomy.

Endocrinology

In nondomestic birds, seasonal changes in reproductive hormonal levels interact with and lead to profound physiological, anatomical, and behavioral changes (Dittami, 1981; Groscolas et al., 1986). Reproductive success depends on integrating signals from the neural and endocrine systems (Kobayashi and Wada, 1973; El Halawani et al., 1980a, b; van Tienhoven, 1980; El Halawani et al., 1982; Oksche, 1983). For more detailed information on the pituitary and hypothalamus, consult Kobayashi and Wada (1973), Tixier-Vidal and Follett (1973), Gorbman et al. (1983), and Scanes (1986). Many gonadotrophins and other hormones interact to either potentiate or negate each other, supplying an internal control over the reproductive effort. Also, the gonadotrophins, prolactin, and possibly others exist in several isohormone forms. Investigators identified some isohormone forms in chickens that may have different potencies and effects in control of the reproductive system (Proudman, 1987; Corcoran and Proudman, 1991).

Outside forces such as daylength, temperature, presence of a mate, humidity or rainfall, food supply, and chick rearing interact with endogenous hormonal rhythms (Scanes et al., 1983; Hector et al., 1986a). These start or end reproductive activity in birds (Dittami, 1981; Cheng and Balthazart, 1982; Wingfield, 1984a, b, c; Dittami et al., 1986). Although not yet identified as a controlling gland, the pineal gland may control the bird's interaction with outside stimuli (timing of endogenous rhythms, and response to unfavorable reproductive conditions) (Ueck and Umar, 1983). External stimuli that adversely affect behavioral or physiological mechanisms can reduce or stop reproduction (Evans, 1980; Bluhm, 1985b; Vleck and Priedkalns, 1985).

The gonadotrophins, other pituitary and hypothalamic hormones, and gonadal steroids decline after the reproductive season in most birds (Tixier-Vidal and Follett, 1973). But before declining in some nondomestic birds, adrenal steroids and prolactin rise for some period after the reproductive season (Payne, 1972; Peczely, 1985; Scanes, 1986). The gonadotrophin and gonadal steroid levels begin to rise again in the fall or winter and reach reproductive levels in the spring in most seasonal breeders (Table 14.1). In the male, these elevated hormone levels stabilize or decline gradually for the dura-

Table 14.1
General Scheme of Changes in Avian Hormonal Levels*

Hormonal levels	Season			
	Fall	Winter	Spring	Summer
Androgens	-	+	+ +	- -
Corticosterone	- -	- (++)**	+	+ +
Estrogen	- -	+	+ +	- -
FSH	-	+	+ +	- -
LH	-	+	+ +	- -
Prolactin	- -	-	+	+ +
Thyroxine	-	+ (++)**	+	- -

- - depressed
- somewhat depressed
+ somewhat elevated
+ + elevated
*   Fits no one species, intended only to show trend.
** May be elevated in cold stress.

Table 14.2
Transient Increased Plasma Hormonal Concentrations
Associated With Ovulation and Oviposition*

Hormone	Prior to Ovulation (Hours)		After	
	–20 to –10	–10 to 0	Ovulation	Oviposition
Androgen	+	+	+	
Corticosterone	+	+		+
Estrogen**		+		
LH		+		
Progesterone		+	+	
Oxytocin				+
Prostaglandins		+	+	+
Vasotocin				+

+ Increased level
* Generally found in studies with domestic fowl, comparative studies in other species needed.
**Levels stay elevated throughout the egg production cycle.

tion of the reproductive season. In the female, however, an elaborate symphony of cyclical changes occurs with most of the reproductive hormones (Table 14.2). These changes induce differentiation of the ovary and oviduct, follicular maturation, ovulation, egg formation, and oviposition (Tanaka and Nakajo, 1962; van Tienhoven, 1980; Kamiyoshi and Tanaka, 1983; Wang and Bahr, 1983; Scanes, 1986).

Gonadotrophins. Generally, follicle stimulating hormone (FSH) induces follicular development and growth of the oviduct, and luteinizing hormone (LH) stimulates ovulation and the production of progesterone and other gonadal steroids. The hypothalamus controls FSH and LH release by a decapeptide hypothalamic gonadotrophin (luteinizing hormone releasing hormone [LHRH] or gonadotrophin releasing hormone [Gn RH]) (Bluhm, 1985a; Scanes, 1986). Neural structures control the complex secretory pattern for LHRH by integrating phases of the life cycle, external neural senses, and circulating levels of steroid hormones (Cheng and Balthazart, 1982; Bluhm et al., 1983; Hiatt et al., 1987). The sex steroids control the action of LHRH on FSH and LH secretions, and of FSH and LH on the target tissues. Also, the gonadotrophins act in concert with prolactin and a variety of other reproductive or related hormones

(Table 14.1) in the target tissues (Lofts and Murton, 1973; Pavgi and Chandola, 1981).

Estrogen. Estrogen from the ovary prepares and stimulates oviduct growth, differentiation, and function (Johnson, 1986a; Scanes, 1986). Estrogen also increases vitellogenesis and growth of the ovarian follicle (Lofts and Murton, 1973; Johnson, 1986a). Also, estrogen prepares the female's body for reproduction by increasing deposition of fat, medullary bone, and oviductal and yolk precursor proteins. Estrogen titers rise in early stages of ovarian follicle development. When follicular development is obvious, hyperossification of medullary bone and increased fat deposits are obvious as well. Even in the young chick, when endogenous FSH and LH levels are very low, exogenous estrogen can increase oviduct weight (Lofts and Murton, 1973; Johnson, 1986a).

Estrogens help support the oviduct and ovary during the active reproductive phase and help control FSH and LH synthesis and release through feedback mechanisms in the hypothalamus (Pavgi and Chandola, 1981; Scanes, 1986). During egg formation, blood levels of calcium, phosphorous, lipids, and proteins rise in response to elevated estrogen levels (Lofts and Murton, 1973). The bird's elevated blood calcium used to form the egg shell comes from diet and hyperossified bone. Exogenous estrogen alone produces hyperossification in mature birds such as the quail (*Coturnix coturnix*), pigeon (*Columba livia*), and sparrow (*Passer domesticus*) (Marshall, 1961b; Baksi and Kenny, 1977). Elevated estrogen levels decrease the release of prolactin from the pituitary and induce the production of progesterone from the mature follicle (Sturkie, 1965b). The bird maintains uniformly elevated plasma estrogen throughout most of the egg production cycle (van Tienhoven, 1980).

Although estrogen is responsible for feminization, development of secondary sexual characteristics can result from androgens, estrogens, or genetic traits (Lofts and Murton, 1973). Estrogens are responsible for some variations in feather shape, plumage pattern, bill color, body size and shape, and voice (Lofts and Murton, 1973). Carlson (pers. comm.) uses voice prints to sex immature and adult cranes.

In pigeons, canvasbacks (*Aythya valisineria*), and mallards (*Anas platyrhynchos*), estrogen interacts with environmental cues to induce proper sexual behavior such as nest building. Also, estrogen can delay or end broodiness (Slater, 1978; Bluhm et al., 1983; Bluhm, 1985b). In pigeons, estrogen stimulates parental and mating behavior such as squatting, copulation, food begging, stooping, and the care and protection of chicks (Slater, 1978; Chadwick, 1983).

Androgens. Female androgens, produced primarily by the ovary, contribute to the normal cyclic phenomenon associated with egg production. Androgens also contribute to the expression of sexual characteristics, the reversal of sex roles during the nonreproductive season (Hohn and Cheng, 1967; Lofts and Murton, 1973; Slater, 1978; Wingfield, 1984a; Johnson, 1986a), and the establishment of higher rank and territorial defense by the female (Wingfield, 1983). During the breeding season, androgen levels are lower in the female than in the male. When progesterone synthesis increases, follicular androgen synthesis increases from a few hours before to a few hours after ovulation (van Tienhoven, 1980; Kamiyoshi and Tanaka, 1983; Johnson, 1986a). Androgen production peaks again 20 hours before ovulation (Shahabi et al., 1975). Androgens are necessary for estrogens to be effective in the cyclic production of eggs. Although the exact androgen role is unknown, an androgen rise always precedes the LH surge associated with ovulation (van Tienhoven, 1980; Kamiyoshi and Tanaka, 1983; Johnson, 1986a).

Progesterone. The largest, most rapidly-growing follicles (birds do not form corpora lutea) produce progesterone. Progesterone induces oviduct differentiation, controls oviduct function, and takes part in the timing of ovulation (Bahr et al., 1983; Johnson, 1986a). The peak progesterone synthesis interval begins six hours before ovulation and ends a few hours after ovulation, coinciding with elevated plasma progesterone levels (van Tienhoven, 1980; Kamiyoshi and Tanaka, 1983; Johnson, 1986a). Progesterone participates in a variety of synergistic actions with the gonadotropins, estrogen, and prolactin (Lofts and Murton, 1973).

Corticosterone. Adrenal cortical hormones help to integrate seasonal events like migration. They also help to integrate the normal cyclical phenomena associated with ovulation, egg formation, and oviposition during the breeding season (van Tienhoven, 1980; Deviche, 1983). The adrenal cortical hormones, especially corticosterone, may induce (Peczely, 1985) or delay reproduction (Deviche, 1983; Ghosh and Banerjee, 1983). Investigators (van Tienhoven, 1980) observed elevated plasma corticosterone levels during oviposition in the normal cycle of doves (Columbidae) and domestic fowl In the domestic fowl, the elevated corticosterone level occurs at the predicted time for oviposition without an egg in the uterus (after premature surgical removal) (Peczely and Pethes, 1980; van Tienhoven, 1980). Therefore, the plasma rise that coincides with oviposition does not have to be associated with the stress of oviposition.

Corticosterone is the primary stress related hormone produced by birds (Siegel, 1971; Deviche, 1983). The stress induced by the reproductive effort may be related to some changes in corticosterone levels (Deviche, 1983; Mallick and Sarkar, 1985). Corticosterone levels rise in some species (chicken, duck [*Anatinae*], brown pelican) during the winter and may reflect the birds' response to cold stress (Siegel, 1971; Assenmacher, 1973). Investigators observed an elevated corticosterone level before the start of the reproductive season (blossomheaded parakeet *Psittacula cyanocephala*, Maitra, 1987), during the reproductive season (common myna *Acridotheres tristis*, Mallick and Sarkar, 1985), or during the fall migration (white-throated sparrow *Zonotrichia albicollis*, Deviche, 1983). In other species, like the collared dove (*Streptopella decaocto*), plasma corticosterone levels rise during the reproductive season. Low levels of plasma corticosterone found at the time of the first egg rise to higher levels during incubation (Peczely and Pethes, 1980). Investigators (Bluhm et al., 1983; Deviche, 1983; Ghosh and Banerjee, 1983) have associated high corticosterone levels in some species (pigeon, chicken, duck, canary [*Serinus canaria*]) with delays in the reproductive season. In some species (duck, tree sparrow [*Spizella arborea*], pigeon) researchers used exogenous corticosterone to interfere with the reproductive effort (Bluhm et al., 1983; Deviche, 1983; Ghosh and Banerjee, 1983).

Some researchers of white-throated sparrow relate the onset of reproduction to phase angle difference between circadian rhythms of corticosterone and prolactin. In the reproductive season, a difference of 12 hours exists between the peak blood plasma corticosterone level and peak plasma prolactin level. At other times a difference of six hours exists between the peak levels (Meier et al., 1980; Deviche, 1983). Corticosterone levels in not all, but many birds (duck, canary, sparrow, chicken, dove) decrease when androgen or estrogen levels increase and increase when thyroxine (T_4) levels increase (Assenmacher, 1973; Pecezely and Pethes, 1980). Uniform results from studies of plasma corticosterone are difficult to obtain because handling increases circulating corticosterone levels (Dittami, 1981). There are some intriguing suggestions in the corticosterone relationships, but they are more difficult to interpret than the simplified version discussed above (Opel and Proudman, 1988, 1989). In birds, corticosterone seems to have a role not only in stress and gonadal development, but also in fat storage, molt, and migratory behavior (Deviche, 1983).

Prolactin. Prolactin induces and maintains incubation and stimulates migration (El Halawani et al., 1980a; Dittami, 1981; Hector et al., 1986b; Hiatt et al., 1987; Proudman, 1991). Prolactin maintains the crop sac response in pigeons and doves (Clarke and Bern, 1980; Chadwick, 1983; Scanes, 1986). Others related the antigonadal effect of increased plasma levels of prolactin to the suppression of LH levels (Scanes, 1986) and to molt in other birds (chickens, geese, pigeons, sparrows) (Payne, 1972; van Tienhoven, 1980; Dittami, 1981). Moderately elevated plasma prolactin levels are compatible with ovarian function but higher levels may block ovarian function (Dawson et al., 1984). Also, estrogen and prolactin interact to form the brood patch found in many birds like the canary (Steel and Hind, 1963). Stress and photoperiod without other environmental stimuli may induce elevated plasma prolactin in some species (turkey, white-crowned sparrow [*Zonotrichia leucophrys*]) (Opel and Proudman, 1986; Hiatt et al., 1987).

Thyroxine. Thyroid function, depending on species, may promote or inhibit gonadal development (Silverin, 1983; Kar and Chandola, 1985) and molt (Assenmacher and Jallageas, 1980). Assenmacher (1973) and Dawson et al. (1984) found that some species (like the chicken) need thyroid hormone for normal gonad development, and other species (like the pigeon) do not. Chickens, ducks, house sparrows, and the male collared dove belong to the group that needs elevated thyroid activity. The European starling (*Sturnus vulgaris*), Japanese white-eyes (*Zosterops japonica*), female collared dove, Baya weaver (*Ploceus philippinus*), red avadavat (*Amandava amandava*), and the chestnut maniken (*Lonchura malacca*) do not need elevated thyroid activity to maintain gonadal development (Assenmacher, 1973; Peczely and Pethes, 1980). Also, the ratio of triiodothyronine (T_3) and T_4 may be an important mitigating influence in the control of the reproductive cycle (Chandola et al., 1983; Kar and Chandola, 1985; Sharp and Klandorf, 1985).

Oxytocin and vasotocin. Although oviposition may involve vasotocin and oxytocin, vasotocin seems to have the greater effect. Vasotocin produces the most powerful contractions of the oviduct and the most rapid onset of oviposition (Kobayashi and Wada, 1973). Birds produce both hormones in the hypothalamus and store them in the neural lobe of the pituitary. Therefore, removal of the neural lobe does not lead to deficiency in vasotocin or oxytocin (van Tienhoven, 1980). Vasotocin increases 20-fold in the plasma of a hen during oviposition, but the rise in oxytocin levels is only slight (Sturkie and Lin, 1966; van Tienhoven, 1980). The decrease in vasotocin in the neural lobe after oviposition is marked (Tanaka and Nakajo, 1962).

Prostaglandins. Prostaglandins (PG), especially PGF_{22}, take part in oviposition in domestic fowl (Hertelendy 1974; Day and Nalbandov, 1977; Poyser and Pharm, 1981). How PGs interact with vasotocin and other hormonal factors responsible for oviposition is unclear. PGs increase fourfold in the preovulatory follicle four to six hours before ovulation (Hertelendy et al., 1974; van Tienhoven, 1980). PGs in the postovulatory follicular sheath increase 100-fold during the 24 hours following ovulation. PGs reach their peak concentrations two hours before the next oviposition (Day and Nalbandov, 1977; Poyser and Pharm, 1981). Exogenous PGs are more effective than oxytocin in producing premature oviposition in domestic fowl (Hertelendy et al., 1974; Hargrove and Ottinger, 1991). Also, the oviduct produces PGs, PGF_{22} being two to eight times greater than PGE (van Tienhoven, 1980). PGE, a calcium mobilizing hormone, may be responsible in some way for eggshell calcification (Poyser and Pharm, 1981).

Reproductive Physiology of the Avian Male

The avian male produces semen in synchrony with the egg production season, and most share responsibility in nest building, incubation, and rearing of the young.

Functional Anatomy

The male reproductive tract has paired testis, simple epididymides, and ductus deferens (Sturkie, 1965a; Lake, 1981; Johnson, 1986b). The testes are above the abdominal air sacs and ventral to the cephalic end of the kidneys. The epididymis, in the hilar part of the testes, is rudimentary compared with the mammalian system. Sperm when entering the ductus deferens can fertilize ova and need to undergo no further maturation. In galliformes, the ductus deferens is a highly-coiled duct which acts as a sperm storage site. The ductus deferens continue into the urodeum as small papillae. Sperm collect in the simple epididymis on the caudal wall of the testis and need one to four days to pass through the ductus deferens (Munro, 1938). Accessory seminal fluids come directly from reproductive tract secretions and from lymph folds surrounding the terminal parts of the reproductive tract (Sturkie, 1965a, b). Although most birds store semen in the ductus deferens in the body cavity, passerines store semen in the cloacal protuberance. The cloacal protuberance contains the coiled vas deferens under the skin above the dorsal lip of the cloaca (Howell and Bartholomew, 1952; Wolfson, 1952, 1960b; Salt, 1954; Middleton, 1974).

A few birds have an intromittent organ to help in copulation (ratites and waterfowl), an extension of the rudimentary phallus found in other birds (Bump and Bump, 1969; Skinner, 1974; Fujihara et al., 1976). These birds release semen at the base of the phallus and use the phallus to guide the semen into the female (Bump and Bump, 1969; Skinner, 1974; Fujihara et al., 1976). In most waterfowl, the phallus is a highly-coiled ribbon containing many papillae on its surface when erect (Fujihara et al., 1976; King, 1981b). In ratites, the addition of many collagenous support structures gives the phallus rigidity.

Sperm morphology varies from species to species and shows a phylogenetic relation. The simple sauropsid form is typical of the less advanced species (nonpasserines), and the more elaborate helical form is typical of the more advanced species (Vireonidae and Fringillidae) (McFarlane, 1962, 1971). The American kestrel may be an exception because the primary shape of the spermatozoa seems round or oval (Bird and Lague, 1977).

Besides the lymph-like fluid produced and secreted during ejaculation, obvious cloacal secretions are uncommon in most birds. Yet, there are some notable exceptions (Quay, 1967). In the Japanese quail, the proctodeal glands on the dorsal wall of the cloaca produce a frothy mucoid secretion; the ani (*Crotophage ani*), a copious mucoid secretion; and the ratites, a waxy or greasy material. The importance of these secretions to normal reproductive activities is unclear. Nalbandov (1958), Quay (1967), Lofts and Murton (1973), King (1981a, b), Lake (1981), and Johnson (1986b) provide detailed descriptions of avian male anatomy.

Endocrinology

Both sexes use like mechanisms to control their reproductive endocrinology (Hiatt et al., 1987). Two notable exceptions are:

(1) the relative levels of androgens and estrogens vary between sexes, and (2) males lack the cyclic hormonal variations associated with ovulation and oviposition in the female.

Gonadotrophins. Both FSH and LH regulate the maturation and function of the male reproductive tract. FSH induces spermatogenesis in the Sertoli cells of the seminiferous tubules (Lofts and Murton, 1973; Johnson, 1986b). LH induces androgen production from the interstitial (Leydig) cells (Lofts and Murton, 1973; Maung and Follett, 1978; Johnson, 1986b). FSH and LH plasma levels rise in the spring and fall to basal levels in summer in seasonal breeders (Lofts and Murton, 1973; Dittami, 1981; Dufty and Wingfield, 1986b). The gonadotrophins in most species stay at basal plasma levels in the fall and winter (Chadwick, 1983; Farner et al., 1983; Haase, 1983; Wada, 1984, 1985; Chakroborty et al., 1985; Hegner and Wingfield, 1986; Hiatt et al., 1987; Williams et al., 1987). During the reproductive season in species like ring doves (*Streptoplia risoria*), rooks (*Corvus frugilagus*), white-crowned sparrows, and pied flycatcher (*Ficeduila hypoleuca*), LH and androgen levels rise in the copulatory and early nesting season and then decline during the incubation and brooding phases of reproduction. In species that renest (mallards, white-crowned sparrows, and ring doves), LH and androgen levels rise with the onset of renesting. In species that do not nest (brood parasites) like the brown-headed cowbird (*Melothrus ater*), LH and androgen levels stay elevated during the prolonged egg laying (and mate guarding) season (Lofts and Murton, 1973; Davies et al., 1976; Dittami, 1981; Silverin, 1984; Bluhm, 1985; Dufty and Wingfield, 1986b). In a few species of biennial breeders like the grey-headed albatross (*Diomedea chrysostoma*) and the wandering albatross (*D. exulans*), gonadotrophin levels increase in association with the reproductive cycle (Hector et al., 1986a, b).

Gonadotrophins also affect nonreproductive tract tissues, either indirectly through other hormones, or directly on target tissues. LH produces changes in plumage and beak color, as evident in the paradise whydah (*Vidua paradisaea*), the red-billed (*Quela quela*) and tropical weaver birds (Lofts and Murton, 1973; Deviche, 1982; Chakrovorty et al., 1985). LH also can increase reproductive displays and improve social status in many birds like the European starling and the red-billed weaver (Lofts and Murton, 1973; Deviche, 1982; Chakrovorty et al., 1985).

Androgens. Androgens induce growth and maintenance of the reproductive tract in response to LH stimulation (Lofts and Murton, 1973; Dittami, 1981; Wada, 1983; Johnson, 1986a). Androgens also increase masculine reproductive behavior (Adkins-Regan, 1981; Balthazart, 1982, 1983; Akesson and Raveling, 1983; Ottinger, 1983) and secondary sexual characteristics (Lofts and Murton, 1973). The cloacal protuberance in passerines enlarges profoundly in response to elevated androgen titers throughout the year (Wilson, 1986). Rising androgen levels increase aggressive behavior in both sexes and contribute to male dominance in most species. Aggressive meetings with conspecific males or, sometimes, presence of the female increase androgen levels (Dufty and Wingfield, 1986a; Wingfield et al., 1987). The neural-endocrine interaction continues until the bird establishes territory and begins nesting. With the new social order associated with nesting, androgen levels decline and the incubation and rearing phases of reproduction begin (Wingfield, 1984a, b, c; Wingfield, 1985b; Wingfield et al., 1987).

Estrogens and progestins. Besides androgens, the testes produce estrogens and progestins (Lofts and Murton, 1973). Progesterone acts synergistically with the other reproductive hormones. In different species, progesterone seems to have different plasma level patterns during the reproductive cycle (Lofts and Murton, 1973; Balthazart, 1982; Chadwick, 1983; Hector et al., 1986 a, b). In the male white-crowned sparrow, the dove, and the domestic duck (*Anas platyrhynchos*), progesterone levels are constant throughout the reproductive cycle (Silver et al., 1974; Donham, 1979; Balthazart, 1983). In the ring dove, large increases in plasma progesterone levels occur in the later stages of egg production and in the wandering albatross in the chick-rearing stage (Chadwick, 1983; Hector et al., 1986a). In the black-browed (*Diomedea melanophris*) and the grey-headed albatross, progesterone reaches elevated levels in both sexes during the prelaying season and, in males, remains high for most of the chick-rearing phase (Hector et al., 1986a, b). In young male zebra finches (*Taeniopygia guttata*) estrogen and other hormones may prevent sexual imprinting during the sensitive phase (Prove, 1985).

Prolactin. A prolactin-releasing factor from the hypothalamus controls prolactin secretion (Harvey et al., 1982) and may maintain a strong circadian rhythm (see earlier corticosterone and prolactin discussion). Prolactin, with or without support from progestins and androgens (Macularia et al., 1984), induces and maintains incubation and brooding in species like turkey (*Meleagris gallapavo*), rook and bar-headed goose (*Anser indicus*), and crop gland secretion in pigeons and doves (Columbiformes) (Clarke and Bern, 1980; El Halawani et al., 1980a; Haase, 1983). Prolactin supports fattening and migratory restlessness in passerines like the white-throated sparrow (Meier and Farner, 1964; Meier et al., 1971; Tixier-Vidal and Follett, 1973; Clarke and Bern, 1980; Goldsmith, 1983). In some birds such as the white-crowned and white-throated sparrows, and California quail (*Callipepla californica*), testes function is tolerant of high prolactin levels (Meier et al., 1969; Clarke and Bern, 1980; Meier et al., 1980; Hiatt et al., 1987). Yet, increased prolactin suppresses spermatogenesis and induces testicular collapse in many other birds like the pigeon, European starling, mallard duck, and pied flycatcher (Clarke and Bern, 1980; Goldsmith, 1983; Haase, 1983; Sharp et al., 1986; Hiatt et al., 1987).

Artificial Insemination In Nondomestic Birds

Artificial insemination (AI) developed in response to a variety of needs in aviculture (Smyth, 1968; Martin, 1975; Cooper, 1977; Gee and Temple, 1978; Gee, 1983). Natural copulation can be difficult because of differences in body size, injury or deformity, and aberrant behavior. Also, AI allows propagators to keep females in separate pens or at a distant location, and to get fertile eggs by transferring semen. AI is useful in carrying out the breeding goals for captive propagation, and in collecting semen for laboratory evaluations and in cryopreserving semen (Gee et al., 1985; Gee, 1986). Infertility, a common problem in captive birds, may be corrected with AI if a semen source is available (Szumowski et al., 1976; Sexton, 1977; Lake, 1978; Gee, 1983). Although AI corrects some infertility, one should consider other choices first because AI is labor-intensive and time-consuming.

The names of the three AI techniques (cooperative, massage, and electroejaculation) reflect the degrees of cooperation by the birds with the technician. In an earlier version of the cooperative technique, technicians intercepted semen during natural copulation with other birds or dummies (Smyth, 1968; Tan, 1980). Falconers perfected cooperative semen collection and insemination with sexually-imprinted birds of prey (Hammerstrom, 1970; Berry, 1972; Temple, 1972; Grier, 1973). Technicians encourage the unrestrained male to copulate, and to deposit semen in or on a suitable receptacle (Boyd and Boyd, 1976; Boyd, 1978). Handlers encourage the female birds to assume copulatory positions. Technicians deposit semen in the cloaca or everted oviduct of the receptive bird (Berry, 1972; Temple, 1972; Boyd et al., 1977). Cooperative semen collection and insemination call for opportune timing to obtain an adequate number of samples and to get fertile eggs.

Aviculturists have used the massage collection technique (Quinn and Burrows, 1936) for decades with domestic poultry and recently with nondomestic birds (Gee, 1983). In nondomestic birds an assistant holds and massages the bird while an operator massages and collects the sample or inseminates. The bird responds to massage by a partial eversion of the cloaca (occasionally ejaculation). The operator collects the semen from the ventral lip of the vent in a cup or a funnel. Researchers developed a variety of holding devices to handle dangerous birds or to enable one person to collect and inseminate (Smyth, 1968).

Electroejaculation, although a common practice in domestic mammals, is not a common method for collecting avian semen. Several investigators prefer electroejaculation of domestic ducks and geese, and psittacines (cockatiels [*Leptolophus*], budgarigars [*Melopsottacus undulatus*], macaws [*Ata*]) to other methods of collection (Serebrovski and Sokolovskaja, 1934, Watanabe, 1957; Chelmonska and Geborska-Dymkowska, 1980; Harrison, 1982). Duck semen collected by electroejaculation contained more spermatozoa and greater volume than that collected by the conventional massage technique (Watanabe, 1957). Electroejaculation may become a more common form of collection if aviculturists can apply its reported advantages (greater volume and concentration) to other birds.

It is difficult to stimulate and collect semen from songbirds because of their small size. Yet, during the reproductive season, song birds store semen in a well-developed cloacal protuberance, an evagination of the dorsal lip of the cloaca containing the distal segments of the ductus deferens (Howell and Bartholomew, 1952; Wolfson, 1952, 1960b; Salt, 1954; Middleton, 1974). Small quantities of semen can be collected from many passerines by applying gentle pressure to the protuberance.

The copulatory organ (phallus) in waterfowl, ratites, and tinamous (*Nothura, Rhynchotis, Nothoprocata*) (Bump and Bump,

1969) uncoils as it erects during sexual excitation. It carries semen along a twisted groove that runs the length of the organ. Early in the massage collection process, the operator everts the phallus (Smyth, 1968; Skinner, 1974). After ejaculation, the operator collects the semen at the base and tip of the phallus with a small funnel, tube, or suction device. The copulatory organ is very delicate and rough treatment should be avoided or injury may result (Smyth, 1968). The phallus' irregular surface and groove hold semen and can interfere with semen collection in species that yield small semen samples. Gentle manipulation of the vent permits collection of the semen without everting the phallus. This maneuver prevents spreading the semen over the irregular surface of the phallus.

The female, stimulated by massage, responds with a partial eversion of the oviduct. A deep vaginal insemination is usually preferable to a cloacal insemination (Lorenz, 1969; Ogasawara and Fuqua, 1972), because the oviduct stores sperm in the sperm host glands at the uterovaginal junction (Bobr et al., 1962). Still, a moderate depth of insemination gives satisfactory results (Smyth, 1968; Wentworth et al., 1975; Boyd et al., 1977). Propagators should avoid injury by gently inserting the inseminating device because injury can interfere with production and fertility (Ogasawara and Fuqua, 1972; Wentworth et al., 1975). When depositing semen in the cloaca instead of the oviduct, inseminations should be more frequent and timed to coincide with oviposition (Berry, 1972; Temple, 1972; Grier, 1973; Archibald, 1974; Gee, 1983).

The frequency of insemination is dependent on many things including semen quality, duration of fertility, age, and stage of egg production. Recommended insemination frequency varies from every other day in Japanese quail (Lepore and Marks, 1966) to every other week in turkeys (Smyth, 1968). The duration of fertility varies from 4 to 5 days for Japanese quail (Wentworth and Mellen, 1963) and 6 to 8 days in some raptors (Grier, 1973; Bird et al., 1976; Boyd et al., 1977) to 21 days in Temminck's tragopan (Durrant et al., 1988) and 45 days in turkeys (Lorenz et al., 1959; Smyth, 1968) (Table 14.3). Also, several repeated inseminations before the onset of egg production improve later fertility (Smyth, 1968). Semen volumes vary from 5 to 10 μl for small birds, to 1 to 5 ml for very large birds, and sperm concentration varies from $2x10^7$ (Hargrove, 1986) to $10x10^9$ cells per ml. (Gee, 1983).

Semen volume deposited per insemination depends on the sperm concentration and capacity of the reproductive tract to retain the semen. Often, semen volume and concentration are adequate to

Table 14.3
Semen Volume, Sperm Concentration, and Duration of Fertility for Variety of Birds*

Species	Volume	Concentration[1]	Fertility (days)	References
Domestic				
Canary	=10 μl		10–13	Griffith (pers. comm.)
Chicken	0.5–0.8 ml	3.5x10⁹	8	Smyth (1968)
Duck	0.2–0.4 ml	2–9x10⁹	8–16	Johnson (1986b), Watanabe (1957)
Goose	10–800 μl			Gee and Temple (1978), Oliver (1971), Johnson (1954)
Japanese Quail	10 μl	5x10⁹	4–5	Smyth (1968)
Pigeon	10–20 μl			Owen (1941)
Ring-necked Pheasant	50–250 μl	10x10⁹	11	Smyth (1968), Cain (1978)
Turkey	0.2–0.3 ml	8x10⁹	45	Smyth (1968)
Nondomestic				
American Kestrel	14 μl		8	Bird et al. (1976)
Brewer's Blackbird	=10 μl	+		Wolfson (1960b)
Eclectus Parrot	50–100 μl	-		Gee and Beall (unpublished)
Goshawk	20–30 μl			Berry (1972)
House Finch	10 μl	+		Griffith (per. comm.)
Prairie Falcon	50–100 μl	0.02x10⁹	6–8	Boyd (1978), Boyd et al. (1977)
Red-tailed Hawk	0.1 ml		6	Gee and Temple (1978)
Swamp Sparrow	=10 ml	+		Wolfson (1952)
Sandhill Crane	10–200 μl	0.3x10⁹	10	Gee and Temple (1978), Putnam (1982)
Temminck's Tragopan	33 ml	1.28x10⁹	21	Durrant et al. (1988)
Andean Condor	0.1–0.2 ml			Gee (unpublished)
Wood Thrush	10 ml	+		Wolfson (1960b)
Wattled Cassowary	1–5 ml	-		Pickett (pers. comm.)
House Sparrow	=10 μl	+		Gee (unpublished)
Seaside Sparrow	=10 μl	+		Gee (unpublished)
Golden Eagle	0.2 ml		9	Grier (1973), Grier et al. (1973)
Cockatiel	50 ml			Harrison (pers. comm.)
Budgerigar	5.4±1.1 μl	2.5x10⁷		Hargrove (1986)

+   greater than the domestic chicken   =   approximate
-   less than the domestic chicken   *   Modified from Gee (1983).
[1]   # spermatozoa/ml of semen

inseminate several females from each ejaculation. Investigators know little about spermatozoa concentration needed per insemination in nondomestic birds, but many recommend between 80 and 100 million in chickens and turkeys (Sexton, 1977; Lake and Steward, 1978). For nondomestic birds, inseminators should adjust the frequency of insemination to reach a satisfactory fertility rate (Gee, 1983).

Semen characteristics can be evaluated, but the most reliable test of viability is the production of fertile eggs. Before insemination, researchers often evaluate samples for sperm concentration, percentage of progressive motility, morphology, live-dead ratio, metabolic rate, and semen composition.

Light and Reproduction

Since the late 1800s, biologists believed photoperiod controlled avian reproductive periodicity (Farner, 1986). Rowan (1925, 1926, 1929) linked length of day with reproductive control in birds (Marshall, 1961b). Since then, every bird tested from the north temperate zone and some from the equatorial regions have exhibited photoperiod control of reproduction (Immelmann, 1971; Gwinner and Dittami, 1985; Wada, 1985).

Avian physiologists have classified the factors that influence reproduction into two groups ("proximate" and "ultimate"). Ultimate factors are those "which give survival value to the adaptation of the bird's cycle to that of the environment" and proximate factors are those "which provide the actual timing that brings the adaptation into play" (Thomson, 1950, pp. 174–175). Ultimate factors such as food supply, nesting conditions, competition, predator pressure, and inclement weather act before the birds lay. Ultimate factors can start or stop the reproductive effort (Marshall, 1961a, b; Immelmann, 1971; El Halawani et al., 1980a, 1984; Wingfield, 1983, 1985a, b; Farner, 1986). The proximate factors act early in the reproductive cycle. Proximate factors act by entraining and strengthening the bird's own endogenous rhythms (Nalbandov, 1958; Marshall, 1959; Scanes et al., 1983; Wada, 1983, 1984; Tewarty et al., 1984). Many excellent reviews contain information on proximate factors such as photoperiod, rainfall, water level, territory, nest site, state of nutrition, temperature, social interactions, and food supply (Marshall, 1959; Immelmann, 1971, 1972; Murton and Westwood, 1977; Wingfield, 1983; Wada, 1984). Light is the most effective and universal proximate reproductive factor in birds of the north temperate zone (Farner, 1986).

Birds can be classified by their response to photoperiod in their native habitat. Under captive conditions, photoperiod may exert an influence not normally encountered in the wild, such as reproductive stimulations by long light days in some equatorial birds (Singh and Chandola, 1981; Tewarty and Dixit, 1986). Some birds may be insensitive to photoperiod or may not respond to small changes they experience in their native habitat. Examples of photoperiod-insensitive birds include: (1) continuous breeders of equatorial rain forests and tropical islands, (2) sea birds, and (3) nonannual breeders of equatorial habitats, tropical sea birds, and Australian birds (Immelmann, 1971). Some birds respond to small increases in photoperiod (short day) such as the crow (*Corvus*) and the Nene goose (*Branta sandvicensis*), and some need large increases in photoperiod (long day) to trigger the reproductive effort such as the bobolink (*Dolichonyx oryzivorus*), junco (*Junco*), and wading birds of the Arctic. Some birds such as many north temperate zone passerines that first respond to photoperiod, eventually become refractory to it and end reproduction at earlier stimulatory photoperiods (Engles, 1969; Pavgi and Chandola, 1981; Falk and Gwinner, 1983; Tewarty and Tripathi, 1983).

The photorefractory period may be directly related to LH or LHRH cycles in birds (Wingfield et al., 1981, Kant and Saxena, 1982; Dawson et al., 1984). Photorefractoriness is species specific (some photosensitive species have none, some have short and others long refractory periods) and probably has multiple origins and controls (Lofts and Murton, 1973; Farner et al., 1983). The relation between peak diel levels in corticosterone, thyroxine, and prolactin may be responsible for the LH response of photorefractoriness in some birds (Jallageas and Assenmacher, 1974; Deviche, 1983; Goldsmith, 1984; Lal and Thapliyal, 1985; Nicholls et al., 1985). In others, negative feedback of gonadal steroids may be responsible (Cusick and Wilson, 1972; Davies et al., 1976; Haase, 1983). More information on photoperiod is in Burger (1949), Farner (1959, 1961, 1964, 1986), Wolfson (1959, 1960a), Marshall (1961a, b), Lofts and Murton (1968), Farner and Lewis (1971), Immelmann (1971), and Murton and Westwood (1977).

Cryopreservation

Frozen gametes and embryos can aid captive propagation and scientific studies, assist with gene flow between disjunct populations, and can help protect the gene pool. Protecting genetic diversity with a frozen gene pool supports the genetic base necessary for survival (Graham et al., 1978; Senner, 1980; Soulé, 1980; Terbough and Winter, 1980). Also, genetic diversity provides a pool of genetic variation upon which future choices may operate (Mettler and Gregg, 1969). If an endangered bird loses diversity, it cannot be restored without a frozen gene pool.

Aviculturists cannot keep all endangered birds in captivity (Conway, 1980), but they can help greater numbers through cryopreservation programs (Gee, 1986; Durrant, 1990). Conservationists must take advantage of cryopreservation and other new technologies soon, before many vulnerable birds are beyond rescue (National Research Council, 1978).

Today, aviculturists can store frozen semen, and eventually they may also store frozen eggs and embryos. Semen stored in liquid nitrogen (–196° C) stops metabolic activity, and viability persist for long periods, possibly centuries (Mazur, 1980). Freezing semen from nondomestic birds was impractical until the mid-1970s when the Beltsville Agricultural Research Center froze chicken semen in dimethylsulfoxide (DMSO) (Sexton, 1976). Researchers had to remove glycerol, the cryprotectant used before DMSO, from the semen before inseminating (Sexton, 1979). Semen with glycerol at cryoprotectant levels has a contraceptive effect in birds (Lake, 1978). With DMSO, small semen samples can be handled quickly and birds inseminated without removing the DMSO.

Frozen gene pools should include all animals, even if the fertility rates of a few are lower than others in the population. The aviculturists should collect and store more semen from these animals to compensate for their lower fertility rates. The frozen gene pool should contain every founder line in a captive endangered species population, and a representative sample of unrelated lines in a captive nonendangered species population. Frozen banks are inexpensive compared with an active captive propagation program. The space for a frozen gene pool and the cost of storage varies with the availability of the semen and of liquid nitrogen, the containers used, and the number and size of the samples stored.

The greatest expense in cryopreservation is the time, people, animals, and facilities to develop a suitable freezing technique for each species (Gee, 1986; Durrant, 1990). Costs for collection are smallest if donor animals are available. Combining frozen gene pools with existing programs may make it possible to preserve small populations that are otherwise destined for extinction. Frozen banks are useful for many purposes: to provide semen out-of-season, to overcome deleterious alleles, to satisfy quarantine restrictions, and to aid in a variety of mating schemes.

The Patuxent Wildlife Research Center of the U.S. Fish and Wildlife Service and the Beltsville Agricultural Research Center of the Agricultural Research Service started cooperative research on freezing crane semen in 1976 (Sexton and Gee, 1978). Since then, they have produced fertile eggs and young from cranes, geese, sparrows, and kestrels inseminated with frozen-thawed semen. Although fertility rates in the early studies start at 10% to 30% (Sexton and Gee, 1978), fertility rates of 50% or more are possible from cranes, geese, and kestrels (Gee et al., 1985; Gee and Sexton, 1990; Gee et al., 1993).

Technical detail is essential for successful cryopreservation of bird semen. Hargrove and Gee expect fertility rates above 50% when the semen of sandhill (*Grus canadensis*) and white-naped (*G. vipio*) cranes is diluted 1:2 and frozen in 6% or 8% DMSO (Gee et al., 1985; Hargrove and Gee, unpublished). Fertility in the endangered Aleutian Canada goose (*Branta canadensis leucopareia*) exceeded 50% when semen was diluted 1:2 and frozen in 7% DMSO. Fertility from frozen fecal- and urate-contaminated semen was less than fertility from frozen clean semen (Gee and Sexton, 1990). Also, Gee et al. (1993) expect fertility rates above 50% from the American kestrel (*Falco sparverius*) when the semen is diluted 1:0.5 and frozen in 6%, 8%, or 10% DMSO. These investigators froze goose, kestrel, and sparrow semen at the same rate described for cranes and held it in liquid nitrogen. The semen from all four species was thawed for three minutes in an ice bath and the birds inseminated a few minutes after the semen was thawed. Birds were inseminated Monday, Wednesday, and Friday and after each oviposition. The birds were not inseminated when the uterus contained a palpable egg. Also, others have frozen semen successfully in the crane (Gruidae), Impeyan pheasant (*Lophophorus impeyanus*), Temminck's tragopan (*Tragopan temmincki*), and budgarigars (*Melopsottacus undulatus*) with DMSO and in the kestrel with glycerol and dimethylacetamide (Brock, 1986; Hargrove, 1986; Parks et al., 1986; Gale, 1987; Samour et al., 1988; Durrant and Burch, 1991).

Conclusion

Knowledge of the many physiological factors associated with egg production, fertility, incubation, and brooding in nondomestic birds is limited. Science knows even less about reproduction in most of the 238 endangered or threatened birds. This discussion uses studies of nondomestic and, when necessary, domestic birds to describe physiological control of reproduction. Studies of the few nondomestic avian species show large variation in physiological control of reproduction. Aviculturists, in order to successfully propagate an endangered bird, must understand the bird's reproductive peculiarities. First, investigators can do studies with carefully chosen surrogate species, but eventually they need to confirm the results in the target endangered bird. Studies of reproduction in nondomestic birds increased in the last decade. Still, scientists need to do more comparative studies to understand the mechanisms that control reproduction in birds.

New technologies are making it possible to study reproductive physiology of nondomestic species in less limiting ways. These technologies include telemetry to collect information without inducing stress on captives (Howey et al., 1987; Klugman, 1987), new tests for most of the humoral factors associated with reproduction, and the skill to collect small samples and manipulate birds without disrupting the physiological mechanisms (Bercovitz et al., 1985). Managers are using knowledge from these studies to improve propagation in zoological parks, private and public propagation facilities, and research institutions.

Researchers need to study the control of ovulation, egg formation, and oviposition in the species of nondomestic birds that lay very few eggs in a season, hold eggs in the oviduct for longer intervals, or differ in other ways from the more thoroughly studied domestic birds. Other techniques that would enhance propagation for nondomestic birds include tissue culture of cloned embryonic cells, cryopreservation of embryos and gametes, embryo transplant, DNA analysis and manipulation, disease screening and control, and improved release conditioning methods.

15

Behavioral Considerations in the Captive Management, Propagation, and Reintroduction of Endangered Birds

*Michael Hutchins, Christine Sheppard,
Anna Marie Lyles, and Gerard Casadei*

A knowledge of animal behavior is fundamental to the *ex situ* conservation of endangered birds. By helping to identify a species' unique social and environmental requirements, the discipline is critical to the success of long-term captive breeding programs and to the release of captive-bred individuals into the wild. Behavioral research can also provide zoo educators with basic data on avian lifestyles—the information through which people come to perceive birds as living, intrinsically valuable creatures—instead of ornaments, curiosities, or status symbols.

The purpose of this chapter is to discuss how a knowledge of behavior can be applied to the exhibition, care, propagation, and reintroduction of endangered or threatened birds. Our intention is not to provide a comprehensive review of these topics, but rather to introduce aviculturists to a broad range of relevant issues. Also included is a review of some of the research methods currently employed in behavioral studies of captive birds.

Scope of Existing Field Studies

Most behavioral studies originate as attempts to answer basic questions about the way animals interact with one another and with their environment; the purpose being to gain an understanding of complex organismal, ecological, and evolutionary processes. Much of the existing literature has therefore been conducted on common, easily accessible species; especially ring doves, ducks, pigeons, finches, chickens, sparrows, and starlings. In contrast, endangered species are often difficult to study because they occur in small numbers, are located in remote areas, or inhabit unusual ecological niches. Governmental restrictions on the capture, marking, or disturbance of endangered wildlife further limits any research potential (Ralls and Brownell, 1989). A significant exception are studies initiated by the U.S. Fish and Wildlife Service and the U.S. Forest Service on endangered native birds, such as the whooping crane (*Grus americana*), peregrine falcon (*Falco peregrinus*), red-cockaded woodpecker (*Picoides borealis*), California condor (*Gymnogyps californianus*), and northern spotted owl (*Strix occidentalis*) (e.g., Kepler, 1976, 1978; Wilbur, 1978; Derrickson, 1980; Lennartz et al., 1987; Carey et al., 1990).

Methods of Research in Captivity

Identification and Marking Techniques

The ability to identify individuals quickly and reliably is essential for the collection of valid behavioral data. Identification methods must therefore be conspicuous and unique enough to allow for rapid discrimination. Microchip transponders can be implanted under the skin as a method of permanent identification (Elbin, 1990). However, the reading device must be within a few inches of the implantation site to be effective, thus precluding their use in observational research.

Leg bands, neck bands or wing (patagial) tags are commonly used to identify individual birds (Marion and Shamis, 1977). It is often desirable that marking techniques do not restrict flight, and tags or bands must therefore be constructed out of a strong, light material, such as plastic or aluminum. For example, numbered metal leg bands are often used in avian population, migration, or habitat utilization studies. However, unless the subjects can be approached very closely or remain still long enough for examination with binoculars, the small numbers stamped on these bands are useless for behavioral studies. In some cases, leg bands made with polyvinyl chloride (PVC) and engraved with larger numbers can help alleviate this problem (Ogilvie, 1972). Colored bands or combinations of colored bands are also a possibility, because they can be used to identify individuals from greater distances. It should be noted, however, that this marking technique has the potential to affect both behavior and demography. Burley et al. (1982, 1986) found that female zebra finches (*Poephila guttata*) preferred to mate with red-banded males over unbanded ones, and avoided those wearing light blue and light green bands. Incidence of nestling mortality in captive zebra finches and free-ranging red-cockaded woodpeckers is also known to be correlated with band-color (Burley, 1985; Hagan and Reed, 1988). The reasons for such phenomena are not well understood. Red is a signal for aggression in woodpeckers and red-banded males may incite more aggression from other conspecifics, thus reducing their ability to care for nestlings (Hagan and Reed, 1988). However, it should also be noted that no such relationship between band color and nesting success was found for red-winged blackbirds (*Agelaius phoeniceus*), therefore challenging the generality of Burley's results (Beletsky and Orians, 1989). Researchers who use color-banding to identify individuals can minimize possible deleterious effects by: (1) avoiding the use of colors which accentuate conspecific colors, and (2) by applying colors randomly so that the possible impact of such practices can be evaluated (Hagan and Reed, 1988).

Wing tags have also been shown to have adverse effects on pairing, reproductive performance, and survivability in free-ranging birds (Kinkel, 1989; Southern and Southern, 1989). The impact on captive birds may not be comparable. However, considerable thought should be given to the marking techniques employed; especially when working with endangered species.

Data Collection Techniques

Sampling techniques used to study avian behavior are essentially the same as those used to study other animals (see Lehner, 1979; Gittleman and McMillan, chap. 19, this volume; Martin and Bateson, 1986). However, birds tend to be more mobile and active than many other organisms, perhaps as a result of their higher metabolism and ability to fly. Changes in behavior and location are therefore likely to come comparatively rapidly, thus making reliable data collection difficult. When birds are maintained in large flight cages, the animals' mobility can be a problem as observing behavior is dependent on the subjects being in sight. Within a few seconds a flying bird can cover the length of even the largest enclosure, therefore making it difficult to track. Larger, more naturalistic zoo enclosures pose many of the same logistical problems as fieldwork, and there is no easy way to avoid this problem. If data are collected by hand, it is advisable to keep the ethogram and coding system simple. If more complex schemes are used, videotaped or filmed sequences are helpful; as is the use of automated data collection devices or audio tape recorders (Lehner, 1979; MacNamara and Lalina, 1981).

Bird physiology and behavior can be monitored remotely using biotelemetric devices. Movement patterns, activity budgets, heart rates, and temperature can be monitored on larger, terrestrial species (e.g., ostriches, currassows, raptors, cranes), and recent advances in electronics have even made it possible to employ some of these techniques on smaller species (e.g., Great tit *Parus major*, East and Hofer, 1986). Biotelemetric devices have allowed ornithologists to document heretofore unknown aspects of avian behavior, but they are also known to have many deleterious side effects; including an increased risk of predation (Sorenson, 1989), weight loss, skin irritations (e.g., Greenwood and Sargeant, 1973), decreased flight speed, greater energy expenditure (Geesaman and Nagy, 1988), and alterations of behavior (Massey et al., 1988, Wanless et al., 1988). Studies of incubation behavior have been enhanced greatly by biotelemetric techniques. Stetton et al. (1989) monitored the incubation temperatures and egg-turning behavior of cranes using a biotelemetric egg. Such findings may be critical to the development of effective methods of artificial incubation.

Breeding birds or birds recently brought into captivity may be stressed by the presence of humans; necessitating the use of blinds or similar structures to conceal the observer. Stress can result in lowered breeding success in wild, unhabituated birds (see Westmoreland and Best, 1985; Pierce and Simons, 1986). In addition, the presence of an observer may alter behavior and bring the validity of the study into question (Lehner, 1979). Some birds will habituate to humans with time, but others may not—depending on the individual, species, or reproductive condition. When habituation proves impossible, closed circuit television (CCTV) can sometimes be employed to either reduce or eliminate interactions with humans. CCTV is very useful for observing nesting birds. Hutchins (1976) reported on the use of CCTV to monitor nesting hornbills, and Worth et al. (1991) used CCTV and a time-lapse video recorder to study nest attendance patterns in a female red bird of paradise (*Paradisea rubra*).

Behavior, Captive Management, and Propagation

Social Organization

An understanding of avian social systems is critical for successful captive management and propagation. Improper composition of the social unit that serves as a breeding nucleus may affect behavior and ultimately contribute to reproductive failure. Some birds, such as hummingbirds, are primarily solitary and may be stressed by forced proximity to conspecifics (Johnsgard, 1983c). Others, like flamingos, spoonbills, and ibises, are extremely social and seem to require the presence of large numbers of conspecifics before they will breed (Duplaix-Hall and Kear, 1975; Luthin et al., 1986). In some social species, development of normal behavior may also depend on an association with the parents or other adult birds during particular stages of maturation (see sections on parental care, and foraging behavior, this chapter).

It is estimated that about 95 percent of all bird species mate monogamously (Lack, 1968). Yet monogamy has many variations, all of which can be found among birds. Large, long-lived species, such as cranes, hornbills, condors and swans, most closely approximate the model many humans prefer to think of as monogamy. Once pairs are formed, mates usually stay together until the death of the partner ("permanent monogamy" after Wittenberger, 1981). Pairs do split up ("divorce") on occasion, but birds without mates will re-pair whenever possible (Harris et al., 1986, Rohwer and Anderson, 1988). Other species, including most passerines, pair for a single breeding season, but tend to change mates every year ("serial monogamy" after Wittenberger, 1981). Such pair bonds may endure only through egg-laying (e.g., in ducks; Johnsgard, 1965), or may include substantial investment by the male in nest building, incubation, and chick rearing (Breitwisch, 1989). It should be noted that monogamy does not necessarily imply complete fidelity. Indeed, extra-pair copulations and forced copulations are common phenomena in many species (Barash, 1977, Beecher and Beecher, 1979).

A bird can have more than one mate during a single breeding season. Polygyny (one male mates with more than one female) is much more common than polyandry (one female mates with more than one male), but both systems occur in birds and many variations exist. In "territorial harem polygyny" (Wittenberger, 1981), for example, males defend habitats where females congregate (e.g., red-winged blackbirds; Orians, 1980).

Some birds are promiscuous (i.e., there is no prolonged association between the sexes) and members of at least one sex engage in multiple matings. A prime example of this mating system is "arena promiscuity" (Wittenberger, 1981), where males defend a display area or lek that is used exclusively for attracting mates. Such systems occur in many types of birds, including ruffs, hummingbirds, grouse, and birds of paradise. After mating females depart, laying eggs and rearing young without paternal assistance (Bradbury, 1981).

Although it is important to understand the social systems characteristic of various species, it is not always possible to simulate the naturally occurring social milieu under captive conditions. In addition, some avian mating systems are variable given certain ecological conditions. Free-ranging dunnocks (*Prunella modularis*), for instance, may exhibit either monogamy or various degrees of polygyny depending on ecological conditions (Davies and Lundberg, 1984).

Each social system represents a unique challenge for aviculturists. For example, depending on the species, monogamous birds may nest in separate territories or in colonies. Differences in the spacing of pairs can have a significant bearing on the design of facilities, and on husbandry and/or breeding techniques. Thus, it is frequently impossible to maintain breeding pairs of monogamous, territorial species (such as cranes) in the same enclosure or even in visual contact, as they will spend excessive amounts of time engaged in aggressive behavior. One common solution to this problem is to place an empty pen, or one containing an unrelated species, between two conspecific pairs (Carpenter, 1986). In contrast, multiple pairs of colonial species, such as flamingoes or ibis, can be kept in the same space required by a single pair of cranes. Colonial species are therefore much more economical to maintain (Conway, 1987).

Restricted space is a common theme in any discussion of the problems of captive management. For species in which the male does not normally assist with care of offspring, the continued presence of males may disrupt reproduction. Females of lek-forming species, such as ruffs or some birds of paradise, may be inhibited from nesting by the presence of males (Searle, 1980; Todd and Berry, 1980). In addition, aggressive interactions among communally-displaying males generally precludes the formation of true leks in captivity. Thus, keeping males in adjacent cages can stimulate display behavior and perhaps enhance male libido, although formation of a normal dominance hierarchy is impossible. This tactic has proven to be successful with red birds of paradise. Females are kept in separate cages, placed with males when they begin nest building, and isolated again after mating has taken place (Hundgen and Bruning, 1989; Worth et al., 1991).

Reproductive Behavior

Because it is so closely tied to reproduction, behavior associated with courtship, mate selection, copulation, nest building, incubation, and parental care is of great relevance to avicultural practices. In particular, the social and physical environments of young birds may have subtle, yet pervasive, influences on later behavior.

Courtship Behavior, Pair Formation, and Reproductive Synchrony. Among the vast majority of birds, male courtship displays probably serve to attract females as well as to repel other males. Thus, females may use male displays as one means by which they assess the appropriateness (i.e., same species) and quality (i.e., vigor, health, etc.) of potential mates (Barash, 1982). It is known for some birds that appropriate, species-typical courtship behavior triggers hormonal and behavioral changes which are critical for normal reproduction (Lehrman, 1958; Warren and Hinde, 1961; Brockway, 1965).

In some cases, the ability of males to perform courtship displays can be limited by the physical characteristics of captive environments. Some species of birds, such as sandpipers of the subfamily Calidridinae, engage in distinctive aerial displays during the breeding season (Miller, 1983). Unless enclosures offer sufficient vertical and horizontal space, it may be impossible for the birds to express their full behavioral repertoire. Theoretically this could also disrupt normal reproductive cycles. Ground- or perch-displaying species may be similarly affected. Horning et al. (1987) suggested that open spaces might be necessary for normal courtship display by common trumpeters (*Psophia crepitans*). Males of this terrestrial, neotropical species display in open areas on the forest floor, and their active and exaggerated courtship may require a minimum amount of space to be performed. Male manakins (*Manacus spp.*) display on leks, and the courtship arenas of these birds are not established at random. The degree of illumination at particular times of the day is an important factor influencing lek site selection and display rates in these birds (Thery, 1990). Thus, many aspects of the captive environment, including patterns of artificial lighting, have the potential to affect courtship activities.

Certain management protocols can also influence a male's ability to exhibit appropriate courtship behavior. Wing clipping (pinioning) in order to prevent escape would certainly inhibit displays that involve flight and might also impact other types of behavior, such as mounting. Whereas visual displays in birds may be relatively "hard-wired," the males of some species learn their species-typical songs during a so-called sensitive period early in development (Baptista and Petrinovitch, 1984; Bohner, 1990). When some birds are reared in isolation from conspecifics (either alone, by humans, or by or near other species), it may have long-term effects on song characteristics and perhaps also inhibit future breeding success (see section on mate preferences, this chapter).

Courtship behavior is essential to the establishment of pair bonds in monogamous birds. Initially, unfamiliar individuals are often intolerant or indifferent to one another, but become progressively less so as the bond strengthens (Caryl, 1976; Silcox and Evans, 1982). Ideally, subadult birds could be placed in larger flocks and allowed to select their own mates, as has been suggested for cranes (Derrickson and Carpenter, 1987) and hornbills (Sheppard, 1988b). But this is not always possible; especially when pairings are determined on the basis of genetic and demographic considerations.

Familiarity seems to be an important component of successful pair formation and may also facilitate coordination of reproductive behavior (Yamamoto et al., 1989). Thus, problems of incompatibility or aggression may arise as a result of "forced" pairings. Because fighting can lead to injury or stress, males and females are typically introduced while they are in visual, as opposed to in physical contact (i.e., in separate cages). Pairs should only be placed together when they cease to perform threat displays, synchronize their activities, regularly maintain close proximity, and/or exhibit courtship behavior. However, even seemingly compatible pairs may fail to breed as a consequence of behavioral factors. Kepler (1976, 1978) noted that male dominance over the female was critical for successful reproduction in captive whooping cranes. It was also noted that when a female failed to exhibit appropriate submission postures, males also failed to achieve copulation. This was true even in pairs that showed no overt aggression and otherwise seemed completely compatible. Research aimed at developing objective and simple measures of pair compatibility (i.e., strength of pair-bonding) would be useful for a number of endangered species.

Courtship may also help to synchronize a pair's breeding cycle, so that a normal sequence of behavioral and physiological events can ensue (Lehrman, 1958). The importance of reproductive synchrony may not be as widely appreciated among aviculturists as it should be. Birds are often shipped from various localities to be placed in captive breeding programs, and when this occurs subtle differences in behavior and physiology can result in a lack of breeding success. Depending on the species, such differences may be difficult or even impossible to overcome. For example, Fentzloff (1984) formed pairs of white-tailed sea eagles (*Haliaeetus albicilla*) with the objective of starting a captive breeding program. Wild birds were captured in areas only six to seven degrees latitude apart. It soon became evident, however, that many randomly-formed pairs were not synchronized in their breeding activities, resulting in a lack of reproduction. Interestingly, birds from one cline never adapted to the cycle of another even after six to ten years of continuous exposure. Only after pairing individuals on the basis of geographical origin and degree of behavioral synchronization was successful reproduction achieved.

Successful captive breeding programs also require that the sex of a bird be determined so that proper pairing can occur. Unfortunately, many birds are sexually monomorphic and, when this occurs, it is often impossible to sex individuals on the basis of external cues. The problem has been solved in recent years with the development of laproscopic, genetic, and hormonal methods of sex determination (Hungerford et al., 1966; Bush et al., 1978; Bercovitz, 1987; Bercovitz and Sarver, 1988). However, behavioral differences can sometimes be employed to differentiate the sexes, and this method is comparatively less expensive and risky than other techniques. In most species of cranes, for example, visual and vocal components of certain displays differ between males and females, and this can be used to determine sex (Kepler, 1978; Derrickson and Carpenter, 1987).

Manipulation of courtship and/or sexual behavior has also been used to augment artificial insemination programs. One of the biggest problems to overcome is the collection of semen from males without risky chemical immobilization or stressful manual capture and restraint. Male goshawks (*Accipiter gentilis*) have been taught to mate voluntarily with a keeper's hand, thereby facilitating semen collection (Berry, 1972). Archibald (1982) was able to induce an imprinted female whooping crane to lay eggs fertilized by artificial insemination. He accomplished this by performing the spring courtship dance and subsequently developing a "pair bond" with the bird. Although a bit unorthodox, the technique resulted in a healthy chick.

Mate Preferences. Cues used by birds during mate selection are highly varied, and the reader should recognize that it is often impossible to generalize from one species to another. However, an understanding of such factors might help to explain why certain species are extremely difficult to breed under captive conditions or why a particular pair of birds experiences reproductive failure. It is not uncommon for captive managers to pair birds with impeccable genetic backgrounds, only to find that they have little or no interest in one another (e.g., pink pigeons [*Columba mayeri*], Bruning, 1988).

Some female birds reportedly choose mates based on the quality of a male's territory rather than on morphological or behavioral characteristics (Nagata, 1986). In other cases, physical characters or behavior may be extremely important. Plumage coloration, for example, is correlated with assortative or nonrandom mating patterns in some birds (e.g., lesser snow geese [*Anser c. caerulescens*], Cooke and McNally, 1975; brant geese [*Branta bernicla*], Abraham et al., 1983).

Reproductive isolation between color morphs may also occasionally be based on subtle differences in courtship behavior. Among western grebes (*Aechmophorus occidentalis*) for example, interbreeding between color morphs was found to be rare (Nuechterlein, 1981). Although there were no differences in the form, frequency, or duration of visual courtship displays, there was evidence that a distinctive call, which apparently functions in mate attraction, differed between the two morphs.

Male song is thought to be an important factor influencing female mate recognition and choice in a number of species (Marler and Tamura, 1962; Miller, 1979; Loffredo and Borgia, 1986). Although this topic has received little attention from aviculturists, it could explain some cases of breeding failure in captive birds. When breeding pairs of wild-caught birds are formed, curators often have no knowledge of capture location or even of the subspecific status of specimens. Subtle geographical or subspecific differences in courtship behavior or male song characteristics could conceivably affect mate choice and/or compatibility and thus lead to reproductive failure. Though difficult to test conclusively (Petrinovitch et al., 1981) and even repudiated for some species (Baptista and Morton, 1982), it has been suggested that differences in male song characteristics may function as reproductive isolating mechanisms, both between and within species (Baker and Mewaldt, 1978; King et al., 1980a; Tomback and Baker, 1984; Baker et al., 1987).

Assortative mating has been documented based on age and breeding experience in birds. Numerous authors have noted that pairs of breeding birds are frequently of similar age, and it has been suggested that pair complementarity may be a factor in mate selection (Marzluff and Balda, 1988; Reid, 1988). Complementarity can imply either similarity or dissimilarity between partners. Among feral pigeons, for example, older and more experienced individuals of both sexes appeared to be preferred as mates (Burley and Moran, 1979). Breeding experience may be a strong determinant of reproductive potential. Indeed, sexually naive cockatiels (*Nymphicus hollandicus*) have much lower reproductive success than those which have experienced at least one reproductive cycle (Myers et al., 1988). Perhaps aviculturists should take such factors into account when pairing birds.

Nest Building, Egg-Laying, Incubation, and Hatching. Although it is possible to remove eggs or nestlings for artificial incubation or hand-rearing, such practices create abnormal rearing environments which can influence later behavior (see section on parental behavior, this chapter). Therefore, it is usually desirable to allow captive birds to rear their offspring as naturally as possible. Thus, a parent's ability to build a nest, lay eggs and incubate them properly become critical factors influencing reproductive success. In addition, a chick's ability to escape from its egg shell and to show appropriate behavior immediately posthatching are also important, as are the reactions of other cage mates towards nests, eggs, and chicks.

Nest building is nearly universal among birds, although the form and complexity of these structures may vary considerably (see Collias and Collias, 1984). Some species lay their eggs in a simple scrape on the ground (e.g., gulls), whereas others build huge and complex structures, some of which may be one to two meters thick and up to nine meters long (e.g., sociable weaverbirds [*Philetairus socius*], Collias and Collias, 1984). Nest building behavior is triggered largely by hormonal factors and appears to have a strong genetic component. In fact, the structure of nests is often used as a taxonomic indicator (e.g., weaverbirds; Collias and Collias, 1984). Like many other aspects of bird behavior, nest building can be affected by early experience, and the lack of a normal rearing environment can therefore lead to abnormalities. When reared in the absence of a nest or appropriate building materials, some birds fail to construct nests as adults (Scott, 1902, 1904; Collias and Collias, 1973). Nest site selection can also be influenced by early experience. For example, some raptors reportedly choose nest sites similar to those in which they were reared (Shutt and Bird, 1985).

The lack of an appropriate nest site, building materials, or environment can lead to reproductive failure, and aviculturists need to be familiar enough with a species' breeding biology to provide the necessary conditions (see O'Donnell, 1989). Coulter (1980) suggested that stones are an important stimulus for incubation in gulls and terns, and mud is often incorporated into the nest entrance walls built by captive hornbills (Hutchins, 1976). For some cavity-nesting species, it has been suggested that the act of opening or widening the cavity may also help to stimulate courtship or aid in pair-bond formation (e.g., toco toucan [*Ramphastos toco*], Seibels, 1979; emerald toucanet [*Aulachorynchus prasinus*], Jennings, 1981). Thus, provision of an uncompleted nest cavity may help to facilitate breeding. In addition, rainfall and flooding have been implicated as important environmental cues for nesting in both free-ranging and captive flamingos (Duplaix-Hall and Kear, 1975; Brown et al., 1983). However, these and many other hypotheses about avicultural practices and bird behavior have yet to be tested experimentally.

Other behaviors which occur at or around nesting can lead to reproductive failure. A behavior known as siblicide or "cainism" occurs in a wide variety of birds (Mallet, 1977; Stinson, 1979; Mock, 1984) and has important implications for captive management. In siblicidal species, two or more eggs are laid asynchronously over a period of days. The parents begin incubation as soon as the first egg is laid and, as a result, the eggs hatch asynchronously. Another result of this staggered development is that older chicks become substantially larger than their younger siblings, thus placing the latter at a competitive disadvantage (Edwards and Collopy, 1983). When food is in short supply, starvation may be the end result for the young chicks. In some species, however, aggression extends beyond competition for food. Older chicks may injure, cannibalize, or push their weaker siblings out of the nest (Meyberg, 1984; Mock, 1984). In some cases, this behavior is obligate, rather than facultative, as reported in white boobies (*Sula dactylatra*) which typically lay two eggs, but raise only one chick regardless of how much food is available (Nelson, 1989).

In birds that show sibling aggression or siblicide, chick mortality will be high if nature is left to run its course, and the significance for captive breeding programs is obvious. In facultative siblicidal species, the factor most commonly controlling sibling aggression is food availability (Proctor, 1975). It should be possible to minimize nestling loss in captivity through proper monitoring and provisioning, but other forms of intervention might be desirable in species that are obligatory in their siblicidal behavior. For instance, second or third eggs in a clutch could be removed for artificial incubation or transferred to a nest occupied by another pair with infertile eggs (Meyberg, 1983). An additional option is to prevent contact between siblings by placing a physical barrier in the nest (Thaler and Pechlaner, 1980), or to separate the chicks temporarily until the younger individuals become large and strong enough to defend themselves (Sauey and Brown, 1977).

Unrelated adults can also pose a threat to eggs or chicks. For example inter- and intra-species ovicide and infanticide have been documented in a wide variety of species (Mock, 1984). Some birds commonly destroy the nests and eggs of conspecifics breeding in the immediate area (Picman, 1977; Vehrencamp, 1977; Goldstein et al., 1986; Emlen et al., 1989). Such behavior may represent a form of reproductive competition through which future competitors are eliminated (Barash, 1982). Newly immigrated adults may also procure mates by interrupting the breeding cycles of already established individuals (Crook and Shields, 1985; Freed, 1986; Robertson and Stutchbury, 1988). There are few reports of this behavior occurring in captive birds, but in the case of endangered species kept in mixed species exhibits or exhibits housing more than a pair of conspecifics, it is always wise to take precautions to prevent its occurrence.

Parental Behavior. Parental care is generally well-developed in birds and may be either indirect (e.g., territorial defense) or direct (e.g., antipredator behavior, feeding the young, brooding the young). Nevertheless, great variation exists in the type and duration of care provided, and in the number and identity of caretakers across various avian species. At one extreme is the polygynous malee fowl (*Leipoa ocellata*). Chicks of this species never interact with their parents and are completely independent from the moment they hatch (Frith, 1962). In monogamous birds, the male and female typically share parental duties, though not necessarily equally (e.g., Adelie penguins [*Pygoscelis adeliae*], Ainley et al., 1983). In polygynous or promiscuous species, females may care for the young without male assistance (e.g., red bird of paradise; Frith, 1976) or the male may provide only rudimentary aid (e.g., red-winged blackbirds; Orians, 1980). Complete reversal of sex roles is seen in polyandrous species, with males being the exclusive caretakers (e.g., American jacana [*Jacana spinosa*], Jenni and Betts, 1978). In some cases, the parents may be assisted by other individuals. These "helpers at the nest" are typically older offspring of the adult pair; however, there are cases of unrelated individuals helping (e.g., Florida scrub jay [*Aphelocoma coerulescens*], Woolfenden, 1975). Care patterns can also differ in species that produce altricial versus precocial young. In any event, knowing the normal behavior of a species is essential for developing effective management strategies.

Abnormal parental behavior can result in increased chick mortality and therefore threaten a captive breeding program. Although parental infanticide (i.e., direct killing of chicks) has been documented in wild birds (e.g., white spoonbills [*Palatalea leucorodia*], Aguilera, 1990), it is apparently extremely rare. There are, however, several reports of parental ovicide and infanticide among captive birds. Kovisto (1977) described a mixed-species exhibit in which spotted redshanks (*Tringa erythropus*) and ruffs (*Philomachus pugnax*) apparently destroyed, and in some instances ate, their own eggs. In addition, parent birds are known to either abandon or trample their eggs or chicks as a result of disturbances (e.g., Fyfe, 1975; Samour et al., 1983). Certain raptors will apparently kill and sometimes even cannibalize their young under captive conditions (Porter and Wiemeyer, 1970; Wylie, 1977; Steenberg, 1981), and some captive birds, such as endangered pink pigeons, are notoriously bad parents (Bruning, 1989). It is sometimes difficult to pinpoint the reasons for such behavior, but it may occur as a result of nutritional or behavioral stress, or an abnormal rearing experience (Porter and Wiemeyer, 1970). In the case of endangered varieties, it appears to be advisable to monitor parental behavior closely and to remove the chicks for hand- or foster-rearing if abnormal parental behavior is detected.

When chicks are removed due to abnormal parental care, aviculturists are faced with other problems, including the potential that young birds will become sexually imprinted on their human caretakers (Hediger, 1950). Fortunately, some techniques have been developed to help alleviate this problem. One of the more innovative approaches is the use of artificial parents, as described by Bruning (1983) for Andean condors (*Vultur gryphus*). Hand-reared condor chicks were initially fed with a forceps by keepers, but eventually these birds became strongly imprinted on humans. In an effort to avoid this problem, hand puppets were fashioned in the likeness of adults and used to pass food to the chicks. Every effort was made to restrict contact with people, and the technique appeared to be successful. Birds reared in this manner preferred the company of conspecifics to that of humans. In some cases, chicks can be fostered to closely-related species. Pink pigeons have been raised successfully by doves (Bruning, 1989), but it is important to note that sexual imprinting on the foster species can also occur and this may influence future reproductive success (see section on reintroduction, this chapter).

In some cases, the effects of imprinting might also be minimized by restricting contact with humans either before or after some critical point in the chick's development. Cade and Fyfe (1977) noted considerable variation in the degree of later sexual competence in hand-raised peregrine falcons. Chicks removed from the nest at an earlier age tended to develop more problems, but some individuals still became competent breeders as adults. The authors emphasized the importance of determining an optimum age of removal—one that would allow normal sociosexual development to occur. Of course, it is not always possible to remove young at optimal times, especially when parents abandon or abuse their young. On the other hand, chicks are sometimes removed earlier than normal, so that parental reproduction can be maximized (i.e., "double-clutching," Dixon, 1986). In such cases, determination of optimal removal times is more likely to be critical. Contact with humans can also be avoided or at least minimized by peer-rearing. Many birds apparently gain essential experience through interaction with siblings or peers (see Sherrod, 1974). In the case of Andean condors, hand-reared birds became sexually imprinted on humans, but individuals reared with peers preferred members of their own species (Bruning, 1983).

Although abuse or neglect are the most common forms of abnormal parental behavior, it is interesting to note that mortality can also result when parents are abnormally solicitous. Among captive Adelie penguins for example, adults appeared unable to refuse to feed their growing chicks. Because normal dispersal could not occur, adults fed their offspring well beyond the time that the chicks would have separated from their parents. This resulted in the death of at least one molting adult. Thus, curators found it necessary to separate adults and juveniles to assure that the parent-offspring bond was broken at about the same time it would occur in nature (Penny, 1978). This example highlights the importance of knowing when the parent-offspring bond typically breaks down.

Some species of birds show prolonged parental care and continue to associate with their chicks long after leaving the nest (e.g., geese and swans, Kear, 1970). In such cases, premature removal of the young may prove detrimental. For example, it has been suggested that such prolonged associations are necessary for the young to perfect specialized foraging skills (Ashmole and Tovar, 1968) or receive protection from other conspecifics so that they may forage more efficiently (Turcotte and Bedard, 1989).

It is not always reasonable to assume that all behavioral changes due to captivity are going to be detrimental. Under natural conditions, Adelie penguins incubate their eggs for about 34 days. After laying, the female returns to the sea to feed for approximately two weeks, while the male incubates. When the female returns, the male goes to sea, and the female completes another shorter trip prior to hatching (Davis, 1982). Conversely, in captivity, artificially provisioned birds do not make long foraging trips and, consequently, more time is available for social interaction. Captive pairs that spent more nonincubating time together at the nest during the incubation period had significantly higher reproductive success. Successful birds also spent considerably longer periods at the nest site after nest relief, suggesting that the behavioral cohesiveness of a pair is a critical factor affecting reproductive output, even under captive conditions (Ellis-Joseph, 1988).

Foraging Behavior

Wild birds spend much of the day looking for food, and at the same time they must avoid becoming food for other animals. Although captive foraging is much less hazardous, feeding time may be the most significant event in a captive bird's day. Because aviculturists usually cannot replicate a species' natural diet, substitute foods are used. While the nutritional content, convenience, and economy of artificial diets is improving continually (Snyder, 1978; Sheppard, 1982), there is a danger that such rations may leave animals behaviorally deprived. The diet of captive birds not only influences their physical well-being, but also their psychological health, activity patterns, and social interactions.

Improving Diets

Getting captive birds to accept new foods can be difficult, and this is essentially a behavioral problem. Highly insectivorous birds may be the most difficult to maintain in captivity because many never learn to eat artificial diets (Muller, 1976). Although problems may be more acute in dietary specialists, many species are reluctant to eat novel foods or foods presented in novel ways (Conway, 1957; Rabinowitch, 1968; Desforges and Wood-Gush, 1975; Sheppard, 1982; Heinrich, 1988). In social species, observational learning often plays an important role, and the acceptance of new foods in a flock may be initiated by a single bold individual (Mason and Reidinger, 1981; Heinrich, 1988). In other cases, gradual transition may successfully shift adults onto new foods. For those species in which adults never learn to eat artificial foods, it may be possible to teach hand-raised nestlings to accept substitutes (Conway, 1957).

Artificial diets are often monotonous compared to natural ones (Hediger, 1950), yet provision of a mixed diet does not ensure that birds will make a nutritionally adequate selection. Captive ovenbirds (*Seiurus aurocapillus*) fed an abundance of preferred food items, chose their favorite foods almost exclusively (Zach and Falls, 1978). When favored items are low in nutrition, such choices may lead to unbalanced diets. White-quilled black bustards (*Eupodotis afraoides*) chose raw meat almost exclusively from their pans, even though they were offered other items; resulting in a diet that was too high in phosphorous (Sheppard, 1982). Apparently, devising substitute foods is not enough. Aviculturists also need to understand the cues that birds use to recognize and select food items. Such cues could theoretically be used to attract birds to certain foods, and to promote balanced diets when a variety of foods are offered.

Birds probably use multiple cues to recognize food; including appearance, composition, sound, taste, and smell. Food appearance can be broken down into color, shape, size, and movement. Birds have good color discrimination in the red wavelengths, and many frugivorous birds are attracted by red and/or purple-black fruits (Gautier-Hion et al., 1985). However, there appear to be no universal preferences for food color. For example, insectivores avoid brightly-colored, noxious prey (Muller, 1976), and young waterfowl prefer to peck at yellow and green items (Kear, 1976). Size and shape of a food item can also be important, as is the case with ducklings which prefer curved, worm-like shapes (Kear, 1976).

Provided a food item can be swallowed, bigger seems to be better, at least for some captive insectivores (Muller, 1976). Movement is a critical stimulus for some birds, such as young waterfowl (Kear, 1976) and bee-eaters (Fry, 1984). Thus, moving artificial foods may stimulate some captive birds to feed (Hediger, 1950).

There is little information about the role of taste and texture in avian food choice. Sweetness is favored by some birds, although the ability to distinguish small differences in sugar concentration varies, even among frugivores (Levey, 1987). Most food preference studies essentially compare "apples with oranges" and note the birds' choices. Such studies have shown cases of preferences for fresh over older or freeze-dried, preserved fruits, and for ripe over unripe fruits (Moerman and Denslow, 1983; Wheelwright, 1988). Similarly, folivorous hoatzins (*Opisthocomus hoazin*) prefer newly-grown plant material over old growth (Grajal et al., 1989).

Other sensory cues, such as temperature (Hediger, 1950) or smell, could also be important in food recognition and choice. Birds are generally assumed to have a poor sense of smell (Welty, 1979). Yet even passerines, which are presumed to have the poorest ability to detect odors, have been shown to have fairly sophisticated olfactory abilities that can be used to locate food (Buitron and Nuechterlein, 1985; Clark and Mason, 1987).

Birds routinely eat less-preferred items if favored items are difficult to obtain or widely dispersed (Moerman and Denslow, 1983; Levey et al., 1984; Whelan, 1989b). Similarly, the more processing a food item requires (e.g., removal of shells, seeds, skins, exoskeletons), the less appealing it becomes (Zach and Falls, 1978; Moerman and Denslow, 1983). Aviculturists can take advantage of these traits by spreading out treats among separate food pans, or by making "junk food" more difficult to eat.

Producing Appropriate Activity

The majority of wild birds spend most of their waking hours foraging. However, in captivity they are typically provided with abundant food at regular times, and there may be a mismatch between natural and artificial feeding times and feeding opportunities (Hediger, 1950). Avian meal spacing has more to do with how quickly the digestive system processes food than with energetic or nutritional needs (Savory, 1980). Therefore, birds that can process larger meals or store food may require less frequent feedings. Husbandry of small birds which process and store small quantities is more difficult, and frequent feedings may be an unavoidable requirement of maintaining such species.

Psychological requirements should also be considered when planning a feeding regime. Captive birds tend to have long periods of inactivity or other nonforaging behaviors, punctuated by a few bursts of scheduled feeding activity. When deprived of an opportunity to forage, captive birds probably compensate by increasing other behaviors, both desirable and undesirable. Chamove et al. (1982) demonstrated that nonhuman primates occupied in searching for grain hidden in floor litter showed significant decreases in aggression, manipulation of the environment, play, and abnormal behaviors. Similar studies should be conducted on birds. Feeders could be designed to slow food consumption and occupy birds in foraging tasks. Partridge and Green (1987) developed three feeders that required corvids to lift flaps, probe, or perch in order to obtain food. These feeders occupied the birds for considerable amounts of time and were also sturdy enough to withstand months of use.

Reducing Aggression and Competition

Much as feedings tend to be unnaturally spaced during the day, artificial feeders tend to concentrate food items into clumps. Territorial birds normally defend concentrations of resources, and under captive conditions such behavior can be greatly accentuated. Submarine foraging alcids engage in numerous attacks and chases around feeding areas as they attempt to steal food from one another (Duffey et al., 1987). Thus, clumping food can foster competition and increase the probability that subordinate individuals do not receive adequate nutrition (Feare and Inglis, 1979). Indeed, Swingland (1975) found that subordinate rooks (*Corvus frugilegus*) died when a captive flock was provisioned in a restricted place. To reduce aggressive interactions and promote feeding by subordinates, feeders can be spread further apart, increased in number, or made larger, so that they can be utilized by more individuals (Duffey et al., 1987). Frequent changes in feeder locations might also help to reduce competition.

In mixed-species exhibits, birds that would normally reduce competition by utilizing different "niches" may be forced to use the same one. Waterfowl which normally gather food on or below the surface may be out-competed at shore feeders; providing food in the water greatly reduces any problems (Kear, 1976). In any event, methods of food presentation should be compatible with a species' normal feeding behavior.

Rearing Normal Chicks

The food that is provided to chicks by their parents or keepers is important for both physical and behavioral development. The dietary needs of chicks change rapidly over time, as do their preferences for certain foods. Although the acquisition of food habits is not well understood, some learning is almost certainly involved. Most young birds probably learn to recognize and acquire food items by pecking at and picking up the same items as their parents. If the initial pecking and ingestion of an item has no adverse effects, the peck rate may increase and the chick may develop a preference for that food. If the experience is unrewarding or unpleasant, then the peck rate may decrease and the chick will avoid that food (Hale and Green, 1988). Precocial chicks probably learn to select appropriate foods within the first few days by sampling what the parents eat, and altricial chicks probably learn in a similar fashion after leaving the nest.

The ability to recognize food is distinct from the skills necessary to obtain it. Naive birds probably learn many foraging techniques through trial and error (Kamil and Yoerg, 1982). However, the learning of specialized food handling techniques may have sensitive periods for development, and the appropriate experiences must occur before a certain age. For example, reed warblers, (*Acrocephalus scirpaceus*) may need to learn to manipulate insects before structural maturation of the bill is complete (Davies and Green, 1976). In some species, observational learning also plays some role in the development of proper foraging techniques; such as in domestic chickens (Hale and Green, 1988), ospreys (*Pandion haliaetus*) (Edwards, 1989), and oystercatchers (*Haematopus ostralegus*) (Norton-Griffiths, 1969).

Reintroduction

A major goal of modern captive breeding programs is the reestablishment of extirpated or reduced wild animal populations (Brambell, 1977). Bird reintroductions are among the earliest and most successful attempts at population restoration (Fyfe, 1977). They have taught us much about the role of genetics, disease, habitat suitability, physical condition, social organization, and behavior in the success or failure of various release techniques. A full review of this topic is beyond the scope of this chapter and, instead, we refer the reader to several relevant reviews (Fyfe, 1977; Conway, 1989; Stanley-Price, 1989a). The present discussion is focused specifically on behavioral aspects of avian reintroduction programs.

Phases of Reintroduction

Captive breeding and reintroduction of endangered birds can be broken into four behaviorally important phases: (1) chick rearing, (2) prerelease preparation, (3) release, and (4) postrelease survival and breeding. Captive-bred birds are either hand- or parent-reared before being moved to the release site. They are then held at the site for a period of acclimatization and training. The release itself generally involves little more than opening the cage door, but food is often provided at the site. This provisioning of food serves the dual purpose of providing the animals with an adequate diet during the transition and facilitating postrelease monitoring by inhibiting immediate dispersal (see section on social skills and reintroduction, this chapter).

The protocols used in each of these phases must be adjusted to the species and sometimes even to the individuals being reintroduced. The prerelease period may be one of the most critical from a behavioral viewpoint. Behavioral attributes, such as tameness, that are adaptive in captivity, may be maladaptive in the wild. For example, hand-reared birds are not as wary as wild-reared birds and they suffer higher hunter and predator-related mortality (e.g., mallard ducks [*Anas platyrhynchos*], Brakhage, 1953). Hand-reared thick-billed parrots (*Rhynchopsitta pachyrhyncha*) exhibited no signs of vigilance against avian predators, even though they had many opportunities to observe the reactions of wild conspecifics to raptors flying overhead (Snyder et al., 1989). Wariness was "taught" in one elaborate prerelease training program involving a human foster parent dressed in a crane costume. Sandhill crane (*Grus canadensis*) chicks were harassed and chased by humans, and then "saved" by their foster parent (Horwich, 1989). Although apparently successful, the effectiveness of this experiment is difficult to evaluate because of the lack of controls.

Malnutrition is common in released birds, which may have difficulty recognizing or locating novel, natural food items (Klimstra and Scott, 1973). During experimental releases on the Island of Mauritius, pink pigeons were provisioned with familiar foods while they gradually added unfamiliar, natural foods to their diets. The birds were observed tentatively pecking at various objects, some of which were eventually eaten (Todd, 1984). Prerelease training of birds could help to familiarize naive individuals with natural food items. Similarly, released birds may need to develop aversions to toxic items. Studies of food aversion suggest that color cues might be useful in teaching avoidance of certain items, but considerable research remains to be done (Mason and Reidinger, 1983).

"Gentle-release," a protocol for housing birds at the release site for a period of acclimation, increases waterfowl survival (Brakhage, 1953). This may be because birds are more willing to remain in the release area, which is usually relatively safe. Todd (1984) found that pink pigeons were more likely to stay near the release site if they were held and fed for several weeks, and then starved for two or more days before release. Upon release the birds were more likely to feed immediately rather than fly away. Similarly, the survival of reintroduced, captive-reared barn owls (*Tyto alba*), seems to improve when they are kept confined until they have chicks (Scott, 1989). The chicks provide a strong inducement for the adults to remain near the release site.

Optimal Timing of Release

Adaptive behaviors are basic to successful reintroductions. A certain proportion of bird behavior is innate and inflexible. Innate behaviors can either facilitate or frustrate reintroduction efforts, and each program should therefore be planned to take advantage of species-typical behavior. Other behaviors, such as foraging skills, are largely learned and flexible (see section on foraging behavior, this chapter). Birds also appear to be programmed to learn or to express certain behaviors during critical periods in their development. For example, Horwich (1989) described a second "imprinting" period at 3–4 months in sandhill cranes (*Garus canadensis*), during which released birds were attracted to conspecifics and successfully joined a flock.

"Programmed learning" can play an important role in the planning and timing of an avian release program. Fledgling peregrine falcons normally learn self-sufficiency through interaction with their parents. However, hand-reared young, if released at the time when they would normally become independent, seem to develop in a similar way and on a similar schedule as parent-reared birds (Cade et al., 1988). Wallace and Temple (1987) took advantage of their knowledge of condor behavioral development to reintroduce post-fledging birds into the wild. Young condors gradually increase their foraging area, and if they fail to locate a carcass, will return to the nest site to be fed by the parents. Similarly, young, captive-bred condors will return to the release site for many weeks while they learn foraging and flying skills. They can eventually be led further from the site by provisioning them with carcasses (Wallace and Temple, 1987). Condors released at fledging also tended to be more socially cohesive than year-old birds, and thus easier to control and monitor.

Loss of Culture and Reintroduction

When birds learn through association with their elders, they may be acquiring cultural or traditional behavior patterns. Types of behaviors that often have cultural components in birds include song dialects, alarm calls, foraging techniques, mobbing behavior, and locations of migratory routes and breeding sites (Bonner, 1980; Mundinger, 1980). Unfortunately, culturally acquired behavior patterns are likely to be lost or severely altered during captive breeding or fostering/cross-fostering programs. For animals with learned (flexible) behavior, loss of "culture" may pose the most significant barrier to successful reintroductions (May and Lyles, 1987). For example, the foraging behavior of cranes can be changed as a result of captive-rearing, and this can affect the success of reintroduction programs. Young cranes follow their parents for an extended period of time, learning what to eat by observing the habits of adults. They are notoriously conservative in their selection of foods, generally choosing items that they grew up eating. Reintroduced sandhill cranes, which were raised on grains, such as maize, foraged in grain crops extensively, rather than adopting the more varied foraging patterns of wild adults (Zwank et al., 1988). It is unknown how long it might take for the birds to broaden their feeding preferences, or if they ever will. In the meantime, they are likely to become significant agricultural pests—a situation which may threaten their long-term survival.

Many species, even wayfaring ones, tend to return to breed in the same area that they were reared. This "site tenacity" seems to make good evolutionary sense, in that locations that have proven to be successful in the past often continue to be good bets in the present. However, when conditions change at a site (e.g., due to habitat alteration or pollution), it can lead to massive reproductive failure. Furthermore, philopatry may prevent free-ranging birds from recolonizing vacant, but appropriate, habitats. An understanding of this behavioral phenomenon has aided in the successful restoration of philopatric species, such as peregrine falcons (Cade et al., 1988) and bald eagles (*Haliaeetus leucocephalus*) (Simons et al., 1988). In such cases, captive-raised fledglings are held at a "hacking site" where they are released and provisioned, and where they later return to breed (Temple, 1977b).

Location and timing of releases may also be critical for facilitating natural migratory behavior. It certainly would be desirable for captive-reared birds to participate in normal, species-typical migrations once they are released. Migratory behavior in many bird species is generally thought to be controlled largely by physiological mechanisms, with seasonal changes in the photoperiod being considered a particularly important stimulus (see Farner et al., 1983). Other species appear to possess an endogenous circannual rhythm, in that they will exhibit seasonal physiological indices of the migratory cycle even when maintained under constant daylength (Gwinner, 1986). More recently, it has been shown that experience can alter migratory cycles, and that arrival at and recognition of a traditional breeding site may serve as a signal which terminates migration. For example, migratory restlessness and its associated physiological changes can, in some cases, be completely suppressed by confinement, even when the subjects are maintained on a natural light cycle. It is possible that site familiarity may be responsible for this phenomenon, in that the birds already perceive themselves as being at their migratory destination (Ketterson and Nolan, 1987; Sniegowski et al., 1988). Thus, there is a possibility that captive-reared birds will exhibit abnormal migratory behavior, because they have no knowledge of traditional destination sites for that species. Techniques are currently being developed to overcome this problem. In one interesting case, Canada geese (*Branta canadensis*) were imprinted on an ultralight aircraft, which they subsequently followed (Walsh, 1990). The intent of this project was to provide a means by which captive-reared trumpeter swans (*Olor buccinator*) could be taught their traditional migratory routes and destinations. The method has considerable promise and could help to reestablish many species of migratory waterfowl.

A knowledge of migration and philopatry can be used to manipulate the behavior of birds and promote their conservation. An interesting and apparently successful set of Swedish reintroduction experiments changed the migratory routes of the bean-goose (*Anser fabalis*) and the lesser white-fronted goose (*A. erythropus*) by taking advantage of philopatry and cross-fostering (Morner, 1986). Both species had declined rapidly, largely due to overhunting on their unprotected wintering grounds in southern Europe. The goal was to change the wintering site to safer locations in western Europe. Eggs were placed with foster parents of the species *Branta canadensis* and *B. leucopsis*, respectively. After hatching at the breeding stations, whole families were transferred to northern lakes where the goslings were raised. The families migrated together to west European wintering grounds, but in the following years the foster parents returned to the breeding stations while the released species returned to breed in the northern lakes where they were reared.

Social Skills and Reintroduction

Released birds that survive to reproductive age will not necessarily have the social skills required to reproduce under natural conditions, especially if they have been reared artificially. In British releases of some 3,400 hand-reared, six-week-old ring-necked pheasants (*Phasianus colchicus*) the breeding success of wild males was two to five times that of hand-reared males, in part, because hand-reared males were not as successful in establishing territories. Similarly, the productivity of wild females was about four times that of hand-reared females. Although both groups made the same number of nesting attempts, hand-reared females were three times more vulnerable to predation (Hill and Robertson, 1988). Behavioral deficiencies (e.g., those related to territorial defense or nest site selection) could account for these results. Unlike wild birds, hand-reared thick-billed parrots showed no tendency to flock after release, thus making it difficult to create normal breeding groups (Snyder et al., 1989).

The use of artificial parents and peer-rearing have already been discussed as methods by which the effects of hand-rearing can be minimized. However, another way to reduce the behavioral effects of early experience is to employ fostering techniques, wherein the clutches of free-ranging birds are expanded by adding eggs produced by captive birds. Fostering has been used to decrease postrelease mortality in European eagle owls (*Bubo bubo*) (Frankenberg et al., 1984). Typically, the foster parents are artificially provisioned, so that they can provide for a larger clutch. Fostering holds some promise for release programs, but its success is contingent on the foster parents accepting unrelated eggs or chicks. Some species have the ability to recognize their own eggs and chicks (Beecher et al., 1986; Arnold, 1987c), and this might limit the effectiveness of such techniques.

Interspecies rearing or "cross-fostering" has proven to be less successful. Drewien and Bizeau (1977) suggested that cross-fostering to sandhill cranes is a viable technique for reintroducing endangered whooping cranes to new geographical areas. Cross-fostered whooping cranes survived, migrated, and even flocked with conspecifics. However, there are indications that their long-term reproductive success may be compromised as a result of behavioral factors. Despite many successful rearings by sandhill cranes since 1975, no cross-fostered whooping crane has yet successfully reproduced (Brownlie, 1987). Behavior, including that associated with species recognition and mate choice, are known to be affected by early experience and this may account, at least in part, for the lack of reproduction in cross-fostered birds (Brownlie, 1987).

Some bird species seem to require large groupings for survival and/or reproduction. In fact, the statistical probability of a successful release or translocation increases with the number of individuals released (Griffith et al., 1989). The reasons may have something to do with the probability of finding mates, and the role of social interactions in facilitating reproduction (Lande, 1988; Dobson and Lyles, 1989). For reintroductions, this may require that cohesive groups of birds be released together, as has been suggested for thick-billed parrots (Snyder et al., 1989). Another option is to release captive-reared birds along with wild-born individuals, or to incorporate the former into already existing wild groups. The release of a captive-bred female into the territory of a wild male was successful on at least one occasion for the endangered Lord Howe Island woodhen (*Tricholimnas sylvestris*); the new pair reared 16 chicks during the following 18 months (Fullagar, 1985). It is important to note here that the strategy of mixing captive-reared with wild birds carries certain risks, such as introducing diseases or causing social stress in already reduced wild populations (see Woodford and Kock, 1991; Griffith et al., 1993). However, it should be possible to overcome such problems with careful medical management and planning.

Obviously, the more that is known about the behavioral biology of a species, whether in captivity or in the wild, the easier it will be to plan a reintroduction program. Scott and Carpenter (1987) point out that most of the numerous avian releases have been poorly documented, and that studies are desperately needed to judge the effectiveness of various reintroduction techniques. More often than not, release protocols evolve in a trial and error fashion, rather than on the basis of careful systematic study. Postrelease monitoring of reintroduced birds, as for example with radiotelemetry (see Ridley, 1986), will therefore be critical for the development of effective technologies.

Summary and Conclusions

An understanding of behavioral phenomena has been shown to be of great importance in formulating methods of exhibition, care, captive breeding, and reintroduction for endangered birds. Of particular importance are an understanding of avian social organization, courtship behavior and mate selection, nest building and associated activities, parental care, behavioral development, and foraging behavior. Zoos with serious captive breeding efforts and government wildlife agencies could therefore profit from placing behavioral scientists on staff. Despite great progress in the last decade, aviculturists have barely scratched the surface when it comes to documenting the behavioral requirements of specific species in captivity, or to developing effective technologies for the release of captive-reared birds. Considering that at least 5% of the world's 9,000 species of birds are considered endangered (IUCN, 1993), there is much work to be done and little time left in which to accomplish it.

Acknowledgments

N. Fascione deserves thanks for reading and commenting on an earlier draft of this manuscript. B. Bohmke, S. Johnson, C. Mirande, S. Ellis, E. Paul, and K. Cox helped with the literature search.

16

Captive Design for Endangered Birds

Bruce W. Bohmke

Prior to the early 1970s, there was little difference between designing a captive environment for an endangered species or a more commonly displayed species. Rare birds were perhaps highlighted, but still exhibited like the rest of the collection (Kennon, 1931). Most zoological collections exhibited individuals from as wide a variety of species as possible (Anonymous, 1960; Polakowski, 1987), and if pairs were exhibited it was often to indicate dimorphism. The last fifteen years has seen a major shift in exhibit philosophy for birds in general and endangered species in particular.

Gradually the concepts of mixed species display (Reed, 1966), zoogeographic grouping (Conway, 1966), and naturalistic exhibits (Wylie, 1981) became more important design criteria. Reproduction was recognized as a legitimate goal for both economic reasons and conservation purposes (Wayre, 1969). Captive design started to reflect this new thinking, and limited resources were put into nonpublic cages expressly for reproduction (McGill-Harelstad, 1987).

Endangered birds are currently housed in a wide variety of environments which are dependent on the goals of the holding institution. There are a number of institutions that focus on certain groups of birds such as cranes and birds of prey (Conway, 1978; Cade, 1986a) while others specialize in species suited to the particular climate of captive facilities (Todd, 1978). The Florida location of breeders of endangered amazons (*Amazona spp.*) is a good example of matching the species with the environment (Noegel, 1979). Most zoos, however, still attempt to display and reproduce a wide variety of bird species, an increasing number of which are endangered (King, 1979).

Economics of Captive Design

Spatial and Monetary Restrictions

The amount of space and money needed to both construct and operate a facility for birds varies widely. If the facility will be closed to the public, then human aesthetics can be ignored and practicality can dictate the design. Generally, enclosures not open to public viewing can be reduced in size, constructed of less expensive materials, and operated more efficiently. Reproduction has often occurred in exhibits considered small by human standards (Todd, 1972; Wylie, 1977). One pair of an endangered crane species may breed in a pen of 200 m^2, but for public display considerations such as human-animal flight distance, visual barriers, and landscaping may increase the required space to 800 m^2 or more (Archibald, 1974). Endangered Amazon parrots have been bred in cages with a total volume of 7 m^3 (Risser, 1978), but most zoo exhibits of Amazons are at least 2–3 times this volume. Endangered species on public display must have a cage size sufficiently large to satisfy not only the bird's needs, but also the visitor's idea of adequate space. Many large raptors are housed in displays 6 to 9 m high (Kish, 1970; Wylie, 1973), despite the fact that increased height does not alter activity or cage use. The excessive heights of large exhibits are usually more satisfying to the zoo visitor than to the birds. On the other hand, giving a bird sufficient space to feel completely at ease may result in a poor visual display. A pair of pheasants in a heavily planted exhibit will be out of view much of the time (Todd, 1982). Often visibility is the justification for more expensive exhibits, even though they may not improve the bird's condition. Cranes, for example, can be exhibited behind a chain link fence quite adequately (Sheppard, 1989). A shallow moat combined with a low barrier, while more expensive, allows visitors an unimpeded view of the birds.

When new construction for endangered species is planned, every attempt should be made to include multiple pairs of each endangered species (Durrell, 1976). Such an arrangement provides opportunities to manipulate pairings and allows for intraspecies stimulation where necessary. This type of vocal stimulation seems to be important for some parrots such as Cuban amazon, (*Amazona leucocephala*) (Noegel, 1979) while visual stimulation is critical for some birds of paradise (Hundgen and Bruning, 1988).

Design, Animal Health, and Animal Replacement

Whether dealing with endangered or common species, design is critical to the health of the birds. Certain design features are universal for cleanliness and sanitation. Type of substrate, ease of cleaning, and proper placement of drains are all important (Todd, 1982). Pest exclusion may be very important with some species. In addition to traditional disease vectors (such as rats, mice, roaches, sparrows, pigeons, and starlings), mosquitoes or other insects may also have to be excluded (Risdon, 1975). Mosquitoes are thought to expose certain birds to blood parasites previously unknown in their native environments (Weaver and Cade, 1983). Superior water quality is essential with many marine species. Proper design of filtration and water handling systems seems to be one of the keys to successful husbandry programs with penguins, alcids, and other marine birds (Swennen, 1977).

Health factors are especially important with endangered species because many endangered birds are impossible to replace. Examples include the Micronesian kingfisher (*Halcyon cinnamomina cinnamomina*) (Shelton, 1986) and the California condor (*Gymnogyps californianus*) (Snyder, 1983) which are presently extinct in the wild. Endangered species found in greater numbers in the wild may still be extremely difficult to acquire. Philippine monkey-eating eagle (*Pithecophaga jefferyi*), Imperial Amazon (*Amazona imperialis*), and black-necked crane (*Grus nigricollis*) are species still found in the wild but few, if any, are available for captive programs (Nichols, 1977; Cade, 1986; Mirande, 1988). On the other hand, some endangered species, such as nene goose (*Branta sandvicensis*) and Elliot's pheasant (*Syrmaticus ellioti*) breed so freely in captivity that reproduction must be controlled (Kear and Berber, 1980; Grahame, 1983).

Keeper Work Efficiency

Bird enclosures should be designed for maximum keeper efficiency. Poorly designed exhibits necessitate excessive keeper time spent cleaning, which translates into more money spent per exhibit. Small diameter drains cause pools to drain slowly and clog frequently. Low water pressure extends time spent cleaning and filling pools (Muller, 1975; Todd, 1982). Small keeper access doors make changing substrate, plants, and perches unnecessarily difficult. However, designing small access doors adjacent to feeding sites eliminates the need to enter the enclosure. When this method of feeding is available, stress to the animals can be reduced and keeper work efficiency can be increased (Weaver and Cade, 1983). Another common design flaw involves too few keeper service areas that cause needless trips back and forth to a central tool repository. Keeper work efficiency can also be impacted by other aspects of cage design. Without an efficient method of capture, much time can be wasted bringing a bird inside for the night, for the winter, or for health reasons. Enclosing a preferred perch or feeding area, leaving only a trap door entrance, serves to catch birds with a minimum of stress (Olney, 1975). This should be a design feature of all large aviaries (Bohmke and Healy, 1985). Automatic sprinkler systems can cut down on time spent watering essential exhibit plantings. All parts of the keeper's daily routine should be carefully examined to determine how design will impact efficiency.

Captive Design and Security

Three major security risks must be addressed: danger from vandals or thieves, danger from predators, and danger of escape. Their rare status makes some endangered species targets for theft and vandalism. Standard procedures, such as secure locks, alarms, and security personnel are the only practical solutions to this problem. Danger from predators is a somewhat more difficult problem. The risk may be eliminated by housing the animals indoors, but many birds are best kept outdoors. Fox, mink, raccoon, opossum, owl, crow, night heron, snake, dog, and cat are some of the more common problem predators (Todd, 1979). Outdoor pens should have 0.6 m of wire mesh underground to frustrate digging predators and an additional 0.3 m of wire turned out. Electrified wires around the top of the pen will help discourage climbing mammals (Delacour, 1973; Committee on Birds, 1977), and netting over an open pen is an effective way to eliminate an owl threat (Coe, 1980). Predator control design features will help reduce losses. Many ducks, geese, and swans seek the safe haven of an island to nest and roost, while planting low overhanging shrubs gives some protection from aerial predators. Egg and chick-eating snakes can get through very small mesh wire and, consequently, small birds vulnerable to snake predation are best kept indoors (Frampton, 1988). Some birds may be killed by predators if they nest or roost adjacent to a single barrier. Double wire or a solid barrier are the only sure solutions to such a problem (Low, 1972).

Bird escape can also be eliminated by careful design. All exhibits housing flighted birds should have a safety area between the exhibit and freedom (Bates and Busenbark, 1970; Todd, 1982), consisting of an enclosed space which has the access door to the cage on one side and an exit door to the outside on the other side. An exhibit should have sufficient height to allow birds to perch above the door. This simple design criteria will allow the bird to "escape" above the keeper's head instead of out the door (Committee on Birds, 1977). The condition of large trees adjacent to enclosures should also be continually monitored. In high winds, a large falling limb or tree can create sudden escape opportunities.

Species Considerations in Captive Design

Abiotic Factors

Temperature. With approximately 8,900 different species of birds (Clements, 1974) inhabiting almost the entire globe, the variety of environmental conditions birds are adapted for is extremely wide. Ranges vary from −57° C recorded for some passerine species to 45° C for some desert species (Serventy, 1971; Calder and King, 1974). Most birds from temperate and tropical areas will adapt quite well to a temperature range of 10–32° C (Rutgers and Norris, 1977). In fact, bird species from temperate climates can acclimate to below zero temperatures (Delacour, 1977). Some species, such as tropical storks, adapt very poorly to cold climates and must be housed indoors during winter (Coulter et al., 1989).

Precipitation and wind can also influence a bird's ability to adapt to cold. Providing a heated night enclosure, bedding materials over snow, windbreaks, and water artificially kept from freezing will improve some species' ability to withstand cold (Rutgers and Norris, 1977). In an outdoor enclosure, it is relatively simple to provide supplemental heat for birds because most will have a preferred roosting location. The addition of a heat source at the roost will provide heat during cooler nocturnal hours (Risdon, 1975). Attempting to reduce temperatures is more difficult. Penguins, alcids, and other birds which live in colder temperate climates may suffer ill effects from constant high temperatures. The most efficient method is to take advantage of microclimates in designing the exhibit. Locating exhibits near a body of water, under existing shade trees, or in a valley exposed to reduced hours of sunlight can all help to reduce exposure to high temperatures. In many cases, however, indoor enclosures with artificial climate controls are the only solutions to this problem. In addition, backup systems provide a measure of security against loss of climate control ability.

Illumination. Light intensity and duration requirements also vary tremendously among bird species. In general, birds from temperate areas rely heavily on light cycles for timing of biological events such as breeding and migration (Welty, 1975). These birds' reproductive efforts can be manipulated by changes in day length. Some birds such as hooded cranes (*Grus monacha*) which breed in high latitudes, may need artificially extended day lengths to successfully breed in captivity (Johnsgard, 1983b).

Most tropical species seem to depend on other types of cues, such as rainfall or fruit abundance to stimulate breeding behavior (Immelmann, 1965; Wheelwright, 1983; Leighton, 1986). Some species which are forest-dwelling, such as peacock pheasants of the genus *Polyplectron*, may prefer to nest in reduced light intensity areas, and this need can be accommodated by providing a darkened nesting chamber or heavily planted section of the exhibit (Low, 1972; Delacour, 1973; Orejuela, 1980; Heston, 1987). In a totally artificially fixed light schedule, some tropical birds may breed at any time of the year. If artificial lights are the only source of illumination, lighting should attempt to duplicate a natural spectrum as closely as possible (Committee on Birds, 1977).

Quality and Quantity of Space. Most birds, including endangered species, are exhibited in planted, naturalistic displays. These "soft" environments contain ample space, adequate visual barriers, and "natural" cage furniture. Birds of prey and parrots are often kept in a "harder" environment with few visual barriers, few live plants, and an obvious enclosure system such as chain link wire. Hard environments characterize birds that are destructive of their exhibits. Another reason for the prevalence of the hard enclosure is that some birds do not require a soft environment to settle in and be comfortable on display. Species such as bald eagle (*Haliaeetus leucocephalus*), Andean condor (*Vultur gryphus*), hyacinth macaw (*Anodorhynchus hyacinthinus*), and salmon-crested cockatoo (*Cacatua moluccensis*) may live long lives and even reproduce with little more than a suitable nest and adequate perches in the exhibit (Todd, 1972; Wylie, 1977; Berry, 1981; Cade, 1986). In an off-display facility designed for breeding, the design criteria will generally be more simplistic and less expensive. The addition of even a simple visual barrier can mean the difference between success and failure of a captive design as measured by longevity and reproduction. Such barriers have proven effective at reducing periodic aggression in Oriental white storks (*Ciconia boyciana*) (King, 1990).

Given their ability to fly, birds generally make use of all three dimensions of any exhibit. Even birds which are mainly terrestrial may roost off the ground at night. Some birds seldom go to the ground. In this case special consideration must be given to the placement of food and water (Committee on Birds, 1977). Diving birds also need three-dimensional space. Penguins, alcids, grebes, and other aquatic species make very efficient use of underwater space, if available (Flieg et al., 1971).

Biotic Factors

Food and Water. Ideally, diets for birds in captivity should provide all nutritional ingredients essential to maintain good health. Many exhibits incorporate plant material so that birds may supplement their diets. Most displays for geese have a portion of the exhibit planted in grass, which geese will readily consume. Many pheasants including brown-eared pheasant (*Crossoptilon montchuricum*), Elliot's Pheasant (*Syrmaticus ellioti*), and Palawan peacock pheasant (*Polyplectron emphanum*) will graze on tender plant shoots and buds. Exhibits should be designed to allow for this type of consumption and avoid potentially toxic plants (Delacour, 1973). Frequently, in a poorly designed exhibit, birds will destroy the plant material and perches. Parrots, such as white cockatoo (*Cacatua alba*), Hyacinth macaw (*Anodorhynchus hyacinthinus*), and thick billed parrot (*Rhynchopsitta pachyrhyncha*) are well known for this propensity (Berry, 1981). Careful placement of the perches away from live plants will slow the destruction. Regular replacement of "cage furniture" may also be attempted (Strasser, 1982).

Many otherwise well designed exhibits fail to provide proper conditions for feeding. Inappropriate placement of food sites can result in competition and food contamination. To avoid competition, food should be offered at multiple sites and at different heights (Committee on Birds, 1977). Feeding sites with visual barriers may also reduce competition.

Social Considerations. Many zoos house birds in pairs. In some cases, maintaining a larger group creates the possibility for intraspecific aggression. This is of particular concern with endangered species that are irreplaceable. Even species that are social all or part of the year in the wild may become aggressive during breeding season. Some species, such as the Guam rail (*Rallus owstoni*) are so aggressive that it is a challenge to successfully introduce birds for pairing without mortality or injury (Derrickson, 1986). In this case, birds are held in adjacent cages until the female produces eggs. This is taken as an indication that pairing has occurred. The technique of housing young birds together until pair bonds have formed has also been used successfully in cranes, including the white-nape crane (*Grus vipio*) (Derrickson and Carpenter, 1987; Sheppard, 1989). The introduction of new birds to an exhibit is a dangerous period and traumatic injuries may easily occur as dominance hierarchies are adjusted and feed stations located. Much of the stress associated with introductions can be relieved by housing new birds in an adjacent exhibit with visual and auditory interchange with prospective cagemates for a period of several days. A refinement of this procedure is the use of a "howdy" cage. This is a small, easily moved cage placed within an exhibit with the new bird inside. Within several days the old inhabitants adjust to the newcomer, and vice versa. The door to the cage is opened and the bird allowed to come out at its own pace. Such "howdy" cages should be built into new aviaries (Bohmke and Healy, 1985).

Truly social birds, such as wading birds and sea birds, may need the stimulation of conspecifics to facilitate breeding (Hirsch, 1978; Coulter et al., 1989). There may even be a critical lower limit that must be surpassed for reproduction to be successful (Ogilvie and Ogilvie, 1986). Exhibit design needs to factor in the flock size needed for successful reproduction. Mixed-species displays featuring endangered or rare species are not practical in most cases. Birds are often easily disturbed by even the most benign cage mate. Exceptions to this rule include birds with mutually exclusive lifestyles, gregarious birds, and aggressive species. For example, the combination of a completely terrestrial species with a totally arboreal species may be successful. In this case there would be no competition for feeding, roosting, or nesting sites. This combination has worked successfully with the Guam rail, and the Guam kingfisher (*Halcyon c. cinnamomina*) (Derrickson, pers. comm.). Some gregarious waterfowl and pheasants have successfully reproduced while in mixed-species displays. Examples include marbled teal (*Marmaronetta angustirostris*) and peacock pheasants (*Polyplectron spp.*) (Delacour, 1977; Lindholm, 1991). Multiple nest sites, feed stations, and roosting perches must be provided. Visual barriers and refuges are also essential (Schmitt, 1984; Bohmke and Healy,

1985). The idea that endangered species may be displayed in mixed-species enclosures as long as the display has been designed specifically for the endangered species is a dangerous concept. Due to unanticipated interactions, there are few situations where this idea is practical. If longevity and reproduction of the endangered species are the goals, the target species should generally be housed alone (Bohmke and Healy, 1985).

Enclosures of predator and prey should generally be separated at least visually. Predatory birds do not seem to be bothered by the close proximity of prey species (Todd, 1972), but prey species may be placed under unusual stress without visual barriers. Moreover, if predator and prey species are exhibited adjacent to one another, a possibility is created for traumatic injury resulting from sudden panic. This response to a perceived threat is especially great with species in the Order Galliformes (Delacour, 1977).

Captive Design and Animal Health

Injuries Due to Faulty Design

Injuries can occur to birds for which there is no obvious explanation. Some injuries, however, are directly attributed to exhibit design flaws. For instance, when excited, a bird will often try to fly through glass even though it may have previously been habituated to this type of barrier (Risdon, 1975). If the exhibit is too large, the bird can build up enough flight speed to severely injure itself (Bohmke, 1984). If the sides of the pool are steep the bird may be unable to get out and thus drown. The vertical steel wire cage system commonly known as "piano" or "harp" wire may allow birds to fly into the wires and get caught. If unable to escape the entanglement, injury or death may result. Any protrusions into the living space, such as faucets, wire, pipes, or nails may also injure a bird. Such protrusions should be removed or shielded (Committee on Birds, 1977). Highly territorial birds are capable of injuring each other through large mesh fencing. Suitable visual barriers or a buffer zone between exhibits are simple solutions to this design problem (Kepler, 1978; Derrickson and Carpenter, 1987). All pools should have a gradual slope to allow birds to walk in and out of the water (Bohmke, 1984).

The substrate may also impact on avian health. Many aquatic birds including penguins, pelicans, and waterfowl are susceptible to infections involving the feet. Many foot problems begin or are exacerbated by certain substrate such as concrete. Zoos have experimented with rubber mats, sand, kitty litter, fiberglass, and other substrates in an attempt to avoid problems. Generally a surface which is easily cleaned and dries quickly is most desirable for susceptible aquatic species.

Quarantine and Isolation of Injured or Sick Animals

Once a bird has become injured or sick it is usually isolated from cagemates. This is done not only to limit exposure of other birds to contagious diseases, but also to protect the sick bird from peer aggression. An obviously injured or ill member of a group of birds is usually driven away from the flock. In captivity, a bird unable to escape persecution from cagemates may be harassed to death.

The type of cage used for isolation should be constructed out of metal, fiberglass, plastic, sealed concrete, or other easily disinfected material. All quarantine and isolation cages should be as small as possible to help restrict movement and reduce the stress of routine capture for treatments. In addition, quarantine and isolation areas should be as quiet and disturbance free as possible. Stress reduction will facilitate recovery from illness and improve a bird's ability to adapt to the new environment (International Bird Rescue Research Center, 1978).

Animal Hospitals

Birds kept in animal hospitals are usually housed alone. The effect of social isolation on most birds is minimal, but for those species that are highly social, housing conspecifics within visual and/or vocal range will reduce the effects of the physical isolation. When birds are ill or injured, their activity level declines. Small, easily cleaned cages can reduce stress during daily cleaning, facilitate capture for medication, and reduce energy expended in foraging. Once a bird has recovered from illness, reintroduction into the customary exhibit should be accomplished gradually. Housing the recently recovered specimen in an adjacent enclosure for several days will ease tension and allow former cagemates to become reacquainted.

Captive Design and Conservation

Design of captive enclosures with the goal of introduction to the wild requires a different perspective. Longevity, public display, or reproduction are no longer primary concerns. The most important focus becomes the identification of design features that will en-hance fitness in the wild. The need to potentially release birds to the wild is the major cause for differences in design for endangered versus nonendangered birds. Additional factors that must be con-sidered include species recognition, control of disease introduction, imprinting on humans, and optimizing physical condition.

Some design criteria involve improvement of the animal's physical condition, for example, a simple design technique to im-prove plumage by reducing contact with wire caging is to cover the wire with burlap or tar paper (Ellis et al., 1978). Providing suffi-cient space and proper perching to encourage flying builds flight endurance (Snyder, 1987). Providing general experience necessary for long-term survival in the wild may, in fact, involve a great deal of space. Recognition of wild foods in a natural setting may demand an enclosure many times the size ordinarily needed to house the target species. Clever design of facilities has allowed some species to forage at liberty for short training periods (Ellis et al., 1978). Construction of aviaries near remaining wild populations, as has been done with the Puerto Rican parrot, is felt to be important for handling field emergencies where eggs, chicks or adults need tem-porary assistance (Wiley, 1983).

Birds reared for release into the wild may require other ex-hibit modifications. Visual and auditory isolation from humans may be desired. The use of shift cage, single direction viewing glass, visual barriers, and sound buffers all act to prevent familiarization and imprinting with humans (Berger, 1978a; Derrickson and Car-penter, 1987). Appropriate social responses to conspecifics are equally critical to survival in the wild. Social species must respond correctly to other individuals or they may not be accepted into the flock (Low, 1972; Snyder, 1987). Multiple enclosure units that al-low a gradual increase of visual and auditory contact can be useful in this regard (Mitchell and Zwank, 1987). Large enclosures that accommodate multiple pairs of birds at the same time may be necessary. A large enclosure with ample cover may also help to initiate instinctual predator avoidance responses (Berger, 1978b).

Specialized structures have been designed for unique release methods. The "hack tower" is a proven method for the release of various birds of prey into the wild (Temple, 1978). This technique is unlikely to have widespread use with other types of birds but does illustrate the concept of unique design demands. Finally, an often overlooked problem is the introduction of disease into the wild population. Exhibits must be designed to reduce or eliminate parasites and diseases in captive birds about to be released,

especially those diseases previously unknown in the wild population (Berger, 1978b; van Riper et al., 1986).

Conclusions

Captive design concerns of the future will be directed by the goals
that managers are attempting to satisfy. Foremost among these
goals will be the effort to salvage endangered species through maintenance of captive populations. Many zoos have already taken the
first steps down this road by building off-exhibit breeding centers,
redesigning enclosures to maximize reproduction, and experiment-
ing with captive designs which train birds for release to the wild
(Mirande, 1985; McGill-Harelstad, 1987). Flexibility is an important design criteria to accommodate changing species priorities.
The accelerating rate of avian extinctions underscores the importance of this work (Temple, 1986).

Another primary goal of zoos is and will be to provide a pleasant experience for visitors while imparting information about animals. Design of captive environments will become increasingly
sophisticated at immersing visitors in a seemingly natural setting
while observing birds. Educational opportunities will continue to
be an important component of design. The current use of temporary exhibits for endangered species such as pandas and koalas
may point the way to a more novel method of operation—one that
emulates the tactic used by museums. Temporary loans and rotating exhibits, while necessitating more off-exhibit holding, allows
greatly expanded educational opportunities within a single institution.

Some future design challenges can be anticipated. More species will be produced in captivity for release to the wild, and this
will necessitate innovative design of prerelease training enclosures.
Cooperative interactions between captive facilities and large natural wildlife preserves will result in facilities designed to serve both
interests at the same site. Design of successful captive environments for difficult-to-maintain groups, such as lek-breeding species, nectar feeding species, grebes, and swallows is still in the
future (Sheppard, 1985). Design of avian environments will be important in meeting the challenges of captive conservation in the
next century.

V

Mammals
(Excluding Marine Mammals and Primates)

Introduction of Authors
and Chapter Previews

Reginald Hoyt, curator of Collections at the Phoenix Zoo, focuses on the captive conservation of mammals with an emphasis on species poorly represented in captive collections. Of particular interest to him are the Orders Pholidota and Chiroptera. His current research deals with the feasibility of the long-term captive propagation of the kangaroo rat (*Dipodomys deserti*), with the goal of developing techniques for the translocation and reintroduction of endangered forms of *Dipodomys*. His long-term goals include a broader level of collaboration between the academic and zoo communities on behalf of species at risk.

The status and captive successes of representative species from thirteen mammalian orders are discussed by Mr. Hoyt in his chapter. The triage system for captive conservation programs, espoused by this author, will factor the level of endangerment of a species with effective utilization of space and wise expenditure of funds when selecting a species for intensive conservation effort.

Reproductive physiology of endangered species is discussed by Barbara Durrant. As head of the reproductive physiology division of the Center for the Reproduction of Endangered Species at the Zoological Society of San Diego, she conducts research on semen collection, evaluation, and cryopreservation in a number of mammalian and avian species. *In vitro* assessment of the potential fertilizability of fresh and frozen sperm is a major area of research. The hormonal control of estrus and ovulation and artificial insemination in equids and felids (especially the Przewalski's horse and the cheetah) are of particular interest. Isolation of preantral ovarian follicles, *in vitro* growth, maturation, and fertilization is a current project aimed at rescuing germplasm from endangered species postmortem.

Dr. Durrant emphasizes the need for integrated knowledge of the affects of multiple factors (genetics, behavior, health, nutrition, endocrinology, and physiology) on the reproduction of endangered species in captivity. She urges conservationists to carefully evaluate a species' need for artificial reproductive techniques prior to embarking on expensive, infrequently successful high-technology methodologies.

Mammalian behavior is reviewed by John Gittleman and Greta C. McMillan, both from Knoxville, Tennessee. Dr. Gittleman is associate professor in the Department of Zoology and assistant director of the Graduate Program in Ethology, both of the University of Tennessee. He conducts research in phylogeny, evolutionary biology, and the comparative method. The interrelationships of size and phylogenetic constraints on adaptive trait variation is a special interest. In conservation biology, he is mainly involved in applications of comparative biology to management and preservation of carnivores. Ms. McMillan occupies the position of conservation resarch coordinator at the Knoxville Zoological Gardens. Her field research experience took her to Belize, Barbados, and Southern Florida. The primary focus of her zoo-based research is the behavior and reproductive physiology of the red panda. Her capacity as editor of the International Indian lion studbook and role of biologist at the Indian lion Population Habitat and Viability Analyses (PHVA) workshop in Baroda, India, reflects a continuing interest in small population biology and management.

The authors encourage the coordination of field and captive behavior studies through discussion of how selected behavioral problems (i.e., antipredatory behavior, mother-infant interactions, and mating relationships) may be better understood by complementary studies. They do warn, however, that extrapolation between captive and field studies must be constantly verified as patterns observed in either setting may not be reproduced in the other.

The mammal captive design chapter was prepared by four coauthors: Debra Forthman, Rita McManomon, Uriel Levi, and Gail Bruner. Dr. Forthman is coordinator of Scientific Programs in the Conservation and Research Department at Zoo Atlanta. She facilitates research endeavors by Zoo Atlanta staff, visiting scientists and students, and serves as cochair of the zoo's design and behavioral enrichment committees. Dr. Forthman is also adjunct assistant professor of Psychology at Georgia Institute of Technology. In addition to pursuing research interests in behavioral enrichment, the development and social behavior of species not well studied in the wild, feeding ecology and applied conditioned taste aversion, she is developing a field project on the behavioral ecology of an orphaned population of African elephants in Akagera National Park, Rwanda. As senior vice-president of Veterinary Services, Dr. McManamon oversees the Animal Health and Commissary Departments at Zoo Atlanta, as well as performing other senior administrative duties. She participates actively in exhibit design, and frequently consults on projects involving facility design for local and international wildlife rehabilitation projects. She also serves as the veterinary advisor for the AZA Orangutan Species Survival Program. Her professional interests include behavioral enrichment and training as well as clinical exotic animal medicine, nutrition, neonatology, and dentistry. Uriel Levi began his involvement with interactive environments at the Boston Museum School. He became interested in ecological principles of design and their application in the development of places that encourage creative interaction as a graduate student and fellow at the Massachusetts Institute of Technology Center for Advanced Visual Studies. Dr. Levi's recently completed dissertation focused on species appropriate space-use patterns and their application in bioexhibit design. Combined with a background in fine arts and multimedia computing, his eclectic interests have found a comfortable convergence in bioexhibit design. As zoo biologist, Gail Bruner operated as liaison between zoo staff, architects, and construction teams on design and construction matters in the redevelopment of animal exhibits at the Atlanta Zoo. She has recently become an ecotourism consultant after completion of a master's degree in Technology and Science Policy at Georgia Institute of Technology, in which she evaluated the impact of ecotourism on local populations living on the periphery of the Community Baboon Sanctuary, Belize.

In their chapter, these authors urge design teams to ask two fundamental questions when planning a new exhibit: What is the species' natural social organization? What are the species' primary modes of communication? Consideration for the animals' behavioral (social) needs is evident throughout this chapter as is the authors' belief that the public must be educated about all aspects of animal exhibition.

17

The Status and Challenges of the Conservation of Mammals in Captivity

Reginald A. Hoyt

The current rate of extinction is unprecedented in the history of the planet. Of the 3,968 species of mammals (excluding primates and marine mammals) recognized by Corbett and Hill (1986), 431 forms may be identified as at risk. In this chapter, "at risk" is defined as those species appearing on the International Union for the Conservation of Nature and Natural Resources Red List (IUCN, 1993), excluding those taxa denoted as extinct (Ex) or as insufficiently known (K); listed in Convention for the International Trade of Endangered Species (CITES), Appendix I or II (U.S. Fish and Wildlife Service 1990a); or the U.S. Fish and Wildlife Service Endangered Species List (1990b).

Species Status in the Wild

The major causes for the global decline of mammal populations can be directly attributed to human activity. These activities include habitat destruction, hunting or direct persecution, and commercial trade. Habitat loss is of the greatest consequence for most species. However, over-hunting continues to be a major threat for those species used as food by growing human populations. Persecution remains a threat to large carnivores, and while commercial trade has been reduced by CITES regulations, there is still considerable illegal trade in those species considered to be of economic importance.

It has been the role of organizations such as the IUCN, World-wide Fund for Nature (WWF), Conservation International (CI), and Wildlife Conservation International (WCI) to monitor the status of wild species and to suggest and implement conservation programs. The IUCN has been particularly active in the development of action plans which are discussed in this chapter. Each of these action plans identifies threats to species and provides recommended conservation action.

Conservation Programs In Captivity

Table 17.1 outlines the status of those mammals listed as at risk and currently held in captivity. While much of this information was gleaned from the records of the International Species Inventory System (ISIS), and the International Zoo Yearbook (Olney, 1986, 1987a, and 1987b), the literature has been used to augment these records.

Order Monotremata

Of the three species with this Order, the long-nosed echidna (*Zaglossus bruijni*) is the only species currently listed as endangered. Although Flower (1931) reported remarkable captive longevities (31+ years), captive reproduction has not been reported. Recent management successes with the short-nosed echidna (*Tachyglossus aculeatus*) reported by Boisvert and Grisham (1988), Dee (1990), and George (1990) provide some hope for the successful breeding of the long-nosed echidna, assuming sufficient numbers can be recruited into the captive population. The American Zoo and Aquariums Association (AZA) has recently formed a Taxon Advisory Group (TAG) for the marsupials and monotremes, in hopes of better coordinating efforts in North America.

Order Marsupialia

A diverse Order (270 species), there are 54 species (20%) listed as at risk. Of those threatened species, 46% (N=25) are currently held in captive collections and 39% (N=21) have been recently bred. The macropods have the largest captive populations. Tree kangaroos, although popular in zoos, have a poor captive record with only the Goodfellow's (*Dendrolagus goodfellowi*), grizzled grey (*D. inustus*), and Doria's (*D. dorianus notatus*) tree kangaroos being currently bred in captivity. However, none have self-sustaining captive populations.

Table 17.1
Species Considered at Risk That Are
Currently Held in Captive Collections

(Note: Species with captive populations exceeding 50 individuals are denoted by a *, and those with captive populations exceeding 100 individuals are denoted by a +. Those species for which captive programs have been reported, but no recent data could confirm the continued existence of the colony, have been denoted by a ?).

Scientific Name/Common Name	Captive	Bred
ORDER MONOTREMATA		
Zaglossus bruijni/Long-nosed echidna	X	
ORDER MARSUPIALIA		
Dasyurus viverrinus/Quoll	X	X
Myrmecobius fasciatus/Numbat	X	X
Macrotis lagotis/Rabbit bandicoot	X	X
Phalanger maculatus/Spotted cuscus	X	
P. orientalus/Gray cuscus	X	
Gymnobelideus leadbeateri/Leadbeater's possum	X*	X
Burramys parvus/Mountain pygmy possum	X	X
Bettongia gaimardi/Gaimard's bettong	X	X
B. penicillata/Brush-tailed bettong	X+	X
Caloprymnus campestris/Desert rat-kangaroo	X	X
Dendrolagus dorianus notatus/Doria's tree kangaroo	X?	X
D. goodfellowi shawmayer/Goodfellow's tree kangaroo	X	X
D. inustus/Grizzled gray tree kangaroo	X	X
D. lumholtzi/Lumholtz's tree kangaroo	X	
D. ursinus/Black tree kangaroo	X	
Lagorchestes hirsutus/Western hare wallaby	X	X
Lagostrophus fasciatus/Banded hare wallaby	X	X
Macropus fuliginosus/Western gray kangaroo	X+	X
M. giganteus/Eastern gray kangaroo	X	X
M. parma/Parma wallaby	X+	X
M. rufus/Red kangaroo	X+	X
Onychogales fraenata/Brindled nail-tailed wallaby	X?	X
Petrogale xanthopus/Yellow-footed rock wallaby	X*	X
Potorous longipes/Long-footed potoroo	X	X
Setonix brachyurus/Quokka	X	X
ORDER INSECTIVORA		
Atelerix frontais/South African hedgehog	X	X
Podogymnura truei/Mindanao moonrat	X	X
Solenodon paradoxus/Haitian solenodon	X	
Desman moschata/Russian desman	X	

Table 17.1 *continued*

Scientific Name/Common Name	Captive	Bred
ORDER CHIROPTERA		
Pteropus livingstonii/Comoro Island fruit bat	X	
P. rodricensis/Rodriques fruit bat	X+	X
Macroderma gigas/Ghost bat	X	X
ORDER EDENTATA		
Myrmecophaga tridactyla/Giant anteater	X+	X
Tamandua tetradactyla chapadensis/Tamandua	X?	X
ORDER PHOLIDOTA		
Manis crassicaudata/Indian pangolin	X	
M. pentadactyla/Chinese pangolin	X	
M. temmincki/Cape pangolin	X	
ORDER LAGOMORPHA		
Bunolagus monticularis/Riverine rabbig	X	X
Romerolagus diazi/Volcano rabbit	X+	X
ORDER RODENTIA		
Marmota vancouverensis/Vancouver Island marmot	X?	
Ratufa affinis/Cream-coloured giant squirrel	X	
R. bicolor/Black giant squirrel	X	X
R. indica/Indian giant squirrel	X	X
Dipodomys heermanni morroensis/Morro Bay kangaroo rat	X	X
Chinchilla lanigera/Long-tailed chinchilla	X+	X
Geocapromys brownii/Jamaican hutia	X*	X
G. ingrahami/Bahamian hutia	X?	
Plagiodontia aedium/Hispaniolan hutia	X?	
ORDER CARNIVORA		
Canis lupus/Gray wolf	X+	X
C. rufus/Red wolf	X+	X
Chrysocyon brachyurus/Maned wolf	X+	X
Cuon alpinus/Dhole	X	X
Dusicyon culpaeus/Culepo	X	X
Lycaon pictus/African hunting dog	X+	X
Speothos venaticus/Bush dog	X+	X

Table 17.1 *continued*

Scientific Name/Common Name	Captive	Bred
ORDER CARNIVORA *(continued)*		
Vulpes macrotis mutica/San Joaquin kit fox	X	
V. velox hebes/Swift fox	X*	X
Ailuropoda melanoleuca/Giant panda	X	X
Helarctos malayanus/Sun bear	X+	X
Melursus ursinus/Sloth bear	X*	X
Selenarcotos thibetanus/Asian black bear	X+	X
Tremarctos ornatus/Spectacled bear	X+	X
Ursus arctos/Brown bear	X+	X
U. maritimus/Polar bear	X+	X
Ailurus fulgens/Lesser panda	X+	X
Aonyx capensis/African clawless otter	X	X
A. cinerea/Oriental small-clawed otter	X+	X
Enhydra lutris/Sea otter	X	X
Gulo gulo/Wolverine	X	X
Lutra canadensis/Canadian otter	X+	X
L. longicaudis/Long-tailed otter	X	
L. lutra/European river otter	X+	X
L. maculicollis/Spotted-necked otter	X	X
L. perspicillata/Smooth-coated otter	X	
Mustela lutreola/European mink	X	X
M. nigripes/Black-footed ferret	X+	X
Pteronura brasiliensis/Giant otter	X	X
Cryptoprocta ferox/Fossa	X	X
Fossa fossa/Malagasy civet	X	X
Hemigalus derbyanus/Banded palm civet	X	X
Macrogalidia musschenbroekii/Sulawesi palm civet	X	
Prionodon linsang/Banded linsang	X	X
P. pardicolor/Spotted linsang	X	X
Liberiictis kuhni/Liberian mongoose	X	
Hyaena brunnea/Brown hyaena	X*	X
Acinonyx jubatus/Cheetah	X+	X
Felis bengalensis/Leopard cat	X*	X
F. canadensis/Canadian lynx	X*	X
F. caracal/Caracal	X+	X
F. chaus/Jungle cat	X*	X
F. colocolo/Pampas cat	X*	X
F. concolor/Cougar	X+	X
F. geoffroyi/Geoffroy's cat	X*	X
F. iriomotensis/Iriomote cat	X	
F. libyca/African wild cat	X	X

Table 17.1 *continued*

Scientific Name/Common Name	Captive	Bred
ORDER CARNIVORA *(continued)*		
F. lynx/Lynx	X*	X
F. manul/Pallas's cat	X	X
F. margarita/Sand cat	X	X
F. marmorata/Marbled cat	X	X
F. nigripes/Black-footed cat	X	X
F. pardalis/Ocelot	X+	X
F. pardina/Spanish lynx	X	
F. planiceps/Flat-headed cat	X	
F. rubiginosa/Indian rusty spotted cat	X	X
F. rufus/Bobcat	X+	X
F. serval/Serval	X+	X
F. silvestris/Wild cat	X	X
F. temmincki/Temminck's golden cat	X	X
F. tigrinus/Tiger cat	X	X
F. viverrinus/Fishing cat	X	X
F. wiedii/Margay	X+	X
F. yagouaroundi/Jaguarundi	X*	X
Neofelis nebulosa/Clouded leopard	X+	X
Panthera leo/lion	X+	X
P. onca/Jaguar	X+	X
P. pardus/Leopard	X+	X
P. tigris/Tiger	X+	X
P. uncia/Snow leopard	X+	X
ORDER TUBULIDENTATA		
Orycteropus afer/Aardvark	X	X
ORDER PROBOSCIDEA		
Elephas maximus/Asian elephant	X+	X
Loxodonta africana/African elephant	X+	X
ORDER PERISSODACTYLA		
Equus africanus/African wild ass	X+	X
E. grevyi/Grevy's zebra	X+	X
E. hemionus/Asian wild ass	X	X
E. kiang/Kiang	X	X
E. przewalskii/Przewalski's horse	X+	X
E. zebra hartmannae/Hartmann's mountain zebra	X+	X
Tapirus bairdii/Baird's tapir	X	X

Table 17.1 *continued*

Scientific Name/Common Name	Captive	Bred
ORDER PERISSODACTYLA *(continued)*		
T. indicus/Malayan tapir	X+	X
T. pinchaque/Mountain tapir	X	X
T. terrestris/South American tapir	X+	X
Ceratotherium simum/White rhinoceros	X+	X
Didermocerus sumatrensis/Sumatran rhinoceros	X	X
Diceros bicornis/Black rhinoceros	X+	X
Rhinoceros unicornis/Indian rhinoceros	X*	X
ORDER ARTIODACTYLA		
Choeropsis liberiensis/Pygmy hippopotamas	X+	X
Babyrousa babyrussa/Babirusa	X*	X
Sus salvanius/Pygmy hog	X?	X
S. scrofa riukiuanus/Ryukyu Island's wild pig	X	X
S. verrucosus/Javan warty pig	X	X
Catagonus wagneri/Chacoan peccary	X	X
Tayassu pecari/White-lipped peccary	X	X
T. tajacu/Collared peccary (outside U.S.)	X*?	X
Camelus bactrianus/Wild bactrian camel	X*	X
Lama guanicoe/Guanaco	X+	X
Vicugna vicugna/Vicuna	X	X
Blastocerus dichotomus/Marsh deer	X	X
Cervus albirostris/Thorold's deer	X	X
C. calamianensis/Philippine hog deer	X	X
C. duvauceli/Barasingha	X+	X
C. elaphus bactrianus/Bactrian deer	X	X
C. e. barbarus/Barbary stag	X	X
C. e. corsicanus/Corsican red deer	X	X
C. e. hanglu/Kashmir deer	X	X
C. e. macneilli/McNeill's deer	X*	X
C. e. yarkandensis/Yarkand red deer	X*	X
C. eldi/Eld's brow-antlered deer	X+	X
C. kuhli/Bawean hog deer	X*	X
C. mesopotamica/Persian fallow deer	X	X
C. nippon keramae/Ryukuyu sika deer	X	
C. n. mandarinus/North China sika deer	X	X
C. n. taiouanus/Formosan sika deer	X*	X
C. porcinus/Indochina hog deer	X+	X
Elaphurus davidianus/Père David's deer	X+	X
Hippocamelus antisensis/North Andean huemal	X	
Moschus chrysogaster/Forest musk deer	X	

Table 17.1 *continued*

Scientific Name/Common Name	Captive	Bred
ORDER ARTIODACTYLA *(continued)*		
M. moschiferus/Siberian musk deer	X	X
Muntiacus crinifrons/Black muntjac	X	X
M. feae/Fea's muntjac	X	X
Odocoileus. v. leucura/Columbian white-tailed deer	X	X
Ozotoceros bezoarticus/Pampas deer	X	X
Pudu pudu/Southern pudu	X*	X
Rangifer tarandus caribou/Woodland caribou	X*	X
Taurotragus d. derbianus/Western giant eland	X	X
Addax nasomaculatus/Addax	X+	X
Oryx dammah/Scimitar-horned oryx	X+	X
O. leucoryx/Arabian oryx	X+	X
Hippotragus equinus/Roan antelope	X+	X
Kobus leche/Red lechwe	X+	X
Damaliscus dorcas dorcas/Bontebok	X*	X
D. hunteri/Hunter's hartebeest	X	X
Aepyceros melampus petersi/Black-faced impala	X	X
Gazella cuvieri/Cuvier's gazelle	X*	X
G. dama/Dama gazelle	X+	X
G. dorcas/Dorcas gazelle	X+	X
G. gazella/Mountain gazelle	X*	X
G. leptoceros/Slender-horned gazelle	X*	X
G. rufifrons/Red-fronted gazelle	X	X
G. soemmerringi/Soemmerring's gazelle	X	X
G. spekei/Speke's gazelle	X	X
G. subgutturosa marica/Sand gazelle	X*	X
Cephalophus dorsalis/Bay duiker	X	X
C. jentinki/Jentink's duiker	X	X
C. monticola/Blue duiker	X*	X
C. sylvicultor/Yellow-backed duiker	X	X
C. zebra/Zebra-backed duiker	X	X
Ammotragus lervia/Aoudad	X+	X
Capra falconeri/Markhor	X+	X
C. walie/Walia ibex	X	X
Capricornis crispus swinhoei/Formosan serow	X	X
C. sumatraensis/Sumatran serow	X	X
Hemitragus hylocrius/Nilgiri tahr	X	X
H. jayakari/Arabian tahr	X+	X
Nemorhaedus goral / Goral	X	X
Ovis ammon/Argali	X	X
O. canadensis/North American bighorn sheep	X+	X

Table 17.1 *continued*

Scientific Name/Common Name	Captive	Bred
ORDER ARTIODACTYLA *(continued)*		
O. orientalis musimon/Mouflon	X+	X
Ovis o. ophion/Cyprian red sheep	X	X
Budorcas taxicolor/Takin	X	X
Rupricapra pyrenaica ornata/Apennian chamois	X	X
Bison bison athabascae/Wood bison	X*	X
B. bonasus/European bison	X+	X
Bos gaurus/Gaur	X+	X
B. grunniens mutus/Wild yak	X	X
B. javanicus/Banteng	X+	X
Bubalus bubalus/Wild Asiatic water buffalo	X*	X
B. depressicornis/Lowland anoa	X	X
B. mindorensis/Tamaraw	X	X
B. quarlesi/Mountain anoa	X	X

Small marsupial species that are relatively well represented in captivity include the Leadbeater's opossum (*Gymnobelideus leadbeateri*), and the brush-tailed bettong (*Bettongia penicillata*). While a cooperative captive conservation program between the Perth Zoo and the Western Australia Department of Conservation and Land Management has been developed to benefit the numbat (*Myrmecobius fasciatus*), the program is struggling with various husbandry problems (DeJose, 1988). The hare wallabies (*Lagorchestes hirsutus*) and *L. fasciatus* (Burton and Pearson, 1987) as well as *Onychogales fraenata* (Thornback and Jenkins, 1984) are also subjects of breeding programs, with *L. fasciatus* being reintroduced to Dirk Hartog Island, Australia in 1974 (Burton and Pearson, 1987).

Numerous authors (Collins, 1973; Aslin, 1982; Bennet et al., 1982; Wooley, 1982; Bryant, 1988; Conway, 1988) have described their experiences with the propagation of Dasyurids. Hulbert (1982) had considerable success with the care and breeding of the bilby (*Macrotis lagotis*), and although there has been little experience with the Queensland hairy-nosed wombat (*Lasciorhinus krefftii*), Gaughwin (1982) and Presidente (1982) have described their work with the closely related common (*Vombatus ursinus*) and southern hairy-nosed (*L. latifrons*) wombats. Other studies include George's

(1982) work with members of the Phalangeridae, Fairfax's (1982) attempts at breeding the scaly-tailed opossum (*Wyulda squamicaudata*), Thomas's (1982) studies of the mountain pygmy opossum (*Burramys parvus*), Rose's (1982) success with Gaimard's bettong (*Bettongia gaimardi*), and Tyndale-Biscoe's (1968) work with Lesueur's bettong (*B. lesueur*).

For a review of the captive management of Australian mammals and current breeding programs in Australia, the reader is referred to Evans (1982) and George (1990), respectively. The formation of the AZA's Monotreme/Marsupial Taxon Advisory Group will improve captive management in North America. However, unless the legal pathways for the exportation of native wildlife from Australia are streamlined, the prospects for meaningful conservation programs outside of that country are limited.

Order Insectivora

This large Order (349 species) has only 15 threatened forms (4%), and is poorly represented in captivity, with only the Russian desman (*Desman moschata*), South African hedgehog (*Atelerix frontalis*) (Smithers, 1986), Mindanao moonrat (*Podogymnura truei*), and the Haitian solenodon (*Solenodon paradoxus*) known to be in captive collections. However, there is a large body of literature concerning the husbandry of various Insectivore species (e.g., golden moles [*Chrysochloridae*], Bateman, 1959; Holm, 1969; Meester, 1972; long-tailed tenrec [*Microgale*], Eisenberg and Gould, 1967, 1970; Eisenberg and Maliniak, 1974; shrew [*Crocidura*], Marlow, 1955; Meester, 1963; Ansell, 1964; Hellwing, 1973; Vlasak, 1973; Grunwald and Mohres, 1974; Godfrey, 1975; and long-tailed shrew [*Sorex longirostris*], Odum, 1944). More recently, a long-eared tenrec (*Geogale a. aurita*) was held at the Parc Botanique et Zoologique de Tsimbazaza, Madagascar, with a longevity of 25 months being recorded (Nicoll, pers. comm.). In addition, a male web-footed tenrec (*Limnogale mergulus*) was collected by the staff of the U.S. National Zoological Park, and successfully maintained at the Parc Botanique et Zoologique de Tsimbazaza for three weeks before being released (Gould, pers. comm.).

At the Fifth World Conference on Breeding Endangered Species in Captivity, Ottenwalder (1988) reported on a cooperative program to study *Solenodon paradoxus* in the wild and attempts at establishing a captive colony. His review of the history of captive husbandry over the last 100 years revealed that there has been only one captive birth of *Solenodon*, which did not survive.

Order Chiroptera

Although the second largest Order of mammals (988 species), only 32 forms (3%) are recognized as at risk, most of which are island forms of the genus *Pteropus*. However, only three endangered bat species are currently held and bred in captivity (Table 17.1). The large captive populations of the nonendangered flying fox (*Pteropus giganteus*), and the success of the Jersey Wildlife Preservation Trust's program for the Rodrigues flying fox (*P. rodricensis*), attest to the potential for captive propagation of this genus (Carroll, 1990). Attempting to follow through on its previous success, the Jersey Wildlife Preservation Trust (McNicholas, 1989) is initiating a captive propagation effort for the Comoro Island flying fox (*P. livingstonii*). In addition, a cooperative program involving the IUCN, the Zoological Society for the Conservation of Species and Populations, and the Phoenix Zoo is being developed to propagate the Pemba flying fox (*P. voeltzkowi*) in captivity, while simultaneously implementing *in situ* conservation efforts.

While the island forms of bats hold the greatest potential for *ex situ* conservation efforts, many of the frugivorous New World bats (Microchiroptera) are equally suited to captive propagation (Rasweiler, 1977). The insectivorous bats of the Vespertilionidae seldom reproduce in captivity (Constantine, 1986), and are likely less well suited to captive propagation programs than the frugivorous bats. The AZA has formed a Chiropteran Taxon Advisory Group to help coordinate efforts with this poorly represented order and to help develop improved husbandry technologies.

Order Edentata

This small Order (29 species) has eight species (28%) that are at risk. Of the endangered edentates only the giant anteater (*Myrmecophaga tridactyla*), with a large (i.e., 107 specimens) captive population, and the tamandua (*Tamandua tetradactyla*) are presently held and bred in captivity. The remaining rare edentates have poor captive husbandry histories. Members of the genus *Bradypus* (three-toed sloths) seldom survive more than a few months in captivity (Meritt, 1977). The fairy armadillos (*Chlamyphorus truncatus* and *C. retusus*), and giant armadillo (*Priodontes maximus*) are rarely exhibited by zoos, and have never bred in captivity (Burton and Pearson, 1987). The AZA has formed a Taxon Advisory Group to aid in the coordination of efforts with this Order.

Order Pholidota

Four of the seven extant pangolin species are considered at risk and are among the rarest of zoo specimens. Heath and Vanderlip (1988) recently described husbandry techniques for the Chinese pangolin (*Manis pentadactyla*), while Hoyt (1987) found that historically, 71% of all captive specimens did not survive more than six months. Although no recent captive breedings of pangolins have been reported, the Indian (*Manis crassicaudata*) and Cape pangolins (*M. temmincki*) have been bred in the past (Van Ee, 1966 and 1978; Acharjyo and Mohapatra, 1978; respectively). The Chipangali Wildlife Trust of Zimbabwe attempted a captive propagation program for the Cape pangolin (*M. temmincki*), but results were disappointing (Cross, pers. comm.).

Order Lagomorpha

Of this Order's 59 species, only 14% (N=8) are considered at risk, with only two species having conservation programs in place (Chapman and Flux, 1990). In 1987 the National Zoo of South Africa, in cooperation with the Mammal Research Institution of the Wildlife Society of Southern African and the South African Nature Foundation, began a captive propagation program for the riverine rabbit (*Bunolagus monticularis*) with the goal of establishing a breeding population in Karoo National Park by 1990 (Labuschagne, 1989). In 1968 the Jersey Wildlife Preservation Trust initiated a program for the captive propagation of the volcano rabbit (*Romerolagus diazi*). However, the most successful captive colony was that established at the Chapultepec Zoo in 1984 (Hoth and Granadas, 1987). In lieu of this success, the distribution of the Tehuentepec hare (*Lepus flavigularis*) within Mexico, and the availability of suitable models (*L. californicus* and *L. alleni*) would make this species an excellent candidate for captive propagation.

Order Rodentia

Rodentia, the largest of all mammalian Orders (1738 species), has relatively few endangered species (N=62). The IUCN/Species Survival Commission (SSC) has, however, produced a survey of those rodent species which are of concern based upon a regional format (Lidicker, 1989). Nearly all of the North American forms at risk (N=36) have considerable potential for captive propagation based upon experiences with laboratory colonies of closely related forms.

There have been few efforts to implement captive conservation programs for endangered squirrels. Notable exceptions include
recent efforts to breed the giant squirrels (*Ratufa*) (Willis, 1980;
Paulraj, 1988a, b), a pair of Vancouver Island marmots (*Marmota
vancouverensis*) reportedly held in British Columbia (Thornback
and Jenkins, 1984), and the recovery program described by Burton
and Pearson (1987) involving a small captive population of Utah
prairie dog (*Cynomys parvidens*).

The Heteromyid rodents are endemic to North America and
several species of *Dipodomys* have been bred in captivity (Chew,
1958; Pfeiffer, 1960; Butterworth, 1961; Eisenberg and Isaac, 1963;
Behrends, 1981; Daly et al., 1984; Wilson et al., 1985a). Hall (1985),
referring to southwestern North America, identified this genus as
of extreme regional concern. However, the Morro Bay kangaroo rat
(*Dipodomys heermanni morroensis*) is the only endangered form
known to have a small captive population at this time (Roest, 1987,
1988). While no members of the genera *Conilurus*, *Leporillus*,
Notomys, *Pseudomys*, *Xeromys*, and *Zyzomys* are currently known
in captive collections, Watts (1982) has reviewed the captive husbandry of these Australian murids.

Several species of hutia have been held in captivity (Radden,
1968; Howe and Clough, 1971; Clough, 1976; Oliver, 1977). The
first Jamaican hutias (*Geocapromys brownii*) were acquired in 1972,
with 111 offspring being produced in 14 years. By 1986 the first
attempts at reintroducing this species had begun (Anonymous,
1987a).

Order Carnivora

Thirty-eight percent (N=102) of the 268 carnivore species are considered at risk. However, excluding the families Mustelidae,
Viverridae, and Herpestidae, the endangered Carnivora are generally well represented in captivity. Sixty-nine percent (N=70) of all
endangered carnivores are held by zoos, and 61% are being bred.
Seven of the nine endangered canid species currently benefit from
cooperative captive management programs (West, 1989). Of the
IUCN's Canid Action Plan conservation priorities (Ginsberg et al.,
1989); which include the African wild dog (*Lycaon pictus*), red wolf
(*Canis rufus*), and Simien jackal (*Canis simensis*); only the Simien
jackal is not currently held in captivity. Recovery plans have been
developed for the Mexican wolf (*Canis lupus baileyi*) and red
wolf (*Canis rufus*) by the U.S. Fish and Wildlife Service, and

reintroductions of the red wolf in the U.S. (Smith, 1989, 1990), and the swift fox (*Vulpes velox hebes*) in Canada (Schroeder, 1982; Herrero et al., 1986; Stromberg and Boyce, 1986) have occurred.

Although there has been considerable emphasis placed on propagation programs for the giant panda (*Ailuropoda melanoleuca*), this species is not self-sustaining in captivity. Current research focuses on the development of artificial means of reproduction (Masui et al., 1989).

Mustelids, other than otters and some social Viverrids, are poorly represented in captivity. For example, the birth of banded linsangs (*Prionodon linsang*) at the Cincinnati Zoo represented the first captive birth of the species in North America, and only the second worldwide (Brady, 1989). Metro Toronto Zoo is attempting to establish a breeding program for the Liberian mongoose (*Liberiictis kuhni*). However, only a single male has been acquired to date (Carnio, 1990). IUCN's Action Plan for mustelids and viverrids (Schreiber et al., 1989) and otters (Foster-Turley et al., 1990) identifies species in immediate danger of extinction. It designates the fossa (*Cryptoprocta ferox*), black-footed ferret (*Mustela nigripes*), and wolverine (*Gulo gulo*) as priorities as these species are currently held in captivity in some numbers. The rediscovery of the black-footed ferret, and the role captive conservation has played in its preservation, are outlined by Seal et al. (1989). In 1988, the captive colony in Wyoming was subdivided to prevent a catastrophic loss. Experimental reintroductions began in 1991, the goal is to establish populations in the wild by 1996 (Wyoming Game and Fish Department, 1987). Finally, recent success with the fisher (*Martes pennanti*) may serve as a model for future work with endangered forms of *Martes* (LaBarge et al., 1990).

Felids are generally well represented in captivity, with the large cats being the most numerous. However, the Florida panther (*Felis concolor coryi*) is of particular concern in the United States (Ballou et al., 1989). Seal et al. (1987) and Seal (1989) have produced management plans for the tiger (*Panthera tigris*), and fourteen cat species have studbooks or coordinated management groups (West, 1989). Many other species, however, are poorly coordinated. The small cats are seldom exhibited, with some species being better represented in private collections than in zoological parks. Artificial means of captive reproduction of felids are currently being developed (Hoage, 1987; Dresser and Pope, 1989).

Many carnivore species have large captive populations, yet they are not free of management problems. Examples include the maned wolf (*Chrysocyon brachyurus*) (Rodden, 1989), lesser panda (*Ailurus fulgens*) (Roberts, 1989), brown hyaena (*Hyaena brunnea*, Shoemaker, 1983, 1988), and cheetah (*Acinonyx jubatus*) (Grisham, 1989; Marker and O'Brien, 1989; and Millard, 1989). With the formation of Taxon Advisory Groups for canids, felids, and bears by the AZA, perhaps answers can be found to some of the current management questions.

Order Tublidentata

The aardvark (*Orycteropus afer*) is the sole representative of the Order Tubulidentata and was first bred in captivity in 1962 (Goldman, 1986). However, the first mother-reared offspring was not reported in North America until 1982 (DiSabato, 1982). Although the propagation of this species has improved, the captive population remains low.

Order Proboscidea

Both elephant species are currently recognized as endangered, and an IUCN Action Plan for the Asian elephant has been produced (Santiapillai and Jackson, 1990). ISIS reported 192 African elephants (*Loxodonta africana*) in 1988, and 239 Asian elephants (*Elaphas maximus*) are listed in the 1989 North American Regional Studbook. While there were no African elephant births recorded by ISIS for 1988, there have been many recent successes. Likewise, while there were only 25 Asian elephant births recorded between 1980 and 1988 (Tuttle, 1988), captive reproduction has improved considerably in more recent years. Research is currently underway on genetics, health care, nutrition, and artificial means of reproduction (Howard et al., 1986; Balke et al., 1987, 1988; and Tuttle, 1989a). Elephant management commands considerable public attention, and the wide variety of cooperative propagation programs for the Asian elephant (West, 1989), including the Species Survival Plan of the AZA, are faced with the difficult task of developing long-term captive management plans for elephants.

Order Perissodactyla

For a small Order consisting of 18 species the Perissodactyla has a high percentage of endangered species (78%). The Equidae (N=9), in particular, includes seven endangered species (78%). Fortunately, 88% of the forms at risk are in captivity and being bred, and all but the kiang (*Equus kiang*) have captive populations exceeding 100 individuals. Several cooperative programs are in place for equids (West, 1989), and international efforts are underway for the reintroduction of the Przewalski horse (*Equus przewalskii*) to the wild (Bouman-Heinsdijk, 1982; Kreeger, 1991; Houpt and Boyd, 1994). The Tapiridae is also well represented in captivity, and cooperative programs and studbooks are in place for most species (West, 1989).

Other than the Javan rhino (*Rhinoceros sondaicus*), there are captive representatives of each of the rhino species, and a wide variety of programs are in place to coordinate captive efforts (West, 1989). In addition, Action Plans have been formulated by the IUCN/SSC for both the African (Cumming et al., 1989), and Asian rhinos (Momin Khan, 1988). The white rhino (*Ceratotherium simum*) is the most well represented rhino species in captivity. Although the northern subspecies (*C. s. cottoni*) is represented by only 12 individuals, an Action Plan has been formulated by the IUCN's Captive Breeding Specialist Group (CBSG) for this subspecies. Two distinct subspecies of the black rhino (*Diceros bicornis*) are also recognized and are being managed separately. Hemolytic anemia in black rhinos is the subject of intense research at this time, as this disease may constitute a severe threat to their survival (Dresser and Maruska, 1988).

The Indian rhino's (*Rhinoceros unicornis*) numbers in both the wild and captivity appear to be on the rise (Dee, 1987), while the Javan rhino is the rarest (N=30–50 specimens), with none in captivity. However, a collaborative Action Plan has been formulated, although not yet funded, that calls for the removal of 10–12 animals from the Ujung Kulan National Park for placement in a captive breeding situation (Thomas, 1989b). The captive status of the Sumatran rhino (*Didermocerus sumatrensis*) is also of great concern, because the birth at the Melaka Zoo of Peninsula Malaysia in 1987 was the first for this species in over a century (Foose, 1987a). After several years of intensive negotiations, the Sumatran Rhino Trust has finalized plans for a cooperative conservation program involving field research and *ex situ* propagation (Thomas, 1987b). In 1989 the first two Sumatran rhinos benefitting from this program arrived in North America (Thomas, 1989a).

Order Artiodactyla

More than 60% of the 192 extant species within this Order are considered at risk. Of the species at risk, 80 are currently held in captivity (68%), and 79 are breeding. Thirty-seven taxa have captive populations exceeding 50 individuals, of which 21 are represented by more than 100 individuals. Thirty-two forms also have studbooks and/or cooperative breeding programs in place (West, 1989). A historical perspective of rare ruminants in captivity may be found in Thomas et al. (1986), and Sausman (1989) has produced a survey of the Artiodactyla currently in captivity.

Action Plans have been formulated by the IUCN/SSC Antelope Specialist Group for the antelopes of Africa (East, 1988, 1989, 1990), and the AZA has formed a Taxon Advisory Group in the hope of better coordinating conservation efforts for this Order. Although the Artiodactyls generally do well under captive conditions, representation is not evenly distributed among the taxa. The Suidae (pigs), Antilocapridae (pronghorns), and Cephalopinae (duikers) are clearly underrepresented in captive collections (Table 17.1), with the Cervidae (deer), Tragelaphinae (kudu, nyala), Alcelaphinae (hartebeests), and Caprinae (goats and sheep) also having small captive populations.

The cervids often breed well in captivity, but few are held in numbers sufficient to maintain viable captive populations. Many of the rarer forms have seldom made their way into collections in the United States. For example, Penny (1989) reported the first captive birth of the Bawean deer (*Cervus kuhli*) in the Western Hemisphere. Foose (1987b) estimated that the carrying capacity for deer in the world's zoos is sufficient to maintain 31 species at populations of 250 individuals per species. Currently, there are only four endangered forms with captive populations exceeding 100 individuals (Table 17.1). The Père David's deer (*Elaphurus davidianus*) reflects the captive propagation potential of this family. Formerly extinct in the wild, it was reintroduced to China in 1987 (Thouless et al., 1988).

With the exception of the giant sable (*Hippotragus niger variani*), the members of the Hippotraginae have benefitted greatly from captive propagation. Dixon and Jones (1988) have reviewed the history of the Arabian oryx (*Oryx leucoryx*), from the establishment of the "World Herd" at the Phoenix Zoo, to the return of the species to Oman twenty years later. Stanley Price (1989b) provides a more in depth review of this species' reintroduction. A second release program into Jordan began in 1983 (Abu Jafar and Hays-Shahin, 1988), and plans are underway for releases in Saudi Arabia (Abu-Zinada et al., 1988; Asmode, 1989). These reintroductions may serve as a model for the addax (*Addax nasomaculatus*) and scimitar-horned oryx (*Oryx damah*). Addax have been returned to Tunisia for reintroduction (Hanscom, 1988), and plans are being formulated for a release in Niger (Foose, 1989). In addition, a plan is being developed to reintroduce the scimitar-horned oryx to Niger (Tuttle, 1989b), and animals have been returned to Tunisia for release into the Bou-Hedna National Park (Bertram, 1988).

In 1989, an Arid-Land Antelope Workshop was held to develop more comprehensive and coordinated conservation strategies for this highly endangered group (Foose, 1989b). The Arabian oryx, addax, and scimitar-horned oryx were the primary focus, but attention also turned to arid-land gazelles. A reintroduction project for the Mhorr gazelle (*Gazella dama mhorr*) was discussed. However, for some species, conservation endeavors may be complicated by taxonomic uncertainties (Kingswood and Kumamoto, 1988; Foose, 1989b).

Conservation efforts are also underway for several species that are currently not held in zoos. The Chacoan peccary (*Catagonius wagneri*), thought extinct until 1972, is part of a cooperative program involving a consortium of U.S. zoos and the Paraguayan Government (Benirschke, 1987). Starting with four pairs of animals, the first captive birth for the species was reported in 1989 (Benirschke, 1989). An AZA Species Survival Plan is already in place for this species (Foose, 1988). Efforts continue to develop a kouprey (*Bos sauveli*) propagation program (Simmons, 1990). To date, there are no kouprey in captivity. However, a Kouprey Action Plan has been formulated by the IUCN (MacKinnon and Stuart, 1988), and a Species Survival Plan is in place. The tamaraw (*Bubalus mindorensis*) is also not held by zoos, but 14 individuals are enclosed in a large parcel of forest in the Philippines in preparation for *ex situ* conservation action.

Problems Facing Conservation Programs in Captivity

Perry et al. (1972) reported that of 291 rare mammal species, 162 (56%) were in zoos, with only 73 (25%) having been bred at some point in time. Pinder and Barkham (1978) came to similar conclusions. In the present report, 431 forms are listed as at risk, with 219 (51%) currently known to be held in captivity. Of those taxa held in captivity, 89% (195) have been recently bred. In addition, 100 forms (46% of those held in captivity) have captive populations exceeding 50 individuals, with 68 of those being represented by more than 100 individuals. Eighty-four species are currently monitored by studbooks and/or regional management plans (West, 1989).

Clearly, great strides have been made in the captive management of rare and endangered species during the last ten years, but there are still many problems to be resolved.

Ex Situ Conservation and Triage

Webster's New World Dictionary (Neufeldt and Guralnik, 1988) defines triage as "any system of establishing the order in which acts of assistance are to be carried out in an emergency." However, to date, there is no clear system of triage for the captive conservation of endangered species, although both the CBSG and the AZA are attempting to set conservation priorities. Western (1986b, p. 17) suggested that the triage criteria for the captive management of endangered species should " ... forge links between species (and ecosystems) conservation, ecological theory, and captive management constraints."

While the issue of species selection for conservation action is being addressed by the IUCN's Red List and Action Plans, there are other criteria that must be addressed as "captive management constraints." Among the numerous factors that must be taken into consideration when initiating ex situ conservation efforts are: the current knowledge of a species' husbandry, availability of specimens, spatial requirements and availability, financial considerations, and the potential for the coordination of both in situ and ex situ conservation efforts.

Ex situ conservation programs are initially concerned with two basic constraints. Firstly, not all species are equally suited for captive conservation. For example, the natural history and basic biology of many specialized forms are too poorly known for there to be much hope of success, and for some, like the baleen whales, there are other practical constraints. A second factor is availability of specimens. The SSPs of the AZA were designed to better manage collections of endangered species already in captivity. Therefore, species have generally not been selected solely on the basis of need, but have depended upon the availability of specimens. There are notable exceptions, however, such as the Sumatran rhino, black-footed ferret, and Rodrigues fruit bat. Programs for the more critically endangered species that are not currently held in captive collections must be developed, and should be coordinated with in situ research and conservation efforts.

Because husbandry problems even plague programs for which there are available specimens (e.g., maned wolf, African hunting dog, giant panda, lesser panda, brown hyaena, cheetah, elephants, rhinos, and hartebeest), research must continue in the areas of genetics, physiology, ethology, nutrition, and veterinary medicine (Benirschke, 1983a). In addition, small population genetic management techniques and population databases (e.g., ISIS; Animal Record Keeping System, ARKS; Medical Animal Record Keeping System, MEDARKS; and Single Population Animal Record Keeping System, SPARKS) must be fully utilized so that captive populations may be managed effectively (Foose and Ballou, 1988; Flesness and Mace, 1988). Efforts must also be made to prepare husbandry protocols for endangered species, or closely related nonthreatened taxa that have historically performed poorly in captivity before wild populations are so low that emergency action must be taken (e.g., Arabian oryx and black-footed ferret).

The spatial requirements for holding genetically viable captive populations of endangered species have been the subject of considerable discussion (Frankel and Soulé, 1981; Foose, 1983; Seal, 1985; Conway, 1986a; Western, 1986b; Maguire and Lacy, 1990). While it is clear that there is not enough space in zoos to maintain self-sustaining, genetically viable populations of every endangered species, more endangered taxa may be accommodated than are presently held. For example, Foose (1987b) estimated that there are currently 44,106 spaces available worldwide for members of the Artiodactyla. Assuming that 250 individuals would be sufficient for a genetically self-sustaining population for each taxa, he calculates that 176 forms could be maintained. There are 118 endangered forms of Artiodactyla identified here as at risk. If these species were to replace more common forms, hypothetically all of the endangered Artiodactyla could be accommodated. Furthermore, if nonzoo spaces are taken into consideration, the capacity for hoofed mammals alone increases many fold. Estes (1990b) reported that there may be as many as 147,000 spaces on Texas ranches alone for exotic Artiodactyls. While the management of these species may be complicated by the involvement of the private sector, there is great potential for the expansion of available spaces for endangered species, with considerable savings in operational costs for zoos (Tuttle, 1989b; Estes, 1990a). The implementation of growing technologies in genetic management (Benirschke, 1977, 1985; Mace, 1986; and Ryder, 1986), and artificial reproduction (Durrant and Benirschke, 1981; Ralls and Ballou, 1983; Wildt and Bush, 1984; Polge, 1985; Dresser, 1986; Hearn, 1986b; Summers, 1986; Wildt, 1989) should assist in the effective use of limited space. Future plans must also address the possibilities for the exchange of specimens between wild and captive populations. The resulting reduction of the minimum viable population required per species would free space for many more taxa, as well as insuring that the captive population more accurately reflects the genetic makeup of the wild population.

Monetary constraints are also of primary concern when determining conservation priorities. Limited budgets must be used in more effective ways. Conway (1986a) demonstrated that herbivores cost less to feed than carnivores, social species are less expensive to manage than asocial species, and larger numbers of animals are more economical to care for per animal than small numbers. In addition, species from geographic regions that are ill-adapted to the climate of the institution (e.g., tropical species in northern zoos) are more expensive to care for than species adapted to a climate similar to the holding institution. Where facilities and expertise exist, it would be more economical for *ex situ* conservation efforts to be undertaken within a threatened species' country of origin.

The potential for the coordination of efforts is an important aspect of triage. The coordination of programs has increased dramatically in recent years (Glatston, 1986), and it is clear that an interdisciplinary approach is required at both national and international levels (Mallinson, 1986). The CBSG of the IUCN/SSC and the International Union of Directors of Zoological Gardens were formed to provide international forums for the development of collaborative captive propagation programs, while the Taxon Advisory Groups of the AZA were formed to coordinate efforts within North America. In the future there must be a coordination of efforts among the IUCN, zoos, conservation organizations, researchers, wildlife law enforcement agencies, and the countries of origin if we are to effectively utilize the limited resources (Mallison, 1988). Conservation strategies for endangered species in the wild and in captivity cannot be independent nor competitive (Western, 1986b).

A triage system for captive conservation programs based upon the above factors, among others, should result in the development of a comprehensive long-range plan for the preservation of endangered species which reacts not only to the needs of species at risk, but also takes into account physical, financial, and philosophical realities.

Conclusions

From this summary of the captive status of rare and endangered mammals, excluding primates and marine mammals, it is clear that great progress has been achieved in the last decade. However, many problems have yet to be resolved, including the need for a system of triage.

This triage system must not only take into account the level of endangerment of a species, but must also balance other factors important to the efficient use of limited resources. Effective utilization of captive space must be a priority, and conservation dollars must be spent wisely. Husbandry techniques must be improved for many species currently held in captivity and developed for poorly known species that are in need of *ex situ* conservation. The further development of reproductive technologies will be of great benefit and should be pursued with vigor. The coordinated management of wild and captive populations as a single entity is desirable and will require unprecedented coordination of *in situ* and *ex situ* conservation efforts. The numbers of cooperative programs must continue to increase and take a multidisciplinary approach. Although *in situ* conservation of endangered species is always preferable to *ex situ* preservation, there is often no choice. The future of the world's fauna depends upon our willingness and ability to meet the challenges of the task ahead.

18

Reproduction in Mammals: Captive Perspectives

Barbara S. Durrant

It has been stated that reduction in the biological diversity of this planet is the most basic issue of our time, and that slowing this process of "biotic impoverishment" is a great challenge to the ingenuity of biologists (Lovejoy, 1980a). Extinction of a species represents the loss of a resource that has evolved through thousands, perhaps millions, of years of selection and mutation. The genetic diversity that now exists in captive exotic animals will steadily dwindle with decreasing input from wild populations. The National Research Council (1978) has stressed the importance of conserving this genetic material and emphasized that if immediate action is not taken, much of this vital resource will be depleted in the near future. Because the majority of captive species are within a few generations of genetic input from the wild, the most immediate need is to preserve the genetic diversity that currently exists in captive populations. This goal will be accomplished through captive reproduction and long-term storage of germplasm resources.

Physiological Considerations

Successful reproduction is dependent upon the harmonious operation of myriad physiological processes. Beginning with the genetic assignment of sex and migration of the primordial germ cells through gonadal and tubular differentiation, the stage is set early in life for procreation. Maturation of reproductive organs in concert with hormonal stimulation of gametogenesis is contingent in large part upon adequate health and nutrition. Union of gametes occurs in the absence of anatomical or behavioral impediments and in the presence of functional gamete transport systems. The processes controlling maternal recognition and maintenance of pregnancy, parturition, and lactation are hormonally directed and nutritionally sanctioned.

Understanding the complexities of mammalian reproduction, in its infinite variety, is the challenge confronting conservationists whose goal is self-sustaining wildlife populations. Only well-designed strategies for the evaluation of reproductive potential in individuals, groups, or species will result in consistently successful captive propagation of endangered animals. The plan must include analysis of the following six physiological parameters: (1) genetics, (2) anatomy, (3) health and nutrition, (4) hormonal competency, (5) production, release, and transport of viable gametes, and (6) pregnancy maintenance.

Genetics

It is incumbent upon zoos, as stewards of a large proportion of the earth's captive species, to maintain them in sufficient numbers to assure that genetic variability is adequate for continuing selection (Lovejoy, 1980). Soulé et al. (1986) have estimated that 29–1000 individuals (depending on the generation time and the number of founders) are required to maintain 90% of a species' genetic diversity for the next 200 years. Due to severe spatial, financial, and personnel limitations in zoos and animal parks, this ideal genetic state may not be attainable for most of the species we are attempting to save from extinction. Long-term germplasm storage minimizes holding space requirements, thereby increasing the number of species conservable through captive breeding. The judicious assimilation of genetic material from frozen reserves into extant breeding populations will assure continuance of genetically healthy species in captivity. Thoughtful genetic management will mitigate the deleterious forces of founder effect, inbreeding, selection, drift, and introgression (Benirschke, 1985) that threaten the genetic health of captive populations.

For the many captive species now extinct in the wild, the heterozygosity inherent in the founder animals will forever prescribe the limits of genetic variability in their descendants. Thus, equal representation of founders in the gene pool is the ideal condition for minimizing the founder effect (Ballou, 1984). If equalization can be realized or approximated, a founder population as small as twenty may provide adequate genetic variation with which to preserve a species (Soulé et al., 1986)—assuming that they are not inbred or related (Foose et al., 1986).

The reproductive consequences of the loss of heterozygosity known as inbreeding are well documented in domestic and laboratory species (Land, 1984). Breeding related individuals in zoos has been implicated in increased neonatal and juvenile mortality in gazelles (Dorcas [*Gazella dorcas*], Ralls et al., 1980 and Speke's [*Gazella spekei*], Templeton and Read, 1983), eland (*Taurotragus oryx*, Treus and Lobanov, 1971) and various other ungulates (Ralls et al., 1979), decreased cub survival in Asian lions (*Panthera leo*) (Ballou, 1984), and reduced fertility of inbred Przewalski's mares (*Equus przewalskii*) (Bowman, 1977).

The European bison (*Bison bonasus*) was poached nearly to extinction in the early 1900s. Of the 17 animals surviving, only 12 "outbred" genomes contributed to successive generations. Reproductive comparisons between the founders and their inbred offspring (Slatis, 1960) revealed no loss of fertility in the latter females. Perinatal and juvenile deaths were actually reduced in the inbred populations. This fascinating discovery demonstrated the adaptability of this species to what would be normally considered a pernicious genetic predicament.

Thus, in extreme circumstances, when a species is restricted to a severely limited founder number, mating of related individuals is unavoidable. In such a case, the population may be intentionally inbred to reduce the genetic load of lethal genes (Frankham et al., 1986). Increasing homozygosity will necessarily pair normally recessive lethal alleles, thereby eliminating them through the death of the carrier. Living inbred individuals are considered adapted to inbreeding and are used as parents of the next generation. Templeton and Read (1983) successfully selected a nucleus group of Speke's gazelle for inbreeding tolerance while equalizing founder contributions to the gene pool. The resulting population exhibited slightly increased birth weight and enhanced neonatal survival compared to the original, unselected inbred group.

Unintentional selection of zoo specimens for adaptation to captivity can significantly alter the gene pool. This selection may improve captive reproduction and increase tameness, but may concomitantly impair survival upon reintroduction into the wild (Frankham et al., 1986).

Genetic drift occurs in small populations as the result of decreased effective population size. The Przewalski's horse serves as a cogent illustration of genetic drift separating two breeding groups (Ryder et al., 1981). Electrophoretic analysis of the two lines separated for five generations revealed genetic divergence as great as that found between some rodent species.

To minimize genetic drift in small populations, a species should reach an effective population size of 200–300 within a few generations (Soulé et al., 1986). The captive population can then be considered a single interbreeding unit if at least one reproducing individual is exchanged between groups each generation (Allendorf, 1983).

Introgression is the introduction of the genes of one species (or subspecies) into the gene pool of another. Specific or subspecific hybridization exacerbates the effects of genetic drift by dramatically altering gene frequencies. The intentional introgression of domestic horse genes into one Przewalski's horse group undoubtedly contributed to the significant divarication of the two lines. In addition to the loss of "pure" species or subspecies, introgression may negatively impact reproduction. For example, sterile hybrid dik-dik (*Madoqua spp.*) have been produced by the inadvertent pairing of multiple subspecies (Ryder et al., 1989).

Meticulous breeding records or studbooks are the framework upon which pedigrees are constructed. Pedigrees, then, provide genetic and demographic data necessary to avoid inbreeding and genetic drift (Ryder, 1986). Unfortunately, studbooks for many species are incomplete or inaccurate, and pedigrees formulated from them lead to inappropriate pairings. Genetic evaluation of individuals whose relatedness is not certain can provide the information needed to complete or correct a pedigree. To that end, karyotypic analysis can confirm parentage, as in a pygmy chimpanzee (*Pan paniscus*) with two potential sires (Benirschke and Kumamoto, 1983).

Recent or historical introgressions resulting in taxonomic chaos and, in some instances, impaired reproductive function, have been brought to light by examination of the chromosomes of species such as the Soemmerring's gazelle (*Gazella soemmerringi*) (Benirschke et al., 1984), sand gazelle (*Gazella subgutturosa marica*), and dik-dik (Benirschke and Kumamoto, 1987). To avoid further adulteration of these forms, future pairings should be arranged according to karyotypic compatibility.

Biochemical and molecular genetic techniques such as electrophoretic separation and identification of blood protein allozymes, isoelectric focusing, blood typing, mitochondrial DNA and DNA fingerprinting add new dimensions to the genetic analysis of endangered species. The techniques are used to determine levels of genetic variability (O'Brien et al., 1983), paternity, identification of hybrid individuals (Gentz and Yates, 1986), and separation of discrete genetic subpopulations (Brisbin, 1980).

The preceding review of genetic factors affecting captive populations serves to remind researchers that it is imprudent to attempt to utilize state-of-the-art technology to solve reproductive problems in a species for which the genetic contribution to reproductive failure is unknown. Thus, the factors affecting the genetic health of a population should be evaluated prior to undertaking an extensive reproductive research program.

Reproductive Physiology

A comprehensive discussion of the anatomy, physiology, and endocrinology of reproduction for all mammals other than primates and marine forms is beyond the scope of this chapter. Approximately 3,870 species comprise the 15 orders of mammals, and the melange of their reproductive strategies has been organized only superficially. The subtleties of variation in the progenitive systems of this extensive group are largely unexplored; scant knowledge overshadowed by widespread ignorance. However, reproductive research in exotic species is a rapidly growing field of endeavor and ten years hence this chapter will be greatly expanded.

Female Anatomy

Knowledge of the reproductive anatomy of a species is essential for successful application of artificial reproduction techniques. Vaginal length, cervical conformation, and placement of the urethral orifice must be considered when attempting artificial insemination (AI). Add uterine body and horn structure to the list of prerequisites for nonsurgical embryo recovery or transfer (ET), and rectal palpation or ultrasound for evaluation of ovarian activity and pregnancy determination.

From the simplex uterus of some bats to the complex arrangement of marsupial tubular structures, variety of form seems to be the rule in mammalian reproductive anatomy. The anatomy of an exotic species is generally similar in form to the domestic species to which it is most closely related. However, anatomical identity with domestics or even closely related exotics cannot be assumed. Hradecky (1982) described the reproductive anatomy of female antelope as compared with the domestic cow. Bipartite uterine morphology was similar, and he found cervical uniformity in certain Alcelaphinae (hartebeests), Tragelaphinae (kudu, nyala), Reduncinae (kob, waterbuck), Antilopinae (gazelles), and Aepycerotinae (impala) species and further speculated that an undivided cervix also exists in Neotraginae (dwarf antelope), Cephalophinae (duikers), and other Tragelaphinae. However, a partially divided cervix was found in four Hippotraginae (oryx) and three Alcelaphinae species. Three Artiodactyl species (pronghorn antelope [*Antilocapra americana*]; mule deer [*Odocoileus hemionus*]; pygmy goat [*Capra hircus*]) had similar bipartite uterine morphologies and a single cervical canal (Kanagawa and Hafez, 1973).

Kanagawa and Hafez (1973) found cervical morphologies similar to marsupials and rabbits in three wild rodent species. The muskrat (*Ondatra zibethicus*), wood rat (*Neotoma fuscipes*), and ground squirrel (*Citellus tridecemlineatus*) exhibited fully separated cervical canals unlike most rodent species. The same authors studied the American badger (*Taxidea taxus*), the American black bear (*Euarctos americanus)*, the red fox (*Vulpes vulpes*), and the timber wolf (*Canis lupus*). All were found to possess a simple cervix with a single canal and a bipartite uterus like the domestic dog (*Canis familiaris*), as does the raccoon dog (*Nyctereutes procyonides*) (Valtonen et al., 1977).

Also similar to its domestic counterpart *Sus scrofa,* the collared peccary (*Tayassu tajacu*) possesses a bicornate uterus. However, Wislocki (1931) found differences in the conformation of the uteri, ovaries, and oviducts of the two species. The bison-like musk ox (*Ovibos moschatus*), placed taxonomically in the subfamily Caprinae, has a reproductive tract very similar in form to its sheep and goat relatives (Rowell et al., 1987).

The variability of cervical division between individuals of the same species was demonstrated by Stover (1987). In six white-tailed gnu (*Connochaetes gnou*), 36% to 100% of the length of the cervix was divided; one female exhibited the two external ossa of a duplex cervix. It is not difficult to imagine how this lack of anatomical consistency could thwart artificial reproductive protocols requiring passage of an insemination rod or embryo catheter through the cervix. Placement of trans-cervical instruments cannot be confirmed via rectal palpation in small species, thus tortuous or unpredictable cervices may be avoided by surgical insemination or embryo recovery/transfer.

Some Antelopinae exhibit asymmetry of a bicornate uterus with enlargement of the right horn in the Uganda kob (*Adenota kob*) (Buechner, 1961), the impala (*Aepyceros melampus*) (Mossman and Mossman, 1962), the common duiker (*Sylvicapra grimmia*) (Child and Mossman, 1965), and the springbok (*Antidorcas marsupialis*) (Els, 1981). This anatomical feature is concomitant with increased placentome number in the right horn in the kob, impala and, inconsistently, the springbok. Of these antelope species, the duiker and kob exhibit right horn implantation only. Spinage (1969) found that although the left ovary is more active than the right in the waterbuck (*Kobus defassa ugandae*), 92% of embryo implantations occur in the right uterine horn. The opposite is found in the female dromedary (*Camelus dromedarius*) where the left uterine horn is nearly 50% larger than the right and contains more than 99% of the pregnancies (ElWishy, 1988).

Other taxonomic groups display laterally unequal reproductive function. For example, Clough (1969) found that the left ovary of the warthog (*Phacochoerus aethiopicus pallus*) is slightly more active than the right and the left horn is the preferred implantation site. Hellwing and Funkenstein (1977) observed that, like natural ovulation, induced ovulation in the shrew (*Crocidura russula monacha*) resulted in left ovarian dominance with equal distribution of blastocysts in both uterine horns.

Preferential lateral reproduction is taken to an extreme in the platypus (*Ornithorhynchis anatinus*) whose right ovary is nonfunctional. Although destined never to transport gametes, the less-developed right oviduct exhibits uterine glands during the breeding season when the right ovary and both uteri enlarge (Griffiths, 1978). The uteri communicate separately with one urogenital sinus, hence the Monotremata designation of the Order (from the Greek meaning "one hole"). Unlike the platypus, the echidnas (*Tachyglossus aculeatus* and *Zaglossus bruijnii*) exhibit bilaterally well-developed ovaries and uteri that produce ova and carry eggs, respectively (Griffiths, 1978).

In some Chiroptera (i.e., the Japanese greater horseshoe bat [*Rhinolophus ferrumequinum nippon*], Oh et al., 1985; black mastiff bat [*Molossus ater*], Rasweiler, 1988), only the right ovary supports the growth and maintenance of a Graafian follicle. In other bats (long-winged [*Miniopterus schreibersii*] and little bent-winged [*M. australis*]), ovulation always occurs from the left ovary and implantation is always in the right uterine horn (Richardson, 1977).

Marsupial reproductive anatomy, unique in class Mammalia, is reviewed by Tyndale-Biscoe and Renfree (1987). The paired uteri are separate and the duplex cervices lead into lateral vaginae that open into a urogenital sinus. In some species a median vagina is present and acts as the birth canal. In others, a pseudovaginal canal is formed just prior to parturition and may remain patent after the first offspring (Benett's wallaby [*Macropus rufogriseus*]) or may close after each birth (Grey kangaroo [*M. giganteus*]). The vaginal complex of opossums (*Didelphis virginiana*) enlarges as the female approaches estrus, then subsides (Barbour, 1977).

Unlike any other mammalian species, the external genitalia of the female spotted hyena (*Crocuta crocuta*) closely resembles that of the male (Kingdon, 1977). The elongated clitoris resembles a penis in size and placement and is capable of erection. Two fibrous tissue-filled pockets are located in a scrotal position and resemble testes. This unique masculinization may be related to unusually high androstenedione levels in female spotted hyenas, especially during infancy (Glickman et al., 1987).

Clearly, a consistently successful program of AI and ET depends on a thorough knowledge of functional reproductive anatomy. For many endangered or threatened species there is no domestic counterpart from which to glean even general anatomical information. For these species a literature search may not uncover the detail required, and only painstaking evaluation of reproductive tracts at necropsy will provide researchers with sufficient knowledge to undertake a program of artificial reproduction.

Female Endocrinology: Cycles and Seasons

Circulating levels of reproductive hormones have long been utilized to monitor folliculogenesis, ovulation, corpus luteum function and regression, pregnancy and impending parturition, and testicular function in humans and domestic animals. The application of blood assay techniques to endangered species has been limited by the infrequency with which most exotic animals can be chemically or physically restrained for blood collection. Thus, the development of assays for excreted hormone metabolites has granted zoo researchers the opportunity to characterize reproductive events in a growing number of species without the stress that may alter normal hormone profiles (Wesson et al., 1979).

Table 18.1 depicts a representative sample of exotic species whose estrous cycles have been described through direct hormone analysis (blood and urine assays) and indirect estrogen analysis (vaginal cytology). Corroborating behavioral evidence of cyclicity

Table 18.1

Estrous Cycles of Selected Exotic Mammals

Species	Mean Cycle length (days)	Method*	Season+	Reference
Pere David's deer *Elephurus davidianus*	19.5	*P*	s.p.	Curlewis et al., 1988
Eld's deer *Cervus eldi*	18.5	PdG, E1, LH,P	s.p.	Monfort et al., 1990
Red deer *Cervus elaphus*	21	*P*	s.p.	Adams et al., 1985
Muskox *Ovibos moschatus*	19.6	*P,E2,LH*	s.p.	Rowell and Flood, 1988
Okapi *Okapia johnstoni*	14.5	PdG		Loskutoff et al., 1982
Giraffe *Giraffa camelopardalis*	15	PdG		Loskutoff et al., 1986
Scimitar oryx *Oryx damma*	22	PdG		Loskutoff et al., 1983
Blackbuck *Antilope cervicapra*	17	PdG		Holt et al., 1988

Table 18.1 continued

Species	Mean Cycle length (days)	Method*	Season+	Reference
North American bison *Bison bison*	23	PdG	s.p.	Kirkpatrick et al., 1991
Camel *Camelus dromedarius*	23	*P,E,LH*		Homeida et al., 1988
Wooly opossum *Caluromys philander*	28–45	VC, *P*		Perret and Atramentowicz, 1989
Giant Panda *Ailuropoda melanoleuca*	monoestrus	PdG, El, *P*	spring	Hodges et al., 1984
Clouded leopard *Neofelis nebulosa*	29	VC, Beh		Yamada and Durrant, 1989
Jaguar *Pantera onca*	47	*P,LH* LAP, Beh		Wildt et al., 1979
Leopard *Panthera pardus*	21–28 no ov. 49 with ov.	E2, *P*		Schmidt et al., 1988
Puma *Felis concolor*	—	E2, *P*, LAP		Bonney et al., 1980
Wolf *Canis lupus*	monoestrus	*P,E2,LH* VC, Beh	Jan–April	Seal et al., 1979

Species	Cycle	Hormones	Season	Reference
Black bear *Ursus americanus*	*monoestrus*	*P*		Foresman and Daniel, 1983
Lion *Panthera leo*	monoestrus	E2, P		Schmidt et al., 1979
Cape hunting dog *Lycaon pictus*	monoestrus	E2, P	Jan–May	van Heerden and Kuhn, 1985
Tayra *Tayra barbara*	52–56	VC, Beh		Poglayan-Newall et al., 1989
Siberian tiger *Panthera tigris*	25	E2, P, LH	s.p.	Seal et al., 1985
River otter *Lutra canadensis*	monoestrus	VC		Stenson, 1988
Steppe polecat *Mustela eversmanni*	monoestrus	E1, VC		Mead et al., 1990
Indian Rhinoceros *Rhinoceros unicornis*	48	PdG, E1		Kasman et al., 1986
Asian elephant *Elephas maximus*	112	P, E2, LH		Hess et al., 1983
African elephant *Loxodonta africana*	112	P, LH		Plotka et al., 1988

*P = serum progesterone, E = total serum estrogens, E1 = urinary estrone, E2 = serum estradiol, LH = serum luteinizing hormone, PdG = urinary pregnanediol-3-glucuronide, VC = vaginal cytology, Beh = behavior, LAP = laparoscopy
+ s.p. = seasonally polyestrus

has been included when reported. To date, urinary hormone analysis has been restricted to steroid metabolites. The development of gonadotrophic hormone assays for urine, feces, or saliva will greatly enhance our understanding of the events surrounding ovulation and will allow greater precision in ovulation prediction/detection for artificial insemination.

Fecal steroid analysis is emerging as such an important adjunct to serum hormone assays that an international symposium on fecal steroid monitoring in zoo animals was held in 1992. Hoppen et al. (1992) reported there that fecal pregnanediol and 20α-hydroprogesterone were well correlated with plasma progesterone in Asian elephants (*Elephas maximus*). Because steroids are excreted primarily in feces in carnivores, the development of fecal assays is especially valuable in these taxa. Serum and fecal estradiol and progesterone concentrations were positively correlated in six carnivore species (Gross, 1992) including the cheetah (*Acinonyx jubatus*), maned wolf (*Chrysocynon brachyurus*), black-footed ferret (*Mustela nigripes*), two otter species (*Lutra canadensis* and *Aonyx cinerea*), and tigers (*Panthera tigris*).

Pregnancy determination and prediction of parturition increase in importance when animals are bred in captivity. In many species, successful reproduction is of such monumental significance that the process must be monitored throughout. Special attention must be arranged at parturition so offspring born to inexperienced mothers can be removed for hand-rearing should rejection occur. Noninvasive techniques are obviously highly desirable for pregnancy determination in untractable animals. Urinary progesterone metabolite profiles in pregnancy have been elucidated for the giant panda (*Ailuropoda melanoleuca*) (Hodges et al., 1984), Indian rhinoceros (*Rhinoceros unicornis*) (Kasman et al., 1986), giraffe (*Giraffa camelopardalis*) and okapi (*Okapi johnstoni*) (Loskutoff et al., 1986), and the black rhinoceros (*Diceros bicornis*) (Ramsey et al., 1987). Urinary estrogen profiles during pregnancy have been elucidated for Malayan and Brazilian tapirs (*Tapirus indicus* and *T. terrestris*) (Kasman et al., 1985), blackbuck (*Antilope cervicapra*) (Holt et al., 1988), Przewalski's horse and Hartman's mountain zebra (*Equus zebra hartmannae*) (Czekala et al., 1990), Eld's deer (*Cervus eldi thamin*) (Monfort et al., 1990), and Asian elephant (Mainka and Lathrop, 1990). Bamberg and Mostl (1988) found fecal estrogens diagnostic of pregnancy in the Przewalski's horse, Mhorr gazelle (*Gazella dama mhorr*), and Malayan tapir as did Safar-Hermann et al.

(1987) in the Grevy's zebra (*Equus grevyi*) and Nubian ibex (*Capra ibex nubiana*).

The literature regarding seasonality in mammals is immense and cannot be adequately discussed here. However, an interesting collection of articles dealing with exotic species was edited by Perry and Rowlands (1973). Reviews of seasonal reproduction in monotremes (Griffiths, 1984), marsupials (Tyndale-Biscoe, 1984), and nonprimate eutherians (Rowlands and Weir, 1984) cover virtually all orders of mammals other than primates and marine forms. Cervid seasons are more extensively discussed by Sadleir (1987). In an excellent recent review, Bronson (1988) comments that inadequate attention has been paid to nonphotoperiodic regulation of seasonal reproduction.

Social control of reproduction is most vividly expressed in species manifesting reproductive suppression. Three nonprimate mammalian species exhibiting this trait are the naked mole rat (*Heterocephalus glaber*) (Faulkes et al., 1990), the wolf (*Canis lupus*) (Seal et al., 1979), and the dwarf mongoose (*Helogale parvula*) (Creel et al., 1992). The mechanism of suppression differs between sexes and species. Subordinate female wolves and males of all three species are suppressed behaviorally (prevented from breeding) while female mongooses and mole rats are repressed endocrinologically.

Hormonal Manipulation and Artificial Reproduction

It is possible to manipulate the estrous cycle of an animal whose cycle is largely unknown. This apparent paradox occurs when species are (correctly) assumed to be similar to those of closely related domestic species. Thus, estrus synchronization and ovulation have been successful in a number of antelope species through the application of estrus synchronization techniques developed for domestic cattle.

Table 18.2 summarizes the majority of the successful artificial reproduction efforts in exotic mammals. One assumes that failed ET or AI attempts are not reported, thus an accurate overview of artificial reproductive activity and success rates is not possible. Documentation of such "negative data" would enhance reproductive technology for exotic species by reducing or eliminating the costly replication of failed methodologies.

Endocrinological data insufficient to predict ovulation no doubt explains the rather surprising dearth of successful artificial

Table 18.2
Successful Artificial Insemination and Embryo Transfer in Exotic Mammals

Species	Estrus/ovulation Induction	AI: F/C*	ET: F/C (recipient)	Reference
Mouflon *Ovis musimon*	—	—	F, inter (domestic sheep)	Bunch et al., 1977
Gaur *Bos gaurus*	—	C[b]	[a]F, inter (domestic cow)	[a]Stover & Evans, 1984 [b]Junior et al., 1990
Bongo *Tragelaphus euryceros*	+[ab]	—	[a]F, intra, inter (eland)	[a]Dresser et al., 1984b [b]Schiewe et al., 1988
Eland *Taurotragus oryx*	+[ab]	—	[c]C, F, intra	[a]Dresser et al., 1982b [b]Schiewe et al., 1988 [c]Dresser et al., 1984a
Przewalski's horse *Equus przewalskii*	+[a]	—	[b]F, inter (domestic horse)	[a]Durrant & Hoge, 1988 [b]Kydd et al., 1985
Zebra *Equus burchelli*	—	—	F, inter [a](domestic horse) [b](domestic donkey)	[a]Bennett & Foster, 1986 [b]Summers, 1986
Addax *Addax nasomaculatus*	+	C	—	Densmore et al., 1987

Species				References
Blackbuck *Antilope cervicapra*	+	C	—	Holt et al., 1988
Wapiti *Cervus elephus*	+[b]	C[ab]	—	[a]Kelly & Moore, 1981 [b]Haigh et al., 1984a
White-tailed deer *Dama virginianus*	+[ab]	C[a]	**F**, intra[b]	[a]Jacobson et al., 1989 [b]Waldhalm et al., 1989
Fallow deer *Dama dama*	+	C	—	Asher et al., 1990
Scimitar-horned oryx *Oryx damma*	+[ab]	C[c]	**F**, intra[d] C, intra[e]	[a]Durrant, 1983 [b]Schiewe et al., 1988 [c]Garland (pers. comm.) [d]Pope et al., 1991 [e]Schmitt, 1986
Camel *Camelus dromedarius*[a] *Camelus bactrianus*[b]	+[a]	**F**[b]	—	[a]Elias et al., 1985 [b]Chen et al., 1985
Duiker *Cephalophus sylvicultor*	+	—	—	Pope et al., 1988
Suni *Neotragus moschatus*	+	—	—	Raphael et al., 1988
Père David's deer *Elaphurus davidianus*	+[a]	C[b]	—	[a]McLeod et al., 1989 [b]Asher et al., 1988

Table 18.2 *continued*

Species	Estrus/ovulation Induction	AI: F/C*	ET: F/C (recipient)	Reference
Reindeer *Rangifer tarandus*	—	C	—	Dott and Utsi, *1973*
Wolf *Canis lupus*	—	C	—	Seager et al., 1975b
Fox *Vulpes vulpes*	—	C	—	Aamdel et al., 1972
Lion *Panthera leo*	+[abc]	F[c]	—	[a]Rowlands & Sadleir, 1968 [b]Phillips et al., 1982 [c]Dresser et al., 1981
Puma *Felis concolor*	+[abc]	F[a]	—	[a]Moore et al., 1981 [b]Phillips et al., 1982 [c]Miller et al., 1990
Leopard *Panthera pardus*	+[ab]	F[b]	—	[a]Phillips et al., 1982 [b]Dresser et al., 1982a
Cheetah *Acinonyx jubatus*	+[abc]	C[d]	—	[a]Wildt et al., 1981 [b]Phillips et al., 1982 [c]Lindburg et al., 1985 [d]Howard et al., 1992

Species	AI*		+ET	References
Tiger *Panthera tigris*	+[ab]	F[b]	F, intra[c]	[a]Phillips et al., 1982 [b]Dresser et al., 1981 [c]Donoghue et al., 1990
Indian desert cat *Felis silvestris ornata*	+[a]	—	F, inter[a] (domestic cat)	[a]Pope et al., 1989
Ferret *Mustela putorius*	+[a]	C[b]	—	[a]Mead & Neirinckx, 1989 [b]Howard et al., 1991

*AI = artificial insemination, F = fresh semen, C = cryopreserved semen

+ET = embryo transfer, F = fresh embryo, C = cryopreserved embryo, (recipient): inter = interspecies recipient, intra = intraspecies transfer

inseminations in exotic species. Likewise, interspecies ET has not been consistently successful. Most authors report only single offspring following multiple ET attempts. A better understanding of the endocrinology and physiology of these species will undoubtedly enhance the efficacy of artificial reproduction techniques.

Summers (1986) summarized the major impediments to interspecies embryo transfer as: blocking the luteolytic pathway (maternal recognition of pregnancy), implanting, preventing immunological rejection, and initiating parturition. Of these, perhaps only implantation success can be predicted by comparing placental morphology and attachment in the donor and recipient species. Hradecky (1983) reported gross anatomical features of the giraffe and several antelope species. In a more detailed histological study of the eland, bongo, okapi, and giraffe, Hradecky et al. (1987) suggested that close similarity in the structure of the chorionic villi of the two antelope species contributed to the success of ET between the bongo and the eland. The authors cautioned against ET between the okapi and the giraffe, however, based on cotyledonary dissimilarities. Benirschke (1983b) discussed the importance of placentation studies in an interspecies ET program.

Determination of exact timing of ovulation is difficult, if not impossible, in exotic species, thus uterine synchronization between donor and recipient is likely to be a common cause of ET failure. Donor-recipient asynchrony would theoretically be minimized in species experiencing embryonic diapause. Interspecies ET may hold promise for the rarer delayed implanters (some bears, giant pandas). However, significant differences can exist between even closely related species and extensive knowledge of both donor and recipient diapause characteristics would be essential. Details of hormonal and environmental control of diapause are discussed by Flink et al. (1981). Other theoretical aspects of interspecies ET are discussed in a review by Gibbons and Durrant (1987).

Male Anatomy

Male tubular reproductive anatomy (vas deferens and ampullae) is at least as varied as the female's. The prostate is the only accessory gland present in virtually all mammals but most also have at least one pair of bulbourethral glands (Setchell and Brooks, 1988). The number of these glands and the presence or absence of seminal vesicles differs between and within mammalian orders. Some species also possess coagulating glands (Mann and Lutwak-Mann, 1981).

As with the females, the morphology of a male's reproductive tract frequently resembles his most closely related domestic counterpart. Thus, the male collared peccary anatomy is virtually the same as the domestic boar (Low, 1970). Most Bovids resemble the domestic bull, and exotic sheep, goats, and horses reflect the anatomy of their domestic analogues.

It can also be said that penile anatomy conforms to the reproductive tract of the female of the species. Indeed, the corkscrew peccary penis fits the spiral cervical canal of the female. The bifid penis of the monotremes and marsupials (except kangaroos; Barbour, 1977) is not unexpected given the dual reproductive organs of the female.

The function of the penile spines seen throughout the family Felidae is unknown, but has been theorized to enhance vaginal/cervical stimulation in induced ovulators or to anchor the penis in the female reproductive tract during fleeting copulatory episodes (Milligan, 1982).

As female marsupials show unique reproductive anatomy, so do the males of this order. The prepenial position of the marsupial scrotum is found only in two other mammalian groups; lagomorphs and certain myomorph rodents (Tyndale-Biscoe and Renfree, 1987). The large prostate and multiple, paired bulbourethral glands of marsupials are unaccompanied by seminal vesicles, coagulating glands, or ampullae. The prostate of some marsupials (i.e., brush-tailed possum [*Trichosura vulpecula*]) becomes so large during the breeding season that it fills the lower abdominal cavity (Gilmore, 1969). In most species the testes are permanently scrotal but in the marsupial mole (*Notoryctes typhlops*) they remain undescended. A breeding season descent of abdominal testes characterizes the wombats (Barbour, 1977).

Testicond mammals are rare. In addition to the aforementioned monotremes and marsupials, elephants (*Elephas maximus* and *Loxodonta africana*; Short et al., 1967) hyrax (*Procavia capensis*; Glover and Sale, 1968), and certain families of Edentata and Insectivora are the only representatives.

The bulbourethral glands of the platypus exhibit seasonal enlargement, but their disseminate urethral glands (analogous to a marsupial prostate) do not (Griffiths, 1978). In this species the abdominal testes also increase in size and weight during the breeding season. The breeding season of the rock hyrax (*Procavia capensis*) is marked by a tremendous increase in the weight of the testes, seminal vesicles, and bulbourethral gland (Millar and Glover, 1970).

The size and function of the combined accessory glands account for the tremendous range in ejaculate volume and chemical composition among mammals. An individual's fluctuations in semen parameters over time combined with the scarcity of semen samples for most exotic species complicates the formulation of normal spermiograms. However, familiarity with a species' reproductive anatomy and its seasonal permutations will shed some light on expected ejaculate quantity and quality, and is essential knowledge for maximum efficiency of electroejaculation. The positioning of electrodes during this artificial semen collection technique is a critical factor in the contribution of each accessory gland's fluid to the ejaculate.

Male Endocrinology: Cycles and Seasons

With the exception of the antler cycle in Cervids (roe deer [*Capreolus capreolus*], Gimenez et al., 1975; black-tailed deer [*Odocoileus hemionus columbianus*], West and Nordan, 1976; reindeer [*Rangifer tarandrus*], Stokkan et al., 1980; wapiti [*Cervus elephus*], Haigh et al., 1984b; fallow deer [*Dama dama*], Rolf and Fischer, 1987), relatively few papers describe male reproductive hormone cycles in exotic species.

Social status has been linked to hormone levels in some species. Illius et al. (1983) measured higher plasma testosterone response to gonadotrophin releasing hormone (GnRH) in territorial male impala and blesbok (*Damaliscus dorcas*) than in bachelors. Similarly, Chaudhuri and Ginsberg (1990) found that urinary androgens were correlated with social status in two species of free-ranging zebras (*Equus burchelli* and *E. grevyi*). In both species, breeding males had higher androgen concentrations than nonbreeding stallions. Dominant male collared peccaries exhibited higher testosterone levels than subordinate males, the latter also failing to show seasonal cyclic hormone profiles (Hellgren et al., 1989).

Musth, the period of increased temporal gland secretion and aggression in mature Asian elephant bulls, has been shown to be correlated with elevated serum testosterone (Cooper et al., 1990). Testosterone levels of one Asian bull normally rose one to four weeks prior to visible signs of musth, thereby providing a practical gauge of aggressive behavior. Although 90% of captive Asian bulls experience musth annually or biannually, the phenomenon has been reported in less than 5% of captive African elephant bulls (Rasmussen et al., 1984).

Photoperiodic cues in seasonal breeders of both sexes are melatonin-dependent and mediated through the pineal gland (Arendt, 1986). Induction of normal spermatogenesis out of season has been achieved with melatonin implants in the fox (Forsberg et al., 1990). Although refractoriness to melatonin has been demonstrated in this species and in the domestic ram (*Ovis aries*) (Lincoln and Ebling, 1985), interval administration of the hormone may be useful in the captive reproduction of related endangered species. Spermatogenesis induced out of season could provide semen for cryopreservation and viability studies, and the opportunity to bank semen for future insemination.

Histological examination of testes throughout the year has, in the past, been the experimental method of choice to describe spermatogenic cycles (Blackshaw, 1977). Sacrifice of individuals for such studies is no longer an acceptable experimental design. Testicular biopsy is intricate and may result in permanent damage to the gonad. Instead, electroejaculation repeated throughout the year may define seasonality of spermatogenesis. Testicular measurements and abdominal ultrasound examination may also be helpful in species that show great seasonal variation in gonad and/or accessory gland size.

Semen Collection, Evaluation, and Cryopreservation

Electroejaculation (EE) has become the standard semen collection technique in zoos and primate centers due to the intractable nature of most exotic animals. The physiological mechanisms of EE are well understood (Martin, 1978), and the prerequisite tranquilization/immobilization appears to be the most significant health concern associated with the procedure. The small body of literature describing the influence of anesthesia on EE must be greatly expanded to provide guidelines for exotic species.

Semen collection with an artificial vagina (AV) offers the advantage of frequent sampling without the stress of chemical or physical restraint (Durrant et al., 1985). However, the contact required to train a male to service an AV excludes all but the most tractable animals. In contrast, postmortem extraction of sperm can be developed as an important source of germplasm. Sperm frozen as long as 12 hours after death has shown acceptable postthaw motility, and the ability to penetrate hamster ova *in vitro* (Durrant, 1987).

Male fertility is a complex continuum that begins with spermatogenesis and proceeds to sperm maturation, ejaculation, sperm transport through the female reproductive tract and, finally, penetration of the ovum. Infertility is still not well understood even in the most extensively studied species. The ultimate demonstration of male fertility is conception and is difficult or impossible to examine *in vivo* on a routine basis in exotic animals. Therefore, researchers have attempted to develop laboratory tests of semen quality that can be correlated with fertility (Durrant, 1990).

Traditional parameters of sperm quality include volume, motility, concentration, and morphology. As single predictors of fertility, none of these measurements is sufficiently sensitive. When these parameters are combined, the accuracy of fertility assessment is enhanced but still incomplete as none of these criteria can predict the ability of sperm to perform effectively in the female reproductive tract. Truly comprehensive semen analysis involves evaluation of the ability of sperm to reach the site of fertilization, undergo capacitation and the acrosome reaction, penetrate the zone pellucida, fuse with the oolemma, and decondense (Bedford, 1981). *In vitro* tests have been developed for human sperm for each of the above parameters and their correlation with fertility has been the much disputed topic of many research reports (Durrant, 1990). One assay commonly used to assess potential fertility in human subjects is the sperm penetration assay (SPA) that measures sperm's ability to penetrate hamster ova. Although the sperm of numerous exotic species has been reported to penetrate hamster ova with varying success (bat, Lambert, 1981; tiger, Post et al., 1987; cheetah, Durrant et al., 1989), no attempt has been made to correlate the SPA with fertility in any of these species.

The acrosome reaction is considered an end point of successful sperm capacitation and occurs *in vivo* when sperm contact the zona pellucida. Loss of the acrosome in the absence of capacitation is associated with sperm degeneration and renders the sperm incapable of zona penetration. Morphological assessment of acrosomal integrity in ejaculated sperm, and as a means to compare various cryopreservation protocols, can be accomplished only in species with acrosomes of sufficient dimension to allow reasonably accurate scoring (African elephant, Howard et al., 1986; wapiti, Haigh et al., 1986; various ungulates, Howard et al., 1981 and ferrets [*Mustela putorius*], Howard et al., 1989). For others, staining techniques must be employed for visualization of the acrosome (Pratt et al., 1991; Durrant et al., 1992b).

Analysis of sperm morphology has long been part of traditional semen evaluation. Individual males with high proportions of severe sperm anomalies, such as detached heads, would be expected to be subfertile due to impaired motility. The relationships between less serious sperm defects and fertility are not clear. Freeranging and captive cheetahs have uniformly poor semen quality including a large percentage of morphological abnormalities (Wildt et al., 1983; Durrant et al., 1985). All proven cheetah sires at the San Diego Wild Animal Park exhibit these semen characteristics that, if observed in domestic felids, would signal potential infertility. These cheetahs, however, when properly managed, breed and sire offspring at a rate considered normal for fertile populations of other mammals (Lindburg et al., 1993). Two clouded leopard (*Neofelis nebulosa*) males of proven fertility had extremely high proportions of sperm abnormalities as did six other males of unknown fertility (Wildt et al., 1986). These examples are provided as a caution that prediction of the potential fertility or sterility of exotic animals cannot be based on spermiograms constructed for related domestic animals. Normal sperm parameters must be compiled for each species.

It has been stated that the most efficient method for preserving gene pools is semen cryopreservation (Gee, 1984). Semen is less problematic to collect than ova or embryos; thus, more samples can be made available for cryopreservation studies. In addition, semen thawing and AI require less training and equipment than embryo thawing and ET. Therefore, AI is feasible for more zoological institution personnel. Although numerous reports claim the successful freezing of semen of exotic species (Graham et al., 1978; Wildt, 1986), the end point of most of these early experiments was the demonstration of postthaw motility, however slight. Semen cryopreservation protocols have been validated by the birth of offspring or sophisticated *in vitro* testing for an extremely limited number of exotic species (Table 18.2).

For some exotic species, semen freezing techniques will be similar to those developed for closely related domestic species. For example, studies with antelope or gazelle semen will logically begin with cryopreservation techniques developed for domestic cattle, and human semen freezing methods will serve as models for primate sperm. At least one exception to this "rule of thumb" has been illustrated by Durrant and co-workers (1992a) who conducted semen cryopreservation studies in the Przewalski's horse. They found that replication of freezing techniques proven successful for the domestic horse were not appropriate for the closely related Przewalski's. This study suggests that scientists must proceed with caution when extrapolating semen freezing protocols between species as significant modification may be required. Taxonomically unique species, such as the cheetah, however, may require extensive research to elucidate appropriate protocols. Comprehensive evaluation of sperm through the application of multiple analyses both before and after freezing is essential to the development of freezing protocols as well as the identification of appropriate evaluative procedures for sperm of each species.

Conclusion

An integrated knowledge of the effects of genetics, anatomy, environment, behavior, health, nutrition, endocrinology, and physiology on reproduction is essential for the creation of self-sustaining captive populations of endangered species.

Artificial reproduction can play a crucial role in the maintenance of these populations through transport of genetic material through time and space, and by accelerating propagation of genetically valuable individuals through germplasm cryopreservation, artificial insemination, and embryo transfer. However, until basic physiological mechanisms of reproduction are elucidated for each species, artificial reproduction will remain experimental, lacking the consistent success required for its incorporation into routine exotic animal management practices.

19

Mammalian Behavior:
Lessons from Captive Studies

John L. Gittleman and Greta C. McMillan

At present, even though a sizable literature exists on behavioral research, application of behavioral principles to captive management has reached only a fairly elementary level as far as *most* endangered mammalian species are concerned (Eisenberg and Kleiman, 1977; Erwin and Deni, 1979; Kleiman, 1980). Application has progressed with respect to some carnivore, ungulate, and rodent taxa, and we will selectively review examples mainly from these taxa to indicate the direction this development has taken. We wish to emphasize throughout this chapter that behavioral factors must not be considered in isolation from other species-typical traits, but as integral parts of a complete set of physiological, ecological, and phylogenetic characteristics. It is imperative to recognize that the primary condition for successful captive management of mammals is the provisioning of suitable food, living space, and social needs in terms of species-typical ecological requirements. Only when this condition has been met can behavioral information begin to play a useful role.

Rationale for Behavioral Studies on
Endangered Species in Captivity

Relative Number of Field Studies

We have included in this discussion a diversity of taxa, many of which have not been singled-out for protective status. There are several reasons why we adopt this strategy. First, we primarily use studies that reflect a conceptual or theoretical point that will assist in learning more about breeding endangered mammals. Second, for taxonomic inclusion we prefer a broad rather than a restrictive view of endangered species because species numbers are constantly fluctuating and the degree to which an individual species should be included on a list will often change more rapidly than bureaucratic decision-making policies (Gittleman and Pimm, 1991; Pimm and Gittleman, 1992). Further, recent discussion questions whether our general approach to conservation "lists" is useful (Diamond, 1988), implying as they do that all remaining species are secure.

Scope of Existing Field Studies

Studies of endangered mammals have passed through a renaissance due to a number of developments in field biology. New advances in radio telemetry reveal information on individual spacing patterns, day range movements, population density, habitat selection, and a range of physiological parameters (see Amlaner and Macdonald, 1979; Cheeseman and Mitson, 1982; Mech, 1983; Mech et al., 1984). Chemical analyses (gas chromatography-mass spectrometry) are useful for identifying sex-specificity and breeding condition in scent mark secretions (see Hefetz et al., 1984; Gorman and Trowbridge, 1989). Traditional field techniques, such as mark-recapture for censusing or pugmark tracings for identification of individual characteristics (sex, age, size), are more carefully scrutinized for accuracy (see for example, Karanth, 1987). Furthermore, physiological measures of oxygen consumption, metabolic rate or heart rate are collected in concert with behavioral data using revolutionary methods of doubly-labeled water or telemetric adaptors (see Bennett, 1986; Loudon and Racey, 1987; Nagy, 1987; Gittleman and Thompson, 1988; Kunz and Nagy, 1988; Speakman and Racey, 1988). The importance of formulating an ecological and/or evolutionary theoretical framework *prior to* marching out in the field is now accepted protocol, even in more applied areas of wildlife ecology and conservation biology (see Kleiman, 1980; Soulé and Wilcox, 1980; Robbins, 1983; Schaller et al., 1985; Soulé, 1986; Simberloff, 1988; VanBlaricom and Estes, 1988; Sunquist and Sunquist, 1989). In addition, nonapplied areas of behavioral and evolutionary ecology (e.g, optimal foraging theory, sex ratio evolution) have begun to use information from captive mammal populations as well as apply theoretical constructs to captive management problems (Kleiman, 1980; Clutton-Brock and Iason, 1986; Metcalfe and Monaghan, 1987).

As a consequence of such trends toward interdisciplinary field study, long-term field research devoted to management of endangered mammal species has developed more pluralistic approaches than previously used. Schaller et al.'s (1985, 1989) studies of the giant panda (*Ailuropoda melanoleuca*) illustrate this approach. Realizing that the giant panda is taxonomically a carnivore, thus possessing a typical digestive system (simple stomach, short intestine, no caecum) for processing primarily meat, Schaller and colleagues analyzed the plight of this species in terms of the nutritional constraints of primarily foraging on bamboo. This involved detailed chemical and digestive analyses (e.g., chemical constituents during various seasons, passage rate and energy available per kg of bamboo) to evaluate energetic efficiency and the consequences to home range movements, day range lengths, and activity cycles. For example, after concluding that pandas require up to 10–18 (avg. 12.5 fresh weight) kg of bamboo per day or up to 45% of total body weight, the activity time budget of foraging more than 50% of the day is clearly understandable. Similar investigation by Clemens and Maloiy (1982) on the comparative digestive physiology of the elephant (*Loxodonta africana*), black rhinoceros (*Diceros bicornis*) and hippopotamus (*Hippopotamus amphibius*) shows the influence of digestive efficiency on species differences in feeding behavior. Additional field studies of other endangered mammals convincingly demonstrate that analyzing behavioral and ecological characteristics from one perspective, or inferring conservation guidelines from data collected on one population parameter (e.g., changes in population density; decline in reproduction), will likely restrict our ability to understand critical needs of endangered mammals (as examples of this new wave in field study, see the following: sea otter [*Enhydra lutris*], VanBlaricom and Estes, 1988; tiger [*Panthera tigris*], Tilson and Seal, 1987; jaguar, [*Panthera onca*], Rabinowitz and Nottingham, 1986; snow leopard, [*Panthera uncia*], Blomqvist, 1984; Clark's gazelle or dibatag [*Ammodorcas clarkei*], Leuthold, 1977; Caprinae: Soma, 1987).

Nevertheless, specific inferences for conservation management drawn from field studies of behavioral and ecological attributes must be assessed on a species-by-species basis. Some mammals are narrowly adapted to fine grained ecological needs (e.g., giant pandas feeding on seasonally flowering bamboo) in which a species' physiology, life history, and behavior are very sensitive to ecological fluctuation. Moreover, effects of phylogenetic history, genetic bottlenecks, morphological constraints, or mating systems may also influence adaptive flexibility. By contrast, other species, though showing similar declines in population, are less tied into one or a few critical resources and thus possess greater flexibility to resist ecological hardship. Even though individual species must be carefully studied in their natural habitat to truly evaluate where it falls on such a "flexibility continuum," captive studies provide a first step toward assessing this capacity. For example, trends in breeding success of endangered ungulates reveal one type of flexibility. Although the ecological division of deer is admittedly a superficial one, grass eaters appear to present considerably fewer problems than highly selective browsers (Leuthold, 1977; Fradrich, 1980). It is therefore not surprising that, with the possible exception of pampas deer (*Ozotoceros bezoarticus*), the species doing well in captivity belong to the grazing form (see Thomas et al., 1986).

Controlled Behavioral Studies

Planning meaningful conservation programs and establishing successful captive breeding facilities demand a certain resolution in understanding patterns of variation, both among individuals within a species and between species. In natural populations, level of resolution generally increases with length of study, number of individuals and populations observed, systematic controls for confounding variables, and so on. For example, Moehlman (1979) initially observed in black-backed jackals (*Canis mesomelas*) that the number of pups surviving past 14 weeks of age (the most vulnerable period for the young) increased significantly with the number of adult helpers attending the neonatal den. With a sample size of 15 litters, this study was criticized for failing to control for litter size and observing young through to weaning, perhaps a better developmental marker of survivorship (Montgomerie, 1981). However, subsequent data collected over a 10-year-period substantiated the claim of direct benefits by helpers and further detailed: (1) specific roles that individual helpers contribute to a litter (e.g., antipredatory vigilance, food provisioning for young), (2) sexual dimorphism in helping behavior, (3) quantitative measures of helping, and (4) various ecological and allometric effects of these behavioral trends (Moehlman, 1986, 1987, 1989; see also Table 19.1 for further examples of long-term field studies revealing progressively finer resolution in data collection, results, and explanatory power).

Table 19.1
Examples of Longitudinal Field Studies Revealing
Progressively More Detailed Data Collection.

Species	Reference
African lion, *Panthera leo*	Packer & Pusey (1982, 1983a, b)
Tiger, *Panthera tigris*	McDougal (1977); Smith et al. (1987b); Sunquist (1981); Sunquist & Sunquist (1989)
Cheetah, *Acinonyx jubatus*	Caro & Collins (1986, 1987); Ashwood & Gittleman (1989)
Dwarf mongoose, *Helogale parvula*	Rasa (1987); Rood (1980, 1983, 1986)
Brown hyena, *Hyaena brunnea*	Mills (1982, 1989); Owens & Owens (1982)
Spotted hyena, *Crocuta crocuta*	Frank (1986a, b)
Gray wolf, *Canis lupus*	Harrington & Paquet (1982)

Long-term field studies are the best means for describing species requirements under natural ecological conditions and, in some cases, may allow for judgment and predictions regarding the adaptability of particular species to harsh or changing environmental conditions. However, because ecological forces are essentially stochastic, specific causal factors critical to breeding endangered species are more completely isolated through: (1) experiments in the field, showing correlational relationships between behavioral and environmental characteristics, and (2) carefully controlled experimental procedures in captive surroundings. Ideally, captive studies and field studies should be complementary. In the following, we describe various behavioral problems that illustrate the potential value of coordinating captive and field approaches.

Antipredatory Behavior. Most small mammals which are common prey species show specific antipredatory defenses, depending on the severity of threat and/or particular predator. Smith et al. (1977) identified seven vocalizations of black-tailed prairie dogs (*Cynomys ludovicianus*) in the field, and were able to verify contextual information in a zoo population after changing various social and predatory cues. Essentially, vocal responses to potential predators and conspecific interactions were similar in both settings, though vocalizations in the field were more intense in some calls.

Mother-Infant Interactions. Leuthold (1977) generally described a sequential pattern of nursing interactions in bovids. He suggested that the initiation of nursing shows that, as nursing time approaches, the cow wanders toward the hiding place, stops about 10–30 meters away and vocalizes; the calf, which may vocalize in reply, then stands and approaches its mother. Specific behavioral changes are difficult to quantify in the field because of various observational obstructions. Thus, Murdock et al. (1983) tested Leuthold's predictions in a captive herd of sable antelope (*Hippotragus niger*) and confirmed that mother-infant interactions appear in the predicted sequential pattern.

Based on general field observations, ungulates are commonly classified into "followers," in which young initially stay close to their mother, and "hiders," in which young remain at some distance from the mother, often concealed in vegetation (Walther, 1965; Lent, 1974; Leuthold, 1977). Ralls et al. (1986b) analyzed four measures of mother-young associations for 59 mother-young pairs belonging to 22 species and seven families of ungulates. Using cluster analyses, the 22 species essentially pattern the follower/hider dichotomy reported in the literature. However, due to the capability of quantitatively measuring in captive populations various changes in association during development, Ralls et al. (1987) further showed that this simple dichotomous classification obscures considerable variation in mother-young behavior among species within each taxonomic group. In follower species, two measures of mother-infant association decreased over time; in hiders, contact between mother and young did not increase over time although the distance between them, while both were lying, decreased (see Fig. 19.1). Carl and Robbins (1988) also showed the relative energetic costs of neonatal hiders versus followers.

Mating Relationships. In many social mammals which live in permanent reproductive groups, often comprised of extended families, individuals are organized in hierarchies that reflect potential reproductive performance. A dominant breeding pair hold alpha status over lower ranking, subordinate individuals and thus achieves a significantly greater proportion of matings (e.g., gray wolf [*Canis lupus*], Mech, 1970; dwarf mongoose [*Helogale parvula*], Rood, 1980). Although the behavioral mechanisms causing reproductive suppression may sometimes be observed from field study, other less accessible factors often require close study in captives. For example, Rood (1980) observed in dwarf mongooses that the alpha female in a pack produces litters at regular intervals, usually three times a

Mother-young Relationships in Captive Ungulates

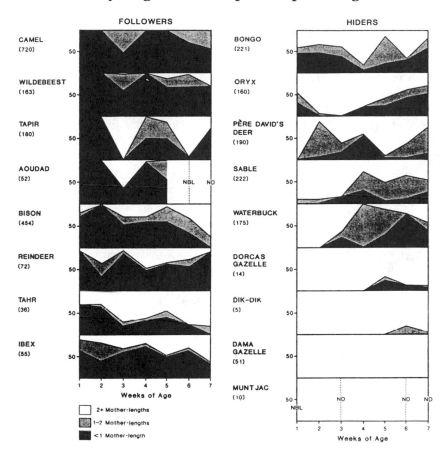

Figure 19.1. Percentage of time mother and young were both lying and: <1 mother-length apart, 1 to 2 mother-lengths apart, or greater than 2 mother-lengths apart. Five species are not included: Nile and pygmy hipopotami because they were scored as "inactive' rather than lying; giraffe because the mothers never lay down; and zebra and onager, because the mothers lay for a total of only 4 and 5 min, respectively, during the entire 7 week study period. Approximate adult female weights (kg) are shown beneath the name of each species. ND = no data; NBL = never both lying. From: Ralls et al. (1987).

year. Although it appeared that other sexually mature females came into estrus in synchrony with the alpha female and thus were suppressed behaviorally, detailed analyses of estrous cycling in three captive groups studied over 30 cycling periods indicate that subordinates cycled only eight times in comparison with 29 times for alpha females (Rasa, 1987), and that the average frequency of estrus/subordinate female was 0.66 compared with 9.66 for alpha females. Thus, behavior patterns closely tied to physiological or hormonal factors are frequently more recognizable in captive individuals (see also, Frank et al., 1985; Packard et al., 1985; Glickman et al., 1987).

Two reservations, however, must be borne in mind when drawing conclusions from data collected in both captive and field settings. First, patterns observed in captivity may not be precisely reflected in the wild, particularly when highly artificial conditions surround the study animal. Thus, extrapolating between captive and field studies should be constantly verified. Second, certain kinds of explanation will probably not be helped by merging field and captive perspectives, such as understanding individual changes in daily food intake, medical history, or reactions to visiting public.

Functions of Behavioral Research in Captivity

Public Education

Heini Hediger wrote that " . . . an essential feature of the development of living animals in the zoo is to show the visitor, in the best way possible, a careful selection of species in near-natural spatial areas, as a natural social group with near-natural feeding and treatment, rather than to present as many animals as possible, singly, in more or less abstract jail-like rooms" (1970, p. 523).

A significant trend has developed in conveying species richness and community ecology to the viewing public through mixed-species exhibits. Such mixed-species exhibits and resulting behavioral analyses may inform the viewing public about: (1) mammalian evolutionary history through presentation of taxonomic and phylogenetic description, (2) communication in mammals from observable displays and vocalizations, and (3) community ecology through natural presentation of community assemblages.

Obviously, many difficulties are inherent in this approach, the most common being increased aggression. Careful behavioral analysis, however, lends itself to increased knowledge about the animals and to effective management decisions. For example, five ungulate species housed in an area (e.g., white rhino [*Ceratothenum simum*], Grevy's zebra [*Equus grevyi*], axis deer [*Axis axis*]) were studied in relation to aggressive contact, chases, displacement, and threats (Popp, 1984). From analyses of species pairwise comparisons, aggression was found to be the highest among distantly related species. The inability of taxonomically distant species to recognize the threat of another species may explain this trend. Mixed-species exhibitry may also elucidate predator-prey interactions. For example, five ungulate species housed near a natural predator species, the African lion (*Panthera leo*), showed significantly less time in nonvigilance behaviors (lying down, feeding, drinking, sniffing ground, sniffing each other, defecating, urinating) when the predator was visually present (Stanley and Aspey, 1984). These changes in captive ungulate behavior indicate an awareness of the predator and a general increase in predator surveillance without producing deleterious effects in the ungulates.

Although behavioral assessment of endangered mammals has vastly improved many areas of captive management and educational presentation, there remains considerable room for improvement. One priority must lie in the display of natural mating systems and social organization because of their fundamental influence on breeding success (see e.g., Eisenberg and Kleiman, 1977; Kleiman, 1980; Eisenberg, 1981; Clutton-Brock, 1991). Unfortunately, most endangered mammals possess mating systems that are subtle and less well-studied. For example, in the Carnivora, over 80% of the species are strictly solitary, males and females remaining in distant spatial relations during most of the year except for short breeding periods (Ewer, 1973; Gittleman, 1989c; Sandell, 1989). This bias in our knowledge of mammalian mating systems influences both captive management and the presentation of supposed "near-natural" behavior to the viewing public. One survey of over 70 zoos breeding a total of 16 species of small felids (e.g., caracal [*Felis caracal*], Geoffroy's cat [*Leopardus geoffroyi*], fishing cat [*Prionailurus viverrinus*]) revealed that a significant number are housed in pairs or larger groups, and few zoos keep the female separated from the male outside of the breeding season (Eaton, 1984). In natural populations, these species show strictly maternal care and males rarely remain in close proximity to females. Thus, the consequences of such mating arrangements are that: (1) the visiting public experiences unnatural social settings, (2) cannibalism of young (and occasionally mates) occurs unnecessarily (see Packer and Pusey, 1984), and (3) stress from frequent social encounters, such as food competition, probably causes ill-health. A more accurate alternative would be to arrange carnivore species along gradations of sociality ranging from strictly solitary (e.g., snow leopard) to monogamous pair bonding (e.g., maned wolf [*Chrysocyon brachyurus*]) to large social groups (e.g., spotted hyena [*Crocuta crocuta*]).

One further point is necessary concerning the current state of public education in zoos. Generally, endangered species arouse public interest in direct correspondence with how particular species are portrayed in the media. For example, giant pandas are cute and cuddly while wolves are bad and sagacious. Zoos frequently pander to the popular mythology of these animals in complete disregard of their biology. Moreover, zoo collections still do not generally reflect diversity and richness of mammals. For instance, small mammals (less than 0.5 m in length) comprise 87% of the 4008 species recognized by Corbett and Hill (1980). Yet, in proportion to larger species (ranging 0.5–5.0 m in length), small mammals represent only 32% of species held in captivity (see Fig. 19.2, taken from Bertram, 1986). Of the species identified as threatened in the *Red Data Book* (through 1982), only 3% fall in the small size category (see Fig. 19.2). Zoos must improve upon this misrepresentation of the distribution and diversity of mammals. Indeed, in terms of daily management decisions, financial costs, and the capacity to replicate natural lifestyles of mammals (see Conway, 1986a), small sized animals rather than large bodied species would probably be a welcomed change in most zoos.

Husbandry

Thus far, the primary functions of behavioral studies of captive endangered mammals have been to: (1) identify and interpret various pathologies in captive settings, and (2) improve captive management and reintroduction in the wild (Eisenberg and Kleiman, 1977). It is also necessary to point out that in some cases behavioral study in captivity is the only route for learning about a species because they are to the best of our knowledge extinct (or very close to) in the wild (e.g., Père David's deer [*Elaphurus davidianus*], Beck and Wemmer, 1983; black-footed ferret [*Mustela nigripes*], Clark et al., 1986; Clark, 1989; Seal et al., 1989).

Early mammal behavior studies in captivity were frequently used to indicate changes in health, stress, or reproductive state

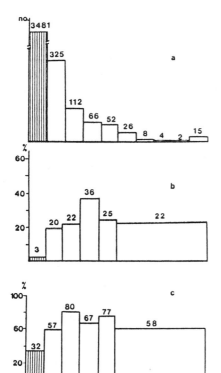

Figure 19.2. Number of mammalian species in each size class based on head-and-body length (as calculated from Nowak & Paradiso, 1983); b. percentage of species in each group which is defined as threatened in the *Red data book*; c. percentage of the threatened species held in capitivity. The data on numbers in captivity are taken from the *Yearbook* Rare animal census as at January 1981 (volume 22). The column for 'small' mammals, i.e. those with a head-and-body length of <0.5 m, is vertically hatched. From: Bertram (1986).

(see Hediger, 1950; Meyer-Holzapfel, 1957; Eisenberg, 1966; Beck, 1975; Burghardt, 1975; Snyder, 1975). In this review, we will not address all of the problems or perspectives in using behavioral studies as indicators for other characteristics; more thorough, updated reviews are found elsewhere (see Erwin and Deni, 1979; Eisenberg, 1981; Stoskopf, 1983; Walther et al., 1983; Quick, 1984; Monaghan, 1984). Rather, we concentrate on particular studies concerning the usefulness of interpreting changes in social and spatial behaviors.

Social Behavior. Many changes in social behavior reflect individual idiosyncrasies (e.g., prior mating history) that are difficult to forecast in unpredictable environments (Slater, 1981; Macdonald, 1983). Nevertheless, fundamental species-typical traits related to social behavior are quite predictable and may profoundly influence other features. Mammals develop social bonds that strongly influence mate selection, breeding success, and rearing of offspring

(Vehrencamp, 1979; Bell, 1983; Dunbar, 1983; Vehrencamp and Bradbury, 1984; Gittleman, 1985; Clutton-Brock, 1991). The introduction of unfamiliar individuals into social units after bonds have been established, such that social interactions are significantly altered, may produce immediate physiological effects (see Schnell et al., 1985 for a statistical model for analyzing change in associations among individuals). For example, in many small mammals (e.g., *Microtus, Pitymys, Lagurus*) the introduction of an unfamiliar male in early to midlactation will cause rapid termination of pregnancy by abortion (Stehn and Jannett, 1981). Generally, it is unknown how prevalent this phenomenon (often referred to as the "Bruce effect") is across taxa, either in captivity or in wild populations.

Introduction and maintenance of social groups (including appropriate sex ratio composition) is generally more critical for highly territorial species. In ungulate species such as Indian blackbuck antelope (*Antilope cervicapra*) or Thomson's gazelle (*Gazella thomsoni*) where territory size is comparatively small, only one male may reside within a given enclosure representing a territory. Introduction of additional males creates increased aggression and possible injury (Walther et al., 1983). Increased aggression due to improper sex ratios of adults, overcrowding, or conflict over food resources has been reported for a number of species (e.g., crab-eating fox [*Cerdocyon thous*], Biben, 1982; gray wolf [*Canis lupus*], Mech, 1970). Increased aggression may also relate to level of sociality in some mammalian groups (e.g., carnivores; Kleiman and Eisenberg, 1973), thus classification of social systems in the wild is helpful for predicting potential aggression in captivity.

Changes in social behavior may also be useful for detecting sensitive periods during reproduction. Territorial disputes during breeding, copulation efforts, and postcopulatory guarding are all periods of intense stress and aggression. Parental care is also an extremely stressful period both behaviorally (Gubernick and Klopfer, 1981; Gittleman, 1988; Clutton-Brock, 1991) and physiologically (Gittleman and Thompson, 1988), especially in species in which females solely feed and protect young. In some species which are usually docile (e.g., echidna [*Tachyglssus aculeatus*]; red panda [*Ailurus fulgens*]), females markedly increase aggression toward intruders in the neonatal denning area (Augee et al., 1978; Roberts and Gittleman, 1984).

In general, the highest incidence of mortality for many species in captivity is during the parental care period (e.g., lutrinae; Mason and Macdonald, 1986). It is critical that all forms of social behavior (parental, adult conspecific, with viewing public) be monitored closely for dramatic changes, as aggression due to improper levels of social encounters may rapidly lead to injury or even death. This is especially relevant for solitary species. Even commonly kept species like the European otter (*Lutra lutra*), Canadian otter (*Lutra canadensis*), and Oriental small-clawed otter (*Amblonyx cinerea*) show very low reproductive success partly as a result of failing to protect individuals during sensitive periods (e.g., see Mason and Macdonald, 1986).

Spatial Behavior. In zoos, consideration of spatial requirements usually involves determining proper enclosure size or niche characteristics. For example, in ungulate species (e.g., blackbuck, Thomson's gazelle) where territory size is comparatively small and only one male can become territorial in an enclosure, a single male will take all of the space available, the outdoor runs as well as the stall (Leuthold, 1977; Walther et al., 1983). If there are conspecific males above the age of adolescence and occasionally of juvenile age, the alpha male harasses them continually. In addition to fighting and chasing them, a territorial male under spatial limitations of captivity may be much more detrimental than in the wild, for he may prevent them from feeding, resting, and using shelter during inclement weather. Some measures may, however, be employed if larger spatial areas are available: (1) avoidance of sharp and right angle corners in the fence line so that subordinates cannot be cornered, (2) arrangement of several widely distributed feeding places that may be filled simultaneously so that subordinates have a chance to feed undisturbed, and (3) separation of males into individual stalls during certain periods of the day.

Generally, the zoo literature is replete with similar examples of how animals respond to various spatial parameters, yet there are no detailed studies of the development of spatial needs nor studies of changes in behavior with systematic manipulations of the spatial environment. Such an experimental approach would be useful for designing enclosures, particularly for species that do not readily adjust to varying environmental conditions. Toward this end, Innis et al. (1985) formulated a model based on intragroup dispersion and nearest neighbor distances that offers some guidelines for approximating the amount of space desirable for a captive group of animals.

Specific niche requirements, such as denning areas, feeding locations, or tree climbing opportunities, are as important to successful maintenance and propagation as absolute space. For example, female red pandas require multiple nesting sites to move young around during the nestbound stage. If insufficient nesting areas are available, the female may carry the young around excessively, eventually risking the health of the young through dropping, neck lacerations, or exposure (Roberts and Gittleman, 1984). Periodic tendency to change the location of the maternal den has been observed in a number of carnivore and marsupial species (e.g., gray wolf, red fox [*Vulpes vulpes*], spotted hyena, fat-tailed dunnart [*Sminthopsis crassicaudata*]), and may relate to the natural need for females to change dens as food resources become depleted in a given area (Ewer, 1973). In captivity such behavior may also be a response to the constant stress of confinement, but the provisioning of several nesting sites can prevent cannibalism or other pathological behavior directed towards the young.

Special niche requirements are often not obvious and, in the absence of field data, manipulations of cage artifacts may be necessary before a final cage design can be adopted. For instance, in the case of the giant panda, it was found that with no grass substrate or tubs of soil, individuals spent little time autogrooming which eventually led to poor fur condition (Kleiman, 1983). Provisioning of such basic artifacts may lead to more species-typical behavior.

Reintroduction into the Wild

Brambell (1977) defines reintroduction as "the process of reestablishing a population of animals within the area of its natural habitat" (p. 112). As defined, reintroduction involves careful consideration of many factors such as carrying capacity in the species' natural habitat, characteristics of captive-bred stock to be reintroduced (e.g., subspeciation and genetic suitability, physiological and behavioral suitability), and the process of reintroduction (see e.g., Ralls et al., 1983; VanBlaricom and Estes, 1988). In addition, many mammals are locked into specialized dietary, spatial, habitat, or other ecological needs which may fluctuate or reach critical thresholds in the wild. Either these species will have to be taught behavioral flexibility, or reintroduction programs should emphasize intrinsically adaptable species. For example, although many large carnivores and ungulates require extensive home range areas, they show considerable behavioral and ecological flexibility in movement, activity, and feeding patterns which indicate the adaptive capability of reintroduction (e.g., European otter, Mason and Macdonald, 1986; jaguar, Rabinowitz and Nottingham, 1986; gray wolf, Pulliainen, 1982; oryx, [*Oryx leuoryx*] Stanley Price, 1986). Nevertheless, for larger carnivores reared strictly in captivity some training is probably required at least for acquiring prey. There are no reports of trained individual carnivores that have eventually been released and then followed in the wild. Through initial exposure to prey in off-exhibit enclosures and then behavioral modification techniques, predatory movements and successful hunting may be taught (e.g., mountain lion, [*Puma concolor*] Bogue and Ferrari, 1978; snow leopard, Nardelli, 1984; see also Lindburg, 1988).

Other species-typical characteristics that are often considered more "hard-wired" may also demand captive instruction (Brambell, 1977; Frankel and Soulé, 1981). Kleiman (1980) discusses various captive-induced behavioral changes that make reintroduction difficult. For example, in some hider ungulates (e.g., sable antelope) which use crypsis to avoid predation, parent-offspring interactions are more conspicuous in captivity. The increased initiation of nursing bouts and resting with young (Hnida, 1985) could deleteriously affect the outcome of attempts at reintroducing hider species into areas supporting predator populations.

Even though behavioral changes occur in captivity, it is often difficult to pinpoint which physical and/or biological conditions produce the lack of continuity in captive and field populations. An important step would be to draw upon field studies for estimating the level of behavioral variability among populations of a given species in a variety of ecological conditions (Clutton-Brock et al., 1982; Bekoff et al., 1984). Comparative studies may provide complementary data for revealing the effects of different captive conditions. In the end, it is critical that follow-up studies be carried out once captives have been released in the wild.

Methods of Captive Research

Identification and Marking Techniques

Various marking techniques are currently used: ear tags, leg bands, or dyes (Biben, 1983; DonCarlos et al., 1986; Green, 1986; Bennett and Fewell, 1987), radio collars (Rothman and Mech, 1979; Bekoff and Wells, 1986), and natural marks such as coat or vibrissa-spot patterns (Ough, 1982; Asa et al., 1985; Bekoff and Wells, 1986; Ralls et al., 1987; Stuwe and Grodinsky, 1987; Blasetti et al., 1988). Captive behavioral studies of mammals use more direct observational techniques due to greater potential of manipulating animals for identification, close-up viewing, and repetitive observations. Thus, detailed analyses of such captive data permit testing of differences in the development and form of individual variation more than most field studies (see e.g., Ralls et al., 1987). Natural variation in morphological characters (e.g., coat patterning, individual scars) are predominantly used for discriminating among captive individuals (see Benson and Smith, 1975; Aquilina, 1981; Mellen et al., 1981; Stuwe and Grodinsky, 1987; Blasetti et al., 1988; Conover, 1988). Behavioral studies of individual variation in mammalian neonates may be hampered by homogeneity of size, color, or even behaviors; use of dyeing techniques and color-marked ear tags are often used for studies of neonatal behavior (e.g., Biben, 1983; Seiber, 1986; Bennett and Fewell, 1987).

Data Collection Techniques

Sampling. Depending upon the particular questions and behaviors involved, one or a combination of scan, focal animal, all-inclusive occurrences, and sequence sampling techniques may be employed (for reviews see Altmann, 1974; Lehner, 1979; Martin and Bateson, 1986). Focal animal sampling, in which one or two animals are monitored in a predetermined time frame, is frequently used in captive mammalian research because it requires close distance viewing and generates detailed, rigorous information on sequential patterns of differences among individuals, often with small samples sizes. Due to the flight distance of particular species (e.g., some ungulate species, Walther et al., 1983) or sensitivity to human presence (e.g., some carnivores, Gittleman, 1988a), observations on some species are even restricted in captivity. For example, in a study of changes in feeding behavior during lactation in the red panda, Gittleman (1988a) found that different indices of feeding behavior (e.g., duration of feeding bouts, interval between feeds) could not be simultaneously monitored because individual animals avoided observers and often were obscured by trees. Scan sampling (or instantaneous sampling), in which larger numbers of animals are observed at preselected time intervals (e.g., every minute on the minute throughout the day), may be more appropriate for obtaining data on group characteristics, such as variation in group size parameters of individuals residing in adjacent enclosures (Benson and Smith, 1975) or species housed in large groups (Read and Frueh, 1980).

Recording Instruments. Tools for collection of behavioral data range from simple descriptive note taking and checksheets to sophisticated portable computers. While the use of video cameras (Hudson and Distel, 1982), audio recorders (Brady, 1981; Seiber, 1986), and ultrasonic detectors and computers (Ralls et al., 1986b) is becoming increasingly common, the checksheet remains the standard technique for data collection, even when recording equipment is employed. Kleiman (1974) classified two forms of checksheets: time sample—used for focal animal samples of brief duration extended over a long observation period (5 min/hr across several months); and all occurrence—used for longer sampling periods for brief observation period (30–60 min/day for one month). Regardless of the format of checksheet, it is imperative that behavioral categories be complete, clear and concise; all behaviors must be well-defined (preferably mutually exclusive) and identifiable by all those participating in the research.

One of the benefits of carrying out behavioral research on captive mammals, both from the institution's perspective and the observer's, is that there is always an abundant and enthusiastic population of volunteers on hand. Although this vastly increases opportunities for collecting large amounts of information, it presents serious potential for gathering unreliable or spurious data when volunteers are unfamiliar with systematic research. Even so, if careful instructions are given concerning all phases of the research (i.e., problem, data collection, benefits of research) prior to data collection, the study will be more valuable (Crockett Wilson, 1978). Ralls et al. (1982) statistically examined interobserver reliability among 50 volunteers who gathered data on mother-young interactions in captive ungulates. They concluded that: (1) variability of data collected by two or more observers was no greater than data collected by a single observer, (2) the variability of data on species for which there were multiple mother-young pairs was no higher than that on species for which only one pair was observed, and (3) observations made during two times of the day contained about the same degree of variability. In essence, this study emphasizes the value of presenting clear checksheets and periodic retraining sessions for producing high interobserver reliability.

Physiological Techniques. Physiological data can also provide information about behavioral characteristics. The doubly-labeled water technique has been used for estimating milk composition (Oftedal, 1984, 1985; Gittleman and Oftedal, 1987) or overall energy usage (Nagy, 1987; Speakman and Racey, 1988), both of which influence such behaviors as duration of nursing, foraging behavior, or reproductive performance (for review, see Gittleman and Thompson, 1988).

Another physiological device currently used for captive endangered species is the oxygen analyzer, which provides information on basal metabolic rate and thermoregulatory abilities (see e.g., Hennemann et al., 1983; Muller and Rost, 1983; Costa and Kooyman, 1984; Muller and Lojewski, 1986; for review see McNab, 1986, 1989). The primary constraint in applying these techniques is that animals must be easily transferable (or retrappable) and, with the oxygen analyzer, must remain relatively immobile for designated periods (time frame depends on body size).

Problems of Research in Captivity

Generally, problems that influence captive studies include: (1) artificially imposed social groupings, (2) absence or reduction of home range movements, (3) presence of keepers and viewing public, (4) relatively sterile housing conditions, and (5) scheduled feeding regimes (Burghardt, 1975; Markowitz, 1975; Sadleir, 1975; Eisenberg and Kleiman, 1977). Abnormal behavior or poor breeding success in many captive mammals may be due to one or a combination of these factors. We discuss a few of the salient problems below.

Social Structure

The social structure of captive mammals is frequently based on availability of animals or space within a facility. Groupings that deviate from that of the wild condition may profoundly affect individual behavior patterns. Primarily solitary species are adversely affected by the presence of conspecifics during parturition and rearing. Aggression from conspecifics toward mating pairs frequently disrupts breeding performance (maned wolf [*Chrysocyon brachyurus*], Brady and Dilton, 1979; Hartmann's mountain zebra [*Equus zebra*], Dolan, 1977; Sierra Leone striped squirrel [*Funisciurus pyrrhopus*], Mallinson, 1975), and females which normally raise their young alone or apart from the population group often kill or abandon their litters when conspecifics are in close proximity (spectacled bear [*Tremarctos ornatus*], Peel et al., 1979; Aquilina, 1981; European bison [*Bison bonasus*], Dolan, 1977; maned wolf, Brady and Dilton, 1979; Speke's gazelle [*Gazella spekei*], Read and Frueh, 1980). Similar problems are also exhibited by social species in the absence of conspecifics. Breeding behavior may be induced in either males or females by the presence of aggression in groups of the opposite sex (Przewalski horse [*Equus przewalskii*],

Bouman, 1977; Asiatic wild ass [*Equus hemionus*], Dolan, 1977; white rhinoceros, [*Ceratotherioum simum*], Dolan, 1977; cheetah, Benson and Smith, 1974, 1975). Thus, inadequate social groupings may negatively affect breeding performance.

Spatial Requirements

Hediger's (1950, 1955) concept of "flight distance" emphasized the importance of adequate enclosure size in both physical and psychological needs. Adjustments to the reduction of relative home range movements in captivity may contribute to poor reproductive success. Several species require "distant visibility," or the capacity to look beyond their enclosures at surrogate escape routes or possible prey (pronghorn [*Antilocapra americana*], Moore, 1987a; cheetah, Tong, 1974; polar bear [*Thalarctos maritimus*], Van Keulen-Kromhout, 1978). The increase of perceptual stimulation may facilitate successful breeding performance in some species (see Tong, 1974).

A vexing problem in management decisions of endangered mammals is that spatial and social requirements of a species are closely interrelated. Among group living species, the structure of the group is often a function of the amount of space available. Overcrowding can lead to the breakdown of hierarchical relationships, thus raising levels of aggression and subsequently leading to poor maternal care, abortion of young, or flight-related deaths (cervids, Fradrich, 1980; dwarf mongoose, Rasa, 1975; Hartmann's mountain zebra, Dolan, 1977; Speke's gazelle, Read and Frueh, 1980).

Inbreeding

Species in which reduced heterozygosity has been demonstrated show higher incidences of juvenile mortality and decreased fertility (Przewalski horse, Fisher et al., 1979; dorcas gazelle [*Gazella dorcas*], Ralls et al., 1980). Ralls et al. (1979) found in 15 ungulate species a significant increase in mortality and a decrease in female fertility in 19 of 25 individuals. Further analyses of the data eliminated potential confounding variables (variation in management practices, birth order, and birth season) as contributing to the higher mortality rates of inbred young, thus pinpointing the severe impact effects of inbreeding. Although inbreeding effects on behavior have not been well-studied in endangered species, decline in maternal ability and lack of mate receptivity have generally been attributed to a decrease in genetic heterogeneity in other mammals (Lasley, 1978; Shoemaker, 1982; Hillman and Carpenter, 1983).

Handrearing

The removal of mammalian neonates from natural rearing conditions requires a series of difficult decisions. Neonates may be removed due to neglect or abuse by the mother, for research opportunities, or to facilitate the taming process so that an animal is more easily managed (see National Zoological Park Handrearing Facility Handbook [NZPHFH], 1987). Successful handrearing procedures (e.g., composition of milk formulas, feeding techniques, housing arrangements) are outlined in various sources (see *International Zoo Yearbooks*; or *Zoo Biology*; Taylor and Bietz, 1979; NZPHFH).

Although handrearing procedures may be successful in terms of neonatal survival, deleterious effects are often observed subsequent to handrearing. Handreared individuals may be incompatible with conspecifics, exhibit poor breeding performance, or lack appropriate maternal skills (e.g., leopard [*Panthera pardus*], Shoemaker, 1982; dwarf mongoose, Rasa, 1975; jungle cat [*Felis chaus*], Jayewardene, 1975; little spotted cat [*F. tigrinus*], Quillen, 1981). Food supplementation of the young while they remain with the mother may be a better alternative if the mother is accepting. Another technique is to handrear young in litter groups (if young are of roughly the same developmental age), thus minimizing the amount of "imprinting effects" from human intervention. Both techniques are preferable to the handrearing of young in solitary because they increase the likelihood the neonate will develop species-typical social skills.

Conclusions

Behavioral research on captive endangered mammals is passing through an exciting and rapidly moving period. Interdisciplinary research with conservation biologists, wildlife ecologists, physiological ecologists, and behavioral ecologists is generating new ideas which will vastly increase our knowledge of endangered species and in turn favorably affect conservation strategies. Three developing areas of research are particularly important for this interdisciplinary trend.

First, studies of the physiological capacities of mammals are extremely informative for: (1) providing preliminary data on diet, social behavior, activity cycles, and geographical distribution when field data are lacking (e.g., Hennemann et al., 1983; McNab, 1983, 1986), (2) setting guidelines for handrearing programs (e.g., calculating milk dosages and compositions) and captive diets, and (3) educating the public about the general physiological adaptability (scope) of different endangered mammals.

Second, the capacity to manipulate species which are difficult, if not impossible, to study in the wild should increase the value of behavioral studies on captive mammals. As one fascinating example, the naked mole rat (*Cryptomys hottentotus*) is the only known mammal to have a social structure similar to that of social insects. Within each colony only a single pair breeds; the remaining males and females belong to castes which are distinguishable by differences in size and by the tasks they perform (Jarvis, 1981). Unfortunately, the naked mole rat is strictly fossorial, utilizing extensive tunnels below ground which are inaccessible to observation. Recent studies using experimental tunnel systems reveal a sophisticated mode of communication among individuals that aids in coordinating activity and burrowing movements (Hickman, 1980; see also Rado et al., 1987). Presumably, such communication influences the unusual form of reproduction shown in this species. Further experimental type behavioral study, combined with physiological approaches (see Lovegrove and Wissel, 1988), is a key for unraveling the evolution of this hymenopteran mammal. Similar captive studies of endangered mammals should be focused on species which are largely unobservable in the wild (e.g., nocturnal, arboreal, aquatic, fossorial).

Finally, as a result of many years of data collection, both from captive and field populations, massive data banks are available on a multitude of behavioral, ecological, and life history variables across diverse mammalian taxa (see Eisenberg, 1981). Recent quantitative techniques for analyzing comparative relationships have made empirical tests and predictions of broad scale behavior patterns more rigorous (Harvey and Mace, 1982; Clutton-Brock and Harvey, 1984; Gittleman, 1989a; Burghardt and Gittleman, 1990; Brooks and McLennan, 1991; Harvey and Pagel, 1991; Gittleman and Luh, 1992). Although resolution of these comparative findings are often not helpful for planning captive management, they may be used for preliminary decisions, especially when information is unavailable for certain species. For example, by calculating the correlation coefficient ($r^2 = 0.71$), slope (0.11), and intercept (4.02) for the allometric relationship of gestation length and body weight in carnivores (see

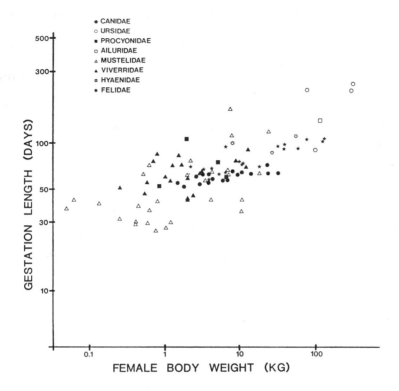

Figure 19.3. Gestation length plotted against female body weight for taxonomic families within the order Carnivora. Species values, data sources, and statistical analyses are given in Gittleman (1986).

Fig. 19.3), we can predict with a relative degree of certainty the gestation length of a given carnivore if we know its body size (see Gittleman, 1986, 1992). Clearly, the predictive power of such comparative findings rests with the quality of data, statistical analyses, taxa concerned, intraspecific variation, and various other methodological problems (see Kiltie, 1982; Clutton-Brock and Harvey, 1984; Gittleman, 1989a). Nevertheless, with the paucity of basic information on endangered mammals, the comparative approach should be coopted for initially informing about diet (Lee and Cockburn, 1985; Oftedal, 1985), neonatal growth rate (Gittleman and Oftedal, 1987), basal metabolic rate (McNab, 1986, 1989), life history traits (Eisenberg, 1981, 1986; Harvey and Clutton-Brock, 1985; Gittleman, 1986; Boyce, 1988; Bronson, 1989), social behavior (Moehlman, 1986; Packer, 1986; Gittleman, 1989b, c; Sandell, 1989), and parental care (Kleiman and Malcolm, 1981; Gittleman, 1985).

20

Interdisciplinary Issues in the Design of Mammal Exhibits (Excluding Marine Mammals and Primates)

Debra L. Forthman, Rita McManamon,
Uriel A. Levi, and Gail Y. Bruner

The history and philosophy of design of captive environments for mammals have been discussed extensively, perhaps most frequently with respect to nonhuman primates. In general, historical trends in exhibit design for nonhuman primates are comparable to those for many other large mammals (Hediger, 1964, 1968, 1969; Sommer, 1974; Michelmore, 1975, 1976, 1980; Campbell, 1984; Coe, 1985; Maple and Finlay, 1986; Polakowski, 1987; Finlay et al., 1988; Shettell-Neuber, 1988; Ogden, 1992; Lindburg and Coe, chap. 28, this volume).

There are three points regarding the history of captive design that should be emphasized. First, preference has been given to large, "dramatic" species (e.g., carnivores, primates, and hoofed mammals), over the small, crepuscular, or nocturnal species that comprise the majority of the class Mammalia (Orders Rodentia, Chiroptera, Insectivora, and smaller species of Carnivora; Morris, 1961; Nowak and Paradiso, 1983; see also Hoyt, chap. 17, this volume). These Orders will probably continue to be underrepresented, despite the fact that the important messages of conservation, adaptation, behavior, and biogeography may be illustrated with small mammals, in less space and sometimes at less expense than is possible with larger species (Conway, 1968).

Second, during all phases in the architectural evolution of zoos, designers have attempted to create a generic exhibit applicable, with minor modifications, to most species. First these were "boxes," which Hediger deplored (1969), followed by circular, moated, grottos (Hagenbeck, 1912). In recent years, the integration of data from captive and field studies has led to much progress in the design of functional, species-typical interior exhibit spaces (Crandall, 1964; Ewer, 1973; Crowcroft, 1975; Hutchins et al., 1978, 1979, 1984; Hancocks, 1980; Mellen et al., 1981; Markowitz, 1982; Nowak and Paradiso, 1983; Forthman Quick, 1984; Shepherdson, 1989a, b; Carlstead et al., 1991; Perkins, 1992).

Nonetheless, most exhibits can be reduced to a simple form, either the cube or the sphere. The point is that the exterior configuration of exhibits and both exterior and interior layout of holding facilities have not progressed far during the past century, despite the fact that few animals in nature inhabit simple spherical spaces (see section on future directions, this chapter).

Third, while the same design criteria usually apply whether a species is endangered or not (see section on reintroduction, this chapter), history has shown that it is extremely important to design exhibit, propagation, holding (including long-term retirement; e.g., Lindburg, 1991a), and veterinary facilities with as much flexibility as possible. Once construction is complete, the effective lifespan of an exhibit may be 25–30 years. This is more than enough time for exhibit and propagation priorities to change due to drastic declines in wild populations (e.g., black rhinoceros [*Diceros bicornis*]), and for research to identify exhibit characteristics that will improve a species' health (Schmidt and Markowitz, 1977; Markowitz et al., 1978; Wallach and Boever, 1983b; Langman et al., 1990), propagation (Meyer-Holzapfel, 1968; Wemmer, 1974; Jacobi, 1975; Roberts, 1975), well-being (Rosenthal, 1975; Wemmer and Fleming, 1975; Mellen et al., 1981; Chamove et al., 1982; Forthman Quick and Pappas, 1986; Dow, 1987), and educational impact (Rasa, 1975; Markowitz and Stevens, 1978; Foster-Turley and Markowitz, 1978, 1982; Shepherdson et al., 1989a; Snowden and Savage, 1989; Carlstead et al., 1991; Forthman et al., 1992).

While this discussion focuses on design optima rather than minima, zoo exhibit design has been influenced to a considerable degree in recent years by governmental regulatory agencies, such as the U.S. Department of Agriculture/Animal and Plant Health Inspection Service (USDA/APHIS), which have been required to undertake the definition and enforcement of minimal care standards for captive animals. The public has, to some extent, focused the attention of these entities on "charismatic mega-mammals." In general, such agencies are ill-prepared to define the parameters of environmental variables as they affect individual species. Their problem, and that of proactive zoo professionals, is a difficult one.

There is an enormous body of basic research dispersed over a number of fields which may neither share a common language, nor have an immediately obvious impact on animal management or zoological design. Yet, were it possible to access these literatures effectively, there is much knowledge that could facilitate work with exotic species in complex social settings (Forthman and Ogden, 1992; Glickman and Caldwell, 1994). Ideally, professional reaction to regulations created by well-intentioned guesswork will promote interdisciplinary evaluations of the impact of abiotic and biotic environmental variables on the physiology, behavior, and psychology of captive animals. Fields relevant to such inquiry include user-centered design (Mikellides, 1980; Norman and Draper, 1986; Lang, 1987; Rouse and Boff, 1987; Norman, 1988), psychoneuroimmunology (Ader, 1981, 1985; Moberg, 1985), and psychoneuroendocrinology (Stoskopf, 1983; Moberg, 1985; Line, 1987; Pereira, 1989; see also Stoskopf and Gibbons, 1994).

Finally, large system studies such as those undertaken in restoration ecology (Jordan et al., 1987) provide useful models for deriving necessary and sufficient conditions for the re-creation and "transposition of natural conditions" (Hediger, 1964). In effect, such replication of an organism's physical and behavioral ecology would help to forestall premature exhibit obsolescence. The users' (i.e., animal occupants, keepers, researchers, and visitors) interfaces would be designed as integrated aspects of this replication, with appropriate levels of access provided for each user group. Much of what follows is a set of considerations that have accumulated through collective experience and sharply focused, but largely disconnected, research. Ideally, what will emerge from this chapter is the framework for a coherent interdisciplinary approach to future design research, and execution and evaluation of zoological exhibits.

Economics of Captive Design

Spatial and Monetary Restrictions

Because a number of economic decisions must be made by zoo design teams involved in reclaimation or reconstruction of mammal exhibits, a flow chart strategy may be useful in the initial stages of planning. An example of some major decisions that must be considered with respect to the physical size, location, and financial strength of an institution is presented below. First, there is the decision to renovate or reconstruct. Although renovation is usually less expensive in the short-run, it may not be cost-effective long-term, particularly as building codes and mammal housing standards have changed dramatically and frequently since many existing zoo structures were initially built. A mixed strategy of renovating some exhibits and reconstructing others is often a viable solution. This leads to the decision to use contracted or in-house construction teams. A general contractor is most expensive, but is usually essential for major reconstruction and within zoological parks that are unionized. For small or simple exhibits, however, staff or volunteer labor may be employed effectively (e.g., Bauer and Geise, 1988). For example, many exhibits in Zoo Atlanta's existing reptile house have been ably renovated by staff and volunteers as an interim strategy pending construction of a new facility. Similar reconstructions have taken place in mammal exhibits, such as the Cincinnati Zoo's "cat house."

Obviously, naturalistic exhibits are more expensive because higher-priced materials are generally required (e.g., decorated concrete wall at $20/linear ft vs. chain link fence at $5/linear ft) and furnishings (artificial trees vs. milled poles; "streams" vs. troughs). Finally, the most expensive exhibits are those that are naturalistic and "high tech" (i.e., incorporating computerized interactive graphics, sound, light and misting systems, and feeding devices; Conway, 1986c). It is essential that budgets include funds for subsequent operation, maintenance, and enhancement of such exhibitry.

Where increased knowledge of a species' natural history necessitates alterations in group size (e.g., elephants), new and larger exhibitry means not only additional financial expense, but also additional commitment of land. In particular, small to midsized urban zoos face difficult decisions with respect to which species to exhibit. Most have a long history of displaying single individuals of many species, with the concomitant public affection for those well-known individuals. Further, the trend towards biome displays limits the number of species per taxonomic group that a single zoo can display. For example, the old zoo "cat house" may be reduced to a small group of lions in "Africa," and pairs of jaguars and tigers in "South America" and "Asia," respectively.

A major cost factor in the decision of which species to exhibit involves the zoo's geographic location. This is one situation in which the "right" choice happens to be the most cost-effective, but one of the more difficult to sell to the public. It is simply a fact that polar exhibits which are cost-effective, high in quality, and functional from the standpoint of all users (i.e., animals, staff, public) cannot be constructed in tropical or semitropical climates; the converse also holds. One of the best re-creations of a polar environment is the Penguin Encounter at Sea World in San Diego. However, the cost of building and maintaining that exhibit would be prohibitive for most dedicated zoological parks. The alternative—tropical rain forest exhibits in Florida and tundra exhibits in Minnesota—is obviously more realistic. Construction and maintenance budgets are reduced, and the local availability of appropriate landscaping and supplementary foods is maximized. However, this strategy must be marketed carefully to a public that is accustomed to seeing the complete spectrum of wildlife in the neighborhood zoo.

It might also be worthwhile for some zoos to invest in species that occupy more vertical than horizontal space, even though cost per square foot is high in multistoried exhibitry with subterranean holding facilities. If urban-dwelling humans are forced to build up, why not urban zoos (e.g., Hancocks, 1971)? Finally, not every species requires an expensive exhibit; many walk-through aviaries and indoor exhibits have incorporated "free-ranging" small mammals successfully (e.g., free-flying bats at Jungle World; sloths, small cervids and antelope in aviaries; immature bovids and antelope in contact areas).

Animal Health and Replacement Costs

Improved husbandry and veterinary care is largely responsible for the trend towards self-sustaining captive populations. Increased ability to maintain healthy captive animals translates into a greater financial investment in state-of-the-art health care, holding facilities and support systems that employ the most knowledgeable designers and highest-quality materials. Some of this investment is mandated by stricter governmental standards, such as those that necessitate the installation of costly heating, ventilation and air conditioning (HVAC) or water filtration and purification systems. In some cases, such as the Toledo and Woodland Park Zoos, additional staff were required to operate such equipment.

Facilities for physical restraint of, or "restricted contact" from, large mammals are also expensive but necessary additions to facility design and will soon be required by the American Association of Zoological Parks and Aquariums (AAZPA). These will not only safeguard animal health by providing a humane system for routine handling, transport, veterinary care, and research, but will greatly improve keeper safety and reduce insurance costs. Good security (see below) is also important in maintaining animal health and reducing replacement costs.

Security

The importance of professionally constructed and installed, pre-tested, and redundant security systems cannot be overemphasized. Many zoos have suffered losses, in genetic potential, revenue, and bad publicity when individuals of an endangered species die or must be destroyed after escape. The use of CAD (computer-aided design) software during the design process may help staff and architects pinpoint "blind" areas of exhibits and holding areas, as well as the optimal placement of keeper escape areas in facilities for more dangerous species. Redundant systems with signs, alarms, and closed-circuit television monitors can help reduce the incidence of escapes and injuries (both to occupants and staff) due to human error (see section on cognitive engineering, this chapter). Just as important, the choice of materials (20-year life vs. 5-year life) can have critical effects on security. The opposite side of the security issue concerns the widespread practice of confining animals to holding areas for 12–16 hours out of every 24 hours. Clearly, training animals to come in daily for inspection, for monitoring food intake, and for providing veterinary care is optimal. Moreover, the public must be protected from dangerous animals and vice versa. In addition, continuous occupation of exhibits would lead to further enclosure degradation, and would shorten their effective lifespans. Nonetheless, perhaps the amount of time animals spend indoors could be reduced with redundant exhibitry or outdoor, off-exhibit holding space.

Keeper Efficiency

At least three factors increase the cost of building or maintaining facilities. The first is nonanimal spaces in holding facilities, such as storage and food preparation areas, restrooms with showers, offices, and research space. These areas often fall victim to "value-engineering," greatly compromising keeper efficiency in the process. Second, consideration of normal patterns of animal movement, and the special needs associated with animal training is essential in the initial design process of interior spaces. Examples include employment of rounded chutes for artiodactylids, sufficient numbers of squeeze cages with metabolic trays located in entry and exitways, and shift cages (with rounded corners in flooring and exterior drains) that provide varied views, degrees of privacy, and light patterns. Some shift cages should feature access ports that allow keepers to easily reinforce animals' behaviors during training. All of these design features will serve to reduce the chance of animal injury, but the latter two will facilitate training, cleaning, treatment of, and biological sample collection from individuals. These items are expensive and also vulnerable to "value-engineering," but ultimately save medical and labor costs.

Species Considerations in Captive Design

Stress and the degree to which an animal's behavior affects the rewards and punishments it receives are relevant to all that follows. Designers today are more aware of stress as an issue, but decades of research on the effects of an animal's ability to influence its environment (Seligman and Weiss, 1980; Moberg, 1985) have only recently been applied in zoos (Markowitz, 1982; Carlstead et al., 1991; Forthman and Ogden, 1992).

Stress

In design terminology, stress is "the action on a body of any system of balanced forces whereby strain or deformation results," or "the internal resistance or reaction of an elastic body to the external forces applied to it" (Anonymous, 1972). Engineers refer to the former as a stressor, a stimulus impinging on an organism, while the latter emphasizes the organism's response to a stressor. Stressors may be acute, such as confinement in a squeeze cage; chronic, such as the inadequacy of artificial light sources (which may have cumulative effects); or synergistic, when two stressors, such as a veterinary procedure and poor cardiovascular fitness, combine to elicit a stress response greater than that produced by either alone. The responses described above may be called "distress"—those that "deform" the organism's equilibrium. Selye (1974) also proposed the term "eustress" to describe stress responses, such as adrenocortical feedback processes that serve to maintain homeostasis (Ewbank, 1985). Danzer and Mormede (1985) and Novak and Drewson (1989) discussed the problems with simple definitions of stress and well-being for captive animals.

Control

The study of species-typical coping responses to environmental events over which organisms have varying control has produced an enormous body of literature (e.g., Breland and Breland, 1961, 1966; Neuringer, 1969; Bolles, 1972; Jenkins and Moore, 1973; Moore, 1973; Hanson et al., 1976; Seligman and Binik, 1977; Carder and Berkowitz, 1979; Foster-Turley and Markowitz, 1982; Moberg, 1985; Mineka et al., 1986; Markowitz and Line, 1989). Such studies show that animals exhibit more adaptive responses to stressors over which they exert control. In the absence of control, "maladaptive" behaviors are exhibited that in fact serve to reduce potentially damaging physiological stress responses (Brett and Levine, 1979). These behaviors, often appetitive in nature (e.g., pacing), are performed when a normal consummatory response (e.g., prey-killing and feeding) is delayed or prevented. Species have evolved to perform a linked set of responses, such as foraging prior to feeding, and adapt with difficulty to disruptions in that linkage.

Much of the "maladaptive" behavior of captive mammals attests to the fact that designers often fail to develop and construct exhibits that provide animals with a responsive living place. Again, Hediger (1964, p. 72) was right: "Naturalness in the sense of biologically correct type of space, is not the result of an attempt at imitation, but of an adequate transposition of natural conditions."

Abiotic Factors

Although behavioral physiology is a subject of theoretical interest and applied research (Western, 1979; Calder, 1984), transfer of this knowledge to zoo professionals appears to be sporadic (Besch and Kollias, 1994; Stoskopf and Gibbons, 1994).

Temperature and Humidity. Most mammalian species are small, and thus function best within a narrower range of temperatures than larger mammals (Calder, 1984). When humidity is factored in to obtain a heat index or measure of "apparent temperature," that range narrows even more. Considerations of temperature and humidity optima are important in any exhibit design, and are critical for species at either end of the size continuum. Yet, they are frequently the subject of cursory analysis for large species. The risk of hyperthermia in large mammals, and in those from polar regions (e.g., Van Keulen-Kromhout, 1978), should be of equal concern to designers as is the risk of hypothermia in small species.

USDA's (1991) requirement for "shade" for animals has underscored the difficulty of defining physical comfort in terms so nebulous. If, for example, shelter from direct sun (i.e., "shade") is provided in an area in which the heat index is higher than in direct sun, due to poorer air circulation or higher relative humidity, "shade" alone is insufficient to describe the physical parameters necessary to reduce thermal load in large mammals. Langman (Langman, 1977, 1985, 1990) has quantified the thermal relationship between large mammals and their environments (Porter and Gates, 1969). Specifications on the thermal performance of building materials and designs are available (e.g., Watson and Labs, 1983; Anonymous, 1989b). The problem is communicating to designers the link between the biophysics of animal thermoregulation and the thermal performance of materials and buildings. For example, preliminary data suggest that large structural areas of gunite, often used in zoos, may be inappropriate in exhibits designed for large mammals; as gunite's heat absorptive and reflective properties may contribute significantly to thermal distress (Langman et al., 1990; Forthman and Bakeman., 1992). Thermal evaluations should be a routine aspect of the design process.

Illumination. Behavioral periodicity in temperate and polar mammals, endogenously controlled by the endocrine system, is largely entrained by circadian and seasonal variations in quality, intensity, and length of illumination (Gwinner, 1977; Jander, 1977; Goss, 1983). Endocrine function in turn regulates physiological and behavioral patterns, such as hair, antler and gonadal growth, activity cycles, migration, food hoarding, hibernation, and mating and parturition. For crepuscular species, periods of rising and falling light intensity are probably crucial even for adequate adaptation to captivity, because many essential maintenance, feeding, and social behaviors are selectively performed under particular light intensities (Helfman, 1979, 1981). Such transitional photoperiods have only recently begun to be reproduced artificially, but are of particular importance when species are maintained indoors (e.g., Anonymous, 1987c).

Sound. Sound, like light, is a critical environmental variable to consider in design of captive mammal facilities. Like light, its deleterious effects are pervasive and can be profound (Peterson, 1980; Stoskopf, 1983; Krause, 1989). The influences of sound stimuli have only recently begun to be quantified within the zoological community. Generally, studies have focused on the variable of intensity

(Stoskopf, 1983). Deleterious physiological and behavioral effects of loud noise are well-documented (Barrett and Stockham, 1963; Peterson, 1980; Gamble, 1982; deBoer et al., 1989; Gold and Ogden, 1991; cf., Thomas et al., 1990). Periodicity effects have also been shown in that intermittent loud sounds are less distressing than constant ones (Ising, 1981; deBoer et al., 1988), and predictable loud sounds (for which anticipatory responses may be made) are the least disruptive (see refs. in control section above). Frequency is another variable that profoundly influences the psychoneuroendocrine and immune axes of animals. Much of animal communication is acoustic in nature (Marler, 1967; Sebeok, 1968; Macedonia, 1986; Pereira, 1986). Some of that acoustic communication occurs within the range of human hearing, so that if, for example, sound levels in an exhibit or holding area mask animals' contact vocalizations, managers may recognize that there is an acoustic problem in the design. It is also necessary, however, to evaluate effects of background noise on acoustic signals of animals that locate prey, communicate, or navigate via ultrasound and infrasound frequencies (Payne et al., 1986; Poole et al., 1988; Gibbons and Stoskopf, 1989). Finally, as Stoskopf (1983) wrote, content must be considered in design, as sound recordings with public educational value may be distressful to the animals exhibited (Ogden, 1992; cf., Maples and Haraway, 1982; Shepherdson et al., 1989b).

Quality and Quantity of Space. Most professionals are in agreement with Yerkes (1925), Hediger (1969), Markowitz (1982), and others who have long emphasized that the quality of space is far more important to captive animals than the quantity of space. However, the degree to which such agreement is reflected in design varies enormously. Certainly there are allometric and ecological constraints on quantity of space—an elephant occupies more volume than a mouse. However, just because bears are large does not mean that they require spacious dens; in fact, studies have shown the opposite to be true (Wemmer, 1974; Jacobi, 1975; Van Keulen-Kromhout, 1978). Physical and psychological effects of long-term indoor housing and/or restricted activity have been documented (Pereira et al., 1989; Beck, 1991). Variables relevant to the naturalistic display, health, survivorship, and propagation of captive animals must continue to be quantified and, most importantly, factored into design (Besch and Kollias, 1994; Glickman and Caldwell, 1994). For example, exhibits that require frequent cleaning subject animals such as pandas, which use chemical sign-posts to delimit their territories and regulate reproduction, to chronic stress that may result in excessive levels of scent-marking. Further, it would certainly be educational and perhaps necessary for the proper physical development of captive cheetahs if their exhibits enabled them to achieve their maximum straight-line running speed. Here the quantity and configuration of the space is important.

Hard vs. Soft. While "hard" vs. "soft" environments obviously provide animals with different tactile sensations, they also differ on many of the abiotic dimensions discussed above. Because this subject has received so much attention in the literature (e.g., Sommer, 1974; Brenner, 1994; Glickman and Caldwell, 1994), suffice it to say that "soft" environments should be the standard for holding facilities as well as exhibits.

The ability to achieve "softness" in relatively small enclosures would be greatly enhanced were zoo professionals able to maintain in them more living trees, shrubs, and herbaceous material, without constantly battling exhibit degradation from overuse. As mentioned above, adequate shift spaces improve efficiency in holding facilities. An extremely valuable feature of interior and exterior design often eliminated by cost and land restrictions is the agricultural concept of "rotating pastures." The ability to rotate exhibit and holding space increases novelty, reduces parasite loads and damage to exhibit plantings, and may permit regrowth of desirable food items. This in turn reduces landscaping costs and improves exhibit aesthetics. Animals shift foraging areas in the wild, and prevention of movement leads to habitat degradation. Such an important ecological concept can and should be communicated to the public.

Configuration and Layout. As mentioned before, interior configurations tend to be cubic, and exterior layouts tend to be spherical. However, these are not necessarily the preference of the animal inhabitants or their managers. It is initially less expensive and simpler to design and build in familiar, linear patterns, particularly with respect to the installation of plumbing, electrical, and HVAC systems. It may be productive, however, to reexamine these concepts more innovatively with each species, and to experiment with varied configurations (Glickman and Caldwell, 1994). Organisms occupy a certain volume; therefore, design should always be three-dimensional in nature, emphasizing appropriateness of features within an exhibit's volume to the species in question. Design for terrestrial species is easiest for humans to accomplish well, although the importance of vertical space to primarily terrestrial mammals is sometimes overlooked. For example, provision of numerous, multilevel perches in domestic catteries reduces aggression (see also de Waal, 1989) and increases breeding success.

Failure most often occurs, however, in designs for arboreal and fossorial mammals. For example, while most designs for arboreal species provide numerous opportunities for species-typical locomotion, some still require the animals to be fed on the ground, thus eliminating a primary motivation for arboreality.

Similarly, the type of substrate and design features are important to the behavioral adaptation and effective exhibition of species such as aardvarks (*Orycteropus after*), meerkats (*Suricata suricatta*), and naked mole rats (*Heterocephalus glaber*), which in nature construct extensive warrens of burrows interconnected by subterranean tunnels and surface trails. Usually, when the larger, nocturnal species are permitted to burrow, they are inaccessible to the public. Nocturnal exhibits with subterranean views, such as are found for beavers, otters, mustelids, and rodents, are the ideal but must be designed and constructed with care to prevent tunnels from collapsing or flooding, or the viewing port from being obstructed. The Toledo Zoo has had excellent results with a naked mole rat exhibit, which is constructed like a large ant-farm, with the addition of shock absorbers to prevent the animals from being disturbed by vibrations caused by the public (Winslow, pers. comm.).

Biotic Factors

Foods and feeding methods are probably the most important aspects of maintaining captive animals appropriately, yet with a few exceptions, proper management and husbandry are more crucial than design (Fiennes, 1966; Hediger, 1966; Dittrich, 1971).

Food and Water. With respect to design issues, safe and species-appropriate water sources are critical. The tendency to incorporate large, deep bodies of water in exhibits as aesthetic barriers has been used somewhat indiscriminately, with the result that animals have drowned. For species that acquire water from moisture on foliage or in tree cavities, misters may be perfectly adequate sources of drinking water. Mechanical waterers should be used only with watering systems that are closed to prevent bacterial contamination and with species that can operate them reliably (Lindburg and Coe, chap. 28, this volume). With respect to foraging, design is important in selection of appropriate substrates, plantings, and materials for interior furnishings (Hutchins et al., 1983, 1984). Ideally, it is suggested that design teams think in terms of creating exhibits that first reduce to a minimum the necessity for holding areas and time spent in them, and second, incorporate dynamic and renewable interior spaces, rather than fixed and permanent ones (Doherty and Gibbons, 1994). Clearly this does not apply to such features as barriers and hardware, which may in fact have to be made more durable to achieve the first goal.

Methods of Feeding. With the exception of folivores and large carnivores, most species spend more time in foraging and feeding than in any other activity (Forthman Quick, 1986; Forthman Quick and Demment, 1988). Although feeding methods are primarily husbandry issues, designers should incorporate, or provide for the installation of, devices to promote appropriate methods of feeding and prevent postconstruction installation of obtrusive, unaesthetic, and inconvenient feeding devices. Further, an important and often overlooked aspect of design for large mammal exhibits is the degree and ease of postconstruction access to the exhibit by machinery (e.g., cranes, bulldozers, roto-tillers). Good access facilitates maintenance, modification, and replacement of exhibit furnishings, substrates, feeders, and supplemental foods, such as felled trees with foliage, live trees, and herbaceous plants.

Social Considerations. Design teams must ask at least two fundamental questions when contemplating a new exhibit. First, what is the species' natural social organization, and second, what are its primary modes of communication? If the species' normal grouping is highly social and nomadic or migratory (e.g., wolf [*Canis lupus*], African wild dog [*Lycaon pictus*]), or highly gregarious (e.g., giant eland [*Tauotragus derbianus*]), designers should think carefully whether the zoological park has sufficient space, in quantity and quality, to exhibit such species. For example, small or recently established wolf packs require larger interpersonal spaces than do larger, established packs (Knick and Mech, 1980). Further, most nomadic carnivores confined to small areas have a strong tendency to develop locomotor stereotypes that are distressing to observe. Herd ungulates, if exhibited in appropriately-sized groups, require sufficient space to prevent "desertification" of their exhibit by overgrazing and overbrowsing. If plans for exhibition include captive propagation, as they normally should with endangered mammals, the issue of social mechanisms of reproductive suppression becomes an important consideration (Packard et al., 1983; Asa, 1987; Jenks and Ginsburg, 1987). At least two exhibits will be necessary to optimize breeding through separation of subordinates and maturing offspring. Conversely, among species that communicate primarily by chemosensory channels, proximity has been observed to influence behavior; in particular the social facilitation of reproduction. For example, male felids may initiate copulation with anestrus females when an adjacent pair, even of another species, is breeding (Mellen, pers. comm.).

Natural Social Groupings. Giving animals some control over their social partners is also important. For example, instead of managing bears, or other "solitary" species always as pairs, or always alone, an exhibit might be designed so a subordinate animal has controlled access to a conspecific through the use of interconnecting doors operable only from the subordinate's side of the exhibit.

Mixed-species Designs. Although they present the best educational message, most closely approximate natural conditions, and can save exhibit space (Partridge, 1990), it appears that in most current enclosures, actual rather than virtual mixed-species exhibits are more often unsuccessful than successful. The problems associated with designing multiple, species-appropriate holding facilities, with the means for sorting each species into its holding area are considerable, although not insurmountable. Exhibit design must also be flexible enough to contain both the largest or strongest, as well as the smallest animal. This often presents a challenge in the selection of barriers, as what is safe and appropriate for one species (e.g., mountain zebra [*Equus zebra*]) may fail to contain another (e.g., bontebok [*Damaliscus dorcas*]). Social incompatibility in multispecies exhibits is also frequently a problem and in this regard, design of the interior space of an exhibit is crucial for long-term success. The converse is the potential for undesirable hybridization in such exhibits. This is not to say that successful multispecies exhibits do not exist. Partridge (1990) discusses two exhibits he considered successful: (1) alpaca, (*Lama pacos*), Patagonian cavy (*Dolichotis sp.*), prairie dog (*Cynomys ludovicianus*), rhea, penguin together, and (2) agoutis (*Dasyprocta sp.*) and tapirs (*Tapirus sp.*) together. These were not without problems, many of which illustrate the more important design details. Zoo Atlanta has a fairly successful Masai Mara exhibit that combines birds (ostrich, secretary birds, storks, various ducks) with zebra, giraffe (*Giraffa camelopardalis*), impala (*Aepyceros melampus*), and Thompson's gazelle (*Gazella thomsoni*). While this exhibit does show an array of savannah species, the numbers and sex ratios of impala,

gazelle, and zebra exhibited do not illustrate natural social groupings in the wild. Another quite successful mixed-species exhibit at
the Los Angeles Zoo that more closely approximates normal group
sizes features bongos (*Tragelaphus euryceros*), yellow-backed duikers (*Cephalophus sylvicultor*), and bat-eared foxes (*Otocyon megalotis*).
Numerous rock and log exclosures in both of the latter exhibits
provide refuge for the smaller species, and the bat-eared foxes at
Los Angeles constructed a series of dens within one such exclosure.
Crotty (1981) described other mixed-species exhibits at the Los
Angeles Zoo.

Adjacent Predator-prey Exhibits. The jury is still out on the effects
of adjacent exhibits on predators and prey. In a carefully-designed
study at Columbus Zoo, Stanley and Aspey (1984) demonstrated
that visual presence of lions significantly restricted the behavioral
repertoire of a wide variety of ungulates in adjacent exhibits. However, the behaviors reduced were exhibited at low frequencies when
predators were not visible, so that the well-being of the prey was
not demonstrably compromised. Anecdotes from South African cheetah breeders indicate that the visual presence of prey has a positive influence on the predators' behavior. Considerably more research on this subject is required before firm design recommendations may be made.

Captive Design and Animal Health

One point to keep in mind is the fact that the USDA/APHIS and
AZA regulations change frequently, so design requirements are
also in flux. It is incumbent upon zoo professionals to not only
remain abreast of regulatory standards, but also to be proactive in
offering input on the standardization process (Annelli and Mandrell,
1994; Besch and Kollias, 1994). For example, one design feature
that has received little attention, and yet could benefit greatly from
interinstitutional communication and standardization, is the issue
of filtration systems. With the exception of highly regulated animals like marine mammals, the USDA and animal managers have
not established specific water quality standards. It is reasonable to
presume that some high level of coliform bacteria would be harmful to an animal, but it is also reasonable to presume that all
mammals may not require highly chlorinated systems. Further,
most recirculating systems in exhibits have limited filtration, if
any. Objective comparison, testing, and establishment of reasonably

cost-effective and safe water quality designs would be helpful to all zoo managers.

Another issue relevant to animal health, which has been little explored to date, is the need for ecologically sound pest management in zoos, and the potential for applied conditioned taste aversion to fill that need. Successful applications of taste aversion would have implications for the design and placement of feeders for exhibit animals, and the installation of feeders on exhibit perimeters and in holding areas accessible to avian, mammalian, and arthropod pests (Forthman and Ogden, 1992; Brenner, 1994).

Injuries Due to Faulty Design

The use of high-quality materials, such as nonslip flooring, full-spectrum lighting (or skylights), stainless steel hardware, and hydraulic doors, greatly reduces the risk of animal and staff injuries attributable to faulty design. Species-appropriate materials are also important in reducing injuries and chronic disease processes; for example, chain-link fencing may not be the best choice for horned ungulates, as injuries and fatalities may result if horns become caught in the mesh. Similarly, inappropriate substrates can induce chronic foot problems in some hoofed stock. Finally, when the materials used in an exhibit are not able to withstand the strength or ingenuity of the occupants, injuries and/or escapes may result from broken fixtures and barriers.

Hospital, Quarantine, and Holding Facilities

Within medical and quarantine facilities the requirements for disinfection and frequent visual inspection of patients with minimal handling are often in direct conflict with goals of "softer" and more responsive features of housing. Because quarantine regulations often require biohazard-level disposal or incineration of all objects removed from a cage, daily provision of large amounts of bedding material is prohibitive, and may be unsafe for handlers. Within these constraints, however, thoughtful designers and managers can and should provide opportunities for multipurpose and species customized caging. A bank of uniformly sized, stainless steel cages is less useful than having cages that can be adjusted in size or configuration, possibly with interconnecting tunnels or refuges that may still be viewed. For territorial and solitary species, shiny metal cages can be very stressful to an animal constantly exposed to its reflection; for social species, they can be soothing.

Proactive design and placement of quarantine and nursery rearing areas can significantly aid animal management, and might reduce the perception that quarantine is inherently "stressful" and interferes with breeding programs. In many cases, use of multiple quarantine and nursery facilities placed adjacent to exhibit holding areas can reduce the perceived isolation and facilitate introduction or reintroduction of separated animals. The use of clear or one-way visual panels could permit visual access and habituation of separated animals, without compromising quarantine, as long as HVAC and plumbing systems are kept separate. For some species (small felids) or age classes (very young or elderly animals), however, true separation, including olfactory and auditory stimulation, is necessary or desirable. Again, designing flexible facilities permits such objective evaluations to be made on an individual and species basis.

Observational Reactions to Others' Distress

Such responses can be profound with respect to conditioned fears, such as observation of another individual's reaction to restraint, painful stimulation, or handling. Perhaps designers could incorporate tunnels that lead from hospital holding to treatment areas, to minimize the trauma to other patients when an animal must be removed for treatment (Garcia et al., 1984).

Conditioned Fears

One design factor that might reduce the incidence or strength of conditioned emotional responses is to attempt to design hospital facilities so that levels of olfactory, visual, and auditory stimulation may be maintained below those that elicit alarm and cause sensitization, rather than habituation.

Captive Design and Conservation

Facilities for Potential Reintroductees

Most decisions about reintroduction facilities relate to management and husbandry issues. The principal design issues with respect to mammal facilities for potential reintroductees are whether to construct such facilities as on-site exhibits, off-exhibit facilities, or off-site. A related consideration is whether holding facilities that permit daily access to the animals are necessary. This will depend upon whether or not management maintains a "hands-off" policy with such individuals. In the case of mammal species whose survivorship after reintroduction may be compromised by excessive familiarity with humans (e.g., large and small carnivores, large ungulates), facilities that permit keepers to carry out their duties with limited exposure to the animals may be advisable. On the other hand, Beck (pers. comm.) reported that, in experience with golden lion tamarins (*Leontopithecus rosalia*) at least, captive-bred animals are expendable; if they survive long enough to reproduce, their offspring are indistinguishable from those of wild-born parents. This suggests that it may be optimal to manage potential reintroductees more intensively, with respect to nutrition and preventive health care (Strum, pers. comm.). If reintroductees are in peak physical condition when released, they have a higher probability of surviving to reproduce.

Experiences in Reintroduction Facilities

Probably the most critical aspect of the design of reintroduction facilities is that they permit a species to perform its full behavioral repertoire, as determined from field studies. For example, for some species, predator identification occurs without prior experience, while for others, experience with potential predators is required (Mineka et al., 1980). This introduces a problem associated with a major feature of vertebrate ecology and sociobiology—predator-prey relationships. As the management of zoo exhibits develops, both the costs (in labor and resources expended) and consequences (behavioral, nutritional, sociobiological, and genetic) of insulating the public from the reality of predation will emerge as significant, and lead to the reevaluation of this nearly universal practice. Ultimately, zoo participation in reintroduction efforts will force policymakers to confront the task of fostering public awareness and understanding of the role of predators, a factor which is crucial to the acceptance and success of reintroduction programs (Durrell and Mallinson, 1987). The extirpation of keystone species (frequently predators) from most of the continental U.S. has significantly reduced overall species diversity and the genetic health of prey populations (e.g., Diamond, 1992).

Finally, studies have made it clear that when animals become familiar with a particular range of variables in their rearing environment, these most frequently translate into strong preferences in adulthood (Ogden, 1989; Beck, 1991). For example, preference for concrete, wire mesh, and lumber perches of captive environments may lead to strong neophobia for, and physical incompetence in, locomotion in grass, bushes and trees (Ogden, 1989; Beck, 1991). Obviously, physical fitness is a factor as well as familiarity—it is more difficult to locomote on flimsy, flexible branches than on solid wood perches or static mesh. One might presume that the resolution of such problems is simply a matter of adjustment through experience and practice in temporary housing at the release site. However, Beck's (1991) findings suggest otherwise and bring to mind research on the persistent influences of early environmental experience on neural organization (Berkson et al., 1963; Rosenzweig and Bennett, 1978). In this regard, designs that use only natural materials and facilitate the staff's ability to provide complexity and to vary the captive environment are probably key in the production of behaviorally flexible, fit, and competent animals for reintroduction.

Conclusions: Future Directions

As in the past, numerous challenges will shape the design of future zoos. Today, animal welfare organizations prioritize individual well-being, biologists are concerned with preservation of biodiversity, ecologists stress system integrity, and the public demands educational and recreational resources. What will change is the manner in which these challenges are met. Most design, management, and policy decisions have been made by individuals, with the experiential and personal biases inherent in individual decision-making. Henceforth, decision-makers have the opportunity and responsibility to consult a dynamic knowledge base before implementing changes that affect the lives of exhibit animals and the way in which the public is exposed to them.

A working model of the future zoo is one that maintains genetically and demographically viable populations of healthy individuals exhibiting species-appropriate behavior within a subset of a functioning ecosystem. This model delivers educational and recreational opportunities through exhibit interfaces that engage visitors in the ordered complexity of the relationships among individuals, populations, and ecosystems.

In this view, the design of future zoological exhibits will emerge from the convergence of three methodological approaches: (1) "mesocosm" thematic models, (2) "syntactic" configuration and layout, and (3) cognitively-engineered user interfaces.

Mesocosms

Odum (1984, p. 558) introduced the term "mesocosm" or "middle-sized world" to describe an "environment where parts (populations) and wholes (ecosystems) can be investigated simultaneously..." in a replication positioned between the microcosms of the laboratory and the macrocosms of nature. Zoo exhibits, no matter how complex, are not self-sustaining. Properly implemented, however, they can be aesthetic, functional subsets of a replicated ecosystem. Some mesocosm-type exhibits may require technologically sophisticated infrastructures. For example, an artificial spring flowing into a fish pool in a fishing cat exhibit must be recirculated and filtered as a substitute for natural water cycles. An interpretive display of the artificial water system provides an educational opportunity if it is juxtaposed with a graphic illustrating the natural process that it replaces.

Space Syntax

Space syntax theory (Hillier and Hanson, 1984) identifies patterns in the arrangement of human habitation space and suggests that the nature of these patterns is structured (syntactic) and that they remain constant with transformation (topological). The theory also identifies correspondences between these patterns and the social structure of the cultures that produce them. Field research has identified mechanisms that explain how social organization reinforces the space-use patterns it produces. Similar relationships may exist in nonhuman cultures. Recent work (Levi, 1993) illustrates how space syntax may provide a framework to address space-use issues in zoological exhibitry. For example, structures of sociospace identified in mammals as diverse as wolves (Rothman and Mech, 1979; Knick and Mech, 1980; Harrington, 1983) and naked mole rats (Sherman et al., 1992), and expressed in the relationships between convex (e.g., denning, nesting sites) and axial spaces (e.g., trails, tunnels), can serve to guide site planning for animal-visitor and animal-caretaker exhibit interfaces.

Cognitive Engineering

The term "cognitive engineering" (Norman and Draper, 1986) is used to describe the study of: (1) human action and performance as they relate to interfaces between people and complex systems, and (2) the application of these principles to provide "pleasurable engagement" with complex systems.

Norman (1988) operationalized the task of user-centered design as principles that transform difficult tasks into simple ones. These: (1) use both perceived (in the world) and encoded (in the head) knowledge, (2) simplify task structure, (3) make things (information, constraints, and affordances) visible, (4) achieve correspondence between perception, cognition, and action, (5) use natural (e.g., maximum jumping distances) and artificial (e.g., one-way electrical connections) constraints to limit choices to those which produce desired actions, and (6) design for error. When all else fails, standardize. These principles can be applied to everything from tamper-proof cage doors and clear signage to computer-based interpretive graphics.

Most developments in the field have emerged from research on human-computer interaction. The recent convergence of computer graphics, image processing, and display and network technology has made it possible to channel enormous quantities of data into sounds and pictures. These have the ability to represent the immediate past state(s) of any or all of the components in a complex system accurately. Because each member of an organization develops an idiosyncratic view of its operation, the ability for users to configure a view or level-of-detail according to individual priorities has significance within and among multifaceted organizations such as zoos. When conferring or reporting, two or more parties can simultaneously consult images that display each party's perspective of the situation. Proposed changes, whether structural or procedural, may then be evaluated cooperatively from each viewpoint. For example, an animal area workstation would have a screen displaying a digitized image of each individual animal. A keeper could access feeding, veterinary, and research records for any individual simply by "clicking" on the animal's icon. Advisories concerning that animal would appear along with the records, and if crucial, would cause the image of the animal to flash or change color. These messages could originate from any other staff member or from automated sensors in exhibit areas.

The next generation of zoological exhibits, therefore, is likely to combine characteristics of Robinson's (1988b, 1989) "bioexhibits" and of small-scale, intensively-managed nature preserves ("bioreserves"). To achieve the latter, zoo professionals and private landowners must coordinate effectively to establish large, regional wildlife conservation consortia. In such conservation parks, zoos will concentrate (within acceptable limits of security from catastrophic events) on those endangered species that can be best managed in captivity only in large facilities (the social or wide-ranging "mega-fauna," such as rhinoceros, tigers, and Przewalski's horses). This strategy would delegate to smaller facilities the task of conserving the myriad examples of smaller species, such as marsupials, rodents, and small ungulates and carnivores. Both "bioreserves" and "bioexhibits" will rely upon and contribute to a knowledge base that maintains strong connections to the disciplines of wildlife and sociobiology, and behavioral and restoration ecology. They will become increasingly involved with decisions of environmental policy, and will come under increasing public, political, and professional scrutiny (Wilson, 1989). Apart from size, the fundamental distinction between dedicated "bioreserves" and "bioexhibits" will be in the nature and degree of the visitor interface. Most reserves will seek to minimize human impact, while exhibits will strive to enhance the visitor experience.

The appearance of exhibits in zoological parks may change dramatically, so that circulation patterns for visitors and animals are consistent with the syntactic and topological properties of space-use patterns among free-ranging animals in bioreserves. Consider the example of a savannah exhibit. In the traditional approach, a series of circular enclosures might individually display several plains species. Each would typically be surrounded by public spaces that encourage static clusters of visitors around the perimeter of and mass movements between enclosures. Instead, for example, one might construct a mixed-species savannah "mesocosm" composed of multiple convex (water hole, salt lick, foraging areas, dens) and axial (trails between resource areas) spaces. The configuration of these convex and axial spaces presumes the absence of any cul-de-sacs. This exhibit might be inhabited by species such as zebra, impala, ostrich, bat-eared fox, jackal, and mongoose. Circadian rhythms and interspecific dominance relationships would modulate space-use in the various resource areas. The site plan would integrate visitors into the environment in a manner that minimizes disturbance of the animals' behavior and space-use patterns and maximizes visitors' opportunities for brief, but intense, encounters adjacent to axial animal spaces (narrow boardwalks and trails) and prolonged observation at resting sites (benches, tables) some distance from convex spaces.

In conclusion, Odum (1983, p. ix, Preface) states: "If the bewildering complexity of human knowledge developed in the twentieth century is to be retained and well-used, unifying concepts are needed to consolidate the understanding of systems of many kinds and to simplify the teaching of general principles." To realize the "bioexhibit" of the future as envisioned here, zoo professionals must follow his prescription. In so doing, the product achieved will serve to further contribute to the explication of unifying concepts and general principles of the natural world.

Acknowledgments

We thank the following colleagues who have provided us with critical comments, or examples from their own experience: E.F. Gibbons, Jr., K.C. Gold, N. Lash, L.A. Perkins, C.D. Schaaf, E.F. Stevens, and S.W. Winslow.

VI

Marine Mammals

Introduction of Authors
and Chapter Previews

Sam Ridgway, author of the conservation of marine mammals chapter, is a senior scientist in Animal Care at the Naval Ocean Systems Center in San Diego, California. He also holds an adjunct professorship in the Department of Veterinary Physiology and Pharmacology at Texas A & M University and serves on the Boards of Veterinary Medical Examiners in both Texas and California. Dr. Ridgway is responsible for the world-wide medical care program for all Navy marine mammals, including the biomedical research that supports that program. His volumes *Mammals of the Sea: Biology and Medicine* (Thomas, Springfield, Il.) and *Handbook of Marine Mammals*, Vols. I & II (with R.J. Harrison, coeditor; Academic Press, London) have been major sources for understanding the physiologic and behavioral functioning of these animals.

In his chapter, Dr. Ridgway reviews the current status of wild and captive populations of Cetacea, Sirenia, and marine mammal representatives of the Order Carnivora. He recognizes that difficulties in housing the larger Cetacean species coupled with the lack of knowledge regarding the natural history of marine mammals in the wild will complicate captive breeding efforts for many species. To facilitate the preservation of these highly visible mammals, Dr. Ridgway calls for cooperation between conservationists and animal rights activists.

The reproductive physiology of marine mammals chapter was prepared by J. Pete Schroeder. Dr. Schroeder has been research/attending veterinarian at Sea World San Diego, Scripps Institute of Oceanography Physiological Research Laboratory, Naval Ocean Systems Center (NOSC) Hawaii Laboratory and Ocean Park, Hong Kong. As manager of the NOSC captive breeding research program, he developed semen collection and artificial insemination techniques for dolphins. He directed the preventive medicine program at NOSC Hawaii from 1981 to 1992 and is currently a private consultant in marine mammal breeding at Schroeder Research Associates in Washington.

Dr. Schroeder has chosen to discuss the relatively well documented reproductive physiology of the bottlenose dolphin as a model for endangered cetacean species. He illustrates how husbandry and training techniques facilitate the noninvasive collection of blood and urine for hormone analysis and semen for cryopreservation studies and artificial insemination.

The behavior of marine mammals is discussed by Susie Ellis, program officer for the Captive Breeding Specialist Group of the IUCN—The World Conservation Union's Species Survival commission. Dr. Ellis, a comparative psychologist by training, has carried out behavioral research with birds, primates, and marine mammals. Her approach to the present chapter is, therefore, applied in nature. She views research in captivity as essential in providing insight concerning the basic biology of species. It is Dr. Ellis' opinion that collaborative research programs, both *in situ* and *ex situ*, with vigorous interdisciplinary exchange and cooperation between researchers in the field and in zoological facilities will be an essential key in conserving endangered species. She feels that these programs are the only means by which adequate information can be obtained to allow informed decision-making for species conservation.

In her chapter, Dr. Ellis emphasizes the importance of normal social groups for captive marine mammals, explaining that, although the behavior of one individual is not necessarily an accurate reflection of the physiological status of the group, the behavior of the group can often be assessed to learn about the status of individuals. She discusses the types of behavioral research that can be pursued most effectively in captive settings and how training marine mammals can facilitate studies on cognitive behavior and sensory abilities.

The marine mammal captive design chapter is coauthored by Jay Sweeney and Terry Samansky. Dr. Sweeney, chief veterinarian at Veterinary Consultant Services, has been extensively involved in the conduct and support of clinical research projects involving marine mammals. His scientific emphasis has been on the development of advanced information on diseases, diagnostic therapeutic techniques, and preventive medicine. Dr. Sweeney's present interests include the development of new concepts in display facility design and operations for marine mammals. Mr. Samansky, curator of Marine Mammals at Marine World Africa, U.S.A., has conducted research in the medical care and rehabilitation of stranded marine mammals. He recognizes that through the effective exhibition of marine mammals in captivity, advances will be made in public education, research, and conservation which will help to preserve wild populations and their habitats.

These authors express their enthusiasm for the innovations in marine mammal exhibit design that are playing an important role in the increased health and survival rates of captive species. In addition, modern exhibit design and management practices enhance the visitor experience, thus increasing the public's knowledge and appreciation of marine mammals as integral components of the earth's marine environment.

21

The Tides of Change: Conservation of Marine Mammals

Sam H. Ridgway

Marine mammals are represented in three taxonomic Orders of mammals: Cetacea, Sirenia, and Carnivora. Normally spending their entire lives in water, all extant members of Cetacea and Sirenia arc designated marine mammals and include both fresh and salt water species. Some of the Order Carnivora spend considerable periods of time (many months) in the water, but none are totally aquatic. Within the Order Carnivora there are several families that include marine mammals: Otariidae or eared seals (fur seals and sea lions), Odobenidae (walrus), Phocidae (true seals), Mustelidae (chungungo and sea otters), and one member of the family Ursidae (polar bears).

In the United States, all marine mammals are legally protected by the Marine Mammal Protection Act of 1972. The U.S. Fish and Wildlife Service (FWS) of the U.S. Department of the Interior is responsible for administering regulations under this Act for polar bears, walrus, manatees, and sea otters, while the National Marine Fisheries Service of the U.S. Department of Commerce is responsible for all whales, dolphins, seals, sea lions, and other marine mammals not regulated by FWS. In addition, another independent body, the Marine Mammal Commission, maintains a scientific committee to advise on scientific issues related to marine mammal conservation. Those species designated as endangered are further protected under the Endangered Species Act of 1973.

Pressures that affect marine mammal populations worldwide are many and include fishing (gill nets, drift nets, ghost nets, the yellowfin tuna purse-seine fishery, rolling hooks), pollution (agricultural run-off, industrial waste, petroleum spills, trash dumping), deforestation and development of the rain forests, damming, oil field development, mining, and other human actions.

Status in the Wild

The Cetacea: Whales, Dolphins, and Porpoises

The larger cetaceans include Physeteroidea (sperm whales), Ziphoidea (beaked whales and bottlenose whales), and Suborder Mysticeti (baleen whales). Eight of the eleven species of large whales appeared on the 1987 U.S. List of "Endangered and Threatened Wildlife" including the sperm (*Physeter macrocephalus*), blue (*Balaenoptera musculus*), finback (*Balaenoptera physalus*), bowhead (*Balaena mysticetus*), sei (*Balaenoptera borealis*), gray (*Eschrichtius robustus*), humpback (*Megaptera novaeangliae*), and right (*Eubalaena glacialis*).

The sperm whale (see Rice, 1989) has been listed on the U.S. Endangered Species List, even though there may be about 1.5 million sperm whales in the world's oceans where they are probably of great ecological significance (Kanwisher and Ridgway, 1983). The great baleen whales have been the mainstays of the whaling industry of the past. Because of their past exploitation by whalers and recent publicity regarding this exploitation, most are assumed by the public to be endangered species; however, in the absence of the resumption of full commercial whaling, these larger cetaceans are in reality not endangered—including those that appear on the endangered species list. Some of these species have been completely protected for many years and all are currently protected by the moratorium on commercial whaling promulgated by the International Whaling Commission (IWC). Brownell et al. (1989) suggest that some of these large whales be removed from the endangered species list while some small cetaceans should be added to the list. In fact, the 1994 IUCN Red List of Threatened Animals lists only the right and blue whales as endangered species (IUCN, 1993).

The arctic white whale or beluga (*Delphinapterus leucas*), is still hunted by natives of the far north, but the major depletion was probably caused by past exploitation (Klinowska, 1991). Because white whales migrate to a relatively few estuaries and river mouths for calving, some populations could be impacted by development in such areas. Human activities such as oil and gas development, mining, hydroelectric plant construction, and increased commercial fishing may be leading to changes in white whale distribution (Hazard, 1988; Smith et al., 1990). Some populations are far below historic levels (Braham, 1984). Accurate surveys and population estimates are necessary for effective management of the species.

Recently down listed from endangered to vulnerable, the bowhead whale is an example of successful management, especially in Alaska where there has been cooperative catch monitoring. Although subsistence hunting of the bowhead continues, the involvement of the local people in the management of the species has resulted in a limited take which will probably not threaten the species.

There are more than 40 species of smaller cetaceans, dolphins, and porpoises found worldwide. While no cetacean species has been driven yet to extinction by human endeavors (Perrin, 1988), four species of the smaller cetaceans are in jeopardy in the coming decades if some human activities in their habitats are not changed (Brownell, 1991; Norris, 1992). These include the baiji (*Lipotes vexillifer*), the black dolphin (*Cephalorhynchus eutropia*), the Indus dolphin (*Plantanista minor*), and the vaquita (*Phocoena sinus*).

The most seriously threatened cetacean species belong to Superfamily Platanistoidea, which is made up of mostly river dolphins. All living genera of the Platanistidae: Ganges dolphin (*Plantanista gangetica*), Indus dolphin, baiji, and franciscana (*Pontoporia blainvillei*), are threatened by human activities including damming, development, pollution, habitat encroachment, and fishing.

Living only in the Yangtze River system of central China (Chen, 1989), the baiji may be the most endangered of all cetacean species. It is possible that less than 200 individuals remain (Norris, 1992) due to development, fishing practices, collisions with boats, use of explosives, extensive habitat damage, and possible food shortage (Perrin et al., 1989; Klinowska, 1991). Recently, baiji have been afforded the highest level of protection by the Chinese government. This protection, in concert with worldwide and community support, may result in saving the species.

Also threatened by fishing, the franciscana of coastal South America are often caught in gill nets set by shark fishermen, but there is too little information about the population to determine whether the animal is endangered (see Brownell, 1989). On the most recent expedition to the coast of Chile to find black dolphins, only two small groups were found (Norris, 1992). These charcoal and white dolphins are being harpooned to serve as crab bait for a fishery that may also target Commerson's dolphin (*Cephalorhynchus commersonii*). Although protected by law since 1977, these species depend on law enforcement as well as an alternative source of bait (Klinowska, 1991). Living in the Amazon and Orinoco Rivers of South America, the boto (*Inia geoffrensis*), and tucuxi (*Sotalia fluviatilis*), may be seriously threatened by the deforestation and development of the rain forests, especially by the damming of river systems (Klinowska, 1991).

In Southern Asia, the Ganges dolphin and the Indus dolphin are threatened by gill net fishing, illegal capture, construction of dams or irrigation barrages, loss of habitat, and pollution of the rivers (Perrin et al., 1989; Reeves and Brownell, 1989; Reeves et al., 1991). The Indus dolphin population is estimated to be 500 individuals (Reeves et al., 1991).

Only one small cetacean species from the Superfamily Delphinoidea appears immediately vulnerable to extinction—the vaquita or Gulf of California harbor porpoise. The vaquita population is severely depleted apparently due to its entrapment in fishing gear (Barlow, 1986; Brownell, 1986).

Populations of a million or so of the fast-moving, striking black and white Dall's porpoise (*Phocoenoides dalli*), found in the North Pacific may have declined sharply in recent years. As the supply of whale meat decreased, fishing pressure on these animals increased; 40,000 were taken in 1988 (Norris, 1992). After a study by Dr. Toshio Kasuya showed that continued pressure would severely threaten the population, the Japanese government demanded a sharp decline in the catch. However, it is possible that even with the 15% planned reduction of catches for 1990, the take will be too much to sustain the population (Klinowska, 1991). A similar situation has threatened the finless porpoise (*Neophocaena phocaenoides*). In the absence of a rapid reversal of these trends some dolphins and porpoises face extinction in this century or early in the next century.

The Sirenia: Dugongs and Manatees

Although they receive much less attention by the media, the Sirenia are probably more endangered than any of the great whales with the possible exception of right whales. In fact, a sirenian species has become extinct in modern times. In 1841 Georg Wilhelm Steller, a member of the Bering expedition in the North Pacific, wrote of the sea cows found on Bering Island in the Commander Islands off Kamchatka. These sea cows probably grew to lengths of more than

8 m and weights of nearly 3600 kg. The heart of a single animal weighed as much as 16 kg. Steller and the group of stranded explorers enjoyed the tender meat of the large and docile mammals later called the great northern sea cow or Steller's sea cow (*Hydrodamalis gigas*). The men with Steller may have eaten the sea cows only to survive, but by 1868 hunters had apparently destroyed the last of the remaining great northern sea cows (Nishiwaki and Marsh, 1985). Dugongs and manatees are the two living genera of Sirenia and represent two distinct families of plant grazing marine mammals that are found in separate parts of the world.

The dugong is the only surviving member of its family; the other four subfamilies are extinct. Viewed dorsally, the dugong appears like a rather rotund dolphin; dugong tail flukes resemble those of dolphins and other small whales (see Nishiwaki and Marsh, 1985 for an excellent review of this species). Dugongs occur in tropical and subtropical shallows of the Indo-Pacific where they graze on sea grasses and algae. Dugong meat is appreciated in many human cultures and dugong oil is prized for medicinal properties. Although the animals are still hunted over most of their range, much of this hunting is now illegal.

There may be some 70,000 dugongs in the waters of northern Australia (Brownell, 1991). Small populations are scattered around Indonesia with an area of abundance around the Aru Islands. Dugong populations are sparse or greatly reduced around Sri Lanka, India, the Arabian Peninsula, and along most of the east African coast and Madagascar. However, there are areas of abundance off southern Somalia and the southern end of the State of Bahrain in the Arabian (Persian) Gulf. A natural dugong reserve has been established along the Guangxi coast of China (Zhou, 1991).

Other than the dugong, the elephant and the hyrax are the closest living relatives of the manatee. The geographic ranges of manatees and dugongs do not overlap; distinguishing the two living genera of sirenians may be mainly of taxonomic interest. The most obvious physical distinction between manatees and dugongs is that the manatee has flattened, rounded flukes, whereas dugongs have flukes resembling those of dolphins and other small whales.

There are three living species of manatees: The West Indian or Florida manatee (*Trichechus manatus*), the African manatee (*T. senegalensis*), and the Amazonian manatee (*T. inunguis*). Manatees seem to prefer shallow estuaries and swampy areas where aquatic plants are abundant (Caldwell and Caldwell, 1985). They are at times found in fresh water, brackish water, or marine waters.

West Indian manatees range from about Georgia on the coast of the U.S. to the coast of Brazil; however, there is a very patchy distribution over this wide range. The population in the southeastern United States is one of the most endangered marine mammal populations in coastal waters of the United States and is estimated to number at least 1,200 animals (1990 report to the Marine Mammal Commission). Steps are being taken to restore manatee populations in Florida. These include: (1) defining manatee habitat use patterns and key population parameters, (2) identifying areas where manatees are most likely to be struck by boats, (3) implementing site-specific protection measures to reduce vessel-related deaths, (4) reducing potentially hazardous development in essential manatee habitat, and (5) acquiring additional manatee habitat for incorporation into existing protected areas. (See Marine Mammal Commission, 1991 for details of this program.)

The African manatee is generally rare in its West African range from the Senegal River in the north to the Cuanza River of Angola in the south. The area of greatest abundance is apparently the Niger river and its tributaries (Nishiwaki et al., 1982); however, there are areas of density along the coast of Sierra Leone. Even though protected by law, African manatees are still caught in fishermen's gill nets and trapped for food (Reeves et al., 1988). The Amazonian manatee is found in the Amazon basin and possibly parts of the Orinoco river system as well.

The Carnivora: Pinnipeds, Otters, and Bears

While cetaceans and sirenians are totally aquatic, the marine Carnivora all spend some time on land to breed and bear their young. The breeding areas are therefore especially sensitive to human encroachment. As with cetaceans, there are species that live in fresh water as well as in the sea. Marine mammals in the Order Carnivora include fur seals and sea lions, true seals, walrus, chungungo and sea otters, and polar bears.

Pinnipeds. Pinniped means "feather footed," and the Suborder Pinnipedia includes three families: Otariidae (fur seals and sea lions), Phocidae (true seals), and Odobenidae (walrus). Pinnipeds account for 28% of marine mammal species. While most pinniped species are usually found in salt water, a few are found in fresh water lakes. Historically, almost all pinnipeds have been hunted at one time for fur, meat, oil, or ivory. Brownell (1991) suggests that during the 1990s, while most pinniped species will probably experience an increase in number, at least three species: northern fur seal (*Callorhinus ursinus*), Steller's sea lion (*Eumetopias jubatus*), and monk seal (*Monachus monachus*), will continue to decline in the absence of stronger corrective measures. One pinniped species, the West Indian monk seal (*Monachus tropicalis*), has apparently become extinct during this century.

Fur Seals and Sea Lions. Northern fur seal populations have declined but still number more than one million. A decline in pup production of as much as 50% between the late 1950s and the 1980s has been attributed to harvest of female fur seals from 1956 to 1968, and in recent years to entanglement in fishing gear and marine debris (Brownell, 1991). Populations of southern fur seals of the genus *Arctocephalus* appear to be on the increase.

The Steller's sea lion population of the North Pacific has been in decline. Counts in 1985 were more than 80% less than counts taken in 1958 (from about 250,000 to 68,000 individuals). Causes of the decline probably include catches incidental to fishing (hooks, nets, entanglement in gear), shooting, and scarcity of the animal's prey species (Brownell, 1991).

The California sea lion (*Zalophus californianus*), historically is probably the best known of all marine mammals because it is quite common in exhibits around the world. In the wild, the California population is very robust and the Galapagos population is persevering; however, the Japanese population is severely endangered or extinct in the wild. There are rumors of sea lions living under Korean cliffs (King, 1983), but there have been no recent confirmed sightings.

The Australian sea lion (*Neophoca cinerea*), numbers perhaps a few thousand individuals off southern and western Australia; the New Zealand sea lion (*Phocarctos hookeri*), also has a small population.

True Seals. Some true seals or phocids live in temperate and even tropical areas; however, it is near the frozen poles that they are most numerous. Those species occurring at the two poles are separate and distinct. Only the more temperate-dwelling elephant seal (genus *Mirounga*) lives on both sides of the equator. The harbor seal or common seal (*Phoca vitulina*) is found in more temperate areas of the northern hemisphere. Although much attention has been focused on the harp seal (*Phoca groenlandica*) because pictures of hunters clubbing the snow-white pups appeal so strongly to human emotions, the most endangered of the phocids are the monk seals.

The status of the world's populations of monk seals is precarious. The Caribbean monk seal (*Monachus tropicalis*) is considered to be extinct. Population estimates for the Mediterranean monk seal (*Monachus monachus*) appear to be around 500 and declining (Brownell, 1991). Pollution, human disturbance, heavy boat traffic, reduction in food sources, and competition for a failing fishery are all contributing to this reduction in numbers.

Recovery efforts with the Hawaiian monk seal (*Monachus schauinslandi*) have been more successful. Found mostly in the northwestern Hawaiian Islands, the Hawaiian monk seal population declined on some islands by about 50% between the late 1950s and the late 1970s (Johnson et al., 1982). In 1981 the National Marine Fisheries Service (NMFS) and the Southwest Fisheries Center Honolulu laboratory (SWFC), initiated recovery efforts on several of the islands (see Gilmartin, 1988). On Kure Atoll a project nicknamed "Head Start" was begun. One of the most seriously depleted, the Kure population primarily consisted of adult animals. Juvenile seals were seldom seen on the beach. Additionally, the sex ratio was biased towards males. In the head start program, female pups were placed in protective care in natural ocean and beach enclosures for the first few months following weaning. Under this protection they learned how to catch live reef fish, and were released when natural seasonal pressures that included shark predation and adult male monk seal aggression were reduced. Results have been encouraging. In 1987 one of the first pups in the head start project gave birth. In 1992, 8 of the 14 females that pupped on Kure had been participants in this program (Swensen, pers. comm.). In 1992, the Coast Guard's almost 30 year presence on the small atoll ended, leaving a recovering population behind. Without human disturbance on the atoll, it is hoped the population will continue its recovery. One of the known pressures still plaguing monk seal populations on all the islands is potential entanglement in marine debris, especially fishing nets and lines. A mysterious reduction in pup production throughout the entire range of the Hawaiian monk seal during 1990, and the recent decline of the once recovering population on French Frigate Shoals also shadow the recovery process (Gilmartin et al., 1990).

Walrus. The walrus (*Odobenus rosmarus*) is the only living member of the family Odobenidae. Walrus have traits in common with sea lions and seals. Similar to the sea lions, walrus can use rear flippers to move upright across rocky shores or ice floes; however, a trait they share with true seals is the absence of external ear pinna. In the wild, walrus dive in the seas of the far north to feed on benthic fauna including bivalve mollusks and other invertebrates that they locate with sensitive whiskers (Kastelein et al., 1990a) and rake with their giant tusks. When housed in concrete tanks, this natural behavior can become a problem, resulting in tusk wear and perhaps dento-alveolar abscesses (Brown, 1962). The Pacific walrus population appears to be fairly robust (about 250,000 animals) but the Atlantic population is about one-quarter as large (Sease and Chapman, 1988).

Sea Otters and Polar Bears. The sea otter of the North Pacific (*Enhydra lutris*) is a coastal animal that is often associated with kelp beds just off the coast of California, British Columbia, and Alaska. Recently, one population of sea otters was threatened by the huge oil spill that occurred with the grounding of the tanker Exxon Valdez in Alaska. Otters are more likely to be killed by oil spills than any other marine mammal because of their narrow coastal habitats and because their fur must maintain a layer of air to keep its insulating properties. Oil can disrupt this essential fur insulation and the otter may soon die from hypothermia.

The marine otter of the coasts of Peru and Chile, chungungo (*Lutra felina*), is severely endangered because the animals are hunted for their prized pelts on the Chilean coast, and because Peruvians often shoot them as a menace to fishing. Although the animals have been legally protected for many years, this protection has apparently not been effective (Miller et al., 1983). Another large otter (*Lutra longicaudis*) of northeast Brazil is threatened by fishing, clandestine hunting, and habitat degradation (Almeida et al., 1991).

The polar bear from the family Ursidae preys primarily on ringed seals, but other marine mammals such as the bearded seal (*Erignathus barbatus*), the white whale, and the narwhal (*Monodon monoceros*), are also taken. Although polar bears have been seen some distance at sea, they spend most of their time on ice (where they hunt seals in dens or ice holes) or on land. In the past, polar bears were hunted for sport and for hides, but now they are almost totally protected in the U.S. and are not considered to be endangered.

In Canada, hunting continues but is carefully managed (Amstrup and DeMaster, 1988).

Conservation Programs in Captivity

The Cetacea: Whales, Dolphins, Porpoises

For some small cetacean species, captive breeding may be a partial solution to ensure their survival. The International Union for Conservation of Nature and Natural Resources policy statement on captive breeding (IUCN, 1988b) recommends the establishment of supporting captive populations. Ideally, these breeding programs would be established when the wild population is still in the thousands. Some cetacean species are not viable candidates for such a program because their large size or temperament make them unsuitable for maintenance with present methods. For the majority of cetacean species, very little is known about them either in the wild or under human care. For some species like the baiji and the Indus dolphin, captive breeding programs could probably save them from extinction.

A majority of cetacean species have been kept for only short periods of time—often a result of stranding. Much of what is known about some cetaceans has been gleaned through such encounters. This is true of the beaked whales, Ziphoidea. Next to the sperm whale, the beaked whales are the largest toothed whales. There are 18 species of these beaked whales for which relatively few scientific data are available (see Balcomb, 1989; Heyning, 1989; Mead 1989a, b, c). Only occasional stranded individuals have been kept for short periods. With our present capabilities and poor knowledge base, large size precludes most if not all of the beaked whales from captive breeding.

A few stranded sperm whale calves have been kept alive in oceanarium tanks for a few days or weeks, but no adults have been in human care. Adults and calves of pygmy sperm whales (*Kogia breviceps* and *K. simus*) have also been subjects of rescue attempts after stranding but none have been kept for long periods.

A number of small cetacean species have been kept for varying periods of time in aquaria, oceanaria, and research laboratories. The genus *Stenella* comprises mostly open ocean dolphins that have been difficult to keep. The Atlantic spotted dolphin (*S. frontalis*) has been kept with some success in Florida, and the spinner dolphin (*S. longirostris*) has been kept in Hawaii. There have been a few captive births but none lived for long. A similar situation is true of Fraser's dolphin (*Lagenodelphis hosei*) and northern and southern right whale dolphins (*Lissodelphis borealis* and *L. peronii*). Dall porpoise have been kept in California, but have never reproduced successfully (Ridgway, 1966; Walker, 1975). The Pacific white-sided dolphin (*Lagenorhynchus obliquidens*) has bred in captivity, but has not reared offspring. The common dolphin (*Delphinus delphis*) and the Indo-Pacific hump-backed dolphin (*Sousa chinensis*) have been kept under human care but have never bred, and Risso's dolphin (*Grampus griseus*), short-finned pilot whale (*Globicephala macrorhynchus*), and the false killer whale (*Pseudorca crassidens*) have produced hybrid calves with the bottlenose dolphin (*Tursiops truncatus*). The tucuxi has been kept at several oceanaria. The riverine variety of tucuxi has never survived very long in captivity; however, displays of the marine variety in Western Europe have been more successful (Terry, 1986). One dolphin was born at the Nuremberg Zoo but did not survive. Over 107 finless porpoise have been kept in Japan, China, and Java. There has been breeding at three Japanese establishments, resulting in at least two successful births (Kasuya et al., 1986).

A captive pair of baiji has been held at the Institute of Hydrobiology at Wuhan, China near the center of this dolphin's range. The conditions for the Wuhan pair were inadequate because the water supply could not be rapidly exchanged and a filtration system was not available to maintain sanitary water quality. Despite these drawbacks, a male has survived for about nine years in Wuhan (as of this writing) after extensive treatment of severe rolling hook wounds received from entanglement in fishing gear. Hopefully the Chinese can modernize their facilities and enhance their capability to rescue animals that are injured in the future.

In November 1986, scientists and conservationists met in Wuhan, China to assess the status of platanistoid dolphins, and to discuss means of saving these endangered animals from extinction. The proceedings of this conference have now been published (Perrin and Brownell, 1989). Proposals for the rescue of the baiji put forth at the Wuhan meeting in 1986 included the establishment of semi-natural reserves. Two reserves are currently being developed in an effort to promote the survival and recovery of the wild population of baiji (Baiji Research Group, 1989; Zhou, 1989a). In these reserves, the animals remain in the waters of the Yangtze River, but barriers prevent their escape from the safety of the reserve. Under this protection and the guidelines of a semicaptive breeding program (see Ralls 1989 for an outline of this program), the population can be monitored and studied. If the rescue scheme is adopted by the People's Republic of China, the effort will represent the first official and direct attempt to save an endangered cetacean by such means. A similar program may also benefit the Indus dolphin (Reeves et al., 1991). Immediate action is crucial. Development of semicaptive reserves and breeding colonies will take time—time that may not be available unless dolphin mortality incidental to fishing and other human activities in the river can be eliminated.

The development of techniques for propagating the river dolphins may become the single most important key to ensure the survival of the rapidly decreasing wild populations (Ridgway et al., 1989). To date, few platanistoid dolphins have been born in captivity and there is no established record of husbandry or research to provide guidelines for propagating them. The few baiji that have been kept at Wuhan were, out of necessity, maintained in inadequate facilities. These facilities must be upgraded before more attempts are made to keep baiji. The boto (*Inia geoffrensis*) is more numerous than some of the other platanistoids and it has been kept in captivity. Perhaps this species could serve as a model for developing techniques for propagation of the more endangered platanistoids. Captive breeding to maintain and restore wild populations of river dolphins may be much needed insurance against natural or man-made disasters.

Some cetacean species have bred successfully in human care; however, most are from the Superfamily Delphinoidea. These species include the bottlenose dolphin, Commerson's dolphin, and killer whale (*Orcinus orca*), which have bred at Sea World in San Diego, California (Joseph et al., 1987; Cornell et al., 1988b). Several small white whale (*Delphinapterus leucas*) groups are maintained in the U.S. and there are others in Canada, Europe, Japan, and the Soviet Union. White whales have successfully bred at the Vancouver Public Aquarium, at the Aquarium for Wildlife Conservation (New York), the Tacoma Zoo, and at the Sea Worlds in San Diego and San Antonio. As of this writing, two calves survive in New York and one in San Antonio. The Irrawaddy dolphin (*Orcaella brevirostris*) has been kept and successfully bred at the Jaya Oncol Oceanarium in Indonesia (Marsh et al., 1989).

Delphinid species in several locations have produced crossbred offspring. All of these crosses have involved bottlenose dolphins and pilot whales, rough-toothed dolphins (*Steno bredanensis*), false killer whales, or Risso's dolphins. A "wolfon," a cross between a bottlenose dolphin and a false killer whale at Sea Life Park in Hawaii, produced two live calves—the first at five years of age. The first calf died soon after birth, but the second survived and is over a year of age at this writing. These events prove that this "wolfon" hybrid is fertile.

From September 1985 until the end of 1991, there have been eight births of killer whales at Sea World parks in California, Texas, and Florida. At this writing, six of these offspring are alive and well and over one year of age. In three different Canadian aquaria, there have been six births with three still alive. With a birth weight of about 150 kg, these killer whale calves are the largest mammals to be born to animals in human care (also see Duffield and Miller, 1988).

The greatest breeding success can be claimed by those who keep bottlenose dolphins. A plentiful small toothed whale, the bottlenose dolphin has been successfully bred in many countries. By 1975, over 150 bottlenose dolphins had been born in collections worldwide (Ridgway and Benirschke, 1977). Second generation offspring have been produced in a few locations. In North America alone, 204 successful births occurred from 1976 to 1990 (Asper et al., 1990a). The first successful long-term breeding occurred at Marineland of Florida where there were 40 births between 1939 and 1969 of which 30% of the calves survived more than one year. By the mid-1980s, this overall survival rate more than doubled in North American oceanaria (Cornell et al., 1987; DeMaster and Drevenak, 1988), and the rate of stillbirths was also reduced (Schroeder, 1990b).

In the past, most of the dolphin breeding occurred in large tanks or enclosures with several adult females and usually just one adult male. Births occurred in the same group. At the time of birth and soon afterward, aggression may have occurred in groups, especially if males were present. Bull dolphins have been found to be aggressive toward each other and sometimes towards mothers and calves (McBride and Hebb, 1948; Essapian, 1963; Wood, 1977; Zeiller, 1977). It is possible that this male aggression and competition between some of the females resulted in the high incidence of reported stillbirths and calf mortality. Because these earlier groupings were successful in breeding dolphins but not in rearing them, new strategies were devised in some collections. Pregnant females were moved alone or with other compatible females to "nursery" tanks or pens. At Sea World in San Diego, more than 40 pregnancies have been handled in this manner and a majority of the calves survived to be weaned. At the Naval Ocean Systems Center (NOSC) facilities in San Diego and Hawaii, there have been at least 10 bottlenose dolphin pregnancies in which the mother was separated from all other dolphins (personal observation). In each case the offspring survived past weaning age, and one female reared in this way became pregnant at age 11 and reared her own first offspring. Evidently, a dolphin mother does not require an "auntie" dolphin to assist in rearing her young nor does isolation with its mother for the first year have any obvious negative influences on the calf.

Bottlenose dolphins as young as 7 years and as old as 36 years have borne calves, although females (on the average) do not fully mature until around age 12 and males a year or two older (Sergeant et al., 1973). Bottlenose dolphin births have occurred during every month of the year although peak calving periods have been observed during spring and fall. Dolphin females that have had stillbirths have calved again in as little as 13 months (Ridgway and Benirschke, 1977; Cornell et al., 1987). When births and rearing have been successful, in the U.S. the minimum calving interval has been just over two years but three or more years has been most usual (Cornell et al., 1987). At Sea World of Australia, one female produced live calves at intervals of only 20 and 15 months (Hayes-Lovell, pers. comm.). The mothers and calves are not normally handled until the calf is one-year-old, however, some ill calves have been successfully handled and treated. Photographic methods have been used to measure growth rates of some calves (Scott, pers. comm.). A comparison of survival rates and other demographic features of captive bottlenose dolphins with a wild population off Sarasota, Florida, suggests that values for reproductive parameters may favor the captive population (Duffield and Wells, 1991)—further emphasizing that the species might serve as a model for breeding other cetaceans in the future.

The Sirenia: Dugongs and Manatees

About 30 dugongs have been captured for display but few have survived. This species' low survival rate may be due to the young age of captured animals, because many were not yet weaned (Nishiwaki and Marsh, 1985). Two dugongs were kept at the Marine Fisheries Institute at Cochin, India, for 11 years. Others were kept at Toba Aquarium in Japan, at Jaya Ancol Oceanarium near Jakarta, Indonesia, and at Expo Aquarium in Okinawa (Uchida, 1991). There is not much information available about the husbandry of these animals.

Some injured manatees are treated and rehabilitated at oceanaria such as Miami Seaquarium and Sea World in Orlando, Florida.

Manatees have been held in both fresh and saline waters for considerable periods of time. One was maintained at Bradenton, Florida for 29 years (Brownell and Ralls, 1981). Miami Seaquarium has had a small but successful breeding program (White, 1984 b, c) and Sea World of Florida has recently had successful captive births. Mexico traded two manatees for two giant pandas. The manatees have produced two young at the Bejing zoo, one of which survived (Zhou, 1991). Twins were born at Expo Aquarium in Okinawa but died after 34 and 37 days (Uchida, 1991).

The Carnivora: Pinnipeds, Otters, Bears

From 1976 to 1990, 884 California sea lions were born in the world's zoos and oceanaria (Asper et al., 1990a). As a result of this prolific captive breeding and the successful salvage efforts for the numerous sea lions that were found beached in a sick and dying condition, very few sea lions have been taken from the wild for exhibit in recent years.

Both southern (with the exception of *Arctocephalus phillippii*) and northern fur seals have been held at various zoos and oceanaria around the world. They have adapted well to captivity and have often bred (Bonner, 1981).

The Australian sea lion (*Neophoca cinerea*) has been kept successfully in several locations including Atlantis Marine Park near Perth. Reportedly, the New Zealand sea lion (*Phocarctos hookeri*) has not been held in captivity since four were taken to the London Zoo in 1887 (Walker and Ling, 1981). The large South American sea lion (*Otaria flavescens*) has been successfully bred at the Montevideo Zoo (Vas-Ferreira, 1981).

Walrus have been kept quite successfully at a number of zoos. In 1990, there were 22 in zoos and oceanaria worldwide (Asper et al., 1990a). Harbor seals are also found abundantly in aquaria and zoological parks where captive breeding has been very successful. Indeed, from 1979–1983, 50% of acquired harbor seals came from captive breeding programs (Asper et al., 1988). Further, both extant species of monk seal have been kept at various zoos and aquaria. A rescue and research program keeps several seals at Sea Life Park, Hawaii. There are no captive breeding programs established for monk seals.

Sea otters have been kept at several zoos and aquaria. They have a high metabolic rate, their food is relatively expensive, and are not easy to maintain. Finally, polar bears have been kept and bred successfully in many zoos.

Problems Facing Conservation Programs in Captivity

Lack of knowledge regarding the natural history of marine mammals in the wild is one of the greatest problems facing captive conservation programs. Monetary and educational support for further research of marine mammal species both in the wild and in human care is urgently needed. An additional negative force is placed on zoological parks, aquaria, and research facilities by animal activist groups with an anthropomorphic view of the animals, especially cetaceans. In the most severe cases these groups cause closure of the very institutions that are working to learn more about these animals. Precious time and money is spent defending such institutions against law suits and against publicized claims of abuse that are usually contrived and unfounded. It is time that conservation groups and those providing care for cetaceans work together for the benefit of these species.

Conclusions: The Future

The existence of marine mammals in the direct care of humans is a recent development on a worldwide basis. In the past 30 years, much progress has been made in understanding marine mammal biology through the study of sea mammals in human care. Millions of people who otherwise would have no proximate experience with these sea mammals have appreciated and learned about them. Further, some sea mammals have become symbols and vehicles for educating the public about the world's oceans and their ecosystems. Protection of ocean ecosystems must be a high priority as we look toward the twenty-first century. At the top of the ocean food chain, the fish-eating sea mammals may be important indicator species for understanding the effects of some human activities on the ocean environment. With the exception of the endangered river dolphins, breeding marine mammals in captivity to replace depleted stocks in the wild is not a likely alternative in the near future. In a few instances, small numbers of captive-born animals might be released to join wild stocks. This might happen with, for example, manatees. Unfortunately, in many cases, we have little experience in the captive care of the species most severely threatened. For now, captive rehabilitation of injured or ill wild animals appears much more important than captive breeding in the protection and augmentation of wild populations of marine mammals.

Zoos, marine parks, aquaria, and research laboratories housing marine mammals often take an active role in rehabilitating beached or stranded marine mammals (precautions must be taken so that ill animals do not infect healthy individuals being kept permanently). Marine mammal stranding networks have been set up in many coastal areas of the United States to retrieve and rehabilitate beached or stranded marine mammals. In this process, we can gain valuable information about the threats in the marine environment of today. As new knowledge is acquired the public can be informed about threats to marine mammal populations from human activities such as boating, water pollution, and from various fishing methods (for example, drift nets, gill nets, seines, and rolling hooks) that kill marine mammals incidentally.

Progress must continue in all fields of marine mammal biology. We can enhance the condition and extend the lifespan of animals in our care. Preventive medicine, improved disease treatment through better medications such as new antibiotics, and improved methods for anesthesia and surgery should be more widely practiced.

Regional and international studbooks are being developed. In Europe, a studbook has already been developed for bottlenose dolphins; a studbook for California sea lions is in preparation. In Japan, studbooks have been developed for the bottlenose dolphin, South American sea lion, largha seal (*Phoca largha*), Kuril harbor seal (*P. vitulina kurilensis*), California seal lion, sea otter, and harbor seal. The American Zoo and Aquariums Association (AZA) has formally adopted similar recommendations for its member institutions and has recently formed a Marine Mammal Taxon Advisory Group. As of 1992, studbooks have been developed in North America for the bottlenose dolphin and the West Indian manatee; stud-books are in various stages of development for the Pacific white-sided dolphin, walrus, northern fur seal, harbor seal, gray seal (*Halichoerus grypus*), California sea lion, white whale, and the killer whale. By sharing data, zoological facilities should be able to maximize genetic diversity and make major advances in the management for marine mammal taxa.

Those of us who keep sea mammals must develop partnerships not only with our colleagues, but also with the general public, the governmental agencies that are concerned with animals and the environment, and with environmental and wildlife organizations. Professional organizations in the marine mammal field include the Society for Marine Mammalogy, the International Marine

Mammal Trainers Association, and the International Association for Aquatic Animal Medicine. Also active in seal mammal conservation efforts are the International Whaling Commission through its scientific committee and the International Union for Conservation of Nature (IUCN) through the Captive Breeding Specialist Group (CBSG, Apple Valley Minnesota, U.S.A.) and the Cetacean Specialist Group (CSG, Ocean Park, Hong Kong).

A great deal of what is known about sea mammals derives from animals in human care. The sonar of dolphins, the special diving physiology of seals, and the cooperative nature of killer whales are but a few examples of scientific understanding that resulted from work with sea mammals in our care. Those oceanaria, aquaria, zoos, and other institutions who keep sea mammals have contributed to their revered standing and protected status in most of the modern industrialized countries today. Despite this fact, professionals and organizations keeping sea mammals often are attacked as exploiters. We need to continue to improve our abilities and facilities for keeping sea mammals, but especially we must do a better job of public education to gain a broader basis of support from environmental and conservation organizations. So far, marine mammal research has only scratched the surface and needs to continue if we are to protect marine mammals and their ecosystems in this world of expanding human populations.

22

Marine Mammal Reproductive Physiology

J. Pete Schroeder

The study of the reproductive physiology of marine mammals has complications not encountered in terrestrial animals: the aquatic environment, small total numbers of subjects, and relatively small variety of species in captivity are factors that limit physiological studies. This section primarily presents recent findings in captive breeding research with *Tursiops truncatus,* and applicability of those efforts to reproduction of endangered species of cetacea. Reviews of pinniped (Schroeder, 1990a), sirenian (Nishiwaki and Marsh, 1985; Caldwell and Caldwell, 1985; White and Floyd, 1990), and sea otter (Kenyon, 1981) reproduction are suggested for current information on reproduction of additional species of aquatic mammals.

The most common species of cetacean in captivity is the bottlenose dolphin (*Tursiops truncatus*) which is fortunately not an endangered species. When considering captive breeding of an endangered species, it is advisable to begin with studies of related common species that can provide a model system (Wildt et al., 1986). The bottlenose dolphin is the logical choice. The reproductive cycle of the male bottlenose dolphin has been defined (Schroeder and Keller, 1989) and techniques of artificial insemination (AI) have been developed (Schroeder, 1985; Schroeder and Keller, 1990); thus providing the bottlenose dolphin as a model for captive or seminatural breeding programs of endangered species of dolphins and porpoises. Necessary physiological information includes male and female anatomy, endocrinology (as it relates to reproductive cycles, especially estrus and ovulation), semen collection and cryopreservation, ovulation (spontaneous or induced), sexual and reproductive maturity, pregnancy diagnosis, gestation, parturition, and the intercalf interval. Meaningful physiological studies and breeding programs with captive marine mammals require extensive logistical and financial support. Additionally, a preventive medicine program must be in place to ensure the longevity of the breeding animals and survival of their progeny.

Consideration must also be given to the genetic problems of maintaining small numbers of marine mammals for captive breeding programs. What number of founders from an endangered species is necessary to provide long-term conservation? Is the objective to be release back into the wild, or to build and sustain a captive population of rare marine mammals not presently capable of self-sustaining reproduction in the wild? Selection of breeding stock for appearance, tameness, and adaptation to captivity is not always possible in a severely limited population.

Breeding plans based on population parameters should be followed regardless of the numbers of animals available. For example, the characteristics of free-ranging populations are typically subjected to stabilizing selection. Where the environment is heterogeneous, characters may be subjected to disruptive selection. Selection in captive populations should attempt to mimic this aspect of natural selection. This should take the form of selection against outliers for morphological characters and reproductive fitness characters (Frankham et al., 1986).

Ideally, the breeding sex ratio and social groups in the captive breeding programs should resemble those in the wild. As little is known about the reproductive and social behavior of most marine and aquatic mammals, it would be desirable to begin studies of the wild population to fill this gap in our knowledge (Ralls, 1989). For instance, the current estimated population of the baiji (*Lipotes vexillifer*) is approximately 200 individuals and is continuously declining (Chen et al., 1992). Their territory extends for 1,645 km, they are commonly seen in schools and are divided into 20 subgroups over their range (Lin et al., 1986; Chen and Hua, 1989). The social structure of the captive group should resemble, as closely as possible, a wild subgroup.

The reproductive physiology and biology of the bottlenose dolphin serves as the model system for the following discussion. Further study will illuminate its applicability to the survival of the platanistoid dolphins, the most endangered of the small odontocetes.

Reproductive Anatomy and Physiology
of the Female Tursiops

Anatomy

The ventrum of the female dolphin has one continuous ano-genital slit, with one mammary gland on each side under a short slit one to two cm lateral to the ano-genital slit (Harrison, 1969; Green, 1972, 1977). The female dolphin has a bicornate uterus very similar in appearance to those of the horse, dog and cow, but the dolphin has a unique pseudo cervix, combined with the true cervix, forming a spermathecal recess in the upper vagina. Some authors consider this cervix/pseudocervix as a true folding of the vaginal wall within a spermathecal recess (Harrison, 1969; Green 1972, 1977). Dissections of the female reproductive tracts of Pacific white-sided dolphins (*Lagenorhynchus obliquidens*), common dolphins (*Delphinus delphis*), harbor porpoises (*Phocoena*), striped dolphins (*Stenella coeruleoalba*), spinner dolphins (*Stenella longirostris*), and beluga whales (*Delphinapterus leucas*) all reveal the presence of a pseudocervix and spermathecal recess (Schroeder, 1985). Recently the dissection of a mature false killer whale (*Pseudorca crassidens*) revealed the same anatomical structures (Schroeder, Brook and Chow, unpublished data). The folds of the pseudocervix contain some muscle bundles and appear capable of movement (Harrison, 1969). The upper section of the vagina described in one of the platanistoid dolphins, the baiji, is covered with thin leaf-like folds. In addition to these, there are several rings of transverse folds facing the lower section of the vagina (Chen et al., 1984). Regardless of terminology (folds, rings, or pseudocervix), it is clear that the vaginas of these small odontocetes contain a remarkable anatomical adaptation for breeding in the marine environment. This "compartment," or spermathecal recess/space between the true cervix and the pseudocervix, is not as well defined in mammals that breed on land. The sow has a corkscrew-like (10–23 cm) cervix with 2–3 annular rings and the cow an 8–10 cm cervix with 3–4 annular rings (McDonald, 1977), indicating a commonalty with the cetacean. Perhaps a primitive common ancestor, a member of an archaic ungulate group Mesonychidae that lived some 60 million years ago (Wood, 1975) provided the evolutionary precursor of the cetacean cervix.

Endocrinology

Cycles and Seasons. A normal reproductive year for captive bottlenose dolphins in Hawaii includes two to three ovulations, during
August to November. The length of the estrous cycles, anestrus to
anestrus, in these bottlenose dolphins is 25 to 32 days (Schroeder,
1990b). Females start reproductive cycles at four to five years of
age and, as in the case of a dolphin born in 1953 at Seaquarium,
Florida, can successfully deliver a healthy calf at 36 years of age.
The optimal dolphin breeding season varies geographically, and it
should be noted that captive dolphin births occur in all months of
the year (Cornell and Asper, 1978). All wild populations of delphinids
studied to date have been found to mate and calve seasonally (Perrin
and Reilly, 1984).

The bottlenose dolphin was suggested to be a reflex ovulator
by some investigators (Harrison and Ridgway, 1971; Harrison, 1977).
Evidence from histological examinations of ovaries in conjunction
with specified uterine sections from spinner and striped dolphins
supports the theory that dolphins of the genus *Stenella* may sometimes ovulate spontaneously (Benirschke et al., 1980). Also, levels
of progesterone and total immunoreactive estrogens have provided
hormonal evidence of spontaneous ovulation in captive dolphins of
the genera *Tursiops* and *Delphinus* (Kirby and Ridgway, 1984) and
the species *Stenella longirostris* (Wells, 1984). Our findings have
confirmed those results and indicated that in some bottlenose dolphins spontaneous ovulation could be detected up to seven times in
a thirteen-month period (Schroeder, 1990).

The ability to monitor the onset and duration of estrus is
important to a successful breeding program, whether that program
is based on natural or artificial insemination. However, estrus is
difficult, sometimes impossible, to detect in many animals. The
phenomenon of "silent heat" is well known in domestic animals and
"estrus" behavior is not necessarily accompanied by a normal "heat"
period including ovulation (Britt et al., 1981). Appearance of external genitalia, increased secretions and/or behavioral changes are
the most obvious, but not always the most reliable signs indicating
estrus in most domestic animals. Wild animals present problems of
estrus detection not only because there are generally few individuals in any single captive colony, but also because the normal cycling of physiological events can be disrupted by the conditions of
captivity. Just as the reproductive efficiency of domestic animals is
affected by season, temperature, confinement, group size, pen struc-

ture, and other factors, it is reasonable to expect that breeding groups of captive dolphins are affected by such factors.

The female dolphin's genital slit is generally under water, making the detection of estrus more complicated for the investigator than it is in terrestrial animals. Behavioral signs, including male dolphin acoustic activity, are used in some cases to infer that captive dolphins are in estrus (Wood, 1953; Tavolga and Essapian, 1957). In our studies and observations, we found no consistent and objective criterion of behavior or appearance to judge whether or not a female dolphin is in estrus. The conditions sometimes taken to be indicative of dolphin estrus include an increased pinkness of the abdomen, the female positioning close or swimming closer than usual to the male in the area, two females, in the absence of a male, becoming more tactile than usual with each other, enlarged or puffy-appearing external genitalia, and periodic anorexia. However, these did not correlate with induced or spontaneous ovulations. In no case did we observe a strong correlation between any of these conditions or behaviors and the detection of estrus through radioimmunoassay (RIA) or serum estrogen and progesterone levels (Schroeder, 1990b).

RIA of serum progesterone and total estrogens will classify reproductive conditions of female dolphins. A baseline below 1 ng/ml of progesterone indicates that the female is anestrus or nonpregnant. Ovulations are indicated by episodic total estrogen levels above 120 pg/ml and/or episodic "spikes" of serum progesterone levels greater than 1 ng/ml. Progesterone levels during gestation are greater than 2 ng/ml, ranging from 2 to 56 ng/ml (Schroeder, 1990b). The most promising new technique for detecting the onset of estrus and even more importantly, ovulation, is the analysis of urinary estrone conjugates (Loskutoff et al., 1983; Czekala et al., 1986; Walker et al., 1988). Walker et al. (1988) followed urinary steroid levels in six female killer whales for periods ranging from 11 to 16 months and characterized normal estrus, anestrus, fertilization, and pregnancy by analyzing urine obtained from animals conditioned to deliver samples on cue (Krames, 1984). Robeck et al. (1990) continued this research for an additional three years, using analysis of urinary steroids to assess seasonality, length of gestation, intra- and inter-individual estrous cycle variations, and dates of conception. In studies involving the analysis of urinary steroids, it is required that the marine mammals be trained for routine urine collection.

Pregnancy Determination, and Prediction of Parturition

Early pregnancy diagnosis is an important management tool in all breeding programs and is possible in captive marine mammals. A negative pregnancy diagnosis allows rebreeding during the current breeding season. If the test is positive, adjustments for prenatal care and feeding can be made. Serum progesterone levels have been monitored intermittently from 28 pregnant cetaceans including 24 *Tursiops spp.*, one Pacific white-sided dolphin (*Lagenorhynchus obliquidens*), one pilot whale (*Globicephala macrorhynchus*), two killer whales, and monthly from four bottlenose dolphins (Schroeder and Keller, 1990). Five additional *Tursiops truncatus spp. aduncus* housed at Ocean Park, Hong Kong, have been monitored monthly during gestation with comparable results. When the serum progesterone level is between 3 and 52 ng/ml on three tests separated by two weeks, birth has followed 100% of the time. Three consecutive progesterone levels above 3 ng/ml at two-week intervals (starting as early as the first week after breeding) indicates pregnancy, but another confirming progesterone test 4 to 6 months into the pregnancy is recommended. For early pregnancy diagnosis (1 to 2 weeks after breeding) a progesterone level of <1 ng/ml indicates an anestrus, nonpregnant female. The diagnostic "gray area" from >1 ng/ml to <3 ng/ml indicates the need for further testing.

Pregnancy can be confirmed at 4 to 5 months of gestation with a doppler stethoscope. The fetal heartbeat ranges from 130 to 140 beats a minute, approximately twice that of the dam's. A doppler examination should be done if there is any question of fetal viability during a pregnancy (Cornell et al., 1987; Schroeder, 1990b). Our most consistent fetal heart monitoring results are from the left side, mid to lower abdomen, 8 to 20 cm posterior to a line extending from the posterior insertion of the dorsal fin to the ventral midline.

Pregnancy diagnosis as early as one month may be possible using ultrasound. This technique can be applied to a female dolphin while she is restrained in the water or trained to station for the examination (Williamson et al., 1990). Good ultrasound equipment is expensive, and experience is necessary for the proper use and interpretation of results.

Early pregnancy diagnosis allows nutritional changes to be made as soon as possible. Our pregnant dolphins are fed *ad lib.* a mixture of 10% mackerel, 70% smelt, and 20% herring at least three times daily. Their usual multivitamin mineral supplement is also adjusted to provide a calcium phosphorous ration of 1.25:1.

A pregnant female's weight may be monitored once monthly. For 6 females delivering normal calves of 30 to 35 pounds, an average gestational weight gain of 96.7 pounds (range 68 to 133) has been recorded. In this author's experience (Schroeder, unpublished data), neonatal mortality (within 24 hours) is associated with lower gestational weight gains (68 to 79 pounds). The female dolphins delivering calves living longer than 2 years gain 39% to 61% of their weight in the last trimester, while females delivering calves surviving <24 hours gain only 10% to 27% during the same time period. In each of six gestations monitored monthly for weight gains, there has been a weight loss (of 2 to 10 lbs) during the first 6 months.

If the above-mentioned techniques are not available for early pregnancy diagnosis, the physical appearance of the female may give impressions of pregnancy during the last trimester (last 4 months). During that time, weight gain and obvious swelling of the mammary tissue cause a characteristic "step-like" appearance near the genital slit (McBride and Kritzler, 1951). Caution is advised, however, as near term to term births have occurred without physical signs of pregnancy being noted. This can occur when groups of animals are housed together, and a first-time pregnant (primigravida) dolphin does not gain enough weight to develop the step-like appearance.

Hormonal Manipulation of the Ovary and Estrous Cycle

It is possible to regulate estrus by the injection of exogenous hormones or to monitor each individual female's serum progesterone level allowing breeding at an opportune time (Schroeder and Keller, 1990). In our experience, a reproductively mature male and a reproductively mature female can be housed together, separated from other pairs, for over seven years without producing young. We have housed three male-female pairs of dolphins together for 4–8 years without pregnancy. On the other hand, placement of a reproductively mature male with a reproductively mature female, when the pair has not been housed together previously, usually results in conception at the next ovulation.

Ovulation induction through intramuscular injections of pregnant mare serum gonadotropin (PMSG) followed by human chorionic gonadotropin (HCG) is an experimental procedure that may be advantageous in captive dolphin programs by regulating the estrous cycle (Sawyer-Steffan et al., 1983; Schroeder and Keller, 1990). The author was able to induce ovulation in 14 of 20 trials

(Schroeder and Keller, 1990). The optimum dose and interval to induce follicle growth is 1600 IU of PMSG intramuscular injection, followed in 48 hours by a second PMSG injection of 800 to 1000 IU, followed in 120 hours by an intramuscular injection of 3,000 IU of HCG, causing ovulation of the developed ovum. This procedure is feasible in oceanaria if facilitated by training the female dolphin to present her flukes for blood sampling. Unless there is a shallow restraint area available, training this behavior is essential.

Puberty

The development and application of RIA over the last quarter-century (Lasley, 1980) makes it possible to directly measure hormone levels in biological fluids which, in turn, reflect specific physiological states. Using RIA analysis of serum progesterone levels, we determined that puberty in female dolphins starts at 4–7 years of age (Schroeder, 1990b). The female would be receptive to a male and could conceive if breeding were to occur at this age. In this regard, it is important to distinguish between sexual maturity (puberty) and reproductive maturity. The latter occurs when the female is cycling on a regular basis and has attained her adult size. Reproductive maturity may be more important for successful births in terrestrial animals than in cetaceans due to the latter's lack of a pelvic girdle. However, breeding a female dolphin before she has attained her mature size may result in a difficult birth, stillbirth or other problems associated with pregnancy in a system that is not fully developed, as well as a lack of mothering skills. In nature, or in a seminatural breeding environment, the nulliparous female may gain mothering skills by observing older females and their calves.

Reproductive maturity occurs between 7 and 11 years of age. Managed breeding of dolphins in this age range should result in fewer stillbirths, better maternal care, and healthier calves. Data on dolphin births in captivity prior to 1975 indicate approximately 40% were stillbirths (Ridgway and Benirschke, 1977). More recently, the rate of stillbirths has decreased to approximately 20% (Couver and Schroeder, 1984). This decrease is due to a number of factors: (1) collections avoid capturing pregnant females who often experience stillbirths of that calf, (2) captive dolphin colonies are being managed more carefully to prevent young (sexually mature but not reproductively mature) female dolphins from becoming pregnant, and (3) the nutrition provided to pregnant dolphins has become better as captive marine mammal husbandry practices and knowledge of nutrition have improved.

Gestation Lengths

The bottlenose dolphin's gestation period averages 12 months (plus or minus 2 weeks) and lactation continues for 18 to 24 months. Boto (*Inia geoffrensis*) and tuxuci (*Sotalia fluviatills*) have a calculated gestation length of 10.2 months (Best and DaSilva, 1984). Baiji (*Lipotes vexillfer*) has a gestation period of 10–11 months (Liu, 1988). *Orcinus orca* has a gestation length of 17–18 months (Walker et al., 1988).

Artificial Insemination (AI)

The AI of bottlenose dolphins is an experimental procedure developed at Naval Ocean System Center's Hawaii Laboratory (Schroeder et al., 1983, 1985; Schroeder and Keller, 1990). Among the advantages of AI in captive cetacea: (1) the genetic improvement of captive dolphins can be achieved through careful selection for desirable characteristics; (2) inbreeding can be avoided; (3) frozen semen from a desirable captive male dolphin can be shipped to facilities housing only female dolphins or unsuitable or immature male dolphins, saving the expense of transporting animals for breeding from one facility to another; and (4) behavioral problems caused by the actions taken by overly aggressive male dolphins against female dolphins can be avoided.

For insemination of a female dolphin, freshly collected semen or a sample of frozen semen pellets, thawed as rapidly and gently as possible in a 37° C water bath, was placed in the reproductive tract of the female dolphin eight hours and 24 hours following induced ovulation (Schroeder, 1985; Schroeder and Keller, 1990). Two of four AI procedures resulted in pregnancies, one of 10 weeks duration and one of one week duration; both terminated spontaneously (Schroeder and Keller, 1990). Further studies are necessary to determine the optimum time of insemination relative to time of ovulation. An application of AI, using the bottlenose dolphin model, may be possible for endangered species of small odontocetes, such as the baiji (Chinese river dolphin), but additional studies are necessary to prove that AI will result in a live birth of a dolphin.

Embryo Transfer

Embryo transfer technology is well defined and applied successfully to humans and some domestic animals. It may involve the use of cryopreserved semen from the subject species, a technology which is available for dolphins (Schroeder and Keller, 1990). The more difficult technology of superovulation of the dolphin and collection of oocyte-cumulus complexes does not currently exist. It presents an excellent subject for research and is one that should be vigorously pursued. Capacitated dolphin sperm (Fleming et al., 1981) exposed to dolphin ova on homologous oviductal monolayers may result in formation of a pronucleus leading to a viable embryo. The methodology of inserting that viable egg into the uterus of a dolphin of the same or different species should be possible using techniques similar to those used in AI.

The recent successful intercontinental transport of porcine embryos, properly buffered at 36.5° C, has further extended the possibilities of embryo transplantation (Niemann et al., 1989). The development of freezing methods allows easy and rapid shipment of bovine, ovine, and caprine embryos; an encouraging development, and one which may be applicable to dolphin breeding.

Parturition

The birth of captive *Tursiops* has been described by several authors (Essapian, 1953; Tavolga, 1966; Cornell et al., 1987; Schroeder, 1990b). As the mother-to-be approaches term, the size of her abdomen enlarges and her mammary glands enlarge rapidly 2 to 3 days before delivery. Behavioral changes and a 24-hour-period of inappetence usually precede delivery. The female may hunch and arch her back and produce loud, forceful exhalations just before the usually rapid underwater delivery. Birth may occur any time of the day (usually at night in the Hawaii facility). The placenta is usually passed within an hour of the twenty minute to four-hour-delivery period.

Reproductive Anatomy and Physiology of the Male *Tursiops*

Anatomy

The bottlenose dolphin's penis is enclosed within the genital groove. The testes are retained in the abdominal cavity throughout life and vary in size seasonally in small odontocetes (Ridgway and Green, 1967; Collet, 1981). When the male dolphin is viewed from below, the genital groove is seen approximately 4–5 cm anterior to another small slit, the anal opening. This separation between the genital and anal slits is the most obvious external difference between the male and the female bottlenose dolphin. The female genital slit is continuous with the anal slit. Two small pores are present on the male, between the two slits, one on each side of an imaginary line joining the back of the genital slit to the front of the anal slit. These may be vestigial scent glands, such as are seen in the dog or the skunk, and they could serve a pheromonal function. However, in this author's opinion, these pores are vestigial small openings to vestigial mammary glands. The penis of the dolphin (and other cetaceans) is of the fibroelastic type found in ruminants (Slijper, 1972). The cetacean penis has its origin by crura from the median surfaces of the pelvic bones. These crura fuse into a long, firm, rope-like body, round to oval in cross section, forming a distinct sigmoid flexure lying in a horizontal plane (Green, 1972). The distal portion of the dolphin's penis tapers to a very small, sharply tapered tip which seems to be well adapted to couple with the uniquely configured cervix of the female. Most descriptions of the accessory reproductive organs in male cetaceans include only the prostate gland, which surrounds the urethra a short distance posterior to the urinary bladder (Green, 1972).

Endocrinology

Reports on male dolphin reproductive cycles and seasonality have been based on data obtained by RIA of serum testosterone levels and measurements and histological examinations of gonads (Ridgway and Green, 1967; Collet and Saint Groins, 1984; Wells, 1984; Hohn et al., 1985). To examine a male dolphin's reproductive cycle, a mature bottlenose dolphin was trained to provide semen samples on command (Keller, 1987). After completion of the ten-week training period, semen was collected twice weekly and blood was sampled twice monthly for a period of 28 months. Total sperm per ejaculate ranged from no sperm (in off breeding season samples) to 54.6×10^9. Sperm densities of each session (multiple ejaculates collected during a session) ranged from zero to $1,587 \times 10^6$ sperm/ml (n=241). Testosterone levels ranged from 1.1 to 54.4 ng/ml (n=79) (Schroeder and Keller, 1989). Seasonal variations were observed in total sperm per ejaculate, sperm density per ml of ejaculate, and serum testosterone levels. Peak sperm densities were detected during September and October of three consecutive breeding seasons. Serum testosterone levels peaked in June, decreased during July and August, and were lowest in September and October, the period of greatest sperm density. Peak sperm production and density were coincident with the peak period of breeding activity but at a time when serum testosterone levels were lowest (Schroeder and Keller, 1989, 1990).

Maturation

Male bottlenose dolphins are precocious at birth. Reflex penile erections occur in male *Tursiops* within 48 hours of birth. Puberty in male dolphins is often classified on the basis of serum testosterone levels, and is identified by testosterone levels of 3–5 ng/ml in *Tursiops* 8 to 14 years old. Lower levels indicate immaturity and higher levels in older males indicate reproductive maturity. It is necessary to take multiple testosterone samples to determine breeding status. During his breeding season, a mature male dolphin's serum testosterone levels can be less than 5 ng/ml (Schroeder and Keller, 1989). However, an immature male's serum testosterone of more than 5 ng/ml has not been recorded. Although at 15 years a male is reproductively mature, a nine-year-old male is able to produce viable sperm. Optimum breeding efficiency will be obtained using males 15 years or older.

Semen Collection, Evaluation and Cryopreservation

Freshly collected semen should be evaluated as outlined by Seager et al. (1975) and Seager and Platz (1977). The semen should be evaluated by volume, total sperm count (by hemocytometer), morphology, percent motility, and progressive motility (rapid forward movement). Additionally, evaluation of sperm density, the number of sperm/ml of ejaculate (Linde et al., 1981), should be recorded.

Electroejaculation has become the standard semen collection technique in zoos and primate centers (Durrant, 1990). However, because of diminished sperm motility in most electrostimulated ejaculates (Hirsch et al., 1990) and ease of collection, we opted for manually collected samples from a dolphin trained to station in the water, as previously mentioned, avoiding the use of electroejaculation. Semen collection and cyropreservation studies are indicated for additional species of cetacea, especially the platanistoid dolphins.

Environmental and Social Influences

If the total population of a species in the natural environment reaches a nonsustainable point, extinction will follow. Estimation of the minimum viable population size required for long-term survival of a given species is complex, but the best estimates for many animal species are rarely lower than several hundred individuals (Soulé and Simberloff, 1986). A total population number under 200 dolphins, for example, may have 100 females, fewer than 50% of which may be capable of becoming pregnant. Successful reproduction requires female dolphins of the proper age and stage of their estrous cycle. Conception requires a healthy and receptive female and successful gestation requires adequate nutrition and freedom from accidents. A few females, widely distributed in nature, with a seasonal breeding pattern, have seriously reduced chances of meeting a suitable male at the optimum time. This meeting becomes more unlikely as population numbers continue to decrease.

Possibly complicating the issue are peaks and troughs in the age structure of the population. Unfavorable conditions can cause reproduction to cease or to be inhibited and/or can cause calf mortality to be high. The intercalf interval in dolphins (three years for *Tursiops*) could also produce irregular recruitment if the females tend to breed in synchrony.

Information on baiji suggest that they may be springtime seasonal breeders (Brownell, 1984); as inferred from observation of young calves with their mothers, and the examination of two recovered pregnant females in January with nearly fully developed fetuses (Chen et al., 1984). Research on the behavior of *Lipotes* in captivity and in the wild indicate two sexual peaks, one in fall and one in spring, with a two-year intercalf interval (Liu, 1988). Two strategies for captive breeding programs are possible: (1) a captive research program similar to that used for the bottlenose dolphin, and (2) the establishment of a reserve in which the endangered dolphin can breed under semicaptive conditions in an optimal natural habitat. Each alternative presents the need to determine the number of founders based on the principles of population genetics and demography. With proper planning and luck, dolphins in captive or semicaptive conditions will have a genotype preadapted for breeding under these existing conditions. This would be desirable for behavioral reasons, as many mammals exhibit individual preferences and are not equally likely to mate with all members of the opposite sex. AI is an alternative to behavioral reluctance to breed if genetic compatibility has been determined.

It is always wise to have as many founders as possible to provide maximum genetic viability. Soulé and Simberloff (1986) suggest at least 25 individuals. Genetic objectives could be achieved

by having more females than males in the breeding program's population, and periodically replacing the breeding males with new animals captured from the wild (Ralls, 1989). Wells et al. (1987) reported on a relatively closed community of feral bottlenose dolphins
in Sarasota, Florida. In spite of the closed nature of the community, genetic heterogeneity within the community was high (Duffield
and Wells, 1986). These Sarasota dolphins have not exhibited any
patterns of long-term pair bonding between adult males and females that would be diagnostic of a monogamous system, and a
number of facts argue for a polygamous or promiscuous breeding
strategy (Wells et al., 1987). Using that study group as a model
would indicate that the initial group of dolphins should have a
predominance of females of breeding age, and that males could
be rotated periodically into the population. The collection and
cryopreservation of semen from each male is a top priority.

Conclusions

Ideal husbandry and training techniques in captive or semicaptive
breeding programs include: (1) training for medical examination
with the dolphin remaining in the water, (2) blood collection from
the flukes, and (3) collection of urine and semen. The addition of
inhouse enzyme linked immunosorbent assay (ELISA) of urinary
estrogen levels, the results of which would be used to schedule
semen collection and insemination with freshly collected semen,
would present the optimum conditions for successful artificial
insemination.

More than 40 species of dolphins and porpoises thrive, but
several species number in the hundreds and are endangered due to
increasing degradation of their limited environment, overfishing of
their prey, and accidental death in nets and hooks. Among these
are Vaquita (*Phocoena sinus*), Indus river dolphin (*Platanista minor*), Ganges river dolphin (*Platanista gangetica*), and the baiji.

Presently, the baiji is listed as a rare and endangered species
(Perrin, 1988), the rarest small cetacean in the world (Zhou, 1989b),
and has not bred successfully in captivity or in semicaptivity. Recent development and application of photo-identification techniques
suggest that the baiji population density of the lower Yangtze is
about 1 per 14 km, half of previous estimates. If this estimate is
also appropriate for the baiji population in the middle reaches of
the Yangtze, we can assume that the dolphin's number has fallen

to less than 200 individuals (Zhou et al., 1992). A population and habitat viability analysis workshop (a collaboration of the Mammalian Society of China, IUCN/SSC Cetacean Specialist Group and the Captive Breeding Specialist Group) has recommended immediate commencement of captive breeding of the baiji to prevent its extinction.

Caution, therefore, must be exercised in recommending that baiji be captured for experimental artificial insemination—even though a male baiji, QiQi, has been housed successfully in captivity since 1980 (Chen and Liu, 1989). On the other hand, capture may be the only way to intervene at this time. Captive breeding programs with bottlenose dolphins have produced 204 dolphins in the last 14 years. The existence of second generation captive-born individuals indicates that relatively stress free captive environments (Ames, 1991) are possible and may indicate the direction for survival of the baiji and other endangered dolphins.

A unique combination of captive and seminatural environments have been created since 1986 to enhance survival of the baiji in China. Seminatural areas of the Yangtze have been fenced off from the main channel of the river, one near Wuhan and the other near Tongling. Additionally, the 135.5 km Xin-Luo section of the Yangtze has been designated as a natural preserve, providing a natural area for reintroduction of baiji (Chen et al., 1992). The author, in May 1992, conducted a survey of the captive facilities for baiji at Wuhan and Tongling. Excellent facilities are nearing completion, and their locations will facilitate the transition of newly captured baiji from the river to captivity, then to seminatural areas, and eventually back to the river. In Wuhan, QiQi is successfully being trained for semen collection and is thriving in captivity.

It must be noted, however, that the principal cause of most species' decline is habitat destruction. Where there is a viable captive population of a species, the lack of available suitable habitat is the single major reason for ruling out a reintroduction program (Kleiman, 1989).

The finless porpoise (*Neophocena phocaenoides*), though usually marine, has a population seen as far up the Yangtze as Tung Ting Lake (Nishiwaki, 1972). This porpoise, not as endangered as the baiji, is providing an acceptable research bridge from the bottlenosed dolphin to the baiji. There are currently three in captivity at Tongling and five at the seminatural preserve site west of Wuhan. A key consideration, however, is just how long the current population of baiji can survive in the deteriorating environment of the Yangtze river. Reproductive data are reported for *Inia* (Best and DaSilva, 1984), and they are kept in collections in Sea World in San Diego, Pittsburgh, Duisberg, West Germany, and Venezuela. There is a collection of *Orcaella* successfully maintained and reproducing at the Jaya Ancol Oceanarium in Indonesia (Marsh et al., 1989). A tucuxi dolphin (*Soralia fiuviatilis*) was born on March 30, 1991 at a 10-acre sanctuary in Sete Lagoas, Minas Gerais, Brazil. One must conclude that *Lipotes* could be similarly maintained in semicaptivity or captivity as a last resort.

The best option for many endangered species of marine mammals may be to capture group representatives to preserve gene pools for the future. For *Lipotes*, that will be a difficult and controversial decision, similar to the problems surrounding the California condor project. Programs using procedures outlined above have produced viable progeny of *Tursiops*. Application of those techniques, along with continued basic research, will maximize the probability of a successful captive endangered cetacean species breeding program. Combining studies of induced reproductive cycle events (Schroeder, 1984; Schroeder and Keller, 1990) with current veterinary medical and husbandry knowledge of platanistoid dolphins (Chen and Liu, 1989; Ridgway et al., 1989) is important for the conservation of the baiji in its wild environment. Several specific conservation projects and their costs have been identified (Perrin, 1988) for the baiji. An *Action Plan for the Conservation of Biological Diversity of Dolphins, Porpoises and Whales* (Perrin, 1989) is highly recommended for additional information on this critical issue.

23

Marine Mammal Behavior: Conservation Through Research

Susie Ellis

In recent years, increasing concern for the preservation of rare, threatened, and endangered species has prompted zoos, aquariums, and marine zoological parks to increase participation in programs for behavioral and physiological research, wildlife management, and captive propagation. Increasingly, opportunities for conducting research, both basic and applied in nature, have become available in zoological facilities. Some taxa, particularly mammals, have been well-studied in captivity, adding to a broad base of integrative knowledge concerning many species.

Among mammalian species, few are intrinsically valued and held in awe by humans as much as those that live in the sea, particularly cetaceans (Jenkins, 1987, 1991; Golden, 1989). Cetaceans, beyond other marine mammals, possess a highly developed cerebral cortex and large, convoluted brains (Flanigan, 1972) which are believed to be indicative of a high level of intelligence. These indications have generated considerable interest, and as Gaskin (1982) points out, in recent years no research on cetaceans has attracted more public attention than that which focuses on behavior, communication, and levels of intelligence.

Rationale for Behavioral Studies on Endangered Species in Captivity

Scope of Existing Field Studies

Field studies on endangered species of marine mammals are few, reflecting both the small number of species currently classified as endangered as well as the difficulty of studying marine mammals, regardless of status, in nature. Among cetaceans, humpback whales (*Megaptera novaeangliae*) (e.g., Katona et al., 1980; Darling and Juracz, 1983; Baker et al., 1985), killer whales (*Orcinus orca*) (e.g., Kirkevold and Lockard, 1986), and bottlenose dolphins (*Tursiops truncatus spp.*) (e.g., Bryden and Harrison, 1986; Shane et al., 1986; Leatherwood and Reeves, 1990; Pryor and Norris, 1991) are probably the best-known and most studied species. Of pinnipeds, the endangered Mediterranean monk seal (*Monachus monachus*) (e.g., van Bree, 1979; Reijnders et al., 1988; Anselin et al., 1990; Vedder and t'Hart, 1990; Vlachoutsikou and Cebrian, 1992) has received a great deal of recent attention, as has the endangered Hawaiian monk seal (*Monachus schauinslandi*) (e.g., Gilmartin, 1982, 1983, 1987, 1988; Alcorn, 1984; Alcorn and Henderson, 1984; Johanos, 1984; Alcorn et al., 1988; Eliason et al., 1990; Henderson and Finnegan, 1990), and the once near-extinct northern elephant seal (*Mirounga angustirostrus*) (e.g., Bartholomew, 1952; LeBouef and Peterson, 1969; LeBouef et al., 1972; LeBouef et al., 1974).

Traditionally, the scope of the majority of marine mammal field studies has not emphasized endangered species. Rather, attention has been directed toward those species that are more easily observed. A few studies are of broad focus (e.g., Bartholomew, 1952; Goodall et al., 1985; Ljungblad et al., 1986; Santos and Lacerda, 1987), but many are more specialized, discussing phenomena such as distribution and feeding behavior (Leatherwood, 1975; Wells et al., 1980; Dorsey, 1983; Hall, 1986; Felleman et al., 1991), growth analysis (Heimlich-Boran, 1986a), thermoregulatory behavior (Whittow, 1978), communication (LeBoeuf and Peterson, 1969; Tyack, 1976; Ford and Fisher, 1982), or parent-offspring behavior (Thomas and Taber, 1984; Thomas, 1987a; Gisiner and Schusterman, 1991).

Need for Controlled Studies

Successful captive management of animals, endangered or not, demands a thorough familiarity with the animal in the context of its natural habitat (Maple, 1986). Information provided from field studies combined with research carried out in zoological facilities has added considerably to our understanding of marine mammals. One of the basic advantages of captive research is that it allows close examination of phenomena that in many cases cannot be observed in nature.

To date, the largest body of research produced in captivity has been in the study of the bottlenose dolphin. As Wood (1986) pointed out, just 50 years ago virtually nothing was known about the social behavior of dolphins. The first dolphins were displayed at Marine Studios in Florida in 1938 (Tavolga, 1966; Powell, 1986), and from this group came early classical studies on social behavior (McBride and Hebb, 1948; Tavolga, 1966), parturition, and mother-infant behavior (McBride and Kritzler, 1951; Tavolga and Essapian, 1957; Essapian, 1963).

Other important contributions from this facility were early works on audition in dolphins by Kellogg and Kohler (1952), Schevill and Lawrence (1953), and Lawrence and Schevill (1954). Investigations on audition, communication, and echolocation abilities have continued to be popular topics for captive research (Table 23.1). The majority of studies have been carried out with bottlenose dolphins.

Many recent studies have focused on cognitive abilities in marine mammals, and some have investigated "language" abilities. In one of the earliest studies, a food reward for each of two dolphins was made contingent on an apparent cooperative transmission of information between the pair (Bastian, 1967). Herman and his colleagues have provided a great deal of information on artificial language and cognition in bottlenose dolphins (cf., Herman, 1980, 1986, 1987, 1991; Herman et al., 1982, 1984; Richards et al., 1984). Schusterman and his associates have reported on cognition and syntax comprehension in California sea lions and bottlenose dolphins (Schusterman and Krieger, 1984, 1986; Schusterman and Gisiner, 1988).

The social behavior of marine mammals in zoological facilities has not been given a great deal of attention. Notable exceptions are early papers by McBride and Hebb (1948) and Tavolga (1966) in which the social behavior of bottlenose dolphins was discussed at length. Ethograms have been developed (e.g., DeFran and Pryor, 1980; Rector et al., 1986; Morris, 1988), but have not often been published or utilized in a standard way in a wide number of studies. In a report on the little-known Orinoco river dolphin (*Inia geoffrensis humboldtiana*), Sylvestre (1985) described locomotion, respiration, senses, feeding, play, and sexual behavior in captivity. Terry (1983, 1984, 1986, 1989) reported on the behavior and surveyed the trainability of the endangered tucuxi (*Sotalia fluviatilis*) in European zoological facilities. More recently, Östman (1991) reported on quantitative changes in aggressive and social behavior

Table 23.1
**Representative Studies on Echolocation, Audition, and
Communication in Marine Mammals from 1961 to 1991.**

Author/Year	Species/Subject
Norris et al., 1961	*Tursiops truncatus*
Evans et al., 1964	*T. truncatus*
Norris, 1964, 1968, 1969	general
Kellogg & Rice, 1966	*T. truncatus*
Norris & Evans, 1966	*Stenella brenadensis*
Evans & Powell, 1967	*T. truncatus*
Evans & Bastian, 1969	general
Gurevich, 1969	*Delphinus spp.*
Herman et al., 1969	*T. truncatus*
LeBouef & Peterson, 1969	*Mirounga angustirostrus*
Pryor et al., 1969	*T. truncatus*
Beach & Pepper, 1972	*T. truncatus*
Lilly, 1975	*T. truncatus*
Renaud & Popper, 1975	*T. truncatus*
Herman, 1980	*Zalophus californianus*
Schusterman, 1980	general
Bain & Allen, 1982	*Orcinus orca*
Herman et al., 1982	*T. truncatus*
Hult, 1982	*T. truncatus*
Patterson, 1983	*T. truncatus*
Richards et al., 1984	*T. truncatus*
Schusterman & Krieger, 1984	*Z. californianus*
Tyack, 1985	*T. truncatus*
Herman, 1986	*T. truncatus*
Johnson, 1986	*T. truncatus*
Schusterman & Krieger, 1986	*Z. californianus*
Brill et al., 1988	*T. truncatus*
Schusterman & Gisiner, 1988	*Z. californianus*
Schusterman & Gisiner, 1989	general
Marrin-Cooney, 1989	*T. truncatus*
Tyack & Sayigh, 1989	*T. truncatus*
Klishlin et al., 1990	*Trichechus inguinus*
Gisiner & Schusterman, 1991	*Z. californianus*
Herman, 1991	*T. truncatus*
Moore, 1991	*T. truncatus*

between two male bottlenose dolphins. Considering the number of animals available for study as well as the number of social groupings, research on the social behavior of marine mammals in captive environments has been very poorly represented in the literature and needs more emphasis.

A number of studies on the development of marine mammals have been carried out in zoological facilities. For example, the social development in grey seal (*Halichoerus grypus*) pups was chronicled by several groups (Wilson et al., 1985b; Kastelein and Wiepkema, 1988, 1990). Development of bottlenose dolphin calves housed in social groups, a study not easily undertaken under field conditions, has been described by Eastcott and Dickinson (1987) and Chirighin (1987). Joseph et al. (1987) briefly described development of the first Commerson's dolphin (*Cephalorhynchus commersonii*) calf born in captivity; observations were conducted from underwater public viewing areas. Issues of imprinting and its interaction with learning have been discussed by Schusterman (1986), Hanggi et al. (1986), and Gisiner and Schusterman (1991). Attachment, well-studied in other mammalian taxa such as primates and ungulates, has not been investigated in marine mammals.

Functions of Behavioral Research in Captivity

Public Education

All animals housed in zoological facilities have the potential to provide a unique educational opportunity for the public. Because of the nature of the aquatic habitat, most people do not have the opportunity to view marine mammals in the wild. Even when marine mammals are opportunistically seen in nature, the majority of behaviors in an animal's repertoire are not readily observable. When maintained in social groupings that approximate those found in nature and in thoughtfully-designed habitats that provide opportunity for expression of species-typical behavior, marine mammals housed in zoological facilities readily exhibit most behaviors reported in the wild.

One of contemporary zoological facilities' primary strengths as well as responsibilities is in providing visitors with synthesized lessons about animal anatomy, physiology, ecology, and behavior—ultimately instilling an appreciation of a species and its particular adaptations to the natural environment. For much of the public, interest in marine mammals, initially fostered by anthropomorphic television programs such as "Flipper," is now more sophisticated. Presently, most of the zoo-going public tends to be fairly knowledgeable about nature, primed before visiting the zoo by television programs that have introduced the plight of many exotic animal species (Serrell, 1982). Education efforts in zoological facilities can reinforce this antecedent knowledge by using and redefining already familiar themes such as adaptation and communication (Serrell, 1982).

While visitors may come to a zoological facility with a relatively sophisticated knowledge of marine mammals, the unique experience of closeness that these settings provide can promote a far deeper appreciation and understanding than is possible through any other means. For example, in July and August 1992, visitors at the Minnesota Zoo were able to witness the births of bottlenose dolphin calves from underwater viewing windows. Similarly, in September 1988, an estimated 2,000 visitors watched in fascination as a killer whale gave birth at Sea World in San Diego, California (Antrim, pers. comm.). In both these cases, visitors and animal managers had the opportunity to see something that few, if any, field researchers have ever witnessed. Each person that saw these events will likely never forget their experience. Additional millions of people have been able to witness these and other cetacean births on national television broadcasts.

Apart from special events like births, daily activities of marine mammals can also foster appreciation. Dolphins can inspire awe as they leap and dive deep into a crystal-clear pool. The visitor who sees a sea otter break open a sea urchin with a rock, much as it would in the wild, gains an appreciation of the species' dexterity that can otherwise only be touched on through nonexperiential media. Situations like this, in which animals have the opportunity to engage in species-typical behaviors, are some of the most basic and important means by which zoological facilities can foster public appreciation for wildlife by providing a "personal" experience with animals.

At present, there are few representative species of marine mammals in North American zoological facilities (Asper et al., 1990a; Andrews and Duffield, 1992). However, many of the nonrepresented species, especially those that are rare or less cosmopolitan in distribution, have gained protection and appreciation through limited public exposure to a few nonendangered species. Campaigns for curtailment of whaling, for example, likely receive a great deal of funding from people whose initial interest was enlisted by watching nonendangered odontocetes such as killer whales and bottlenose dolphins in zoological facilities, but who may have never seen any of the endangered baleen whales or river dolphins. As such, zoological facilities, with attendance of over 100 million visitors per year (Joseph, 1993), are singularly capable of enhancing and enlisting public support not only for their own conservation and research programs but also for conservation and research efforts with marine mammals in the wild.

Ironically, while zoological facilities were among the first to appreciate and call the attention of the public to the uniqueness of marine mammals, they now find themselves defending their very existence under controversy and close scrutiny by animal rights proponents (e.g., Cherfas, 1984; Pilleri, 1984, 1987; Lawson and Parker, 1990) and legislators. This is particularly enigmatic in light of the fact that zoological facilities have rarely collected from populations of threatened or endangered marine species for breeding programs or for exhibition; those species have diminished in number via other human activities such as harvesting by fisheries, pollution, and ecological degradation.

Some of the objections to maintaining marine mammals in zoological facilities have been perpetuated by films and shows designed to entertain rather than educate the public. Too often these media events have emphasized human-like qualities and human-animal "relationships," depicting marine mammals in other than a species-typical manner. The popularization of flagship species, chosen by zoological facilities because of their marketing appeal, also have encouraged many of the misconceptions surrounding marine mammals (Jenkins, 1991). As such, zoological facilities themselves have contributed greatly, albeit inadvertently, to the almost "religious" (Jenkins, 1987) reverence for marine mammals and their personification as exemplified by the most extreme faction of animal rights groups.

Husbandry

The maintenance of marine mammals in captivity is a monumental task with regard to ongoing financial commitment, staff support, physical facilities, and logistics. Assumption of this task brings the responsibility not only to house animals in behaviorally relevant facilities and in species-appropriate social groups, but also to provide proper husbandry techniques, veterinary care, and a healthy living space.

Because of the nature of the ocean environment and its abundant predators, marine mammals have evolved an ability to mask signs of injury or illness (Cornell, 1982), often appearing to behave normally while illness is manifested internally. For this reason, it is imperative that staff working with marine mammals be highly trained and attuned to slight variations in behavior, posture, respiration, appetite, and physical appearance, both for individuals as well as for social groups. Early detection of any variation in behavioral or physiological status can enable veterinary treatment before problems become visible or insurmountable.

When animals are housed in social groups, the behavior of one individual is not necessarily an accurate reflection of the physiological status of the group; however, the behavior of the group often gives insight into the status of individuals. For example, spatial behavior can lend insight into physiological processes. In cetaceans, isolation from the social group is often a sign of impending parturition. Pod configuration and swimming patterns may reflect hormonal activity (Wells, 1984). A study by Gibbons and Stoskopf (1989) addressed health problems manifested in newly introduced bottlenose dolphins by identifying and treating not only physical problems but also contributory environmental and social influences, as quantified by behavioral research. Information obtained through applied behavioral research can objectively complement observations of those individuals responsible for the physical care and well-being of animals, such as trainers, keepers, and veterinarians, thus maximally contributing to comprehensive husbandry and management programs.

Within the last decade, the maintenance and husbandry of marine mammals in zoos has passed from its infancy to its adolescence. These strides are perhaps best reflected by successful self-sustaining breeding programs involving sea lions (Captive Breeding Specialist Group, 1990; Asper et al., 1990a, Andrews and Duffield, 1992), seals (Captive Breeding Specialist Group, 1990; Asper et al., 1990a; Andrews and Duffield, 1992), bottlenose dolphins (Cornell et al., 1987; Asper et al., 1990a; Andrews and Duffield, 1992), and recent killer whale births in several marine zoological parks (Asper et al., 1990a; Andrews and Duffield, 1992). In 1992, more than 90 percent of cetaceans in current populations were reported to be housed in breeding or potential breeding situations (Andrews and Duffield, 1992). Successful reproduction is perhaps one of the best measures of a captive management program, indicating that at least the basic environmental and social needs of a species are being met.

Methods of Research in Captivity

Identification and Marking Techniques

A necessary requisite for most behavioral studies, beyond initial stages, is that the observer be able to recognize individuals (Lehner, 1979). For some species, such as killer whales and bottlenose dolphins, individuals can often be identified by characteristics of pigmentation patterns, dorsal fin size and shape, and the presence of scratches or scars on the dorsal fin and back (Bigg et al., 1976; Würsig and Würsig, 1977; Bigg, 1982; Heimlich-Boran, 1986b; Bigg et al., 1987, Santos and Lacerda, 1987; Katona, 1989). Sizes, shapes, color patterns, and distribution of external parasites also have been used to identify individual baleen whales (e.g., Price and Winn, 1981; Dorsey, 1983; Payne et al., 1983; Payne, 1986). Photographs of animals in social groups in the wild and in captivity have been catalogued and used to recognize individuals (Katona et al., 1980; Balcomb and Bigg, 1986; Kraus et al., 1986; Bigg et al., 1987; Sears, 1987; Kastelein and Dokter, 1988).

Permanent marking of marine mammals for long-term study and management has been addressed in a variety of ways. Baleen and sperm whales have been tagged with "discovery-type" tags (Rayner, 1940; Clark, 1962; Mackintosh, 1965) that have provided valuable information on migration, distribution, and other aspects of life history. Scott et al. (1990) presented an excellent overview and history of marking techniques that have been used with small cetaceans. Orr and Hiatt-Saif (1992) reported on a clear polyurethane, flattened flipper band that was tested with beluga whales. Small cetaceans have also been tagged using a number of methods that are now not often utilized including: circular plastic "button" tags (Norris and Pryor, 1970), vinyl "spaghetti" tags (Sergeant and Brodie, 1969; Evans et al., 1972), and underwater paint (Watkins and Scheville, 1976). Radio and theodolite tracking (e.g., Evans, 1974; Würsig and Würsig, 1980; Würsig et al., 1991) are now more commonly used.

Cryogenic marking also has been done on cetaceans, in the wild as well as in zoological facilities, as marks are less obtrusive and avoid problems associated with superficial tagging, such as tag removal or secondary infection associated with insertion (Macpherson and Penner, 1967; Evans et al., 1972; Cornell, 1978; Irvine et al., 1982). Pinnipeds have been marked using cryogenic methods (Macpherson and Penner, 1967) and cattle-type ear tags inserted through the flipper.

Sea otters present a special problem in marking as they are capable of removing flipper tags with their forelimbs. Cryogenic marking is presently not suitable for this species because of its potential effect on thermoregulation. Thomas et al. (1987) and Williams (1988) described the use of subcutaneously implanted transponder chips to identify individual sea otters. This method has been used successfully with manatees (Andrews, pers. commun.), and with penguins in a marine zoological park (pers. obs.). A drawback to this technique is that the observer must be within 5–38 cm of the animal in order to achieve an accurate scanner reading (Captive Breeding Specialist Group, 1991). While captive animals may be tolerant of readings at these distances, use with wild marine mammals would require capture and restraint. With further refinement of scanning capacity, however, this method shows great promise for use in the field.

Data Collection Techniques

As a rule, most behavioral studies carried out with captive marine mammals have been short-term in nature (cf., Essapian, 1963; Tavolga, 1966; DeFran et al., 1983; Brill et al., 1988; Kastelein and Wiepkema, 1988, 1990). In zoological facilities, social groupings and dynamics may change as animals are added or moved from groups according to husbandry requirements. As such, short-term research questions can often be addressed more realistically than can long-term questions, unless a facility is philosophically committed to a particular longitudinal research program. When plausible, long-term research programs have the advantage of contributing to knowledge of lifespan development, which to date has not been systematically documented in marine mammals.

Methods used for collection of behavioral data on marine mammals have changed a great deal from the *ad libitum* sampling characteristic of classical early studies (cf., McBride and Hebb, 1948; Essapian, 1963; Caldwell and Caldwell, 1964; Tavolga, 1966). Many contemporary studies employ standardized behavioral checklists (Wilson et al., 1985; Eastcott and Dickinson, 1987). Kleiman (1974) described two types of checksheets (time-sample and all-occurrence sampling) that can be easily adapted for use in the behavioral study of marine mammals. Other methods that are particularly suitable for use in study of marine mammals housed in zoological facilities include video-recording (Hutchins and

Gledhill, 1978), audio-recording, and microprocessors. These devices have many uses. For example, Kastelein and Wiepkema (1988, 1990) used video-recording to monitor interactions in a grey seal mother-infant dyad; Morton et al. (1986) recorded killer whale vocalizations and behavioral observations on each of two channels on a tape recorder to correlate sounds with particular behavioral states; and Chirighin (1987) used a microprocessor to collect data in a study of mother-calf behavior in bottlenose dolphins.

In addition to providing insight into behavioral phenomena, captive research has contributed greatly to the physiological database so vital to conservation programs. From research carried out in zoological facilities there is now a rich body of literature on normative anatomical and physiological parameters of marine mammals (e.g., Ridgway et al., 1970; Geraci, 1978; Geraci and Sweeney, 1978; Medway and Geraci, 1978; Cornell, 1983; Bryden and Harrison, 1986; Cornell et al., 1988a; Asper et al., 1990b; Bossart and Dierauf, 1990; O'Shea and Reep, 1990). Studies carried out in captivity have provided a greater understanding of marine mammal sensory abilities (e.g., Kuznetsov, 1974; Johnson, 1986; Brill et al., 1988; Marrin-Cooney, 1989). Hormonal studies of marine mammals have led to an increased understanding of normative reproductive cycles. These investigations are of critical importance to the growing body of scientific knowledge about marine mammals, and have significant implications for their management and conservation both in nature and in zoological facilities.

Problems and Advantages of Research in Captivity

In a recent survey, 41% of 58 responding zoological facilities reported conducting research with marine mammals in their care (American Association of Zoological Parks and Aquariums, 1990). Most zoological facilities recognize a need for research that will provide basic information about the behavior, biology, and general requirements of animal species in captivity. While part of this information may be gained by studying species in the wild, much of the information regarding basic biology and behavior can only be gained through captive research. Direct application of field research to captive management situations and vice versa, however, must be prudent. Constraints inherent in each environment may make clear quantitative assessment of the effects of each environment extremely difficult.

For the behavioral study of marine mammals, the nature of the aquatic habitat precludes observation of many behaviors in animals' repertoires in the wild. Observation of marine mammal species commonly seen in the wild is often very difficult for many reasons, including basic ones such as unfavorable weather conditions and difficulty in maintaining contact with animals for extended periods of time (Chirighin, 1987). Compounded with difficulties in locating less-plentiful populations, the study of threatened and endangered species, particularly cetaceans, is often unfeasible.

Problems of Validity

In order to contribute to conservation, behavioral studies must be relevant and valid. Beyond the normal difficulties encountered in attempting to measure behavior, the study of marine mammals presents problems with regard to validity. Chirighin (1987) points out that studies of behavior conducted in the wild tend to be high in external validity in that behaviors recorded are those exhibited in a natural environment, but nevertheless low in internal validity because of increased difficulty in systematically gathering concise data. Studies performed in captivity, on the other hand, are apt to be higher in internal validity as they are more accurate and systematic as far as the data-gathering process is concerned, but probable changes brought about by captivity may make them lower in external validity. Gaskin (1982) suggests that when data from studies on wild marine mammal populations can be compared to data from captive studies, the latter can be validated.

Nonetheless, field and captive behavioral research are each valid and strongly complement one another. Information provided by each is critical to a broader science of marine mammal study. Field and captive researchers tend to adopt different techniques of achieving perspective, analogous to "zooming in" and "zooming out" with a lens (Menzel, 1969). Field investigation offers an opportunity to observe, from a broad perspective, the animal's full pattern of activities from various approaches. In the captive or laboratory situation, in contrast, it is possible to focus on specialized questions, pursuing them in detail and under conditions involving refined controls (Schnierla, 1950). Each approach focuses attention on different aspects of the same phenomenon, and are inextricably entwined and vital to one another.

Advantages of Research in Captivity

The distinction between captivity and the wild is not a dichotomous one; these environments are part of a continuum of variable environments to which animals adapt. A captive environment is another ecological niche, to be adapted to and utilized by a population. Behavioral data drawn from studies in zoological facilities, especially when supported with data from nature, have the potential to show us an animal's capacity for adaptation (i.e., how they adapt to changes in the environment, in essence illustrating degrees of behavioral plasticity).

Captive research facilitates the investigation of basic biological and behavioral questions that might not be feasible to address in the wild. Populations and individuals housed in zoological facilities are usually readily identifiable and, particularly if captive-born, of known age, as well as medical and familial history. As such, captive populations lend themselves well to longitudinal study. Another advantage is that captive animals generally have a decreased flight distance. Captive animals do not disappear mysteriously, as is sometimes the case with wild subjects. Although marine mammal stranding networks can provide some information, complete gross and histologic postmortem examinations are rarely possible when an animal dies in the wild. Postmortem examination of captive animals facilitates greater insight into both physiology and behavior.

Where data from the field are available for one species, there may be a tendency to apply that information to the management of a second closely-related species, even though application of such data may not be appropriate (Eisenberg and Kleiman, 1977). It is imperative that studies performed both in captivity and in the field are evaluated on a species-by-species basis and generalizations cautiously made, when applicable.

In the case of endangered marine mammals, generalizations are particularly difficult. Even when closely related species occasionally have been maintained in zoological facilities, little research traditionally has been conducted. When endangered species, such as river dolphins, are present in zoological facilities, populations generally consist of a few animals, and most research has been limited to noninterventive observation to reduce the risk of interfering with potential reproduction. Regardless, any contribution gained from research on common or endangered marine mammal species helps to build a foundation from which basic understanding of the species can be drawn; including essential requirements for maintenance, propagation, and conservation.

Limitations of Research in Captivity

Although captive research confers several advantages over field research, there are also factors that define the limitations of research in this setting. Subjects in a captive setting are kept in a constrained environment that, by definition, can affect behavior; particularly if key social and environmental elements necessary to the display of species-typical behavior are absent. For example, it is only within the past decade that killer whales have been housed in social units that approximate the group structure of wild pods (pers. obs.). Even so, the capacity for interaction with regard to number of available partners is reduced from what it would be in nature, and this may affect behavior. Depending on the species and appropriateness of the environment, however, the effect of captivity on behavior is not necessarily detrimental (Ellis-Joseph, 1988).

In response to animal management decisions, unexpected changes in social groups under study, such as removal of animals for medical reasons, also may occur. For example, the logistics of treatment for a single marine mammal, which might involve partial draining of a pool or require physical restraint, may preclude this animal from remaining with the social unit under study. These and other factors present in a captive situation must be acknowledged and realistically accepted as uncontrolled intervening variables. Some, such as nonemergency changes in social groupings, can be minimized by an institutional commitment to a particular longitudinal research program. While administrative, medical, and management variables are important, they do not in any way obscure the contribution of captive research to a synthesized understanding of marine mammal taxa.

Training and Behavior

One unique factor that must be considered in the study of marine mammals, particularly cetaceans, is that the majority of animals maintained in zoological facilities are managed in a very "hands-on" manner. Most captive-housed marine mammals participate regularly in operant conditioning or training exercises, whether for demonstrations or to facilitate husbandry practices. Hediger (1955) viewed such training as "disciplined play," or "occupational therapy" which can assist in "brightening up the daily existence of animals . . . giving the animal the necessary amount of exercise and occupation" (p.139).

A review by DeFran and Pryor (1980) discussed responses to training in most species of cetaceans and rated their respective "trainability." Advantages of working with animals that are accustomed to training are many, and are best illustrated by the types of studies that have been made possible by utilizing trained marine mammals. For example, in one of many investigations of semantic comprehension, Schusterman and Krieger (1982) trained California sea lions in a symbolic matching paradigm. Other investigations of cognition such as one performed by Herman and Forestell (1985) have investigated transmission of information about symbolically referenced objects in trained bottlenose dolphins. Assessment of the cognitive abilities of these animals has been greatly facilitated by the use of operant techniques.

Investigations of other sensory abilities in marine mammals also have been carried out using operant techniques. Tyack (1991) was able to identify which dolphin within a group produced a sound with a vocalight telemetry device that was attached to the dolphin's head with a suction cup. Marrin-Cooney (1989) described a research breakthrough in which a bottlenose dolphin was trained to accept a fiber optic scope inside its nasal passage, obtaining video and audio recordings while the dolphin performed an echolocation task. Brill et al. (1988) conducted a study on echolocation "jaw hearing" theory with a dolphin trained to locate objects in the water while its eyes were covered. Wearing soft rubber eye cups, the dolphin was unable to locate the objects when its jaw also was covered with a neoprene barrier through which echolocation clicks could not pass. Operant procedures were used by Sokolov and Volkova (1973) and Kuznetsov (1974) in tests of taste discrimination in trained bottlenose dolphins. Hall and Richards (1982) performed a study on taste discrimination using an operant paradigm in a Pacific bottlenose dolphin (*T. t. gilli*) and a California sea lion.

In all of the above cases, the primary advantage allowed by training was that it facilitated calm investigation of basic research questions that would be difficult, if not impossible, to study in untrained animals. In particular, these studies are unique in that operant conditioning was used to investigate behavioral and physiological responses that would be unfeasible to study in the wild or in many captive situations, particularly with endangered marine mammal species.

Hand-rearing and Natural Behavior

Another factor that may also affect behavior is an animal's rearing history. While maternal rearing is always preferable, occasionally situations arise that dictate that an animal be reared by humans. Such situations may include beaching or stranding of wild-born animals, inadequate maternal care, or health problems either on the part of the mother or offspring. Beyond the challenge of simply keeping a young animal alive, zoological facilities are charged with providing an environment that fosters normal development and the expression of species-typical tendencies for hand-reared animals (Ellis-Joseph, unpub.).

Neonatal marine mammals, particularly cetaceans, are rarely removed from their mothers for hand-rearing except as a last resort. To date, only a few successes have been reported, including a baby California gray whale (*Escrichtius robustus*) that was collected, successfully hand-reared, and released at approximately one year of age (pers. obs.; Coerr and Evans, 1980). Recently, two stranded harbor porpoises (*Phocoena phocoena*) were successfully hand-reared from approximately four to five days of age (Andrews and Otjen, pers. comm.). At another facility, a hybrid bottlenose dolphin x false killer whale (*Pseudorca crassidens*) had a calf sired by a bottlenose dolphin. Staff were able to train the mother to allow milking and, for the first few days of its life, were able to exclusively tube-feed mother's milk to the calf. Over the following two months, the calf was fed mother's milk that was mixed with formula (Jones, pers. comm.). Other success stories include at least two bottlenose dolphins that were hand-reared from a few days of age (Joseph, pers. comm.), a six-month-old orphaned bottlenose dolphin (Goodall, 1988), and another bottlenose dolphin of the same age that was hand-reared in another zoological facility after its mother died (Joseph, pers. comm.). Other near successes have also been reported. For example, a baby killer whale that did not establish an appropriate nursing interaction with its mother survived 46 days while being bottle-fed by human caretakers (Desmond and Rutherford, 1982). A stranded baby pilot whale (*Globicephala spp.*) was successfully hand-reared and weaned to solid food but did not survive to adulthood due to injuries it received from adult conspecifics (Andrews, pers. comm.).

While techniques for hand-rearing cetaceans still pose great difficulty, there exists potential for refinement of these techniques via contributions afforded by captive-housed and captive-born animals. For example, postpartum milk samples are routinely obtained from unrestrained mother killer whales at three Sea World parks for compositional analysis (Andrews, pers. comm.). Similarly, milk samples were analyzed from the hybrid dolphin x false killer whale discussed previously (Jones, pers. comm.). These analyses may allow closer duplication of cetacean milk should hand-rearing efforts be necessary in the future. Such information also allows systematic examination of changes in milk composition that may be associated with calf development.

In contrast to cetacean hand-rearing efforts, pinniped hand-rearing programs have been very successful (e.g., Otten and Andrews, 1976; Otten et al., 1977; Dinnes and Gage, 1984; Gage et al., 1985; Gage, 1986, 1987, 1990a; Steele, 1986). Stranded California sea lions and harbor seals have been routinely hand-reared and released as part of marine mammal recovery programs (Dinnes and Gage, 1984; Gage et al., 1985; Gage, 1986, 1987, 1990; see also Odell, 1992). At present, quantitative data are not available regarding reproductive success of pinnipeds reared in such programs.

Hand-reared animals of other mammalian species often sexually imprint on human caretakers. Although not an indication of eventual reproductive success, copulation in hand-reared walruses (*Odobenus rosmarus*) is common in zoological facilities (pers. obs.), suggesting that for at least one pinniped species hand-rearing does not preclude normal sexual behavior. One hand-reared female has given birth to two offspring; one did not survive (Lack and Lotshaw, pers. comm.) and one had to be removed for hand-rearing (Campbell, pers. comm.). Most pinnipeds are hand-reared in peer-groups, which may help to attenuate any deleterious effects of human-rearing. Orphaned sea otters also have been successfully hand-reared (Williams, 1983b; Tyler, 1986), but have not been rehabilitated and reintroduced into wild populations in great numbers.

Influencing Social Factors on Conservation in Captivity

Social Behavior and Conservation in Captivity

While social behavior has not been well-studied in marine mammals housed in zoological facilities, reproductive behavior has been more widely examined, particularly in some of the early studies on bottlenose dolphins by McBride and Kritzler (1951), Tavolga and Essapian (1957) and Essapian (1963). Most recent reports have concentrated on cetaceans (e.g., Caldwell and Caldwell, 1975; Amundin, 1986; Lowenstein-Whaley and Cardeilhac, 1988). Other investigators have studied reproductive behavior in killer whales (e.g., Desmond and Rutherford, 1982) and Commerson's dolphin (Joseph et al., 1987). In one of the few interdisciplinary studies, Wells (1984) compared behavior patterns and steroid hormone concentrations in a captive colony of Hawaiian spinner dolphins (*Stenella longirostris*), linking frequencies of several behaviors to changes in reproductive hormone levels. One factor that has contributed to the relative paucity of reports on reproductive behavior has been husbandry, which in only the last two decades has advanced to the point that regular reproductive success is achieved in breeding programs for captive-housed cetaceans.

Research on basic social organization has the potential to provide information particularly pertinent to captive propagation and conservation programs. If animals are collected to supplement captive populations or to establish new groups in the future, it will be important to consider what field research as well as captive research has shown about the social organization and interactions of the species in question. Particularly for long-lived social species, issues such as the consequences of removal of an individual from its social unit will have to be considered, especially in light of criticism from proponents of animal rights. For example, killer whales in the Puget Sound, Vancouver Island area are known to occur both in relatively large stable social groups with limited overlapping ranges and in widely ranging transient pods of small numbers (Bigg et al., 1976; Balcomb et al., 1980; Bigg, 1982; Ford and Fisher, 1982). Long-term studies of bottlenose dolphin in Sarasota, Florida (Wells et al., 1987; Wells, 1991) and studies of bottlenose dolphin in the Gulf of California (Ballance, 1990) described the fluidity of social group associations. Wells has also reported a polygynous mating system for the Sarasota population. Both Hawaiian spinner dolphins (Wells et al., 1987) and Argentine bottlenose dolphins (Würsig and Würsig, 1977) are reported to show more fluidity in group association than the Sarasota population. Information regarding social systems and the demographics of social groups in the wild is of critical importance so that facilities establishing or maintaining marine mammals can better provide for each species' social needs.

Kirkevold (1986) suggested that collection of killer whales for public display and research should be limited to groups (rather than random individuals) whose social structure is well documented and whose demographic factors are sufficiently appraised. She suggested that after the collection of a group, effective programs should then monitor the remaining population. This logistically complex alternative has been suggested to avoid the potential disruption of the previously reported bonds of stable social groupings character- istic of animals such as killer whales (Bigg et al., 1976; Bigg, 1982; Balcomb and Bigg, 1986; Matkin and Leatherwood, 1986), although no ill effects from such disruptions have been quantified. Beyond logistic complexity, a significant drawback to this method is the likelihood of increased degrees of relatedness of group founders, and the decreasing genetic variability in subsequent generations. The killer whale social structure described by Bigg et al. (1987) implies very high levels of inbreeding, with very low dispersal rates (Hoezel et al., 1991). Highly inbred animals are generally not desir- able for captive breeding programs due to reduced fecundity (Ralls and Ballou, 1982; Ralls et al., 1986a). New reports of DNA finger- printing to determine paternity in captive killer whales (Hoezel et al., 1991) may someday have to be applied to wild populations, and may be helpful in guiding the establishment of any new groups of small cetaceans.

On the other hand, social groups of animals are not unac- customed to the disappearance of single animals due to illness, death, or emigration, and resultant changes in pod configura- tion. Thus, standard collection practices, in which one or two animals are removed from a social group, may in some way mimic the natural departure of pod members. New groups formed with animals collected in this way are likely to have more genetic variability than those collected as intact groups (see Bigg et al., 1987; Hoezel et al., 1991), thus minimizing potential inbreeding effects. Particularly for threatened and endangered species, good genetic variability is critical to successful captive management and conservation programs. As new animals are collected for zoological facilities, the merits of both Kirkevold's (1986) ap- proach and the standard collection practices will have to be weighed, and advantages of each discussed on a case-by-case basis—depending on the species and concomitant long-range cap- tive management and conservation goals. With either approach, further research is needed on genetic variability, behavior, and social organization of wild populations.

Conclusions

A clear need exists for continuation and expansion of study on marine mammals both in the field and in zoological facilities. At the most basic level, research should aid in clarifying our understanding of marine mammals and in elucidating basic behavioral and physiological processes. On a more applied level, research contributes to improving husbandry, propagation, and management, as well as the psychological well-being of extant captive-housed populations. Toward the goal of public education, zoological facilities are in a singularly powerful position to contribute to and to promote public appreciation of the uniqueness of marine mammals through scientific research. Emphasizing and elucidating specialized adaptations and characteristics of marine mammal species, without romanticizing or attributing human-like qualities to them, zoological facilities can actively enlist the support of their visitors for marine mammal research and conservation programs.

For marine mammal taxa, studies that merit immediate attention in the field may require a different focus than those that merit immediate attention in captivity. Beyond basic behavioral observation, the focus of field research should be multifaceted, including reliable information on population demographics and trends, genetics, social organization, diet, migration, fisheries interactions, harvesting by whalers and sealers, as well as the effects of pollutants and other marine perturbations. The focus of captive research also must be multifaceted, augmenting topics listed above as well as systematically determining how the captive environment affects the animal. Captive research programs should attempt to gather information via behavioral and physiological research that is basic as well as applied in nature, with the aim of elucidating the basic biology of the species, as well as enhancing our ability to maintain and propagate animals already housed in zoological parks. In light of the relative paucity of field research on the majority of marine mammal taxa, more substantial investigation of those species thought to be critically endangered or extremely vulnerable is called for before groups are collected for captive propagation and research programs. Husbandry techniques for those species may be modeled, where appropriate, from other closely related species whose populations would not be detrimentally affected by removal of small numbers of individuals for such programs.

Citing the recent successful introduction and breeding of Commerson's dolphins (Joseph et al., 1987; Cornell et al., 1988b), Asper et al. (1990) suggests that, given proper conditions, it is possible to constitute breeding colonies of cetaceans that can become reproductively active in a short period of time. Asper et al. (1990) suggest that zoological facilities examine current collections and, given the concern over global ecosystem degradation, look into expanding or reconstituting current marine mammal collections. If this is to happen, then it is imperative that all zoological facilities participate in regional as well as global collaborative breeding and research programs; thereby taking responsibility for strengthening and supporting current research programs to include comprehensive field and captive research with many species, not just the more common ones. Information from these research directions will provide a complementary and synthesized base of information upon which comprehensive global conservation and management policies can be developed both in nature and in zoological facilities.

Captive breeding programs are not meant to be a substitute for adequate habitat preservation. Especially for critically endangered species, however, they present a workable and valuable "banking" system for species' genetic material until such time when habitat degradation or other environmental pressures are under control. Realistically, the majority of marine mammal species will likely never be present in zoological collections, and still fewer will be propagated for the express purpose of reintroduction to the wild. However, the creation of future breeding programs with the eventual goal of reestablishment of endemic populations may be a realistic possibility, particularly for some smaller species.

To date, there has been only one documented successful reintroduction involving small cetaceans. As a segment of a two-part research project studying the processing of sonar information, Wells (pers. comm.) collected and returned two young male bottlenose dolphins to Tampa Bay in Florida, where the animals appear to have integrated into the local dolphin population. Wells cautions, however, that this was a special case and that this success does not indicate that release is feasible for every dolphin. Rather, release attempts must be considered on an individual basis, taking into consideration a myriad of factors such as the length of time in captivity, age, sex, health status, region of origin, and behavioral plasticity. As future reintroduction programs are developed, however, there is a clear need for concomitant incorporation of active and integrated research on marine mammal immunology, disease etiology and transmission so that existing wild groups are not harmed by the introduction of new animals. Such programs would likely involve reintroduction of F_1 or F_2 offspring, before any genetic adaptation to captivity that might take place can have progressed very far.

Some species on this planet, not yet even classified, will likely be extinct before we know them scientifically (Wilcox, 1988). Until habitat is restored, overexploitation stopped, and management errors corrected, captive populations may provide a means to buy time for some species (Flesness and Foose, 1990). Beyond preserving some of the wonder of the natural world for future generations, captive populations may also be a vehicle for mitigation of natural and human-caused disasters. We do not know, for example, the long-term ramifications of recent oil spills in the Persian Gulf and in Prince William sound. It is likely that the already endangered Persian Gulf population of dugongs (*Dugong dugon*), estimated to be 3,000–7,000 individuals (Anonymous, 1991b), was deleteriously affected by the recent spill. Although not considered endangered, it is estimated that one-fourth of the Alaskan sea otter population was depleted by the oil spill in Prince William Sound (Lemonick, 1989). Numerous otters were rescued and rehabilitated using a deoiling protocol developed during a pilot study carried out in conjunction with a marine zoological park (Davis et al., 1986; Joseph et al., 1986). Although neither the Persian Gulf or Prince William Sound oil spills are worst-case scenarios, had populations of these species been present and reproducing in zoological facilities, husbandry techniques and genetic material could have been readily available to help assuage the effects of these disasters, had they been needed. This kind of "banking" is particularly important for species whose populations number in the hundreds, such as the baiji, estimated at no more than 200 animals (Zhou, 1986, 1989; IUCN, 1987; Chen et al., 1992; Zhou and Wang, 1992; see also Schroeder, chap. 22, this volume). When population numbers reach such low levels, an entire population could be devastated by a single catastrophic event.

Realistically, intensive captive management programs are best initiated when populations still number in the thousands. All too typically, however, as in the black-footed ferret (*Mustela nigripes*) and California condor (*Gymnogyps californianus*) cases, captive options have been resisted until the wild population is less than 20, genetic erosion has already begun, and the population is at maximum risk (Flesness and Foose, 1990). At this point, there is no room or time for error, or for learning captive husbandry requirements (Flesness and Foose, 1990).

Given current and predicted levels of habitat degradation, it is not an unrealistic possibility that at some point, captive populations may provide the last bastion for a select few marine mammal species. If so, then we must become knowledgeable in all aspects of marine mammal behavior and biology, and the effects of human management on behavior, genetics, and biology, including long-term reproduction and survival. This goal can be best served by the development of strong and active *in situ* and *ex situ* collaborative research programs that are supported by zoological facilities. This scientific approach would facilitate vigorous interdisciplinary exchange, and would foster cooperation between researchers in the field and in zoological facilities. In an uncertain world, it is only through vigorous teamwork on all fronts that adequate information can be obtained to allow informed decision-making for strategies leading to protracted species conservation.

Acknowledgments

I would like to thank B. Andrews, R. Brill, B. Joseph, J. Mellen, and D. Odell for helpful comments on early drafts of the manuscript. I am grateful to J. Shaw, librarian at the Lincoln Park Zoo, and to the library staff at the John G. Shedd Aquarium for valuable assistance. Finally, I thank J. Demarest for his assistance in improving this manuscript during all phases of its development.

24

Elements of Successful Facility Design: Marine Mammals

Jay Sweeney and Terry Samansky

Until the 1980's, water spaces for marine mammals were designed with an emphasis on maintenance and operational simplicity while holding to a rather static state-of-the-art in facility size and configuration. Beginning in the 1980s, a surge in new facilities resulted in a significantly larger size and vastly increased versatility in exhibit design (Krajniak, 1984; Murphy, 1984; Charfauros, 1986; Hewlett, 1986; Hewlett and Hewlett, 1986; Jones, 1986; Proctor, 1986; Hausknecht, 1987). The emphasis has been on providing naturalistic habitats and increased behavioral enrichment. While the costs associated with construction and maintenance of these facilities has greatly escalated (Hewlett, 1986; Jones, 1986), so too has the visiting public's knowledge and appreciation of these animals as integral components of the earth's total marine environment.

Economics of Facility Design

Most of the facilities designed and constructed in the 1980s have included budget allocations well into the millions of dollars (Proctor, 1986; Hausknecht, 1987). For small cetaceans, such as bottlenose dolphins (*Tursiops truncatus*), facilities holding between 500,000 and 1,000,000 gallons of water carry a price tag of between 2 and 5 million dollars, which includes the life support system structures that are required for suitable maintenance of water quality. In locales where a structural pool covering is required, buildings with full visitor amenities have become the norm resulting in budgets that are often more than doubled, compared to pool and life-support systems alone. Pinniped pools equipped with free formed rock work, and ranging in size between 50,000 and 250,000 gallons of water, carry a price tag of at least 1 to 2 million dollars, including life-support system. Even the costs required to renovate existing facilities can easily run into the millions of dollars (Hausknecht, 1987; Judges, 1988). Such financial commitments will undoubtedly increase as designers are given free hand in both size and structural versatility. Because of escalating costs, some facilities in construction have realized significant savings by contracting value engineering study specialists to evaluate design specifications and to identify areas of unnecessary costs. In addition, increased requirements for design versatility and creativity have spurred the accepted use of the design consultant team approach (McCusker and Larson, 1986). By utilizing specialists (e.g., veterinarians, behaviorists, and zoologists), a higher level of habitat detail can be achieved without accruing major additional costs.

The increased level of commitment required for state-of-the-art marine mammal displays is high, it is accepted because these animals maintain a strong public appeal, are often difficult to acquire, and tend to thrive in well-designed and managed facilities. Advances in marine mammal medicine have resulted in design of back areas which emphasize, in structural elements, a commitment to medical support. Up to 20% of a facility's cost is now accounted for by back area support capabilities.

The increased level of commitment has been very worthwhile. In the recent past, we have seen substantial variation in marine mammal survival rates among various institutions, and a significant rise in these rates among some captive marine mammal species (Bain, 1987; DeMaster and Drevenak, 1988). For example, studies by DeMaster and Drevenak (1988) found that the survival of bottlenose dolphins in captivity was significantly higher between 1980–1984 than during the previous 5-year-period. These variations can, in part, be attributed to an increased investment in husbandry and medical support. In the same study (DeMaster and Drevenak, 1988), a captive annual survival rate of .93 (i.e., 93% of all individuals in captivity are expected to still be alive at the end of any given year) for *Tursiops truncatus* has been calculated using data beginning at capture or birth. This corresponds favorably with Wells' and Scott's (1990) data for a wild *Tursiops truncatus* population with an average annual survival rate of .961, including individuals beginning at one year of age (thus not accounting for the relatively high mortality experienced in the first year of life).

As a result of better water filtration systems, more efficient skimmer design, strategic placement of drains and water hose bibs, and more efficient access for maintenance personnel, the newer design facilities are also more easily maintained. With less time allotted to maintenance, there is greater opportunity for research, exhibit programming and, where training of animals is concerned, behavioral conditioning and show presentation. Increasingly, the value of keeper/trainer input into the design of exhibits is being recognized (Brisby, 1985; Valleriani, 1985). In addition to planning for the routine maintenance requirements of an exhibit, insights into personnel support needs (e.g., lockers, showers, and laundry) can help maintain a motivated staff; thereby reducing employee turnover rates and the associated costs of hiring and training personnel and related impact on animal care and health.

Means for protection of captive animals from abuse by the public are required by the rules for care and handling of marine mammals as published by the U.S. Department of Agriculture (USDA) (Jenkins, 1990; USDA, 1992). Additionally, a security plan is required as part of every marine mammal permit application that is filed with the National Marine Fisheries Service of the U.S. Department of Commerce. Generally, a security plan includes preventive barriers and on-site security personnel during public access periods. All security provisions are examined regularly by inspectors of the USDA as part of their routine site inspections required for licensure.

Species Considerations In Facility Design

Abiotic Factors

USDA regulations (USDA, 1992, p. 87) require that captive marine mammals not be subjected to "rapid changes in air and water temperatures" or temperatures that would "adversely affect their health and comfort." Although specific temperature ranges have not been addressed by government regulations, there nevertheless remain empirically derived criteria for temperature requirements for certain species (Geraci, 1986a; Dierauf, 1990a; Faulk, 1990; White and Francis-Floyd, 1990; Williams, 1990; Worthy, 1990). An example of temperature ranges, successfully utilized and recommended by the authors, is listed in Table 24.1.

Table 24.1
Water Temperature Range Guidelines for Marine Mammals

	Max. Temp. F°/C°	Min. Temp. F°/C°	Mean Temp. F°/C°
Polar Species, Cetaceans	75/24	40/4	55/13
Polar Species, Pinnipeds	75/24	32/0	55/13
Temperate Species, Cetaceans	80/27	45/7	60/16
Temperate Species, Pinnipeds	80/27	45/7	70/21
Tropical Species, Cetaceans	85/29	55/13	75/24
Tropical Species, Pinnipeds	85/29	55/13	75/24

In those locales where ambient water temperatures range to the extreme, it is now considered necessary for facilities responsible for the above species to provide heating or cooling in order to suitably maintain these animals.

Government regulations (USDA, 1992, p. 87) also require that "at no time shall (habitat) lighting be such that it will cause the animal discomfort or trauma," and in some cases, access to protection from direct sunlight may be required. In addition, indoor facilities must provide "ample lighting, by natural or artificial means, or both, of a quality, distribution, and duration which is appropriate for the species involved" and sufficient for "inspections, observations, and cleaning." It is generally considered desirable to provide natural light for animal enclosures. Where this is not possible, a mixture of candescent and incandescent light is desirable in a periodicity equivalent to the animal's natural habitat (Geraci, 1986a). For polar species, local ambient cycles are generally utilized without discernible adverse consequences. Walruses (*Odobenus rosmarus*), for example, have successfully reproduced within the continental United States at latitudes far below their natural distribution (Walsh et al., 1990a). Most facilities, therefore, provide a light cycle similar to that of seasonal ambient lighting.

In addition to environmental configuration, the maintenance of a high standard of water quality is primary to the success of marine mammal exhibits (Geraci, 1986a), and is especially important in the husbandry of sea otters (Hewlett, 1983; Farwell and Hymer, 1988; Farwell et al., 1988; Williams, 1990). USDA (1992) standards require that water samples be taken from primary marine mammal enclosures and tested at least daily for pH, chlorine, and any other chemicals added to maintain water quality standards, and at least weekly for coliform bacteria counts. By current USDA (1992) standards, the most probable number (MPN) for coliform bacteria counts must not exceed 1,000 per 100 ml of water, though in practice, coliform counts above 100 per 100 ml of water may signify problems in water sanitation procedures. To achieve acceptable standards of microbiological sanitation, water clarity, and biochemical homeostasis, a variety of filtration and chemical treatment techniques have been devised. Table 24.2 contains a list of the various water treatment mechanisms in use today (Rubin, 1975; Spotte, 1979b, 1992; Geraci, 1986a; Sieswerda, 1986; Van der Toorn, 1987; Faulk, 1990). Each item on the list is an individually selected procedure used for the water treatment indicated. Some procedures may be more efficient when used in combination. For example, chlorine and ozone together may control algae and bacteria more effectively at lower concentrations than if one or the other were used independently. Some procedures, however, are incompatible. Utilization of chlorine and biological filtration together, for example, may result in each eliminating the beneficial effect of the other. Experienced water quality engineers usually provide the detailed expertise in this very technical area of design, including an analysis of relative cost-effectiveness and for acceptable ranges of quality control, these being very much dependent upon the demands of each system.

The design of facilities for marine mammals in the 1980s has seen a trend away from the linear dimensions of traditional marine mammal exhibits (hard environments) toward an attempt to reproduce natural (soft) environments (Coe, 1988). While this has been especially true of exhibits designed for pinnipeds (Jones, 1986; Hausknecht, 1987; Krajniak, 1987) and otters (Hewlett, 1983; Farwell and Hymer, 1988; Farwell et al., 1988), some cetacean exhibits are now beginning to follow this trend (Hewlett, 1986; Proctor, 1986; Hausknecht, 1987; Krajniak, 1987). In recent years, exhibit designers have emphasized naturalistic habitat as the primary theme factor in the design of these facilities. Animals are exhibited in habitats resembling those in which they are found in nature. This allows for a much higher degree of versatility relative to species selection and may offer the opportunity for providing mixed species exhibits. Larger and more diverse environments provide for a greater degree of socialization and positive behavioral interactions among individuals and species (Geraci, 1986a; Sweeney, 1990). Furthermore, because marine mammal exhibits nearly always contain a water body, there is, by definition, a three-dimensional

Table 24.2
Outline of Water Quality Management for Marine Mammals

I.   Control of Bacteria
  A. Chlorination
  B. Ozone
  C. Copper
  D. Copper/Silver
  E. Biological Filtration
  F. Mechanical Filtration*
  G. Ultraviolet Light
  H. Water Exchange

II. Removal of Particulates
  A. Mechanical Filtration*
  B. Ozone
  C. Flocculents
  D. Water Exchange

III. Removal of Biological Wastes
  A. Chlorination—Trace or Breakpoint
  B. Chlorination—Shock
  C. Ozone
  D. Activated Carbon
  E. Biological Filtration
  F. Water Exchange

IV. Control of Algae
  A. Chlorination
  B. Copper
  C. Ozone
  D. Herbicides
  E. Avoidance of Ultraviolet Light
  F. Biological Filtration
  G. Water Exchange

V.   Removal of Organic/Inorganic Colors
  A. Chlorination—Shock
  B. Mechanical Filtration*
  C. Ozone
  D. Copper
  E. Activated Carbon
  F. Water Exchange

---

* Mechanical Filtration
  —Pressure Sand Filters
  —Diatomaceous Earth Filters
  —Gravity Feed Sand Filters

character to these sorts of exhibits. Where older facilities provided merely a uniform length, width, and depth feature to an exhibit, modern designs include more interesting dimensional features like depth contouring. The three-dimensional character of the exhibits is now highlighted by offering underwater viewing of rocks, caves, ledges, peepholes, tunnels, rubbing posts, cascading water, and wave action. While these features certainly make the exhibit more aesthetically pleasing to visitors, they also provide beneficial opportunities for animals to interact and control elements of their environments (Markowitz, 1990; Sweeney, 1990).

Biotic Factors

In healthy marine mammals, the metabolic requirements for water are generally satisfied through the consumption of food via preformed moisture and the hydrolysis of fat (Ridgway, 1972; White and Francis-Floyd, 1988; Dierauf, 1990a; Riedman, 1990; Worthy, 1990). Anorexic and otherwise dehydrated animals often require supplemental fluid therapy (Sweeney and Ridgway, 1975; White and Francis-Floyd, 1988; Walsh et al., 1989), and some species (e.g., walruses, seals, and sea lions) have been observed drinking fresh water or eating ice (Flynn, 1987; Turley, 1988; Dierauf, 1990a; Riedman, 1990; Worthy, 1990). To satisfy occasional freshwater needs, portable trays or tubs can be utilized in pinniped and otter facilities. Cetaceans undergoing dehydration may be successfully rehydrated by means of medical or other pools designed for variable salinity control (Walsh et al., 1989).

With the exception of the herbivorous Sirenian Order (Best, 1981; White and Francis-Floyd, 1990), the diet of most captive marine mammals consists of various fish and marine invertebrates; items particularly susceptible to contamination, spoilage, and nutrient loss (Geraci, 1986b; White and Francis-Floyd, 1988). Federal law (USDA, 1992, p. 95) requires that food fed to marine mammals be "wholesome, palatable, and free from contamination" and that frozen food be "maintained at a maximum temperature of -18° C (0° F)." Food preparation areas must be designed with an emphasis on hygiene (e.g., ease of cleaning, proper storage, and effective waste disposal).

Importance should also be placed on the provisional control of food and associated record keeping (Geraci, 1986a, b). Accurate distribution, detailed food charts (Hecker, 1985), and computerized databases (Williams and Ghebremeskel, 1988) help to maintain proper diets. Utilization of food as a positive reinforcer in the training of marine mammals is well established (Pryor, 1984), and even among nonperforming animals, behavioral control has been demonstrated to be very beneficial in socialization (Desmond and Laule, 1987) and husbandry management (Andrews, 1986; Stephens, 1986; Skaar, 1987; Sweeney, 1990). In designing facilities, thought should be given to feeding stations, slide out areas, stretcher stations, and other environmental elements to enhance the effectiveness of training programs.

To achieve compatible social groupings, it is important to consider how the animals interact in free living groups and a review of relevant field literature is recommended. Some species, for example, exhibit extreme male territorial aggression (King, 1983; Sweeney, 1990) during certain times of the year. In some groups (e.g., some pinniped species) the number of allowable males in a given habitat may be limited relative to the size and/or spatial orientation of the facility. Providing access to visual separation between adult males, for example, may help to reduce aggressive interactions. In other groups that are largely matriarchal (e.g., bottlenose dolphins; Wells et al., 1980; Wells, 1991), attention must be paid to the sex and age makeup of long-standing adult groups. There must be planning for incorporation of juveniles into this group because nonrelated juveniles are not normally observed in adult groupings (Wells et al., 1980; Shane et al., 1986; Wells, 1991). Failure to pay attention to these matters can result not only in breaks in behavioral stability, but can also lead to problems associated with animal health (Geraci, 1986a; Dierauf, 1990b; Sweeney, 1990).

A current trend in zoological design and management is toward multispecies exhibits. Attempts to exhibit mixed-species of marine mammals (e.g., bottlenose dolphins, Pacific white-sided dolphins [*Lagenorhynchus obliquidens*], Risso's dolphins [*Grampus griseus*], and false killer whales [*Psuedorca crassidens*]) within the same habitat has, in general, met with widespread success (Hewlett and Newman, 1968; Neugebauer, 1967; Caldwell and Caldwell, 1972; Flynn, 1987). With marine mammals, there has been a wide range of mixed-species compatibility, providing that ample volume and structural variability is provided to allow some natural separation of habitat space. Many species of cetaceans and pinnipeds cohabit the same natural environment and, in fact, are commonly seen in mixed-species groupings (King, 1983; Minasian et al., 1984; Polacheck, 1987). In some exhibits, species compatibility is such that interspecies breeding has been observed (Burgess, 1968), and in some cases hybrid offspring (e.g., *Tursiops* x *Grampus*, and

Tursiops x *Psuedorca*) have been the result (Nishiwaki and Tobayama, 1982; Sylvestre and Tasaka, 1985; Duffield, 1990). Interspecific hybrids have also been recorded in the wild (Sylvestre and Tasaka, 1985; Duffield, 1990), and while this situation may indicate social compatibility, hybridization should be avoided when managing endangered species. As has been observed in the wild, social and/or territorial dominance tend to be exhibited throughout the captive habitat irrespective of the species involved. Where facilities provide inadequate space for the animals, there have been instances where dominant species have displayed traumatic aggression toward their subdominant counterparts (e.g., walrus towards harbor seals [*Phoca vitulina*], bottlenose dolphins towards Pacific white-sided dolphins or common dolphins [*Delphinus delphis*]) as well as toward their conspecifics (Geraci, 1986a).

Facility Design and Animal Health

Errors in design may serve as an important factor in the onset of health related problems. Failure to provide ample space for normal behavioral variability and expression, for example, may lead to stereotypic behavior. This activity may be progressive and could lead to functional alterations of behavior that may have very definite health consequences. These include problems of aggression/submission, aberrant sexual activity, reproductive failure, nervousness, self-inflicted trauma, and pathological behavior (e.g., vomiting and foreign body consumption) (Gaskin, 1982; Amundin, 1986; Dierauf, 1990b; Sweeney, 1990).

Injuries and/or illness can also result directly or indirectly from defects associated with the configuration of the pool environment. For example, consumption of pool components may occur as portions of the pool disintegrate or as animals disassemble portions of their environment (Sweeney, 1990). Where drain covers are not securely attached to the bottom drain, animals frequently investigate and may remove the cover. In this situation, animals may be sucked into the drain and are then unable to withdraw, resulting in drowning. Drains should be secured to the bottom structure. Animals may also jump or be pushed out of pools while engaged in play or aggressive behavior if they are allowed close approximation to the pool edge and when this edge is close in elevation to the water level. This can be prevented by building a ledge or fence barrier.

Animals may abrade skin and other body parts on sharp edges or on surfaces that are rough to passing contact. In particular, cetaceans may traumatize appendages on environmental overhangs which do not make contact with the water surface. In contrast, the animals can readily navigate to avoid structures that are in the water.

Where inadequate ventilation is provided, chlorine fumes as well as other heavier-than-air noxious gases can accumulate at the water surface where they are taken in by the animals through the exchange of respiratory gases. Air exchanges within enclosed structures are necessary as per civil codes, but here it is important to assure that flushing at water level is effectively maintained (Amundin, 1986; Geraci, 1986a).

Care should be taken to avoid the inflow of surface contamination into the main pool body. Drains can be positioned in such a way that contaminating materials are washed away from the animal's environment. This is especially relevant for pinniped facilities where feces are normally deposited upon the haul-out space (Dierauf, 1990a). In order for proper cleaning and surface sanitation, access to all portions of the habitat is necessary. While the benefits of newer naturalistic rockwork habitats are readily apparent, it must be stated that the rough surfaces of such materials may also contribute to increased opportunity for excess algae and bacterial growth (Farwell and Hymer, 1988; Farwell et al., 1988); a situation that, if not corrected, could lead to serious health problems.

At times it is necessary to remove animals from the general environment for isolation and medical treatment (Geraci, 1986a). In part, the successful treatment of infirmed animals depends upon the efficient configuration of the medical pool complex (see Figure 24.1).

The facility represented in Figure 24.1 provides for ease of access to sick animals for treatment, for variable water depth, and provides options for both salt and freshwater maintenance. With pinnipeds, back area holding facilities should be provided that allow for isolation and communal living. Such areas may be used for night holding of the entire stock, thereby reducing the impact of night time depositions of excrements on the exhibit haul-out space and water bodies. They may also be used for back area training or they may serve for medical treatment and for the provision of a secure area for reproduction and early rearing of the young. It should be noted here that medical services for marine mammals, including diagnostic and most therapeutic procedures, are performed

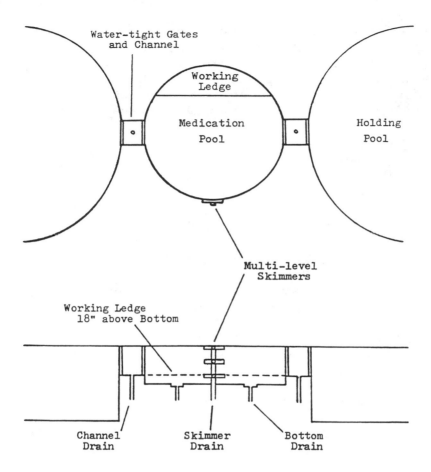

Figure 24.1. Medication and Isolation Pool for Cetaceans

at pool or holding facility sites. In light of this, it is necessary to design these areas for access and use of medical equipment and medical procedures.

Facility Design and Conservation

The marine mammal display community has had a long history of commitment to conservation. Much of the knowledge required to successfully manage wild populations has been gained as a direct result of cooperation between the display and scientific communities

(Norris, 1991). Research is vital to any effective conservation program and should be included in the design of marine mammal facilities. Above and below water observation areas, video and hydrophone access, weighing stations, on site data labs, and equipment storage space are some examples of design elements that can be incorporated for the enhancement of conservation related research.

Many display and research institutions devote considerable resources to the ongoing rehabilitation and release of sick, injured, orphaned, and otherwise stranded animals, and respond in times of ecological emergency (e.g., hurricanes, mass strandings, and oil spills) (Barrett, 1990; Dierauf, 1990c; Gage, 1990b; Walsh et al., 1990b; White and Francis-Floyd, 1990; Williams, 1990a). The 1989 Exxon Valdez disaster is one example of the conservation, research, and display communities working together to resolve a complex environmental problem (Davis, 1990; Williams, 1990a).

Long before the 1988 amendments to the Marine Mammal Protection Act required applicants for public display permits to offer education or conservation programs (Hoffman, 1989), much of the emphasis in design was directed towards expanding the public's knowledge and appreciation of marine mammals, and the crucial role that preservation of habitats plays in the long-term survival of species. To this end, many facilities are utilizing naturalistic settings, multispecies exhibits, interpretive graphics, and high-tech audio and video displays to present the animals as integral components of their particular ecosystems (Krajniak, 1984; Murphy, 1984; Charfauros, 1986; Hewlett, 1986; Hewlett and Hewlett, 1986; Jones, 1986; Proctor, 1986; Hausknecht, 1987). This commitment to education and conservation is reflected in changing attitudes, both in the United States and overseas (Glass and Englund, 1989), and has resulted in increased public interest and support for marine mammal conservation.

The international conservation community is beginning to accept the importance of captive propagation of endangered species (Conway, 1986a; Seal, 1986a). Captive breeding of marine mammals has been quite successful (Duffield, 1990), and in some facilities, birth control measures have actually been adopted to prevent the overpopulation of some species (e.g., California sea lions [*Zalophus californianus*]) (Dierauf, 1990d; Schroeder, 1990a). The successful captive reproduction of marine mammal species designated as threatened or endangered (IUCN, 1988a; Jenkins, 1990; Roletto and Mazzeo, 1990) include: sea otters [*Enhydra lutris*] (Williams, 1990b), Steller sea lions [*Eumetopias jubatus*] (Kastelein et al., 1990b), and manatees [*Trichechus manatus*] (White and Francis-Floyd, 1990). While still in their infancy, complex captive breeding and repopulation programs for marine mammals hold much promise for the future (Avella, 1986; Seal, 1986b; Joseph et al., 1987; Ames, 1991). In the mean time, by understanding the captive husbandry and reproductive requirements of non-endangered model species (e.g., California sea lions, harbor seals, bottlenose dolphins and killer whales [*Orcinus orca*]) the scientific, display, and conservation communities will be better prepared to enact well-planned cooperative captive propagation and reintroduction programs for those related species that are endangered (Bertram, 1986; Joseph et al., 1987; Ames, 1991).

Conclusions

The design of zoological displays for marine mammals has advanced in recent years with an emphasis on the provision of an environment compatible with the biological, social, and health requirements of these animals. Facilities have been designed with specific attention to the configuration of the natural habitat of the species, both for the enrichment of the animal's existence, and for the visitor's education, enjoyment, and appreciation of the animals within their natural environment. While acknowledging that nature cannot be totally recreated, modern design and management practices are utilizing the findings from field ecology studies to an ever greater degree. Much attention has been paid to efficient exhibit maintenance, better medical care, and the reproductive needs of the animals. Recent successes in habitat design and in the exhibition and propagation of a wide variety of species have cultivated a creative opportunity that should encourage even more interesting environments for the future.

Acknowledgments

The authors would like to thank Dr. Randall Wells, Dr. David Bain, Mr. Michael Demetrios, and Mr. Sonny Allen for their critical reviews and editorial assistance.

VII

Primates

Introduction of Authors
and Chapter Previews

The conservation chapter was authored by Edward F. Gibbons, Jr., director of the Center for Science and Technology, Briarcliffe College. Dr. Gibbons' research in zoos and aquariums has involved a variety of reptilian, avian, and mammalian species. His focus has been the application of animal behavior science to enhance the biological and psychological functioning of exotic animals in captivity. In addition to this volume, the book *Naturalistic Environments in Captivity for Animal Behavior Research* (with E. J. Wyers, E. Waters, and E. W. Menzel, Jr.) was recently published by the State University of New York Press. Dr. Gibbons' current research interest involves the application of behavioral medicine to the health and well-being of animals in captivity.

In his chapter, Dr. Gibbons analyzes International Species Inventory System records of primates in captivity and notes that the majority of specimens and captive births represent very few species. He warns that the disproportionate growth of a few taxa may skew the allocation of conservation resources to these few highly represented taxa which may inhibit population growth of other species and subspecies.

S. Kolkute and W. Richard Dukelow coauthored the primate reproductive physiology chapter. Dr. Kholkute is affiliated with the Institute for Research in Reproduction (ICMR) in Bombay, India as senior research officer. At present, he is working as a visiting scientist at the Endocrine Research Center of Michigan State University which is directed by Dr. Dukelow. Dr. Dukelow is also professor of Physiology and Animal Science at Michigan State University. He is a former president of both the American Society of Primatologists and the International Primatological Society. Both Kholkute

481

and Dukelow have worked extensively with a variety of primate species including marmosets, squirrel monkeys, bonnet macaques, and baboons. Their research has been focused on the understanding of physiological processes that affect or control reproduction in primates.

Drs. Kholkute and Dukelow review in detail the reproductive physiology of some representative primate species from which inferences can be made about other, more endangered forms. The authors are encouraged that progress in assisted reproductive technology for humans will benefit the captive propagation of endangered primate species.

The primate behavior chapter was coauthored by Douglas Candland, professor of Animal Behavior and Psychology at Bucknell University, and Sarah L. Bush, a Marshall Scholar presently studying at the University of East Anglia, United Kingdom and at the Jersey Preservation Trust, Channel Islands. Dr. Candland works with two long-standing social groups of Japanese macaques and hamadryas baboons housed for twenty-five years on the Bucknell campus. His current research program concerns how primates form visual categories, and he has published a book entitled *The Silent Mind* (Oxford University Press). After earning a B.S. in Animal Behavior at Bucknell, Ms. Bush now focuses her research on the principles of reproduction and captive breeding.

In their chapter, the authors provide an interesting review of the history of field research on primates. They also describe several significant translocated primate populations, emphasizing differences in behavior between captive and endemic situations, especially in vocalizations and the seasonal patterns of behavior.

The primate captive design chapter was prepared by Donald Lindburg, behaviorist at the Center for Reproduction of Endangered Species at the Zoological Society of San Diego, and Jon Coe, an architect with Coe, Lee, Robinson & Roesch. Dr. Lindburg, who edits the journal *Zoo Biology,* heads a behavior program that is aimed at increasing understanding of the ways in which environmental factors impact the reproduction and psychological health of captive wildlife. The scope of these investigations includes the design of optimum conditions for eliciting reproduction. Mr. Coe and his firm are among the leading innovators in the design of environments for zoo and aquarium animals. They have designed facilities for great apes and other primates at several of the nation's best known zoos. Coe is recognized for his emphasis on habitat simulation in outdoor areas and for integrated environmental enrichment throughout captive facilities.

These authors begin their chapter with a discussion of the history of maintaining primates in captivity and progress to a review of recent advances in captive design. They point out that habitats that are designed with the biology of the animal in mind are more likely to elicit behaviors that are both aesthetically pleasing and educational for the visitor.

25

Conservation of Primates in Captivity

Edward F. Gibbons, Jr.

Wild primate populations are on a decline worldwide. Of the approximately 236 primate species, 100 species and subspecies are declared either endangered, vulnerable, or rare by the International Union for Conservation of Nature and Natural Resources (Harcourt and Thornback, 1990; IUCN, 1993). In addition, the IUCN classifies another 13 species and subspecies as known or suspected to be endangered, vulnerable, or rare pending further determination of their status in the wild (see Table 25.1). A similar classification has been compiled by the United States Fish and Wildlife Service (1992). Of the 113 primate taxa in the *IUCN Red List of Threatened Animals*, 17 are of such low numbers that it is doubtful they will survive into the 21st Century. Three taxa: the hairy-eared dwarf lemur (*Allocebus trichotis*), Perrier's sifaka (*Propithecus diadema perrieri*), and the tonkin snub-nosed monkey (*Pygathrix avunculus*) may be declared extinct in the near future (Mittermeier et al., 1986).

The demise of the world's wild primate populations can be attributed to three categories of human activity: (1) deforestation, (2) hunting, and (3) commercial trade. On a global scale, the destruction of rain forests is by far the greatest threat to wild primate populations (Mittermeier et al., 1986; Johns and Skorupa, 1987). Approximately 90% of all primate species occur in rain forests and about 200,000 km^2 of this habitat is converted annually for human use (Myers, 1980, 1986, 1987b; McNeely et al., 1990). The agricultural and lumber industries are the primary harvesters of rain forests (Terborgh, 1986; Marsh et al., 1987; Mather, 1990; Gómez-Pompa and Burley, 1991).

Hunting also contributes to the decline of wild primate populations. Mittermeier (1987) provides a review of this topic, and cites eight reasons for the hunting of primates: (1) as a food source, (2) for medicinal purposes, (3) as bait to hunt other species, (4) as evil omens, (5) for ornamentation, (6) as agricultural pests, (7) for "sport," and (8) as pets. The influence of hunting on primate populations, however, varies according to cultural attitudes of specific regions (Mittermeier et al., 1986). Primates endemic to the Amazon, and West and Central Africa are heavily affected by hunting (e.g., Peres, 1990). The black-and-white colobus (*Colobus guerza*), for example, has suffered significant population losses due to use of their skins for ornamentation (Mittermeier, 1973; Oates, 1977). In contrast, the hunting of primates in many regions of Asia is rare because of religious beliefs by Buddhists, Hindus, and Muslims (Mittermeier, 1987). Asian primates, however, are hunted by aboriginal societies and the Chinese. In China, primates are killed for food and for use in traditional medicine (Wang and Quan, 1986; Mittermeier, 1987; Bleisch and Nan, 1990).

The decline of wild primate populations may also be attributed to the international trade. Each year thousands of primates are captured and sold for the pet trade, to zoos and menageries, and for use in biomedical research (Mack and Eudey, 1984; Mack and Mittermeier, 1984; Kavanagh et al., 1987; Cater and McGreal, 1991; Speart, 1992). The commercial trade of wild caught primates, however, is decreasing due to export bans by many native countries (e.g., Colombia, India, Peru, Thailand, and Malaysia), and greater enforcement of regulations such as those developed by the *Convention on International Trade in Endangered Species of Wild Fauna and Flora* (Kavanagh and Bennett, 1984; Kavanagh et al., 1987; CITES, 1992). The decrease in primate importations has necessitated that biomedical and zoological research institutions improve their animal care/use practices which, in turn, has further reduced the need to import primates from the wild (PAHO/WHO, 1976; Prasad and Anand Kumar, 1977; ILAR, 1980, 1985; Vickers, 1983; Gay, 1986; Johnsen and Whitehair, 1986; Driscoll, 1989; McPherson, 1980; Snowdon, 1989, 1994; Novak et al., 1994).

Species Status in the Wild

A number of reports have provided detailed accounts on the status of wild primate populations (e.g., Richard, 1982; Wolfheim, 1983;

Table 25.1
Endangered and Threatened Primate Taxa

Taxa[a]	Conservation Regions[b]	Status[c]	ISIS Institutions No. Maintained 1994 N	%	No. Bred 1989–1994 N	%
Family Cheirogaleidae						
Allocebus trichotis	M*	E	59	2.36	31	1.43
Microcebus conquereli	M*	V				
Phaner furcifer	M*	R				
Family Lemuridae						
Eulemur coronatus	M*	E				
Eulemus fulvus albocollaris	M*	+				
Eulemur fulvus mayottensis	M*	+				
Eulemur macaco	M*	V	636	25.46	478	22.03
Eulemur mongoz	M*	E	14	0.56	85	3.92
Eulemur rubriventer	M	V	30	1.20	21	0.97
Hapalemur aureus	M*	E				
Hapalemur griseus alaotrensis	M*	+	8	0.32	2	0.09
Hapalemur griseus occidentalis	M*	+	1	0.04	1	0.05
Hapalemur simus	M*	E	4	0.16	0	0.00
Lemur catta	M*	V	960	38.43	918	42.30
Varecia variegata	M*	E	711	28.46	608	28.02
Family Megaladapidae						
Lepilemur dorsalis	M	V				
Lepilemur edwardsi	M	R				
Lepilemur leucopus	M	R				
Lepilemur microdon	M	R				
Lepilemur mustelinus	M	R				
Lepilemur ruficaudatus	M	R				
Lepilemur septentrionalis	M	V				
Family Indridae						
Avahi laniger	M*	V				
Indri indri	M*	E				
Propithecus diadema	M*	V	2	0.08	0	0.00
Propithecus tattersalli	M*	E	5	0.20	21	0.97
Propithecus verreauxi	M*	V	53	2.12	2	0.09
Family Daubentoniidae						
Daubentonia madagascariensis	M*	E	15	0.60	3	0.14
Total, Malagasy Primates			**2498**	**100.00**	**2170**	**100.00**

Table 25.1 *continued*

Taxa[a]	Conservation Regions[b]	Status[c]	ISIS Institutions No. Maintained 1994 N	%	No. Bred 1989–1994 N	%
Family Lorisidae						
Arctocebus calabarensis	Af*	V				
Loris tardigradus	As*	+	77	34.38	77	50.33
Nycticebus pygmaeus	As*	V	139	62.05	71	46.41
Family Galagidae						
Galago matschiei	Af	V				
Galago thomasi	Af	K				
Galago zanzibaricus	Af*	V				
Family Tarsiidae						
Tarsius dianae	As	I				
Tarsius spectrum	As*	K				
Tarsius syrichta	As*	+	8	3.57	5	3.27
Tarsius pumilus	As*	I				
Total, Lorisidae, Galagidae, Tarsiidae			224	100.00	153	100.0
Family Callitrichidae						
Callimico goeldii	NW	R	297	11.35	388	13.26
Callithrix aurita	NW	E				
Callithrix chrysoleuca	NW	V				
Callithrix flaviceps	NW	E				
Callithrix geoffroyi	NW	V	195	7.45	303	10.35
Callithrix intermedia	NW	V				
Callithrix kuhll	NW	V				
Callithrix nigriceps	NW	V				
Leontopithecus caissara	NW	E				
Leontopithecus chrysomelas	NW	E	304	11.62	354	12.09
Leontopithecus chrysopygus	NW	E	19	0.73	21	0.72
Leontopithecus rosalia	NW	E	315	12.04	379	12.95
Saguinus leucopus	NW	E	4	0.15	0	0.00
Saguinus oedipus	NW	E	631	24.11	1032	35.26
Saguinus tripartitus	NW	K				
Family Cebidae						
Alouatta fusca	NW	V				
Alouatta pigra	NW	K				

Table 25.1 *continued*

Taxa[a]	Conservation Regions[b]	Status[c]	No. Maintained 1994 N	No. Maintained 1994 %	No. Bred 1989–1994 N	No. Bred 1989–1994 %
Family Cebidae *(continued)*						
Aotus brumbacki	NW	V				
Aotus miconax	NW	V				
Ateles belzebuth	NW	V	33	1.26	13	0.44
Ateles fusciceps	NW	V	143	5.46	88	3.01
Ateles geoffroyi	NW	V	482	18.42	250	8.54
Ateles paniscus	NW	V	104	3.97	55	1.88
Brachyteles arachnoides	NW	E				
Cacajao calvus	NW	E	3	0.11	0	0.00
Cacajao melanocephalus	NW	E				
Callicebus oenanthe	NW	V				
Callicebus olallae	NW	I				
Callicebus personatus	NW	V				
Cebus kaapori	NW	E				
Chiropotes albinasus	NW	V	2	0.08	0	0.00
Lagothrix flavicauda	NW	E				
Lagothrix lagothricha	NW	V	82	3.13	44	1.50
Pithecia aequatorialis	NW	V				
Saimiri oerstedii	NW	E	3	0.11	0	0.00
Saimiri vanzolinii	NW	V				
Total, New World Monkeys			**2617**	**100.00**	**2927**	**100.00**
Family Cercopithecidae						
Allenopithecus nigroviridis	Af*	K				
Cercocebus aterrimus	Af*	K	43	1.49	16	0.92
Cercocebus galeritus	Af*	+	66	2.29	23	1.32
Cercocebus torquatus	Af*	+	99	3.44	76	4.37
Cercopithecus diana	Af*	V	152	5.28	55	3.16
Cercopithecus dryas	Af*	K				
Cercopithecus erythrogaster	Af*	E	1	0.03	0	0.00
Cercopithecus erythrotis	Af*	V				
Cercopithecus hamlyni	Af*	V	53	1.84	15	0.86
Cercopithecus l'hoesti	Af*	V	31	1.08	24	1.38
Cercopithecus preussi	Af*	E				
Cercopithecus sclateri	Af*	E				
Cercopithecus solatus	Af	E				
Colobus polykomos	Af*	V	76	2.64	82	4.71
Colobus satanas	Af*	E				

Table 25.1 *continued*

Taxa[a]	Conservation Regions[b]	Status[c]	ISIS Institutions			
			No. Maintained 1994		No. Bred 1989–1994	
			N	%	N	%
Family Cercopithecidae *(continued)*						
Colobus vellerosus	Af*	V				
Macaca arctoides	As*	K	63	2.19	14	0.80
Macaca brunnescens	As*	+				
Macaca cyclopsis	As*	V	40	1.39	21	1.21
Macaca fuscata	As*	V	433	15.05	289	16.61
Macaca hecki	As*	+				
Macaca maura	As*	V				
Macaca nigra	As*	I	218	7.58	46	2.64
Macaca nigrescens	As*	+				
Macaca ochreata	As*	+				
Macaca pagensis	As*	+				
Macaca silenus	As*	E	339	11.78	191	10.98
Macaca sylvanus	Af*	V	144	5.01	125	7.18
Macaca thibetana	As*	K	2	0.07	1	0.06
Macaca tonkeana	As*	+				
Mandrillus leucophaeus	Af*	E	44	1.53	19	1.09
Mandrillus sphinx	Af*	V	378	13.14	278	15.98
Miopithecus talapoin	Af*	+	54	1.88	14	0.80
Nasalis larvatus	As*	V	12	0.42	7	0.40
Presbytis comata	As*	E				
Presbytis potenziani	As*	E	1	0.03	0	0.00
Procolobus verus	Af*	V				
Procolobus [badius] badius	Af*	+				
Procolobus [badius] gordonorum	Af*	+				
Procolobus [badius] kirkii	Af*	+				
Procolobus [badius] pennanti	Af*	+				
Procolobus [badius] rufomitratus	Af*	+				
Pygathrix avunculus	As*	E				
Pygathrix bieti	As*	+				
Pygathrix brelichi	As*	E				
Pygathrix nemaeus	As*	E	29	1.01	28	1.61
Pygathrix nigripes	As*	+				
Pygathrix roxellanae	As*	V				

Table 25.1 *continued*

Taxa[a]	Conservation Regions[b]	Status[c]	ISIS Institutions No. Maintained 1994 N	%	No. Bred 1989–1994 N	%
Family Cercopithecidae (*continued*)						
Papio hamadryas	Af*	+	543	18.87	371	21.32
Papio papio	Af*	+				
Simias concolor	As*	E				
Theropithcus gelada	Af*	R	56	1.95	45	2.59
Trachypithecus francoisi	As*	E				
Trachypithecus geei	As	R				
Trachypithecus johnii	As*	I				
Trachypithecus vatulus	As*	+				
Total, Old World Monkeys			**2877**	**100.00**	**1740**	**100.00**
Family Hylobatidae						
Hylobates concolor	As*	E	141	3.50	39	3.13
Hylobates hoolock	As*	E	1	0.02	0	0.00
Hylobates klossii	As*	E	1	0.02	0	0.00
Hylobates moloch	As*	E	62	1.54	30	2.41
Hylobates pileatus	As*	E	39	0.97	5	0.40
Family Pongidae						
Gorilla gorilla	Af*	V	595	14.78	179	14.38
Pan paniscus	Af*	V	89	2.21	36	2.89
Pan troglodytes	Af*	V	2539	63.05	821	65.94
Pongo pygmaeus	As*	E	560	13.91	135	10.84
Total, Apes			**4027**	**100.00**	**1245**	**100.00**

a Included in this table are 25 taxa assigned conservation priority status in the African, Asian, and Lemur Action Plans, but are not listed as threatened by the IUCN. These species are indicated by a + in the **Conservation Status** column.

b The **Regions** where primates occur are as follows: Af = Africa, As = Asia, M = Madagascar, NW = New World. An * following a region indicates that the species was assigned conservation priority status in either the African, Asian, or Lemur Action Plans.

c The **Conservation Status** of the various species are indicated as follows: E = Endangered, V = Vulnerable, R = Rare, K = Known to be threatened, and I = Suspected to be threatened.

Mittermeier et al., 1986; Southwick et al., 1986; Happel et al., 1987; Petter and Andriatsarafara, 1987; Lee et al., 1988; Harcourt and Thornback, 1990; Pearl, 1992). A document of particular importance is the *Global Strategy For Primate Conservation* developed by the IUCN/SSC Primate Specialist Group (Mittermeier, 1978). This Global Strategy was one of the first attempts to prioritize primate conservation efforts worldwide. It also advocated the development of improved educational programs in primate conservation, and the need for humans to curtail encroachment upon primate habitat. Stemming from this Global Strategy, action plans either have or will be developed for the major geographic regions where primates occur: Africa, Asia, Madagascar, and the Neotropics. Action plans have been published for African (Oates, 1986) and Asian (Eudey, 1987) primates as well as for the Lemurs of Madagascar (Mittermeier et al., 1992a).

The three published action plans outline overall conservation priorities for species and projects in the respective geographic regions. All species are rated based on their degree of threat, taxonomic uniqueness, and ecological association with other endangered primates. Projects are rated as to the critical status of the habitat, number of endangered primate species affected by demise of the habitat, total number of primate species in the project area, and number of primate species endemic to the project area.

Oates (1986) in his *Action Plan For African Primates: 1986–1990* classified a total of 63 African species, of which 34 (54%) are in need of immediate conservation action. Of these 34 species, 5 are listed as endangered, 14 vulnerable, 1 rare, and 3 as known to be threatened by the IUCN (1993) (Table 25.1). Ten taxa are not included in the 1993 *IUCN Red List*, and they are also listed in Table 25.1. The remaining species, Harrison's monkey (*Cercopithecus ? sp.*) from Gabon, was discovered in 1984. Little information is available on its taxonomic status and distribution in the wild (Oates, 1986). Finally, of the six species that were assigned the highest conservation priority rating in the *Action Plan for African Primates*, only the drill baboon (*Mandrillus leucophaeus*), Preuss's monkey (*Cercopithecus preussi*), and Sclater's guenon (*Cercopithecus ? sclateri*) are listed as endangered by the IUCN (1993). Of the three remaining species, the gorilla from equatorial Africa (*Gorilla gorilla*), and the pygmy chimpanzee (*Pan paniscus*) are listed as vulnerable, while the Uehehe red colobus (*Procolobus [badius] gordonorum*) is not included in the *1994 IUCN Red List of Threatened Animals*.

The *Action Plan For Asian Primate Conservation: 1987–91* classified a total of 63 Asian species with 37 (59%) in need of immediate conservation action (Eudey, 1987). Of these 37 species, the IUCN (1993) listed 14 as endangered, 6 vulnerable, 3 known and 3 suspected to be threatened (Table 25.1). The remaining eleven species are not listed in the *1994 IUCN Red List of Threatened Animals*; however, they are listed in Table 25.1. Of the seven species assigned highest conservation priority in the *Action Plan For Asian Primate Conservation*, the black snub-nosed monkey (*Pygathrix bieti*) and the black-shanked monkey (*Pygathrix nigripes*) were not listed as threatened by the IUCN (1993).

An *Action Plan for the Lemurs of Madagascar* has also been published (Mittermeier et al., 1992a). As a zoogeographic group, the Malagasy primates are the most endangered taxon within the Order Primates. Forty-six of fifty species and subspecies (92%) are listed either in the *1994 IUCN Red List of Threatened Animals* or in the 1990 IUCN Red Data Book entitled: *The Lemurs of Madagascar and The Comoros* (Harcourt and Thornback, 1990). The lemurs may very well be the most endangered zoogeographic group among all higher mammals (Richard and Sussman, 1975; Jolly, 1986; Meier and Albignac, 1991). Indeed, of the thirty species and subspecies assigned conservation priority in the Lemurs of Madagascar Action Plan (Mittermeier et al., 1992a), the *1994 IUCN Red List of Threatened Animals* and the *1990 IUCN Red Data Book* classifies 17 (57%) as endangered, 9 (30%) as vulnerable, and 4 (13%) as rare. Further, taxa such as the hairy-eared dwarf lemur (*Allocebus trichotis*), the aye-aye (*Daubentonia madagascariensis*), the broad-nosed gentle lemur (*Hapalemur simus*), the golden bamboo lemur (*Hapalemur aureus*), Perrieri's sifaka (*Propithecus diadema perrieri*), and Tattersall's sifaka (*Propithecus tattersalli*) may be extinct within the next decade (Richard, 1982; Jolly, 1986; Pollock, 1986; Meier et al., 1987; Simons, 1988; Meier and Albignac, 1991; Mittermeier et al., 1992a). Extreme endemism along with habitat destruction are the primary reasons for the decline of the Malagasy primates (Richard and Sussman, 1987).

The Action Plan for New World monkeys is in preparation. Present taxonomic classifications recognize 79 species (e.g., Mittermeier et al., 1988; Mittermeier et al., 1992b), of which 36 are listed in the *1994 IUCN Red List of Threatened Animals* (Table 25.1). A few of these species are of special conservation concern due to their taxonomic uniqueness (Mittermeier, 1986a, b): (1) the muriqui (*Brachyteles arachnoides*), of which between 300–400 exist in the wild (Strier, 1991); (2) four species of lion tamarins: *Leontopithecus rosalia*, *L. chrysopygus*, *L. chrysomelas*, and *L. caissara*, of which the latter two are thought to be the rarest of all New World primates; and (3) the yellow-tailed woolly monkey (*Lagothrix flavicauda*).

Conservation Programs in Captivity

The International Species Inventory System (ISIS) is a program whose purpose is to keep census and demographic information on wild animals in zoos (Seal et al., 1976, 1977). Since its inception in 1975, the number of institutions reporting to ISIS has grown to well over 400, and includes research institutions and universities throughout North America as well as many South American and European zoos. Zoological institutions in Australia and India also contribute demographic information to ISIS (Seal, 1986a). Although not a complete listing of all primates in captivity, ISIS is the most thorough and up-to-date source of information on primate species maintained and bred in captivity (Flesness, 1986).

According to the 30 June 1994 listing of ISIS there exist 19905 individual primates comprising 130 species. This number represents approximately 55% of the total species classified in the Order Primates. Of these 130 species, 63 taxa are listed by the IUCN (1993) as threatened. This constitutes 56% of the 113 threatened primate taxa recognized by the IUCN, and 47% (N=47) of the 101 taxa assigned conservation priority in the *African, Asian*, and *Lemur Action Plans* (Oates, 1986; Eudey, 1987; Mittermeier et al., 1992a). However, it should be noted that ISIS institutions maintain and breed 8 species that are of conservation priority in the African, Asian and Lemur Action Plans, but are not listed as threatened by the IUCN (1993). These 8 species are included in Table 25.1.

Table 25.1 summarizes the ISIS distribution of taxa and specimens among the Malagasy primates, other prosimians, Old and New World monkeys, and the apes. To be emphasized is the disproportionate number of ape specimens (N=4027, 32.9% of specimens from threatened ISIS taxa) relative to the number of ape species and sub-species (N=9, 14.3% of threatened ISIS taxa). In particular, the chimpanzee (*Pan troglodytes*) accounts for 20.7% (N=2539) of the total ISIS primate population.

Analysis of ISIS indicates that a couple of species account for the majority of specimens and captive births within each zoogeographic group. In the Malagasy primates, for example, the ring-tailed (*Lemur catta*, N=960), ruffed (*Varecia variegatas*, N=711), and black (*Eulemur macaco*, N=636) lemurs account for 92.4% of the group's threatened ISIS population. From 1989 to 1994 these three species produced 92.4% (N=2004) of the births from threatened Malagasy species. Similarly, the cotton-top tamarin (*Saguinus oedipus*, N=631), the spider monkey (*Ateles geoffroyi*, N=482), the golden lion tamarin (*Leontopithecus rosalia*, N=315), and the golden-headed lion tamarin (*Leontopithecus chrysomelas*, N=304) comprise 66.2% of the threatened New World ISIS population, and 68.8% (N=2015) of births from 1989 to 1994. Similar findings exist for Old World primates and apes (Table 25.1).

The unequal distribution of individual primates and births among threatened taxa raises concern as to the extent ISIS populations can meet genetic criteria for effective captive populations (Franklin, 1980; Soulé, 1980; Frankel and Soulé, 1981; McNeely et al., 1990). Specifically, there should be a minimum effective population size (N_e) of 100 in order to maintain 90% of the founder group's genetic diversity for at least the next 200 years and most likely for 500–1000 years; the duration of "demographic winter" on earth. The period of "demographic winter" will be characterized by the extinction of one-fourth to one-half of all plant and animal species. The major factors contributing to this loss of biodiversity will be human population growth and the continued need to develop natural habitat (Foose et al., 1986, 1987; Soulé et al., 1986; McNeely et al., 1990). Flesness (1986) provided a crude estimate of N_e for primates using pedigree data abstracted from 1984 ISIS records. His analyses indicated that only 9 species met the criteria for an effective captive population, and only 4 of these species were listed as endangered by the IUCN.

Examination of 1994 ISIS records suggest that most captive primate populations are unlikely to be genetically self-sustaining. Of the 63 threatened taxa in ISIS institutions, only 23 have population sizes greater than 100. Fourteen of these 23 taxa were assigned conservation priority in the *African, Asian* and *Lemur Action Plans* (Oates, 1986; Eudey, 1987; Mittermeier et al., 1992a) (Table 25.1). Another taxon, the hamadryas baboon (*Papio hamadryas*), not listed as threatened by the IUCN but given conservation priority in the *African Action Plan* has an ISIS population of 543. Further, because the number of specimens of Pygmy loris (*Nycticebus pygmaeus*, N=139); brown-headed spider monkey (*Ateles fusciceps*, N=143), black spider monkey (*Ateles paniscus*, N=104), diana guenon (*Cercopithecus diana*, N=152), Barbary macaque *(Macaca sylvanus*, N=144), and black gibbon (*Hylobates concolor*, N=141) is not much greater than 100, it is doubtful that they have genetically effective population sizes. At most 17 ISIS taxa (including 11 priority taxa from *African, Asian,* and *Lemur Action Plans*) meet the criteria for genetically self-sustaining populations. These amount to 12% of the primate species and subspecies listed in the *1994 IUCN Red List of Threatened Animals* or assigned conservation priority in the *African, Asian,* and *Lemur Action Plans* (Oates, 1986; Eudey, 1987; Mittermeier, 1992b). It is clear that ISIS institutions need to better evaluate the primate taxa they maintain and breed.

Problems Facing Conservation Programs in Captivity

The establishment of genetically self-sustaining populations is clearly an important priority in conservation programs for primates in captivity. There exist, however, additional problems that must be addressed if captive programs are to have a significant impact on primate conservation. These problems include: (a) taxonomy and population demographics, (b) preventive health care, (c) spatial requirements, and (d) monetary needs.

Taxonomy and Population Demographics

To know precisely what is being preserved is of fundamental importance to any conservation program. For primates, knowledge of what is to be conserved is sometimes unclear because of: (1) uncertainties in taxonomic classification (e.g., Mittermeier and Coimbra-Filho, 1981; Ford, 1986; Schwartz, 1986; Mittermeier et al., 1988), and (2) indecision as to which taxa are to be included in the conservation ark (e.g., Mittermeier, 1986; Rabb et al., 1986). The first problem emphasizes the need for basic taxonomic research, especially with regard to its role in the biodiversity crisis (e.g., Benirschke, 1983; Konstant, 1986; Schwartz, 1986; Eldridge, 1992; Rojas, 1992; and see Futuyma, 1979; Mayr, 1982; Wiens, 1982; May, 1990; Qumsiyeh, 1990 for issues on the taxonomic classification of species and subspecies). Interdisciplinary investigations into areas such as protein sequencing, electrophoresis, immunology, morphometrics, and breeding behavior should help to resolve questions involving primate taxonomy (Chambers and Bayless, 1983). It is also imperative that the zoological community keep abreast of advances in primate taxonomy, and that these findings are re-flected in their record keeping systems and educational displays. In this regard, there is some divergence in the taxonomy and nomen-clature used by ISIS and that used by the IUCN.

The second concern involves the taxa to which conservation efforts in captivity should be devoted (e.g., Foose et al., 1986). Cap-tive programs cannot be established for all primate species and subspecies. For which taxa, then, are programs to be established, and by what criteria is the decision to be made? Solutions to these problems have been discussed by a number of authors, and have included the following species' characteristics: (1) degree of threat in the wild, (2) taxonomic uniqueness, and (3) suitability for cap-tive maintenance and breeding programs (e.g. Lovejoy, 1980; Mittermeier, 1986; Seal, 1986b; Woodruff, 1989).

A fourth consideration in the selection of species for captive programs involves the preservation of ecosystems, the ultimate goal of conservation biology (Slobodkin, 1986; Western, 1986a, b). Cap-tive conservation programs can help to preserve ecosystems through the breeding of taxa to reinforce wild populations (criteria 1 to 3), and through the development of education programs that teach the concept of ecosystems and the value of their preservation (Conway, 1985a; Foose, 1986). This breeding/educational objective can be at-tained by the exhibition of "charismatic" primate taxa in context with their native flora and fauna (see Lindburg and Coe, chap. 28, this volume). In such simulated environments, the ecological roles of primates and other species are re-created for the education of the public. The inclusion of human artifacts from the region and exhibit graphics can extend this educational experience to include the relationship between culture and conservation. The education of humans as to the need to preserve ecosystems should be an objective of every primate conservation program.

Conservation programs in captivity will also have to be con-cerned with changes in population demographics. Much discussion has focused on the effects of inbreeding and outbreeding of captive populations, and the importance of maintaining stable age/sex class distributions (e.g., Goodman, 1980; Ralls and Ballou, 1982; Foose, 1983; Ryman and Laikre, 1991). The continued development of regional and international studbooks as well as species survival plans will help to address these breeding and demographic con-cerns (Conway, 1985b; Glatston, 1986; Foose et al., 1987). However, it must be emphasized that the maintenance of stable age distribu-tions will be of central importance to captive breeding programs because it can be expected that as husbandry and veterinary procedures improve there will be a shift to more aged captive populations. The increased agedness of captive populations poses concern regarding the allocation of conservation resources to animals with limited reproductive potential. An increase in the relative percentage of aged animals will place emphasis on research involving lifespan problems, including infant development and maternal care.

Preventive Health Care

In order to ensure the long-term health of primates it is imperative that their health status be regularly monitored and medical problems dealt with in a timely and cost-effective manner. Preventive health care, however, extends beyond providing regular physical examinations, innoculations, medication, and corrective therapy. It also involves defining those environmental and social influences that could lead to a health problem. This component of preventive health care can be referred to as "comparative behavioral medicine" after the burgeoning field of behavioral medicine for humans (e.g., Schwartz and Weiss, 1977; Pomerleau and Brady, 1979; Melamed and Siegel, 1980; Pinkerton et al., 1982; Linden, 1988).

Comparative behavioral medicine is an interdisciplinary study of disease and trauma conducted with the intention of identifying a priori situations detrimental to health. The early identification of factors that influence health will minimize animal medical and replacement costs, and will promote the effective management and husbandry of endangered primates in captivity. Gibbons and Stoskopf (1989) and Gibbons et al. (1992) provide examples of how this approach can enhance the medical care of exotic animals in captivity.

Spatial Requirements

Another area of concern is the need for space that meets the biological and psychological requirements of the respective primate species (Conway, 1986a; Coe, 1989; Gibbons et al., 1994). Lindburg and Coe, chap. 28, this volume, discuss the spatial requirements for primates in captivity. At this point it should be emphasized that in order to maximize the effective use of space (and other limited conservation resources) it will be important for each zoological institution to specialize in the primate taxa they can effectively maintain and breed.

Institutional specialization, however, should not preclude the exchange of animals among institutions. An optimal subdivision of a captive population among geographically proximate facilities can enhance genetic management, reduce the probability that nongenetic factors (e.g., accidents and disease) may contribute to the extinction of a captive population, and, in general, provide for cost-effective management programs for primates (Foose et al., 1986; Ralls and Ballou, 1986).

Monetary Needs

If primate conservation programs in captivity are to be effective there must be greater monetary support, and a more equal distribution of these funds among participating institutions. Funds are needed for basic husbandry and medical care, to up-grade enclosures, to establish breeding colonies, and to finance research projects necessary for the implementation and evaluation of conservation programs. The development of an endowment fund for primate conservation in captivity will go far towards meeting these needs (Short, 1986).

Increased financial support will depend on the continued education of the legislative and public sectors of society. Conservation work with primates will have an important role in this process because of their phylogenetic, morphological, and behavioral similarities with humans. It is because of such similarities that academic and zoological institutions can arouse public interest in primates, and through education programs convey the conservation message and the need for financial support.

Conclusion

The continued decline of wild primate populations will result in a greater emphasis being placed on technological and scientific advancements in many diverse fields associated with conservation biology (Conway, 1986b, 1989; Wildt and Seal, 1988). The ultimate success of such endeavors will depend on the integration of disciplines to address, in a cost-effective manner, complex biological problems (Bartholomew, 1982). An interdisciplinary approach to primate conservation biology will provide greater insight into problems than would have been achieved by focusing within one discipline.

The success of an interdisciplinary approach to primate conservation in captivity, however, will be limited unless there is a dramatic increase in the availability of resources, especially space.

Conway (1986a) has calculated that there exist enough captive space to preserve 330 mammalian species at population levels of about 275 for 200 years. As primates comprise 15.2% of the mammalian taxa listed as threatened by the IUCN (1993), this will be enough space for only 50 primate species. It can be projected that most, if not all, of the 236 primate species will require assistance from captive programs. In order to meet this need, the amount of space in captivity will have to be at least quadrupled. An adequate supply of other resources (e.g., funding and personnel) will also be of importance to promote effective conservation programs.

The problem of limited conservation resources must be addressed with regard to distribution among primate taxa. Among ISIS institutions, species such as the spider monkey, the gorilla, the ring-tailed lemur, the golden-lion tamarin, and the chimpanzee are overrepresented in relation to other threatened species. While there is a need for growth among all captive populations, growth must be relatively uniform across taxa. The disproportionate growth of a few taxa will skew the allocation of conservation resources to a few highly represented taxa, and will inhibit population growth of other species and subspecies. The development of programs for primate taxa not presently represented in ISIS institutions will also be affected by the accelerated growth of a few taxa.

The unequal representation of animals across taxa will also hinder the advancement of scientific knowledge within primate conservation biology. Much needs to be learned in disciplines such as behavior, environmental design, and reproductive physiology. Among ISIS institutions, small numbers of primates, within and between taxa, combined with the physiological, morphological, and behavioral diversity within the Order Primates will affect the internal and external validity of empirical findings derived from these taxa (e.g., Sokal and Rohlf, 1969; Hays, 1973). Empirical findings from small sample sizes may also lead to the development of erroneous hypotheses that may affect management decisions for endangered primates in captivity (e.g., Root-Bernstein, 1989). These and similar methodological problems will affect scientific development within primate conservation biology.

The area to which primate conservation in captivity can have the greatest impact is public education. As already noted, humans are acutely interested in primates, and it is through this attraction that primates can serve as effective educational tools to teach the importance of species and ecosystem conservation (e.g. Conway, 1985a). Just as primates serve as "flagship" species for conservation in the wild, so too can they serve as educational "flagship" species for conservation in captivity. It is only through education that there can be any hope for the long-term preservation of the earth's natural heritage. As noted in the Chinese proverb: "... if you plan for this year you plant rice, if you plan for 10 years you plant trees, if you plan for 100 years you educate...." (cited in Besh, 1987, p. 50). Public education and changing of cultural attitudes toward biological conservation is the most important function of conservation programs for primates in captivity.

Acknowledgments

The author would like to thank Jennifer White, Department of Ecology and Evolution, State University of New York at Stony Brook and an anonymous reviewer for their helpful comments on earlier versions of this manuscript. Mr. Stephen Nash of Conservation International and the Department of Anatomical Sciences, State University of New York at Stony Brook, and Nilda Ferrer of the Wildlife Conservation Society are also acknowledged for their help throughout the preparation of this manuscript.

26

Comparative Reproductive Physiology of Female and Male Nonhuman Primates

S. D. Kholkute and W. Richard Dukelow

The gradual encroachment of man on the natural habitat of many nonhuman primates has resulted in a gradual decline of populations and the near extinction of some species. In recent years, the increased knowledge of the basic reproductive biology of nonhuman primates has resulted in more judicious use of these animals in research, improved breeding in captivity, and more effective conservation programs for both endangered and nonendangered species (Bercovitch and Ziegler, 1989; Lindburg et al., 1989).

To establish captive reservoirs of primate species, it is of utmost importance to have self-sustaining captive breeding colonies. Demographically, one would prefer a steady population growth which would become stable in just a few generations.

The criteria for a captive, self-sustaining population should be established in terms of the genetic diversity retained. Arbitrarily, 90% of the initial diversity of the founder stock should be preserved for 200 years. It is also important to know how many founders have contributed to the captive population. For example, a widespread effect of inbreeding depression has been reported for 16 groups of captive primates (Ralls and Ballou, 1982). Available evidence suggests that inbreeding reduces individual survival, and a breeding program based on inbreeding results in the highest possible rate of loss of genetic variation from the population. Hence, if the conservation aims are to preserve the original gene pool, inbreeding should be held to a minimum. In free ranging colonies, inbreeding is minimized naturally by the emigration of males or females to other groups soon after reaching sexual maturity and also by the periodic change in dominance rank. For captive species founded by only a few individuals, it is desirable to equalize founder contributions, monitor sex ratios, and enhance the reproductive opportunities for individuals with reduced fecundity. Methods such as the controlled elimination of inbreeding depression should also be considered (Templeton and Read, 1983).

Reproductive Physiology of the Female

Anatomy

In general, the reproductive tract consists of ovaries that perform the dual role of gametogenesis and steroidogenesis, oviducts, uterus lined with glandular endometrium, the cervix and the vagina.

The size of the ovaries shows tremendous variation. The ovaries of prosimians, catyrrhines, and some of the great apes are relatively small. The ovaries of platyrrhines and gibbons are usually thick, compact, and much larger. This is mainly due to the presence of large amounts of interstitial luteal tissue. Follicles exist simultaneously in various stages and, depending on structure, are termed primary or secondary follicles. Only a few follicles will reach maximum size followed by ovulation. Ova are shed at species-specific intervals. Ovulation transforms the follicle into the corpus luteum (CL). The microscopic nature of the corpus luteum changes during the cycle, and it has a definite species-specific lifespan. If fertilization does not occur, the corpus luteum regresses and the cycle starts over. The cyclical events can be divided into the follicular and luteal phases. The follicular phase is further subdivided (early, mid, late) into stages based on the growth rates of follicles. Microscopic anatomical criteria allow subdivision of the luteal phase into early, mature, or senescent stages. The endocrine profile also changes during the phases of ovarian/menstrual cycles. The histological structure of the ovary, follicular development and atresia, and endocrinology in nonhuman primates have been extensively reviewed (Greenwald, 1978; Koering, 1978; Robinson and Goy, 1986).

The oviducts are usually coiled in lower primates (loris, lemur). However, they are almost straight in the squirrel monkey (*Saimiri sciureus*) and marmosets (*Callithricidae spp.*). In tarsiers (*Tarsius*), the degree of coiling varies with the stage of the ovarian cycle and is most pronounced in the follicular phase (Hill, 1953).

A bicornuate uterus is found throughout the prosimians, whereas higher primates have a simplex uterus. The uterus of the macaque (*Macaca mulatta*) is roughly divided into an upper segment consisting of the body and fundus and the lower portion formed by a thick walled and highly convoluted cervix. The uterus of the gorilla (*Gorilla gorilla*) is much larger than in women, while that of the chimpanzee (*Pan spp.*) is smaller. Most of the New World monkeys, such as marmosets (*Callithrix spp.*), squirrel monkeys, and tamarins (*Saguinus spp.*), lack menstruation; however, the cebus monkey (*Cebus apela*) shows slight bleeding. The cellular structure of the endometrium and its cyclical changes have been extensively studied (Eckstein and Zuckerman, 1956), and changes in the vaginal cytology are used to ascertain cycle stage.

The cervix is more developed in macaques (Demers et al., 1972) than in anthropoids. The cervix is a complex and convoluted structure in rhesus (*Macaca mulata*), cynomolgus (*M. fascicularis*), and bonnet macaques (*M. radiata*). In the bonnet macaque, the cervix consists of highly glandular epithelium and produces copious amounts of cervical mucus (McArthur et al., 1972; Kholkute et al., 1981a). In baboons (*Papio*), langurs (*Presbytis entellus*), marmosets, patas monkeys (*Erythrocebus patas*), and anthropoids, the cervical canal is straight (Doyle and Chandler, 1973).

The vagina in lemurs is a flattened tube. The cyclical changes in vaginal epithelium of galago (*Galago crassicudatus*) are comparable to laboratory rodents. A conical cervix is found in tarsiers and cyclical changes in the vagina have also been reported in this species (Catchpole and Fulton, 1943). The vagina in macaques is thick walled and muscular with extensively folded mucosa.

Endocrinology

Cycles and seasons. The endocrine cycle in rhesus monkeys has been extensively reviewed (Knobil, 1971; Knobil and Plant, 1978). Estradiol-17β rises from days 1 to 6 (Day 1 = first day of menstruation) from 50-75 to 150 pg/ml on day 9. There is a sharp rise to about 350 pg/ml by day 11 followed by a fall to 20 pg/ml by day 13 or 14. This is followed by a small rise in estradiol believed to be associated with implantation about 7-8 days after ovulation. Estrone levels are about one-fifth of the estradiol levels and they follow the same pattern. Progesterone levels during the follicular phase are low (0.2 ng/ml) and reach maximal levels (4.6 ng/ml) about day 15. They remain high for seven days but are undetectable by 3 days prior to the next menses. Luteinizing hormone (LH) starts to rise about day 10 of the cycle and peaks on day 11 at a level 20 to 30 times that of baseline levels. A rat interstitial cell bioassay has been correlated with LH in rhesus and humans (Dufau et al., 1977). Follicle stimulating hormone (FSH) levels also peak about the same time as LH. Resko et al. (1974) have demonstrated that the rise of FSH during the late luteal and early follicular phases was not due to declining levels of progesterone or 20-α-ol progesterone. In the rhesus, estrone is the principal urinary estrogen and it has been shown to be associated with ovulation (Hopper and Tulner, 1970). The day of the LH surge/cycle length ratio approximates 0.43 to 0.44 in stumptailed macaques (Macaca arctoides) and rhesus (Dukelow and Bruggemann, 1979).

Progesterone secretion during the luteal phase is not correlated with any LH changes and the corpus luteum lifespan is not affected by uterine factors. Hysterectomized rhesus females cycle normally (Neill et al., 1969a). In intact females, if conception occurs, the corpus luteum is rescued 9 to 11 days after ovulation with a progesterone surge that lasts about ten days (Neill et al., 1969b). This progesterone secretion is stimulated by gonadotropin secretion by the blastocyst and is accompanied by an increase in serum estrogen levels (Atkinson et al., 1971; Neill and Knobil, 1972).

Similar patterns exist in most macaques and baboons as well. Baboon estrone levels are lower than for humans and there is no evidence of a secondary estrone peak (Kling and Westfahl, 1978) even though such a peak is found in rhesus, orangutans (Pongo spp.), and gorillas (Bosu et al., 1972; Collin et al., 1975; Nadler et al., 1979). Chimpanzees show endocrinological patterns similar to humans (Howland et al., 1971; Graham, 1973; Winter et al., 1975).

New World primates show extremely high levels of circulating steroids. Estrogen levels in Callithrix approximate 2.3 ng/ml with a rise to 6.2 ng/ml (Hampton and Hampton, 1974). Progesterone levels range from 20 to 140 ng/ml (Abbott and Hearn, 1978; Hearn, 1986a) in the common marmoset (Callithrix jacchus), and are as high as 273 ng/ml in the cotton-top marmoset (Saguinus oedipus). These values are mimicked in the urine and feces (Ziegler et al., 1989). In the squirrel monkey, extremely high levels of steroid hormones have been found. The estradiol peak approximates 503 ng/ml and the progesterone peak is nearly 400 ng/ml (Wolf et al., 1977). Cortisol approaches baseline levels of 405 μg/100 ml in the squirrel monkey, and the comparative value in the cotton-top marmoset is 98 to 200 μg/100 ml (Brown et al., 1970; Yamamoto et al., 1977).

The estrogen values for ringtailed lemurs (Lemur catta) range from 20 to 120 pg/ml, and the progesterone value is about 3.3 ng/ml on the day of estrogen peak. The latter rises to a level of 93 ng/ml 26 days later (Van Horn and Resko, 1977).

Seasonality is affected, directly or indirectly, by environmental changes (Lindburg, 1987). Some species, such as the cynomolgus macaque, stumptailed macaque, pigtailed macaque (*M. nemestrina*), spider monkeys, and the common marmoset adapt quickly to captivity and soon cycle and breed throughout the year. In other species, such as the Japanese macaque (*M. fuscata*), patterns of breeding cyclicity from the wild are often continued for years in captivity. Many individual rhesus monkeys will experience an anovulatory period during the summer in captivity. Generally, photoperiod is not the main controlling factor in primate seasonality. In ringtailed lemurs and mouse lemurs (*Microcebus murinus*), however, photoperiod does play a role in both sexes (Van Horn, 1975, 1980; Bogart et al., 1977).

Pregnancy Determination and Prediction of Parturition. The human blastocyst begins to implant about 7.5 days after fertilization (Beck, 1976). Histotropic nutrition of the embryo then begins. In Old World primates, the epithelial plaques are the source of the histotroph. In marmosets, proliferation of the trophoblast cells is much greater than in Old World primates and humans. Chorionic gonadotropin (CG) secretion is similar in both human and nonhuman primates. Chimpanzee CG concentrations are similar to those of human term placentae (Hobson, 1975). These levels are significantly higher than for Callithrix and rhesus monkeys (Hearn, 1986a; Hearn and Webley, 1987; Hearn et al., 1988a, b). CG is secreted for a limited period of pregnancy in *M. mulata*, and represents a difference from the longer period of production in higher catarrhine and platyrrhine primates (Tullner, 1971). CG has been detected at the time of implantation in both the blood and urine of macaques, baboons, chimpanzees, and orangutans. CG extracted from human, rhesus macaque, and common marmoset placentae have antigenic determinants in common and give similar slopes in radioimmunoassays for human CG (Hobson and Wide, 1972). Widespread use of this principal as a "pregnancy test kit" in a variety of species has greatly benefited breeding programs of *M. mulata* and higher primates.

The steroids of primate pregnancy have been reviewed (Soloman and Leung, 1971; Ryan and Hopper, 1974) and therefore only a brief discussion will be given here. In the human, progesterone levels at term are about 290 mg/ml but are lower in chimpanzees and are much lower in rhesus macaques. In the common marmoset LH/CG, androstenedione, and testosterone rise in early pregnancy to peak at 6-10 weeks (Hearn and Webley, 1987). Estradiol and progesterone rise after ovulation and remain high throughout pregnancy. The latter declines about 2 weeks before parturition (Chambers and Hearn, 1979).

Hormonal Manipulation of the Cycle. Administration of exogenous hormones has been used experimentally to study endocrinological change in the normal cycle. The use of progesterone to block the midcycle estrogen surge has been used in cycling females.

Ovulation induction in nonhuman primates has been extensively reviewed (van Wagenen, 1968; Dukelow, 1983, 1985; Dukelow, et al., 1986; Cranfield et al., 1989). Standard human ovulation induction regimens are effective in nonhuman primates like the squirrel (Dukelow, 1970) and rhesus monkeys (van Wagenen, 1968). The use of synthetic LH-releasing hormone (LHRH) to elicit an LH response has been reported in a number of different primates (Yen et al., 1972). Interestingly, an insensitivity to this compound has been reported in rhesus (Ehara et al., 1972) and bonnet macaques (Shah et al., 1976). Baboons, chimpanzees, and pigtailed macaques have all been reported to respond to LHRH (Koyama 1976; Hobson and Fuller, 1977; Graham et al., 1979).

Puberty

Puberty in female common marmosets and tamarins occurs at 16-18 months, 3 to 4 years in most of the macaques and baboons and 8 to 11 years in chimpanzees and gorillas. Puberty is accompanied by development of the mammary glands, appearance of the sex skin, and perineal swelling or swelling of the vulva. For several months after sexual maturity, females exhibit irregular and anovulatory cycles. The ages at which some of the nonhuman primates attain puberty is given in Table 26.1.

Gestation Length. The length of gestation varies considerably between primates. It is affected by age, weight, and general physiological conditions of the mother and the size and weight of the fetus. An extensive list of gestation lengths in various nonhuman primates was published by Ardito (1976).

In Vitro Fertilization and Embryo Transfer. Since 1978, the possibility of *in vitro* fertilization (IVF) and embryo transfer in primates

Table 26.1
Age at puberty and breeding season in some
nonhuman primates.

Species	Age at Puberty	Breeding Season
Common marmoset	14–18 months	all year
Tamarin	12 months	all year
Squirrel monkey	2–3 years	June–September
Owl monkey	10–14 months	all year
African green monkey	2 years	April–October
Rhesus macaque	3–4 years	October–April
Bonnet macaque	3–4 years	all year
Japanese macaque	3–4 years	October–April
Langur	4–5 years	all year
Baboon	3–4 years	all year
Chimpanzee	8–11 years	all year
Gorilla	7–8 years	all year
Orangutan	7–10 years	all year

has stimulated much research (Dukelow and Bruggemann, 1979). IVF has been achieved in five nonhuman primate species: squirrel monkey, marmoset, baboon, rhesus and cynomolgus macaque. The first successful IVF was by Kraemer in 1972 (pers. comm.) in the baboon. Unfortunately, this work was not published. Later in 1972 two authors reported IVF in the squirrel monkey (Cline et al., 1972; Johnson et al., 1972). In 1982, Kreitman et al. reported IVF in the cynomolgus macaque and in 1983, Bavister et al. reported the same for the rhesus macaque. The first live birth by IVF and embryo transfer was a baboon in 1983 (Clayton and Kuehl, 1984). A review of IVF technology, relative to the conservation of endangered primates, has recently been published (Bavister and Boatman, 1989).

Initial experimentation with embryo transfer involved naturally fertilized embryos that were recovered surgically. These embryo transfer experiments have been summarized by Kraemer et al (1979). The first successful surgical transfer was in a baboon by Kraemer et al. (1976). In the rhesus monkey, a simple surgical flushing procedure was developed by Hurst et al. (1976). Marston et al. (1977) used this procedure to transfer embryos from one oviduct to the opposite oviduct and these resulted in pregnancy. The need for a nonsurgical method of embryo recovery and transfer lead Pope et al. (1980) to utilize an endometrial cell sampler to recover embryos which were then transferred to baboons with subsequent live births (Pope et al., 1983). Embryo transfer and pregnancy have resulted in live births only in the marmoset among New World species (Lopata et al., 1988), but more IVF New World primate embryos have been utilized in a variety of experiments relating to temporal, chromosomal, and biochemical developmental normality than embryos extracted from Old World species. These studies have been summarized by Dukelow (1983) and Dukelow et al. (1986). Implantation has not been examined in detail in endangered species, but has been extensively described in other primates (Enders and Schlafke, 1986; Smith et al., 1987a).

Parturition. Because many morphological, mechanical, nutritional, endocrinological, and neural factors are involved in the maintenance of pregnancy, it is logical to assume that normal parturition requires synchronization of these factors. In spite of recent advances in the field of reproductive physiology, the precise mechanisms in the initiation of parturition are still not clear.

In late pregnancy there is an increase in the production of prostaglandins in rhesus monkeys. Increased myometrial activity following exogenous administration of prostaglandins is also observed (Thorburn and Challis, 1979). Progesterone is mainly of placental origin and there is no decrease of circulating levels of progesterone in macaques or chimpanzees before parturition (Thorburn and Challis, 1979). In rhesus monkeys, estrogens are formed by placental aromatization of C_{19} steroids derived from the fetal zone of the fetal adrenal. There is a prepartum rise in estradiol in the rhesus monkey that may be involved in parturition (Sholl et al., 1979).

It has been speculated that progesterone and estradiol influence lysosomal stability and thereby phospholipase A_2 activity and prostaglandin production. It is suggested that progesterone stabilizes while estrogen labilizes the lysosomes. Alterations in the concentrations of these steroid hormones could lead to parturition. Support for the involvement of estrogen in parturition of primates is further strengthened by the observation of prolonged pregnancy in women with placental sulphase deficiency, resulting in lowered unconjugated estrogens in the circulation (France et al., 1973).

The exact mechanism that triggers parturition is unknown. Prostaglandins do have a specific effect on CL lifespan if given at specific times of the cycle (Kirton et al., 1970; Spilman, 1977). A prepartum rise in estradiol in the rhesus may be involved in parturition (Sholl et al., 1979). Finally, the fetal adrenal has been implicated in the initiation of parturition of several nonprimates and man (Walsh et al., 1978). The rhesus fetal adrenal has the steroidogenenic capacity to maintain fetal and maternal plasma levels of estrogen and cortisol (Walsh et al., 1979).

The role of the fetus in parturition is not fully understood. A rise in fetal cortisol output occurs throughout the second half of gestation (Jaffe et al., 1977). This may be associated with changes in the enzymatic potential of the adrenal gland as in the baboon (Pepe et al., 1977). Fetal decapitation in monkeys prolongs gestation (Noy et al., 1977). Endocrine function of the fetal adrenal is suppressed by dexamethasone, but the adrenal responds to adrenocorticotrophic hormone administration by producing an increase in the concentration of dehydroepiandrosterone sulfate in fetal plasma. There is also an increase in maternal estrone and estradiol and in fetal estrone (Walsh et al., 1978). The pattern of fetal adrenal steroidogenesis is altered in favor of other C_{19} steroid secretions during late pregnancy (Jaffe et al., 1980). Quantitative measurements of behavioral and physiological changes during parturition are reported for several nonhuman primate species; e.g., baboons (Love, 1975), squirrel monkeys (Bowden et al., 1967), lemurs (Richard, 1976), gorilla (Nadler, 1974), chimpanzee (Goodall and Athumani, 1980), and pig-tailed macaques (Goodlin and Sackett, 1983). The typical primate pattern for time of delivery seems to be soon after nightfall (Jolly, 1972).

Reproductive Physiology of the Male

Anatomy

The testes are located within the scrotum in all primates except some prosimians in which they descend only during the active breeding season. In most prosimians and monkeys, the testes are relatively large compared to the body weight, whereas in anthropoid apes, other than chimpanzees, the testes are small relative to body weight. In sagittal section, the tunica albuginea divides the testis into lobules and compartments. Each lobule consists of seminiferous tubules that produce spermatozoa. The diameter of seminiferous tubules varies by species (van Wagenen and Simpson, 1954; Ramakrishha and Prasad, 1967; Kholkute et al., 1987). The spermatozoa are passed through the rete testes into the efferent tubules. The efferent tubules then join to form the epididymis. The lower portion of the ductal system becomes the vas deferens that passes through the inguinal canal into the pelvic cavity. The vas deferens enlarges, forming the ampulla. Each ampulla then joins to the ducts of the ipsilateral seminal vesicle and forms an ejaculatory duct. These ducts enter the caudal prostate and open into the urethra. Accessory glands located distal to the prostate (e.g., cowper's gland, intraepithelial and periurethral glands) empty their contents into the urethra.

The testes and male reproductive tract secrete fluids. The testicular fluid is secreted primarily by the Sertoli cells. This fluid is distinctly different in concentrations of sodium and potassium compared to blood and lymph that drain the testes (Waites and Einer-Jensen, 1974). The epididymal fluid is involved in maturation of spermatozoa and is important for their storage. The fluid of the ejaculate is contributed mainly by seminal vesicles followed by secretion of the prostate. For a detailed review of the male reproductive tract and fluids in nonhuman primates, refer to Harrison and Lewis (1986).

Spermatogenesis is composed of three main processes: (1) mitosis, by which spermatogonia divide either to renew or proliferate their number and to produce spermatocytes (two types of spermatogonia, A and B, have been identified [Clermont, 1972]), (2) meiosis by which the diploid primary spermatocytes (derived from type B spermatozoa) divide and produce haploid spematids, and (3) spermiogenesis in which spermatids are transformed into testicular spermatozoa. After they are released into the lumen of the tubules, the spermatozoa begin their passage through a series of ducts and are finally stored in the cauda epididymis prior to ejaculation.

Spermatogenesis has been investigated in detail in the rhesus macaque (Clermont and LeBlond, 1959; Barr, 1973), stumptailed macaque (Clermont and Antar, 1973), vervet monkey (*Cercopithecus alliops*; Clermont, 1969), baboon (Barr, 1973; Chowdhury, 1978), and squirrel monkey (Clermont, 1969). The cycle duration is between 9 to 12 days and the duration of spermatogenesis is from 36 to 48 days. The overall similarity of cell types, cellular association, and kinetics of spermatogenesis suggests similar hormonal regulation in several primate species.

The Sertoli cells are large, slender cells that extend from the basement membrane of the tubule to the luminal area. They provide the "blood-testis" barrier (Dym, 1973). The size of Sertoli cells and their nuclei varies according to the stage of spermatogenesis and the male's reproductive status (Aumuller et al., 1975). The Sertoli cells also are the main source of testosterone-estrogen-binding globulins in monkeys and man (Vigersky et al., 1976).

The space between the seminiferous tubules (interstitial space) contains connective tissue, blood vessels, lymphatics, and the Leydig cells (Bourne and Bourne, 1975). LH stimulates the Leydig cells to produce testosterone. In seasonal breeders like squirrel monkeys, seasonal factors have a profound effect on the tubular diameter and interstitium. In primates with relatively large testis compared to body weight (e.g., chimpanzees, macaques, and baboons), there are proportionately more tubular elements than interstitial tissues. Gorillas have small testes with few, small tubules and correspondingly large interstitial tissues (Wislocki, 1942; Hall-Craggs, 1962). In chimpanzees, however, the bulk of testicular tissue consists of seminiferous tubules (Martin and Gould, 1981).

Endocrinology (Seasonal aspects)

Numerous investigators have reported pronounced seasonal variations in reproduction in primates (Ewing, 1982). Among New World primate species, the squirrel monkey shows distinct seasonal variations in sexual and social behavior (Coe and Rosenblum, 1976; Mendoza et al., 1978). Individually housed males fail to show circannual variation in plasma androgen levels; however, there is distinct annual cyclicity in weight gain and sexual behavior is observed (Wilson et al., 1978). Under natural conditions, squirrel monkeys are seasonal breeders with distinct mating and birth peaks (DuMond, 1968; Baldwin, 1970). The birth period lasts 3-4 months and usually coincides in the wild with the season of highest rainfall. Most adult males will show an annual weight gain ("fatting") which begins 2-3 months before mating activity. There is also increased dominance and aggression (Coe et al., 1983). Mendoza and coworkers (1978) demonstrated dissociation in testosterone secretion and change in body weight. Castrated males also showed a small incremental gain in body weight (Coe and Rosenblum, 1976), indicating that testosterone is not the only factor in controlling "fatting" in male squirrel monkeys. Male squirrel monkeys, during mating season, showed highest testosterone levels at 0800 h (Mendoza et al., 1978). Furthermore, Coe et al. (1983) demonstrated strikingly different patterns in the daily variations in testosterone levels during the mating and nonmating seasons. Finally, though data from field studies are not extensive, common marmosets breed throughout the year in captivity (Hearn and Lunn, 1975; Kholkute, 1984), and show no circannual testosterone rhythm.

Sade (1964) showed that there is a seasonal variation in the size of the testes of rhesus monkeys. This change correlates with spermatogenesis throughout the year (Conaway and Sade, 1965). In rhesus monkeys maintained under controlled conditions, Richter et al. (1978) studied the annual cycle of morphological events which included regression and degeneration of the germinal epithelium, reduction in the tubular diameter, total depopulation of the tubules, recrudescence starting in July, and the presence of complete spermatogenesis by September. In accord with these changes in testicular volume (Wickings and Nieschlag, 1980), changes in sperm counts have also been reported (Zamboni et al., 1974). The first evidence that seasonal variation in testis size and spermatogenesis is under the control of cyclic production of testosterone was provided by Sade (1964). Direct measurement of peripheral testosterone levels in male macaques subsequently confirmed this finding (Plant et al., 1974; Gordon et al., 1976; Michael and Bonsall, 1977; Glick, 1979; Wickings and Nieschlag, 1980).

In sexually quiescent rhesus macaques, few LH peaks are observed. Furthermore, the distinct diurnal testosterone rhythm is lacking during this period. During recrudescence, basal LH levels increase to reach breeding season concentrations (Plant, 1980; Wickings et al., 1981). Although the pituitary responds to exogenous LHRH stimulation, a markedly dampened response is observed during the nonbreeding season (Wickings et al., 1986). Together, these findings indicate reduced hypothalamic activity during the nonbreeding season and a testicular quiescent period in adult male rhesus monkeys.

The Leydig cells respond to trophic stimuli in both breeding and nonbreeding seasons. However, during the breeding season, small amounts of LH are sufficient to elicit a larger increase in testosterone (Nieschlag and Wickings, 1980). Testosterone production rates are lowest during quiescence (Wickings and Nieschlag, 1977). Wickings et al. (1981) could induce full testicular function even in the quiescent period by administration of low pulsatile doses of LHRH.

Comparatively little information is available on other nonhuman primates. In stumptailed macaques, Slob et al. (1979) observed circannual fluctuations in serum testosterone levels with a nadir in September and a peak in June. However, birth occurs throughout the year in this species (MacDonald, 1971). Baboons breed and give birth throughout the year (Kraemer et al., 1975), and there is no circannual testosterone rhythm in adult males of this species (Castracane et al., 1981). Bonnet monkeys also failed to show any distinct circannual testosterone rhythm (Kholkute et al., unpub.).

Physiology

Active spermatogenesis begins at 3 years of age in rhesus monkeys and baboons and at 10 years in chimpanzees. Langur males attain complete adulthood at 6 to 7 years, while common marmosets attain sexual maturity by 18 to 24 months of age.

The endocrinological changes that occur during puberty have been studied in some primate species; e.g., common marmoset (Abbott and Hearn, 1978), squirrel monkey (Coe and Levine, 1981), rhesus monkey (Arslan, et al., 1986), cynomolgus macaques (Steiner and Bremner, 1981), baboon (Castracane, et al., 1986), Japanese macaque (Niji et al., 1980) and chimpanzee (Hobson et al., 1980). During infancy, gonadotropin concentrations are high (Robinson and Bridson, 1978; Frawley and Neill, 1979; Steiner and Bremner, 1981). High levels of circulating testosterone during the first three months of life have also been reported. The gonadal steroidogenic apparatus is competent and the response to LHRH during infancy is more similar to that of adults than to prepubertal animals (Hobson et al., 1980). In cynomolgus macaques (Steiner and Bremner, 1981), testis size increases gradually with age and body weight until 36 months (3 kg body weight) which is followed by a phase of rapid testicular growth. By 52 months this growth spurt is complete. In baboons, a linear increase in body weight over the first 3 years is followed by a more rapid increase between 3 to 4 years. Castracane et al. (1986) and Cutler and Loriaux (1980) reported that chimpanzees undergo adrenarche prior to puberty. No such "adrenarche" was observed in either rhesus macaques (Cutler and Loriaux, 1980) or baboons (Castracane et al., 1986). Studies carried out on chimpanzees indicated that during prepuberty the block in endocrine function is exerted at the hypothalamic level mainly due to hyposecretion of LHRH (Hobson et al., 1980).

Artificial Insemination. The procedures for successful semen collection and artificial insemination were developed for most primate species in the 1960s and 1970s (Dukelow, 1971) and have recently been reviewed by Schaffer et al. (1989). Semen of nearly all primates is characterized by rapid coagulation after collection. Autolysis of this coagulum is extremely slow at 37°C. In the rhesus, a 4 to 5 gm ejaculate will autolyze 0.5 to 0.7 ml of sperm-rich fluid after 30-40 minutes.

Semen is normally collected by electroejaculation (Wildt, 1986). Basically, a rigid probe containing silver, platinum, copper, or stainless steel electrodes (Warner et al., 1974; Gould et al., 1978) is inserted just past the anal sphincter to a position just over the accessory sex glands. Electrical current directions and patterns have been described by Warner et al. (1974). A second method involves the penile electrode technique of Mastroianni and Manson (1963). In this procedure, foil strips are placed at the base and tip of the penis and light current is applied.

Artificial insemination of primates usually involves fresh semen samples. Occasional reports of success with frozen semen have not been confirmed. Four species of primates have been successfully artificially inseminated: macaque, baboon, chimpanzee, and squirrel monkey. Artificial insemination has resulted in live births in only the first three of these species. Generally, insemination is most successful when the time of ovulation can be predicted or controlled (van Wagenen, 1968; Dukelow, 1983, 1985; Dukelow et al., 1986). Due to the ease of natural mating of most captive primate species, artificial insemination has been less extensively used in breeding of nonhuman primates.

Environmental and Social Influences

Reproduction is exquisitely sensitive to environmental perturbations. Social subordinance, stressors, and overcrowding can disrupt reproduction in various nonhuman primate species. The influence of environmental cues in regulation of seasonal breeding in captive as well as free-ranging rhesus macaques has been recognized (Carpenter, 1942; Koford, 1965; Southwick et al., 1965; Vandenberg, 1973; Van Horn, 1980; Smith, 1984b; Rawlins and Kessler, 1985). A consistent relationship between the onset of mating and decreasing day length as a function of latitude has implicated photoperiod as the principle control for reproduction (Van Horn, 1980). However, experimentally, the influence of photoperiodicity in regulating reproduction in macaques could not be corroborated (Barsetti et al., 1980; Gordon, 1981). Koford (1965) observed that photoperiodicity, average daily temperature, and annual average daily temperature could not be distinguished for their relative influences on reproduction at two sites in Puerto Rico. The distinctive patterns of rainfall and subsequent vegetation growth at these two locations were reported to be associated with the onset of reproductive activity (Koford, 1965; Vandenberg and Vessey, 1968) and this was confirmed by subsequent studies (Varley and Vessey, 1977). However, studies by Drickamer (1974) failed to find any correlation between the timing of birth season and peak rainfall. Rawlins and Kessler (1985) systematically evaluated variations in temperature, humidity, and rainfall as environmental cues for reproductive activity. This study ruled out the influence of temperature and humidity and suggested that the commencement of spring rainfall was the main environmental cue for the onset of reproductive activity. The effect of photoperiodicity on captive baboon females has also been studied, and it was reported that exposure to constant light had no effect on menstrual cycle, ovulation, or corpus luteum function.

Various primate species show distinct circadian rhythms in male plasma testosterone levels (Goodman et al., 1974; Mukku et al., 1976; Beattie and Bullock, 1978; Kholkute et al., 1981b). However, the role of environmental cues in determining this rhythm is not known. In bonnet monkeys, the nocturnal rise in testosterone levels was abolished when animals were exposed to constant light for 15 days (Mukku et al., 1976). However, when rhesus macaques were exposed to continuous light, it failed to abolish the normal diurnal testosterone rhythm (Dubey et al., 1983). Exposure of adult male marmosets to continuous light for 60 days had no effect on circadian rhythmicity of testosterone levels, spermatogenesis, or fertility (Kholkute et al., 1987). These results indicate that photoperiodicity is not the main environmental determinant that regulates reproduction in male marmosets.

The social suppression of fertility in individuals by other group members in primate species is emerging as a basic factor controlling the breeding strategies (Southwick et al., 1965; Rowell, 1970; Drickamer, 1974; Abbott and Hearn, 1978; Bowman et al., 1978; Keverne, 1979). In marmosets and tamarins, reproduction is often the exclusive right of one male and one female in each group (Dawson and Dukelow, 1976). In females, these effects are mediated through alterations of the endocrine system. Subordinate females in peer groups show reduced estrogen excretion compared to dominant females (Lunn, 1978) and also exhibit low and anovulatory progesterone profiles (Abbott et al., 1981). Similarly, in cottontop tamarins, specific social environments are associated with reduced, noncyclic patterns of estrogen excretion (French et al., 1984).

Removal of the subordinate female from this social environment leads to a rapid rise in her urinary estrogen excretion. This phenomenon has also been observed in common marmosets (Abbott and Hearn, 1978).

In free-ranging rhesus monkeys, male sexual behavior and testosterone production can be returned to mating season levels during the nonbreeding season by exposure to estrogen treated females (Vandenbergh and Drickamer, 1974; Bernstein et al., 1978). Sexually inactive rhesus males display an initiation of testicular activity and sexual behavior when exposed to females (Vandenbergh, 1969).

Carpenter (1942) reported that females were frequently the objects of aggression from other females during periods of increased sexual interaction with the male. In a group of male talapoin monkeys (*Miopithecus talapoin*), dominance-related differences in testosterone response have been observed. These findings suggest that social factors may contribute significantly to the endocrine response of primates (Eberhart and Keverne, 1979; Keverne, 1979). Studies by Glick (1984) in cynomolgus macaques further support the hypothesis of social environmental mediation of male hormonal responses to females. A positive relationship between adrenocortical responsiveness and social subordinance has also been proposed for rhesus monkeys (Chamove and Bowman, 1978). It also has been observed that social defeat and ensuing subordinate status in rhesus and talapoin monkeys induced decreases in plasma testosterone (Sade, 1964; Eberhart and Keverne, 1979).

Conclusions

Early scientific and field studies of primates were limited to a very few species. This greatly limited comparative research and the determination of general rules of procedure that would allow extension of findings to other rarer and more endangered species.

The export embargoes of the 1960s coupled with man's gradual encroachment on the native habitat of many primate species, have forced us to undertake more refined examination of basic primate reproductive physiology. This has, in the past decade, provided us with an appreciation of similarities and dissimilarities between species.

Additionally, many advances in the field of medicine, especially infertility treatment in humans, have provided us with many new techniques for saving endangered species. Such techniques have included artificial insemination, hormonal control of cycles, *in vitro* fertilization, and embryo transfer. Certainly, the more modern biotechnological procedures of embryo splitting, gene splicing, and recombinant DNA technology will soon find application to primates. Because of restrictions on the usage of endangered species, we must use more common primate species to elucidate basic reproductive mechanisms and for this reason the present review has concentrated on the use of models for endangered species.

The future is bright, even for endangered primate species. Modern science progresses rapidly and the development of applications could/may be equally rapid. Genetic control will continue to be an issue. Artificial reproduction techniques have done little to reduce captive inbreeding, but by adhering to some of the basic genetic principles mentioned in this chapter, future progress should be stimulating.

27

Primates and Behavior

Douglas K. Candland and Sarah L. Bush

Captivity may be expected to have profound effects on the behavior of primates. If for no other reason than that primates are highly social animals for whom any restriction can be expected to alter their sociality, the single most significant aspect of their behavior. Captive conditions may result in inappropriate reproductive behaviors, infant care, social relationships, hormonal output, aggression, and may affect longevity and morbidity. People who study wild primates write of animals in the captive state as living in an environment that is socially bereft. The artificiality of the captive environment, it is said, takes from the primate the opportunity to respond appropriately and intelligently to its environment. Those who study captive primates, to the contrary, point out that the behavior of such animals may provide important information on reactions and abilities not seen in the wild state. This may be attributable to the limited observational conditions imposed on human observers or because, in captivity, the animals, being freed from the time-consuming need to find nourishment, become inventive with the space and objects provided (Beck, 1980; Bernstein and Williams, 1986; Caminiti, 1986; Shapiro and Mitchell, 1986; Candland, 1987; Boysen et al., 1989; U.S. Department of Agriculture, 1988; American Journal of Primatology, 1989).[1]

A Rationale for Captivity

Populations of primates have been made captive in many ways and for many purposes. (1) By becoming companions or workers, as

suggested by Egyptian drawings of everyday life. (2) By translocation to nonendemic habitats both accidentally and to remove them
from areas in which they are at risk and where they have become
pests to human beings. (3) To establish populations specifically for
display and research purposes.

For primates, the conditions comprising captivity are diverse.
They range from laboratory and zoo housing in which individuals
are assigned to solitary cages, to large, open-air but contained facilities that encourage groups and troops to live together (sometimes over many generations), to situations permitting large numbers of primates to live without human-made barriers. Each
situation describes a form of captivity because humans have imposed constraint upon the species either by building confined areas, such as cages, or by providing environmentally confined areas,
as in transport from an ecologically diverse continent to an island.
Free-ranging groups may be domesticated in some behavior due to
the needs of the research designed to investigate their "natural"
behavior. When humans feed or follow primates, we can expect the
animals' behavior to be altered, usually in ways that benefit humans. Every published study in the field can be said, therefore, to
require some type of captive condition, however modest, and behavior may be expected to vary as a result of the type of captivity to
which the animals are subjected.

The advantages to systematic research offered for human beings by captive, semifree ranging populations include the availability of the known history of the animals, and the opportunity to
compare demographic and social structures with populations in the
wild. Observations in this habitat may be easier, due to environmental simplicity and the limited range of the animals. The disadvantages of using semifree ranging populations are, as in field
studies, the difficulty in controlling and manipulating variables
and observational conditions.

When endangered species are translocated to captivity, the
rationale is that few animals are to be found, that the habitat is
no longer suitable, and that translocation offers the only opportunity for survival and successful breeding. Reproductive behavior
is of the greatest interest in these cases, while in some situations
there is time to undertake longer-term investigations of various
aspects of the species' behavior. It is instructive as well to study
translocated captive populations of primates for whom translocation has negated or transformed their endangered status. Several
such groups have been studied extensively and over sufficient

time to permit behavior and morphological change to be measured. These groups are representative of the variety of situations and are not inclusive. (For a more complete description, see Southwick and Smith, 1986; for an editorial questioning reintroduction, see Lindburg, 1992a).

(1) The St. Kitts' vervets (*Cercopithecus aethiops*) originated in West Africa and were taken to the Caribbean islands of St. Kitts, Nevis, and Barbados over 300 years ago. There have been no outside additions to the population other than a few monkeys released after 1700. Some questions to consider in reading this chapter: When may we say that the population has become indigenous to these islands? May we compare the behavior of these animals to those of their native Africa? If so, what factors have led to differences in behavior between the captive and wild populations?

(2) The rhesus macaques (*Macaca mulatta*) of Cayo Santiago, Puerto Rico, are descended from 409 monkeys captured in India by C. R. Carpenter in 1938, in anticipation of the disruption of field research to be caused by World War II, and released on the island for purposes of conservation and research. Following Carpenter's (1942a, b) studies, the population was not systematically investigated until S. Altmann began work in 1956 (Rawlins and Kessler, 1986a). Comparison of the behavior with that of the Indian population can be made, as can studies in physiology which are possible only under captive conditions. The collection also may be of interest to historians of life science, as these animals have been under U.S. federal jurisdiction of different sorts for half a century—the sociology of changing cultural views on the husbandry of these animals is a worthwhile study of human and animal interaction.

(3) The Barbary macaques (*Macaca sylvanus*) on Gibraltar were brought to that area most probably from North Africa, although there has been no importation since World War II. Extensive contact with both tourists and with the Gibraltar regiment of the British Army, who provision them with one-third of their diet, has enabled close observation and continuous recording of the population since the early 1940s. Observations of the Barbary macaques have been conducted by MacRoberts and MacRoberts (1966) and Burton (1972).

(4) The Arashiyama West troop of Japanese macaques (*Macaca fuscata*) was moved from Japan to a ranch near Laredo, Texas in 1972, following the fissioning of the large Arashiyama (Japan) troop (Fedigan, 1976). The troop had been studied since 1954 but had become an agricultural pest in local Japanese communities. The U.S. monkeys are contained in a 42.4 ha enclosure which is surrounded by an electric fence, and are minimally provisioned with food. As is true of the Cayo Santiago macaques, the *M. fuscata* have survived under different human administrative arrangements and form a resource for sociological and historical study. Chapters on *M. fuscata* behavior by workers at this site appear in a book edited by Fedigan and Asquith, 1991. Another troop of *M. fuscata* was moved from Japan to the Oregon Regional Primate Research Center (U.S.) in 1965, while the Minoo troop in Japan have long been studied in terms of their behavior and reproductive strategies (Ehara et al., 1991; see also Perloe, 1991.)

Other captive populations of interest either because of unique facilities (special caging or special forms of captivity) or long-term programs (some social groups are in their fifth generation) include the golden lion tamarin (*Leontopithecus rosalia*) based at the National Zoological Park, Washington D.C.; the gorilla (*Gorilla g. gorilla*) housings in various zoos throughout the world, but especially at San Diego, California, and the Jersey Wildlife Preservation Trust, Jersey, Channel Islands, U.K.; *Macaca arctoides* at the University of California at Riverside; and *Papio hamadryas* and *Macaca fuscata* at Bucknell University (Lewisburg, Pennsylvania). Many zoos throughout the world have long-standing collections or unusual captive conditions as do the U.S. federal primate centers (see the *International Zoo Yearbook* for descriptions of zoo facilities; and for a description of U.S. federal Primate Centers see National Institutes of Health, 1978).

History and Scope of Existing Field Studies

The most comprehensive analysis of behavioral field studies of nonhuman primates is that of Smuts et al. (1987). Candland (1988), in reviewing the book, counted mention of 172 species, a number that may be compared to the 54 species discussed in the pioneer work edited by DeVore twenty years previously (1965). We estimate that

41 of 79 (52%) subspecies of primates regarded as endangered have received some attention or description in the wild state. That high percentage of the Order is, no doubt, a record representation for any Order. Oddly, the high percentage is a product of the last twenty years, these being two decades marked by intense investigation of primate species. Before the 1960s, our knowledge of primates, captive or wild, was slight. It remains a mystery as to why humans took so long to invest in the study of their nearest animal relatives. One result is that our understanding of primate forms is somewhat Europeanized. Although Europe and North America are bereft of native nonhuman primates, it is these peoples, and their own social structures and languages, that contribute significantly to what we know about primates, and whose own cultural views shape the questions we ask and the answers we give about nonhuman primate behavior.

The undernoticed commentaries by Garner (1892, 1896a, b) and Marais (1975) provide the first European/North American views of both captive and wild primate behavior. In a lifetime of work that appears to be unknown to many scholars, Garner examined primates in U.S. zoos (Cincinnati, Chicago, Washington, D.C., and New York City) with a special interest in primate vocalizations. He appears to have invented the procedure of playing self and species-mates' vocalizations to a primate by means of the then new phonograph. His investigations of chimpanzees in French Gabon (now Gabon) were remarkable in that he erected as his living quarters a cage in which he lived for three months while observing the wild primates. Garner's interest in speech included his attempts to teach several captive chimpanzees to speak in sounds understandable to humans. Garner's work may be seen as a major precursor to present-day research with primates whose goal is to establish human-animal means of communication. The idea of making the human observer captive while leaving the primates to range was put into practice in the 1930s by the DuMond family who established a facility, "Monkey Jungle," in south Florida that grew and evolved by the 1960s into a rain forest for new world primates. Visitors walked through screened trails while the primates were free within the confines of the acreage (DuMond, 1955, 1967).

Marais, a journalist and lawyer, returned to southern Africa at the time of the Boer War to work on the side of his countrymen. Finding himself in Waterberg, he studied Chacma baboons (*Papio ursinus*) over a long period of time and published the first book concerned with long-term behavior of primates. (Marais, 1975).

The first generation of European and North American directed field studies through the onset of World War I emphasized (to the European/American eyes) the human-like qualities of primates. Some reports were anecdotes, important if unique findings can be made general, misleading if not. Other observations were refined measures of the kinds and frequencies of behavior relevant to specific theoretical issues. Nomenclature was incomplete and unsettled. Discovery of the human-like qualities of the primate was of greatest importance; recognition of its specific abilities and behaviors was secondary.

The second generation of fieldwork took its impetus (at least in European languages) from the scholarship of R. Yerkes and A. Yerkes (1929), who reviewed studies of the great apes from antiquity to that present time. Ada Yerkes' grasp of medieval scholarship is unparalleled, but often copied, in the history of the study of primates. This generation of fieldwork initiated, sponsored, or prompted by R. Yerkes from 1910–1940 had as its purpose the categorization of behavior, emphasizing the location and identification of species, along with estimates of the frequencies of patterns of behavior. Research on captive primates, work beginning seriously with Garner, was underway in Russia, the U.S., and Germany by the onset of World War I. The pioneer names include Kots-Ladygin (Kots-Ladygin, 1923) in Russia, Wolfgang Köhler (1927) in Germany and Tenerife, and, in North America, Edward Lee Thorndike, Robert Yerkes, Milton Edward Haggerty, and Gilbert van Tassel Hamilton in addition to Garner. The questions investigated included whether monkeys could learn by imitation, whether they were tool-makers and tool-users, how they mapped locations, the kinds of learning processes used to solve problems, and, to some degree, where they could be placed on a scale of mental ability that included humans and animals. The argument that studies of captive animals were unreliable in comparison to observations of wild primates was put forward then as now, in an instructive exchange between the captivity-endorser, Thorndike (1898) and the Canadian naturalist and psychologist, T. W. Mills (1898).

The Focus of Studies in Captivity

Science begins with nomenclature, and the science of living beings begins with categorization of the kinds and frequencies of behavior.

The success of these studies was made possible by the organization and development of the Yale sponsored Institute of Primatology at Orange Park, Florida, which later was renamed for Yerkes and moved to Georgia. From this Institute, work on captive primates was undertaken and field studies were encouraged in both hemispheres. World War II ended fieldwork and severely restricted research on captive species. A combination of factors—economic, cultural, and educational—came together in the 1960s, leading to the construction and long-term funding in the U.S. of regional primate centers. The chief task of these federal centers was investigations of captive primates. Much of the work was chiefly of medical interest. Some centers had as their goal the clarification of nomenclature, anatomy, and physiology, and some focused directly on behavior. There is no simple way to assess the overall effects of these centers in studying the behavior of captive primates, as the goals and directives of the centers have changed and drifted in response to national needs. Nonetheless, their establishment marked national recognition of the appropriateness of governmental support of behavioral research on primate species. This brought the Order itself to a degree of prominence unmatched by any other Order, by any government, at any time.

From approximately 1970 to the present, a generation of captive and field studies appeared that may be distinguished by their increasing sensitivity to experimental methodologies. The result has been a productive if uneven synthesis of ethology and comparative psychology, and of captive and field studies, that encouraged observers to examine primates in social environments in preference to solitary environments. The sociality of primates itself became an object of study. The next generation of studies, one now well underway, is assessing directly the similarities and distinctions between primate behavior conducted in field and primate behavior observed during various kinds of captive conditions. A major impetus for this goal, at least in the U.S., is the development of laws and inspections governing noncommercial facilities that demand concern for the psychological welfare of primates.

A significant portion of the information now available from captive-social primates appears to be related more to the dramatic change in primate housing in zoos than to any planned program of research. Such conditions have encouraged more naturalistic behavior in the captive-social environment and, consequently, contemporary captive research has acquired both a broader focus and a continuing synthesis of ethology and comparative psychology. Twenty years ago, metal bars confined the primates, while social interactions were denied or limited to a potential mate or to human visitors. Today, caging displayed to the public is designed to maximize the natural activity of nonhuman primates. Such design has made possible the sort of systematic examination of specific kinds of behavior such as play, development, and tool-use whose variables could not be easily manipulated in the wild. If the themes of the past were those of the fenceless compound, one that emphasized naturalistic-looking backgrounds and barriers natural to the animals, along with the displaying and, perhaps, the breeding, of endangered and threatened species; the theme of the future may be that of "mixed species," of displaying together species which normally inhabit the same environment. To do so successfully on a large scale is a daunting undertaking and might involve, for example, information on mixed-species displays that are currently in use. An example of a modest start in a zoo is described by Xanten (1990) using as example the marmoset.

Work on primates in captive-social conditions is not sparse, but neither has it been well-focused or coordinated. Much of importance that is published arises from unexpected and casual conditions as well as from the straightforward testing of productive hypotheses. In part, this ambiguity of purpose reflects the obligations of zoos, the places in which captive-social conditions are most common. In their attempt to attract and educate the public and to care for the welfare of their animal populations, zoos have many priorities that must appear ahead of basic research (Durrell, 1976b; Essock and Rumbaugh, 1977; Markowitz and Stevens, 1978; Mallinson, 1980, 1991; Durrell, 1986; Mittermeier, 1989; Mallison and Redshaw, 1992). In contrast to the older notion that zoos exist to display one or two members of each species, modern zoos have adopted a conservation-oriented approach to guide the acquisition of species. In regard to this approach, zoos should build breeding and socialized collections of rare, threatened, and endangered species. The several publications of the International Union for Conservation of Nature and Natural Resources (IUCN) have made possible international agreements on the status of animal populations (IUCN, 1987, 1988a). Savage (1988) reviewed the nature of the collaborative endeavors among zoos, and provided a useful listing of the names and address of primate centers and primatological societies throughout the world. A comprehensive description of such centers has been compiled by the Wisconsin Regional Primate Research Center (International Directory of Primatology, 1992).

Some Functions of Research in Captivity

Public Education

As it is claimed that more people visit zoos in a year than attend professional sporting events, the display of captive animals provides an unmatched opportunity for education regarding animal life. Zoos are converting their housing facilities to follow the often praised designs and demonstrations of Hagenbeck (1910) and Hediger (1950, 1964) in which the means by which primates are kept captive are not made obvious to human visitors. Such human-made "natural environments" (e.g., deep moats [sometimes electrified], unscalable cliffs, and the use of plastic forms to represent natural-appearing stone and barriers) act to maintain the animals in captive conditions (see Lindburg and Coe, chap. 28, this volume). A sound design is one that encourages the behavior seen in the wild state and that educates the public about the nature of the species' environment.

A minimally acceptable enclosure will permit social groups and individuals to show the behavior seen in the wild state at similar frequencies. The enclosure serves to make the animal visible to humans and, thereby, to educate visitors about the presumably normal activities and interactions of the species. The enclosure also provides an opportunity for the naturalist and scientist to learn about the physiology and behavior of animals. There is a tacit belief that all is known about the anatomy, physiology, nomenclature, and evolution of primates, perhaps because we, as humans, are members of the Order and we assume that we know much about those most like us. But the truth is otherwise; for example, we know almost nothing about the nature and likelihood of diseases being transferred between animal and humankind. Any understanding we may acquire will almost certainly be based on information from captive animals.

Reintroduction Efforts

Until it is possible to recover extinct species by gene-splicing, freezing, or some such technique, once extinction occurs, the species is irreplaceable. Emphasis on conservation, therefore, is placed on preventing extinction by removing animals from the habitat in which factors are working toward extinction of animal species. When removal is accomplished, two general possibilities exist: (1) the animals are placed in a synthetic environment which is modeled after the original environment in ways important to the animals' reproductive success; and/or (2) plans are made to rehabilitate the environment so that at some future time members of the species may be returned to it.

The problems inherent in each approach are many: capture of the threatened species is often very difficult; if captured, the appropriate social or physical conditions for maintenance away from the established habitat is not always known; and reestablishment of a physical environment is a complex task with no guarantee of continued care. The difficulties are multiplied in the case of primate species by their sociality. Two model programs have attracted professional and public education within recent decades. One of these, the removal, reestablishment, and reintroduction of *Leontopithecus rosalia* into coastal Brazil was begun at a conference at the National Zoo (Smithsonian), advanced at what is now the DuMond Conservancy in Florida (DuMond, 1971), and promulgated by the National Zoo (Kleiman, 1978, 1989; Kleiman and Jones, 1978; Kleiman et al., 1986). This work, extending now over a twenty-year-period, has served as a model and prototype for other reintroduction efforts. As is to be expected when undertaking such work, where the problems themselves were to be discovered, both successes and failures are instructive. One lesson, to be sure, relates to the amount of time required to mount such a program. For primates, by the time the degree of endangerment is noted, it may be too late to establish a successful program. We do not always know enough about the causes of extinction to be able to intervene in time.

A second program, funded for several decades by the Wildlife Preservation Trust of the United Kingdom (and supported by like trusts in the U.S. and in Canada), has emphasized the captive breeding of endangered species at facilities on the island of Jersey, the Channel Islands, U.K., and of like, but on site, breeding facilities in various countries. Some of the funds are acquired by charging tourists to see the facilities, a policy that has both financial and educational benefits (Mallinson, 1991). This program has succeeded in providing much useful data and information on captive breeding, and the possibility of reintroduction from a variety of species.

Methods of Research in Captivity

Data Collection Techniques: Generality and Reliability

The two basic questions to be asked when studying captive populations are: (1) to what population are the findings to be generalized,
and (2) to what degree are the observations reliable? Reliability
refers to whether repeated observations would yield like data. Most
field studies and, alas, many laboratory studies fail to design the
schedule of observations so that reliability may be assessed. Or, if
reliability measures are available between or among observers, the
reliability is rarely reported. Such is inexcusable, as there exist
easy but refined methods for estimating reliability even under the
unique and seemingly unrepeatable conditions to be found in field
research (Kazdin, 1982).

Generality refers to the difference between the sample observed and the population one wishes to describe. Does study of a
collection of five primates permit the observer to comment on: (1)
all members of the genus and species, wherever they may live;
(2) all members who live in captive environments; (3) all groups of
the same size; or (4) smaller or larger groups as well? As captive
groups are rarely, if ever, comparable in demography, it follows
that each captive group is a unique set. However suggestive and
revealing such comparisons may be, they are usually untested
statistically and therefore unwarranted. Consider an example: Hamadryas baboons (*Papio hamadryas*) will choose cliffs or rocks on
which to sleep if such are available in nature (Kummer, 1968;
Abegglen, 1984). They do not, of course, select rocks as sleeping
places if none are available. A careful observer will be unacquainted
with the choice unless the field conditions permit the alternatives. Do they select cliffs in captivity as well? Yes, if they are
available in the captive environment (Michelmore and Bath, 1978).
Note that even a careful observer may conclude that wild *P. hamadryas* are rock sleepers, or that they may be (if seen without
rocks available), or that they are in the captive environment, or
are not (if rocks are not available in the captive state). If we
conclude that they are rock sleepers, we are suggesting the presence of a trait; if they are such sleepers under one condition, but
not under another, we may decide that the trait is environmentally bound, and thereby not a strong one, or that there is no such
trait. The lesson is that we cannot make the observation general
without the necessary control conditions, and surely not without

providing experimental alternatives whose selection dictates our answer. The possibility of generality between behavior seen in the field and in the captive state depends on additional factors, such as the size of the sample, the independence of the behavior of members of the sample, and the comparableness of the environments.

Traits notwithstanding, primates are adaptable. Berman's (1980) comparison of mother-infant interactions of the *Macaca mulatta* on Cayo Santiago with caged colonies in Madingley, England is instructive of attempts to generalize between the two kinds of samples. Although the behavioral frequencies were qualitatively and quantitatively similar between the two populations, there were significant differences that emphasize the environmental impact on the social interactions of infants. Compared to Madingley mothers, Cayo Santiago mothers rejected a higher proportion of the attempts of infants for nipple contact. Cayo Santiago infants spent more time off their mothers, and were more responsible for maintaining proximity with their mothers than were Madingley infants. Berman (1980) concluded that the differences in the mother-infant interactions between the two populations were due to differences among the mothers, rather than among the infants. Caged mothers were more protective of their infants and encouraged independence at a later age than were Cayo Santiago mothers. The conclusion emphasizes the point that different forms of captivity might affect behavior in different ways.

Often enough, the effect of a shift in kind of captivity is transitory and a reflection of the initial impact of a change in environment. For example, in the Berman (1980) comparison, there was also evidence that the Madingley animals were becoming more like the Cayo Santiago animals during captivity. Earlier in the formation of the Madingley colonies, the infants played a smaller role in maintaining proximity to their mothers. Over time, the Madingley mothers became less protective and the responsibility of the infants for maintaining maternal proximity increased. Berman (1980) suggested that the most plausible explanation for the change in mother-infant relationships is the formation of kinship clusters. As the Madingley colonies aged, the number of related animals per colony increased, perhaps enabling mothers to raise their infants in a more relaxed atmosphere surrounded by kin. While it is vital to assess generality of findings under degrees of captive conditions, it is also true that assessment of the degree of the generality can tell us much about the effects of captivity.

The kind and degree of variation observed may say more about the behavioral and genetic potential of the species than does a strict comparison of frequencies of behavior under varying environmental conditions. An instructive example of the problem is this: primate communication is often most easily studied in a captive environment in which vocalizations can be conveniently recorded and analyzed. Generalizations to wild populations become difficult, however, due to the unknown effect of the unnatural environment on the vocal repertoire. McGuire (1974), for example, compared communication in the vervets of St. Kitts and Amboseli. The St. Kitts population exhibited only 81% of the communicative gestures and 56% of the vocalizations recorded by Struhsaker (1967a, b) at Amboseli. Both the frequency and variety of vocalizations were low among the St. Kitts vervets. An interesting discovery was that most of the vocalizations not heard at St. Kitts were associated with behaviors not observed in that population, suggesting that the correlation between vocalization and behavior is highly specific. Only two vocalizations heard at St. Kitts were not recorded at Amboseli. In addition, six of the vocalizations common to both populations were performed in different environmental situations. On the one hand, we may wish to assess the degree of similarity between the two groups, groups of the same genetic stock but with longstanding differences in ecology. On the other, differences found may tell us much about basic issues of primate behavior, as in this example, the relationship between vocalizations and behavior.

Data Collection Techniques: Observation and Hypothesis Testing

A different matter to consider is whether human observation of primates alters the behavior of the primates. As fundamental and simple as the statement is, the question is given slight consideration by human researchers, probably because the asking of the question brings all that has been learned through observation into question. The notion that human beings can be "accepted" by primate populations is longstanding in literature, and of more recent origin in behavioral science (Garner, 1896a, b; Goodall, 1986). "Acceptability" may imply tameness and domestication or that the behavior is unchanged. It is usually assumed that the presence of a human observer alters wild primate behavior at first, but that the animals later adapt; that is, their behavior becomes as it was without human intervention. There are no data based on wild animals to support any view.

For captive animals, the presence of human observers is known to alter behavior. Working with socially housed *Saimiri*, and recording behavior both without the presence of humans and with people watching the primates on closed-circuit TV, Candland et al. (1972) found that although the animals had been observed systematically for five years, they reacted to the presence of human observers with increases in drinking water, waiting, and sexual activity. While these enhanced frequencies may return to the rate recorded when human observers are not present, there were no indications that such was occurring during the course of study of these often observed animals. Caine (1990), when studying the reactions of socially housed tamarins (*Saguinas labiatus*) to potential predators, found no evidence of habituation to such stimuli when in the presence of human observers. Caine writes: " . . . the remarks that many investigators make about habituation should be made with circumspection" (1990, p. 196). We have much to learn about the habituation, if any, of both captive and wild primates to human beings. Such studies ought to be a staple of research done under captive conditions.

When observing either captive or wild populations, it is rarely possible to observe all animals and all interactions simultaneously. No one can follow the movements and behavior patterns of larger groups without error, and arboreal primates are often out of human sight. The restrictions of data collection, therefore, necessitates the generalization from a small sample to a larger one. Thus, the population of animals selected for observation and the abstracting of their behavior constitutes the fundamental problem of research. Observers have developed several methods to sample individual animals or selected portions of groups that permit one to generalize from a small sample to a larger one. For example, in focal sampling, the observer watches a preselected animal for a preselected amount of time, then, by design, turns the attention to another animal, and so on. A second method is to watch for a preselected behavior, such as grooming. Here the observer watches first for the behavior, rather than the animal. There are a number of modifications and variations on these basic forms of sampling, each of which has benefits and costs relative to the research question being asked. For example, extrapolation will not determine whether a specific behavior is practiced away from human presence, never performed, or performed only in human presence (Altmann, 1974; Lehner, 1979).

The Lehner book (1970) and a monograph published by the National Research Council (1981) provide the best single sources of descriptions of data collection techniques and analysis and of their costs and benefits. An excellent technique for instruction is provided by Mellen (1983) who prepared two videotapes that demonstrate these methods with captive animals, including some primates, at the Minnesota Zoological Garden. Segal (1989) has edited contributions on the requirements for psychological well-being of captive primates.

When sufficient normative data are established, investigators turn to the manipulation of conditions and the testing of hypotheses. One example is the contemporary interest in hypotheses derived from "kin selection" theory, a theory which suggests that animals behave toward one another in ways that maximize their inclusive fitness. Although some of these hypotheses require nothing more than a redefinition of observational categories (e.g., is it the case that individuals act altruistically toward other animals to the degree that they are genetically related to them?), others may require the introduction of independent variables. In this way theory is tested and, by the introduction of experimental procedures, refined and assessed. The dilemma is that when captive animals are chosen to test a hypothesis that demands the manipulation of an independent variable, the investigator accepts the uncertainties of generality to the wild population in order to control the independent variables. Alternately, if one chooses to observe wild animals to test theory, one trades the exact knowledge of animals, conditions, and experimental procedure for the freedom of the natural state.

Data Collection Techniques: Instrumentation

Early studies of primate populations involved the collection of normative data regarding the occurrence and frequencies of specific kinds of behavior. Although the study of primate behavior rarely resulted in the production of new forms of instrumentation, many products developed for commercial or military purposes have come to be used by researchers. These include, for example, laptop computers, videotape, frequency counters, long-range audio equipment, and telescopes able to aid night vision. The need to locate, observe, and record is basic to all research on behavior, and the development of any instrument that assists any of these processes is promptly incorporated into research plans.

A research instrument whose value is sometimes overlooked is the statistical device. As formulae are developed to permit generalization from few cases to the many, so they may be employed to use data from small groups, or a few individuals within a group, to generalize to a far larger sample. One advantage of such techniques is that, when properly applied, they may lead to validity using a smaller number of subjects than might be expected. If the original population to be studied is chosen with regard to how well it represents the larger sample, the clever researcher can discover valid relationships by using a small, but well-identified sample. In contrast, when an investigator does not know the relevant variables, or how to select a sample population, the temptation is to select as many subjects as possible, an approach that is at once wasteful of the animals and likely to produce false generalities.

Identification and Marking Techniques

Records of primates maintained under captive conditions are rarely complete. Although noncommercial facilities report their census of illnesses, death, and births to the U.S. Department of Agriculture, the fact that most captive primates have been captured somewhere, transported, and sold or traded means that there is ample room for records to be incomplete and erroneous (see especially, National Research Council, 1981).

Tattooing is a permanent means of identification, but it is not useful for prompt identification from a distance and is quickly obscured by hair growth. Other common means are the use of beaded necklaces on smaller primates, patterns of ear snips that form a code, or the use of paint to form recognizable patterns. Each system has drawbacks. Animals lose beads or, worse, the size of the animal's neck grows while the beads do not; the application of ear snips is painful to the animal and, in any case, difficult to read at a distance; paint patterns may lead to mistreatment from other animals and, in any event, wear off. Many observers rely on coming to know the animals by sight and name or number. Although this procedure requires initial effort and provides ample opportunity for error, especially in larger groups, it is the method used most frequently, perhaps because it avoids the need to restrain the animal while identifying marks are made. A record of pictures of each animal in different poses is helpful. All considered, no means has been determined that leads to errorless and quick identification of animals from a distance.

Husbandry

An important aspect of animal husbandry is appropriate cage design—appropriate, to be sure, to the animal inhabiting it, for that which is beautiful to the human observer may be uninteresting to the captive animal. Animals in captive environments have far less to do than in the wild. In captivity, food and water are provided, while in the wild, the acquisition of these often occupy 90% of the day. Idle minds and idle hands may lead to exaggerated social behavior: play, tool-making, and sexual activity appear to be far different in captive conditions than in wild situations (Candland et al., 1972). Sexual activity, for example, is evidently far more frequent in captivity than in the wild, or alternatively, far less frequent or absent, depending upon the species, individual history, and the environment (Hediger, 1950). Mating is among the most fragile of activities for primates and it is fair to argue that a captive environment is not a successful one if mating does not occur.

Successful care of offspring is also a requirement of sound captive design. A common husbandry problem among captive social groups involves attacks by males on either animals of low status or on infants (Itani, 1982). However, the conditions that promote this activity are often unclear, as the time and place are often unknown. An area into which the mother and infant may retreat or an area that larger animals cannot enter is often built; however, a mother with an infant is defenseless against the interests of a mob. Captive conditions restrict animals under attack from leaving the troop for a time or staying out of harm. Designing areas to which they can retreat is a dilemma, for while one wants an area in which the animal can feel safe, one does not want an area in which a sick animal can hide and not be reached or attended.

Those familiar with captive primates rate conditions on the combined physical and mental health of the animal more than on the specific characteristics of the environment. Although the present standards for animal care set by the U.S. Department of Agriculture concentrate on the specific requirements of the enclosure, such as volume of space available and type of construction materials used, experienced caretakers look for the following behavioral aspects, among others, that indicate something of the physical and psychological health of the primate: (1) the animal uses its senses (it watches, smells, hears, tastes); (2) the animal communicates vocally—in appropriate conditions it gives warning calls and alarms; (3) the animal is active; the eyes turn toward novelty (compare: the eyes are fixed and staring, irrespective of what is happening); (4) the fur is clean and has sheen, and does not show signs of being repeatedly rubbed against some part of the enclosure; (5) the animal interacts with other animals in ways appropriate to its age; (6) the animal breeds, delivers young, and cares for them; (7) the animal does not pace nor show other stereotypic behaviors. It would appear that captivity extends the lifespan for many primates. Whether it does so for all, or whether the infant mortality rate in captivity is greater than that in the wild, is not established. These data are difficult to obtain, as the birthdate of wild animals is frequently unknown, and those who are moved into captivity are of uncertain age.

Endangered primate species are often beyond the "crash point" in numbers when the problem of survival is recognized. Captivity assures that minimal variability of the gene pool is available. Knowledge of the reproductive physiology of rare species may be minimal. The result is that husbandry must be learned under conditions already desperate. Under these conditions, there is little opportunity to try alternative procedures or to gain the basic knowledge of diet, climate, social, and behavioral needs requisite for survival and reproduction. Indeed, successful reproduction and care is sufficiently rare that few generalities are known.

Problems in Research in Captivity

The research advantages offered for humans by captive, semifree ranging populations include the availability of the known history of the animals and the opportunity to compare demographic and social structures with populations in the wild. The disadvantages of using semifree ranging populations are, as in field studies, the difficulties in controlling and manipulating variables and observational conditions. A discussion of some problems follows.

Population Density

In captivity, as in the wild, resource limitations may regulate population size through decreased fecundity, increased aggression, and susceptibility to disease (Geller and Christian, 1982). Provisioning of captive populations enables the environment to support a much higher density of animals than in the wild. The density of rhesus monkeys on Cayo Santiago, Puerto Rico, in 1983, for instance, was six times that of wild populations (Rawlins and Kessler, 1986b).

High-density captive populations can affect both the behavior and health of the animals. Alexander and Bowers (1967) found evidence that high density results in hyperaggression. The Oregon troop of *Macaca fuscata,* in comparison to wild troops, exhibited more severe injuries as a result of agonistic encounters, more frequent group attacks, and seemingly random attacks on a series of different monkeys. Kawai et al. (1967) also blamed increased density for the high frequency of agonistic interactions in a troop of Japanese macaques that had been transplanted to a small island.

Disruptions in the social behavior of males are often indicative of overcrowding. Rhesus males, as is true of other macaque species, may leave their natal troops during the mating season and either join other troops or remain solitary. On Cayo Santiago, only one permanent transfer was observed by Altmann (1962) during a 1956–1958 study. The population expanded, and between 1960 and 1963 there were 301 observed changes in troop membership (Koford, 1966). Although troop affiliations change in wild populations, Boelkins and Wilson (1972) have suggested that the high frequency of transfers on Cayo Santiago may be due to the unnaturally high density of monkeys on the island.

Upon arriving in Texas, the 150 Arashiyama West *Macaca fuscata* were initially confined to a one-acre enclosure in which aggression was promptly directed against the peripheral males of the troop (Fedigan, 1976). A few of these males escaped over the electric fence, others were removed from the enclosure, and two died of stress related conditions. Primates maintained under captive conditions should have ample space available in order for peripheral males to separate themselves from the troop. Otherwise, culling of juvenile males may be necessary to reduce the number of peripheral males and the frequency and severity of aggressive interactions, as has been practiced on the *M. sylvanus* of Gibraltar (Fa, 1984).

Alexander and Bowers (1967) have proposed several reasons that explain why high density is often correlated with hyperaggression. First, the troop leader normally initiates and guides the movements of the troop. Both the lack of space and the ready availability of resources reduces the directive role of the troop leader resulting in a disruption of the troop's organization and leading to tension and aggression between troop members. Second, aggressiveness may also be a response to the relatively boring and static environment provided to captive animals. A third result of hyperaggression is the skewed sex ratio often present in captive populations. Solitarization in wild *M. fuscata* males results in an unequal sex ratio, as much as 2:1 in favor of females (Tokuda, 1961–1962). In captivity, the inability of captive males to leave the natal troop increases the ratio of males to females, an imbalance from the natural social structure of the species that may lead to hyperaggression.

Intergroup spacing also affects the behavior of captive primates. Kleiman (1978a) has found a tendency for female *L. rosalia* in auditory and olfactory contact to stimulate each other's reproductive cycles. Mating and birth were synchronized in groups living in close proximity. DuMond's (1971) theory that a cage represents a group's territory was used by Fontaine and Hench (1982) in the housing of golden lion tamarins. Because the walls of the cage are the boundaries of the territory, conspecifics were not kept in adjacent wire-mesh cages without a buffer zone in between. Intraspecies aggression was reduced, although conflicts between *L. rosalia* and the *Saguinus* species that were housed in the buffer zones remained. In addition, noncontact aggressive interactions with conspecifics persisted through visual and auditory exchanges. When stress from intergroup fighting between cages was believed to be contributing to a high frequency of miscarriages, a second wire-mesh barrier was installed which may have been partly responsible for the reduced rate of stillbirths that followed.

Maternal Behavior

A major block in breeding captive primates, particularly gorillas, is the likelihood that the female will not appropriately care for her infant. This problem has been attributed to the lack of opportunities for females to learn maternal behavior. Under natural social conditions, adolescent females are thought to observe the behavior of older females, thereby gaining experience in handling and caring for infants (Schaller, 1963; Beck, 1984 and Nadler, 1974). The inability of most zoos to imitate natural social conditions for gorillas diminishes the probability that a female will respond appropriately to her infant. The problem is self-perpetuating, because a gorilla raised by human beings may be improperly socialized and therefore less likely to care for her own offspring, who may in turn need to be raised by humans. Nadler (1981, 1984, 1989) has provided model work in his instructive analyses of the maternal behavior of captive great apes.

Allowing females to raise and interact socially with their offspring may be necessary for the long-term captive survival of the species. There is recent interest in educating female gorillas by exposing them to maternal stimuli during pregnancy. The Apenheul Sanctuary for Gorillas and South American Monkeys in Apeldoorn, Netherlands, has attributed the successful rearing of an infant by a female gorilla to a maternal education program (Mager, 1981). This program is based on the belief that inexperienced mothers abandon their newborns because they are frightened by the movements and sounds of the infant. In an attempt to familiarize a nulliparous pregnant gorilla with infants, she was introduced to a young hand-raised black spider monkey (*Ateles paniscus*). The twenty-minute sessions were repeated at three-day intervals until an interest in touching and smelling the monkey replaced her fear. The gorilla exhibited appropriate maternal behavior following the birth of her own infant, although the extent to which her training was responsible for the success cannot be determined.

A different approach for inducing maternal behavior has been tried at the San Diego Wild Animal Park (Joines, 1977). Because the female, Dolly, had rejected her first infant, a program to teach appropriate behavior was initiated during her second pregnancy. Attempts to show her movies of female gorillas interacting with infants proved unsuccessful due to Dolly's short attention span and the distraction of the projector. The second phase of the training program involved a cloth surrogate of a baby gorilla. Dolly was taught four verbal commands and was rewarded for responding appropriately to "Turn the baby around, Dolly;" "Pick up the baby, Dolly;" "Be nice to the baby, Dolly;" and "Show me the baby, Dolly." The gorilla learned these commands by daily practice over a period of two months. She held and fed her baby immediately following parturition, and only required the voice commands to dispel her confusion the first time the infant cried.

A similar training program attempted by Keiter and Pichette (1977) at the Woodland Park Zoo in Seattle met with less success. The gorilla failed to pick up the surrogate infant and thus never learned the commands for holding the baby properly. She did appear, however, to have learned how to position and support the infant through observation of her trainers. Nevertheless, she dropped her baby on its fifth day and it subsequently died of hyaline membrane disease. Although maternal training programs are too few in number to permit an accurate assessment of their worth, the importance of properly socialized infants requires that these and other approaches to stimulating maternal behavior be investigated.

Dominance

In both field and captive conditions, the criteria used to determine dominance must be defined explicitly. Kawai (1965) divided dominance relations into two types. An animal's basic rank was determined by looking only at the relationship between the two individuals directly involved in the interaction. As dominance, by definition, is often related to aggressive behavior in both captivity and field conditions, an understanding of its permanence or prediction of its change is useful to successful captive conservation. An animal's dependent rank takes into consideration the involvement of other animals in the interaction between two individuals. The latter category can be further divided into primary dependent rank, based on kinship ties, and secondary dependent rank, based on social ties.

Most studies of dominance relations in primates measure the frequency of dyadic encounters in which one individual performs a submissive behavior in response to the aggressive behavior of another individual. Or, as stated clearly by Sade (1967, p. 107), dominance can be determined by the outcome of a fight, defined as ". . .an interaction in which an attack of any intensity is followed by a flight of any intensity." Missakian (1972) used these criteria of dominance interactions to study the behavior of the Cayo Santiago *M. mulatta*. Among females, a linear relationship existed in which mothers outranked all their offspring until the sons were in their sixth year. At this age, males either left their natal troop or rose in dominance status. The adult males possessed a linear dominance hierarchy that was separate from that of the females. In contrast to the female hierarchy, however, the male hierarchy was unstable, probably due to deaths, migrations into and out of the social group, and rank reversals between older and younger brothers. Missakian (1972) suggested that the instability of the male hierarchy indicates the role of the females in maintaining group stability over time.

Gender differences are also apparent when the dominance hierarchy is compared with social behavior. Sade (1972) found a positive correlation between dominance and grooming status (as measured by the number and grooming status of the monkeys who groomed the subject) in female *M. mulatta*. This observation indicates that females which possess the highest dominance status also occupy the central positions of the grooming network. No correlation between dominance and grooming status was found among male rhesus macaques. Sade (1972) suggests that these data indicate the less homogeneous relationships of males to the social group than those of females.

Analysis of dominance hierarchies is useful in the study of population dynamics. Sade et al. (1976) found that higher ranking genealogies of *M. mulatta* increased in numbers at faster rates than lower ranking genealogies. Priority of access to resources was not considered a factor, due to the abundant and well distributed food supply on the provisioned island. The correlation between genealogy, dominance and rate of increase is more likely due to the earlier onset of reproduction in females of high ranking genealogies.

Recognized changes in dominance hierarchy may be a means of viewing the social structure in relation to the size of a primate troop. Kawamura (1965) predicted that the decrease in number of interactions between any two individuals in a large troop would result in the disappearance of clear dominance relations within the troop. Missakian (1972), however, did not find this relationship to be true in her study of a large troop of Cayo Santiago rhesus macaques. The linear cross-genealogical hierarchy was maintained following troop fission. That is, the genealogies within both new troops were ranked relative to one another, as they had been when the two troops were combined. This study emphasizes the strength of the stable hierarchies in maintaining the social structure of the troop.

In captive populations, the dominance hierarchy of a troop can be manipulated by human interference. In the *M. sylvanus* of Gibraltar, for instance, if the caretakers decide that a change in leadership would benefit by reducing aggression or increasing the gene pool of the troop, they capture the dominant male and transfer him to a zoo. The younger male then takes over the role of protecting and controlling the movements of the troop (Burton, 1972).

Human interference has also made possible a study of the role of the dominant male in captive gorilla societies. Hoff et al. (1982) observed the effect on social behavior of removing the male from a troop of three females and infants. In the absence of the dominant male, the females exhibited increases in aggression, spatial proximity, physical activity, and both ventroventral and nipple contact with infants. Infants remained in closer proximity to their mothers and infant play behavior decreased in frequency. Upon reintroduction, male aggression increased sharply from the preremoval frequencies, and female aggression began to decline. All behavior returned to approximately baseline frequencies within two weeks of the return of the male. This study suggests the role of aggression by the dominant male in maintaining social stability and mediating intragroup aggression (Hoff et al., 1982).

The role of the dominant male may also be important in infant development and socialization. Burton (1972) described interactions among *M. sylvanus* in which the dominant male initiated walking in young infants. After placing an infant on the ground, the male lowered his head and backed up while chattering to the infant, who chattered in response and crawled toward the male. The dominant male assisted in the development of motor activities that later enabled the infant to engage in social interactions within the troop. This study emphasizes the importance of maintaining natural social conditions in captive populations to ensure proper socialization of infants into the troop.

An important confounding variable in studies of dominance is the differential visibility of the animals to the observer. Dominant individuals, for instance, may be more easily observed than individuals likely to remain on the periphery of the troop. Sade (1972) acknowledged the bias of differential observability in his study of the Cayo Santiago *M. mulatta* by performing test observations to determine which individuals were visible during randomly sampled time intervals. A significant correlation between an individual's rank in observability and a particular behavior indicated that the data for that behavior may have been biased by the differential visibility of the animals. The confounding variables of age and relatedness should also be controlled in studies of primate dominance rank (Colvin, 1983). A means of removing the effects of the former variable is to use subjects of the same age, providing the study population is sufficiently large. Reducing the possible effects of relatedness is more difficult due to the often complex genealogies of primate societies.

Communication

The small communicative repertoire of the St. Kitts vervets may be attributed to a relatively simple environment (McGuire, 1974). Compared to Amboseli vervets, St. Kitts vervets are exposed to fewer predators and less intense competition for resources. More complex environments may require more complex patterns of communication. McGuire (1974) has suggested that animals have the potential to perform a limited number of behaviors. The type and frequency of the behaviors actually performed are determined by the environment. Amboseli vervets, for instance, emit a progression

grunt, which is thought to coordinate troop movement when cross-
ing large, short-grassed areas (Struhsaker, 1967a). St. Kitts vervets
rarely cross such areas and have not been known to use this vocalization. When traveling through tall grass, however, St. Kitts vervets
raise their tails above their backs and expose their white chests.
These behaviors may be adaptations that serve the same function
as the progression grunt (Poirier, 1972). It is possible that environmental conditions have reshaped the vocal and behavioral repertoires of the vervets on St. Kitts. Researchers must be cautious
when drawing conclusions from vocalizations of captive animals, as
the observable vocal repertoire may have been altered by the captive environment.

Primate vocalizations, once thought to convey only emotional
or motivational states, have recently been shown to function
representationally, containing information about both social relationships and external objects (Seyfarth et al., 1980a, b; Cheney
and Seyfarth, 1982; Gouzoules et al., 1986). When examining the
responses of Cayo Santiago rhesus females to the recordings of
juvenile scream vocalizations, it was found that females reacted
differentially to both the type of call and the identity of the caller.
Screams associated with contact from higher ranking opponents,
for instance, elicit a stronger response when the caller was closely
rather than distantly related to the female. No kin discrimination
was made in response to calls that were associated with noncontact
aggression from lower ranking opponents. This research suggests
that rhesus are able to discriminate between categories of social
and kin relationships purely on the basis of vocal cues. The well-
documented history of the Cayo Santiago rhesus made this study
possible. The genealogies of wild populations are rarely sufficiently
well known to examine categories of kin relationships.

Some species of primates use scent-marking as a form of olfactory communication. L. rosalia, for example, possess both ster-
nal and circumgenital glands, which are dragged or rubbed on
objects in the animal's environment. The frequency of scent-marking behavior has been shown to vary with the reproductive state of
the female (Kleiman, 1978a). Scent-marking frequency in females
is very low during periods of peak mating activity, but increases
throughout the following week and during pregnancy. Males also
scent-mark more frequently following periods of increased sexual
activity, though the variation in frequency over the estrous cycle is
much smaller than in females. Kleiman (1978a) suggests that the
sudden drop in female scent-marking behavior during mating

periods functions to prevent males outside the pair-bond from sensing the receptive state of the female and interrupting the mating activities. Scent-marking behavior is difficult to study in the wild due to the decreased visibility of the subjects. The captive environment enables researchers to obtain accurate measurements of the frequency of scent-marking behavior while varying the social and physical environments.

Conservation in Captivity: Nonsocial Factors

Hormones

Hormonal assessments of urine samples have made it possible to diagnose and monitor the pregnancies of captive gorillas. The Jersey Wildlife Preservation Trust, in collaboration with Wellcome Laboratories, began a great ape hormone monitoring program in 1974. Analysis of daily urinary estrogens is used to determine the reproductive cycle of each gorilla. The test for pregnancy is based on levels of chorionic gonadotrophin and is effective in diagnosing pregnancy within a month of conception (Martin et al., 1977). The small amount of urine required for the tests can be collected with minimal disturbance to the animals. In addition to diagnosing pregnancies and predicting birth dates, hormonal assays can be used to monitor pubertal changes and to check for hormonal imbalances that may be responsible for reduced breeding success in either males or females (Martin et al., 1977; Mallinson, 1982). Several months of daily sampling, for instance, can detect irregular menstrual cycles in female gorillas (Martin et al., 1977).

Urinary hormone levels were found to be associated with gorilla sexual behavior at the Los Angeles Zoo. Mitchell et al. (1985) found that frequencies of female presentations were significantly correlated with estrogen production. Copulations occurred on only three days of the female reproductive cycle, peaking on the same day as estrogen excretion. Shideler and Lasley (1982) also noted more frequent copulations during the estrogen peak, and suggest that estrogen production is correlated with female attractiveness in stimulating male sexual behavior. Estrogen, the predominant reproductive hormone prior to ovulation, is thought to enhance the morphological and behavioral changes that are associated with attractiveness, such as vaginal opening, sex skin swelling, and proliferation of the endometrium (Shideler and Lasley, 1982).

Diet and Nutrition

Specific dietary requirements may pose problems in the captive maintenance of certain species. Although commercially available primate diets are usually supplemented with fruits and vegetables, certain Cercopithedae may also require fresh browse from trees, and both callitrichids and prosimians may require live prey such as crickets or mealworms. The quality and quantity of the diet have been found to influence both survival and reproduction of captive primates. For instance, the first successes in the captive survival and reproduction of gorillas were partially attributed to changes in their diets (Maple and Hoff, 1982). But, improved nutrition in the golden lion tamarin may have a detrimental impact on a captive population. Kleiman (1978b) noted that overproduction is a problem in older females, many of whom are producing triplets twice a year, rather than the annual twin births observed in the wild. The increased reproductive rate is a burden to the female, often resulting in a higher mortality rate in both infants and mothers. Epple (1970) suggested that the increased occurrence of triplets in captivity may be a result of the highly nutritious captive diet. It may be necessary to separate the pair for six months to give the female a break from reproduction.

The arrangement of the food in a captive environment may influence the observed social structure. For example, Fedigan's (1976) study of the Arashiyama West macaques supports the observations of Miyadi (1964), Yamada (1966), and Sugiyama (1960) that wild troops in Japan possess a central-peripheral social structure. The dominant male is surrounded by high ranking males and females. Other females, lower ranking males, and juveniles occupy the next concentric ring, and solitary or semisolitary males form the periphery of the troop. Alexander and Bowers (1967), however, suggested that this ring-like stratification is an artifact of environmental factors, including the arrangement of the provisioned food. Their observations of the Oregon troop of Japanese macaques indicated that the central-peripheral structure formed only when the food was arranged in a small circle. This structure was replaced by a random pattern when the food was spread over a wider area.

Daily and Seasonal Behavior

Seasonal patterns of behavior in some primate species appear to be influenced by the geographic location of the captive environment. *L. rosalia* maintained in the northern hemisphere typically give birth between March and August, in contrast to the September to March birth season of wild *L. rosalia* in Brazil (Kleiman, 1978a). It is supposed that the seasonality of breeding behavior is determined by photoperiod, weather patterns, social influences, or a combination of factors.

Van Horn (1980) analyzed the birth data of wild populations of *M. fuscata* and noted a significant correlation between latitude and conception. Earlier conceptions occurred in the more northern latitudes, suggesting that the reproductive cycle is affected by day length. Eaton et al. (1987), however, found that the mean conception date of *M. fuscata* in Oregon is nearly three months later than would be predicted based on photoperiod. Furthermore, the Arashiyama West troop of *M. fuscata* maintained the May birth peak of the Arashiyama troop in Japan, although the change in latitude would suggest a later birth season (Gouzoules et al., 1981). Further evidence against photoperiod is provided by Varley and Vessey (1977), who studied a population of Cayo Santiago rhesus that had been translocated to La Parguera, Puerto Rico. They found that the birth peak shifted by ninety days within two years of the translocation, even though the two populations are at the same latitude. These studies suggest that there are factors other than photoperiod involved in determining reproductive seasons in primates.

There is also some evidence that breeding behavior is affected by weather patterns. The birth season of the St. Kitts vervets occurs from late May through early July (Poirier, 1972), and that of wild vervets in Africa from October through March (Struhsaker, 1967a). Both birth periods correspond to the rainy season and times of increasing food supplies in the respective habitats. For both the Cayo Santiago rhesus and wild *M. mulatta* in India, it is the breeding period that is correlated with the wet season (Koford, 1965). Koford (1965) has suggested that weather patterns only indirectly affect breeding seasons and that a combination of nutritional and social factors triggers the onset of mating. The distribution of rainfall determines the abundance and composition of the natural food supply, which may influence the production of sex hormones. This explanation, however, does not account for the behavior of the Oregon troop of *M. fuscata*. Rainfall in Oregon rises sharply during the breeding season, in contrast to a decrease in precipitation during the breeding season in Japan (MacRoberts and MacRoberts, 1966).

Vandenbergh (1973) has implicated a combination of factors in the onset of seasonal reproduction. It is claimed that environmental conditions such as day length set the stage for breeding behavior, and that social stimuli within a breeding population act to coordinate mating activities. Regional differences in the timing of reproductive cycles may be due to differences in the social conditions of the population. Thus, the similarity between the birth seasons of the Arashiyama West and Japanese troops of *M. fuscata* may be attributed to a lack of social pressures to alter the reproductive cycle (Gouzoules et al., 1981). MacRoberts and MacRoberts (1966) claim that decreasing temperature and decreasing day length are the most important factors influencing the timing of the mating season. They point to evidence that the Barbary macaques of Gibraltar, wild *M. fuscata*, and *M. fuscata* in Oregon all breed when these conditions are met. It is likely that there is a variety of factors affecting the reproductive cycle, with various ecological and social conditions affecting each population to a different degree.

Some primate species also exhibit seasonality in nonreproductive behavior. Eaton et al. (1987) studied the effect of captivity on seasonal aggression in the Oregon *M. fuscata*. Males were most aggressive during the mating season, and females were most aggressive toward other females during the nonmating season, but toward males during the mating season. The correlation between male aggression and the mating season is presumably related to high levels of testosterone. The high frequency of female-female aggression during the nonmating season is thought to be the result of social factors such as the conflict between maternal protectiveness and the attractiveness of the infants (Eaton et al., 1981 and Eaton et al., 1987). Eaton et al. (1987) have concluded that the nature of seasonal behavior such as aggression is not affected by captivity because seasonal behavior is closely tied to the yearly reproductive cycle.

Primate behavior can be strongly influenced by the daily routines of captive management. Boelkins and Wilson (1972) describe a typical morning provisioning of the Cayo Santiago rhesus macaques. The boat is met by a throng of excited, chattering, monkeys who fight over spilled food and who follow the caretakers to the feeding locations. Social structure is altered by the expectation of food imposed by a regular feeding schedule. As has been previously mentioned, the provisioning of captive primates may also alter the frequency of certain behavior by providing the animals with extra time that would otherwise have been spent foraging. McGuire (1974) found a positive correlation between simple day research observation plans and high tension (as measured by the mean flight distance from human observers) in the St. Kitts vervets. That is, the greater the tension level within the troop, the more limited was the variety of behavior performed by the monkeys. Thus, it is difficult to compare daily activity patterns of captive primates to those of wild populations, or even to those of other captive populations. However, daily activity profiles can be used as a behavioral assay to compare the frequencies of kinds of behavior at different times or under different captive conditions.

Conclusions

A number of kinds of captive environments can be identified ranging from island refuges to acre enclosures to small exhibits that represent the human observer's concept of the animals' original environment. The appropriate test of the efficacy of a captive environment would appear to be the primate societies' reaction to it. The continuation of societal and reproductive strategies in the captive environment are appropriate measures of success.

Primates are social animals. It is appropriate to think of the natural environment as including conspecifics within a broad demographic range. Captive conditions should imitate these ranges if one is interested in assessing behavior or exhibiting the animals in ways that show their abilities and opportunism. Although it may be necessary to house primates in single cages for studies of, say, immune responses or the like, such environments deprive the animal of common responses and impose unnatural conditions on the animal.

Several longstanding groups of primates have lived in translocated conditions. We mention the St. Kitts vervets, the rhesus of Cayo Santiago, the Barbary macaques, the Japanese snow monkey, the gorilla, and the golden lion tamarin. The nature of the translocated environments is instructive, as some differences between captive behavior and behavior in the endemic situation has been often noted, especially in vocalizations and the seasonal patterns of behavior.

For some primates, captive conditions are essential, as the endemic situation is changing in ways that lead to a threat to the survival of the species. The imminent danger means that there is rarely time for adequate research on the results of varying kinds of captive conditions.

The design of successful and unsuccessful captive conditions is lore rather than established fact. Nonetheless, the availability of some studies that compare captive and endemic populations permits generalization among and between genera and species. The task of the conservator is to assess the behavior seen in the natural state to be sure that the effects of constraint on sociality are minimal.

Note

The references are chosen to guide the reader to important examples and extensions of the point being made in the text. The published literature in this field is difficult to document as many fine reports appear in the newsletters issued by zoos. These documents have a limited distribution, and while they are usually noted in bibliographies, they are rarely kept by libraries. Such papers are of contemporary significance, but because of the nature of their publication, they are not often available as archival material. Readers interested in specialized examples might consult back issues of Zoologische Jahrbücher, Zoo Biology (both periodicals), and, the International Zoo Yearbook, which is published in book, not periodical, form.

Acknowledgment

We thank Bucknell students Becky Addington, Amy Galloway, Jon Laguna, Thomas Lomax, Thomas Mollerus, Douglas Sumerford, and Beau Beegle Vent for their very thoughtful readings of the manuscript.

28

Ark Design Update: Primate Needs and Requirements

Donald G. Lindburg and Jon Coe

Endangered primates reside for the most part in zoological gardens. Some notable exceptions are found at more scientifically oriented facilities such as the prosimian collection at Duke University and the great apes held at the Yerkes Regional Primate Research Center. Major differences between the goals of the two types of facilities affect the design of living quarters. For example, primates in research facilities are not usually on public display, and conservation goals may be secondary to scientific ones. Zoos, on the other hand, may be less constrained by economics and by scientific requirements. While recognizing an overlap between zoos and research facilities, in this chapter we address primarily the design concerns of zoos.

Primates have been taken into captivity since ancient Egyptian times. Their inclusion in the menageries of royalty seems to have been a feature of most if not all civilizations (Cherfas, 1984). A notable aspect of 18th and 19th century exhibition was the high rates of mortality during transit or soon after arrival in captivity, caused by the stresses of capture and transport or by diseases contracted from humans. Poor nutrition and husbandry techniques, stress from boredom, and close confinement insured a relatively short lifespan for even the hardiest of species (Mallinson, 1980; Maple and Hoff, 1982).

Since the early 1900s primates have been maintained in relatively large numbers in both research facilities and zoological gardens. Initially, improved sanitation and diets led to enhanced survivorship, and some species were even induced to reproduce. However, the drive to reduce mortality and, in zoos, concern with viewer convenience, gave emphasis to semi-sterile, indestructible, and easily sanitized design features. Elements such as light, temperature, humidity, ventilation levels, and feeding and cleaning schedules were strongly influenced by human needs and human convenience. In addition, the consequences of social isolation on infant development (Harlow and Harlow, 1962) were as yet unrecognized. In the hard-surface, sterile environments of the day there was much evidence of boredom, social conflict, and abnormal motor activity. Above all, reproductive rates remained distressingly low (Maple and Finley, 1989).

Following the concept pioneered by Carl Hagenbeck (Hagenbeck, 1909), some zoological parks began displaying primates on islands. These exhibits were considered naturalistic (Coe, 1987, 1989), and represented a significant step to an environment intermediate between natural and highly artificial conditions. Others adopted an increasingly "high-tech" approach, with complex apparatuses of steel pipe and rope substituting for the arboreal substrates of the natural world. More recent "natural habitat" exhibits, having their roots in Hagenbeck's ideas, have attempted to simulate native habitats as closely as possible, with the expectation that they will more adequately meet the biological requirements of the animals (Coe and Maple, 1984; Coe, 1985, 1987). "Natural habitat" exhibits are distinguished by having large, outdoor areas of living vegetation that are used for cover, exercise, and limited natural foraging, while at the same time giving visitors the experience of seemingly encountering the animal in its wilderness home. While the result often appears pristine and primitive, the horticultural and exhibitry methods used to achieve this effect may be very "high-tech" (Coe, 1983). Good examples of this approach are the great ape exhibits at Woodland Park Zoo in Seattle, Zoo Atlanta (Coe and Maple, 1984), and the Dallas and San Diego Zoos. Jungle World at the Bronx Zoo has used the "natural habitat" design in preparing exhibits for colobine monkeys and gibbons.

Economics of Captive Design

Outdoor Exhibits and Activity Areas

A "natural habitat" approach is typically utilized for the more terrestrial primates where large outdoor areas are available for construction. Containment structures are usually the highest cost elements. The selection of barrier type (Table 28.1) is dictated by species requirements, enclosure function (exhibition, research), site details, and cost. Smaller areas, either outdoors or in large conservatory-like spaces, for particularly agile and arboreal species, are effectively enclosed by an architectural structure of wire mesh. Such structures may be supported by either a rigid framework or a more flexible tensile or tent-like structure. The latter is more compatible with naturalistic settings but, in either case, total containment gives arboreal primates greater usable volume of space with reduced concern for escape.

Plantings and Their Protection

The more active primates usually cause considerable plant damage by eating leaves and bark, breaking branches, and compacting soil. Damage can be minimized by planting fast growing or unpalatable but nontoxic species, and by providing rapidly draining soil, ideally with underdrainage and irrigation (Coe, 1989). However, even under these conditions plantings will eventually be destroyed if too many individuals occupy an area for too long a time. Low density per unit of space and rotation between areas gives plants a better opportunity to regenerate. A major consideration in the use of naturally planted exhibits is a construction schedule that allows the vegetation to become firmly established before occupation. Because most primates find buds and new leaves especially palatable, access to natural plantings should be postponed until after new leaves are fully developed. Subsequently, access should be limited to the growing season. While much remains to be learned about the use of natural vegetation in primate exhibits, lists of species currently being used are available (Harke et al., 1985). Primate field reports provide lists of plant foods for which local equivalents can sometimes be found. Plants known to have toxic effects on humans and other animals are identified in Kingsbury (1964) and in Lampe and McCann (1985).

Electrified wires, mesh wraps, simulated fiberglass tree trunks, thorn and metal barriers, and water areas have been used to protect plantings. Developmental research continues for repellent chemicals. In selecting among available approaches, one must ask: (1) are they humane, (2) are they effective, (3) do they inhibit nominal and desirable behavior and, (4) are they visible and distracting to the public? Without special protection or limited access, it is impossible to keep trees alive over the long-term in exhibits holding large-sized primates (macaques and larger).

Indoor plantings are especially problematic because space is usually more limited than in outdoor areas. These plantings also require abundant light with appropriate wavelengths and a suitable period of acclimatization (Ortho Books, 1975; Morrison, 1984). Because of the difficulties involved, especially with the more destructive primates, many zoos forego the attempt to maintain permanent indoor plantings and rely instead on provisioning of browse and/or artificial elements.

Indoor Holding, and Activity Areas

Since most primates are of tropical origin, they require a climate-controlled environment to escape cold in temperate-zone facilities. Confinement indoors for up to 30-40 percent of the year, and the multiple functions of indoor quarters as exhibit, living environment, and holding area (bedroom or day room), requires a more equitable expenditure of facility funds on both indoor and outdoor aspects. Indoor quarters tend to be hard-textured, inflexible, and devoid of novelty—concessions to sanitary considerations and the high cost of construction. Some zoos (e.g., Minnesota, Bronx, Arnhem) have solved this problem by enclosing huge areas as "tropical" habitats that are large enough to permit several species to experience "outdoor" living throughout the year. With this approach, the wintertime visitor to the zoo is spared the often unpleasant experience (and associated, undesirable educational messages) of seeing highly sentient mammals in small, relatively barren, nonstimulating conditions. This is an aspect of facility design that deserves much more attention from zoos in designing for the future.

Design and Caregiver Efficiency

A useful approach in designing a functional unit is to encourage experienced caregivers to participate fully in the design process. Architects have found it extremely useful to prepare models of proposed facilities that allow staff to simulate daily routines or emergency procedures. This process also helps to develop a sense that those who must work in the area have contributed to the final product. To protect against the tendency to emphasize human convenience over animal requirements, input from individuals having

Table 28.1
Summary of Barrier Types

Type of Construction	Relative Cost	Remarks
Smooth masonry or poured concrete walls and moats.	High	Very durable, usually unsightly, emphasize confinement, not suitable for natural habitat exhibits.
Textured concrete (gunite, shotcrete, made to resemble natural rock or banks.	Higher	Very durable, suitable for natural habitat exhibits.
Cast concrete shells over structural wall.	Highest	Very durable, suitable for natural habitat exhibits.
Mesh fence with smooth overhang on primate side.	Moderate	Practical but unsightly unless hidden in ditch or behind berm.
Mesh fence with electric shocking devices (hotwire).	Moderate	Practical but unsightly unless hidden in ditch or behind berm. Depends on constant electrical supply.
Low "electronet" type of electrified fence (2 meters high).	Low	Assumes animals will not jump over. Useful for subdivisions in larger yards.
Water moats, with outer wall. Concrete construction.	High	Suitable for nonswimming animals. Drowning is a risk. Can be attractive.
Water moats with clay or artificial membrane (no outer wall).	Moderate	Suitable for nonswimming animals. Drowning is a risk. Can be attractive, but difficult to sanitize.

first hand knowledge of the species in the wild is highly desirable. It is inevitable that human and animal requirements will conflict at some points, but dialogue at an early stage of the design process will lead to innovations that brings about compatibility between diverse requirements (Wallace, 1982). In addition, this process reduces the prospect of costly modifications to correct design flaws at a later time.

Security. Even small prosimians can inflict painful injuries, and pound for pound the monkey is much stronger and quicker than its keepers. Furthermore, some primates have the intelligence to plan and carry out group escapes, assisting each other in the process. Many species have the dexterity, intellect and, in some cases, the strength to systematically dismantle apparatuses and control devices, or to lure the unsuspecting human within reach of their powerful grasp. The risk to caregivers can be reduced by incorporating a number of proven safety factors into the design of primate facilities.

SAFETY ZONES. Animals should be kept in areas of primary security, with secondary human access and, in the case of potentially dangerous species, tertiary human work areas (kitchens, offices, etc.). Each zone should provide an unobstructed view of the entire area of adjacent higher security zones. Each zone should be separated by a secure and lockable door. There should be at least three such doors between potentially dangerous animals and the public or nonkeeper staff.

DOORS. Doors normally swing into animal areas so that charging animals cannot push them open. Caregivers entering animal areas, especially in outdoor habitats, must be able to secure all animal gates into the area so that animals cannot be inadvertently allowed to enter while keepers are present.

CONTROL GATES. The gate operator should have a clear view of both sides of the gate and be able to obtain easy confirmation that the gate is locked. Gates and controls must be clearly labeled and interrelated.

Escapes or unintended contacts with animals are potentially costly for both animals and humans. No dollar value can be attached to human death or injury resulting from poor design, and design features that result in the destruction of escapees must be avoided.

Species Considerations in Captive Design

Abiotic Factors

Temperature. As creatures from tropical environments, most primates require temperatures in the 20–30°C range. However, with gradual acclimatization, many primates can tolerate outdoor temperatures down to freezing on sunny days, provided they are protected from wind and have access to heated perches. As a rule, primates should have the option of entering shelter when they desire warmth, though care must be taken to prevent socially ostracized individuals from becoming hypothermic. Some facilities maintain indoor temperatures during cooler seasons that are below the thermal comfort range of the animals. It has been shown that primates that are physiologically adapted to cooler temperatures are less likely to chill if not subjected to extreme daily fluctuations in temperature (Mager and Griede, 1986; Kopff and Mager, 1990).

Ventilation. Laboratory facilities that hold large numbers of primates in individual units typically maintain 15 air changes per hour (AAALAC Animal Care Regulations). However, this is excessive where the cubic area of space available per animal is large, as is usually the case in zoos. Also, the heating or cooling of such large volumes of air is costly.

Lighting. In circumstances requiring long-term exposure to artificial light, particular care must be given to the implications for primate health (e.g., metabolic bone diseases), and, in many species, to the influence of light on the timing of reproductive events. Designers are advised to consult the technical literature for guidance in installing illumination (see for example, Wurtman et al., 1985; Gehrmann, 1987; Erkert, 1989).

Acoustic Environment. The sounds experienced by captive primates deserve consideration from three perspectives: aversive sounds which increase corticosteroid levels and are therefore stressful (Tempest, 1985); sounds of human activity, such as food preparation, which may result in undesired conditioned responses; and the use of sound for its positive effects (i.e., for auditory enrichment). The statement by Anthony (1963) that no acoustical criteria for noise tolerance in captive animals have been developed would appear to be true today. Also, we know of no studies on the implications of auditory conditioning, even though it is found in every captive colony. Studies of the importance of exposure to ecologically relevant sounds for their psychological benefits have only recently been initiated (Shepherdson et al., 1989b; Ogden and Lindburg, 1991).

Incidental Radiation. Most of the electromagnetic spectrum is beyond primate sensory awareness. However, recent studies with captive baboons indicate that exposure to unnatural levels of electromagnetism or to radio and microwave radiation can produce undesirable effects on mood or behavior (Easley et al., 1990). Very small primates may be adversely affected by close proximity to the transformers in common fluorescent lighting fixtures. Where necessary, the "clean room" technology developed in silica chip manufacturing plants can be employed to shield primate facilities from these types of exposure.

Space. The relationship of enclosure size to the activities of its inhabitants is complex, and precludes the development of general rules that can be broadly applied (Erwin, 1979; Crockett, 1987; Snowdon, 1994). It is obvious that large-bodied species need more area in which to express normal locomotor and social behavior than small-bodied ones, and troop-living species may have greater spatial requirements than monogamous species. If density is too high, such that aggression becomes overly frequent or plantings are destroyed, reduction in the number of occupants may be a less desirable alternative than increasing the accessible space. Cost probably deters most zoos from building for groups of 10 or more individuals, even though adequate infant socialization and an enriched social experience (hence, better viewing by the public) would result.

Internal Furnishings and Spatial Configuration. Recent reports on the relationship of space to the expression of species-typical behavior rather conclusively demonstrate that shape and internal amenities of the environment are more important than quantity of space (Erwin, 1979; Maple and Finley, 1986; de Waal, 1989). Departure from the cube design, described by Hediger (1969) as the most unbiological of all shapes, is an encouraging trend in recently completed outdoor facilities. Undulating terrain and vegetative barriers provide opportunities for seclusion and add aesthetic value. It is unfortunate, however, that most exhibits encourage terrestrial living, regardless of species preferences. Providing vertical space does not suffice by itself, if above-ground areas hold little interest for the animals. Placement of food and water above ground, if combined with canopy-level viewing, holds the potential for an enriched experience for both the animals and the visiting public.

The incorporation of perches, poles, climbing structures, water elements, etc., in accordance with the animals' characteristics has become a common practice in captive housing (see, for example, Segal, 1989; Gibbons et al., 1994). One of the principal occupations of many species is to modify their habitat by a variety of means, including bending, tearing, chewing, dismantling, scent-marking, and bark-stripping. Soft furnishings such as branches, bamboo poles, logs, coarse fabrics, and vines are admirably suited to these needs. In prosimians and several New World primates scent-marking of structures serves an important communicative function. At the Duke University Primate Center limbs used for scent-marking are occasionally cleaned and are replaced several times a year. According to Izard and Pereira (1994), properly maintained wood substrates have been used at the Center for up to 20 years with no indications that they harbor harmful pathogens. Some regulations discourage the use of noncleanable materials such as wood or rope in primate enclosures. In our opinion these proscriptions work against the overall welfare and especially the psychological health of captive primates.

Dead trees or treetops placed either horizontally or vertically provide bouncy, resilient surfaces that encourage the development of locomotor skills. These structures are also suited for resting and the expression of habitual behaviors. (Designers are encouraged to consult Ripley [1967] for an outstanding example of the use of activity-specific structures by a wild-living primate.) These kinds of structures are functionally superior to fabricated ones (even when made of natural materials), are cheaper, and pose no health risks. Further softening of quarters may be achieved by placing various kinds of litter over hard floor surfaces (Chamove et al., 1982; McKenzie et al., 1986). Bedding is particularly important in the case of animals that must spend the winter months indoors. Apart from the properties of the bedding itself, it is important that such indoor facilities be designed to provide for its easy addition and removal and for essential drainage.

Biotic Factors

Food and Water. According to Ullrey (1986, p. 823), "species differences in dietary habits in the wild and in morphology of the gut lead one to conclude that all captive primates should not be fed in the same way." In addition, differences in feeding styles, from the "banqueting" of folivores to the more demanding tasks of foraging by those preferring fruits or insects (Oates, 1987), and the concomitant differences in the substrates that are negotiated by wild living primates (Lindburg, 1991b) are variables of importance. The provisioning of captives therefore poses a complex array of design considerations if nutritional, psychological, and locomotor requirements of this diverse Order are to be adequately met.

Commercially available primate biscuits, garden variety fruits and vegetables, prey (or meat products), and browse comprise the main components of diets fed by zoos. Assuming nutritionally appropriate foods are selected for the species in question, the design of dispensing equipment should take into consideration the need for equal access to food items by group members, the protection of food from body wastes or other contaminants, the stimulation of species-typical feeding activity, and consumption. The widespread presence of "kitchens" and the extensive amount of "food prep" that is practiced in captive provisioning suggests that some aspects may be anthropomorphically determined. Interestingly, the common practice of scattering food items on the floor or ground is a notable exception.

The design and placement of dispensers to accommodate food types as well as social and sanitation requirements has received relatively little attention from architects or from commercial suppliers of primate equipment. More often one sees innovations that are added to existing facilities by caregivers or researchers. Examples of devices that have been employed with the foregoing goals in mind are termite mounds for chimpanzees (Nash, 1982), food puzzles for chimpanzees (Bloomstrand et al., 1986; Brent and Eichberg, 1991) and gorillas (Cole, 1987), gum trees for marmosets (McGrew et al., 1986), feeders suspended from ceilings for marmosets (Molzen and French, 1989) and macaques (Shumaker, pers. commun.), and foraging racks attached at various heights to cage walls for macaques (Beckley and Novak, 1988). Feeders that would accommodate the dispensing of garden foods in intact form have apparently not been developed, even though this form of provisioning has been shown to have beneficial effects in a study of highly competitive macaques (Smith et al., 1989). Work in progress by the first author indicates that lion-tailed macaques respond with higher levels of activity and feeding to cut browse presented in a fixed, upright position than when tossed on the ground or floor. Whether fed as an essential diet item or for its psychological benefits, it would appear that designing for the regular feeding of browse would be a significant addition to the facilities of most primates (Shepherdson, 1989). For this to become a reality, zoos will have to find the means to overcome the problem of seasonal availability.

All primates require ready access to water. Use of pressure sensitive devices such as "lixits" reduces contamination and cleaning requirements. However, some prosimians are limited in their ability to manipulate automatic watering devices or even to drink from water bottles, and must therefore be provisioned with shallow containers (Izard and Pereira, 1994). New arrivals should be monitored closely to insure that they learn to utilize available water sources. For animals in quarantine, it may be desirable to use marked water bottles in order to monitor intake.

Social Considerations

Grouping Patterns. The diverse expressions of social life found in the primates have far-reaching implications for management and for the design of good living environments. Emulation of natural grouping and dispersal patterns where possible is an encouraging trend. A notable exception is the reduction of multi-male groups for species such as macaques and baboons to a single-male composition, with consequent reduction in space requirements. Unfortunately, some zoos reduce extrafamilial type primates to pairs or trios, thereby risking the production of peer-deprived offspring and atypical social relationships. In a number of prosimians and the orangutan, adults typically live apart in nature but can be housed socially in captivity, apparently without detriment (Maple, 1980; Pereira et al., 1989). However, Nadler (1982) found that the use of small passageways that allowed female orangutans to regulate their contact with separately housed males resulted in an increased pregnancy rate. In several callitrichid species, functional space should be sufficient to accommodate the retention of several successive litters in order to insure that youngsters gain essential parenting skills (Snowdon, 1994). In species having a steep dominance gradient, the space must be adequate in both size and configuration to keep aggression within manageable levels. In addition to the potential for undesired trauma or infanticide, females chronically subjected to excessive aggression may become reproductively suppressed (see Tilson, 1986 for examples). Chimpanzee males, at about one year of age, begin to acquire essential sexual experience by mounting estrous females (King et al., 1980b), and should be kept in a group situation during their formative years. The provision of facilities that are adequate for the maintenance of species-typical groupings ameliorate many of the undesirable consequences of the cramped, sterile facilities of a bygone era. However, as the foregoing examples illustrate, deficiencies may yet result if certain social aspects are overlooked.

Interactions between social groups comprise an important aspect of life in the wild state. Where zoos maintain multiple groups of the same species, opportunities for the expression of unique intergroup behaviors may be realized. At Zoo Atlanta four gorilla enclosures are juxtaposed so as to encourage natural displays between groups. Also, the habitats for adult male orangutans are located on opposite sides of a larger female enclosure with the hope of encouraging long calls by males (Coe and Maple, 1984). The Bronx Zoo has recently constructed a habitat containing multiple harems of gelada monkeys, designed in a manner that elicits some of the highly colorful and visible displays of males (Doherty, 1991). One may expect that exhibit designs that encourage such rarely seen behaviors are useful in incurring public support for the preservation of endangered species.

Captive Design and Animal Health

Effects of Social Isolation

It is recognized that separation of individual primates from their social milieu for treatment of health problems is an unavoidable aspect of life in captivity. At the same time, the research literature amply confirms that prolonged separation of very young individuals may result in undesirable behavior patterns and compromised breeding potential. Short-term social isolation of infants and the separation of older animals for treatment may have only transient effects on behavior, even though the experience may be highly stressful. Although difficult to measure in the specific case, separation stress probably slows the progress of recovery or contributes to death in severely afflicted individuals. Designing health facilities to minimize separation effects is therefore a desirable goal.

Facilities that allow mothers of nursing infants to accompany them during hospitalization (unless precluded by risks from infectious diseases or the problems this would pose logistically, e.g., very large primates) would help to alleviate separation-induced stress. Providing a familiar, compatible companion during the hospitalization of juveniles or adults is rarely attempted even when doing so poses no risk to health or interference with treatment. Unnecessary separation occurs when animals are held for medicating that could be as easily accomplished within the confines of the group, or within adjacent, short-term holding cages (Jones, 1981). Wherever possible, every effort should be made to design in ways that bring the treatment to the animal, instead of the reverse. Removal for any purpose exposes the animal to overly novel, frequently noxious, and always stressful, stimuli. The increase in cost of facilities incurred by these approaches may be outweighed, particularly in the case of the highly endangered, by increased rates of survival.

Changing the Social Configuration of Groups

The periodic transfer of individuals between collections to meet genetic or reproductive requirements is a common, albeit socially disruptive, event. While the design of facilities is often influenced by the need for periodic restraint or capture of individuals, less attention has been given to structures that would accommodate releases. The frequently severe consequences of introductions of new breeders can be partially alleviated by transferring the sex that normally migrates in the wild. Managing the aggression attendant to introductions of new stock is, nevertheless, a major challenge, and requires the development of varied strategies (Lindburg and Robinson, 1986).

At the San Diego Zoo a process is used with macaques that allows the pace of assimilation to be determined by the animals themselves. New males are placed in an adjoining pen, with access limited via a wire-mesh tunnel with openings at each end restricted initially to permit passage of the smaller, immature individuals. Size of the aperture at each end is gradually increased to allow larger sized individuals to visit the new male. Placement of these tunnels at the top of cage walls gives visiting individuals an advantage in retreating if males react aggressively. Using this method, eight different males have been introduced to established groups without injury.

The integration of young individuals that have been taken for hand-rearing is a most problematic procedure. The risks attendant to this event are exacerbated by the common practice of confinement in nurseries that are spatially removed from one's conspecifics. Incorporation of hand-rearing modules within the living environment of the animals in question permits exposure during early infancy to the sight, sound, and smell of one's own kind, while simultaneously permitting easy removal for feeding or treatment. (This approach may also be useful in improving the future mothering behavior of naive females.) Interconnected passageways of limited size may be used to encourage physical contact with potential peers. A portable design reduces cost, because the module can be moved to different locations as needed. A unit of this type has been successfully used with macaques at the San Diego Zoo.

Quarantine and Postoperative Recovery

As with other aspects of health maintenance, in quarantine and postoperative facilities the treatment or prevention of health problems takes precedence over all other considerations. These are invariably hard-textured environments, with easily sanitizable surfaces throughout. The boredom that ensues from such sterile living conditions may be further exacerbated by lengthy separation of up to six months (Martin, 1986) from conspecifics. Perhaps the most that can be hoped, given the particularly stringent health requirements of these facilities, is that every effort is made to design in ways that minimize the fear and discomfort experienced by their occupants. Some useful directions would be to design for quick, efficient capture and restraint, muffle noxious sounds, make human monitoring unobtrusive, and encourage appropriate enrichment through food, sanitizable objects, and perhaps sound. All captive environments provide experiences that are to some extent insulting, and, out of necessity, health facilities provide these in the most concentrated and severe forms. They are locations, furthermore, in which the individual spends a relatively small portion of its life, hence, contain aversively high levels of novelty. Sensitivity of staff to the many sources of fear and pain experienced by a wild animal can never make the hospital stay pleasant, only more or less tolerable.

Captive Design and Conservation

Preparing for Reintroduction

It should be recognized at the outset that relatively few primates will be candidates for reintroduction to wild habitat. Because they are logistically complex, reintroductions are best justified when wild populations no longer exist (but suitable habitat remains), or where they are so drastically reduced that augmentation with captive-bred individuals would help to insure survival in wild habitat. Also, support for introduction of surplus captives can perhaps be justified on grounds of information banking (Lindburg, 1992a) in cases where wild populations are declining but not yet at critically low levels (e.g., lion-tailed or Sulawesi macaques). To date, a credible case has been made, and a scientifically based protocol put in place, only for the golden-lion tamarin (Kleiman et al., 1986).

Having so little experience with reintroductions, primatologists know very little about the range of skills that may have to be taught if captive born individuals, reared in the simplified, protective embrace of a zoo, are to survive in the wild. As the tamarin example revealed (Kleiman et al., 1986), finding food in a strange locale was only a small part of the problem. The animals first had to be taught to recognize foods appropriate for eating as well as ways of extracting them from the environment. Also, they must be able to overcome their "psychological cages" (Beck and Castro, 1994), acquire a new "sense of place", recognize and avoid predators, and learn ways of traveling efficiently and safely through the habitat. Prerelease preparations can and should be attempted (see Price, 1992, for a recent example), despite the fact that much of the learning relevant to survival will have to be site-specific. In terms of facility design, Snowdon (1994, p. 223) has emphasized the importance of naturalistic features in contributing to the development of " . . . motoric, social, cognitive, and other skills that would be needed by the animals to survive in the wild if they were to be reintroduced." His claim is reinforced by the observation that, unless an adolescent tamarin acquires leaping ability at the right developmental age, it will never do so (Grand, 1992). If the goal is return to wild habitat, it seems unlikely that a naturalistic exhibit would contain all the features needed to prepare captive born individuals for that experience. Guidelines to designing for this purpose are to be found in Beck et al., 1991, and Bronikowski et al., (1989).

Visitor Education

Designing for conservation also embraces goals of educating visitors about zoo animals' wild counterparts. Exhibits that have the power to transport visitors to the animals' native habitat, and to communicate at both emotional and intellectual levels, may also have the power to change people's attitudes about wildlife conservation (Coe, 1985; Finlay et al., 1988). Conversely, exhibits that present wildlife as totally dependent upon human care and technology may

propagate the message that wildlife habitat conservation is unnecessary because animals live very well at the zoo (Coe, 1987). But
educational opportunities exist in designs that encompass more
than construction of a wonderfully naturalistic exhibit. Those that
incorporate information on natural and evolutionary history, and
on the species' interactions with a wild community that includes
humans and other species of wildlife, will give added value to conservationist goals (Robinson, 1988).

Conservation-Relevant Research

Acquiring knowledge of a species' biology is yet another conserva-
tion-relevant activity having design implications. For this purpose,
facilities should be designed to optimize the recording of species-
typical behaviors and the nontraumatic collection of samples of
tissue or excreta. The importance of this information to genetic,
reproductive, and social management of captives, and to the conserving of wild populations, has been amply demonstrated (Lasley
et al., 1981; Benirschke, 1983a; Hutchins, 1988).

Conclusions: Future Directions

Zoos of the future will be more likely to attain their goal of preserving wildlife if they adopt approaches that enhance the experiences
of both animal and viewer. The majority of patrons have entertainment on their minds when they visit the zoo or park. They desire to
see species-typical activities in naturalistic surroundings. This is a
reasonable expectation, for normally expressed behavior is inherently interesting. Poorly designed facilities result in behaviors that
are often abnormal or absent. The interaction of the animal with
its environment is a dynamic process. Conceptual designs that begin with the biology of the animal in mind (Lindburg, 1992b) will
be more likely to elicit the desired activities, and offer the best
prospect of being aesthetically and educationally valued by the
visitor. Facilities that are designed preeminently for the animal
allow it greater freedom to act in its own self-interest. They are
habitats that provide for choice among a range of activities—to
explore, play, groom, or rest as their needs dictate, and to do so at
locations that are sunny or shaded, warm or cool, or at varied
locations. They are habitats that impart to the animal a sense of
having some control over daily events (Snowdon and Savage, 1989).
These considerations underscore the point that provision of acces-

sible space is not sufficient by itself. For example, a chimpanzee in a large field of grass is unlikely to find such surroundings either functional or interesting.

We anticipate a greater role for scientifically based criteria in the design and operation of zoos in the future. For example, the role of nurseries should decline as the causes of maternal insufficiency are better understood. Alternatives to human parenting of the orphaned, sickly, abandoned, or abused primate infant already exist (Smith, 1986; Lindburg and Fitch-Snyder, 1988; Lindburg, 1992b). Zoos simply have not invested much effort in their utilization.

Zoos of the future have the option of greater utilization of recently developed technology to good advantage. The application of technologies developed in human medical practice to the treatment of animal health problems is now commonplace (see examples in Ryder and Byrd, 1984). Less widely used but nevertheless potentially important applications pertain to the area of behavioral enrichment (Markowitz, 1982). Although anthropoids are visually oriented animals, introduction of ecologically relevant, high quality sound holds promise for the enrichment of both animal and zoo visitor (Ogden and Lindburg, 1991).

Video monitoring in the management of crisis episodes such as parturition or the integration of new individuals is a useful technology that is underutilized. Because primates usually give birth at night, this phase of the reproductive process is not routinely observed. Intervention of veterinary staff in problem deliveries depends on monitoring (Fitch-Snyder and Lindburg, 1990), and this is best achieved without a potentially stressful human presence.

Substantial progress has been made in the captive conservation of endangered primates in the last two decades. These fast paced developments are fueled by the urgent need for captive populations to become reproductively self-sufficient in the shadow of continued human decimation of wild populations (Benirschke, 1986; Hutchins, 1989). Because primate reproduction and psychological well-being are closely linked, both causes must be actively advanced. The pace of this advance must, of course, depend upon funding which in turn often follows successful enterprise. Future improvements will most likely be seen in refining techniques already under development and in greater integration of elements now scattered throughout the primate conservation field. For example, further field research will make possible more realistic and appropriate living environments in captivity, better interpretive elements, and improved husbandry. Exhibits will be better able to support behavioral observations and passive research, while improvements in the design of holding areas will make possible the routine collection of physiological information. Sound systems will simulate a realistic, interactive, acoustic environment for both visitors and animals.

Successful captive preservation practices will allow the selective return of groups to wild habitat, but for most species we must look toward a very long period of captive maintenance (Soulé et al., 1986). We must plan, design, build, and operate for the long-term, developing techniques which maximize genetic diversity while maintaining behavior fitness, not for the convenience of management, but for ultimate self-reliance of primate species.

Conclusion

Endangered Species in Captivity:
Scientific Discipline and Taxonomic Synthesis

Volume Editors

The long-term conservation of endangered species is threefold: (1) protection of *in situ* populations, (2) captive proliferation of severely compromised species, and (3) reintroduction of expatriated species. In the most optimistic scenario, all three strategies would be employed with shifting emphasis over time. Although this volume has focused on *ex situ* propagation, captive breeding success must not be allowed to mislead the public into believing that habitat preservation is no longer a priority. However, with the ever increasing rate of habitat destruction, it is likely that the number of species conserved through *ex situ* efforts will increase in future years.

The preceding chapters have rather thoroughly reviewed the literature on conservation, reproductive physiology, behavior, and captive design of endangered species. No single area of research will provide sufficient knowledge or understanding of all a species' requirements for captive reproduction. Combining the four disciplines explored in this volume with the information in existing volumes on genetics, nutrition, and medicine (including pathology) comprises the interdisciplinary foundation necessary to build self-sustaining captive populations. The following scientific discipline and taxonomic overviews will highlight important issues discussed in the preceding 28 chapters.

Scientific Discipline Overview

Conservation

Reintroduction of captive bred populations and, more rarely, removal of a species from the wild for captive propagation has far-reaching ramifications because animals do not exist in an ecological void. The effects on the ecological niche filled by reintroduced animals is at least as important as the preservation of individual species. For example, introduced species were implicated in 27 of the 40 fish extinctions in North America in the last century.

As emphasized in many of the conservation chapters (e.g., invertebrates, fish and marine mammals), *ex situ* conservation is not considered a viable adjunct to habitat preservation. However, since one-third of all avian species reside in tropical forests, and 90% of their habitat will be destroyed by the beginning of the next century, captive breeding may be essential to the survival of many bird species. "Head-starting" tortoises and gharials has proven to be a successful alternative to strictly captive breeding. To minimize the stresses of reintroduction, captive breeding should be undertaken in the country of species' origin to facilitate re-creation of weather conditions, photoperiodic cycles, and native vegetation.

Conservation efforts have been thwarted by a range of problems such as incomplete description of the taxon and extreme plant-host specificity (especially in invertebrates), taxonomic confusion and uneven captive representation of species, and inability to routinely produce offspring. The fact that the geographic distribution of the world's population of biologists is inversely proportionate to the majority of animal and plant species compounds the political, cultural, and economic impact of conservation plans (see Robinson chap. 1, this volume).

Because zoos cannot preserve all endangered species through captive breeding, a triage system has been proposed for assigning species conservation priorities. A system based on degree of endangerment, management protocols, spatial requirements, monetary concerns, and coordination of efforts would assuage many of the problems facing today's conservationists.

Reproductive Physiology

Reproductive physiology research is a high-profile field of endeavor currently receiving a great deal of popular press. However, despite some notable successes, authors in this volume agree that very little is known about the reproductive processes of the majority of endangered species. Although many species reproduce readily in captivity, others have not yet been successful. A system of assigning research priorities based on population size and captive propagation potential would be of great benefit in this field.

The dearth of empirically derived information concerning endangered species is emphasized in this volume by the use of models based on research with nonthreatened species thought to be applicable to endangered "target" animals. This approach will not always be successful as many species exhibit unique physiologies and responses to captivity (e.g. stress-induced suppression of reproduction).

Progress in this field is slowed by logistical difficulties in gathering physiological data, challenging scientists to develop non-invasive methods (e.g., quantification of hormone metabolites in urine and feces). Insufficient knowledge concerning the effects of genetics, nutrition, and health on reproduction is a significant impediment to research and propagation in captivity. In addition, the astounding array of reproductive strategies (sex-reversal in fishes, parthenogenesis in invertebrates, pair-bonding in birds, and dissociated sexual cycles in reptiles) discourages extrapolation of data between and even within taxa.

The need for basic research to elucidate the mechanisms of reproduction in endangered species is universal across taxa. Once the normal processes of reproduction are understood, captive breeding may be enhanced through superovulation, artificial insemination, embryo transfer, and gamete and embryo cryopreservation. The latter promises the potential to exponentially increase the number of individuals (and, hence, genetic diversity) preserved in captivity, either extant or in the form of frozen germplasm.

Behavior

The authors contributing behavior chapters express the importance of well-designed studies of behavior in free-ranging populations with which to compare the behavior of specimens in captivity. Studies involving captive endangered species range from nonexistent (invertebrates) to extensive (primates). In the most thoroughly studied Order, half of the primate species listed as endangered or threatened have been described at least preliminarily in the wild, thus providing the framework for constructing ethograms for captive populations. The more a species is perceived to differ morphologically or cognitively from humans, the smaller the body of literature concerning its behavior. This predictable bias may be corrected as the integral part each species plays in its ecosystem is understood and communicated.

Proponents of behavioral research in captivity state that the ability to closely observe animals allows the documentation of more behaviors than can be seen in wild populations. In addition, variables affecting behavior can be manipulated within certain limits. Critics, on the other hand, point out that artificial habitats prevent animals from responding appropriately to their environment. The location and ingestion of food comprises a significant behavioral investment (occupying up to 90% of an animal's time) and a wide array of cognitive, social, and locomotor skills. Current methods of provisioning animals in captivity may deleteriously alter entire social and/or nonsocial behavioral repertoires necessary for survival of reintroduced specimens. Predator avoidance is a survival necessity for most free-ranging animals. However, captive specimens rarely or never exposed to natural predators may not recognize dangerous animals and therefore fail to flee when reintroduced into the wild. For example, as discussed by Francis-Floyd and Williams (chap. 7, this volume) captive-reared fish that did not learn to school were lost upon reintroduction. Thus, the alteration of behavior in captivity impacts not only captive breeding but also a species' prognosis for survival upon reintroduction. The analysis of behavior is, therefore, a most important factor in assessing the appropriateness of the captive environment.

Captive Design

The unique positioning of zoos as entertainment facilities as well as centers for education, conservation, and research necessitates the incorporation of an enclosure's appeal to the public in its design. The movement from strictly functional spaces to naturalistic environments improves visitor experience thereby enhancing the conservation message and elevating revenues for conservation efforts. However, the modern zoo enclosure built to accommodate the special needs of each species as well as research, veterinary care, population growth, and public appeal requires a more thoughtful and expensive design.

The social needs of individual species dictate enclosure design for reproductive groups (e.g., facilities to separate and rejoin the sexes in solitary species). Often the most efficient design for high volume captive propagation is not pleasing to the public, therefore the construction of lower cost but psychologically adequate breeding facilities off-exhibit provide an alternative or adjunct to high cost exhibit areas. Flexibility in exhibit design allows for the concurrent or serial exhibition of more than one species, thereby promoting public awareness of ecological relationships between species while reducing long-term costs per enclosure.

With greater emphasis on reintroduction, *in situ* and *ex situ* prerelease enclosures are a growing need. Habitats that "train" groups of animals for release into the wild incorporate mechanisms to reduce interaction with human caregivers, to provision animals with natural diets in more challenging ways, and to simulate the climate to be encountered upon reintroduction.

Taxonomic Overview

Invertebrates

With the majority of the estimated 15–30 million species in this taxon scientifically unknown, captive breeding cannot be expected to significantly subsidize *in situ* conservation of invertebrates. Faunal surveys in high species density areas must be undertaken to assess the degree of loss of biological diversity. A concerted educational effort is needed to replace the public perception of invertebrates as pests with a deeper understanding of the significant role they play in virtually all ecosystems.

Fish

Commercial fisheries provide excellent models for the aquaculture of endangered fish. In fact, approximately 50 of the 89 fish species listed by ISIS as endangered and threatened are held in captivity and recovery plans have been formulated for 41 species (see Kohler, chap. 5, this volume). For some species, limited knowledge of the environmental requirements and the inability to achieve appropriate facility scale and complexity lower the expectation that captive reproduction will be effective in a multigenerational program. It is therefore understood why current research focuses on reintroduction programs.

Reptiles and Amphibians

Although less than 10% of the 10,000 reptile and amphibian species have been bred in captivity, relatively few species have passed the threshold beyond which they can be saved only by captive breeding. A great deal is known about the reproductive processes of a few reptile species and that information may be used to enhance captive propagation of certain closely related, more severely endangered forms.

Birds

Captive breeding is seen as an essential part of avian conservation, especially for tropical forest birds. Unfortunately, zoos currently have spaces sufficient to preserve only about 300 of the 9,000 bird species (see Sheppard, chap. 13, this volume). Clearly, a system for assigning species' priorities must be instituted in the near future. Reintroductions of captive bred individuals have been among the first and most successful attempts at population restoration. A program combining captive propagation of severely endangered birds with well-orchestrated reintroductions holds the promise of success for many species.

Mammals (Excluding Marine Mammals and Primates)

Because of popular appeal and press coverage, public awareness of the plight of mammalian species is higher than for other taxonomic groups. This extensive and varied group of animals is comprised of 87% "small" mammals. However, of the 11% of the mammal species that are listed as endangered or threatened, nearly 85% are "large" in size. Further, of the 431 endangered and threatened mammalian species listed by ISIS, 51% are held in captivity, 89% of which breed regularly. A desirable balance of species in captivity can be produced using the aforementioned triage system to assign conservation priorities.

Marine Mammals

Research on captive, nonendangered species is thought to be of great value to endangered marine mammals. Although some species are in such severe peril that captive breeding may be their only hope (e.g., river dolphins; see Ridgway, chap. 21, this volume), for most, species protection in the wild will be the primary form of conservation. Because of the charismatic appeal of marine mammals and their trainability, captive specimens play a significant role in the education of the public to the issues of conservation.

Primates

This taxon represents the most severely endangered group of species with 47.9% listed as endangered or threatened. The majority of the captive specimens are members of only thirteen genera, again indicating the need for more informed selection of species to be bred in captivity. Their likeness to humans has led to primate utilization as laboratory specimens which, until recently, has contributed to declining numbers in the wild. This research, however has provided the most detailed physiological and behavioral data of all taxonomic groups. Primate similarities to humans highlight them in the public eye, and it behooves conservationists to present them for maximum educational impact in the captive forum.

Captive Conservation and Scientific Creativity

George Bartholomew (1982), in his past-presidential address to the American Society of Zoologists, outlined four requisites for promoting scientific innovation and creativity: " . . . (1) to ask new and incisive questions, (2) to form new hypotheses, (3) to examine old questions in new ways or with new techniques, and (4) to perceive previously unnoticed relationships" (p. 231). He recommended that in order for creativity to flourish, an interdisciplinary approach must be applied to the art and business of doing science. An interdisciplinary approach to science requires an integration of disciplines and a conjugation of philosophical paradigms (Gibbons and Stoskopf, 1983).

There is no doubt that the challenges facing conservation biologists requires creative and interdisciplinary solutions to complex problems. The science of conservation must consider not only the unique genetic, physiological, and cognitive processes inherent within individuals of a species, but also the role of individuals and species within their ecosystems (Western et al., 1989). In addition, the local and global cultural, economic, and political consequences of species loss or proliferation must be considered when designing and prioritizing conservation programs.

The disciplines discussed within the seven taxonomic groups represent an additional step toward the development of a truly interdisciplinary approach to *ex situ* conservation. The content presented in each of the disciplines complements an already extensive body of knowledge in fields such as genetics, nutrition, and veterinary medicine. Further, the content presented in some chapters will substantially add to a limited literature regarding a discipline and the conservation of a taxonomic group in captivity (e.g., the invertebrate behavior chapter by Demarest and Bradley).

It is also important to comment on the structure of the present volume and the value it may have for the development of an interdisciplinary approach to *ex situ* conservation. The volume is represented by seven taxonomic sections with each containing chapters on the same four disciplines. Within each discipline and across taxonomic groups, the chapters are organized by similar headings and subheadings. It is because of this organization that readers of this volume can make comparisons within disciplines and between taxonomic groups. The comparative value of the volume's organizational structure is further enhanced by an extensive bibliography; thereby facilitating the conceptualization of interdisciplinary hypotheses. Thus, through inductive and deductive reasoning, hypotheses can be initially developed within taxonomic groups and disciplines and subsequently expanded to include other taxonomic groups and disciplines (cf., Root-Bernstein, 1989).

As scientists continue to expand the base of knowledge regarding disciplines and taxonomic groups, it is important to consider that the advances made by modern scientists are the cumulative products of other scientists—past and present, and from within and between disciplines (e.g., Hull, 1988). It is from these longitudinal and cross-sectional perspectives that scientists will develop creative interdisciplinary solutions to the complex problems of preserving wildlife. The scientific task is monumental and the time is limited, but the preservation of the earth's biodiversity is perhaps the most important issue of our time. It is hoped that this volume brings us closer to that goal.

References

Aamdal, J., K. Anderson and J.A. Fougner. 1972. Insemination with frozen semen in the blue fox. *VII Congr. on Anim. Reprod. Artif. Insem.* 2:1713–1716.

Abbott, D.H. and J.P. Hearn. 1978. Physical, hormonal and behavioral aspects of development in the marmoset monkey, *Callithrix jacchus*. *J. Reprod. Fertil.* 53:155–166.

Abbott, D.H., A.S. McNeilly, S.F. Lunn, M.J. Hulme and F.J. Burden. 1981. Inhibition of ovarian function in the subordinate female marmoset monkey (*Callithrix jacchus*). *J. Reprod. Fertil.* 63:335–345.

Abegglen, J. 1984. *On socialization in hamadryas baboons: A field study*. Bucknell Univ. Press, Lewisburg, PA.

Abraham, K.F., C.D. Ankey and H. Boyd. 1983. Assortative by brant. *Auk* 100:201–203.

Abu-Jafer, M.Z. and C. Hays-Shahin. 1988. Reintroduction of the Arabian oryx into Jordan. Pp. 35–40 in A. Dixon and D. Jones, eds. *Conservation and biology of desert antelopes*. Christopher Helm, London, England.

Abu-Zinada, A.H., K. Habibi and R. Seitre. 1988. The Arabian oryx programme in Saudi Arabia. Pp. 41–46 in A. Dixon and D. Jones, eds. *Conservation and biology of desert antelopes*. Christopher Helm, London, England.

Acharjyo, L.N. and S. Mahaptra. 1978. A note on the breeding and longevity of the Indian pangolin (*Manis crassicaudata*) in captivity. *J. Bombay Natur. Hist. Soc.* 75:921–922.

Adams, C.L., C.E. Moir and T. Atkinson. 1985. Plasma concentrations of progesterone in female red deer (*Cervus elaphus*) during the breeding season, pregnancy and anoestrus. *J. Reprod. Fertil.* 74:631–636.

Ader, R. 1985. Conditioned taste aversions and immunopharmacology. Pp. 293–307 in N.S. Braveman and P. Bronstein, eds. *Experimental assessments and clinical applications of conditioned food aversions. Annals New York Acad. of Sci.* 443, New York, NY.

Ader, R. and N. Cohen. 1981. Conditioned immunopharmacologic responses. Pp. 281–320 in R. Ader, ed. *Psychoneuroimmunology*. Academic Press, New York, NY.

Adey, W.M. and K. Loveland. 1991. *Dynamic aquaria: Building living ecosystems*. Academic Press, New York, NY.

Adiyodi, K.G. and R.G. Adiyodi, eds. 1983. *Reproductive biology of invertebrates, Vol. 1: Oogenesis, oviposition and oosorption*. John Wiley & Sons, New York, NY.

Adiyodi, K.G. and R.G. Adiyodi, eds. 1984. *Reproductive biology of invertebrates, Vol. 2: Spermatogenesis and sperm function*. John Wiley & Sons, New York, NY.

Adiyodi, K.G. and R.G. Adiyodi, eds. 1988. *Reproductive biology of invertebrates, Vol. 3: Accessory sex glands*. John Wiley & Sons, New York, NY.

Adiyodi, K.G. and R.G. Adiyodi, eds. 1989. *Reproductive biology of invertebrates, Vol. 4, Part A: Fertilization, embryonic development and parental care*. John Wiley & Sons, New York, NY.

Adkins-Regan, E. 1981. Effect of sex steroids on the reproductive behavior of castrated male ring doves (*Streptopelia* sp.). *Physiol. Behav.* 26:561–565.

Aguilera, E. 1990. Parental infanticide by white spoonbills, *Platalea leucorodia*. *Ibis* 132:124–125.

Ahsan, F. 1984. Study of *Trionyx nigricans* in Bangladesh. *Hamadryad* 9:19.

Ainley, D.G., R.E. LeResche and W.J.L. Sladen. 1983. *Breeding biology of the Adelie penquin*. Univ. of California Press, Berkeley, CA.

Akesson, T.R. and D.G. Raveling. 1983. Endocrine and behavioral correlates of nesting Canada geese. *Can. J. Zool.* 62:845–850.

Alberts, A.C. 1989. Ultraviolet visual sensitivity in desert iguanas: Implications for pheromone detection. *Anim. Behav.* 38:129–137.

Alberts, A.C., N.C. Pratt and J.A. Phillips. 1992. Seasonal productivity of lizard femoral glands: Relationship to social dominance and androgen levels. *Physiol. Behav.* 51:729–733.

Alcock, J. 1987. Leks and hilltopping in insects. *J. Natur. Hist.* 21:319–328.

Alcock, J. and A.P. Smith. 1987. Hilltopping, leks and female choice in the carpenter bee, *Xylocopa (Neoxylocopa) varipuncta. J. Zool.* 211:1–10.

Alcorn, D. 1984. *The Hawaiian monk seal on Laysan Island: 1982*. NOAA technical memo NMFS, NOAA-TM-NMFS-SWFC-42, U.S. Dept. Commer., Washington, DC.

Alcorn, D.J. and J.R. Henderson. 1984. Resumption of nursing in "weaned" Hawaiian monk seal. *Elapio* 45:11–12.

Alcorn, D.J., R.G. Forsyth and R.L. Westlake. 1988. *Hawaiian monk seal research on Lisianski Island, 1985 and 1986.* NOAA technical memo NMFS, NOAA-TM-NMFS-SWFC-120, U.S. Dept. Commer., Washington, DC.

Alderete, M.R., R.R. Tokarz and D. Crews. 1980. Luteinizing hormone-releasing hormone (LHRH) and thyrotropin releasing hormone (TRH) induction of female sexual receptivity in the lizard, *Anolis carolinesis. Neuroendocrinol.* 30:200–205.

Aldridge, R.D. 1975. Environmental control of spermatogenesis in the rattlesnake *Crotalus viridis. Copeia* 1975:493–496.

Aldridge, R.D. 1979. Female reproductive cycles of the snakes *Arizona elegans* and *Crotalus viridis. Herpetol.* 35:256–261.

Alexander, B.K. and J.M. Bowers. 1967. The social structure of the Oregon troop of Japanese macaques. *Primates* 8:333–340.

Allen, M.E., O.T. Oftedal and D.I. Werner. 1990. Management of the green iguana *(Iguana iguana)* in Central America. *Proc. Amer. Assoc. Zoo Vets.* 1990:19–22.

Allendorf, F.W. 1983. Isolation, gene flow, and genetic differentiation among populations. Pp. 51–65 in C.M. Schonewald-Cox, S.M. Chambers, B. MacBryde and W.L. Thomas, eds. *Genetics and conservation: A reference for managing wild animal and plant populations.* Benjamin/Cummings, Menlo Park, CA.

Almeida, R.T., G.P. Pimentel and F.J.L. Silva. 1991. Occurrence of otter *Lutra longicaudis* (Mammalia-Mustelidae) in mangrove area Pernambuco State, N.E. Brazil. *Proc. 9th Bienn. Conf. Biol. Marine Mamm.* 1991:1 (Abstr.). Chicago Zool. Soc., Chicago, IL.

Altaba, C.R. 1990. The last known population of the freshwater mussel *Margaritafera auricularia* (Bivalvia, Unionoidae): A conservation priority. *Biol. Conserv.* 52:271–286.

Altmann J. 1974. Observational study of behavior: Sampling methods. *Behaviour* 49:227–267.

Altmann, S.A. 1962. A field study of the sociobiology of rhesus monkeys, *Macaca mulatta. Annals New York Acad. Sci.* 102:338–435.

Amano, M., K. Okuzawa, T. Yanagisawa, Y. Hasegawa and K. Aida. 1992. Immunoreactive gonadotropin–releasing hormone (Ir-GnRH) in the carp brain. *Nippon Suisan Gakkaishi* 58:593.

Amano, M., Y. Oka, K. Aida, N. Okumoto, S. Kawashima and Y. Hasegawa. 1991. Immunocytochemical demonstration of salmon GnRH and chicken GnRH-II in the brain of Masu salmon, *Oncorhynchus masou*. *J. Comp. Neurol.* 314:587–597.

American Association of Zoological Parks and Aquariums. 1990. *The status of AAZPA's marine mammal conservation education and research programs*. Amer. Assoc. Zool. Parks Aquar., Wheeling, WV.

American Journal of Primatology. 1989. Suppl. 1, 1989: *Psychological well-being and environmental enrichment*. John Wiley & Sons, New York.

Ames, M.H. 1991. Saving some cetaceans may require breeding in captivity: Work on bottlenose dolphin may be applied to the baiji. *BioScience* 41:746–749.

Amlaner, C.J. and D.W. MacDonald, eds. 1979. *A handbook on biotelemetry and radio tracking*. Pergamon Press, New York, NY.

Amstrup, S.C. and D.P. DeMaster. 1988. Polar bear *Ursus maritimus*. Pp. 39–56 in J.W. Lentfer, ed. *Selected marine mammals of Alaska: Species accounts with research and management recommendations*. Report No. PB88178462. Marine Mamm. Commiss., Washington, DC.

Amundin, M. 1986. Breeding the bottle-nose dolphin *Tursiops truncatus* at the Kolmarden Dolphinarium. *Int'l. Zoo Yb.* 24/25:263–271.

Anderson, D.J. 1990. Evolution of obligate siblicide in boobies. *Amer. Natural.* 135:334–350.

Andrews, B. 1986. Marine mammal husbandry and training. *Regional Proc. Amer. Assoc. Zool. Parks Aquar.* 1986:318–319.

Andrews, H. 1988. A bumper crop of mugger. *Hamadryad* 13:3–4.

Angelini, F. and G. Ghiara. 1984. Reproductive modes and strategies in vertebrate evolution. *Boll. Zool.* 51:121–203.

Annelli, J.F. and T.D. Mandrell. 1994. USDA inspection procedures: Nonstandard facilities, site visits, waivers, and enforcement. Pp. 53–61 in E.F. Gibbons, Jr., E.J. Wyers, E.J. Waters and E.W. Menzel, Jr., eds. *Naturalistic environments in captivity for animal behavior research*. State Univ. New York Press, Albany, NY.

Anonymous. 1960. Tropical rain forest at San Diego Zoo. *Int'l Zoo Yb.* 2:67–68.

Anonymous. 1972. *Random House College Dictionary*. 1972. Random House, New York, NY.

Anonymous. 1980. India. *IUCN Crocodile Specialist Group Newsletter* June 18:1.

Anonymous. 1983. Stop press. World's rarest turtle (we think) lays eggs in captivity. *Hamadryad* 8:13.

Anonymous. 1987a. Jamaican hutias (*Geocapromys brownii*). *Wildl. Preserv. Trust* 1985/1986:21.

Anonymous. 1987b. Blues for a butterfly. *Time Mag.* April:87.

Anonymous. 1987c. Rodruguez fruit bat protocol. *Jersey Wildlife Preservation Trust December*:87. Jersey, United Kingdom.

Anonymous. 1989a. Pp. 1–9 in minutes from the paramyxovirus meeting. Audubon Zoo, New Orleans, LA.

Anonymous. 1989b. *American society for heating, refrigerating and air conditioning engineers handbook and product directory. Fundamentals volume.* Amer. Soc. Heat., Refrig., Air Cond. Engnrs., Atlanta, GA.

Anonymous. 1991a. Spix's macaw update. *World Birdwatch* 13:4.

Anonymous. 1991b. Tragedy in a delicate ecosystem: The Persian Gulf oil spills. *Whale News* 45:2.

Anselin, A., M.D.N. van der Elst, R.C. Beudels and P. Devillers. 1990. *Analyse descriptive et project pilote preparatoire a une strategie pour la conservation du phoque moine en Mediterranee (Monachus monachus).* Rapport a la direction generale de l'environnement, de la protection des consommateurs et de la Securite Nucleaire de la Commission des Communautes Europeenees. I.R.S.N.B. Contract 6611/28.

Ansell, W.F.H. 1964. Captive behavior and post-natal development of the shrew *Crocidura bicolar*. *Proc. Zool. Soc. London* 142:123–127.

Anthony, A. 1963. Criteria for acoustics in animal housing. *Lab. Anim. Care* 23:340–350.

Antivenom Index. 1989. Amer. Assoc. Zool. Parks Aquar. and Amer. Assoc. Poison Control Centers. Rio Grande Zoo, Albuquerque, NM.

Aquilina, G.D. 1981. Stimulation of maternal behaviours in the spectacled bear, *Tremarctos ornatus* at Buffalo zoo. *Int'l. Zoo Yb.* 21:143–145.

Arad, Z., P. Raber and Y.L. Werner. 1989. Selected body temperature in diurnal and nocturnal forms of *Ptyodactylus* (Reptilia: Gekkoninae) in a photothermal gradient. *J. Herpetol.* 23:103–108.

Archibald, G. 1974. Methods for breeding and rearing cranes in captivity. *Int'l. Zoo Yb.* 14:147–155.

Archibald, G. 1982. Gee whiz! ICF hatches a whooper. *The ICF Bugle* 8:1–4.

Archibald, G. and D.L. Viess. 1979. Captive propagation at the International Crane Foundation, 1973–1978. Pp. 51–74 in C. Lewis, ed. *Proc. 1978 Crane Workshop.* Colorado State Univ., Fort Collins, CO.

Archibald, G., Y. Siigeta, K. Matsumoto and K. Momose. 1980. Endangered cranes. Pp. 1–2 in J. Lewis and H. Masatomi, eds. *Crane research around the world*. Int'l. Crane Found., Baraboo, WI.

Ardelt, T.C. 1986. Effects of behavioral stress on *Cichlasoma nigrofasciatum* infected with *Aeromonas hydrophila*. Master's Thesis. Illinois State University, Normal, IL.

Ardito, G. 1976. Check-list of the data on the gestation length of primates. *J. Human Evol*. 5:213–222.

Arendt, J. 1986. Role of the pineal gland and melatonin in seasonal reproductive function in mammals. *Oxford Rev. Reprod. Biol*. 8:266–320.

Arnold, R.A. 1981a. A review of endangered species legislation in the U.S.A. and preliminary research on 6 endangered California butterflies (Lepidoptera: Lycaenidae). *Beih. Veroff. Naturschutz Landschaftpflege Badi.-Wurtt*. 21:79–96.

Arnold, R.A. 1981b. *Captive breeding of the endangered Lange's Metalmark butterfly, Apodemia normo langei*. Final report for U.S. Fish and Wildlife Service, Office of Endangered Species, Sacramento, CA.

Arnold, R.A. 1983a. *Ecological studies of six endangered butterflies (Lepidoptera: Lycaenidae): Island biogeography, patch dynamic, and the design of habitat preserves*. Univ. of California Pubs. in Entomol., No. 99. Berkeley, CA.

Arnold, R.A. 1983b. Conservation and management of the endangered Smith's blue butterfly, *Euphilotes enoptes smithi* (Lepidoptera: Lycaenidae). *J. Res. Lepidopt*. 22:135–153.

Arnold, R.A. 1983c. Biological studies of the Delta green ground beetle, *Elaphrus viridis* Horn (Coleoptera: Carabidae) at Jepson Prairie Preserve in 1983. Unpublished report produced for the Nature Conservancy, Arlington, VA.

Arnold, R.A. 1984. *Valley elderberry longhorn beetle recovery plan*. U. S. Fish and Wildlife Service, Portland, OR.

Arnold, R.A. 1985a. *Recovery plan for the lotis blue butterfly*. U. S. Fish and Wildlife Service, Portland, OR.

Arnold, R.A. 1985b. *Delta green ground beetle and Solano grass recovery plan*. U. S. Fish and Wildlife Service, Portland, OR.

Arnold, R.A. 1985c. *Private and government-funded conservation programs for endangered insects in California. Natur. Areas J*. 5:28–38.

Arnold, R.A. 1986. *Studies of the El Segundo blue butterfly*. California Dept. Fish & Game, Inland Fish. Admin. Report No. 86–4. Sacramento, CA.

Arnold, R.A. 1987a. Decline of the endangered Palos Verdes blue butterfly in California. *Biol. Conserv.* 40:203–217.

Arnold, R.A. 1987b. The mission blue butterfly. Pp. 371–378 in R.L. Di Silvestro, ed. *Audubon Wildlife Report*. Academic Press, New York, NY.

Arnold, R.A. 1988a. *Ecological and behavioral studies on the threatened Oregon silverspot butterfly at its Rock Creek, Cascade Head, Mt. Hebo, and Clatsop Plains populations in Oregon*. U. S. Fish and Wildlife Service, Portland, OR.

Arnold, R.A. 1988b. *Computer programs for the analysis of capture-recapture data of open populations*. Package of computer programs. Entomol. Consult. Serv., Pleasant Hill, CA.

Arnold, R.A. and A.E. Goins. 1987. Habitat enhancement techniques for the El Segundo blue butterfly: An urban endangered species. Pp. 173–181 in L.W. Adams and D.L. Leedy eds. *Integrating man and nature in the metropolitan environment*. Nat'l Instit. for Urban Wildl., Columbia, MD.

Arnold, S.J. 1977. Polymorphism and geographic variation in the feeding behavior of the garter snake, *Thamnophis elegans*. *Science* 197:676–678.

Arnold, S.J. 1978. Some effects of early experience on feeding responses in the common garter snake, *Thamnophis sirtalis*. *Anim. Behav.* 26:455–462.

Arnold, T.W. 1987c. Conspecific egg discrimination in American coots. *Condor* 89:675–676.

Arslan, M., S. Mahmood, S. Khurshid, S.M.S. Naqui, M.A. Afzal and S.M. Baig. 1986. Changes in circulating levels of immunoreactive follicle stimulating hormone, luteinizing hormone, and testosterone during sexual development in the rhesus monkey (*Macaca mulatta*). *J. Med. Primatol.* 15:351–360.

Asa, C.S. 1987. Reproduction in carnivores and ungulates. Pp. 258–290 in E. Crews, ed. *Psychobiology of reproductive behavior: An evolutionary perspective*. Prentice-Hall, Englewood Cliffs, NJ.

Asa, C., L.D. Mech and U.S. Seal. 1985. The use of urine, feces, and anal-gland secretions in scent-marking by a captive wolf *Canis lupus* pack. *Anim. Behav.* 33:1034–1036.

Asher, G.W., D.D. Kraemer, S.J. Magyar, M. Brunner, R. Moerbe and M. Giaquinto. 1990. Intrauterine insemination of farmed fallow deer (*Dama dama*) with frozen-thawed semen via laparoscopy. *Theriogenology* 34:569–577.

Asher, G.W., J.L. Adam, W. Otway, P. Bowman, G. van Reenan, C.G. Mackintosh and P. Dratch. 1988. Hybridization of Pere David's deer (*Elaphurus davidianus*) and red deer (*Cervus elephus*) by artificial insemination. *J. Zool. London* 215:197–203.

Ashmole, N.P and H. Tovar. 1968. Prolonged parental care in royal terns and other birds. *Auk* 85:90–100.

Ashton, P.S. 1988. Conservation of biological diversity in botanical gardens Pp. 269–278 in E.O. Wilson, ed. *Biodiversity*. Nat'l. Acad. Press, Washington, DC.

Aslin, H.J. 1982. Small dasyurid marsupials: Their maintenance and breeding in captivity. Pp. 22–26 in D.D. Evan, ed. *The management of Australian mammals in captivity. Proc. Aust. Mamm. Soc.*, 1979. Ramsey Ware Stockland, Victoria, Australia.

Asmode, J.F. 1989. Arabian Oryx in Saudi Arabia. *Gnusletter* 8:6.

Asper, E.D., L.H. Cornell, D.A. Duffield and N. Dimeo–Ediger. 1988. Marine mammals in zoos, aquaria and marine zoological parks in North America: 1983 census report. *Int'l. Zoo Yb.* 27:287–294.

Asper, E.D., D.A. Duffield, N. Dimeo–Ediger and D. Shell. 1990a. Marine mammals in zoos, aquaria and marine zoological parks in North America: 1990 census report. *Int'l. Zoo Yb.* 29:179–187.

Asper, E.D., L.H. Cornell, D.A. Duffield, B.E. Joseph, B. Stark and C. Perry. 1990b. Hematology and serum chemistry values in bottlenose dolphins. Pp. 475–485 in S. Leatherwood and R. Reeves, eds. *The bottlenose dolphin*. Harcourt, Brace, Jovanovich, Orlando, FL.

Assenmacher, I. 1973. The peripheral endocrine glands. Pp. 183–286 in D.S. Farner and J.R. King, eds. *Avian Biology*, Vol. III. Academic Press, New York, NY.

Assenmacher, I. and M. Jallageas. 1980. Adaptive aspects of endocrine regulations in birds. Pp. 93–102 in S. Ishi, T. Hurano and M. Wada, eds. *Hormones, adaptions, and evolution*. Japan Sci. Soc. Press Tokyo, Japan/Springer-Verlag, Berlin, Germany.

Atkinson, L.E., J. Hotchkiss, G.R. Fritz, A.S. Surve and E. Knobil. 1971. Circulating levels of luteinizing hormone, chorionic gonadotropin, estrogens and progesterone during pregnancy in the rhesus monkey. *Biol. Reprod.* 5:95 (Abstr.).

Audet, C., G. Fitzgerald and H. Guderly. 1985. Homing behavior noted for Colorado squawfish. *Copeia* 1985:213–215.

Auffenberg, W. 1977. Display behavior in tortoises. *Amer. Zool.* 17:241–250.

Auffenberg, W. 1981. *The behavioral ecology of the Komodo monitor.* Univ. Press Florida, Gainesville, FL.

Auffenberg, W. 1988. *Gray's monitor lizard.* Univ. Press Florida, Gainesville, FL.

Augee, M.L., T.J. Bergin and C. Morris. 1978. Observations on behaviors of echidnas at Taronga Zoo. Pp. 121–129 in M.L. Augee, ed. *Monotreme Biology.* The Royal Zoological Society of N.S.W., Mosman, N.S.W., Australia.

Aumuller, A., B. Schenck and F. Neumann. 1975. Fine structure of monkey *(Macaca mulatta)* sertoli cells after treatment with cyproterone. *Andrologia* 7:317–328.

Avella, F.J. 1986. A plan for the reintroduction of the monk seal *(Monachus monachus)* in the Archipelago of Cabrera (Balearic Islands, Spain). *Aquat. Mamm.* 12:43–48.

Avery, M. 1984. Lekking in birds: Choice, competition and reproductive constraints. *Ibis* 126:177–187.

Axelrod, H. 1976. *Breeding aquarium fishes,* Book 4. T.F.H. Pubs., Neptune City, NJ.

Baggerman, B. 1990. Sticklebacks. Pp. 79–107 in A.D. Munro, A.P. Scott and T.J. Lam, eds. *Reproductive seasonality in teleosts: Environmental influences.* CRC Press, Boca Raton, FL.

Bahr, J.M., S.C. Wang, M.Y. Huang and F.O. Calvo. 1983. Steroid concentrations in isolated theca and granulosa layers of preovulatory follicles during the ovulatory cycle of the domestic hen. *Biol. Reprod.* 29:326–334.

Baiji Research Group. 1989. A proposal for establishment of a semi-natural reserve at Shishou for conservation and management of the Baiji *(Lipotes vexillifer).* Pp. 21–22 in W.F. Perrin, R.L. Brownell, Jr., K.Y. Zhou and R.J. Liu, eds. *Biology and conservation of the river dolphins.* Int'l. Union Conserv. Nature & Natur. Resour. Species Survival Commiss. Occasional Paper 3. Gland, Switzerland.

Bailey, W.J. and T.J. Ridsdill-Smith, eds. 1991. *Reproductive behavior of insects: Individuals and populations.* Chapman and Hall, New York, NY.

Bain, D. 1987. A journey through the National Marine Fisheries Service marine mammal inventory. *Proc. Int'l. Marine Anim. Trainers Assoc.* 1987:103–130.

Bain, D. and S. Allen. 1982. Interactions of a killer whale from Iceland with one from northern Vancouver Island. *Proc. Int'l. Marine Anim. Trainers Assoc.* 1982:83 (Abstr.).

Bakeman, R. and J.M. Gottman. 1986. *Observing interaction: An introduction to sequential analysis*. Cambridge Univ. Press, New York, NY.

Baker, C.S., L.M. Herman, A. Perry, W.S. Lawton, W.S. Straley and J.H. Straley. 1985. Population charateristics and migration of summer and late-season humpback whales *Magaptera novaengliae*, in southeastern Alaska. *Marine Mamm. Sci.* 1:304–323.

Baker, M.C. and L.R. Mewaldt. 1978. Song dialects as barriers to dispersal in white-crowned sparrows, *Zonotricha leucophys nuttalli*. *Evolution* 32:712–722.

Baker, M.C., T.K. Bjerke, H.U. Lampe and Y.O. Espmark. 1987. Sexual response of female yellowhammers to differences in regional song dialects and repertoire sizes. *Anim. Behav.* 35:395–401.

Baksi, S.N. and A.D. Kenny. 1977. Vitamin D_3 metabolism in immature Japanese quail: Effects of ovarian hormones. *Endocrinology* 101:1216–1220.

Bakst, M.R. 1988. Duration of fertility of turkeys inseminated at different times after the onset of photostimulation. *J. Reprod. Fertil.* 84:531–537.

Bakst, M.R. and D.M. Bird. 1987. Localization of oviductal sperm-storage tubules in the Americn kestrel (*Falco sparverius*). *Auk* 104:321–324.

Balance, A. 1990. *Giant weta captive breeding programme*. Fauna & Flora Preserv. Soc. Project No. 87/55/23. Brighton, England.

Balcomb, K.C. 1989. Baird's beaked whale, *Berardius bairdii* Stejneger, 1883: Arnoux's beaked whale *Berardius arnuxii* Duvernoy, 1851. Pp. 261–288 in S.H. Ridgway and R.J. Harrison, eds. *Handbook of marine mammals, Vol. 4: River dolphins and the larger toothed whales*. Academic Press, London, England.

Balcomb, K.C. and M.A. Bigg. 1986. Population biology of the three resident killer whale pods in Puget Sound and off southern Vancouver Island. Pp. 85–96 in B.C. Kirkevold and J.S. Lockard eds. *Behavioral biology of killer whales*. Alan Liss, New York, NY.

Balcomb, K.C., J.R. Boran, R.W. Osborne and N.J. Haenel. 1980. *Observations of killer whales (Orcinus orca) in Greater Puget Sound, State of Washington*. Report No. MM1300731-7, U.S. Marine Mamm. Commiss., Washington, DC.

Baldwin, J.D. 1970. Reproductive synchronization in squirrel monkeys (*Saimiri sciureus*). *Primates* 11:317–326.

Balke, J.M.E., I.K. Barker, M.K. Hackenberger, R. McManamon and W.J. Boever. 1988. Reproductive anatomy of three nulliparous female Asian elephants: The development of artificial breeding techniques. *Zoo Biol.* 7:99–113.

Balke, J.M.E., B.W. Read, W.J. Boever, D. Gibson, R.E. Miller, R.E. Junge, U.S. Seal and E.D. Plotka. 1987. Artificial insemination in elephants. *Regional Proc. Amer. Assoc. Zool. Parks Aquar.* 1987:652–658.

Ball, S.G. 1990. Recorder: An attempt to provide a biological recording package for widely dispersed use in the United Kingdom. Pp. 29–32 in *Colloquy on the Berne convention on invertebrates and their conservation.* Council of Europe, Strasburg, France.

Ballance, L.T. 1990. Residence patterns, group organization, and surfacing associations of bottlenose dolphins in Kino Bay, Gulf of California, Mexico. Pp. 267–283 in S. Leatherwood and R. Reeves, eds. *The bottlenose dolphin.* Academic Press, San Diego, CA.

Ballou, J.D. 1984. Strategies for maintaining genetic diversity in captive populations through reproductive technology *Zoo Biol.* 3:311–323.

Ballou, J.D., T.J. Foose, R.C. Lacy and U.S. Seal. 1989. *Florida panther, Felis concolor coryi, population viability analysis and recommendations.* Captive Breeding Specialist Group, Apple Valley, MN.

Balthazart, J. 1982. Steroid receptors and behavior. Pp. 141–151 in C.B. Scanes, A. Epple and M.H. Stetson, eds. *Aspects of avian endocrinology: Practical and theoretical implications.* Grad. Studies, Texas Tech. Univ. 26.

Balthazart, J. 1983. Hormonal correlates of behavior. Pp. 221–365 in D.S. Farner, J.R. King, and K.C. Parkes, eds. *Avian Biology,* Vol. VII. Academic Press, New York, NY.

Bamberg, E. and E. Mostl. 1988. Pregnancy test in zoo animals by EIA of estrogens in faeces. *Proc. 11th Int'l. Congr. Anim. Reprod. Artif. Insem.* 1988:82 (Abstr.). Univ. College, Dublin, Ireland.

Banks, B. and T.J.C. Beebee. 1986. Climatic effects on calling and spawning of the natterjack toad *Bufo calamita:* Discriminant analyses and applications for conservation monitoring. *Biol. Conserv.* 36:339–350.

Baptista, L.F. and M.L. Morton. 1982. Song dialects and mate selection in montane white-crowned sparrows. *Auk* 99:537–547.

Baptista, L.F. and L. Petrinovich. 1984. Social interaction, sensitive phases, and the song template hypothesis in the white-crowned sparrow. *Anim. Behav.* 32:172–181.

Barash, D.P. 1977. Sociobiology of rape in mallards *Anas platyrhynchos:* Responses of the mated male. *Science* 197:788–789.

Barash, D.P. 1982. *Sociobiology and behavior,* 2nd Ed. Elsevier, Amsterdam, Netherlands.

Barbour, R.A. 1977. Anatomy of marsupials. Pp. 237–305 in B. Stonehouse and D. Gilmore, eds. *The biology of marsupials.* MacMillan, London, England.

Barclay, J. and T. Cade. 1983. Restoration of the peregrine falcon in the eastern United States. Pp. 3–40 in S. Temple, ed. *Bird conservation.* Cambridge Univ. Press, New York, NY.

Barinaga, M. 1990. Where have all the froggies gone? *Science* 247:1033–1034.

Barker, D.G., J.B. Murphy and K.W. Smith. 1979. Social behavior in a captive group of Indian pythons, *Python molurus* (Serpentes, Boidae) with formation of a linear social hierarchy. *Copeia* 1979:466–471.

Barker, J.F. and W.S. Herman. 1976. Effect of photoperiod and temperature on reproduction of the monarch butterfly, *Danaus plexippus. J. Insect Physiol.* 22:1565–1568.

Barlow, G. 1961. Social behavior of the desert pupfish, *Cyprinodon macularuius,* in the field and in the aquarium. *Amer. Midland Natural.* 65:339–359.

Barlow, J. 1986. *Factors affecting the recovery of Phocoena sinus, the vaquita or Gulf of California harbor porpoise.* S.W. Fish. Center Admin. Report. LJ-86-37, La Jolla, CA.

Barr, A.B. 1973. Timing of spermatogenesis in four nonhuman primates species. *Fertil. Steril.* 24:381–389.

Barrett, A.M. and M.A. Stockham. 1963. The effect of housing conditions and simple experimental procedures upon corticosterone level in plasma of rats. *J. Endocrinol.* 26:97–105.

Barrett, P. 1991. *Keeping wetas in captivity.* Wellington Zoological Garden, Nelson, New Zealand.

Barrett, P.C. 1990. Marine mammal rehabilitation centers. Pp. 693–698 in L.A. Dierauf, ed. *CRC handbook of marine mammal medicine: Health, disease and rehabilitation.* CRC Press, Boca Raton, FL.

Barrows, E.M. 1976. Mating behavior in halactine bees (Hymenoptera: Halictidae): I. Patrolling and age specific behavior in males. *J. Kansas Entomol. Soc.* 49:105–119.

Barrows, E.M. 1986. A hornet, paperwasps, and yellowjackets (Hymenoptera: Vespidae) in suburban habitats of the Washington, D. C. area. *Proc. Entomol. Soc. of Wash.* 88:237–243.

Barrows, E.M., J.S. DeFilippo and M. Tavallali. 1983. Urban community gardener knowledge of arthropods in vegetable gardens in Washington, DC. Pp. 107–126 in G.W. Frankie and C.S. Koehler, eds. *Urban entomology: Interdisciplinary perspectives.* Praeger, Westport, CT.

Barsetti, D.A., L.J. Abrahamson, R.J. Marlar and R.J. Allen. 1980. Effects of climate controlled housing on reproductive potential of rhesus monkeys. *J. Reprod. Fertil.* 59:15–20.

Bartholomew, G.A. 1952. Reproductive and social behavior of the northern elephant seal. *Univ. California Pub. in Zool.* 47:369–472.

Bartholomew, G.A. 1982. Scientific innovation and creativity: A zoologist's point of view. *Amer. Zool.* 22:227–235.

Bartlett, A.C. 1985. Guidelines for genetic diversity in laboratory colony establishment and maintenance. Pp. 7–17 in P. Singh and R.F. Moore, eds. *Handbook of insect rearing,* Vol. I. Elsevier, Amsterdam, Netherlands.

Bastian, J. 1967. The transmission of arbitrary environmental information between bottlenosed dolphin. Pp. 803–873 in R.G. Busnel, ed. *Animal sonar systems,* Vol. II. Laboratoire de Physiologie Acoustique, Jouy-en-Josa, France.

Bateman, J.A. 1959. Laboratory studies of the golden mole and mole-rat. *Afr. Wildl.* 13:65–71.

Bates, H. and R. Busenbark. 1970. Pp. 47–76 in *Finches and soft-billed birds*. T.F.H. Pubs., Neptune City, NJ.

Bauer, A.M. and G.B. Geise. 1988. Binder Park: The zoo that youth built. *Proc. Amer. Assoc. Zool. Parks Aquar.* 1988:143–155.

Baugh, T. and J. Deacon. 1983. Maintaining the Devils Hole pupfish, *Cyprinodon diabolis* Wales in aquaria. *J. Aquaricult. Aquat. Sci.* 3:73–75.

Baugh, T.M. and J.E. Deacon. 1988. Evaluation of the role of refugia in conservation efforts for the Devils Hole pupfish, *Cyprinodon diabolis* Wales. *Zoo Biol.* 7:351–358.

Baugh, T.M., J.E. Deacon and P. Fitzpatrick. 1987. Reproduction and growth of the Pahrunp pupfish (*Empetrichthys latos latos* Miller) in the laboratory and nature. *J. Aquaricult. Aquat. Sci.* 5:1–5.

Baugh, T.M., J.E. Deacon and D. Withers. 1985. Conservation efforts with the Hiko White River springfish *Crenicthys baileyi grandis*. (Williams and Wilde). *J. Aquaricult. Aquat. Sci.* 4:49–53.

Bavister, B.D. and D.E. Boatman. 1989. *In vitro* fertilization and embryo transfer technology as an aid to the conservation of endangered primates. *Zoo Biol.* Suppl. 1:21–31.

Bavister, B.D., D.E. Boatman, L. Leibfried, M. Loose and M.W. Vernon. 1983. Fertilization and cleavage of rhesus monkey oocytes *in vitro*. *Biol. Reprod.* 28:983–999.

Baylis, M. and N.E. Pierce. 1991. The effect of host plant quality on the survival of larvae and oviposition by adults of an ant-tended lycaenid butterfly *Jalmenus evagoras*. *Ecol. Entomol.* 16:1–9.

Beach, F.A. and R.L. Pepper. 1972. Operant responding in the bottlenose dolphin, *Tursiops truncatus*. *J. Exp. Anal. Behav.* 17:159–160.

Beaman, K.R., F. Caporaso, S. McKeown and M. Graff, eds. 1990. *First International Symposium on turtles and tortoises: Conservation and captive husbandry.* Chapman Univ., Orange, CA.

Beattie, C.W. and B.C. Bullock. 1978. Diurnal variations of serum androgen and estradiol-17β in the adult male green monkey (*Cercopithecus sp.*) *Biol. Reprod.* 19:36–39.

Beaver, R.A. 1979. Host specificity of temperate and tropical animals. *Nature* 281:139–141.

Bechler, D. 1983. The evolution of agonistic behavior in amblyopsid fishes. *Behav. Ecol. Sociobiol.* 12:35–42.

Beck, B.B. 1975. Student behavioral research in zoos. Pp. 91–102 in National Academy of Sciences, eds. *Research in Zoos and Aquariums.* National Academy of Sciences, Washington, DC.

Beck, B.B. 1980. *Animal tool behavior: The use and manufacture of tools by animals.* Garland, New York, NY.

Beck, B.B. 1984. The birth of a lowland gorilla in captivity. *Primates* 25:378–383.

Beck, B.B. 1991. Managing zoo environments for reintroduction. *Proc. Amer. Assoc. Zool. Parks Aquar.* 1991:436–440.

Beck, B.B. and M.I. Castro. 1994. Environments for endangered primates. Pp 259–270 in E.F. Gibbons, Jr., E.J. Wyers, E.J. Waters and E.W. Menzel, Jr., eds. *Naturalistic environments in captivity for animal behavior research.* State Univ. New York Press, Albany, NY.

Beck, B.B. and C. Wemmer, eds. 1983. *The biology and management of an extinct species, Pere David's deer.* Noyes Publications, Park Ridge, NJ..

Beck, B.B., D.G. Kleiman, J.M. Dietz, I. Castro, C. Carvalho, A. Martins and B. Retburg-Beck. 1991. Losses and reproduction in golden lion tamarins *Leontopithecus rosalia. Dodo* 27:50–61.

Beck, F. 1976. Comparative placental morphology and function. *Environ. Health Perspect.* 18:5.

Beckley, S. and M. Novak. 1988. An examination of various foraging components and their suitability as enrichment tools for captively housed primates. *Amer. J. Primat.* 14:409 (Abstr.).

Bedford, J.M. 1981. Why mammalian gametes don't mix. *Nature* 291:286–288.

Beecher, M.D. and I.M. Beecher. 1979. Sociobiology of bank swallows: Reproductive strategy of the male. *Science* 205:1282–1285.

Beecher, M.D., M.B. Medvin, P.K. Stoddard and T. Loesche. 1986. Acoustic adaptations for parent-offspring recognition in swallows. *J. Exp. Biol.* 45:179–193.

Beehler, B. 1983. Frugivory and polygamy in birds of paradise. *Auk* 100:1–12.

Beehler, B. 1985. Conservation of New Guinea rainforest birds. Pp 233–248 in A. Diamond and T. Lovejoy, eds. *Conservation of tropical forest birds.* Proc. XVIII World Confr. Int'l. Council Bird Preserv. Page Bros., Norwich, England.

Beehler, B. and M. Foster. 1988. Hotshots, hotspots, and female preference in the organization of lek mating systems. *Amer. Natural.* 131:203–219.

Behler, J.L. 1987. Ultraviolet light and reptile propagation. *Proc. Amer. Assoc. Zool. Parks Aquar.* 1987:162–169.

Behler, J.L. 1989. The status of wild crocodilians and their captive culture. *Proc. Amer. Assoc. Zoo Vet.* 1989:127–138.

Behler, J.L. 1991. Chinese alligator *(Alligator sinenus). Amer. Assoc. Zool. Parks Aquar. Ann. Report on Conservation and Science.* 1990–1991:171–172.

Behler, J.L. and T. Joanen. 1982. Captive management of the Chinese alligator. *Proc. Amer. Assoc. Zool. Parks Aquar.* 1982:424–429.

Behrends, P. R. 1981. Copulatory behavior of *Dipodomys microps* (Heteomyidae). *S.W. Natural.* 25:562–563.

Bekoff, M. and M.C. Wells. 1986. Social ecology and behavior in coyotes. *Adv. Study Behav.* 16:251–338.

Bekoff, M., T.J. Daniels and J.L. Gittleman. 1984. Life history patterns and the comparative social ecology of carnivores. *Ann. Rev. Ecol. Syst.* 15:191–232.

Beleau, S. 1988. Water quality. Pp. 293–304 in M.K. Stoskopf, ed. *Tropical fish medicine. Veterinary Clinics of North America: Small animal.* W. B. Saunders, Philadelphia, PA.

Beletsky, L.D. and G.H. Orians. 1989. Red bands and red-winged blackbirds. *Condor* 91:993–995.

Bell, D.J. 1983. Mate choice in the European rabbit. Pp. 211–223 in P. Bateson, ed. *Mate choice.* Cambridge University Press, New York, NY.

Bell, W.J. 1990. Searching behavior patterns in insects. *Ann. Rev. Entomol.* 35:447–467.

Bell, W.J. 1991. *Searching behaviour: The behavioural ecology of finding resources.* Chapman and Hall, London, England.

Beltz-Decker, E., ed. 1989. *Care in captivity. Husbandry techniques for amphibians and reptiles.* Chicago Herpetol. Soc., Chicago, IL.

Benirschke, K. 1977. Genetic management. *Int'l. Zoo Yb.* 17:50–60.

Benirschke, K. 1983a. The impact of research on propagation of endangered species in zoos. Pp. 402–413 in C.M. Schonewald-Cox, S.M. Chambers, B. MacBryde and W.L. Thomas, eds. *Genetics and conservation: A reference for managing wild animal and plant populations.* Benjamin/Cummings, Menlo Park, CA.

Benirschke, K. 1983b. Placentation. *J. Exp. Zool.* 228:385–389.

Benirschke, K. 1985. The genetic management of exotic animals. *Symp. Zool. Soc. London* 54:71–87.

Benirschke, K., ed. 1986. *Primates: The road to self-sustaining populations.* Springer-Verlag, New York, NY.

Benirschke, K. 1987. Chacoan Peccary SSP Report. *Amer. Assoc. Zool. Parks Aquar. Newsletter* 28:6.

Benirschke, K. 1989. Chacoan peccary born. *Amer. Assoc. Zool. Parks Aquar. Newsletter* 30:16.

Benirschke, K. and A.T. Kumamoto. 1983. Paternity diagnosis in pygmy chimpanzees. *Int'l. Zoo Yb.* 23:220–223.

Benirschke, K. and A.T. Kumamoto. 1987. Challenges of artiodactyl cytogenetics. *La Kromosomo II* 45:1468–1478.

Benirschke, K., M.L. Johnson and R.V. Benirschke. 1980. Is ovulation in dolphins, *Stenella longrostris* and *Stenella attenuata*, always copulation induced? *Fish. Bull.* 78:507–528.

Benirschke, K., A.T. Kumamoto, J.H. Olsen, M.M. Williams and J. Oosterhuis. 1984. On the chromosomes of *Gazella soemmeringi* Cretzschmar, 1926. *Z. Sauegetierk* 49:368–373.

Bennett, A.F. 1986. Measuring behavioral energetics. Pp. 69–81 in M.E. Feder and G.V. Lauder, eds. *Predator-prey relationships.* Chicago University Press, Chicago, IL.

Bennett, B. and J.H. Fewell. 1987. Play frequencies in captive and free-ranging bighorn lambs *Ovis canadensis canadensis. Zoo Biol.* 6:237–242.

Bennett, J.H., M.J. Smith, R.M. Hope and C.M. Chesson. 1982. Fat-tailed dunnart *Sminthopsis crassicaudata*: Establishment and maintenance of a laboratory colony. Pp.38–44 in D.D. Evans, ed. *Management of Australian mammals in captivity.* Proc. Aust. Mamma. Soc. 1979, Ramsay Ware Stockland, Victoria, Australia.

Bennett, S.D. and W.R. Foster. 1986. Successful transfer of a zebra embryo to a domestic horse. *Equine Vet. J. Suppl.* 3:78–79.

Benoit, D.A. and G.W. Holcombe. 1978. Toxic effects of zinc on fathead minnows *Pimephales promelas* in soft water. *J. Fish Biol.* 13:701–708.

Benson, T.A. and R.F. Smith. 1974. Male dominance hierarchies and their possible effects upon breeding in cheetahs, *Acinonyx jubatus. Int'l. Zoo Yb.* 14:174–179.

Benson, T.A. and R.F. Smith. 1975. A case of programmed cheetah, *Acinonyx jubatus,* breeding. *Int'l. Zoo Yb.* 15:154–157.

Benz, G. 1963. Genetic diseases and aberrations. Pp. 161–184 in E.A. Steinhaus, ed. *Insect pathology.* Academic Press, New York, NY.

Bercovitch, F.B. and T.E. Ziegler. 1989. Reproductive strategies and primate conservation. *Zoo Biol.* Suppl. 1:163–168.

Bercovitz, A.B. 1987. Avian sex identification techniques. Pp. 197–203 in E.L. Burr, ed. *Companion bird medicine.* Iowa State Univ. Press, Ames, IA.

Bercovitz, A.B. and P.L. Sarver. 1988. Comparative sex-related differences of excretory sex steroids from day-old Andean condors *(Vultur gryphus)* and peregrine falcons *(Falco peregrinus)*: Non-invasive monitoring of neonatal endocrinology. *Zoo Biol.* 7:147–153.

Bercovitz, A.B., A. Mirsky and F. Frye, Jr. 1985. Non-invasive assessment of endocrine differences in day-old chicks *(Gallus domesticus)* by analysis of the immunoreactive oestrogen excreted in the egg. *J. Reprod. Fertil.* 74:681–686.

Berger, A.J. 1978a. A reintroduction of Hawaiian geese. Pp. 342–343 in S. A. Temple, ed. *Endangered species.* Univ. Wisconsin Press, Madison, WI.

Berger, A.J. 1978b. Fitness of offspring from captive populations. Pp. 315–320 in S. A. Temple, ed. *Endangered species.* Univ. Wisconsin Press, Madison, WI.

Berger, A.J. 1981. *Hawaiian birdlife,* 2nd Ed. Univ. Hawaii Press, Honolulu, HI.

Berger, J.J., ed. 1990. *Environmental restoration.* Island Press, Washington, DC.

Berkson, G., W.A. Mason and S.V. Saxon. 1963. Situation and stimulus effects on stereotyped behaviors and chimpanzees. *J. Comp. Physiol. Psychol.* 56:786–792.

Berman, C.M. 1980. Mother-infant relationships among free-ranging rhesus monkeys on Cayo Santiago: A comparison with captive pairs. *Anim. Behav.* 28:860–873.

Bernstein, I.S. and L.E. Williams. 1986. The study of social organization. Pp. 195–216 in G. Mitchell and J. Erwin, eds. *Comparative primate biology, 2A: Behavior, conservation and ecology.* Alan Liss, New York, NY.

Bernstein, I.S., T.P. Gordon, R.M. Rose and M.S. Peterson. 1978. Influences of sexual and social stimuli upon circulating levels of testosterone in male pigtail macaques. *Behav. Biol.* 24:400–404.

Berry, C. 1988. Effects of cold shock in Colorado squawfish larvae. *S.W. Natural.* 33:193–197.

Berry, K.H. 1974. The ecology and social behavior of the chuckwalla, *Sauromalus obesus obesus* Baird. *Univ. California Publ. Zool.* 101:1–60.

Berry, K.H. 1986. Desert tortoise *Gopherus agassizii* relocation: Implications of social behavior and movements. *Herpetologica.* 42:113–125.

Berry, R.B. 1972. Reproduction by artificial insemination in captive American goshawks. *J. Wildl. Manage.* 36:1283–1288.

Berry, R.J. 1981. Breeding cockatoos and macaws in captivity. *Amer. Fed. Avicult. Watchbird* Feb./Mar.:10–17.

Bertram, B.C.R. 1986. Endangered small mammals in zoos. *Int'l. Zoo Yb.* 24/25:99–106.

Bertram, B.C.R. 1988. Re-introducing scimitar-horned oryx into Tunisia. Pp.136–145 in A. Dixon and D. Jones, eds. *Conservation and biology of desert antelopes.* Christopher Helm, London, England.

Bertsch, J.A. 1987. HLA typing using nonisotopic M13 probes for genetic analysis. *Amer. Biotech. Lab.* 52:55–57.

Besch, E.L. and G.V. Kollias, Jr. 1994. Physical, chemical and behavioral factors in large, low density naturalistic animal facilities. Pp. 77–96 in E.F. Gibbons, Jr., E.J. Wyers, E.J. Waters and E.W. Menzel, Jr., eds. *Naturalistic environments in captivity for animal behavior research.* State Univ. New York Press, Albany, NY.

Besh, D.A. 1987. Animaline. *Animal Kingdom* 90:50.

Best, R.C. 1981. Foods and feeding habits of wild and captive Sirenia. *Mamm. Rev.* 11:3–29.

Best, R.C. and V.M.F. DaSilva. 1984. Preliminary analysis of reproductive parameters of the Boutu, *Inia geoffrensis*, and the Tucuxi, *Sotalia fluviatilis*, in the Amazon River system. Pp. 361–369 in *Report Int'l. Whaling Commiss.* Spec. Issue 6. Cambridge, England.

Biben, M. 1982. Urine-marking during agonistic encounters in the bush dog *Speothos venaticus. Zoo Biol.* 6:359–362.

Biben, M. 1983. Comparative ontogeny of social behavior in three South American canids, the maned wolf, crab-eating fox and bush dog: Implications for sociality. *Anim. Behav.* 31:814–826.

Bigg, M.A. 1982. An assessment of killer whale *Orcinus orca* stocks off Vancouver Island, British Columbia. *Report Int'l. Whaling Commiss.* 32:655–666. Cambridge, England.

Bigg, M.A., I.B. MacAskie and G. Ellis. 1976. *Abundance and movements of killer whales off eastern and southern Vancouver Island, with comments on management.* Arctic Biological Station, Ste. Ann de Bellevue, Quebec, Canada.

Bigg, M.A., G.M. Ellis, J.K.B. Ford and K.C. Balcomb. 1987. *Killer whales: A study of their identification, genealogy, and natural history in British Columbia and Washington State.* Phantom Press, Nanaimo, British Columbia.

Billard, R., A. Fostier, C. Weil and B. Breton. 1982. Endocrine control of spermatogenesis in teleost fish. *Can. J. Fish. Aquat. Sci.* 39:65–79.

Bird, D.M. and P.C. Lague. 1977. Semen production of the American kestrel. *Can. J. Zool.* 55:1351–1358.

Bird, D.M., P.C. Lague and R.B. Buckland. 1976. Artificial insemination vs. natural mating in captive American kestrels. *Can. J. Zool.* 54:1183–1191.

Birkhead, T.R. 1987. Sperm-storage glands in a passerine: The zebra finch, *Poephila gutta* (Estrildidae). *J. Zool.* 212:103–108.

Birkhead, T.R., J. Pellatt and F.M. Hunter. 1988. Extra-pair copulation and sperm competition in the zebra finch. *Nature* 334:60–62.

Bishop, K.A. and J.D. Bell. 1978. Aspects of the biology of the Australian grayling *Prototroctes maraena* Gunther (Pisces: Prototroctidae). *Aust. J. Marine Freshwater Res.* 29:743–761.

Black, T. and R. Bulkley. 1985a. Growth rate of yearling Colorado squawfish at different water temperatures. *S.W. Natural.* 30:253–257.

Black, T. and R. Bulkley. 1985b. Preferred temperature of yearling Colorado squawfish. *S.W. Natural.* 30:95–100.

Blackburn, D., L.J. Vitt and C.A. Beuchat. 1984. Eutherian-like reproductive specializations in a viviparous lizard. *Proc. Nat'l. Acad. Sci. U.S.A.* 81:4860–4863.

Blackshaw, A.W. 1977. Temperature and seasonal influences. Pp. 517–545 in A.D. Johnson and W.R. Gomes, eds. *The testis,* Vol. IV. Academic Press, New York, NY.

Blair, W.F. 1960. *The rusty lizard: A population study.* Univ. Texas Press, Austin, TX.

Blasetti, A., L. Boitani, M.C. Riviello and E. Visalberghi. 1988. Activity budgets and use of enclosed space by wild boars *Sus scrofa* in captivity. *Zoo Biol.* 7:69–79.

Blaustein, A.R. and B. Waldman. 1992. Kin recognition in anuran amphibians. *Anim. Behav.* 44:207–221.

Bleisch, W. and C. Nan. 1990. Conservation of the black-crested gibbon in China. *Oryx* 24:147–156.

Blomqvist, L. 1984. Conservation measurements taken for the captive snow leopard *Panthera uncia* population and a report of the fluctuations in the stock in 1983. *Int'l. Pedigree. Book of Snow Leopards* 4:55–71.

Bloomstrand, M., K. Riddle, P. Alford and T.L. Maple. 1986. Objective evaluation of a behavioral enrichment device for captive chimpanzees *Pan troglodytes*. *Zoo Biol.* 5:293–300.

Bloxam, Q.M.C. and S.J. Tonge. 1986. Breeding programmes for reptiles and snails at Jersey Zoo: An appraisal. *Int'l. Zoo Yb.* 24/25:49–56.

Bluhm, C.K. 1985a. Seasonal variation in pituitary responsiveness to luteinizing hormone-releasing hormone of mallards and canvasbacks. *Gen. Comp. Endocrinol.* 58:487–491.

Bluhm, C.K. 1985b. Social factors regulating avian endocrinology and reproduction. Pp. 247–264 in B.K. Follett, S. Ishii, and A. Chandola, eds. *The endocrine system and the environment.* Japan Sci. Soc. Press, Tokyo, Japan/Springer-Verlag, Berlin, Germany.

Bluhm, C.K., R.E. Phillips and W.H. Burke. 1983. Serum levels of luteinizing hormone, prolactin, estradiol, and progesterone in laying and nonlaying mallards *Anas platyrhynchos*. *Biol. Reprod.* 28:295–305.

Blum, M.S. and N.A. Blum, eds. 1979. *Sexual selection and reproductive competition in insects.* Academic Press, New York, NY.

Boardman, W.S.J. and M.D. Sibley. 1991. The captive management, diseases and veterinary care of tuatara. *Proc. Amer. Assoc. Zoo Vets.* 1991:159–167.

Bobr, L.W., F.W. Lorenz and F.X. Ogasawara. 1962. The role of the uterovaginal junction in storage of cock spermatozoa. *Poultry Sci.* 41:1628 (Abstr.).

Boccone, V. and T. Mills. 1979. Spawning behavior and spawning substrate preference of the Madoc sucker *Catostomas microps* (Rutter). Inland Fish. Endanger. Species Progr. Spec. Pub. 79–2. State of CA Dept. of Fish & Game, Sacramento, CA.

Bock, B.C. 1984. Movement patterns relative to nesting site locations in a population of green iguanas *(Iguana iguana)* in Panama. Ph.D. Dissertation, University of Tennessee, Knoxville, TN.

Bodson, L. 1984. Living reptiles in captivity: A historical survey from the origins to the end of the XVIIIth century. *Acta Zool. Path.* 78:15–32.

Boelkins, R.C. and A.P. Wilson. 1972. Intergroup social dynamics of the Cayo Santiago rhesus (*Macaca mulatta*) with special reference to changes in group membership by males. *Primates* 13:125–140.

Bogart, M.H., A.T. Kumamoto and B.L. Lasley. 1977. A comparison of the reproductive cycle of three species of lemur. *Folia Primatol.* 28:134–143.

Bogerd, J., K.W. Li, C. Janssen-Dommerholt and H. Goos. 1992. Two gonadotropin-releasing hormones from African catfish (*Clarias gariepinus*). *Biochem. Biophys. Res. Commit.* 187:127–134.

Bogue, G., and M. Ferrari. 1978. The predatory "training" of captive-reared pumas. *The World's Cats* 3:35–52.

Bohmke, B.W. 1984. Avian mortality analysis. *Regional Proc. Amer. Assoc. Zool. Parks Aquar.* 1984:395–402.

Bohmke, B.W. and M. Healy. 1985. Mixed species walk-through aviaries: Blessing or burden? *Proc. Amer. Assoc. Zool. Parks Aquar.* 1985:288–293.

Bohner, J. 1990. Early acquisition of song in the zebra finch *Taeniopygua guttata*. *Anim. Behav.* 39:369–374.

Boice, R. 1980. Domestication and degeneracy. Pp. 84–99 in M.R. Denny, ed. *Comparative psychology: An evolutionary analysis of animal behavior*. John Wiley & Sons, New York, NY.

Boice, R. 1981. Captivity and feralization. *Psychol. Bull.* 89:407–421.

Boisvert, M. and J. Grisham. 1988. Reproduction of the short-nosed echidna *Tachyglossus aculeatus* at the Oklahoma City Zoo. *Int'l. Zoo Yb.* 27:103–106.

Bok, A.H. and H.W. Heard. 1982. Induced spawing of *Barbus trevelyani* (Pisces, Cyprinidae). *S. Afr. J. Wildl. Res.* 12:106–108.

Boller, E. 1972. Behavioral aspects of mass-rearing of insects. *Entomophaga* 17:9–25.

Bolles, R.C. 1972. Reinforcement, expectancy, and learning. *Psychol. Rev.* 79:394–409.

Bolze, D. 1992. When a bird in the hand means none in the bush: A call to stop the current practices of the wild bird trade. An issue analysis by the New York Zool. Soc. & Wildl. Conserv. Int'l., New York Zool. Soc., New York, NY.

Bona-Gallo, A. and P. Licht. 1983. Effects of temperature on sexual receptivity and ovarian recrudescence in the garter snake *Thamnophis sirtalis parietalis*. *Herpetologica* 39:173–182.

Bona-Gallo, A., P. Licht, D.S. MacKenzie and B. Lofts. 1980. Annual cycles in levels of pituitary and plasma gonadotropin, gonadal steroids, and thyroid activity in the Chinese cobra (*Naja naja*). *Gen. Comp. Endocrinol.* 42:477–493.

Bonner, J.T. 1980. *The evolution of culture in animals.* Princeton Univ. Press, Princeton, NJ.

Bonner, W.N. 1981. Southern fur seals. Pp. 161-208 in S.H. Ridgway and R.J. Harrison, eds. *Handbook of marine mammals. Vol. 1: The walrus, sea lions, fur seals, sea otter.* Academic Press, London, England.

Bonney, R.C., H.D.M. Moore and D.M. Jones. 1980. Plasma concentrations of oestradiol-17β and progesterone, and laparoscopic observations of the ovary in the puma (*Felis concolor*) during oestrus, pseudopregnancy and pregnancy. *J. Reprod. Fertil.* 63:523–531.

Borror, D.J. and D.M. DeLong. 1971. *An introduction to the study of insects.* Holt, Rinehart & Winston, New York, NY.

Bortolotti, G.K., K.L. Wiebe and W.M. Iko. 1991. Cannibalism of nestling American kestrels by their parents and siblings. *Can. J. Zool.* 69:1447–1453.

Boschung, H. 1976. An evaluation of the slackwater darter, *Etheostoma boschungi*, relative to its range, critical habitat and reproductive habitat in the Cypress Creek watershed and adjacent stream systems. U.S. Dept. Agricult. Soil Conserv. Serv., Auburn, AL.

Bossart, G.D. and L.A. Dierauf. 1990. Marine mammal clinical laboratory medicine. Pp. 1–52 in L.A. Dierauf, ed. *Handbook of marine mammal medicine: Health, disease and rehabilitation.* CRC Press, Boca Raton, FL.

BOSTID/NAS. 1983. *Butterfly farming in Papua New Guinea.* Report Ad Hoc Panel Advisory Committee on Technology Innovation. Board on Science and Technology for Internal Development Office of International Affairs, National Academy Press, Washington, DC.

Bosu, W.T.K., T.H. Holmdahl, E.D.B. Johansson and C. Gemzell. 1972. Peripheral plasma levels of oestrogens, progesterone and 17-α-hydroxyprogesterone during the menstrual cycle of the rhesus monkey. *Acta Endocrinol.* 71:755–764.

Bouman, J. 1977. The future of Przewalski horses *Equus przewalskii* in captivity. *Int'l. Zoo Yb.* 17:63–68.

Bouman-Heinsdijk, I. 1982. Semi-reserves for Przewalski horse as an intermediary stop between captivity and reintroduction into the wild and an international stallion exchange strategy for reducing inbreeding in captivity. Pp. 221–229 F. Bouman, I Bouman and A. Groeneveld, eds.

Breeding Przewalski horses in captivity for release in the wild. Found. Preserv. Protect. Przewalski Horse, Rotterdam, Netherlands.

Bourn, N.A.D. and J.A. Thomas. 1993. The ecology and conservation of the brown argus butterfly *Aricia agestis* in Britain. *Biol. Conserv.* 63:67–74.

Bourne, A.R., J.L. Taylor and T.G. Watson. 1985. Identification of epitestosterone in the plasma and testis of the lizard *Tiliquia (Trachysaurus) rugosa. Gen. Comp. Endocrinol.* 58:394–401.

Bourne, M.N.G. and G.H. Bourne. 1975. Histology and histochemistry of the rhesus monkey: Male reproductive system. Pp. 260–276 in G.H. Bourne, ed. *The rhesus monkey. Vol. 1: Anatomy and physiology.* Academic Press, New York, NY.

Bowden, D., P. Winter and D. Ploog. 1967. Pregnancy and delivery behavior in squirrel monkey *(Saimiri sciureus)* and other primates. *Folia Primatol.* 5:1–42.

Bowers, B.B. and G.M. Burghardt. 1992. The scientist and the snake: Relationships with reptiles. Pp. 250–263 in H. Davis and D. Balfour, eds. *The inevitable bond.* Cambridge Univ. Press, New York, NY.

Bowers, M.D. 1990. Recycling plant natural products for insect defense. Pp. 353–386 in D.L. Evans and J.O. Schmidt, eds. *Insect defenses: Adaptive mechanisms and strategies of prey and predators.* State Univ. New York Press, Albany, NY.

Bowers, W.S. 1980. Chemistry of plant/insect interactions. Pp. 613–633 in M. Locke and D.S. Smith, eds. *Insect biology in the future.* Academic Press, New York, NY.

Bowler, J.K. 1980. Modern management and exhibit techniques for reptiles. Pp. 19–22 in J.B. Murphy and J.T. Collins, eds. *Reproductive biology and diseases of captive reptiles.* Soc. Study Amphib. Reptiles Contrib. Herpetol., Oxford, OH.

Bowman, L.A., S.R. Dilley and E.B. Keverne. 1978. Suppression of estrogen-induced LH surges by social subordination in talapoin monkeys. *Nature* 275:56–58.

Box, H.O. 1991. Training for life after release: Simian primates as examples. *Symp. Zool. Soc. London* 62:111–123.

Boyce, M.S., ed. 1988. *Evolution of life histories of mammals.* Yale Univ. Press, New Haven, CT.

Boycott, R. and O. Bourquin. 1988. *The South African tortoise book.* Southern Book Pub., Johannesburg, South Africa.

Boyd, L.L. 1978. Artificial insemination of falcons. *Symp. Zool. Soc. London* 43:73–80.

Boyd, L.L. and N.S. Boyd. 1976. Hybrid falcon: The sharic at fledging. *Hawk Chalk* 14:53–54.

Boyd, L.L., N.S. Boyd and F.C. Dolber. 1977. Reproduction of prairie falcons by artificial insemination. *J. Wildl. Manage.* 41:266–271.

Boysen, S.T., K.S. Quigley and V.R. Woods. 1989. Primate enrichment: An annotated bibliography. Ohio State Univ. and Columbus Zool. Garden Cooperative Research Program, Appropriate Primate Enrichment (APE) Project. Columbus, OH.

Bradbury, J.W. 1981. The evolution of leks. Pp. 138–169 in R.D. Alexander and D.W. Tinkle, eds. *Natural selection and social behavior: Recent research and new theory*. Chiron Press, New York, NY.

Bradshaw, S. D. 1986. *Ecophysiology of desert reptiles*. Academic Press, Sydney, Australia.

Bradshaw, S.D., C. Gans and H. St. Girons. 1980. Behavioral thermoregulation in a pygopodid lizard, *Lialis burtonis*. *Copeia* 1980:738–743.

Brady, B. 1989. First North American captive birth of banded linsang reported at Cincinnati Zoo. *Amer. Assoc. Zool. Parks Aquar. Newsletter* 30:28.

Brady, C.A. 1981. The vocal repertoires of the bush dog *Speothos venaticus*, the crab-eating fox *Cerdocyon thous* and the maned wolf *Chrysocyon brachyurus*. *Anim. Behav.* 29:649–669.

Brady, C.A. and M.K. Dilton. 1979. Management and breeding of maned wolves *Chrysocyon brachyurus* at National Zoological Park, Washington. *Int'l. Zoo Yb*. 19:171–176.

Braham, H.W. 1984. Review of reproduction in the white whale, *Delphinapterus leucas*, narwhal, *Monodon monoceros,* and Irrawaddy dolphin, *Orcaella brevirostris*, with comments on stock assessment. *Report Int'l. Whaling Commiss.* Spec. Issue 6:81–89. Cambridge, England.

Brakhage, G.K. 1953. Migration and mortality of ducks hand-reared and wild-trapped at Delta Manitoba. *J. Wildl. Manage.* 17:465–477.

Brambell, M.R. 1977. Reintroduction. *Int'l. Zoo Yb.* 17:112–116.

Brattstrom, B.H. 1968. Thermal acclimation in anuran amphibians as a function of latitude and altitude. *Comp. Biochem. Phys.* 24:93–111.

Breder, C.M., Jr. and D.E. Rosen. 1966. *Modes of reproduction in fishes*. T.F.H. Pubs., Neptune City, NJ.

Breitwisch, R. 1989. Mortality patterns, sex ratios and parental investment in monogamous birds. Pp. 1–50 in D.M. Power, ed. *Current ornithology,* Vol. 6. Plenum Press, New York, NY.

Breland, K. and M. Breland. 1961. The misbehavior of organisms. *Amer. Psychol.* 16:661–664.

Breland, K. and M. Breland. 1966. *Animal behavior.* MacMillan, New York, NY.

Brenner, R.J. 1994. Arthropod pests: Varieties, risks, and strategies for control in naturalistic familities. Pp. 97–111 in E.F. Gibbons, Jr., E.J. Wyers, E.J. Waters and E.W. Menzel, Jr., eds. *Naturalistic environments in captivity for animal behavior research.* State Univ. New York Press, Albany, NY.

Brent, L. and J.W. Eichberg. 1991. Primate puzzleboard: A simple environmental enrichment device for captive chimpanzees. *Zoo Biol.* 10:353–360.

Brett, L.P. and S. Levine. 1979. Schedule-induced polydipsia suppressess pituitary-activity in rats. *J. Comp. Physiol. Psychol.* 93:946–956.

Brill, R.L., M.L. Sevenich, T.J. Sullivan, J.D. Sustman and R.E. Witt. 1988. Behavioral evidence for hearing through the lower jaw by an echolocating dolphin *Tursiops truncatus. Marine Mamm. Sci.* 4:223–230.

Brisbin, I.L. 1980. Zoological parks and the conservation of wildlife: An overview of ecological and genetic principles. *Proc. Amer. Assoc. Zool. Parks Aquar.* 1980:22–29.

Brisby, W. 1985. The training of a good keeper. *Regional Proc. Amer. Assoc. Zool. Parks Aquar.* 1985:157–159.

Britt, J.H., N.M. Cox and J.S. Stevenson. 1981. Advances in reproduction in dairy cattle. Paper No. 6657 of the *Journal Series of the North Carolina Agricultural Research Service.* Raleigh, NC.

Brock, M.K. 1986. Cryopreservation of semen of the American kestrel (*Falco sparverius*). Master's Thesis. Macdonald College of McGill Univ., Montreal, Canada.

Brock, P. 1985. *The phasmid rearer's handbook. Vol. 20 of The Amateur Entomologist.* Amat. Entomol. Soc., Feltham, Middlesex, England.

Brockway, B.F. 1965. Stimulation of ovarian development and egg laying by male courtship vocalization in budgerigars *Melopsittacus undulatus. Anim. Behav.* 13:575–578.

Bronikowski, E.J., B.B. Beck and M. Power. 1989. Innovation, exhibition and conservation: Free-ranging tamarins at the National Zoological Park. *Proc. Amer. Assoc. Zool. Parks Aquar.* 1989:540–546.

Bronson, F.H. 1988. Seasonal regulation of reproduction in mammals. Pp. 1831–1871 in E. Knobil and J.D. Neill, eds. *The physiology of reproduction.* Raven Press, New York, NY.

Bronson, F.H. 1989. *Mammalian reproductive biology*. Univ. of Chicago Press, Chicago, IL.

Brooks, D.R. and D.A. McLennan. 1991. *Phylogeny, ecology, and behavior*. University Chicago Press, Chicago, IL.

Brooks, M.A. 1985. Nutrition, cell culture, and symbosis of leafhopper and plant hoppers. Pp. 195–216 in L. R. Nault and J. G. Rodriguiez, eds. *The leafhoppers and planthoppers*. John Wiley & Sons, New York, NY.

Brower, A.V. 1986. Update on conservation from MONCON II: Notes on the Second International Conference on the monarch butterfly and the preservation of overwintering colonies. *Atala* 14:12–14.

Brower, L.P. and S.B. Malcolm. 1989. Endangered phenomena. *Wings* 14:3–9.

Brown, D.H. 1962. The health problems of walrus calves, and remarks on their general progress in captivity. *Int'l. Zoo Yb.* 4:13–23.

Brown, G., P. Shannon and G. Farnell. 1983. Renesting and brooding in the Caribbean flamingo. *Zoo Biol.* 2:137–141.

Brown, G.M., L.J. Grota, D.P. Penny and S. Reichlin. 1970. Pituitary-adrenal function in the squirrel monkey. *Endocrinology* 86:519–529.

Brown, I.L. and P.R. Ehrlich. 1980. Population biology of the checkerspot butterfly *Euphydryas chalcedona*. Structure of the Jasper Ridge colony. *Oecologia* 47:239–251.

Brown, J.H. and C.R. Feldmeth. 1971. Evolution in constant and fluctuating environments: Thermal tolerance of desert pupfish (*Cyprinodon*). *Evolution* 25:390–398.

Brown, J., P. Johansen, P. Colgan and R. Mathers. 1987. Impairment of early feeding behavior of largemouth bass by pentachlorophenol exposure: A preliminary assessment. *Trans. Amer. Fish. Soc.* 116:71–78.

Brownell, R.L., Jr. 1984. Review of reproduction in platanistoid dolphins. *Report Int'l. Whaling Commiss.* Special Issue 6:149–158. Cambridge, England.

Brownell, R.L., Jr. 1986. Distribution of the vaquita, *Phocoena sinus* in Mexican waters. *Marine Mamm. Sci.* 2:299–305.

Brownell, R.L., Jr. 1989. Franciscana, *Pontoporia blainvillei* (Gervais and d'Orbigny, 1844). Pp. 45–67 in S.H. Ridgway and R.J. Harrison, eds. *Handbook of marine mammals, Vol. 4: River dolphins and the larger toothed whales*. Academic Press, London, England.

Brownell, R.L., Jr. 1991. Marine mammal populations in the 1990's: Status, problems and research. *Int'l. Marine Biol. Res. Instit., IBI Report* 2:1–10.

Brownell, R.L., Jr., and K. Ralls, eds. 1981. *The West Indian manatee in Florida*. Workshop proceedings. Florida Dept. Natural. Resources, Tallahassee, FL.

Brownell, R.L., Jr., K. Ralls and W.F. Perrin. 1989. The plight of the "forgotten" whales. *Oceanus* 32:5–11.

Brownlie, S. 1987. Fostering hope for the whooper. *Nat'l. Wildl.* 25:40–43.

Bruce, D. 1992. Habitat enrichment in two species of pheasant. *Shape Enrich. Newsletter* 1:8–9.

Bruning, D. 1983. Breeding condors in captivity for release into the wild. *Zoo Biol.* 2:245–252.

Bruning, D. 1989. Saved! But where to now? *Birds Int'l.* 1:73–78.

Brussard, P.F. and P.R. Ehrlich. 1970. The population structure of *Erebia epipsodea* (Lepidoptera: Satyrinae). *Ecology* 51:119–129.

Bryant, S. 1988. Maintenance and captive breeding of the eastern quoll *Dasyurus viverrinus*. *Int'l. Zoo Yb.* 27:119–124.

Bryden, M.M. and R. Harrison. 1986. *Research on dolphins*. Clarendon Press, Oxford, England.

Buechner, H.K. 1961. Unilateral implantation in the Uganda kob. *Nature* 190:738–739.

Buitron, D. and G.L. Nuechterlein. 1985. Experiments on olfactory detection of food catches by black-billed magpies. *Condor* 87:92–95.

Bump, G. and J.W. Bump. 1969. *A study of the spotted tinamous and the pale spotted tinamous of Argentina*. U.S. Dept. Interior, Fish Wildl. Serv., Bur. Sport Fish. Wildl., Special Scientific Report, Wildlife No. 120.

Bunch, T.E., W.C. Foote, and B. Whitaker. 1977. Interspecies ovum transfer to propagate wild sheep. *J. Wildl. Manage.* 41:726–730.

Burchfield, P.M., C.S. Hairston and S.L. Huntress. 1987. Captive management of the Galapagos tortoise *Geochelone elephantopus ssp.* at the Gladys Porter Zoo. *Proc. Amer. Assoc. Zool. Parks Aquar.* 1987:151–157.

Burger, J.W. 1949. A review of experimental investigations on seasonal reproduction in birds. *Wilson Bull.* 61:211–230.

Burges, H.D. 1973. Enzootic diseases of insects. *Annals New York Acad. of Sci.* 217:31–49.

Burgess, K. 1968. The behaviour and training of a killer whale *Orcinus orca* at San Diego Sea World. *Int'l. Zoo Yb.* 8:202–205.

Burghardt, G.M. 1969. Comparative prey-attack studies in newborn snakes of the genus *Thamnophis*. *Behavior* 33:77–114.

Burghardt, G.M. 1975. Behavioral research on common animals in small zoos. Pp. 103–133 in Instit. Lab. Anim. Resour. and Amer. Assoc. Zool. Parks Aquar., eds. *Research in zoos and aquariums*. National Academy of Sciences, Washington, DC.

Burghardt, G.M. 1977. Learning processes in reptiles. *Biol. Reptiles* 7:555–681.

Burghardt, G.M. 1978. Behavioral ontogeny in reptiles: Whence, whither, and why. Pp. 149–174 in G.M. Burghardt and M. Bekoff, eds. *The development of behavior: Comparative and evolutionary aspects*. Garland, New York, NY.

Burghardt, G.M. 1988. Precocity, play, and the ectotherm—endotherm transition: Profound reorganization or superficial adaptation? Pp. 107–148 in E.M. Blass, ed. *Handbook of behavioral neurobiology*, Vol. 9. Plenum Press, New York, NY.

Burghardt. G.M. 1990. Chemically mediated predation in vertebrates: Diversity, ontogeny, and information. Pp. 475–499 in D. McDonald, D. Muller-Schwarze, and S.E. Natynczuk, eds. *Chemical signals in vertebrates*, Vol. 5. Oxford Univ. Press, New York, NY.

Burghardt, G.M. and L.J. Gittleman. 1990. Comparative behavior and phylogenetic analyses: New wine, old bottles. Pp. 192–225 in M. Bekoff and D. Jamison, eds. *Interpretation and explanation in the study of animal behavior*. Westview Press, Boulder, CO.

Burghardt, G.M. and A.S. Rand, eds. 1982. *Iguanas of the world: Their behavior, ecology and conservation*. Noyes, Park Ridge, NJ.

Burghardt, G.M., B. Allan and H. Frank. 1986. Exploratory tongue flicking by green iguanas in laboratory and field. Pp. 305–321 in D. Duvall, D. Muller-Schwarze, and R.M. Silverstein, eds. *Chemical signals in vertebrates*, Vol. 4. Plenum Press, New York, NY.

Burke, R.L. 1991. Relocations, repatriations, and translocations of amphibians and reptiles: Taking a broader view. *Herpetologica* 47:350–357.

Burke, T. and M.W. Burford. 1987. DNA fingerprinting in birds. *Nature* 327:149–152.

Burley, N. 1985. Leg-band color and mortality patterns in captive breeding populations of zebra finches. *Auk* 102:647–651.

Burley, N. 1986. Comparison of the band-colour preferences of two species of estrildid finches. *Anim. Behav.* 34:1732–1741.

Burley, N. and N. Moran. 1979. The significance of age and reproductive experience in the mate preferences of feral pigeons *Columba livia*. *Anim. Behav.* 27:686–698.

Burley, N., G. Krantzberg and P. Radman. 1982. Influence of colour-banding on the conspecific preferences of zebra finches. *Anim. Behav.* 30:444–455.

Burns, J.R. and K.D. Kallman. 1985. An ovarian regression syndrome in the platyfish *Xiphophorus maculatus*. *J. Exp. Zool.* 233:301–316.

Burton, F.D. 1972. The integration of biology and behavior in the socialization of *Macaca sylvana* of Gibraltar. Pp. 29–62 in F.E. Poirier, ed. *Primate socialization*. Random House, New York, NY.

Burton, J.A. and B. Pearson. 1987. *The Collins guide to the rare mammals of the world*. The Stephen Greene Press, Lexington, MA.

Bury, R.B. and J.A. Whelan. 1984. *Ecology and management of the bullfrog*. U.S. Dept. of the Interior, Fish and Wildlife Service. Resource Publication, Washington, DC.

Busch, G.L. 1969. Sympatric host race formation and speciation in frugivorous flies of the genus *Rhagoletis* (Diptera, Tephritidae). *Evolution* 23:237–251.

Busch, R.L. 1985. Channel catfish culture in ponds. Pp. 13–84 in C.S. Tucker, ed. *Channel catfish culture*. Elsevier, Amsterdam, Netherlands.

Bush, G.L., R.W. Neck and G.B. Kitto. 1976. Screwworm eradication: Inadequate selection for noncompetitive ecotypes during mass rearing. *Science* 193:491–493.

Bush, M., S. Kennedy, D. Wildt and S. Seager. 1978. Sexing birds by laparoscopy. *Int'l. Zoo Yb.* 18:197–198.

Butcher, G.S. 1991. Mate choice in female northern orioles with a consideration of the role of the black male coloration in female choice. *Condor* 93:82–88.

Butterworth, B.B. 1961. The breeding of *Dipodomys deserti* in the laboratory. *J. Mammal.* 42:413–414.

Bye, V.J. 1984. The role of environmental factors in the timing of reproductive cycles. Pp. 187–205 in G.W. Potts and R.J. Wootton, eds. *Fish reproduction: Strategies and tactics*. Academic Press, Orlando, FL.

Bye, V.J. 1990. Temperate marine teleosts. Pp. 125–143 in A.D. Munro, A.P. Scott and T.J. Lam, eds. *Reproductive seasonality in teleosts: Environmental influences*. CRC Press, Boca Raton, FL.

Cade, T.J. 1982. *Falcons of the world*. Comstock/Cornell University Press, Ithaca, N.Y.

Cade, T.J. 1986a. Propagating diurnal raptors in captivity: A review. *Int'l Zoo Yb*. 24/25:1–20.

Cade, T.J. 1986b. Reintroduction as a method of conservation. *Raptor Res. Reports.* 5:72–84.

Cade, T.J. and R.W. Fyfe. 1978. What makes peregrine falcons breed in captivity? Pp. 251–262 in S.A. Temple, ed. *Endangered birds: Management techniques for preserving threatened species.* Univ. Wisconsin. Press, Madison, WI.

Cade, T.J., J.H. Enderson, C.G. Thelander and C.M. White. 1988. Conclusion. Pp.857–861 in T.G. Cade, J.H. Enderson, C.G. Thelaner and C.M. White, eds. *Peregrine falcon populations.* Peregrine Fund, Boise, ID.

Cain, J.R. 1978. Artificial inscmination: A practical method for genetic improvement in ring-necked pheasant, *Phasianus colchius. Symp. Zool. Soc. London* 43:81–88.

Caine, N.G. 1990. Unrecognized anti-predator behavior can bias observational data. *Anim. Behav.* 39:195–197.

Caine, N.G. and V.J. O'Boyle, Jr. 1992. Cage design and forms of play in red-bellied tamarins *Saguinus labiatus. Zoo Biol.* 11:215–220.

Cairns, J., ed. 1988. *Rehabilitating damaged ecosystems.* CRC Press, Boca Raton, FL.

Calder, W.A., III. 1984. *Size, function, and life history.* Harvard Univ. Press, Cambridge, MA.

Calder, W.A. and J.R. King. 1974. Thermal and coloric relations of birds. Pp. 260–393 in D.S. Farner, and J.R. King eds. *Avian biology*, Vol. IV. Academic Press, New York, NY.

Caldwell, D.K. and M.C. Caldwell. 1972. Behavior of marine mammals. Pp. 419–465 in S.H. Ridgway, ed. *Mammals of the sea: Biology and medicine.* Charles Thomas, Springfield, IL.

Caldwell, M.C. and D.K. Caldwell. 1964. Experimental studies on factors involved in care-giving behavior in three species of the cetacean family Delphinidae. *Bull. California Acad. Sci.* 63:1–19.

Caldwell, M.C. and D.K. Caldwell. 1975. Social interactions and reproduction in Atlantic bottlenose dolphins. Pp. 755–789 in S. Ridgway and K. Bernirschke eds. *Breeding dolphins: Present status, suggestions for the future.* Nat'l. Tech. Info. Serv., PB 273. U.S. Dept. Commer., Washington, DC.

Caldwell, M.C. and D.K. Caldwell. 1985. Manatees, *Trichechus manatus* Linnaeus, 1758; *Trichechus senegalensis* Link, 1795 and *Trichechus linunquis* (Natterer, 1883). Pp. 33–66 in S.H. Ridgway and R.J. Harrison, eds. *Handbook of marine mammals, Vol.3: The sirenians and baleen whales.* Academic Press, London, England.

Callard, I.P., L. Kosterman and G.V. Callard. 1988. Reproductive physiology. Pp. 277–317 in T.J. Shuttleworth, ed. *Physiology of elasmobranch fishes*. Springer-Verlag, New York, NY.

Calvert, W.H. and L.P. Brower. 1986. The location of monarch butterfly *Danaus plexippus L.* overwintering colonies in Mexico in relation to topography and climate. *J. Lepidopt. Soc.* 40:164–187.

Caminiti, B. 1986. *Cages, corrals and consequences: Housing of monkeys in the lab colony: A bibliography, 1976–1986.* Primate Information Center, Regional Primate Research Center, Univ. Washington, Seattle, WA.

Campbell, J.A. and E.D. Brodie, eds. 1992. *Biology of the pit vipers.* Selva, Tyler, TX.

Campbell, S. 1984. A new zoo? *Zoonooz* 55:4–7.

Candland, D.K. 1987. Tool use in behavior, cognition, and motivation. Pp. 85–103 in G. Mitchell and J. Erwin, eds. *Comparative primate biology,* Vol. 2B. Alan Liss, New York, NY.

Candland, D.K. 1988. A primer of primate society. *Contemp. Psychol.* 33:578–580.

Candland, D.K., L. Dresdale, J. Leiphart and C. Johnson. 1972. Videotape as a replacement for the human observer in studies of nonhuman primate behavior. *Behav. Res. Meth. Instruct.* 4:24–26.

Captive Breeding Specialist Group. 1990. Report from the marine mammal working group. *Captive Breed. Spec. Group News* 1:11.

Captive Breeding Specialist Group. 1991. Final report on transponder system testing and product choice as a global standard for zoological specimens. *Captive Breed. Spec. Group News* 2:3–4.

Carayon, J. 1964. Un cas d'offrande nuptiale chez les Hetcropteres. *C. R. Acad. Sci. (Paris)* 259:4815–4818.

Carder, B. and K. Berkowitz. 1979. Rats preference for earned in comparison with free food. *Science* 167:1273–1274.

Carey, A.B., J.A. Reid and S.P. Horton. 1990. Spotted owl home range and habitat use in southern Oregon coast ranges. *J. Wildl. Manage.* 54:11–17.

Carl, G.R. and C.T. Robbins. 1988. The energetic cost of predator avoidance in neonatal ungulates: Hiding versus following. *Can. J. Zool.* 66:239–246.

Carlstead, K., J. Seidensticker and R. Baldwin. 1991. Environmental enrichment for zoo bears. *Zoo Biol.* 10:3–16.

Carmignani, G.M. and J.P. Bennett. 1976. Leaching of plastics used in closed aquaculture systems. *Aquaculture* 7:89–91.

Carnio, J. 1990. Metropolitan Toronto Zoo: 1990 Liberian mongoose research. *Mustelid and Viverrid Conservation* 1990:17.

Caro, T.M. and D.A. Collins. 1986. Male cheetahs of the Serengeti. *Nat'l. Geogr. Res.* 2:75–86.

Caro, T.M. and D.A. Collins. 1987. Ecological characteristics of territories of male cheetahs *Acinonyx jubatus. J. Zool. Lond.* 211:89–105.

Carpenter, C.C. 1967. Aggression and social structure of iguanid lizards. Pp. 87–105 in W.W. Milstead, ed. *Lizard ecology: A symposium.* Univ. Missouri Press, Columbia, MO.

Carpenter, C.C. 1977. Communication and displays of snakes. *Amer. Zool.* 17:217–223.

Carpenter, C.C. 1980. An ethological approach to reproductive success in reptiles. Pp. 33–48 in J.B Murphy and J.T. Collins, eds. *Reproductive biology and diseases of captive reptiles.* Soc. Study Amphib. Reptiles Contrib. Herpetol., Oxford, OH.

Carpenter, C.C. 1982. The aggressive displays of iguanine lizards. Pp. 215–231 in G.M. Burghardt and A.S. Rand, eds. *Iguanas of the world: Their behavior, ecology, and conservation.* Noyes, Park Ridge, NJ.

Carpenter, C.C. 1984. Dominance in snakes. Pp. 195–202 in R.A. Seigel, L.E. Hunt, J.L. Knight, L. Malaret and N.I. Zuschlag, eds. *Vertebrate ecology and systematics: A tribute to Henry S. Fitch.* Univ. Kan. Mus. Natur. Hist. Spec. Publ. 10. Lawrence, KS.

Carpenter, C.R. 1942a. Sexual behavior of free-ranging rhesus monkeys *(Macaca mulatta)*: I. Specimens, procedures and behavioral characteristics of estrus. *J. Comp. Psychol.* 33:113–142.

Carpenter, C.R. 1942b. Sexual behavior of free-ranging rhesus monkeys *(Macaca mulatta)*: II. Periodicity of estrus, homosexual, autoerotic and non-conformist behavior. *J. Comp. Psychol.* 33:143–162.

Carpenter, J.W. 1986. Cranes (Order Gruiformes). Pp. 316–326 in M.E. Fowler, ed. *Zoo and wild animal medicine.* W.B. Saunders, Philadelphia, PA.

Carpenter, J.W. and S.R. Derrickson. 1981. The role of captive propagation in preserving endangered species. Pp. 109–113 in R.R. Odom and J.W. Guthrie, eds. *Proc. Nongame Endang. Wildl. Symp.* Georgia Dept. Natur. Resour., Game and Fish Div. Tech. Bull. WL5. Athens, GA.

Carroll, J.B. 1990. Rodriques fruit bat. *Amer. Assoc. Zool. Parks Aquar. Communique.* January:4–5.

Carthy, J.D. 1958. *An introduction to the behavior of invertebrates.* George Allen & Unwin, London, England.

Caryl, P.G. 1976. Sexual behaviour in the zebra finch *Taeniopygia guttata*: Response to familiar and novel partners. *Anim. Behav.* 24:93–107.

Case, T.J., D.T. Bolger and A.D. Richman. 1992. Reptilian extinctions: The last 10,000 years. Pp. 91–113 in P.L. Fiedler and S.K. Jain, eds. *Conservation biology*. Chapman & Hall, New York, NY.

Castleberry, D.T. and J.J. Cech, Jr. 1986. Physiological responses of a native and an introduced desert fish to environmental stresses. *Ecology* 67:912–918.

Castracane, V.D., K.C. Copeland, P. Reyes and T.J. Kuehl. 1986. Pubertal endocrinology of yellow baboon *Papio cynocephalus*: Plasma testosterone, testis size, body weight and crown-rump length in males. *Amer. J. Primatol.* 11:263–270.

Castracane, V.D., T. Kyle, E. Wright and D. Martinez. 1981. Episodic, circadian and circannual patterns of plasma testosterone in the male baboon. *Amer. J. Primatol.* 1:345 (Abstr.).

Castro, A. 1983a. Steinhart Aquarium log for Devils Hole pupfish colony, *Cyprinodon diabolis*. In E.P. Pister, ed. *Proc. Desert Fish. Council*, Vol. III–IX:30–31.

Castro, A. 1983b. Progress report by cooperating aquarists. In E.P. Pister, ed. *Proc. Desert Fish. Council*, Vol. III–IX:68.

Castro, A. 1983c. Preservation programs at Steinhart Aquarium. In E.P. Pister, ed. *Proc. Desert Fish. Council*, Vol. III–IX:124.

Catchpole, H.R. and J.F. Fulton. 1943. The oestrous cycle in Tarsius: Observations on a captive pair. *J. Mammal.* 24:90–93.

Cater, B. and S. McGreal. 1991. The case of the bartered babies. *BBC Wildl.* 9:254–260.

Cayrol, C.I., D.H. Garnier and P. Deparis. 1985. Comparative plasma levels of androgens and 17α-estradiol in the diploid and triploid newt, *Pleurodeles waltl*. *Gen. Comp. Endocrinol* 58:342–346.

Chadwick, A. 1983. Endocrinology of reproduction. Pp. 55–72 in M. Abs, ed. *Physiology and behavior of the pigeon*. Academic Press, New York, NY.

Chakroborty, K., K.K. Sharma, D. Bhatt and A. Chandola. 1985. Control of seasonal reproduction in tropical weaver bird. Pp. 157–165 in B.K. Follett, S. Ishii and A. Chandola, eds. *The endocrine system and the environment*. Japan Sci. Soc. Press, Tokyo, Japan/Springer-Verlag, Berlin, Germany.

Chambers, P.L. and J.P. Hearn. 1979. Peripheral plasma levels of progesterone, oestradiol-17β, oestrone, testosterone, androsterone and chorionic gonadotropin during pregnancy in the marmoset monkey *Callithrix jacchus*. *J. Reprod. Fertil.* 56:23–32.

Chambers, S.M. and J.W. Bayless. 1983. Systematics, conservation, and the measurement of genetic diversity. Pp. 349–363 in C.M. Schonewald-Cox, S.M. Chambers, B. MacBryde and W.L. Thomas, eds. *Genetics and conservation: A reference for managing wild animal and plant populations.* Benjamin/Cummings, Menlo Park, CA.

Chamove, A.S and R.E. Bowman. 1978. Rhesus plasma cortisol response at four dominance positions. *Aggress. Behav.* 4:43–55.

Chamove, A.S., J.R. Anderson, S.C. Morgan-Jones and S.P. Jones. 1982. Deep woodchip litter: Hygiene, feeding, and behavioural enhancement in eight primate species. *Int'l. J. Study Anim. Prob.* 3:308–318.

Chandola, A., D. Bhatt and V.K. Pathak. 1983. Environmental manipulation of seasonal reproduction in spotted munia *Lonchura punctulata.* Pp. 229–242 in S. Mikami, K. Homma and M. Wada, eds. *Avian endocrinology: Environmental and ecological perspectives.* Japan Sci. Soc. Press, Tokyo, Japan/Springer-Verlag, Berlin, Germany.

Chang, J.P., B. Wildman and F. Van Goor. 1991. Lack of involvement of arachidonic acid metabolism in chicken gonadotropin-releasing hormone II (cGnRH-II) stimulation of gonadotropin secretion in dispersed pituitary cells of goldfish, *Carrassius auratus.* Identification of a major difference in salmon GnRH and chicken GnRH-II mechanisms of action. *Mol. Cell. Endocrinol.* 79:75–83.

Chang, W.Y.B. 1986. Biological principles of pond culture: An overview. Pp. 1–5 in J.E. Lannan, R. Oneal Smitherman and G. Tchobanoglous, eds. *Principles and practices of pond aquaculture.* Oregon State Univ. Press, Corvallis, OR.

Chao, N.H., W.C. Chao, K.C. Liu and I.C. Liao. 1987. The properties of tilapia sperm and cryopreservation. *J. Fish Biol.* 30:107–118.

Chapman, J.A. and J.E.C. Flux. 1990. *Rabbits, hares and pikas: Status survey and conservation action plan.* Int'l. Union Nature & Natur. Resour., Gland, Switzerland.

Chapman, R.F. 1971. *The insects: Structure and function.* American Elsevier, New York, NY.

Charfauros, V. 1986. Benefits of a natural presentation in a zoo environment. *Proc. Int'l. Marine Anim. Trainers Assoc.* 1986:49–50.

Chatto, D. 1979. Effects of salinity or hatching success of the Cui-ui. *Progr. Fish Cultur.* 41:82–85.

Chaudhuri, M. and J.R. Ginsberg. 1990. Urinary androgen concentrations and social status in two species of free ranging zebra (*Equus burchelli* and *E. grevyi*). *J. Reprod. Fertil.* 88:127–133.

Cheeseman, C.L. and R.B. Mitson. 1982. *Telemetric studies of vertebrates.* Symp. Zool. Soc. Lond. 49.

Chelmonska, B. and B. Geborska-Dymkowska. 1980. The appraisal of musk drake semen obtained by electroejaculation method. *Medycyna Weterymaryjna* 36:414–417.

Chen, B.X., Z.X. Yuen and G.W. Pan. 1985. Semen-induced ovulation in the bactrian camel (*Camelus bactrianus*). *J. Reprod. Fertil.* 74:335–339.

Chen, P.S. 1984. The functional morphology and biochemistry of insect male accessory glands and their secretions. *Ann. Rev. Entomol.* 29:233–255.

Chen, P.X. 1989. Baiji, *Lipotes vexillifer* Miller, 1918. Pp. 25–43 in S.H. Ridgway and J.R. Harrison, eds. *Handbook of marine mammals, Vol. 4: River dolphins and the larger toothed whales.* Academic Press, London, England.

Chen, P.X. and Y.Y. Hua. 1989. Distribution, population size and protection of *Lipotes vexillifer*. Pp. 81–85 in W.F. Perrin, R.L. Brownell, Jr., K.Y. Zhou and R.J. Liu, eds. *Biology and conservation of the river dolphins.* Occasional paper of the Int'l. Union Conserv. Nature & Natur. Resour., Species Survival Commission No. 3. Allen Press, Lawrence, KS.

Chen, P.X. and R.J. Liu. 1989. Captive husbandry of the baiji. Pp. 146–149 in W.F. Perrin, R.L. Brownell, Jr., K.Y. Zhou and R.J. Liu, eds. *Biology and conservation of the river dolphins.* Occasional paper of the Int'l. Union Conserv. Nature & Natur. Resour., Species Survival Commission No. 3. Allen Press, Lawrence, KS.

Chen, P.X., R.J. Liu and K.J. Lin. 1984. Reproduction and the reproductive system in the Beiji *Lipotes vexillifer*. Pp. 445–450 in W.R Perrin, R.L. Brownell and D.P. DeMaster, eds. *Reproduction in whales, dolphins and porpoises.* Int'l. Whaling Commiss., Special Issue 6.

Chen, P.X., X.F. Zhang and D. Wang. 1992. Conservation of the endangered baiji, *Lipotes vexillifer*, in China. *Proc. Int'l. Assoc. Aquatic Anim. Med.* 32:2–7

Cheney, D.L. and R.M. Seyfarth. 1982. Recognition of individuals within and between groups of free-ranging vervet monkeys. *Amer. Zool.* 22:519–529.

Cheng, M.F. and J. Balthazart. 1982. The role of nest-building activity in gonadotrophin secretions and the reproductive success of ring doves (*Streptopelia risorial*). *J. Comp. Physiol. Psychol.* 96:307–324.

Cherfas, J. 1984. *Zoo 2000: A look beyond the bars.* British Broadcasting Corporation, London, England.

Chew, R.M. 1958. Reproduction by *Dipodomys merriami* in captivity. *J. Mammal.* 39:597–598.

Child, G. and A.S. Mossman. 1965. Right horn implantation in the common duiker. *Science* 149:1265–1266.

Chirighin, L. 1987. Mother-calf spatial relationships and calf development in the captive bottlenose dolphin *Tursiops truncatus*. *Aquat. Mamm.* 13:5–15.

Chiszar, D., C.W. Radcliffe, T. Boyer and J.L. Behler. 1987. Cover–seeking behavior in red spitting cobras *Naja mossambica pallida*: Effects of tactile cues and darkness. *Zoo Biol.* 6:161–167.

Chiszar, D., B. O'Connell, R. Greenlee, B. Demeter, T. Walsh, J. Chiszar, K. Moran and H.M. Smith. 1985. Duration of strike-induced chemosensory searching in long-term captive ratlesnakes at National Zoo, Audubon Zoo, and San Diego Zoo. *Zoo Biol.* 4:291–294.

Choudhury, B.C. 1981. Mugger (*Crocodylus palustris*) releases in Andhra Prodesh and Tamil Nadu. *Hamadryad* 6:10–11.

Chowdhury, A. 1978. Studies on mammalian spermatogenesis. The baboon—a model for the study of human spermatogenesis. Pp. 385–395 in N.J. Alexander, ed. *Animal models for research on contraception and fertility.* Harper & Row, London, England.

Ciarcia, G., F. Angelini, A. Polzonetti, M. Zerani and V. Botte. 1986. Hormones and reproduction in the lizard *Podarcis s. sicula* RAF. Pp. 95–100 in I. Assenmacher, and J. Boissin, eds. *Endocrine regulations as adaptive mechanisms to the environment.* Coll. Inter. Cen. d'Etudes Biol. Anim. Sauv. Foret de Chize, France.

CITES. 1984. *Protected species: Appendices, I, II, and III.* Secretariat of the Convention Laujanne Switzer. U. S. Dept. Interior, Fish Wildl. Serv., Washington, DC.

CITES. 1990. *Convention on international trade in endangered species: Appendices I, II, and III.* U.S. Dept. Interior, Fish Wildl. Serv., Washington, DC.

CITES. 1992. *Convention on international trade in endangered species: Appendices I, II, and III.* U.S. Dept. Interior, Fish Wildl. Serv., Washington, DC.

Clark, H.F., J.C. Brennan, R.F. Zeigel and D.T. Karzon. 1968. Isolation and characterization of viruses from the kidneys of *Rana pipiens* with renal adenocarcinoma before and after passage in the red eft *Triturus viridescens. J. Virol.* 2:629–640.

Clark, K.V. 1967. Insects and temperature. Pp. 293–352 in A.H. Rose, ed. *Thermobiology.* Academic Press, New York, NY.

Clark, L. and R. Mason. 1987. Olfactory discrimination of plant volatiles by the European starling. *Anim. Behav.* 35:227–235.

Clark, R. 1962. Whale observation and whale marking off the coast of Chile in 1958, and from Equador towards and beyond the Galapagos Islands in 1959. *Norwegian Whaling Gazette* 51:265–287.

Clark, T.W. 1989. *Conservation biology of the black-footed ferret Mustela nigripes*. Wildl. Preserv. Trust Spec. Sci. Report #3. Wildl. Preserv. Trust Int'l., Philadelphia, PA.

Clark, T.W., L. Richardson, S.C. Forrest, D.E. Casey and T.M. Campbell. 1986. Descriptive ethology and activity patterns of black-footed ferrets. *Great Basin Natural. Memoirs* 8:115–134.

Clarke, C.A. 1977. Breeding the large blue butterfly *Maculinea arion* and the swallowtail buttefly *Papilo machaon* in captivity. *Int'l. Zoo Yb.* 17:60–62.

Clarke, C.A. and P.M. Sheppard. 1956. Hand-pairing of butterflies. *Lepidopt. News* 10:47–53.

Clarke, R.F. 1965. An ethological study of the iguanid lizard genera *Callisaurus, Cophosaurus* and *Holbrookia. Emporia State Res. Studies* 13:1–66.

Clarke, W.C. and H.A. Bern. 1980. Comparative endocrinology of prolactin. Pp. 106–197 in C.H. Li, ed. *Hormonal proteins and peptides, Vol. VIII: Prolactin*. Academic Press, New York, NY.

Clayton, O. and T.J. Kuehl. 1984. The first successful *in vitro* fertilization and embryo transfer in a nonhuman primate. *Theriogenology* 21:228 (Abstr.).

Clemens, E.T. and G.M.O. Maloiy. 1982. The digestive physiology of three east African herbivores: The elephant, rhinoceros, and hippopotamus. *J. Zool. Lond.* 198:141–156.

Clements, R.J. 1974. *Birds of the world: A checklist*. Two Continents, New York, NY.

Clermont, Y. 1969. Two classes of spermatogonial stem cells in the monkey *Cercopithecus aetiops. Amer. J. Anat.* 126:57–72.

Clermont, Y. 1972. Kinetics of spermatogenesis in mammals: Seminiferous epithelium cycle and spermatogonial renewal. *Physiol. Rev.* 52:198–235.

Clermont, Y. and M. Antar. 1973. Duration of the cycle of the seminiferous epithelium and the spermatogonial renewal in the monkey *(Macaca arctoides). Amer. J. Anat.* 136:153–166.

Clermont, Y. and C.P. LeBlond. 1959. Differentiation and renewal of spermatogenesis in the monkey *Macaca rhesus. Amer. J. Anat.* 104:237–273.

Cline, E.M., K.G. Gould and C.W. Foley. 1972. Regulation of ovulation, recovery of mature ova and fertilization *in vitro* of mature ova of the squirrel monkey *(Saimiri sciureus). Feder. Proc.* 31:277 (Abstr.).

Clough, G. 1969. Some preliminary observations on reproduction in the warthog, *Phacochoerus aethiopicus pallas. J. Reprod. Fertil.* Suppl. 6:323–337.

Clough, G.C. 1976. Current status of two endangered Caribbean rodents. *Biol. Conserv.* 10:43–47.

Clubb, S.L. 1987. The pet bird industry—past, present and future. *Proc. Amer. Assoc. Avian Vet.* 1987:233–242.

Clutton-Brock, T.H. 1991. *The evolution of parental care.* Princeton Univ. Press, Princeton, NJ.

Clutton-Brock, T.H. and P.H. Harvey. 1984. Comparative approaches to investigating adaptation. Pp. 7–29 in J.R. Krebs and N.B. Davies, eds. *Behavioural ecology: An evolutionary approach.* Sinaur, Sunderland, MA.

Clutton-Brock, T.H. and G.R. Iason. 1986. Sex ratio variation in mammals. *Quart. Rev. Biol.* 61:339–374.

Clutton-Brock, T.H., F.E. Guinness and S.D. Albon. 1982. *Red deer: Behavior and ecology of two sexes.* Univ. Chicago Press, Chicago, IL.

Cochran, R.C. 1992. *In vivo* and *in vitro* evidence for the role of hormones in fish spermatogenesis. *J. Exp. Zool.* 261:143–150.

Coe, C.L. and S. Levine. 1981. Psychoendocrine relationship underlying reproductive behavior in the squirrel monkey. *Int'l. J. Mental Health* 10:22–42.

Coe, C.L. and L.A. Rosenblum. 1976. Annual reproductive strategy of the squirrel monkey *(Saimiri sciureus). Folia Primatol.* 29:19–42.

Coe, C.L., E.R. Smith, S.P. Mendoza and S. Levine. 1983. Varying influence of social status on hormone levels in male squirrel monkeys. Pp. 7–32 in S.A. Kling and H. Steklis, eds. *Hormones, drugs and social behavior.* Spectrum, New York, NY.

Coe, J.C. 1980. The waterfowl exhibit at Woodland Park Zoo Seattle. *Int'l. Zoo Yb.* 20:282–286.

Coe, J.C. 1983. A greensward for gorillas: Adventures in zoo horticulture. *Proc. Amer. Assoc. Zool. Parks Aquar.* 1983:177–185.

Coe, J.C. 1985. Design and perception: Making the zoo experience real. *Zoo Biol.* 4:197–208.

Coe, J.C. 1987. In search of Eden: A brief history of great ape exhibits. *Proc. Amer. Assoc. Zool. Parks Aquar.* 1987:628–638.

Coe, J.C. 1988. How should we manage the new exhibit technology? "Soft technology". *Proc. Amer. Assoc. Zool. Parks Aquar.* 1988:51–58.

Coe, J.C. 1989. Naturalizing habitats for captive primates. *Zoo Biol.* Suppl. 1:117–125.

Coe, J.C. and T. Maple. 1984. Approaching Eden: A behavioral approach to great ape exhibits. *Proc. Amer. Assoc. Zool. Parks Aquar.* 1985:117–128.

Coerr, E. and W.E. Evans. 1980. *Gigi: A baby whale borrowed for science and returned to the sea.* G. Putnam's Sons, New York, NY.

Cole, K.S. and R.J.F. Smith. 1992. Attraction of female fathead minnows, *Pimephales promelas*, to chemical stimuli from breeding males. *J. Chem. Ecol.* 18:1269–1284.

Cole, M. 1987. How we keep gorillas occupied. *Animal Keepers' Forum* 14:401–403.

Colgan, P. 1983. *Comparative social recognition.* Univ. Chicago Press, Chicago, IL.

Collet, A. 1981. Biology of the common dolphin, *Delphinus delphis*, in the N.E. Atlantic. Ph.D. Dissert. L'Universite de Poitiers, Poitiers, France.

Collet, A. and H. Saint Groins. 1984. Preliminary study of the male reproductive cycle in common dolphins, *Delphinus delphis*, in the eastern north Atlantic. Pp. 355–360 in W.F. Perrin, R.L. Brownell and D.P. DeMaster, eds. *Reproduction in whales, dolphins and porpoises.* Int'l. Whaling Commiss. Spec. Issue 6. Cambridge, England.

Collias, E.C. and N.E. Collias. 1973. Further studies on the development of nest-building behaviour in a weaverbird (*Ploceus cucullatus*). *Anim. Behav.* 21:371–382.

Collias, N.E. and E.C. Collias. 1984. *Nest building and bird behavior.* Princeton Univ. Press, Princeton, NJ.

Collins, D.C., C.E. Graham and J.R.K. Preedy. 1975. Identification and measurement of urinary estrone, estradiol–17β, estriol, pregnanediol and androsterone during the menstrual cycle of the orangutan. *Endocrinology* 96:93–101.

Collins, L. 1973. Pp. 84–87 in *Monotremes and marsupials: A reference for zoological institutions.* Smithsonian Instit. Press., Washington, DC.

Collins, N.M. 1987. *Butterfly houses in Britain—the conservation implications.* Int'l. Union Conserv. Nature & Natur. Resour. Report. Cambridge, England.

Collins, N.M., ed. 1990. *The management and welfare of invertebrates in captivity.* Nat'l. Fed. Zool. Garden, London, England.

Collins, N.M. and J.A. Thomas. 1991. *The conservation of insects and their habitats.* Academic Press, London, England.

Collins, N.M., J.A. Sayer and T.C. Whitmore, eds. 1991. *The conservation atlas of tropical forests: Asia and the Pacific.* MacMillan, London, England.

Colt, J. 1986. Pond culture practices. Pp. 191–203 in J.E. Lannan, R. Oneal Smiterman and G. Tchobanoglous, eds. *Principles and practices of pond aquaculture.* Oregon State Univ. Press, Corvallis, OR.

Colvin, J. 1983. Rank influences rhesus male peer relationships. Pp. 57–64 in R.A. Hinde, ed. *Primate social relationships: An integrated approach.* Sinauer Assoc., Sunderland, MA.

Colyn, M., A. Gautier-Hion and D. Thys van den Audenaerde. 1991. *Cercopithecus dryas* Schwartz 1932 and *C. salongo* Thys van den Audenaerde 1977 are the same species with an age-related coat pattern. *Folia Primatol.* 56:167–170.

Committee on birds. 1977. *Laboratory animal management: Wild birds.* National Res. Council. Nat'l. Acad. Sci., Washington, DC.

Conant, R. 1971. Reptile and amphibian management practices at Philadelphia Zoo. *Int'l. Zoo Yb.* 11:224–230.

Conant, R. 1980. The reproductive biology of reptiles: An historical perspective. Pp. 3–5 in J.B. Murphy and J.T. Collins, eds. *Reproductive biology and diseases of captive reptiles.* Soc. Study Amphib. Reptiles Contrib. Herpetol., Oxford, OH.

Conant, S. 1988. Saving endangered species by translocation: Are we tinkering with evolution? *BioScience* 38:254–257.

Conaway, C.H. and D.S. Sade. 1965. The seasonal spermatogenic cycle of free-ranging rhesus monkeys. *Folia Primatol.* 3:1–12.

Conner, W.E., T. Eisner, R.K. Vander Meer, A. Guerrero and J. Meinwald. 1981. Precopulatory sexual interaction in the arctiid moth (*Utetheisa ornatrix*): Role of a pheromone derived from dietary alkaloids. *Behav. Ecology Sociobiol.* 9:227–235.

Conover, G.K. 1988. Aspects of reproductive behavior in captive red pandas, *Ailurus fulgens.* Master's Thesis. Univ. Tenn., Knoxville, TN.

Constantine, D.G. 1986. Insectivorous bats. Pp. 650–655 in M.E. Fowler, ed. *Zoo and wild animal medicine,* 2nd Ed. W.B. Saunders, Philadelphia, PA.

Constantz, G.D. 1975. Behavioral ecology of mating in the male Gila topminnow, *Poeciliopsis occidentalis* (Cyprinodontiformes: Poeciliidae). *Ecology* 56:966–973.

Conway, K. 1988. Captive management and breeding of the tiger quoll *Dasyurus maculatus*. *Int'l. Zoo Yb.* 27:108–119.

Conway, W.G. 1957. Kingfishers are "problem birds". *Anim. Kingdom* 60:148–150.

Conway, W.G. 1966. A new exhibit for waterbirds at the New York Zoological Park. *Int'l. Zoo Yb.* 6:131–134.

Conway, W.G. 1968. How to exhibit a bullfrog: A bed-time story for zoo men. *Curator* 11:310–318.

Conway, W.G. 1978. Breeding endangered birds in captivity: The last resort. Pp. 225–229 in S.A. Temple, ed. *Endangered birds: Management techniques for preserving threatened species.* Univ. Wisconsin. Press, Madison, WI.

Conway, W.G. 1980. An overview of captive propagation. Pp. 199–208 in M.E. Soulé and B.A. Wilcox, eds. *Conservation biology: An evolutionary-ecological perspective.* Sinauer Assoc., Sunderland, MA.

Conway, W.G. 1985a. Saving the lion-tailed macaque. Pp. 1–12 in P.G. Heltine, ed. *The lion-tailed macaque: Status and conservation.* Alan Liss, New York, NY.

Conway, W.G. 1985b. The species survival plan and the conference on reproductive strategies for endangered wildlife. *Zoo Biol.* 4:219–223.

Conway, W.G. 1986a. The practical difficulties and financial implications of endangered species breeding programmes. *Int'l. Zoo Yb.* 24/25:210–219.

Conway, W.G. 1986b. Can technology aid species preservation? Pp. 263–268 in E.O. Wilson, ed. *Biodiversity.* Nat'l. Acad. Press, Washington, DC.

Conway, W.G. 1986c. Jungleworld, concept and execution. *Proc. Amer. Assoc. Zool. Parks Aquar.* 1986:325–333.

Conway, W.G. 1987. Species carrying capacity in the zoo alone. A species selection masterplan. *Proc. Amer. Assoc. Zool. Parks Aquar.* 1987:20–32.

Conway, W.G. 1989. The prospects of sustaining species and their evolution. Pp. 199–209 in D. Western and M.C. Pearl, eds. *Conservation for the twenty-first century.* Oxford Univ. Press, New York, NY.

Cooke, F. and C.M. McNally. 1975. Mate selection and colour preferences in lesser snow geese. *Behavior* 53:151–170.

Cooper, D.M. 1977. Artificial insemination. Pp. 302–307 in R.F. Gordon, ed. *Poultry disease.* Bailliere Tindall, London, England.

Cooper, K.A., J.D. Harder, D.H. Clawson, D.L. Fredrick, G.A. Lodge, H.C. Peachey, T.J. Spellmire and D.P. Winstel. 1990. Serum testosterone and musth in captive male African and Asian elephants. *Zoo Biol.* 9:297–306.

Cooper, W.E., Jr. and L.E. Vitt. 1987. Ethological isolation, sexual behavior and pheromones in *Fasciatus* species group of the lizard genus *Eumeces*. *Ethology* 75:328–336.

Cooper, W.E., Jr., M.T. Mendonca and L.J. Vitt. 1986. Induction of sexual receptivity in the female broad-headed skink, *Eumeces laticeps*, by estradiol-17β. *Horm. Behav.* 20:235–242.

Copeland, P.A. and P. Thomas. 1989. Purification of maturational gonadotropin from Atlantic croaker (*Micropogonias undulatus*) and development of a radioimmunoassay. *Gen. Comp. Endocrinol.* 73:425–441.

Copenhagen Zoo. 1990. *Behavioral enrichment—a catalog of ideas.* Copenhagen Zoo, Copenhagen, Denmark.

Copeyon, C., J. Walters and J. Carter, III. 1991. Induction of red cockaded woodpecker group formation by artificial cavity construction. *J. Wildl. Manage.* 55:549–556.

Corbett, G.B. and J.E. Hill. 1980. *A world list of mammalian species.* British Mus. Natur. Hist., London, England.

Corbett, G.B. and J.E. Hill. 1986. *A world list of mammalian species.* British Mus. Natur. Hist., London, England.

Corcoran, D.H. and J.A. Proudman. 1991. Isoforms of turkey prolactin: Evidence for differences in glycosylation and in tryptic peptide mapping. *Comp. Biochem. Physiol.* 99B:563–570.

Cornell, L.H. 1978. Capture, transportation, restraint, and marking. Pp. 573–580 in M.E. Fowler, ed. *Zoo and wild animal medicine.* W.B. Saunders, Philadelphia, PA.

Cornell, L.H. 1982. Husbandry of marine mammals. Pp. 283–287 in K. Sausman, ed. *Zoological park and aquarium fundamentals.* Amer. Assoc. Zool. Parks Aquar., Wheeling, WV.

Cornell, L.H. 1983. Hematology and clinical chemistry values in the killer whale, *Orcinus orca.* *J. Wildl. Dis.* 19:259–264.

Cornell, L.H. and E.D. Asper. 1978. A census of captive marine mammals in North America. *Int'l. Zoo Yb.* 18:220–224.

Cornell, L.H., D.A. Duffield, B.E. Joseph and B. Stark. 1988a. Hematology and serum chemistry values in the beluga (*Delphinapterus leucas*). *J. Wildl. Dis.* 24:220–224.

Cornell, L.H., J.E. Antrim, E.D. Asper and B.J. Pincheira. 1988b. Commerson's dolpins (*Cephalorhynchus commersoni*) live-captured from the Strait of Magellan, Chile. *Report Int'l. Whaling Comm.* Special Issue 8:183–194.

Cornell, L.H., E.D. Asper, J.E. Antrim, S.S. Searles, W.G. Young and T. Goff. 1987. Progress report: Results of a long-range captive breeding program for the bottlenose dolphin, *Tursiops truncatus* and *Tursiops truncatus gilli*. *Zoo Biol.* 6:41–53.

Costa, D.P. and G.L. Kooyman. 1984. Contribution of specific dynamic action to heat balance and thermoregulation in the sea otter *Enhydra lutris*. *Physiol. Zool.* 57:199–203.

Coulter, M.C. 1980. Stones: An important incubation stimulus for gulls and terns. *Auk* 97:898–899.

Coulter, M.C., S. Balzano and R.E. Johnson. 1989. Pp. 12–15 in C.E. King and P.W. Shannon, eds. *Conservation and captive management of storks*. New York Zoological Society, New York, NY.

Courtenay, W.R., Jr. and C.C. Kohler. 1986. Exotic fishes in North American fisheries management. Pp. 401–413 in R.H. Stroud, ed. *Fish culture in fisheries management*. Amer. Fish. Soc., Bethesda, MD.

Courtenay, W.R., Jr. and J.R. Stauffer, eds. 1984. *Distribution, biology, and management of exotic fishes*. The Johns Hopkins Univ. Press, Baltimore, MD.

Couver, R.L. and J.P. Schroeder. 1984. A status report on a survey of *Tursiops* breeding programs. Programmes and summaries. *Ann. Symp. European Assoc. Aquat. Mamm.* 1984:34 (Abstr.).

Cowles, R.B. and C.M. Bogert. 1944. A preliminary study of the thermal requirements of desert reptiles. *Bull. Amer. Mus. Natur. Hist.* 83:265–296.

Crandall, L.S. 1964. *Management of wild animals in captivity*. Univ. Chicago Press, Chicago, IL.

Cranfield, M.R., N. Schaffer, B.D. Bavister, N. Berger, D.E. Boatman, S. Kempske, N. Miner, M. Panos, J. Adams and P.M. Morgan. 1989. Assessment of oocytes retrieved from stimulated and unstimulated ovaries of pig-tailed macaques (*Macaca nemistrina*) as a model to enhance the genetic diversity of captive lion-tailed macaque (*Macaca silenus*). *Zoo Biol* Suppl. 1:33–46.

Crawford, M.A., ed. 1968. *Comparative nutrition of wild animals*. Academic Press, New York, NY.

Crear, D. and I. Haydock. 1971. Laboratory rearing of the desert pupfish, *Cyrinodon macularus*. *Fish. Bull.* 69:151–156.

Creel, S., N. Creel, D.E. Wildt and S.L. Monfort. 1992. Behavioural and endocrine mechanisms of reproductive suppression in Serengeti dwarf mongooses. *Anim. Behav.* 43:231–245.

Crews, D. and L.D. Garrick. 1980. Methods of inducing reproduction in captive reptiles. Pp. 49–70 in J.B. Murphy and J.T. Collins, eds. *Reproductive biology and diseases of captive reptiles*. Soc. Study Amphib. Reptiles Contrib. Herpetol., Oxford, OH.

Crews, D. and W.R. Gartska. 1982. The ecological physiology of a garter snake. *Sci. Amer.* 247:158–168.

Crews, D. and M.C. Moore. 1986. Evolution of mechanisms controlling mating behavior. *Science* 231:121–125.

Crews, D. and M.C. Moore. 1993. Reproductive psychobiology of parthenogenetic whiptail lizards. Pp. 257–282 in J.W. Wright and L.J. Vitt, eds. *Biology of whiptail lizards (genus Cnemidophorus)*. Oklahoma Mus. Nat. Hist., Norman, OK.

Crews, D. and R. Silver. 1985. Reproductive physiology and behavior interactions in nonmammalian vertebrates. Pp. 101–182 in N. Adler, D. Pfaff and R.W. Goy, eds. *Handbook of behavioral neurobiology*, Vol. 7. Plenum Press, New York, N.Y.

Crim, L.W. 1982. Environmental modulation of annual and daily rhythms associated with reproduction in teleost fishes. *Can. J. Fish. Aquat. Sci.* 39:17–21.

Crockett, C. 1987. Behavioral research and zoo enclosure design. Pp. 1–21 in *Applying behavioral research to zoo animal management*. Woodland Park Zoo, Seattle, WA.

Crockett Wilson, C. 1978. Methods of observational research in the zoo setting. Pp. 51–73 in C. Crockett and H. Hutchins, eds. *Applied behavioral research at the Woodland Park Zoological Gardens, Seattle, Washington*. Pika Press, Seattle, WA.

Crook, J.R. and W.M. Shields. 1985. Sexually selected infanticide by adult male barn swallows. *Anim. Behav.* 33:754–761.

Crotty, M.J. 1981. Mixed exhibits or "What's that funny looking animal in with the monkeys?" *Int'l. Zoo Yb.* 21:203–206.

Crowcroft, W.P. 1975. A new building for small cats. Pp. 345–349 in R.D. Martin, ed. *Breeding endangered species in captivity*. Academic Press, New York, NY.

Crowder, L.B. 1980. Alewife, rainbow smelt and native fishes in Lake Michigan: Competition or predation? *Environ. Biol. Fish.* 5:225–233.

Crump, M.L., F.R. Hensley and K.L. Clark. 1992. Apparent decline of the golden toad: Underground or extinct? *Copeia* 1992:413–420.

Culley, D.D., Jr. 1981. Have we turned the corner on bullfrog culture? *Aquacult. Mag.* 7:20–24.

Cullum, L. and J.T. Justus. 1973. Housing for aquatic animals. *Lab. Anim. Sci.* 23:126–129.

Cumming, D.H., R.F. du Toit and S.N. Stuart. 1989. *African elephants and rhinos. Status and conservation action plan.* Int'l. Union Nature & Natur. Resour., Gland, Switzerland.

Curlewis, J.D., A.S.I. Loudon and A.P.M. Coleman. 1988. Oestrous cycles and the breeding season of the Père David's deer hind (*Elaphurus davidianus*). *J. Reprod. Fertil.* 82:119–126.

Cusick, E.K. and F.E. Wilson. 1972. On control of spontaneous testicular regression in three sparrows. (*Spezella arborea*). *Gen. Comp. Endocrinol.* 19:441–456.

Cutler, A.B., Jr. and D.L. Loriaux. 1980. Adrenarche and its relationship to the onset of puberty. *Fed. Proc.* 39:2384–2390.

Czekala, N.M., S. Galluser, J.E. Meier and B.L. Lasley. 1986. The development and application of an enzyme immunoassay for urinary estrone conjugates. *Zoo Biol.* 5:1–61.

Czekala, N.M., L.H. Kasman, J. Allen, J. Oosterhuis and B.L. Lasley. 1990. Urinary steroid evaluations to monitor ovarian function in exotic ungulates. VI: Pregnancy detection in exotic equidae. *Zoo Biol.* 9:43–48.

Dalrymple, G.H. and N.G. Reichenbach. 1984. Management of an endangered species of snake in Ohio, U.S.A. *Biol. Conserv.* 30:195–200.

Daly, M., M.I. Wilson and P. Behrends. 1984. Breeding of captive kangaroo rats, *Dipodomys merriami* and *D. microps*. *J. Mammal.* 65:338–341.

Danzer, R. and P. Mormede. 1985. Stress in domestic animals: A psychoneuroendocrine approach. Pp. 81–96 in G.P. Moberg, ed. *Animal stress.* Amer. Physiol. Soc., Bethesda, MD.

Darevsky, I.S., L.A. Kupriyanova and T. Uzzell. 1985. Parthenogenesis in reptiles. Pp. 411–526 in C. Gans and F. Billett, eds. *Biology of the reptilia,* Vol 15B. John Wiley & Sons, New York, NY.

Darling, J.D. and C.M. Juracz. 1983. Migratory destinations of North Pacific humpback whales (*Megaptera novaeangliae*). Pp. 359–368 in R. Payne, ed. *Communication and behavior of whales.* Westview Press, Boulder, CO.

da Silva, H.R., M. De Britto-Pereira and U. Caramaschi. 1989. Frugivory and seed dispersal by *Hyla truncata*, a neotropical treefrog. *Copeia* 1989:781–783.

Davey, K.G. 1965. *Reproduction in the insects.* Oliver & Boyd, Edinburgh, Scotland.

Davey, K.G. 1967. The physiology of reproduction: Some lessons from insects. Pp. 351–364 in J.W.L. Beament and J.E. Treherne, eds. *Insects and physiology*. Elsevier, Amsterdam, Netherlands.

Davies, D.J., L.P. Goulden, B.K. Follett and N.L. Brown. 1976. Testosterone feedback on luteinizing hormone (LH) secretion during a photoperiodically-induced breeding cycle in Japanese quail. *Gen. Comp. Endocrinol.* 30:477–486.

Davies, N.B. and R.E. Green. 1976. The development and ecological significance of feeding techniques in the reed warbler (*Acrocephalus scirpaceus*). *Anim. Behav.* 24:213–229.

Davies, N.B. and A. Lundberg. 1984. Food distribution and a variable mating system in the dunncok, *Prunella modularis*. *J. Anim. Ecol.* 53:895–912.

Davis, L.S. 1982. Timing of nest relief and its effect on breeding success in Adelie penguins (*Phgoscelis adeliae*). *Condor* 84:178–183.

Davis, M. and R.D. Fernald. 1990. Social control of neuronal soma size. *J. Neurobiol.* 21:1180–1188.

Davis, R.W. 1990. Advances in rehabilitating oiled sea otters: The Valdez experience. Symp. on the effects of oil on wildlife. *Int'l. Wildl. Rehab. Council* 1990:171–186.

Davis, R.W., J.A. Thomas, T.D. Williams and R.A. Kastelein. 1986. *Assessment of cleaning and rehabilitation procedures using live sea otters. Sea otter oil spill mitigation study*. Minerals Manage. Serv., U.S. Dept. Interior, Contract No. 14-12-0001-31057.

Dawson, A., B.K. Follett, A.R. Goldsmith and T.J. Nichols. 1984. Hypothalamic gonadotrophin-releasing hormone and pituitary and plasma FSH and prolactin during photo stimulation and photo refractoriness in intact and thyroidectomized starlings, (*Sturnus vulgaris*). *J. Endocrinol.* 105:71–77.

Dawson, G.A. and W.R. Dukelow. 1976. Reproductive characteristics of free-ranging Panamanian tamarins (*Saguinus oedipus geoffroyi*). *J. Med. Primatol.* 5:266–275.

Day, S.L. and A.V. Nalbandov. 1977. Presence of prostaglandin F (PGF) in hen follicles and its physiological role in ovulation and oviposition. *Biol. Reprod.* 16:486–494.

Deacon, J.E., G. Kobetich, J.D. Williams, S. Contreras and members of the Endangered Species Committee of the American Fisheries Society. 1979. Fishes of North America endangered, threatened or of special concern. *Fisheries* 4:29–44.

Deacon, J., P. Schumann and E. Stuenkel. 1987. Thermal tolerances and preferences of fishes of the Virgin River system (Utah, Arizona, Nevada). *Great Basin Natural.* 47:538–546.

deBoer, S.F., J.L. Slangen and J. van der Gugten. 1988. Adaptation of plasma catecholamine and corticosterone responses to short-term repeated noise stress in rats. *Physiol. Behav.* 44:273–280.

deBoer, S.F., J. van der Gugten and J.L. Slangen. 1989. Plasma catecholamine and corticosterone responses to predictable and unpredictable noise stress in rats. *Physiol. Behav.* 45:795–798.

Dee, M. 1987. Indian rhino SSP report. *Amer. Assoc. Zool. Parks Aquar. Newsletter* 28:16–17.

Dee, M. 1990. Los Angeles Zoo reports hatching of an echidna. *Amer. Assoc. Zool. Parks Aquar. Communique.* Nov:26.

DeFran, R.H. and K.W. Pryor. 1980. The behavior and training of cetaceans in captivity. Pp. 319–362 in L.M. Herman, ed. *Cetacean behavior.* John Wiley & Sons, New York, NY.

DeJose, J. 1988. Captive breeding of the numbat. Pp. 501–509 in *Proc. 5th World Conf. Breed. Endang. Species in Captivity.* Cincinnati Zoo & Botanical Gardens, Cincinnati, OH.

Delacour, J. 1973. Pp. 55–79 in *Pheasant breeding and care,* 5th Ed. T.F.H. Pubs., Neptune City, NJ.

Delacour, J. 1977. P. 32 in *The pheasants of the world.* Spur Publications, Hants, England.

DeLuca, H.F. 1982. New developments in the vitamin D endocrine system. *J. Amer. Diet. Assoc.* 80:231–236.

DeMaster, D.P. and J.K. Drevinak. 1988. Survivorship patterns in three species of captive cetaceans. *Marine Mamm. Sci.* 4:297–311.

Demers, L.M., G.J. MacDonald, A.T. Hertig, N.W. King and J.J. Mackey. 1972. The cervix uteri in *Macaca mulatta, Macaca arctoides,* and *Macaca fascicularis.* A comparative anatomic study with special reference to *Macaca arctoides* as a unique model for endometrial study. *Fertil. Steril.* 23:529–534.

Demski, L.S. 1983. Behavioral effects of electrical stimulation of the brain. Pp. 317–359 in R.E. Davis and R.G. Northcutt, eds. *Fish neurobiology,* Vol. 2. Univ. Michigan Press, Ann Arbor, MI.

Demski, L.S. 1987. Diversity in reproductive patterns and behavior in teleost fishes. Pp. 1–27 in D. Crews, ed. *Psychobiology of reproductive behavior.* Prentice-Hall, Englewood Cliffs, NJ..

Demski, L.S. 1989a. Neuroendocrine mechanisms of sexual development and behavior of sharks and rays. *J. Aquaricult. Aquat. Sci.* 5:53–67.

Demski, L.S. 1989b. Pathways for GnRH control of elasmobranch reproductive physiology and behavior. *J. Exp. Zool.* Suppl. 2:4–11.

Demski, L.S. 1989c. Neural substrates for photic control of elasmobranch sexual development and behavior. *J. Exp. Zool.* Suppl. 5:121–129.

Demski, L.S. 1989d. Elasmobranch reproductive biology: Implications for captive breeding. *J. Aquaricult. Aquat. Sci.* 5:84–95.

Demski, L.S. and J.G. Dulka. 1986. Thalamic stimulation evokes sex-color change and gamete release in a synchronous hermaphroditic sea bass. *Experimentia* 42:1285–1287.

Demski, L.S. and P.J. Hornby. 1982. Hormonal control of fish reproductive behavior: Brain-gonadal steroid interactions. *Can. J. Fish. Aquat. Sci.* 39:36–47.

Demski, L.S. and H.E. Sloan. 1985. A direct magnocellular-preopticospinal pathway in goldfish: Implications for control of sex behavior. *Neurosci. Lett.* 55:283–288.

Densmore, M.A., M.J. Bowen, S.J. Magyar, M.S. Amoss, Jr., R.M. Robinson, P.G. Harms and D.C. Kraemer. 1987. Artificial insemination with frozen, thawed semen and pregnancy diagnosis in addax (*Addax nasomaculatus*). *Zoo Biol.* 6:21–29.

Derrickson, S.R. 1980. *Whooping crane recovery plan.* U.S. Dept. Interior, Fish Wildl. Serv., Washington, DC.

Derrickson, S.R. 1986. Propagation of the Guam rail—an update. P. 19 in L.E. Shelton, ed. *Philadelphia Zoo Review,* Vol. II, No. 2. Philadelphia Zoological Garden, Philadelphia, PA.

Derrickson, S.R. and J.W. Carpenter. 1987. Behavioral management of captive cranes—factors influencing propagation and reintroduction. Pp. 493–509 in G.W. Archibald and R. Pasquier, eds. *Proc. 1983 Int'l. Crane Workshop,* Int'l. Crane Found., Baraboo, WI.

Desforges, M.F. and D.G.M. Wood-Gush. 1975. A behavioral comparison of mallard ducks. Habituation and flight reactions. *Anim. Behav.* 23:692–697.

Desmond, T. and G. Laule. 1987. Husbandry training: A gateway to enhanced socialization. *Proc. Int'l. Marine Anim. Trainers Assoc.* 1987:55–62.

Desmond, T. and S. Rutherford. 1982. Corky's fourth calf. *Proc. Int'l. Marine Anim. Trainers Assoc.* 1982:59–67.

Dethier, V.G. 1957. Communication by insects: Physiology of dancing. *Science* 125:331–336.

Deviche, P. 1982. Are gonadotrophins directly involved in the control of avian activities? In C.G. Scanes, A. Epple and M.H. Stetson, eds. Aspects of avian endocrinology: Practical and theoretical implications. *Grad. Studies Texas Tech. Univ.* 26:105–106.

Deviche, P. 1983. Interactions between adrenal function and reproduction in male birds. Pp. 243–254 in S. Mikami, K. Homma and M. Wada, eds. *Avian endocrinology: Environment and ecological perspectives.* Japan Sci. Soc. Press, Tokyo, Japan/Springer-Verlag, Berlin, Germany.

de Vlaming, V.L. 1974. Environmental and endocrine control of teleost reproduction. Pp. 13–83 in C.B. Schreck, ed. *Control of sex in fishes.* Virginia Polytechnic Instit., Blacksburg, VA.

de Vlaming, V.L. 1983. Oocyte development patterns and hormonal involvements among teleosts. Pp. 176–199 in J.C. Rankin, T.J. Pitcher and R.T. Duggan, eds. *Control processes in fish physiology.* John Wiley & Sons, New York, NY.

Devore, I., ed. 1965. *Primate behavior: Field studies of monkeys and apes.* Holt, Rinehart & Winston, New York, NY.

de Vosjoli, P. 1978. On the use of vita lite for the maintenance of herptiles in captivity. *Chamaeleon Res. Cent.* Jour. No. 1:40–43.

DeVries, P.J. 1990. Enhancement of symbiosis between butterfly caterpillars and ants by vibrational communication. *Science* 248:1104–1106.

de Waal, F.B.M. 1989. The myth of a simple relation between space and aggression in captive primates. *Zoo Biol.* Suppl. 1:141–148.

DeWitt, C.B. 1967. Precision of thermoregulation and its relation to environmental factors in the desert iguana, *Dipsosaurus dorsalis. Phys. Zool.* 40:49–66.

Diamond, A. 1985a. Preface. In A. Diamond and T. Lovejoy, eds. *Conservation of tropical forest birds.* Int'l. Council Bird Preserv. Page Bros. Ltd., Norwich, England.

Diamond, J.M. 1985b. Population processes in island birds: Immigration, extinction and fluctuations. Pp. 17–22 in P.J. Moors, ed. *Conservation of island birds.* Int'l. Council Bird Preserv., Tech. Pub. No. 3. Page Bros. Ltd, Norwich, England.

Diamond, J.M. 1988. Red books or green lists? *Nature* 332:304–305.

Diamond, J.M. 1992. Must we shoot deer to save nature? *Natur. Hist.* 101:2–8.

Diefenbach, C.O. 1975. Thermal preferences and thermoregulation in *Caiman crocodilus. Copeia* 1975:530–540.

Dierauf, L.A. 1990a. Pinniped husbandry. Pp. 553–590 in L.A. Dierauf, ed. *CRC handbook of marine mammal medicine: Health, disease and rehabilitation.* CRC Press, Boca Raton, FL.

Dierauf, L.A. 1990b. Stress in marine mammals. Pp. 295–301 in L.A. Dierauf, ed. *CRC handbook of marine mammal medicine: Health, disease and rehabilitation.* CRC Press, Boca Raton, FL.

Dierauf, L.A. 1990c. Marine mammal stranding networks. Pp. 667–672 in L.A. Dierauf, ed. *CRC handbook of marine mammal medicine: Health, disease and rehabilitation*. CRC Press, Boca Raton, FL.

Dierauf, L.A. 1990d. Disposition of marine mammals. Pp. 267–284 in L.A. Dierauf, ed. *CRC handbook of marine mammal medicine: Health, disease and rehabilitation*. CRC Press, Boca Raton, FL.

Dierenfeld, E.S., N. Katz, J. Pearson, F. Murru and E.D. Asper. 1991. Retinol and alpha-tocopherol concentrations in whole fish commonly fed in zoos and aquariums. *Zoo Biol*. 10:119–125.

Dinnes, M.R. and L.J. Gage. 1984. Hand rearing pinniped pups. *Proc. Amer. Assoc. Zoo Vets*. 1984:32–33.

DiSabato, L. 1982. First mother-reared, captive-born aardvark born at San Antonio Zoo. *Amer. Assoc. Zool. Parks Aquar. Newsletter* 26:17.

Disney, R.H.L. 1968. Observations on a zoonosis: Leishmaniasis in British Hondurus. *J. Appl. Ecol*. 5:1–59.

Disney, R.H.L. 1976. Notes on crab-phoretic Diptera (Chironimidae and Simuliidae) and their hosts in Cameroon. *Entomol. Month. Mag*. 111:131–136.

Disney, R.H.L., Y.Z. Erzinclioglu, D.J. deC Henshaw, D. Howse, D.M. Unwin, P. Withers and A. Woods. 1982. Collecting methods and the adequacy of attempted fauna surveys, with reference to the Diptera. *Field Studies* 5:607–621.

Dittami, J.P. 1981. Seasonal changes in the behavior and plasma titers of various hormones in barheaded geese, *Anser indicus*. *Z. Tierpsychol*. 55:289–324.

Dittami, J.P., J. Wozniak, G. Ganshirt, M. Hall and E. Gwinner. 1986. Effects of females and nestboxes on the reproductive condition of male European starlings, *Sturnus vulgaris*, during the breeding cycle. *Die Vogelwarte* 33:226–231.

Dittrich, L. 1971. Food presentation in relation to behaviour in ungulates. *Int'l. Zoo Yb*. 16:48–54.

Dixon, A. and D. Jones, eds. 1988. *Conservation and biology of desert antelopes*. Christopher Helm, London, England.

Dixon, A.R. 1986. Captive management and the conservation of birds. *Int'l. Zoo Yb*. 24/25:45–49.

Dobson, A.P. and A.M. Lyles. 1989. The population dynamics and conservation of primate populations. *Cons. Biol*. 3:362–380.

Dodd, C.K., Jr. and R.A. Seigal. 1991. Relocation, repatriation, and translocation of amphibians and reptiles: Are they conservation strategies that work? *Herpetologica*. 47:336–350.

Doherty, J.G. 1991. The exhibition and management of geladas in the Baboon Reserve at the New York Zoological Park. *Proc. Amer. Assoc. Zool. Parks Aquar.* 1991:599–605.

Doherty, J.G. and E.F. Gibbons, Jr. 1994. Managing naturalistic environments in captivity. Pp. 125–141 in E.F. Gibbons, Jr., E.J. Wyers, E.J. Waters and E.W. Menzel, Jr., eds. *Naturalistic environments in captivity for animal behavior research.* State Univ. New York Press, Albany, NY.

Dolan, J. 1977. The saiga, *Saiga tatarica*, a review as a model for the management of endangered species. *Int'l. Zoo Yb.* 17:25–32.

Donaldson, E.M. and G.A. Hunter. 1983. Induced final maturation, ovulation, and spermiation in cultured fish. Pp. 351–403 in W.S Hoar, D.J. Randall and E.M. Donaldson, eds. *Fish physiology,* Vol. IXB. Academic Press, New York, NY.

DonCarlos, M.W., J.S. Peterson and R.L. Tilson. 1986. Captive biology of an asocial mustelid, *Mustela ermina*. *Zoo Biol.* 5:363–370.

Donham, R.S. 1979. Annual cycles of plasma luteinizing hormone and sex hormones in male and female mallards (*Anas platyrhynchos*). *Biol. Reprod.* 21:1273–1285.

Donoghue, A.M., L.A. Johnston, U.S. Seal, D.L. Armstrong, R.L. Tilson, P. Wolf, K. Petrini, L.G. Simmons, T. Gross and D.E. Wildt. 1990. *In vitro* fertilization and embryo development *in vitro* and *in vivo* in the tiger (*Panthera tigris*). *Biol Reprod.* 43:733–744.

Dorsey, E.M. 1983. Exclusive adjoining ranges in individually identified minke whales (*Balaenoptera acutorostrata*) in Washington state. *Can. J. Zool.* 61:174–181.

Dott, H.M. and M.N.P. Utsi. 1973. Artificial insemination of reindeer (*Rangifer tarandus*). *J. Zool. London* 170:505–508.

Dow, S.M. 1987. Environmental enrichment for captive primates and foxes. *Appl. Anim. Behav. Sci.* 18:383–390.

Doyle, L.L. and Chandler, G. 1973. *Erythrocebus patas*—an anatomically suitable primate model for reproductive studies. *Fertil. Steril.* 24:648–651.

Dresser, B. 1986. Embryo transfer in exotic bovids. *Int'l. Zoo Yb.* 24/25:138–142.

Dresser, B. and E. Maruska. 1988. Black rhino SSP report. *Amer. Assoc. Zool. Parks Aquar. Newsletter* 29:13–14.

Dresser, B. and E. Pope. 1989. Indian desert cats born to domestic cat at Cincinnati Zoo. *Amer. Assoc. Zool. Parks Aquar. Newsletter* 30:21.

Dresser, B.L., L. Kramer, B. Reece and P.T. Russell. 1982a. Induction of ovulation and successful artificial insemination in a Persian leopard (*Panthera pardus saxicolor*). *Zoo Biol.* 1:55–57.

Dresser, B.L., L. Kramer, R.D. Dahlhausen, C.E. Pope and R.D. Baker. 1984a. Cryopreservation followed by successful transfer of African eland antelope (*Tragelaphus oryx*) embryos. *Proc. 10th Int'l. Congr. Anim. Reprod. Artif. Insem.* 1984:191 (Abstr.). Univ. Ill., Urbana-Champaign, IL.

Dresser, B.L., L. Kramer, C.E. Pope, R.D. Dahlhausen and C. Blauser. 1982b. Superovulation of African eland (*Taurotragus oryx*) and interspecies embryo transfer to Holstein cattle. *Theriogenology* 17:86 (Abstr.).

Dresser, B., L. Kramer, P. Russell, G. Reed and B. Reece. 1981. Superovulation and artificial insemination in bengal tigers (*Panthera tigris*), African lions (*Panthera leo*) and a Persian leopard (*Panthera pardus saxicolor*). *Proc. Amer. Assoc. Zool. Parks Aquar.* 1981:149.

Dresser, B.L., C.E. Pope, L. Kramer, G. Kuehn, R.D. Dahlhausen and W.D. Thomas. 1984b. Superovulation of bongo antelope (*Tragelaphus euryceros*) and interspecies embryo transfer to African eland (*Tragelaphus oryx*). *Theriogenology* 21:232 (Abstr.).

Drewien, R.C. and E.G. Bizeau. 1977. Cross-fostering whooping cranes to sandhill crane foster parents. Pp. 201–222 in S.A. Temple, ed. *Endangered birds: Management techniques for preserving threatened species.* Univ. Wisconsin. Press, Madison, WI.

Drickamer, L.C. 1974. A ten-year summary of reproductive data for free-ranging *Macaca mulatta. Folia Primatol.* 21:61–80.

Drieschman, W.S. 1982. Zoo design III. *Proc. 3rd. Int'l. Symp. Zoo Design Construct.* Herbert Whitley Trust, Publ. 1982:48–51.

Driscoll, J., ed. 1989. *Animal care and use in behavioral research: Regulations, issues, and applications.* Anim. Inform. Center, U.S. Dept. Agricult., Washington, DC.

Drummond, B.A. 1984. Multiple mating and sperm competition in the Lepidoptera. Pp. 291–370 in R.L. Smith, ed. *Sperm competition and the evolution of animal mating systems.* Academic Press, New York, NY.

Drummond, H.D. 1983. Aquatic foraging in garter snakes: A comparison of specialists and generalists. *Behaviour* 8:1–30.

Dubey, A.K., C.P. Puri, V. Puri and R.C. Anand Kumar. 1983. Day and night levels of hormones in male rhesus monkeys kept under controlled or constant environmental light. *Experimentia* 39:207–209.

du Bois, T. 1991. Behavioral enrichment: Labors of love. *ZooView* 25:8–11.

du Bois, T. 1992. Los Angeles Zoo environmental enrichment program: We get a lot of help from our friends. *Proc. Amer. Assoc. Zool. Parks Aquar.* 1992:112–119.

Dubourg, P., E. Burzawa-Gerard, P. Chambolle and O. Kah. 1985. Light and electron microscopic identification of gonadotropic cells in the pituitary gland of the goldfish by means of immunocytchemistry. *Gen. Comp. Endocrinol.* 59:472–481.

Duellman, W.E. 1987. Lizards in an Amazonian rainforest community: Resource utilization and abundance. *Nat'l. Geogr. Res.* 3:489–500.

Duellman, W.E. and L. Trueb. 1986. *Biology of amphibians*. McGraw-Hill, New York, NY.

Dufau, M.L., G.D. Hodgen, A.L. Goodman and K.J. Catt. 1977. Bioassay of circulating luteinizing hormone in the rhesus monkey: Comparison with radioimmunoassay during physiological changes. *Endocrinolology* 100:1557–1565.

Duffey, D.C., F.S. Todd and W.R. Siegfried. 1987. Submarine foraging behavior of alcids in the artificial environment. *Zoo Biol.* 6:373–378.

Duffey, E. 1971. The management of Woodwalton Fen: A multidisciplinary approach. Pp. 581–597 in E. Duffey and A.S. Watt, eds. *The scientific management of animal and plant communities for conservation*. Symp. 11 of the British Ecol. Soc. Blackwell Sci. Pubs., Oxford, England.

Duffield, D.A. 1990. Genetic and physiological research applications in marine mammal medicine. Pp. 371–380 in L.A. Dierauf, ed. *CRC handbook of marine mammal medicine: Health, disease and rehabilitation*. CRC Press, Boca Raton, FL.

Duffield, D.A. and K.W. Miller. 1988. Demographic features of killer whales in oceanaria in the United States and Canada, 1965–1987. *Rit Fiskideildar* II:297–306.

Duffield, D.A. and R.S. Wells. 1986. *Population structure of bottlenose dolphins: (2) Genetic studies of bottlenose dolphins along the central west coast of Florida*. Pp. 1–10 in Final report to Nat'l. Marine Fish. Serv. S.E. Fish. Center. Contract #45-WCNF-5-00366. Miami, FL.

Duffield, D.A. and R.S. Wells. 1991. Bottlenose dolphins: Comparison of census data from dolphins in captivity with a wild population. *Int'l. Marine Anim. Trainers Assoc. Soundings*. Spring 1991:11–15.

Dufty, A.M., Jr. and J.C. Wingfield. 1986a. The influence of social cues on the reproductive endocrinology of male brown-headed cowbirds: Field and laboratory studies. *Hormones and Behav.* 20:222–234.

Dufty, A.M., Jr. and J.C. Wingfield. 1986b. Temporal patterns of circulating LH and steroid hormones in a brood parasite, the brown-headed cowbird, *Molothrus ater.* I. Males. *J. Zool. London* 208:191–203.

Dugan, B. 1982. The mating behavior of the green iguana *Iguana iguana.* Pp. 320–339 in G.M. Burghardt and A.S. Rand, eds. *Iguanas of the world: Their behavior, ecology, and conservation.* Noyes, Park Ridge, NJ.

Dukelow, W.R. 1970. Induction and timing of single and multiple ovulation in the squirrel monkey (*Saimiri sciureus*). *J. Reprod. Fertil.* 22:303–309.

Dukelow, W.R. 1971. Semen and artificial insemination. Pp. 115–127 in E.S.E. Hafez, ed. *Comparative reproduction of nonhuman primates.* C.C. Thomas, Springfield, IL.

Dukelow, W.R. 1983. The squirrel monkey (*Saimiri sciureus*). Pp. 149–179 in J.P. Hearn, ed. *Reproduction in New World primates.* MTP Press, Lancaster, England.

Dukelow, W.R. 1985. Reproductive cyclicity and breeding in the squirrel monkey. Pp. 169–190 in L.A. Rosenblum and C.L. Coe., eds. *Handbook of squirrel monkey research.* Plenum Press, New York, NY.

Dukelow, W.R. and S. Bruggemann. 1979. Characteristics of the menstrual cycle in nonhuman primates. II: Ovulation and optimal mating times in macaques. *J. Med. Primatol.* 8:79–87.

Dukelow, W.R., B. Fan and A.G. Sacco. 1986. Ovulation and corpus luteum formation. Pp. 263–275 in W.R. Dukelow and J. Erwin, eds. *Comparative Primate Biology, Vol 3: Reproduction and development.* Alan Liss, New York, NY.

Dulka, J.G. and L.S. Demski. 1986. Sperm duct contractions mediate centrally evoked sperm release in goldfish. *J. Exp. Zool.* 237:271–279.

Dulka, J.G., N.E. Stacey, P.W. Sorensen, G.J. Van Der Kraak and T.A. Marchant. 1987. A sex pheromone system in goldfish: Is the nervus terminalis involved? *Annals New York Acad. Sci.* 519:411–420.

DuMond, F.V. 1967. Semi free-ranging colonies of monkeys at Goulds Monkey Jungle. *Int'l. Zoo Yb.* 7:202–207.

DuMond, F.V. 1968. The squirrel monkey in a semi-natural environment. Pp. 87–145 in L.A. Rosenblum and R.W. Cooper, eds. *The squirrel monkey.* Academic Press, New York, NY.

DuMond, F.V. 1971. Comments on minimum requirements in the husbandry of the golden marmoset (*Leontopithecus rosalia*). *Lab. Primate Newsletter* 10:30–37.

DuMond, G. 1955. Typescript draft of the history of Monkey Jungle. Courtesy of the author, Monkey Jungle, Goulds, Florida.

Dunbar, R.I.M. 1983. Life history tactics and alternative strategies of reproduction. Pp. 423–433 in P. Bateson, ed. *Mate choice*. Cambridge Univ. Press, New York, NY.

Dunson, W.A., ed. 1975. *The biology of sea snakes*. Univ. Park Press, Baltimore, MD.

Duplaix-Hall, N. and J. Kear. 1975. Breeding requirements in captivity. Pp. 131–141 in J. Kear and N. Duplaix-Hall. *Flamingos*. T. & A.D. Poyser, Hertfordshire, England.

Durrant, B.S. 1983. Reproductive studies of the oryx. *Zoo Biol.* 2:191–197.

Durrant, B.S. 1987. Penetration of hamster ova by non-human primate spermatozoa. *J. Androl.* 8:27P (Abstr.).

Durrant, B.S. 1990. Semen collection, evaluation and cryopreservation in exotic animal species: Maximizing reproductive potential. *Instit. Lab. Anim. Resour. News* 32:2–9.

Durrant, B. and K. Benirschke. 1981. Embryo transfer in exotic animals. *Theriogenology* 15:77–83.

Durrant, B. and C. Burch. 1991. Successful artificial insemination of cryopreserved pheasant semen. *J. Androl.* 12:56 (Abstr.).

Durrant, B.S. and M.L. Hoge. 1988. Ultrasonography in Przewalski's horse mare, *Equus przewalskii*. *Theriogenology* 29:240 (Abstr.).

Durrant, B., T. Schuerman and S. Millard. 1985. Non-invasive semen collection in the cheetah (*Acinonyx jubatus*). *Proc. Amer. Assoc. Zool. Parks Aquar.* 1985:564–567.

Durrant, B.S., J.K. Yamada and S.E. Millard. 1989. Development of a semen cryopreservation protocol for the cheetah. *Cryobiol.* 26:542–543 (Abstr.).

Durrant, B.S., K.A. Biery, M.L. Patton and V. Smith. 1992a. Effects of prefreeze citrate exposure, cooling and thaw techniques on the cryosurvival of sperm from domestic and exotic equids. *J. Androl.* 13 Suppl. 1:71 (Abstr.).

Durrant, B.S., M.L. Patton, N.C. Pratt and K.A. Biery. 1992b. Effect of pre-freeze cooling and packaging on cryosurvival of cheetah sperm. *Biol. Reprod.* 46 Suppl 1:95 (Abstr.)

Durrant, B., P. Sarver, J. Yamada and J. Good. 1988. Semen evaluation and artificial insemination in pheasants. *Proc. Amer. Assoc. Zool. Parks Aquar.* 1988:27–30.

Durrell, G. 1976a. Pp. 80–85 in *The stationary ark*. Simon & Schuster, New York, NY.

Durrell, G. 1976b. *The stationary ark*. Simon & Schuster, New York, NY.

Durrell, L. 1986. *State of the ark*. Bodley Head, London, England.

Durrell, L. and J. Mallinson. 1987. Reintroduction as a political and educational tool for conservation. *Dodo* 24:6–19.

Duvall, D., B.M. Graves and G.C. Carpenter. 1987. Visual and chemical composite signaling effects of *Sceioporus* lizard fecal boli. *Copeia* 1987:1028–1031.

Duvall, D., L.J. Guillette, Jr. and R.E. Jones. 1984. Environmental control of reptilian reproductive cycles. Pp. 201–231 in C. Gans and F.H. Pough, eds. *Biology of the Reptilia*, Vol. 13. Academic Press, London, England.

Dwyer, W. and B. Rosenlund. 1988. Role of fish culture in the reestablishment of greenback cutthroat trout. *Amer. Fish. Soc. Symp.* 4:75–80.

Dym, M. 1973. The fine structure of the monkey (*Macaca*) sertoli cell and its role in maintaining the blood testis barrier. *Anat. Rec.* 175:639–656.

Easley, S.P., A.M. Coelho, W.R. Rogers and L.L. Taylor. 1990. Effects of 60-Hz electric field exposure on the social behavior of baboons: 60 kV/m. *Amer. J. Primatol.* 20:187–188 (Abstr.).

East, M.L. and H. Hofer. 1986. The use of radio-tracking for monitoring great tit, *Parus major*, behaviour: A pilot study. *Ibis* 128:103–114.

East, R. 1988. Antelopes. *Global survey and regional action plans. Part 1: East and northeast Africa*. Int'l. Union Conserv. Nature & Natur. Resour., Gland, Switzerland.

East, R. 1989. Antelopes. *Global survey and regional action plans. Part 2: Southern and south-eastern Africa*. Int'l. Union Conserv. Nature & Natur. Resour., Gland, Switzerland.

East, R. 1990. *Antelopes. Global survey and regional action plans. Part 3: West and central Africa*. Int'l. Union Conserv. Nature & Natur. Resour., Gland, Switzerland.

Eastcott, A. and T. Dickinson. 1987. Underwater observations of the suckling and social behavior of a new-born bottlenose dolphin (*Tursiops truncatus*). *Aquat. Mamm.* 13:51–56.

Eaton, G.G., K.B. Modahl and D.F. Johnson. 1981. Aggressive behavior in a confined troop of Japanese macaques: Effects of density, season, and gender. *Aggress. Behav.* 7:145–164.

Eaton, G.G., D.C. Rostal, B.B. Glick and J.W. Senner. 1987. Seasonal behavior in a confined troop of Japanese macaques (*Macaca fuscata*). In T. Miura, ed. Seasonal effects on reproduction, infection and psychoses. *Prog. Biometeorol.* 5:29–40.

Eaton, R.L. 1984. Survey of smaller felid breeding. *Zool. Garten N.F.* 54:101–120.

Eberhart, J.A. and E.B. Keverne. 1979. Influences of the dominance hierarchy on luteinizing hormone, testosterone and prolactin in male talapoin monkeys. *J. Endocrinol.* 83:42P–43P.

Echelle, A. 1973. Behavior of the pupfish, *Cyprinodon rubrofluviatilis*. *Copeia* 1973:68–76.

Echelle, A., C. Hubbs and A. Echelle. 1972. Developmental rates and tolerances of the Red River pupfish *Cyprinodon rubrofluviatilis*. *S.W. Natural.* 17:55–60.

Echelle, A., S. Wilson and L. Hill. 1973. The effects of four temperatures—day length combinations on ovogenesis in the Red River pupfish. *Cyprinodon rubrofluviatilis* (Cyprinodontidae). *S.W. Natural.* 18:229–239.

Eckstein, P. and S. Zuckerman. 1956. Morphology of the reproductive tract. Pp. 43–155 in G.E. Lamming, ed. *Marshall's physiology of reproduction,* Vol. 1., 3rd Ed. Longmans, Green & Co., London, England.

Edwards, D.R., W.A. Dickerson and N.C. Leppla. 1987. *Arthropod species in culture.* Entomol. Soc. Amer., College Park, MD.

Edwards, M.A. and U. McDonnell, eds. 1982. *Animal disease in relation to animal conservation. Symp. Zool. Soc. London,* Number 50. Academic Press, New York, NY.

Edwards, T.C., Jr. 1989. Similarities in the development of foraging mechanics among sibling ospreys. *Condor* 91:30–36.

Edwards, T.T. and M.W. Collopy. 1983. Obligate and facultative brood reduction in eagles: An examination of factors that influence fratricide. *Auk* 100:630–635.

Eems, M., R. Pinxten and R.F. Verheyen. 1991. Male song as a cue for mate choice in the European starling. *Behaviour* 116:210–238.

Ehara, A., T. Kimura, O. Takenaka and M. Iwamoto. 1991. Primatology today. *Proc. XIII Congr. Int'l. Primatol. Soc.* 1991:18–24. Elsevier, New York, NY.

Ehara, Y., K.J. Ryan and S.S.C. Yen. 1972. Insensitivity of synthetic LRF in LH-release of rhesus monkey. *Contraception* 6:465–478.

Ehrlich, P.R. 1965. The population biology of the butterfly, *Euphydryas editha,* II. The structure of the Jasper Ridge colony. *Evolution* 19:327–336.

Ehrlich, P.R. 1984. The structure and dynamics of butterfly populations. Pp. 25–40 in R.I. Vane-Wright and P.R. Ackery, eds. *The biology of butterflies: Symposium of the Royal Entomological Society of London,* No. 11. Academic Press, London, England.

Ehrlich, P.R. and L.C. Birch. 1967. The "balance of nature" and "population control." *Amer. Natural.* 101:97–107.

Ehrlich, P.R. and S.E. Davidson. 1960. Techniques for capture–recapture studies of Lepidoptera populations. *J. Lepidopt. Soc.* 14:227–229.

Ehrlich, P.R. and D.D. Murphy. 1987. Conservation lessons from long-term studies of checkerspot butterflies. *Conserv. Biol.* 1:122–131.

Ehrlich, P.R. and E.O. Wilson. 1991. Biodiversity studies: Science and policy. *Science* 253:758–761.

Ehrlich, P.R., D.D. Murphy and B.A. Wilcox. 1988. Islands in the desert. *Natur. Hist.* 97:59–64.

Ehrlich, P.R., R.R. White, M.C. Singer, S.W. McKechnie and L.E. Gilbert. 1975. Checkerspot butterflies: A historical perspective. *Science* 188:221–228.

Eisenbeis, G. and W. Wichard. 1987. *Atlas of the biology of soil arthropods.* Springer-Verlag, New York, NY.

Eisenberg, J.F. 1966. The social organization of mammals. *Handbk. Zool.* 39:1–92.

Eisenberg, J.F. 1981. *The mammalian radiations.* Univ. Chicago Press, Chicago, IL.

Eisenberg, J.F. 1986. Life history strategies of the Felidae: Variations on a common theme. Pp. 293–303 in S.D. Miller and D.D. Everett, eds. *Cats of the world.* Nat'l. Wildl. Fed., Washington, DC.

Eisenberg, J.F. and E. Gould. 1967. The maintenance of tenrecoid insectivores in captivity. *Int'l. Zoo Yb.* 7:194–196.

Eisenberg, J.F. and E. Gould. 1970. The tenrecs: A study in mammalian behavior and evolution. *Smithson. Contrib. Zool.* 27:1–137.

Eisenberg, J.F. and D.E. Isaac. 1963. The reproduction of heteromyid rodents in captivity. *J. Mammal.* 44:61–67.

Eisenberg, J.F. and D.G. Kleiman. 1977. The usefulness of behaviour studies in developing captive breeding programmes for mammals. *Int'l. Zoo Yb.* 17:81–89.

Eisenberg, J.F. and E. Maliniak. 1974. The reproduction of the genus *Microgale* in captivity. *Int'l. Zoo Yb.* 14:108–110.

Eisner, T. 1970. Chemical defense against predation in arthropods. Pp. 157–218 in E. Sondheimer and J.B. Simeone, eds. *Chemical ecology.* Academic Press, New York, NY.

Eisner, T. 1980. Chemistry, defense and survival: Case studies and selected topics. Pp. 847–878 in M. Locke and D.S. Smith, eds. *Insect biology in the future*. Academic Press, New York, NY.

Elbin, S.B. 1990. Multiple methods of identifying individual Waldrapp ibis *Geronticus eremita*. *Proc. Amer. Assoc. Zool. Parks Aquar*. 1990:208–215.

Eldredge, N., ed. 1992. *Systematics, ecology, and the biodiversity crisis*. Columbia Univ. Press, New York, NY.

El Halawani, M.E., W.H. Burke and P.T. Dennison. 1980a. Effect of nest-deprivation on serum prolactin level in nesting female turkeys. *Biol. Reprod*. 23:118–123.

El Halawani, M.E., W.H. Burke and L.A. Ogren. 1980b. Involvement of catecholaminergic mechanisms in the photoperiodically-induced rise in serum luteinizing hormone of Japanese quail (*Coturnix coturnix japonica*). *Gen. Comp. Endocrinol*. 41:14–21.

El Halawani, M.E., W.H. Burke, P.T. Dennison and J.L Silsby. 1982. Neuropharmacological aspects of neural regulation of avian endocrine function. In C.G. Scanes, A. Epple and M.H. Stetson, eds. Aspects of avian endocrinology: Practical and theoretical implications. *Grad. Studies Texas Tech. Univ*. 26:33–40.

El Halawani, M.E., W.H. Burke, J.L. Silsby, E.J. Behnke and S.C. Fehrer. 1984. Effect of ambient temperature on serum prolactin and luteinizing hormone levels during the reproductive cycle of the female turkey (*Meleagris gallopavo*). *Biol Reprod*. 30:809–815.

Elias, E., E. Bedrak and D. Cohen. 1985. Induction of oestrus in the camel (*Camelus dromedarius*) during seasonal anoestrus. *J. Reprod. Fertil*. 74:519–525.

Elliason, J.J., T.C. Johanos and M.A. Webber. 1990. Parturition in the Hawaiian monk seal (*Monachus schauinslani*). *Marine Mamm. Sci*. 6:145–151.

Ellis, D.H., S.J. Dobrett and J.G. Goodwin. 1978. Reintroduction techniques for masked bobwhites. Pp. 345–353 in S.A. Temple, ed. *Endangered birds: Management techniques for preserving threatened species*. Univ. Wisconsin. Press, Madison, WI.

Ellis-Joseph, S.A. 1988. Factors contributing to reproductive success in Adelie penguins (*Pygoscelis adeliae*) housed in a controlled environment. Ph.D. Dissertation. Univ. California, Davis, CA.

Ellis-Joseph, S. 1990. Patterns of incubation behavior in captive-housed Adelie penguins: Implications for long-term penguin breeding programs. *Regional Proc. Amer. Assoc. Zool. Parks Aquar*. 1990:115–120.

Els, D.A. 1981. The anatomy of the female reproductive tract of the springbok (*Antidorcas marsupials*). *J. S. Afr. Vet. Assoc.* 52:29–32.

ElWishy, A.B. 1988. A study of the genital organs of the female dromedary (*Camelus dromedarius*). *J. Reprod. Fertil.* 73:337–342.

Emlen, S.T. 1976. Lek organization and mating strategies in the bullfrog. *Behav. Ecol. Sociobiol.* 1:283–313.

Emlen, S.T., N.J. Demong and D.J. Emlen. 1989. Experimental induction of infanticide in female wattled jacanas. *Auk* 106:1–7.

Emmel, T.C. and R. Boender. 1991. Wings in paradise: Florida's Butterfly World. *Wings* 15:7–12.

Enders, A.C. and S. Schlafke. 1986. Implantation in nonhuman primates and in the human. Pp. 291–310 in W.R. Dukelow and J. Erwin, eds. *Comparative Primate Biology, Vol 3: Reproduction and development.* Alan Liss, New York, NY.

Engelmann, F. 1970. *The physiology of insect reproduction.* Pergamon Press, Oxford, England.

Engles, W.L. 1969. Photoperiodically-induced testicular recrudescence in the transequatorial migrant dolichonyx relative to natural photoperiods. *Biol. Bull.* 137:256–264.

Epple, G. 1970. Maintenance, breeding and development of marmoset monkeys (Callithricidae) in captivity. *Folia Primatol.* 12:56–76.

Erickson, R.C. 1968. A federal research program for endangered wildlife. *Trans. 33rd N. Amer. Wildl. Nat'l. Resource Confr.* 1968:418–433.

Erkert, H.G. 1989. Lighting requirements of nocturnal primates in captivity: A chronological approach. *Zoo Biol.* 8:179–191.

Erwin, J. 1979. Aggression in captive macaques: Interaction of social and spatial factors. Pp. 139–171 in J. Erwin, T. Maple and G. Mitchell, eds. *Captivity and behavior.* Van Nostrand, New York, NY.

Erwin, J. and R. Deni. 1979. Strangers in a strange land: Abnormal behaviors or abnormal environments? Pp. 1–28 in J. Erwin, T. Maple and G. Mitchell, eds. *Captivity and behavior.* Van Nostrand Reinhold, New York, NY.

Erwin, T. 1982. Tropical forests: Their richness in Coleoptera and other arthropod species. *The Coleopt. Bull.* 36:74–75.

Erwin, T. 1983a. Tropical forest canopies: The last biotic frontier. *Bull. Entomol. Soc. Amer.* 29:14–19.

Erwin, T. 1983b. Beetles and other insects of tropical forest canopies at Manaus, Brazil, samples by insecticidal fogging. Pp. 59–75 in S.L. Sutton,

T.C. Whitmore and A.C. Chadwick, eds. *Tropical rain forest: Ecology and management*. Blackwell Sci. Pubs, Edinburgh, Scotland.

Essapian, F.S. 1953. The birth and growth of a porpoise. *Natur. Hist.* 62:392–399.

Essapian, F.S. 1963. Observation on abnormalities of parturition in captive bottlenosed dolphins, *Tursiops truncatus*, and concurrent behavior of other porpoises. *J. Mammal.* 44:405–414.

Essock, S.M. and D.M. Rumbaugh. 1977. Development and measurement of cognitive capabilities in captive nonhuman primates. Pp. 47–61 in H. Markowitz and V.J. Stevens, eds. *Behavior of captive wild animals*. Nelson-Hall, Chicago, IL.

Estes, R.D. 1990a. USA: Texas, land of exotic ungulates. *Antelope Spec. Group Gnusletter* 9:12–13.

Estes, R.D. 1990b. Captive breeding; breeding endangered species on ranches. *Antelope Spec. Group Gnusletter* 9:8–9.

Eudey, A.A. 1987. *Action plan for Asian primate conservation: 1987–91*. Int'l. Union Conserv. Nature & Natur. Resour./Species Survival Commiss. Primate Specialist Group. Stony Brook, NY.

Evans, D.D., ed. 1982. *The management of Australian mammals in captivity*. Proc. Aust. Mamm. Soc., 1979. Ramsey Ware Stockland, Victoria, Australia.

Evans, D.L. and J.O. Schmidt, eds. 1990. *Insect defenses: Adaptive mechanisms and strategies of prey and predators*. State Univ. New York Press, Albany, NY.

Evans, R.M. 1980. Colony desertion and reproductive synchrony of black-billed gulls *Larus bulleri*. *Ibis* 124:491–501.

Evans, W.E. 1974. Radio-telemetric studies of two species of small odontocete cetaceans. Pp. 385–394 in W.E. Schevill, ed. *The whale problem*. Harvard Univ. Press, Cambridge, MA.

Evans, W.E. and J. Bastian. 1969. Marine mammal communication: Social and ecological factors. Pp. 425–474 in H.T. Andersen, ed. *The biology of marine mammals*. Academic Press, New York, NY.

Evans, W.E. and B.A. Powell. 1967. Discrimination of different metallic plates by an echolocating Delphinid. Pp. 363–383 in R.G. Busnel, ed. *Animal sonar systems: Biology and bionics*. Laboratoire de Physiologie Acoustique, Jouy-en-Josas, France.

Evans, W.E., W.W. Sutherland and R.G. Berl. 1964. The directional characteristics of Delphinid sounds. Pp. 353–372 in W.N. Tavolga, ed. *Marine bioacoustics*. Pergamon Press, New York, NY.

642 *References*

Evans, W.E., J.D. Hall, A.B. Irvine and J.S. Leatherwood. 1972. Methods for tagging small cetaceans. *Fish. Bull.* 70:61–65.

Ewbank, R. 1985. Behavioral response to stress in farm animals. Pp. 71–80 in G.P. Moberg, ed. *Animal stress.* Amer. Physiol. Soc., Bethesda, MD.

Ewer, R.F. 1973. *The Carnivores.* Cornell Univ. Press, Ithaca, NY.

Ewing, L.L. 1982. Seasonal variation in primate fertility with an emphasis on the male. *Amer. J. Primatol.* Suppl. 1:145–160.

Fa, J.E. 1984. Structure and dynamics of the Barbary macaque population in Gibralter. Pp. 263–306 in J.E. Fa, ed. *The Barbary macaque: A case study in conservation.* Plenum Press, New York, NY.

Fairfax, R.Z. 1982. Notes on the scaly-tailed possum *Wyulda squamicaudata* in captivity. Pp. 73–74 in D.D. Evans, ed. *The management of Australian mammals in captivity.* Proc. Austral. Mamm. Soc. 1979. Ramsey Ware Stockland, Victoria, Australia.

Falk, H. and E. Gwinner. 1983. Photoperiodic control of testicular regression in the European starling. *Die Naturwissenschaften* 70:257–258.

FAO (Food and Agriculture Organization). 1986. *Farming snails.* Food and Agricult. Organ. Econ. and Soc. Develop. Series. No. 3/33. Rome, Italy.

Farner, D.S. 1959. Photoperiodic control of annual gonadal cycles in birds. Pp. 716–750 in *Photoperiodism and related phenomena in plants and animals.* Publ. No. 55. Amer. Assoc. Advance. Sci. Washington, DC.

Farner, D.S. 1961. Comparative physiology: Photoperiodicity. *Ann. Rev. Physiol.* 23:71–96.

Farner, D.S. 1964. The photoperiodic control of reproductive cycles in birds. *Amer. Sci.* 52:137–156.

Farner, D.S. 1986. Generation and regulation of annual cycles in migratory passerine birds. *Amer. Zool* 26:493–501.

Farner, D.S. and R.A. Lewis. 1971. Photoperiodism and reproductive cycles in birds. Pp. 325–370 in A.C. Giese, ed. *Current topics in photobiology and photochemistry,* Vol. 6. Academic Press, New York, NY.

Farner, D.S., R.S. Donham, K.S. Matt, P.W. Mattocks, Jr., M.C. Moore and J.C. Wingfield. 1983. The nature of photorefractoriness. Pp. 149–166 in S. Mikami, K. Homma and M. Wada, eds. *Avian endocrinology: Environmental and ecological perspectives.* Japan Sci. Soc. Press, Tokyo, Japan/ Springer-Verlag, Berlin, Germany.

Farrell, B.D. and T.L. Erwin. 1988. Leaf-beetle community structure in an Amazonian rainforest canopy. Pp. 73–90 in P. Jolivet, E. Petitpierre and T.H. Hsiao, eds. *Biology of Chrysomelidae.* Kluvier Academic, The Hague, Netherlands.

Farwell, C.J. and J. Hymer. 1988. Sea otter water quality management with regard to coliforms. *Proc. Amer. Assoc. Zool. Parks Aquar.* 1988:344–348.

Farwell, C.J., T. Williams and J. Hymer. 1988. Deviations in water quality data for the Monteray Bay Aquarium sea otter display. *Proc. Int'l. Assoc. Aquat. Anim. Med.* 1988:72–74.

Fast, A.W. 1986. Pond production systems: Water quality management practices. Pp. 141–167 in J.E. Lannan, R. Oneal Smitherman and G. Tchobanoglous, eds. *Principles and practices of pond aquaculture.* Oregon State Univ. Press, Corvallis, OR.

Faulk, E.Y. 1990. Water quality considerations for marine mammals. Pp. 537–542 in L.A. Dierauf, ed. *CRC handbook of marine mammal medicine: Health, disease and rehabilitation.* CRC Press, Boca Raton, FL.

Faulkes, C.G., D.H. Abbott and J.U.M. Jarvis. 1990. Social suppression of ovarian cyclicity in captive and wild colonies of naked mole-rats, *Heterocephalus glaber. J. Reprod. Fertil.* 88:559–568.

Feare, C.J. and I.R. Inglis. 1979. The effects of reduction of feeding space on the behaviour of captive starlings, *Sternus vulgarus. Ornis Scand.* 10:42–47.

Fedigan, L.M. 1976. A study of roles in the Arashiyama West troop of Japanese monkeys (*Macaca fuscata*). *Contr. Primatol.* 9:1–95.

Fedigan, L.M. and P.J. Asquith. 1991. *The monkeys of Arashiyama, thirty-five years of research in Japan and the west.* State Univ. New York Press, Albany, NY.

Feldmeth, C.R. and J. Basken. 1976. Thermal and respiratory studies with reference to temperature and oxygen tolerance for the unarmored stickleback, *Gasterosteus aculeatus williamsoni* Hubbs. *Bull. S. California Acad. Sci.* 75:127–131.

Feldmeth, C.R., D. Soltz, L. McClanahan, J. Jones and J. Irwin. 1985. Natural resources of the Lake Seep system (China Lake, CA.) with special emphasis on the Mojave chub (*Gila bicolor mohavensis*). *Proc. Desert Fish. Council* 15:356–358.

Felleman, F.L., J.R. Heimlich-Boran, and R.W. Osborne. 1991. The feeding ecology of killer whales (*Orcinus orca*) in the Pacific northwest. Pp. 113–147 in K. Pryor and K.S. Norris, eds. *Dolphin Societies.* Univ. California Press, Berkeley, CA

Fentzloff, C. 1984. Breeding, artificial incubation and release of white-tailed sea eagles, *Haliaeetus albicilla. Int'l. Zoo Yb.* 23:18–35.

Ferguson, M.W.J. 1989. Birth defects in American alligators. P. 98 in C.A. Ross, ed. *Crocodiles and alligators.* Facts on File, Inc., New York, NY.

Ferner, J.W. 1979. *A review of marking techniques for amphibians and reptiles.* Soc. Study Amphib. Reptiles Contrib. Herpetol., Oxford, OH.

Fiennes, R. 1966. Feeding animals in captivity. *Int'l. Zoo Yb.* 6:58–67.

Fine, M.L., H.E. Winn and B.I. Olla. 1977. Communication in fishes. Pp. 472–518 in T.A. Sebeok, ed. *How animals communicate.* Indiana Univ. Press, Bloomington, IN.

Finlay, T.W. and T.L. Maple. 1986. A survey of research in American zoos and aquariums. *Zoo Biol.* 5:261–268.

Finlay, T.W., L.R. James and T.L. Maple. 1988. People's perception of animals: The influence of zoo environments. *Environ. Behav.* 20:508–528.

Fisher, R.A., W. Putt, A.M. Scott, C.M. Hawkey, P.D. Butcher, D.G. Ashton and P. Bircher. 1979. Gene markers in 40 Przewalski horses, *Equus przewalskii. Int'l. Zoo Yb.* 19:228–235.

Fisher, W.R. and N.C. Leppla. 1985. Insectary design and operation. Pp. 167–183 in P. Singh and R.F. Moore, eds. *Handbook of insect rearing,* Vol. 1. Elsevier, Amsterdam, Netherlands.

Fitch, H.S. 1954. Life history and ecology of the five-lined skink, *Eumeces fasciatus. Univ. Kans. Mus. Natur. Hist. Pub.* 8:1–156.

Fitch, H.S. 1956. An ecological study of the collared lizard (*Crotophytus collaris*). *Univ. Kans. Mus. Natur. Hist. Pub.* 8:213–274.

Fitch, H.S. 1970. Reproductive cycles of lizards and snakes. *Univ. Kans. Mus. Natur. Hist. Misc. Pub.* 52:1–247.

Fitch-Snyder, H. and D.G. Lindburg. 1990. Nighttime is the norm: Labor and birth in the lion-tailed macaque. *Zoonooz* 63:13–14.

Flanigan, M.J. 1972. Marine mammals: The central nervous system. Pp. 215–246 in S. Ridgway, ed. *Mammals of the sea: Biology and medicine.* Charles C. Thomas, Springfield, IL.

Fleming, A.D., R. Yanagimachi and H. Yanagimachi. 1981. Spermatozoa of the Atlantic bottlenose dolphin *Tursiops truncatus. J. Reprod. Fertil.* 63:509–514.

Flesness, N.R. 1986. Captive status and genetic considerations. Pp. 845–856 in K. Benirschke, ed. *Primates: The road to self-sustaining populations.* Springer-Verlag, New York, NY.

Flesness, N.R. and T.J. Foose. 1990. The role of captive breeding in the conservation of species. Pp. xi–xv in *1990 IUCN red list of threatened animals.* Int'l. Union Conserv. Nature & Natur. Resources Monitoring Centre, Cambridge, England.

Flesness, N.R. and G.M. Mace. 1988. Population databases and zoological conservation. *Int'l. Zoo Yb.* 27:42–49.

Fletcher, L.W., H.V. Claborn, J.P. Turner and E. Lopez. 1968. Difference in response of two strains of screw-worm flies to male pheromones. *J. Econ. Entomol.* 61:1386–1388.

Fletcher, W.J. and A.J. Underwood. 1987. Interspecific competition among subtidal limpets: Effect of substratum heterogeneity. *Ecology* 68:387–400.

Flieg, G.M., H. Foerster and H. Sanders. 1971. Penguin exhibit at St. Louis Zoo. *Int'l. Zoo Yb.* 11:67–73.

Flink, A.P.F., M.B. Renfree and B.J. Weir, eds. 1981. Embryonic diapause in mammals. *J. Reprod. Fertil.* Suppl. 29.

Flower, S.S. 1931. Contributions to our knowledge of the duration of life in vertebrate animals, 5: Mammals. *Proc. Zool. Soc. London* 5:145–234.

Floyd, D. 1987. *Keeping stick insects.* Floyd Pub., Nottingham, England.

Flynn, T. 1987. Conditions and treatment of an eating disorder in a Pacific walrus — an anecdotal report. *Proc. Int'l. Marine Anim. Trainers Assoc.* 1987:39–46.

Fontaine, M. 1976. Hormones and the control of reproduction in aquaculture. *J. Fish. Res. Board Canada* 33:922–939.

Fontaine, R. and M. Hench. 1982. Breeding New World monkeys at Miami's Monkey Jungle. *Int'l. Zoo Yb.* 22:77–84.

Foose, T.J. 1983. The relevance of captive populations to the conservation of biotic diversity. Pp. 374–401 in C.M. Schonewald-Cox, S. Chambers, B. MacBride and W.L. Thomas, eds. *Genetics and conservation: A reference for managing wild animal and plant populations.* Benjamin Cummings, London, England.

Foose, T.J. 1986. Riders of the last ark: The role of captive breeding in conservation strategies. Pp. 141–165 in L. Kaufman and K. Mallory, ed. *The last extinction.* Mass. Instit. Tech. Press, Cambridge, MA.

Foose, T.J. 1987a. Sumatran rhino born at Melake Zoo in Malaysia. *Amer. Assoc. Zool. Parks Aquar. Newsletter* 28:22.

Foose, T.J. 1987b. A strategic view of the history, status and prospects of Cervidae in captivity. Pp. 467–479 in C. Wemmer, ed. *Biology and management of the Cervidae.* Smithsonian Instit. Press, Washington, DC.

Foose, T.J. 1988. Conservation coordinator's report. *Amer. Assoc. Zool. Parks Aquar. Newsletter* 29:5.

Foose, T.J. 1989. Conservation director's report. *Amer. Assoc. Zool. Parks Aquar. Newsletter* 30:12.

Foose, T.J. and J.D. Ballou. 1988. Management of small populations. *Int'l. Zoo Yb.* 27:26–41.

Foose, T.J., U.S. Seal and N.R. Flesness. 1987. Captive propagation as a component of conservation strategies for endangered primates. Pp. 263–299 in C.W. March and R.A. Mittermeier, eds. *Primate conservation in the tropical rain forest.* Alan Liss, New York, NY.

Foose, T.J., R. Lande, N.R. Flesness, G. Rabb and B. Read. 1986. Propagation plans. *Zoo Biol.* 5:139–146.

Ford, D. 1981. Small aquaria. Pp. 149–170 in A.D. Hawkins, ed. *Aquarium systems.* Academic Press, New York, NY.

Ford, J.K. and H.D. Fisher, 1982. Killer whale (*Orcinus orca*) dialects as an indicator of stocks in British Columbia. *Report Int'l. Whaling Commiss.* 32:671–680. Cambridge, England.

Ford, S.M. 1986. Systematics of the New World monkeys. Pp. 73–135 in D.R. Swindler and J. Erwin, eds. *Comparative primate biology, Vol. 1: Systematics, evolution, and anatomy.* Alan Liss, New York, NY.

Foresman, K.R. and J.C. Daniel. 1983. Plasma progesterone concentrations in pregnant and non-pregnant black bears (*Ursus americanus*). *J. Reprod. Fertil.* 68:235–239.

Forsberg, M., J.A. Fougner, P.O. Hofmo and E.J. Einarsson. 1990. Effect of melatonin implants on reproduction in the male silver fox (*Vulpes vulpes*). *J. Reprod. Fertil.* 88:383–388.

Forthman, D.L. and R. Bakeman. 1992. Environmental and social influences on enclosure use and activity patterns of captive sloth bears (*Ursus ursinus*). *Zoo Biol.* 11:405–415.

Forthman, D.L. and J.J. Ogden. 1992. The role of behavior analysis in zoo management: Today and tomorrow. *J. Appl. Behav. Anal.* 25:647–652.

Forthman, D.L., S.D. Elder, R. Bakeman, T.W. Kurkowski, C.C. Noble and S.W. Winslow. 1992. Effects of feeding enrichment on behavior of three species of captive bears. *Zoo Biol.* 11:187–195.

Forthman Quick, D.L. 1984. An integrative approach to environmental engineering in zoos. *Zoo Biol.* 3:65–77.

Forthman Quick, D.L. 1986. Activity budgets and the consumption of human foods in two troops of baboons (*Papio anubis*) at Gilgil, Kenya. Pp. 221–228 in J.C. Else and P.C. Lee, eds. *Proc. Xth Congr. Int'l. Primatol. Soc. Vol. 2: Primate ecology and conservation.* Cambridge Univ. Press, New York, NY.

Forthman Quick, D.L. and M.W. Demment. 1988. The dynamics of exploitation: Differential energetic adaptations of two troops of baboons to recent human contact. Pp. 25–51 in J.E. Fa and C.H. Southwick, eds. *The ecology and behaviour of food enhanced primate groups.* Alan Liss, New York, NY.

Forthman Quick, D.L. and T.C. Pappas. 1986. Enclosure utilization, activity budgets and social behavior of captive chamois (*Rupicapra rupicapra*) during the rut. *Zoo Biol.* 5:281–292.

Foster-Turley, P. and H. Markowitz. 1982. A captive behavioral enrichment study with Asian small-clawed river otters (*Aonyx cinerea*). *Zoo Biol.* 1:29–43.

Foster-Turley, P., S. Macdonald and C. Mason. 1990. *Otters: An action plan for their conservation*. Int'l. Union Conserv. Nature & Natur. Resour., Gland, Switzerland.

Fostier, A., B. Jalabert, R. Billard, B. Breton and Y. Zohar. 1983. The gonadal steroids. Pp. 277–372 in W.S. Hoar, D.J. Randall and E.M. Donaldson, eds. *Fish physiology,* Vol. IXA. Academic Press, New York, NY.

Fox, H. 1923. *Disease in captive wild mammals and birds: Incidence, description, comparison.* J.P. Lippincott, Philadelphia, PA.

Fox, H. 1977. The urogenital system of reptiles. Pp. 1–158 in C. Gans and T.S. Parsons, eds. *Biology of the reptilia,* Vol. 6. Academic Press, New York, NY.

Fradrich, H. 1980. Breeding endangered cervids in captivity. *Int'l. Zoo Yb.* 20:80–89.

Fraenkel, G. and D.L. Gunn. 1940. *The orientation of animals.* Monographs in Animal Behavior. Clarendon Press, Oxford, England.

Frakes, T.A. and J.R. Hoff. 1983. Mass propagation techniques currently being used in the spawning and rearing of marine fish species. *Zoo Biol.* 2:225–234.

Frampton, T. 1989. Captive breeding of black-bellied seed crackers. *Int'l. Zoo Yb.* 27:270–272.

France, J.J., R.J. Seddon and G.C. Liggins. 1973. A study of a pregnancy with low estrogen production due to placental sulfatase deficiency. *J. Clin. Endocrinol. Metab.* 36:1–9.

Francis-Floyd, R. 1988. Behavioral diagnosis. In M.K. Stoskopf, ed. Tropical fish medicine. *Vet. Clinics of North America: Small Anim. Practice* 18:305–316.

Frank, L.G. 1986a. Social organization of the spotted hyaena (*Crocuta crocuta*). I: Demography. *Anim. Behav.* 34:1500–1509.

Frank, L.G. 1986b. Social organization of the spotted hyaena (*Crocuta crocuta*). II: Dominance and reproduction. *Anim. Behav.* 34:1510–1527.

Frank, L.G., J.M. Davidson and E.R. Smith. 1985. Androgen levels in the spotted hyaena *Crocuta crocuta*: The influence of social factors. *J. Zool. Soc. London* 206:525–531.

Frankel, O.H. and M.E. Soulé. 1981. *Conservation and evolution*. Cambridge Univ. Press, New York, NY.

Frankenberg, O., E. von Herrlinger and W. Bergerhausen. 1984. Reintroduction of the European eagle owl *Bubo b. bubo* in the Federal Republic of Germany. *Int'l. Zoo Yb.* 23:95–100.

Frankham, R., H. Hemmer, O.A. Ryder, E.G. Cothran, M.E. Soulé, N.D. Murray and M. Snyder. 1986. Selection in captive populations. *Zoo Biol.* 5:127–138.

Franklin, I. 1980. Evolutionary change in small populations. Pp. 135–149 in M.E. Soulé and B.A. Wilcox, eds. *Conservation biology: An evolutionary-ecological perspective*. Sinauer Assoc., Sunderland, MA.

Frawley, L.S. and J.D. Neill. 1979. Age-related changes in serum levels of gonadotropins and testosterone in infantile male rhesus monkeys. *Biol. Reprod.* 20:1147–1155.

Free, J.B. 1982. *Bees and mankind*. George Allan & Unwin, London, England.

Freed, L.A. 1986. Territory takeover and sexually selected infanticide in tropical house wrens. *Behav. Ecol. Sociobiol.* 19:197–206.

French, J.A., D.H. Abbott and C.T. Snowdon. 1984. The effect of social environment on estrogen excretion, scent marking, and sociosexual behavior in tamarins (*Saguinus oedipus*). *Amer. J. Primatol.* 6:155–167.

Frith, C.B. 1962. *The Malee-fowl*. Angus & Robertson, Sydney, Australia.

Frith, C.B. 1976. Displays of the red bird of paradise *Paradisaea rubra* and their significance, with a discussion on displays and systematics of the other Paradisaeidae. *Emu* 76:69–78.

Frohlich, D.R. and V.J. Tepedino. 1986. Sex ratio, parental investment and interparent variability in nesting success in a solitary bee. *Evolution* 40:142–151.

Fry, C.H. 1984. *The bee-eaters*. Buteo Books, Vermillion, SD.

Frye, F.L. 1973. *Husbandry, medicine and surgery in captive reptiles*. V.M. Pub., Bonner Springs, KS.

Frye, F.L. 1984. Nutritional disorders in reptiles. Pp. 633–660 in G.L. Hoff, F.L. Frye and E.R. Jacobson, eds. *Diseases of amphibians and reptiles*. Plenum Press, New York, NY.

Frye, F.L. 1992. *Captive invertebrates: A guide to their biology and husbandry*. Krieger Pub., Malabar, FL.

Fujihara, N., H. Nishiyama and N. Nakashima. 1976. Studies on the accessory reproductive organs in the drake. 2: Macroscopic and microscopic observations on the cloaca of the drake with special reference to the ejaculatory groove region. *Poult. Sci.* 55:927–935.

Fullagar, P.J. 1985. The woodhens of Lord Howe Island. *Avicult. Mag.* 91:15–30.

Furse, M.T., J.F. Wright, P.D. Armitage and D. Moss. 1981. An appraisal of pond-net samples for biological monitoring of lotic macro-invertebrates. *Water Resour.* 15:679–689.

Futuyma, D.J. 1979. *Evolutionary biology.* Sinauer Assoc., Sunderland, MA.

Fyfe, R.W. 1975. Breeding peregrine and prairie falcons in captivity. Pp. 134–141 in R.D. Martin, ed. *Breeding endangered species in captivity.* Academic Press, London, England.

Fyfe, R.W. 1978. Reintroducing birds into the wild. Pp. 323–329 in S.A. Temple, ed. *Endangered birds: Management techniques for preserving threatened species.* Univ. Wisconsin. Press, Madison, WI.

Gage, L.J. 1986. The California marine mammal center: Operation of a rehabilitation center for pinnipeds. *Proc. Amer. Assoc. Zoo Vet.* 1986:105 (Abstr.).

Gage, L.J. 1987. Hand rearing pinniped pups. *Proc. 1st Int'l Conf. Zool. & Avian Med.* 1987:396 (Abstr.).

Gage, L.J. 1990a. Hand rearing pinniped pups. Pp. 533–535 in L.A. Dierauf, ed. *Handbook of marine mammal medicine: Health, disease, and rehabilitation.* CRC Press, Boca Raton, FL.

Gage, L.J. 1990b. Rescue and rehabilitation of cetaceans. Pp. 685–692 in L.A. Dierauf, ed. *CRC handbook of marine mammal medicine: Health, disease and rehabilitation.* CRC Press, Boca Raton, FL.

Gage, L.J., D. Vandenbroek and L. Amaya. 1985. Common medical problems encountered in pinnipeds at the California marine mammal center. *Proc. Int'l. Assoc. Aquatic Anim. Med.* 1985:42–43.

Gagne, W.C. 1988. Conservation priorities in Hawaiian natural systems. *BioScience* 38:264–271.

Gale, J.R. 1987. Cryopreservation of semen from endangered crane species. Master's Thesis, Univ. Wisconsin, Madison, WI.

Gall, L.F. 1984a. The effects of capturing and marking on subsequent activity in *Boloria acrocnema* (Lepidoptera; Nymphalidae), with a comparison of different numerical models that estimate population size. *Biol. Conserv.* 28:139–154.

Gall, L.F. 1984b. Population structure and recommendations for conservation of the narrowly endemic alpine butterfly, *Boloria acrocnema* (Lepidoptera: Nymphalidae). *Biol. Conserv.* 28:111–138.

Gamble, M.R. 1982. Sound and its significance for laboratory animals. *Biol. Rev.* 57:395–421.

Gans, C. and others. 1969–1992. *Biology of reptilia* series. Vol. 1–13, Academic Press, New York, NY.; Vol. 14–16, John Wiley & Sons, New York, NY.; Vol. 17–18, Univ. Chicago Press, Chicago, IL.

Gans, C., J.D. Gillingham and D.L. Clark. 1984. Courtship, mating and male combat in tuatara, *Sphenodon punctatus. J. Herpetol.* 18:194–197.

Ganzhorn, D. and P. Licht. 1983. Regulation of seasonal gonadal cycles by temperature in the painted turtle *Chrysemys picta. Copeia* 1983:347–358.

Garcia, J., D.L. Forthman Quick and B. White. 1984. Conditioned fear and disgust from mollusk to monkey. Pp. 47–61 in E.L. Alkon and J. Farley, eds. *Primary neural substrates of learning and behavioral change.* Cambridge Univ. Press, New York, NY.

Garner, R.L. 1892. *The speech of monkeys (Die Sprache der Affen).* Webster, New York, NY.

Garner, R.L. 1896a. *Gorillas and chimpanzees.* Osgood and McIlvaine, London, England.

Garner, R.L. 1896b. *Apes and monkeys; their life and language.* Ginn & Co., Boston, MA.

Garnier, D.H. 1985a. Androgen and estrogen levels in the plasma of *Pleurodeles waltl*, Michah, during the annual cycle. I. Male cycle. *Gen. Comp. Endocrinol.* 58:376–385.

Garnier, D.H. 1985b. Androgen and estrogen levels in the plasma of *Pleurodeles waltl*, Michah, during the annual cycle. II. Female cycle. *Gen. Comp. Endocrinol.* 60:414–418.

Garnier, D.H. and J. Joly. 1980. Preliminary investigations on estrogen levels in *Pleurodeles waltl* and *Salamandra salamandra* (Amphibia: Caudata). *Gen. Comp. Endocrinol.* 40:321–322 (Abstr.).

Gaskin, D.E. 1982. *The ecology of whales and dolphins.* Heinemann Educational Books, London, England.

Gatten, R.E., Jr. 1974. Effect of nutritional status on the preferred body temperature of the turtles *Pseudemys scripta* and *Terrapene ornata. Copeia* 1974:912–917.

Gaughwin, M.D. 1982. Southern hairy-nosed wombat *Lasiorhinus latifrons*: Its maintenance, behaviour and reproduction in captivity. Pp. 144–155 in D.D. Evans, ed. *Management of Australian mammals in captivity. Proc. Aust. Mamm. Soc., 1979.* Ramsey Ware Stockland, Victoria, Australia.

Gaugler, R. and H.K. Kaya. 1991. *Entomopathogenic nematodes in biological control.* CRC Press, Boca Raton, FL.

Gautier-Hion, A., J.M. Duplantier, R. Quris, F. Freer, C. Sourd, J.P. Decoux, G. Dubost, L. Emmons, C. Erard, P. Hecketsweiler, A. Moungazi, C. Roussilhon and J.M. Thiollay. 1985. Fruit characters as a basis of fruit choice and seed dispersal in a tropical forest vertebrate community. *Oecologica* 65:324–337.

Gavaud, J. and F. Xavier. 1986. The possible significance of hibernation in the determinism of the reptilian reproductive cycle. Pp. 251–261 in I. Assenmacer and J. Boissin, eds. *Endocrine regulation as adaptive mechanisms to the environment*. CNRD, Paris, France.

Gay, W.I. 1986. Research uses and projections of nonhuman primates. Pp. 513–520 in K. Benirschke, ed. *Primates: The road to self-sustaining populations*. Springer-Verlag, New York, NY.

Gee, G.F. 1983. Avian artificial insemination and semen preservation. Pp. 375–398 in J. Delacour, ed. *IFCB Symp. on breeding birds in captivity*. Int'l. Found. Conserv. Birds. N. Hollywood, CA.

Gee, G.F. 1984. Value of frozen tissue collections for gene pool preservation. Pp. 14–16 in H.C. Dessauer and M.S. Hafner, eds. *Collection of frozen tissues: Value, management, field, and laboratory procedures, and directory of existing conditions*. Assoc. System. Collect., Lawrence, KS.

Gee, G.F. 1986. Frozen gene pools. A future for species otherwise destined for extinction. *Proc. Regional. Conf. Amer. Assoc. Zool. Parks Aquar.* 1986:80–87.

Gee, G.F. and T.J. Sexton. 1990. Cryogenic preservation of semen from the Aleutian Canada goose. *Zoo Biol.* 9:361–371.

Gee, G.F. and S.A. Temple. 1978. Artificial insemination for breeding non-domestic birds. *Symp. Zool. Soc. London* 43:51–72.

Gee, G.F., M.R. Bakst and T.J. Sexton. 1985. Cryogenic preservation of semen from the greater sandhill crane. *J. Wildl. Manage.* 49:480–484.

Gee, G.F., C.A. Morrell, J.C. Franson and O.H. Pattee. 1993. Cryopreservation of American kestrel semen with dimethylsulfoxide. *J. Raptor Res.* 27:21–25.

Gehlbach, F., C. Bryan and H. Reno. 1978. Thermal ecological feature of *Cyprinodon elegans* and *Gambusia nobilis*, endangered Texas fishes. *Texas J. Sci.* 30:99–101.

Gehrmann, W.H. 1971. Influence of constant illumination on thermal preference in the immature water snake, *Natrix erythrogaster transversa*. *Phys. Zool.* 44:84–89.

Gehrmann, W.H. 1987. Ultraviolet irradiances of various lamps used in animal husbandry. *Zoo Biol.* 6:117–127.

Geller, M.D. and Christian, J.J. 1982. Population dynamics, adrenocortical function and pathology in *Microtus pennsylvanicus*. *J. Mammal.* 63:85–95.

Gentz, E.J. and T.L. Yates. 1986. Genetic identification of hybrid camelids. *Zoo Biol.* 5:349–354.

George, G.G. 1982. *Cuscus phalanger*: Their management in captivity. Pp. 67–72 in D.D. Evans, ed. *The management of Australian mammals in captivity. Proc. Aust. Mamm. Soc. 1979.* Ramsey Ware Stockland, Victoria, Australia.

George, G.G. 1990. Monotreme and marsupial breeding programs in Australian zoos. *Aust. J. Zool.* 37:181–205.

Geraci, J.R. 1978. Marine mammals: Introduction and identification. Pp. 555–563 in M.E. Fowler, ed. *Zoo and wild animal medicine.* W.B. Saunders, Philadelphia, PA.

Geraci, J.R. 1986a. Husbandry. Pp. 757–760 in M.E. Fowler, ed. *Zoo and wild animal medicine.*, 2nd Ed. W.B. Saunders, Philadelphia, PA.

Geraci, J.R. 1986b. Nutrition and nutritional disorders. Pp. 760–764 in M.E. Fowler, ed. *Zoo and wild animal medicine,* 2nd Ed. W.B. Saunders, Philadelphia, PA.

Geraci, J.R. and J.C. Sweeney. 1978. Marine mammals: Clinical techniques. Pp. 580–587 in M.E. Fowler, ed. *Zoo and wild animal medicine.* W.B. Saunders, Philadelphia, PA.

Gern, W.A., J.M. Nervina and S.S. Greenhouse. 1987. Pineal involvement in seasonality of reproduction. Pp. 433–460 in D.O. Norris and R.E. Jones, eds. *Hormones and reproduction in fishes, amphibians and reptiles.* Plenum Press, New York, NY.

Gershoff, S.N. 1981. Vitamin D. Pp. 1–3 in *Nutrition of dogs and cats.* Ralston Purina, Co., St. Louis, MO.

Gertstung, E. 1988. Status, life history, and management of the Lohontan cutthroat trout. *Amer. Fish. Soc. Symp.* No. 4, 1988:93–106.

Gessaman, J.A. and K.A. Nagy. 1988. Transmitter loads affect the flight speed and metabolism of homing pigeons. *Condor* 90:662–668.

Ghiselin, M.T. 1974. *The economy of nature and the evolution of sex.* Univ. California Press, Berkeley, CA.

Ghosh, A. and J. Banerjee. 1983. Effect of population stress on the histophysiology of avian endocrine organs. *J. Yamashima Instit. Ornithol.* 15:156–166.

Gibbons, E.F., Jr. and B.S. Durrant. 1987. Behavior and development of offspring from interspecies embryo transfer: Theoretical issues. *Appl. Anim. Behav. Sci.* 18:105–118.

Gibbons, E.F., Jr. and M.K. Stoskopf. 1983. Foreward. Baltimore conference on the conservation of endangered species in zoological parks and aquariums. *Zoo Biol.* 2:163–164.

Gibbons, E.F.., Jr. and M.K. Stoskopf. 1989. An interdisciplinary approach to animal medical problems. Pp. 60–68 in J.W. Driscoll, ed. *Animal care and use in behavior research: Regulations, issues and applications.* Anim. Welfare Inform. Center, U.S. Dept. Agricult., Washington, DC.

Gibbons, E.F., Jr., F.W. Koontz, R. Cook and M.K. Stoskopf. 1992. Behavioral medicine in zoological parks and aquariums. *Proc. Soc. Behav. Med.* 1992:119 (Abstr.).

Gibbons, E.F., Jr., E.J. Wyers, E.J. Waters and E.W. Menzel, Jr., eds. 1994. *Naturalistic environments in captivity for animal behavior research.* State Univ. New York Press, Albany, NY.

Gibbons, J.W., ed. 1990. *Life history and ecology of the slider turtle.* Smithsonian Instit. Press, Washington, DC.

Gibbons, J.W. and R.D. Semlitsch. 1987. Activity patterns. Pp. 396–421 in R.A. Seigel, J.T. Collins and S.S. Novak, eds. *Snakes: Ecology and evolutionary biology.* MacMillan, New York, NY.

Gilbert, L.E. 1972. Pollen feeding and reproductive biology of *Heliconius* butterflies. *Proc. Nat'l. Acad. Sci.* 69:1403–1407.

Gilbert, L.E. 1977. The role of insect-plant coevolution in the organization of ecosystems. Pp. 399–413 in V. Labeyrie, ed. *Comportement des insects et miliue trophique.* Colloques Int'l. CNRS, Paris, France.

Gilmartin, W.G. 1982. The Hawaiian monk seal: Behaviors that may affect survival. *Proc. Int'l. Marine Anim. Trainers Assoc.* 1982:68 (Abstr.).

Gilmartin, W.G. 1983. *Recovery plan for the Hawaiian monk seal, Monachus schauinslandi.* S.W. Region, Nat'l. Marine Fish. Serv., NOAA, La Jolla, CA.

Gilmartin, W.G. 1987. *Hawaiian monk seal die-off response plan, a workshop report.* S.W. Fish. Central Admin. Report H-87-19. Nat'l. Marine Fish. Serv., NOAA, Honolulu, HI.

Gilmartin, W.G. 1988. *The Hawaiian monk seal: Population status and current research activities.* S.W. Fish. Center Admin. Report H-88-17. Honolulu, HI.

Gilmartin, W.G., T.J. Ragen, T.C. Johanos and M.P. Craig. 1991. Catastrophic events observed in Hawaiian monk seal populations, 1990–1991. *9th Bienn. Conf. Biol. Marine Mamm.* 1991:27 (Abstr.).

Gilmore, D.P. 1969. Seasonal reproductive periodicity in the male Australian brush-tailed possum (*Trichosurus vulpecula*). *J. Zool. London* 157:75–98.

Gimenez, T., D. Barth, B. Hoffman and A. Karg. 1975. Blood levels of testosterone in the roe deer (*Capreolus capreolus*) in relationship to the season. *Acta Endocrinol.* Suppl. 193:59 (Abstr.).

Ginsberg, J.R., O.W. Macdonald and L.D. Mech. 1989. *Foxes, wolves, jackals and dogs: An action plan for the conservation of canids*. Int'l. Union Conserv. Nature & Natur. Resour., Gland, Switzerland.

Gipps, J.H.W. 1991. *Beyond captive breeding*. Clarendon Press, Oxford, England.

Girin, M. 1979. Feeding problems and the technology of rearing marine fish larvae. Pp. 359–368 in K. Tiews, ed. *Proc. World Symp. Finfish Nutri. Fishfeed Technol.* Heenemann Verlagsgesellschaft, Berlin, Germany.

Gisiner, R. and R.J. Schusterman. 1991. California sea lion pups play an active role in reunions with their mothers. *Anim. Behav.* 41:364–366.

Gissis, A., B. Levavi-Sivan, H. Rubin-Kedem, M. Ofir and Z. Yaron. 1991. The effect of gonadotropin releasing hormone superactive analog and dopamine antagonists on gonadotropin level and ovulation in Tilapia hybrids. *Israeli J. Aquacult.-Bamidgeh* 43:123–136.

Gist, D.H. and J.M. Jones. 1987. Storage of sperm in the reptilian oviduct. *Scanning Microsc.* 1:1839–1849.

Gittleman, J.L. 1985. Functions of communal care in mammals. Pp. 187–205 in P.J. Greenwood, P.H. Harvey and M. Slatkin, eds. *Evolution: Essays in honour of John Maynard Smith*. Cambridge Univ. Press, New York, NY.

Gittleman, J.L. 1986. Carnivore life history patterns: Allometric, phylogenetic, and ecological associations. *Amer. Natural.* 127:744–771.

Gittleman, J.L. 1988. Behavioral energetics of lactation in a herbivorous carnivore, the red panda (*Ailurus fulgens*). *Ethology* 79:13–24.

Gittleman, J.L. 1989a. The comparative approach in ethology: Aims and limitations. Pp. 55–83 in P.P.G. Bateson and P.H. Klopfer, eds. *Perspectives in ethology*, Vol 8. Plenum Press, New York, NY.

Gittleman, J.L., ed. 1989b. *Carnivore behavior, ecology and evolution*. Cornell Univ. Press, Ithaca, NY.

Gittleman, J.L. 1989c. Carnivore group living: Comparative trends. Pp. 183–207 in J.L. Gittleman, ed. *Carnivore behavior, ecology and evolution*. Cornell Univ. Press, Ithaca, NY.

Gittleman, J.L. 1993. Carnivore life histories: A reanalysis in the light of new models. Pp. 64–86 in N. Dunstone and M. Gorman, eds. *Mammals as predators*. Oxford Univ. Press, Oxford, England.

Gittleman, J.L. and H.K. Luh. 1992. On comparing comparative methods. *Ann. Rev. Ecol. Syst.* 23:383–404.

Gittleman, J.L. and O.T. Oftedal. 1987. Comparative growth and lactation energetics in carnivores. *Symp. Zool. Soc. London* 57:41–77.

Gittleman, J.L. and S.L. Pimm. 1991. Crying wolf in North America. *Nature* 351:524–525.

Gittleman, J.L. and S.D. Thompson. 1988. Energy allocation in mammalian reproduction. *Amer. Zool.* 28:863–875.

Glass, K. and K. Englund. 1989. A view from the other side: Why the Japanese are so stubborn about whaling. *Oceanus* 32:45–51.

Glatston, A.R. 1986. Studbooks: The basis of breeding programmes. *Int'l. Zoo Yb.* 24/25:162–167.

Glick, B.B. 1979. Testicular size, testosterone level and body weight in male *Macaca radiata*. Maturational and seasonal effects. *Folia. Primatol.* 32:268–289.

Glick, B.B. 1984. Male endocrine responses to females: Effects of social cues in cynomolgus macaques. *Amer. J. Primatol.* 6:229–239.

Glickman, S.E. and G.S. Caldwell. 1994. Studying natural behaviors in artificial environments: The problem of "salient" dimensions. Pp. 207–226 in E.F. Gibbons, Jr., E.J. Wyers, E.J. Waters and E.W. Menzel, Jr., eds. *Naturalistic environments in captivity for animal behavior research.* State Univ. New York Press, Albany, NY.

Glickman, S.E., L.G. Frank, J.M. Davidson, E.R. Smith and P.K. Siiteri. 1987. Androstenedione may organize or activate sex-reversed traits in female spotted hyenas. *Proc. Nat'l. Acad. Sci.* 84:3444–3447.

Glover, T.D. and J.B. Sale. 1968. The reproductive system of male rock hyrax (*Procavis* and *Heterohyrax*). *J. Zool. Soc. London* 156:351–362.

Gloyd, H.K. and R. Conant. 1990. *Snakes of the Agkistrodon complex: A monographic review.* Soc. Study Amphib. Reptiles Contrib. Herpetol., Oxford, OH.

Glynn, P.W. 1985a. Corallivore population sizes and feeding effects following el Niño (1982–1983) associated coral mortality in Panama. *Proc. 5th Int'l. Coral Reef Congress* 4:183–188.

Glynn, P.W. 1985b. El Niño-associated disturbance to coral reefs and post disturbance mortality by *Acanthaster planci*. *Marine Ecol—Progress Series* 26:295–300.

Godfrey, G.K. 1975. Controlled breeding of the lesser white-toothed shrew (*Crocidura suaveolens* Pallas, 1811) in Jersey. *Jersey Wildl. Preserv. Trust Ann. Report* 1975:52–54.

Goetz, F.W. 1983. Hormonal control of oocyte final maturation and ovulation in fishes. Pp. 117–170 in W.S. Hoar, D.J. Randall and E.M. Donaldson, eds. *Fish physiology*. Vol. IXB. Academic Press, New York, NY.

Gold, K.C. and J.J. Ogden. 1991. Effects of construction noise on captive lowland gorillas (*Gorilla gorilla gorilla*). *J. Primatol*. 1991:104 (Abstr.).

Golden, F. 1989. Introduction: Facts and fantasy. *Oceanus* 32:3–4.

Goldman, C.A. 1986. A review of the management of the aardvark, *Orycterus afer*, in captivity. *Int'l. Zoo Yb*. 24/25:286–294.

Goldsmith, A.R. 1983. Prolactin in avian reproductive cycles. Pp. 375–387 in J. Balthazart, E. Prove and R. Gilles, eds. *Hormones and behaviour in higher vertebrates*. Springer-Verlag, New York, NY.

Goldsmith, A.R. 1984. Influences of photoperiod and incubation upon prolactin secretion. *J. Steroid Biochem*. 20:1545 (Abstr.).

Goldsmith, B., ed. 1991. *Monitoring for conservation and ecology*. Chapman and Hill, New York, NY.

Goldstein, H., D. Eisikovitz and Y. Yom-Tov. 1986. Infanticide in the Palestine sunbird. *Condor* 88:528–529.

Gomez-Pompa, A. and F.W. Burley. 1991. The management of natural tropical forests. Pp. 3–18 in A. Gomez-Pompa, T.C. Whitmore and M. Hadley, eds. *Rain forest regeneration and management*. Casterton Hall, Carnforth, England.

Goodall, J. 1986. *The chimpanzees of Gombe*. Harvard Univ. Press, Cambridge, MA.

Goodall, J. and J. Athumani. 1980. An observed birth in a free-living chimpanzee (*Pan troglodytes*) in Gombe National Park, Tanzania. *Primates* 21:545–547.

Goodall, R.M.P., A.R. Galeazzi, I.S. Cameron and A.P. Sobral. 1985. Studies on Commerson's dolphin, *Cephalorhynchus commersonii*, off Tierra del Fuego. *Report Int'l. Whaling Commiss*. Sci. Committ. No. SC/36/SM WP3. Int'l. Whaling Commiss., Cambridge, England.

Goodall, S.H. 1988. Notes on the rearing of an orphaned bottlenosed dolphin (*Tursiops truncatus*). Pp. 137–139 in M.L. Augee, ed. *Marine mammals of Australasia: Field biology and captive management*. Royal Zool. Soc. New South Wales, Mosman, N.S.W., Australia.

Goodenough, J.L. and C.B. Parnell. 1985. Basic engineering design requirements for ventilation, heating, cooling and humidification of insect rearing facilities. Pp. 137–155 in P. Singh and R.F. Moore, eds. *Handbook of insect rearing*, Vol. 1. Elsevier, Amsterdam, Netherlands.

Goodlin, B.L. and G.P. Sackett. 1983. Parturition in *Macaca nemestrina*. *Amer. J. Primatol*. 4:283–307.

Goodman, D. 1980. Demographic intervention for closely managed populations. Pp. 171–195 in M.E. Soulé and B.A. Wilcox, eds. *Conservation biology: An evolutionary-ecological perspective*. Sinauer Assoc., Sunderland, MA.

Goodman, R.L., J. Hotchkiss, F.J. Karsch and E. Knobil. 1974. Diurnal variations in the serum testosterone concentrations in the adult male rhesus monkey. *Biol. Reprod*. 11:624–630.

Goodwin, R.H. 1984. Recognition and diagnosis of disease in insectaries and the effects of disease agents on insect biology. Pp. 96–129 in E.G. King and N.C. Leppla, eds. *Advances and challenges in insect rearing*. U.S. Dept. Agricult., Anim. Resource Serv., Washington, DC.

Gorbman, A., W.W. Dickhoff, S.R. Vigna, N.B. Clark and C.L. Ralph. 1983. *Comparative endocrinology*. John Wiley & Sons, New York, NY.

Gordon, T.P. 1981. Reproductive behavior in the rhesus monkey: Social and endocrine variables. *Amer. Zool*. 21:185–195.

Gordon, T.P., R.M. Rose and I.S. Bernstein. 1976. Seasonal rhythm in plasma testosterone levels in rhesus monkey (*Macaca mulatta*). *Horm. and Behav*. 7:229–243.

Gorman, G.C., P. Licht and F. McCollum. 1981. Annual reproductive patterns in three species of marine snakes from the central Phillippines. *J. Herpetol*. 15:335–354.

Gorman, M.L. and B.J. Trowbridge. 1989. The role of odor in the social lives of carnivores. Pp. 57–88 in J.L. Gittleman, ed. *Carnivore behavior, ecology and evolution*. Cornell Univ. Press, Ithaca, NY.

Goss, R.J. 1983. Control of deer antler cycles by the photoperiod. Pp. 1–14 in R.D. Brown, ed. *Antler development in Cervidae*. Caesar Kleberg Wildl. Res. Instit., Kingsville, TX.

Gould, K.G., H. Warner and D.E. Martin. 1978. Rectal probe electro-ejaculation of primates. *J. Med. Primatol*. 7:213–222.

Gouzoules, H., S. Gouzoules and L. Fedigan. 1981. Japanese monkey group translocation: Effects on seasonal breeding. *Int'l. J. Primatol*. 2:323–334.

Gouzoules, H., S. Gouzoules and P. Marler. 1986. Vocal communication: A vehicle for the study of social relationships. Pp. 111–130 in R.G. Rawlins, M.J. Kessler, eds. *The Cayo Santiago macaques: History, behavior, and biology*. State Univ. New York Press, Albany, NY.

Gowen, R. L. 1988. Amer. Fed. Herpetocult. interview: Sean McKeown. *Vivarium (Amer. Fed. Herpetocult.)* 1:14–17.

Gowen, R.L., ed. 1989. *Captive propagation and husbandry of reptiles and amphibians.* N. California Herp. Soc. Spec. Publ. #5.

Graham, C.E. 1973. Chimpanzee endometrium and sexual swelling during menstrual cycle or hormone administration. *Folia Primatol.* 19:458–468.

Graham, C.E., K.G. Gould, D.C. Collins and J.R.K. Preedy. 1979. Regulation of gonadotropin release by luteinizing hormone-releasing hormone and estrogen in chimpanzees. *Endocrinology* 105:269–275.

Graham, E.F., M.K.L. Schnell, B.K. Evensen and D.S. Nelson. 1978. Semen preservation in non-domestic mammals. *Symp. Zool. Soc. London* 43:153–173.

Grahame, D. 1983. The world pheasant situation. Captive status and future policy. Pp. 359–373 in A. Risser and F. Todd, eds. *Proc. J. Delacour IFCB Symp. on breeding birds in captivity.* Int'l. Found. Conserv. Birds, N. Hollywood, CA.

Grajal, A., S.D. Strahl, R. Parra, M.G. Dominguez and A. Neher. 1989. Foregut fermentation in the hoatzin, a neotropical leaf-eating bird. *Science* 245:1236–1238.

Grand, T.I. 1992. Altricial and precocial mammals: A model of neural and muscular development. *Zoo Biol.* 11:3–15.

Granoff, A. 1969. Viruses of amphibia. *Current Topics Microbiol. Immunol.* 50:107–137.

Graves, R.G. 1990. Animal facilities: Planning for flexibility. *Lab. Anim.* 19:29–50.

Green, R.F. 1972. Observations on the anatomy of some cetaceans and pinnipeds. Pp. 247–297 in S.H. Ridgway, ed. *Mammals of the sea: Biology and medicine.* Chas. C. Thomas, Springfield, IL.

Green, R.F. 1977. Anatomy of the reproductive organs in dolphins. Pp. 185–194 in S.H. Ridgway and K. Benirschke, eds. *Breeding dolphins: Present status, suggestion for the future.* U.S. Dept. Commer. Nat'l. Tech. Info. Serv., PB 273, Washington, DC.

Green, W.C.H. 1986. Age-related differences in nursing behavior among American bison cows (*Bison bison*). *J. Mammal.* 67:739–741.

Greenberg, N. 1977. An ethogram of the blue spiny lizard, *Sceloporus cyanogenys* (Reptilia, Lacertilia, Iguanidae). *J. Herpetol.* 11:177–195.

Greenberg, N. and P.D. McLean, eds. 1978. *Behavior and neurology of lizards.* Pub. DHEW-(ADM) 77-491. U.S. Dept. Health, Educ. Welfare, Washington, DC.

Greenberg, N. and J.C. Wingfield. 1987. Stress and reproduction: Reciprocal relationships. Pp. 461–503 in D.O. Norris and R.E. Jones, eds. *Hor-*

mones and reproduction in fishes, amphibians, and reptiles. Plenum Press, New York, NY.

Greenberg, N., G.M. Burghardt, D. Crews, E. Font, R. Jones and G. Vaughn. 1989. Reptile models for biomedical research. Pp. 289–308 in A.D. Woodhead, ed. *Animal models in biomedical research*, Vol 1. CRC Press, New York, NY.

Greene, H.W. 1977. Phylogeny, convergence, and snake behavior. Ph.D. Dissertation. Univ. Tenn., Knoxville, TN.

Greene, H.W. 1987. Antipredator behavior in reptiles. *Biol. Reptiles* 16:1–153.

Greenslade, P.J.M. 1964. The distribution, dispersal and size of a population of *Nebria brevicollis* (F.), with comparative studies on three other Carabidae. *J. Anim. Ecol.* 33:311–333.

Greenwald, G.S. 1978. Comparative aspects of antral follicular development during the menstrual and estrous cycle. Pp. 178–186 in N.J. Alexander, ed. *Animal models for research on contraception and fertility.* Harper & Row, London, England.

Greenwood, R.J. and A.B. Sargeant. 1973. Influence of radio packs on captive mallards and blue-winged teal. *J. Wildl. Manage.* 37:3–9.

Gregor, P. and J. Deacon. 1982. Observations on woundfin spawning and growth in an outdoor experimental stream. *Great Basin Natural.* 42:549–552.

Grier, H.J. 1981. Cellular organization of the testis and spermatogenesis in fishes. *Amer. Zool.* 21:345–357.

Grier, H.J. 1992. Chordate testis: The extracellular matrix hypothesis. *J. Exp. Zool.* 261:151–160.

Grier, H.J., J.R. Linton, J.F. Leatherland and V.L. de Vlaming. 1980. Structural evidence for two different testicular types in teleost fishes. *Amer. J. Anat.* 159:331–345.

Grier, J.W. 1973. Techniques and results of artificial insemination with golden eagles. *Raptor Res.* 7:1–2.

Grier, J.W., R.B. Berry and S.A. Temple. 1973. Artificial insemination with imprinted raptors. *J. N. Amer. Falconers' Assoc.* 11:45–55.

Griffith, B., J.M. Scott, J.W. Carpenter and C. Reed. 1989. Translocation as a species conservation tool: Status and strategy. *Science* 245:477–480.

Griffith, B., J.M. Scott, J.W. Carpenter and C. Reed. 1993. Animal translocations and potential disease transmission. *J. Zoo Wildl. Med.* 24:231–236.

Griffiths, M. 1978. *The biology of the monotremes.* Academic Press, New York, NY.

Griffiths, M. 1984. Mammals: Monotremes. Pp. 351–385 in G.E. Lamming, ed. *Marshall's physiology of reproduction, Vol 1. Reproductive cycles of vertebrates*. Churchill Livingston, New York, NY.

Grisham, J. 1989. Cheetah Species Survival Plan report. *Amer. Assoc. Zool. Parks Aquar. Newsletter* 30:8–9.

Groombridge, G. 1982. *The IUCN amphibia-reptilia red data book, Part 1: Testudines, Crocodylia, Rhynchocephalia*. Int'l. Union Conserv. Nature & Natur. Resour., Gland, Switzerland.

Groscolas, R.M., A. Jallageas, A. Goldsmith and I. Assenmacher. 1986. The endocrine control of reproduction and molt in male and female emperor (*Aptenodytes forsteri*) and Adelie (*Pugoscelis adeliae*) penguins, 1: Annual changes in plasma levels of gonadal steroids and LH. *Gen. Comp. Endocrinol*. 62:43–53.

Gross, M.R. 1984. Sunfish, salmon, and the evolution of alternative reproduction strategies and tactics in fishes. Pp. 55–75 in G.W. Potts and R.J. Wootten, eds. *Fish reproduction: Strategies and tactics*. Academic Press, Orlando, FL.

Gross, T. 1992. Development and use of faecal steroid analysis in several carnivore species. *Proc. 1st Int'l. Symp. Faecal Steroid Monitor. Zoo Anim*. 1992:55.

Grunwald, A., and F.P. Mohres. 1974. Beobachtungen zur Jugendentwicklung und Kadawanenbildung bei weisszahnspitz mausen (Soricidae-Crocidurinae). *Z. Saugetierkd*. 39:321–337.

Gubernick, D.J. and P.H. Klopfer, eds. 1981 *Parental care in mammals*. Plenum Press, New York, NY.

Guillette, L.J., Jr. 1987. The evolution of viviparity in fishes, amphibians and reptiles: An endocrine approach. Pp. 523–562 in D.O. Norris and R.E. Jones, eds. *Hormones and reproduction in fishes, amphibians and reptiles*. Plenum Press, New York, NY.

Gurevich, V.S. 1969. Ability of the dolphin *Delphinus* to distinguish geometric shapes by means of echo-location. *Zestnik Biologii Mgu M.M. Lomonosov* 24:109.

Guthrie, W.D., J.L. Jarvis and G.L. Reed. 1984. Leaf-feeding damage by European corn borer (Lepidoptera: Pyralidae) larvae reared one generation each year on dent maize and eight generations each year on a meridic diet (for eight years) and then reared continuously on a meridic diet for eight additional years. *J. Kansas Entomol. Soc*. 57:352–354.

Guthrie, W.D., J.L. Jarvis, G.L. Reed and M.L. Lodholz. 1982. Plant damage and survival of European corn borer cultures reared for 16 generations on maize plants and for 120 generations on a meridic diet (one generation per year on resistant or susceptible maize plants, eight generations per year on the diet). *J. Econ. Entomol.* 75:134–136.

Gwinner, E. 1977. Biological clocks. Pp. 187–198 in B. Grzimek, ed. *Grzimek's encyclopedia of ethology*. Van Nostrand Reinhold, New York, NY.

Gwinner, E. 1986. Circannual rhythms in the control of avian migrations. *Adv. Stud. Behav.* 16:191–228.

Gwinner, E. and J. Dittami. 1985. Photoperiodic responses in temperate zone and equatorial stonechats: A contribution to the problem of photoperiodism in tropical organisms. Pp. 279–294 in B.K. Follett, S. Ishii and A. Chandola, eds. *The endocrine system and the environment*. Japan. Sci. Soc. Press, Tokyo, Japan/Springer-Verlag, Berlin, Germany.

Gwynne, D.T. 1984. Male mating effort, confidence of paternity, and insect sperm competition. Pp. 117–149 in R.L. Smith, ed. *Sperm competition and the evolution of animal mating systems*. Academic Press, Orlando, FL.

Haase, E. 1983. The annual reproductive cycle in mallards. *J. Steroid Biochem.* 19:731–737.

Habibi, H.R., G. Van Der Kraak, R. Fraser and R.E. Peter. 1989. Effect of a teleost GnRH analog on steroidogenesis by the follicle-enclosed goldfish oocytes, *in vitro. Gen. Comp. Endocrinol.* 76:95–105.

Hagan, J.M. and J.M. Reed. 1988. Red color bands reduce fledging success in red-cockaded woodpeckers. *Auk* 105:498–503.

Hagenbeck, K. 1912. *Beasts and men*. Longmans, Green, London, England.

Haigh, J.C., A.D. Barth and P.A. Bowman. 1986. An evaluation of extenders for wapiti, *Cervus elaphus*, semen. *J. Zoo. Anim. Med.* 17:129–132.

Haigh, J.C., M.P. Shadbolt and G.J. Glover. 1984a. Artificial insemination of wapiti (*Cervus elephus*). *Proc. Amer. Assoc. Zoo Vets.* 1984:173.

Haigh, J.C., W.F. Cates, G.J. Glover and N.C. Rawlings. 1984b. Relationships between seasonal changes in serum testosterone concentrations, scrotal circumference and sperm morphology of male wapiti (*Cervus elephus*). *J. Reprod. Fertil.* 70:413–418.

Hale, C. and L. Green. 1988. Effects of early ingestional experiences on the acquisition of appropriate food selection by young chicks. *Anim. Behav.* 36:211–224.

Hall, D.D., G.L. Cromwell and T.S. Stahly. 1985. Hemorrhagic syndrome induced by high dietary calcium levels in growing pigs. *J. Anim. Sci.* 61:319–320.

Hall, J.D. 1986. Notes on the distribution and feeding behavior of killer whales in Prince William Sound, Alaska. Pp. 69–83 in B.C. Kirkevold and J.S. Lockard, eds. *Behavioral biology of killer whales.* Zoo Biol. Monogr., Vol. 1. Alan Liss, New York, NY.

Hall, J.G. 1985. Rodents of concern in southwestern North America. Pp. 4–7 in W.Z. Lidicker, Jr., ed. *Rodents: A world survey of species of conservation concern.* Int'l. Union Nature & Natur. Resour., Gland, Switzerland.

Hall, R.W. and J.L. Richards. 1982. Conditioning a Pacific bottlenose dolphin and a California sea lion in a test experiment. *Proc. Int'l. Marine Anim. Trainers Assoc.* 1982:79–82

Hall-Craggs, E.C.B. 1962. The testis of *Gorilla gorilla beringei. Proc. Zool. Soc. London* 139:511–514.

Halliday, T. 1980. The extinction of the passenger pigeon *Ectopistes migratorius* and its relevance to contemporary conservation. *Biol. Conserv.* 17:157–162.

Hamman, R.L. 1981a. Hybridization of three species of chub in a hatchery. *Progress. Fish Cultur.* 43:140–141.

Hamman, R.L. 1981b. Spawning and culture of Colorado squawfish in raceways. *Progress. Fish Cultur.* 43:173–177.

Hamman, R.L. 1982a. Spawning and culture of humpback chub. *Progress. Fish Cultur.* 44:213–216.

Hamman, R.L. 1982b. Induced spawning and culture of bonytail chub. *Progress. Fish Cultur.* 44:201–203.

Hamman, R.L. 1985a. Induced spawning of hatchery-reared razorback sucker. *Progress. Fish Cultur.* 47:187–189.

Hamman, R.L. 1985b. Induced spawning of hatchery-reared bonytail. *Progress. Fish Cultur.* 47:239–241.

Hamman, R.L. 1986. Induced spawning of hatchery-reared Colorado squawfish. *Progress. Fish. Cultur.* 48:72–74.

Hammerstrom, F. 1970. *An eagle to the sky.* Iowa Univ. Press, Ames, IA.

Hampton, J.K. and S.H. Hampton. 1974. Some expected and unexpected characteristics of reproduction in Callithricidae. *Lab. Anim. Handbk.* 6:235–239.

Hancocks, D. 1971. *Animals and architecture.* Praeger, New York, NY.

Hancocks, D. 1980. Bringing nature into the zoo: Inexpensive solutions for zoo environments. *Int'l. J. Study Anim. Prob.* 1:170–177.

Hanggi, E., M. Jeffries, R. Gisiner and R.J. Schusterman. 1986. Facilitation of learning through imprinting in a captive-born sea lion pup. *Proc. Int'l. Marine Anim. Trainers Assoc.* 1986:16–19.

Hanscom, T. 1988. San Diego Wild Animal Park sends addax to Tunisia. *Amer. Assoc. Zool. Parks Aquar. Newsletter* 29:22.

Hanson, J.P., M.E. Larson and C.T. Snowdon. 1976. The effects of control over high intensity noise on plasma cortisol levels in rhesus monkeys. *Behav. Biol.* 16:333–340.

Happ, G.M. 1992. Maturation of the male reproductive system and its endocrine regulation. *Ann. Rev. Entomol.* 37:303–320.

Happel, R.E., J.F. Noss and C.W. Marsh. 1987. Distribution, abundance, and endangerment of primates. Pp. 63–82 in C.W. Marsh and R.A. Mittermeier, eds. *Primate conservation in the tropical rain forest*. Alan Liss, New York, NY.

Harcourt, C. and J. Thornback. 1990. *Lemurs of Madagascar and the Comoros. IUCN red data book*. Int'l. Union Conserv. Nature & Natur. Resour., Gland, Switzerland.

Harder, W. 1975. *Anatomy of fishes*. E. Schweizerbart'sche Verlagsbuchhandlung, Stuttgart, Germany.

Hargrove, T.L. 1986. Cryogenic preservation of budgerigar, *Melopsittacus undulatus*, semen. Master's Thesis. Florida Atlantic Univ., Boca Raton, FL.

Hargrove, T.L. and M.A. Ottinger. 1991. Induced oviposition of precalcified eggs following prostaglandin administration. *Poult. Sci.* 71:548–552.

Harke, C., S. Maloney and J. Steinberg. 1985. *Plant research team primate survey results*. Woodland Park. Zool. Gardens, Seattle, WA

Harlow, H.S. and M.K. Harlow. 1962. Social deprivation in monkeys. *Sci. Amer.* 207:137–146.

Harlow, P. and G. Grigg. 1984. Shivering thermogenesis in a brooding diamond python, *Python spilotes spilotes. Copeia* 1984:959–965.

Harmin, S.A. and L.W. Crim. 1992. Gonadotropic hormone-releasing hormone analog (GnRH-A) induced ovulation and spawning in female winter flounder, *Pseudopleuronectes americanus* (Walbaum). *Aquacult.* 104:375–390.

Harrington, F.H. 1983. Wolf pack spacing: Howling as a territory-independent spacing mechanism in a territorial population. *Behav. Ecol. Sociobiol.* 12:161–168.

Harrington, F.H. and P.C. Paquet, eds. 1982. *Wolves of the world*. Noyes, Park Ridge, NJ.

Harris, M.P., U.N. Safriel, M. De L. Brooke and C.K. Britton. 1986. The pair bond and divorce among oystercatchers *Haematopus ostralegus* on Skokholm Island, Wales. *Ibis* 129:45–57.

Harrison, G.J. 1982. First psittacine produced by artificial insemination. *Amer. Fed. Avicult. Watchbird* Aug/Sept:36.

Harrison, R.J. 1969. Reproduction and reproductive organs. Pp. 253–348 in H.R. Anderson, ed. *Biology of marine mammals.* Academic Press, New York, NY.

Harrison, R.J. 1977. Ovarian appearances and histology in *Tursiops truncatus.* Pp. 195–204 in S.H. Ridgway and K. Benirschke, eds. *Breeding dolphins, present status, suggestions for the future.* U.S. Dept. Commer. Nat'l. Tech. Info. Serv., PB 273, Washington, DC.

Harrison, R.J. and S.H. Ridgway. 1971. Gonadal activity in some bottlenose dolphins (*Tursiops truncatus*). *J. Zool. Soc. London* 165:355–366.

Harrison, R.M., and R.W. Lewis. 1986. The male reproductive tract and its fluids. Pp. 101–148 in W.R. Dukelow and J. Erwin, eds. *Comparative Primate Biology, Vol 3: Reproduction and development.* Alan Liss, New York, NY.

Harte, J. and E. Hoffman. 1989. Possible effects of acidic deposition on a rocky mountain population of the tiger salamander *Ambystoma tigrinum. Conserv. Biol.* 3:149–158.

Hartl, D.L. 1980. *Principles of population genetics.* Sinauer Assoc., Sunderland, MA.

Harvey, P.H. and T.H. Clutton-Brock. 1985. Life history variation in primates. *Evolution* 39:559–581.

Harvey, P.H. and G.M. Mace. 1982. Comparisons between taxa and adaptive trends: Problems of methodology. Pp. 343–361 in King's College Sociobiology Group, ed. *Current problems in sociobiology.* Cambridge Univ. Press, New York, NY.

Harvey, P.H. and M.D. Pagel. 1991. *The comparative method in evolutionary biology.* Oxford Univ. Press, New York, NY.

Harvey, S., A. Chadwick, G. Border, C.G. Scanes and J.G. Phillips. 1982. Neuroendocrine control of prolactin secretion. In C.G. Scanes, A. Epple and M.H. Stetson eds. Aspects of avian endocrinology: Practical and theoretic implications. *Grad. Studies, Texas Tech. Univ.* 26:41–60.

Hatch, S.A. 1983. Mechanism and ecological significance of sperm storage in the northern fulmar with reference to its occurrence in other birds. *Auk* 100:593–600.

Hausknecht, E. 1987. A new larger Seven Seas unfolds at Brookfield Zoo. *Regional Proc. Amer. Assoc. Zool. Parks Aquar.* 1987:562–565.

Havelka, M., C. Booth, K. Whitney and C. Whitney. 1982. Growth and population structure of the Mojave tui chub. *CA-NV Wildl. Trans.* 1982:9–15.

Hawkins, A.D. and P.D. Anthony. 1981. Aquarium design and construction. Pp. 1–46 in A.D. Hawkins, ed. *Aquarium systems.* Academic Press, New York, NY.

Hawkins, A.D. and R. Lloyd. 1981. Materials for the aquarium. Pp. 171–222 in A.D. Hawkins, ed. *Aquarium systems.* Academic Press, New York, NY.

Hays, W.L. 1973. *Statistics for the social sciences,* 2nd Ed. Holt, Rinehart & Winston, New York, NY.

Hazard, K. 1988. Beluga whale, *Delphinapterus leucas.* Pp. 195–235 in J.W. Lentfer, ed. *Selected marine mammals of Alaska: Species accounts with research and management recommendations.* U.S. Marine Mamm. Commiss. PB 88178462. Washington, DC.

Hearn, J.P. 1986a. The embryo-maternal dialogue during early pregnancy in primates. *J. Reprod. Fertil.* 76:809–819.

Hearn, J.P. 1986b. Artificial manipulation of reproduction: Priorities and practicalities in the next decade. *Int'l. Zoo Yb.* 24/25:148–157.

Hearn, J.P. and S.F. Lunn. 1975. The reproductive biology of the marmoset monkey, *Callithrix jacchus.* Pp. 191–202 in F.T. Perkins and P.N. O'Donague, eds. *Breeding simians for developmental biology.* Laboratory Animals, Ltd., London, England.

Hearn, J.P. and G.E. Webley. 1987. Regulation of the corpus luteum of early pregnancy in the marmoset monkey: Local interactions of luteotropic and luteolytic hormones *in vivo* and their effect on the secretion of progesterone. *J. Endocrinol.* 114:231–239.

Hearn, J.P., J.K. Hodges and S. Gems. 1988a. Early secretion of chorionic gonadotropin by marmoset embryos *in vivo* and *in vitro. J. Endocrinol.* 119:249–255.

Hearn, J.P., A.A. Gidley-Baird, J.K. Hodges, P.M. Summers and G.E. Webley. 1988b. Embryonic signals during the peri-implantation period in primates. *J. Reprod. Fertil.* Suppl. 36:49–58.

Heath, M.S. and S.L. Vanderlip. 1988. Biology, husbandry and veterinary care of Chinese pangolins, *Manis pentadactyla. Zoo Biol.* 7:293–312.

Hecker, N.F. 1985. An updated model of the food requirements of captive California sea lions, *Zalophus californianus. Regional Proc. Amer. Assoc. Zool. Parks Aquar.* 1985:441–452.

Hector, J.A.L., J.P. Croxall and B.K. Follett. 1986a. Reproductive endocrinology in the wandering albatross *Diomedia exulans* in relation to biennial breeding and deferred sexual maturity. *Ibis* 128:9–22.

Hector, J.A.L., B.D. Follett and P.A. Prince. 1986b. Reproductive endocrinology of the black-browed albatross *Diomedea malanophris* and the grey-headed albatross *D. chrysostoma. J. Zool. Soc. London* 208:237–253.

Hediger, H. 1950. *Wild Animals in captivity*. Butterworth, London, England.

Hediger, H. 1955. *Psychology and behavior of captive animals in zoos and circuses*. Butterworth, London, England.

Hediger, H. 1964. *Wild animals in captivity*. Dover, New York, NY.

Hediger, H. 1966. Diet of animals in captivity. *Int'l. Zoo Yb*. 6:37–57.

Hediger, H. 1968. *The psychology and behaviour of animals in zoos and circuses*. Dover, New York, NY.

Hediger, H. 1969. *Man and animal in the zoo: Zoo biology*. Delacorte Press, New York, NY.

Hediger, H. 1970. The development of the presentation and the viewing of animals in zoological gardens. Pp. 519–528 in L.R. Aronson, E. Toback, D. Lehrman and J. Rosenblatt, eds. *Development and evolution of behavior: Essays in memory of T.C. Schneirla*. W.H. Freeman, San Francisco, CA.

Hefetz, A., R. Ben-Yaacov and Y. Yom-Tov. 1984. Sex specificity in the anal gland secretion of the Egyptian mongoose *Herpestes ichneumon*. *J. Zool. Soc. London* 203:205–209.

Hegner, R.E. and J.C. Wingfield. 1986. Gonadal development during autumn and winter in house sparrows. *Condor* 88:269–278.

Heimlich-Boran, J.R. 1986a. Photogrammetric analysis of growth in Puget Sound *Orcinus orca*. Pp. 97–112 in B.C. Kirkevold and J.S. Lockard, eds. *Behavioral biology of killer whales*. Zoo Biol. Monogr., Vol. 1. Alan Liss, New York, NY.

Heimlich-Boran, J.R. 1986b. Fishery correlations with the occurrences of killer whales in greater Puget Sound. Pp. 113–131 in B.C. Kirkevold and J.S. Lockard, eds. *Behavioral biology of killer whales*. Zoo Biol. Monogr., Vol. 1. Alan Liss, New York, NY.

Heinrich, B. 1988. Why do ravens fear their food? *Condor* 90:950–952.

Helfman, G.S. 1979. Twilight activities of yellow perch, *Perca flavescens*. *J. Fish. Res. Board Canada* 36:173–179.

Helfman, G.S. 1981. Twilight activities and temporal structure in a freshwater fish community. *Can. J. Fish. Aquat. Sci.* 38:1405–1420.

Heller, H. 1972. The effect of neurohypophyseal hormones on the female reproductive tract of lower vertebrates. *Gen. Comp. Endocrinol.* Suppl. 3:703–714.

Hellgren, E.C., R.L. Lochmiller, M.S. Amoss, S.W.J. Seager, S.J. Magyar, K.P. Coscarelli and W.E. Grant. 1989. Seasonal variation in serum testosterone, testicular measurements and semen characteristics in the collared peccary (*Tayassu tajacu*). *J. Reprod. Fertil.* 85:677–686.

Hellwing, S. 1973. Husbandry and breeding of white-toothed shrews (Crocindurinae) in the Research Zoo of the Tel-Aviv University. *Int'l. Zoo Yb.* 13:127–134.

Hellwing, S. and B. Funkenstein. 1977. Ovarian asymmetry in the shrew, *Crocidura russula monacha. J. Reprod. Fertil.* 49:163–165.

Henderson, H. 1980. Behavioral adjustment of fishes to release into a new habitat. In J.E. Bardach, J.J. Magnuson, R.C. May and J.M. Reinhart, eds. Fish behavior and its use in the capture and culture of fishes. *Proc. 5th Conf. Int'l. Center Living Aquat. Res. Manage.* 1980:331–344.

Henderson, J.R. and M.R. Finnegan. 1990. *Population monitoring of the Hawaiian monk seal, Monachus schauinslandi, and captive maintenance project at Kure Atoll, 1988.* NOAA technical memo, NMFS-SWSFC-150, U.S. Dept. Commer., Washington, DC.

Hennemann, W.W., S.D. Thompson and M.J. Konecny. 1983. Metabolism of crab-eating foxes, *Cerdocyon thous*: Ecological influences on the energetics of canids. *Physiol. Zool.* 56:319–324.

Herman, L.M. 1980. Cognitive characteristics of dolphins. Pp. 363–429 in L.M. Herman, ed. *Cetacean behavior: Mechanism and functions.* John Wiley & Sons, New York, NY.

Herman, L.M. 1986. Cognition and language competencies of bottlenose dolphins. Pp. 221–252 in R.J. Schusterman and F.G. Wood, ed. *Dolphin cognition and behavior: A comparative approach.* Lawrence Earlbaum, Hillsdale, NJ.

Herman, L.M. 1991. What the dolphin knows, or might know, in its natural world. Pp. 349–363 in K. Pryor and K.S. Norris, eds. *Dolphin Societies.* Univ. of California Press, Berkeley, CA.

Herman, L.M. and P.H. Forestell. 1985. Reporting presence or absence of named objects by a language-trained dolphin. *Neurosci. Biobehav. Rev.* 9:667–681.

Herman, L.M., D.G. Richards and J.P. Wolz. 1984. Comprehension of sentences by bottlenosed dolphins. *Cognition* 16:129–219

Herman, L.M., J.P. Wolz and D.G. Richards. 1982. Comprehension of sentences by bottlenosed dolphins. *Proc. Int'l. Marine Anim. Trainers Assoc.* 1982:102 (Abstr.).

Herman, L.M., F.A. Beach, R.L. Pepper and R.B. Stalling. 1969. Learning set performance in the bottlenosed dolphin. *Psychonomic Sci.* 14:98–99.

Herman, W.S. 1981. Studies on the adult reproductive diapause of the monarch butterfly, *Danaus plexippus. Biol. Bull.* 160:89–106.

Herman, W.S. 1985. Hormonally mediated events in adult monarch butterflies. In M.A. Rankin, ed. Migration: Mechanisms and adaptive significance. *Contrib. Marine Sci.* 27:799–815.

Herman, W.S. and J.F. Barker. 1977. Effect of mating on monarch butterfly oogenesis. *Experientia* 22:688–689.

Herman, W.S., L.P. Brower and W.H. Calvert. 1989. Reproductive tract
development in monarch butterflies overwintering in California and
Mexico. *J. Lepidopt. Soc.* 43:50–58.

Herrero, S., C. Schroeder and M. Scott-Brown. 1986. Are Canadian foxes
swift enough? *Biol. Conserv.* 36:159–167.

Hertelendy, F., M. Yek and H.V. Biellier. 1974. Induction of oviposition in the domestic hen by prostaglandins. *Gen. Comp. Endocrinol.*
22:529–531.

Herzog, H.A., Jr. and G.M. Burghardt. 1977. Vocal communication signals
in juvenile crocodilians. *Z. Tierpsychol.* 44:294–304.

Herzog, H.A., Jr. and G.M. Burghardt. 1988. Development of antipreditor
responses in snakes, III: Stability of individual and litter differences
over the first year of life. *Ethology* 77:250–258.

Herzog, H.A., Jr., B.B. Bowers and G.M. Burghardt. 1989. Stimulus control of antipredator behavior in juvenile garter snakes (*Thamnophis*). *J.
Comp. Psychol.* 103:233–242.

Heston, J. 1987. Captive propagation and management of the Guinea turaco.
Amer. Fed. Avicult. Watchbird 13:46–51.

Hess, D.L., A.M. Schmidt and M.J. Schmidt. 1983. Reproductive cycle of
the Asian elephant (*Elephus maximus*) in captivity. *Biol. Reprod.* 28:767–
773.

Hewlett, K.G. and M.A. Newman. 1968. "Skana" the killer whale *Orcinus
orca* at Vancouver Public Aquarium. *Int'l. Zoo Yb.* 8:209–211.

Hewlett, S. 1983. A decade of sea otters, (*Enhydra lutris*). *Proc. Amer.
Assoc. Zool. Parks Aquar.* 1983:224–228.

Hewlett, S. 1986. A "new" approach to exhibiting cetaceans in captivity.
Proc. Amer. Assoc. Zool. Parks Aquar. 1986:691–694

Hewlett, S. and K.G. Hewlett. 1986. Killer whale habitat: A new approach to
cetacean exhibits. *Proc. Int'l. Marine Anim. Trainers Assoc.* 1986:11–13.

Heyning, J.E. 1989. Cuvier's beaked whale, *Ziphius cavirostris* G. Cuvier,
1823. Pp. 289–308 in S.H. Ridgway and R.J. Harrison. *Handbook of
marine mammals, Vol. 4: River dolphins and the larger toothed whales.*
Academic Press, London, England.

Hiatt, E.S., A.R. Goldsmith and D.S. Farner. 1987. Plasma levels of prolactin and gonadotrophins during the reproductive cycle of white-crowned sparrows (*Zonotrichia leucophrys*). *Auk* 104:208–217.

Hickman, G. and R. Fitz. 1978. *A report on the conservation and ecology of the snail darter (Percina tanasi, Etnier) 1975–1977*. Tennessee Valley Authority, Div. Forest., Fish. Wildl. Dev. Norris, TN.

Hickman, G.C. 1980. Locomotory activity of captive *Cryptomys hottentotus*, (Mammalia: Bathyergidae), a fossorial rodent. *J. Zool. Soc. London* 192:225–235.

Highfield, A.C. 1988. Notes on the dietary constituents for herbivorous terrestrial chelonians and their effect on growth and development. *J. Assoc. Study Reptiles Amphib.* 3:7–19.

Hill, D. and P. Robertson. 1988. Breeding success of wild and hand-reared ring-necked pheasants. *J. Wildl. Manage.* 52:446–450.

Hill, L. and J. Holland. 1971. Preference behavior of the Red River pupfish, *Cyprinodon rubrofluviatilis*, (Cyprinodontidae), to acclimation salinities. *S.W. Natural.* 16:55–63.

Hill, W.C.O. 1953. The female reproductive organ of tarsius, with observations on the physiological changes therein. *J. Zool. Soc. London* 123:589–598.

Hill, W.G. 1987. DNA fingerprints applied to animal and bird populations. *Nature* 327:98–99.

Hillier, B. and J. Hansen. 1984. *The social logic of space*. Cambridge Univ. Press, New York, NY.

Hillman, C.N. and J.W. Carpenter. 1983. Breeding biology and behaviour of captive black-footed ferrets, *Mustela nigripes*. *Int'l. Zoo Yb.* 23:186–191.

Hinegardner, R.T. 1981. *Laboratory animal management: Marine invertebrates*. Committee on Marine Invert. Nat'l. Acad. Press, Washington, DC.

Hinton, H.E. 1951. *Myrmecophilous lycaenidae* and other Lepidoptera. A summary. *Proc. S. London Entomol. Natur. Hist. Soc.* 1949–1950:111–175.

Hirsch, I.M., S.W.J. Seager, J. Sedor, L. King and W.C. Stass, Jr. 1990. Electroejaculatory stimulation of a quadraplegic man resulting in pregnancy. *Arch. Phys. Med. Rehab.* 71:54–57.

Hirsch, U. 1978. Artificial nest ledges for bald ibis. Pp. 61–69 in S.A. Temple, ed. *Endangered birds: Management techniques for preserving threatened species*. Univ. Wisconsin. Press, Madison, WI.

Hnida, J.A. 1985. Mother-infant and infant-infant interactions in captive sable antelope: Evidence for plasticity in a hider species. *Zoo. Biol.* 4:339–349.

Ho, S. 1987. Endocrinology of vitellogenesis. Pp. 145–169 in D.O. Norris and R.E. Jones, eds. *Hormones and reproduction in fishes, amphibians, and reptiles.* Plenum Press, New York, NY.

Hoage, R. 1987. Domestic cats produced through *in vitro* fertilization techniques. *Amer. Assoc. Zool. Parks Aquar. Newsletter* 28:23.

Hobson, B.M. 1975. Chorionic gonadotropin in the placenta of a chimpanzee *(Pan troglodytes)*. *Folia Primatol.* 23:135–139.

Hobson, B.M. and L. Wide. 1972. A comparison between chorionic gonadotrophins extracted from human, rhesus monkey and marmoset placentae. *J. Endocrinol.* 55:363–369.

Hobson, E.S. 1965. Diurnal-nocturnal activity of some inshore fishes in the Gulf of California. *Copeia* 1965:291–302.

Hobson, W. and G.B. Fuller. 1977. LH-RH induced gonadotropin release in chimpanzees. *Biol. Reprod.* 17:294–297.

Hobson, W., J.S.D. Winter, F.I. Reyes, G.B. Fuller and C.C. Faiman. 1980. Non-human primates as models for studies on puberty. Pp. 409–421 in M. Serio and L. Martini, eds. *Animal models in human reproduction.* Raven Press, New York, NY.

Hodges, J.K., D.J. Bevan, M. Celma, J.P. Hearn, D.M. Jones, D.G. Kleiman, J.A. Knight and H.D.M. Moore. 1984. Aspects of the reproductive endocrinology of the female giant panda *(Ailuropoda melanoleuca)* in captivity with special reference to the detection of ovulation and pregnancy. *J. Zool. Soc. London* 203:253–268.

Hodson, P.V., U. Borgmann and H. Shear. 1979. Toxicity of copper to aquatic biota. Pp. 348–360 in J.O. Nriagu, ed. *Copper in the environment, Vol. II: Health effects.* John Wiley & Sons, New York, NY.

Hoezel, A.R., J.K.B. Ford and G.A. Dover. 1991. A paternity test case for the killer whale *(Orcinus orca)* by DNA fingerprinting. *Marine Mamm. Sci.* 7:35–43.

Hoff, G.L. and D.M. Hoff. 1984. *Salmonella* and *Arizona*. Pp. 69–82 in G.L. Hoff, F.L. Frye and E.R. Jacobson, eds. *Diseases of amphibians and reptiles.* Plenum Press, New York, NY.

Hoff, M.P., R.D. Nadler and T.L. Maple. 1982. Control role of an adult male in a captive group of lowland gorillas. *Folia Primatol.* 38:72–85.

Hoffman, R.J. 1989. The marine mammal protection act: A first of its kind anywhere. *Oceanus* 32:21–25.

Hohn, A.A., S.J. Chivers and J. Barlow. 1985. Reproductive maturity and seasonality of male spotted dolpins, *Stenella attenuata,* in the eastern tropical Pacific. *Marine Mamm. Sci.* 1:273–293.

Hohn, E.O. and S.C. Cheng. 1967. Gonadal hormones in Wilson's phalarope (*Steranapas tricolor*) and other birds in relation to plumage and sex behavior. *Gen. Comp. Endocrinol.* 8:1–11

Holm, E. 1969. Contributions to the knowledge of the biology of Namib Desert golden mole (*Eremitalpa granti namibensis,* Bauer and Neithammer 1959). *Sci. Pap. Namib Desert Res. Stn.* 41:37–42.

Holt, W.V., H.D.M. Moore, R.D. North, T.D. Hartman and J.K. Hodges. 1988. Oestrus detection, artificial insemination and pregnancy monitoring in the blackbuck, *Antilope cervicapra. Proc. 11th Int'l. Congr. Anim. Reprod. Artif. Insem.* 1988:255. Univ. College, Dublin, Ireland.

Homeida, A.M., M.G.R. Khalil and A.A.M. Taha. 1988. Plasma concentrations of progesterone, oestrogens, testosterone and LH-like activity during the oestrous cycle of the camel (*Camelus dromedarius*). *J. Reprod. Fertil.* 83:593–598.

Honegger, R.E. 1975. Breeding and maintaining reptiles in captivity. Pp. 1–12 in R.D. Martin, ed. *Breeding endangered species in captivity.* Academic Press, New York, NY.

Hontela, A. and R.E. Peter. 1983. Characteristics and functional significance of daily cycles in serum gonadotropin hormone levels in the goldfish. *J. Exp. Zool.* 228:543–550.

Hontela, A. and N.E. Stacey. 1990. Cyprinidae. Pp. 53–77 in A.D. Numro, A.P. Scott and T.J. Lam, eds. *Reproductive seasonality in teleosts: Environmental influences.* CRC Press, Boca Raton, FL.

Hoppen, H.O., L. Diaz de Aguirre, D. Hagenbeck, M. Boer and F. Schwarzenberger. 1992. Progesterone metabolites in elephants faeces. *Proc. 1st Int'l. Symp. Faecal Steroid Monitor. Zoo Anim.* 1992:51.

Hopper, B. and W.W. Tullner. 1970. Urinary estrone and plasma progesterone levels during the menstrual cycle of the rhesus monkey. *Endocrinology* 86:1225–1230.

Horning, C.L., M. Hutchins and W. English. 1987. Breeding and management of the common trumpeter (*Psophia crepitans*). *Zoo Biol.* 7:193–210.

Horst, K. 1978. Pests and diseases. Pp. 153–166 in R.W. Langhans, ed. *A growth chamber manual.* Comstock, Cornell Univ. Press, Ithaca, NY.

Horwich, R.H. 1989. Use of surrogate parental models and age periods in a successful release of hand-reared sandhill cranes. *Zoo Biol.* 8:379–390.

Hoth, J. and H. Granadas. 1987. A preliminary report on the breeding of the volcano rabbit *Romerolagus diazi* at the Chapultepec Zoo, Mexico City. *Int'l. Zoo Yb.* 26:261–265.

Houck, L.D. 1977. Reproductive biology of a neotropical salamander, *Bolitoglossa rostrata. Copeia* 1977:70–83.

Houpt, K. and L. Boyd, eds. 1994 *The Przewalski horse: History and biology of an endangered species.* State Univ. New York Press, Albany, NY.

Howard, J.G., V.G. Pursel, D.E. Wildt and M. Bush. 1981. Comparison of various extenders for freeze-preservation of semen from selected captive wild ungulates. *J. Amer. Vet. Med. Assoc.* 179:1157–1161.

Howard, J.G., M. Bush, C. Morton, F. Morton, K. Wentzel and D.E. Wildt. 1991. Comparative semen cryopreservation in ferrets (*Mustela putorius furo*) and pregnancies after laparoscopic intrauterine insemination with frozen-thawed spermatozoa. *J. Reprod. Fertil.* 92:109–118.

Howard, J.G., M. Bush, V. de Vos, M.C. Schiewe, V.G. Pursel and D.E. Wildt. 1986. Influence of cryoprotective diluent on post-thaw viability and acrosomal integrity of spermatozoa of the African elephant *Loxodonta africana. J. Reprod. Fertil.* 78:295–306.

Howard, J.G., S.L. Hurlbut, C. Morton, F. Morton, M. Bush and D.E. Wildt. 1989. Pregnancies in the domestic ferret after laparoscopic artificial insemination with frozen-thawed spermatozoa. *J. Androl* 10:52P (Abstr.).

Howard, J.G., A.M. Donoghue, M.A. Barone, K.L. Goodrowe, E.S. Blumer, K. Snodgrass, D. Starnes, M. Tucker, M. Bush and D.E. Wildt. 1992. Successful induction of ovarian activity and laparoscopic intrauterine artificial insemination in the cheetah (*Acinonyx jubatus*). *J. Zoo Wildl. Med.* 23:288–300.

Howard, R.D. 1978a. The evolution of mating strategies in bullfrogs, *Rana catesbeiana. Evolution* 32:850–871.

Howard, R.D. 1978b. The influence of male-defended oviposition sites on early embryo mortality in bullfrogs. *Ecology* 59:789–798.

Howe, R. and G.C. Clough. 1971. The Bahaman hutia *Geocapromys ingrami* in captivity. *Int'l. Zoo Yb.* 11:89–93.

Howell, T.R. and G.A. Bartholomew, Jr. 1952. Experiments on the mating behavior of the Brewer blackbird. *Condor* 54:140–151.

Howey, P.W., T.W. Strikwerda, S. Mantel, M.R. Fuller, G.F. Gee, S.S. Klugman, W.S. Seeger and P.F. Ward. 1987. A system for acquiring physiological and environmental telemetry data. *Biotelemetry* 1:347–350.

Howland, B.E., C. Faiman and T.M. Butler. 1971. Serum levels of FSH and LH during the menstrual cycle of the chimpanzee. *Biol. Reprod.* 4:101–105.

Hoyt, R.A. 1987. Pangolins: Past, present and future. *Proc. Amer. Assoc. Zool. Parks Aquar.* 1987:107–134

Hradecky, P. 1982. Uterine morphology in some African antelopes. *J. Zoo Anim. Med.* 13:132–136.

Hradecky, P. 1983. Placental morphology in African antelopes and giraffes. *Theriogenology* 20:725–734.

Hradecky, P., K. Benirschke and G.G. Stott. 1987. Implications of the placental structure compatibility for interspecies embryo transfer. *Theriogenology* 28:737–746.

Hubbs, C. 1967. Geographic variations in survival of hybrids between Etheostomatine fishes. *Bull. Texas Mem. Mus.* 13:1–72.

Hubbs, C. 1971. Competition and isolation mechanisms in the *Gambusia affinis* x *G. heterochir* hybrid swarm. *Bull. Texas Mem. Mus.* 19:1–47.

Hubbs, C. and H. Brodrick. 1963. Current abundance of *Gambusia gagei*, an endangered fish species. *S.W. Natural.* 8:46–48.

Hubbs, C. and G. Drewry. 1962. Artificial hybridization of *Crenichthys baileyi* with related cyprinodont fishes. *Texas J. Sci.* 14:107–110.

Hubbs, C. and B. Jensen. 1984. Extinction of *Gambusia amistadensis*, an endangered fish. *Copeia* 1984:529–530.

Hubbs, C. and V. Springer. 1957. A revision of the *Gambusia nobilis* species group, with descriptions of three new species, and notes on their variation, ecology, and evolution. *Texas J. Sci.* 9:279–327.

Hudson, R. and H. Distel. 1982. The pattern of behaviour of rabbit pups in the nest. *Behaviour* 79:255–271.

Huettel, M.D. 1986. *Evolutionary genetics of invertebrate behavior.* Plenum Press, New York, NY.

Huey, R.B., E.R. Pianka and T.W. Schoener, eds. 1983. *Lizard ecology: Studies of a model organism.* Harvard Univ. Press, Cambridge, MA.

Huff, T.A. 1980. Captive propagation of the subfamily Boinae with emphasis on the genus *Epicrates.* Pp. 125–134 in J.B. Murphy and J.T. Collins, eds. *Reproductive biology and diseases of captive reptiles.* Soc. Study Amphib. Reptiles, Oxford, OH.

Hughes, D.G. and P.M. Bennett. 1991. Captive breeding and the conservation of invertebrates. *Int'l. Zoo Yb.* 31:45–51.

Hulbert, A.J. 1982. Notes on the management of a captive breeding colony of the greater bilby *Macrotis lagotis.* P. 53 in D.D. Evans, ed. *The management of Australian mammals in captivity. Proc. Aust. Mamm. Soc. 1979.* Ramsey Ware Stockland, Victoria, Australia.

Hulings, N.C. 1985. Activity patterns of homing in two intertidal limpets, Jordan Gulf of Aqaba. *Nautilus* 99:75–80.

Hull, D.L. 1988. *Science as a process: An evolutionary account of the social and conceptual development of science.* Univ. Chicago Press, Chicago, IL.

Hult, R.W. 1982. Another function of echolocation for bottle-nosed dolphins *(Tursiops truncatus)*. *Proc. Int'l. Marine Anim. Trainers Assoc.* 1982:88–95.

Hundgen, K. and D. Bruning. 1988. Propagation techniques for birds of paradise at the New York Zoological Park. *Proc. Amer. Assoc. Zool. Parks Aquar.* 1988:14–20.

Hundgen, K., M. Hutchins, C. Sheppard, D. Bruning and W. Worth. 1990. Management and breeding of the red bird of paradise *Paradisaea rubra* at the New York Zoological Park. *Int'l. Zoo Yb*. 30:192–198.

Hungerford, D.A., R.L. Snyder and J.A. Griswold. 1966. Chromosome analysis and sex identification in the management and conservation of birds. *J. Wildl. Manage*. 30:707–712.

Hunt, R.H. 1987. The Morelet's crocodile project of Zoo Atlanta. *Proc. Amer. Assoc. Zool. Parks Aquar.* 1987:158–161.

Hunt, R.H. 1975. Maternal behavior in the Morelet's crocodile, *Crocodylus moreleti*. *Copeia* 1975:763–764.

Hunter, G.A. and E.M. Donaldson. 1983. Hormonal sex control and its application to fish culture. Pp. 223–303 in W.S. Hoar, D.J. Randall and E.M. Donaldson, eds. *Fish physiology*, Vol. IXB. Academic Press, New York, NY.

Hurst, P.R., K. Jefferies, P. Eckstein and A.G. Wheeler. 1976. Recovery of uterine embryos in rhesus monkeys. *Biol. Reprod.* 15:429–434.

Hutchins, M. 1976. Breeding biology and behaviour in the Indian-pied hornbill, *Anthracoceros malibaricus malabalicus*. *Int'l. Zoo Yb*. 16:99–104.

Hutchins, M. 1988. On the design of zoo research programmes. *Int'l. Zoo Yb*. 27:9–19

Hutchins, M. 1989. Wildlife conservation and zoos. *Zoo Biol.* 8:391–395.

Hutchins, M. and N. Fascione. 1991. Ethical issues facing modern zoos. *Proc. Amer. Assoc. Zoo Vets.* 1991:56–64.

Hutchins, M. and L. Gledhill. 1978. The use of closed circuit television for research, education, and animal management in a zoo setting. Pp. 25–50 in C. Crockett and M. Hutchins, eds. *Applied behavioral research*. Pika Press, Seattle, WA.

Hutchins, M., D. Hancocks and T. Calip. 1978. Behavioral engineering in the zoo: A critique. Parts I and II. *Int'l. Zoo News*. 25:18–23

Hutchins, M., D. Hancocks and T. Calip. 1979. Behavioral engineering in the zoo: A critique. Part III. *Int'l. Zoo News*. 26:20–27.

Hutchins, M., D. Hancocks and C. Crockett. 1983. Naturalistic solutions to the behavioral problems of captive animals. Part I. *Der Zool. Garten* 53:1–15.

Hutchins, M., D. Hancocks and C. Crockett. 1984. Naturalistic solutions to the behavioral problems of captive animals. Part II. *Der Zool. Garten* 54:28–42.

Idler, D.R. and T.B. Ng. 1983. Teleost gonadotropins: Isolation, biochemistry, and function. Pp. 187–221 in W.S. Hoar, D.J. Randall and E.M. Donaldson, eds. *Fish physiology*, Vol. IXA. Academic Press, New York, NY.

Idler, D.R., L.W. Crim and J.M. Walsh, eds. 1987. *Proc. 3rd Int'l. Symp. Reprod. Physiol. Fish*. Memorial Univ. Press, St. John's, Newfoundland.

Iela, L., R.K. Rostogi, G. Delrio and J.T. Bagnara. 1986. Reproduction in the Mexican leaf frog, *Pachymedusa dacnicolor*. III: The female. *Gen. Comp. Endocrinol*. 63:381–392.

Illius, A.W., N.B. Haynes, G.E. Lamming, C.M. Howles, N. Fairall and R.P. Millar. 1983. Evaluation of LH-RH stimulation of testosterone as an index of reproductive status in rams and its application in wild antelope. *J. Reprod. Fertil*. 68:105–112.

Immelmann, K. 1965. Pp. 136–146 in *Australian finches*. Angus & Robertson, Sydney, Australia.

Immelmann, K. 1971. Ecological aspects of periodic reproduction. Pp. 341–389 in D.S. Farner and J.R. King, eds. *Avian biology*, Vol. I. Academic Press, New York, NY.

Immelmann, K. 1972. Role of environment in reproduction as source of "predictive information." Pp. 121–147 in D.S. Farner, ed. *Breeding biology of birds*. Nat'l. Acad. Sci., Washington, DC.

Innis, G.S., M.H. Balph and D.F. Balph. 1985. On spatial requirements of captive social animals. *Anim. Behav*. 33:680–682.

Institute of Laboratory Animal Resources. 1980. Laboratory animal management: Nonhuman primate. *ILAR News* 23:1–44.

Institute of Laboratory Animal Resources. 1985. *Guide for the care and use of laboratory animals*. NIH Pub. 85–23. U.S. Dept. Health and Human Services, Washington, DC.

International Bird Rescue Research Center. 1978. Pp. 8–12 in A. Berkner and K. Hay, eds. *Saving oiled seabirds*. Amer. Petro. Institute, Washington, DC.

International Directory of Primatology. 1992. Pub. 32–010, Wisconsin Regional Primate Research Center, Madison, WI.

Irvine, A.B., R.S. Wells and M.D. Scott. 1982. An evaluation of techniques for tagging small odontocete cetaceans. *Fish. Bull.* 80:135–143.

Ising, H. 1981. Interaction of noise-induced stress and Mg decrease. *Artery* 9:205–211.

Isom, B.G. and R.G. Hudson. 1982. *In vitro* culture of parasitic freshwater mussel glochidia. *Nautilus* 96:147–151.

Itani, J. 1982. Intraspecific killing among non-human primates. *J. Soc. Biol. Struct.* 5:361–368.

IUCN (International Union for the Conservation of Nature and Natural Resources). 1983. *The IUCN Invertebrate Red Data Book*. Int'l. Union Conserv. Nature & Natur. Resour., Gland, Switzerland.

IUCN. 1985. List of threatened taxa. Int'l. Union Conserv. Nature & Natur. Resour. Conserv. Monitor. Centre's Anim. Data Base. Unpubl. Oct. 1985.

IUCN. 1986. *1986 IUCN Red list of threatened animals*. Int'l. Union Conserv. Nature & Natur. Resour., Gland, Switzerland.

IUCN. 1987. *The IUCN policy statement on captive breeding*. Int'l. Union Conserv. Nature & Natur. Resour., Gland, Switzerland.

IUCN. 1988a. *1988 IUCN Red list of threatened animals*. Int'l. Union Conserv. Nature & Natur. Resour., Gland, Switzerland.

IUCN. 1988b. *Captive breeding — the IUCN policy statement. Species.* Pp. 1027–1028. Int'l. Union Conserv. Nature & Natur. Resour., Gland, Switzerland.

IUCN. 1989. *Tortoises and freshwater turtles. An action plan for the conservation of biological diversity.* Int'l. Union Conserv. Nature & Natur. Resour./ Species Surviv. Commiss. Tortoise and Freshwater Turtle Specialist Group. Int'l. Union Conserv. Nature & Natur. Resour., Gland, Switzerland.

IUCN. 1990. *1990 IUCN Red list of threatened animals*. Int'l. Union Conserv. Nature & Natur. Resour., Gland, Switzerland.

IUCN. 1993. *1994 IUCN Red List of Threatened Animals.* Int'l. Union Conserv. Nature of Natur. Resour., Gland, Switzerland and Cambridge, United Kingdom.

IUCN/UNEP/WWF (International Union for the Conservation of Nature and Natural Resources/United Nations Environmental Program/World Wildlife Fund). 1980. *World conservation strategy: Living resource conservation for sustainable development.* Int'l. Union Conserv. Nature & Natur. Resour., Gland, Switzerland.

Iverson, J.B. 1978. The impact of feral cats and dogs on populations of the West Indian rock iguana, *Cyclura carinata*. *Biol. Conserv.* 14:63–73.

Iverson, J.B. 1979. Behavior and ecology of the rock iguana, *Cyclura carinata*. *Bull. Flor. State. Mus. Biol. Sci.* 24:175–358.

Iwamatsu, T. 1978a. Studies on oocyte maturation of the medaka, *Oryzias latipes*,V: On the structure of steroids that induce maturation *in vitro*. *J. Exp. Zool.* 204:401–408.

Iwamatsu, T. 1978b. Studies on oocyte maturation of the medaka, *Oryzias latipes*, VI: Relationship between the circadian cycles of oocyte maturation and activity of the pituitary gland. *J. Exp. Zool.* 206:355–364.

Izard, M.K. and M.E. Pereira. 1994. Design of indoor housing for a breeding and research colony of prosimian primates. Pp. 111–125 in E.F. Gibbons, Jr., E.J. Wyers, E.J. Waters and E.W. Menzel, Jr., eds. *Naturalistic environments in captivity for animal behavior research*. State Univ. New York Press, Albany, NY.

Jacob, J.S. and C.W. Painter. 1980. Overwinter thermal ecology of *Crotalus viridis* in the north-central plains of New Mexico. *Copeia* 1980:799–805.

Jacobi, E.F. 1975. Breeding sloth bears in Amsterdam zoo. Pp. 351–356 in R.D. Martin, ed. *Breeding endangered species in captivity*. Academic Press, London, England.

Jacobson, E.R. 1984. *Pseudomonas*. Pp. 37–47 in G.L. Hoff, F.L. Frye and E.R. Jacobson, eds. *Diseases of amphibians and reptiles*. Plenum Press, New York, NY.

Jacobson, H.A., H.J. Bearden and D.B. Whitehouse. 1989. Artificial insemination trials with white-tailed deer. *J. Wildl. Manage.* 53:224–227.

Jaenike, J. 1990. Host specialization in phytophagous insects. *Ann. Rev. Ecol. Sys.* 21:243–273.

Jaffe, R.B., M. Seron-Ferre, I. Huhtaniemi and C. Karenbrot. 1977. Regulation of the primate fetal adrenal gland and testis *in vitro* and *in vivo*. *J. Steroid Biochem.* 9:479–490.

Jaffe, R.B., M. Seron-Ferre, B.F. Mitchell and D. Koritnik. 1980. Adrenal and gonadal regulation and function in the primate fetus and infant. Pp. 359–378 in M. Serio and L. Martini, eds. *Animal models in human reproduction*. Raven Press, New York, NY.

Jallageas, M. and I. Assenmacher. 1974. Thyroid gonadal interactions in the male domestic duck in relationship with the sexual cycle. *Gen. Comp. Endocrinol.* 22:13–20.

Jander, R. 1977. Orientation ecology. Pp. 145–163 in B. Grzimek, ed. *Grzimek's encyclopedia of ethology*. Van Nostrand Reinhold, New York, NY.

Janzen, D.H. 1966. Why mountain passes are higher in the tropics. *Amer. Natural.* 101:233–249.

Jarchow, J.L. 1988. Hospital care of the reptile patient. Pp. 19–34 in E.R. Jacobson and G.V. Kollias, Jr., eds. *Exotic animals*. Churchill Livingstone, New York, NY.

Jarchow, J.L., H.K. McCrystal and D.F. Retes. 1991. Reptiles in captivity: A roundtable discussion. *Sonoran Herp.* 4:200–206.

Jarvis, J.U.M. 1981. Eusociality in a mammal: Cooperative breeding in naked mole-rat colonies. *Science* 212:571–573.

Jayewardene, E.D.W. 1975. Breeding the fishing cat, *Felis viverrina*, in captivity. *Int'l. Zoo Yb.* 15:150–152.

Jenkins, H. and B. Moore. 1973. The form of the auto-shaped response with food or water reinforcers. *J. Exp. Anal. Behav.* 20:163–181.

Jenkins, R.L. 1987. Of dolphins, men, and gods. *Proc. Int'l. Assoc. Aquat. Anim. Med.* 1987:194–198.

Jenkins, R.L. 1990. Federal legislation governing marine mammals. Pp. 469–482 in L.A. Dierauf, ed. *CRC handbook of marine mammal medicine: Health, disease and rehabilitation*. CRC Press, Boca Raton, FL.

Jenkins, R.L. 1991. Quips and quotes: An analysis of marine mammal display problems in the media. *Proc. Int'l. Marine Anim. Trainers Assoc.* 1991:194–198

Jenks, S.M. and B.E. Ginsburg. 1987. Socio-sexual dynamics in a captive wolf pack. Pp. 375–399 in H. Frank, ed. *Man and wolf: Advances, issues and problems in captive wolf research*. Dr. W. Junk, Dordrecht, Netherlands.

Jenni, D. and B. Betts. 1978. Sex differences in nest construction, incubation and parental behavior in the polyandrous American jacana (*Jacana spinosa*). *Anim. Behav.* 26:207–218.

Jennings, H.S. 1923. *The behavior of the lower organisms*. Columbia Univ. Press, New York, NY.

Jennings, J. 1981. First captive breeding of the emerald toucanet. *Amer. Fed. Avicult. Watchbird* Feb/Mar:22–24.

Jenssen, T.A. 1970. The ethoecology of *Anolis nebulosis* (Sauria, Iguanidae). *J. Herpetol.* 4:1–38.

Johanos, T.C. 1984. Hawaiian monk seal association patterns on Lisianski Island: 1982 pilot study results. S.W. Fish. Center Admin. Report H-84-18. Nat'l. Marine Fish. Serv., NOAA, Honolulu, HI.

Johns, A.D. and J.P. Skorupa. 1987. Responses of rain-forest primates to habitat disturbance: A review. *Int'l. J. Primatol.* 8:157–191.

Johnsen, D.V. and L.A. Whitehair. 1986. Research facility breeding. Pp. 499–511 in K. Benirschke, ed. *Primates: The road to self-sustaining populations*. Springer-Verlag, New York, NY.

Johnsgard, P.A. 1965. *Handbook of waterfowl behavior*. Cornell Univ. Press, Ithaca, NY.

Johnsgard, P.A. 1983a. *Cranes of the world*. Indiana Univ. Press, Bloomington, IN.

Johnsgard, P.A. 1983b. P. 52 in *Cranes of the world*. Indiana Univ. Press, Bloomington, IN

Johnsgard, P.A. 1983c. *Hummingbirds of North America*. Smithsonian Institution Press, Washington, DC.

Johnson, A.L. 1986a. Reproduction in the female. Pp. 403–431 in P.D. Sturkie, ed. *Avian physiology*, 4th Ed. Springer-Verlag, New York, NY.

Johnson, A.L. 1986b. Reproduction in the male. Pp. 432–451 in P.D. Sturkie, ed. *Avian physiology*, 4th Ed. Springer-Verlag, New York, NY.

Johnson, A.M., R.L. DeLong, C.H. Fiscus and K.W. Kenyon. 1982. Population status of the Hawaiian monk seal (*Monachus shauinslandi*), 1978. *J. Mammal.* 63:415–421.

Johnson, A.S. 1954. Artificial insemination and duration of fertility in geese. *Poult. Sci.* 33:638–640.

Johnson, C.R., G.J.W. Webb and C. Johnson. 1975. Thermoregulation in pythons — III: Thermal ecology and behavior of the black-headed rock python, *Aspidites melanocephalus*. *Herpetologica.* 31:326–332.

Johnson, C.S. 1986. Dolphin audition and echolocation capacities. Pp. 115–136 in R.J. Schusterman, J.A. Thomas and F.G. Wood, eds. *Dolphin cognition and behavior: A comparative approach*. Lawrence Earlbaum, Hillside, NJ.

Johnson, J.E. 1987. *Protected fishes of the United States and Canada*. Amer. Fish. Soc., Bethesda, MD.

Johnson, J.E. and B.L. Jensen. 1991. Hatcheries for endangered freshwater fishes. Pp. 199–217 in W.L. Minckley and J.E. Deacon, eds. *Battle against extinction—native fish management in the American West*. Univ. Arizona Press, Tucson, AZ.

Johnson, M.J., R.M. Harrison and W.R. Dukelow. 1972. Studies on oviductal fluid and *in vitro* fertilization in rabbits and nonhuman primates. *Fed. Proc.* 31:278. (Abstr.)

Joines, S. 1977. A training programme designed to induce maternal behaviour in a multiparous female lowland gorilla, *Gorilla g. gorilla*, at the San Diego Wild Animal Park. *Int'l. Zoo Yb.* 17:185–188.

Joint Herpetological Societies. 1987. Guidelines for use of live amphibians and reptiles in field research. *J. Herpetol.* Suppl. 4:1–14.

Jolly, A. 1972. Hour of birth in primates and man. *Folia Primatol.* 18:108–121.

Jolly, A. 1986. Lemur survival. Pp. 71–98 in K. Benirschke, ed. *Primates: The road to self-sustaining populations.* Springer-Verlag, New York, NY.

Jones, D.M. 1981. Veterinary care of non-domestic animals. *Int'l. Zoo News* 28:12–21.

Jones, G.E. 1987a. *The conservation of ecosystems and species.* Croom Helm, London, England.

Jones, J. 1986. Captive pinnipeds without blue swimming pools. *Proc. Amer. Assoc. Zool. Parks Aquar.* 1986:341–347.

Jones, R.E. 1987b. Ovulation: Insights about the mechanisms based on a comparative approach. Pp. 203–240 in D.O. Norris and R.E. Jones, eds. *Hormones and reproduction in fishes, amphibians, and reptiles.* Plenum Press, New York, NY.

Jordan, D. 1891. Report of explorations in Colorado and Utah during the summer of 1889, with an account of fishes in each of the river basins examined. *Bull. U.S. Fish Commiss.* 89:1–40.

Jordan, R.H. and G.M. Burghardt. 1986. Employing an ethogram to detect reactivity of black bears (*Ursus americanus*) to the presence of humans. *Ethology* 73:89–115.

Jordan, W.R., III., M.E. Gilpin and J.D. Aber. 1987. *Restoration ecology: A synthetic approach to ecological research.* Cambridge Univ. Press, New York, NY.

Jordano, D. and C.D. Thomas. 1992. Specificity of an ant-lycaenid interaction. *Oecologia* 91:431–438.

Jordano, D., J. R. Rodriguez, C.D. Thomas, J. Fernandez Haeger. 1992. The distribution and density of a lycaenid butterfly in relation to *Lasius* ant. *Oecologia* 91:439–446.

Joseph, B.E., J.E. Antrim, L.H. Cornell. 1987. Commerson's dolphin (*Cephalorhynchus commersonii*): A discussion of the first live birth within a marine zoological park. *Zoo Biol.* 6:69–77.

Joseph, B.E., L.H. Cornell and T.D. Williams. 1986. Chemical sedation in sea otters. Sea otter oil spill mitigation study. Minerals Manage. Serv., U.S. Dept. Interior, Contract No. 14-12-0001-31057.

Judges, M.K. 1988. National Aquarium in Baltimore—marine mammal system renovation. *Proc. Amer. Assoc. Zool. Parks Aquar.* 1988:336–343.

Junior, S.M., D.L. Armstrong, S.H. Hopkins, L.G. Simmons, M.C. Schiewe and T.S. Gross. 1990. Semen cryopreservation and the first successful artificial insemination of gaur (*Bos gaurus*). *Theriogenology* 33:262 (Abstr.).

Kadzen, A.E. 1982. *Single-case research designs: Methods for clinical and applied settings*. Oxford Univ. Press, London, England.

Kamil, A.C. and S.I. Yoerg. 1982. Learning and foraging behavior. Pp. 325–364 in P.P.G. Bateson and P.H. Klopfer, eds. *Perspectives in ethology, Vol V: Ontogeny*. Plenum Press, New York, NY.

Kamiyoshi, M. and K. Tanaka. 1983. Endocrine control of ovulatory sequence in domestic fowl. Pp. 167–177 in S. Mikami, K. Homma and M. Wada, eds. *Avian endocrinology: Environmental and ecological perspectives*. Japan Sci. Soc. Press, Tokyo, Japan/Springer-Verlag, Berlin, Germany.

Kanagawa, H. and E.S.E. Hafez. 1973. Morphology of cervix uteri of Rodentia, Carnivora and Artiodactyla. *Acta Anat.* 84:118–128.

Kant, R. and R.N. Saxena. 1982. Stimulatory and inhibitory effects of synthetic luteinizing hormone releasing hormone (Syn-LHRH) on reproductive activity of the male Indian weaver bird *Ploceus philippinus*. *Indian J. Exp. Biol.* 21:8–11.

Kanwisher, J.W. and S.H. Ridgway. 1983. The physiological ecology of whales and porpoises. *Sci. Amer.* 248:110–120.

Kar, A. and A. Chandola. 1985. Seasonality in birds and reptiles: The involvement of thyroxine and triiodothyroxine. Pp. 117–126 in B.K. Follett, S. Ishii and A. Chandola, eds. *The endocrine system and the environment*. Japan Sci. Soc. Press, Tokyo, Japan/Springer-Verlag, Berlin, Germany.

Karanth, K.U. 1987. Tigers in India: A critical review of field censuses. Pp. 118–132 in R.L. Tilson and U.S. Seal, eds. *Tigers of the world*. Noyes, Park Ridge, NJ.

Kardon, A. 1981. Reptile breeding techniques used at the San Antonio zoo: Emphasis on temperature and photoperiod manipulation. Pp. 83–85 in *5th Ann. Reptile Symp. on Captive Prop. and Husband*. Zool. Consortium, Thurmond, MD.

Karp, C. and H. Tyus. 1990. Behavioral interactions between young Colorado squawfish and six fish species. *Copeia* 1990:25–34.

Kasman, L.H., B. McCowan and B.L. Lasley. 1985. Pregnancy detection in tapirs by direct urinary estrone sulfate analysis. *Zoo Biol.* 4:301–306.

Kasman, L.H., E.C. Ramsey and B.L. Lasley. 1986. Urinary steroid evaluations to monitor ovarian function in exotic ungulates: III Estrone sulfate and pregnanediol-3-glucuronide excretion in the Indian rhinoceros (*Rhinoceros unicornis*). *Zoo Biol.* 5:355–361.

Kastelein, R.A. and T. Dokter. 1988. A safe and standardized technique to identify individual dolphins in human care. *Aquat. Mamm.* 14:13–20.

Kastelein, R.A. and P.R. Wiepkema. 1988. Case study of the neonatal period of a grey seal pup (*Halichoerus grypus*) in captivity. *Aquat. Mamm.* 14:33–38.

Kastelein, R.A. and P.R. Wiepkema. 1990. The suckling period of a grey seal (*Halichoerus grypus*) while confined to an outdoor land area. *Aquat. Mamm.* 16:120–128.

Kastelein, R.A., S. Stevens and P. Mosterd. 1990a. The tactile sensitivity of the mystacial vibrissae of a Pacific walrus (*Odobenus rosmarus divergens*). Part 2: Masking. *Aquat. Mamm.* 16:78–87.

Kastelein, R.A., N. Vaughan and P.R. Wiepkema. 1990b. The food consumption of Steller sea lions (*Eumetopias jubatus*). *Aquat. Mamm.* 15:137–144.

Kasuya, T., T. Tobayama, T. Saiga and T. Kataoka. 1986. Perinatal growth of Delphinoides: Information from aquarium reared bottlenose dolphins and finless porpoises. *Sci. Report Whales Res. Instit. Tokyo* 37:85–97.

Katona, S.K. 1989. Getting to know you. *Oceanus* 32:37–44.

Katona, S.K., P. Harcourt, J. Perkins and S. Kraus. 1980. *Humpback whales in the western North Atlantic ocean: A fluke catalog of individuals identified by means of fluke photographs*, 2nd Ed., College of the Atlantic, Bar Harbor, ME.

Kauffeld, C. 1969. The effect of altitude, ultra-violet light, and humidity on captive reptiles. *Int'l. Zoo Yb.* 9:8–9.

Kavanagh, M. and E. Bennett. 1984. A synopsis of legislation and the primate trade in habitat and user countries. Pp. 19–48 in D. Mack and R.A. Mittermeier, eds. *The international primate trade*, Vol. 1 TRAFFIC (USA). World Wildl. Fund-U.S. & Int'l. Union Conserv. Nat. & Nat. Resour./Species Survival Commiss. Specialist Group, Washington, DC.

Kavanagh, M., A.A. Eudey and D. Mack. 1987. The effects of live trapping and trade on primate populations. Pp. 147–177 in C.W. Marsh and R.A. Mittermeier, eds. *Primate conservation in the tropical rain forest*. Alan Liss, New York, NY.

Kawai, M. 1965. On the system of social ranks in a natural troop of Japanese monkeys: I. Basic rank and dependent rank. Pp. 66–86 in S.A. Altmann, ed. *Japanese monkeys: A collection of translations*. S.A. Altmann, Yerkes Region. Primate Ctr., Emory Univ., Atlanta, GA.

Kawai, M., S. Azuma and K. Yoshiba. 1967. Ecological studies of reproduction in Japanese monkeys (*Macaca fuscata*), I: Problems of the birth season. *Primates* 8:35–74.

Kawamura, S. 1965. Matriarchal social ranks in the Minoo-B troop: A study of the rank system of Japanese monkeys. Pp. 105–112 in S.A. Altmann, ed. *Japanese monkeys: A collection of translations*. S.A. Altmann, Yerkes Region. Primate Ctr., Emory Univ., Atlanta, GA.

Kear, J. 1970. The adaptive radiation of parental care in waterfowl. Pp. 357–392 in J.H. Crook, ed. *Social behaviour in birds and mammals*. Academic Press, London, England.

Kear, J. 1976. The presentation of food to captive waterfowl in relation to their natural behaviour. *Int'l. Zoo Yb*. 16:25–32.

Kear, J. and A.J. Berger. 1980. P. 76 in *The Hawaiian goose*. Buteo Books, Vermillion, SD.

Keeton, W.T. 1967. P. 895 in *Biological science*. W.W. Norton, New York, NY.

Keiter, M. and P. Pichette. 1977. Surrogate infant prepares a lowland gorilla, *Gorilla g. gorilla*, for motherhood. *Int'l. Zoo Yb*. 17:188–189.

Keller, E.C., R.H.T. Mattoni and M.S.B. Seiger. 1966. Preferential return of artifically displaced butterflies. *Anim. Behav*. 14:197–200.

Keller, K.V. 1987. Training of Atlantic bottlenose dolphins, *Tursiops truncatus*, for artificial insemination. *Proc. Int'l. Marine Anim. Trainers Assoc*. 1987:22–24.

Kellogg, W.N. and R. Kohler. 1952. Reactions of the porpoise to ultrasonic frequencies. *Science* 116:250–252.

Kellogg, W.N. and C.E. Rice. 1966. Visual discrimination and problem solving in a bottlenose dolphin. Pp. 731–754 in K.S. Norris, ed. *Whales, dolphins and porpoises*. Univ. California Press, Berkeley, CA.

Kelly, R.W. and G. Moore. 1981. Artificial insemination of red deer. New Zealand Min. Agric., Ann. Report 1980/81, Aukland, New Zealand.

Kennedy, S.E. 1977. Life history of the Leon Springs pupfish, *Cyprinodon bovinus*. *Copeia* 1977:93–103.

Kennon, H.M. 1931. The new bird house at St. Louis. *Avicult. Mag*. 37:37–43.

Kenyon, K.W. 1977. Caribbean monk seal extinct. *J. Mammal*. 58:97–98.

Kenyon, K.W. 1981. Sea otter *Enhydra lutris* (Linnaeus, 1758). Pp. 209–223 in S.H. Ridgway and R.J. Harrison, eds. *Handbook of marine mammals*, Vol 1. Academic Press, New York, NY.

Kepler, C.B. 1976. Dominance and dominance-related behavior in the whooping crane. Pp. 177–196 in J.C. Lewis, ed. *Proc. Int'l. Crane Workshop*. Oklahoma State Univ., Stillwater, OK.

Kepler, C.B. 1978. Captive propagation of whooping cranes, a behavioral approach. Pp. 231–241 in S.A. Temple, ed. *Endangered birds: Manage-*

ment techniques for preserving threatened species. Univ. Wisconsin. Press, Madison, WI.

Ketterson, E.D. and V. Nolan, Jr. 1987. Spring and summer confinement of dark-eyed juncos at autumn migratory destination suppresses normal autumn behavior. *Anim. Behav*. 35:1744–1753.

Keverne, E.B. 1979. Sexual and aggressive behavior in social groups of talapoin monkeys. Pp. 271–297 in *Sex, hormones and behavior*. Ciba Found. Symp. Vol 62, Excerpta Medica, Amsterdam, Netherlands.

Kholkute, S.D. 1984. Diurnal and annual variations in plasma androgen levels in the adult male marmoset (*Callithrix jacchus*). *Int'l. J. Androl*. 7:431–438.

Kholkute, S.D., S. Jayaraman, R. Asok Kumar and C.P. Puri. 1987. Continuous light environment has no effect on circadian testosterone rhythm, spermatogenesis or fertility of the marmoset (*Callithrix jacchus*). *Int'l. J. Androl*. 10:635–644.

Kholkute, S.D., R. Joseph, U.M. Joshi and S.R. Munshi. 1981a. Some characteristics of the normal menstrual cycle of the bonnet monkey (*Macaca radiata*). *Primates* 22:399–403.

Kholkute, S.D., R. Joseph, U.M. Joshi and S.R. Munshi. 1981b. Diurnal variations of serum testosterone levels in the male bonnet monkey (*Macaca radiata*). *Primates* 22:427–430.

Kiltie, R.A. 1982. Intraspecific variaton in the mammalian gestation period. *J. Mammal*. 63:646–652.

King, A.P., M.J. West and D.H. Eastzer. 1980a. Song structure and song development as potential contributors to reproductive isolation in cowbirds (*Molothrus ater*). *J. Comp. Physiol*. 94:1028–1039.

King, A.S. 1981a. Cloaca. Pp. 63–105 in A.S. King and J. McLelland, eds. *Form and function in birds*, Vol. 2. Academic Press, New York, NY.

King, A.S. 1981b. Phallus. Pp. 107–147 in A.S. King and J. McLelland, eds. *Form and function in birds*, Vol. 2. Academic Press, New York, NY.

King, C. 1990. Reproductive management of the Oriental white stork in captivity. *Int'l. Zoo Yb*. 29:85–90.

King, E.G. and N.C. Leppla, eds. 1984. Advances and challenges in insect rearing. Agricult. Research Serv., U.S. Dept. Agricult. Tech Bull., U.S. Govern. Print. Office, Washington, DC.

King, J.A., S. Dufour, Y.A. Fontaine and R.P. Millar. 1990. Chromatographic and immunological evidence for mammalian GnRH and chicken GnRH II in eel (*Anguilla anguilla*) brain and pituitary. *Peptides* 11:507–514.

King, J.E. 1983. *Seals of the world*, 2nd Ed. Cornell Univ. Press, Ithaca, NY.

King, N.E., V.J. Stevens and J.D. Mellen. 1980b. Social behavior in a captive chimpanzee (*Pan troglodytes*) group. *Primates* 21:198–210.

King, W.B. 1978. Endangered birds of the world and current efforts toward managing them. Pp. 9–17 in S.A. Temple, ed. *Endangered birds: Management techniques for preserving threatened species*. Univ. Wisconsin. Press, Madison, WI.

King, W.B., ed. 1979. *Red data book. Vol. 2: Aves*. Int'l. Union for Conserv. Nature & Natur. Resour., Morges, Switzerland.

King, W.B. 1985. Island birds: Will the future repeat the past? Pp. 3–15 in P.J. Moors, ed. *Conservation of island birds*. Tech. Pub. No. 3, Int'l. Council Bird Preserv. Page Bros., Norwich, England.

Kingdon, J. 1977. Carnivores. P. 475 in *East African mammals. An atlas of evolution in Africa*, IIIA. Academic Press, London, England.

Kingsbury, J.M. 1964. *Poisonous plants of the United States and Canada*. Prentice Hall, Englewood Cliffs, NJ.

Kingswood, S.C. and A.T. Kumamoto. 1988. Research and management of Arabian sand gazelle in the U.S.A. Pp. 221–226 in A. Dixon, and D. Jones, eds. *Conservation and biology of desert antelopes*. Cristopher Helm, London, England.

Kinkel, L.K. 1989. Lasting effects of wing tags on ring-billed gulls. *Auk* 106:619–624.

Kinne, O., ed. 1980. *Diseases of marine animals*, Vols. I–IV. John Wiley & Sons, New York, NY.

Kinney, S. 1980. *Partula* project: Moorea and Tahitian land snails. *Water Shed* 1980:June. Shedd Aquarium, Chicago, IL.

Kirby, V.L. and S.H Ridgway. 1984. Hormonal evidence of spontaneous ovulation in captive dolphins, *Tursiops truncatus* and *Delphinus delphi*. Pp. 459–464 in W.F. Perrin, R.L. Brownell and D.F. DeMasters, eds. *Reproduction in whales, dolphins and porpoises*. Int'l. Whaling Commiss. Spec. Issue 6. Cambridge, England.

Kirkevold, B.C. 1986. Introduction and management issues of wild and captive killer whales. Pp. 3–16 in B.S. Kirkevold and J.S. Lockard, eds. *Behavioral biology of killer whales*. Zoo Biol. Monogr. Vol. 1. Alan Liss, New York, NY.

Kirkevold, B.C. and J.S. Lockard, eds. 1986. *Behavioral biology of killer whales*. Zoo Biol. Monogr. Vol. 1. Alan Liss, New York, NY.

Kirkpatrick, J.F., V. Kincy, K. Bancroft, S.E. Shideler and B.L. Lasley. 1991. Oestrous cycle of the North American bison (*Bison bison*) characterized by urinary pregnanediol-3-glucuronide. *J. Reprod. Fertil.* 93:541–547.

Kirton, K.T., G.G. Niswender, A.R. Midgley, Jr, R.B. Jaffe and A.D. Forbes. 1970. Serum luteinizing hormone and progesterone concentration during the menstrual cycle of the rhesus monkey. *J. Clin. Endocrinol.* 30:105–110.

Kish, F. 1970. Egg laying and incubation by American golden eagles. *Int'l. Zoo Yb.* 10:26–29.

Kleiman, D.G. 1974. Activity rhythms in the giant panda *Ailuropoda melanoleuca*: An example of the use of checksheets for recording behaviour data in zoos. *Int'l. Zoo Yb.* 14:165–169.

Kleiman, D.G. 1978. Characteristics of reproduction and sociosexual interactions in pairs of lion tamarins (*Leontopithecus rosalia*) during the reproductive cycle. Pp. 181–190 in D.G. Kleiman, ed. *The biology and conservation of the Callitrichidae.* Smithsonian Instit. Press, Washington, DC.

Kleiman, D.G. 1980. The sociobiology of captive propagation. Pp. 243–261 in M.E. Soulé and B.A. Wilcox, eds. *Conservation biology: An evolutionary-ecological perspective.* Sinauer Assoc., Sunderland, MA.

Kleiman, D.G. 1983. Ethology and reproduction of captive giant pandas (*Ailuropoda melanoleuca*). *Z. Tierpsychol.* 62:1–46.

Kleiman, D.G. 1985. Criteria for the evaluation of zoo research projects. *Zoo Biol.* 4:93–98.

Kleiman, D.G. 1989. Reintroduction of captive mammals for conservation: Guidelines for reintroducing endangered species into the wild. *BioScience* 39:152–159.

Kleiman, D.G. and J.F. Eisenberg. 1973. Comparisons of canid and felid social systems from an evolutionary perspective. *Anim. Behav.* 21:637–659.

Kleiman, D.G. and M. Jones. 1978. The current status of *Leontopithecus rosalia* in captivity with comments on breeding success at the National Zoological Park. Pp. 215–218 in D.G. Kleiman, ed. *The biology and conservation of the Callitrichidae.* Smithsonian Instit. Press, Washington, DC.

Kleiman, D.G. and J.R. Malcolm. 1981. The evolution of male parental investment in mammals. Pp. 347–387 in D.J. Gubernick and P.H. Klopfer, eds. *Parental care in mammals.* Plenum Press, New York, NY.

Kleiman, D.G., B.B. Beck, J.M. Dietz, L.A. Dietz, J.D. Ballou and A.F. Coimbra-Filho. 1986. Conservation program for the golden lion tamarin: Captive research and management, ecological studies, educational strategies and reintroduction. Pp. 959–979 in K. Benirschke, ed. *Primates: The road to self-sustaining populations*. Springer-Verlag, New York, NY.

Klimstra, W.D. and T.G. Scott. 1973. Adaptation of pen-reared bobwhites to foods in a natural environment. *J. Wildl. Manage*. 37:492–494.

Kling, O.R. and P.K. Westfahl. 1978. Steroid changes during the menstrual cycle of the baboon (*Papio cynocephalus*) and human. *Biol. Reprod*. 18:392–400.

Klinowska, M. 1991. *Dolphins, porpoises, and whales of the world. IUCN red data book*. Int'l. Union Conserv. Nature & Natur. Resour., Gland, Switzerland and Cambridge, U.K.

Klishin, V.O., R.P. Diaz, V.V. Popov and A.Y. Supin. 1990. Some characteristics of hearing in the Brazilian manatee, *Trichechus inguinus. Aquat. Mamm*. 16:129–144.

Kluger, M.J., D.H. Ringler and M.R. Anver. 1975. Fever and survival. *Science* 188:166–168.

Klugman, S.S. 1987. Response of captive sandhill cranes to management-related disturbances. Master's Thesis, Pennsylvania State Univ., State College, PA.

Knick, S.T. and D.L. Mech. 1980. Sleeping distance in wild wolf packs. *Behav. Neural Biol*. 28:507–511.

Knobil, E. 1971. Hormonal control of the menstrual cycle and ovulation in the rhesus monkey. Pp. 137–144 in *Symposium on the use of nonhuman primates for research on problems of human reproduction*. World Health Org., Geneva, Switzerland.

Knobil, E. and T.M. Plant. 1978. Neuroendocrine control of gonadotropin secretion in the female rhesus monkey. *Front. Neuroendocrinol*. 5:249–263.

Kobayashi, H. and M. Wada. 1973. Neuroendocrinology in birds. Pp. 287–347 in D.S. Farner and J.R. King, eds. *Avian biology*, Vol. III. Academic Press, New York, NY.

Kobayashi, H., K. Aida and I. Hanyu. 1986. Annual changes in plasma levels of gonadotropin and steroid hormones in goldfish. *Bull. Japan. Soc. Fish*. 52:1153–1158.

Kobayashi, H., K. Aida and I. Hanyu. 1987. Hormone changes during ovulation and effects of steroid hormones on plasma gonadotropin levels and ovulation in goldfish. *Gen. Comp. Endocrinol*. 67:24–32.

Kobayashi, H., K. Aida and I. Hanyu. 1988. Hormone changes during the ovulatory cycle in goldfish. *Gen Comp. Endocrinol*. 69:301–307.

Koch, D.L. and G.P. Contreras. 1973. Hatching technique for the cui-ui lakesucker (*Chasmistes cujus*, Cope 1883). *Progr. Fish. Cultur.* 35:61–63.

Kodric-Brown, A. 1981. Variable breeding systems in pupfishes (genus *Cyprinodon*): Adaptations to changing environments. Pp. 205–235 in R. Naiman and D. Soltz, eds. *Fishes in North American deserts*. John Wiley & Sons, New York, NY.

Koering, M.J. 1978. Folliculogensis in primates: Process of maturation and atresia. Pp. 187–199 in N.J. Alexander, ed. *Animals models for research on contraception and fertility*. Harper & Row, London, England.

Koford, C.B. 1965. Population dynamics of rhesus monkeys and Cayo Santiago. Pp. 160–174 in I. DeVore, ed. *Primate behavior: Field studies of monkeys and apes*. Holt, Rinehart & Winston, New York, NY.

Koford, C.B. 1966. Population changes in rhesus monkeys: Cayo Santiago, 1960–1964. *Tulane Studies in Zool.* 13:1–7.

Kohler, C.C. and W.R. Courtenay, Jr. 1986. American Fisheries Society position on introductions of aquatic species. *Fisheries* 11:39–42.

Kohler, W. 1927. *The mentality of apes*. Harcourt, Brace, Jovanovich, New York, NY.

Komen, J., G.F. Wiegertjes, V.J.T. van Ginneken, E.H. Eding and C.J.J. Richter. 1992. Gynogenesis in common carp (*Cyprinus carpio* L.), III: The effects of inbreeding on gonadal development of heterozygous and homozygous gynogenetic offspring. *Aquacult.* 104:51–66.

Konstant, W.R. 1986. Considering subspecies in the captive management of *Ateles*. Pp. 911–920 in K. Benirschke, ed. *Primates: The road to self-sustaining populations*. Springer-Verlag, New York, NY.

Kopec, S. 1922. Studies on the necessity of the brain for the inception of insect metamorphosis. *Biol. Bull. Woods Hole* 42:323–342.

Kopff, H.O. and W.B. Mager. 1990. Further developments in the breeding population of lowland gorillas at Aspenheul. *Zoo Biol.* 9:165–170.

Korpi, R., ed. 1991. Spring 1991 whooping crane report. *Nebraska Bird Rev.* 59:61–62.

Kosztareb, M. 1984. A biological survey of the United States. *Science* 223:443.

Kots-Ladygin, N. 1923. N. Untersuchen uber die Erkenntnisfahigkeiten des Schimpansen. Published in Moscow. Cited in 1925 by Yerkes, R.M. in *Almost human*. Century, New York, NY.

Kovisto, I. 1977. The breeding and maintenance of some northern European waders *Charadii* at Helsinki Zoo. *Int'l. Zoo Yb* 17:150–153.

Koyama, T. 1976. Mechanisms of LH release with synthetic LH-RH. *Folia Endocrinol. Japan* 52:881–897.

Kozol, A., M.P. Scott and J.F.A. Traniello. 1988. The American burying beetle, *Niccrophorus americanus*: Studies on the natural history of a declining species. *Psyche* 95:167–176.

Kraemer, D.C., S.S. Kalter and G.T. Moore. 1975. The establishment of non-human primate breeding colonies at the Southwest Foundation for Research and Education. *Lab. Anim. Handbk.* 6:41–47.

Kraemer, D.C., G.T. Moore and M.A. Kramen. 1976. Baboon infant produced by embryo transfer. *Science* 192:1246–1247.

Kraemer, D.C., B.L. Flow, M.D. Schriver, G.M. Kinney and J.W. Pennycock. 1979. Embryo transfer in the nonhuman primate, feline and canine. *Theriogenology* 11:51–62.

Krajniak, E. 1984. A new marine mammal facility for Brookfield Zoo. *Proc. Int'l. Marine Anim. Trainers Assoc.* 1984:56–57.

Krajniak, E.F. 1987. Opening a new marine mammal exhibit. *Proc. Int'l Marine Anim. Trainers Assoc.* 1987:63–66.

Krames, B. 1984. The conditioning of various behaviors for animal husbandry of killer whales. *Proc. Int'l. Marine Anim. Trainers Assoc.* 1984:51–55

Kraus, S.D., K.E. Moore, C.A. Price, M.J. Crone, W.A. Watkins, H.E. Winn and J.H. Prescott. 1986. *The use of photographs to identify individual North Atlantic right whales (Eubalaena glacialis).* Report Int'l. Whaling Commiss. Special Issue D., Cambridge, England.

Krause, B.L. 1989. Habitat ambient sound as a function of transformation for resident animals and visitors at zoos, aquaria, and theme parks: A hypothesis. *Proc. Amer. Assoc. Zool. Parks Aquar.* 1989:415–419.

Kreeger, T.J., cd. 1991. Przewalski's horse global management plan. *Captive Breeding Specialist Group News* 2:10–11.

Kreitmann, O., A. Lynch, W.R. Nixon and G.D. Hodgen. 1982. Ovum collection, induced luteal dysfunction, *in vitro* fertilization, embryo development and low tubal ovum transfer in primates. Pp. 303–324 in E.S.E. Hafez and K. Semm, eds. *In vitro fertilization and embryo transfer.* MTP Press, Lancaster, England.

Kruuk, H. and H. Snell. 1981. Prey selection by feral dogs from a population of marine iguanas (*Amblyrhynchus cristatus*). *J. Applied Ecol.* 18:197–204.

Kuchling, G. 1982. Effect of temperature and photoperiod on spermatogenesis in the tortoise, *Testudo hermanni hermanni* Gremlin. *Amphibia-Reptilia* 2:329–341.

Kuchling, G. 1989. New hope for recovery from the brink of extinction: *Pseudemydura umbrina*, the rarest turtle on earth, breeds again. *Int'l. Union Conserv. Nature & Natur. Resources. Tortoise and Freshwater Turtle Specialist Group Newsletter* September 1989:16–19.

Kuchling, G. and Q.M.C. Bloxam. 1988. Field data on the Madagascan flat tailed tortoise *Pyxis (Acinixys) planicauda. Amphibia-Reptilia* 9:175–180.

Kujala, G.A. 1978. Corticosteroid and neurohypophyseal hormone control of parturition in the guppy, *Poecilia reticulata. Gen. Comp. Endocrinol.* 36:286–296.

Kummer, H. 1968. *Social organization of Hamadryas baboon: A field study.* Univ. Chicago Press, Chicago, IL.

Kunz, T.H. and K.A. Nagy. 1988. Methods of energy budget analysis. Pp. 277–302 in T.H. Kutz, ed. *Ecological and behavioral methods for the study of bats.* Smithsonian Instit. Press, Washington, DC.

Kuznetsov, V.B. 1974. A method of studying chemoreception in Black Sea bottlenose dolphins (*Tursiops truncatus*). Pp. 147–153 in V. Ye. Sokolov, ed. *Morfologiys, fisiologiya i Akustika Morskikh Miekopitayushchikh.* Izdatel'stvo "Nauka." Moscow, Russia.

Kydd, J., M.S. Boyle, W.R. Allen, A. Shephard and P.M. Summers. 1985. Transfer of exotic equine embryos to domestic horses and donkeys. *Equine Vet. J. Suppl.* 3:80–83.

Kyle, A.L., P.W. Sorensen, N.E. Stacey and J.G. Dulka. 1987. Medial olfactory tract pathways controlling sexual reflexes and behavior in teleosts. *Annals New York Acad. Sci.* 519:97–107.

Kyle, A.L., N.E. Stacey, R.E. Peter and R. Billard. 1985. Elevations in gonadotrophin concentrations and milt volumes as a result of spawning behavior in the goldfish. *Gen. Comp. Endocrinol.* 57:10–22.

LaBarge, T., A. Baker and D. Moore. 1990. Fisher (*Martes pennanti*): Birth, growth, and development in captivity. *Mustelid and Viverrid Conserv.* 2:1–3.

Labeyrie, V. 1978. The significance of the environment in the control of insect fecundity. *Ann. Rev. Entomol.* 23:69–89.

Labuschagne, W. 1989. The conservation of biological diversity through co-operation. *Proc. 44th Ann. Conf. Int'l. Union Direct. Zool. Gardens.* 1989:59–69.

Lack, D. 1968. *Ecological adaptations for breeding in birds.* Methuen, London, England.

Lake, P.E. 1978. The principles and practice of semen collection and preservation in birds. *Symp. Zool. Soc. London* 43:31–49.

Lake, P.E. 1981. Male genital organs. Pp. 1–61 in A.S. King and J. McLelland, eds. *Form and function in birds*, Vol. 2. Academic Press, New York, NY.

Lake, P.E. and J.M. Steward. 1978. Artificial insemination in poultry. Bull. Min. Agr. Fish. Fd. No. 213. London, England.

Lal, P. and J.P. Thapliyal. 1985. Photorefractoriness in migratory red-headed buntings *Emberiza buniceps*. Pp. 137–148 in B.K. Follett, S. Ishii and A. Chandola, eds. *The endocrine system and the environment*. Japan. Sci. Soc. Press, Tokyo, Japan/Spinger-Verlag, Berlin, Germany.

Lam, T.J. 1982a. Applications of endocrinology to fish culture. *Can. J. Fish. Aquat. Sci.* 39:111–137.

Lam, T.J. 1982b. Fish culture in southeast Asia. *Can. J. Fish. Aquat. Sci.* 39:138–142.

Lam, T.J. 1983. Environmental influences on gonadal activity in fish. Pp. 65–116 in W.S. Hoar, D.J. Randall and E.M. Donaldson, eds. *Fish physiology*, Vol. IXB. Academic Press, New York, NY.

Lambert, H. 1981. Temperature dependence of capacitation in bat sperm monitored by zona-free hamster ova. *Gamete Res.* 4:525–533.

Lampe, K. and M.A. McCann. 1985. *AMA handbook of poisonous and injurious plants*. Amer. Med. Assoc., Chicago, IL.

Lance, V.A. 1984. Endocrinology of reproduction in male reptiles. *Symp. Zool. Soc. London* 52:357–383.

Lance, V.A. 1989. Reproductive cycle of the American alligator. *Amer. Zool.* 29:999–1018.

Lance, V.A. and R.M. Elsey. 1986. Stress induced suppression of testosterone secretion in male alligators. *J. Exp. Zool.* 239:241–264.

Lance, V., T. Joanen and L. McNease. 1983. Selenium, vitamin E, and trace elements in the plasma of wild and farm-reared alligators during the reproductive cycle. *Can. J. Zool.* 61:1744–1751.

Lance, V.A., K. Vilet and J.L. Bolaffi. 1985. Effect of mammalian luteinizing hormone-releasing hormone on plasma testosterone in male alligators, with observations on the nature of alligator hypothalamic gonadotropin-releasing hormone. *Gen. Comp. Endocrinol.* 60:138–143.

Land, R.B. 1984. Genetics and reproduction. Pp. 62–102 in C.R. Austin and R.V. Short, eds. *Reproduction in mammals: 4. Reproductive fitness*. Cambridge Univ. Press, New York, NY.

Lande, R. 1988. Genetics and demography in biological conservation. *Science* 241:1455–1460.

Lang, J. 1987. *Creating architectural theory: The role of behavioral sciences in environmental design.* Van Nostrand Reinhold, New York, NY.

Lang, J.W. 1989a. Sex determination. P. 120 in C.A. Ross, ed. *Crocodiles and alligators.* Facts on File, New York, NY.

Lang, J.W. 1989b. Social behavior. Pp. 102–116 in *Crocodiles and alligators.* Facts on File, New York, NY.

Langhans, R.W. ed. 1978. *A growth chamber manual: Environmental control for plants.* Comstock, Cornell Univ. Press, Ithaca, NY.

Langman, V.A. 1977. Cow-calf relationships in giraffe. *Zeitschrift Tierphychol.* 43:264–286.

Langman, V.A. 1985. Heat balance in the black rhinoceros (*Diceros bicornis*). *Nat'l. Geogr. Res. Reports* 21:251–254.

Langman, V.A. 1990. Thermal profile of the African elephant enclosure at Zoo Atlanta. Report to Zoo Atlanta, Atlanta, GA.

Langman, V.A., O.S. Bamford and G.M.O. Maloiy. 1982. Respiration and metabolism in the giraffe. *Respir. Physiol.* 50:141–152.

LaRivers, I. 1962. *Fishes and fisheries of Nevada.* Nevada State Game and Fish Commission. Reno, NV.

Larsen, R.E., P.T. Cardeilhac and T.J. Lane. 1984. Semen extenders for artificial insemination in the American alligator. *Aquacult.* 42:141–149.

Larson, B. and J. Vijaya. 1981. Mugger breeding in Nehru Zoological Park, Hyderabad. *Hamadryad* 6:11–12.

Lasley, B.L. 1980. Endocrine research advances in breeding endangered species. *Int'l. Zoo Yb.* 20:166–170.

Lasley, B.L., D.G. Lindburg, P.T. Robinson and K. Benirschke. 1981. Captive breeding of exotic species. *J. Zoo Anim. Med.* 12:67–73.

Lasley, J.F. 1978. *Genetics in livestock improvement.* Prentice-Hall, Englewood Cliffs, NJ.

Laszlo, J. 1969. Observations on two new artificial lights for reptile displays. *Int'l. Zoo Yb.* 9:12–13.

Laszlo, J. 1979. Notes on thermal requirements of reptiles and amphibians in captivity. *3rd Ann. Reptile Symp. Captive Prop. Husbandry.* 1979:24–43.

Lawrence, B. and W.E. Schevill. 1954. *Tursiops* as an experimental subject. *J. Mammal.* 35:225–232.

Lawson, J. and P. Parker. 1990. The Flipper flap. *Florida Environ.* October:1–30.

Laxter, J.H.S. The rearing of larval fish. Pp. 303–324 in A.D Hawkins, ed. *Aquarium systems*. Academic Press, New York, NY.

Leatherwood, S. 1975. Some observations of feeding behavior of bottlenose dolphins (*Tursiops truncatus*) in the northern Gulf of Mexico and (*Tursiops t. gilli*) off southern California, Baja California, and Nayarit, Mexico. *Marine Fish. Rev.* 37:10–16.

Leatherwood, S. and R. Reeves. 1990. *The bottlenose dolphin*. Harcourt, Brace, Jovanovich, Orlando, FL.

Le Boeuf, B.J. and R.S. Peterson. 1969. Dialects in elephant seals. *Science* 166:1654–1656.

Le Boeuf, B.J., D.G. Ainley and T.J. Lewis. 1974. Elephant seals on the Farallones: Population structure of an incipient breeding colony. *J. Mammal*. 55:370–385.

Le Boeuf, B.J., K.W. Kenyon and B. Villa-Ramirez. 1986. The Caribbean monk seal is extinct. *Marine Mamm. Sci*. 2:70–72.

Le Boeuf, B.J., R.J. Whiting and R.F Gantt. 1972. Perinatal behavior of northern elephant seal females and their young. *Behavior* 43:121–156.

Lecouteux, A., D.H. Garnier, T. Bassez and J. Joly. 1985. Seasonal variations of androgens, estrogens, and progesterone in the different lobules of the testis and in the plasma of *Salamandra salamandra*. *Gen. Comp. Endocrinol*. 58:211–221.

LeCroy, M. 1981. The genus *Paradisaea*—display and evolution. *Amer. Mus. Novit*. 2714:1–52.

Lederhouse, R.C. 1990. Avoiding the hunt: Primary defenses of Lepidopteran caterpillars. Pp. 175–189 in D.L. Evans and J.O. Schmidt, eds. *Insect defenses: Adaptive mechanisms and strategies of prey and predators*. State Univ. New York Press, Albany, NY.

Lederhouse, R.C., M.P. Ayres and J.M. Scriber. 1990. Adult nutrition affects male virility in *Papilio glaucus*. *Funct. Ecol*. 4:743–751.

Lee, A.K. and A. Cockburn. 1985. *The evolutionary ecology of marsupials*. Cambridge Univ. Press, New York, NY.

Lee, C.S., C.S. Tamaru, C.D. Kelley, G.T. Miyamoto and A.M. Moriwake. 1992. The minimum effective dosage of 17α-methyltestosterone for induction of testicular maturation in the striped mullet, *Mugil cephalus* L. *Aquacult*.104:183–191.

Lee, P.C., J. Thornback and E.L. Bennett. 1988. *Threatened primates of Africa: The IUCN red data book*. Int'l. Union Conserv. Nature & Natur. Resour., Gland, Switzerland.

Lehner, P.N. 1979. *Handbook of ethological methods*. Garland, New York, NY.

Lehrman, D.S. 1958. Induction of broodiness by participation in courtship and nest-building in the ring dove (*Streptopelia risoria*). *J. Comp. Physiol. Psychol*. 51:32–36.

Leighton, M. 1986. Hornbill social dispersion: Variations on a monogamous theme. P. 112 in D.I. Rubenstein and R.W. Wrangham, eds. *Ecological aspects of social evolution*. Princeton Univ. Press, Princeton, NJ.

Lemonick, M.D. 1989. The two Alaskas. *Time* April 17:56–66.

Lennartz, M.R., R.G. Hooper and R.F. Harlow. 1987. Sociality and cooperative breeding of red-cockaded woodpeckers, *Picoides borealis. Behav. Ecol. Sociobiol*. 20:77–88.

Lent, P.C. 1974. Mother-infant relationships in ungulates. Pp. 14–55 in V. Geist and F. Walther, eds. *The behavior of ungulates and its relation to management*. Int'l. Union Conserv. Nature & Natur. Resour., Morges, Switzerland.

Leopold, R.A. 1976. The role of male accessory glands in insect reproduction. *Ann. Rev. Entomol*. 21:199–221.

Lepore, P.D. and A.L. Marks. 1966. Intravaginal insemination of Japanese quail: Factors influencing the basic techniques. *Poult. Sci*. 45:888–891.

Leuthold, W. 1977. *African ungulates*. Springer-Verlag, New York, NY.

Levey, D.J. 1987. Sugar-tasting ability and fruit selection in tropical fruit-eating birds. *Auk* 104:173–179.

Levey, D.J., T.C. Moerman and J.S. Denslow. 1984. Fruit choice in neotropical birds: The effect of distance between fruits on preference patterns. *Ecology* 65:844–850.

Levi, U.A. 1993. Spatial logic of animal culture: Implications for bioexhibit design. Ph.D. Dissertation. Georgia Institute of Technology, Atlanta, GA.

Lewis, M. 1978. Acute toxicity of copper, zinc and manganese in single and mixed salt solutions to juvenile longfin dace, *Agosia chrysogaster. J. Fish. Biol*. 13:695–700.

Li-Chan, E. and S. Naki. 1989. Biochemical basis for the properties of egg white. Pp. 21–58 in R.R. Dietert, ed. *Reviews in poultry biology*, Vol. 2, Issue 1. CRC Press, Boca Raton, FL.

Licht, P. 1965. The relation between preferred body temperatures and testicular heat sensitivity in lizards. *Copeia* 1965:428–436.

Licht, P. 1970. Effects of mammalian gonadotropins (ovine FSH and LH) in female lizards. *Gen. Comp. Endocrinol*. 14:98–106.

Licht, P. 1972. Actions of mammalian pituitary gonadotropins (FSH and LH) in reptiles. II: Turtles. *Gen. Comp. Endocrinol.* 19:282–289.

Licht, P. 1973. Thermal and photic influences on reptilian reproduction. Int'l. Endocrinol. Congr., Washington, DC., *Excerpta Med. Int'l. Congr. Serv.* 273:185–190.

Licht, P. 1975. Temperature dependence of the actions of mammalian and reptilian gonadotropins in a lizard. *Comp. Biochem. Physiol.* 50A:221–222.

Licht, P. 1979. Reproductive endocrinology of reptiles and amphibians. *Ann. Rev. Physiol.* 41:337–351.

Licht, P. 1980. Evolutionary and functional aspects of pituitary gonadotropins in the green turtle, *Chelonia mydas*. *Amer. Zool.* 20:565–574.

Licht, P. 1984. Reptiles. Pp. 206–282 in G.E. Lamming, ed. *Marshall's physiology of reproduction*. Churchill Livingstone, New York, NY.

Licht, P. and H. Papkoff. 1976. Species specificity in the response of an *in vitro* amphibian (*Xenopus laevis*) ovulation assay to mammalian luteinizing hormones. *Gen. Comp. Endocrinol.* 29:552–555.

Licht, P. and H. Papkoff. 1985. Reevaluation of the relative activities of the pituitary glycoprotein hormones (follicle stimulating hormone, luteinizing hormone and thyrotrophin) from the green sea turtle, *Chelonia mydas*. *Gen. Comp. Endocrinol.* 58:443–451.

Licht, P. and D.A. Porter. 1987. Role of gonadotropin-releasing hormone in regulation of gonadotropin secretion from amphibian and reptilian pituitaries. Pp. 61–85 in D. Norris and R.E. Jones, eds. *Hormones and reproduction in fishes*. Plenum Press, New York, NY.

Licht, P., G.L. Breitenbach and J.D. Congdon. 1985. Seasonal cycles in testicular activity, gonadotropin and thyroxine in the painted turtle, *Chrysemys picta*, under natural conditions. *Gen. Comp. Endocrinol.* 59:130–139.

Licht, P., S.W. Farmer and H. Papkoff. 1976. Further studies on the chemical nature of reptilian gonadotropins: FSH and LH in the American alligator and green sea turtle. *Biol. Reprod.* 14:222–232.

Licht, P., D. Porter and R.P. Millar. 1987. Specificity of amphibian and reptilian pituitaries for various forms of gonadotropin-releasing hormones *in vitro*. *Gen. Comp. Endocrinol.* 66:248–255.

Licht, P., W. Rainey and K. Cliffton. 1980. Serum gonadotropin and steroids associated with breeding activities in the green sea turtle, *Chelonia mydas*. II: Mating and nesting in natural populations. *Gen. Comp. Endocrinol.* 40:116–122.

Licht, P., S.W. Farmer, A. Bona-Gallo and H. Papkoff. 1979a. Pituitary gonadotropins in snakes. *Gen. Comp. Endocrinol.* 39:34–52.

Licht, P., B.R. McCreery, R. Barnes and R. Pang. 1983. Seasonal and stress related changes in plasma gonadotropins, sex steroids, and corticosterone in the bullfrog, *Rana catesbeiana. Gen. Comp. Endocrinol.* 50:124–145.

Licht, P., D.W. Owen, K. Cliffton and C. Penaflores. 1982. Changes in LH and progesterone associated with the nesting cycle of the olive ridley sea turtle, *Lepidochelys olivacea. Gen. Comp. Endocrinol.* 48:247–253.

Licht, P., J. Wood, D.W. Owens and F. Wood. 1979b. Serum gonadotropins and steroids associated with breeding activities in the green turtle *Chelonia mydas.* I: Captive animals. *Gen. Comp. Endocrinol.* 39:274–289.

Licht, P., R. Millar, J.A. King, B.R. McCreery, M.T. Mendonca, A. Bona-Gallo and B. Lofts. 1984. Effects of chicken and mammalian gonadotropin-releasing hormones (GnRH) on *in vivo* pituitary gonadotropin release in amphibians and reptiles. *Gen. Comp. Endocrinol.* 54:89–96.

Lidicker, W.Z. 1989. Rodents: *A world survey of species of conservation concern.* Int'l. Union Conserv. Nature & Natur. Resour., Gland, Switzerland.

Lieberman, A., J.W. Wiley, J.V. Rodriguez and J.M. Paez. 1991. The first experimental reintroduction of captive-reared Andean condors (*Vultur gryphus*) into Columbia, South America. *Proc. Amer. Assoc. Zool. Parks Aquar.* 1991:129–136.

Liewes, E.W. 1984. *Culture, feeding and diseases of commercial flatfish species.* A. A. Balkema, Boston, MA.

Light, P., W.R. Dawson, V.H. Shoemaker and A.R. Main. 1966. Observations on the thermal relations of western Australian lizards. *Copeia* 1966:97–110.

Light, R., P. Adler and D. Arnold. 1983. Evaluation of gastric lavage for stomach analysis. *N. Amer. J. Fish. Manage.* 3:81–85.

Liley, N.R. and N.E. Stacey. 1983. Hormones, pheromones, and reproductive behavior in fish. Pp. 1–63 in W.S. Hoar, D.J. Randall and E.M. Donaldson, eds. *Fish physiology*, Vol. IXB. Academic Press, New York, NY.

Liley, N.R., B. Breton, A. Fostier and E.S.P. Tan. 1986a. Endocrine changes associated with spawning behavior and social stimuli in a wild population of rainbow trout (*Salmo gairdneri*), I: Males. *Gen. Comp. Endocrinol.* 62:145–156.

Liley, N.R., A. Fostier, B. Breton and E.S.P. Tan. 1986b. Endocrine changes associated with spawning behavior and social stimuli in a wild population of rainbow trout (*Salmo gairdneri*), II: Females. *Gen. Comp. Endocrinol.* 62:157–167.

Lilly, J.C. 1975. *Lilly on dolphins*. Anchor Press/Doubleday, New York, NY.

Lin, H.R., C. Peng, G. Van Der Kraak and R.E. Peter 1989. Dopamine inhibits gonadotropin secretion in the Chinese loach (*Paramisgurnus dabryanus*) *Fish Physiol. Biochem.* 6:285–288.

Lin, H.R., M.L. Zhang, S.M. Zhang, G. Van Der Kraak and R.E. Peter. 1991a. Stimulation of pituitary gonadotropin and ovarian development by chronic administration of testosterone in female Japanese silver eel, *Anguilla japonica. Aquacult.* 96:87–95.

Lin, H.R., M.L. Zhang, S.M. Zhang, G. Van Der Kraak and R.E. Peter. 1991b. Effects of gonadotropin-releasing hormone agonists and dopamine antagonists on gonadotropin secretion and ovulation in Chinese loach, *Paramisgurnus dabryanus. Aquacult.* 95:139–147.

Lin, K.J., P.X. Chen and Y.Y. Hua. 1986. Population size and conservation of *Lipotes vexillifer*. Southwest Fisheries Center, Nat'l. Marine Fish. Serv. Administrative Report LJ-86-27. La Jolla, CA.

Lin, Y.W.P., B.A. Rupnow, D.A. Price, R.M. Greenberg and R.A. Wallace. 1992. *Fundulus heteroclitus* gonadotropins. 3: Cloning and sequencing of gonadotropic hormone (GTH) I and II β–subunits using the polymerase chain reaction. *Mol. Cell. Endocrinol.* 85:127–139.

Lincoln, G.A. and F.J.P. Ebling. 1985. Effect of constant-release implants of melatonin on seasonal cycles in reproduction, prolactin secretion and moulting in rams. *J. Reprod. Fertil.* 73:241–253.

Lindburg, D.G. 1988. Improving the feeding of captive felines through application of field data. *Zoo Biol.* 7:211–218.

Lindburg, D.G. 1991a. Zoos and the "surplus" problem. *Zoo Biol.* 10:1–2.

Lindburg, D.G. 1991b. Ecological requirements of macaques. *Lab. Anim. Sci.* 41:315–322.

Lindburg, D.G. 1992a. Are wildlife reintroductions worth the cost? *Zoo Biol.* 11:1–2.

Lindburg, D.G. 1992b. Facilities for the propagation of endangered primates. Pp. 89–93 in J. Erwin and J.C. Landon, eds. *Chimpanzee conservation and public health: Environments for the future*. Diagnon/Bioqual, Rockville, MD.

Lindburg, D.G. and H. Fitch-Snyder. 1988. Priorities and directions in zoo behavioral research. *Proc. Amer. Assoc. Zool. Parks Aquar.* 1988:380–386.

Lindburg, D.G. and P.T. Robinson. 1986. Animal introductions: Some suggestions for easing the trauma. *Anim. Keepers Forum* 13:8–11.

Lindburg, D.G., A.M. Lyles and N.M. Czekala. 1989. Status and reproductive potential of lion-tailed macaques in captivity. *Zoo Biol.* Suppl. 1:5–16.

Lindburg, D.G., S. Millard and B. Lasley. 1985. Induced estrus in the cheetah. *Proc. Amer. Assoc. Zool. Parks Aquar.* 1985:560–562.

Lindburg, D.G., B.S. Durrant, S.E. Millard and J.E. Oosterhuis. 1993. Fertility assessment of cheetah males with poor quality semen. *Zoo Biol.* 12:97–103.

Linde, R., G.C. Doelle, N. Alexander, F. Kirschner, W. Vale, J. Rivier and D. Rabin. 1981. Reversible inhibition of testicular steroidogenesis and spermatogenesis by a potent gonadotropin-releasing hormone agonist in men. *New England J. Med.* 305:663–667.

Linden, W., ed. 1988. *Biological barriers in behavioral medicine.* Plenum Press, New York, NY.

Lindholm, J. 1991. The marbled teal, an unheralded achievement of aviculture. *Amer. Fed. Avicult.* 18:24–25.

Line, S.W. 1987. Environmental enrichment for laboratory primates. *J. Amer. Vet. Med. Assoc.* 190:854–859.

Lint, K.C. and A.M. Lint. 1981. *Diets for birds in captivity.* Blandford Press, Poole, England.

Lipa, J.J. 1975. An outline of insect pathology. Foreign Sci. Pub., Dept. Nat'l. Center Sci., Tech., Econ. Infor., Warsaw, Poland. Springfield, VA.

Liu, R.J. 1988. Study on regularity of reproduction in *Lipotes. Aquat. Mamm.* 14:63–68.

Ljungblad, D.K., S.E. Moore and D.R. Van Schoik. 1986. *Seasonal patterns of distribution, abundance, migration and behavior of the Western Arctic stock of bowhead whales, Balaena mysticetus, in Alaska seas.* Report Int'l. Whaling Commiss. Special Issue 8. Cambridge, England.

Loeb, J. 1918. *Forced movements, tropisms and animal conduct.* Lippincott, Philadelphia, PA.

Loffredo, C.A. and G. Borgia. 1986. Sexual selection, mating systems, and the evolution of avian acoustical display. *Amer. Natural.* 128:773–794.

Lofts, B. 1984. Amphibians. Pp. 127–205 in G.E. Lamming, ed. *Marshall's physiology of reproduction,* Vol. 1: Churchill Livingstone, London, England.

Lofts, B. 1987. Testicular function. Pp. 283–325 in D.O. Norris and R.E. Jones, eds. *Hormones and reproduction in fishes, amphibians and reptiles.* Plenum Press, New York, NY.

Lofts, B. and R.K. Murton. 1968. Photoperiodic and physiological adaptations regulating avian breeding cycles and their ecological significance. *J. Zool.* 155:327–394.

Lofts, B. and R.K. Murton. 1973. Reproduction in birds. Pp. 1–107 in D.S. Farner and J.R. King, eds. *Avian biology*, Vol. III: Academic Press, New York, NY.

Longmire, J.L. 1988. Identification and development of breeding population-specific DNA polymorphisms within the genome of the *Falco peregrinus*. Pp. 779–788 in T.J. Cade, J.H. Enderson, C.G. Thelander and C.M.White, eds. *Peregrine falcon populations. Their management and recovery*. Proc. Int'l. Symp. Peregrine Falcon, 1985. The Peregrine Fund, Boise, ID.

Longmire, J.L., G.F. Gee, C.L. Hardekopf and G.A. Mark. 1992. Establishing paternity in whooping cranes (*Grus americana*) by DNA analysis. *Auk* 109:522–529.

Lopata, A., P.M. Summers and J.P. Hearn. 1988. Births following the transfer of cultured embryos obtained by *in vitro* and *in vivo* fertilization in the marmoset monkey. (*Callithrix jacchus*). *Fertil. Steril.* 50:503–509.

Lorenz, F.W. 1969. Reproduction in domestic fowl. Pp. 569–608 in H.H. Cole and P.T. Cupps, eds. *Reproduction in domestic animals*, 2nd Ed. Academic Press, New York, NY.

Lorenz, F.W., V.K. Abott, V.S. Asmundson, H.E. Adler, F.H. Kratzer, F.X. Ogasawara and J.D. Carson. 1959. Turkey fertility. California Agr. Exp. Sta. Ext. Cir. 472. Univ. California, Davis, CA.

Loskutoff, N.M., J.E. Ott and B.L. Lasley. 1982. Urinary steroid evaluations to monitor ovarian function in exotic ungulates. I: Pregnanediol-3-glucoronide immunoreactivity in the okapi (*Okapia johnstoni*). *Zoo Biol.* 1:45–53.

Loskutoff, N.M., J.E. Ott and B.L. Lasley. 1983. Strategies for assessing ovarian function in exotic species. *J. Zoo Anim. Med.* 14:3–12.

Loskutoff, N.M., L. Walker, J.E. Ott-Joslin, B.L. Raphael and B.L. Lasley. 1986. Urinary steroid evaluations to monitor ovarian function in exotic ungulates. II: Comparisons between the giraffe (*Giraffa camelopardalis*) and the okapi (*Okapia johnstoni*). *Zoo. Biol.* 5:331–338.

Lott, D.F. 1991. *Intraspecific variation in the social systems of wild invertebrates*. Cambridge Univ. Press, New York, NY.

Loudon, A. and P.A. Racey, eds. 1987. *The reproductive energetics of mammals*. Oxford Univ. Press, New York, NY.

Love, J.A. 1975. A note on the birth of a baboon (*Papio anubis*). *Folia Primatol.* 29:303–306.

Lovegrove, R.G. and C. Wissel. 1988. Sociality of molerats: Metabolic scaling and the role of risk sensitivity. *Oecologia* 74:600–606.

Lovejoy, T. 1980a. Foreword in M.E. Soulé and B.A. Wilcox, eds. *Conservation biology: An evolutionary-ecological perspective.* Sinauer Assoc., Sunderland, MA.

Lovejoy, T.E. 1980b. Tomorrow's ark: By invitation only. *Int'l. Zoo Yb.* 20:181–183.

Lovejoy, T.E. 1983. Tropical deforestation and North American migrant birds. P. 126–127 in S. Temple, ed. *Bird conservation* 1. Univ. Wisconsin Press, Madison, WI.

Lovejoy, T.E. 1985. Minimum size for bird species and avian habitats. *Proc. Int'l. Ornithol. Congr.* 18:324–327.

Lovejoy, T.E. and D.C. Oren. 1981. Minimum critical size of ecosystems. Pp. 7–12 in R.L. Burgess and D.M. Sharp, eds. Forest island dynamics in man-dominated landscapes. Springer-Verlag, New York, NY.

Low, R. 1972. Pp. 15–37 in *The parrots of South America.* John Gifford, London, England.

Low, R. 1984. *Endangered parrots.* Blandford Press, Poole, England.

Low, W.A. 1970. The influence of aridity on reproduction in the collared peccary (*Dicotyles tajacu* Linn) in Texas. Ph.D. Dissertation, Univ. British Columbia, Vancouver, Canada.

Lowe-McConnell, R.H. 1979. Ecological aspects of seasonality in fishes of tropical waters. *Symp. Zool. Soc. London* 44:219–241.

Lowenstein, L. 1986. Nutritional disorders of birds. Pp. 201–212 in M.E. Fowler, ed. *Zoo and wild animal medicine.* Saunders, Philadelphia, PA.

Lowenstein-Whaley, J. and P. Cardeilhac. 1988. Reproductive parameters for the captive colony of dolphins (*Tursiops truncatus*) at Marineland of Florida. *Proc. Int'l. Marine Anim. Trainers Assoc.* 1988:56–59.

Lunn, S.F. 1978. Urinary estrogen excretion in the common marmoset, *Callithrix jucchus.* Pp. 67–73 in R. Rothe, H.J. Walters and J.P. Hearn, eds. *Biology and behavior of marmosets.* Eigenverlag Rothe, Gottengen, Germany (FRG).

Luthin, C.S., G.W. Archibald, L. Hartman, C.M. Mirande and S. Swengel. 1986. Captive breeding of cranes, storks, ibises and spoonbills. *Int'l. Zoo Yb.* 24/25:25–39.

MacArthur, R.H. and E.O. Wilson. 1967. *The theory of island biogeography.* Princeton Univ. Press, Princeton, NJ.

MacCluer, J.W., J.L. VandeBerg, B. Read and O.A. Ryder. 1986. Pedigree analysis by computer simulation. *Zoo Biol.* 5:147–160.

MacDonald, D., ed. 1985. *Encyclopedia of mammals*. Facts on File, New York, NY.

Macdonald, G.J. 1971. Reproductive patterns of three species of macaques. *Fertil. Steril.* 22:373–377.

Macdonald, K. 1983. Stability of individual differences in behavior in a litter of wolf cubs (*Canis lupus*). *J. Comp. Physiol. Psychol.* 97:99–106.

Mace, G.M. 1986. Genetic management of small populations. *Int'l. Zoo Yb.* 24/25:167–174.

Macedonia, J.M. 1986. Individuality in a contact call of the ringtailed lemur (*Lemur catta*). *Amer. J. Primatol.* 11:163–179.

Mack, D. and A.A. Eudey. 1984. A review of the U.S. primate trade. Pp. 91–136 in D. Mack and R.A. Mittermeier, eds. *The international primate trade*, Vol. 1 TRAFFIC (USA). World Wildlife Fund-US, Int'l. Union Conserv. Nature & Natur. Resour./Species Surviv. Commiss. Primate Specialists Group, Washington, DC.

Mack, D. and R.A. Mittermeier, eds. 1984. *The international primate trade*, Vol. 1. TRAFFIC (USA). World Wildlife Fund-US, Int'l. Union Conserv. Nature & Natur. Resour./Species Surv. Commiss. Primate Specialists Group, Washington, DC.

MacKinnon, J.R. and S.N. Stuart. 1988. *The kouprey: An action plan for its conservation*. Int'l. Union Conserv. Nature & Natur. Resour., Gland, Switzerland.

Mackintosh, N.A. 1965. *The stocks of whales*. Fishing News Limited. London, England.

MacNamara M. and J. Kalina. 1981. Time-lapse video as a tool in behavioral studies. *Int'l. Zoo Yb.* 21:207–210.

Macpherson, J.W. and P. Penner. 1967. Animal identification. II: Freeze branding of seals for laboratory identification. *Can. J. Comp. Vet. Med.* 31:275–276.

MacRoberts, M.H. and B.R. MacRoberts. 1966. The annual reproductive cycle of the Barbary ape (*Macaca sylvana*) in Gibraltar. *Amer. J. Phys. Anthro.* 25:299–304.

Macularia, A., A.J. Fivizzani, L.W. Oring and M. El Halawani. 1984. Prolactin levels associated with incubation in the spotted sandpiper. *Amer. Zool.* 24:71A (Abstr.).

Mager, W. 1981. Stimulating maternal behaviour in the lowland gorilla, *Gorilla g. gorilla*, at Apeldoorn. *Int'l. Zoo Yb.* 21:138–143.

Mager, W.B. and T. Griede. 1986. Using outside areas for tropical primates in the northern hemisphere: *Callitrichidae*, *Saimiri*, and *Gorilla*.

Pp. 471–477 in K. Benirschke, ed. *Primates: The road to self-sustaining populations.* Springer-Verlag, New York, NY.

Magnusson, W.E., K.A. Vliet, A.C. Polley and R. Whitaker. 1989. Reproduction. Pp. 118–135 in C.A. Ross, ed. *Crocodiles and alligators.* Facts on File, New York, NY.

Magri, M.H., A. Solari, R. Billard and P. Reinaud. 1985. Influence of testosterone on precocious sexual development in immature rainbow trout. *Gen. Comp. Endocrinol.* 57:411–421.

Maguire, L.A. and R.C. Lacy. 1990. Allocating scarce resources for conservation of endangered subspecies: Partitioning zoo space for tigers. *Conserv. Biol.* 4:157–166.

Mainka, S.A. and C.D. Lothrop. 1990. Reproductive and hormonal changes during the estrous cycle and pregnancy in Asian elephants (*Elephas maximus*). *Zoo Biol.* 9:411–419.

Maitland, P. and D. Evans. 1986. The role of captive breeding in the conservation of fish species. *Int'l. Zoo Yb.* 24/25:66–74.

Maitra, S.K. 1987. Seasonal changes in the adrenal medulla of male blossomheaded parakeet in relation to environment and reproductive cycles. *J. Interdiscipl. Cycle Res.* 18:43–48.

Malaret, L. and H.S. Fitch. 1984. Effects of overfeeding and underfeeding on reproduction in four speices of reptiles. *Acta Zool. Path.* 78:77–84.

Mallet, M. 1977. Breeding the Waldrapp ibis, *Geronticus eremita* at Jersey Zoo. *Int'l. Zoo Yb.* 17:143–145.

Mallick, B. and A.K. Sarkar. 1985. Studies on the seasonal cyclicity of the testis and adrenal in the common myna (*Acridotheres tristis tristis*). *J. Reprod. Biol. Comp. Endocrinol.* 5:80–88.

Mallinson, J. 1975. Notes on breeding a group of Sierra Leone striped squirrels, *Funisciurus pyrrhopus leonis. Int'l. Zoo Yb.* 15:237–240.

Mallinson, J.J.C. 1980. The concept behind and design of the new gorilla environment at the Jersey Wildlife Trust. *Dodo* 11:79–85.

Mallinson, J.J.C. 1982. The establishment of a self-sustaining breeding population of gorillas in captivity with special reference to the work of the Anthropoid Ape Advisory Panel of the British Isles and Ireland. *Amer. J. Primatol.* Suppl. 1:105–119.

Mallinson, J.J.C. 1986. The importance of an interdisciplinary approach. Pp. 995–1003 in K. Benirschke, ed. *Primates: The road to self-sustaining populations.* Springer-Verlag, New York, NY.

Mallinson, J.J.C. 1988. Collaboration for conservation between the Jersey Wildlife Preservation Trust and countries where species are endangered. *Int'l. Zoo Yb.* 27:176–191.

Mallinson, J.J.C. 1991. Partnerships for conservation between zoos, local governments and non-governmental organizations. *Symp. Zool. Soc. London* 62: 99–106.

Mallinson, J.J.C. and M.E. Redshaw. 1992. Maximizing natural behaviour for primates in captivity. Pp. 179–185 in E.M.C. Stevens, ed. *Proc. 4th Int'l. Symp. on Zoo Design and Construction.* Whitley Wildl. Conserv. Trust, Paignton, England.

Mann, T. and C. Lutwak-Mann. 1981. Male reproductive function and the composition of semen: General considerations. Pp. 1–34 in T. Mann and C. Lutwak-Mann, eds. *Male reproductive function and semen.* Springer-Verlag, New York, NY.

Manuwoto, S. and J.M. Scriber. 1985. Neonate larval survival of European corn borers, *Ostrinia nebales*, on maize: Effects of light intensity and degree of insect inbreeding. *Agric. Ecosys. Environ.* 14:211–236.

Maple, T.L. 1980. *Orang-utan behavior.* Van Nostrand Reinhold, New York, NY.

Maple, T.L. 1986. Series preface. P. xiii in B.C. Kirkevold and J.S. Lockard, eds. *Behavioral biology of killer whales.* Zoo Biol. Monogr. Vol. 1. Alan Liss, New York, NY.

Maple, T.L. and T.W. Finlay. 1986. Evaluating the environments of captive nonhuman primates. Pp. 479–487 in K. Benirschke, ed. *Primates: The road to self-sustaining populations.* Springer-Verlag, New York, NY.

Maple, T.L. and T.W. Finlay. 1989. Applied primatology in the modern zoo. *Zoo Biol.* Suppl 1:101–116.

Maple, T.L. and M.P. Hoff. 1982. *Gorilla behavior.* Van Nostrand Reinhold, New York, NY.

Maples, E.G. and M.M. Haraway. 1982. Taped vocalizations as a reinforcer of vocal behavior in a female agile gibbon (*Hylobates agilis*). *Psychol. Reports.* 51:95–98.

Marais, E. 1975. *My friends the baboons.* Blond and Briggs, London, England.

Marcellini, D. and T. Jenssen. 1988. Visitor behavior in the National Zoo's reptile house. *Zoo Biol.* 7:329–338.

Margulis, L. and K.V. Schwartz. 1988. *Five kingdoms: An illustrated guide to the phyla of life on earth.* 2nd Ed. W.H. Freeman, New York, NY.

Marine Mammal Commission. 1991. Annual report of the Marine Mammal Commission calender year 1990. A report to Congress. U.S. Marine Mamm. Commiss., Washington, DC.

Marion, W.R. and J.D. Shamis. 1977. An annotated bibliography of bird marking techniques. *Bird Banding* 48:42–61.

Marker, L. and S.J. O'Brien. 1989. Captive breeding of the cheetah (*Acinonyx jubatus*) in North American zoos (1871–1986). *Zoo Biol.* 8:3–16.

Markowitz, H. 1975. Analysis and control of behavior in the zoo. Pp. 77–90 in National Academy of Sciences, ed. *Research in zoos and aquariums.* Nat'l. Acad. Sci., Washington, DC.

Markowitz, H. 1982. *Behavioral enrichment in the zoo.* Van Nostrand Reinhold, New York, NY.

Markowitz, H. 1990. Environmental opportunities and health care for marine mammals. Pp. 483–488 in L. A. Dierauf, ed. *CRC Handbook of marine mammal medicine: Health, disease and rehabilitation.* CRC Press, Boca Raton, FL.

Markowitz, H. and S.W. Line. 1989. Primate research models and environmental enrichment. Pp. 203–212 in E.F. Segal, ed. *Housing, care and psychological wellbeing of captive and laboratory primates.* Noyes, Park Ridge, NJ.

Markowitz, H. and V.J. Stevens, eds. 1978. *Behavior of captive wild animals.* Nelson Hall, Chicago, IL.

Markowitz, H., M. Schmidt and A. Moody. 1978. Behavioral engineering and animal health in the zoo. *Int'l. Zoo Yb.* 18:190–194.

Marler, P.R. 1967. Animal communication signals. *Science* 157:769–774.

Marler, P. and M. Tamura. 1962. Song "dialects" in three populations of white crowned sparrows. *Condor* 64:368–377.

Marlow, B.J.G. 1955. Observations on the Herero musk shrew, *Crocidura flavenscens herero* St. Leger, in captivity. *Proc. Zool. Soc. London* 124:805–807.

Marrin-Cooney, D. 1989. Video recording the nasal passage of an echolocating dolphin. *Proc. Int'l. Marine Anim. Trainers Assoc.* 1989:27–30.

Marsh, C.W., A.D. Johns and J.M. Ayres. 1987. Effects of habitat disturbance on rain forest primates. Pp. 83–107 in C.W. Marsh and R.A. Mittermeier, eds. *Primate conservation in the tropical rain forest.* Alan Liss, New York, NY.

Marsh, H., R. Lloze, G.E. Heinsohn and T. Kasuya. 1989. Irrawaddy dolphin *Orcaella brevirostris* (Gray, 1866). Pp. 101–118 in S.H. Ridgway and R. Harrison, eds. *Handbook of marine mammals, Vol. 4. River dolphins and the larger toothed whales*. Academic Press, New York, NY.

Marsh, P. 1985. Effect of incubation temperature on survival of embryos of native Colorado River fishes. *S.W. Natural*. 30:129–140.

Marshall, A.J. 1959. Internal and environmental control of breeding. *Ibis* 101:456–478.

Marshall, A.J. 1961a. Breeding seasons and migration. Pp. 307–339 in A.J. Marshall, ed. *Biology and comparative physiology of birds*, Vol. II. Academic Press, New York, NY.

Marshall, A.J. 1961b. Reproduction. Pp. 169–213 in A.J. Marshall, ed. *Biology and comparative physiology of birds*, Vol. II. Academic Press, New York, NY.

Marshall, N.B. 1972. Influence of male sound production on oviposition in female *Tilapia mossambica* (Pisces, Cichlidae). *Bull. Ecol. Soc. Amer.* 53:29 (Abstr.).

Marston, J.H., R. Penn and P.C. Sivelle. 1977. Successful autotransfer of tubal eggs in the rhesus monkey (*Macaca mulatta*). *J. Reprod. Fertil.* 49:175–176.

Martin, D.P. 1986. Preventive medicine. Pp. 667–669 in M.E. Fowler, ed. *Zoo and wild animal medicine*. 2nd Ed. W.B. Saunders, Philadelphia, PA.

Martin, G.E. and K.G. Gould. 1981. The male ape genital tract and its secretions. Pp. 127–162 in C.E. Graham, ed. *Reproductive biology of the great apes*. Academic Press, New York, NY.

Martin, I.C.A. 1978. The principles and practice of electroejaculation of mammals. *Symp. Zool. Soc. Lond.* 43:127–152.

Martin, P. and P. Bateson. 1986. *Measuring behavior*. Cambridge Univ. Press, New York, NY.

Martin, R.D., ed. 1975. *Breeding endangered species in captivity*. Academic Press, New York, NY.

Martin, R.D., S.R. Kingsley and M. Stavy. 1977. Prospects for coordinated research into breeding of great apes in zoological collections. *Dodo* 14:45–54.

Marzluff, J.M. and R.P. Balda. 1988. Pairing patterns and fitness in a free-ranging population of pinyon jays: What do they reveal about mate choice? *Condor* 90:201–213.

Mason, C.F. and S.M. Macdonald. 1986. *Otters: Ecology and conservation*. Cambridge Univ. Press, New York, NY.

Mason, J.F. and R.F. Reidinger. 1981. Effects of social facilitation and observational learning on feeding behavior of the red-winged blackbird. *Auk* 98:778–784.

Mason, J.F. and R.F. Reidinger. 1983. Importance of color for methiocarb-induced food aversions in red-winged blackbirds. *J. Wildl. Manage.* 47:383–393.

Massey, B.W., K. Keane and C. Boardman. 1988. Adverse effects of radio transmitters on the behavior of nesting least terns. *Condor* 90:945–947.

Masters, A.R., S.B. Malcolm and L.P. Brower. 1988. Monarch butterfly (*Danaus plexippus*) thermoregulatory behavior and adaptations for over-wintering in Mexico. *Ecology* 69:458–467.

Mastroianni, L. and W.A. Manson. 1963. Collection of monkey semen by electroejaculation. *Proc. Soc. Exp. Biol. Med.* 112:1025–1027.

Masui, M., M. Hiramatsu, N. Nose, R. Nakasato, Y. Sagawa, H. Tajima and K. Saito. 1989. Successful artificial insemination in the giant panda (*Ailuropoda melanoleuca*) at Ueno Zoo. *Zoo Biol.* 8:17–26.

Mather, A.S. 1990 *Global forest resources*. Timber Press, Portland, OR.

Matkin, C.O. and S. Leatherwood. 1986. General biology of the killer whale (*Orcinus orca*): A synopsis of knowledge. Pp. 35–68 in B.C. Kirkevold and J.S. Lockard, eds. *Behavioral biology of killer whales*. Zoo Biol. Monogr. Volume I. Alan Liss, New York, NY.

Maung, S.L. and B.K. Follett 1978. The endocrine control by luteinizing hormone of testosterone secretion from the testis of the Japanese quail. *Gen. Comp. Endocrinol.* 36:79–89.

May, M. 1979. Insect thermoregulation. *Ann. Rev. Entomol.* 24:313–349.

May, R.M. 1986. How many species are there? *Nature* 324:514–515.

May, R.M. 1988. Conservation and disease. *Conservation Biology*, Special Section, Volume 2, Number 1.

May, R.M. 1990. Taxonomy as destiny. *Nature* 347:129–130.

May, R.M. and A.M. Lyles 1987. Living latin binomials. *Nature* 326:642–643.

Mayr, E. 1982. Of what use are subspecies? *Auk* 99:593–595.

Mazur, P. 1980. Fundamental aspects of the freezing of cells with emphasis on mammalian ova and embryos. Pp. 99–114 in *Int'l. Congr. Anim. Reprod. Artif. Insem.*, Madrid, Spain.

McArthur, J., J. Ovadia, O. Smith and J.C. Bashir-Farahmand. 1972. The menstrual cycle of the bonnet monkey (*Macaca radiata*): Changes in the cervical mucus secretion, vaginal cytology, sex-skin and urinary estrogen excretion. *Folia Primatol.* 17:107–121.

McBride, A.F. and D.O. Hebb. 1948. Behavior of the captive bottle-nose dolphin, *Tursiops truncatus. J. Comp. Physiol. Psychol.* 41:111–123.

McBride, A.F. and H. Kritzler. 1951. Observations on pregnancy, parturition, and post–natal behavior in the bottlenose dolphin. *J. Mammal.* 32:251–266.

McClanahan, L.L., C.R. Feldmeth, J. Jones and D.L. Soltz. 1986. Energetics, salinity and temperature tolerance in the Mohave chui chub, *Gila bicolor mohavensis. Copeia* 1986:45–52.

McCreery, B.R. and P. Licht. 1983a. Pituitary and gonadal responses to continuous infusion of gonadotropin releasing hormone (GnRH) in the male bullfrog, *Rana catesbeiana. Biol. Reprod.* 29:129–136.

McCreery, B.R. and P. Licht. 1983b. Induced ovulation and changes in pituitary responsiveness to continuous infusion of gonadotropin-releasing hormone (GnRH) during the ovarian cycle in the bullfrog, *Rana catesbeinana. Biol. Reprod.* 29:863–871.

McCrystal, H.K. and J.L. Behler. 1982. Husbandry and reproduction of captive giant ameiva lizards *Ameiva ameiva* at the New York Zoological Park. *Int'l. Zoo Yb.* 22:159–163.

McCusker, J.S. and K.B. Larson. 1986. Contracting zoological and aquarium exhibit design services: The request for proposals and interview process. *Proc. Amer. Assoc. Zool. Parks Aquar.* 1986:314–324.

McDonald, L.E. 1977. Female reproductive system. Pp. 247–303 in L.E. McDonald, ed. *Veterinary endocrinology and reproduction.* Les & Febigler, Philadelphia, PA.

McDougal, C. 1977. *The face of the tiger.* Rivingden Books and Andre Deutsch, London, England.

McFarlane, R.W. 1962. The taxonomic significance of avian sperm. Master's Thesis. Univ. of Florida, Gainesville, FL.

McFarlane, R.W. 1971. The ultrastructure and phylogenetic significance of avian spermatozoa. Ph.D. Dissertation. Univ. of Florida, Gainesville, FL.

McGill-Harelstad, P. 1987. Breeding birds off-exhibit at Brookfield Zoo. Evaluation and Prospects. *Regional Proc. Amer. Assoc. Zool. Parks Aquar.* 1987:614–617.

McGrew, W.C., J.A. Brennan and J. Russell. 1986. An artificial "gum-tree" for marmosets (*Callithrix j. jacchus*). *Zoo Biol.* 5:45–50.

McGuire, M.T. 1974. The St. Kitts vervet. Pp. 1–202 in *Contributions to primatology*, Vol. 1. Karger, Basil.

McKenzie, S.M., A.S. Chamove and A.C. Feistner. 1986. Floor-coverings and hanging screens alter arboreal monkey behavior. *Zoo Biol.* 5:339–348.

McKeown, S. 1984. Management and propagation of the lizard genus *Phelsuma. Acta Zool. Path.* 78:149–162.

McLeod, B.J., A.S.I. Loudon, B.R. Brinklow and J.C. Curlewis. 1988. Induced oestrus in Père David's deer; responsiveness to GnRH. *J. Reprod. Fertil. Abstr. Series* 1:48 (Abstr.).

McNab, B.K. 1983. Ecological and behavioral consequences of adaptation to various food resources. Pp. 664–695 in J.F. Eisenberg and D.G. Kleiman, eds. *Advances in mammalian behavior.* Spec. Publ. Amer. Soc. Mamm. #7. Lawrence, KS.

McNab, B.K. 1986. The influence of food habits on the energetics of eutherian mammals. *Ecol. Monogr.* 56:1–19.

McNab, B.K. 1989. Rate of metabolism, body size and food habits in the order Carnivora. Pp. 335–354 in J.L. Gittleman, ed. *Carnivore behavior, ecology and evolution.* Cornell Univ. Press, Ithaca, NY.

McNeely, J.A., K.R. Miller, W.V. Reid, R.A. Mittermeier and T.B. Werner. 1990. *Conserving the world's biological diversity.* Int'l. Union Conserv. Nature & Natur. Resour., World Resour. Instit., Conserv. Int'l., World Wildl. Fund-U.S., and the World Bank, Gland, Switzerland and Washington, DC.

McNicholas, J. 1989. Comoro Island bat. *Solitaire* 5(Dec.):8–9.

McPherson, C. 1980. Remarks on primate supply. Pp. 3–14 in S.S. Kalter, ed. *The use of nonhuman primates in cardiovascular diseases.* Univ. of Texas Press, Austin, TX.

McPherson, R.J. and K.R. Marion. 1981. Seasonal testicular cycle of the stinkpot turtle (*Sternotherus odoratus*) in central Alabama. *Herpetologica* 37:33–40.

Mead, J.G. 1989a. Shepherd's beaked whale, *Tasmacetus shepherdi* Oliver, 1937. Pp. 309–320 in S.H. Ridgway and R.J. Harrison, eds. *Handbook of marine mammals, Vol 4: River dolphins and the larger toothed whales.* Academic Press, London, England.

Mead, J.G. 1989b. Beaked whales of the genus *Mesoplodon.* Pp. 349–430 in S.H. Ridgway and R.J. Harrison, eds. *Handbook of marine mammals, Vol 4: River dolphins and the larger toothed whales.* Academic Press, London, England.

Mead, J.G. 1989c. Bottlenose whales, *Hyperoodon ampullatus* (Forster, 1770) and *Hyperoodon planifrons,* Flower, 1882. Pp. 321–348 in S.H. Ridgway and R.J. Harrison, eds. *Handbook of marine mammals, Vol 4: River dolphins and the larger toothed whales.* Academic Press, London, England.

Mead, R.A. and S. Keirinckx. 1989. Hormonal induction of oestrus and pregnancy in anoestrus ferrets (*Mustela putorius furo*). *J. Reprod. Fertil.* 86:309–314.

Mead, R.A., S. Keirinckx and N.M. Czekala. 1990. Reproductive cycle of the steppe polecat (*Mustela eversmanni*). *J. Reprod. Fertil.* 88:353–360.

Mech, L.D. 1970. *The wolf: The ecology and behavior of an endangered species.* Natural Hist. Press, New York, NY.

Mech, L.D. 1983. *A handbook of animal radio-tracking.* Univ. Minnesota Press, Minneapolis, MN.

Mech, L.D., R.C. Chapman, W.W. Cochran, L. Simmons and U.S. Seal. 1984. Radio-triggered anesthetic-dart collar for recapturing large mammals. *Wildl. Soc. Bull.* 12:69–74.

Medonca, M.T. and P. Licht. 1986. Photothermal effects on the testicular cycle in the musk turtle, *Sternotherus odoratus. J. Exp. Zool.* 239:117–130.

Medway, W. and J.R. Geraci. 1978. Clinical pathology of marine mammals. Pp. 604–610 in M.E. Fowler, ed. *Zoo and wild animal medicine.* W.B. Saunders, Philadelphia, PA.

Meester, J. 1963. A systematic revision of the shrew genus *Crocidura* in southern Africa. *Transvaal Mus. Mem.* 13:1–16.

Meester, J. 1972. A new golden mole from Transvaal (Mammalia: Chrysochloridae). *Ann. Transvaal Mus.* 28:35–46.

Meffe, G.K. 1986. Conservation genetics and the management of endangered fishes. *Fisheries* 11:14–23.

Meffe, G.K. 1987. Conserving fish genomes: Philosophies and practices. *Envir. Biol. Fishes* 18:3–9.

Meffe, G.K., D.A. Hendrickson, W.L. Minckley and J.N. Rinne. 1983. Factors resulting in decline of the endangered Sonoran topminnow *Poeciliopsis occidentalis* (Atheriniformes: Poeciliidae) in the United States. *Biol. Conserv.* 25:135–159.

Meier, A.H. and D.S. Farner. 1964. A possible endocrine basis for premigratory fattening in the white-crowned sparrow, *Zonotrichia leucophrys gambelii* (Nuttall). *Gen. Comp. Endocrinol.* 4:584–595.

Meier, A.H., J.T. Burns and J.W. Dusseau. 1969. Seasonal variation in the diurnal rhythm of pituitary prolactin content in the white-throated sparrow, *Zonotrichia albicollis. Gen. Comp. Endocrinol.* 12:282–289.

Meier, A.H., B.R. Ferrell and L.J. Miller. 1980. Circadian components of the circannual mechanism in the white-throated sparrow. Pp. 458–462 in R. Nohring, ed. *Acta XVII Congress. Int'l. Ornithol.*, Vol. 1. Deutsche Ornithologen Gesellschaft. Berlin, Germany.

Meier, A.H., D.D. Martin and R. MacGregor. 1971. Temporal synergism of corticosterone and prolactin controlling gonadal growth in sparrows. *Science* 173:1240–1242.

Meier, B. and R. Albignac. 1991. Rediscovery of *Allocebus trichotis* Guther 1875 (Primates) in northeast Madagascar. *Folia Primatol.* 56:57–63.

Meier, B., R. Albignac, A. Peyrieras, Y. Rumpler and P. Wright. 1987. A new species of *Hapalemur* (Primates) from southeast Madagascar. *Folia Primatol.* 48:211–215.

Melamed, B.G. and L.J. Siegel. 1980. *Behavioral medicine: Practical applications in health care.* Springer-Verlag, New York, NY.

Mellen, J. 1983. *Research methods for studying animal behavior, Part I: Introduction to research. Part II: Sampling methods.* Minnesota Zool. Gard., Apple Valley, MN.

Mellen, J.D., V.J. Stevens and H. Markowitz. 1981. Environmental enrichment for servals, *Felis serval*, Indian elephants, *Elephas maximus*, and Canadian otters, *Lutra canadensis* at Washington Park Zoo, Portland. *Int'l. Zoo Yb.* 21:196–201.

Mendonca, M.T. 1987a. Photothermal effects on the ovarian cycle of the musk turtle, *Sternotherus odoratus. Herpetologica* 43:82–90.

Mendonca, M.T. 1987b. Timing of reproductive behaviour in male musk turtles, *Sternotherus odoratus*: Effects of photoperiod, temperature and testosterone. *Anim. Behav.* 35:1002–1014.

Mendonca, M.T. and P. Licht. 1986a. Seasonal cycles in gonadal activity and plasma gonadotropin in the musk turtle, *Sternotherus odoratus. Gen. Comp. Endocrinol.* 62:459–469.

Mendonca, M.T. and P. Licht. 1986b. Photothermal effects on the testicular cycle of the musk turtle, *Sternotherus odoratus. J. Exp. Zool.* 239:117–130.

Mendonca, M.T., P. Licht, M.J. Ryan and R. Barnes. 1984. Changes in hormone levels in relation to breeding behavior in male bullfrogs (*Rana catesbeiana*) at the individual and population levels. *Gen. Comp. Endocrinol.* 58:270–279.

Mendoza, S.P., E.L. Lowe, J.M. Davidson and S. Levine. 1978. Annual cyclicity in the squirrel monkey (*Saimiri sciureus*): The relationship between testosterone, fatting, and sexual behavior. *Horm. and Behav.* 11:295–303.

Menn, J.J. and M. Beroza, eds. 1972. *Insect juvenile hormones, chemistry and action.* Academic Press, New York, NY.

Menzel, E.W., Jr. 1969. Naturalistic and experimental approaches to primate behavior. Pp. 78–121 in E.P. Willems and H.L. Rausch, eds. *Natu-*

ralistic viewpoints in behavioral research. Holt, Rinehart & Winston, New York, NY.

Meritt, D.A. 1977. Edentata nutrition. Pp. 541–547 in M. Recheigl, ed. *CRC handbook series in nutrition and food*, Vol 1. CRC Press, Cleveland.

Merritt, P., ed. 1978. *Aracnology*. Academic Press, New York, NY.

Merritt, R.W. and K.W. Cummins, eds. 1984. *Introduction to the aquatic insects of North America*. Kendall/Hunt Pub. Co., Dubuque, IA.

Mertins, J.W. 1986. Arthropods on the screen. *Bull. Entomol. Soc. Amer.* 1986:85–90.

Metcalfe, N.B. and P. Monaghan. 1987. Behavioral ecology: Theory into practice. *Adv. Study Behav.* 17:85–120.

Mettler, L.D. and T.G. Gregg. 1969. *Population genetics and evolution*. Prentice-Hall, Englewood Cliffs, NJ.

Metz, K.J. and P.J. Weatherhead. 1991. Color bands function as secondary sexual traits in male red-winged blackbirds. *Behav. Ecol. Sociobiol.* 28:23–27.

Meyberg, B. 1984. The significance for captive breeding programmes of fratricide and cainism in birds of prey. *Int'l. Zoo Yb.* 23:110–113.

Meyer-Holzapfel, M. 1957. Das verjalten der baren (Ursidae). *Handbuch Zool.* 8:1–28.

Meyer-Holzapfel, M. 1968. Breeding the European wild cat at Berne Zoo. *Int'l. Zoo Yb.* 8:31–38.

Michael, R.P. and R.D. Bonsall. 1977. A 3-year study of an annual rhythm in plasma androgen levels in male rhesus monkeys (*Macaca mulatta*) in a constant laboratory environment. *J. Reprod. Fertil.* 49:129–131.

Michelmore, A.P.G., ed. 1975. Zoo design. *Proc 1st Int'l. Symp. on Zoo Design and Construction*. Whitley Wildl. Conserv. Trust, Paignton, England.

Michelmore, A.P.G., ed. 1976. Zoo design 2. *Proc. 2nd Int'l. Symp. Zoo Design and Construct*. Whitley Wildl. Conserv. Trust, Paignton, England.

Michelmore, A.P.G., ed. 1980. Zoo design 3. *Proc. 3rd Int'l. Symp. Zoo Design and Construct*. Whitley Wildl. Conserv. Trust, Paignton, England.

Michelmore, A.P.G. and G. Bath. 1978. The baboon rock at Paignton Zoo. *Int'l. Zoo Yb.* 18:216–219.

Middleton, A.L.A. 1974. Spermiation and sperm transport in passerine birds. *J. Reprod. Fertil.* 40:31–37.

Migaki, G., E.R. Jacobson and H.W. Casey. 1984. Fungal diseases of reptiles. Pp. 183–204 in G.L. Hoff, F.L. Frye and E.R. Jacobson, eds. *Diseases of amphibians and reptiles*. Plenum Press, New York, NY.

Mikellides, B. 1980. *Architecture for people*. Holt, Rinehart and Wilson, New York, NY.

Millar, R.P. and T.D. Glover. 1970. Seasonal changes in the reproductive tract of the male rock hyrax, *Procavia capensis. J. Reprod. Fertil.* 23:497–499.

Millard, S. 1989. Cheetah births reported at the San Diego Wild Animal Park. *Amer. Assoc. Zool. Parks Aquar. Newsletter* 30:27.

Miller, A.M., M.E. Roelke, K.L. Goodrowe, J.G. Howard and D.E. Wildt. 1990. Oocyte recovery, maturation and fertilization *in vitro* in the puma (*Felis concolor*). *J. Reprod. Fertil.* 88:249–258.

Miller, D.B. 1979. The acoustic basis of mate recognition by female zebra finches (*Taeniopygia guttata*). *Anim. Behav.* 27:376–380.

Miller, E.H. 1983. The structure of aerial displays in three species of Calidridinae (Scolopacidae). *Auk* 100:440–451.

Miller, M.J. 1980. Current techniques of management and reproduction of gekkonid lizards at the Gekkonidae Breeding Foundation. *4th Ann. Reptile Symp. on Captive Propag. and Husbandry.* 1980:24–35.

Miller, M.J. 1984. Captive husbandry and propagation of geckos. *Proc. N. CA. Herp. Soc., Special Pub. No. 2 and Bull. Chicago Herpetol. Soc.* 19:41–54.

Miller, R. 1961. Man and the changing fish fauna of the American southwest. *Papers Michigan Acad. Sci. Arts Lett.* 46:365–404.

Miller, R., P. Sanchez and D. Soltz. 1985. Fishes and aquatic resources of the Death Valley system California-Nevada, 1878–1984: A bibliography. U.S. Dept. Interior, Nat'l. Park Service, San Francisco, CA.

Miller, R.R., J.D. Williams and J.E. Williams. 1989. Extinctions of North American fishes during the past century. *Fisheries* 14:22–38.

Miller, T.J. 1987. Artificial incubation of eggs of the green iguana (*Iguana iguana*). *Zoo Biol.* 6:225–236.

Miller, W.E. 1989. Reproductive enhancement by adult feeding: Effects of honeydew in imbibed water on spruce budworm. *J. Lepidopt. Soc.* 43:167–177.

Milligan, S.R. 1982. Induced ovulation in mammals. Pp. 1–46 in C.A. Finn, ed. *Oxford reviews of reproductive biology*, Vol 4. Clarendon Press, Oxford, England.

Mills, C.W. 1898. *The nature and development of animal intelligence.* MacMillan, New York, NY.

Mills, M.G.L. 1982. The mating system of the brown hyena *Hyaena brunnea* in the southern Kalahari. *Behav. Ecol. Sociobiol.* 10:131–136.

Mills, M.G.L. 1989. The comparative behavioral ecology of hyenas in the southern Kalahari. Pp. 125–142 in J.L. Gittleman, ed. *Carnivore behavior, ecology and evolution.* Cornell Univ. Press, Ithaca, NY.

Milostan, M.A. 1989. The comparative ontogeny of prey capture and immobilization in *Boa constrictor* and *Elephe obsoleta*, with comments on the origin and evolution of constricting behavior in bold and colubrid snakes. Master's Thesis, Central Michigan Univ., Mount Pleasant, MI.

Minasian, S.M., K.C. Balcomb and L. Foster. 1984. *The world's whales.* Smithsonian Books, Washington, DC.

Minckley, C.H. and J.E. Deacon. 1973. Observations on the reproductive cycle of *Cyprinodon diabolis. Copeia* 1973:610–613.

Minckley, C.H. and J.E. Deacon. 1975. Foods of the Devils Hole pupfish, *Cyprinodon diabolis* (Cyprinodontidae). *S.W. Natural.* 20:105–111.

Minckley, W.L. and J.E. Deacon. 1968. Southwestern fishes and the enigma of "endangered species." *Science* 159:1424.

Mincka, S., M. Gunnar and M. Champoux 1986. Control and early socioemotional development: Infant rhesus monkeys reared in controllable versus uncontrollable environments. *Child Dev.* 57:1241–1256.

Mineka, S., R. Kier and V. Price. 1980. V: Fear of snakes of wild- and lab-reared rhesus monkeys. *Anim. Learn. Behav.* 8:653–663.

Mirande, C. 1985. Captive breeding and reintroduction program for the eastern sarus crane *(Grus antigone sharpii). Proc. Amer. Assoc. Zool. Parks Aquar.* 1985:270–277.

Mirande, C. 1988. Black-necked cranes hatch! *Int'l. Crane Found. Bugle* 14:8.

Mirande, C. 1990. Sexual maturity and pair formation in captive cranes at the International Crane Foundation. *Proc. Amer. Assoc. Zool. Parks Aquar.* 1990:216–225.

Missakian, E.A. 1972. Genealogical and cross-genealogical dominance relations in a group of free-ranging rhesus monkeys *(Macaca mulatta)* on Cayo Santiago. *Primates* 13:169–180.

Mitchell, L.C. and P.J. Zwank. 1987. Comparison of release methods for parent reared Mississippi sandhill cranes. Pp. 399–409 in G.W. Archibald, ed. *Proc. 1983 Int'l. Crane Workshop*, Int'l. Crane Found., Baraboo, WI.

Mitchell, W.R., D.G. Lindburg, S.E. Shideler, S. Presley and B.L. Lasley. 1985. Sexual behavior and urinary ovarian hormone concentrations during the lowland gorilla menstrual cycle. *Int'l. J. Primatol.* 6:161–172.

Mittermeier, R.A. 1973. Colobus monkeys and the tourist trade. *Oryx* 12:113–117.

Mittermeier, R.A. 1978. *Global strategy for primate conservation.* Int'l. Union Conserv. Nature & Natur. Resour./Species Survival Commiss. Primate Specialist Group, Washington, DC.

Mittermeier, R.A. 1986a. Strategies for the conservation of highly endangered primates. Pp. 1013–1022 in K. Benirschke, ed. *Primates: The road to self-sustaining populations.* Springer-Verlag, New York, NY.

Mittermeier, R.A. 1986b. Primate conservation in the neotropical region. Pp. 221–240 in K. Benirschke, ed. *Primates: The road to self-sustaining populations.* Springer-Verlag, New York, NY.

Mittermeier, R.A. 1987. Effects of hunting on rain forest primates. Pp. 109–146 in C.W. Marsh and R.A. Mittermeier, eds. *Primate conservation in the tropical rain forest.* Alan Liss, New York, NY.

Mittermeier, R.A. 1989. Primate conservation. *Orion Nat'l. Quart.* 8:38–43.

Mittermeier, R.A. and A.F. Coimbra-Filho. 1981. Systematics: Species and subspecies. Pp. 29–109 in R.A. Mittermeier and A.F. Coimbra-Filho, eds. *Ecology and behavior of neotropical primates,* Vol. 1. Acad. Brasil. de Ciencias, Rio de Janeiro, Brasil.

Mittermeier, R.A., A.B. Rylands and A. Coimbra-Filho. 1988. Systematics: Species and subspecies—an update. Pp. 13–78 in R. A. Mittermeier, A.B. Rylands, A. Coimbra-Filho and G.A.B. Fonseca, eds. *Ecology and behavior of neotropical primates,* Vol. 2. World Wildlife Fund for Nature, Washington, DC.

Mittermeier, R.A., M. Schwarz and J.M. Ayres. 1992a. A new species of marmoset, Genus *Callithrix* Erxleben, 1777 (Callitrichidae, Primates) from the Rio Maues Region, State of Amazonas, Central Brazilian Amazonia. *Goeld. Zool.* 14:1–17.

Mittermeier, R.A., W.R. Konstant, M.E. Nicoll and O. Langrand. 1992b. *Lemurs of Madagascar: An action plan for their conservation 1993–1999.* Int'l. Union Conserv. Nature & Natur. Resour., Gland, Switzerland.

Mittermeier, R.A., J.F. Oates, A.A. Eudey and J. Thornback. 1986. Primate conservation. Pp. 3–72 in G. Mitchell and J. Erwin, eds. *Comparative primate biology, Vol 2A: Behavior, conservation, and ecology.* Alan Liss, New York, NY.

Miura, T., K. Yamauchi, H. Takahashi and Y. Nagahama. 1991. Hormonal induction of all stages of spermatogenesis *in vitro* in the male Japanese eel (*Anquilla japonica*). *Proc. Nat'l. Acad. Sci. U.S.A.* 88:5774–5778.

Miyadi, D. 1964. Social life of Japanese monkeys. *Science* 143:783–786.

Moberg, G.P., ed. 1985. *Animal stress*. Amer. Physiol. Soc. Bethesda, MD.

Mock, D.W. 1984. Infanticide, siblicide and avian nestling mortality. Pp. 3–30 in G. Hausfater and S.B. Hrdy, eds. *Infanticide: Comparative and evolutionary perspectives*. Aldine Press, New York, NY.

Mock, D.W., H. Drummond and C.H. Stinson. 1990. Avian siblicide. *Amer. Sci*. 135:334–350.

Moe, M.A. 1992. *The marine aquarium reference*, 2nd Ed. Green Turtle Press, Plantation, FL.

Moehlman, P.D. 1979. Jackal helpers and pup survival. *Nature* 277:382–383.

Moehlman, P.D. 1986. Ecology of cooperation in Canidae. Pp. 64–86 in D. Rubenstein and R. Wrangham, eds. *Ecological aspects of social evolution*. Princeton Univ. Press, Princeton, NJ.

Moehlman, P.D. 1987. Social organization in jackals. *Amer. Scient*. 75:366–375.

Moehlman, P.D. 1989. Intraspecific variation in canid social behavior. Pp. 143–163 in J.L. Gittleman, ed. *Carnivore behavior, ecology and evolution*. Cornell Univ. Press, Ithaca, NY.

Moehn, L.D. 1974. The effect of quality of light on agonistic behavior of iguanid and agamid lizards. *J. Herpetol*. 8:175–183.

Moerman, T.C. and J.S. Denslow. 1983. Fruit choice in neotropical birds: Effects of fruit type and accessibility on selectivity. *J. Anim. Ecol*. 52:407–420.

Moll, E.O. 1979. Reproductive cycles and adaptations. Pp. 305–331 in M. Harless and H. Morlock, eds. *Turtles: Perspective and research*. John Wiley & Sons, New York, NY.

Moll, E.O. 1983. IUCN Meeting—Malaysia. Int'l. Union Conserv. Nature & Natur. Resour./Species Survival Commiss. *Freshwater Chelonian Group Newsletter* 5:1–4.

Moll, E.O. and J.M. Legler. 1971. The life history of a neotropical slider turtle *Pseudemys scripta* (Schoepf), in Panama. *Bull. Los Angeles Co. Mus. Natur. Hist. Sci*. No. 11.

Molzen, E.M. and J.A. French. 1989. The problem of foraging in captive callitrichid primates: Behavioral time budgets and foraging skills. Pp. 89–101 in E.F. Segal, ed. *Housing, care and psychological wellbeing of captive and laboratory primates*. Noyes, Park Ridge, NJ.

Moman Khan, M.K. 1988. *Asian rhinos: An action plan for their conservation*. Int'l. Union Conserv. Nature & Natur. Resour., Gland, Switzerland.

Monaghan, P. 1984. Applied ethology. *Anim. Behav.* 32:908–915.

Monfort, S.L., C. Wemmer, T.H. Kepler, M. Bush, J.L. Brown and D.E. Wildt. 1990. Monitoring ovarian function and pregnancy in Eld's deer (*Cervus eldi thamin*) by evaluating urinary steroid metabolite excretion. *J. Reprod. Fertil.* 88:271–281.

Monroe, J. 1966. Population "flushing" with sexually sterile insects. *Science* 151:1536–1538.

Monsma, S.A., H.A. Harada and M.F. Wolfner. 1990. Synthesis of two *Drosophila* male accessory gland proteins and their fate after transfer to the female during mating. *Dev. Biol.* 142:465–475.

Montali, R.J. and G. Migaki, eds. 1980. *The comparative pathology of zoo animals*. Smithsonian Institution Press, Washington, DC.

Montgomerie, R.D. 1981. Why do jackals help their parents? *Nature* 289:824–825.

Moore, B.R. 1973. The role of directed Pavlovian reactions in simple instrumental learning in the pigeon. Pp. 150–188 in R.A. Hinde and J. Stevenson-Hinde, eds. *Constraints on learning: Limitations and predispositions*. Academic Press, New York, NY.

Moore, D. 1987a. The pronghorn (*Antilocapra americana*): A review as a model for development of a "species management plan" format, Part I. *Zoo Biol.* 6:169–182.

Moore, F.L. 1987b. Regulation of reproductive behavior. Pp. 505–522 in D.O. Norris and R.E. Jones, eds. *Hormones and reproduction in fishes, amphibians and reptiles*. Plenum Press, New York, NY.

Moore, F.L., L.J. Miller, S.P. Spielvogel, T. Kubiak and K. Folkers. 1982. Luteinizing hormone-releasing hormone involvement in the reproductive behavior of a male amphibian. *Neuroendocrinol.* 35:212–216.

Moore, H.D.M., R.C. Bonney and D.M. Jones. 1981. Successful induced ovulation and artificial insemination in the puma (*Felis concolor*). *Vet. Record* 108:282–283.

Moore, M.C. and C.A. Marler. 1987. Effects of testosterone manipulations on nonbreeding season territorial aggression in free-living male lizards, *Sceloporus jarrovi*. *Gen. Comp. Endocrinol.* 65:225–232.

Moore, P.W.B. 1991. Dolphin psychophysics: Concepts for the study of dolphin echolocation. Pp. 365–383 in K. Pryor and K.S. Norris, eds., *Dolphin Societies*. Univ. California Press, Berkeley, CA.

Moore, R.F., T.M. O'Dell and C.O. Collins. 1985. Quality assessment in laboratory-reared insects. Pp. 107–135 in P. Singh and R.F. Moore, eds. *Handbook of insect rearing*, Vol I. Elsevier, Amsterdam, Netherlands.

Moore, W.S. 1984. Evolutionary ecology of unisexual fishes. Pp. 329–398 in B.J. Turner, ed. *Evolutionary genetics of fishes*. Plenum Press, New York, NY.

Moran, N.A. 1992. The evolution of aphid life cycles. *Ann. Rev. Entomol.* 37:321–348.

Morner, T. 1986. Zoological gardens and the conservation of wildlife in Sweden. *Int'l. Zoo Yb* 24/25:189–192.

Morreale, S.J., G.J. Ruiz, J.R. Spotila and E.A. Standora. 1982. Temperature-dependent sex determination: Current practices threaten conservation of sea turtles. *Science* 216:1245–1247.

Morris, D. 1961. A new approach to the problem of exhibiting small mammals in zoos. *Int'l. Zoo Yb.* 3:1–9.

Morris, P. 1983. Annotated outline of captive care of snakes and lizards. *Northern California. Herpetol. Soc.*, Special Pub. No. 1. 1983:1–30.

Morris, T. 1988. Social behavior of dolphins at the Living Seas. *Proc. Int'l. Assoc. Aquat. Anim. Med.* 1988:22 (Abstr.).

Morrison, M.K. 1984. *Interior landscaping report for Price Forbes Federale Volkskas, Johannesburg, South Africa*. Mark K. Morrison Assoc., Sharon, CT.

Morton, A.B., J.C. Gale and R.C. Prince. 1986. Sound and behavioral correlations in captive *Orcinus orca*. Pp. 303–334 in B.C. Kirkevold and J.S. Lockard, eds. *Behavioral biology of killer whales*. Zoo Biol. Monogr. Vol. 1. Alan Liss, New York, NY.

Morton, A.C. 1983. Butterfly conservation. The need for a captive breeding institute. *Biol. Conserv.* 25:19–33.

Mossman, A.S. and H.W. Mossman. 1962. Ovulation, implantation and fetal sex ratio in impala. *Science* 137:869.

Mountfort, G. 1988. *Rare birds of the world: A Collins/ICBP handbook*. The Penguin Group, Stephen Greene Press, Lexington, KY.

Mousseau, T.H. and H. Dingle. 1991. Maternal effects in insect life histories. *Ann. Rev. Entomol.* 36:511–534.

Moyle, M. 1989. Vitamin D and UV radiation: Guidelines for the herpetoculturist. *13th Int'l. Herpetol. Symp. on Captive Propagation. and Husbandry*. 1989:61–70.

Moyle, P.B. 1973. Effects of introduced bullfrogs, *Rana catesbeiana*, on the native frogs of the San Joaquin Valley, California. *Copeia* 1973:18–22.

Moyle, P.B and A. Marcioche. 1975. Biology of the Modoc sucker, *Catoslomus mierops* in northeastern California. *Copeia* 1975:556–560.

Muir, R.C. 1958. On the application of the capture-recapture method to an orchard population of *Blepharidopterus angulatus* (Fall.) (Hemiptera-Heteroptera, Miridae). Pp. 140–147 in Annual Report of the East Malling Res. Station-1957. Maidstone, England.

Muirhead-Thompson, R.C., ed. 1991. *Trap responses of flying insects.* Academic Press, New York, NY.

Mukku, V.R., S. Prahalada, and N.R. Moudgal. 1976. Effect of constant light on nychthemeral variation in serum testosterone in male *Macaca radiata. Nature* 260:778–780.

Muller, C.H. 1977. Plasma 5α-dihydrotestosterone and testosterone in the bullfrog, *Rana catesbeiana*: Stimulation by bullfrog LH. *Gen. Comp. Endocrinol.* 33:122–132.

Muller, E.F. and U. Lojewski. 1986. Thermoregulation in the meerkat (*Suricata suricatta* Schreber, 1776). *Comp. Biochem. Physiol.* 83A:217–224.

Muller, E.F. and H. Rost. 1983. Respiratory frequency, total evaporative water loss and heart rate in the kinkajou (*Potos flavus* Schreber). *Z. Sauget.* 48:217–226.

Muller, K.A. 1975. The thematic display as applied to bird exhibits. *Int'l. Zoo Yb.* 15:256–258.

Muller, K.A. 1976. Maintaining insectivorous birds in captivity. *Int'l. Zoo Yb.* 16:32–38.

Muller, K.A., 1984. The strange and wonderful birds of paradise. *Zoonooz* 57:4–9.

Mundinger, P.C. 1980. Animal cultures and a general theory of cultural evolution. *Ethol. Sociobiol.* 1:183–223.

Munn, C.A. 1987. Macaw biology in Manu National Park, Peru. *Parrotletter* 1:18–21.

Munro, A.D. 1990. Tropical freshwater fishes. Pp. 145–239 in A.D. Munro, A.P. Scott and T.J. Lam, eds. *Reproductive seasonality in teleosts: Environmental influences.* CRC Press, Boca Raton, FL.

Munro, A.D., A.P. Scott and T.J. Lam, eds. 1990. *Reproductive seasonality in teleosts: Environmental influences.* CRC Press, Boca Raton, FL.

Munro, S.S. 1938. Functional changes in fowl sperm during their passage through the excurrent ducts of the male. *J. Expl Zool.* 79:71–92.

Murdoch, W.W. 1963. A method for marking Carabidae (Col.). *Entomol. Monthly Mag.* 99:22–24.

Murdock, G.K., W.W. Stine and T.L. Maple. 1983. Observations of maternal-infant interactions in a captive herd of sable antelope, (*Hippotragus niger*). *Zoo Biol.* 2:215–224.

Murphy, D.D. and S.B. Weiss. 1988. Ecological studies on the conservation of the Bay checkerspot butterfly, *Euphydryas editha bayensis*. *Biol. Conser.* 46:183–200.

Murphy, D.D., M.S. Menninger, P.R. Ehrlich and B.A. Wilcox. 1986. Local population dynamics of adult butterflies and the conservation status of two closely related species. *Biol. Conserv.* 37:201–223.

Murphy, J.B. and J.A. Campbell. 1987. Captive maintenance. Pp. 165–181 in R.A. Seigel, J.T. Collins and S.S. Novak, eds. *Snakes: Ecology and evolutionary biology*. MacMillan, New York, NY.

Murphy, J.B. and D. Chiszar. 1989. Herpetological master planning for the 1990s. *Int'l. Zoo Yb.* 28:1–7.

Murphy, J.B. and T. Collins, eds. 1980. *Reproductive biology and diseases of captive reptiles*. Soc. Study Amphib. Reptiles, Oxford, OH.

Murphy, J.B. and L.A. Mitchell. 1989. "The other side": An experiment in reptile appreciation at the Dallas Zoo. *Int'l. Zoo Yb.* 28:205–207.

Murphy, J.B., T. Collins and K. Adler, eds. 1994. *Captive management and conservation of amphibians and reptiles*. Soc. Study Amphib. Reptiles. Contrib. Herpetol., Oxford, OH.

Murphy, K. 1984. The Living Seas Pavillion. *Proc. Int'l Marine Anim. Trainer's Assoc.* 1984:94–100.

Murphy, S.D. 1980. Pesticides. Pp. 357–408 in J. Doull, C.D. Klaassen and M.O. Amdur, eds. *Casarett and Doull's toxicology*. MacMillan, New York, NY.

Murray, J., E. Murray and B. Clarke. 1988. The extinction of *Partula* on Moorea. *Pacific Sci.* 42:150–153.

Murton, R.K. and N.J. Westwood. 1977. *Avian breeding cycles*. Clarendon Press, Oxford, England.

Murty, A.S., ed. 1986. *Toxicity of pesticides to fish*, Vol.II. CRC Press, Boca Raton, FL.

Mushinsky, H.R. and K.H. Lotz. 1980. Chemoreceptive responses of two sympatric water snakes to extracts of commonly ingested prey species: Ontogenetic and ecological considerations. *J. Chem. Ecol.* 6:523–535.

Muth, A. 1977. Thermoregulatory postures and orientation to the sun: A mechanistic evaluation for the zebra-tailed lizard, *Callisaurus draconoides*. *Copeia* 1977:710–720.

Myers, N. 1980. *Conservation of tropical moist forests*. Nat'l. Acad. Sci., Washington, DC.

Myers, N. 1986. Tropical deforestation and a mega-extinction spasm. Pp. 394–409 in M.E. Soulé, ed. *Conservation biology: The science of scarcity and diversity*. Sinauer Assoc., Sunderland, MA.

Myers, N. 1987a. The kill factor. *The Guardian*, October 9, 1987.

Myers, N. 1987b. Trends in the destruction of rain forests. Pp. 3–22 in C.W. Marsh and R.A. Mittermeier, eds. *Primate conservation in the tropical rainforest*. Alan Liss, New York, NY.

Myers, N. 1988. Tropical forests and their species: Going, going . . . ? Pp. 28–35 in E.O. Wilson and F. Peter, eds. *Biodiversity*. National Acad. Press, Washington, DC.

Myers, S.A., J.R. Millam, J.R. Roudybush and C.R. Grau. 1988. Reproductive success of hand-reared vs. parent-reared cockatiels (*Nymphicus hollandicus*). *Auk* 105:536–542.

Nace, G.W. 1968. The amphibian facility of the University of Michigan. *BioScience* 18:767–775.

Nace, G.W., D.D. Culley, M.B. Emmons, E.L. Gibbs, V.H. Hutchison and R.G. McKinnell. 1974. *Amphibians, guidelines for the breeding, care, and management of laboratory animals*. Nat'l. Acad. Sci., Washington, DC.

Nadler, R.D. 1974. Periparturitional behavior of a primiparous lowland gorilla. *Primates* 15:55–73.

Nadler, R.D. 1981. Laboratory research on sexual behavior of the great apes. Pp. 191–238 in C.E. Graham, ed. *Reproductive behavior of the great apes: Comparative and biomedical perspectives*. Academic Press, New York, NY.

Nadler, R.D. 1982. Laboratory research on sexual behavior and reproduction of gorillas and orang-utans. *Amer. J. Primatol.* Suppl. 1:57–66.

Nadler, R.D. 1984. Biological contributions to the maternal behavior of the great apes. Pp. 109–128 in M. Lewis, ed. *Beyond the dyad*. Plenum Press, New York, NY.

Nadler, R.D. 1989. The psychological well-being of captive gorillas. Pp. 416–420 in E.F. Segal, ed. *Housing, care and psychological wellbeing of captive and laboratory primates*. Noyes, Park Ridge, NJ.

Nadler, R.D., C.E. Graham, D.C. Collins and K.G. Gould. 1979. Plasma gonadotropins, prolactin, gonadal steroids and genital swelling during the menstrual cycle of lowland gorillas. *Endocrinology* 105:290–296.

Nagahama, Y. 1983. The functional morphology of teleost gonads. Pp. 223–275 in W.S. Hoar, D.J. Randall and E.M. Donaldson, eds. *Fish physiology*, Vol. IXA. Academic Press, New York, NY.

Nagahama, Y. 1987. Endocrine control of oocyte maturation. Pp. 171–202 in D.O. Norris and R.E. Jones, eds. *Hormones and reproduction in fishes, amphibians and reptiles*. Plenum Press, New York, NY.

Nagahama, Y. and S. Adachi. 1985. Identification of maturation-inducing steroid in a teleost, the amago salmon *(Oncorhynchus rhodurus)*. *Dev. Biol.* 109:428–435.

Nagata, H. 1986. Female choice in Middendorff's grasshopper-warbler *(Locustella ochotensis)*. *Auk* 103:694–700.

Nagy, K.A. 1987. Field metabolic rate and food requirement scaling in mammals and birds. *Ecol. Monogr.* 57:111–128.

Naiman, R.J. and D.L. Soltz, eds. 1981. *Fishes in North American deserts*. John Wiley & Sons, New York, NY.

Nalbandov, A.V. 1958. *Reproductive physiology of mammals and birds. The comparative physiology of domestic and laboratory animals and man.* W.H. Freeman, San Francisco, CA.

Nalleau, G. 1983. The effects of temperature on digestion in *Vipera aspis*. *J. Herpetol.* 17:166–170.

Nalleau, G., F. Fleury and J. Boissin. 1987. Annual cycles in plasma testosterone and thyroxine in male aspic viper *Vipera aspis* L., (Reptilian, Viperidae), in relation to the sexual cycle and hibernation. *Gen. Comp. Endocrinol.* 65:254–263.

Nardelli, F. 1984. The management of snow leopards in captivity at Howletts and Port Lympne. *Int'l. Pedigree Book of Snow Leopards* 4:75–78. Helsinki Zoo, Helsinki, Finland

Nash, V.J. 1982. Tool use by captive chimpanzees at an artificial termite mound. *Zoo Biol.* 1:211–221.

National Academy of Sciences. 1974. *Amphibians: Guidelines for the breeding, care and management of laboratory animals*. Nat'l. Acad. Press, Washington, DC.

National Academy of Sciences. 1975. *Research in zoos and aquariums*. Nat'l. Acad. Press, Washington, DC.

National Academy of Sciences. 1980. Pp. 1–116 in *Research priorities in tropical biology*. Nat'l. Acad. Press, Washington, DC.

National Council on Gene Resources. 1982. *Anadromous salmonid genetic resource, an assessment and plan for California*. California Gene Resources Program, Berkeley, CA.

National Institutes of Health. 1978. *Primate research centers: A major scientific resource*. U.S. Dept. of Health, Educ. and Welfare, Washington, DC.

National Marine Fisheries Service. 1982. *Shortnose sturgeon recovery plan, Acipenser brevirostium* Le Seur 1818. Nat'l. Marine Fish. Ser., Northeast Region, Gloucester, MA.

National Research Council. 1978. *Conservation of Germ Plasm resources: An imperative.* Nat'l. Acad. Sci., Washington, DC.

National Research Council. 1981. *Techniques for the study of primate population ecology.* Nat'l. Acad. Sci, Washington, DC.

National Research Council. 1987. Technologies to maintain biological diversity. U.S. Congress, Office of Technology Assessment, OTA-F-330. U.S. Govern. Print. Office, Washington, DC.

National Zoological Park. 1987. *Handrearing Facility Handbook.* National Zoological Park, Washington, DC.

Neill, J.D. and E. Knobil. 1972. On the nature of the initial luteotropic stimulus of pregnancy in the rhesus monkey. *Endocrinology* 90:34–38.

Neill, J.D., E.D.B. Johansson and E. Knobil. 1969a. Failure of hysterectomy to influence the normal pattern of cyclic progesterone secretion in the rhesus monkey. *Endocrinology* 84:464–465.

Neill, J.D., E.D.B. Johansson and E. Knobil. 1969b. Patterns of circulating progesterone concentrations during the fertile menstrual cycle and the remainder of gestation in the rhesus monkey. *Endocrinology* 84:45–48.

Nelson, B. 1989. Cainism in the Sulidae. *Ibis* 131:609.

Neufeldt, V. and D.B. Guralnik. 1988. P. 1426 in *Webster's new world dictionary*, 3rd College Ed. Simon and Schuster, New York, NY.

Neugebauer, W. 1967. Breeding the southern elephant seal *Mirounga leonia* at Stuttgart Zoo. *Int'l. Zoo Yb.* 7:152–154.

Neuringer, A. 1969. Animals respond for food in the presence of free food. *Science* 166:399–401.

Newman, D.G. 1977. Hamilton's frog. *Wildlife: A review* (New Zealand) 1977:48–53.

Ng, T.B. and D.R. Idler. 1983. Yolk formation and differentiation in teleost fishes. Pp. 373–404 in W.S. Hoar, D.J. Randall and E.M. Donaldson, eds. *Fish Physiology*, Vol. IXA. Academic Press, New York, NY.

Ngamvongchon, S., N.M. Sherwood, C.M. Warby and J.E. Rivier. 1992. Gonadotropin-releasing hormone from Thai catfish: Chromatographic and physiological studies. *Gen. Comp. Endocrinol.* 87:266–274.

Nichols, H. 1978. Captive breeding programs for Amazon parrots. Pp. 263–271 in S.A. Temple, ed. *Endangered birds: Management techniques for preserving threatened species.* Univ. Wisconsin. Press, Madison, WI.

Nicholls, T.J., A.R. Goldsmith, A. Dawson, S. Chakraborty and B.K. Follett. 1985. Involvement of the thyroid glands in photorefractoriness in starlings. Pp. 127–135 in B.K. Follett, S. Ishii and A. Chandola, eds. *The endocrine system and the environment*. Japan Sci. Soc. Press, Tokyo, Japan/Springer-Verlag, Berlin, Germany.

Nieman, H., A. Wust and J.C. Gardon. 1989. Successful intercontinental transport of porcine embryos from Europe to South America. *Theriogenology* 31:525–530.

Nieschlag, E. and E.J. Wickings. 1980. Testicular and adrenal steroids in the adult rhesus monkey and in man. Pp. 136–147 in T.C. Anand Kumar, ed. *Non-human primate models for study of human reproduction*. Karger Verlag, Basel, Switzerland.

Nigi, M., T. Tiba, S. Yamamoto, Y. Floescheim and M.M. Obsawa. 1980. Sexual maturation and seasonal changes in reproductive phenomena of male Japanese monkeys (*Macaca fuscata*) at Takasakiyama. *Primates* 21:230–240.

Nilson, G. 1980. Male reproductive cycle of the European adder, *Vipera berus*, and its relation to annual activity periods. *Copeia* 1980:729–737.

Nilsson, G. 1981. *The bird business. A study of the commercial cage bird trade*. 2nd Ed. Animal Welfare Institute, Washington, DC.

Nishiwaki, M. and H. Marsh. 1985. Dugong *Dugong dugong* (Muller, 1776). Pp. 1–31 in S.H. Ridgway and R.J. Harrison, eds. *Handbook of marine mammals, Vol. 3. The sirenians and baleen whales*. Academic Press, London, England.

Nishiwaki, M. and T. Tobayama. 1982. Hybrids between *Pseudorca crassidens* and *Tursiops truncatus gilli*. *Sci. Report Whales Res. Instit.*, 34:109–121.

Nishiwaki, M., M. Yamaguchi, S. Shikota, S. Uchida and T. Kataoka. 1982. Recent survey on the distribution of African manatee. *Sci. Report Whales Res. Instit.* 34:137–147.

Nocgcl, R. 1979. Amazon husbandry. *Amer. Fed. Avicull. Watchbird* Aug/Sept:10–21.

Norman, D.A. 1988. *The psychology of everyday things*. Basic Books, Inc. New York, NY.

Norman, D.A. and S.W. Draper. 1986. *User centered system design: New perspectives on human-computer interaction*. Lawrence Erlbaum, Hillsdale, NJ.

Norris, D.O. 1987. Regulation of male gonaducts and sex accessory structures. Pp. 327–354 in D. O. Norris and R. E. Jones, eds. *Hormones and reproduction in fishes, amphibians, and reptiles*. Plenum Press, New York, NY.

Norris, D.O., M.F. Norman, M.K. Pancak and D. Duvall. 1985. Seasonal variations in spermatogenesis, testicular weights, vasa deferentia, and androgen levels in neotenic male tiger salamanders, *Ambystoma tigrinum. Gen. Comp. Endocrinol.* 60:51–57.

Norris, K.S. 1964. Some problems of echolocation in cetaceans. Pp. 317–336 in W.N. Tavolga, ed. *Marine Bioacoustics.* Pergamon Press, New York, NY.

Norris, K.S. 1968. The evolution of acoustic mechanisms in odontocete cetaceans. Pp. 297–324 in E.T. Brake, ed. *Evolution and environment.* Yale University Press, New Haven, CT.

Norris, K.S., 1969. The echolocation of marine mammals. Pp. 391–423 in H.T. Andersen, ed. *The biology of marine mammals.* Academic Press, New York, NY.

Norris, K.S. 1992. Dolphins in crisis. *Nat'l. Geogr.* 182:2–35.

Norris, K.S. and W.E. Evans. 1966. Directionality of echolocation clicks in the rough-toothed porpoise *Stenella brenadensis* (Lesson). Pp. 305–316 in W.N. Tavolga, ed. *Marine bioacoustics.* Pergamon Press, New York, NY.

Norris, K.S. and K.W. Pryor. 1970. A tagging method for small cetaceans. *J. Mammal.* 51:609–610.

Norris, K.S., J.H. Prescott, P.V. Asa-Dorian and P. Perkins. 1961. An experimental demonstration of echo-location behavior in the porpoise, *Tursiops truncatus* (Montagu). *Biol. Bull.* 120:163–176.

Norton-Griffiths, M. 1969. The organisation, control and development of parental feeding in the oystercatcher (*Haematopus ostralegus*). *Behaviour* 34:55–114.

Novak, M.A. and K.H. Drewson. 1989. Enriching the lives of captive primates: Issues and problems. Pp. 161–182 in E.F. Segal, ed. *Housing, care, and psychological wellbeing of captive and laboratory primates.* Noyes, Park Ridge, NJ.

Novak, M.A., P. O'Neill, S.A. Beckley and S.J. Suomi. 1994. Naturalistic environments for captive primates. Pp. 236–258 in E.F. Gibbons, Jr., E.J. Wyers, E.J. Waters and E.W. Menzel, Jr., eds. *Naturalistic environments in captivity for animal behavior research.* State Univ. New York Press, Albany, NY.

Nowak, R.M. and J.L. Paradiso, eds. 1983. *Walker's mammals of the world,* 4th Ed. Johns Hopkins Univ. Press, Baltimore, MD.

Noy, M.J., S.W. Walsh and G.W. Klittinger. 1977. Experimental fetal anancephaly in the rhesus monkey—effect on gestational length and fetal and maternal plasma steroids. *J. Clin. Endocrinol. Metab.* 45:1031–1040.

Nuechterlein, G.L. 1981. Courtship behavior and reproductive isolation between western grebe color morphs. *Auk* 98:335–349.

Oates, J.F. 1977. The guerza and man. Pp. 419–467 in Prince Rainier of Monaco and G.H. Bourne, eds. *Primate conservation*. Academic Press, New York, NY.

Oates, J.F. 1986. *Action plan for African primate conservation: 1986–90*. Int'l. Union Conserv. Nature & Natur. Resour./Species Survival Commiss. Primate Specialist Group, Stony Brook, New York, NY.

Oates, J.F. 1987. Food distribution and foraging behavior. Pp. 197–209 in B.B. Smuts, D.L.Cheney, R.M. Seyfarth, R.W. Wrangham and T.T. Struhsaker, eds. *Primate societies*. Univ. Chicago Press, Chicago, IL.

O'Brien, S.J., D.E. Wildt, D. Goldman, C.R. Merril and M. Bush. 1983. The cheetah is depauperate in genetic variation. *Science* 221:459–462.

O'Connell, B., R. Greenlee, J. Bacon and D. Chiszar. 1982. Strike-induced chemosensory searching in Old World vipers and New World pit vipers at San Diego Zoo. *Zoo Biol*. 1:287–294.

Odell, D.K. 1992. Marine mammal stranding networks in the United States. *Proc. Int'l. Assoc. Aquat. Anim. Med*. 1989:29 (Abstr.).

O'Donnell, J. 1989. Characterization of nest sites on three Arctic seabird species with applications for design of exhibits. *Proc. Amer. Assoc. Zool. Parks Aquar*. 1989:272–278.

Odum, E. 1984. The mesocosm. *BioScience* 34:558–562.

Odum, E.P. 1944. *Sorex longirostris* at Mountain Lake, Virginia. *J. Mammal*. 25:196.

Odum, H.T. 1983. *Systems ecology: An introduction*. John Wiley & Sons, New York, NY.

Odum, R.A., J.M. McClain and T.C. Shely. 1983. Hormonally induced breeding and rearing of White's treefrog, *Litoria caerula* (Anura: Pelodryadidae). *Proc. 7th Annual Reptile Symp. on Captive Propagation. & Husbandry*. 1983:42–53.

Oftedal, O.T. 1984. Milk consumption, milk yield and energy output at peak lactation: A comparative review. *Symp. Zool. Soc. Lond*. 51:33–85.

Oftedal, O.T. 1985. Pregnancy and lactation. Pp. 215–238 in R.J. Hudson and R.G. White, eds. *Bioenergetics of wild herbivores*. CRC Press, Boca Raton, FL.

Ogasawara, F.X. and C.L. Fuqua. 1972. The vital importance of the uterovaginal sperm-host glands for the turkey hen. *Poult. Sci*. 51:1035–1039.

Ogden, J.J. 1989. A post-occupancy evaluation: Naturalisic habitats for captive lowland gorillas (*Gorilla gorilla gorilla*). Master's Thesis. Georgia Instit. Tech., Atlanta, GA.

Ogden, J.J. 1992. A comparative evaluation of naturalistic habitats for captive lowland gorillas (*Gorilla gorilla gorilla*). Ph.D. Dissertation, Georgia Instit. Tech., Atlanta, GA.

Ogden, J.J. and D.G. Lindburg. 1991. Do you hear what I hear? The effect of auditory enrichment on zoo animals and visitors. *Proc. Amer. Assoc. Zool. Parks Aquar.* 1991:428–435.

Ogilvie, M.A. 1972. Large numbered leg bands for individual identification of swans. *J. Wildl. Manage.* 36:1261–1265.

Ogilvie, M. and C. Ogilvie. 1986. *Flamingos*. Alan Sutton, Gloucester, England.

Oh, Y.K., T. Mori and T.A. Uchida. 1985. Prolonged survival of the Graafian follicle and fertilization in the Japanese greater horseshoe bat, *Rhinolophus ferrumequinum nippon*. *J. Reprod. Fertil.* 73:121–126.

Oksche, A. 1983. Reflections on the structural basis of avian neuroendocrine systems. Pp. 3–10 in S. Mikami, K. Homma and M. Wada, eds. *Avian endocrinology: Enviromental and ecological perspectives*. Japan Sci. Soc. Press, Tokyo, Japan/Springer-Verlag, Berlin, Germany.

Okuzawa, K., M. Amano, M. Kobayashi, K. Aida, I. Hanyu, Y. Hasegawa and K. Miyamoto. 1990. Differences in salmon GnRH and chicken GnRH-II contents in discrete brain areas of male and female rainbow trout according to age and stage of maturity. *Gen. Comp. Endocrinol.* 80:116–126.

Oliver, M.D. 1971. Artificial insemination and duration of fertility in Chinese geese. *Agroanimalia* 3:79–86.

Oliver, W.L.R. 1977. The butias of the West Indies. *Int'l. Zoo Yb.* 17:14–20.

Olney, P.J.S. 1975. Walk-through aviaries. Pp. 130–135 in A.P.G. Michelmore, ed. *Proc. 1st Int'l. Symp. Zoo Design and Construct*. Whitley Wildl. Conserv. Trust, Paignton, England.

Olney, P.J.S. 1986. Census of rare animals in captivity 1983/1984. *Int'l. Zoo Yb.* 24/25:565–622.

Olney, P.J.S. 1987a. Census of rare animals in captivity 1985. *Int'l. Zoo Yb.* 26:520–546.

Olney, P.J.S. 1987b. Mammals bred in captivity and multiple generation births 1984. *Int'l. Zoo Yb.* 26:467–506.

Olney, P.J.S., P. Ellis and F.A. Fiskin, eds. 1989. Reptiles and amphibians. *Int'l. Zoo Yb.* 28:1–216.

Olsen, R. 1984. Tiny crested toads returned to habitat. *San Juan Star*, May 7, 1984. San Juan, Puerto Rico.

Ono, R.D., J.D. Williams and A. Wagner. 1983. *Vanishing fishes of North America*. Stone Wall Press, Washington, DC.

Opel, H. and J.A. Proudman. 1986. Plasma prolactin response to serial bleeding in turkeys. *Dom. Anim. Endocrinol.* 3:199–207.

Opel, H. and J.A. Proudman. 1988. Effects of poults on plasma concentrations of prolactin in turkey hens incubating without eggs or a nest. *British Poult. Sci.* 29:791–800.

Opel, H. and J.A. Proudman. 1989. Plasma prolactin levels in incubating turkey hens during pipping of the eggs and after introduction of poults into the nest. *Biol. Reprod.* 40:981–987.

Opler, P.A. 1989. Ecological and behavioral aspects of seasonal diphenism in *Eurema daira* (Pieridae, Lepidoptera). Pp. 515–533 in J.H. Bock and Y.B. Linhart, eds. *The evolutionary ecology of plants*. Westview Press, Boulder, CO.

Orejuela, J.E. 1980. Niche relationships between turquoise-browed and blue-crowned motmots in the Yucatan Peninsula, Mexico. *Wilson Bull.* 92:229–244.

Orians, G.H. 1980. *Some adaptations of marsh-nesting blackbirds*. Princeton Univ. Press, Princeton, NJ.

Ortho Books. 1975. *The facts of light about indoor gardening*. Ortho Books, San Francisco, CA.

O'Shea, T.J. and R.L. Reep. 1990. Encephalization quotients and life-history traits in the Sirenia. *J. Mammal.* 71:534–543.

Osmundson, D. 1987. Growth and survival of Colorado squawfish (*Ptychocheilus lucius*) stocked in riverside ponds, with reference to large-mouth (*Micropterus salmoides*) predation. Master's Thesis. Utah State Univ., Logan, UT.

Östman, J. 1991. Changes in aggressive and sexual behavior between two male bottlenose dolphins (*Tursiops truncatus*) in a captive colony. Pp. 305–317 in K. Pryor and K.S. Norris, eds. *Dolphin societies*. Univ. California Press, Berkeley, CA.

Otten, T. and B. Andrews. 1976. Report on the successful rearing of a California sea lion pup. *J. Aquat. Mamm.* 4:21–24.

Otten, T., B. Andrews and D.D. Edwards. 1977. Hand-rearing a California sea lion. *Int'l. Zoo Yb.* 17:215–218.

Ottenwalder, J. 1988. Solenodons in captivity: A review. P. 519 in *Proc. 5th World Conf. Breed. Endang. Species Captivity*. Cincinnati Zoo & Botan. Gardens, Cincinnati, OH. (Abstr.).

Ottinger, M.A. 1983. Hormonal control of reproductive behavior in the avian male. *Poult. Sci.* 62:1690–1699.

Ough, W.D. 1982. Scent-marking by captive racoons. *J. Mammal.* 63:318–319.

Owen, R.D. 1941. Artificial insemination of pigeons and doves. *Poult. Sci.* 20:428–431.

Owens, D.D. and Owens, M.J. 1982. Helping behaviour in brown hyaenas. *Nature* 308:843–845.

Owens, D.W. 1976. Endocrine control of reproduction and growth in the green sea turtle *Chelonia mydas*. Ph.D. Dissertation. Univ. Arizona, Tucson, AZ.

Owens, D.W. 1980. The comparative reproductive physiology of sea turtles. *Amer. Zool.* 20:549–563.

Owens, D.W., J.R. Hendrickson and D.B. Endres. 1979. Somatic and immune responses to bovine growth hormone, bovine prolactin, and diethylstilbestrol in the green sea turtle. *Gen. Comp. Endocrinol.* 38:53–61.

Packard, J.M., L.D. Mech and U.S. Seal. 1983. Social influences on reproduction in wolves. Pp. 78–85 in L.N. Carbyn, ed. *Wolves in Canada and Alaska: Their status, biology and management*. Canadian Wildl. Serv. Report Series No 45.

Packard, J.M., U.S. Seal, L.D. Mech and E.D. Plotka. 1985. Causes of reproductive failure in two family groups of wolves (*Canis lupus*). *Z. Tierpsychol.* 68:24–40.

Packer, C. 1986. The ecology of sociality in felids. Pp. 429–451 in D.I. Rubenstein and R.W. Wrangham, eds. *Ecological aspects of social evolution*. Princeton Univ. Press, Princeton, NJ.

Packer, C. and A.E. Pusey. 1982. Cooperation and competition within coalitions of male lions: Kin selection or game theory? *Nature* 296:740–742.

Packer, C. and A.E. Pusey. 1983a. Adaptations of female lions to infanticide by incoming males. *Amer. Natural.* 121:716–728.

Packer, C. and A.E. Pusey. 1983b. Male takeovers and female reproductive parameters: A simulation of oestrous synchrony in lions (*Panthera leo*). *Anim. Behav.* 31:334–340.

Packer, C. and A.E. Pusey. 1984. Infanticide in carnivores. Pp. 31–42 in G. Hausfater and S.B. Hrdy, eds. *Infanticide: Comparative and evolutionary perspectives*. Aldine Press, New York, NY.

Page, L.A., ed. 1976. *Wildlife diseases*. Plenum Press, New York, NY.

Page, L.M. 1983. *Handbook of darters*. T.F.H. Pubs., Neptune City, NJ.

Page, L.M. 1985. Evolution of reproductive behaviors in percid fishes. *Illinois Natur. Hist. Surv. Bull* 33:275–295.

PAHO/WHO (Pan American Health Organization/World Health Organization). 1976. *First inter-American conference on conservation and utilization of American non-human primates in biomedical research*. Pan Amer. Health Org/World Health Org., Washington, DC.

Palmer, B.D. and L.J. Guillette, Jr. 1988. Histology and functional morphology of the female reproductive tract of the tortoise *Goperus polyphemus*. *Am. J. Anat.* 183:200–211.

Pan, M.L. and G.R. Wyatt. 1971. Juvenile hormone induces vitellogenin synthesis in the monarch butterfly. *Science* 174:503–505.

Parker, G.A. 1970. Sperm competition and the evolutionary consequences in the insects. *Biol. Rev.* 45:525–567.

Parker, N.C., A.E. Giorgi, R.C. Heidinger, D.B. Jester, Jr., E.D. Prince and G.A. Winans, eds. 1990. *Fish-marketing techniques*. Amer. Fish. Symp. 7.

Parker, S.P., ed. 1982. *Synopsis and classification of living organisms*. McGraw-Hill, New York, NY.

Parks, J.E., W.R. Heck and V.A. Hardaswick. 1986. Cryopreservation of peregrine falcon semen and post-thaw dialysis to remove glycerol. *Raptor Res.* 20:15–20.

Parsons, M.J. 1992. Butterfly farming and conservation in the Indo-Australian region. *Trop. Lepidopt.* 3 (Suppl. 1):1–62.

Partridge, J. 1990. Mixed animal exhibits. *Int'l. Zoo News* 371:13–18.

Partridge, L. and P. Green. 1977. An advantage for specialist feeding in jackdaws, *Corvus monedula*. *Anim. Behav.* 35:982–990.

Patterson, S.A. 1983. Training of an echolocation matching-to-sample talk in a bottlenose dolphin, *Tursiops truncatus*. *Proc. Int'l. Marine Anim. Trainers Assoc.* 1983:72–75.

Paulraj, S. 1988a. Breeding the Indian giant squirrel (*Ratufa indica*) in captivity. P. 521 in *Proc. 5th World Conf. Breed. Endang. Species in Captivity*. Cincinnati Zoo & Botan. Gardens, Cincinnati, OH. (Abstr.).

Paulraj, S. 1988b. Breeding behaviour of the Malay giant squirrel *Ratufa bicolor* at Arignar Anna Zoological Park. *Int'l. Zoo Yb.* 27:279–282.

Pavgi, S.S.N. and A. Chandola. 1981. Role of gonadal feedback in annual reproduction of the weaver bird: Interaction with photoperiod. *Gen. Comp. Endocrinol.* 45:521–526.

Pawley, R. 1969. Observations on the reaction of the Mata Mata turtle, *Chelys fimbriata*, to ultra-violet radiation. *Int'l. Zoo Yb.* 9:31–32.

Payne, K.B., W.R. Langbauer and E.M. Thomas. 1986. Infrasonic calls of the Asian elephant *(Elaphas maximus)*. *Behav. Ecol. Sociobiol.* 18:297–301.

Payne, R.B. 1972. Mechanisms and control of molt. Pp. 103–155 in D.S. Farner, J.R. King and K.C. Parkes, eds. *Avian biology*, Vol. II. Academic Press, New York, NY.

Payne, R.D. 1986. *Long term behavioral studies of the southern right whales (Eubalaena australis).* Report Int'l. Whaling Commiss., Spec. Issue 10. Cambridge, England.

Payne, R.D., E.M. Brazier, J.S. Corsey, V.J. Perkins, V.J. Rowntree and A. Titus. 1983. External features in southern right whales *(Eubalaena australis)* and their use in identifying individuals. Pp. 371–445 in R. Payne, ed. *Communication and behavior of whales.* Amer. Assoc. Adv. Sci. Select. Symp. 76., Washington, DC.

Pearl, M.C. 1992. Conservation of Asian primates: Aspects of genetics and behavioral ecology that predict vulnerability. Pp. 297–320 in P.L. Fielder and S.K. Jain, eds. *Conservation biology: The theory and practice of nature conservation, preservation, and management.* Routledge, Chapman & Hall, New York, NY.

Peczely, P. 1985. Adrenocortical adaptations in birds. Pp. 213–220 in B.K. Follett, S. Ishii and A. Chandola, eds. *The endocrine system and the environment.* Japan Sci. Soc. Press, Tokyo, Japan/Springer-Verlag, Berlin, Germany.

Peczely, P. and G. Pethes. 1980. Plasma corticosterone, thyroxine and triiodothroxine level in collared dove *(Streptopelia decaocto)* during the reproductive cycle. *Acta Physiol. Acad. Sci. Hungar.* 56:421–430.

Peel, R.R., J. Price and P. Karsten. 1979. Mother-rearing of a spectacled bear cub, *Tremarctos ornatus*, at the Calgary Zoo. *Int'l. Zoo Yb.* 19:177–182.

Penny, C. 1989. Kuhl's deer born at San Diego Zoo. *Amer. Assoc. Zool. Parks and Aquar. Newsletter* 30:25.

Penny, R.L. 1978. Breeding the Adelie penguins, *Pygoscelis adelinae*, in captivity. *Int'l. Zoo Yb.* 18:13–21.

Pepe, G.J., J.A. Titus and J.D. Townsley. 1977. Increasing fetal adrenal formation of cortisol from pregnenolone during baboon *(Papio papio)* gestation. *Biol. Reprod.* 17:701–705.

Pereira, M.E. 1986. Maternal recognition of juvenile offspring coo vocalizations in Japanese macaques. *Anim. Behav.* 34:935–937.

Pereira, M.E., J.M. Macedonia, D.M. Haring and E.L. Simons. 1989. Maintenance of primates in captivity for research: The need for naturalistic environments. Pp. 40–60 in E. Segal, ed. *Housing, care and psychological wellbeing of captive and laboratory primates.* Noyes, Park Ridge, NJ.

Peres, C.A. 1990. Effects of hunting on western Amazonian primate communities. *Biol. Conserv.* 54:47–59.

Perkins, L.A. 1992. Variables that influence the activity of captive orangutans. *Zoo Biol.* 11:177–186.

Perloe, S.I. 1991. Mate selection and reproductive success among Japanese macaque males in Minoo. Pp. 203–206 in A. Ehara, T. Kimura, O. Takenaka and M. Iwamoto, eds. *Primatology today.* Elsevier, New York, NY.

Perret, M. and M. Atramentowicz. 1989. Plasma concentrations of progesterone and testosterone in captive wooly opossums (*Caluromys philander*). *J. Reprod. Fertil.* 85:31–41.

Perrin, W.F. and R.L. Brownell, Jr. 1989. Report of the workshop on conservation and biology of the plantanistoid dolphins. Pp. 1–22 in W.F. Perrin, R.L. Brownell, Jr., K.Y. Zhou and R.J. Liu, eds. *Biology and conservation of the river dolphins.* Int'l. Union Conserv. Nature & Natur. Resour./Species Survival Commission Occasional Paper No 3. Gland, Switzerland.

Perrin, W.F. and S.B. Reilly. 1984. Reproductive parameters of dolphins and small whales of the family delphinidae. Pp. 97–133 in W.F. Perrin, R.L. Brownell and D.P. DeMasters, eds. *Reproduction in whales, dolphins and porpoises.* Int'l. Whaling Commiss., Special Issue 6.

Perry, J., D. Bridgewater and D. Horseman. 1972. Captive propagation: A progress report. *Zoologica* Fall:109–117.

Perry, J.S. and I.W. Rowlands, eds. 1973. *The environment and reproduction in mammals and birds. J. Reprod. Fertil.* Suppl. 19.

Peter, R.E. 1981. Gonadotropin secretion during reproductive cycles in teleosts: Influences of environmental factors. *Gen. Comp. Endocrinol.* 45:294–305.

Peter, R.E. 1982. Neuroendocrine control of reproduction in teleosts. *Can. J. Fish. Aquat. Sci.* 39:48–55.

Peter, R.E. 1983. The brain and neurohormones in teleost reproduction. Pp. 97–135 in W.S. Hoar, D.J. Randall and E.M. Donaldson, eds. *Fish physiology*, Vol IXA. Academic Press, New York, NY.

Peter, R.E., L. Hao-ren and G. Van Der Kraak. 1987. Drug/hormone induced breeding of Chinese teleosts. Pp. 120–123 in D.R. Idler, L.W. Crim and J.M. Walsh, ed. *Proc. 3rd Int'l. Symp. Reprod. Physiol. Fish.* Memorial Univ. Press, St. John's, Newfoundland.

Peter, R.E., K.L. Yu, T.A. Marchant and P.M. Rosenblum. 1990. Direct neural regulation of the teleost adenohypophysis. *J. Exp. Zool.* Suppl 4:84–89.

Peter, R.E., V.L. Trudeau, B.D. Sloley, C. Pend and C.S. Nahorniak. 1991. Actions of catecholamines, peptides and sex steroids in regulation of gonadotropin-II in the goldfish. Pp. 30–34 in A.P. Scott, J.P. Sumpter, D.E. Kime and M.S. Rolfe, eds. *Proc. 4th Int'l. Symp. on the Reprod. Phys. of Fish.* Univ. E. Anglia Print. Unit, Norwich, England.

Peter, R.E., J.P. Chang, C.S. Nahorniak, R.J. Omeljaniuk, M. Sokolowska, S.H. Shih and R. Billard. 1986. Interactions of catecholamines and GnRH in regulation of gonadotropin secretion in teleost fish. *Recent Progr. Horm. Res.* 42:513–548.

Peters, G., M. Faisal, T. Lang and I. Ahmed. 1988. Stress caused by social interaction and its effect on susceptibility to *Aeromonas hydrophila* infection in rainbow trout *Salmo gairdneri. Diseases Aquat. Org.* 4:83–89.

Peters, R.L. and D.S. Darling. 1985. The greenhouse effect and nature reserves. *BioScience* 35:707–717.

Peterson, A. 1953. *A manual of entomological equipment and methods.* Edwards Brothers, Ann Arbor, MI.

Peterson, E.A. 1980. Noise and laboratory animals. *Lab. Anim. Sci.* 30:422–439.

Petrinovitch, L., T. Patterson and L.F. Baptista. 1981. Song dialects as barriers to dispersal: A reevaluation. *Evolution* 35:180–188.

Petter, J.-J. and F. Andriatsarafara. 1987. Conservation status and distribution of lemurs in the west and northwest of Madagascar. *Primate Conserv.* 8:169–171.

Pfeiffer, E.W. 1960. Cyclic changes in the morphology of the vulva and clitoris of *Dipodomys. J Mammal.* 41:43–48.

Pfleiger, W. 1978. Distribution, status, and life history of the Niangua darter, *Etheostoma nilanguae*. Missouri Dept. Conserv., Aquatic series 16. Jefferson City, MO.

Phillips, J.A. and B.L. Lasley. 1987. Modification of reproductive rhythm of lizards via GnRH therapy. *Annals New York Acad. Sci.* 518:128–136.

Phillips, J.A., A.C. Alberts and N.C. Pratt. 1993. Differential resource use, growth and the ontogeny of social relationships in the green iguana. *Physiol. Behav.* 55:81–88.

Phillips, J.A., N. Alexander, W.B. Karesh, R. Millar and B.L. Lasley. 1985. Stimulating male sexual behavior with repetitive pulses of GnRH in female green iguanas, *Iguana iguana. J. Exp. Zool.* 234:481–484.

Phillips, J.A., F. Frye, Jr., A. Berkovitz, P. Calle, R. Millar, J. Rivier and B.L. Lasley. 1987. Exogenous GnRH overrides the endogenous annual reproductive rhythm in green iguanas, *Iguana iguana. J. Exp. Zool.* 241:227–236.

Phillips, L.G., L.G. Simmons, M. Bush, J.G. Howard and D.E. Wildt. 1982. Gonadotropin regimen for inducing ovarian activity in captive wild felids. *J. Amer. Vet. Med. Assoc.* 181:1246–1250.

Pianka, E.R. 1988. P. 208 in *Ecology and natural history of desert lizards*. Princeton Univ. Press, Princeton, NJ.

Pickford, G.E. and J.W. Atz. 1957. *The physiology of the pituitary gland of fishes*. New York Zoological Society, New York, NY.

Picman, J. 1977. Intraspecific nest destruction in the long-billed marsh wren. *Can. J. Zool.* 55:1997–2003.

Pierantoni, R., B. Varriale, S. Fasano, S. Minucci, L. DiMatteo and G. Chieffi. 1987. Seasonal plasma and intraovarian sex steroid profiles, and influence of temperature on gonadotropin stimulation of *in vitro* estradiol-17β and progesterone production in *Rana esculenta* (Amphibia: Anur). *Gen. Comp. Endocrinol.* 67:163–168.

Pierce, D.J. and T.R. Simons. 1986. The influence of human disturbance on tufted puffin breeding success. *Auk* 103:214–216.

Pierce, N.E. and P.S. Mead. 1981. Parasitoids as selective agents in the symbiosis between lycaenid butterfly larvae and ants. *Science* 211:1185 1187.

Pilleri, G. 1984. Animals on display—educational and scientific impact: Comments on a workshop held at the John G. Shedd Aquarium, Chicago, IL. Pp. 9–17 in G. Pilleri, ed. *Investigations on Cetacea*, Vol XVI. Berne, Switzerland.

Pilleri, G. 1987. Down with dolphin zoos! Pp. 283–288 in G. Pilleri, ed. *Investigations on Cetacea*, Vol XX. Berne, Switzerland.

Pimentel, R. and R. Bulkley. 1983. Concentration of total dissolved solids preferred or avoided by endangered Colorado fishes. *Trans. Amer. Fish. Soc.* 112:595–600.

Pimm, S.L. and J.L. Gittleman. 1992. Biodiversity: Where is it? *Science* 255:940.

Pinder, N.J. and J.P. Barkham. 1978. An assessment of the contribution of captive breeding to the conservation of rare animals. *Biol. Conserv.* 13:187–245.

Pinkerton, S.S., H. Hughes and W.W. Wenrich. 1982. *Behavioral medicine: Clinical applications*. John Wiley & Sons, New York, NY.

Plant, T.M. 1980. The neuroendocrine basis of the diurnal variation of testicular testosterone secretion in the adult rhesus monkey (*Macaca mulatta*). Pp. 419–423 in A. Steinberger and E. Steinberger, eds. *Testicular development, structure and function*. Academic Press, New York, NY.

Plant, T.M., D. Zumpe, M. Sauls and R.P. Michael. 1974. An annual rhythm in the plasma testosterone of adult male rhesus monkeys maintained in the laboratory. *J. Endocrinol.* 62:403–404.

Pliske, T.E. 1975. Courtship behavior and use of chemical communication by males of certain species of ithomiine butterflies (Nymphalidae: Lepidoptera). *Ann. Entomol. Soc. Amer.* 68:935–942.

Plotka, E.D., U.S. Seal, F.R. Zarembka, L.G. Simmons, A. Teare, L.G. Phillips, K.C. Hinshaw and D.G. Wood. 1988. Ovarian function in the elephant: Luteinizing hormone and progesterone cycles in African and Asian elephants. *Biol. Reprod.* 38:309–314.

Plotkin, M.J., R. Medem, R.A. Mittermeier and I.D. Constable. 1983. Distribution and conservation of the black cayman (*Melanosuchus niger*). Pp. 695–705 in A. Rhodin and K. Miyata, eds. *Adv. in Herpetol. and Evol. Biol.* Mus. Comp. Zool., Harvard, MA.

Poglayan-Newall, I., B.S. Durrant, M.L. Swansen, R.C. Williams and R.A. Barnes. 1989. Estrous cycle of the tayra, *Eira barbara. Zoo Biol.* 8:171–177.

Poinar, G.O., Jr. and G.M. Thomas. 1984. *Laboratory guide to insect pathogens and parasites.* Plenum Press, New York, NY.

Poirier, F.E. 1972. The St. Kitts green monkey (*Cercopithecus aethiops sabaeus*): Ecology, population dynamics, and selected behavioral traits. *Folia Primatol.* 17:20–55.

Polacheck, T. 1987. Relative abundance, distribution and inter-specific relationship of cetacean schools in the eastern tropical Pacific. *Marine Mamm. Sci.* 3:54–77.

Polakowski, K.J. 1987. *Zoo design: The reality of wild illusions.* Univ. Michigan, School of Natural Resour. Ann Arbor, MI.

Polge, C. 1985. Embryo manipulation and genetic engineering. *Symp. Zool. Soc. London* 54:123–135.

Polis, G.A. and C.A. Myers. 1985. A survey of intraspecific predation among reptiles and amphibians. *J. Herpetol.* 19:99–107.

Pollack, J.I. 1986. Towards a conservation policy for Madagascar's eastern rain forests. *Primate Conserv.* 7:82–86.

Polzonetti-Magni, A., V. Botte, L. Bellini-Cardellini, A. Gobetti and A. Crasto. 1984. Plasma sex hormones and post-reproductive period in the green frog, *Rana esculenta* Complex. *Gen. Comp. Endocrinol.* 54:372–377.

Pomerleau, O.F. and J.P. Brady, eds. 1979. *Behavioral medicine: Theory and practice.* Williams & Wilkins, Baltimore, MD.

Poole, J.H., K.B. Payne, W.R. Langbauer and C.J. Moss. 1988. The social contexts of some very low frequency calls of African elephants. *Behav. Ecol. Sociobiol.* 22:385–392.

Pope, C.E., V.Z. Pope and L.R. Beck. 1980. Nonsurgical recovery of uterine embryos in the baboon. *Biol. Reprod.* 23:657–662.

Pope, C.E., V.Z. Pope, L.R. Beck. 1983. Successful nonsurgical transfer of a nonsurgically recovered four-cell uterine embryo in the baboon. *Theriogenology* 19:144 (Abstr.).

Pope, C.E., B.L. Dresser, L.W. Kramer and D. Gillespie. 1988. Nonsurgical embryo recovery in the yellow-backed duiker (*Cephalophus sylvicultor*)- A preliminary study. *Proc. 11th Int'l. Congr. Anim. Reprod. and Artif. Insem.* 1988:185(Abstr). Univ. College, Dublin, Ireland.

Pope, C.E., E.J. Gelwicks, M. Burton, R. Reece and B.L. Dresser. 1991. Nonsurgical embryo transfer in the scimitar-horned oryx (*Oryx dammah*): Birth of a live offspring. *Zoo Biol.* 10:43–51.

Pope, C.E., E.J. Gelwicks, K.B. Wachs, G.L. Keller, E.J. Maruska and B.L. Dresser. 1989. Successful interspecies transfer of embryos from the Indian desert cat (*Felis silvestris ornata*) to the domestic cat (*Felis catus*) following *in vitro* fertilization. *Biol. Reprod.* Suppl. 40:61(Abstr).

Popp, J.W. 1984. Interspecific aggression in mixed ungulate species exhibits. *Zoo Biol.* 3: 211–219.

Porter, K. 1982. Basking behaviour in larvae of the butterfly *Euphydryas aurinia*. *Oikos* 38:308–312.

Porter, K.R. 1972. *Herpetology*. W.B. Saunders. Philadelphia, PA.

Porter, W.P. and D.M. Gates. 1969. Thermodynamic equilibria of animals with their environment. *Ecol. Monogr.* 39:227–244.

Post, G.S., H.C. Hensleigh, A.P. Byers, U.S. Seal, T.J. Kreeger, N.J. Reindl and R.L. Tilson. 1987. Penetration of zona-free hamster ova by Siberian tiger sperm. *Zoo Biol.* 6:183–187.

Pough, F.H. 1991. Recommendations for the care of amphibians and reptiles in academic institutions. *Nat'l. Acad. Press* 33:S1–S21.

Powell, B.A. 1986. Marine mammal research opportunities in oceanariums, aquariums, marine parks, and zoos. *Aquat. Mamm.* 12:40–42.

Poyser, N.L. and B. Pharm. 1981. *Prostaglandins in reproduction*. Research Studies Press, John Wiley & Sons, New York, NY.

Prasad, M.R.N. and T.C. Anand Kumar, eds. 1977. *Use of non-human primates in biomedical research*. Indian Nat'l. Sci. Acad., New Delhi, India.

Pratt, N.C., M.L. Patton and B.S. Durrant. 1991. Coomassie staining as a technique for determination of the acrosome reaction in frozen-thawed semen samples. *Proc. Amer. Assoc. Zool. Parks Aquar.* 1991:640 (Abstr.).

Pratt, N.C., A.C. Alberts, K.G. Fulton-Needler and J.A. Phillips. 1992. Behavioral, physiological, and morphological components of dominance and mate attraction in male green iguanas. *Zoo Biol.* 11:153–163.

Presidente, P.J.A. 1982. Common wombat, *Vombatus ursinus*, maintenance in captivity, blood values, infectious and parasitic diseases. Pp. 133–143 in D.D. Evans, ed. *The management of Australian mammals in captivity*. Proc. Aust. Mammal. Soc., 1979. Ramsey Ware Stockland, Victoria, Australia.

Price, C.A. and H.E. Winn. 1981. Development of methodology for identifying individual right whales (*Eubalaena glacialis*) based on bonnet patterns and other markings, with a report on preliminary results. App. A, 1980 CeTad Ann. Report to Bureau of Land Manage. Nat'l. Tech. Info. Serv. PB-83-149905. U.S. Dept. of Commerce, Washington, DC.

Price, E.C. 1992. Adaptation of captive-bred cotton-top tamarins (*Saguinus oedipus*) to a natural environment. *Zoo Biol.* 11:107–120.

Price, P.W., T.M. Lewinsohn, G.W. Fernandes and W.W. Benson. 1991. *Plant-animal interactions: Evolutionary ecology in tropical and temperate regions*. John Wiley & Sons, New York, NY.

Pritchard, P.C.H. 1977. Three, two, one tortoise. *Natur. Hist.* 86:90–100.

Pritchard, P.C.H. 1985. The toughest tortoises in the Galapagos. *Defenders* 60:10–16.

Pritchard, P.C.H. 1988. First captive reproduction of *Podocnemis expansa*. *Int'l. Union Conserv. Nature & Natur. Resour. Tortoise and Freshwater Turtle Specialist Group Newsletter*, December 1988:1.

Pritchard, P.C.H. 1989a. Galapagos tortoises: Captive breeding success. *Int'l. Union Conserv. Nature & Natur. Resour. Tortoise and Freshwater Turtle Specialist Group Newsletter*. September 1989:3.

Pritchard, P.C.H. 1989b. *The alligator snapping turtle: Biology and conservation*. Milwaukee Public Mus., Milwaukee, WI.

Proctor, D.L.C. 1979. Chick loss in south polar skua. *Ibis* 117:452–459.

Proctor, S. 1986. Max Bell Marine Mammal Center at the Vancouver Aquarium. *Proc. Amer. Assoc. Zool. Parks Aquar.* 1986:334–340.

Proudman, J.A. 1987. Purification and partial characterization of isohormone forms of turkey luteinizing hormone. *Poult. Sci.* Suppl. 1 66:161 (Abstr.).

Proudman, J.A. 1991. Daily rhythm of prolactin and corticosterone in unrestrained, incubating turkey hens. *Domestic Anim. Endocrinol.* 8:265–270.

Prove, E. 1985. Steroid hormones as a physiological basis of sexual imprinting in male zebra finches (*Taeniopygia guttata castanotis* Gould).

Pp. 235–245 in B.K. Follett, S. Ishii and A. Chandola, eds. *The endocrine system and the environment.* Japan Sci. Soc. Press, Tokyo, Japan/Springer-Verlag, Berlin, Germany.

Pryor, K. 1984. *Don't shoot the dog.* Simon and Schuster, New York, NY.

Pryor, K. and K.S. Norris. 1991. *Dolphin societies.* Univ. California Press, Berkeley, CA.

Pryor, K.W., R. Haag and J. O'Reilly. 1969. The creative porpoise: Training for novel behavior. *J. Exp. Anal. Behav.* 12:653–661.

Pullianinen, E. 1982. Behavior and structure of an expanding wolf population in Karelia, northern Europe. Pp. 134–145 in F.H. Harrington and P.C. Paquet, eds. *Wolves of the world.* Noyes, Park Ridge, NJ.

Putnam, M.S. 1982. Refined techniques in crane propagation at the International Crane Foundation. Pp. 250–258 in *Proc. 1981 Crane Workshop, Grand Teton Nat'l. Park, WY.*

Pyle, R.M. 1976. Conservation of Lepidoptera in the United States. *Biol. Conserv.* 9:55–75.

Pyle, R.M. 1988. Captive breeding of butterflies for conservation. Pp 423–430 in *Proc. 5th World Conf. Breed. Endang. Species in Captivity.* Cincinnati Zoo & Botan. Gardens, Cincinnati, OH.

Pyle, R.M., M. Bentzien and P. Opler. 1981. Insect conservation. *Ann. Rev. Entomol.* 26:233–258.

Quattro, J.M., J.C. Avise and R.C. Vrijenhoek. 1992. Mode of origin and sources of genotypic diversity in triploid gynogenetic fish clones (Poeciliopsis: Poeciliidae). *Genetics* 130:621–628.

Quay, W.B. 1967. Comparative survey of the anal glands in birds. *Auk* 84:379–389.

Quick, D.L.F. 1984. An integrative approach to environmental engineering in zoos. *Zoo Biol.* 3:65–77.

Quillen, P. 1981. Handrearing the little spotted cat or oncilla, *Felis tigrinus. Int'l. Zoo Yb.* 21:240–242.

Quinn, J.P. and W.H. Burrows. 1936. Artificial insemination of fowls. *J. Hered.* 27:31–37.

Qumsiyeh, M.B. 1990. On the nature of controversies in evolutionary biology. *Perspect. Biol. Med.* 33:421–430.

Rabb, G., K. Milton, A.H. Harcourt, D.A. Meritt, A. Jolly and R.A. Mittermeier. 1986. Strategies for the highly endangered primates. Pp. 1005–1007 in K. Benirschke, ed. *Primates: The road to self-sustaining populations.* Springer-Verlag, New York, NY.

Rabinowitch, V.E. 1968. The role of experience in the development of food preferences in gull chicks. *Anim. Behav.* 16:425–428.

Rabinowitz, A.R. and B.G. Nottingham, Jr. 1986. Ecology and behaviour of the jaguar (*Panthera onca*) in Belize, Central America. *J. Zool.* 210:149–159.

Radden, R.D. 1968. The Dominican Republic hutia, *Plagiodontia aedium hylaeum*, in captivity. Master's Thesis. University of Puget Sound, Tacoma, WA.

Radeleff, R.D. 1970. Pp. 312–313 in *Veterinary toxicology*. Lea & Febiger, Philadelphia, PA.

Rado, R., N. Levi, H. Hauser, J. Witcher, N. Adler, N. Intrator, Z. Wolberg and J. Terkel. 1987. Seismic signaling as a means of communication in a subterranean mammal. *Anim. Behav.* 35:1249–1251.

Raikhel, A.S. and T.S. Dhadialla. 1992. Accumulation of yolk proteins in insect oocytes. *Ann. Rev. Entomol.* 37:217–251.

Ralls, K. 1989. A semi-captive breeding program for the Baiji, *Lipotes vexillifer*: Genetic and demographic considerations. Pp. 150–156 in W.F. Perrin, R.L. Brownell, Jr., K.Y. Zhou and R.J. Liu, eds. *Biology and conservation of the river dolphins*. IUCN Species Survival Commission Occasional Paper No 3. Allen Press, Lawrence, KS.

Ralls, K. and J. Ballou. 1982. Effects of inbreeding on infant mortality in captive primates. *Int'l. J. Primatol.* 3:491–505.

Ralls, K. and J. Ballou. 1983. Extinction: Lessons from zoos. Pp. 164–184 in C.M. Schonewald-Cox, S.M. Chambers, B. MacBryde and W.L. Thomas, eds. *Genetics and conservation: A reference for managing wild animal and plant populations*. Benjamin/Cummings, Menlo Park, CA.

Ralls, K. and J. Ballou. 1986. Preface to the proceedings of the workshop on genetic management of captive populations. *Zoo Biol.* 5:81–86.

Ralls, K. and R.L. Brownell. 1989. Protected species-research permits and the value of basic research. *BioScience* 39:394–396.

Ralls, K., J. Ballou and R.L. Brownell, Jr. 1983. Genetic diversity in California sea otters: Theoretical considerations and management implications. *Biol. Conserv.* 25:209–232.

Ralls, K., K. Brugger and J. Ballou. 1979. Inbreeding and juvenile mortality in small populations of ungulates. *Science* 206:1101–1103.

Ralls, K., K. Brugger and A. Glick. 1980. Deleterious effects of inbreeding in a herd of captive Dorcas gazelles, *Gazella dorcas*. *Int'l. Zoo Yb.* 20:137–146.

Ralls, K., P.H. Harvey and A.M. Lyles. 1986a. Inbreeding in natural populations of birds and mammals. Pp. 35–56 in M.E. Soulé, ed. *Conservation biology: The science of scarcity and diversity.* Sinauer Assoc., Sunderland, MA.

Ralls, K., K. Kranz and B. Lundrigan. 1986b. Mother-young relationships in captive ungulates: Variability and clustering. *Anim. Behav.* 34:134–145.

Ralls, K., B. Lundrigan and K. Kranz. 1982. Variability of behavioral data recorded by volunteer observers. *Int'l. Zoo Yb.* 22:151–156.

Ralls, K., B. Lundrigan and K. Kranz. 1987. Mother-young relationships in captive ungulates: Behavioral changes over time. *Ethology* 75:1–14.

Ramakrishna, P.A. and M.R.N. Prasad. 1967. Changes in the male reproductive organs of *Loris tardigradus lydekkerianus. Folia Primatol.* 5:176–189.

Ramsay, E.C., J.H. Kasman and B.L. Lasley. 1987. Urinary steroid evaluations to monitor ovarian function in exotic ungulates: V. Estrogen and pregnanediol-3-glucuronide excretion in the black rhinoceros (*Diceros bicornis*). *Zoo Biol.* 6:275–282.

Rand, A.S. 1967. Ecology and social organization in the iguanid lizard *Anolis lineatopus. Proc. U.S. Nat'l. Mus.* 122:1–79.

Rand, A.S. 1968. A nesting aggregation of iguanas. *Copeia* 1968:552–561.

Rand, G.M. 1985. Behavior. Pp. 221–263 in G.M. Rand and S.R. Petrocelli, eds. *Fundamentals of aquatic toxicology.* Hemisphere, New York, NY.

Raphael, B.L., N.M. Loskutoff, L.A. Nemec, B.A. Wolfe, J.G. Howard and D.C. Kraemer. 1988. Hormonal characterization and manipulation of the estrous cycle and nonsurgical embryo recovery in suni antelope. *Theriogenology* 29:292 (Abstr.).

Rasa, O.A.E. 1975. Mongoose sociality and behavior as related to zoo exhibition. *Int'l. Zoo Yb.* 15:65–73.

Rasa, O.A.E. 1987. The dwarf mongoose: A study of behavior and social structure in relation to ecology in small, social carnivore. *Adv. Study Behav.* 17:121–163.

Rasmussen, L.E., I.O. Buss, D.L. Hess and M.J. Schmidt. 1984. Testosterone and dihydrotestosterone concentrations in elephant serum and temporal gland secretions. *Biol. Reprod.* 30:352–362.

Rastogi, R.K., L. Iela, G. Delrio and J.T. Bagnara. 1986. Reproduction in the Mexican leaf frog, *Pachymedusa dacnicolor*, II: The male. *Gen. Comp. Endocrinol.* 62:23–35.

Rasweiler, J.J. 1977. The care and management of bats as laboratory animals. Pp. 519–617 in W.A. Wimsatt, ed. *Biology of bats*, Vol III. Academic Press, New York, NY.

Rasweiler, J.J. 1988. Ovarian function in the captive black mastiff bat, *Molossus ater. J. Reprod. Fertil.* 82:97–111.

Ratcliffe, D. 1967. Decrease in eggshell weight in certain birds of prey. *Nature* 215:208–210.

Ratcliffe, D. 1980. *The peregrine falcon.* Buteo Books, Vermillion, SD.

Rauch, N. 1981. Comportamiento reproductivo de las iguanas marinas. *Informe Ann., Charles Darwin Res. Sta., Galapagos.* 1981:136–138.

Raup, D.M. 1986. *The nemesis affair: A story of the death of dinasaurs and the ways of science.* W.W. Norton, New York, NY.

Ravenscroft, N.O.M. 1990. The ecology and conservation of the silver-studded blue butterfly *Plebejus argus* L. on the sandlings of East Anglia, England. *Biol. Conserv.* 53:21–36.

Rawlins, R.G. and M.J. Kessler. 1985. Climate and seasonal reproduction in Cayo Santiago macaques. *Amer. J. Primatol.* 9:87–99.

Rawlins, R.G. and M.J. Kessler, eds. 1986a. *The Cayo Santiago macaques: History, behavior, and biology.* State Univ. New York Press, Albany, NY.

Rawlins, R.G. and M.J. Kessler. 1986b. Demography of the free-ranging Cayo Santiago macaques (1976–1983). Pp. 13–46 in R.G. Rawlins and M.J. Kessler, eds. *The Cayo Santiago macaques: History, behavior, and biology.* State Univ. New York Press, Albany, NY.

Rayner, G.W. 1940. Whale marking, progress, and results in 1939. *Discovery Report* 19:245–284.

Read, B. and R. Frueh. 1980. Management and breeding of Speke's gazelles, *Gazella spekei*, at the St. Louis zoo, with a note on artificial insemination. *Int'l. Zoo Yb.* 20:99–104.

Rector, D.A., G.S. Jacobs and T.G. Hopkins. 1986. The ethogram: Present and future applications. *Proc. Int'l. Marine Anim. Trainers Assoc.* 1986:37–41.

Reddy, M. 1989. Population monitoring of the Hawaiian monk seal, *Monachus schauinslandi*, and captive maintenance project for female pups at Kure Atoll, 1987. National Oceanic Atmospheric Assoc. Tech. Memo., Nat'l. Marine Fish. Serv., S.W. Fish. Center. NOAA-TM-NMFS-SWFC-123, Honolulu, HI.

Reed, T.H. 1966. Remodelled bird house and new great flight cage at the National Zoological Park. *Int'l. Zoo Yb.* 6:129–131.

Reeves, R.R. and R.L. Brownell, Jr. 1989. Susu, *Plantanista gangetica* (Roxburgh, 1801) and *Plananista minor* Owen, 1853. Pp. 69–99 in S.H. Ridgway and R.J. Harrison, eds. *Handbook of marine mammals. Vol. 4: River dolphins and the larger toothed whales.* Academic Press, London, England.

Reeves, R.R., A.A. Chaudhry and U. Khalid. 1991. Competing for water on the Indus Plain: Is there a future for Pakistan's river dolphins? *Environ. Conserv.* 18:341–350.

Reeves, R.R., D. Tuboku-Metzger and R.A. Kapindi. 1988. Distribution and exploitation of manatees in Sierra Leone. *Oryx* 22:75–84.

Regal, P.J. 1980. Temperature and light requirements of captive reptiles. Pp. 79–90 in J.B. Murphy and J.T. Collins, eds. *Reproductive biology and diseases of captive reptiles.* Soc. Study Amphib. and Reptiles, Lawrence, KS.

Reid, W.V. 1988. Age correlations within pairs of breeding birds. *Auk* 105:278–285.

Reijnders, P.J.H., M.N. de Visscher and E.H. Ries. 1988. *The Mediterranean monk seal.* Int'l. Union Conserv. Nature & Natur. Resour., Gland, Switzerland.

Reinert, H.K. 1991. Translocations as a conservation strategy for amphibians and reptiles: Some comments, concerns, and observations. *Herpetologica* 47:357–363.

Renaud, D.L. and A.N. Popper. 1975. Sound localization by the bottlenose porpoise *Tursiops truncatus. J. Exp. Biol.* 63:569–585.

Resink, J.W., P.K. Voorthuis, R. Van den Hurk, H.G.B. Vullings and P.G.W.J. Van Oordt. 1989. Pheromone detection and olfactory pathways in the brain of the female African catfish, *Clarias gariepinus. Cell Tiss. Res.* 256:337–345.

Resko, J.A., R.L. Norman, G.D. Niswender and H.G. Spies. 1974. The relationship between progestins and gonadotropins during the late luteal phase of the menstrual cycle in rhesus monkeys. *Endocrinology* 94:128–135.

Reynolds, R. 1982. Some observations on the captive management of Galapagos tortoises and land iguanas at the Darwin Station and suggestions for the future. *Inform. Ann., Charles Darwin Res. Sta., Galapagos* 1982:115–123.

Rhodin, A.G.R. and R.A. Mittermeier. 1983. Conservation and status of chelid turtles. Proc. of Freshwater Chelonian Subgroup Report, Int'l. Union Conserv. Nature & Natur. Resour./Species Survival Commiss. *Hamadryad* 8:43–44.

Rice, D.W. 1973. Caribbean monk seal *Monachus tropicalis.* IUCN Survival Service Commission. *Int'l. Union Conserv. Nature & Natur. Resour. Publ. New Ser. Suppl. Pap.* 39:98–112.

Rice, D.W. 1989. Sperm whale, *Physeter macrocephalus* Linnaeus, 1758. Pp. 177–233 in S.H. Ridgway and R.J. Harrison, eds. *Handbook of marine mammals. Vol 4: River dolphins and the larger toothed whales.* Academic Press, London, England.

Richard, A.F. 1976. Preliminary observations on the birth and development of *Propithecus verrawxi* to the age of six months. *Primates* 17:357–366.

Richard, A.F. 1982. The world's endangered primate species: A case study on the lemur fauna of Madagascar. Pp. 23–30 in R.A. Mittermeier and M.J. Plotkin, eds. *Primates and the tropical forest.* L.S.B. Leakey Found., Pasadena, CA and World Wildl. Fund-U.S., Washington DC.

Richard, A.F. and R.W. Sussman. 1975. Future of the Malagasy lemurs: Conservation or extinction? Pp. 335–350 in I. Tattersall and R.W. Sussman, eds. *Lemur biology.* Plenum Press, New York, NY.

Richard, A.F. and R.W. Sussman. 1987. Framework for primate conservation in Madagascar. Pp. 329–341 in C.W. Marsh and R.A. Mittermeier, eds. *Primate conservation in the tropical rain forest.* Alan Liss., New York, NY.

Richards, D.G., J.P. Wolz and L.M. Herman. 1984. Vocal mimicry of computer generated sounds and vocal labeling of objects by a bottlenose dolphin, *Tursiops truncatus. J. Comp. Psychol.* 98:10–28.

Richardson, C.H. 1925. The ovipositon responses of insects. Bull. No. 1324. U.S. Dept. Agric., Washington, DC.

Richardson, E.G. 1977. The biology and evolution of the reproductive cycle of *Miniopterus schreibersii* and *M. australis* (Chiroptera: Vespertilionidae). *J. Zool. London* 183:353–375.

Richter, K.D., R. Korte and T. Senge. 1978. Morpho-funktionelle studies on hoden gesunder Rhesusaffen. Pp. 41–46 in T. Senge, F. Neumann and U.W. Tunn, eds. *Physiologie and pathophysiologie des hodens.* Thieme–Verlag, Stuttgart, Germany.

Ricklefs, R.E. and G.W. Cox. 1972. Taxon cycles in the West India avifauna. *Amer. Natural.* 106:195–219.

Ridgway, S.H. 1966. Dall porpoise, *Phocoenoides dalli* (True): Observations in captivity and at sea. *Norsk. Hvalfangst-Tidende* 55:97–110.

Ridgway, S.H. 1972. Homeostasis in the aquatic environment. Pp. 590–747 in S.H. Ridgway, ed. *Mammals of the sea: Biology and medicine.* Charles Thomas, Springfield, IL.

Ridgway, S.H. and K. Benirschke, eds. 1977. Breeding dolphins: Present status, suggestions for the future. U.S. Dept. Commer., Nat'l. Info. Tech. Info. Serv., PB 273–673. Washington, DC.

Ridgway, S.H. and R.F. Green. 1967. Evidence for a sexual rhythm in male porpoises, *Lagenorhynchus obliquidens* and *Delphinus delphis baidi. Norsk Hvalfangst-Tidende* 1:1–8.

Ridgway, S.H., K.S. Norris and L.H. Cornell. 1989. Some considerations for those wishing to propagate platanistoid dolphins. Pp. 159–167 in W.F. Perrin, R.L. Brownell, Jr., K.Y. Zhou and R.J. Liu, eds. *Biology and conservation of the river dolphins*. Occasional papers of the Int'l. Union Conserv. Nature & Natur. Resour./Species Survival Commission, No. 3. Allen Press, Lawrence, KS.

Ridgway, S.H., J.G. Simpson, G.S. Patton and W.G. Gilmartin. 1970. Hematologic findings in certain small cetaceans. *J. Amer. Vet. Med. Assoc.* 157:566–575.

Ridley, M.W. 1986. Captive breeding and reintroduction of pheasants. *Int'l. Zoo Yb.* 24/25:40–44.

Rinne, J.N. 1980. Spawning habitat and behavior of Gila trout, a rare salmonid of the southeastern United States. *Trans. Amer. Fish. Soc.* 109:83–91.

Rinne, J.N., J.E. Johnson, B.L. Jensen, A.W. Ruger and R. Soreson. 1986. The role of hatcheries in the management and recovery of threatened and endangered fishes. Pp. 271–285 in R. Stroud, ed. *Fish culture in fisheries management*. Amer. Fish. Soc., Bethesda, MD.

Ripley, S. 1967. The leaping of langurs: A problem in the study of locomotor adaptation. *Amer. J. Phys. Anthro.* 26:149–170.

Risdon, D.H.S. 1975. Aviary design and construction. Pp. 122–129 in A.P.G. Michelmore, ed. *Proc. 1st Int'l. Symp. Zoo Design and Construct*. Whitley Wildl. Conserv. Trust, Paignton, England.

Risser, A.C. 1978. *Amazons*. Zoonooz 51:13.

Robbins, C.T. 1983. *Wildlife feeding and nutrition*. Academic Press, New York, NY.

Robeck, T.R., J.F. McBain, L.M. Dalton, M.T. Welsh, N. Czekala and D.C. Kraemer. 1990. Monitoring reproductive endocrinology of captive killer whales, *Orcinus orca*. *Proc. Int'l. Assoc. Aquat. Anim. Med.* 1990:48–54.

Roberts, M.S. 1975. Growth and development of mother-reared red pandas, *Ailurus fulgens*. *Int'l. Zoo Yb.* 15:57–63.

Roberts, M.S. 1989. Red Panda Species Survival Plan Report. *Amer. Assoc. Zool. Parks Aquar. Newsletter* 30:10–11.

Roberts, M.S. and J.L. Gittleman. 1984. *Ailurus fulgens. Mammalian Species Account* 222:1–8. Am. Soc. Mamm., Lawrence, KS.

Robertson, R.J. and B.J. Stutchbury. 1988. Experimental evidence for sexually selected infanticide in tree swallows. *Anim. Behav.* 36:749–753.

Robinson, J.A. and W.E. Bridson. 1978. Neonatal hormone patterns in the macaque, I: Steroids. *Biol. Reprod.* 19:773–778.

Robinson, J.A. and R.W. Goy. 1986. Steroid hormones and the ovarian cycle. Pp. 63–91 in W.R. Dukelow and J. Erwin, eds. *Comparative Primate Biology, Vol 3: Reproduction and development.* Alan Liss, New York, NY.

Robinson, M.H. 1969. The defensive behavior of some orthopteroid insects from Panama. *Trans. Roy. Entomol. Soc. London* 121:281–303.

Robinson, M.H. 1978. Culture techniques for *Acanthops falcata,* a neotropical mantid suitable for biological studies (with notes on raising web building spiders). *Psyche* 844:225–232.

Robinson, M.H. 1982. The philosophy and practice of environmental education in the tropics: A critical assessment. *Proc. Delhi Conf. on Environ. Educ., Indian Environ. Soc.* 1982:145–163.

Robinson, M.H. 1985. Predator-prey interactions, informational complexity, and the origins of intelligence. *J. Wash. Acad. Sci.* 75:91–104.

Robinson, M.H. 1987. Beyond the zoo: The biopark. *Defend. Wildl. Mag.* 62:10.

Robinson, M.H. 1988a. Overture to a new zoo: The National Zoo's invertebrate house. *Freshwater and Marine Aquar.* 12:104–134.

Robinson, M.H. 1988b. Bioscience education through bioparks. *BioScience* 38:630–634.

Robinson, M.H. 1989. Networking the world of the bioexhibit. *Proc. Amer. Assoc. Zool. Parks Aquar.* 1989:303–309.

Robinson, M.H. 1991a. Animal rights, objections to zoos, and the evolution of bioparks. *Proc. Int'l. Union Direct. Zool Gardens.* 1990:18–45.

Robinson, M.H. 1991b. Invertebrates: Exhibiting the silent majority. *Int'l. Zoo Yb.* 30:1–7.

Roca, P., F. Sainz, M. Gonzalez and M. Alemany. 1984. Stucture and composition of the eggs from several avian species. *Comp. Biochem. Physiol.* 77:307–310.

Rockey, S.J., J.H. Hainze and J.M. Scriber. 1987. A latitudinal and obligatory diapause response in three subspecies of the eastern tiger swallowtail *Papilio glaucus* (Lepidoptera: Papilionidae). *Amer. Midl. Natural.* 118:162–168.

Rodda, G.W. 1992. The mating behavior of *Iguana iguana. Smith. Contrib. Zool.* 534:1–40.

Rodda, G.W. and T.H. Fritts. 1992. The impact of the introduction of the colubrid snake, *Bioga irregularis*, on Guam's lizards. *J. Herpetol.* 26:166–174.

Rodda, G.W., B.C. Bock, G.M. Burghardt and A.S. Rand. 1988. Techniques for identifying individual lizards at a distance reveal influences of handling. *Copeia* 1988:905–913.

Rodden, M. 1989. Maned Wolf Species Survival Plan Report. *Amer. Assoc. Zool. Parks Aquar. Newsletter* 30:12–14.

Rodriguez, J.G. 1979. *Recent advances in acarology*, Vol II. Academic Press, New York, NY.

Roest, A.I. 1987. Morro Bay kangaroo rat captive breeding project. Annual Report No. 3. U.S. Fish and Wildlife Service, Sacramento, CA.

Roest, A.I. 1988. Morro Bay kangaroo rat captive breeding project. Final summary report. U.S. Fish and Wildlife Service, Sacramento, CA.

Rohwer, F. and M.G. Anderson. 1988. Female based philopatry, monogamy, and the timing of pair formation in migratory waterfowl. Pp. 187–221 in R.F. Johnston, ed. *Current ornithology*, Vol. 5. Plenum Press, New York, NY.

Rojas, M. 1992. The species problem and conservation: What are we protecting? *Conserv. Biol.* 6:170–178.

Roletto, J. and J. Mazzeo. 1990. Identification of North American marine mammals. Pp. 399–468 in L.A. Dierauf, ed. *CRC Handbook of marine mammal medicine: Health, disease and rehabilitation.* CRC Press, Boca Raton, FL.

Rolf, H.J. and K. Fischer. 1987. Annual periodicity of blood testosterone and 5-α-DHT levels in the adult male fallow deer *(Dama dama)*. *Acta Endocrinol. Copenh.* 114(Suppl. 283):178. (Abstr.).

Rood, J.P. 1980. Mating relationships and breeding suppression in the dwarf mongoose. *Anim. Behav.* 28:143–150.

Rood, J.P. 1983. The social system of the dwarf mongoose. Pp. 454–488 in J.F. Eisenberg and D.G. Kleimanm eds. *Recent advances in the study of mammalian behavior.* Spec. Pub #7. Amer. Soc. Mammal, Lawrence, KS.

Rood, J.P. 1986. Ecology and social evolution in the mongooses. Pp. 131–152 in D.I. Rubenstein and R.W. Wrangham, eds. *Ecological aspects of social evolution.* Princeton Univ. Press, Princeton, NJ.

Root-Bernstein, R.S. 1989. How scientists really think. *Perspect. Biol. Med.* 32:472–488.

Rose, R.W. 1982. Tasmanian bettong, *Bettongia giamardi:* Maintenance and breeding in captivity. Pp.108–110 in D.D. Evans, ed. *The manage-*

ment of Australian mammals in captivity. Proc. Aust. Mammal. Soc., 1979. Ramsey Ware Stockland, Victoria, Australia.

Rosenthal, M.A. 1975. Observtions on the water opposum or yapok in captivity. *Int'l. Zoo Yb.* 15:4–6.

Rosenzweig, M.R. and E.L. Bennett. 1978. Experiential influences on brain anatomy and brain chemistry in rodents. Pp. 287–327 in G. Gottlieb, ed. *Early influences: Studies on the development of behavior and the nervous system.* Academic Press, New York, NY.

Ross, R.A. and G. Marzec. 1991. *The reproductive husbandry of pythons and boas.* Institute for Herpetological Research, Stanford, CA.

Rothman, R.J. and L.D. Mech. 1979. Scent-marking in lone wolves and newly formed pairs. *Anim. Behav.* 27:750–760.

Rothschild, M. and C. Farrell. 1983. *The butterfly gardner.* Michael Joseph Ltd. & Rainbird Pub. Group, London, England.

Rouse, W.B. and K.R. Boff. 1987. *System design: Behavioral perspectives on designers, tools, and organizations.* North-Holland, New York, NY.

Rowan, W. 1925. Relation of light to bird migration and developmental changes. *Nature* 115:494–495.

Rowan, W. 1926. On photoperiodism, reproductive periodicity and annual migration of birds and certain fishes. *Proc. Boston Soc. Nat. Hist.* 38:147–189.

Rowan, W. 1929. Experiments in bird migration. 1. Manipulations of the reproductive cycle: Seasonal histological changes in the gonads. *Proc. Boston. Soc. Nat. Hist.* 39:151–208.

Rowell, J.E. and P.E. Flood. 1988. Progesterone, oestradiol-17β and LH during the oestrus cycle of muskoxen (*Ovibos moschatus*). *J. Reprod. Fertil.* 84:117–122.

Rowell, J.E., K.J. Betteridge, G.C.B. Randall and J.C. Fenwick. 1987. Anatomy of the reproductive tract of the female muskox (*Ovibos moschatus*). *J. Reprod. Fertil.* 80:431–444.

Rowell, T.E. 1970. Baboon menstrual cycles affected by social environment. *J. Reprod. Fertil.* 21:133–141.

Rowlands, I.W. and R.M.F.S. Sadleir. 1986. Induction of ovulation in the lion (*Panthera leo*). *J. Reprod. Fertil.* 16:105–111.

Rowlands, I.W. and B.J. Weir. 1984. Mammals: Non-primate eutherians. Pp. 455–658 in G.E. Lamming, ed. *Marshall's physiology of reproduction, Vol 1: Reproductive cycles of vertebrates.* Churchill Livingstone, New York, NY.

Rubin, A.J. 1975. *Chemistry of water supply treatment and distribution.* Ann Arbor Science, Ann Arbor, MI.

Rutgers, A. and K.A. Norris. 1977. *Encyclopedia of aviculture,* Vol. 3. Blandford Press, Dorset, England.

Ryan, K.J. and B.R. Hopper. 1974. Placental biosynthesis and metabolism of steroid hormones in primates. *Contrib. Primatol.* 3:258–269.

Ryan, M.J. 1985. *The tungera frog: A study in sexual selection and communication.* Univ. Chicago Press, Chicago, IL.

Ryder, O.A. 1986. Genetic investigations: Tools for supporting breeding programme goals. *Int'l. Zoo Yb.* 24/25:157–162.

Ryder, O.A. and M.L. Byrd. 1984. *One medicine.* Springer-Verlag, New York, NY.

Ryder, O.A., P.C. Brisbin, A.T. Bowling and E.A. Wedemeyer. 1981. Monitoring genetic variation in endangered species. Pp. 417–424 in G.G.E. Scudder and J.L. Reveal, eds. *Evolution today.* Proc. 2nd Int'l. Congr. Syst. & Evol. Biol. Carnegie-Mellon Univ., Pittsburg, PA.

Ryder, O.A., A.T. Kumamoto, B.S. Durrant and K. Benirschke. 1989. Chromosomal divergence and reproductive isolation in dik-diks. Pp. 208–225 in D. Otte and J.A. Endler, eds. *Speciation and its consequences.* Sinauer Assoc., Sunderland, MA.

Ryman, N. and L. Laikre. 1991. Effects of supportive breeding on the genetically effective population size. *Conserv. Biol.* 5:325–329.

Ryman, N. and F. Utter, eds. 1987. *Population genetics and fishery management.* Univ. Washington Press, Seattle, WA.

Ryon, M.G. 1986. The life history and ecology of *Etheostoma trisella* (Pisces: Percidae). *Amer. Midl. Natur.* 115:73–86.

Sade, D.S. 1964. Seasonal cycle in size of testes of free-ranging *Macaca mulatta. Folia Primatol.* 2:171–180.

Sade, D.S. 1967. Determinants of dominance in a group of free-ranging rhesus monkeys. Pp. 99–114 in S.A. Altmann, ed. *Social communication among primates.* Univ. Chicago Press, Chicago, IL.

Sade, D.S. 1972. Sociometrics of *Macaca mulatta*: I. Linkages and cliques in grooming matrices. *Folia Primatol.* 18:196–223.

Sade, D.S., K. Cushing, P. Cushing, J. Dunaif, A. Figueroa, J.R. Kaplan, C. Lauer, D. Rhodes and J. Schneider. 1976. Population dynamics in relation to social structure on Cayo Santiago. *Yb. Phys. Anthro.* 20:253–262.

Sadleir, R.M.F.S. 1975. Role of the environment in the reproduction of mammals in zoos. Pp. 151–156 in *Research in zoos and aquariums*. Nat'l. Acad. Sci., Washington, DC.

Sadleir, R.M.F.S. 1987. Reproduction of female cervids. Pp. 123–144 in C.M. Wemmer, ed. *Biology and management of the Cervidae*. Smithsonian Instit. Press, Washington, DC.

Safar-Hermann, N., M.N. Ismail, H.S. Choi, E. Mostl and E. Bamberg. 1987. Pregnancy diagnosis in zoo animals by estrogen determination in feces. *Zoo Biol*. 6:189–193.

Sajdak, R.A. 1983. Herpetological research in zoos: A literature survey, 1977–1981. *Zoo Biol*. 2:149–152.

Salt, W.R. 1954. The structure of the cloacal protuberance of the vesper sparrow (*Pooecetes gramineuns*) and certain other passerine birds. *Auk* 71:64–73.

Samour, J.H., J.A. Markham and H.D.M. Moore. 1988. Semen cryopreservation and artificial insemination in budgerigars (*Melopsittacus undulatus*). *J. Zool. London* 216:169–176.

Samour, J.H., P.J.S. Olney, D. Herbert, R. Smith, J. White and D. Wood. 1983. Breeding and hand-rearing the Andean condor, *Vultur gryphus* at London Zoo. *Int'l. Zoo Yb*. 23:7–11.

Sandell, M. 1989. Mating tactics and spacing patterns in solitary carnivores. Pp. 164–182 in J.L. Gittleman, ed. *Carnivore behavior, ecology, and evolution*. Cornell Univ. Press, Ithaca, NY.

Santiapillai, C. and P. Jackson. 1990. *The Asian elephant: An action plan for its conservation*. Int'l. Union Conserv. Nature & Natur. Resour., Gland, Switzerland.

Santos, A.J.G., K. Furukawa, M. Kobayashi, K. Bando, K. Aida and I. Hanyu. 1986. Plasma gonadotropin and steroid hormone profiles during ovulation in the carp *Cyprinus carpio*. *Bull. Japan. Soc. Sci. Fish*. 52:1159–1166.

Santos, dos M.E. and Lacerda, M. 1987. Preliminary observations of the bottlenose dolphin (*Tursiops truncatus*) in the Sado estuary. *Aquat. Mamm*. 13:65–80.

Sauey, R.T. and C.B. Brown. 1977. The captive management of cranes. *Int'l. Zoo Yb*. 17:89–92.

Saul, L. 1992. Captive husbandry of selective species or Orthoptera for public exhibits. *Regional Proc. Amer. Assoc. Zool. Parks and Aquar*. 1992:280–287.

Sausman, K. 1989. Surveys of artiodactyls in captivity. Unpublished document of the Captive Breeding Special. Group. Apple Valley, MN.

Savage, A. 1988. Collaboration between research institutions and zoos for primate conservation. *Int'l. Zoo Yb.* 27:140–148.

Savory, C.J. 1980. Meal occurrence in Japanese quail in relation to particle size and nutrient density. *Anim. Behav.* 28:160–171.

Sawyer-Steffan, J.E., V.L. Kirby and W.G. Gilmartin. 1983. Progesterone and estrogens in the pregnant and non-pregnant dolphin, *Tursiops truncatus*, and the effect of induced ovulation. *Biol. Reprod.* 28:897–901.

Sayer, J.A. and T.C. Whitmore. 1991. Tropical moist forests: Destruction and species extinction. *Biol. Conserv.* 55:199–213.

Scanes, C.G. 1986. Pituitary gland. Pp. 383–402 in P.D. Sturkie, ed. *Avian physiology*, 4th Ed. Springer-Verlag, New York, NY.

Scanes, C.G., T.J. Lauterio and F.C. Buonomo. 1983. Annual, developmental, and diurnal cycles of pituitary hormone secretion. Pp. 307–326 in S. Mikami, K. Homma, M. Wada, eds. *Avian endocrinology: Environmental and ecological perspectives*. Japan Sci. Soc. Press, Tokyo, Japan/Springer-Verlag, Berlin, Germany.

Schaaf, C.D. 1984. Animal behavior and the captive management of wild animals: A personal view. *Zoo Biol.* 3:373–377.

Schafer, S.F. and C. O'Neill Krekorian. 1983. Agonistic behavior of the Galapagos tortoise, *Geochelone elephantopus*, with emphasis on its relationship to saddle-backed shell shape. *Herpetologica* 39:448–456.

Schaffer, N., M. Cranfield, T. Meehan and S. Kempske. 1989. Semen collection and analysis in the conservation of endangered nonhuman primates. *Zoo Biol.* Suppl. 1:47–60.

Schaller, G.B. 1963. *The mountain gorilla: Ecology and behavior.* Univ. of Chicago Press, Chicago, IL.

Schaller, G.B., H. Jinchu, P. Wenshi and Z. Jing. 1985. *The giant pandas of Wolong.* Univ. of Chicago Press, Chicago, IL.

Schaller, G.B., T. Qitao, K.G. Johnson, W. Xiaming, S. Heming and H. Jinchu. 1989. Feeding ecology of giant panda and Asiatic black bear in the Tangjiahe Reserve, China. Pp. 212–241 in J.L. Gittleman, ed. *Carnivore behavior, ecology, and evolution.* Cornell Univ. Press, Ithaca, NY.

Schapiro, S. and G. Mitchell. 1986. Primate behavior in captive or confined free-range settings. Pp. 93–140 in G. Mitchell and J. Erwin, eds. *Comparative primate biology, 2A, Behavior, conservation and ecology.* Alan Liss, New York, NY.

Schenck, J.R. and B.G. Whiteside. 1977a. Reproduction, fecundity, sexual dimorphism and sex ratio of *Etheostoma fonticola* (Osteichthyes: Percidae). *Am. Midl. Nat.* 98:365–375.

Schenck, J.R. and B.G. Whiteside. 1977b. Food habits and feeding behavior of the fountain darter, *Etheostoma fonticola* (Osteichthyes: Percidae). *S.W. Natural.* 21:487–492.

Schevill, W.E. and B. Lawrence. 1953. Auditory response of a bottlenosed porpoise, *Tursiops truncatus*, to frequencies above 100 KC. *J. Exp. Zool.* 124:147–165.

Schiewe, M.C., M. Bush, L.G. Phillips and D.E. Wildt. 1988. Variables influencing the collection and cryopreservation of embryos from nondomestic hoofed species. *Proc.11th Int'l. Congr. Anim. Reprod. Artif. Insem.* 1988:190 (Abstr.). Univ. College, Dublin, Ireland.

Schmidt, A.M., L.A. Nadal, M.J. Schmidt and N.B. Beamer. 1979. Serum concentrations of estradiol and progesterone during the normal oestrous cycle and early pregnancy in the lion (*Panthera leo*). *J. Reprod. Fertil.* 57:267–272.

Schmidt, A.M., D.L. Hess, M.J. Schmidt, R.C. Smith and C.R. Lewis. 1988. Serum concentrations of oestradiol and progesterone and sexual behavior during the normal oestrous cycle in the leopard (*Panthera pardus*). *J. Reprod. Fertil.* 82:43–49.

Schmidt, J.O. 1990. Evolution of major defensive ensembles. Pp. 1–2 in D.L. Evans and J.O. Schmidt, eds. *Insect defenses: Adaptive mechanisms and strategies of prey and predators.* State Univ. New York Press, Albany, NY.

Schmidt, M.J. and H. Markowitz. 1977. Behavioral engineering as an aid in the maintenance of healthy zoo animals. *J. Amer. Vet. Med. Assoc.* 171:966–969.

Schmitt, D.L. 1986. Nonsurgical embryo transfer in scimitar-horned oryx. *Proc. Amer. Assoc. Zoo Vets.* 1986:10–11.

Schmitt, E.C. 1984. Indoor aviary maintenance. *Regional Proc. Amer. Assoc. Zool. Parks Aquar.* 1984:408–412.

Schnierla, T.C. 1950. The relationship between observation and experimentation in the field study of behavior. *Annals New York Acad. Sci.* 51:3–29.

Schneirla, T.C. 1958. The study of animal behavior: Its history and relation to the museum (Part I). *Curator* 1:17–35.

Schneirla, T.C. 1959. The study of animal behavior: Its history and relation to the museum (Part II). *Curator* 2:27–48.

Schnell, G.D., D.J. Watt and M.E. Douglas. 1985. Statistical comparison of proximity matrices: Applications in animal behaviour. *Anim. Behav.* 33:239–253.

Schoenherr, A.A. 1977. Density dependent and density independent regulation of reproduction in the Gila topminnow, *Poeciliopsis occidentalis* (Baird and Girard). *Ecology* 58:438–444.

Schoenwald-Cox, C.M., S.M. Chambers, B. MacBryde and W.L. Thomas, eds. 1983. *Genetics and conservation.* Benjamin/Cummings, Menlo Park, CA.

Schreck, C.B. 1974. Hormonal treatment and sex manipulation in fishes. Pp. 84–106 in C.B. Schreck, ed. *Control of sex in fishes.* Virginia Polytech. Instit., Blacksburg, VA.

Schreck, C.B. 1981. Stress and compensation in teleostean fishes: Responses to social and physical factors. Pp. 295–321 in A.D. Pickering, ed. *Stress and fish.* Academic Press, New York, NY.

Schreck, C.B. and M.L. Hopwood. 1974. Seasonal androgen and estrogen patterns in the goldfish, *Carassius auratus. Trans. Amer. Fish. Soc.* 93:375–378.

Schreiber, A., R. Wirth, M. Riffel and H. Van Rompaey. 1989. *Weasels, civets, mongooses and their relatives: An action plan for the conservation of mustelids and viverrids.* Int'l. Union Conserv. Nature & Natur. Resour., Gland, Switzerland.

Schreibman, M.P., H. Margolis-Nunno and L. Halpern-Sebold. 1987. Aging of the neuroendocrine system. Pp. 563–584 in D.O. Norris and R.E. Jones, eds. *Hormones and reproduction in fishes, amphibians and reptiles.* Plenum Press, New York, NY.

Schroeder, C. 1982. A cooperative propagation and release program for the endangered swift fox (*Vulpes velox hebes*). *Regional Proc. Amer. Assoc. Zool. Parks Aquar.* 1982:287–295.

Schroeder, J.P. 1984. Induced reproductive cycle events in *Tursips truncatus.* P. 438 (Abstr.) in W.F. Perrin, R.L. Brownell and D.P. DeMaster, eds. *Reproduction in whales, dolphins, and porpoises.* Int'l. Whaling Commiss., Special Issue 6.

Schroeder, J.P. 1985. Artificial insemination of the bottlenose dolphin, *Tursiops truncatus. Proc. Amer. Assoc. Zoo Vet.* 1985:122–124.

Schroeder, J.P. 1990a. Reproductive aspects of marine mammals. Pp. 353–369 in L. Dierauf, ed. *CRC Handbook of marine mammal medicine: Health, disease and rehabilitation.* CRC Press, Boca Raton, FL.

Schroeder, J.P. 1990b. Breeding bottlenose dolphins in captivity. Pp. 435–446 in J.S. Leatherwood and R. Reeves, eds. *The bottlenose dolphin: Recent progress in research.* Academic Press, New York, NY.

Schroeder, J.P. and K.V. Keller. 1989. Seasonality of serum testosterone levels and sperm density in *Tursiops truncatus. J. Exp. Zool.* 249:316–321.

Schroeder, J.P., and K.V. Keller. 1990. Artificial insemination of bottlenose dolphins. Pp. 447–460 in S. Leatherwood and R.R. Reeves, eds. *Bottlenose dolphins: Recent progress in research.* Academic Press, New York, NY.

Schroeder, J.P., K.V. Keller and V.L. Kirby. 1983. Testosterone levels and sperm production in *Tursiops truncatus. 5th Bienn. Conf. Biol. Marine Mammals* 1983:91 (Abstr.).

Schulz, R.W., M. Andriske, P.J. Lambke and V. Blum. 1992. Effect of salmon gonadotropic hormone on sex steroids in male rainbow trout: Plasma levels and testicular secretion *in vitro. J. Comp. Physiol.* B 162:224–230.

Schuster, R. and P.W. Murphy. 1991. *The acari: Reproduction development and life history strategies.* Chapman and Hall, London, England.

Schusterman, R.J. 1980. Behavioral methodology in echolocation by marine mammals. Pp. 11–41 in R.G. Busnel and J.F. Fish, eds. *Animal sonar systems.* Plenum Press, New York, NY.

Schusterman, R.J. 1986. California sea lions (*Zalophus californianus*) imprint on human voices. *Proc. Int'l. Marine Mamm. Trainers Assoc.* 1986:14–15.

Schusterman, R.J. and R.C. Gisiner. 1988. Artificial language comprehension in dolphins and sea lions: The essential cognitive skills. *Psychol. Rec.* 38:311–348.

Schusterman, R.J. and R. C. Gisiner. 1989. Please parse the sentence: Animal cognition in the procrustean bed of linguistics. *Psychol. Rec.* 39:3–18.

Schusterman, R.J. and K. Krieger. 1982. Teaching sea lions that signals represent objects, object qualities, and behaviors. *Proc. Int'l. Marine Anim. Trainers Assoc.* 1982:99–101.

Schusterman, R.J. and K. Krieger. 1984. California sea lions are capable of semantic comprehension. *Psychol. Rec.* 34:3–23.

Schusterman, R.J. and K. Krieger. 1986. Artificial language comprehension and size transposition by a California sea lion (*Zalophus californianus*). *J. Comp. Psychol.* 100:348–355.

Schwartz, A., J. Weaver, N. Scott and T. Cade. 1977. Measuring the temperature of eggs during incubation under captive falcons. *J. Wildl. Manage.* 41:12–17.

Schwartz, G.E. and S.M. Weiss. 1977. What is behavioral medicine? *Psychosom. Med.* 39:377–381.

Schwartz, J.H. 1986. Primate systematics and a classification of the Order. Pp. 1–41 in D.R. Swindler and J. Erwin, eds. *Comparative primate biology, Vol. I: Systematics, evolution, and anatomy.* Alan Liss, New York, NY.

Scott, A.P. 1987. Reproductive endocrinology of fish. Pp. 223–256 in I. Chester-Jones, P.M. Ingleton and J.G. Phillips, eds. *Fundamentals of comparative vertebrate endocrinology*. Plenum Press, New York, NY.

Scott, A.P. 1990. Salmonids. Pp. 33–51 in A.D. Munro, A.P. Scott and T.J. Lam, eds. *Reproductive seasonality in teleosts: Environmental influences*. CRC Press, Boca Raton, FL.

Scott, A.P. and S.M. Baynes. 1980. A review of the biology, handling and storage of salmonid spermatozoa. *J. Fish. Biol.* 17:707–739.

Scott, A.P. and A.V.M. Canario. 1987. Status of oocyte maturation-inducing steroids in teleosts. Pp. 224–234 in D.R. Idler, L.W. Crim and J.M. Walsh, eds. *Proc. 3rd Int'l. Symp. Reprod. Physiol. Fish*. Memorial Univ. Press, St. John's, Newfoundland.

Scott, A.P. and J.P. Sumpter. 1983. The control of trout reproduction: Basic and applied research on hormones. Pp. 200–220 in J.C. Rankin, T.J. Pitcher and R.T. Duggan, eds. *Control processes in fish physiology*. John Wiley & Sons, New York, NY.

Scott, A.P. and J.P. Sumpter. 1989. Seasonal variations in testicular cell stages and in plasma concentrations of sex steroids in male rainbow trout (*Salmo gairdneri*) maturing at 2 years old. *Gen. Comp. Endocrinol.* 73:46–58.

Scott, A.P., V.J. Bye, S.M. Baynes and J.R.C. Springer. 1980. Seasonal variations in plasma concentrations of 11-ketotestosterone and testosterone in male rainbow trout, *Salmo gairdneri* Richardson. *J. Fish. Biol.* 17:495–505.

Scott, J.A. 1968. Hilltopping as a mating mechanism to aid the survival of low density species. *J. Res. Lepidopt.* 7:191–204.

Scott, J.A. 1973. Convergence of population biology and adult behaviour in two sympatric butterflies, *Neominois ridingsii* (Palilionidea: Nymphalidae) and *Amblyscirtes simius* (Hesperioidea: Hesperiidae). *J. Anim. Ecol.* 42:663–672.

Scott, J.A. 1975. Flight patterns among eleven species of diurnal Lepidoptera. *Ecology* 56:1367–1377.

Scott, J.M. and J.W. Carpenter. 1987. Release of captive-reared or translocated endangered birds: What do we need to know? *Auk* 104:544–545.

Scott, J.M., C. Kepler, C. van Riper III and S.I. Fever. 1988. Conservation of Hawaii's vanishing avifauna. *BioScience* 38:238–253.

Scott, J.M., S. Mountainspring, F.L. Ramsey and C.B. Kepler. 1986. *Forest bird communities of the Hawaiian Islands: Their dynamics, ecology, and conservation*. Allen Press, Lawrence, KS.

Scott, M. 1989. Unhappy homecomings. *British Broadcasting Company Wildlife* 7:824–828.

Scott, M.D., R.S. Wells, A.B. Irvine and B.R. Mate. 1990. Tagging and marking studies on small cetaceans. Pp. 489–514 in S. Leatherwood and R. Reeves, eds. *The bottlenose dolphin*. Academic Press, New York, NY.

Scott, W.E.D. 1902. Instinct in song birds: Methods of breeding in hand-reared robins (*Merula migratoria*). *Science* 16:70–71.

Scott, W.E.D. 1904. The inheritance of song in passerine birds: Further observations on the development of song and nest-building in hand-reared rose-breasted grosbeaks. *Zamelodia ludoviciana* (Linneaus). *Science* 20:282–283.

Scriber, J.M. 1977. Limiting effects of low leaf-water content on the nitrogen utilization, energy budget, and larval growth of *Hyalophora cecropia* (Lepidoptera: Saturnaidae). *Oecologia* 28:269–287.

Scriber, J.M. 1986. Local foodplant specialization in the natural field populations of the southern armyworm, *Spodoptera eridania* (Lepidoptera: Noctuidae). *Entomol. News* 97:183–185.

Scriber, J.M. and R.C. Lederhouse. 1991. Thermal units as a resource dictating geographic pattern of feeding specialization of insect herbevores. Pp. 429–466 in M.R. Hunter, T. Ohguishi and P.W. Price, eds. *Resource distribution and animal-plant interactions*. Academic Press, New York, NY.

Scriber, J.M. and F. Slansky. 1981. The nutritional ecology of immature insects. *Ann. Rev. Entomol.* 26:183–211.

Scriber, J.M., B.L. Giebink and D. Snider. 1991. Reciprocal latitudinal clines of oviposition behavior of *Papilia glaucus* and *P. canadensis* across the Great Lakes hybrid zone: Possible sex-linkage of oviposition preferences. *Oecologia* 87:360–368.

Seager, S.W.J. and C.C. Platz. 1977. Collection and evaluation of canine semen. *Vet. Clincs of N. Amer.* 7:765 (Abstr.).

Seager, S.W.J., C.C. Platz and W.S. Fletcher. 1975a. Conception rates and related data using frozen dog semen. *J. Reprod. Fertil.* 45:189 (Abstr.).

Seager, S.W.J., C.C. Platz and W. Hodge. 1975b. Successful pregnancy using frozen semen in the wolf. *Int'l. Zoo Yb.* 15:140–143.

Seal, U.S. 1985. The realities of preserving species in captivity. Pp. 71–95 in R.J. Hoaje, ed. *Animal extinctions: What everyone should know*. Smithsonian Instit. Press, Washington, DC.

Seal, U.S. 1986a. Goals of captive propagation programmes for the conservation of endangered species. *Int'l. Zoo Yb.* 24/25:174–179.

Seal, U.S. 1986b. How zoos and aquariums can help to maintain biological diversity. *Proc. Amer. Assoc. Zool. Parks and Aquar.* 1986:70–76.

Seal, U.S. 1986c. Intensive technology in the care of *ex situ* populations of vanishing species. Pp. 289–295 in E.O. Wilson, ed. *Biodiversity.* Nat'l. Acad. Sci., Washington, DC.

Seal, U.S. 1989. Tiger SSP Report. *Amer. Assoc. Zool. Parks Aquar. Newsletter* 30:5–8.

Seal, U.S., P. Jackson and R.C. Tilson. 1987. A global tiger conservation plan. Pp. 487–498 in R.C. Tilson and U.S. Seal, eds. *Tigers of the world: The biology, biopolitics, management and conservation of an endangered species.* Noyes Publ., Park Ridge, NJ.

Seal, U.S., D.G. Makey and L.E. Murtfeldt. 1976. ISIS: An animal census system. *Int'l. Zoo Yb.* 16:180–184.

Seal, U.S., E.D. Plotka, J.M Packard and L.D. Mech. 1979. Endocrine correlates of reproduction in the wolf. I: Serum progesterone, estradiol and LH during the estrous cycle. *Biol Reprod.* 21:1057–1066.

Seal, U.S., E.T. Thorne, M.A. Bogan and S.H. Anderson, eds. 1989. *Conservation biology and the black-footed ferret.* Yale Univ. Press, New Haven, CT.

Seal, U.S., D.G. Makey, D. Bridgewater, L. Simmons and L. Murtfeldt. 1977. ISIS: A computerised record system for the management of wild animals in captivity. *Int'l. Zoo Yb.* 17:68–70.

Seal, U.S., E.D. Plotka, J.D. Smith, F.H. Wright, N.J. Reindl, R.S. Taylor and M.F. Seal. 1985. Immunoreactive luteinizing hormone, estradiol, progesterone, testosterone, and androstenedione levels during the breeding season and anestrus in Siberian tigers. *Biol Reprod.* 32:361–368.

Searle, K.C. 1980. Breeding Count Raggi's bird of paradise *Paradisaea raggiaisa salvadorii* at Hong Kong. *Int'l. Zoo Yb.* 20:210–214.

Sears, R. 1987. Photographic identification of individual blue whales (*Balaenoptera musculus*) in the Sea of Cortez. *Cetus* 7:14–17.

Sease, J.L. and D.G. Chapman. 1988. Pacific walrus, *Odobenus rosmarus divergens.* Pp. 17–38 in J.W. Lentfer, ed. *Selected marine mammals of Alaska: Species accounts with research and management recommendations.* Marine Mamm. Commiss. Rept. PB88178462. Washington, DC.

Sebeok, T.A., ed. 1968. *Animal communication: Techniques of study and results of research.* Indiana Univ. Press, Bloomington, IN.

Segal, E.F., ed. 1989. *The housing, care and psychological wellbeing of captive and laboratory primates.* Noyes Pub., Park Ridge, NJ.

Seibels, R.E. 1979. Breeding the toco toucan, *Ramfastos toco. Amer. Fed. Avicult. Watchbird* Feb/Mar:30–32.

Seiber, O.J. 1986. Acoustic recognition between mother and cubs in raccoons (*Procyon lotor*). *Behaviour* 96:130–163.

Seigel, R.A. 1986. Ecology and conservation of an endangered rattlesnake, *Sistrurus catenatus*, in Missouri, U.S.A. *Biol. Conserv.* 35:333–346.

Seigel, R.A., J.T. Collins and S.S. Novak, eds. 1987. *Snakes: Ecology and evolutionary biology*. MacMillan, New York, NY.

Seigel, R.A., L.E. Hunt, J.L. Knight, L. Malaret and N.L. Zuschlag, eds. 1984. *Vertebrate ecology and systematics: A tribute to Henry S. Fitch*. Univ. Kansas Mus. Hist. Spec. Publ. 10. Lawrence, KS.

Seligman, M.E.P. and Y.M. Binik. 1977. The safety signal hypothesis. Pp. 165–187 in H. Davis and H.M.B. Hurwitz, eds. *Operant-Pavlovian interactions*. Lawrence Erlbaum, Hillside, NJ.

Seligman, M.E.P. and J. Weiss. 1980. Coping behavior: Learned helplessness, physiological activity, and learned inactivity. *Beh. Res. Therapy* 18:459–512.

Selye, H. 1974. *Stress without distress*. Hodder & Stoughton, London, England.

Senner, J.W. 1980. Inbreeding depression and the survival of zoo populations. Pp. 209–224 in M.F. Soulé and B.A. Wilcox, eds. *Conservation biology*. Sinauer Assoc., Sunderland, MA.

Serebrovski, A.S. and I.I. Sokolovskaja. 1934. Electroejakuljacia. *Anim. Breed Abstr.* 3:73–74.

Sergeant, D.E. and P.F. Brodie. 1969. Tagging white whales in the Canadian Arctic. *J. Fish. Res. Board. Can.* 25:2201–2205.

Sergeant, D.E., D.K. Caldwell and M.C. Caldwell. 1973. Age, growth and maturity of bottlenose dolphins *Tursiops truncatus* from northeast Florida. *J. Fish. Res. Board Can.* 30:1009–1011.

Serrell, B.A. 1982. Education in zoos and aquariums. Pp. 13–17 in K. Sausman, ed. *Zoological park and aquarium fundamentals*. Amer. Assoc. Zool. Parks Aquar., Wheeling, WV.

Serventy, S.L. 1971. Biology of desert birds. Pp. 317–331 in D.S. Farner and J.R. King, eds. *Avian biology*, Vol. 1. Academic Press, New York, NY.

Setchell, B.D. and D.E. Brooks. 1988. Anatomy, vasculature, innervation and fluids of the male reproductive tract. Pp. 753–836 in E. Knobil and J.D. Neill, eds. *The physiology of reproduction*. Raven Press, New York, NY.

Sexton, T.J. 1976. Studies on the fertility of frozen fowl semen. *VIII Int'l. Congr. Anim. Reprod. Artif. Insem.* 4:1079–1082.

Sexton, T.J. 1977. Relationship between number of sperm inseminated and fertility of turkey hens at various stages of production. *Poult. Sci.* 56:1054–1056.

Sexton, T.J. 1979. Preservation of poultry semen-review. In H. Hawk, ed. *Animal reproduction. Beltsville Agric. Res. Symp.* 3:159–170.

Sexton, T.J. and G.F. Gee. 1978. A comparative study on the cryogenic preservation of semen from the sandhill crane and the domestic fowl. Pp. 89–95 in F. Watson, ed. *Artificial Breeding of Non-Domestic Animals.* Symp. #43 of Zool. Soc. London. Academic Press, New York, NY.

Seyfarth, R.M., D.L. Cheney and P. Marler. 1980a. Vervet monkey alarm calls: Semantic communication in a free-ranging primate. *Anim. Behav.* 28:1070–1094.

Seyfarth, R.M., D.L. Cheney and P. Marler. 1980b. Monkey responses to three different alarm calls: Evidence of predator classification and semantic communication. *Science* 210:801–803.

Shah, R.S., A.R. Sheth, B.A. Godgil and X.R. Swamy. 1976. Effect of LH/FSH-RH on circulating serum gonadotropins in the bonnet monkey. *Indian J. Exp. Biol.* 14:171–174.

Shahabi, N.A., H.W. Norton and A.V. Nalbandov. 1975. Steroid levels in follicles and the plasma of hens during the ovulatory cycle. *Endocrinology* 96:962–968.

Shane, S.H., R.S. Wells and B. Würsig. 1986. Ecology, behavior and social organization of the bottlenose dolphin: A review. *Marine Mam. Sci.* 2:34–63.

Sharma, R.K. 1987. Captive rearing of the gharial (*Gavialis gangeticus*) in Madhya Pradesh. *Hamadryad* 12:19.

Sharp, P.J. and H. Klandorf. 1985. Environmental and physiological factors controlling thyroid function in galliformes. Pp. 175–188 in B.K. Follet, S. Ishii and A. Chandola, eds. *The endocrine system and the environment.* Japan. Sci. Soc. Press, Tokyo, Japan/Springer-Verlag, Berlin, Germany.

Sharp, P.J., H. Klandorf and A.S. McNeilly. 1986. Plasma prolactin, thyroxine, triiodothyroxine, testosterone, and luteinizing hormone during a photoinduced reproductive cycle in mallard drakes. *J. Exp. Zool.* 238:409–413.

Shelton, L.C. 1986. Captive propagation of the Micronesian kingfisher. *Philadel. Zoo Rev.* 2:28.

Shepherdson, D.J. 1989a. Review of environmental enrichment in zoos: 1. *Ratel* 16:35–40.

Shepherdson, D.J. 1989b. Environmental enrichment in zoos: 2. *Ratel* 16:68–72.

Shepherdson, D.J, T. Brownback and A. James. 1989a. A mealworm dispenser for the slender-tailed meerkat (*Suricata suricata*) at London Zoo. *Int'l. Zoo Yb*. 28:268–271.

Shepherdson, D.J., N. Bemment, N. Carman and S. Reynolds. 1989b. Auditory enrichment of lar gibbon, *Hylobates lar*, at London Zoo. *Int'l. Zoo Yb*. 28:256–260.

Sheppard, C. 1982. How to eat like a bird. *Anim. Kingdom* 85:32–39.

Sheppard, C. 1985. Population management for birds: A growing need. *Proc. Amer. Assoc. Zool. Parks Aquar*. 1985:38–42.

Sheppard, C. 1988a. Planning long-term captive management for the white-naped crane, *Grus vipio. Int'l. Zoo Yb*. 27:58–69.

Sheppard, C., ed. 1988b. Breeding hornbills in captivity: Panel discussion. *Regional Conf. Proc. Amer. Assoc. Zool. Parks Aquar*. 1988:490–495.

Sheppard, C. 1989. P. 15 in *Crane masterplan*. New York Zool. Soc., New York, NY.

Sheppard, C. and D. Bruning. 1983. Development of techniques to aid the long-term survival of white-naped and other rare crane species. *Proc. Amer. Assoc. Zool. Parks Aquar*. 1983:203–207.

Sherman, P.W., J.U.M. Jarvis and S.H. Braude. 1992. Naked mole rats. *Sci. Amer*. 267:72–78.

Sherrod, L. 1974. The role of sibling associations in the formation of social and sexual companion preferences in ducks (*Anas platyrhychos*): An investigation of the "primacy vs. recency" question. *Z. Teirpsychol*. 34:247–264.

Sherwood, N.M., R. DeLeeuw and H. Goos. 1989. A new member of the gonadotropin-releasing hormone family in teleosts: Catfish gonadotropin-releasing hormone. *Gen. Comp. Endocrinol*. 75:427–436.

Shettell-Neuber, M.J. 1988. Second- and third-generation zoo exhibits: A comparison of visitor, staff, and animal responses. *Environ. Behav*. 20:452–473.

Shideler, S.E. and B.L. Lasley. 1982. A comparison of primate ovarian cycles. *Amer. J. Primatol*. Suppl. 1:171–180.

Shields, O. 1967. Hilltopping. *J. Res. Lepidopt*. 6:69–78.

Shine, R. 1983. Reptilian reproductive modes: The oviparity-viviparity continuum. *Herpetologica* 39:1–8.

Shoemaker, A.H. 1982. The effect of inbreeding and management on propagation of pedigree leopards, *Panthera pardus spp. Int'l. Zoo Yb*. 22:124–127.

Shoemaker, A.H. 1983. 1982 studbook report on the brown hyaena, *Hyaena brunnea:* Decline of a pedigree species. *Zoo Biol.* 2:133–136.

Shoemaker, A.H. 1988. *1988 international brown hyaena studbook.* Riverbanks Zool. Park, Charleston, S.C.

Sholl, S.A., J.A. Robinson and R.C. Wolf. 1979. Estrone, 17β-estradiol and cortisol in serum of peripartum rhesus monkeys. *Endocrinology* 104:1274–1278.

Short, R.V. 1986. Primate ethics. Pp. 1–11 in K. Benirschke, ed. *Primates: The road to self-sustaining populations.* Springer-Verlag, New York, NY.

Short, R.V., T. Mann and M.F. Hay. 1967. Male reproductive organs of the African elephant, *Loxodonta africana. J. Reprod. Fertil.* 13:517–536.

Shotts, E.B., Jr. 1984. *Aeromonas.* Pp. 49–57 in G.L. Hoff, F.L. Frye and E.R. Jacobson, eds. *Diseases of amphibians and reptiles.* Plenum Press, New York, NY.

Shumaker, R.W. 1987. The effect of artificial feeders on a captive group of *Macaca nigra.* Report to the National Zoo. National Zoological Park, Washington, DC.

Shuster, S.M. 1981a. Sexual selection in the Socorro isopod, *Thermosphaeroma thermophilum* (Cole) (Crustacea: Peracarida). *Anim. Behav.* 29:698–707.

Shuster, S.M. 1981b. Life history characteristics of *Thermosphaeroma thermaphilum*, the Socorro isopod (Crustacea: Peracarida). *Biol. Bull.* 161:291–302.

Shutt, L.J. and D.M. Bird. 1985. Influence of nesting experience on nest-type selection in captive kestrals. *Anim. Behav.* 33:1028–1030.

Siegel, H.S. 1971. Adrenals, stress, and the environment. *World's Poult. Sci. J.* 27:327–349.

Sieswerda, P.L. 1986. Filtration enhancement (trickle filters and ozonation). *Proc. Amer. Assoc. Zool. Parks Aquar.* 1986:705–708.

Sikorowski, P.P. and R.H. Goodwin. 1985. Contaminant control and disease recognition in laboratory colonies. Pp. 85–105 in P. Singh and R.F. Moore, eds. *Handbook of insect rearing*, Vol 1. Elsevier, Amsterdam, Netherlands.

Silcox, A.P. and S.M. Evans. 1982. Factors affecting the formation and maintenance of pair bonds in the zebra finch, *Taeniopygia guttata. Anim. Behav.* 30:1237–1243.

Silver, R., C. Reboulleau, D.S. Lehrman and H.H. Feder. 1974. Radioimmunoassay of plasma progesterone during the reproductive cycle of male and female ring doves (*Streptopelia risoria*). *J. Endocrinol.* 94:1547–1554.

Silverin, B. 1983. Population endocrinology and gonadal activities of the male pied flycatcher (*Ficedula hypoleuca*). Pp. 289–305 in S. Mikami, K. Homma and M. Wada, eds. *Avian endocrinology: Environmental and ecological perspectives*. Japan. Sci. Soc. Press, Tokyo, Japan/Springer-Verlag, Berlin, Germany.

Silverin, B. 1984. Annual gonadotrophin and testosterone cycles in free-living male birds. *J. Exp. Zool.* 232:581–587.

Simberloff, D. 1988. The contribution of population and community biology to conservation science. *Ann. Rev. Ecol. Syst.* 19:473–511.

Simmons, E.L. 1988. A new species of *Propithecus* (Primates) from northeast Madagascar. *Folia Primatol.* 50:143–151.

Simmons, L. 1990. Update on kouprey conservation efforts. *Captive Breed. Special. Group News* 1:13.

Simons, R., S.K. Sherrod, M.W. Collopy and M.A. Jenkins. 1988. Restoring the bald eagle. *Amer. Sci.* 76:253–260.

Singer, M.C. 1986. The definition and measurement of oviposition preference in plant-feeding insects. Pp. 65–94 in J. Miller and T.A. Miller, eds. *Insect-plant relations*. Springer-Verlag, New York, NY.

Singh, S.N.P. and A. Chandola. 1981. Photoperiodic control of seasonal reproduction in tropical weaver bird. *J. Exp. Zool.* 216:292–298.

Skaar, D. 1987. Stretcher training for handling whales and dolphins. *Proc. Int'l. Marine Mamm. Trainers Assoc.* 1987:35–38.

Skinner, J.L. 1974. Infertility and artificial insemination. Pp. 147–152 in D.O. Hyde, ed. *Raising wild ducks in captivity*. E.P. Dutton, New York, NY.

Slansky, F., Jr. and J.G. Rodriguez. 1987a. Nutritional ecology of insects, mites, spiders, and related invertebrates: An overview. Pp. 1–69 in F. Slansky, Jr. and J.G. Rodriguez, eds. *Nutritional ecology of insects, mites, spiders and related invertebrates*. John Wiley & Sons, New York, NY.

Slansky, F., Jr. and J.G. Rodriguez, eds. 1987b. *Nutritional ecology of insects, mites, spiders and related invertebrates*. John Wiley & Sons, New York, NY.

Slansky, F. and J.M. Scriber. 1985. Food consumption and utilization Pp. 87–163 in G.A. Kerkut and L.I. Gilbert, eds. *Comprehensive insect physiology, biochemistry and pharmacology*, Vol 4. Pergamon Press, Oxford, England.

Slater, P.J.B. 1978. *Sex hormones and behaviour*. Instit. Biol., Studies in Biol. No 103. E. Arnold, London, England.

Slater, P.J.B. 1981. Individual differences in animal behavior. Pp. 35–49 in P.P.G. Bateson and P.H. Klopfer. *Perspectives in ethology*, Vol 4. Plenum Press, New York, NY.

Slatis, H.M. 1960. An analysis of inbreeding in the European bison. *Genetics* 45:275–287.

Slijper, E.J. 1972. *Whales*, 2nd Ed. Cornell Univ. Press, Ithaca, NY.

Sloan, H.E. and L.S. Demski. 1987. Studies on the terminal nerve and its central connections in goldfish. *Annals New York Acad. Sci.* 519:421–432.

Slob, A.K., M.P. Ooms and J.T.M. Vreeburg. 1979. Annual changes in serum testosterone in laboratory housed male stumptailed macaques (*Macaca arctoides*). *Biol. Reprod.* 20:981–984.

Slobodkin, L.B. 1986. On the susceptibility of different species to extinction: Elementary instructions for owners of a world. Pp. 226–242 in B.G. Norton, ed. *Preservation of species: Value of biological diversity*. Princeton Univ. Press, Princeton, NJ.

Sloley, B.D., O. Kah, V.L. Trudeau, J.G. Dulka and R.E. Peter. 1992. Amino acid neurotransmitters and dopamine in brain and pituitary of the goldfish: Involvement in the regulation of gonadotropin secretion. *J. Neurochem.* 58:2254–2262.

Smith, A., D.G. Lindburg and S. Vehrencamp. 1989. Effect of food preparation on feeding behavior of lion-tailed macaques. *Zoo Biol* 8:57–65.

Smith, C. 1992. Herpetological literature in the International Zoo Yearbook, Volumes 19–29 (1979–1990). *Herpetol. Rev.* 23:71–74.

Smith, C.A., H.D.M. Moore and J.P. Hearn. 1987a. The ultrastructure of early implantation in the marmoset monkey (*Callithrix jacchus*). *Anat. Embryol.* 175:399–410.

Smith, C.N. 1966. *Insect colonization and mass production*. Academic Press, New York, NY.

Smith, E.O. 1984a. Non-seasonal breeding patterns in stumptailed macaques (*Macaca arctoides*). *Primates* 25:117–122.

Smith, G.R. and J.P. Hearn, eds. 1988. *Reproduction and disease in captive and wild animals. Symp. Zool. Soc. London,* Number 60, Clarendon Press, Oxford, England.

Smith, H.M. and R.B. Smith. 1980. *Synopsis of the herpetofauna of Mexico. VI: Guide to Mexican turtles*. J. Johnson, North Bennington, VT.

Smith, H.M., G. Sinelik, J.D. Fawcett and R.E. Jones. 1972. A survey of the chronology of ovulation in anoline lizard genera. *Trans. Kansas Acad. Sci.* 75:107–120.

Smith, J.L.D., C.W. McDougal and M.E. Sunquist. 1987b. Female land tenure system in tigers. Pp. 97–109 in R.L. Tilson and U.S. Seal, eds. *Tigers of the world*. Noyes, Park Ridge, NJ.

Smith, L.S. 1982. *Introduction to fish physiology*. T.F.H. Pubs., Neptune City, NJ.

Smith, N.G. 1983. Host plant toxicity and migration in the day-flying moth *Urania*. *Florida Entomol*. 66:76–85.

Smith, R. 1989. Red wolf Species Survival Plan report. *Amer. Assoc. Zool. Parks Aquar. Newsletter* 30:5.

Smith, R. 1990. Red wolf Species Survival Plan report. *Amer. Assoc. Zool. Parks Aquar. Communique*. April:9–10.

Smith, R.F., T.E. Mittler and C.N. Smith, eds. 1973. *History of entomology*. Annual Review, Palo Alto, CA.

Smith, R.L., ed. 1984b. *Sperm competition and the evolution of animal mating systems*. Academic Press, Orlando, FL.

Smith, S. 1986. Infant cross-fostering in rhesus monkeys (*Macaca mulatta*): A procedure for the long-term management of captive populations. *Amer. J. Primatol*. 11:229–237.

Smith, S.H. 1968. Species succession and fishery exploitation in the Great Lakes. *J. Fish. Res. Board Can*. 25:667–693.

Smith, T., W. Jenkins, W. Oldland and R. Hamilton. 1986. Development of nursery systems for shortnose sturgeon, *Acipenser brevirostrum*. *Proc. Ann. Conf. S.E. Assoc. Fish and Wildl. Agen*. 40:169–177.

Smith, T., E. Dingley, R. Lindsey, S. Van Sant, R. Smiley and A. Stokes. 1985. Spawning and culture of the shortnose sturgeon, *Acipenser brevirostrum*. *J. World Maricult. Soc*. 16:104–113.

Smith, T.G., D.J. St. Aubin and J.R. Geraci. 1990. Research on beluga whales, *Delphinapterus leucas*: Introduction and overview. Pp. 1–6 in T.G. Smith, D.J. St. Aubin and J.R. Geraci, eds. *Advances in research on the beluga whale, Delphinapterus leucas. Can. Bull. Fisheries and Aquat. Sci*. Vol. 224.

Smith, W.J., S.L. Smith, E.C. Oppenheimer and J.G. Devilla. 1977. Vocalizations of the black-tailed prairie dog, *Cynomys ludovicianus*. *Anim. Behav*. 25:152–164.

Smithers, R.H.N. 1986. South African red data book-Terrestrial mammals. *S. African Natur. Sci. Programmes Report*. 125:1–216.

Smuts, B.B., D.L. Cheney, R.M. Seyfarth, R.W. Wrangham and T.T. Struksaker. 1987. *Primate societies*. Univ. Chicago Press, Chicago, IL.

Smyth, J.R., Jr. 1968. Poultry. Pp. 258–300 in E.J. Perry, ed. *The artificial insemination of farm animals*. Rutgers Univ. Press, New Brunswick, NJ.

Snelson, F.F., Jr. 1971. *Notropis mekistocholas*, a new herbivorous cyprinid fish endemic to Cape Fear River basin, North Carolina. *Copeia* 1971:449–462.

Snelson, F.F., Jr. and R.E. Jenkins. 1973. *Notropis perpallidus*, a cyprind fish from south-central United States: Description, distribution and life history aspects. *S.W. Natural.* 18:291–304.

Sniegoowski, P.D., E.D. Ketterson and V. Nolan, Jr. 1988. Can experience alter the avian annual cycle? Results of migration experiments with indigo buntings. *Ethology* 79:333–341.

Snodgrass, R.E. 1935. *Principles of insect morphology*. McGraw-Hill Book Co., New York, NY.

Snowdon, C.T. 1989. The criteria for successful captive propagation of endangered primates. *Zoo Biol.* Suppl. 1:149–161.

Snowdon, C.T. 1994. The significance of naturalistic environments for primate behavioral research. Pp. 217–235 in E.F. Gibbons, Jr., E.J. Wyers, E.J. Waters and E.W. Menzel, Jr., eds. *Naturalistic environments in captivity for animal behavior research*. State Univ. New York Press, Albany, NY.

Snowdon, C. and A. Savage. 1989. Psychological well-being of captive primates: General considerations and examples from callitrichids. Pp. 75–88 in E.F. Segal, ed. *Housing, care and psychological wellbeing of captive and laboratory primates*. Noyes, Park Ridge, NJ.

Snyder, N.F. 1974. Breeding biology of swallow-tailed kites in Florida. *Living Bird* 13:73–97.

Snyder, N.F. 1983. Establishment of a viable captive population of California condors. Pp. 333–337 in A. Risser and F. Todd, eds. *Symposium on breeding birds in captivity*. Int'l. Found. Conserv. Birds. North Hollywood, CA.

Snyder, N.F. 1987. Thick-billed parrot release in Arizona. Pp. 360–384 in A. Risser, ed. *Symposium on breeding birds in captivity*. Int'l. Found. Conserv. Birds. North Hollywood, CA.

Snyder, N.F., H.A. Snyder and T.B. Johnson. 1989. Parrots return to the Arizona skies. *Birds Int'l.* 1:41–52.

Snyder, R.L. 1975. Behavioral stress in captive animals. Pp. 41–76 in *Research in zoos and aquariums*. Nat'l. Acad. Sci., Washington, DC.

Snyder, R.L. 1978. Feeding and nutrition. Pp. 296–302 in M.E. Fowler, ed. *Zoo and wild animal medicine*. W.B. Saunders, Philadelphia, PA.

Sokal, R.R. and F.J. Rohlf. 1969. *Biometry*. W.H. Freeman, San Francisco, CA.

Sokol, O. 1954. To the desert for fishes. *Aquar. J.* 25:178–182.

Sokolov, V.Ye. and O.V. Volkova. 1973. Structure of the dolphin's tongue. Pp. 119–127 in K.K. Chapskii and V.Ye. Sokolov, eds. *Morphology and evolution of marine mammals: Seals, dolphins, and porpoises.* J. Wiley & Sons, New York, NY.

Soloman, S. and K. Leung. 1971. Steroid hormones in nonhuman primates during pregnancy. Pp. 178–190 in *Symposium on the use of nonhuman primates for research on problems of human reproduction.* World Health Organization, Geneva, Switzerland.

Soltz, D. 1974. Variation in life history and social organization of some populations of Nevada pupfish, *Cyprinodon nevadensis.* Ph.D. Dissertation. Univ. California, Los Angeles, CA.

Soma, H., ed. 1987. *The biology and management of Capricornis and related mountain antelopes.* Croom Helm, London, England.

Sommer, R. 1974. *Tight spaces: Hard architecture and how to humanize it.* Prentice Hall, Englewood Cliffs, NJ.

Sorensen, M.D. 1989. Effects of neck collar radios on female redheads. *J. Field Ornithol.* 60:523–528.

Sorensen, P.W., T.J. Hara and N.E. Stacey. 1991. Sex pheromones selectively stimulate the medial olfactory tracts of male goldfish. *Brain Res.* 558:343–347.

Sorensen, P.W., N.E. Stacey and K.J. Chamberlain. 1989. Differing behavioral and endocrinological effects of two female sex pheromones on male goldfish. *Horm. Behav.* 23:317–332.

Sorensen, P.W., T.J. Hara, N.E. Stacey and J.G. Dulka. 1990. Extreme olfactory specificity of male goldfish to the preovulatory steroidal pheromone 17α, 20β-dihydroxy-4-pregen-3-one. *J. Comp. Physiol. A.* 166: 373–383.

Sorensen, P.W., T.J. Hara, N.E. Stacey and F.W. Goetz. 1988. F prostaglandins function as potent olfactory stimulants which comprise the postovulatory female sex pheromone in goldfish. *Biol. Reprod.* 39:1039–1050.

Soulé, M.E. 1980. Thresholds for survival: Maintaining fitness and evolutionary potential. Pp. 151–169 in M.E. Soule and B.A. Wilcox, eds. *Conservation biology: An evolutionary-ecological perspective.* Sinauer Assoc., Sunderland, MA.

Soulé, M.E., ed. 1986. *Conservation biology.* Sinauer Assoc., Sunderland, MA.

Soulé, M.E. 1987. *Viable populations for conservation.* Cambridge Univ. Press, Cambridge, MA.

Soulé, M.E. and D. Simberloff. 1986. What do genetics and ecology tell us about the design of nature reserves? *Biol. Conserv.* 35:19–40.

Soulé, M.E. and B.A. Wilcox, eds. 1980. *Conservation biology: An evolutionary-ecological perspective.* Sinauer Assoc., Sunderland, MA.

Soulé, M., M. Gilpin, W. Conway and T. Foose. 1986. The millenium ark: How long a voyage, how many staterooms, how many passengers? *Zoo Biol.* 5:101–113.

Southern, L.K. and W.E. Southern. 1989. Some effects of wing tags on breeding ring-billed gulls. *Auk* 102:38–42.

Southwick, C.H. and R.B. Smith. 1986. The growth of primate field studies. Pp. 73–92 in G. Mitchell and J. Erwin, eds. *Comparative primate biology, 2A, Behavior, conservation, and ecology.* Alan Liss, New York, NY.

Southwick, C.H., M.A. Beg and M.R. Siddiqi. 1965. Rhesus monkeys in North India. Pp. 111–159 in I. DeVore, ed. *Primate behavior: Field studies of monkeys and apes.* Holt, Rinehart & Winston, New York, NY.

Southwick, C.H., R.A. Mittermeier, J.G. Robinson and R.A. Tenaza. 1986. Conservation note: Report of the American Society of Primatologists subcommittee on the status of primates in the wild. *Amer. J. Primatol.* 10:371–378.

Southwood, T.R.E. 1977. Entomology and mankind. *Amer. Sci.* 65:30–39.

Southwood, T.R.E. 1978a. *Ecological methods with particular references to the study of insect populations,* 2nd Ed. Chapman & Hall, London, England.

Southwood, T.R.E. 1978b. Marking invertebrates. Pp. 102–106 in B. Stonehouse, ed. *Animal marking: Recognition marking of animals in research.* Univ. Park Press, Baltimore, MD.

Speakman, J.R. and P.A. Racey. 1988. The doubly-labelled water technique for measurement of energy expenditure in free-living animals. *Sci. Prog. Oxf.* 72:227–237.

Speart, J. 1992. Orang odyssey. *Wildl. Conserv.* 95:18–25.

Specker, J.L. and F.L. Moore. 1980. Annual cycle of plasma androgens and testicular composition in the rough-skinned newt, *Taricha granulosa. Gen. Comp. Endocrinol.* 42:297–303.

Spilman, C.H., D.C. Beuving, A.D. Forbes and F.A. Kimball. 1977. Effects of PGF and PGF 2α, 1,15 lactone on the corpus luteum and on early pregnancy in the rhesus monkey. *Prostaglandins* 14:477–488.

Spinage, G.A. 1969. Reproduction in the Uganda defassa waterbuck, *Kobus defassa ugandae* Neumann. *J. Reprod. Fertil.* 18:445–457.

Spotte, S. 1979a. *Fish and invertebrate culture: Water management in closed systems*, 2nd Ed. John Wiley & Sons, New York, NY.

Spotte, S. 1979b. *Seawater aquariums, the captive environment.* John Wiley & Sons, New York, NY.

Spotte, S. 1991. *Sterilization of marine mammal pool waters-theoretical and health considerations.* U.S. Dept. Agricult., Anim. and Plant Inspect. Serv. Tech. Bull. No. 1797, 10–1991.

Spotte, S. 1992. *Captive seawater fishes.* John Wiley & Sons, New York, NY.

Stacey, N.E. 1984. Control of the timing of ovulation by exogenous and endogenous factors. Pp. 207–222 in G.W. Potts and R.J. Wootten, eds. *Fish reproduction: Strategies and tactics.* Academic Press, Orlando, FL.

Stacey, N.E. 1987. Roles of hormones and pheromones in fish reproductive behavior. Pp. 28–60 in D. Crews, ed. *Psychobiology of reproductive behavior.* Prentice-Hall, Englewood Cliffs, NJ.

Stacey, N.E. and F.W. Goetz. 1982. Role of prostaglandins in fish reproduction. *Can. J. Fish. Aquat. Sci.* 39:92–98.

Stacey, N.E., A.F. Cook and R.E. Peter. 1979. Spontaneous and gonadotropin-induced ovulation in the goldfish, *Carassius auratus* L: Effects of external factors. *J. Fish Biol.* 15:349–361.

Stacey, N.E., P.W. Sorensen, G.J. Van Der Kraak and J.G. Dulka. 1989. Direct evidence that $17\alpha,20\beta$-dihydroxy-4-pregnen-3-one functions as a goldfish primer pheromone: Preovulatory release is closly associated with male endocrine responses. *Gen. Comp. Endocrinol.* 75:62–70.

Stacey, N.E., D.S. MacKenzie, T.A. Marchant, A.L. Kyle and R.E. Peter. 1984. Endocrine changes during natural spawning in the white sucker, *Catostomus commersoni.* I. Gonadotropin, growth hormone, and thyroid hormones. *Gen. Comp. Endocrinol.* 56:333–348.

Stanley, M.E. and W.P. Aspey. 1984. An ethometric analysis in a zoological garden: Modification of ungulate behavior by the visual presence of a predator. *Zoo Biol.* 3:89–109.

Stanley-Price, M.R. 1986. The reintroduction of the Arabian oryx, *Oryx leucoryx* into Oman. *Int'l. Zoo Yb.* 24/25: 179–188.

Stanley-Price, M.R. 1989a. Reconstructing ecosystems. Pp. 210–218 in D. Western and M. Pearl, eds. *Conservation for the twenty-first century.* Oxford Univ. Press, New York, NY.

Stanley-Price, M.R. 1989b. *Animal reintroductions: The Arabian oryx in Oman.* Cambridge Univ. Press, New York, NY.

Starnes, W. 1977. The ecology and life history of the endangered snail darter, *Percina (imostoma) tanasi* Etnier. Tennessee Wildl. Res. Agency Tech. Report No. 77–52. Univ. Tenn., Knoxville, TN.

Steel, E.A. and R.A. Hinde. 1963. Hormonal control of brood patch and oviduct development in domesticated canaries. *J. Endocrinol.* 26:11–24.

Steele, G.D. 1986. Rehabilitation and conditioning of stranded leopard seals. *Proc. Int'l. Marine Mamm. Trainers Assoc.* 1986:51–55.

Steenberg, J. 1981. Captive breeding of American golden eagles, *Aquila chrysaelis canadensis*, at Topeka Zoo between 1969 and 1976. *Int'l. Zoo Yb.* 21:109–115.

Stehn, R.A. and F.J. Jannett, Jr. 1981. Male-induced abortion in various microtine rodents. *J. Mammal.* 62.369–372.

Steiner, R.A. and W.J. Bremner. 1981. Endocrine correlates of sexual development in the male monkey, *Macaca fascicularis*. *Endocrinology* 109:914–919.

Steinhaus, E.A. 1958. Stress as a factor in insect disease. *Proc. 10th Int'l. Congr. Entomol.* 4:725–730.

Steinhaus, E.A. 1963. Introduction. Pp. 1–27 in E.A. Steinhaus, ed. *Insect Pathology*. Academic Press, New York, NY.

Stenhouse, S.L., N.C. Hairston and A.E. Cobey. 1983. Predation and competition in *Ambystoma* larvae: Field and laboratory experiments. *J. Herpetol* 17:210–220.

Stenson, G.B. 1988. Oestrus and the vaginal smear cycle of the river otter, *Lutra canadensis. J. Reprod. Fertil.* 83:605–610.

Stetton, G., F. Koontz, C. Sheppard and C. Koontz. 1989. Biotelemetric monitoring of white-naped crane *(Grus vipio)* nest microclimate in captivity. *Proc. Amer. Assoc. Zool. Parks Aquar.* 1989:264–271.

Stevens, B. 1986. Conditioning behavior for husbandry purposes. *Proc. Amer. Assoc. Zool. Parks Aquar.* 1986:216–217.

Stevenson, R.A. 1972. Regulation of feeding behavior of bicolor damselfish *(Eupomacentrus partitus poey)* by environmental factors. Pp. 278–302 in *Behavior of marine animals, Vol 2: Vertebrates*. Plenum Press, New York, NY.

St. Girons, H. 1982. Reproductive cycles of male snakes and their relationships with climate and female reproductive cycles. *Herpetologica.* 38:5–15.

St. Girons, H. 1985. Comparative data on lepidosauian reproduction and some time tables. Pp. 35–58 in C. Gans and F. Billett, eds. *Biology of the reptilia*, Vol 15B. John Wiley & Sons, New York, NY.

Stickney, R.R. and C.C. Kohler. 1990. Maintaining fishes for research and teaching. Pp. 633–663 in C.B. Schreck and P.B. Moye, eds. *Methods for fish biology*. Amer. Fish. Soc., Bethesda, MD.

Stinson, C.H. 1979. On the selective advantage of fratricide in raptors. *Evolution* 33:1219–1225.

Stokkan, K.-A., K. Hove and W.R. Carr. 1980. Plasma concentrations of testosterone and luteinizing hormone in rutting reindeer bulls (*Rangifer tarandrus*). *Can. J. Zool.* 58:2081–2083.

Storey, K.B. 1989. Freeze tolerance and winter survival in terrestrially hibernating reptiles and amphibians. *Proc. Amer. Soc. Ichthy. Herpetol. and Amer. Elasmo. Soc.,*. 1989:150 (Abstr.). San Francisco State Univ. and Cal. Acad. Sci.

Storey, K.B. and J.M. Storey. 1990. Frozen and alive. *Sci. Amer.* December:92–97.

Stork, N.E. 1987. Arthropod faunal similarity of Bornean rain forest trees. *Ecol. Entomol.* 12:219–226.

Stoskopf, M.K. 1983. The physiological effects of psychological stress. *Zoo Biol.* 2:179–190.

Stoskopf, M.K. 1992. Hospitalization. Pp. 98–112 in M.K. Stoskopf, ed. *Fish medicine*. W.B. Saunders, Philadelphia, PA.

Stoskopf, M.K. and E.F. Gibbons, Jr. 1994. Quantitative evaluation of the effects of environmental parameters on the physiology, behavior, and health of animals in naturalistic captive environments. Pp. 142–166 in E.F. Gibbons, Jr., E.J. Wyers, E.J. Waters and E.W. Menzel, Jr., eds. *Naturalistic environments in captivity for animal behavior research*. State Univ. New York Press, Albany, NY.

Stoskopf, M.K. and R. Hudson. 1982. Commercial feed frogs as a source of trematode infection in reptile collections. *Herpetol. Rev.* 13:125.

Stoss, J. 1983. Fish gamete preservation and spermatozoan physiology. Pp. 305–350 in W.S. Hoar, D.J. Randall and E.M. Donaldson, eds. *Fish physiology*, Vol IXB. Academic Press, New York, NY.

Stover, J. 1987. Variability of uterine cervical anatomy in the white-tailed gnu (*Connochaetes gnou*). *Zoo Biol.* 6:265–271.

Stover, J. and J. Evans. 1984. Interspecies embryo transfer from gaur (*Bos gaurus*) to domestic Holstein cattle (*Bos taurus*) at the New York Zoological Park. *Proc. 10th Int'l. Congr. Anim. Reprod. Artif. Insem.* 2:243 (Abstr.). Univ. Ill., Urbana-Champaign, IL.

Strasser, P. 1982. Plush crested jays at Audubon Zoo. *Amer. Fed. Avicult. Watchbird* Feb/Mar 9:22–25.

Strier, K.B. 1991. Demography and conservation of an endangered primate, *Brachyteles arachnoides*. *Conserv. Biol.* 5:214–218.

Stromberg, M.R. and M.S. Boyce. 1986. Systematics and conservation of the swift fox, (*Vulpes velox*), in North America. *Biol. Conserv.* 35:97–110.

Struhsaker, T.T. 1967a. Auditory communication among vervet monkeys (*Cercopithecus aethiops*). Pp. 281–324 in S. Altmann, ed. *Social communication among primates*. Univ. Chicago Press, Chicago, IL.

Struhsaker, T.T. 1967b. Behavior of vervet monkeys (*Cercopithecus aethiops*) *Univ. California Pub. Zool.* 82:1–74.

Stuart, H. and J.E. Johnson. 1981. A refuge for southwestern fish. *New Mex. Wildl.* 26:2–5.

Sturkie, P.D. 1965a. Reproduction in the male, fertilization, and early embryonic development. Pp. 515–533 in P.D. Sturkie, ed. *Avian physiology*, 2nd Ed. Comstock, Cornell Univ. Press, Ithaca, NY.

Sturkie, P.D. 1965b. Gonadal hormones. Pp. 568–591 in P.D. Sturkie, ed. *Avian physiology*, 2nd Ed. Comstock, Cornell Univ. Press, Ithaca, NY.

Sturkie, P.D. and Y. Lin. 1966. Release of vasotocin and oviposition in the hen. *J. Endocrinol.* 35:325–326.

Stuwe, M. and C. Grodinsky. 1987. Reproductive biology of captive alpine ibex (*Capra i. ibex*). *Zoo Biol.* 6:331–339.

Sugarman, R.A. and R.A. Hacker. 1980. Observer effects on collared lizards. *J. Herpetol.* 14:188–190.

Sugiyama, Y. 1960. On the division of a natural troop of Japanese monkeys at Takasakiyama. *Primates* 2:109–148.

Sullivan, A.L. and M.L. Shaffer. 1975. Biogeography of the megazoo. *Science* 189:13–17.

Summers, P.M. 1986. Collection, storage and use of mammalian embryos. *Int'l. Zoo Yb.* 24/25:131–138.

Sumpter, J. 1990. General concepts of seasonal reproduction. Pp. 13–31 in A.D. Munro, A.P. Scott and T.J. Lam, eds. *Reproductive seasonality in teleosts: Environmental influences*. CRC Press, Boca Raton, FL.

Sunquist, M.E. 1981. *The social organization of tigers (Panthera tigrus) in Royal Chitwan National Park, Nepal*. Smithsonian Contr. to Zool., Vol. 336.

Sunquist, M.E. and F. Sunquist. 1989. Ecological constraints on predation by large felids. Pp. 283–300 in J.L. Gittleman, ed. *Carnivore behavior, ecology, and evolution*. Cornell Univ. Press, Ithaca, NY.

Suzuki, K., H. Kawauchi and Y. Nagahama. 1988a. Isolation and characterization of two distinct gonadotropins from chum salmon pituitary glands. *Gen. Comp. Endocrinol.* 71:292–301.

Suzuki, K., H. Kawauchi and Y. Nagahama. 1988b. Isolation and characterization of subunits from two distinct salmon gonadotropins. *Gen. Comp. Endocrinol.* 71:302–306.

Suzuki, M., S. Hyodo, M. Kobayashi, K. Aida and A. Urano. 1992. Characterization and localization of mRNA encoding the salmon-type gonadotrophin-releasing hormone precursor of the masu salmon. *J. Mol. Endocrinol.* 9:73–82.

Sved, J.A. 1979. The hybrid dysgenesis syndrome in *Drosophila melanogaster*. *Bioscience* 29:659–664.

Swanson, P., K. Suzuki, H. Kawauchi and W.W. Dickhoff. 1991. Isolation and characterization of two coho salmon gonadotropins, GTH I and GTH II. *Biol. Reprod.* 44:29–38.

Sweeney, J.C. 1990. Marine mammal behavioral diagnostics. Pp. 53–72 in L.A. Dierauf, ed. *CRC Handbook of marine mammal medicine: Health, disease and rehabilitation.* CRC Press, Boca Raton, FL.

Sweeney, J.C. and S.H. Ridgway. 1975. Procedures for the clinical management of small cetaceans. *J. Amer. Vet. Med. Assoc.* 16:540–545.

Swennen, C. 1977. *Laboratory research on sea birds.* Netherlands Institute for Sea Res., Texel, Netherlands.

Swingland, I.R. 1975. The influence of weather and individual interactions on the food intake of captive rooks (*Corvus frugilegus*). *Physiol. Zool.* 48:295–302.

Sylvester, J.R., L.E. Holland and T.K. Kammer. 1984. Observations on burrowing rates and comments on host specificity in the endangered mussel, *Lamsilis higginsi*. *J. Freshwater Ecol.* 2:555–560.

Sylvestre, J.P. 1985. Some observations on behaviour of two Orinoco dolphins *Inia geoffrensis humboldtiana*, (Pilleri and Gihr 1977), in captivity, at Duisburg Zoo. *Aquat. Mamm.* 11:58–65.

Sylvestre, J. and S. Tasaka. 1985. On the intergeneric hybrids in cetaceans. *Aquat. Mamm.* 11:101–108.

Szumowski, P., M. Theset and B. Denis. 1976. Semen and artificial insemination of pigeons. *Proc. VIII Int'l. Congr. Anim. Reprod. Artif. Insem.* 1976:256 (Abstr.).

Tan, N.S. 1980. The frequency of collection and semen production in muscovy ducks. *Brit. Poult. Sci.* 21:265–272.

Tanaka, K. and S. Nakajo. 1962. Participation of neurohypophyseal hormone in oviposition in the hen. *Endocrinology* 70:453–458.

Tauber, M.J., C.A. Tauber and S. Masaki. 1986. *Seasonal adaptations of insects*. Oxford Univ. Press., New York, NY.

Tavolga, M.C. 1966. Behavior of the bottlenose dolphin (*Tursiops truncatus*): Social interactions in a captive colony. Pp. 718–730 in K.S. Norris, ed. *Whales, dolphins and porpoises*. Univ. California Press, Berkeley, CA.

Tavolga, M.C. and F.S. Essapian. 1957. The behavior of the bottlenosed dolphin (*Tursiops truncatus*): Mating, pregnancy, parturition, and mother-infant behavior. *Zoologica* 42:11–31.

Taylor, F. 1981. Ecology and evolution of physiological time in insects. *Amer. Natural*. 117:1–23.

Taylor, F. 1982. Sensitivity of physiological time in arthropods to variation of its parameters. *Environ. Entomol*. 11:573–577.

Taylor, J. 1984. Iron accumulation in avian species in captivity. *Dodo* 21:126–131.

Taylor, M.H. 1990. Estuarine and intertidal teleosts. Pp. 109–124 in A.D. Munro, A.P. Scott and T.J. Lam, eds. *Reproductive seasonality in teleosts: Environmental influences*. CRC Press, Boca Raton, FL.

Taylor, S. and A. Bietz. *Infant diet / care notebook*. Amer. Assoc. Zool. Parks Aquar., Wheeling, WV.

Tekulsky, M. 1985. *The butterfly garden*. Harvard Common Press, Boston, MA.

Tempest, W., ed. 1985. *The noise handbook*. Academic Press, London, England.

Temple, S.A. 1972. Artificial insemination with imprinted birds of prey. *Nature* 237:287–288.

Temple, S.A. 1978a. The concept of managing endangered birds. P. 3–8 in S.A. Temple, ed. *Endangered birds: Management techniques for preserving threatened species*. Univ. Wisconsin. Press, Madison, WI.

Temple, S.A. 1978b. Reintroducing birds of prey to the wild. Pp. 355–363 in S.A. Temple, ed. *Endangered birds: Management techniques for preserving threatened species*. Univ. Wisconsin. Press, Madison, WI.

Temple, S.A. 1986. The problem of avian extinctions. Pp. 453–485 in R. Johnson, ed. *Current ornithology*, Vol 3. Plenum Press, New York, NY.

Templeton, A.R. 1986. Coadaptation and outbreeding depression. Pp. 105–121 in M.E. Soulé, ed. *Conservation biology: The science of scarcity and diversity*. Sinauer Assoc., Sunderland, MA.

Templeton, A.R. and B. Read. 1983. The elimination of inbreeding depression in a captive herd of Speke's gazelle. Pp. 241–261 in C.M. Schonewald-Cox, S.M. Chambers, B. MacBryde and W.L. Thomas, eds. *Genetics and conservation: A reference for managing wild animal and plant populations.* Benjamin/Cummings, Menlo Park, CA.

Terborgh, J. 1986. Conserving New World primates: Present problems and future solutions. Pp. 355–366 in J.G. Else and P.C. Lee, eds. *Primate ecology and conservation.* Cambridge Univ. Press, New York, NY.

Terborgh, J. and B. Winter. 1980. Some causes of extinction. Pp. 119–133 in M.E. Soulé and B.A. Wilcox, eds. *Conservation biology: An evolutionary-ecological perspective.* Sinauer Assoc., Sunderland, MA.

Terry, R.P. 1983. Observations on the captive behavior of *Sotalia fluviatilis guianensis. Aquat. Mamm.* 10:95–105.

Terry, R.P. 1984. Intergeneric behavior between *Sotalia fluviatilis guianensis* and *Tursiops truncatus* in captivity. *Zeits. Sauget.* 49:290–299.

Terry, R.P. 1986. The behaviour and trainability of *Sotalia fluviatilis guianensis* in captivity: A survey. *Aquat. Mamm.* 12:71–79.

Terry, R.P. 1989. A short guide to the biology of the tucuxi: Lessons from captivity and the wild. *Proc. Int'l. Marine Mamm. Trainers Assoc.* 1989:43–59.

Terry, W.R. 1990. Evolution of digestive systems of insects. *Ann. Rev. Entomol.* 35:181–200.

Tewary, P.D. and A.S. Dixit. 1986. Photoperiodic regulation of reproduction in subtropical female yellow-throated sparrows (*Gymnorhis zanthocollis*). *Condor* 88:70–73.

Tewary, P.D. and B.K. Tripathi. 1983. Photoperiodic control of reproduction in a female migratory bunting (*Emberiza bruniceos*). *J. Exp. Zool.* 226:269–272.

Tewary, P.D., A.S. Dixit and V. Kumar. 1984. Circadian rhythmicity and the initiation of reproductive functions in female passerines. *Physiol. Zool.* 57:563–566.

Thaler, E. and H. Pechlaner. 1980. Cainism in the Lammergeier or bearded vulture, *Gypaetus barbatus aureus*, at Innsbruck, Alpenzoo. *Int'l. Zoo Yb.* 20:278–280.

Thery, M. 1990. Influence de la lumiere sur le choix de l'habitat et le comportement sexuel des Pipridae (Aves: Passeriformes) en Guyane Francaise. *Rev. Ecol.* (Terre Vie) 45:215–236.

Thiel, A.J. 1989. *Advanced reef keeping.* Aarvark Press, Mesillia Park, NM.

Thomas, D.E. 1982. Notes on the behaviour of the mountain pygmy-possum *Burramys parvus* in captivity. Pp. 85–86 in D.D. Evans, ed. *Management of Australian mammals in captivity*. Proc. Aust. Mamm. Soc., 1979. Ramsey Ware Stockland, Victoria, Australia.

Thomas, J.A. 1980. Why did the large blue become extinct in Britain? *Oryx* 15:243–247.

Thomas, J.A. 1984. The conservation of butterflies in temperate countries: Past efforts and lessons for the future. *Symp. Royal Entomol. Soc. London* 11:333–353.

Thomas, J.A. 1991. Rare species conservation: Case studies of European butterflies. Pp. 149–197 in I.F. Spellerberg, F.B. Goldsmith and M.G. Morris, eds. *Scientific management of temperate communities for conservation*. Blackwell Sci. Pubs., Oxford, England.

Thomas, J.A., R.A. Kastelein and F.T. Awbrey. 1990. Behavior and blood catecholamines of captive belugas during playbacks of noise from an oil drilling platform. *Zoo Biol.* 9:393–402.

Thomas, J.A., L.H. Cornell, B.E. Joseph, T.D. Williams and S. Drieschman. 1987. An implanted transponder chip used as a tag for sea otters (*Enhydra lutris*). *Marine Mamm. Sci.* 3:271–274.

Thomas, P. and J.M. Trant. 1989. Evidence that 17α, 20β, 21-trihydroxy-4-pregnen-3-one is a maturation-inducing steroid in spotted seatrout. *Fish Physiol. Biochem.* 7:185–191.

Thomas, P.O. 1987a. Social behavior, habitat use and inter-specific interactions of the southern right whale, *Eubalaena australis*, mother-calf pairs. Dissertation Abstr. Int'l. 1987:48 (Abstr.).

Thomas, P.O. and S.M. Taber. 1984. Mother-infant interaction and behavioral development in southern right whales, *Eubalaena australis*. *Behaviour* 88:42–60.

Thomas, W. 1987b. Sumatran rhino Species Survival Plan report. *Amer. Assoc. Zool. Parks Aquar. Newsletter* 28:8–9.

Thomas, W. 1989a. Sumatran rhino Species Survival Plan report. *Amer. Assoc. Zool. Parks Aquar. Newsletter* 30:15.

Thomas, W. 1989b. Conservation director's report: Sumatran and Javan rhino. *Amer. Assoc. Zool. Parks Aquar. Newsletter* 30:9–10.

Thomas, W.D., R. Barnes, M. Crotty and M. Jones. 1986. An historical overview of selected rare ruminants in captivity. *Int'l. Zoo Yb.* 24/25: 77–99.

Thomsen, J.B. and C.A. Munn. 1987. *Cyanopsitta spixii*: A non-recovery report. *Parrotletter* 1:6–7.

Thomson, A.L. 1950. Factors determining the breeding season of birds: An introductory review. *Ibis* 92:173–184.

Thorburn, G.D. and J.R.G. Challis. 1979. Endocrine control of parturition. *Physiol. Rev.* 59:863–918.

Thorgaard, G.H. 1983. Chromosome set manipulation and sex control in fish. Pp. 405–434 in W.S. Hoar, D.J. Randall and E.M. Donaldson, eds. *Fish physiology*, Vol IXB. Academic Press, New York, NY.

Thornback, J. and M. Jenkins. 1984. *The IUCN Mammal red data book*, Part 1. Int'l. Union Conserv. Nature & Natur. Resour., Gland, Switzerland.

Thorndike, R.L. 1898. Animal intelligence: An experimental study of the associative processes in animals. *Psychol. Rev. Monograph* Suppl. No. 15.

Thorne, G. 1961. *Principles of nematology*. McGraw Hill, New York, NY.

Thornhill, R. and J. Alcock. 1983. *The evolution of insect mating systems*. Harvard Univ. Press, Cambridge, MA.

Thouless, C.R., Liang C.Q. and A.S.I Loudon. 1988. The milu or Père David's deer *Elaphurus davidianus* reintroduction project at Da Feng. *Int'l. Zoo Yb.* 27:223–230.

Thresher, R.E. 1984. *Reproduction in reef fishes*. T.F.H. Pubs., Neptune City, NJ.

Tilson, R.L. 1986. Primate mating systems and their consequences for captive management. Pp. 361–373 in K. Benirschke, ed. *Primates: The road to self-sustaining populations*. Springer-Verlag, New York, NY.

Tilson, R.L. and U.S. Seal, eds. 1987. *Tigers of the world*. Noyes, Park Ridge, NJ.

Tinkle, D.W. 1967. The life and demography of the side-blotched lizard, *Uta stansburiana. Misc. Pub. Mus. Zool. Univ. Michigan* 32:1–182.

Tixier-Vidal, A. and B.K. Follett. 1973. The adenohypophysis. Pp. 109–182 in D.S. Farner and J.R. King, eds. *Avian biology*, Vol III. Academic Press, New York, NY.

Todd, D.M. 1984. The release of pink pigeons *Columba (Nesoenas) mayeri* at Pamplemousses, Mauritius. A progress report. *Dodo* 21:43–57.

Todd, F.S. 1972. Captive breeding of harpy eagles. *Raptor Res.* 6:137–143.

Todd, F.S. 1978. *Penguin husbandry and breeding at Sea World*. Sea World Press, San Diego, CA.

Todd, F.S. 1979. *Waterfowl, ducks, geese and swans of the world*. Sea World Press, San Diego, CA.

Todd, F.S. 1982. Design features of bird exhibits. Pp. 77–90 in *Zoological park and aquarium fundamentals*. Amer. Assoc. Zool. Parks and Aquar. Wheeling, WV.

Todd, W. and R.J. Berry. 1980. Breeding the red bird of paradise, *Paradisaea rubra*, at the Houston Zoo. *Int'l. Zoo Yb.* 20:206–210.

Tokarz, R.R. 1978. Oogonial proliferation, oogenesis, and folliculogenesis in nonmammalian vertebrates. Pp. 145–173 in R.E. Jones, ed. *The vertebrate ovary*. Plenum Press, New York, NY.

Tokuda, K. 1961–1962. A study of the sexual behavior in the Japanese monkey troop. *Primates* 3:1–40.

Tomback, D.F. and M.C. Baker. 1984. Assortive mating by white-crowned sparrows at song dialect boundaries. *Anim. Behav.* 32:465–469.

Toney, D.P. 1974. Observations on the propagation and rearing of two endangered fish species in a hatchery environment. *Proc. West. Assoc. State Game & Fish Commiss.* 54:252–259.

Tong, J.R. 1974. Breeding cheetahs, *Acinonyx jubatus*, at the Beekse Bergen Safari Park. *Int'l. Zoo Yb.* 14:129–131.

Torrans, E.L. 1986. Fish/plankton interactions. Pp. 67–81 in J.E. Lannan, R. Oneal Smitherman and G. Tchobanoglous, eds. *Principles and practices of pond aquaculture*. Oregon State Univ. Press, Corvallis, OR.

Townsend, C.R. and C.J. Cole. 1985. Additional notes on requirements of captive whiptail lizards (*Cnemidophorus*), with emphasis on ultraviolet radiation. *Zoo Biol.* 4:49–55.

Trant, J.M. and P. Thomas. 1988. Structure-activity relationships of steroids in inducing germinal vesicle breakdown in Atlantic croaker oocytes *in vitro*. *Gen. Comp. Endocrinol.* 71:307–317.

Trant, J.M., P. Thomas and C.H.L. Shackleton. 1986. Identification of 17α, 20β, 21-trihydroxy-4-pregnen-3-one as the major ovarian steroid produced by the telost *Micropogonias undulatus* during final oocyte maturation. *Steroids* 47:89–99.

Treus, V.D. and N.V. Lobanov. 1971. Acclimatisation and domestication of the eland, *Taurotragus oryx* at Askanya-Nova Zoo. *Int'l. Zoo Yb.* 11:147–156.

Trudeau, V.L., R.E. Peter and B.D. Sloley. 1991. Testosterone and estradiol potentiate the serum gonadotropin response to gonadotropin-releasing hormone in goldfish. *Biol. Reprod.* 44:951–960.

Tryon, B. 1979. Literature of the International Zoo Yearbook Volumes 1–18 (1959–1978). *Herpetol. Rev.* 10:87–90.

Tryon, B. 1980. Observations on reproduction in the West African dwarf crocodile with a description of parental behavior. Pp. 167–185 in J.B.

Murphy and J.T. Collins. *Reproductive biology and diseases of captive reptiles*. Soc. Study Amphib. Reptiles. Contrib. Herpetol., Oxford, OH.

Tsai, J.H. 1982. Entomology in the People's Republic of China. *J. New York Entomol. Soc.* 90:186–212.

Tubbs, A.A. 1976. Effects of artificial crowding on behavior, growth and survival of juvenile spiny lizards. *Copeia* 1976:820–823.

Tullner, W.W. 1971. Chorionic gonadotropin in nonhuman primates. Pp. 200–213 in *Symposium on the use of nonhuman primates for research on problems of human reproduction*. World Health Org., Geneva, Switzerland.

Turcotte, Y. and J. Bedard. 1989. Prolonged parental care and foraging in greater snow goose juveniles. *Wilson Bull.* 101:500–503.

Turley, P. 1988. The iceman cometh: A technique for weaning sea lion pups. *Soundings, Int'l. Marine Anim. Trainers Assoc.* 13:8.

Turner, F.B., ed. 1986. Management of the desert tortoise in California. *Herpetologica* 42:56–134.

Turney, L.D. and V.H. Hutchison. 1974. Metabolic scope, oxygen debt and the diurnal oxygen consumption cycle of the leopard frog, *Rana pipiens*. *Comp. Biochem. Phys.* 49:583–601.

Tuskes, P.M. 1981. Population structure and biology of *Liguus* tree snails on Lignumvitae Key, Florida. *Nautilus* 95:162–169.

Tuttle, D. 1988. Asian elephant SSP report. *Amer. Assoc. Zool. Parks Aquar. Newsletter* 29:7–8.

Tuttle, D. 1989a. Asian elephant SSP report. *Amer. Assoc. Zool. Parks Aquar. Newsletter* 30:9–10.

Tuttle, D. 1989b. Scimitar-horned oryx SSP report. *Amer. Assoc. Zool. Parks Aquar. Newsletter* 30:10.

Tyack, P.T. 1976. Patterns of vocalization in wild *Tursiops truncatus*. Senior Thesis, Harvard Univ., Cambridge, MA.

Tyack, P.T. 1991. Use of a telemetry device to identify which dolphin produces a sound. Pp. 319–344 in K. Pryor and K.S. Norris, eds. *Dolphin societies*. Univ. California Press, Berkeley, CA.

Tyack, P.T. and L.S. Sayigh. 1989. Those dolphins aren't just whistling in the dark. *Oceanus* 32:80–83.

Tyler, D. 1986. Infant sea otter finds home. *Proc. Int'l. Marine Anim. Trainers Assoc.* 1986:97–100.

Tyler, M.J. 1991. Where have all the frogs gone? *Aust. Natural Hist.* 23:618–624.

Tyndale-Biscoe, C.H. 1968. Reproduction and post-natal development in the marsupial *Bettongia lesueur* (Quay and Gaimard). *Aust. J. Zool.* 16:577–602.

Tyndale-Biscoe, C.H. 1984. Mammals: Marsupials. Pp. 386–454 in G.E. Lamming, ed. *Marshall's physiology of reproduction. Vol I: Reproductive cycles of vertebrates.* Churchill Livingstone, New York, NY.

Tyndale-Biscoe, H. and M. Renfree. 1987. *Reproductive physiology of marsupials.* Cambridge Univ. Press, New York, NY.

Tyus, H.M. 1987. Distribution, reproduction, and habitat use of the razorback sucker in the Green River, Utah, 1979–1986. *Trans. Amer. Fish. Soc.* 116:111–116.

Uchida, S. 1991. Research on Sirenians and the role of aquaria for it. *Int'l. Marine Biol. Res. Instit. Rept.* 2:47–59.

Ueck, M. and H. Umar. 1983. Environmental, neural, and endocrine influences on the parenchyma of the avian pineal organ and its various responses. Pp. 201–215 in S. Mikami, K. Homma and M. Wada, eds. *Avian Endocrinology: Environmental and ecological perspectives.* Japan Sci. Soc. Press, Tokyo, Japan/ Springer/Verlag, Berlin, Germany.

Ueda, H., A. Kambegawa and Y. Nagahama. 1985. Involvement of gonadotropin and steroid hormones in spermiation in the amago salmon *Oncorhynchus rhodurus*, and goldfish, *Carassius auratus*. *Gen. Comp. Endocrinol.* 59:24–30.

Ullrey, D.E. 1986. Nutrition of primates in captivity. Pp. 823–835 in K. Benirschke, ed. *Primates: The road to self-sustaining populations.* Springer-Verlag, New York, NY.

Urquhart, F.A. and N.R. Urquhart. 1976. The overwintering site of the eastern population of the monarch butterfly (*Danaus p. plexippus*; Danaidae) in southern Mexico. *J. Lepidopt. Soc.* 30:153–158.

U.S. Department of Agriculture. 1988. Quick bibliography series: Welfare of experimental animals, 1979–1987. Prepared by J.A. Larson and L. Reynnells. QB 88-17 NAL-BIBL., U.S. Govern. Print. Office, Washington, DC.

U.S. Department of Agriculture. 1991. Animal welfare, 9 CFR. *Federal Register* 56:6426. U.S. Govern. Print. Office, Washington, DC.

U.S. Department of Agriculture. 1992. Animal Welfare Regulations, 9 CFR Chapter 1, 1-1-1992. Anim. and Plant Health Inspect. Serv. U.S. Govern. Print. Office, Washington, DC.

U.S. Fish and Wildlife Service. 1978. *Colorado squawfish recovery plan.* U.S. Fish and Wildl. Serv., Washington, DC.

U.S. Fish and Wildlife Service. 1979. *Humpback chub recovery plan.* U.S. Fish and Wildl. Serv., Washington, DC.

U.S. Fish and Wildlife Service. 1980a. *Devil's Hole pupfish recovery plan.* U.S. Fish and Wildl. Serv., Denver, CO.

U.S. Fish and Wildlife Service. 1980b. *Clear Creek Gambusia (Gambusia heterochir) recovery plan.* U.S. Fish and Wildl. Serv., Albuquerque, NM.

U.S. Fish and Wildlife Service. 1983a. *Moapa Dace recovery plan.* U.S. Fish and Wildl. Serv., Portland, OR.

U.S. Fish and Wildlife Service. 1983b. *Gila trout recovery plan.* U.S. Fish and Wildl. Serv., Albuquerque, NM.

U.S. Fish and Wildlife Service. 1984. *Big Bend Gambusia recovery plan.* U.S. Fish and Wildl. Serv., Albuquerque, NM.

U.S. Fish and Wildlife Service. 1987a. *Recovery plan for the Borax Lake chub, Gila boraxobius.* U.S. Fish and Wildl. Serv., Portland, OR.

U.S. Fish and Wildlife Service. 1987b. *Endangered and threatened wildlife and plants.* U.S. Fish and Wildl. Serv., Washington, DC.

U.S. Fish and Wildlife Service. 1989. *Endangered and threatened wildlife and plants.* 50 CFR 17.11 and 17.12. U.S. Fish.and Wildl. Serv., Washington, DC.

U.S. Fish and Wildlife Service. 1990a. *Appendices I, II and III to the Convention on International Trade in Endangered Species of Wild Fauna and Flora. Protected species.* 50 CFR 23.23. U.S. Govern. Print. Office, Washington, DC.

U.S. Fish and Wildlife Service. 1990b. *Endangered and threatened wildlife and plants.* U.S. Fish. Wildl. Serv., Washington, DC.

U.S. Fish and Wildlife Service. 1991. Box score of listings and recovery plans. *Endangered Species Tech. Bull* 14:12.

U.S. Fish and Wildlife Service. 1992. *Endangered and threatened wildlife and plants.* Office on Endang. Species, U.S. Dept. Interior, Washington, DC.

Usher, M.B. 1986. *Wildlife conservation evaluation.* Chapman and Hall, New York, NY.

Val Giddings, L., K.Y. Kaneshiro and W.W. Anderson, eds. 1989. *Genetics, speciation, and the founder principle.* Oxford Univ. Press, New York, NY.

Valleriani, M. 1985. Exhibit design and management of a breeding captive sea lion, *Zalophus californianus*, population. *Proc. Amer. Assoc. Zool. Parks Aquar.* 1985:436–440.

Valtonen, M.H., E.J. Rajakoski and J.I. Makela. 1977. Reproductive features in the female raccoon dog (*Nyctereutes procyonides*). *J. Reprod. Fertil.* 51:517–518.

VanBlaricom, G.R. and J.A. Estes, eds. 1988. *The community ecology of sea otters*. Springer-Verlag, New York, NY.

van Bree, P.J.H. 1979. Notes on the differences between monk seals from the Atlantic and the Western Mediterranean. Pp. 99 in K. Ronald and R. Duguy, eds. *The Mediterranean monk seal*. Proc. 1st. Int'l. Confr., Vol. 1. United Nations Environment Programme, Oxford, England.

Vandenbergh, J.G. 1969. Endocrine coordination in monkeys: Male sexual response to the female. *Physiol. Behav.* 4:261–264.

Vandenbergh, J.G. 1973. Environmental influences on breeding in rhesus monkeys. *Symp. IVth Int'l. Congr. Primatol.* 2:1–19.

Vandenbergh, J.G. and Drickamer, L.C. 1974. Reproductive coordination among free-ranging rhesus monkeys. *Physiol. Behav.* 13:373–376.

Vandenbergh, J.G. and S. Vessey. 1968. Seasonal breeding of free-ranging monkeys and related ecological factors. *J. Reprod. Fertil.* 15:71–79.

Van Den Hurk, R. and J.W. Resink. 1992. Male reproductive system as sex pheromone producer in teleost fish. *J. Exp. Zool.* 261:204–213.

Van Der Kraak, G., P.W. Sorensen, N.E. Stacey and J.G. Dulka. 1989. Periovulatory female goldfish release three potential pheromones: 17α, 20β-dihydroxyprogesterone, 17α, 20β-dihydroxyprogesterone glucuronide and 17α-hydroxyprogesterone. *Gen. Comp. Endocrinol.* 73:452–457.

Van Der Kraak, G., K. Suzuki, R.E. Peter, H. Itoh and H. Kawauchi. 1992. Properties of common carp gonadotropin I and gonadotropin II. *Gen. Comp. Endocrinol.* 85:217–229.

Van der Toorn, J. 1987. A biological approach to dolphinarium water purification. *Proc. Int'l. Marine Mamm. Trainers Assoc.* 1987:131–132.

Van Ee, C.A. 1966. A note on breeding the Cape pangolin *Manis temmincki* at Bloemfontein Zoo. *Int'l. Zoo Yb.* 6:163–164.

Van Ee, C.A. 1978. Pangolins can't be bred in captivity. *Afr. Wildl.* 32:24–25.

van Heerden, J. and F. Kuhn. 1985. Reproduction in captive hunting dogs *Lycaon pictus*. *S. Afr. J. Wildl. Res.* 15:80–84.

Van Horn, R.N. 1975. Primate breeding season: Photoperiodic regulation in captive *Lemur catta*. *Folia Primatol.* 245:203–220.

Van Horn, R.N. 1980. Seasonal reproductive patterns in primates. *Progr. Reprod. Biol.* 5:181–221.

Van Horn, R.N. and J.A. Resko. 1977. The reproductive cycle of the ring-tailed lemur (*Lemur catta*): Sex steroid levels and sexual receptivity under controlled photoperiods. *Endocrinology* 101:1579–1586.

Van Keulen-Kromhout, G. 1978. Zoo enclosures for bears, Ursidae: Their influence on captive behaviour and reproduction. *Int'l. Zoo Yb.* 18:177–186.

van Mierop, L.H.S. and E.L. Bessette. 1981. Reproduction of the ball python (*Python regius*) in captivity. *Herpetol. Rev.* 12:20–22.

van Riper, C., S.G. van Riper, M.L. Goff and M. Laird. 1986. The epizootiology and ecological significance of malaria in Hawaiian land birds. *Ecol. Monogr.* 56:327–344.

van Tienhoven, A. 1980. Neuroendocrinology of avian reproduction, with special emphasis on the reproductive cycle of the fowl (*Gallus domesticus*). *World's Poult. Sci. J.* 37:156–176.

van Tienhoven, A. 1983. *Reproductive physiology of vertebrates.* Cornell Univ. Press, Ithaca, NY.

van Wagenen, G.W. 1968. Induction of ovulation in *Macaca mulatta*. *Fertil. Steril.* 19:15–29.

van Wagenen, G.W. and M.E. Simpson. 1954. Testicular development in the rhesus monkey. *Anat. Rec.* 118:231–251.

Varley, M.A. and S.H. Vessey. 1977. Effects of geographic transfer on the timing of seasonal breeding of rhesus monkeys. *Folia Primatol.* 28:52–59.

Varona, L.S. 1980. Protection in Cuba. *Oryx* 15:282–284.

Varriale, B., R. Pierantoni, L. DiMatteo, S. Minucci, S. Fasano, M. D'Antonio and G. Chieffi. 1986. Plasma and testicular estradiol and plasma androgen profile in the male frog *Rana esculenta* during the annual cycle. *Gen. Comp. Endocrinol.* 64:401–404.

Vaughn, L.K., H.A. Bernheim and M.J. Kluger. 1974. Fever in the lizard, *Dipsosaurus dorsalis. Nature* 252:473–474.

Vaz-Ferreira, R. 1981. South American sea lion, *Otaria flavenscens* (Shaw, 1800). Pp. 39–65 in S.H. Ridgway and R.J. Harrison, eds. *Handbook of marine mammals. Vol. 1: The walrus, sea lions, fur seals, sea otter.* Academic Press, London, England.

Vedder, E.J. and L. t'Hart. 1990. *The rehabilitation of two newborn Mediterranean monk seals (Monachus schauinslandi) in the Seal Rehabilitation and Research Centre (SSRC) in Peiterburen, Netherlands.* Report prepared for the European Commission. DCXI.

Vehrencamp, S.L. 1977. Relative fecundity and parental effort in communially nesting anis *Crotophaga sulcirostris. Science* 197:403–405.

Vehrencamp, S.L. 1979. The roles of individual, kin, and group selection in the evolution of sociality. Pp. 351–394 in P. Marler and J.G. Vandenbergh. *Handbook of behavioral neurobiology*, Vol 3. Plenum Press, New York, NY.

Vehrencamp, S.L. and J.W. Bradbury. 1984. Mating systems and ecology. Pp. 251–278 in J.R. Krebs and N.B. Davies. *Behavioural ecology*, 2nd Ed. Sinauer Assoc., Sunderland, MA.

Verner, J., M.L. Morrison and C.J. Ralph, eds. 1986. *Wildlife 2000: Modelling habitat relationships of terrestrial vertebrates.* Univ. Wisconsin Press, Madison, WI.

Verrell, P.A. and A. Donovan. 1991. Male-male aggression in the plethodontid salamander *Desmognathus ochrophaeus. J. Zool.* 223:203–212.

Via, S. 1990. Ecological genetics and host adaptation in herbivorous insects: The experimental study of evolution in natural and agricultural systems. *Ann. Rev. Entomol.* 35:421–446.

Vickers, J.H. 1983. FDA regulatory use of nonhuman primates. *Lab. Anim. Sci.* 12:28–34.

Vigersky, R.A., D.L. Loriaux, S.S. Howards, G.B. Hodgen, M.B.A. Lipsett and A. Chamback. 1976. Androgen binding proteins of testis, epididymis and plasma in man and monkey. *J. Clin. Invest.* 58:1061–1068.

Vijaya, J. 1984. Cane turtle (*Geoemyda silvatica*) study project in Kerala. *Hamadryad* 9:4.

Vincent, R. 1960. Some influences of domestication upon three stocks of brook trout (*Salvelinus fontinalis* Mitchill). *Trans. Amer. Fish. Soc.* 89:35–52.

Vinegar, A., V.H. Hutchison and H.G. Dowling. 1970. Metabolism, energetics and thermoregulation during brooding of snakes of the Genus *Python* (Reptilia, Boidae). *Zoologica* 55:19–48.

Vlachoutsikou,A. and D. Cebrian. 1992. Population status, habitat use, interaction with fishery and biology study of the Mediterranean monk seals on Zakynthos Island, Greece. Monk Seal Conservation in the Eastern Mediterranean. World Wildlife Fund Project 3871 Greece.

Vlasak, P. 1973. Vergleich der postnatalen Entwicklung der Arten *Sorex araneus* L. und *Crocidura suaveolens* (Pall.) mit Bemerkungen zur Methodick der Laborzucht (Insectivora: Soricidae). *Vestn. Cesk. Spol. Zool.* 3:222–233.

Vleck, C.M. and J. Priedkalns. 1985. Reproduction in zebra finches: Hormone levels and effect of dehydration. *Cooper Ornithol. Soc.* 87:37–46.

Vogel, M. 1984. WNY-born Caribbean toads jump at chance to go home. *The Buffalo News* April 28, 1984. Buffalo, NY.

von Achen, P.H. and J.L. Rakestraw. 1984. The role of chemoreception in the prey selection of neonate reptiles. Pp. 163–172 in R.A. Siegel, L.E. Hunt, J.L. Knight, L. Malaret and N.L. Zuschlag, eds. *Vertebrate ecology and systematics: A tribute to Henry S. Fitch*. Univ. Kansas Mus. Natur. Hist. Spec. Pub. 10. Lawrence, KS.

Voss, R.S. 1976. Observations of the ecology of the Florida tree snail *Liguus fasciatus* (Muller). *Nautilus* 90:65–69.

Vrijenhoek, R.C. 1984. The evolution of clonal diversity in *Poeciliopsis*. Pp. 399–430 in B.J. Turner, ed.. *Evolutionary genetics of fishes*. Plenum Press, New York, NY.

Wada, M. 1983. Environmental cycles, circadian clock, and androgen-dependent behavior in birds. Pp. 191–200 in S. Mikami, K. Homma and M. Wada, eds. *Avian endocrinology and ecological perspectives*. Japan Sci. Soc. Press, Tokyo, Japan/Springer-Verlag, Berlin, Germany.

Wada, M. 1984. Photoperiodism in avian reproduction. Pp. 101–113 in K. Ochiai, Y. Arai, T. Shioda, M. Takahashi, eds. *Endocrine correlates of reproduction*. Japan Sci. Soc. Press, Tokyo, Japan/Springer-Verlag, Berlin, Germany.

Wada, M. 1985. Reproductive behavior in birds. Pp. 295–306 in B.K. Follett, S. Ishii and A. Chandola, eds. *The endocrine system and the environment*. Japan Sci. Soc. Press, Tokyo, Japan/Springer-Verlag, Berlin, Germany.

Waites, G.M.H. and Einer-Jensen, N. 1974. Collection and analysis of rete testis fluid from macaque monkeys. *J. Reprod. Fertil.* 41:505–508.

Waldhalm, S.J., H.A. Jacobson, S.K. Dhungel and H.J. Bearden. 1989. Embryo transfer in the white-tailed deer: A reproductive model for endangered deer species of the world. *Theriogenology* 31:437–450.

Walker, G.E. and J.K. Ling. 1981. Australian sea lion, *Neophoca cinerea* (Peron, 1816). Pp. 99–117 in S.H. Ridgway and R.J. Harrison, eds. *Handbook of marine mammals. Vol 1: The walrus, sea lions, fur seals, sea otter*. Academic Press, London, England.

Walker, L.A., L. Cornell, K.D. Dahl, N.M. Czekala, C.M. Dargen, B. Joseph, A.J.W. Hsueh and B.L. Lasley. 1988. Urinary concentrations of ovarian steroid hormone metabolites and bioactive follicle-stimulating hormone in killer whales (*Orcinus orchus*) during ovarian cycles and pregnancy. *Biol. Reprod.* 39:1013–1020.

Walker, W.A. 1975. Techniques of live capture of smaller Cetacea. *J. Fish. Res. Board. Can.* 32:197–211.

Wallace, M.E. 1982. Thoughts on the laboratory cage design process. *Int'l. J. Study Anim. Prob.* 8:234–242.

Wallace, M.P. and S.A. Temple. 1987. Releasing captive-reared Andean condors to the wild. *J. Wildl. Manage.* 51:541–550.

Wallace, R.A. and K. Selmon. 1981. Cellular and dynamic aspects of oocyte growth in teleosts. *Amer. Zool.* 21:325–343.

Wallach, J.D. and W.J. Boever. 1983a. *Diseases of exotic animals: Medical and surgical management*. W.B. Saunders, Philadelphia, PA.

Wallach, J.D. and W.J. Boever. 1983b. Ruminants. Pp. 197–345 in *Diseases of exotic animals: Medical and surgical management*. W.B. Saunders, Philadelphia, PA.

Walsh, M.W. 1990. Teaching swans instinct. *San Francisco Chronicle*. Sept. 25:B3,B6.

Walsh, M.T., L.M. Dalton and J.F. McBain. 1989. Electrolyte imbalances in cetaceans: Pathogenesis and treatment. *Proc. Int'l. Assoc. Aquat. Anim. Med.* 20:65.

Walsh, M.T., E.D. Asper, B.F. Andrews and J.E. Antrim. 1990a. Walrus biology and medicine. Pp. 591–599 in L.A. Dierauf, ed. *CRC Handbook of marine mammal medicine: Health, disease and rehabilitation*. CRC Press, Boca Raton, FL.

Walsh, M.T., D.K. Odell, G. Young, E.D. Asper and G. Bossart. 1990b. Mass strandings of cetaceans. Pp. 673–683 in L.A. Dierauf, ed. *CRC Handbook of marine mammal medicine: Health, disease and rehabilitation*. CRC Press, Boca Raton, FL.

Walsh, S.W., R.L. Norman and M.J. Novy. 1979. In utero regulation of rhesus monkey fetal adrenals: Effects of dexamethasone, adrenocorticotropin, thyrotropin-releasing hormone, prolactin, human chorionic gonadotropin and a melanocyte-stimulating hormone on fetal and maternal plasma steroids. *Endocrinology* 104:1805–1813.

Walsh, S.W., J.A. Resko and M.J. Novy. 1978. Role of the fetal adrenal in estrogen biosynthesis as studied in chronically catheterized rhesus monkeys. *Proc. 60th Ann. Mtg. Endocrine Soc.* 1978:346 (Abstr.).

Walther, F.R. 1965. Verhaltensstudien an der Grantgazelle (*Gazella granti* Brooke, 1872) im Ngorongoro-Krater. *Z. Tierpsychol.* 21:871–890.

Walther, F.R., E.C. Mungall and G.A. Grau. 1983. *Gazelles and their relatives*. Noyes, Park Ridge, NJ.

Wang, S. and G. Quan. 1986. Primate status and conservation in China. Pp. 213–220 in K. Benirschke, ed. *Primates: The road to self-sustaining populations*. Springer-Verlag, New York, NY.

Wang, S.C. and J.M. Bahr. 1983. Estradiol secretion by theca cells of the domestic hen during the ovulatory cycle. *Biol Reprod.* 26:618–621.

Wanless, S., M.P. Harris and J.A. Morris. 1988. The effect of radio transmitters on the behavior of common murres and razorbills during chick rearing. *Condor* 90:816–823.

Warburton, G., C. Hubbs and D.W. Hagen. 1957. Reproductive behavior of *Gambusia heterochir*. *Copeia* 1957:299–300.

Warner, H., D.E. Martin and M.E. Keeling. 1974. Electroejaculation of the great apes. *Ann. Biomed. Engineer.* 2:419–432.

Warren, M.S. 1991. The successful conservation of an endangered species, the heath fritillary butterfly *Mellicta athalia* in Britain. *Biol. Conserv.* 55:37–56.

Warren, M.S., C.D. Thomas and J.A. Thomas. 1984. The status of the heath fritillary butterfly *Mellicta athalia* Rott. in Britain. *Biol. Conserv.* 29:287–305.

Warren, R.P. and R.A. Hinde. 1961. Roles of the male and the nest-cup in controlling the reproduction of female canaries. *Anim. Behav.* 9:64–67.

Wasserzug, R.J. 1973. Aspects of social behavior in anuran larvae. Pp. 273–297 in J.L. Vial, ed. *Evolutionary biology of the anurans*. Univ. Missouri Press, Columbia, MO.

Watanabe, M. 1957. An improved technique of the artificial insemination in ducks. *J. Fac. Fish. Anim. Husb.* 1:363–370.

Watkins, W.A. and W.E. Schevill. 1976. Underwater print markings of porpoises. *Fish. Bull.* 74:687–689.

Watson, D. and K. Labs. 1983. *Climatic design*. McGraw Hill, New York, NY.

Watt, W.B., F.S. Chew, L.R.G. Synder, A.B. Watt and D.E. Rothschild. 1977. Population structure of pierid butterflies. I. Numbers and movements of some montane *Colias* species. *Oecologia* 27:1–22.

Watts, C.H.S. 1982. Australina hydromyine rodents: Maintenance of captive colonies. Pp. 180–184 in D.D. Evans, ed. *Management of Australian mammals in captivity*. Proc. Aust. Mamm. Soc., 1979. Ramsey Ware Stockland, Victoria, Australia.

Wayre, P. 1969. Captive breeding as an aid to practical conservation. *Pheasant Trust Ann. Report* 1969:24–28.

Weathers, W.W. and G.K. Snyder. 1977. Relation of oxygen consumption to temperature and time of day in tropical anuran amphibians. *Aust. J. Zool.* 25:19–24.

Weaver, J. and T. Cade, eds. 1983 *Falcon propagation: A manual on captive breeding*. The Peregrine Fund, Ithaca, NY.

Weil, C. 1981. La fonction gonadotrope de l'hypophyse au cours du cycle sexuel de la Carpe et de la Truite; son controle par l'hypothalamus, les gonades et les facteurs externes. These Doct. Sci. Univ. Paris VI, France.

Weiss, S.B., D.D. Murphy and R.R. White. 1988. Sun, slope and butterflies: Topographic determinants of habitat quality for *Euphydryas editha*. *Ecology* 69:1486–1496.

Weiss, S.B., R.R. White, D.D. Murphy and P.R. Ehrlich. 1987. Growth and dispersal of larvae of the checkerspot butterfly *Euphydryas editha*. *Oikos* 50:161–166.

Welcomme, R.L. 1986. International measures for the control of introductions of aquatic organisms. *Fisheries* 11:4–9.

Weldon, P.J. and G.M. Burghardt. 1984. Deception divergence and sexual selection. *Z. Teirpsych*. 65:89–102.

Weldon, P.J., T.S. Walsh and J.S.E. Kleister. 1994. Chemoreception in the feeding behavior of reptiles: Relevance to maintenance and management. Pp. 61–70 in J.B. Murphy, J.T. Collins and K. Adler, eds. *Captive management and conservation of amphibians and reptiles*. Soc. Study Amphib. and Reptiles. Contrib. Herpetol., Oxford, OH.

Wells, D. 1985. The forest avifauna of western Malasia and its conservation. Pp. 213–232 in A. Diamond and T. Lovejoy, eds. *Conservation of tropical forest birds*. Page Bros, Norwich, England.

Wells, L. and A.L. MacLain. 1972. Lake Michigan: Effects of exploitation, introductions, and eutrophication on the salmonid community. *J. Fish. Res. Board Can*. 29:889–898.

Wells, R.S. 1984. Reproductive behavior and hormonal correlates in Hawaiian spinner dolphins, *Stenella longirostris*. Pp. 465–472 in W.F. Perrin, R.L. Brownell, Jr. and D.P. DeMasters, eds. *Reproduction in whales, dolphins and porpoises*. Report Int'l. Whaling Commiss., Special Issue No. 6. Cambridge, England.

Wells, R.S. 1991. The role of long-term study in understanding the social structure of a bottlenose dolphin community. Pp. 199–226 in K. Pryor and K.S. Norris, eds. *Dolphin societies*. Univ. California Press, Berkeley, CA.

Wells, R.S. and M.D. Scott. 1990. Estimating bottlenose dolphin population parameters from individual identification and capture-release techniques. *Report Int'l. Whaling Commiss*. Spec. Issue No 12. 1990:407–415. Cambridge, England.

Wells, R.S., A.B. Irvine and M.D. Scott. 1980. The social ecology of inshore Odontocetes. Pp. 263–318 in L.M. Herman, ed. *Cetacean behavior*. John Wiley & Sons, New York, NY.

Wells, S.M., R.M. Pyle and N.M. Collins. 1983. *The IUCN Invertebrate Red Data Book*. Int'l. Union Conserv. Nature & Natur. Resour., Gland, Switzerland.

Wells, S., M.D. Scott and A.B. Irvine. 1987. The social structure of free-ranging bottlenose dolphins. Pp. 247–303 in H.H. Genoways, ed. *Current mammalogy*, Vol I. Plenum Press, New York, NY.

Welsh, H.H., Jr. 1990. Relictual amphibians and old-growth forests. *Conserv. Biol.* 4:309–319.

Welsh, J.H. 1969. Mussels on the move. *Natural Hist.* 78:56–59.

Welty, J.C. 1975. Pp. 134–160 in *The life of birds*, 2nd Ed. W.B. Saunders, Philadelphia, PA.

Welty, J.C. 1979. P. 73 in *The life of birds,* 2nd Ed. W.B. Saunders, Philadelphia, PA.

Wemmer, C. 1974. Design for polar bear maternity dens. *Int'l. Zoo Yb.* 14:222–223.

Wemmer, C. and S. Derrickson. 1987. Reintroduction: The zoobiologists' dream. Prospects and problems of reintroducing captive bred wildlife. *Proc. Amer. Assoc. Zool. Parks Aquar.* 1987:48–65.

Wemmer, C. and M.J. Fleming. 1975. Management of meerkats in captivity. *Int'l. Zoo Yb.* 15:73–77.

Wentworth, B.C. and W.J. Mellen. 1963. Egg production and fertility following various methods of insemination in Japanese quail (*Cortunix cortunix japonica*). *J. Reprod. Fertil.* 6:215–220.

Wentworth, B.C., M.J. Wineland and G.D. Paton. 1975. Fertility of turkey hens correlated with depth of insemination. *Poult. Sci.* 54:682–687.

Werner, D.I. 1991. The rational use of green iguanas. Pp. 181–201 in J.G. Robinson and K.H. Redford, eds. *Neotropical wildlife use and conservation.* Univ. Chicago Press, Chicago, IL.

Werner, D.I. and T.J. Miller. 1984. Artificial nests for female green iguanas. *Herpetol. Rev.* 15:57–58.

Wesson, J.A., P.F. Scanlon, R.L. Kirkpatrick, H.S. Mosby and R.L. Butcher. 1979. Influence of chemical immobilization and physical restraint on steroid hormone levels in blood of white-tailed deer. *Can. J. Zool.* 57:768–776.

West, C. 1989. *World species list of propagation programs.* Captive Breeding Specialist Group Annual Report. Apple Valley, MN.

West, N.O. and H.C. Nordan. 1976. Hormonal regulation of reproduction and the antler cycle in the male Columbian black-tailed deer, (*Odocoileus hemionus columbianus*). Part. I. Seasonal changes in the histology of the reproductive organs, serum testosterone, sperm production and the antler cycle. *Can. J. Zool.* 54:1617–1636.

Western, D. 1979. Size, life history, and ecology in mammals. *Afr. J. Ecol.* 17:185–204.

Western, D. 1986a. Introduction: Primate conservation in the broader realm. Pp. 343–353 in J.G. Else and P.C. Lee, eds. *Primate ecology and conservation.* Cambridge Univ. Press, New York, NY.

Western, D. 1986b. The role of captive populations in global conservation. Pp. 13–20 in K. Benirschke, ed. *Primates: The road to self-sustaining populations*. Springer–Verlag, New York, NY.

Western, D. and M.C. Pearl, eds. 1989. *Conservation for the twenty-first century*. Oxford Univ. Press, New York, NY.

Western, D., M.C. Pearl, S.L. Pimm, B. Walker, I. Atkinson and D.S. Woodruff. 1989. An agenda for conservation action. Pp. 304–323 in D. Western and M.C. Pearl, eds. *Conservation for the twenty-first century*. Oxford Univ. Press, New York, NY.

Westmoreland, D. and L.B. Best. 1985. The effect of disturbance on mourning dove nesting success. *Auk* 102:774–780.

Wetton, J.H., R.E. Carter, D.T. Parkin and D. Walters. 1987. Demographic study of a wild house sparrow population by DNA fingerprinting. *Nature* 327:147–149.

Wheaton, F.W. 1977a. Ponds, tanks and other impounding structures. Pp. 414–462 in *Aquacultural engineering*. John Wiley & Sons, New York, NY.

Wheaton, F.W. 1977b. Energy in aquatic systems. Pp. 64–113 in *Aquacultural engineering*. John Wiley & Sons, New York, NY.

Wheelwright, N.T. 1983. Fruits and ecology of resplendent quetzals. *Auk* 100:286–301.

Wheelwright, N.T. 1988. Seasonal changes in food preferences of American robins in captivity. *Auk* 105:374–378.

Whelan, C.J. 1989. Avian foliage structure preference for foraging and the effect of prey biomass. *Anim. Behav.* 38:839–846.

Whitaker, R. 1982. Bangladesh: A general survey. *Hamadryad* 7:4–12.

White, F.H. 1984a. *Edwardsiella tarda*. Pp. 83–92 in G.L. Hoff, F.L. Frye and E.R. Jacobson, eds. *Diseases of amphibians and reptiles*. Plenum Press, New York, NY.

White, J. and D.L. Marcellini. 1986. HERPlab: A family learning centre at the National Zoological Park. *Int'l. Zoo Yb.* 24/25:340–343.

White, J.R. 1984b. Man can save the manatee. *Nat'l. Geogr.* 166:414–418.

White, J.R. 1984c. Born captive, released in the wild. *Sea Frontiers* 30:369–375.

White, J.R. and R. Francis-Floyd. 1988. Nutritional management of marine mammals. *Proc. Int'l. Assoc. Aquat. Anim. Med.* 19:5–15.

White, J.R. and R. Francis-Floyd. 1990. Manatee biology and medicine. Pp. 601–623 in L.A. Dierauf, ed. *CRC Handbook of marine mammal medicine: Health, disease and rehabilitation*. CRC Press, Boca Raton, FL.

White, R.R. and M.C. Singer. 1987. Larval marking technique. *Pan Pacific Entomol.* 63:341–344.

Whittaker, R.H. 1970. *Communities and ecosystems.* MacMillan, New York, NY.

Whittier, J.M. and D. Crews. 1986. Ovarian development in red-sided garter snakes, *Thamnophis sirtalis parietalis*: Relationship to mating. *Gen. Comp. Endocrinol.* 61:5–12.

Whittier, J.M. and D. Crews. 1987. Seasonal reproduction: Patterns and control. Pp. 385–409 in D.O. Norris and R.E. Jones, eds. *Hormones and reproduction in fishes, amphibians, and reptiles.* Plenum Press, New York, NY.

Whittier, J.M., R.T. Mason, D. Crews and P. Licht. 1987. Role of light and temperature in the regulation of reproduction in the red-sided garter snake *Thamnophis sirtalis parietalis. Can. J. Zool.* 65:2090–2096.

Whittow, G.C. 1978. Thermoregulatory behavior of the Hawaiian monk seal (*Monachus schauinslandi*). *Pacific Sci.* 32:47–60.

Wibbels, T., D.W. Owens and M.S. Amoss. 1987b. Seasonal changes in the serum testosterone titers of loggerhead sea turtles captured along the Atlantic coast of the US. Pp. 59–64 in W.N. Witzell, ed. *Ecology of East Florida sea turtles.* U.S. Dept. Commer., NOAA Tech. Report NMFS 53. Washington, DC.

Wibbels, T., D.W. Owens, Y.A. Morris and M.S. Amoss. 1987a. Sexing techniques and sex ratios for immature loggerhead sea turtles captured along the Atlantic Coast of the U.S. Pp. 65–74 in W.N. Witzell, ed. *Ecology of East Florida sea turtles.* U.S. Dept. Commer., NOAA Tech. Report NMFS 53. Washington, DC.

Wickings, E.J. and E. Nieschlag. 1977. Testosterone production and metabolism in laboratory maintained male rhesus monkeys. *Int'l. J. Fertil.* 22:56–59.

Wickings, E.J. and E. Nieschlag. 1980. Seasonality in endocrine and exocrine testicular function of the adult rhesus monkey (*Macaca mulatta*) maintained in a controlled laboratory environment. *Int'l. J. Androl.* 3:87–104.

Wickings, E.J., G.R. Marshall and E. Nieschlag. 1986. Endocrine regulation of male reproduction. Pp. 149–170 in W.R. Dukelow and J. Erwin, eds. *Comparative Primate Biology, Vol 3: Reproduction and development.* Alan Liss, New York, NY.

Wickings, E.J., P. Zaidi, G. Brabant and E. Nieschlag. 1981. Stimulation of pituitary and testicular functions with LH-RH agonist or pulsatile LH-RH treatment in the rhesus monkey during the non-breeding season. *J. Reprod. Fertil.* 63:129–136.

Wiens, J.A. 1982. Forum: Avian subspecies in the 1980s. *Auk* 99:593.

Wieser, W. 1973. Temperature relations of ectotherms: A speculative review. Pp. 1–23 in W. Wieser, ed. *Effects of temperature on ectothermic organisms: Ecological implications and mechanisms of compensation.* Springer-Verlag, New York, NY.

Wiewandt, T.A. 1969. Vocalization, aggressive behavior, and territoriality in the bullfrog, *Rana catesbeiana. Copeia* 1969:276–285.

Wigglesworth, V.B. 1933. The physiology of the cuticle and of ecdysis in *Rhodnius prolixus* (Triatomidae, Hemiptera); with special reference to the function of the oenocytes and of the dermal glands. *Quart. J. Microbiol. Sci.* 76:269–318.

Wigglesworth, V.B. 1936. The function of the corpus allatum in the growth and reproduction of *Rhodnius prolixus* (Hemiptera). *Quart. J. Microbiol. Sci.* 79:91–121.

Wigglesworth, V.B. 1970. *Insect hormones.* W.H. Freeman, San Francisco, CA.

Wigglesworth, V.B. 1972. *The principles of insect physiology,* 7th ed. Chapman and Hall, London, England.

Wilbur, H.M. 1972. Competition, predation, and the structure of the Ambystoma-*Rana sylvatica* community. *Ecology* 53:3–21.

Wilbur, S.R. 1978. *The California condor, 1966–1976; a look at its past and future.* U.S. Dept. Interior, Fish & Wildl. Service, Washington, DC.

Wilcox, B.A. 1988. Tropical deforestation and extinction. *1988 Red list of threatened animals.* Int'l. Union Conserv. Nature & Natur. Resour. Conservation Monitoring Centre, Cambridge, England.

Wildt, D.E. 1986. Spermatozoa: Collection, evaluation, metabolism, freezing and artificial insemination. Pp. 171–193 in *Comparative primate biology, Vol. 3: Reproduction and development.* Alan Liss, New York, NY.

Wildt, D.E. 1989. Strategies for the practical application of reproductive technologies to endangered species. *Zoo Biol. Suppl.* 1:17–20.

Wildt, D.E. and M. Bush. 1984. Reproductive physiology studies in zoological species: Concerns and strategies. *Zoo Biol.* 3:363–372.

Wildt, D.E. and U.S. Seal, eds. 1988. *Research priorities for single species conservation biology.* National Science Foundation and National Zool. Park, Washington, DC.

Wildt, D.E., J.G. Howard, L.L. Hall and M. Bush. 1986. Reproductive physiology of the clouded leopard: I. Electroejaculates contain high proportions of pleiomorphic spermatozoa throughout the year. *Biol Reprod.* 34:937–947.

Wildt, D.E., C.C. Platz, P.K. Chakraborty and S.W.J. Seager. 1979. Oestrus and ovarian activity in a female jaguar (*Panthera onca*). *J. Reprod. Fertil.* 56:555–558.

Wildt, D.E., C.C. Platz, S.W.J. Seager and M. Bush. 1981. Induction of ovarian activity in the cheetah (*Acinonyx jubatus*). *Biol Reprod.* 24:217–222.

Wildt, D.E., M. Bush, J.G. Howard, S.J. O'Brien, D. Meltzer, A. Van Dyk, H. Ebedes and D.J. Brand. 1983. Unique seminal quality in the South African cheetah and a comparative evaluation in the domestic cat. *Biol. Reprod.* 29:1019–1025.

Wildt, D.E., M.C. Schiewe, P.M. Schmidt, K.I. Goodrowe, J.G. Howard, I.G. Phillips, S.J. O'Brien and M. Bush. 1986. Developing animal model systems for embryo technologies in rare and endangered wildlife. *Theriogenology* 25:33–51.

Wiley, J.W. 1983. The role of captive propagation in the conservation of the Puerto Rican parrot. Pp. 441–451 in A. Risser and F. Todd, eds. *Proc. Symp. on Breeding Birds in Captivity.* Int'l. Found. Conserv. Birds. North Hollywood, CA.

Wiley, S. 1978. A review of techniques in the maintenance and propagation of cranes. Pp. 15–27 in A. Risser, L. Baptista, S. Wiley and N. Gale, eds. *Proc. Symp. on Breeding Birds in Captivity.* Int'l. Found. Conserv. Birds. North Hollywood, CA.

Williams, G. and K. Ghebremeskel. 1988. The use of a computerized database in the nutritional management of captive animals. *Proc. Amer. Assoc. Zool. Parks Aquar.* 1988:478–481.

Williams, J. 1977. *Observations on the status of the Devil's Hole pupfish in the Hoover Dam refugium.* Bureau of Reclamation. REC-ERC-77-11. Denver, CO.

Williams, J. 1980. Systematics and ecology of chubs (*Gila*: Cyprinidae) of the Alvord Basin, Oregon and Nevada. Ph.D. Dissertation, Oregon State Univ., Corvallis, OR.

Williams, J. 1983a. *Gila boraxobius* Williams and Bond, Borax Lake chub. Pp. 161–165 in D.S. Lee, C.R. Gilbert, C.H. Hocutt, R.E. Jenkins, D.E. McAllister and J.R. Stauffer, Jr., eds. *Atlas of North American freshwater fishes* (suppl). N.C. State Mus. Natur. History, Raleigh, NC.

Williams, J. and C. Bond. 1983. Status and life history notes on the native fishes of the Alvord Basin, Oregon and Nevada. *Great Basin Natural.* 43:409–420.

Williams, J. and C. Williams. 1980. Feeding ecology of *Gila boraxobius* (Osteichthyes: Cyprinidae) endemic to a thermal lake in southeastern Oregon. *Great Basin Natural.* 40:101–114.

Williams, J.E., D.W. Sada, C.D. Williams and other members of the Western Division Endangered Species Committee. 1988. American Fisheries Society guidelines for introductions of threatened and endangered fishes. *Fisheries* 13:5–11.

Williams, J.E., J.E. Johnson, D.A. Hendrickson, S. Contreras-Balderas, J.D. Williams, M. Navarro-Mendoza, D.E. McAllister and J.E. Deacon. 1989. Fishes of North America endangered, threatened or of special concern: 1989. *Fisheries* 14:2–20.

Williams, T.D. 1983b. Sea otter rescue: Preparing for disaster. *Proc. Amer. Assoc. Zoo Vet.* 1983:45–46.

Williams, T.D. 1988. An implanted transponder chip used as a tag for sea otters. *Marine Mamm. Sci.* 3:271–274.

Williams, T.D. 1990a. Sea otter biology and medicine. Pp. 625–648 in L.A. Dierauf, ed. *CRC Handbook of marine mammal medicine: Health, disease and rehabilitation*. CRC Press, Boca Raton, FL.

Williams, T.D., A. Dawson, T.J. Nicholls and A.R. Goldsmith. 1987. Short days induce premature reproductive maturation in juvenile starlings, *Sturnus vulgaris*. *J. Reprod. Fertil.* 80:327–333.

Williams, T.M. 1990b. Evaluating the long term effects of crude oil exposure in sea otters: Laboratory and field observations. In *Effect of oil on wildlife. Proc. 13th Ann. Conf. Int'l. Wildl. Rehab. Council.* 1990:187–195.

Williamson, P., N.J. Gales and S. Lister. 1990. Use of real-time B-mode ultrasound for pregnancy diagnosis and measurements of fetal growth rate in captive bottlenose dolphins (*Tursips truncatus*). *J. Reprod. Fertil.* 88:543–548.

Willis, J.H. 1974. Morphogenetic action of insect hormones. *Ann. Rev. Entomol.* 19:97–116.

Willis, K., R. Wiese and M. Hutchins. 1992. AAZPA Conservation Guide. *Amer. Assoc. Zool. Parks and Aquar.* Bethesda, MD.

Willis, R.B. 1980. Breeding the Malayan giant squirrel (*Ratufa bicolor*) at the London Zoo. *Int'l. Zoo Yb.* 20:218–220.

Willis, Y.L., D.L. Moyle and T.S. Baskett. 1956. Emergence, breeding, hibernation, movements and transformation of the bullfrog, *Rana catesbeiana*, in Missouri. *Copeia* 1956:30–41.

Wilson, E.O. 1961. The nature of the taxon cycle in the Melanesian ant fauna. *Amer. Natural.* 95:169–193.

Wilson, E.O. 1971. *The insect societies*. Belknap Press, Cambridge, MA.

Wilson, E.O. 1985. The biological diversity crisis: A challenge to science. *Issues Sci. Tech.* 2:20–29.

Wilson, E.O. 1987a. The arboreal ant fauna of Peruvian Amazon forests: A first assessment. *Biotropica* 19:245–251.

Wilson, E.O. 1987b. The little things that run the world (The importance and conservation of invertebrates). *Conserv. Biol.* 1:344–346.

Wilson, E.O., ed. 1988a. *Biodiversity*. Nat'l. Acad. Press, Washington, DC.

Wilson, E.O. 1988b. The current state of biological diversity. Pp. 3–18 in E.O. Wilson, ed. *Biodiversity*. Nat'l. Acad. Press, Washington, DC.

Wilson, E.O. 1989. Conservation: The next hundred years. Pp. 1–10 in D. Western and M. Pearl, eds. *Conservation for the twenty-first century*. Oxford Univ. Press, New York, NY.

Wilson, F.E. 1986. Testosterone sensitivity of the seminal sacs of tree sparrows (*Spizella arborea*) in different reproductive states. *J. Endocrinol.* 109:125–131.

Wilson, M., M. Daly and P. Behrends. 1985a. The estrous cycle of two species of kangaroo rats (*Dipodomys microps* and *D. merriami*). *J. Mammal.* 66:726–732.

Wilson, M.I., G.M. Brown and D. Wilson. 1978. Annual and diurnal changes in plasma androgen and cortisol in adult male squirrel monkey (*Saimiri sciureus*) studied longitudinally. *Acta Endocrinol.* 87:424–433.

Wilson, S., L. Miller, M. Hursey, M. Frantz and J. Gorte. 1985b. The social development of a captive grey seal (*Halichoerus grypus*) pup for the first six months. *Aquat. Mamm.* 11:89–100.

Wingfield, J.C. 1983. Environmental and endocrine control of avian reproduction: An ecological approach. Pp. 265–288 in S. Mikami, K. Homma and M. Wada, eds. *Avian endocrinology and ecological perspectives*. Japan Sci. Soc. Press, Tokyo, Japan/Springer-Verlag, Berlin, Germany.

Wingfield, J.C. 1984a. Androgens and mating systems: Testosterone-induced polygyny in normally monogamous birds. *Auk* 101:665–671.

Wingfield, J.C. 1984b. Environmental and endocrine control of reproduction in the song sparrow, *Melospiza melodia*. I. Temporal organization of the breeding cycle. *Gen. Comp. Endocrinol.* 56:406–416.

Wingfield, J.C. 1984c. Environmental and endocrine control of reproduction in the song sparrow, *Melospiza melodia*. II: Agonistic interactions as environmental information stimulating secretion of testosterone. *Gen. Comp. Endocrinol.* 56:417–424.

Wingfield, J.C. 1985a. Influences of weather on reproductive function in male song sparrows, *Melospiza melodia*. *J. Zool. London* 205:525–544.

Wingfield, J.C. 1985b. Environmental and endocrine control of territorial behavior in birds. Pp. 265–277 in B.K. Follett, S. Ishii and A. Chandola, eds. *The endocrine system and the environment*. Japan Sci. Soc. Press, Tokyo, Japan/Springer-Verlag, Berlin, Germany.

Wingfield, J.C., C.M. Vleck and D.S. Farner. 1981. Effect of day length and reproductive state on diel rhythyms of luteinizing hormone levels in the plasma of white-crowned sparrows, *Zonotrichia leucophrys gambelii*. *J. Exp. Zool.* 217:261–264.

Wingfield, J.C., G.F. Ball, A.M. Dufty, Jr., R.E. Hegner and M. Ramenofsky. 1987. Testosterone and aggression in birds. *Amer. Sci.* 75:602–608.

Winter, J.S.D., C. Faiman, W.C. Hobson, A.V. Prasad and F.I. Reyes. 1975. Pituitary-gonadal relations in infancy. I. Patterns of serum gonadotropin concentrations from birth to four years of age in man and chimpanzee. *J. Clin. Endocrinol.* 40:545–551.

Wislocki, G.B. 1931. Notes on the female reproductive tract (ovaries, uterus and placenta) of the collared peccary (*Pecari angulatus bangsi* Goldman). *J. Mammal.* 12:143–149.

Wislocki, G.B. 1942. Size, weight and histology of the testis in the gorilla. *J. Mammal.* 23:281–287.

Wittenberger, J.F. 1981. *Animal social behavior*. Duxbury, Boston, MA.

Wolf, R.C., R.F. O'Connor and J.A. Robinson. 1977. Cyclic changes in plasma progestins and estrogens in squirrel monkeys. *Biol. Reprod.* 17:228–231.

Wolfheim, J.H. 1983. *Primates of the world: Distribution, abundance, and conservation*. Univ. Washington Press, Seattle, WA.

Wolfson, A. 1952. The cloacal protuberance as means for determining breeding condition in live male passerines. *Bird Banding* 23:159–165.

Wolfson, A. 1959. Role of light and darkness in the regulation of the annual stimulus for spring migration and reproductive cycles. Pp. 679–716 in R.B. Withrow, ed. *Photoperiodism and related phenomena in plants and animals*. Amer. Assoc. Advan. Sci. Pub. 55. Washington, DC.

Wolfson, A. 1960a. Regulation of annual periodicity in the migration and reproduction in birds. *Cold Spring Harbor Symp. Quant. Biol.* 25:507–514.

Wolfson, A. 1960b. The ejaculate and the nature of coition in some passerine birds. *Ibis* 102:124–125.

Wood, F.G. 1953. Underwater sound production and concurrent behavior of captive porpoises, *Tursiops truncatus* and *Stenella plagiodon*. *Bull. Marine Sci., Gulf and Caribbean* 32:120–133.

Wood, F.G. 1977. Birth of porpoises at Marineland, FL 1939–1969, and comments on problems involved in captive breeding of small Cetacea. Pp. 47–60 in S.H. Ridgway and K. Benirschke, eds. *Breeding dolphins:*

Present status, suggestions for the future. U.S. Dept. Commer., Nat'l. Tech. Info. Serv., PB–273. Washington, DC.

Wood, F.G. 1986. Social behavior and foraging strategies of dolphins. Pp. 331–333 in J. Thomas and F.G. Wood, eds. *Dolphin cognition and behavior: A comparative study.* Lawrence Earlbaum, Hillsdale, NJ.

Wood, G.L. 1976. P. 201 in *The Guiness book of animal facts and feats*, 2nd Ed. Guiness Superlatives, Enfield, England.

Wood, J.R. and F.E. Wood. 1980. Reproductive biology of captive green sea turtles *Chelonia mydas. Am Zool.* 20:499–506.

Wood, J.R. and F.E. Wood. 1984. Captive breeding of the Kemp's ridley. *Marine Turtle Newsletter* 29:12.

Woodford, M.H. and R.A. Kock. 1991. Veterinary considerations in reintroduction and translocation projects. Pp. 101–108 in J.H.W. Gipps, ed. *Beyond captive breeding.* Clarendon Press, Oxford, England.

Woodruff, D.S. 1989. The problems of conserving genes and species. Pp. 76–88 in D. Western and M.C. Pearl, eds. *Conservation for the twenty-first century.* Oxford Univ. Press, New York, NY.

Woodward, D., A. Farag, E. Little, B. Steadman and R. Yancik. 1991. Sensitivity of greenback cutthroat trout to acid pH and elevated aluminum. *Trans. Amer. Fish. Soc.* 120:34–42.

Woodward, F.R. 1990. Problems in the control of exploitation of freshwater mussels with particular reference to *Margaritafera.* Pp. 52–54 in *Colloquy on the Berne Convent. on Invert. and their Conserv.* Council of Europe, Strassburg, France.

Wooley, P.A. 1982. Laboratory maintenance of dasyurid marsupials. Pp. 13–21 in D.D. Evans, ed. *The management of Australian mammals in captivity.* Proc. Aust. Mamm. Soc., 1979. Ramsey Ware Stockland, Victoria, Australia.

Woolfenden, G.E. 1975. Florida scrub jays helpers at the nest. *Auk* 92:1–15.

Worrest, R.C. and D.J. Kimeldorf. 1976. Distortions in amphibian development induced by ultraviolet-B enhancement (290–315 nm) of a simulated solar spectrum. *Photochem. Photobiol.* 24:377–382.

Worth, W., M. Hutchins, C. Sheppard, D. Bruning, J. Gonzales and T. McNamara. 1991. Hand-rearing, growth, and development of red birds of paradise (*Paradisaea rubra*) at the New York Zoological Park. *Zoo Biol.* 10:17–33.

Worthy, G.A.J. 1990. Nutritional energetics for marine mammals; addendums. Pp. 489–520 in L.A. Dierauf, ed. *CRC Handbook of marine mammal medicine: Health, disease and rehabilitation.* CRC Press, Boca Raton, FL.

Wourms, J.P. 1981. Viviparity: The maternal-fetal relationship in fishes. *Amer. Zool*. 21:473–515.

Wourms, J.P., B.D. Grove and J. Lombardi. 1988. The maternal-embryonic relationship in viviparous fishes. Pp. 1–134 in W.S. Hoar and D.J. Randall, eds. *Fish physiology. Vol XI: The physiology of developing fish: Part B. Viviparity and posthatching juveniles*. Academic Press, New York, NY.

Wright, D.P. 1985. *Spodoptera eridania*. Pp. 459–464 in P. Singh and R.F. Moore, ed. *Handbook of insect rearing*, Vol. II. Elsevier, Amsterdam, Netherlands.

Würsig, B. and M. Würsig 1977. The photographic determination of group size, composition, and stability of coastal porpoises (*Tursiops truncatus*). *Science* 198:755–756.

Würsig, B. and M. Würsig. 1979. Behavior and ecology of the bottlenose dolphin, *Tursiops truncatus*, in the south Atlantic. *Fish. Bull*. 77:399–412.

Würsig, B. and M. Würsig. 1980. Behavior and ecology of the dusky dolphin *Lagenorhynchus obscurus*, in the south Atlantic. *Fish. Bull*. 77:871–890.

Würsig, B., F. Cipriano and M. Würsig. 1991. Dolphin movement patterns: Information from radio and theodolite tracking studies. Pp. 79–112 in K. Pryor and K.S. Norris, eds. *Dolphin societies*. Univ. California Press, Berkeley, CA.

Wurtman, R.J., M.J. Baum and J.T. Potts, Jr., eds. 1985. *The medical and biological effects of light*. New York Acad. Sci., New York, NY.

Wylie, S.R. 1973. Breeding the white-tailed sea eagle at Kansas City Zoo. *Int'l. Zoo Yb*. 13:115–116.

Wylie, S.R. 1977. Breeding the bateleur eagle *Terathopius ecaudatus* at the St. Louis Zoo. *Int'l. Zoo Yb*. 17:146–147.

Wylie, S.R. 1981. Notes from the St. Louis Zoological Park, U.S.A. *Avicult. Mag*. 87:175.

Wyman, R.L. 1990a. What's happening to the amphibians. *Conserv. Biol*. 4:350–352.

Wyman, R.L. 1990b. Amphibian declines, possible contributing or causative factors. Unpub. address to Soc. Study Amphib. Reptile Symp., New Orleans, LA.

Wyoming Game and Fish Department. 1987. *A strategic plan for the management of black-footed ferrets in Wyoming*. Wyoming Fish and Game Dept., Laramie, WY.

Xanten, W.A. 1990. Marmoset behaviour in mixed-species exhibits at the National Zoological Park, Washington. *Int'l. Zoo Yb*. 19:143–148.

Xavier, F. 1987. Functional morphology and regulation of the corpus luteum. Pp. 241–282 in D.O. Norris and R.E. Jones, eds. *Hormones and reproduction in fishes, amphibians, and reptiles.* Plenum Press, New York, NY.

Xerces Society and Smithsonian Institution. 1990. *Butterfly gardening: Creating summer magic in your garden.* Sierra Club Books, San Francisco, in association with the Nat'l. Wildl. Fed., Washington, DC.

Yamada, J.K. and B.S. Durrant. 1989. Reproductive parameters of clouded leopards (*Neofelis nebulosa*). *Zoo Biol.* 8:223–231.

Yamada, M. 1966. Five natural troops of Japanese monkeys in Shodoshima Island, I: Distribution and social organization. *Primates* 7:315–362.

Yamamoto, J.T., K.M. Shields, J.R. Millam, T.E. Roudybush and C.R. Garu. 1989. Reproductive activity of force-paired cockatiels (*Nymphicus hollandicus*) *Auk* 106:86–93.

Yamamoto, S., S. Utsu, Y. Tanioka and N. Ohasawa. 1977. Extremely high levels of corticosteroids and low levels of corticosteroid binding macromolecule in plasma of marmoset monkeys. *Acta Endocrinol.* 85:398–405.

Yamashita, M., S. Fakada, M. Yoshikuni, P. Bulet, T. Hirai, A. Yamaguchi, Y.H. Lou, Z. Zhao and Y. Nagahama. 1992. Purification and characterization of maturation-promoting factor in fish. *Dev. Biol.* 149:8–15.

Yamazaki, F. and E.M. Donaldson. 1969. Involvement of gonadotropin and steroid hormones in the spermiation of the goldfish (*Carassius auratus*). *Gen. Comp. Endocrinol.* 12:491–497.

Yan, H.Y. and P. Thomas. 1991. Histochemical and immunocyto-chemical identification of the pituitary cell types in three sciaenid fishes: Atlantic croaker (*Micropogonias undulatus*), spotted seatrout (*Cynoscion nebulosus*), and red drum (*Sciaenops ocellatus*). *Gen. Comp. Endocrinol.* 84:389–400.

Yan, L., P. Swanson and W.W. Dickhoff. 1992. A two-receptor model for salmon gonadotropins (GTH I and GTH II). *Biol. Reprod.* 47:418–427.

Yardley, D. and C. Hubbs. 1976. An electrophoretic study of two species of mosquitofishes with notes on genetic subdivision. *Copeia* 1976:117–120.

Yaron, Z. 1985. Reptilian placentation and gestation: Structure, function, and endocrine control. Pp. 527–604 in C. Gans and F. Billett, eds. *Biology of Reptilia*, Vol 15B. John Wiley & Sons, New York, NY.

Yen, S.S.C., R. Rebar, G. Vandenburg, F. Naftolin, Y. Ehara, S. Engblom, K.J. Ryan and K. Benirschke. 1972. Synthetic luteinizing hormone-releasing factor: A potent stimulator of gonadotropin release in man. *J. Clin. Endocrinol.* 34:1108–1111.

Yerkes, R.M. 1925. *Almost human*. Johnathan Cope, London, England.

Yerkes, R.M. and A.W. Yerkes. 1929. *The great apes: A study of anthropoid life*. Yale Univ. Press, New Haven, CT.

Young, M. and J. Williams. 1983. The status and conservation of the freshwater pearl mussel *Margaritifera margaritifera* Linn. in Great Britain. *Biol. Conserv.* 25:35–52.

Yu, K.L. and R.E. Peter 1992. Adrenergic and dopaminergic regulation of gonadotropin-releasing hormone release from goldfish preoptic-anterior hypothalamus and pituitary *in vitro*. *Gen. Comp. Endocrinol.* 85:138–146.

Yu, K.L., N.M. Sherwood and R.E. Peter. 1988. Differential distribution of two molecular forms of gonadotropin-releasing hormone in discrete brain areas of goldfish (*Carassius auratus*). *Peptides* 9:625–630.

Zach, R. and J.B. Falls. 1978. Prey selection by captive ovenbirds (Aves: Parulidae). *J. Anim. Ecol.* 47:929–943.

Zamboni, L, C.H. Conaway and L. Van Pelt. 1974. Seasonal changes in production of semen in free-ranging rhesus monkeys. *Biol Reprod.* 11:251–267.

Zavaleta, D. and F. Ogasawara. 1987. A review of the mechanism of the release of spermatozoa from storage tubules in the fowl and turkey oviduct. *World's Poult. Sci. J.* 43:132–139.

Zeiller, W. 1977. Miami Seaquarium dolphin breeding program. Pp. 61–65 in S.H. Ridgway and K. Benirschke, eds. *Breeding dolphins: Present status, suggestions for the future*. U.S. Dept. Commer. Nat'l. Tech. Info. Serv., PB 273, Washington, DC.

Zhou, K.Y. 1989a. Progress report on the semi-natural reserve at Tongling. Pp. 19–20 in W.F. Perrin, R.L. Brownell, Jr., K.Y. Zhou and R.J. Liu, eds. *Biology and conservation of the river dolphins*. Occasional papers of the Int'l. Union Conserv. Nature & Natur. Resour./Species Survival Commission, No. 3. Allen Press, Lawrence, KS.

Zhou, K.Y. 1989b. Review of studies of structure and function of the baiji, *Lipoites vexillifer*. Pp. 99–113 in W.F. Perrin, R.L. Brownell, Jr., K.Y. Zhou and R.J. Liu, eds. *Biology and conservation of the river dolphins*. Occasional papers of the Int'l. Union Conserv. Nature & Natur. Resour./ Species Survival Commission, No. 3. Allen Press, Lawrence, KS.

Zhou, K.Y. 1991. Marine mammal studies in China. *Int'l. Marine Biol. Res. Instit. Report* 2:11–20.

Zhou, K.Y., J. Sun, Y.Y. Hua and A. Gao. 1992. Population monitoring and photo-identification study of the baiji, *Lipotes vexillifer*, in the lower Yangtze. *Proc. Int.l. Assoc. Aquat. Anim. Conf.* 23:30 (Abstr.).

Ziegler, T.A., S.A. Scholl, G. Scheffler, M.A. Haggerty and B.L. Lasley. 1989. Excretion of estrone, estradiol and progesterone in the urine and feces of the female cotton-top tamarin (*Saquinus oedipus oedipus*). *Amer. J. Primatol.* 17:185–195.

Zimmermann, E. 1986. *Breeding terrarium animals*. T.F.H. Pubs., Neptune City, NJ.

Zuagg, W.S. 1981. Advanced photoperiod and water temperature effects of gill Na+-K+ adenosine triphosphatase activity and migration of juvenile steelhead (*Salmo gairdneri*). *Can. J. Fish. Aquat. Sci.* 38:758–764.

Zwank, P.J., J.P. Geaghan and D.A. Dewhurst. 1988. Foraging differences between native and released Mississippi sandhill cranes: Implications for conservation. *Conserv. Biol.* 2:386–390.

Contributors

Dr. Richard A. Arnold
  Entomological Consulting
    Services, Ltd.
  104 Mountain View Court
  Pleasant Hill,
    California 94523

Bruce W. Bohmke
  Phoenix Zoo
  P.O. Box 5155
  Phoenix, Arizona 85010

Dr. Marcia Bradley
  Department of Science
  Ocean County College
  P.O. Box 2001
  Toms River,
    New Jersey 08754

Gail Y. Bruner
  Atlanta/Fulton County Zoo, Inc.
  800 Cherokee Avenue, S.E.
  Atlanta, Georgia 30315

Dr. Gordon M. Burghardt
  Departments of Psychology
    and Zoology
  307 Austin Peay Bldg.
  University of Tennessee
  Knoxville, Tennessee 37996

Sarah L. Bush
  Program in Animal Behavior
  Bucknell University
  Lewisburg,
    Pennsylvania 17837

Dr. Dourglas K. Candland
  Program in Animal Behavior
  Bucknell University
  Lewisburg,
    Pennsylvania 17837

Gerard Casadei
  Department of Ornithology
  Wildlife Conservation Society
  185th. Street and Southern
    Boulevard
  Bronx, New York 10460

Jon C. Coe
  Coe, Lee, Robinson & Roesch
  115 N. 3rd. St.
  Philadelphia, Pennsylvania
    19106

Dr. Jack Demarest
  Department of Psychology
  Monmouth College
  West Long Branch,
    New Jersey 07764

Dr. Leo S. Demski
Department of Biology
New College
University of South Florida
5700 N. Pamiami Trail
Sarasota, Florida 34243

Dr. Boyce A. Drummond
Natural Perspectives
1762 Upper Twinrock Road
Florissant,
   Colorado 80816-9256

Dr. W. Richard Dukelow
Endocrine Research Center
Michigan State University
East Lansing, Michigan 48824

Dr. Barbara S. Durrant
Center for Reproduction of
   Endangered Species
Zoological Society of San Diego
P.O. Box 551
San Diego, California 92112

Dr. Susie Ellis
IUCN/SSC Captive Breeding
   Specialist Group
1201 Johnny Cake Ridge Road
Apple Valley, Minnesota 55124

Dr. Debra L. Forthman
Atlanta/Fulton County Zoo, Inc.
800 Cherokee Avenue, S.E.
Atlanta, Georgia 30315

Dr. Ruth Francis-Floyd
Department of Fisheries and
   Aquatic Sciences
College of Veterinary Medicine
University of Florida
7922 Northwest 71st. Street
Gainesville, Florida 32606

Dr. George F. Gee
Captive Propagation Research
   Group
Endangered Species Research
   Branch
U.S. Fish and Wildlife Service
Patuxent Wildlife Research
   Center
Laurel, Maryland 20708

Dr. Edward F. Gibbons, Jr.
Center for Science and Technology
Briarcliffe College
250 Crossways Park Drive
Woodbury, New York 11797

Dr. John L. Gittleman
Department of Zoology
University of Tennessee
Knoxville, Tennessee 37996

Reginald A. Hoyt[1]
Phoenix Zoo
P.O. Box 5155
Phoenix, Arizona 85010
   [1]Present Address:
   Conservation Cooperative
   304 Center St.
   Bangor, Maine 04401

Dr. Michael Hutchins
Conservation and Science
AZA Conservation Center
7970 Old Georgetown Road
Bethesda, Maryland 20814

Craig S. Ivanyi
Department of Herpetology
   and Ichthyology
Arizona Sonora Desert
   Museum
2021 North Kinney Road
Tucson, Arizona 85743

Dr. S.D. Kholkute
 Endocrine Research Center
 Michigan State University
 East Lansing, Michigan 48824

Dr. Christopher C. Kohler
 Cooperative Fisheries
  Research Laboratory
 and
 Department of Zoology
 Southern Illinois University
 Carbondale, Illinois 62901

Uriel A. Levi
 School of Architecture
 Georgia Institute of Technology
 Atlanta, Georgia 30332

Dr. Paul Licht
 Department of Integrative
  Biology
 University of California at
  Berkeley
 Berkeley, California 94720

Dr. Donald G. Lindburg
 Center for Reproduction of
  Endangered Species
 Zoological Society of San Diego
 P.O. Box 551
 San Diego, California 92112

Dr. Anna Marie Lyles
 Department of Ornithology
 Wildlife Conservation Society
 185th. Street and Southern
  Boulevard
 Bronx, New York 10460

Dr. Rita McManamon
 Atlanta/Fulton County Zoo, Inc.
 800 Cherokee Avenue, S.E.
 Atlanta, Georgia 30315

Greta C. McMillan
 Knoxville Zoological Gardens
 P.O. Box 6040
 Knoxville, Tennessee 37914

Dr. Mark A. Milostan
 Department of Science and
  Mathematics
 Alpena Community College
 666 Johnson St.
 Alpena, Michigan 49707

Janice J. Perry-Richardson
 Department of Herpetology
  and Ichthyology
 Arizona Sonora Desert Museum
 2021 North Kinney Road
 Tucson, Arizona 85743

Dr. Peter C.H. Pritchard
 Florida Audubon Society
 460 Highway, 436 #200
 Casselberry, Florida 32707

Dr. Sam H. Ridgway
 Naval Ocean Systems Center
 San Diego, California 92152

Dr. Michael H. Robinson
 National Zoological Park
 3000 Block of Connecticut Ave.
 Washington, D.C. 20008

Terry Samansky
 Marine World Africa, U.S.A.
 Vallejo, California 94589

Leslie S. Saul-Gershenz
 Insect Zoo
 San Francisco Zoological
  Gardens
 1 Zoo Road
 San Francisco, California 94132

Dr. J. Pete Schroeder
  Veterinary Consultant
    Services
  620 W. Anderson Road
  Sequim, Washington 98382

Dr. J. Mark Scriber
  Department of Entomology
  Michigan State University
  East Lansing, Michigan 48824

Dr. Christine Sheppard
  Department of Ornithology
  Wildlife Conservation Society
  185th. Street and Southern Blvd.
  Bronx, New York 10460

Dr. Michael K. Stoskopf
  Department of Wildlife and
    Aquatic Medicine
  College of Veterinary Medicine
  4700 Hillsboro Street
  North Carolina State
    University
  Raleigh, North Carolina 27606

Dr. Jay Sweeney
  Aquatic and Exotic Animal
    Medicine
  4467 Saratoga
  San Diego, California 92187

Dr. James D. Williams
  U.S. Fish and Wildlife Service
  National Fisheries Research
    Center
  7920 N.W. 71st. Street
  Gainesville, Florida 32606

Index